THE OXFORD HISTORY OF POETRY IN ENGLISH

General Editor

PATRICK CHENEY

Coordinating Editors

ROBERT R. EDWARDS
LAURA L. KNOPPERS
STEPHEN REGAN
VINAY DHARWADKER

Dedicated to the Beloved Memory of
Michael O'Neill
1953–2018
Professor of English, University of Durham, United Kingdom
Founding Coordinating Editor, OHOPE,
Great Romantics Scholar and Distinguished British Poet

THE OXFORD HISTORY OF POETRY IN ENGLISH

The Oxford History of Poetry in English (*OHOPE*) is designed to offer a fresh, multi-voiced, and comprehensive analysis of 'poetry': from Anglo-Saxon culture through contemporary British, Irish, American, and Global culture, including English, Scottish, and Welsh poetry, Anglo-American colonial and post-colonial poetry, and poetry in Canada, Australia, New Zealand, the Caribbean, India, Africa, Asia, and other international locales. *OHOPE* both synthesises existing scholarship and presents cutting-edge research, employing a global team of expert contributors for each of the fourteen volumes.

1. *Medieval Poetry: c.670–1100*
2. *Medieval Poetry: 1100–1400*
3. *Medieval Poetry: 1400–1500*
4. *Sixteenth-Century British Poetry*
5. *Seventeenth-Century British Poetry*
6. *Eighteenth-Century British Poetry*
7. *Romantic Poetry*
8. *Victorian Poetry*
9. *Modern British and Irish Poetry: Twentieth Century to Today*
10. *American Poetry: First Encounters to 1865*
11. *American Poetry: 1865–1939*
12. *American Poetry: 1939–present*
13. *Poetry in Canada, Australia, New Zealand, and Oceania*
14. *Poetry in Asia, Africa, and the Caribbean*

The Oxford History of Poetry in English

Medieval Poetry: 1100–1400

Volume 2

Edited by

HELEN COOPER
AND
ROBERT R. EDWARDS

Great Clarendon Street, Oxford, OX2 6DP,
United Kingdom

Oxford University Press is a department of the University of Oxford.
It furthers the University's objective of excellence in research, scholarship,
and education by publishing worldwide. Oxford is a registered trade mark of
Oxford University Press in the UK and in certain other countries

© The several contributors 2023

The moral rights of the authors have been asserted

All rights reserved. No part of this publication may be reproduced, stored in
a retrieval system, or transmitted, in any form or by any means, without the
prior permission in writing of Oxford University Press, or as expressly permitted
by law, by licence or under terms agreed with the appropriate reprographics
rights organization. Enquiries concerning reproduction outside the scope of the
above should be sent to the Rights Department, Oxford University Press, at the
address above

You must not circulate this work in any other form
and you must impose this same condition on any acquirer

Published in the United States of America by Oxford University Press
198 Madison Avenue, New York, NY 10016, United States of America

British Library Cataloguing in Publication Data

Data available

Library of Congress Control Number: 2022944322

ISBN 978–0–19–882742–9

DOI: 10.1093/oso/9780198827429.001.0001

Printed and bound by
CPI Group (UK) Ltd, Croydon, CR0 4YY

Links to third party websites are provided by Oxford in good faith and
for information only. Oxford disclaims any responsibility for the materials
contained in any third party website referenced in this work.

In memory of Derek Pearsall
Scholar, teacher, colleague, and friend

General Editor's Preface

The Oxford History of Poetry in English (*OHOPE*) aims to offer a fresh, multi-voiced, and comprehensive survey of its vast and complicated topic: from Anglo-Saxon poetry through contemporary British, Irish, American, and Global poetry, including English, Scottish, and Welsh poetry, Anglo-American colonial and post-colonial poetry, and poetry in Canada, Australia, New Zealand, the Caribbean, India, Africa, Asia, and other locales.

By 'poetry in English', we mean, quite simply, *poetry written in the English language*: Old English, Middle English, Early Modern English, Modern English. 'English' poetry certainly emerges in Anglo-Saxon England, around the sixth century CE; but, as 'poetry in English' develops, it extends beyond the geographical boundaries of England. Today, poetry in English is planetary. While *OHOPE* necessarily limits the coverage, if not the scope, simply to come into existence, hopefully the Series will join other international projects in the world-service of 'poetry'.

What do we mean by 'poetry'? While we believe that most readers will know what we mean, the topic is intricate, so much so that a quick definition proves elusive. For example, the *Oxford English Dictionary* (*OED*) offers six major definitions, with seven sub-definitions, bringing the total to thirteen. The definitions range from 'Imaginative or creative literature in general; fable, fiction', to 'The art or work of a poet', and can include even 'A treatise on the art of poetry', or, '*figurative*. Something comparable to poetry in its beauty or emotional impact; a poetic quality of beauty and intensity of emotion; the poetic quality *of* something'. The earliest attested use of the word 'poetry' traces to the 1380s, in contexts that emphasise the contested truth claims of figurative representation. In Chaucer's *House of Fame*, one of the rivalrous authorities on the Troy story 'seyde that Omer made lyes, / Feynynge in hys poetries' (1477–8). The ending of *Troilus and Criseyde* includes a valediction for 'the forme of olde clerkis speche / In poetrie' (5.1854–5). John Trevisa's translation of Ranulf Higden's *Polychronicon* (finished in 1387) connects idolatry and poetry: 'Of þe bryngynge forþ of mawmetrie com wel nyh al þe feyninge of poetrie' (2.279). In the 1390s, by contrast, Chaucer's Clerk sees poetry as an authoritative, illustrious tradition embodied in 'Fraunceys Petrak, the lauriat poete, / … whos rethorike sweete / Enlumyned al Ytaille of poetrie' (*Canterbury Tales* IV.31–3). Intriguingly, none of the *OED* definitions speaks of metre, let alone rhyme, and there is no suggestion that poetry includes different 'kinds' (or forms or genres). The authoritative *Princeton Encyclopedia of Poetry and Poetics* (2012), perhaps wisely, does not include an entry on 'poetry' itself. Because poetry remains such an elusive concept—and can include language in distinct metres (such as iambic pentameter) and rhymes (such as the 'Shakespearean' sonnet, rhyming *abab cdcd efef gg*, or three quatrains and a couplet)—we might remain content simply to open the concept up, and let the volumes in the Series speak on their own.

Yet *OHOPE* does proceed through a general rubric. We have encouraged our contributors to address their project through the following formula: *poetry as poetry*—rather than, say, poetry *as context* or *in context*. The goal is to highlight the art of poetry itself, as it unfolds historically in time, across idioms, forms, nations, and so forth. Yet we do not think such a goal at odds with context, nor should it be. Each volume is thus free to situate poetry historically, ideologically, as the editors see fit.

Precisely because 'Poetry in English' spans some fifteen centuries, develops in four major historical 'languages' (Old, Middle, Early Modern, Modern), spread across multiple nations (ever-changing), and includes countless poets, both men and women, the fourteen-volume *Oxford History of Poetry in English* cannot succeed in mapping the full terrain. That has never been the goal. In keeping with the Press's Oxford Series template, the volumes remain necessarily selective: no satisfactorily comprehensive 'coverage' is possible, or perhaps desirable. Each volume does the best it can to remain representative, and fair.

We believe that *OHOPE* fills a gap in the available scholarship and criticism. At present, there is no authoritative history of poetry in English covering British, Irish, American, and Global poetry from the medieval through the modern eras. Readers might like to know that the origins of the present history evidently began with Alexander Pope. In the eighteenth century, Pope *conceived* of a history of 'British' poetry, but it took Thomas Warton to begin writing one, which he left unfinished at his death, still at work on the English Renaissance. Accordingly, the first to complete a comprehensive *History of British Poetry* was W. J. Courthope, who published a six-volume, single-authored work between 1895 and 1905. Other histories followed: in 1947, Herbert Grierson and J. C. Smith co-authored a one-volume *Critical History of English Poetry* (Oxford); in 1961, James Reeves published *A Short History of English Poetry from 1340–1940* (New York); in 1962, Kenneth Hopkins published *English Poetry: A Short History* (London); and in 1981, G. S. Fraser produced *A Short History of English Poetry* (Shepton Mallet). Between 1977 and 1981, Routledge began a *History of English Poetry*, but evidently the series was never completed; only three volumes are in print: *Old English and Middle English Poetry*, edited by Derek A. Pearsall; *Restoration and Eighteenth Century Poetry 1660–1780*, edited by Eric Rothstein; and *Poetry of the Romantic Period*, edited by J. R. de J. Jackson. In 1994, Carl Woodring, working with James Shapiro as Associate Editor, published *The Columbia History of British Poetry*, a one-volume edited collection beginning with Old English Poetry and ending in 1990. In 2010, the most recent attempt at such a history appeared, edited by the late Michael O'Neill, *The Cambridge History of English Poetry*, another single-volume collection, covering England, Scotland, Ireland, and Wales, with all chapters devoted to a single author or a small group of authors.

As for histories of American poetry, in 1993 Jay Parini published an edited *Columbia History of American Poetry*, making Columbia the first press to print a history of poetry combining 'British' and 'American'—anticipating the present *Oxford History*, yet on a much-reduced scale, minus Global poetry, and now thirty years from its publication date. Earlier histories in American poetry include Horace Gregory and Marya Zaturenska's 1946 *History of American Poetry 1900–1940* (Harcourt Brace) and Donald Barlow Stauffer's 1974 *Short History of American Poetry* (Dutton). No histories of Global poetry in English exist. Consequently, the field remains wide open for a comprehensive history that includes Global, American, and British and Irish poetry, medieval to modern.

The target audience for *OHOPE* is similarly complex, to include the general reader of poetry, students at several levels (upper-division secondary school, undergraduate, graduate), teachers at all levels, literary critics, and textual scholars: effectively, anyone interested in poetry in English. Each chapter aims to meet the primary criterion required for this readership: a combination of both a general orientation to its topic and a fresh approach and contribution to the field. A comprehensive Bibliography will be printed at the back of each volume.

Moreover, each volume aims to feature a stable set of chapters. Not simply will there be chapters on major poets ('Milton'), but each volume aims to include chapters on the following topics, geared to the particular era or century it covers:

- The nature of authorship and literary career, as well as the role of the poet in society.
- Imitation and intertextuality.
- Prosody, poetics, and the nature of literary theory.
- Figuration and allusiveness.
- Modes of representation (e.g., allegory, ekphrasis, and blazon during the Renaissance).
- Genre, mode, and form.
- Translation.
- The material production and circulation of poetry (manuscript, performance, print), including the role of patronage.

OHOPE pays significant attention to such major cultural vectors as religion/theology, politics/nationalism, race/class, and gender/sexuality. However, the goal will be unusual in today's critical climate: to connect such vectors to the *matter of poetry* itself; to discuss 'history' and the 'material' insofar as it allows for the historicisation of poetry *as an art*. Above all, *The Oxford History of Poetry in English* aims to provide an authoritative, useful helpmeet for enjoying and embracing one of the seminal achievements of world-art.

Patrick Cheney

Acknowledgements

The Oxford History of Poetry in English (*OHOPE*) has had a long history. Formally, it began on 16 April 2008, when Andrew McNeillie, then Senior Commissioning Editor of Literature at Oxford University Press, invited Patrick Cheney to be General Editor of the Series. The history continued when Penn State University offered its support—in particular, when the Head of the English Department at the time, Robin Schulze, offered financial and administrative aid. Cheney then appointed four Coordinating Editors to manage the wide range of coverage for the Series, and we remain indebted to their early work and support: along with Professor Schulze, Robert R. Edwards, Laura L. Knoppers, and Robert Caserio. The Penn State team produced a detailed proposal to the Press, which in turn produced a series of readers' reports, including recommendations for revision, one of which was to widen the leadership of the project. At this point, a new set of Coordinating Editors was appointed: along with Professor Edwards for Medieval and Professor Knoppers for Early Modern (now at the University of Notre Dame), Michael O'Neill of the University of Durham for Modern British and Irish, Langdon Hammer of Yale for American, and Vinay Dharwadker of the University of Wisconsin for Global. A revised proposal then went to Press readers, to whom again we remain grateful. When Professor O'Neill passed away in 2018, his colleague at Durham, Stephen Regan, was appointed Coordinating Editor of Modern British and Irish. Recently, as well, Professor Hammer has stepped down, and new appointments are underway. We wish to express our gratitude to all these early begetters of *OHOPE*.

For Volume 2, the editors would like to express their gratitude to Professor Mark Morrisson, Head of the Department of English at Penn State, for his ongoing support of the project. They also wish to thank the Research Assistants who have contributed their work on the volume: Theodore Chelis, Maria Isabel Maza, Danielle Ryle, Mattison Schuknecht, and Audrey Saxton.

OHOPE is dedicated to the memory of Michael O'Neill, who sadly passed away on 21 December 2018. Not merely was Michael a distinguished Romantics scholar and British poet, he was also a Coordinating Editor of the Modern British and Irish unit of *OHOPE*, for which he provided expert, collegial leadership. For Volume 2 of *OHOPE*, the editors wish to dedicate the volume on Middle English poetry to the memory of Derek Pearsall, whose influential contributions to the field ranged over criticism, literary history, biography, textual editing, and manuscript culture.

Contents

List of Abbreviations	xix
List of Contributors	xxi
Editorial Note	xxiii

1. Introduction   1
   Helen Cooper and Robert R. Edwards

PART I CONTEXTS

2. Historical and Political Changes: The Norman Conquest to the
   Hundred Years' War   15
   Laura Ashe

3. Poetic Sites   37
   Ralph Hanna

4. Manuscripts: The Textual Record of Middle English Poetry   54
   Simon Horobin

PART II LITERARY CULTURE

5. The Poetic Field, I: Old and Middle English Language and Poetry   71
   Richard Dance

6. The Poetic Field, II: Anglo-Latin   88
   Siân Echard

7. The Poetic Field, III: Anglo-French   104
   Keith Busby

8. The Poetic Field, IV: Welsh   118
   Victoria Flood

9. Verse Forms   128
   Ad Putter

10. Poetic and Literary Theory   145
    Andrew Galloway

xvi CONTENTS

PART III 'MATERE'

11. Poetry and National History   167
Caroline D. Eckhardt

12. Poetry in Its Age: Satire and Complaint   187
Craig E. Bertolet

13. Doctrine and Learning   200
Stephen M. Yeager

14. Poetry and the Bible   212
Jacqueline Tasioulas

15. Saints' Lives and Sacred Biography   227
Karen A. Winstead

PART IV GENRE POETICS

16. Narrative on the Margins: Tales and Fabliaux   245
Christopher Cannon

17. Religious and Didactic Lyrics   257
Denis Renevey

18. Secular Lyrics   274
Susanna Fein

19. Non-Cyclic Romances of Love   294
Rhiannon Purdie

20. Romances of the Ancient World   309
Wolfram R. Keller

21. The Matter of Britain   323
Elizabeth Archibald

22. Crusade Romances and the Matter of France   339
Marcel Elias

23. The 'Matter of England'   356
Andrew James Johnston

PART V THE RICARDIAN POETS

24. *Piers Plowman* 375
    Nicolette Zeeman

25. The *Gawain*-Poet 392
    Helen Cooper

26. Chaucer's Courtly Poetry 409
    David Lawton

27. *The Canterbury Tales* 425
    Barry Windeatt

28. John Gower 440
    R. F. Yeager

29. Reception of the Middle English Poetic Tradition 457
    Julia Boffey

Complete Bibliography 470
Index 517

List of Abbreviations

AND	*Anglo-Norman Dictionary*
ANTS	Anglo-Norman Text Society
DIMEV	*Digital Index of Middle English Verse*
DOE	*Dictionary of Old English*, ed. Angus Cameron et al.
DOEWC	*Dictionary of Old English Web Corpus*
EETS	Early English Text Society
e.s.	extra series
IMEV	*Index of Middle English Verse*, ed. Carleton Brown and Rossell Hope Robbins
LAEME	*A Linguistic Atlas of Early Middle English*
LALME	*A Linguistic Atlas of Late Mediaeval English*
ME	Middle English
MED	*Middle English Dictionary*, ed. Sherman Kuhn, Hans Kurath, and Robert E. Lewis
MS	manuscript
NIMEV	*New Index of Middle English Verse*, ed. Julia Boffey and A. S. G. Edwards
OE	Old English
OED	*Oxford English Dictionary*
n.s.	new series
o.s.	original series
PL	Patrologia Latina (Patrologiae Cursus Completus. Series Latina)
SATF	Société des anciens textes français
s.s.	supplementary series
STS	Scottish Text Society

List of Contributors

Elizabeth Archibald *Durham University*

Laura Ashe *University of Oxford*

Craig E. Bertolet *Auburn University*

Julia Boffey *Queen Mary University of London*

Keith Busby *University of Wisconsin–Madison*

Christopher Cannon *Johns Hopkins University*

Helen Cooper *University of Cambridge*

Richard Dance *University of Cambridge*

Siân Echard *University of British Columbia*

Caroline D. Eckhardt *Pennsylvania State University*

Robert R. Edwards *Pennsylvania State University*

Marcel Elias *Yale University*

Susanna Fein *Kent State University*

Victoria Flood *University of Birmingham*

Andrew Galloway *Cornell University*

Ralph Hanna *University of Oxford*

Simon Horobin *University of Oxford*

Andrew James Johnston *Freie Universität Berlin*

Wolfram R. Keller *Freie Universität Berlin*

David Lawton *Durham University*

Rhiannon Purdie *University of St Andrews*

Ad Putter *University of Bristol*

Denis Renevey *Université de Lausanne*

Jacqueline Tasioulas *University of Cambridge*

Barry Windeatt *Emmanuel College, Cambridge*

Karen A. Winstead *Ohio State University*

R. F. Yeager *University of West Florida*

Stephen M. Yeager *Concordia University*

Nicolette Zeeman *University of Cambridge*

Editorial Note

All *OHOPE* volumes work from the Series Style Guide, a modified version of the one used by Oxford University Press for humanities publications. Individual *OHOPE* volumes may further modify the Style Guide according to needs—for instance, the need to print and translate Old and Middle English in Volumes 1–3, and early modern Scots in Volume 4. Because of the linguistic diversity of poetry in Middle English, the editors of Volume 2 have followed the judgement of contributors in matters of quotation and orthography.

Where feasible, then, the standard editions of all authors have been quoted and cited. Primary texts are cited in full in the notes on their first occurrence, with abbreviated in-text citations thereafter. Secondary texts are cited in full in the notes on their first occurrence, with an abbreviated endnote thereafter.

When difficult words or phrases appear in the quotation of primary texts, they will be marked with an asterisk (*) and supported by a marginal gloss.

Quotations from classical authors generally come from the Loeb Classical Library. For convenience, all Greek words quoted in the texts are transliterated. All Latin quotations are translated into English.

Each *OHOPE* volume concludes with a detailed, alphabetised Bibliography, combining primary and secondary sources, and citing works identified in the individual chapters themselves.

1

Introduction

Helen Cooper and Robert R. Edwards

The terminal dates of this volume—1100–1400—mark a pivotal phase in the overall project of writing a history of poetry in English. It is in this period that vernacular writing in English emerges for a second time and offers the topics, forms, and means of expression that will comprise something approaching a recognised national tradition in the fifteenth and sixteenth centuries. These developments are by no means uniform or neatly ordered, yet by the end of the period key features have been established. Linguistic changes in morphology and lexicon have generated distinctive registers of diction and style in English usage. Native poetic forms have incorporated models from Latin and French with their different metrical bases, their reliance on rhyme and stanza, and their broader generic range. The materials adapted to composition have expanded the imaginative and practical scope of poetry in a national vernacular still marked by regional features. The terminal date for our volume—1400—anticipates the death in 1408 of John Gower, the great contemporary of Geoffrey Chaucer. By then, this period has by convention become the Age of Chaucer, and the influence of Chaucer as the father of English poetry continues unbroken through Spenser and Shakespeare (James Joyce used the epithet with enthusiasm). But as this volume demonstrates, the entire age was still richer and vastly more diverse than even its iconic poet.

The history of poetry in this period is at once discontinuous and distinctive. The Norman Conquest of 1066 did not abolish poetry in English. Before the Conquest, late Old English poetry was already in competition with works in Latin and Old Norse at the Anglo-Danish court (1018–42), and it developed in a didactic and panegyric vein that was distinguishable stylistically and thematically from the 'classical' poetics of *Beowulf* and the elegies preserved in the great codices assembled around the year 1000. As one instance, the entry for 1087 in the Peterborough Chronicle, which records William the Conqueror's death, includes an Old English poem ('The Rime of King William') in the new form of rhyming couplets enumerating his public acts and failings. In monastic culture, Old English endured into the thirteenth century in the antiquarian glossing of the Tremulous Hand of Worcester. Rather than end poetry in English, the Conquest disrupted the administrative and ecclesiastical structures supporting textual culture altogether; it shifted quickly to Latin and then to French in the next century as the language of governance and cultural authority. It thus truncated the record, if not the practice, of poetry in English. The post-Conquest history of English poetry is of necessity an account of emerging vernacular practices on multiple fronts, derived from a partial, chance record of composition, transmission, and reception, both oral and written.

The changes in language and culture that accompanied the emergence of Middle English poetry have governed a number of the editorial decisions made for this volume. First, we take the series title as a governing premise. This is a history of poetry, not of literature more broadly; and so the emphasis falls more on poetics than on the theoretical, political, and historical questions that have recently dominated much broader literary history.

Helen Cooper and Robert R. Edwards, *Introduction*. In: *The Oxford History of Poetry in English*. Edited by Helen Cooper and Robert R. Edwards, Oxford University Press. © Helen Cooper and Robert R. Edwards (2023).
DOI: 10.1093/oso/9780198827429.003.0001

Those questions cannot, of course, be overlooked; our initial chapters address them as necessary contexts, and later chapters bring them to bear on the poetry as needed. But they are not the sole or primary focus of this volume. By emphasising poetics, we mean to foreground both the imaginative representation of materials (often received materials) and formal expression in metre, poetic form, vocabulary, and aesthetic structure. This emphasis results, we believe, in less of a narrowing of focus than would be true for later periods, since poetry in Middle English covered many areas that were later taken over by prose: it was regularly used for biblical and fictional narrative, doctrinal works, much practical or mnemonic material, and history that moved more towards legend than chronicle.

Second, this is a history of poetry *in English*, not of poetry in England. Recent literary history has rightly emphasised how much was written in the other languages of the trilingual country that England became after the Norman Conquest: French in increasingly distinct insular versions and Latin as both a living tradition and source for classical 'auctores' in the schools. Although a large proportion of Middle English texts was derived from French or Latin originals, if a writer were aiming for close translation of the source, the chosen medium would almost always be prose, not poetry. A poem of any length is much more a matter of adaptation, often such free adaptation as to amount to an original work. The French poetry written in England in the twelfth century was in many respects precocious, setting the pace for writing on the Continent; but its influence on Middle English poetry deserves analysis on its own terms, work by work, and the chapters in this volume that consider French focus their study on what effect it had on the changes and achievements of English-language poetics. The enlarging vocabulary of English into new etymological areas during the period demonstrates how people thought, spoke, and on occasion wrote in more than one language, John Gower being a prime example. They were ready, too, to mix English with other languages in macaronic poetry. The fifteenth century, covered in Volume 3 of this series, marks the first period when English poetry drew on its own linguistic predecessors for sources or models, broadly on Geoffrey Chaucer and Gower, and on William Langland in a narrower sphere of protest and reform poetry. In the twentieth century, as English was becoming a dominant world language, 'poetry in English' itself became a worldwide movement, when other cultures absorbed and transformed it; in the Middle Ages, English was the subaltern language, with negligible wider influence beyond the Channel (Gower was the first English poet to be translated, into Portuguese and Spanish). The very terms of the series title—a history of poetry in English—thus encode a steadily enlarging set of meanings across its fourteen volumes, with the medieval centuries foundational, if not revolutionary, in that process.

Third, we have accepted periodisation in a qualified and pragmatic sense. If the narrative arc of this volume ends with metropolitan writers poised to be joined together in a tradition of English poetry that they could not fully foresee, what lies before and between involves fractures, relocations of time, and significant epicycles. There is no narrative moving towards consolidation. The earliest Middle English texts, such as *The Proverbs of Alfred*, *Poema Morale*, the *Ormulum*, and Laȝamon's *Brut*, had specific, local audiences; they could imagine their fictional origins with sophistication and literary self-consciousness (as in Alfred's summoning the powerful and learned of the realm to an assembly at Seaford for moral instruction, or Laȝamon's setting Wace's *Roman de Brut* between Bede and other sources as he compiles his poem); they generated chains of reception and reuse, yet remain curiously isolated as points of origin. These discontinuities of time in the poetic record have their counterparts in the regional character of much Middle English poetry, though networks of circulation carry poems beyond their places of composition, often transformed in content and language during the process. In this respect, the circulation of works in manuscripts creates a form of periodisation, as poems move across the boundaries of dialects and reading communities in successive stages of transmission. From the thirteenth century onwards, English poetry establishes a more expansive record of composition and transmission, particularly for romances and lyrics, at times in miscellanies and anthologies with a mixture of languages. In the second half of the fourteenth century, poets choose both to write major works in English and to exert a measure of control over their poetic canons. The latter aim can be seen variously in Langland's versions of *Piers Plowman*, Chaucer's Prologues to the *Legend of Good Women* and 'Retraction', and Gower's control over the production of his works and the topics of his final poems, which form a coda to his trilingual corpus.

The chapters of this volume follow the general plan for the series, which is to give readers an overview of their respective topics and to make original contributions to commentary on the poetry. We have asked our contributors to be selective and incisive rather than comprehensive. The chapters typically frame the large issues and then deal with specific examples in detail, focusing on the imaginative and formal dimensions. We have likewise exercised selection in designing the volume, aiming to show what poetry can achieve as a medium in this period rather than all that it covers. One issue that remains prominent but unresolved is the place of gender within the history of poetry in this period. Marie de France and Clemence of Barking produce notable works in French in the twelfth century, and Katherine Sutton has been credited with directing Latin liturgical drama at Barking Abbey in the late fourteenth century, but there is no direct evidence of women as poets in English, despite their considerable influence as patrons and readers.

In the remainder of this chapter, we review the materials and plan of the volume, and end with a brief example of poetry's imaginative and expressive capacity as it emerges over the three centuries we cover.

Contexts

The opening chapters of this volume address the contexts in which poetry in English re-emerges and develops. Laura Ashe argues in Chapter 2 that English was ubiquitous and largely 'inevitable' in Anglo-Norman England: though a subaltern language, it was always linked to politics and cultural power in the public sphere. Didactic poetry, devotional and secular lyric, and chronicle narrative and romance in English cohabit with similar works in Latin and French; we have in all three languages adjacent traditions with differential uses and prestige at any given point. Before the late fourteenth century, as Ralph Hanna (Chapter 3) demonstrates, the geography of English writing is largely regional or local, centred on communities of readers and the coteries of clerical and lay households. Composition serves specific, isolated needs, while the later circulation of works can bear the marks of adaptation to the dialects of scribes and other copyists. One consequence for poems attaining a wide circulation is that a work becomes known only in the singularities of textual transmission. The life of the poem is consequently the received form in which readers happen to encounter it. Manuscripts with poetry in English reflect what Simon Horobin (Chapter 4) terms 'localised literary culture'. Many take the form of assemblages of individual poems and groups of compositions. Scribal production in notable collections such as the Harley, Digby, and Vernon manuscripts frequently incorporates a principle of organisation. Some manuscripts were clearly produced by gathering booklets as required

4 MEDIEVAL POETRY: 1100–1400

for bespoke production. Late in the period, major works in English occupy whole codices; presumably copied from exemplars in a similar format, they suggest canonical status for poets. In addition, such manuscripts in deluxe format may create a secondary demand for other compositions outside the immediate audience, as seems the case for assembling the minor works of Chaucer and Lydgate in the fifteenth century.

Literary Culture

The literary languages of medieval England comprise a dynamic poetic field rather than isolated traditions. English poems, including those that hover on the border of Old and Middle English, involve a diversity of grammatical forms and lexical resources, though the wide adoption of French loan words is more a feature of the fourteenth century than those immediately following the Conquest. The crucial dynamic, as Richard Dance (Chapter 5) points out, is that, within the overall linguistic developments of English, poets, even in the earliest surviving texts, find occasions to make innovations with lasting impact on their traditions and on the language they employ. Anglo-Latin poetry, as Siân Echard (Chapter 6) remarks, introduces developments in style, voice, and authority that are shared by writers in English and English writers in Latin. It joins the works of classical and Continental writers as part of the school curriculum and offers literary models in genres, such as heroic poems, satires, and legends, as well as formal features, such as rhyme and stanzas, for non-narrative works. Insular productions in French, long recognised by scholars for their early achievements, decisively shift the poetic field for post-Conquest English poets. Keith Busby (Chapter 7) contends that they reflect, on the one hand, a narrowing range of commissions, patronage, and presentation to the *langue d'oïl* (the forms of medieval French in central and northern France); on the other, they foster genres outside native English traditions, such as the *chanson de geste* (medieval epic), *roman antique* (vernacular rewriting of classical materials), and romance, as well as religious and didactic topics, and introduce new possibilities in metre (notably, tetrameter lines) and verse form (notably, through the introduction of rhyme and stanzas). English, French, and Latin poetry share manuscript contexts in a number of significant collections; English works from French and Latin sources are more often adaptations than translations. Welsh poetry, by contrast, has a limited influence in loan words and names. Victoria Flood (Chapter 8) remarks that the reciprocal influence of English on Welsh lyric can be seen in borrowings of vocabulary, adaptations, macaronic works, and poetic experiments. Outside the lyric, French and Latin are the likely intermediaries for Welsh materials in Arthurian romance. Anglo-Scottish poetry produced few examples in this period—its first great age came in the fifteenth century—so it is not given a chapter of its own here, though mention is made of John Barbour's *Brut* and the *Scottish Legendary*; fuller attention is given to it in Volume 3. Nor have we provided a separate treatment of the little Middle English poetry written in Ireland (the 'Kildare' and 'Luscombe' poems).

In original compositions and adaptations, poets work in verse forms broadly based on the regularity of beats within individual lines, and in this respect medieval poetry marks the transition to the new forms of prosody that characterise English poetry down to the emergence of free verse. Early Middle English poetry was written without line division: the change to a lineated verse layout came about only in the course of the thirteenth century. The manuscript layout of poems, especially when they are written continuously as prose, can obscure the metrical patterns for works that base metre on stressed syllables.

For an early work like the *Ormulum*, the septenary verses (lines of seven feet with a caesura) depend, as in its Latin models, on the systematic alternation of stressed and unstressed syllables; other works can take less regular patterns. By the fourteenth century, four-beat lines, which remain distinct from regular octosyllabic lines in French poetry, are one norm of versification. Gower and Chaucer display metrical regularity, Gower writing consistent iambic tetrameter and Chaucer writing pentameter with somewhat greater flexibility for unstressed syllables, notably in trochaic inversion. Chaucer's variations, as Ad Putter (Chapter 9) observes, allow an approximation to 'living speech'. Rhyme, as the example from the Peterborough Chronicle indicates, appears in Old English verse, but Middle English poets adapt it from Latin and French models and use it in both couplets and stanzaic forms, including tail-rhyme stanzas (a form typically of six or twelve lines in which a short line follows two rhyming couplets and links the three-line units in the stanza: for example, *aabccb* or *aabccbddbeeb*). As with metre, manuscript transmission and the layering of scribal dialects in a text can at times obscure rhyme. Alliteration by itself and in combination with rhyme appears as a formal device from the earliest poems to the formal achievements of Langland and the *Gawain*-poet in the later fourteenth century. Because alliteration has an extensive historical and regional span and so has a place in a range of chapters within this volume, we have not included a separate discussion of the Alliterative Revival postulated for the second half of the fourteenth century.

The theoretical concerns that underlie and shape poetry in English are less easily located than the practical techniques and models for composing verse. Their sources lie in pedagogy, scriptural commentary, and the requirements for clerical instruction in grammar and doctrine promulgated in Canon 11 of the Fourth Lateran Council in 1215. Orm, Laȝamon, and the anonymous poet of *The Owl and the Nightingale* write English poems within ecclesiastical culture, and they are alive to its textual machinery and broad concerns with authorship, signification, allegory, and forms of discourse. Later writers adapt and fully display features such as prologues, glosses, and appeals to authority and tradition. Translation is a conspicuous site of self-reflexive commentary on writing; at the same time, the large theoretical issues—the truth claims of fiction, the power of language to represent, the poet's relation to literary antecedents—surface as themes and topics within the poems themselves. There are no Middle English equivalents to the poetic handbooks composed for languages such as Provençal, French, or Welsh until the sixteenth century. What we might identify as a vernacular engagement with theory becomes fully visible in the fifteenth century, yet the influence clearly emerges earlier in what Andrew Galloway (Chapter 10) describes as a 'set of emphases' rather than prescriptions that were adapted and enacted by poets writing in English, as they were by poets in Latin and other vernaculars in England and Europe.

'Matere'

A striking feature of the re-emergence of poetry in English is the range of topics—'matere'— that provide fit subjects for verse. Part III begins with materials close to human experience and ways of living. Caroline D. Eckhardt (Chapter 11) explores the fabrication of a comprehensive national history in the *Brut*-narratives, which reach beyond the limits of earlier chronicle histories to connect legendary origins to contemporary events through 'a reiterative web of translations, borrowings, adaptations, and new contributions' from multiple sources. Composed between the late twelfth and early fourteenth centuries, the poems register a continuing influence in their later circulation and share 'sibling similarities' with romance in their topics and literary uses. Satire and complaint are the two genres that Craig E. Bertolet (Chapter 12) examines as poetry specific to its age. He distinguishes satire, as writing directed against persons, from complaint, which addresses the social issues driven by the shifts from production and labour towards a money economy. This tradition of topical commentary employs alliterative lines, stanzas of various forms, and word play, and it shares manuscript contexts with later poems addressing contemporary conditions. Stephen M. Yeager's discussion (Chapter 13) of doctrine and learning divides the materials of orthodox belief from the 'lore' of science and nature. In both domains, poetry serves the practical aims of memory and recovery for specialists and lay audiences through the formal structuring of knowledge and the powers of institutional authority. If the received 'matere' is fixed in content and purpose, the poetry remains open to formal innovations and challenges.

Authoritative narratives in religious and spiritual life are the topics of the two following chapters. Jacqueline Tasioulas (Chapter 14) approaches biblical poetry as a process of composition that enhances Scripture 'by moralisation, commentary, and amplification'. Serving salvation without any anxiety about committing sacrilege, biblical verse in the vernacular can paraphrase, interpret, and add examples to its source. Following the model of Peter Comestor, English poets expect the Bible to be supplemented by other works from a variety of sources, including secular and apocryphal materials. Their treatments feature ingenuity, formal variety, and a fascination with language itself as a means and object of understanding. Saints' lives and sacred biography, as Karen A. Winstead (Chapter 15) shows, offer poets remarkable possibilities for invention and expression. The Katherine Group stands on the border of poetry and prose, its alliteration a feature of both modes. Collections such as the *South English Legendary* are evolving compilations, generally in septenary couplets. Other collections employ tetrameter couplets and stanzaic forms. In the varying treatments of the legend of St Margaret, the selection of detail and verse form aims to produce markedly different effects while retaining a focus on narrative action. In the late fourteenth century, legends and miracle stories prove a rich ground for experiments in theme and technique.

Genre Poetics

Just as there is no writing on poetic technique in Middle English, there is no theoretical writing on genre: what we think of as genre was recognised and distinguished by content, by its subject matter, rather than by a categorising label. Genre became one of the defining and vitalising characteristics of English poetry from the sixteenth century onwards, but what might seem a lack of interest earlier does not mean a lack of awareness. One question that both lyric and narrative verse continually advance has to do with fiction as a discursive mode within poetry. The issue is epitomised by the tales discussed by Christopher Cannon (Chapter 16), which address the nature of 'genre poetics' across the whole period. Cannon reviews the classical and medieval disavowals of fictional narrative as neither truthful nor verisimilar. He finds that in tales and fabliaux plot serves not only as a mechanism of narrative action but also as a rhetorical 'colour' that amplifies meaning. Plot-driven tales prove useful as a device in devotional literature and sermons and stand by themselves in a small body of poetic works, trading on well-crafted action and verbal wit, that appears in the late thirteenth and early fourteenth centuries. By the end of the fourteenth century, English poets adapt the resources of plot to generate other narratives, to gather a series of tales within a narrative frame, and to anchor tales that reflect on the nature and claims of their own art.

Religious poems, by any definition or measure, dominate the corpus of Middle English poetry, both in narrative and in lyric. Religious lyrics are works of celebration, praise, teaching, devotion, penance, liturgical adornment, and spiritual reflection. Denis Renevey (Chapter 17) finds in their speakers—whether cast as male or female, religious or lay—not just an expression of subjective experience but a 'public interiority', a performative quality that allows individual readers and communities to resituate and renew the works, adding resonance to their meaning. Moreover, in their manuscript contexts, the poems show patterns of aesthetic structure and ordering that make meaning; here, too, they move across languages and draw selectively on resources such as biblical and courtly diction and the formal devices of native, French, and Latin composition.

Secular lyrics, by contrast, comprise a notably smaller corpus than religious lyrics. A seemingly miscellaneous array in a wide variety of verse forms, they have frequently been categorised by topic and theme or divided into roughly popular and courtly works. Susanna Fein (Chapter 18) contends, however, that as an ensemble the secular lyrics record 'moments in the life of the body' that register both sensation and experience in the material world. Some survive by chance in margins, flyleaves, and inserts, but many overlap and interact with religious writing in anthologies and miscellanies. As with religious lyrics, a whole-manuscript approach reveals that secular lyrics migrate across the literary languages of England and multiple contexts of use and meaning. Their links to embodied life extend as well to music, dance, and performance.

Like the lyric, the romance is a signature genre of Middle English poetry. We begin discussion of the romance by standing to the side of its most often-cited description—Jean Bodel's thirteenth-century division of romance into the great 'matters' of France, Britain, and Rome. Jean provides a partial, overly influential, account of the topics represented by the genre: Rhiannon Purdie (Chapter 19) notes that roughly one third of the extant English romances deal with other topics. She proposes that suspending the expectations associated with narratives traditionally focused on Charlemagne, Arthur, and classical antiquity may, in fact, have freed poets to revise conventions such as love and friendship or to change narrative point of view by reversing gender perspectives. Moreover, the formal resources of the English romances—greater and more accomplished than that parodied as the 'rym doggerel' in Chaucer's 'Tale of Sir Thopas' (VII.925)—extend outwards to include other verse forms and long alliterative lines, and to achieve memorable effects in the repetition of episodes, themes, and language that colour emotions and establish patterns of significance.

The next three chapters return to the 'three great matters', but we have reversed Jean's sequence to follow a chronology that recognises the foundational roles of romance narratives in national and dynastic mythologies. The romances of antiquity present, as Wolfram R. Keller (Chapter 20) observes, a contested tradition and heroic genealogy from Thebes to Troy and Rome and onwards to the Alexander romances. Troy and Alexander are the prominent topics for English writers because the *translatio imperii* (successive relocations of empire) after Troy's downfall end in England, and Alexander provides a monitory example to nations and princes of worldly achievement and catastrophe. The multiple sources of both topics offer as well an occasion for English poets to establish their claims to authorship through compilation and invention and to apply the formal resources of the romance genre to epic materials.

The Arthurian tales that would follow the matter of antiquity chronologically in a master narrative present similar choices to English poets. Elizabeth Archibald (Chapter 21) examines their decisions to draw on chronicle and romance treatments, the former focused on the king and politics, the latter on individual knights and their adventures. The reshaping of narratives, she shows, occurs within a poetics of belatedness, with a different outlook and sensibility from twelfth-century French and Latin works; nevertheless, it involves an active engagement with the sources, perceptive mediation with romance tradition, and significant decisions about verse forms to adapt and reimagine the materials. The matter of France, like the Arthurian materials, requires poets writing in English to reconsider the scope of literary production. Marcel Elias (Chapter 22) argues that the crusade romances closely aligned with Charlemagne negotiate contemporary anxieties about the crusades as a beleaguered project. In so doing, they unsettle established oppositions between Muslims and Christians, faith and virtue, divine sanction and human failures, and just war and illegitimate violence. As works of translation, they seek innovative solutions to thematic problems inherited from the *chansons de geste*, to aesthetic ambiguity and nuanced characterisation, and to the technical problems of rendering the narratives in rhymed couplets and tail-rhyme stanzas with concomitant effects on action and dialogue.

The matter of England romances have entered the history of English poetry as a supplement to or extension of the established romance topics. As Andrew James Johnston (Chapter 23) contends, however, their claims to status as a genre with a defining horizon of expectations are early (*King Horn* and *Havelok* are the earliest extant romances in English) and substantial: their imaginative world is a pre-Conquest England, the dynastic and political tensions they explore have a resonance with contemporary audiences, they combine folk and hagiographic motifs, and their narratives depend on structural and narrative repetitions. In addition, the poems combine gestures towards oral performance with references to written texts in order to foreground a self-reflexive awareness of literary production that belies the long-standing dismissal of the aesthetic quality of the poems.

The Ricardian Poets

We know the identities of only a handful of poets from the early Middle English period, and with the exceptions of Orm and Laȝamon, few of the ones we do know wrote anything substantial. That changes in the late fourteenth century, with the four who have been labelled after the reign of Richard II as the 'Ricardian poets'; and only two of those—Geoffrey Chaucer and John Gower—went to any effort to record their names. 'William Langland' is largely an inference from within the poem, plus a scribal note in one manuscript; the *Gawain*-poet remains unidentified except by the epithet given by scholars, even the canon of his works being unprovable. The 'Ricardians' never formed a school: with the exception of Gower and Chaucer, who certainly knew each other's work, how far they had any acquaintance with each other's works remains a matter of conjecture. Despite overlaps of interest and content common to their age, they wrote in different contexts, different dialect areas, and different poetic forms. The one characteristic they share is the high quality of what they wrote, though they worked with very different ideas of poetry and what it could do.

As described here by Nicolette Zeeman (Chapter 24), Langland probably started the earliest, though he seems to have spent most of his life writing and rewriting his single work, *Piers Plowman*. Although it may have been partly or mostly written in London, it is a West Country poem in both dialect (West Midland) and poetic medium (alliterative verse). It takes the form of a series of dreams, their number enabling Langland to range over a multitude of topics, social, political, ethical, and religious; he is concerned with the good ordering of society, good government, economics, and the nature of salvation. Much of it is modelled as a debate between exemplary or allegorical personifications, where decisive answers are rarely given, and the 'I' who is the central consciousness (usually the dreamer, but sometimes Langland himself in the role of authoritative moralist) is engaged in a lifelong and unresolved quest. The period of its composition can be traced through its engagement with the labour unrest following on the Black Death, its concern with the rise of the cash economy, the relations between king, parliament, and commons, and the increasing theological disputes within the Church. Langland inspired just a few followers in the fifteenth century, but the popularity of the poem itself, as measured by the number of surviving manuscripts, is indisputable, even though its language and form meant that except for a brief revival in the mid-sixteenth century it largely disappeared from sight until revived by modern scholarly interests to take its place at the forefront of Middle English literature.

Much less well known in his own lifetime but rated equally highly now is the *Gawain*-poet, the presumed author of the four poems contained in British Library MS Cotton Nero A.x. None is given a title in the manuscript, though the editorial ones assigned to them have become accepted. Their common authorship is suggested not only by their presence in a single manuscript but by their high poetic quality, their shared dialect (north-west Midlands), and a range of shared points of interest, though three are broadly devotional and one is a secular romance. *Patience* and *Cleanness* are biblically based poems of ethical instruction in alliterative verse; *Sir Gawain and the Green Knight* is also alliterative, but its lines are grouped into long irregular stanzas that end with a bob and wheel (one two-syllable line followed by four three-stress lines rhyming *ababa*). *Pearl* combines a lament for a lost child, apparently the poet's daughter, with a lesson on salvation, written in a demanding stanza form that is also rich in alliteration. *Gawain* is courtly in orientation and profoundly concerned with what the implications of romance might be, in a way that sets it apart from the rest of Middle English romance. More strikingly than the other poems, it represents the high point of alliterative writing in Middle English, demonstrating all the virtues available to the form, though as Helen Cooper notes (Chapter 25), many of those virtues are unique to the way the English language had developed.

In contrast to Langland and the poet of Cotton Nero, Chaucer and Gower were rapidly acknowledged as the models for later poetry in English, and Chaucer's primacy of place is still widely recognised. English had by this date acquired dominance over French not just as the standard vernacular but as the leading one, though it was an English massively enriched by the absorption of vocabulary from Continental and Anglo-French and from Latin. Chaucer deployed those different etymological registers with supreme skill, to a point that enabled him to be regarded as single-handedly responsible for establishing English as the prestige language for poetry. The scope of his work, its generic range (he is the first person in English to engage directly with generic differences and definitions), its variety of subject matter, and its prosodic innovation require at least the two chapters he is given here. David Lawton (Chapter 26) is concerned with his more courtly poetry, the first body of work in English to which that epithet can be safely applied: the dream poems and *Troilus and Criseyde*, all masterpieces of voicing. Barry Windeatt (Chapter 27) focuses on the *Canterbury Tales*, a story collection that brings together in a single work much of what Middle English poetry had achieved earlier and adds to it a brilliance of style and range that set a new model of poetics for the modern world. In some respects, it has rarely been imitated, not least in the social nature of that poetics as conveyed through its various narrators. It is one of the paradoxes of the *Tales* that it is so difficult to identify an authentic inner Chaucerian voice within its ventriloquist acrobatics, however distinctive the Chaucerian quality of that voice may be.

10 MEDIEVAL POETRY: 1100–1400

The volume's survey of Middle English poetry ends where its origins lie, in an England of three languages, in John Gower's deliberate and unique choice to write in all three. He composed both a substantial major work and shorter ones in each of Latin, French, and English, and he writes moreover predominantly in their own prosodic forms: hexameters in Latin, rhyming stanzas in French, octosyllabic couplets—as distinct from the looser tetrameter couplet widely found elsewhere—in English. His poems share an interest in the ordering of society and in good public and private behaviour addressed to society at large and its constituent elements, though the fiction of the English *Confessio Amantis* is that this instruction is given to a single person, represented by a figure for Gower himself, in a series of exemplary tales. In contrast to the highly rhetorical form of his Latin poems, the *Confessio* is written without any such distracting fireworks, and, as R. F. Yeager notes (Chapter 28), is admired for precisely that.

The volume concludes with Julia Boffey's survey (Chapter 29) of how all this poetry travelled into the fifteenth century, in a fresh tradition that incorporated an explicit acknowledgement of its English foundations. French and Latin continued to supply content and models, but now Chaucer and Gower were added in a manner that established English poetry as a self-aware tradition in its own right that looked to its roots in its own language. Furthermore, a substantial amount of poetry from earlier in the Middle Ages continued to be copied, and was often therefore both preserved and imitated, in the course of this century, ready to be transmitted forwards to the future.

Middle English in Practice

The history of Middle English poetry is not, however, a teleological one, for all Chaucer's dominance by the end of the period. There were certainly massively significant changes, not least in the status and increasing richness of the language; but that does not mean that its poetry progressed towards a greater perfection, although later critics often assumed so. A four-line thirteenth-century lyric shows in miniature what Middle English poetry could achieve:

Now goth sonne* under wod*:	*sun/son*; *wood/cross*
Me reweth*, Marye, thi faire rode*.	*I pity*; *face/cross*
Now goth sonne under tree*:	*tree/cross*
Me reweth, Marye, thi sone and thee.[1]	

This was one of the most widely copied of Middle English lyrics; often written as prose, it appears in forty-one manuscripts of a devotional treatise ascribed to St Edmund Rich of Canterbury, which exists in versions in French (*Merure de Seinte Eglise*), Latin (*Speculum Ecclesiae*), and English (*Myrour of seint Edmund* or *Myrour of holi chirche*). In all those sources, it figures as functional poetry, explicitly as a focus for affective meditation. Regardless of the language of the surrounding text, it is always in English, and has to be so—its word play would be impossible to replicate in any Romance language. That word play too works differently from the wit, let alone the comedy, later associated with puns. The close repetitions are deepening, never merely tautologous. Its vocabulary draws solely on powerfully monosyllabic Old English, but it packs the language with meanings beyond the literal surface. What we might now regard as the Romanticism of its landscape is not the point.

---

[1] Text in Douglas Gray (ed.), *A Selection of Religious Lyrics* (Oxford, 1975), 17.

Through its creation of a strong visual picture of the sun setting behind a wood, it recalls metaphorically both the occlusion of the sun at the Crucifixion and the Virgin's grief at her dying son, a grief with which the reader, like the speaker, is called on to identify. It is an extraordinary piece of poetry; it is impossible to prove that the poet intended every effect, but it is still more impossible to assume that they did not. It is easy to think of English poetry of the Middle Ages as undergoing a process of evolution, which ever since Darwin has been equated with greater complexity. In many respects, and for some poetry, that is true; but lines such as these have already reached their own perfection. We hope that this volume will encourage more readers to respond to the whole range of Middle English poetry in fresher and fuller ways.

PART I
CONTEXTS

2

Historical and Political Changes

The Norman Conquest to the Hundred Years' War

Laura Ashe

On 26 January 1340, King Edward III of England publicly assumed the title and arms of king of France. This strategic gambit established the terms of what would become the Hundred Years' War, the protracted and bloody culmination of the kings of England's centuries-long involvement with their southern neighbour. Almost 300 years earlier, with the accession of Edward the Confessor in 1042, England's orientation in the world had fundamentally, if at first imperceptibly, changed. Early-eleventh-century England was part of the Scandinavian world, with a long history of North Sea warfare; across its archipelago England was the greatest power, but all borders were in flux: there were multiple warring kings and shifting territories in Wales, Ireland, and Scotland, and waves of invasion, raiding, and settlement from Denmark and Norway. England had been subject to Danish rule with the conquest of King Cnut in 1016, and the last serious threat of Danish invasion came as late as 1085.[1] King Æthelred II had married Emma of Normandy in 1002, and she had spectacularly followed the main chance by marrying Cnut on his accession, leaving her children by Æthelred in exile in Normandy. But when her son Edward the Confessor returned to England amid another succession dispute, apparently restoring the West Saxon royal line, he nevertheless brought with him the seeds of another world. Edward had spent his adult life in Normandy; he appointed his follower Robert of Jumièges archbishop of Canterbury in 1051, and although he was locked in a constant struggle for power with the rapacious Anglo-Danish family of Earl Godwine, and married Edith, sister of Harold Godwineson, the marriage produced no children. There is no doubt that Edward flirted with the possibility of a Norman successor, and when he died and Harold seized the crown, Duke William of Normandy launched his invasion under the papal banner and a claim of rightful inheritance.[2]

From Christmas Day 1066, when William the Conqueror was crowned, England's turn to the south had properly begun. But from a literary point of view change and development could not happen with such pinpoint focus. The great Old English poetic codices had been copied either side of the millennium, but in the ensuing decades new poetic composition in English appears to have been vanishingly rare: the Anglo-Danish court (and particularly queens) patronised elegant Latin verse and prose, which coexisted with the intricate praise poetry of the Old Norse skalds.[3] The fate of Old English as a language of governance and

---

[1] J. R. Maddicott, 'Responses to the Threat of Invasion, 1085', *English Historical Review*, 122 (2007), 986–97.

[2] On Edward's vacillation, see Stephen Baxter, 'Edward the Confessor and the Succession Question', in Richard Mortimer (ed.), *Edward the Confessor: The Man and the Legend* (Woodbridge, 2009), 77–118.

[3] See Elizabeth M. Tyler, *England in Europe: English Royal Women and Literary Patronage, c. 1000–c. 1150* (Toronto, 2017); Matthew Townend, 'Contextualizing the *Knútsdrápur*: Skaldic Praise-Poetry at the Court of Cnut', *Anglo-Saxon England*, 30 (2001), 145–79; Laura Ashe, *The Oxford English Literary History vol. 1: 1000–1350 Conquest and Transformation* (Oxford, 2017), 11–63.

Laura Ashe, *Historical and Political Changes*. In: *The Oxford History of Poetry in English.* Edited by Helen Cooper and Robert R. Edwards, Oxford University Press. © Laura Ashe (2023). DOI: 10.1093/oso/9780198827429.003.0002

16 MEDIEVAL POETRY: 1100–1400

administration is well known: after an initial attempt to take over the machinery as he found it, from around 1070 William ceased to issue royal writs in English, and the Latin, which had always functioned alongside written English as the language of authority, became virtually its sole vehicle for the next century or more.[4] As Domesday Book reveals, this was the linguistic marker of a wholesale transfer of property and power from the English to William's followers: Normans, French, Bretons, and Flemish.[5] Their written language was Latin; their shared spoken vernacular was French. But they did not have a written vernacular tradition.

French poetry emerged in England in the early twelfth century, nourished by the patronage of French-speaking aristocrats, evidently conditioned by awareness of the vernacular English literature which had flourished before the Conquest. The earliest major work of French verse which survives (in England or France) is Geffrei Gaimar's poetic chronicle *Estoire des Engleis*, which is an embellished translation of some version of the Anglo-Saxon Chronicles.[6] Before this insular development only one dialect of Old French had appeared in written poetry, around 1100: the Occitan verses of the troubadours, from much further south. When the Conqueror's great-grandson Henry of Anjou became Henry II of England in 1154, at the end of a long period of civil war between the Conqueror's grandchildren King Stephen and Henry's mother the Empress Matilda, he brought with him his formidable wife Eleanor, duchess of Aquitaine, granddaughter of one of the earliest known troubadours. Henry II became overlord of vast territories from Scotland to the Pyrenees; more profoundly and lastingly, this political alignment sealed the place of the French in England's literatures, as it did the cultural influence of the Francophone chivalric world.[7]

Twelfth- and thirteenth-century England under the Norman and Plantagenet kings saw the explosion of a documentary culture:[8] governmental bureaucracy expanded exponentially, in Latin and then increasingly in French as well, while literary developments saw an efflorescence of Latin history and chronicle, satire, poetry, philosophy, and religious writings of all kinds—and the rapid emergence of French verse (and later prose) in romance, hagiography, chronicle, and multiple other genres. Meanwhile, Old English continued to be written and copied in the twelfth century in some few circumstances: chiefly the continuation of the Peterborough manuscript of the Anglo-Saxon Chronicles to 1154, and the reproduction of the sermons and homilies of Ælfric and others, for use in preaching and pastoral care. But the era of Old English poetry was over. The form of Old English used in poetic composition had been a literary vernacular, highly standardised and formalised, and separate from the many different dialects of spoken English; with the end of governmental and institutional use and support of English in official contexts, that standard was lost.

However, English was never displaced as the language of the vast majority of the population. The clergy were trained in Latin, and the aristocracy and anyone with upwardly mobile pretensions learned to read and speak French, but from very soon after the Conquest,

---

[4] M. T. Clanchy, *From Memory to Written Record: England 1066–1307*, 3rd edn. (Chichester, 2013), 24–5.

[5] For an account of the few English landholders surviving in the 1086 survey, see Ann Williams, *The English and the Norman Conquest* (Woodbridge, 1995), 76–97.

[6] Geffrei Gaimar, in Ian Short (ed. and trans.), *Estoire des Engleis* (Oxford, 2009). On the inventive precocity of England's French literature, see Ian Short, 'Patrons and Polyglots: French Literature in Twelfth-Century England', *Anglo-Norman Studies*, 14 (1991), 229–49.

[7] For the strongest argument that French would have fallen out of literary use without the Angevin succession, see Bruce O'Brien, *Reversing Babel: Translation among the English During an Age of Conquests, c. 800 to c. 1200* (Newark, DE, 2011), chapter 6.

[8] The classic and indispensable study is Clanchy, *From Memory to Written Record*.

everyone's first language was English.[9] Moreover, and despite the intricate involvement of English and Continental politics, English society and culture were characterised throughout this period by a strong thread of xenophobia, and particularly (often voiced in raucous, unironic French) Francophobia.[10] After the loss of Normandy in 1204, English territories in France were concentrated in the south-west, and Henry III's reliance on his Poitevin and Savoyard allies and followers was a key focus for complaints about 'aliens'.[11] Edward I (r. 1272–1307) was forced once again into war with the French in 1294, when Philippe IV sought to exert greater control as overlord of the English-held territories, and as part of the peace agreement Edward married the French king's sister Margaret in 1299, while negotiations for the marriage of his son to the French princess Isabella began as early as 1298. Before and after the French war Edward spent his military and political energies on insular campaigns, defeating the Welsh and asserting overlordship of Scotland. His son Edward II (r. 1307–27) and Isabella were married in 1308, and in 1312 the future king Edward III was born, in a time of sustained peaceful relations between the two neighbours. But when the crisis came in English politics and burst into near-civil war in the 1320s, with bitter aristocratic factions turned against the unpredictable Edward II, Queen Isabella was instrumental in her husband's deposition in favour of his son, supported by her brother Charles IV and other Continental allies. By the time of Edward III's declaration of his claim to the French throne, the relationship between the two countries was irreducibly complex, both separate from—and yet inescapably negotiated through—the interactions of the two vernaculars.[12]

Against this background of cacophonous hybridity, much of our understanding of the place and importance of the earliest Middle English poetry must come from detective work, and from speculation. Focusing only upon what remains extant, present in fragments and margins and idiosyncratic experiments from the mid-twelfth century onward, risks occluding the mechanisms by which English poetry was able to re-appear at all, within a fully functioning literary culture dominated by two other high-status languages. I suggest that, in fact, this re-appearance was inevitable, but not for any single or simple reason. To some extent the nexus of cultural, social, and political circumstances that nurtured the earliest Middle English poetry can be teased out of historical anecdote, the local example which adumbrates an overarching pattern. More profoundly, the texts that survive speak to the context and the intertexts of their making, and so reveal, in part, the shadows cast by those that are lost, or were never written down.

Politics and English Poetry

One famous anecdote can help illuminate the public and political role throughout this period of English, of oral culture, and of ordinary people. On Thursday 18 October, 1191, William de Longchamp, chancellor of England, was ignominiously captured and imprisoned, seized by townspeople on the beach at Dover as he tried to flee to the Continent.

---

[9] See Ian Short, 'On Bilingualism in Anglo-Norman England', *Romance Philology*, 33 (1980), 467–79; Hugh M. Thomas, *The English and the Normans: Ethnic Hostility, Assimilation, and Identity 1066–c. 1220* (Oxford, 2003), 377–90.

[10] See Tim William Machan, *English in the Middle Ages* (Oxford, 2003), 39–54; Ashe, *Conquest and Transformation*, 406–11.

[11] See David Carpenter, 'King Henry III's "Statute" against Aliens: July 1263', *English Historical Review*, 107 (1992), 925–44.

[12] See Ardis Butterfield, *The Familiar Enemy: Chaucer, Language, and Nation in the Hundred Years War* (Oxford, 2009), 17–23, and more broadly *passim*.

18 MEDIEVAL POETRY: 1100–1400

William had been appointed to govern England during Richard I's absence on crusade, but he had made some influential enemies, and Richard's ambitious brother John led a group of magnates who deprived William of his office during a vituperative meeting in London on 10 October.[13] William fled to Dover and attempted to cross the Channel unrecognised by disguising himself as a woman; but he was caught out on the shore by a growing crowd and hustled off to be locked in a cellar in the town, while the news made its way to John and his followers.

Modern historians have recounted this as little more than a colourful story,[14] but it might be regarded as an embryonic constitutional crisis.[15] Contemporary accounts made the most of William's humiliation, but for our purposes what matters is the political seriousness of an event in which ordinary people were closely involved, combined with the light the episode throws on the languages of public discourse. The chroniclers tell us that French-born William was unable to talk his way out of trouble on the beach because 'he was completely ignorant of the English language' ('linguam Anglicanam prorsus ignorabat'). His tyrannical abuses of power apparently included 'contempt of the English in all things' ('spreta in omnibus gente Anglorum') and advancement of his low-born French family and cronies. Mocking these humble origins and William's attempts to disguise them, one writer complained that the chancellor surrounded himself with sycophantic minstrels and jesters, whom he paid to sing songs praising his name and fame ('ad augmentum et famam sui nominis emendicata carmina et rhythmos adulatorios comparabat') in the streets and market squares, attracting a crowd of them into his service from France.[16]

William de Longchamp's unpopularity could not disguise the arbitrary and illegal nature of his deposition, and another chronicler gave him a defiant speech in protest: 'de nulla administratione mihi a rege tradita me depono ... ego, cancellarius regis et regni justiciarius, contra formam totius juris judicatus, quia necesse est, fortioribus cedo'[17] ('I do not depose myself from any office conferred upon me by the king ... I, the king's chancellor and the kingdom's justiciar, am condemned against all form of law. It is under compulsion that I give way to greater strength'). The situation was febrile; William continued to serve Richard I on the Continent, and was even reinstated as chancellor in 1194. But this comparatively minor event nonetheless illuminates a constitutional difficulty which would effloresce into political action within decades. The mechanisms of power at issue here can be seen in the provisions and enforcement of Magna Carta; in outright civil war in 1215–17 and 1264–7; and ultimately in the depositions of Edward II and Richard II. Kings' deputies could abuse their power; but so could kings themselves. On battlefields, in charters, and in the growing institution of parliament, the English hammered out the idea that the king was subject to the law; that loyalty was due to the crown, rather than the person of the king; and that it was the duty and prerogative of the 'community of the realm' to establish what was in its own interests, and hence fitting for the crown.[18] These developments had their roots in ideas established long before the Conquest, and were nurtured in the hybrid political cultures of Anglo-Norman England.[19]

---

[13] Ralph V. Turner, 'Longchamp, William de (d. 1197)', *ODNB*.

[14] See, e.g., the brief but vivid account of John Gillingham, *Richard I* (New Haven, CT, 1999), 227–9.

[15] William Stubbs (ed.), *Chronica magistri Rogeri de Houedene*, 4 vols. (London, 1868–71), 3.lxxxiii–lxxxiv.

[16] Roger of Howden (unattrib.), in William Stubbs (ed.), *Gesta regis Henrici Secundi Benedicti abbatis*, 2 vols. (London, 1867), 2:216.

[17] Richard of Devizes, *The Chronicle of Richard of Devizes*, in Richard Howlett (ed.), *Chronicles of the Reigns of Stephen, Henry II., and Richard I.*, 4 vols. (London, 1884–9), 3.418.

[18] See Ashe, *Conquest and Transformation*, 369–76, 416–26.

[19] Ashe, *Conquest and Transformation*, 110–16.

In their minor details and wider implications, the chroniclers' descriptions of William de Longchamp's fall have much to tell us about the situation of English poetry in the two centuries following the Conquest. The French chancellor was caught on Dover beach because he could not speak English—an incapacity for which his accuser mocks him. French was the shared language of the English and Continental aristocracy, but when Richard I raised his Continental followers to positions of great power in England, they were perceived as foreign, and any controversial action would see them subject to xenophobic attack. The ability to speak English emerges here as the key marker of English identity, because it was the first language of English-born people at all levels of society: and indeed, it had been so for decades beforehand. Meanwhile, for the overwhelming majority of the population, it was the only language in daily use. Taken together, these facts mean that the composition of English poetry and songs must have been a ubiquitous fact of everyday life; and that this oral-popular world was not closed to those who inhabited the learned and literate world. At first appearing alongside, and often in the (literal and cultural) margins of clerkly authoritative Latin and aristocratic-aspirational French, English was always profoundly intertwined with these artificially learned languages, and essentially prior to them in shaping the minds of bi- and trilingual authors. As literacy and documentary culture reached further into all strata of society, it was all but inevitable that the writing down and preservation of English poetry would grow and accelerate, and that over the centuries the majority vernacular and ubiquitous first language would gradually become an equal, and ultimately the foremost, partner in English literature's multilingual tradition.

A second aspect of relevance is the claim that William de Longchamp employed jesters and minstrels to sing his praises in the streets and marketplaces. The author sneers that he paid followers from France, but this seems of a piece with his xenophobic attack. For William's songs to make any impression on the townspeople, they would need to be in English; if his minstrels indeed sang in French in the market square, then William becomes an even more ridiculous figure. But perhaps the songs were in English; others certainly were; and either way, this gives us insight into an important social reality. The twelfth and thirteenth centuries saw the growing development of a politicised 'public sphere', a self-aware population engaged with current events, concerned with the machinery of government, and opinionated on the conduct of the powerful.[20] Richard of Devizes tells us that huge crowds attended the meeting in London where William was deposed, which took place in an open field to the east of the city: 'The nobles stood in the centre, close around whom was a circle of citizens, with a watchful public behind them, thought to be as many as ten thousand people'.[21] This number is clearly exaggerated, but certainly news must have spread fast, and widely: William had been made to surrender his office in London only a week before he was apprehended by the townspeople of Dover, imprisoning the man who had been their lord. English poetry played a self-conscious role in the development of this political consciousness, as Robert Mannyng observed a century later in his early-fourteenth-century rhymed chronicle, stating that he wrote:

> not for þe lerid bot for þe lewed
> ffor þo þat in þis land won
> þat þe Latyn no Frankys con,
> ffor to haf solace & gamen
> in felawschip when þai sitt samen.

[20] Ashe, *Conquest and Transformation*, 124–6, 300–5, 397–426.
[21] *Chronicle of Richard of Devizes*, 3.417: 'Tenuerunt majores medium, circa quos proxima fuit corona Quiritum, et populus spectans erat deorsum, ut æstimabatur, ad decem millia hominum'.

20 MEDIEVAL POETRY: 1100–1400

> And it is wisdom forto wytten
> þe state of þe land & haf it wryten:
> what manere of folk first it wan
> & of what kynde it first began.
> And gude it is for many thynges
> for to here þe dedis of kynges,
> whilk were foles & whilk were wyse,
> & whilk of þam couth mast quantyse,
> and whilk did wrong & whilk ryght,
> & whilk mayntend pes & fyght.[22]

(not for the learned but for the uneducated, for those who live in this land that know no Latin or French, to give them pleasure and entertainment when they sit companionably together. And it is wise to have knowledge of the state of the land, and to have it written down: to know what kind of people first conquered it, and what its origins are. And it is good for many reasons to hear of the deeds of kings: which were fools and which were wise, which of them was the most ingenious, and who did wrong and who did right, and who maintained peace or pursued warfare.)

Vernacular English discourse was never divided from the high politics of the realm. Regional jurors in the Domesday inquest of 1086 dated local happenings in Herefordshire and Norfolk to the time 'when Godwine and Harold were outlawed'—in London in 1051—and when 'Earl Tostig left England'—from Northumbria in 1065. In 1275, similarly, a Worcestershire jury dated an illicit burial to the time 'between the two battles in the 48th year of King Henry III'—Northampton and Lewes, 5 April and 14 May 1264, respectively.[23] Throughout this period national news was known nationally, with some precision: and it must have been passed on—from market, to tavern, to churchyard, in stories, anecdotes, and songs—in English.

As we see sharply increasing volumes of English poetic writing surviving from the late thirteenth and beginning of the fourteenth century, it appears in all contemporary genres which worked to shape society and public opinion—as chronicle, satire, debate, fantasy, fable, complaint, and parody. This was not the rebellion of an oppressed linguistic group against foreign rule; when English poetry voices condemnation of the powerful, it joins French and Latin writings in a shared chorus of political commentary and complaint—and that is only one mode of English poetry in the period.[24] Early-fourteenth-century poetry is characteristically experimental, adaptive, and appropriative; English is fully intertwined with French and Latin, in its manuscript contexts, and in its sources, models, and analogues—and often literally and minutely so, in macaronic verse. But more than a hundred years before this great expansion and acceleration, English poetry had re-emerged from the late twelfth century onward to make a substantial mark in the extant written record. These works stand as the surviving evidence of a thriving oral culture, which in a world of shared, functional, and community literacy gradually began to transform the written record.

The earliest Middle English poetry is found in three distinct and vitally important genres. First, the didactic poetry of preaching and pastoral instruction; second, the lyric of devotional and, though much less well preserved, of secular song; third, the narrative of

---

[22] Robert Mannyng of Brunne, in Idelle Sullens (ed.), *Chronicle* (Binghamton, NY, 1996), lines 6–20.
[23] J. R. Maddicott, 'Politics and the People in Thirteenth-Century England', *Thirteenth-Century Studies*, 14 (2013), 1–13 at 3.
[24] See Ashe, *Conquest and Transformation*, 419–29.

chronicle and romance. The earliest examples are sparse, but they are in no sense isolated:[25] they represent the rise in written English of genres which proliferated in French and Latin writing, and which aurally and orally animated the social and cultural lives of English speakers, in public and domestic spaces across the land. The very fact that some of the earliest surviving examples of Middle English poetry are geographically disparate, radically varied, and yet major poetic undertakings tells its own story. This was not the embryonic emergence of a new literature from a low-status vernacular, but the ambitious re-invention of adjacent, multilingual poetic forms in a rapidly shifting, regionally varied language: a vernacular that still carried the traces of its precocious literary past, and that was available to the whole population of a country self-consciously shaping its present and future.

English Poetry and Pastoral Care

The earliest substantial Middle English poem which now survives is very little read. Orm, an Augustinian canon most likely based in Bourne in Lincolnshire, undertook as early as the 1160s to produce a vast work of gospel paraphrase in English verse.[26] This was a period when surviving writing in English can almost always be associated with the demand for religious instruction in the majority vernacular; homiletic and hagiographical material was copied and circulated to supply an evident pastoral need, while little else survives.[27] Much of this material pre-dated the Conquest—many of Ælfric's homilies appear, often with active linguistic updating—but there also survive sermons with no known source, and some identifiable translations from contemporary French and Latin works. Nonetheless, most of this material is in prose. When Orm decided to render the gospels into English verse, he adopted a strict syllabic metre borrowed from clerical Latin, the iambic septenary (unstressed and stressed syllables indicated by x and /, respectively, in the passage below). Within this—and in support of it—he created his own spelling system, doubling consonants to indicate shortened vowels (regardless of stress).[28] Orm addresses the dedication of the work to his brother Walter:

> x / x / x / x /   x / x / x / x
>
> Icc hafe wennd inntill Ennglissh   Goddspelless hallȝhe lare,
>
> Affterr þatt little witt þatt me   Min Drihhtin hafeþþ lenedd.
>
> Þu þohhtesst tatt itt mihhte wel   Till mikell frame turrnenn,
>
> Ȝiff Ennglissh follc, forr lufe off Crist,   Itt wollde ȝerne lernnen,
>
> & follȝhenn itt, & fillenn itt   Wiþþ þohht, wiþþ word, wiþþ dede.[29]

---

[25] *Contra* Christopher Cannon, *The Grounds of English Literature* (Oxford, 2004).

[26] See M. B. Parkes, 'On the Presumed Date and Possible Origin of the Manuscript of the *Ormulum*: Oxford, Bodleian Library, MS Junius 1', in E. G. Stanley and Douglas Gray (eds), *Five Hundred Years of Words and Sounds: A Festschrift for Eric Dobson* (Cambridge, 1983), 115–27; rpt. in Parkes, *Scribes, Scripts and Readers: Studies in the Communication, Presentation and Dissemination of Medieval Texts* (London, 1991), 187–200.

[27] See Mary Swan and Elaine Treharne, (eds), *Rewriting Old English in the Twelfth Century* (Cambridge, 2000); Aidan Conti, 'The Circulation of the Old English Homily in the Twelfth Century: New Evidence from Oxford, Bodleian Library, MS Bodley 343', in Aaron J. Kleist (ed.), *The Old English Homily: Precedent, Practice, and Appropriation* (Turnhout, 2007), 365–402; Mary Swan, 'Preaching Past the Conquest: Lambeth Palace 487 and Cotton Vespasian A.XXII', in Kleist (ed.), *The Old English Homily*, 403–23; Mark Faulkner, 'Archaism, Belatedness and Modernisation: "Old" English in the Twelfth Century', *Review of English Studies*, 63 (2011), 179–203.

[28] See further on Orm's versification Chapter 10, and on his vocabulary and spelling system, Chapter 4.

[29] Orm, *Ormulum*, in Robert Holt and R. M. White (eds), *The Ormulum*, 2 vols. (Oxford, 1878), lines D13–22 (printed in long lines with caesurae rather than the editors' short lines, here and throughout). The dedication is

22 MEDIEVAL POETRY: 1100–1400

(I have turned the holy teaching of the Gospels into English, using the little intelligence that my Lord has entrusted me with. You thought that it might well be put to great profit, if English people would eagerly learn it for the love of Christ, and follow it, and fulfil it, in thought, in word, in deed.)

The *Ormulum*, as Orm himself named it, extends over more than 10,000 long lines of striking regularity,[30] and that represents only a fraction of the full programme he proposes at the outset of what must have been his life's work. Critics have largely engaged with the text only in terms of its role in a self-conscious development of vernacularity (and as a highly experimental linguistic phenomenon), but I have argued elsewhere that Orm's work displays genuine exegetical originality, and a thorough engagement with contemporary theological and pastoral developments.[31] The point is that this vast outpouring of Middle English verse comes in response to a particular nexus of social conditions, contingent not least upon a growing competition for the care of souls. As an Augustinian canon, Orm was a member of the new orders created with the express purpose of expanding pastoral care: preaching to the laity, providing them with the sacraments, aiding them with spiritual guidance, and increasingly regularising their access to confession. In England as elsewhere, Benedictine monks had long provided these services, and monastic houses had benefited greatly from the charitable donations of the grateful laity. It was the Benedictines who were responsible for most of the twelfth century's English-language homiletic compilations; they had no intention of giving up their lucrative role in the care of souls.[32] Orm's long poetic work stands as a competitive bid for the laity's attention and engagement: he uses English verse in apparently unprecedented ways, which must nonetheless reflect not only the Latin he encountered daily but also the oral world of English rhythmic song which surrounded him. And in the neglected content of the work, Orm is engaged in a wholesale campaign to win the souls of his parishioners, and to establish the supremacy of pastoral priests above all others, as guides and teachers who work for the whole community's salvation.

Orm explains his own highly idiosyncratic hierarchy of the faithful:

Þe maste lott tatt heȝhesst iss   Iss þatt lærede genge,

Þatt iss ȝuw sett abufenn ȝuw   To ȝemenn & to lærenn,

To spellenn ȝuw off Cristenndom,   To shrifenn ȝuw & huslenn,

To birrȝenn ȝuw i kirrkegærd,   To biddenn forr þe sawle.

Þiss lott off all Crisstene follc   Iss heȝhesst unnderr Criste,

Forr itt iss set her att te ster   To sterenn baþe þoþre.

Þat oþerr lott iss all þatt follc   Þatt lifeþþ i clænnesse,

I maȝȝþhad & i widdwesshad   I minnstress & i tuness.

---

numbered separately and its line numbers are indicated with a D. The preface and all the ensuing homilies are line-numbered continuously.

[30] See Elizabeth Solopova, 'The Metre of the *Ormulum*', in M. J. Toswell and E. M. Tyler (eds), *Studies in English Language and Literature: 'Doubt Wisely'—Papers in Honour of E. G. Stanley* (London, 1996), 423–38: 'unparalleled in Middle English' (423).

[31] Laura Ashe, 'The Originality of the *Ormulum*', *Early Middle English*, 1 (2019), 35–54; references to earlier studies at note 8.

[32] See George Younge, 'Monks, Money, and the End of Old English', *New Medieval Literatures*, 16 (2016), 39–82 at 41–4.

Þiss lott iss heh biforenn Godd,   Forr þatt itt here onn erþe

Stannt inn to follȝhenn engleþed   Þurrh soþ clænnessess bisne ...

Þe þridde lott iss all þatt follc   Þatt wiþþ weddlac iss bundenn;

Þiss follc iss laȝhest, & tiss lott   Addleþþ þe læste mede,

Forr þatt teȝȝ hafenn allre masst   Off þeȝȝre flæshess wille,

& tohh swa þehh, ȝiff þeȝȝ weddlac   Rihht laȝhelike follȝhenn,

Þeȝȝ addlenn unnderr Crisstenndom   To brukenn eche blisse. (15,248–83)

(The great group that is highest is the host of the learned, who are set above you to lead and to teach, to instruct you in Christianity, to confess and absolve you, to bury you in the churchyard, to pray for your soul. This group of all Christian people is the highest under Christ, for they are set here at the helm to govern both the others. The next group is all the people who live pure lives, in virginity and in widowhood, in monasteries and in towns. This group is high before God, because here on earth they strive to imitate the angels in their example of true purity ... The third group is all the people who are bound in wedlock; these people are the lowest, and this group earns the least reward, because they have the greatest part of their fleshly desires. But even so, if they live fully lawfully in wedlock, they will earn enough in Christendom to enjoy eternal bliss.)

For Orm, monks have nothing to do with the pastoral mission; their chaste and harsh existence earns them a heavenly reward, 'ȝiff þatt itt iss haldenn rihht' (6298: 'if it is rightly undertaken'), but their lives are essentially and properly confined to the cloister; they must entirely flee the business of the world, and occupy themselves with prayers, fasting, vigils, and scourging their own flesh.[33]

In fact, by explaining that the second rank of the faithful includes all those who live chastely—monks in their monasteries and the unmarried or widowed in towns—Orm makes an almost revolutionary claim. With this outright rearrangement of accepted hierarchies, he effectively launches a broadside attack on the Benedictines' claim to instruct the laity; and he elevates the spiritual ambitions of laypeople to new heights. He furthermore does so while showing, in great contrast with his portrayal of monasticism, how closely involved the parish priest is with his people. He offers an education in the Christian life, describing love as the root of all, and as a doctrine of real action in the world: '& her þu mihht nu sen full wel Þatt lufe iss all i dedess: / Forr maȝȝ na lufe berrȝhenn þe Wiþþutenn gode dedess' (5260–3: 'And here you can now see clearly that love is all in actions, for you cannot sustain love without good deeds'). And although Orm explicitly sets the priest over all others in his role as guide and teacher, the reciprocity implicit in his supreme doctrine of love—the shared duty of each to all others—is properly fulfilled as he describes what the laity should expect from their priest, balancing the relationship between pastor and flock as one of shared endeavour:

Nu loke ȝure preost tatt   he ȝuw bliþelike spelle,

Þatt he ȝuw illke Sunenndaȝȝ   Att allre læste lære,

Off all hu ȝuw birrþ ledenn ȝuw   & lefenn uppo Criste,

---

[33] Lines 6320–65; Ashe, 'Originality of the *Ormulum*', 42–3.

24 MEDIEVAL POETRY: 1100–1400

> & lufenn Godd & lufenn mann   & Godess laȝhess haldenn;
>
> & ȝuw birrþ swiþe bliþeliȝ   ȝuw turrnenn till hiss lare ...
>
> Nu ȝiff þatt ȝure preost &   ȝe Þus farenn ȝuw bitwenenn,
>
> Þa maȝȝ ben god till ȝure preost   & till ȝuw sellfenn baþe. (934–49)

(Now look to your priest that he preaches to you joyfully; that every Sunday he teaches you at the very least about how you should lead your life, and put your faith in Christ, and love God and love man, and uphold God's laws. And it is your duty most joyfully to submit to his teaching ... Now if you and your priest work together like this, you can benefit both your priest and yourself.)

And alongside his comfortable advice and humane guidance, Orm also shows himself to be in the vanguard of contemporary theological developments, as in his reference to the as yet ill-defined doctrine of the post-mortem purging of sins:[34]

> & ȝet we muȝhenn, þurrh þatt fir   Þatt Sannt Johan Bapptisste
>
> Spacc offe to þa sanderrmenn,   All full wel unnderrstanndenn
>
> Þatt fir þatt iss inn oþerr lif   To clennsenn menness sawless.
>
> Forr here uss clennseþþ Haliȝ Gast   Þurrh fulluhht & þurrh trowwþe,
>
> & tær þatt fir, ȝiff þatt we rihht   Her endenn unnderr shriffte. (10,464–73)

(And yet, by that fire of which St John the Baptist spoke to the messengers, we must full well understand that fire which is in the other life, to cleanse men's souls. For here the Holy Spirit cleanses us through baptism and through faith, and there that fire cleanses us, if we end our lives properly with confession.)

Orm's importance as an innovator in English poetry—like his precocious theological awareness—has been critically underestimated because the strictness of his syllable-counting metre has a potentially monotonous effect, only heightened by his frequent repetitions and multiple re-phrasings of the same thought. But we might make some unexpected comparisons, and see Orm's achievement in a different light. In an acknowledged masterpiece such as the French-language epic *The Song of Roland* (c 1100, surviving in a twelfth-century English manuscript)[35]—a sweeping account of Charlemagne's battles with the Muslims in Spain, centred on the death of the eponymous hero—the repetition and recasting of events in sequences of *laisses similaires*, monorhymed stanzas of variable length, is admired as an artistic and pragmatic tactic. It is a recursive narrative mode which gives depth and nuance to events shown from multiple perspectives, and allows for an inattentive audience—warriors in the hall—to grasp what matters, and never to lose sight of the work's core significance. Orm's work is no competition for *Roland*, to be clear, but he too is building an epic structure of meaning, addressing his message to everyone, repeating his explanations from different angles. He builds from the ground up, imbricating the daily lives of his flock with the lived experience of Christ's followers, and all earthly experience with the eternal reality which lies behind and illuminates human history: and all in a verse form designed to resound and engrain itself in the consciousness, rhythm like a chant, a pulse.

---

[34] Ashe, 'Originality of the *Ormulum*', 50–2.

[35] Oxford, Bodleian Library, MS Digby 23; bequeathed to Osney Abbey near Oxford by Master Henry of Langley (d. ?1263).

To be precise about this collocation, Orm's meaning and purpose are only, necessarily, given flesh in his writing of English verse. Both form and content embody an English community of the faithful: the pastor speaking directly to his flock, opening up Scripture in vernacular rhythms of speech, and promising his unlearned English audience that this simple knowledge can lead them to salvation. And just as Orm's poetic achievement stands alone for decades, so too is he precociously unorthodox in his generosity with and sensitivity to the complexities of lay lives, and in his responsiveness to changes happening around him as he wrote. When he states that those who live 'lawfully in wedlock' will earn eternity in bliss, he goes further than any orthodox pronouncement of his time; not until the canons of the Fourth Lateran Council in 1215 did a pope explicitly offer the promise of salvation to married Christians.[36] When Orm speaks of the possibility of confession's enabling purgatorial fire to purify us of our sins after death, he heralds a development which would be seized by the laity in the following century with unquenchable enthusiasm. Theological and doctrinal change in this period was debated and codified by popes and their most learned advisors, but changes in devotional practice were driven from the ground upwards. It is not accidental that the urgency of Orm's mission to save souls should issue in this great innovation in English poetry, and in the first significant poem to be written in Middle English. The mission and the poem were both essential developments, demanded by ordinary people. Reading Orm's autograph manuscript now is a humbling experience because it is all too clear that it may never have reached its intended audience; it is a much-corrected, still unfinished, radically chaotic draft, and it was never copied or, to our knowledge, circulated.[37] But it exists, and its magnitude—in several senses—is unarguable.

The fifteen-syllable long line Orm pioneered was widely used, adorned with rhyme. Closely contemporary with Orm, probably composed around the time of his death in the late twelfth century, is the verse sermon *Poema morale* (also known, at the suggestion of its most prominent scholar, as 'The Conduct of Life').[38] This poem survives in seven manuscripts, testifying to genuine influence and popularity, and quotations from it appear in multiple places. It is supremely designed to be memorable, to exercise the cadences of proverb and tag, tapping its rhythm out in rhyming couplets:

> Alto lome ich habbe igult a werke and a worde.
> Alto muchel ic habbe ispend to litel ileid on horde.[39]
> (All too often I have done wrong, in works and in words. All too much
> I have wastefully spent, too little safely saved.)
>
> Þe wel ne deð þe hwile he mai wel ofte hit sal him rewen.
> Þan alle men sulle ripen þat hie ar sewen. (21–2)
> (He who doesn't do right when he can shall evermore regret it. Then all
> men will reap what they have sowed.)
>
> Se man þe nafre nele don god ne nafre god lif lade.
> Are deað and dom cumeð to his dure he maiȝ him sore adrade. (123–4)

---

[36] See Ashe, *Conquest and Transformation*, 333–5, 181–3.

[37] Oxford, Bodleian Library, MS Junius 1, fully digitised at digital.bodleian.ox.ac.uk/inquire/p/90a06f70-880a-4b5b-bd30-798710afff11 [accessed August 2019].

[38] Betty Hill, 'The Twelfth-Century *Conduct of Life*, Formerly the *Poema morale* or *A Moral Ode*', *Leeds Studies in English*, n.s. 9 (1977), 97–144.

[39] Edited from the earliest witness in R. Morris (ed.), *Old English Homilies of the Twelfth Century from the Unique MS B. 14. 52 in the Library of Trinity College, Cambridge*. EETS o.s. 53 (London, 1873), 220–33, lines 11–12.

26 MEDIEVAL POETRY: 1100–1400

(The man who would never do good, never lead a good life, will be stricken
with fear when death and judgement come to his door.)

Ne mai non herte hit þenche ne tunge hit ne mai telle
Hwu muchele pine ne hwu fele senden beoþ in helle. (289–90)
(No heart can understand, nor tongue recount, how much agony there is
in hell, nor how many are sent there.)

These are not nuanced or complex theological statements—though it is striking that hell,
rather than heaven, is said to be beyond description—and notably, there is no concept of
purgatory in this poem at all; its dual theme is the desperate need to act for the soul's good in
this life, and the horrors of hell in the next. In comparison with the *Ormulum* it could even
be described as inhumane: human relationships are dismissed as worthless, as no more than
part of the worldly distraction which keeps us from saving our own souls.[40] But in its form
and effect—and given the undoubted success of both—this poem is an eloquent witness to
the importance of pastoral teaching, in driving English poetic composition, preservation,
and survival.

English Lyric Poetry

Writing in the late 1190s, Gerald of Wales tells an anecdote about a Worcestershire priest
who was kept awake all night by people singing in the churchyard. When he came to the
altar to begin mass in the morning, the song's refrain had fixed itself in his head:

pro salutatione ad populum, scilicet, 'Dominus vobiscum', eandem Anglica lingua
coram omnibus alta voce modulando pronuntiavit in hunc modum: '*Swete lamman
ðhin are*'.[41]

(Instead of the greeting to the people, that is, 'God be with you', in front of everybody he sang the same English phrase in a high voice, like this: 'Sweet lover, your
favour!')

Apparently the local bishop was so scandalised by this that he declared an indefinite anath-
ema on anyone singing the song thereafter. Such is the ephemeral fate of early Middle
English lyrics: we know they must have been ubiquitous, as popular song always has been,
but we have vanishingly little extant (as is also the case for the earlier period; surviving Old English poetry is a highly literary mode, which must have existed alongside a
very different popular tradition).[42] References to (and fragments of) English songs appear
in twelfth-century chronicles and saints' lives;[43] sometimes as jottings in the margins of

---

[40] See lines 29–36, 149–50, and discussion of this idea here and elsewhere in the period in Ashe, *Conquest and Transformation*, 96–8.

[41] *Gemma Ecclesiastica*, in J. S. Brewer, James F. Dimock, and George F. Warner (eds), *Giraldi Cambrensis: Opera*, 8 vols. (London, 1861–91), 2:120. Printed as 'dhin', the initial letter of the English word is evidently ð.

[42] Derek Pearsall, 'Old English and Middle English Poetry', in *The Routledge History of English Poetry vol. 1* (London, 1977), 74.

[43] Famous examples include 'Cnut's song' recorded in the *Liber Eliensis*, two couplets said to be the beginning of a song spontaneously composed by the king as he listened to the monks of Ely sing (*DIMEV* 3487; *IMEV* 2164); and three short songs composed by the hermit Godric of Finchale, preserved by his biographers in several manuscripts (*DIMEV* 980, 4701, 4734; *IMEV* 598, 2988, 3031): see Heather Blurton, 'The Songs of Godric of

manuscripts;[44] and in didactic contexts either of clerical condemnation or via their appropriation as proverbial wisdom for use in sermons.[45] The songs themselves only emerge in any number when they appear, collected together, in multilingual manuscript compilations from the second half of the thirteenth century:[46] and at all points religious lyrics greatly outnumber secular. This anomaly of English (there is no such preponderance of religious material in any other vernacular European lyric)[47] is explained by the circumstances of twelfth- and thirteenth-century patronage and survival. English aristocrats patronised secular poetry in French from at least the 1130s, including chronicle and romance, and despite the linguistic differences between northern (and England's) French and the language of the troubadours, it seems clear that troubadour lyric was well known to the Francophone English from the second half of the twelfth century, not least following the arrival of Queen Eleanor of Aquitaine, wife of Henry II (1154–89).[48] Meanwhile, English poetry before the fourteenth century was largely preserved in clerical contexts, with a resultant emphasis on religious verse. Nonetheless, it cannot be doubted that secular English lyrics and songs were composed, performed, and committed to memory throughout the period, and their eventual preservation in writing was inevitable, a product of the wholly multilingual literary culture which meant that England's poets working with Latin and French were always also thinking in English.

One example of such an author at work is Thomas of Hales, a Franciscan friar who produced a number of works in Latin, French, and English around the middle of the thirteenth century.[49] His English lyric *Love Ron* ('Love-rune') is said in its unique manuscript to have been written 'ad instanciam cuiusdam puelle Deo dicate' ('at the request of a certain young girl dedicated to God').[50] The implication is of the girl's need for a devotional poem in English rather than Latin or French—the same pragmatic consideration which drove Orm nearly a century earlier—but if so, then what matters here is the cultural world the girl is nonetheless presumed to inhabit.

Finchale: Vernacular Liturgy and Literary History', *New Medieval Literatures*, 18 (2018), 75–104, and Chapter 17 in this volume.

[44] One poem generally agreed to be the earliest surviving ME lyric, '[Þe]h þet hi can wittes fule-wis', was pencilled into the margin of an early-twelfth-century Latin MS: London, British Library, MS Royal 8.D.xiii, fol. 25r. See Carleton Brown (ed.), *English Lyrics of the XIIIth Century* (Oxford, 1932), xii–xiii; re-transcribed and translated by Peter Dronke, 'On the Continuity of Medieval English Love-Lyric', in E. Chaney and P. Mack (eds), *England and the Continental Renaissance: Essays in Honour of J. B. Trapp* (Woodbridge, 1990), 7–21, at 8.

[45] The classic study of the poetry we cannot read is R. M. Wilson, *The Lost Literature of Medieval England* (London, 1952); see chapter 9, 'Lyrical Poetry'. For the appearance of fragments of popular verse in sermons, see Siegfried Wenzel, *Verses in Sermons*: Fasciculus Morum *and Its Middle English Poems* (Cambridge, MA, 1978); Wenzel, *Preachers, Poets, and the Early English Lyric* (Princeton, NJ, 1986).

[46] The most important early (pre-1300) MSS collecting English poetry, all of which are multilingual, are: Cambridge, Trinity College MS B.14.39 (formerly MS 323), a late-thirteenth-century verse miscellany containing Latin, English, and French, as well as macaronic texts; London, British Library, Cotton MS Caligula A. IX, *c* 1250–1300, containing Laȝamon's *Brut, The Owl and the Nightingale*, and several shorter ME and French poems; London, British Library, MS Egerton 613, a thirteenth-century miscellany of Latin, French, and English, containing *Poema Morale* and several lyrics; Oxford, Bodleian Library, MS Digby 86, *c* 1275, a miscellany of English, French, and Latin verse and prose; Oxford, Jesus College, MS 29, *c* 1270–1300, which shares English and French material with Cotton Caligula A. IX, above. See John Frankis, 'The Social Context of Vernacular Writing in Thirteenth Century England: The Evidence of the Manuscripts', in P. R. Coss and S. D. Lloyd (eds), *Thirteenth Century England 1: Proceedings of the Newcastle Upon Tyne Conference 1985* (Woodbridge, 1986), 175–84.

[47] See Peter Dronke, *The Medieval Lyric*, 3rd edn. (Woodbridge, 1996), 65.

[48] In this respect it is instructive that troubadours followed the Normans to Sicily, where their influence was formative in the poetry of the Italian trecento.

[49] With firm attributions for the ME lyric *Love Ron*, a French sermon, and a Latin *Vita Mariae*, with other possible works considered, see Sarah M. Horrall, 'Thomas of Hales, O.F.M.: His Life and Works', *Traditio*, 42 (1986), 287–98.

[50] Oxford, Jesus College MS 29, fol. 260r; Brown (ed.), *English Lyrics of the XIIIth Century*, 68–74.

28   MEDIEVAL POETRY: 1100–1400

> Hwer is paris & heleyne
>   þat weren so bryht & feyre on bleo,
> Amadas & dideyne,
>   tristram, yseude and alle þeo,
> Ector, wiþ his scharpe meyne,
>   & cesar, riche of wordes feo.
> Heo beoþ i-glyden vt of þe reyne
>   so þe schef is of þe cleo. (65–72)

(Where are Paris and Helen, who were so bright and fair of face? Amadas and Ydoine, Tristan, Yseut, and all the rest; Hector, with his great prowess, and Caesar, rich in valuable things? They have slipped from the kingdom like a sheaf of grain off a cliff.)[51]

The heroes and lovers of the Trojan War, of French exotically located and Celtic-derived romance, and of classical history are conjured up only to be banished, scattered to the winds. But their usefulness here to both poet and audience reveals to us—at the least—a whole inter- and supra-textual world, one in which anyone might know the significance of the names, even if they knew little more—and at the most, a world in which a monolingual young English woman in the middle of the thirteenth century might know these songs and stories in her own language. If, contrarily, the 'puella' did know French or Latin, then the fact of her request for a poem in English tells its own story: of private devotion being purposely recast in everyone's first language, taking its rightful place in a multilingual discourse. In translations, adaptations, and macaronic combinations of and with French and Latin, energised by a vigorous contact with the popular world that those languages comparatively lacked, English lyric poetry bursts onto the page doing something distinctive, in both religious and secular works.[52]

In this context 'secular' does not only mean love lyric, or the familiar clichés of love-longing which flooded contemporary European lyrics. Perhaps as a result of the absence of canon-forming aristocratic patronage, thirteenth-century English lyrics show some startling idiosyncrasies. One good example is the version of 'Le regret de Maximian' preserved in Oxford, Bodleian Library, MS Digby 86.[53] Usually categorised with religious poems (or at the least as a 'didactic' poem), 'Le regret', as it is titled in the manuscript, is a loose paraphrase of the sixth-century Latin first elegy of 'Maximianus', a text of uncertain authorial provenance but well known in medieval England as a Latin teaching aid.[54] The poem is in the main a series of familiar complaints about the indignities and sorrows of age, in which the speaker longs for death and grieves for his younger self. But in the last two stanzas, something entirely unexpected happens:

---

[51] These last two lines are somewhat obscure, though the general meaning is clear. I have preferred Brown's glosses; cf. the edition and notes of Susanna Greer Fein, in *Moral Love Songs and Laments* (Kalamazoo, MI, 1998).

[52] On the virtues of English religious lyric over its Latin antecedents, see Dronke, *Medieval Lyric*, 63–70, and for a single example favourably compared at length with its Latin and French analogues, Ashe, *Conquest and Transformation*, 317–33.

[53] *DIMEV* 1769 (*IMEV* 1115).

[54] See Susanna Greer Fein, 'Introduction to the Version of the Poem in MS Harley 2253: Article 68, "Herkne to my ron"', in Susanna Fein, David Raybin, and Jan Ziolkowski (ed. and trans.), *The Complete Harley Manuscript, Volume 2* (Kalamazoo, MI, 2014). For Maximianus's place in the thirteenth-century curriculum, see Nicholas Orme, *English Schools in the Middle Ages* (London, 1973), 102–3. For the original Latin, see A. M. Juster (ed. and trans.), *The Elegies of Maximianus* (Philadelphia, PA, 2018).

Reuþfoul is mi reed
Hoe makeþ me selden gled
Mi wif þat sholde be
Of me hoe is al seed
Hoe saiþ ich waste breed
Mine frend me nulleþ i-se
Ich telle me for a queed
Þe wile ich miȝten heueed
I-beten nedde ich hoe[55]
Crist þou do me reed
Me were leuere deed
Þen þus aliue to bee

Iich may seien alas
Þat ich i-boren was
I-liued ich have to longe
Were ich mon so ich was
Min heien so grei so glas
Min her so fair bihonge
And ich hire heuede bi þe trasce
In a derne place
To meken and to monge
Ne sholde hoe neuere atwiten
Min helde ne me befliten
Wel heye I shulde hire honge.[56]

(My state is desperate; she seldom gladdens me, who should be my wife. She is utterly sick of me, she says I'm a waste of bread: my friend will not look at me. I hold myself worthless that while I had the strength I didn't beat her. Christ help me: I'd rather be dead than alive like this. I may say, alas that I was born; I have lived too long. If I were the man I was, my eyes grey as glass, my hair so gorgeous—and I had her by the hair, in a secret place, to force her down and have to do with her—she would never mock my age, nor laugh at me. I would hang her high.)

The Latin elegy has no such passage, and the later version of the poem preserved in Harley 2253 does not contain the most shocking of these lines about beating and rape.[57] With this embittered, violent misogyny the poem's stock figures of life's transitory joys are kicked

---

[55] 'Þe wile ... ich hoe': Both modern editors (see subsequent note) read 'Þe wile ich miȝt en heueed', and Varnhagen reads 'yedde (=hedde)' for MS 'nedde', translating the two lines as 'For as long as I could, I beat her on the head'. The *MED* also suggests 'in the first place' for 'on heueed' (*s.v.* 'hed (n. 1)', 6b); this I ignore. Brown does not offer a translation. I prefer 'miȝten heueed' ('had [the] strength'), not only because that is the clearest MS reading but also on metrical grounds and for simplicity of meaning. In the following line the MS clearly reads 'nedde', and I think the whole context requires the negative, since he rebukes himself in the midst of criticising the woman. For the use of 'hoe' ('she') in the accusative, see *MED s.v.* 'he (pron. 2)'; the word is intended to rhyme with 'bee', so perhaps should be read as 'he(e)'. The MS folio can be viewed at digital.bodleian.ox.ac.uk/inquire/p/1b597c8e-86ea-4e9b-ae1e-7b35ec14dca2 [accessed August 2019].

[56] From 'Le regret de Maximian', in Oxford, Bodleian Library MS Digby 86, fols. 134v–136v (fol. 136vᵃ⁻ᵇ). The poem has been edited twice: Hermann Varnhagen, 'VI. Zu dem klageliede Maximian's', *Anglia*, 3 (1880), 275–85; Brown, *English Lyrics of the XIIIth Century*, 92–100; quoted are Brown's lines 250–73.

[57] The Harley MS version lines 143–53 ('Herkne to my ron', in Fein (ed.), *The Complete Harley Manuscript*) correspond to the penultimate stanza of Digby 86; they wish 'Serewe upon hyre hed!' (149), but there is no

30 MEDIEVAL POETRY: 1100–1400

aside, hijacked by a voice which ventriloquises and performs dark, personal rage. It is just possible for an audience to read against the sentiment by re-contextualising it as the impotent will to harm of repulsive age, but that last line is the violent threat of the powerful, echoed by the tyrants of contemporary romance: 'J shal hangen þe ful heye, / Or Y shal þristen vth þin heie!'[58] In the context of the late-thirteenth-century manuscript, the effect is irretrievably to darken the message of the subsequent (English) poem, *The Thrush and the Nightingale*.[59] Ostensibly this is a light-hearted debate poem (in the ubiquitous Latin and French tradition) about the virtues and vices of women, which is resolved in women's favour by the Nightingale's winning move of citing the Virgin Mary's role in salvation. But after the sheer misogyny of what has come immediately before, it is impossible not to see the imbalance of the argument—the anti-feminist Thrush cites numerous cases of female perfidy derived from the standard examples, while the Nightingale is reduced to repeating that women are nice—and of course the ultimate implicit condemnation of mortal women, which is that Mary is glorified because 'Hoe ne weste of sunne ne of shame' (175: 'She knew nothing of sin or shame').

I have drawn attention to the anomalous voice that bursts into 'Le regret de Maximian' because it bears upon the circumstances in which Middle English lyric poetry was first copied and preserved: which is to say, as the self-conscious product of individual scribes and authors working within, against, and in formation of multiple traditions. This poet chose to break into the conventional paraphrase of Latin commonplaces with a violation, an emotionally charged taboo; in context, a voice of rueful wisdom is transformed into that of an unrepentant sinner. It is poetry's capacity to create rules and expectations, and to break them, that gives it its power; and it is that power which demands to be recorded and preserved.

English Narrative Poetry

In writing about pastoral and lyric poetry, I have emphasised the importance of pragmatism—the necessity of preaching in English—and of broad cultural necessity—the ubiquity of a vernacular popular tradition, slowly but surely entering the surviving written record. The work done by the Middle English lyrics gives power of utterance to multiplicity and anonymity, the unanchored voice of subjectivity without a subject. Turning to early Middle English narrative poetry, in contrast, we encounter at the outset a different paradigm: the author as self-conscious artist. Laʒamon tells us at the beginning of his vast British history, which runs to more than 16,000 long lines, that he was a priest and scholar in Areley Kings, Worcestershire. He wrote around the beginning of the thirteenth century, and two different versions of his poem survive (both late-thirteenth-century manuscripts, derived from a common source which cannot have been the author's original).[60] Laʒamon's work is a poetic translation of Wace's French verse *Brut* of *c* 1155, itself a translation of

---

threat or description of violence. Strangely, Rosemary Woolf misdescribes this crux as merely 'how he would treat his mockers': *The English Religious Lyric in the Middle Ages* (Oxford, 1968), 105. I am not aware of any other discussion of the passage.

[58] G. V. Smithers (ed.), *Havelock* (Oxford, 1987), lines 1152–3: 'I shall hang you from a great height, or I shall put out your eyes'. This late-thirteenth-century romance frequently dramatises the threat of rape of the hero's wife: see Ashe, *Conquest and Transformation*, 383–5. I am reminded of the modern apophthegm attributed to Margaret Atwood: 'Men are afraid that women will laugh at them. Women are afraid that men will kill them'.

[59] *DIMEV* 5052 (*IMEV* 3222); Brown (ed.), *English Lyrics of the XIIIth Century*, 101–7.

[60] E. G. Stanley, 'The Date of Laʒamon's *Brut*', *Notes & Queries*, 15 (1968), 85–8.

Geoffrey of Monmouth's Latin prose *Historia regum Britanniae* (*The History of the Kings of Britain*) of *c* 1136.

It is not the aim of this chapter to attempt to describe the nature of Laʒamon's achievement. What is important for present purposes is its mere existence, and what that indicates about English poetic culture at the time; significance lies in the scale of its ambition and the artistic brilliance of its execution. Orm had produced 10,000 long lines of English verse some decades earlier, but his aims were very different: he sought clarity of communication, transparency of meaning, and memorable effect; poetry was Orm's vehicle for his pastoral teaching. Laʒamon's poetry is itself the purpose: his is an artistic creation, composed of elements which had never before been brought together; it is something new.[61] In contrast with his contemporaries' emulation of Latin and French syllable-counting metres, Laʒamon uses a loosened version of the Old English alliterative metre based on stress rather than syllable count, with a variable number of off-beats; but he does not use alliteration or stresses consistently, he frequently uses rhyme as well, and sometimes his lines do show a syllabic regularity reminiscent of entirely different metrical rules.[62] The longer of the two surviving manuscript versions, in British Library Cotton MS Caligula A. ix, has a markedly low proportion of French or Latin loan words, and has long been regarded as an archaising project,[63] while the revised and abbreviated version in British Library Cotton MS Otho C. xiii shows evidence of linguistic updating in its changes: but these changes are themselves aesthetic in nature, and not a simple matter of cutting or simplifying. The manuscripts cannot be reliably separated in time, and both versions demonstrate serious poetic ambition;[64] nor is it realistic to suggest that the Caligula version could have been perceived as linguistically obsolete in the late thirteenth century, when its manuscript was produced to high and expensive quality, the poem sitting alongside other works in English and French, and decorated in contemporary fashion.[65] Laʒamon's poetic *Brut* (there was also a widely disseminated prose chronicle of the same name) was not an isolated or lost poetic experiment; it has been shown to have influenced numerous later works, including several English verse chronicles and romances (and two items in the Auchinleck Manuscript, which strongly suggests the existence of a *Brut* manuscript in London in the early fourteenth century), and most notably the *Alliterative Morte Arthur*, which has been located in the north-east Midlands, again some distance from the *Brut*'s Worcestershire roots.[66]

Laʒamon's poem is much expanded from Wace's *Brut*, though without making substantive changes to (pseudo-)historical events; W. R. J. Barron and S. C. Weinberg comment on his use of 'a method of redaction which seems, on internal evidence, to have involved reading sections of Wace's text which were then freely re-worked, re-ordered, and expanded,

---

[61] Cf. Eric Weiskott, *English Alliterative Verse: Poetic Tradition and Literary History* (Cambridge, 2016), 89.

[62] For an efficient review of scholarship on the *Brut*'s prosody (which has reached no firm conclusions), followed by technical analysis of Laʒamon's place in the development of English alliterative verse, see Ian Cornelius, *Reconstructing Alliterative Verse: The Pursuit of a Medieval Meter* (Cambridge, 2017), 79–97. For a useful basic introduction to Laʒamon's poetic form and style, see W. R. J. Barron and S. C. Weinberg (ed. and trans.), *Layamon's Arthur: The Arthurian Section of Layamon's Brut* (Exeter, 2001), xlviii–lxv.

[63] The classic argument is E. G. Stanley, 'Laʒamon's Antiquarian Sentiments', *Medium Aevum*, 38 (1969), 23–37, but it has not gone unchallenged: see Cornelius, *Reconstructing Alliterative Verse*, 81.

[64] Stephen M. Yeager argues that the two contemporaneous manuscripts adopted contrasting self-conscious strategies: 'Diplomatic Antiquarianism and the Manuscripts of Laʒamon's Brut', *Arthuriana*, 26 (2016), 124–40.

[65] See Jane Roberts, 'A Preliminary Note on British Library, Cotton MS Caligula A. ix', in Françoise Le Saux (ed.), *The Text and Tradition of Laʒamon's* Brut (Cambridge, 1994), 1–14. On the Caligula MS's high status and (possibly international) decorative milieu, see Elizabeth J. Bryan, 'Laʒamon's *Brut* and the Vernacular Text: Widening the Context', in Rosamund Allen, Jane Roberts, and Carole Weinberg (eds), *Reading Laʒamon's Brut: Approaches and Explorations* (Amsterdam, 2013), 661–89.

[66] See James I. McNelis III, 'Laʒamon as Auctor', in Le Saux (ed.), *Text and Tradition*, 253–72.

32 MEDIEVAL POETRY: 1100–1400

rather than translated line by line, leading to many changes of detail'.[67] He frequently adds dialogue and direct speech; he is famous for his extended, almost epic similes, which have no parallel in Geoffrey or Wace; often he gives voice to his protagonists' thoughts and feelings when his source had made no comment; and he elaborates on whole episodes which become something quite different in his hands—perhaps most famously in the vatic cases of Merlin's declarations and Arthur's dreams, and in violent conflicts such as the chaos which leads to the foundation of the Round Table. In contrast to these well-known interpolations, I want to draw attention to one (no less famous) passage where Laȝamon's interventions are significantly less dramatic, but I suggest no less effective. The story of King Leir and his daughters is my example, demonstrating some of the ways in which Laȝamon's form shapes his content: that is, how he uses his English long-line verse to do things which Wace's French octosyllabic couplet perhaps cannot—and certainly does not—do.

In the midst of Leir's travails with his cruel older daughters, Laȝamon gives an unmistakable echo of Old English poetry, introducing a speech of lamentation: 'and þus seide þe king, sorhful on mode'[68] ('and thus said the king, sorrowful at heart'). 'Sorhful on mode', retained in Otho,[69] is itself a small echo from the prose of Ælfric and his contemporaries, and one preserved locally, in manuscripts held at Worcester and elsewhere.[70] But the work Laȝamon does with this whole episode is not only a matter of his English poetic inheritance. More important is what he does that is new, and the ways in which his adaptation of the British mythical history is in symphonic dialogue with his French and Latin sources and contemporaries. When Leir asks his youngest daughter to echo the empty flattery of her older sisters, Wace has her respond with a strangely discontinuous, rather curt speech, which ends with a derisive proverb:

> Cordeïlle out bien escuté
> E bien out en sun quer noté
> Come les dous sorors parlouent,
> Come lur pere losengouent.
> A sun pere se volt gaber
> E en gabant li volt mustrer
> Que ses filles le blandisseient
> E de losenges le serveient.
> Quant Leïr a raisun la mist
> Come les altres, ele dist:
>
> 'U ad nule fille qui die
> A sun pere par presoncie

---

[67] Laȝamon, *Brut*, in W. R. J. Barron and S. C. Weinberg (eds and trans.), *Brut, or Hystoria Brutonum* (Harlow, 1995), 847 (note to page 89).

[68] Laȝamon, *Brut*, line 1677.

[69] Laȝamon, *Brut*, Otho MS, in G. L. Brook and R. F. Leslie (eds), *Brut: Edited from British Museum MS. Cotton Caligula A. IX and British Museum MS. Cotton Otho C. XIII*, 2 vols. (Oxford, 1963–78), line 1677.

[70] 'Sorhfulle on mode' and variants appear in Ælfric's 'St Agnes' (B 1.3.8) and 'Sermo ad Populum, in Octavis Pentecosten Dicendus' (B 1.4.11), and in the anonymous 'Nativity of Mary the Virgin' (B 3.3.18). All three are preserved in MSS of the eleventh or twelfth centuries; the latter two are in Oxford, Bodleian MSS Hatton 113 and 114, homiliaries prepared for Wulfstan II, Bishop of Worcester 1062–95. Search conducted in the *DOEWC*. For the texts' MSS and provenance, see Orietta Da Rold, Takako Kato, Mary Swan, and Elaine Treharne (eds), *The Production and Use of English Manuscripts 1060 to 1220* (Leicester, 2010–13), le.ac.uk/ee/em1060to1220 [accessed August 2019].

> Qu'ele l'aint plus qu'ele ne deit?
> Ne sai que plus grant amur seit
> Que entre enfant e entre pere,
> E entre enfanz e entre mere.
> Mes peres iés, jo aim tant tei
> Come jo mun pere amer dei.
> E pur faire tei plus certein,
> Tant as, tant vals e jo tant t'aim.'

(Cordeille had listened carefully, and carefully taken note of what her sisters had said and how they deceived their father. She wanted to joke with her father and, in joking, show him how his daughters were flattering him and tricking him with deceit. When Leir spoke to her as he had the others, she said to him: 'Is there anywhere a daughter who arrogantly can tell her father that she loves him more than she should? I don't know of any love greater than that between father and child, or between mother and children. You are my father: I love you as much as I should love my father. And to leave you in no more doubt: you are worth as much as you possess and I love you accordingly.')[71]

'So much you have, so much you're worth: and so much I love you'. The expression is a direct translation of Geoffrey's 'quantum habes tantum uales tantumque te diligo'.[72] The first part of the phrase is ubiquitous: Peter Comester comments 'quia antiquum et verum est proverbium: Quantum habes, tantum vales' ('how ancient and truthful the proverb is: you are worth as much as you have').[73] With Geoffrey's Cordeilla's addition of the ironic declaration of love, and Wace's translation of the whole, however, there appears a new French proverb, which sheds light on the development of both the French language and the temper of its emergent genre, the romance.[74] In the *History of William Marshal* (c 1226) the knight's biographer describes a dramatic change in William's status after he wins a great number of horses and their equipment in a tournament competition:

> Le Mareschal molt ennorerent
> E molt li firent beau semblant,
> Plus k'il n'avoient fait devant.
> A itel paste tel leveim,
> Tant as, tant valz a ge tant t'eim.[75]

(They honoured the Marshal greatly and showed him the fairest treatment, more than they had done before. You get the rise your dough's worth: so much you have, so much you're worth, and so much I love you.)

---

[71] Wace, *Brut*, in Judith Weiss (ed. and trans.), *Wace's Roman de Brut: A History of the British*, rev. edn. (Exeter, 2002), lines 1723–42 (44–5).
[72] Geoffrey of Monmouth, in Michael D. Reeve (ed.) and Neil Wright (trans.), *The History of the Kings of Britain: An Edition and Translation of the* De gestis Britonum [Historia Regum Britanniae] (Woodbridge, 2007), 2.161–2 (39).
[73] Petrus Comestor, *Sermo XXXVII*, in *PL* 198.1809C–D.
[74] It appears, for example, in Chardri, in B. S. Merrilees (ed.), *Le Petit Plet* (Oxford, 1970), line 1642 (witnessed in the *Brut* Caligula MS, fol. 260v[b]); and as 'un proverbe en mon livre' in *Le Dit des Droits*, in Pierre Ruelle (ed.), *Les Dits du Clerc de Vouday* (Brussels, 1969), lines 322–4.
[75] A. J. Holden, S. Gregory, and D. Crouch (ed. and trans.), *History of William Marshal*, 3 vols. (London, 2002–6), lines 1376–80. The translation provided here is my own.

34 MEDIEVAL POETRY: 1100–1400

The huge variability in spelling of Old French means that the verb 'amer', to love, from Latin *amare*,[76] is in many cases indistinguishable from another word, 'asmer', from Latin *aestimare*. This had a variety of closely related meanings: to judge or estimate; to appraise or value—and neutrally 'to value' slides into 'to value (highly)'.[77] Drawn into this lexical field, and sharing meanings with both words, is the ubiquitous *priser*: to value, regard, or estimate; to prize, to hold in high value; to praise or honour.[78] And of course this nexus of meanings is exactly the point of the proverb, and indeed more broadly the point of courtly society, and of the romance genre which idealises it: what is valued is what is loved, and vice versa.

This is in one sense a timeless observation on human society; but more particularly in Wace's poem, and in all the romances which followed in his model, it is an inextricable tangle of values which renders moral worth and human emotion indistinguishable from social status and economic wealth.[79] This is a world that Laȝamon rejects. When he translates Cordoille's speech into English verse, he jettisons the whole derisory force of the French proverb, describing first her clarity of intention, her 'leaffulne huie þat heo liȝen nolden' (1515: 'faithful resolution' [Otho: 'oþ', 'oath'] that she would not lie):

> Þa answarede Cordoille   lude and nowiht stille,
>
> mid gomene and mid lehtre,   to hire fader leue:
>
> 'Þeo art me leof also mi fæder   and ich þe also þi dohter;
>
> ich habbe to þe sohfaste loue,   for we buoð swiþe isibbe.
>
> And, swa ich ibide are,   ich wille þe suge mare:
>
> al swa muchel þu bist woruh   swa þu velden ært,
>
> and al swa muchel swa þu hauest   men þe wllet luuien;
>
> for sone heo bið ilaȝed,   þe mon þe lutel ah.'

(Then Cordoille answered aloud and quite openly, gaily and smilingly, to her beloved father: 'You are dear to me as my father and I to you as your daughter; I have true love for you, for we are close kindred. And, as I hope for mercy, I will say something further to you: you are worth just as much as you are possessed of, and just as much as you possess so much will men love you; for he who possesses little is soon little esteemed.')[80]

Laȝamon's Cordoille is not playing games, but rather demonstrating an easy conscience. She does not close with the mocking proverb of accountable love—or speak of her own love other than as 'sohfaste', 'firm and true'—but with a careful explanation of the social forces which created the proverb. And in its unfolding over three long lines (retained in Otho), all the glib insulting force of the French (and the Latin) is dissipated, replaced with thoughtful wisdom.

---

[76] *AND s.v.* 'amer'.

[77] *AND s.v.* 'asmer'.

[78] *AND s.v.* 'priser', from Latin *pretiare*. On the associations between this cluster of words, see John Orr, 'On Homonymics', in *Studies in French Language and Mediaeval Literature Presented to Professor Mildred K. Pope by Pupils, Colleagues, and Friends* (Manchester, 1939), 253–97 at 277–9.

[79] On Wace as turning point, heralding the courtly romance's deployment of love as a metaphor for social/economic value and personal fulfilment, see Ashe, *Conquest and Transformation*, 244–55.

[80] Laȝamon, *Brut*, in Barron and Weinberg (ed. and trans.), lines 1520–7 (80–1).

The point is that Laȝamon's lexical and prosodic field, his chosen English words and the formations in which he presents them, simply does not trap him in the same cynical nexus as Wace's romance diction and couplets. These contrasts recur when Leir, finally abandoned by his older daughters, reflects on his former folly. Wace's Leir has learnt not only the truth of a proverb but also the indissoluble nature of love, wealth, and power:

> 'Jo n'ai un su apartenant
> Ki d'amur me face semblant.
> Bien me dist veir ma mendre fille,
> Que jo blasmoe, Cordeïlle,
> Ki dist que tant cum jo avreie
> Tant preisiez, tant amez sereie.' (1935–40)

('I haven't a single relation who might pretend to love me. My youngest daughter, Cordeille, whom I reproached, told me the truth when she said that as long as I had possessions, so long I would be esteemed and loved.')

This is a more revealing passage than might be expected, for Geoffrey's Leir thinks much more clearly: 'uisus fui ualere eis qui non michi sed donis meis amici fuerant. Interim dilexerunt me sed magis munera mea' ('I was respected by those who were friendly not to me but to my gifts. For a time they loved me, but really my gifts').[81] Wace's Leir cannot separate *amer* from *aveir*, as is revealed when he laments that he can no longer find anyone who will offer him a performance of love: love only exists in display, in this nexus. 'When I had possessions, then I was loved' is a profoundly different statement from that made by Geoffrey's newly embittered king; it is a half-understanding, shaped and limited by the lexical field of Wace's romance vocabulary.

Laȝamon's Leir, in contrast, gains *muchel wisdom*: and there is an understated dark humour in Laȝamon's rendition of the realities of the situation: 'Now I'm a wretched man, no one loves me for that' (1735: 'Nu ich æm a wrecche mon; ne leouet me no mon for þan'). Another octosyllabic couplet appears to seal Leir's realisation, its chiming rhythm capturing his rueful acknowledgement: 'Ah mi dohtor me seide seoh for nou ich hire ileue inoh' (1736: 'But my daughter told me the truth, for now I quite believe her'). The Otho version intensifies the use of rhyme and quickens the rhythm, heightening the irony of Leir's error of reversal:[82] 'seoþþe ȝeo was me loþest, for ȝeo me seide soþest' (Otho 1729: 'then she was to me most hateful, for she told me the most truth'). The end of Leir's lament produces his crowning realisation, effectively new to Laȝamon, that love is a simple and moral matter:

> And Cordoille mi dohtor   dohȝeþe me seide,
> þat heo me leouede swa feire   swa monnes fader scolde—
> wet wold ich bidde mare   of mire dohter dure! (Caligula 1739–41)

(And my daughter Cordoille spoke for my own good, saying that she loved me as dearly as one should love one's father—what more should I ask of my beloved daughter!)

---

[81] Geoffrey of Monmouth, *History*, II.225–7 (42–3).
[82] Cf. Caligula 1729: 'seoððen heo me wes leaðest for heo me seiden alre sohust'.

36   MEDIEVAL POETRY: 1100–1400

The Otho poet again adds more rhyme and speeds the rhythm,[83] incidentally or purposely getting rid of the word 'dohȝeðe', which was largely obsolete by the fourteenth century.[84] There is a minor irony here because the word is an English example of the kinds of literal and metaphorical (or economic and moral) blending of meaning to be found in the French *biens* and *priser*. It came from the Old English *duguþ*, which had a huge range of meanings: virtue, excellence; power, strength; benefit, good, salvation; wealth, riches; a group of good warriors, an army, the lord's *comitatus*; and even a nation.[85] Here in Leir's recollection of Cordoille's speech that she 'dohȝeþe me seide', it means that she spoke to him of his good, his power, his wealth, his advantage, his possessions—and she did; she showed him that these things were the same, and that to divest himself of what he had was to lose what he thought he was.

Conclusion

The re-emergence of English poetry after the Conquest is partly a matter that requires no explanation: English was everyone's first language, and poetry was always composed. Pastoral care demanded effective communication in English, while dynamic societies produced a world of song, carol, and ballad, which increasingly left its traces in the record. And the culture of post-Conquest England was a great engine of narrative: the home of vernacular chronicle, and creator of the romance; the pathway into the European mainstream of all the vernacular riches of the British past. But that last genre, epitomised by Laȝamon's *Brut*, is also brought to life by a different mechanism: the aesthetic energies of the individual poet. The story of English poetry must be about people as much as about historical and social and institutional change: the poets who chose to write, and the scribes, patrons, and members of communities who chose to record, reproduce, and preserve. Often we witness a self-consciousness about translation, about providing in English something brought from other languages. But the subtle and vital counterpart to this is what English poetry does that is *not* transparently about meaning; what cannot be translated and must instead be created. It is only with that act of creation in mind—and an awareness of what it might have meant to create a poem in English, in deep conversation with a vast, multilingual, hybrid cultural world—that we can begin to understand why 'Hit com him on mode & on his mern þonke. / þet he wolde of Engle þa æðelæn tellen'[86] ('It came to his mind, in his finest thoughts, that he would tell the glories of the English'). Poetry is an act of creation, and that is its own justification.

---

[83] Cf. Otho 1739–41: 'and mi ȝonge dohter Gordoille me seide / þat ȝeo me loue wolde: so man his fader solde. / Wat wolde ich bidde more, of mine dohter deore?'
[84] *MED s.v.* 'dŏuth(e (n.)'; *OED s.v.* '†douth, n'. The Otho MS retains another example of the word at line 13,977, where it means 'army', 'warriors'.
[85] *DOE s.v.* 'duguþ'.
[86] Laȝamon, *Brut*, Caligula MS, in Brook and Leslie (eds), lines 6–7.

3

Poetic Sites

Ralph Hanna

In memory of Anne Middleton

Piers Plowman C is probably the first English poetic text with an immediate public. There is substantial evidence of intensive London circulation by some date in the mid-1390s, certainly within about five years of the latest datable moment alluded to in the poem.[1] Yet aspects of this text indicate that the poet counted upon readers comprehending what his 'published' version (perhaps, as has often been argued, a post-mortem promulgation by an executor), one openly available for dispersed scribal copying, did not include. For portions of Langland's poetic argument would have been resonant only for those who knew what was *not* published; that is, it should have been sensible only to those who had access to what was at that moment largely a private text, the poet's earlier drafts (our modern *Piers Plowman* A and B). So far as one can intuit, in certain passages the poem might have offered its fullest sense only to a coterie, a localised audience conversant with the poet's earlier efforts.[2]

Such an argument illustrates a much larger and more important moment to which *Piers* is equally central: Langland's invention in the 1360s of imaginative poetic fiction in English (as distinct from the largely Anglo-Norman- or French-derived tradition of earlier romance). This is the inception of what would be(come), two centuries down the line, national literary tradition (from the 1400s, associated not with Langland but Chaucer). But the details here illuminate what is at stake in such a creation. Portions of *Piers Plowman* C were, in their fullness, literally illegible in the poem's *public form* as stand-alone text; it could only communicate fully to what its poet must have imagined as audience, as a closet document, shared out among a known small group, one privy to the poet's earlier efforts at actualising his imaginative project.

I take this as a liminal moment, the shift from poem as localised and personalised construct to what Anne Middleton famously identified as 'public poetry'.[3] By this phrase, Middleton meant to identify an address to a broadly conceived community of the realm (Langland's 'commune') on social issues of general import. However, until the 1390s, when

---

[1] See Simon Horobin, '"In London and Opelond": The Dialect and Circulation of the C-Version of Piers *Plowman*', *Medium Ævum*, 74 (2005), 248–69 and 'The Scribe of Bodleian Library, MS Digby 102 and Circulation of the C Text of *Piers Plowman*', *Yearbook of Langland Studies*, 24 (2010), 89–112. One should bring Horobin's demonstration into conjunction with the account of the transmission offered in George Russell and George Kane (eds), *Piers Plowman: The C Version* (London, 1997), especially 41–6, for example, for their demonstration that the early London copies XJH, plausibly of the 1390s, stand at least two scribal generations removed from the archetypal manuscript.

[2] For a fuller version of this argument, with further detail, see Hanna, *Patient Reading/Reading Patience: Oxford Essays on Medieval Literature* (Liverpool, 2017), 346–9.

[3] See 'The Idea of Public Poetry in the Reign of Richard II', *Speculum*, 53 (1978), 94–114. My dedication acknowledges Anne's inspiring companionship and her persistent preoccupation as to what it meant to write in the fourteenth century, notably in two further grand articles: 'The Audience and Public of *Piers Plowman*', in David A. Lawton (ed.), *Middle English Alliterative Poetry and Its Literary Background* (Woodbridge, 1982), 101–23, 147–54; and 'Chaucer's "New Men" and the Good of Literature in the *Canterbury Tales*', in Edward Said (ed.), *Literature and Society*, English Institute Essays 1978 (Baltimore, MD, 1980), 15–56. See also n. 7.

Ralph Hanna, *Poetic Sites*. In: *The Oxford History of Poetry in English*. Edited by Helen Cooper and Robert R. Edwards, Oxford University Press. © Ralph Hanna (2023). DOI: 10.1093/oso/9780198827429.003.0003

38 MEDIEVAL POETRY: 1100–1400

Piers circulation exploded, a success that I would think inspired a variety of comparable efforts, what Langland imagined as he revised *Piers* B, although today the version customarily read, at this point a coterie text, into the publicly circulating C-text was the normal state of things.[4] Before this moment, poetry was sited, local, a matter of known community. No Middle English poet ever wrote anything out of self-satisfaction alone; they always imagined an audience and some means of contacting them. And I would doubt that any medieval poet, even Chaucer, would have imagined the Miltonic sublime of 'leav[ing] something so written to aftertimes as they should not willingly let it die'.[5]

Moreover, it is no accident that promulgating *Piers* C occurred in London—and that it sparked imitation—for until this date such poetic locales or communities were generally elsewhere, and London, as a consequence, what one might imagine empty space, was ripe for development. Before the 1390s, however, poetic locales might be identified in reasonably isolated enclaves and in odd corners of Langland's 'opelond'. It is again no accident that, in all the versions of *Piers Plowman*, the dreamer Will's opening survey of England from a mountain of vision is placed in a locale situated on the boundary, the edge of The March. Or that he is writing within well-recognised provincial/local forms (instructional poetry, alliterative tradition, romance). The remainder of my chapter will examine a few salient examples of such production, the diverse sites from which English poetry had before the 1390s emerged. While the revolution of that decade, the invention or discovery of a literary public, seems to me a seminal one, it is worth noting, as I will sketch out in some respects below, that such public production and dissemination continued for something like three and a half centuries in active competition and interchange with private and isolated efforts.[6]

It is also deeply paradoxical that Langland's C-version provided the stimulus for such public centralised production. For this version is marked by its lengthy and querulous 'autobiographical passage' (C 5.1–96). This turns on the notion, an echo of the 1388 'Statute of Labourers', that everyone has a place, a site all their own. At least in the imaginary of the dreamer Will's chief tormentor/interrogator Reason, this would appear to be somewhere in the fields of one's birth-village. Langland's dreamer is harassed because he has no place and, lacking one, no identity. Although as cleric *manqué* (who can thus claim for himself ubiquity even in the absence of a place-providing benefice), Will continues his poem,

---

[4] Endeavours comparable to Langland's transmission largely cluster in a similar innovation, the slightly later Ricardian investment in translated learned prose: Trevisa's *Polychronicon*, Nicholas Love's *Mirror*, Wycliffite scripture. But cf. the seminal account of activities *c* 1408 involving the more or less standardised London production of Gower's *Confessio Amantis*: A. I. Doyle and Malcolm Parkes, 'The Production of Copies of the *Canterbury Tales* and the *Confessio Amantis* in the Early Fifteenth Century', in Parkes and Andrew G. Watson (eds), *Medieval Scribes, Manuscripts, and Libraries: Essays Presented to N. R. Ker* (London, 1978), 163–210. (One of their scribes, 'D', is responsible for MS J of *Piers Plowman* C, mentioned in n. 1.) Doyle and Parkes's argument is extended, not uncontroversially, in Linne R. Mooney and Estelle Stubbs, *Scribes and the City: London Guildhall Clerks and the Dissemination of Middle English Literature, 1375–1425* (Woodbridge, 2013). (Leaving aside the scribal identifications, the authors' localisation of unique transmissional activity is unconvincing and seems to me deeply improbable in a packed and multi-focused urban environment.)

[5] Whatever the alignment with immortals Chaucer may suggest at *Troilus and Criseyde* 5.1786–99, there is no evidence that he promulgated his text beyond a coterie; the oldest surviving copies (New York, Morgan Library & Museum, M 817 and Cambridge, Corpus Christi College MS 61) postdate both Langland's innovation and the poet's death. Cf. the reference to the Wife of Bath in the lyric Chaucer wrote to a member of his coterie, 'Lenvoy de Chaucer a Bukton', 19.

[6] This interplay between the locally known and 'national literary tradition' is not entirely broken until sometime in the mid-eighteenth century; one late example would be the manuscript texts Pope apparently circulated to his coterie, very different from the printed published versions. For a couple of prominent discussions, see Arthur Marotti, *Manuscript, Print, and the English Renaissance Lyric* (Ithaca, NY, 1995) (although unduly exaggerating the amount of textual disruption introduced) and Harold Love, *Scribal Publication in Seventeenth-Century England* (Oxford, 1993).

it is under qualified auspices. London, stimulated by the apparently immediate success of *Piers Plowman* C, may have been a fifteenth-century book-producer's utopia, but that noun equally designates 'nowhere'. Efficient promulgation to a general nationwide audience represents a step-change in the site of the literary/poetic, and perhaps not one to be applauded without qualification.[7]

It should go without saying that the apparently organised model by which *Piers Plowman* C (and only following it, that poem's earlier avatars) entered the world cannot be applicable to pre-1390s situations. The circulation of Langland's poem throws up one sort of conflation that may be foreign to that earlier situation, that between (canonical?) text and manuscript book. In the case of most copies of *Piers Plowman* C, these might be conceived as coterminous notions, that the text stands alone in a continuously produced independent volume—and thus alien to much medieval book-production, well past the 1390s.[8] There discontinuity and miscellaneity are the rule rather than the exception. Moreover, in imagining sites of poetry in a pre-text era, assuming the equivalence of book and text severely occludes the discussion.

Quite simply, pre-public text communities (and it's important that 'community' and 'communicate' share the same root) are initially recoverable only through the manuscript book. All the tools at one's disposal for first locating, then defining literary sites are predicated on an analysis of information derived from books. First, in the Middle English situation, this involves localisation—initially and most precisely, provenance information (signatures, marks of ownership, and the like); secondarily, evidence provided by the myriad dialectical forms into which text is cast in the course of scribal transmission.[9] In some cases, this data may be precise enough (and enough historical information may survive) to allow some inferential recreation of site, a locale of personalised contact.

Households

The most obvious place to locate such sites would direct attention to a ubiquitous social feature of late medieval England: its profusion of households. As Langland's Reason points out to the dreamer, the most basic unit, to which everyone belongs, is the extended family, a nuclear group, together with some penumbra of blood relations and those 'servants' necessary to support both it and whatever property from which it gains its sustenance: 'hastow londes to lyue by ... or lynage ryche / That fyndeth the thy fode?' (C 5.26–7). Such units begin with the peasant level that Reason most routinely acknowledges. But cultural aspiration and achievement have, of course, always been associated with the upper end of the spectrum, with great houses. These are not necessarily those of the noble or even the titled, and many are familial only in the broad Latinate sense, clerical communities. In such locales, lords and ladies, prelates and clerks, people with some cultural pretensions, an interest in devotion or entertainment, for example, rub shoulders with a considerably more various group.

[7] See Derek Pearsall, 'Langland's London' and Middleton, 'Acts of Vagrancy: The C-Version "Autobiography" and the Statute of 1388', both in Steven Justice and Kathryn Kerby-Fulton (eds), *Written Work: Langland, Labor, and Authorship* (Philadelphia, PA, 1997), 185–207 and 208–317, respectively.

[8] Three quarters of the C-version copies (including A+C 'splices') are devoted to the single text; see Russell-Kane 1–18. The figures are well in excess of those for either A or B versions—and where such presentation occurs there, it may be in imitation of the already circulating C.

[9] Hence the seminal importance of *A Linguistic Atlas of Late Mediaeval English* (*LALME*), now most readily available online, at https://www.lel.ed.ac.uk/ihd/elalme/elalme_frames.html.

40   MEDIEVAL POETRY: 1100–1400

The one common ingredient across all such sites is the need for writers, broadly understood. For all such families depend upon estate-management, the shrewd ability both to organise and to administer properties. In medieval England, these activities customarily involve written record, a great deal of it, from a literary (although not a historical) point of view, thoroughly ephemeral (bills, accounts, rentals, inventories). All these require writers, customarily clerical, both specifically religious (and Latin-trained, which means, until the late fourteenth century, also Anglo-Norman trained) and increasingly, from the later thirteenth century, 'men of affairs', business-writers, attorneys, and perhaps notaries. The attorneys might deserve special notice, since one function of a household servant was, when required, to offer the *paterfamilias*, the lord, 'good counsel', to advise him in his decision-making. Persistently, across the country, one can count upon 'servants', some of more than modest sophistication, who essentially enable a fusion of poetic site in its diverse senses: persons capable, as sumptuary work, moonlighting, of composition (including translation) and copying/transmission (given the prevalence of books in anglicana, the standard business-, not book-hand), with a readily receptive and perhaps commissioning audience at close hand. One scarcely needs to invoke the hoary trope that Chaucer's main value to royalty was not his ability to compose English verse but, *inter alia*, to keep honest customs records in his own hand.[10]

The household may represent a ubiquitous social feature, but in the individual instance, potentially an isolated one, committed to local interests alone. I begin here and hope to develop an argument expansive in nature, ranging from this isolative possibility to considerably more extensive, if perhaps provincial and regionally limited, examples. I hope to map out an expanding locus of engagement, from the negligible, through likely accidental contact, to organised efforts at promulgation.

No one needs to be reminded that English poetry is born, as it were, out of devotion. But one frequently discussed knock-on effect of Innocent III's fourth Lateran council was to draw attention to those in need of informative, largely soul-saving material of an authoritative nature.[11] One central exhibit would be the Englishing of an international devotional classic, Lorens of Orléans's *Somme le roi*, well illustrative of this pre-public landscape. Seventeen such efforts (all but one in prose) survive; they range from Dan Michel of Northgate in 1340 to Caxton's *Royal Book* of 1486 (as well as a slightly later example in Scots).[12] Only one of these, to which I will return, the single verse example, *Speculum Vitae*, had any protracted circulation at all. From this, one might draw two conclusions. First of all, there was a quite substantial number of copies of the French original floating about and in use (indeed, considerably more insularly produced manuscripts of the French *Somme* still survive than do of any English prose version). Second, none of the seventeen original translators was aware of any of the others, since none is likely to have taken up the task were an actual English version at hand.

---

[10] There is, of course, a huge historical literature, of all stripes, on clerical households—bishops' *familiae*, communities of regular clergy (like the Franciscans I will mention in a moment), and the like. For the classic study of lay examples, see G. A. Holmes, *The Estates of the Higher Nobility in Fourteenth-Century England* (Cambridge, 1957), and for provocative thoughts on the relationship of such establishments to literary activity, Elizabeth Salter, *Fourteenth-Century English Poetry: Contexts and Readings* (Oxford, 1983).

[11] For the originary study, drawing attention to specifically English verse materials, see W. A. Pantin, *The English Church in the Fourteenth Century* (Cambridge, 1955), 189–243.

[12] For the original, see Édith Brayer and Anne-Françoise Leurquin-Labie (eds), *La* Somme le roi *par Frère Laurent* SATF (Abbeville, 2008). For English versions, see Ralph Hanna (ed.), *Speculum Vitae: A Reading Edition*, 2 vols., EETS o.s. 331–2 (Oxford, 2008), 1:lxx, esp. n. 42.

The example illustrates a couple of important caveats. First, in its profusion of French readers capable of offering the text in English for the less adept, it testifies to the customarily trilingual state of English medieval culture. Indeed, the demise of Anglo-Norman as an active literary medium probably opened a space to be filled by the profusion of original poetry in English that begins with Langland. In this regard, one might note that two of the prose *Somme*-translations are explicitly language-learning exercises, a mode of preserving fluency, and of personal-use value only. But if such is the case, the broadening public audience associated with writing in English, including poetry, might be perceived as reflecting overt pauperisation, the narrowing of what English literature might mean, so that it would become increasingly monolingual (and impoverished vis-à-vis what an openness to medieval England's other languages might have prioritised).[13] Second, as a linguistic choice English monolingualism is, as it always had been, a pragmatic decision. Whatever the language politics of pre-Plague England, the one thing that had bound any public since the later twelfth century was common access to English—and most texts I will examine are, like *Somme*, most usually expressions of interest in 'common [spiritual] good', not from our perspective imaginative at all.

One prominent subset of this narrative of isolation has always been provided by alliterative poetry, a tradition of great technical and descriptive excellence—but nearly universally attested in unique, presumably household-sponsored manuscripts. As two early examples will indicate, the tradition (all the way to its formal conclusion in the 1508 Edinburgh prints of Chepman and Myllar) is marked by what appears domestic composition and production, for a household audience. 'Winnere and Wastour', for example, parades the heraldry of the Wingfield family (senseless unless one knows them) and includes, in a rather nasty aside, an allusion to Justice Scarisbrook's activities during a Cheshire peasant uprising of the 1350s. The poem itself persistently addresses the dynamics of the household, both in its prologue's interest in witty counsel and in the subsequent debate on issues of household economy. Both references, to Wingfield and to the Cheshire rising, point to authorship and initial promulgation somewhere in the Black Prince's retinue. (Edward was 'Black'—a persistent exploiter of the 'winnings' of others so he could sumptuarially 'waste' them—owing not just to exactions from those revolting Cheshire peasants but also to genocidal extortive efforts in the Limousin.) A similarly early poem, *William of Palerne*, explicitly addresses Humfrey Bohun, earl of Hereford, and was certainly written for and in one of his households.[14] The tradition is marked by learned clerical authors not necessarily engaged with or committed to inherited aristocratic values, but lamenting them, one form of rather indirect counsel (cf. the *Morte Arthure*). Not only were they translators (and perhaps oral readers/reciters), but they or their office colleagues were also presumably the copyists of our surviving manuscripts.[15]

---

[13] Fulfilling John Trevisa's prophecy, in a discussion persistently (yet inaccurately) invoked in triumphalist narratives of English vernacularity; see Kenneth Sisam (ed.), *Fourteenth-Century Verse and Prose* (Oxford, 1921), 148–9.

[14] On the 'site' of 'William', see Thorlac Turville-Petre, *The Alliterative Revival* (Cambridge, 1977), 40–1, 134–5 nn. 31–2. Turville-Petre has also written the most useful account of alliterative poetics, *Description and Narrative in Middle English Alliterative Poetry* (Liverpool, 2018).

[15] Even in its manuscript context, alliterative poetry is typically isolated; 'Winner and Waster', for example, appears in a separable portion of London, British Library, MS Additional 31,042, accompanied only by another alliterative offering, 'The Parliament of the Three Ages'. One might notice in passing the hand of the most famous alliterative scribe, that of the *Gawain*-manuscript, British Library, MS Cotton Nero A.x, so awkward in the small *fere textura* on evidence here that one would suppose him a writer more accustomed to the usual accounts-hand anglicana. As this paragraph implies, it should be unsurprising to find scribes either offering critical commentary, the subject of B. A. Windeatt's seminal 'The Scribes as Chaucer's Early Critics', *Studies in the Age of Chaucer*, 1 (1979), 119–41, or indeed composing themselves.

42 MEDIEVAL POETRY: 1100–1400

Clerical Households—and Others

Clerical orders provide a rather different conception of household, in this instance prominent in producing and promulgating what are customarily taken as the (trilingual) fonts of English poetic tradition. These, with their secular analogues, are overwhelmingly associated with the South-west Midlands (broadly the historical dioceses of Worcester and Hereford).[16] In clerical circles, their bilingualism—Anglo-Norman and Latin—might well be expected, but their English localism is in some sense overdetermined. Its conditions were created by anti-Norman reactions under Bishop Wulfstan II of Worcester, who survived the Conquest by twenty-five years and was an author in English (prose) and apparent sponsor of a sequence of late-eleventh-century English homiliaries, still drawing on pre-Conquest sources.

One excellent example is provided by a true Franciscan *joculator Dei*, William Herebert of the Hereford convent, in his British Library, MS Additional 46919.[17] Herebert not only composed English poems, mainly translations of Latin hymns and presented keyed to the verses of the originals, but also, as a manuscript note indicates, copied them out himself. The audience he imagined must, on several grounds, have been mixed. On the one hand, much of Herebert's transmission, although personal, must have been oral, as a line-by-line gloss (perhaps for responsive oral recitation?) for audiences who heard him preach.[18] On the other hand, Herebert arranged for his book to be communal, conventual property; by bequeathing it to his brethren, he offered them a resource for possible continuing promulgation of his poems, again very likely as oral text.

Herebert's book is also revelatory in its non-English contents, which underwrite the argument of the preceding paragraphs and indicate the power of regional and national networks fostered by well-organised religious orders. In the main, the Additional manuscript is a preacher's sourcebook, one based on Herebert's service before he went to Hereford as convent lector in Oxford. Thus, a considerable portion of the volume is dedicated to sermons in Anglo-Norman verse, materials Herebert probably received directly from their author, his Oxford colleague Nicholas Bozon. Latin portions include Oxonian mendicant staples, for example Walter Map's *Valerius* (now removed from the volume) and Malachy's *De veneno*; portions of these actually appear twice in the book, since Herebert recycles his collected reference materials within the sermons that he delivered (further local oral transmission) and that are also recorded here in Latin, mainly in his own hand.

Similar views would explain a much better-known, slightly later preaching compendium, National Library of Scotland, Advocates' MS 18.2.1 (John of Grimestone's book). Generically, this is an alphabetical book of Latin *distinctiones* (outlines of diverse senses of spiritual lexicon), much more formally and painstakingly produced than Herebert's manuscript. The Latin discussions are original in their local confirmations, yet they clearly rely upon

---

[16] The statistics in Carleton Brown's two anthologies are overwhelming: the relevant books provide two thirds of his volume of thirteenth-century lyrics (not to mention both copies of 'The Owl and the Nightingale') and forty-two of his seventy-six relevant early-fourteenth-century religious lyrics. The only other locale so heavily invested at this period is Anglo-Ireland (British Library, MS Harley 913; and peripherally, Cambridge University Library, MS Gg.1.1). Both are reasonably direct offshoots of areas from which the invaders drew heavily for settlers, in essence exportation of locally familiar culture into an alien colony. See further Angus McIntosh and M. L. Samuels, 'Prologemona to a Study of Medieval Anglo-Irish', *Medium Ævum*, 37 (1968), 1–11.

[17] See Stephen R. Reimer (ed.), *The Works of William Herebert, OFM*, Studies and Texts 81 (Toronto, 1987); the book must predate 1333, the year of the author's death.

[18] Suggested by the *mise en page* of the autograph, reproduced 'Phillipps MS. 8336 ...', Robinson's of Pall Mall catalogue 79 (London, 1950), frontispiece, with the translated English units keyed to brief Latin lemmata from the originals.

standard sources for *praedicabilia* (preaching materials) from a conventual library; however, they are spiced up by around 150 English lyrics. Designed, like Herebert's hymns, for intercalation into delivered sermons, these show every sign of being Grimestone's own. For example, the Advocates' MS presents a revised version of the widely disseminated 'Candet nudatum corpus'; to produce it, Grimestone returned to the original Latin and provided, as no other copy does, a complete rendition of this source. The modest diffusion of some of Grimestone's lyrics across a range of books associable with Franciscan activity so far from the author's King's Lynn neighbourhood as south Yorkshire indicates their (largely oral?) dissemination among his fellow Grey Friars.[19]

But only a minority of these locally concentrated trilingual books clearly reflects the activity of religious orders.[20] The two best-known examples of lay analogues are Bodleian Library, MS Digby 86 and (of course) British Library, MS Harley 2253. The first, simply given the informality of its two scribes, both writing in the business-hand anglicana, is a domestic production for household entertainment, whose precise south Worcestershire provenance has been extensively discussed.[21] The second, as Carter Revard has extensively documented, was copied by a professional Ludlow scribe—mainly attested in legal documents for private parties, but, given his appearance in three books, routinely available for private literary work. The readiest inference, drawn by numerous scholars, would suggest that this is a professionally produced book designed to offer entertainment to a local household. Likely candidates could include either the Mortimers, Marcher lords of Wigmore, or a bishop of Hereford. In either case, Harley 2253 would be associated with figures of national prominence. Such individuals might be expected to have the sort of catholic contacts signalled in the book's contents.[22]

Religious orders offered more or less direct and continuous connections for sharing and transmitting texts, but, as Harley 2253 indicates, much less formal links also operated, joining diverse secular communities, dispersed lay households. The distance some of these acquaintance networks might traverse (and the network, the plurality of contacts that might become peripherally, and very likely ignorantly, impersonally involved with one another) is signalled by passing features of Harley 2253's lyrics. 'When þe nyhtegale singes' contains references to Lincolnshire (notice the Ludlow scribe's retention of the alien North Midlands verbal termination), 'Most I riden by Ribblesdale' points to the North-west, and 'The song of the husbandman' allegedly shows south-eastern language. Local acquaintances formed by land transactions, legal service, and maybe just plain old market-day breaks in the same pub enabled cultural transmission as well.

---

[19] On Grimestone, see Edward Wilson (ed.), *A Descriptive Index of the English Lyrics in John of Grimestone's Preaching Book*, Medium Ævum Monographs n.s. 2 (Oxford, 1973) and the extensive analysis, Siegfried Wenzel, *Preachers, Poets, and the Early English Lyric* (Princeton, NJ, 1986). For his version of 'Candet nudatum corpus', artfully arranged in quatrains of English 'hymn-metre', equally alien to other copies, see Hanna, *Patient Reading*, 78–9. One example of Grimestone's dissemination appears in the south Yorkshire book, New Haven, CT, Yale University Library, MS Takamiya 15. There one of his lyrics appears next to instructions dated 1486 that the book should pass to the Franciscans of Lichfield. For a further example of such production, see Karl Reichl, *Religiöse Dichtung im englischen Hochmittelalter: Untersuchung und Edition der Handschrift B.14.39 der Trinity College in Cambridge* (Munich, 1973).

[20] Regrettably, the definitive demolition of the ancient view that all these volumes reflect mendicant activity remains unpublished: John D. Scahill, 'The Friars' Miscellanies' (PhD Diss., University of Sydney, 1990).

[21] See Judith Tschann and M. B. Parkes (eds), *Facsimile of Oxford, Bodleian Library, MS Digby 86*, EETS s.s. 16 (Oxford, 1996), including abundant further references, and Marilyn Corrie, 'The Compilation of Oxford, Bodleian Library, MS Digby 86', *Medium Ævum*, 66 (1997), 236–49.

[22] See Carter Revard, 'Scribe and Provenance', in Susanna Fein (ed.), *Studies in the Harley Manuscript: The Scribes, Contents, and Social Contexts of British Library MS Harley 2253* (Kalamazoo, MI, 2000), 21–109. Although Ludlow is in southern Shropshire, this was still within the Hereford diocese in the Middle Ages.

44 MEDIEVAL POETRY: 1100–1400

This probable networking appears more flagrantly in the two manuscripts of the most distinguished piece of early Middle English verse, *The Owl and the Nightingale*. British Library, MS Cotton Caligula A.ix and Oxford, Jesus College, MS 29 share not only this poem but also a spectrum of contents, although reproduced in each book in differing orders and with different surrounds. In spite of representing different textual communities, both sets of book-producers had access to the same extensive manuscript (largely Anglo-Norman) as an exemplar. This raises the spectre that not all texts in such a collected volume need necessarily be local products, but rather domestic scribes sharing transmissional roles with those whose work has been received, thereby initiating a new audience.[23]

Yet however extensive and variegated they may be, networks might equally be limited. My analysis of Herebert and Grimestone above is enabled by well-founded expectations about Franciscan behaviour, a homogeneity of occupation and interest. But even a poem so august as *The Owl and the Nightingale*, itself marked linguistically, like Harley 2253's texts, by passage through diverse communities, is isolated. It is not, as is *Piers Plowman* C, a text per se; it is never known outside its miscellaneous appearance as part of the common Caligula and Jesus exemplar inheritance. Moreover, its particular confirmation is unique and locally isolated. Both copies of the poem include other items unique to the individual manuscript (notably, in Caligula, Laȝamon's *Brut*), and although, for example, Cambridge, Trinity College, MS 323 and British Library, MS Egerton 613 are contemporary and from adjacent locales, neither set of these book-producers seems to have known the source manuscript underlying Caligula and Jesus—or if they did, they had no interest in reproducing any part of it.

This will suggest something of the adventitiousness of such sited literary production. Matthew Sullivan offers a provocative hypothesis in this regard. He treats one avenue by which the south Lincolnshire poet Robert Mannyng might have come upon the Anglo-Norman source he translated as *Handling Sin*. It turns on sheer fortuitousness. William of Waddington, the author of the original poem, was the archbishop of York's steward for Southwell Minster (Notts.); Robert's monastic order, the Gilbertines, maintained an altar in that Minster. Clerical chit-chat over table may well have led to a Gilbertine with as yet unfulfilled poetic ambitions undertaking this translated work of instruction. Yet the materials for Mannyng's other major endeavour, *The Chronicle of England*, indicate the shifting nature of his networks. This text probably came to him by more straightforward clerical connections, through the 'Danz Robert of Malton þat ȝe know, [who] Did it wryte ...' (142–3: either 'commanded me to compose' or 'had it written/promulgated'?).[24]

Widening Networks

At the same time, such local networks may have been intense and at least loosely organised. I mentioned earlier the poetic *Speculum Vitae* as the unique success story among Middle English translations of Lorens's *Somme le roi*. Although there are a great many manuscripts

---

[23] See N. R. Ker (ed.), *The Owl and the Nightingale: Reproduced in Facsimile from the Surviving Manuscripts, Jesus College Oxford 29 and British Museum Cotton Caligula A.ix*, EETS o.s. 251 (London, 1963), ix–xi; Caligula reproduces only ten of the thirty-three texts Ker identifies in Jesus.

[24] See Matthew Sullivan, 'The Author of the *Manuel des Péchés*', *Notes & Queries*, 236 (1991), 235–7. Malton, the site of a Gilbertine house, is roughly thirty miles west of Bridlington, home house of the author Mannyng here translates in part, Pierre Langtoft. An alternative suggestion, Andrew W. Taubman, 'New Biographical Notes on Robert Mannyng of Brunne', *Notes & Queries*, n.s. 56 (2009), 197–201, is predicated upon linguistic arguments easily shown from the *LALME* database to be erroneous.

(counting fragments, now about fifty of them known), in fact the majority transmission is highly localised. Although the authorial language reflects the natural usage of the southern Vale of York, the core of transmission is just a bit further north. One imagines that the author, who recycles not simply Lorens but a local Latin *Pater noster* tract as well, and versifies bits from Archbishop Thoresby's vernacular catechism,[25] is a priest, writing in his home dialect—but not necessarily employed in his home country. Given that he knows the slightly earlier and profusely distributed *Prick of Conscience*, his composition may well have represented pure volunteerism, a contribution to the common spiritual good and deliberately designed to avoid (or perhaps more accurately, supplement) pre-existing local instructional products. (*Speculum Vitae* is unique among the sequence of lengthy Northern poems of instruction in directly addressing what evil is/vice and how to live well/virtue.) The prologue's analysis of trilingualism (lines 61–90), the most sophisticated in any of these products, simply settles upon English as the tongue available to all, and the poet's gestures towards an audience would include the most generic Every-person.

However, four of the five most authoritative copies, genetically related against the remaining swarm, cluster in a single locale, a small area between Ripon and Knaresborough, just at the border between Yorkshire's West and North Ridings. Moreover, the most successful of the remaining manuscripts spiral out from this centre in a wide swathe extending up Wensleydale to the north and west. Certainly the area from which the four central copies emerge was filled with aristocratic residences, associated with successful knights and attorneys. Moreover, without exception, these were persons with extensive property holdings (in the case of the lawyers, prosperous clients)—and in all three areas germane to the poem: the southern Vale, where a stay-at-home cleric might have written the poem; the area around and just south of Ripon, packed with prosperous households; and the North Riding, where inevitable connections with the Nevilles's retinue in the Honour of Richmond may well have stimulated the poem's spread. This suggests a compact narrative—the text circulated widely, but within a remarkably confined space, publicised by word of mouth among a local elite and passed great house to great house to domestic copyists—and a text that only by accident may have escaped locality.

This situation might be contrasted with the fate of *The Prick of Conscience*, at least one piece of which offers the most prolific example of organised provincial book-production before 1400.[26] *The Prick* is the most distinguished early example of a local product that in the course of the fifteenth century achieved a truly pan-English circulation. This far outstrips that evident in the poem's original use-community and never involved metropolitan procedures. Of the more than 170 surviving copies, only a single one has London connections, and only about twenty of the survivors were produced in the North, where the text was composed.[27]

How did such a saturation of English reading communities, one that in some cases exceeds Chaucer's mainly south-eastern cultural ambit, come about? At least one process clearly visible is what one might designate 'site-conscious revision'. Transmission here pays

---

[25] A point for which I am grateful to Pamela L. C. Greig, who edited the catechism in an unpublished thesis: 'The "Lay Folks" Catechism—An Edition' (PhD Diss., University of Nottingham, 2018).

[26] A much less extensively recorded transmissional community, apparently somewhere near the Berkshire–Gloucestershire border, awaits detailed analysis. These individuals *c* 1310–20 were engaged in promulgating copies of the *South English Legendary*, in Cambridge, Corpus Christi College, MS 145; British Library, MS Egerton 2891; and fragments at Leicester City Museum and Nottingham University Library.

[27] For the dissemination, see the map at Robert E. Lewis and Angus McIntosh, *A Descriptive Guide to the Manuscripts of the* Prick of Conscience, Medium Ævum Monographs n.s. 12 (Oxford, 1982), 171. The single metropolitan example, Oxford, St John's College, MS 57, was probably copied in the 1440s or 1450s.

46 MEDIEVAL POETRY: 1100–1400

tribute to the power of the work's 'sentence', its instructive value, but alienation from its 'solaas'. *The Prick* required adjustments to communicate properly or attractively in a place differing from that of its original circulation. Here I turn to one of the most clearly documented episodes associated with Yorkshire cultural diffusion, its power predicated upon the persistence with which it went on, over a short and intense period, as well as by care in redacting alien texts, apparently to acclimatise them to new local conditions. These activities were undertaken by what appears a fairly compact scribal (and a less palpable editorial) community in Lichfield. At least one derivative of these export procedures is extremely well known, indeed central to studies of Middle English devotional literature, the texts communicated in the huge Vernon and Simeon manuscripts (Oxford, Bodleian Library, MS Eng. poet. a.1 and British Library, MS Additional 22,283, respectively).

The Example of Lichfield

The Vernon and Simeon MSS are end-products and without progeny, yet they are formidable, indeed inescapable late-fourteenth-century models/monuments of a perceived canonical religious culture in English. And although hugely inclusive/comprehensive and vastly acquisitive in pursuing any useful text,[28] these large volumes include extensive reproduction of earlier Yorkshire literary culture. This is most provocatively displayed in two large blocks of material, common to both books: an enormous grouping of instructional poetry, *The Northern Homilies + Speculum Vitae + The Prick of Conscience* (Vernon, fols. 167ra– 284ra; at the head of Simeon and split, as they are not in Vernon, across a booklet boundary), and Richard Rolle's three English epistles of spiritual counsel (Vernon, fols. 334ra–39ra; at the conclusion of Simeon).[29] All these texts have, in various ways, been subjected to editorial intervention; regardless of its extent in any single text, this is striking enough to distinguish the Northern materials communicated by both books from all other known copies.[30]

---

[28] The one example that has been pursued in any depth, involving expected, quite local exchanges, concerns British Library, MS Additional 37,787 (surveyed as *LALME* LP 7640), from the small Worcestershire Cistercian house at Bordesley. See Nita S. Baugh (ed.), *A Worcestershire Miscellany, Compiled by John Northwood, c. 1400* (Philadelphia, PA, 1956).

[29] The south Yorkshire stanzaic alliterative poem 'Susannah', a rendition of an episode from the biblical Daniel, appears later in the first block, in both books; theirs are the two earliest copies by a far stretch, and the poem now survives in no Northern manuscript. Equally, Rolle's epistles are juxtaposed with a substantial block of texts by Walter Hilton, at this date mainly known from Yorkshire books, as well as the early Yorkshire 'Abbey of the Holy Ghost' (with its sequel, 'The Charter'). For the definitive discussion, with further references, see A. I. Doyle, 'Introduction', in *The Vernon Manuscript: A Facsimile of Bodleian Library, Oxford MS. Eng. poet. a.1* (Cambridge, 1987) and, on one aspect of the collection techniques visible in Simeon but not Vernon, his 'University College, Oxford, MS. 97 and Its Relationship to the Simeon Manuscript (British Library Add. 22283)', in Michael Benskin and M. L. Samuels (eds), *So meny people longages and tonges: Philological Essays in Scots and Mediaeval English Presented to Angus McIntosh* (Edinburgh, 1981), 265–82.

[30] The relevant version of *Cursor Mundi* has long been available (easily comparable with three of the 'original version' manuscripts, all copied three quarters of a century before), in the farthest right column of Richard Morris's edition *Cursor Mundi (The Cursur o the World): A Northumbrian Poem of the XIVth Century in Four Versions*, EETS o.s. 57, 59, 62, 66, 68, 99, 101 (London, 1874–93). This presentation stimulated an important—and subsequently ignored—contribution, Rolf Keiser, *Zur Geographie des mittelenglischen Wortschatzes*, Palaestra 205 (Leipzig, 1937). There is also a full separate edition, *The Southern Version of Cursor Mundi*, gen. ed. Sarah M. Horrall, 5 vols. (Ottawa, 1978–2000). For the local version of *The Prick of Conscience*, see Margaret G. Dareau and Angus McIntosh, 'A Dialect Word in Some West Midland Manuscripts of the *Prick of Conscience*', in A. J. Aitken, Angus McIntosh, and Hermann Pálsson (eds), *Edinburgh Studies in English and Scots* (London, 1971), 20–6; McIntosh, 'Two Unnoticed Interpolations in Four Manuscripts of the *Prick of Conscience*', *Neuphilologische*

A. I. Doyle's studies have shown that, although the scribe most prominently associated with both these books writes the language of northern Worcestershire, these productions are to be associated more narrowly with Lichfield.[31] Rather than a rural locale, the books emanated from a centre, and the patrons who had commissioned these extensive collections remain obscure—although likely a nunnery in the West Midlands or its supporters. However, the materials underlying Vernon and Simeon have a considerable circulation independent of the two anthologies, initially apparent in a small group of books, these offering reiterated evidence for Lichfield-area origins in their common languages. More than that, as the late Jeremy Griffiths first pointed out, two scribes recur across a sequence of volumes with texts related to those of the great anthologies. One of the individuals Griffiths identified ('the Lichfield scribe') appears in at least six books, including distinctive copies of the local versions of both *Cursor Mundi* and *The Prick of Conscience*, as well as contributing to Bodleian Library, MS Rawlinson A.389, a volume with a local version of Rolle's epistles.[32] The second scribe, 'John', perhaps, as Doyle pointed out, to be identified with a Lichfield 'Johannes Scriveyn', appears in at least four books, including the contents table of 'the Vernon manuscript' and portions of two further copies of the local *Prick of Conscience*.[33] Doyle also discusses a note suggesting that he may have produced a further copy of *Speculum Vitae* for a Lichfield Cathedral priest. In addition to this protracted activity, a further scribe, in London, College of Arms, MS Arundel 57, provides both a second copy of the local recension of *Cursor Mundi* and yet another copy of *The Prick of Conscience* recension found elsewhere, again in Lichfield language.

Between them, the two primary scribes show a repeated engagement with a collection of works not native to Lichfield in either composition or intended audience, yet transmitted in distinctive local forms. They bespeak a selective effort at choosing materials—the full range of potential Northern offerings did not pass through this process; for example, they contain no copy of Rolle's English *Prose Psalter*, although there is considerably more surviving evidence for its Northern transmission than there is for his epistles. Equally, so far as the surviving copies offer evidence, patrons exercised some selectivity about texts considered useful; for example, only Vernon and Simeon provide the revised version of *The Northern Homilies* (although it is difficult, in light of the other evidence, to imagine this as anything other than Lichfield work). Similarly, the Vernon-Simeon production teams choose not to provide—or perhaps never acquired separate materials for?—the locally revised *Cursor Mundi*.

For the moment, I defer consideration of the mechanisms effecting transmission, the overlaps among scribes, to consider the poetic site: 'Why Lichfield?' This was a largely unimportant place, but an important transit hub, situated at the juncture of two Roman roads, each entwined with other important connecting roads. Lichfield was always and

---

Mitteilungen, 77 (1976), 63–78; and Robert E. Lewis, 'The Relationship of the Vernon and Simeon Texts of the *Pricke of Conscience*', in Benskin and Samuels (eds), *So meny people*, 251–64.

[31] Vernon is in a single hand, the scribe's language placed in north Worcestershire (*LALME* LP 7360); the contents-table scribe, 'John', is adjacently placed as LP 7670.

[32] The first is Cambridge, Trinity College, MS R.3.8, presented by Morris; the scribe is surveyed from this source, as *LALME* LP 36. For the second, BL Harley 1205, and its form of the text shared with Vernon and Simeon, Lewis-McIntosh's 'Type III' of the text, see their *Descriptive Guide*, 7–8. Harley 1205 is their MV 31; the same scribe also copied MV 54. I am extremely grateful to Bob Lewis for further information on and advice about researching this form of the poem; he tells me that the identification of this recension was entirely Angus McIntosh's work.

[33] These are Lewis and McIntosh's MV 23 and 89. In addition, John copied the cartulary for Stoneleigh abbey (Warwickshire), one of Bordesley abbey's two daughter-houses (cf. n. 27 above).

48 MEDIEVAL POETRY: 1100–1400

only important as an entrepôt, a junction where diverse communities might intersect one another and exchange wares, both mercantile and cultural.[34]

Indeed, Lichfield's development as a place largely depended upon its embeddedness in a transportation network, and one always closely connected to Yorkshire. Moreover, Lichfield was, as it were, a company store. The town was planned, planted, and administered from the 'cathedral of the Mercians', founded from York. There were, for example, no parish churches, only chapels dependent upon the Cathedral. This was a small provincial centre, about the fiftieth most populated place in England. Moreover, although the administrative centre of a diocese that extended from Coventry to Preston, this province appears something of a cultural backwater. Certainly, excepting Ranulf Higden, Benedictine of Chester, the north-west of the diocese was literarily unproductive until very late in the Middle Ages;[35] and the most prominent local author, John Mirk of Lilleshall (a house of Augustinian canons in Shropshire), was probably producing his sermons contemporaneously with these efforts at propagating Northern materials. Like that imagined desert of Anglo-Ireland, into which someone early imported the materials underlying Cambridge University Library, MS Gg.i.1, or, for that matter, late-fourteenth-century London, Lichfield was an English literary void relying on its transport network to bring in materials from more richly endowed neighbourhoods.

Moreover, given the concentration of local sophisticates in the cathedral chapter, this— yet another example of an ecclesiastical household—provides the obvious place to look for agents of cultural transmission. A minor detail suggests that exemplars for all these various works were retained together for a protracted period, presumably to facilitate future demands for copies. The Rolle anthology, Bodleian Library, MS Rawlinson A.389, at fols. 72^v–73^v (along with further notes), includes a series of prophecies added on blank leaves. The same prophecies appear, also added on blank leaves, at Oxford, University College, MS 97, fols. 1–3. As Doyle showed, the latter is the source underlying—indeed, it is probably the exemplar used for—a textual endeavour independent of the Rolle manuscript, religious instructional materials in the Simeon MS (but not included in the companion Vernon). These two books must have been in the same place, and Rawlinson has notes indicating its ownership by identifiable Cathedral canons.

Further, the congregation of scribes I have mentioned represents only the visible end of a considerably protracted process, certainly undertaken before the scribes produced the surviving manuscripts. The Vernon manuscript is conventionally placed c 1390, but, given the limits of palaeographical dating, the book could probably have been in production any time after the early 1380s. The size of the task was daunting, and this single manuscript alone (leaving aside his contributions to its companion Simeon) would have required something like two years of full-time work from its scribe.

But preparation of the redacted texts that formed Vernon's exemplars will obviously have preceded the book itself. As the subsequent discussion will demonstrate, this procedure required extensive work, protracted and detailed, even before the production of fair-copy exemplars, necessary for making the surviving books, could occur. Someone or some group associated with the Cathedral must have been engaged in collecting and preparing the materials underlying Vernon sometime in or before the early 1380s. Because a good many clerics

---

[34] See further Ralph Hanna, 'Lichfield', in David Wallace (ed.), *Europe: A Literary History, 1348–1418*, 2 vols. (Oxford, 2015), 1:279–84, with further references.

[35] I doubt very much that *Gawain and the Green Knight* is the Cheshire product it is often stridently asserted to have been, but to be associated with some large establishment, ecclesiastical or lay.

held positions in both York and Lichfield during the period, there is no dearth of candidates with whom extensive Lichfield transmission of Northern texts—acquisition of Yorkshire *originalia*, inspection (and implicitly rejection) of the textual forms received, and redaction into a version deemed locally acceptable—might be associated.[36]

Because there are ample studies of Lichfield reception and transmission of *Cursor Mundi*, I direct my discussion elsewhere.[37] Just as with Rolle's epistles, transmission through Lichfield was integral to the distribution of *The Prick of Conscience* across western England. In many cases, this appears to have been a benign adventure. A very large number of dispersed 'Type I' copies, the poem's original Northern form, displays South-West Midlands language more or less comparable to that of the Vernon scribe. Apparently, numerous copies of the poem simply passed down the road from Yorkshire into Worcestershire and neighbouring areas with minimal difficulty or textual change.[38]

But considerably more interesting are those copies of the poem produced by local Lichfield scribes, and then subject to further promulgation. All these, as well as Vernon and Simeon, communicate a distinct and meticulous redaction of the text, Lewis–McIntosh's 'Lichfield subgroup'/'Type III'. Apparently initiated in the exemplar used by 'the Lichfield scribe' as source material for British Library, MS Harley 1205, this originally local tradition is extant in nineteen surviving books (and, as Angus McIntosh demonstrated, an original census of at least a hundred), nearly all from Lichfield or its adjacent hinterlands. However, this group of copies also includes a south-western spread, paralleled in other local textual traditions, down one of Lichfield's road links, to Worcester, and beyond its end, to so far away as Devonshire. As one might expect, the textual relations of this version point to alterations made to a copy originating in south Yorkshire; the transmission is thus analogous to that underlying the Vernon and Simeon copies of 'Susannah'. These books form the most protracted and widely dispersed work on *The Prick of Conscience*, excepting 'The Southern Recension'.[39]

---

[36] A few examples, drawn only from among the higher officials of both sees: John Sheppey, chancellor of Lichfield, 1364–77 (also prebendary of York, 1376–8); Francis de Teobalschi, dean of Lichfield, 1371–8 (also prebendary of York, 1370–8); John Carp, treasurer of Lichfield, 1380–7 (also prebendary of York, 1374–97); William de Packington, dean of Lichfield, 1381–90 (also prebendary of York, 1381–90); Nicholas Slake, archdeacon of Chester (in Lichfield diocese), 1385–7 (also prebendary of York, 1396–7). Jonathan Hughes, *Pastors and Visionaries: Religion and Secular Life in Late Medieval Yorkshire* (Woodbridge, 1988) continually insists upon the guiding role he believes was played by Richard Scrope (of the family's Masham branch), who was bishop of Lichfield, 1386–98, and subsequently martyred archbishop of York (see, e.g., 184, 186, 203, 213–14, 221). But, if Vernon was produced *c* 1390, Scrope's move to Lichfield is probably too late to have been anything other than supportive of already ongoing activities.

[37] See Sarah M. Horrall, '"For the commun at understand": *Cursor Mundi* and Its Background', in Michael G. Sargent (ed.), *De cella in seculum: Religious and Secular Life and Devotion in Late Medieval England* (Cambridge, 1989), 97–107 and Horrall, '"Man Yhernes Rimes for to Here": A Biblical History from the Middle Ages', in Carol G. Fisher and Kathleen L. Scott (eds), *Art into Life: Collected Papers from the Kresge Art Museum Medieval Symposia* (East Lansing, MI, 1995), 73–93; John Thompson, 'Textual Instability and the Late Medieval Reputation of Some Middle English Religious Literature', *TEXT*, 5 (1991), 175–94; and Thompson, *The* Cursor Mundi: *Poem, Texts and Contexts*, Medium Ævum Monographs n.s. 19 (Oxford, 1998), esp. 49–56; as well as the caveat, Anne L. Klinck, 'Editing *Cursor Mundi*: Stemmata and the "Open" Text', in Siân Echard and Stephen Partridge (eds), *The Book Unbound: Editing and Reading Medieval Manuscripts and Texts* (Toronto, 2004), 3–13.

[38] Following Lewis and McIntosh, *Descriptive Guide*, most notable would be one related group of six manuscripts generally of Worcester provenance (their MV 3, 9, 10, 87, 90; books 1–2 in MV 24), and one pair (MV 11 and 14). MV 52 is the only other 'Type I' copy without arguable connections to Yorkshire.

[39] See Lewis and McIntosh, *Descriptive Guide*, 7–8, with references to copies, all of which they describe. For the sources of this version, cf. MV 28, 29, 35, 43, 62, 93. For the 'Southern Recension', see Lewis and McIntosh, 9–10, 131–48 (eighteen copies); McIntosh, by tracing dialect relicts, at one time argued in conversation that this recension had been generated from a single East Anglian copy, probably Lichfield Cathedral, MS 50. Now see Jean E. Jost with Hoyt Greeson (eds), *The Pricke of Conscience: An Annotated Edition of the Southern Recension* (Jefferson, NC, 2020).

50 MEDIEVAL POETRY: 1100–1400

In describing and analysing this Lichfield text, I have had necessarily to adopt selective procedures. I limited my study to about 1,100 lines, mainly the poet's discussion of purgatory.[40] In contrast to the well-discussed lexical revisions of the Lichfield *Cursor Mundi*, very little such adjustment appears to have occurred in this recension. One might notice the reviser's avoidance of *Thar* ('need', 2963). *The Prick of Conscience* is probably more restrained in its use of specifically regional dialect than the older poem, and perhaps consequentially there is little evidence of any perceived need for extensive lexical adjustment. A very few items have attracted sporadic revision: *ay* is once retained in rhyme (2878) and sometimes omitted (2869), but elsewhere always *euer* (2673, 2681, 2857, etc.); *sere* has usually been retained in rhyme (3398 and added in the original line 2750), but frequently represented by *sum* (2877, 2885) or *dyuers* (2880), once misread as *sore* (3040); *tite* has always been translated as *sone* (2901, 3727).

But more important—and the sites of continuous detailed correction of the received *Prick of Conscience*—are two fundamentally aesthetic procedures. Obviously enough, the Lichfield editors, followed by a large number of readers, found the poem's doctrine important enough to merit persistent reproduction. But the revised version prepared for Lichfield readers' use often participates in an implicit dialogue with the original presentation of that material. The relative lack of interference with passages offering instructional listings indicates the reviser's respect for the ready and useful doctrine here.[41] But two editorial procedures, both involving radical shortening of the text, persist throughout 'Type III' copies, by means of excisions scattered through the text.[42] Almost invariably these attack the English of the original, and there are only two examples that involve suppressing the author's Latin, one of them the rubric introducing part 4, the discussion of purgatory. On a great many occasions, the reviser suppresses a single couplet. These deletions have apparently been undertaken to reduce repetition, but the revision also inscribes a number of more general objections to the argumentative manner of the original poem. The Lichfield redactor persistently removes materials from the introductory heads and conclusive ends of verse paragraphs in his received text. He displays a pronounced animus against summary reiterative couplets, which for the Yorkshire poet provided generalised statements conceived to drive home his point. The author's infrequent cross-references are always excised. Whatever else he was interested in, the Lichfield reviser was not encouraging consultative topical reading.

These behaviours provide a comprehensive and intelligent reading of the received poem. The poet of *The Prick of Conscience* is committed to 'þe way of wysdom', which the Christian follows by turning their back on the world and its blandishments and by adopting a meek and penitent fear of God (cf. most extensively the prologue, 1–369). This thematic focuses the first three parts of the work, and the presentation of The Four Last Things forces the

---

[40] I have investigated lines 2627–3762 from the parallel versions, Harley 1205, fols. 4–31[v]; Vernon, fols. 270[va]–72[va]. The Vernon facsimile provides an acceptable version of the Lichfield text, most normally in this portion identical with Harley 1205. I have not, as I perhaps should have done, read this text against one of its source copies cited in the preceding note; my discussion characterises materials transmitted from Lichfield, but some of these features may represent inheritances from the reviser's source manuscript.

[41] For example, 3496ff. on the venial sins, or the alignment of deadly sins with diseases at 2987ff.

[42] The 'Southern Recension' (and yet another localised recension, *Speculum huius Vitae*) abbreviates it still more, running to about 11 per cent fewer lines than the 'Type I' version by means of excisions scattered through the text. In the 1,100 lines I surveyed, about 115 have been deliberately cut out, nearly always short passages, on a total of 43 scattered occasions. Another eighteen lines are omitted in places where 'Type III' manuscripts present a revised (sometimes interpolated) text.

poet's point home by describing the horror that awaits those who are not committed to wise behaviours.

However effective as exhortation, there is an imaginative difficulty about the procedures the poet finds most effective. For the greater part of its length, *The Prick of Conscience* addresses situations literally indescribable, the events of The Other World. The poem's opening movement of contempt of the world, essentially an attack on human vanity, demonstrates that healthy behaviour demands a commitment precisely to what is not tangible, and thus (sinfully) attractive, about human experience. As a result, the poet is not readily disposed to indulge in staples of otherworldly narrative, appeals to vision or hearing, for example, and, although examples occur, he is not particularly given to argument by analogy either.

As a result, *The Prick* relies to a large extent on broad, generalised statements, such as that the pains of purgatory are indescribably greater than any pain imaginable in this life. The poem thus tends to fall back upon its frequent citations, for example the clerks who affirm that a single day of purgatorial pain is greater than a year's pain here (2748–57). Having said that, however, the poet then can only reiterate the larger point that the pains of purgatory are very great—and should thus be very terrifying, and thereby encourage the reader's contrition. As a result, the discussion is customarily abstract and generalised, and statements tend to be rather similar, a feature that provokes the Lichfield reviser. His frequently truncated discussions, however, do not form his only acts of abbreviation. Vernon and Harley 1205 probably include only about 75 per cent of the original because, in addition to excision, the reviser has meticulously abbreviated his source, line by line. These procedures required detailed inspection and careful rewriting, since, over the entire 1,100 lines sampled, nearly every one shows some variety of tinkering, most of it designed to remove words deemed extraneous.

At least in part, this behaviour responds to *The Prick of Conscience* in a manner one might take to be counterintuitive, because fundamentally stylistic—and thus literary and poetic. The very few past studies of instructional poems like this one accept their verse form as a given, a form of combatting wasteful romance, perceived to be the model for the literary, on its own ground. Insofar as any critic has ever addressed the issue—that in pan-European literary terms, verse presentation of serious religious materials does not occur elsewhere by the fourteenth century—it is only to suggest that medieval English authors did not routinely consider verse an imaginative medium. But that formulation only reiterates the obvious, that verse was considered an appropriate medium for instruction, although it would seem to us, as it did to Rolle, as well as to most writers after 1380, that prose is both a more accurate and a less distracting form.[43]

But the choice of verse had been deliberate: *The Prick* was versified from antecedent models that were composed in prose. This fact should suggest that form, the intricate reformulation of pre-existing non-English statements into English verse metrical and rhymed, represents a decision taken on some literary grounds. The Yorkshire instructional poets must have understood that verse would add a meaning or provide an attraction not available otherwise, and that technical competence at presenting materials in this form would supplement the doctrinal appeal of their work.

The in-line excision of materials in the Lichfield recension of *The Prick* similarly represents a stylistic response to the presentation of doctrine. Originally, the poem had been

---

[43] One might consider, for a single paired example, the disposition of prose materials among verse in either Chaucer's *Canterbury Tales* or Hoccleve's 'Series', in both instances as the clarified language of 'high sentence'.

52 MEDIEVAL POETRY: 1100–1400

written in a verse form common in Anglo-Norman, although not in Middle English; in this metrical system, a line might be construed as containing four stresses and yet dispose these over as many as eleven syllables. The Lichfield reviser plainly rejects this stylistic choice and embarks on a finicky and purely stylistic overhaul of what he had received; broadly, he attempts to convert a poem in longer, looser lines into conventional Middle English tetrameter verse—peppier to be sure, but also the form most frequent in orally communicated verses within sermons—and supposedly readily memorisable from such a source. Pursuit of this verse form mandates a great many minor changes that characterise this revision. The original poet relies heavily on extended anacrusis to pack in small, grammatically necessary unstressed syllables. To counteract this tendency, there is a considerable amount of head-of-line excision in the Lichfield revision, and line-opening authorial *Until* almost invariably appears in this recension as *Til* (cf. 2952). In addition, the Lichfield reviser makes a sustained effort at reducing words potentially stress-bearing, thereby producing more compact and clearly metrical lines. The reviser also quite systematically removes enjambment, of which *The Prick* has, by medieval standards, quite a bit (3076–7, 3108–9). This process goes hand in hand with a feature I have already noted, the removal of in-couplet repetitions of various sorts.

Textual behaviour like this has recently been associated with 'mouvance', a notion that strikes me as unintelligible. If variation is what is being described, the statement is meaningless, since it is simply in the nature of textual transmission to produce variation.[44] Nor is it clear that medieval texts are in fact more prone to display major variation than those earlier or later.[45] The evidence of *Prick of Conscience* transmission through Lichfield illustrates a more nuanced process: a substantial number of copies, the 'Type I' Worcestershire bunch, testify to reasonably accurate transmission; those subjected to Cathedral revision do not. Furthermore, these different textual strains are complementary rather than competitive, gauged to attract specific differing audiences. Compositions, poetic or prose, appear always to have been understood as site-specific or site-sensitive; even when they provided apparently depersonalised general information of broad potential use, they had been composed with an eye to an immediate local audience,[46] tailored to specific audience expectations and driven by discernible programmes. One can imagine a Lichfield canon muttering, 'Obscure language ... unbearably repetitive ... not recognisably verse'. This is what pre-public literature looks like.

London

In contrast, there is 'nowhere London'. One litmus of this out-of-place-ness, the distance between local site and 'the centre', has always seemed to me the single metropolitan episode in the London Auchinleck manuscript's *Bevis of Hampton*. There (4433–538), in a moment that mixes high hilarity with terrifying danger, the hero's martial capacity, which serves him so well on numerous occasions, is hamstrung in the welter of London lanes, alleyways, and shops. A representative figure from the traditional English form of the genre, the romance

---

[44] Or as James Thorpe once put it in conversation, 'A double-spaced page of A4 holds about 2000 characters. There is only one way to reproduce them all accurately—and an infinity of ways not to'.

[45] Simply consider what used to be called 'the bad quarto' of *Hamlet*—the surviving evidence for what must have been an extensive range of textual versions driven by varying conditions of performance.

[46] Cf. Robert Mannyng's 'men of Bourne' or Michel of Northgate's 'men of Kent'.

of exile, Bevis needs to get home—back to a once-familiar provincial locality—to fulfil his quest, and to secure his identity and heritage.[47]

Although always taken as a crowning glory of early London book-production, and clearly produced for a London patron, it is striking how little of the Auchinleck manuscript actually represents texts certainly produced, as opposed to transmitted, locally. As has been evident since Eugen Kölbing's analysis nearly 150 years ago, the volume's local texts are resolutely historical romance (e.g., *Alisaunder*, *Of Arthour and of Merlin*). The great majority of Auchinleck's contents comprises imports—who can originally have cared about Bevis anywhere but Hampshire/Southampton? They include substantial chunks of material from both the trilingual West Midland locale I have discussed above and from Northern romance (e.g., *Horn Childe and Maiden Rimnild*). No surprises here: two of the scribal languages identified in Auchinleck are placed in Worcestershire (writers who also brought along their local exemplars, thrown into the extensive Auchinleck mix?), and royal clerical staff rode ceaselessly to and from York throughout the early fourteenth century.

Those royal clerks, pulling into some variety of cultural unity a diverse country, are suggestive. Nor is it coincidental that they represent the kingdom's largest household, the royal one, the great generator of service roles, and of parchment record, requiring thousands of writers, all mostly in one place.[48] Moreover, a considerably larger analogue to Lichfield, London, as a port city, had achieved prominence as entrepôt well before the concentration of governmental functions there. In particular, it was the kingdom's central market for sumptuary objects (of which literature is just one). And size is not just evanescent; the density of persons with skills necessary for literary transmission, under-employed royal, municipal, and archiepiscopal scribes, for example, contributes to the efficiency of cultural exchange. As Auchinleck shows, London drew materials in, and—as a place marked by oscillation—expelled them again, to diverse locales.[49] This public production, of course, obliterates the earlier tangible specifics of place/site that had marked earlier production. Yet it also enables what may, except to the most confirmed Brexiteer, represent the gain of Chaucerian cosmopolitanism, enrichment from abroad.

---

[47] Eugen Kölbing (ed.), *The Romance of Sir Beues of Hamtoun*, EETS e.s. 46, 48, 65 (London, 1885–94). See also Susan Wittig, *Stylistic and Narrative Structures in the Middle English Romance* (Austin, TX, 1978), *passim*.

[48] Cf. the arguments advanced about the transmission of local prose texts into a national arena, *c* 1400, Hanna, 'Sir Thomas Berkeley and His Patronage', *Speculum*, 64 (1989), 878–916, at 908–13.

[49] To profound effects, mostly in this case involving Latin texts—in Prague, for example. This dissemination is not simply limited to Wycliffite materials, discussed by Michael Van Dussen, *From England to Bohemia: Heresy and Communication in the Later Middle Ages* (Cambridge, 2012), but involves earlier transmission of relatively benign *praedicabilia*—Fr Herebert's 'De veneno', for example.

4

Manuscripts

The Textual Record of Middle English Poetry

Simon Horobin

Much of the poetry that survives from the early part of this period is extant in unique manuscripts. This does not of course mean that these are the only copies that were produced, since others may have been lost, but it is suggestive of the status of English poetry at this time. During the twelfth and thirteenth centuries, French and Latin functioned as the principal literary languages in England, while English was used more for oral than written communication. Furthermore, because of a lack of a standard literary variety, written English displayed considerable dialectal variation, reflecting its use principally as a means of regional rather than national communication. These factors contributed to the establishment of a series of local vernacular literary cultures focused on ecclesiastical centres and literate clerics; the establishment of a unified national literary culture is a fifteenth-century development. In this chapter, we will investigate the local communities within which texts were copied and consumed and consider the processes that fed into the establishment of a national literary tradition at the end of this period.

An important feature of the transmission of English texts during this time is the way in which they were frequently copied into larger assemblages rather than circulating independently. While modern readers often encounter Middle English verse in an anthology, these collections typically privilege literary works.[1] Alternatively, modern anthologies may be themed around the works of a single author such as Chaucer: either editions of the complete corpus of an author's output or a generic subset of the complete works.[2] Alternatively, an anthology may be thematically focused; examples of such anthologies include ones focusing on travel writing or medieval drama.[3] By contrast, anthologies assembled in the Middle English period typically comprise a much broader and more diverse collection of materials; it is particularly unusual to find a manuscript anthology that brings together the work of a single author. An apparent exception to this is London, British Library, MS Additional 46,919, containing the poetic works of the Franciscan friar William Herebert.[4] But these poems form part of a much more eclectic collection of texts intended to be used by an itinerant preacher; alongside the theological works, we find recipes and remedies. Since the manuscript was copied by Herebert himself, it probably represents a personal collection intended for his own use rather than an attempt to bring together his oeuvre for a wider readership.

---

[1] Examples include J. A. Burrow and Thorlac Turville-Petre (eds), *A Book of Middle English*, 3rd edn. (Oxford, 2004); Elaine Treharne (ed.), *Old and Middle English c.890–c.1450: An Anthology*, 3rd edn. (Oxford, 2009).

[2] For the complete Chaucerian corpus, see Larry D. Benson (ed.), *The Riverside Chaucer* (Boston, MA, 1987); for an example of an edition of part of the Chaucerian corpus, see Helen Phillips and Nick Havely (eds), *Chaucer's Dream Poetry* (London, 1997).

[3] Anthony Bale and Sebastian Sobecki (eds), *Medieval English Travel: A Critical Anthology* (Oxford, 2019); Greg Walker (ed.), *Medieval Drama: An Anthology* (Oxford, 2000).

[4] Stephen R. Reimer (ed.), *The Works of William Herebert, OFM* (Toronto, 1987).

Simon Horobin, *Manuscripts*. In: *The Oxford History of Poetry in English*. Edited by Helen Cooper and Robert R. Edwards, Oxford University Press. © Simon Horobin (2023). DOI: 10.1093/oso/9780198827429.003.0004

Another manuscript collection that is thought to reflect the collected works of a single author is London, British Library, MS Cotton Nero A.x. This is a compendium of four works whose use of the alliterative metre and North-West Midland dialect has led scholars to identify them all as the work of a single poet. But since there is no internal evidence in the manuscript to indicate that the poems are by the same author, and since the putative author remains anonymous, we cannot be certain that the manuscript is not the result of a compiler bringing together a group of poems, *Pearl, Cleanness, Patience*, and *Sir Gawain and the Green Knight*, united by their similar poetic form. Despite being written in the second half of the fourteenth century, Cotton Nero A.x differs from a number of contemporary manuscripts in being written in a textura script with some cursive features, perhaps suggestive of a lack of experience in copying literary texts. The manuscript is also a smaller and much less professional-looking product than the early copies of the poems of Gower, Chaucer, and even Langland, who also wrote in an alliterative metre. Another unusual feature of the Cotton Nero manuscript is the presence of a series of miniatures depicting key events in the texts, although these are rather less accomplished than contemporary instances, further suggestive of provincial manufacture. While some of the earliest manuscripts of the works of Chaucer, Gower, and Langland contain miniatures, these tend to be depictions of the author or the pilgrim narrators rather than episodes from the narrative.[5]

The Case of Harley 2253

More commonly, Middle English anthologies are collections of anonymous works, assembled by one or more unknown compilers. An important instance of this type is London, British Library, MS Harley 2253. This manuscript is best known today for its preservation of a collection of secular lyrics, many of which do not survive in any other manuscript witness. These have been anthologised in collections such as G. L. Brook's edition of *The Harley Lyrics*, which present only the religious and secular love lyrics, ignoring the wealth of other items that appear alongside the lyrics in the original manuscript: debates, fabliaux, legends, prayers, and proverbs.[6] By stripping the lyrics of their original context, these editions place undue emphasis on the manuscript's poetic contents, neglecting their generically diverse accompaniments; Brook's edition even goes so far as to remove the political poems that appear alongside the love poems in the original manuscript. In an important recent development, Susanna Fein has edited the complete contents of the manuscript, allowing modern readers to adopt a more holistic approach to the manuscript and its contents.[7]

Analysing the manuscript in its totality sheds important light on our understanding of the processes of collecting, arranging, and copying textual materials during this period, as well as offering insights into the contexts within which such anthologies were produced and consumed. Although we do not know the identity of the scribe who copied the texts into this manuscript, or the purpose for which it was assembled, we do know a considerable amount about when and where it was produced. The palaeographer N. R. Ker first observed that

---

[5] A. S. G. Edwards, 'The Manuscript: British Library MS Cotton Nero A.x', in D. S. Brewer (ed.), *A Companion to the Gawain-Poet* (Woodbridge, 1998), 197–220.

[6] G. L. Brook (ed.), *The Harley Lyrics: The Middle English Lyrics of Ms. Harley 2253*, 4th edn. (Manchester, 1968).

[7] Susanna Fein with David Raybin and Jan Ziolkowski (eds and trans.), *The Complete Harley 2253 Manuscript*, 3 vols. (Kalamazoo, MI, 2015).

56 MEDIEVAL POETRY: 1100–1400

the scribe who copied Harley 2253 was responsible for a further two manuscripts: London, British Library, MS Royal 12.C.xii and Harley 273.[8] Ker's discoveries were extended by Carter Revard, who identified more than forty legal documents in the same scribe's hand, indicating that the scribe worked as a conveyancer, producing legal charters, between 1314 and 1349, in the area around Ludlow in Shropshire.[9] Although these identifications have not enabled Revard to identify the scribe by name, he was able to make suggestions concerning his affiliations and patronal connections, which appear to point to patronage by the Ludlow family of Stokesay, and specifically by Sir Laurence Ludlow.[10]

Detailed consideration of the three volumes copied by this scribe reveals some clear differences in their contents and their functions. Harley 273, containing instructional and devotional works such as *Manuel des péchés* and the *Purgatoire s. Patrice*, appears to have been collected and partly copied by the scribe around 1314–15 when he was a young priest or chaplain. The inclusion of a work dealing with issues concerning the management of a large household perhaps indicates that he was at that time serving as a household cleric or chaplain. While Royal 12.C.xii has similarly devotional and penitential contents, it includes a more diverse and idiosyncratic collection of works, comprising prophecies, palmistry, recipes, and texts on the interpretation of dreams and romances. Although these works might also have been intended for use with members of a household, the more personal nature of the contents suggests that this manuscript was the scribe's own commonplace book. When compared to these volumes, Harley 2253 differs in containing a much more diverse collection of materials, comprising religious and devotional works and political poems, as well as the secular lyrics for which it is best known today. Another key difference concerns the choice of language. Where most of the texts copied into Royal 12.C.xii are in French or Latin, Harley 2253 includes many more works in English. This difference is well illustrated by the scribe's inclusion in Harley 2253 of *A Bok of Sweuenyng*, an English translation of the Latin *Somnia Danielis*, included in its Latin form in Royal 12.C.xii. These linguistic and generic differences suggest that while Royal 12.C.xii was intended for his own use, Harley 2253 was planned for consumption by a larger, more diverse audience who were not familiar with French or Latin.

There is much debate about the extent of the scribe's putative contribution to the composition, collecting, and arrangement of the Harley lyrics. Early scholars tended to view the manuscript as a haphazard assemblage of materials with no clear principles of inclusion or organisation. Carleton Brown, for instance, claimed, 'No arrangement is discernible in the contents of the book. French and English prose and verse are interspersed without apparent plan. Secular and religious pieces follow indiscriminately'. Revard, however, has argued that, far from being a randomly obtained and assembled collection of works, Harley 2253 is the result of informed and sensitive processes of selection and arrangement. According to Revard, the Harley scribe acted as a compiler; not only did he carefully choose the items for inclusion, he also engaged in judicious organisation of them. The principles underlying such organisation involve the juxtaposition of opposing viewpoints: 'a dialectic arrangement that implies the compiler's ironic awareness of the double view'.[11] Theo Stemmler opted

---

[8] N. R. Ker (intro.), *Facsimile of British Museum MS. Harley 2253*, EETS o.s. 255 (London, 1965).

[9] Carter Revard, 'Scribe and Provenance', in Susanna Fein (ed.), *Studies in the Harley Manuscript: The Scribes, Contents, and Social Contexts of British Library MS Harley 2253* (Kalamazoo, MI, 2000), 21–109.

[10] The Ludlow family connections have been pursued at greater length by John Hines, *Voices in the Past: English Literature and Archaeology* (Woodbridge, 2004).

[11] Carter Revard, '*Gilote et Johane*: An Interlude in B. L. MS. Harley 2253', *Studies in Philology*, 79 (1982), 122–46, at 130.

to take a middle road between these two positions, arguing that the manuscript was neither a miscellany, which he defined as an arbitrary assemblage of randomly chosen texts, nor a carefully selected and tightly organised collection. Instead he categorised the manuscript as an anthology, which he defined as 'a careful collection selected as representative specimens of various genres'.[12] Marilyn Corrie has pointed to similar principles of coherence, arguing that the difference between a miscellany and an anthology is not the degree of organisation but rather the selection of the contents.[13] For Thorlac Turville-Petre, the placement of the lyrics alongside each other in the collection is crucial to their meaning. The texts are deliberately arranged so as to stimulate debate, allowing the discussion and final judgement to be taken up by the manuscript's audience.[14]

Scanning the manuscript's contents in light of these different theories reveals some immediately obvious underlying structural principles: for instance, most of the verse appears in the first half of the manuscript, while the second half consists mostly of prose. These prose texts are predominantly in French and Latin and concerned with religious topics. Such differences imply that, at a macro level, the manuscript's contents were organised according to language, form, and content. There is clear evidence of close linking of texts at a micro level too. This is perhaps most apparent in the juxtaposition of lyrics contrasting secular and spiritual love, such as the pairing of 'The Way of Christ's Love' and 'The Way of Woman's Love'. A similar principle of contrast and juxtaposition is apparent in the pair of French texts praising and abusing women: 'Le Dit des Femmes' and 'Le Blasme des Femmes'.[15] This process of compilation suggests a procedure in which the scribe had access to the texts in advance, enabling him to use his familiarity with their form and content to determine the overall arrangement of the collection. This raises the question of whether the texts were derived from local sources or drawn from ones scattered much more widely. Did they travel as individual items, or were they accessed in larger groups? These questions are important as they help us to determine the extent to which the organisation of the book was the work of the scribe, and the extent to which its organisation was pre-determined by the exemplars he received.

Internal evidence suggests that texts were drawn both from local and from more geographically disparate sources. The manuscript's West Midland connections are apparent from its lives of the saints Ethelbert of Hereford, Etfrid of Leominster, and Wistan of Wistanstow. Some of the English poems, such as the *Song of the Husbandman* ('Ich herde men upon mold'), with its heavy alliteration, appear to be of local West Midland provenance. Revard has even suggested that poems whose dialect is consonant with that of the Ludlow area, such as *Alysoun* ('Bytuene Mersh ant Averil'), may have been the scribe's own compositions. But in other lyrics the place names are suggestive of origins much further afield, such as Ribblesdale in Yorkshire (from the 'Fair Maid of Ribblesdale'). Turville-Petre, building upon his conclusion that at least parts of Harley represent a scribally planned volume,

---

[12] Theo Stemmler, 'Miscellany or Anthology? The Structure of Medieval Manuscripts: MS Harley 2253, for Example', in Susanna Fein (ed.), *Studies in the Harley Manuscript*, 111–20, at 113.

[13] Marilyn Corrie, 'Harley 2253, Digby 86, and the Circulation of Literature in Pre-Chaucerian England', in Susanna Fein (ed.), *Studies in the Harley Manuscript*, 427–43.

[14] Thorlac Turville-Petre, 'Three Languages', in *England the Nation: Language, Literature, and National Identity, 1290–1340* (Oxford, 1996), 181–221. For the importance of debate poetry in medieval English literary culture, see Neil Cartlidge, 'Debate Poetry', in Siân Echard and Robert Rouse (eds), *The Encyclopedia of Medieval British Literature* (Oxford, 2017), 646–9.

[15] Carter Revard, '*Gilote et Johane*: An Interlude in B. L. MS. Harley 2253', *Studies in Philology*, 79 (1982), 122–46.

58 MEDIEVAL POETRY: 1100–1400

concludes that the collection of lyrics represents 'a country-wide selection of the best poems in English'.[16]

Study of the dialects in which the poems were copied suggests that they were sourced in groups from throughout the country, while some travelled in larger units. Frances McSparran's analysis of spellings that are not typical of the scribe's own usage concluded that, while the scribe evidently drew upon a number of different exemplars, some texts travelled as part of larger units containing a sequence of texts. These sequences comprised poems that were composed in a single area and which travelled together, along with others that were later added to them in response to thematic congruities. Others, like the northerly 'Prophecy of Thomas of Erceldoune', were drawn from further afield and may have functioned as fillers.[17]

A useful comparison with Harley 2253 may be made with another trilingual collection of texts produced in the West Midlands in the late thirteenth century: Oxford, Bodleian Library, MS Digby 86.[18] Although the circumstances of their production may differ, there are a number of features that unite Digby 86 and Harley 2253: both include material in English, French, and Latin, texts in verse and prose comprising a variety of genres, both written by a single scribe, and both produced in the West Midlands. The major difference in their contents concerns the lack of political poems in Digby—especially ones relevant to the local area—an important feature of Harley 2253.[19] Digby also has a greater number of pragmatic texts than found in Harley, encompassing charms, medical texts, prognostications, advice on keeping birds of prey, and a poem on avoiding the bad luck consequent on meeting a hare.[20] Although Harley 2253 is more literary in its overall make-up, Digby 86 is important for preserving the unique copies of the English poems *Dame Sirith* and *The Fox and the Wolf*. Similar juxtapositions to those observed in Harley 2253 have been identified in Digby 86. Corrie has noted the way in which a debate poem weighing the merits of chastity and promiscuity is followed by another featuring a dialogue between a body and a damned soul.[21] The compiler of Digby 86 appears to have taken the business of compilation even more seriously, organising his material into sections according to their use of prose or verse and according to the language in which they were written.

Although some sixty years separate their work, the Digby and Harley compilers were drawing upon a similar pool of locally available materials, as well as a corpus of French texts composed on the continent. This is apparent from the fact that both share a number of English texts, including the Sayings of St Bernard, some religious lyrics, Maximian, and Hending, and one in French, 'Le Blasme des femmes'. However, despite the close connection these overlaps imply, the textual affiliations of the works indicate that the scribes did not draw upon the same exemplars; in the case of 'Le Blasme des femmes' and the lyric 'Stond wel, moder, vnder rode', the Harley copies include material not found in the Digby versions. The existence of a common stock of exemplars from which local compilers could draw is further suggested by a collection of English and Latin materials assembled by a fraternal community in Worcester in the 1260s which shares texts with both Digby and Harley, now

---

[16] Turville-Petre, 'Three Languages', 195.

[17] Frances McSparran, 'The Language of the English Poems: The Harley Scribe and His Exemplars', in Susanna Fein (ed.), *Studies in the Harley Manuscript*, 391–426.

[18] On the date and production of Digby 86, see M. B. Parkes and Judith Tschann (intro.), *Facsimile of Oxford, Bodleian Library, MS Digby 86*, EETS e.s. 16 (Oxford, 1996).

[19] See John Scattergood, 'Authority and Resistance: The Political Verse', in Susanna Fein (ed), *Studies in the Harley Manuscript*, 163–201.

[20] For the last of these items, see Margaret Laing, 'Notes on Oxford, Bodleian Library, MS Digby 86, *The Names of a Hare in English*', *Medium Ævum*, 67 (1998), 201–11.

[21] Marilyn Corrie, 'Harley 2253, Digby 86, and the Circulation of Literature'.

Cambridge, Trinity College, MS B.14.39. This manuscript contains the additional two stanzas of 'Stond wel, moder, vnder rode' also attested in Harley 2253, witnessing to a local currency for the Harley version before it was copied by the Harley scribe. Texts in both Digby 86 and Harley 2253 are also shared with Oxford, Jesus College, MS 29, a Herefordshire collection of works copied in the second half of the thirteenth century that includes *The Owl and the Nightingale*. Like Harley 2253 and Digby 86, Jesus 29 brings together poetic works in English and in Anglo-Norman. Jesus 29 shares nine texts with another manuscript produced at the same time in the dialect of nearby Worcestershire, London, British Library, MS Cotton Caligula A.ix.[22] One of these shared texts is *The Owl and the Nightingale*, which is preserved only in these two codices, while others include saints' lives and a debate poem in Anglo-Norman, and six religious lyrics in English. Cotton Caligula A.ix differs from Jesus 29 in including an Anglo-Norman prose chronicle and one of only two surviving copies of the English verse translation of Wace's *Roman de Brut* by the West Midland cleric Laȝamon, who was a priest at Areley Kings in Worcestershire.[23]

While these connections among manuscripts assembled in the South-West Midlands do not rule out a wider circulation for these works, it seems likely that these patterns of attestation between this group of anthologies testify to a localised literary culture that flourished in the late thirteenth and early fourteenth centuries. Neil Cartlidge has suggested that Jesus 29 and Caligula A.ix were produced in a religious house, perhaps one linked to the Premonstratensian house at Titchfield (Hampshire), since a record of 1400 notes the presence of several of their shared texts in the Titchfield library. Access to this exemplar in the West Midlands can be explained by the fact that Titchfield was a colony of the Abbey of Halesowen in Worcestershire, a connection that highlights the monastic networks across which texts and exemplars travelled during this period. In order to assess how representative this localised literary culture was of the nation as a whole, we will compare the evidence of these anthologies with a contemporary London production: Edinburgh, National Library of Scotland, Advocates' MS 19.2.1, the 'Auchinleck' manuscript.

The Case of the Auchinleck Manuscript

Where both Digby 86 and Harley 2253 were the work of single scribes, Auchinleck was copied by six different scribes.[24] Auchinleck also differs from these manuscripts in including a number of miniatures. In its original state, a miniature would have stood at the beginning of each new text; most of these have since been removed, leaving just five intact. It was copied between 1330 and 1340, a date that is based upon the handwriting of the contributing scribes and on references within some of the texts.[25] The Auchinleck manuscript contains the largest collection of Middle English romance among all surviving copies; many of the romances it contains do not survive at all elsewhere, while others appear in their earliest and

[22] Neil Cartlidge, 'The Composition and Social Context of Oxford, Jesus College, MS 29(II) and London, British Library, MS Cotton Caligula A.IX', *Medium Ævum*, 66 (1997), 250–69.

[23] The other manuscript to preserve Laȝamon's *Brut* is London, British Library, MS Cotton Otho C.xiii.

[24] There is some scholarly debate about whether the number of scribes is five or six; this has been resolved by Alison Wiggins, 'Are Auchinleck Manuscript Scribes 1 and 6 the Same Scribe? Whole-Data Analysis and the Advantages of Electronic Texts', *Medium Ævum*, 73 (2004), 10–26.

[25] As well as a reference to the death of Edward II and his son Edward III, who ascended the throne in 1327, the account of how Lancelot held Guinevere in Nottingham Castle suggests the scribe or redactor has merged this legendary story in which Lancelot protected Guinevere in Joyeuse Garde with a historical event when Roger Mortimer and Queen Isabella took shelter in Nottingham Castle in 1330.

60 MEDIEVAL POETRY: 1100–1400

textually most accurate forms in this manuscript.[26] Of its forty-four surviving texts, eighteen are romances; eight of these are in unique versions and all are in their earliest copy, with the one exception of *Floris and Blancheflour*. But, despite its reputation as an important repository of Middle English romances, Auchinleck includes a range of texts in different genres: chronicle, saint's life, religious instruction, satire, and complaint. In this regard it resembles Harley 2253 and Digby 86, further emphasising the way in which Middle English anthologies tend to include more than one genre of writing and both prose and verse. Even among the verse texts we find a mixture of poetic forms; the most common form is couplet and stanzaic verse, but there are some texts that employ the alliterative metre. Like Harley 2253, Auchinleck places different genres in juxtaposition, compelling readers to notice both parallels and contrasts.

In this way, the construction of Auchinleck recalls the organisation underpinning Harley 2253. As we have seen, scholars have characterised the dominant organisational principle underlying Harley 2253 as the construction of oppositions and juxtapositions, intended to contribute to the audience's entertainment or edification. Helen Phillips has argued for a similar policy underlying some of the compilational decisions that are apparent from the construction of the Auchinleck manuscript.[27] For while genre may be an important compilational principle in the production of Auchinleck, as seen in its number of romances, or the hagiographical series represented by the legends of St Margaret, St Katherine, and St Patrick's Purgatory, other works challenge such straightforward categorisations. For instance, a historical text such as the *Short Metrical Chronicle* connects with several of the romances through its representation of Edward I as a chivalric king and its account of the crusading King Richard I.

Despite these similarities, the Auchinleck manuscript differs from Harley 2253 in a number of important ways. One of these is the multiplicity of scribal hands it contains, a phenomenon that led Laura Hibbard Loomis to put forward the theory that the manuscript was produced in a bookshop.[28] This was an important and influential theory since it suggested that this manuscript represented early evidence of the emergence of a secular London book trade. Where manuscripts in the provinces continued to be copied by individual scribes for their own use, or to be consumed by a local household, Auchinleck appeared to indicate that in London book-production had begun to be professionalised. According to Loomis's theory, Auchinleck was the product of a bookshop comprising a group of scribes working alongside other book artisans, such as a limner and illuminator, who would have been responsible for the decoration and illustrations; bookbinders, responsible for binding the book and ensuring that the gatherings were assembled correctly; and stationers taking the commissions, sourcing the exemplars, and overseeing the project. Having identified close linguistic and verbal correspondences between the romances, Loomis posited close collaboration between authors and scribes, suggesting that the bookshop may even have included the translators responsible for the romances, or perhaps that it was the responsibility of the stationer to commission the translations in the first instance.

Loomis's proposal of a large secular bookshop operation was subsequently modified by Pamela Robinson, who posited that Auchinleck was the result of a fascicular mode of

---

[26] For a description of the manuscript, a list of its contents, and a full transcription and facsimile, see David Burnley and Alison Wiggins (eds), *The Auchinleck Manuscript*, http://auchinleck.nls.uk.

[27] Helen Phillips, 'Auchinleck and Chaucer', in Susanna Fein (ed.), *The Auchinleck Manuscript: New Perspectives* (York, 2016), 139–55.

[28] Laura Hibbard Loomis, 'The Auchinleck Manuscript and a Possible London Bookshop of 1330–1340', *PMLA*, 57 (1942), 595–627.

production, in which the manuscript was initially copied as a series of twelve independent booklets, which were bound together at a later stage.[29] According to this model of production, the copying of the individual booklets was begun as a speculative venture; they were only bound together in a single volume at the request of a specific customer who chose the constituent texts and paid for the finished product. Although these two scenarios may seem quite similar, there are significant differences. According to Loomis, it was the customer who was responsible for the contents and arrangement of the entire manuscript. According to Robinson's scenario, the texts had already been copied into the booklets; the customer was responsible only for selecting from the available booklets, and perhaps also for determining the overall shape of the volume. But what unites the two scenarios is the existence of a bookshop, whether it is one in which books were produced entirely to commission or where some initial copying was carried out speculatively.

Later scholars, however, have argued against the existence of secular bookshops in the fourteenth century, as posited by Loomis and Robinson, on various grounds. Focusing on manuscripts produced in the late fourteenth and early fifteenth centuries, A. I. Doyle and M. B. Parkes noted the lack of evidence for collaboration that would be expected in a bookshop environment.[30] The earliest manuscripts of writers such as Chaucer, Gower, and Langland are generally in the hands of single scribes rather than multiple copyists, as might be expected in a bookshop environment. The works of these authors, *Troilus and Criseyde*, the *Canterbury Tales*, *Confessio Amantis*, and *Piers Plowman*, are long, and consequently tend to occupy a complete manuscript on their own.[31] Because of their length, copying these works would have required a considerable investment of time and money. Parcelling out a text to be copied by more than one scribe would be a practical way of getting the copy made as quickly as possible. Most of these manuscripts, however, were copied by a single scribe, implying that—even by the early fifteenth century—scribes worked as independent practitioners. Further evidence in support of this suggestion is found in the appearance of the manuscripts themselves, since they often lay out, organise, and decorate the text in very different ways. If the manuscripts were the product of a single centre, we would expect to see greater evidence of standardisation in the formats they adopt. This diversity of layout and ordering of materials is especially noticeable in manuscripts copied by the same scribe. Two of the earliest and most important copies of Chaucer's *Canterbury Tales*, for instance, were copied by the same scribe, and yet their ordering of the constituent tales and the provision of marginal glosses, decoration, and illustration are very different.[32] Collation of the texts of the poem in the two manuscripts by editors of Chaucer's work has suggested that they were

---

[29] Pamela Robinson, 'A Study of Some Aspects of the Transmission of English Verse Texts in Late Medieval Manuscripts', PhD Diss., University of Oxford, 1972.

[30] A. I. Doyle and M. B. Parkes, 'The Production of Copies of the *Canterbury Tales* and the *Confessio Amantis* in the Early Fifteenth Century', in M. B. Parkes and Andrew G. Watson, (eds), *Mediaeval Scribes, Manuscripts and Libraries: Essays Presented to N. R. Ker* (Aldershot, 1978), 163–203.

[31] Exceptions include the substantial Chaucerian anthology Cambridge, Cambridge University Library, MS Gg.4.27, which includes the *Canterbury Tales*, *Troilus and Criseyde*, and some of the shorter poems. *Piers Plowman* appears in several larger anthologies, such as the substantial manuscript compilation Cambridge, Cambridge University Library, MS Dd.1.17; see Ralph Hanna, 'Cambridge University Library, MS Dd.1.17: Some Historical Notes', *Transactions of the Cambridge Bibliographical Society*, 16.2 (2018), 141–60.

[32] These are the Hengwrt and Ellesmere manuscripts: Aberystwyth, National Library of Wales, MS Peniarth 392D; San Marino, Huntington Library, MS Ellesmere 26.C.9. For the differences between them in terms of their layout, ordering, and text of the *Canterbury Tales*, see Norman F. Blake, 'The Ellesmere Text in Light of the Hengwrt Manuscript', in Martin Stevens and Daniel Woodward (eds), *The Ellesmere Chaucer: Essays in Interpretation* (San Marino, CA, 1995), 205–24, and other essays in that collection. More recently, Linne Mooney and Estelle Stubbs have suggested that these and other manuscripts of works by Gower, Chaucer, and Langland were copied in the London Guildhall. See Linne R. Mooney and Estelle Stubbs, *Scribes and the City: London Guildhall Clerks*

62 MEDIEVAL POETRY: 1100–1400

copied from different exemplars. If they were the product of a bookshop, we would have expected evidence of multiple copies being produced from a single exemplar, but examples of this are only found from the mid-fifteenth century.

A different theory for the production of the Auchinleck manuscript was advanced in a detailed codicological study of the manuscript by Timothy Shonk.[33] Shonk noted that, while the manuscript was copied by a number of scribes, by far the largest amount of copying was carried out by Scribe 1. This uneven distribution led him to suggest that, as well as acting as the principal copyist, Scribe 1 also served as the supervisor, thus combining the roles of scribe, supervisor, and stationer, liaising with the customer over the commission and parcelling out some of the copying tasks to other scribes, but carrying out the majority of the work himself. Evidence for his role as supervisor comes from a number of small details of production that were implemented by him. For instance, he was responsible for supplying the manuscript's catchwords (notes used to help the binder to place the various booklets in the correct order), not only for his own booklets but also for those of the other copyists. This suggests that, once they had completed their copying stint, the other scribes' work on the manuscript was complete. At that point the booklets were returned to Scribe 1, who was responsible for overseeing the subsequent stages in the manuscript's production. Further evidence in support of this scenario is the fact that the Roman numerals that appear at the top of the folios at the beginning of each text are also in Scribe 1's hand, as are the titles of the works themselves. These appear not to have been provided at the time of copying; instead, they were probably incorporated in batches after the rubrication and illumination had been supplied. Shonk further concluded that it was this scribe who liaised with the purchaser, describing him as 'an early entrepreneur who disseminated literature on a contractual basis'.[34] Rather than working in a bookshop, it seems more likely that Scribe 1 was an independent professional who was acting on commission from a wealthy member of the bourgeoisie or gentry. According to this model, it is likely that the manuscript's contents were agreed upon before copying began rather than being a speculative venture that grew organically while the copying process was underway.

Ralph Hanna also considers the Auchinleck manuscript to be the work of Scribe 1, but he differs from Shonk in viewing the manuscript's production as independent booklets to indicate that its contents were not planned in advance.[35] By copying works into separate physical units, the scribe was able to postpone any final decisions about the book's contents or arrangement. Hanna sees the Auchinleck manuscript as a bespoke order that continued to grow as the client requested a number of major romance works, necessitating a format that was expandable. Most importantly, Hanna argues against a scholarly tendency to overstate the Auchinleck manuscript's uniqueness, finding parallels in royal codices and anthologies of legal and historical writings. These other large-scale collections include Cambridge, Corpus Christi College, MS 70, a collection of legal texts in Latin intended to serve as precedents in discussions of city customs, produced for the chamberlain of London, Andrew Horn, c 1310. Like Auchinleck, the manuscript is mostly in the hand of a single scribe, although a second scribe added the laws of Henry II. CCCC 70 further resembles

---

and the Dissemination of Middle English Literature, 1375–1425 (Woodbridge, 2013). This theory has been rejected by Lawrence Warner, *Chaucer's Scribes: London Textual Production, 1384–1432* (Cambridge, 2018).

[33] T. A. Shonk, 'A Study of the Auchinleck Manuscript: Bookmen and Bookmaking in the Early Fourteenth Century', *Speculum*, 60 (1985), 71–91.

[34] Shonk, 'A Study of the Auchinleck Manuscript', 89.

[35] Ralph Hanna III, 'Reconsidering the Auchinleck Manuscript', in Derek Pearsall (ed.), *New Directions in Later Medieval Manuscript Studies: Essays from the 1998 Harvard Conference* (York, 2000), 91–102.

Auchinleck in the way in which decisions about the overall contents and presentation of the manuscript were being made during the production process rather than in advance. The connections with the production of legal books are further suggested by Lynda Dennison's discovery that the artists who provided some of the decoration in Auchinleck belonged to the Queen Mary Psalter workshop, a group of itinerant artists who were based in London in the 1320s when they also decorated a number of substantial legal volumes. A further link with the legal book trade is suggested by the handwriting employed by Scribe 3, which resembles that used in the Chancery by scribes engrossing copies of legal documents. This link with the production of legal books and with scribes working in the offices of the Chancery suggests another connection with Harley 2253, whose scribe was himself a legal scrivener.

While the bookshop theory of production has been discarded in light of subsequent scholarship, it is important not to lose sight of the evident collaboration that went into the Auchinleck manuscript's production. That would have required a number of skilled craftsmen, scribes, rubricators, decorators, and binders; while they may not have inhabited a single workshop, it is likely that they were working in close geographical proximity, probably in the area around St Paul's Cathedral. Derek Pearsall has noted that such a mode of production 'might not be so very different from an extremely ill-organized imaginary bookshop.'[36]

There are other links between Auchinleck and Harley 2253 and Digby 86. While most attention is paid to Auchinleck as a repository of Middle English romance, there are a number of other texts that show connections with these regional anthologies. Auchinleck shares four texts with Digby 86, while its copy of the *Short Metrical Chronicle* is an extended version of that found in Royal 12.C.xii, one of the other manuscripts copied by the Harley 2253 scribe. While Auchinleck is clearly a London book in origin, two of its copyists used a dialect that suggests they received their training in the West Midlands. These are Scribe 2, who copied *Speculum Guy of Warwick* and *The Simonie* in a dialect of the Gloucestershire/Worcestershire/Warwickshire borders, and Scribe 6, who copied *Otuel* in a Worcestershire dialect. These connections suggest that, despite these books appearing to belong to very different regional textual communities, there may have been direct connections between them. Scribes and texts were mobile, with the result that exemplars and copyists often moved between regional communities, thereby disseminating their texts and getting access to additional exemplars. This is also apparent from other relict dialect strata in some Auchinleck texts, which point to exemplars being sourced from beyond the southeast. For instance, its copy of *The Four Foes of Mankind* has a layer of northern dialect forms that indicate it was probably copied from an exemplar derived from the north of England.[37]

While a scholarly consensus has emerged about the production of the Auchinleck manuscript, the patron who was responsible for commissioning the volume remains unknown. There is no coat of arms that would enable us to identify the initial patron, nor are there any inscriptions in the manuscript that would allow identification of its earliest owners. The manuscript's particular mix of contents suggests a readership seeking both edification and entertainment. The large number of romances, all of which are translations of French or Anglo-Norman originals, suggests an upwardly mobile middle-class audience, seeking access to the attractive and high-status world of French romance in

[36] Derek Pearsall, 'The Auchinleck Manuscript Forty Years On', in Fein, *The Auchinleck Manuscript: New Perspectives*, 11–25, at 14.
[37] A. I. McIntosh, 'A Supplementary Note to the Middle English Poem *The Four Foes of Mankind*', *Neuphilologische Mitteilungen*, 94 (1993), 79–81.

64 MEDIEVAL POETRY: 1100–1400

the vernacular. The manuscript's size and presentation suggest a wealthy buyer; the quality of the illustrations and extent of the decoration would perhaps point to a member of the mercantile class rather than an aristocrat. Doyle proposed an audience made up of wealthy Londoners with court connections;[38] Pearsall suggested that the manuscript was intended for the 'coffee-table, or mid-fourteenth-century equivalent thereof, of an aspiring member of the London merchant élite'.[39] Coss, however, has suggested that the book may have been bought by a member of the provincial gentry on a visit to London on judicial or parliamentary business.[40]

Despite the examples we have considered so far, not all texts from this period circulated in anthologies. Several longer poetic works survive in manuscripts in which they are the only or principal item. These works, composed in the fourteenth century, differ from most of the longer poetic works written in the vernacular in the thirteenth century in being extant in large numbers of multiple copies. Although manuscript survival does not necessarily equate to numbers of manuscripts produced, it seems clear from these figures that many more copies of fourteenth-century poems were produced than were made of their predecessors. There are a number of reasons why this may have been the case. The increased importance of English as a literary language is clearly part of the story: many more texts were composed in English in the later fourteenth than in the thirteenth and early fourteenth centuries. The increased status of English as a medium for literary discourse was encouraged by its use by the major poets of the later fourteenth century: Geoffrey Chaucer, William Langland, and the *Gawain*-poet. John Gower wrote works in all three of the languages of medieval England—English, French, and Latin. But while Gower may have seen all three languages as equally available for literary writing, the number of surviving manuscripts suggests that there was a considerably larger audience for the English work, *Confessio Amantis*. Over fifty manuscripts of *Confessio Amantis* survive (including fragments) compared with ten of the Latin *Vox Clamantis*; his French works survive in single copies.[41]

Although the works of Chaucer, Gower, and Langland were composed in the fourteenth century, the majority of their surviving manuscript witnesses were probably produced in the fifteenth century. This may be the result of historical accident—all the earliest copies may have been lost—but it seems likely that this is a genuine reflection of changes in the professionalisation of the book trade and the increased demand for manuscript copies of English verse by a growing reading public. The large temporal gap between the composition of some of these works and their earliest surviving manuscript copies is most apparent in the cases of Chaucer's earliest poems: *Book of the Duchess, House of Fame,* and *Parliament of Fowls*. Although these works were probably composed in the 1370s or 1380s, the earliest copies that survive are found in anthologies produced between 1440 and 1460.[42] This suggests that Chaucer's early works did not circulate in written form during his lifetime; only following the success of his later works, *Troilus and Criseyde* and the *Canterbury Tales*, did a market emerge for manuscript copies of the earlier poems. Chaucer had probably completed

---

[38] A. I. Doyle, 'English Books In and Out of Court from Edward III to Henry VII', in V. J. Scattergood and J. W. Sherborne (eds), *English Court Culture in the Later Middle Ages* (London, 1983), 165.

[39] Derek Pearsall, 'Middle English Romance and Its Audiences', in Mary-Jo Arn and Hanneke Wirtjes with H. Jansen (eds), *Historical and Editorial Studies in Medieval and Early Modern English for Johan Gerritsen* (Groningen, 1985), 37–48, at 42.

[40] P. R. Coss, 'Aspects of Cultural Diffusion in Medieval England: The Early Romances, Local Society and Robin Hood', *Past and Present*, 108 (1985), 35–79, at 64.

[41] Derek Pearsall and Linne R. Mooney, *A Descriptive Catalogue of the English Manuscripts of John Gower's Confessio Amantis* (Woodbridge, 2021).

[42] These Chaucerian works are preserved in three important anthologies: Oxford, Bodleian Library, MSS Fairfax 16, MS Tanner 346, and MS Bodley 638.

Troilus and Criseyde by 1388; its circulation in some form during this period is implied by its dedication to his fellow poet John Gower and to the London lawyer Ralph Strode. Circulation among London readers is further implied by its use by Thomas Usk in his prose work *Testament of Love*. But, despite this, there is no surviving evidence of a manuscript circulation.[43] None of the surviving copies of Chaucer's *Troilus and Criseyde* are thought to have been produced during his lifetime; the earliest and most textually accurate copies Cambridge, Corpus Christi College, MS 61 and New York, Pierpont Morgan, MS M.817, are the product of the 1410s or 1420s. It may be that the earliest written copies of the work have simply been lost, but it may also indicate that circulation during Chaucer's lifetime was through oral performance rather than in manuscript form. The earliest surviving Chaucer manuscripts are copies of the *Canterbury Tales*, a work that Chaucer left unfinished at his death in 1400.[44] Despite recent attempts by scholars to link their production to the author himself,[45] the confusion apparent in the way the earliest copies were assembled strongly suggests that they were posthumous attempts to impose order onto a series of incomplete and inconsistent materials left behind by Chaucer at his death.[46]

A similar chronological gap is apparent in the case of the A-text of *Piers Plowman*, lending support to the claim that there was little appetite for manuscript copies of vernacular poems in the late fourteenth century. While this first version of Langland's poem is considered to have been composed in the 1360s or 1370s, the earliest witnesses are dated to the 1420s. These manuscripts were copied by scribes using regional dialects—Sussex, Norwich, Suffolk—implying production outside the main centre of metropolitan book-production.[47] But there is a significant piece of textual evidence that complicates this explanation: the A-version of *Piers Plowman* is found in the Vernon manuscript, Oxford, Bodleian Library, MS Eng. Poet. a.1, a vast collection of Middle English religious works assembled in the West Midlands at the end of the fourteenth century. This manuscript is one of the largest codices to survive from this period; it comprises around 370 texts written over 350 folios (another 50 or so have been lost). The Vernon manuscript is unusual among manuscript anthologies in having a title for the collection as a whole, which is 'cald in latyn tonge Salus anime and in englyhs tonge Sowlehele'. This broadly captures the range of texts collected together in Vernon, which may all be grouped under the heading of devotional or instructional literature. Some of these are texts that survive in large numbers of copies, such as the *Prick of Conscience, Speculum Vitae*, and Walter Hilton's *Scale of Perfection*, while other texts, such as a sequence of lyrics, are of more restricted distribution. Unusually for a manuscript of this size, the majority of the text is the work of a single individual; the list of contents and the opening text were added slightly later by a second scribe. The financial resources required to assemble a manuscript on this scale, combined with the availability of a single copyist over a protracted period of time, suggest that production took place in a religious house. Possible candidates that have been proposed are the Cistercian houses of Bordesley Abbey

---

[43] Marion Turner, '"Certaynly his noble sayenges can I not amende": Thomas Usk and *Troilus and Criseyde*', *Chaucer Review*, 37 (2002), 26–39. There is also evidence that Thomas Spencer, a London scrivener, owned a copy of the poem in 1394; see Martha Carlin, 'Thomas Spencer, Southwark Scrivener (d. 1428): Owner of a Copy of Chaucer's *Troilus* in 1394?', *Chaucer Review*, 49 (2015), 387–401 (398, 399).

[44] For descriptions of the surviving manuscripts and pre-1500 witnesses of Chaucer's *Canterbury Tales,* see Daniel W. Mosser, *A Digital Catalogue of the Pre-1500 Manuscripts and Incunables of the Canterbury Tales*, 2nd edn., https://www.mossercatalogue.net.

[45] Linne R. Mooney, 'Chaucer's Scribe', *Speculum*, 81 (2006), 97–138.

[46] Simon Horobin, 'Adam Pinkhurst, Geoffrey Chaucer and the Hengwrt Manuscript of the *Canterbury Tales*', *Chaucer Review*, 44 (2010), 351–67.

[47] For the dialects of the manuscripts of *Piers Plowman*, see M. L. Samuels, 'Langland's Dialect', *Medium Ævum*, 54 (1985), 232–47; reprinted in J. J. Smith (ed.), *The English of Chaucer and His Contemporaries* (Aberdeen, 1988), 70–85.

66 MEDIEVAL POETRY: 1100–1400

(Worcestershire) and Stoneleigh Abbey (Warwickshire), although both seem too small to have sustained such an enterprise without external patronage. Another possible location is Lichfield Cathedral, which enjoyed greater financial and human resources, and whose bishop, Richard Scrope, may have been the conduit by which exemplars of northern texts passed to the Vernon copyist. Scrope was descended from a prominent Yorkshire family who actively promoted the cult of Richard Rolle, which could also explain the inclusion of Rolle's English epistles, *Form of Living* and *Ego Dormio*, copied from authoritative exemplars.

Since the Vernon manuscript is a product of the West Midlands, the region in which William Langland himself grew up and the setting for the opening of his poem, it may be that the compiler of Vernon secured access to *Piers Plowman* through local channels. However, there are a number of London spellings in the Vernon copy of *Piers Plowman* that are not part of the scribe's usual West Midlands dialect, and which suggest that it was copied from an exemplar written in the London dialect.[48] This evidence indicates that, rather than obtaining his copy from a local source, the Vernon compiler may have drawn upon London networks, thereby attesting to a London circulation for Langland's earliest version.

While the evidence of the manuscript traditions for these major metropolitan Middle English writers appears to point to a lack of demand for copies of their works in fourteenth-century London, a very different picture emerges from a consideration of a group of anonymous northern works which survive in large numbers of copies. Of these, the *Prick of Conscience* stands out for its more than 100 extant witnesses.[49] This number of surviving copies is surpassed only by two Middle English prose works: the *Brut*, a chronicle of the history of Britain,[50] and the translation of the Bible associated with John Wycliffe.[51] Furthermore, the large number of dialects in which the surviving copies of the *Prick of Conscience* were copied witnesses to the wide geographical spread of its readership, which reached well beyond its northern heartland. As with the works of Chaucer, Langland, and Gower, many of the surviving manuscripts of the *Prick of Conscience* are products of the fifteenth century, but a number of the key witnesses to text of this poem were produced in the fourteenth century. Central to the establishment of its text is London, British Library, MS Cotton Galba E.ix, a large codex copied by three scribes in two columns of 47 to 48 lines, probably produced in Yorkshire. The presence of three scribal hands might appear to point to the kind of cooperative mode of book-production lacking in some of the manuscripts considered earlier; but, once again, the codicological evidence suggests that these scribes were working independently of each other. This independence is suggested by the use of different scripts by the three scribes, combined with the employment of alternative decorative designs and the inclusion of blank pages between scribal stints. The *Prick of Conscience* was copied by Scribe C; Scribe A's contribution is the romance *Ywain and Gawain*, an adaptation of a work by Chrétien de Troyes, and *The Seven Sages of Rome*. Scribe B's stint comprises religious verse and historical poems attributed to Lawrence Minot. This same scribe appears as a contributor to London, British Library, MS Harley 4196, another Yorkshire anthology of similar proportions copied by five scribes and also containing the *Prick of Conscience*,

---

[48] Simon Horobin and Jeremy J. Smith, 'The Language of the Vernon Manuscript', in Wendy Scase (ed.) *A Facsimile Edition of the Vernon Manuscript: A Literary Hoard from Medieval England*, Bodleian Digital Texts (Oxford, 2012).

[49] For a catalogue of the surviving manuscripts, see Robert E. Lewis and Angus McIntosh, *A Descriptive Guide to the Manuscripts of the Prick of Conscience*, Medium Ævum Monographs New Series XII (Oxford, 1982).

[50] For the manuscript tradition of the prose *Brut*, including descriptions of the entire manuscript corpus, see the Imagining History Project at Queen's University Belfast: https://www.manuscriptsonline.org/resources/ih.

[51] On the manuscripts of the Wycliffite Bible, see the various essays in Elizabeth Solopova (ed.), *The Wycliffite Bible: Origin, History and Interpretation*, Medieval and Renaissance Authors and Texts, 16 (Leiden, 2016).

to which he added part of *The Northern Homily Cycle*. Ralph Hanna has suggested that these *Prick of Conscience* manuscripts took their model from Yorkshire copies of the *Cursor Mundi*, a biblical history in verse composed in the early fourteenth century.[52] These manuscripts are London, British Library, MS Cotton Vespasian A.iii; Oxford, Bodleian Library, MS Fairfax 14; and Göttingen, Göttingen Universitätsbibliothek, MS Theol. 107. The *Cursor Mundi* manuscripts share a number of production procedures that recall the later *Prick of Conscience* copies, such as the use of double columns with 40 to 48 lines per column, and similar decorative formats. The connection between these books points to the existence of a local literary community and to a continuity of practices of copying and book-production associated with lengthy instructional works.

The circulation of these Yorkshire texts outside their northern homeland has been sketched by Hanna, who highlights the importance of the Great North road, and Richard Beadle in a study of the transmission of another instructional poem of Yorkshire pedigree, *Speculum Vitae*.[53] But, once again, dialect evidence reminds us that the traffic was likely two-way: the Göttingen manuscript of *Cursor Mundi*, copied by a scribe using spellings typical of the Yorkshire dialect, preserves forms that imply it was copied from an exemplar in the Lincolnshire dialect.[54] It is also important to note that southerly transmission of these Yorkshire works was not solely directed towards London. A number of South-West Midland copies of the *Prick of Conscience* transmit a distinctively Yorkshire form of the poem. Lichfield became a centre for the copying and transmission of a recension of the poem attesting to an additional prologue. This same version of the *Prick of Conscience* is found in the Vernon manuscript, alongside another Lichfield redaction of a northern work, *The Northern Homily Cycle*. A variant version of *Cursor Mundi*, known as the 'Southern recension', was likely produced in Lichfield.

This survey of the transmission and copying of Middle English verse during this period has highlighted the distinctively regional nature of the literary communities in which these texts were reproduced and read. Copyists of the extant anthologies appear to have drawn upon local pools of exemplars when assembling their manuscript collections, carefully arranging them in ways that create productive and provocative dialogues between the texts. We have also noted the heterogeneous nature of such collections, bringing together a diverse group of genres and text-types, in prose as well as verse. But these were not isolated textual enclaves; shared texts and the reuse of exemplars point to direct connections between these regional communities, reminding us of the mobility of both scribes and their exemplars. For much of this period manuscripts were idiosyncratic collections compiled for personal consumption or for the use of a specific household. Towards the end of the period, we begin to see the production of larger numbers of copies of individual texts and their circulation throughout the country. During the late fourteenth century, London began to emerge as a centre for the book trade; but the production of copies of the major vernacular poets, Chaucer, Gower, and Langland, and the consequent emergence of a national literary culture, is a development of the fifteenth century. To understand these Middle English works properly, it is clearly important to pay attention to the manuscript contexts within which they survive, since decisions of layout, script, decoration, illustration, and overall organisation inform our appreciation of the ways in which these texts were copied and read.

---

[52] Ralph Hanna, 'Yorkshire Writers', *Proceedings of the British Academy*, 121 (2003), 91–109.

[53] Richard Beadle, 'Middle English Texts and Their Transmission, 1350–1500: Some Geographical Criteria', in Margaret Laing and Keith Williamson (eds), *Speaking in Our Tongues* (Cambridge, 1994), 69–81.

[54] Angus McIntosh, 'The Textual Transmission of the Alliterative *Morte Arthure*', in Norman Davis and C. L. Wrenn (eds), *English and Medieval Studies Presented to J. R. R. Tolkien* (London, 1962), 231–40.

PART II
LITERARY CULTURE

5

The Poetic Field, I

Old and Middle English Language and Poetry

Richard Dance

In the 'Middle' of English: Diversity and Change

At roughly the mid-point of the Middle English period, a poet in Lincolnshire offers us a nostalgic portrait of ideal kingship:

It was a king bi are-dawes*,		*in days of old*
Þat in his* time were gode lawes		*in whose*
He dede* maken an* ful wel holden.		*caused to; and*
Hym louede yung, him louede holde* —	30	*old*
Erl and barun, dreng* and þayn,		*small landholder*
Knict, bondeman, and swain*,		*squire*
Wydues, maydnes, prestes, and clerkes,		
And al for hise gode werkes.		
He louede god with al his micth*,	35	*might*
And Holi Kirke*, and soth* ant ricth*.		*Church; truth; right*
Ricthwise* men he louede alle,		*righteous*
And oueral made hem* forto calle*.		*them; be summoned*
Wreieres* and wrobberes* made he falle,		*traitors; trouble-makers*
And hated hem so man doth galle*;	40	*poison*
Vtlawes and theues made he bynde,		
Alle þat he micthe fynde,		
And heye hengen on galwe-tre* —		*gallows-tree*
For hem ne yede* gold ne fe*!		*availed; property*
(*Havelok the Dane*, 27–44)[1]		

Havelok the Dane (*c* 1300) constructs a romantic fantasy of the pre-Conquest past, but the kind of English in which it tells its story seems a world away from the language of the Old English period itself. By way of contrast, consider the opening lines of our most famous Old English poem, which paints its own picture of a legendary ruler:

> Hwæt, we Gar-Dena   in geardagum,
>
> þeodcyninga   þrym gefrunon,
>
> hu ða æþelingas   ellen fremedon.

---

[1] G. V. Smithers (ed.), *Havelok* (Oxford, 1987). (I reproduce the editor's italics, marking expanded abbreviations and editorial substitutions.)

Richard Dance, *The Poetic Field, I*. In: *The Oxford History of Poetry in English*. Edited by Helen Cooper and Robert R. Edwards, Oxford University Press. © Richard Dance (2023). DOI: 10.1093/oso/9780198827429.003.0005

72   MEDIEVAL POETRY: 1100–1400

> Oft Scyld Scefing   sceaþena þreatum,
>
> monegum mægþum   meodosetla ofteah,   5
>
> egsode eorl[as],   syððan ærest wearð
>
> feasceaft funden.   He þæs frofre gebad:
>
> weox under wolcnum,   weorðmyndum þah,
>
> oð þæt him æghwylc   þara ymbsittendra
>
> ofer hronrade   hyran scolde,   10
>
> gomban gyldan.   Þæt wæs god cyning.

(Now then, we have heard of the glory of the great kings of the Spear-Danes in days of old, how those princes carried out acts of courage. Scyld Scefing often took away the meadbenches from troops of enemies, from many nations, terrified the warriors, after he was first found destitute. He experienced consolation for that: he grew beneath the skies, prospered in honour, until each one of the neighbouring peoples across the whale-road had to obey him, pay tribute. That was a good king.) (*Beowulf*, 1–11)[2]

Putting these two passages next to one another, it is abundantly clear why we find it useful today on the grounds of grammatical form ('morphology') to distinguish the 'Old' and 'Middle' periods as distinct chronological phases in the story of English—these being the stages with 'full' and 'levelled' inflexional systems, respectively.[3] In *Beowulf*, gender, number, and case are marked on nouns, adjectives, and pronouns: in the first three lines notice *geārdag-um* ('days of old', dative plural), *-Den-a* and *-cyning-a* ('of Danes', 'of kings', both genitive plural), and *æþeling-as* ('princes', nominative plural, and distinctively masculine). Moreover, much of the work of signalling the relationship between words is done by these grammatical endings, with a relatively light use of prepositions, personal pronouns, and articles (compare the modern translation). In the language of *Havelok*, on the other hand, this older system of case and grammatical gender seems to have disappeared: noun plurals are almost uniformly *-es*, whatever their historical gender or role in the sentence (contrast 'bi are-daw-*es*' [*Havelok* 27] with 'in geardag-*um*' [*Beowulf* 1]), and the definite article is the indeclinable *þe* (or assimilated *te*).[4] But morphology is not, of course, the only thing that has changed. As we look back in time from the English of *Havelok* to that of *Beowulf*, differences in all kinds of features are very striking. Together they speak to the many factors—having to do with textual culture and literary tradition as well as language history per se—that had an effect on how English developed and how its varieties were represented in writing. Compared to Old English, chief among our impressions of Middle English today is its *diversity*. This will be one of my themes in the present chapter, where I shall introduce a few of

---

[2] R. D. Fulk, Robert E. Bjork, and John D. Niles (eds), *Klaeber's Beowulf and the Fight at Finnsburg*, 4th edn. (Toronto, 2008). (I have reproduced the edition's square brackets, indicating an editorial addition, but not its length marks or other diacritics.) All translations in this chapter are mine, unless otherwise stated.

[3] The definition here is Henry Sweet's (see especially 'The History of English Sounds', *Transactions of the Philological Society*, 15 [1874], 461–623, at 617–21). For further discussion and references, see Richard Dance, 'Getting a Word In: Contact, Etymology and English Vocabulary in the Twelfth Century', *Journal of the British Academy*, 2 (2014), 153–211, at 157–8.

[4] For introductory remarks on the evolution of English morphology, see Sara M. Pons-Sanz, *The Language of Early English Literature* (Basingstoke, 2014), especially 95–169. The most detailed handbook guides to the spellings, sounds, and grammar of the OE and ME periods are Richard M. Hogg, 'Phonology and Morphology', in Richard M. Hogg (ed.), *The Cambridge History of the English Language*, Volume 1: *The Beginnings to 1066* (Cambridge, 1992), 67–167 and Roger Lass, 'Phonology and Morphology', in Norman Blake (ed.), *The Cambridge History of the English Language*, Volume 2: *1066–1476* (Cambridge, 1992), 23–155.

the ways in which Middle English varied, across both time and space, as well as taking an etymological viewpoint and thinking about the wide range of different origins for the words we meet. As we shall see, however, appreciating the language of this 'Middle' period—not least when it comes to the language of poets—can involve recognising the roles of continuity and similarity alongside change and difference.

Middle English is often characterised as the 'dialectal' stage of English, and there is indeed a great deal to interest us in terms of variation across space. Dialect variety comes to the fore in this period not only because of the greater range of texts which survive from more regions of England than hitherto, but also because of the disintegration of the relatively consistent, 'standard' West Saxon spelling which dominated in manuscripts copied in most of England in the later tenth and eleventh centuries, and which tended to be overlaid onto the spelling of texts of older origin, including *Beowulf*.[5] Between the turn of the twelfth century and the gradual emergence of new 'standards', especially in the south-east of England, in later Middle English, there was an explosion in the linguistic variety represented in manuscripts. The sheer range of different spellings, grammatical forms, and word stems on display, even within one and the same text, is liable to strike modern readers as unpredictable to the point of chaotic—and this impression is often exacerbated by the complex mixture of features which built up as scribes copied and changed their predecessors' work, affected by all manner of social and cultural factors beyond simply geographical space.[6] *Havelok* was probably composed in Lincolnshire, but the scribe of its main surviving manuscript (Oxford, Bodleian Library, Laud Misc. 108), or some previous copyist, has also introduced numerous features of a Norfolk dialect.[7] The difference between authorial and scribal layers can, of course, be particularly accessible to us in a poem, showing up in a now faulty rhyme or piece of scansion. In the passage of *Havelok* above, notice the rhyme of *holden* 'to hold' and *holde* 'old' (29–30), which can be fixed by assuming an authorial (north-east Midland) infinitive form **hold(e)* at line 29.[8]

In etymological terms, the Old English word-hoard was hardly homogeneous. But the vocabulary of *Havelok* is far more diverse in origin than that of *Beowulf*, diagnostic of the many and lasting ways in which contact with the other languages spoken and written in medieval Britain affected the English lexicon.[9] Consider, for instance, *Havelok* lines 31–3, where the all-comers of the poem's imagined social past ('erl and barun ... prestes, and

---

[5] On 'standard' OE and the transmission of OE poetry, see, e.g., Richard Dance, 'The Old English Language and the Alliterative Tradition', in Corinne Saunders (ed.), *A Companion to Medieval Poetry* (Oxford, 2010), 34–50, at 39–42. On the language of *Beowulf*, consult Fulk, Bjork, and Niles (eds), *Klaeber's Beowulf*, cliv–clxii, clxv–clxvii.

[6] The crucial dialect surveys are: Angus McIntosh, M. L. Samuels, and Michael Benskin, *An Electronic Version of A Linguistic Atlas of Late Mediaeval English*, with the assistance of Margaret Laing and Keith Williamson, webscripts by Vasilis Karaiskos and Keith Williamson (Edinburgh, 2013); and Margaret Laing, *A Linguistic Atlas of Early Middle English, 1150–1325*, version 3.2 (introduction by Margaret Laing and Roger Lass, webscripts by Keith Williamson, Vasilis Karaiskos, and Sherrylyn Branchaw) (Edinburgh, 2013–) (hereafter *LAEME*). On the principles and problems of studying linguistic variation in the medieval period, see, e.g., Keith Williamson, 'Middle English: Dialects', in Alexander Bergs and Laurel J. Brinton (eds), *English Historical Linguistics: An International Handbook*, 2 vols. (Berlin, 2012), 1.480–505 and Merja Stenroos, 'Regional Language and Culture: The Geography of Middle English Linguistic Variation', in Tim William Machan (ed.), *Imagining Medieval English: Language Structures and Theories, 500–1500* (Cambridge, 2016), 100–25.

[7] See Smithers, *Havelok*, lxiv–lxxiii, lxxv–lxxxix; Angus McIntosh, 'The Language of the Extant Versions of *Havelok the Dane*', *Medium Ævum*, 45 (1976), 36–49; and the 'Index of Sources' in *LAEME*, index number 285.

[8] As the asterisk indicates, **hold(e)* is a hypothetical form.

[9] For the effects of contact on English vocabulary, see D. Gary Miller, *External Influences on English, from Its Beginnings to the Renaissance* (Oxford, 2012) and Philip Durkin, *Borrowed Words: A History of Loanwords in English* (Oxford, 2014). On multilingualism in medieval Britain, see further, e.g., Dance, 'Getting a Word In'; Ad Putter, 'The Linguistic Repertoire of Medieval England, 1100–1500', in Machan (ed.), *Imagining Medieval English*, 126–44; and Chapter 2 in this volume.

74 MEDIEVAL POETRY: 1100–1400

clerkes') are described using words with a compellingly emblematic, and (for the poet) distinctly contemporary, etymological variety: from Old English we have *þayn*, *knict*, *wydues*, and *maydnes*; *dreng*, *swain*, and *bonde(man)* come from Old Norse, as probably does the meaning of *erl*; *prestes* is an old loan, OE *prēost* < Latin *presbyter* (ultimately < Greek *presbýteros*); and from (Anglo-)French we have *clerkes* (< Latin *clericus*) and *barun* (of obscure ulterior etymology, but perhaps itself from Germanic).[10] It is worth noticing that few of these non-native words are not already recorded in late Old English texts of some kind, even if they are found only rarely in the relatively conservative vocabulary of Old English poetry. As well as *dreng*, *erl*, *prestes*, and *swain*, this is true of other probable Norse borrowings in this passage such as *lawes*, *calle*, and *vtlawe*.[11] But there are some very interesting novelties too, some of them typical regionally, and some of them unique to this text. As well as the loans from (Anglo-)French, *Havelok* contains many instances of Scandinavian input not recorded before Middle English, including an array of rare Norse derivations which may have been native to the poet's own Lincolnshire dialect.[12] One of the most intriguing is the compound *are-dawes* (27), which is attested only here and which may have a distinctively poetic pedigree: its closest Scandinavian analogue is Old Icelandic *árdagar*, which is most often taken to be directly cognate with the OE *geārdagas* found at *Beowulf* 1, an old compound which was always characteristic of verse, and not prose, in the older Germanic languages.[13] And other words recorded for the first time in Middle English are likely to be native in origin: a nice example here is *wrobberes*—not a variant of *robbers*, but a rare word form (unique as an agent noun here) meaning 'speakers of idle tales, stirrers of strife'.[14] All in all, then, the vocabulary of *Havelok* represents very well the diverse etymological mixture of Middle English at large, a vibrant combination of old and new which, as we shall see, provided poets with rich sources of expressive material that could differ considerably between periods and places.

In important respects, then, the language of *Havelok* can be taken as 'typical' of Middle English—and it seems fundamentally distinct from Old English, at least as represented in our most famous Old English poem. But how did we get from one to the other? How much variety and change do we meet in texts from other periods and regions within the (very) broad category of 'Middle' English? And, taking up two keywords from the title of this chapter, just what does an examination of *language* mean for our appreciation of the *poetry* of this period—including the linguistic features distinctive of medieval poetic traditions, and of individual poets? Nothing illustrates the complex interactions of continuity and innovation, diversity and similarity, better than the so-called 'transition' from Old to Middle English. The main focus of this chapter will be upon this early period, with detailed case studies of two poems, from different sides of England. After exploring some of the linguistic resources and expressive choices of these pieces, which (I shall argue) deserve more attention than they have sometimes been afforded, we shall then move forwards in time, looking more briefly at representative features of the language of two famous literary monuments of

[10] See the *Oxford English Dictionary* (Oxford, 1888–; 3rd online edn. in progress) (hereafter *OED*), s.vv. *thane* n.1, *knight* n., *widow* n., *maiden* n. and adj., *dreng* n., *swain* n., *bond* n.2, *bondman* n., *earl* n., *priest* n., *clerk* n., *baron* n.; and on *clerk* notice also Durkin, *Borrowed Words*, 258.

[11] See Sara M. Pons-Sanz, *The Lexical Effects of Anglo-Scandinavian Linguistic Contact on Old English* (Turnhout, 2013), 92–3, 80–1, 30, 84–6, 55, 86–7.

[12] See Smithers, *Havelok*, lxxxiii–lxxxv.

[13] See Matthew Townend, *Antiquity of Diction in Old English and Old Norse Poetry*, E. C. Quiggin Memorial Lectures 17 (Cambridge, 2015), 5–6, 19.

[14] See Smithers, *Havelok*, 158–9; Sherman M. Kuhn, Hans Kurath, and Robert E. Lewis (eds), *Middle English Dictionary* (Ann Arbor, MI, 1956–) (hereafter *MED*), s.v. *wrobber* n.

the later fourteenth century, and how these features contribute to our impressions of these texts' poetic qualities.

The Earliest Middle English: The Same, but Different?

Although we conceive of them typologically as distinct entities, there is in practice no clean chronological division between the records of 'Old' and 'Middle' English. This has to do not only with the gradual nature of the linguistic changes themselves, and how their results varied across space, but also with the complex ways in which the textual witnesses to older and younger traditions overlap. Recopied and recontextualised 'Old English' texts (updated linguistically in sundry and not always consistent ways) are found in manuscripts right up to the early thirteenth century, and the language of some of this material may differ very little from that of the earliest texts which most scholars label as new 'Middle English' compositions, extant from much earlier in the twelfth century.[15] Within this categorical 'grey' period, in fact, there are several texts which could be and have been classed both as (very) late Old English and (very) early Middle English. A case in point is *The Soul's Address to the Body* (hereafter *SAB*), a fragmentary alliterative (and sometimes rhyming) eschatological poem in which a departing soul rails against the body whose sinful excesses have sealed its fate. It survives among the 'Worcester Fragments' now shelved as Worcester, Cathedral Library, F. 174, whose main contents are a linguistically revised copy of the *Grammar and Glossary* (*c* 1000) of Ælfric. *SAB* very much epitomises the period of 'transition' between Old and Middle English—as indicated by the fact that it is cited in both the *Dictionary of Old English* and the *Middle English Dictionary*.[16] Its date of composition is hard to pin down (it is conventionally put in the second half of the twelfth century), but its surviving witness was written at the end of the period when pre-Conquest texts were being copied (and revised), and was produced by the scribe who is best known for his efforts, early in the thirteenth century, to study and make sense of the vocabulary in Old English manuscripts: the so-called 'Tremulous Hand' of Worcester.[17] The English texts copied in this period, especially from the relatively conservative south-west Midlands, are sometimes described by scholars as backward-looking, even antiquarian; many, including *SAB* itself, have little reputation as literary artefacts in their own right. But, linguistically speaking, we can characterise these texts in equal measure as looking forwards, and we do them a disservice if we miss the chance to explore how they stand and speak for themselves, with language choices and stylistic traditions of their own time and place.[18]

As a way of illuminating some of the changes, and the continuities, from earlier English verse evinced by *SAB*, here is an excerpt from it. It is preceded by a passage from an Old

[15] On English textual production during this period, see most notably Mary Swan and Elaine Treharne (eds), *Rewriting Old English in the Twelfth Century* (Cambridge, 2000); and Orietta Da Rold, Takako Kato, Jo Story, Mary Swan, and Elaine Treharne, *The Production and Use of English Manuscripts 1060 to 1220* (Leicester, 2010) (hereafter *EMSS*); for further references, see Dance, 'Getting a Word In', 156–7.

[16] See Angus Cameron, Ashley Crandell Amos, Antonette diPaolo Healey et al. (eds), *Dictionary of Old English: A–I Online* (Toronto, 2018) (hereafter *DOE*), as 'HomU 5.1–5.7 (Buch A–Buch G)'; and *MED*, as 'Body & S.(2) (Wor F.174)'.

[17] For Worcester F.174 and *SAB*, see Douglas Moffat (ed.), *The Soul's Address to the Body: The Worcester Fragments* (East Lansing, MI, 1987), especially 1–25; and Elaine Treharne, 'Worcester, Cathedral Library, F. 174', in *EMSS*. For the Tremulous Hand, see notably Christine Franzen, *The Tremulous Hand of Worcester: A Study of Old English in the Thirteenth Century* (Oxford, 1991).

[18] On *SAB*'s reputation, see Moffat, *Soul's Address*, 33 (and n. 35), and on its twelfth- and thirteenth-century literary contexts, see 39–44; and further, e.g., Seth Lerer, 'Old English and Its Afterlife', in David Wallace (ed.), *The Cambridge History of Medieval English Literature* (Cambridge, 1999), 7–34.

76 MEDIEVAL POETRY: 1100–1400

English poem on the same subject, a piece from the Vercelli Book (Vercelli, Biblioteca Capitolare, CXVII, copied in the second half of the tenth century) known today as *Soul and Body I*:

> Ne eart ðu þon leofra   nænigum lifigendra
> men to gemæccan,   ne meder ne fæder
> ne nænigum gesybban,   þonne se swearta hrefen,
> syððan ic ana of ðe   ut siðode   55
> þurh þæs sylfes hand   þe ic ær onsended wæs.
> Ne magon þe nu heonon adon   hyrsta þa readan
> ne gold ne seolfor   ne þinra goda nan,
> ne þinre bryde beag   ne þin boldwela,
> ne nan þara goda   þe ðu iu ahtest,   60
> ac her sceolon onbidan   ban bereafod,
> besliten synum,   ond þe þin sawl sceal
> minum unwillum   oft gesecan,
> wemman þe mid wordum,   swa ðu worhtest to me.

(You are no more beloved as a companion to any person among the living, to mother or father or any relative, than is the dark raven, since I journeyed out alone from you, through the hand of that very one by whom I was sent before. Now no red treasures can get you away from here, neither gold nor silver nor any of your goods, nor your bride's ring nor your fine house, nor any of the goods which you used to own; but here your bones must remain, stripped and torn away from their sinews, and your soul must, against my will, often seek you out, to revile you with words, according to what you have done to me.) (*Soul and Body I*, 52–64)[19]

> Ʒet sæiþ þeo sowle   soriliche to þen licame:
> 'Ne <þea>rft þu on stirope   stonden mid fotan,
> on nenne goldfohne bowe,   for þu <scal>t faren al to howe
> and þu scalt nu ruglunge   ridæn to þære eorþe,   5
> ut<se>t æt þære dure   (ne þearft þu næffre onʒean cumæn),
> reowliche riden   <son>e beræfed
> a<t> þene eorþliche weole   þe þu iwold ohtest.
> Nu mon mæi <seg>gen bi þe: "Þes mon is iwiten nu her,
> weila, and his weolæn   beoþ her belæfed;   10
> <nol>de he nefre þærof don   his drihtenes wille".
> Ac æfre þu gæderedest   gær<sume o>n þine feonde;
> nulleþ heo nimen gete   hwo hit biʒete;
> nafst þu bute <wei>lawei   þ(et) þu weole heuedest:

---

[19] George Philip Krapp (ed.), *The Vercelli Book* (New York, 1932), 56; and compare Douglas Moffat (ed.), *The Old English Soul and Body* (Woodbridge, 1990), especially 6–19, 41–4 on the history of the text.

al is reowliche þin siþ   efter þin wrecche <lif>.   15

Þeo men beoþ þe bliþre,   þe arisen ær wiþ þe,

þ(et) þin muþ is betuned;   <þu> þeo teone ut lettest

þe heom sore grulde,   þet ham gros þe aȝan ...

(Again the soul speaks sorrowfully to the body: 'You will have no occasion to stand with your feet in stirrups, in no gold-adorned saddlebow, because you must travel utterly into anxiety, and you must now ride backwards into the earth, shut outside at the door (you will never have occasion to come back), grievously ride, immediately deprived of the earthly wealth that you had control over. Now it can be said of you: "This person has now departed from here, alas, and his wealth will be left here; he never wished to do his Lord's will with it". But you always gathered treasure from your enemies; no one will pay attention to who acquired it; you can now only lament that you had this wealth: your departure is utterly grievous, after your wretched life. Those people are happier, who struggled with you before, that your mouth is closed; you let out insults that sorely offended them, that made them afraid of you ...') (*Soul's Address to the Body*, Fragment C, 2–18)[20]

There are clear and important distinctions between the fairly regular late West Saxon of *Soul and Body I* (hereafter *SBI*) in the Vercelli Book and the south-west Midland forms of *c* 1200 which are emerging in our copy of *SAB*.[21] The major orthographic novelty is the systematic distinction of the old insular shape of the letter *g* (<ȝ>, which we call 'yogh') and the caroline *g* (<g>) to represent different sounds; compare, for example, *biȝete* and *gete* (13). There are also regular indications of sound changes, including the rounding of OE /ɑ:/ to (southern and Midland) ME /ɔ:/ evident if we compare *SBI sāwl* (62, 'soul'), *āhtest* (60, 'owned') with *SAB sowle* (2), *ohtest* (8), and other tell-tale signs of recent developments like the monophthongisation of OE /æ:ɑ/ > /ɛ:/ (*SAB* 7 *beræfed*, < OE *berēafod* 'deprived'). The spellings of *SAB* nonetheless show some inconsistencies, with a mixture of some older, West Saxon conventions which persist alongside more modern and/or local forms. Notice, for example, <e> probably for /ɛ:/ in *nenne* (4, 'no') (OE *nænne*), but <æ> in *þære* (6, 'the') (OE *þære*); the West Saxon-looking *gæderedest* (12, 'gathered') with <æ> versus south-west Midland *efter* (15, 'after'), and *heuedest* (14, 'had'), with OE (West Mercian) second fronting of /æ/; and *heom* (18, 'them'), a late Old English plural variant of *him*, next to south-west Midland ME *ham* in the same line. While they may be 'irregular' by modern standards, then, these spellings are not simply an unruly hotch-potch of variants: they have interesting things to tell us about the biography of the text, and about the competing traditions of writing English which have acted upon its copyists.

The most obvious differences between the language of *SBI* and *SAB* are probably in their grammatical forms. The 'full' morphological complexity of the Old English poem (notice, e.g., the dative plus genitive sequence 'nænig*um* lifigend*ra*' [52, '*to none of* the living']) is no longer apparent in *SAB*—and so, if this is our chief reason for classifying by language 'phase', we are justified in calling this 'Middle'. But it may surprise readers more used to the Middle English of *Havelok* (and later) just how much of the Old English inflexional system persists in the language of *SAB*. Hence despite the phonetic reduction in unstressed syllables visible

---

[20] Moffat, *Soul's Address*, 67–8. (I have reproduced the editor's () for expanded abbreviations and <> for emendations, but not his diacritic marks.)

[21] See, e.g., Moffat, *Soul and Body*, 12–16; and Moffat, *Soul's Address*, 7–11, 15–25.

78 MEDIEVAL POETRY: 1100–1400

throughout, there is still some morphological marking of case/number (e.g., dative plural *fot-an* [3, 'feet'], for OE *fōt-um*) and also of grammatical gender (e.g., nominative singular feminine *þeo sowle* [2, 'the soul'], for OE *sēo sāwl*, albeit with analogical levelling of *þ*- for OE *s*-).[22] What is more, there is far less difference between the lexis of *SBI* and *SAB* than one might expect. A few word stems in *SBI* are recorded no later than Old English (here, notice *hyrsta* 57, 'treasures'), but there are very few words and phrases in this passage that would have seemed out of place in the Tremulous Hand's own usage (and compare *SBI* 60b, 61b with *SAB* 7b, 8b). This lexical closeness is no doubt at least partly because *SBI* is not characteristic of the most elaborated tradition of Old English poetic vocabulary of the kind we can see in the opening of *Beowulf* cited above—demonstrating (among other things) the crucial role played by style, and hence that it matters *which* Old English poem we choose as a point of comparison. Old English verse is well known for the copiousness of its word stock, something which developed at least partly for the needs of alliteration and rhythmical variety but which also offered important expressive opportunities in its own right; but no two Old English poets are quite alike in the range of words they employ. Thus *Beowulf* is replete with compounds (including *Gār-Dena* 'Spear-Danes' there are eight nominal or adjectival compounds in the first eleven lines), but *SBI* is relatively sparing in them; and this passage also shows comparatively few distinctly 'poetic' word stems (stems attested only or mainly in verse, like *gombe* 'tribute' and *ellen* 'courage' in our *Beowulf* passage).[23] The hallmarks of Old English poetic diction are perhaps most clearly visible in our *SBI* excerpt in the sequence of words for wealth and treasure items, which include the largely poetic *hyrsta* (attested in poetry and glosses only) and the compound *boldwela* (verse only; emended from manuscript *goldwela*), besides the more quotidian *gold*, *seolfor*, and *bēag*. Old English verse attests an impressive variety of broad synonyms (including numerous compounds) for the idea of material wealth that was so significant in the heroic cultural traditions which underlie the diction of this poetry.[24]

Almost all of the vocabulary found in *SAB* is already recorded in Old English texts. There are no borrowings from (Anglo-)French in this passage, and for that matter no unambiguous instances anywhere in *SAB*. This might seem a surprising lack in a text from this period, more than a hundred years after the Norman Conquest; but as we shall see, it takes much longer than one might expect for French-derived words to build up in significant numbers in English writings. There is nothing to indicate that the lexis of *SAB* is markedly conservative for its time and place, and there are some words here that are novel in the textual record. Notice in particular the Old Norse borrowing *gete* (13), which is first attested in English (as a simplex) here; arguably it was chosen specially for this poetic context, to effect the rhyme with *biȝete*, and it might otherwise not have appeared.[25] Another interesting oddity

---

[22] On the morphology of the text, see further Moffat, *Soul's Address*, 11–15, 24.

[23] For introductions to OE poetic diction, see, e.g., Dance, 'Old English Language', 42–9; Pons-Sanz, *Language of Early English Literature*, 80–4; and on vocabulary and its relationship with alliteration, see further Townend, 'Antiquity of Diction' and references there cited. On *Beowulf* in particular, see Fulk, Bjork, and Niles (eds), *Klaeber's Beowulf*, cxi–cxxi; and on the vocabulary of *SBI*, see Moffat, *Soul and Body*, 16–19.

[24] On words for 'treasure' in OE poetry, see notably Elizabeth M. Tyler, *Old English Poetics: The Aesthetics of the Familiar in Anglo-Saxon England* (York, 2006), especially 25–36. For an impression of the range of words attested in this semantic domain in OE versus later periods, see Christian Kay, Jane Roberts, Michael Samuels, and Irené Wotherspoon (eds), *The Historical Thesaurus of the Oxford English Dictionary*, 2 vols. (Oxford, 2009) (hereafter *HTOED*). Combining 02.06.05.01 ('Wealth/riches') and sub-category 11.01 ('Hoarded wealth > Treasure'), *HTOED* gives thirty items for OE (only), including nineteen compounds.

[25] See *MED* s.v. *gete* n.2; *OED* s.v. *gete* n. On the verse form of *SAB*, see especially Moffat, *Soul's Address*, 25–33; and further Eric Weiskott, *English Alliterative Verse: Poetic Tradition and Literary History* (Cambridge, 2016), 74–6.

is *ruglunge*, a word of native origin which is recorded only here and in the Katherine Group texts, also from the south-west Midlands in the early thirteenth century;[26] it plays a key role in the startling image of 'riding backwards' into the earth, as well as enabling the alliteration in line 5. The reworking of the Old English poetic lexicon is also evident in the words for wealth and treasure in *SAB*. The richness of the Old English verse synonym bank is much reduced in general in early Middle English poetry, and this semantic area is no exception; texts from this period feature hardly any 'treasure' compounds, and the Old English poetic staple *sinc* is moreover never attested in Middle English.[27] In this *SAB* passage, the broad idea of material wealth is expressed repeatedly by the inherited prosaic word *weole*, used three times within seven lines (8, 10, 14, next to the more generic *æihte* 'possessions' elsewhere in the text). Close reiteration of words in this way is a common feature of *SAB*, and other verse from this period, and was evidently a conscious stylistic trait: compare the recurrence in these few lines of the same lexical elements for other key ideas like *riden* (5, 7, 'to ride'), *eorþ-* (5, 8, 'earth'), *weila(-)* (10, 14, 'alas'), and *reowliche* (7, 15, 'grievous(ly)').[28] Some of the variety in the 'treasure' word-field is nonetheless recovered by the use of the Norse borrowing *gærsume* (12, 'treasure, monetary wealth'; it is found three times in *SAB*, including twice in alliterative collocation with the verb *gæderen* 'to gather'); this word is recorded in late Old English, but never before in verse.[29]

To explore further the linguistic diversity of the earliest Middle English verse, let us now move to the other side of England, to a text from the north-east Midlands at more or less the same time. The *Ormulum* is extant in Oxford, Bodleian Library, Junius 1, a peculiarly shaped and scruffy working draft written by a single scribe, apparently its author (Orm), in the period from about 1160 to 1180.[30] Orm's very long and idiosyncratic verse homily collection (more than 20,000 lines survive) occupies a strange place in the story of the English language and of English poetry. It was composed in a new, extremely regular syllabic verse form (the iambic septenary), without either rhyme or alliteration;[31] but it has virtually zero reputation for its poetic artifice, almost always being cited by philologists rather than literary critics.[32] There are a great many 'firsts' in this text, including the earliest attestations of some key words in the history of English; but it is by no means characterisable simply for its innovation, any more than *SAB* incarnates pure conservatism. Let us consider the following excerpts, in which Orm describes the spiritual significance of the gifts of the Magi:

> 3iff þatt tu follȝ[h]esst witt & skill
> & soþ wissdomess le<o>me,
> Þa lakesst tu þe Laferrd Crist   6730
> Wiþþ gold i þine þæwess;
> Forr rihht all swa su*mm* hord off gold
> Mang menn iss horde deresst,

---

[26] See *OED* s.v. *rugling* adv.; *MED* s.v. *ruglinge* adv.

[27] For an impression of early ME, see *HTOED* for the fields given at note 24 above.

[28] On the repetitive style of *SAB*, see Moffat, *Soul's Address*, 33–9.

[29] See *DOE* s.v. *gærsum, gærsuma, gærsume*; *MED* s.v. *gersum(e* n.; Pons-Sanz, *Lexical Effects*, 55–6, 299–300.

[30] See M. B. Parkes, 'On the Presumed Date and Possible Origin of the Manuscript of the "Ormulum": Oxford, Bodleian Library, MS Junius 1', in Eric G. Stanley and Douglas Gray (eds), *Five Hundred Years of Words and Sounds: A Festschrift for Eric Dobson* (Cambridge, 1983), 115–27; the 'Index of Sources' in *LAEME*, index number 301; and Mark Faulkner, 'Oxford, Bodleian Library, Junius 1' in *EMSS*.

[31] See especially Elizabeth Solopova, 'The Metre of the *Ormulum*', in M. J. Toswell and E. M. Tyler (eds), *Studies in English Language and Literature: 'Doubt Wisely', Papers in Honour of E. G. Stanley* (London, 1996), 423–39, and Chapter 9 in this volume.

[32] On Orm's poor reputation as a poet, see, e.g., Christopher Cannon, *The Grounds of English Literature* (Oxford, 2004), 83–5; on his importance and his originality, see further Chapter 2 in this volume, with references.

80 MEDIEVAL POETRY: 1100–1400

> Rihht swa iss allre deresst lac
> Biforenn Godess ehne,   6735
> ʒiff *þatt* we follʒ^henn rihht tatt witt
> Þatt follʒ^heþþ Godess wille,
> Þatt hallʒ^he witt tatt læreþþ uss
> To berrʒ^henn ure sawle.
>
> …
>
> Þeʒʒ brohhtenn Drihhtin þri*nn*e lac
> To don uss tunnderrstanndenn,
> Þatt ure Godd iss þripell Godd   6770
> Inn Allmahhtiʒ þrimmnesse,
> Faderr, & Sune, & Haliʒ Gast,
> An Godd all unntodæledd,
> Þatt æfre wass, & iss, & be<o>þ
> Wiþþ utenn ord & ende,   6775
> & all *þatt* wass, & iss, & be<o>þ,
> He shop, & ah, & ste<o>reþþ.

(If you follow understanding and discernment and true wisdom's radiance, then you make an offering to the Lord Christ with gold in your practices. Because just as a hoard of gold is the most precious of hoards among people, just so it is the most precious offering of all before God's eyes if we follow correctly that understanding which follows God's will, that holy understanding that teaches us how to save our soul … They brought a threefold offering to the Lord to cause us to understand that our God is a triple God in almighty trinity, Father, and Son, and Holy Spirit, one God entirely undivided, that always was, and is, and will be without beginning and end, and all that was, and is, and will be, he created, and possesses, and directs.) (*The Ormulum*, 6728–39, 6768–77)[33]

Orm's innovation is immediately apparent in his famously distinctive spelling, evidently a way of making it as clear as possible how his words should be pronounced. The most striking feature is the doubling of consonants, which is used to signal that the preceding vowel (in a closed syllable) is short.[34] Since this manuscript is an autograph, Orm's preferences are not over-ridden by a subsequent scribe imposing any of his or her own habits. Where there is variation, most notably in the case of <eo> and <e> as reflexes of OE /e:o/ (compare *leome* [6729, 'radiance'], *beoþ* [6774 etc., 'will be'], *steorepþ* [6777, 'directs'], versus *deresst* [6733 etc., 'most precious']), it apparently reflects actual variation in Orm's own dialect, and

---

[33] I have re-edited this passage from digital photographs of the manuscript (columns 167–8; see 'The Ormulum', in *The Digital Bodleian* [Oxford, 2011–]), retaining the lineation, capitalisation, and punctuation of Robert Holt (ed.), *The Ormulum*, with the notes and glossary of R. M. White, 2 vols. (Oxford, 1878), at 1.233–4. Abbreviations are expanded (in italics); <> enclose erasures. Orm's 'flat-topped *g*' (for the sound /g/) is represented simply by <g> (there being no instances here of his 'round *g*', for the sound /dʒ/); the letter 'wynn' is printed as <w>. His superposed <h> in the sequence <ʒ^h> (for the sound /ɣ/) is printed as a superscript letter (Orm consistently differentiates this <ʒ^h> from the <ʒh> in *ʒho* 'she'), but I have not attempted to reproduce his 'stacked' versions of doubled consonants, which are shown here simply as a sequence of two consonants (At the time of writing, a new edition of the *Ormulum* by Nils-Lennart Johannesson and Andrew Cooper for the Early English Text Society is in press.).

[34] On Orm's spelling, see notably R. W. Burchfield, 'The Language and Orthography of the Ormulum MS', *Transactions of the Philological Society*, 55 (1956), 56–87; Meg Worley, 'Using the *Ormulum* to Redefine Vernacularity', in Fiona Somerset and Nicholas Watson (eds), *The Vulgar Tongue: Medieval and Postmedieval Vernacularity* (University Park, PA, 2003), 19–30; and Cannon, *Grounds of English Literature*, 86–97.

THE POETIC FIELD, I   81

(from a diachronic perspective) a change in progress: the unrounding of ME /ø:/ (< OE /e:o/) to /e:/, an East Midland innovation and an important dialect marker in early Middle English (contrast *SAB* spellings in <eo>, e.g., *beoþ* [10]). This change is further evidenced by Orm's going back and painstakingly revising his <eo> spellings to <e> (once he reached about line 13,000 in the extant text), by erasing the <o>.[35] In its grammar, typically for an East Midland dialect, the *Ormulum* looks more 'modern' to us than does *SAB*; see, for instance, the indeclinable singular demonstrative *þe* 'the' (6730), with only a plural form (*þa*) remaining distinct. There is no sign at all of grammatical gender, and very little of case in nouns (though notice *hord-e* possessive plural at 6733, compared to the singular [nominative] in the previous line).[36]

Orm is well known, moreover, for the relative 'modernity' of his vocabulary compared to contemporary texts from the south and west—but only in some respects, and not in others. His poem provides us with some of our earliest attestations of many loans from Old Norse which are commonplace and more widespread later in English, including *skill* (6728), and elsewhere in the text the likes of *bank*, *get*, *ill*, *low*, *meek*, and *seem*, and crucially *they*, *their*, and *them*. It also contains an extensive set of rarer Scandinavian derivations, many of which are scarcely recorded outside the north or north-east Midlands in any period; in this passage, notice *þrinne* (6768, 'three[fold]'), and in particular the conjunction *summ* (6732, 'as'), which is characteristic of dialects where Scandinavian influence was particularly strong.[37] By contrast, there are very few borrowings indeed from (Anglo-)French in the *Ormulum*, despite their occurrence in other twelfth-century texts from the East Midlands (including Orm's near-neighbour, the redactor of the 'second continuation' of the Peterborough Chronicle).[38] But French loans are not altogether absent (notice words like *casstell* 'castle' and *skarnedd* 'scorned'), and occasionally French and/or Latin influence pops up in unexpected places. A remarkable example is *þripell* (6770), which has previously been explained merely as a variant of the later *triple* (< [Anglo-]French *triple* and/or Latin *triplus*), but which I suggest is better understood as a distinct English word stem, with an independent and much earlier line of descent from French or Latin, showing assimilation to the onset *thr-* of Germanic words for 'three'.[39]

While the *Ormulum* has an unenviable reputation as one of the most repetitive and even tedious of Middle English poems, then, there is much of interest in its vocabulary; and Orm's choice of words is, moreover, far from simply an unthinking reflection of 'local' forms unresponsive to poetic context. As in *SAB*, 'treasure' vocabulary can once more be a useful touchstone. Again, the variety of words in this semantic field is much reduced from the rich array of Old English verse: we find generic or representative terms like *hord* (6732–3, 'hoard'), *lac* (6734, 6768, 'offering'), and *gold* (6731–2), and elsewhere in the text *fe* (*fehh*) 'revenue, money', *ahhte* 'possessions', and also *se(o)llþe* (sometimes denoting material

---

[35] See Burchfield, 'Language and Orthography', 74, 80–4 (and 71–84 on Orm's other 'normalisations').

[36] On Orm's nominal morphology, see, e.g., Lass, 'Phonology and Morphology', 109–10.

[37] See *MED* s.vv. *thrin* num., *sum* conj. For discussion of Orm's vocabulary, and further references (especially on Old Norse loans), see Durkin, *Borrowed Words*, 182–6; and Sara M. Pons-Sanz, 'Norse-Derived Terms in Orm's Lexico-Semantic Field of EMOTION', *Journal of English and Germanic Philology*, 114 (2015), 552–86.

[38] See Cecily Clark (ed.), *The Peterborough Chronicle 1070–1154*, 2nd edn. (Oxford, 1970), lxviii. In our 'treasure' word field, these French loans include the first attestation of *tresor* itself, s.a. 1137 (and see *OED* s.v. *treasure* n.; *MED* s.v. *tresour* n.).

[39] *MED* lemmatises Orm's form under *triple* adj., but it long predates the only other attestation of the adjective in the dictionary (in a translation of Chauliac's *Grande Chirurgie*, dated '?a1425'). That Orm's *þripell* represents an etymologically discrete English stem is reinforced by the appearance of the verb *threpild* 'tripled' in the late Middle English poem *The Wars of Alexander* (Hoyt N. Duggan and Thorlac Turville-Petre [eds], *The Wars of Alexander* [Oxford, 1989], line 1599), where initial *thr-* is guaranteed by alliteration.

82 MEDIEVAL POETRY: 1100–1400

riches, but more usually 'happiness, blessing'). The only survivor of the principal treasure words of Old English poetry is *maddmess* ('treasures', plural only, although this is not a 'poetic' word as such, being commonplace in Old English prose too).[40] It is used relatively rarely in Orm's long text, and mainly appears at the end of the second hemistich of his septenary line (i.e., the end of the 'even' verses as printed above), where a disyllabic word is essential to the metre, and hence something like *gold* or *hord* or *fe(hh)* would not work; but it is also found in some repeated constructions, often paired with *lakenn* 'to make an offering (to)'.[41] *Lakenn* is another of Orm's favourite words in this conceptual domain (see 6730, 6763, 6765 in the passage above), and the use of *lak-* as a verb stem is in fact unique to this text in Middle English.[42] There are many other still clearer examples of Orm selecting one of a set of frequently recurring synonyms or by-forms in different metrical positions on the basis of their rhythmical 'shape':[43] in our 'wealth' field, notice *fe* 'revenue, money' (which would be elided with a following word starting with a vowel) versus *fehh* (which would not). In ways remarkably akin to *SAB*, the idiom of Orm's verse is characterised far more by controlled lexical repetition than by the elaboration we associate with Old English poetry. In the first twelve verses of the excerpts above, notice the recurrence of *follȝhen* 'to follow', *witt* 'understanding', *lakenn*, *gold*, *hord*, and *der* 'precious'. This is the crucial driver of the need for regular variants and synonyms to be available, time and time again, to reiterate the same idea under different metrical circumstances; but if this phenomenon, this 'sameness with a difference', is very roughly analogous to the way Old English verse drew on its stock of synonyms to express key concepts in varying sequence, it is independent of it and produces some quite different effects.[44] Orm is also capable of more artfully patterned repetition, as in the last four verses of this excerpt: the threefold statements of eternal existence in the even verses ('Þatt æfre wass, & iss, & beoþ ... & all þatt wass, & iss, & beoþ') are modulated by the threefold *action* of the Trinity in the final one ('He shop, & ah, & steoreþþ'), harnessing the rhythmic potential of the metre and Orm's cumulative reiteration to create a climax focusing on the verb which, apart from anything else, would have been very hard to achieve in the noun-centred diction of an Old English poem.

Later Middle English: Strangers at the Feast

To conclude this short survey, let us jump forwards in time about 200 years, and briefly compare famous passages by two of the best-known Middle English poets of the late fourteenth century. The excerpts below both portray marvellous entrances by uncanny individuals, and in some respects the two scenes are remarkably similar.[45] Moreover, even though the modern reader is liable to find some of the English in the second piece about as weird and exotic as the visitor it depicts, I shall suggest that the linguistic features of these two passages have more in common with one another, and with some later attitudes to poetic language, than one might think at first glance.

---

[40] See Tyler, *Old English Poetics*, 25–7; *MED* s.v. *madmes* pl.

[41] For *maddmess* at the end of the second hemistich, see, e.g., 6471, 7135, 7311, 7356. It collocates with *lakenn* at 7135 and 7311, and also (in different metrical positions) at 6412 and 6491.

[42] See *MED* s.v. *laken* v.; *OED* s.v. *lake* v.2.

[43] See especially Burchfield, 'Language and Orthography', 78; and Chapter 9 in this volume.

[44] On Orm's repetition, see also Cannon, *Grounds of English Literature*, 98–104; and Chapter 2 in this volume.

[45] *Gawain* has sometimes been taken to be Chaucer's direct inspiration; but see Larry D. Benson (ed.), *The Riverside Chaucer*, 3rd edn. (Oxford, 2008), 892.

And so bifel that after the thridde cours,
Whil that this kyng sit thus in his nobleye*,   noble state
Herknynge his mynstralles hir thynges pleye
Biforn hym at the bord deliciously*,   delightfully
In at the halle dore al sodeynly   80
Ther cam a knyght upon a steede of bras,
And in his hand a brood mirour of glas.
Upon his thombe he hadde of gold a ryng,
And by his syde a naked swerd hangyng;
And up he rideth to the heighe bord*.   85   high table
In al the halle ne was ther spoken a word
For merveille of this knyght; hym to biholde
Ful bisily* they wayten*, yonge and olde.   eagerly; watch
This strange knyght, that cam thus sodeynly,
Al armed, save his heed, ful richely,   90
Saleweth* kyng and queene and lordes alle,   greets
By ordre*, as they seten in the halle,   sequentially
With so heigh reverence and obeisaunce,
As wel in speche as in his contenaunce*,   bearing
That Gawayn, with his olde curteisye,   95
Though he were comen ayeyn* out of Fairye,   again
Ne koude hym nat amende with a word.
(Geoffrey Chaucer, 'The Squire's Tale', V.76–97)[46]

Now wyl I of hor seruise say yow no more,   130
For vch wyȝe may wel wit no wont þat þer were.
An oþer noyse ful newe neȝed biliue,
Þat þe lude myȝt haf leue liflode to cach;
For vneþe watz þe noyce not a whyle sesed,
And þe fyrst cource in þe court kyndely serued,   135
Þer hales in at þe halle dor an aghlich mayster,
On þe most on þe molde on mesure hyghe;
Fro þe swyre to þe swange so sware and so þik,
And his lyndes and his lymes so longe and so grete,
Half etayn in erde I hope þat he were,   140
Bot mon most I algate mynn hym to bene,
And þat þe myriest in his muckel þat myȝt ride;
For of bak and of brest al were his bodi sturne,
Both his wombe and his wast were worthily smale,
And alle his fetures folȝande, in forme þat he hade,   145
      ful clene;
For wonder of his hwe men hade,
Set in his semblaunt sene;
He ferde as freke were fade,
And oueral enker-grene.   150

---

[46] Benson, *Riverside Chaucer*, following its glosses (with additions).

84 MEDIEVAL POETRY: 1100–1400

(Now I will tell you no more about the serving of their meal, for everybody can appreciate very well that there was no lack of it. Another very new sound approached quickly, so that the man [i.e., Arthur] might have leave to take sustenance. For the noise [i.e., of the trumpets announcing the first course] had scarcely ceased even for a short time, and the first course been properly served in the court, when there comes in at the hall door a terrible lord, the very largest in the world in his height. From the neck to the waist so squarely built and so stout, and his loins and his limbs so long and so big—I believe that he could be half giant, in fact, but at any rate I declare him to be the largest man, and the most handsome one in his size who could ride. For although his body was formidable in back and chest, both his belly and his waist were becomingly slender, and all his features were in accordance in terms of his form, very elegantly. People marvelled at his colour, plain to see in his appearance; he looked like a man who was bold, and he was completely bright green.) (*Sir Gawain and the Green Knight*, 130–50)[47]

In neither case are spelling or grammar much of a barrier to comprehension by present-day English speakers. Leaving aside the thorns and yoghs (which are used by the scribes of many Chaucer manuscripts too), the *Gawain*-poet has some forms proper to his north-west Midland dialect which are less familiar to us today than are the features of the London variety of Chaucer.[48] Notice, for instance, the *Gawain* forms *wont* (131, 'lack') (with West Midland rounding of OE /ɑ/ before a nasal consonant), *lude* (133, 'man', with the *Gawain* scribe's occasional <u> for the reflex of OE /eːo/), and the Norse loan *fro* as a preposition (138, as opposed to native *from*). In terms of grammar, the change from the language of *SAB* and Orm is very striking. In neither fourteenth-century text is there any trace of grammatical gender, or of case endings in nouns (beyond the *-s* possessive we still use). The morphology of the *Gawain*-poet is in some respects less alien to us than Chaucer's, as in Chaucer's *-eth* for the present third-person singular of verbs (e.g., *rideth* 85), next to *-es* in *Gawain* (e.g., *hales* 136, 'comes'), still a feature of more northern dialects at this period; but in other respects, it is Chaucer's form that we recognise, as in the present participle *-yng* (*hangyng* 84) versus the northern *-ande* in *Gawain* (*folȝande* 145, 'following, in accordance with').

In important respects, these two poets are significantly more alike lexically than either resembles the English of the twelfth century; but they also differ in some telling ways. In terms of their etymological make-up, notably, both poets' vocabularies contain markedly more words of (Anglo-)French origin than we have seen in any of the earlier texts we have examined in this chapter. Chaucer has frequently been stereotyped as a lexical early adopter, a poet with a special penchant for words of Romance origin in particular;[49] and this scene from 'The Squire's Tale' unsurprisingly contains numerous French loans. I count nineteen altogether, none of which is attested in English texts before 1200, and the great majority

---

[47] J. R. R. Tolkien and E. V. Gordon (eds), *Sir Gawain and the Green Knight*, 2nd edn., rev. Norman Davis (Oxford, 1967); and see also the glosses and notes in Ad Putter and Myra Stokes (eds), *The Works of the Gawain Poet: Sir Gawain and the Green Knight, Pearl, Cleanness, Patience* (London, 2014).

[48] On the dialect of the *Gawain*-poet and of the extant manuscript, see especially Ad Putter and Myra Stokes, 'The *Linguistic Atlas* and the Dialect of the *Gawain* Poems', *Journal of English and Germanic Philology*, 106 (2007), 468–91. For Chaucer, see Simon Horobin, *Chaucer's Language* (Basingstoke, 2007), e.g. 44–50 on Chaucer's dialect and the language of the manuscripts. (At 29–30 Horobin also cites most of this passage of *Gawain* and compares some of its features to Chaucer.)

[49] For the dangers of this stereotype, see Horobin, *Chaucer's Language*, 78–90; and on the problems with Chaucer's reputation as innovator, see in particular Christopher Cannon, *The Making of Chaucer's English: A Study of Words* (Cambridge, 1998).

THE POETIC FIELD, I   85

(thirteen) of which are first recorded in the late thirteenth century or afterwards.[50] But all bar two of these words are also found (or closely related to word stems which are found) somewhere in the much shorter oeuvre of the *Gawain*-poet.[51] And, indeed, there are plenty of French derivations in this *Gawain* passage too (thirteen clear instances in total, including the difficult *halen*), all of which are also recorded somewhere in Chaucer—although *halen* is not used by Chaucer in the intransitive sense of someone moving, a meaning which is mainly confined to alliterative verse and which enables the alliteration and striking additional sound play with *halle* at *Gawain* 136 (an effect revisited at line 458 when the Green Knight leaves the hall, head now in hand).[52] Again, few of these thirteen words are found very early in Middle English (only two are recorded before 1200), and some (five this time) are again not known in writing until the later thirteenth century or afterwards.[53] The number of different borrowings from (Anglo-)French increases significantly in English texts during the fourteenth century, and this is a crucial factor in later Middle English 'feeling' to modern readers more like the English we know.[54] In these two passages, notice in particular *delicious, sudden, mirror* (Chaucer), and *service, noise, cease, catch* (*Gawain*), whose shapes and meanings are instantly recognisable. It tends to be in words of non-French origin that the lexis of the two poets is most distinct. Sometimes this is a matter of a word's dialect distribution, as in the case of *swange* 'waist', *etayn* 'giant', *mynn* 'declare', *muckel* 'size', and *fade* 'bold' in our *Gawain* passage; all of these are found mainly in the north or north Midlands by the late fourteenth century.[55] As we noted of *Havelok* and the *Ormulum*, some of these words are of probable Scandinavian origin; some Old Norse input is usually adduced in *swange, mynn*, and *muckel*, as well as in rarer items like the first element of the unique *enker-grene* 'bright green' (though more debatably in this case). But by no means all 'northern' words come from Norse, and not all words normally derived from Norse were 'northern', any more than they are today—consider, for example, *both* and *wont*.[56]

Nonetheless, while the linguistic features of these fourteenth-century authors frequently seem more familiar to present-day speakers than do those of the earliest Middle English poets, this is perhaps not the only reason why the English of Chaucer and *Gawain* appeals to modern readers. Input from (Anglo-)French, and Old Norse, and all the many sources represented in later Middle English lexis feeds the variety, the 'richness' in texture which critics often regard as especially characteristic of both these poets. This is a quality that we far more readily associate with poetic virtuosity, with an individual's artistic flair, than we do the echo and repetition of the likes of *SAB* and Orm, artful though we have seen both earlier poets to be in their deployment of lexical resources. Chaucer's vocabulary is famously

---

[50] For these thirteen words (in the order they appear in this passage), see *MED* s.vv. *cours* n., *noblei(e* n., *deliciousli* adv., *sodeinli* adv., *mirour* n., *merveille* n., *straunge* adj., *sauf* prep., *saluen* v., *reverence* n., *obeisaunce* n., *contenaunce* n., *fairie* n. For the words attested earlier, see *MED* s.vv. *minstral* n., *waiten* v., *armen* v., *ordre* n., *courteisie* n., *amenden* v.; and note that *armed* derives from either French or Latin, or both (*OED* s.v. *arm* v.1).

[51] I include in this figure *deliciousli* (the noun *delyt* is in *Pearl*), *mynstralles* (*mynstralsye* is in *Gawain* and *Cleanness*), and *obeisaunce* (the verb *obe* is in *Pearl*). The two which do not occur in the *Gawain*-poet are *mirour* and *ordre*.

[52] On *halen* (probably via (Anglo-)French *haler*, ultimately < Germanic), see Richard Dance, *Words Derived from Old Norse in Sir Gawain and the Green Knight: An Etymological Survey*, 2 vols. (Chichester, 2019), 2:74.

[53] For the two earliest attested, see *MED* s.vv. *court* n.1, *serven* v.1; for the five later items, see *cesen* v., *cours* n., *halen* v., *squar(e* adj., *feture* n.1; and for the others, see *servis(e* n., *noise* n., *cacchen* v., *mesure* n., *forme* n., *semblaunt* n.

[54] On the attestation of (Anglo-)French loans in ME, see Durkin, *Borrowed Words*, 223–80 (especially 257–63 for a breakdown by period); and Miller, *External Influences*, 148–91.

[55] See *MED* s.vv. *swange* n., *eten* n., *minnen* v.1, *muchel* n., *fad(e* predicate adj.

[56] For discussion of these words, see Dance, *Words Derived from Old Norse in Sir Gawain*, 2:62 (*swange*), 2:292–4 (*mynn*), 2:171–2 (*muckel*), 2:267–8 (*enker-grene*), 2:230–1 (*both*), 2:144 (*wont*).

86 MEDIEVAL POETRY: 1100–1400

capacious, and goes hand in glove with the breadth of subjects and styles for which he is renowned.[57] And it is its range of expression, the sheer number of different lexical stems on display, that modern readers often notice about the language of the *Gawain*-poet.[58] In the case of the latter, some of this multiplicity has to do with the varied and specialist vocabulary of the late Middle English alliterative tradition. It is worth noticing that some of this 'alliterative vocabulary' is very old indeed, and it includes 'poetic words' like *burne* 'man' (< OE *beorn* 'man, warrior') which seem always to have belonged peculiarly to verse in the older Germanic languages, and whose use must somehow therefore have been transmitted from the practices of Old English poetry.[59] But there is also much in the diction of the so-called 'Alliterative Revival' which is new, and shows signs of having developed organically during the Middle English period to meet the special constraints of this verse form. Some of these words seem originally to have belonged to North Midlands or northern dialects, and began to occur in other regions mainly or only in alliterative poetry; thus, for example, *busken* 'to get ready, go', *carpen* 'to speak', both used in *Piers Plowman*. Some items, on the other hand, were apparently always restricted geographically within English— even though in themselves they may be far from parochial in their historical make-up, and showcase some fascinating chains of etymological influence. See, for instance, *tulk*, in (northern) Middle English poetry a synonym simply for 'man' usefully alliterating on *t*-, but one which came to northern English dialects most probably via Old Norse (as in Old Icelandic *tulkr*), and which is ultimately a traveller from even further afield, starting out as a Slavonic or Lithuanian word meaning 'interpreter, spokesman'.[60] Later Middle English alliterative poetry thus favours verbal elaboration of a kind that is to some extent reminiscent of the system of poetic vocabulary known in Old English verse (and the other older Germanic languages) before it. But without the tradition of compounding exploited by Old English poets, allowing more permutations to be made from a smaller number of different stems, the late Middle English alliterative lexicon depended even more strongly on the diversity of its individual word elements. By way of example, in the *Gawain* passage above there are three other words for 'man' from among the extensive set of synonyms in use in alliterative verse: see *wyȝe* (131), *lude* (133), and *freke* (149) (and contrast our Chaucerian excerpt, which manages simply with *knyght*, three times). And let us return once more to our 'treasure' words. The range of broad synonyms in this field in the *Gawain*-poet includes some familiar items, like *wele* and *gold*, beside *sele* 'prosperity' (all of native origin); some we have not seen so far, notably the French borrowing *tresor*, which dominates this field in Chaucer;[61] and one with a new twist, since *garysoun* seems to continue the sense and usage

---

[57] On the breadth of Chaucer's vocabulary, see Horobin, *Chaucer's Language*, 68–93 (including how his choices are conditioned by rhyme). There is a convenient list of all Chaucer's words (9,117 headwords) in Cannon, *Making of Chaucer's English*, 226–416.

[58] Tolkien and Gordon, *Sir Gawain*, rev. Davis, 138 gives the tally as 2,650 different words in the 2,530 lines of this poem.

[59] On the vocabulary of late ME alliterative verse, see notably Marie Borroff, *Sir Gawain and the Green Knight: A Stylistic and Metrical Study* (New Haven, CT, 1962), 52–90; Thorlac Turville-Petre, *The Alliterative Revival* (Cambridge, 1977), 69–83; and Chapter 9 in this volume. On the continuity of this diction from OE (and before), see, e.g., Townend, 'Antiquity of Diction', 20; and Weiskott, *English Alliterative Verse*, especially 95–6.

[60] Dance, *Words Derived from Old Norse in Sir Gawain*, 2:181–2; *MED* s.v. *tulk(e* n.; Borroff, *Sir Gawain*, especially 58–9.

[61] Otherwise, Chaucer has *richesse* beside the more generic *(h)abundaunce*, *suffisaunce*, and *plentee*, and the more specific *gold*. *Wele* generally has more abstract meanings in Chaucer ('joy, good fortune, prosperity, success'). *Havelok*, incidentally, makes do with *gold* and *fe* (as at line 44 quoted above) next to *auhte*, *plente*, and *won* 'abundance'.

of the earlier Norse loan *gærsum(e)* 'treasure' (as in *SAB*), including a longstanding formulaic collocation with *gold* (e.g., *Gawain* 1255, 'Nauþer golde ne garysoun'), but in its form it appears to have been blended with a Middle English loan of the unrelated (Anglo-)French *garisun* 'cure; protection, defence; livelihood, income'.[62] Arguably, then, it is in this literary tradition that we encounter the epitome of the linguistic diversity of Middle English, both etymologically and stylistically; and it is their manipulation of this copiousness which is an essential part of our conception of the art of authors like the *Gawain*-poet.

Change and diversity are, as we have seen, crucial to our impressions of Middle English. Understanding the kinds of differences involved, and their wide array of sources, is vital to appreciating the variety, across space as well as time, of this most varied stage in the history of English. Nonetheless, as we have also seen, understanding the linguistic features of the poems we have examined can involve pursuing continuities just as much as innovations. This is abundantly clear in the complex period of 'transition' from Old English, when earlier forms and conventions so often rub shoulders with newer ones. And the vocabulary of any Middle English poem may combine features of great antiquity with elements recorded in an English text for the first time, and sometimes uniquely visible to us in verse. But, more than this, the language of poetry is never, of course, simply evidence for what went on, where and when, for the effects on language history of 'erl and barun, dreng and þayn', whether 'bi are-dawes' or in the very recent past. For all the apparent flux and unpredictability of this period, the language of Middle English poets does not merely *reflect* the effects of change, reacting unconsciously or spontaneously to the features that became available, any more than the poetic language of any time. If we properly explore the resources available to these poets—in the context of the complex interactions of language, text, tradition and style, paying attention to sameness as well as variety—then their creative use of words and forms is still accessible, even when it comes to poets with far more of a reputation as witnesses to the linguistic nuts and bolts than for the quality of their poetic craftsmanship. This is, as ever, a vital part of reading the choices poets took, and the meanings they made. It plays an essential role in understanding not only how the language of Middle English verse shaped them but also how each of them shaped it.

---

[62] Dance, *Words Derived from Old Norse in Sir Gawain*, 2:210–11.

6

The Poetic Field, II

Anglo-Latin

Siân Echard

And for that fewe men endite
In oure englissh, I thenke make
A bok for Engelondes sake.[1] (Prol. 22–4)

Quam tamen Engisti lingua canit Insula Bruti
Anglica Carmente metra iuuante loquar.
(Let me, in Hengist's tongue, in Brut's isle sung,
With Carmen's help, tell forth my English verse.)[2] (Prol. 3–4)

At the beginning of his Middle English poem the *Confessio Amantis*, John Gower makes two surprising linguistic claims. In English, he suggests that 'few men write poetry in our English, and so I plan to make a book for England's sake'. This is an odd thing to say near the end of the fourteenth century because by the time Gower writes these lines, many people, including his friend and contemporary Geoffrey Chaucer, had written and were writing a great deal of poetry in English. Gower presents himself as a 'burel clerk' (Prol. 52), a simple, unlearned man, so we might imagine that his book for England, in the apparently non-poetic English tongue, is equally simple. The idea that writing in English allows a poet to address a vulgar audience is one of long standing. Robert Mannyng of Brunne says, in the prologue to his verse *Chronicle* (1338), that he is offering an English version of British history 'Not for the lerid bot for the lewed, / For tho that in this land won / That the Latyn no Frankys con' ('Not for the learned, but for the simple; for those people that live in this land who know neither Latin nor French' [7–10]).[3] However, Gower's self-presentation at the outset of the *Confessio* is complicated not only by the patent falsity of his claim about the English poetic landscape but also by what he says, not in English, but in Latin. The *Confessio* is framed throughout by Latin verses and glosses written by Gower himself, and in the first Latin verse he says he is writing in English with the help of Carmenta, the goddess credited with inventing the Latin alphabet. Latin is an essential part of his poem in 'Hengist's tongue' (English). Far from being a 'burel clerk', Gower is a trilingual poet, writing extensive and varied verse in Latin, English, and French, and often, as here in the *Confessio*, combining the languages. He has a clear sense of the differing resources offered by each of his tongues and a clear investment in asserting his facility. The effigy on his self-designed tomb at Southwark Cathedral rests its head on Gower's three main works, one each in French, Latin, and

---

[1] John Gower, *Confessio Amantis*, in G. C. Macaulay (ed.), *The Complete Works of John Gower*, 4 vols. (Oxford, 1899–1902).
[2] Siân Echard and Claire Fanger (trans.), *The Latin Verses in the* Confessio Amantis: *An Annotated Translation* (East Lansing, MI, 1991), 3.
[3] Idelle Sullens (ed.), *Robert Mannyng: The Chronicle* (Binghamton, NY, 1996).

Siân Echard, *The Poetic Field, II*. In: *The Oxford History of Poetry in English*. Edited by Helen Cooper and Robert R. Edwards, Oxford University Press. © Siân Echard (2023). DOI: 10.1093/oso/9780198827429.003.0006

English, and his self-authored (Latin) colophon describes the language, contents, and form of all of these works.

The gap between the claims of the authorial voice in the *Confessio* and Gower the poet's actual practice points to the reason Gower offers an entry into this discussion of the role of Latin in the poetic culture in which he and his fellow Middle English poets worked. Gower was not the only medieval vernacular poet to pillage classical texts for story material, and much has been written about the importance of classical and late antique Latin writers to Gower, Chaucer, and their contemporaries. Less has been said, however, about the specifically poetic issues, by which I mean questions of style, voice, and authority, shared by English vernacular writers and those *other* English writers who also occupied the poetic landscape; that is, by the ones who wrote in Latin rather than in English. The writers dealt with in this chapter were not necessarily sources for Middle English poets, though, as we will see, some of them would have been known to Chaucer, Gower, and their contemporaries. They are, however, poetic voices whose subjects, methods, and preoccupations run parallel to those of vernacular writers.

What Is Anglo-Latin?

I begin by sketching what we mean when we write of Anglo-Latin literature. The term does not refer to classical Latin. Some Middle English poets would have encountered classical texts during their education: Latin grammar was taught through recourse to many classical writers, and instruction in the rhetorical arts often drew on classical examples.[4] French, and later English, translations, often with their own commentary tradition, made authors such as Ovid or Boethius available to English poets. But in addition to these texts, there was an extensive tradition of Latin writing by medieval authors situated in England. This writing begins before the starting point of this volume, and continues into the early modern period, but for our purposes I have concentrated on the twelfth and early thirteenth centuries, a period that saw a significant rise in the quantity, quality, and variety of Latin writing that can be called Anglo-Latin. As A. G. Rigg has pointed out in his detailed overview of post-Conquest Anglo-Latin literature, isolating the 'Anglo' part of the field is difficult.[5] Some Continental Latin writers were enormously influential in England. Immediately after the Norman Conquest, and through the Angevin period, writers moved back and forth across the Channel, so that we have Englishmen such as John of Garland taking up residence in Paris, or Frenchmen such as Reginald of Canterbury moving to an English monastic house. Even when later conflicts curbed some of this easy exchange, Latin, as the lingua franca of the educated across western Europe, was important in part because it was cosmopolitan. At the same time, thanks to the impressively creative period often known as the twelfth-century renaissance, England was particularly fertile ground for Latin writing of all sorts. The authors dealt with in this chapter are only a small sample of this enormous body of texts.

---

[4] Studies of the influence of Latin reading and education on medieval writers include Rita Copeland, *Rhetoric, Hermeneutics, and Translation in the Middle Ages* (Cambridge, 1991); Christopher Baswell, *Virgil in Medieval England: Figuring the Aeneid from the Twelfth Century to Chaucer* (Cambridge, 1995); Domenico Comparetti, *Vergil in the Middle Ages*, trans. E. F. M. Benecke (Princeton, NJ, 1997); Alastair Minnis, *Medieval Theory of Authorship: Scholastic Literary Attitudes in the Later Middle Ages*, 2nd edn. (Philadelphia, PA, 2009); Marjorie Curry Woods, *Classroom Commentaries: Teaching the Poetria Nova across Medieval and Renaissance Europe* (Columbus, OH, 2010); and Amanda Gerber, *Medieval Ovid: Frame Narrative and Political Allegory* (London, 2015).

[5] A. G. Rigg, *A History of Anglo-Latin Literature 1066–1422* (Cambridge, 1992), 5–6.

Epic: Joseph of Exeter and Walter of Châtillon

And ech of these, as have I joye,
Was besy for to bere up Troye.[6] (1471–2)

Wandering through Fame's hall, the dreamer-narrator of Chaucer's *House of Fame* pauses in front of the statues of writers responsible for 'holding up the fame of Troy'. Many Latin texts contributed to medieval authors' understanding of the epic Trojan material, from Virgil's *Aeneid* to the prose accounts of Dares Phrygius and Dictys Cretensis, which were believed to be (unlike Homer) eyewitness accounts of the battle. The idea that Trojan refugees led by Brutus had settled in the island of Britain was laid out by Geoffrey of Monmouth in his twelfth-century Anglo-Latin *History of the Kings of Britain*, and rapidly became a commonplace assumption. But the appeal of the Trojan story was not simply a result of its fame or its (dubious) links to British history. Epic was the supreme expression of poetic high style in the classical period and beyond. It was the target and mark of poetic ambition, and so medieval writers of vernacular and Latin alike were drawn to flex their literary muscles in this arena. The medieval French poet Jean Bodel's three poetic *matières* included the Matter of Rome, subjects drawn from classical antiquity and from the stories of figures such as Alexander the Great. In this section, we will consider two examples of medieval Latin epic in this arena: Joseph of Exeter's *Ylias* and the *Alexandreis* of Walter of Châtillon.

We do not know much about Joseph of Exeter, apart from the fact that he was from Exeter (as indicated by the name Iscanus), that he exchanged letters with Guibert, abbot of Gembloux, and that he praised Baldwin, archbishop of Canterbury from 1185 to 1190, in the prologue to his *Ylias*. That poem, 'the first full-fledged medieval verse epic on Troy', was finished around 1185.[7] It is written in unrhymed hexameter lines, the metre of classical Latin epic, and Joseph deploys it with considerable skill and sophistication. For narrative detail he drew primarily on Dares, though he used Dictys's account as well, but in transforming spare prose into expansive verse he made considerable additions to his sources. His poem consists of six books and includes the pre-story of the Trojan war, in which the insult to Jason and his Argonauts by Laomedon of Troy leads to Hercules sacking the city in retribution and seizing Laomedon's daughter Hesione. Hesione is presented as an unwilling victim of rape, and given a voice to express clearly her view of the situation. By contrast, while Paris is condemned as a rapist in the parallel episode of the seizing of Helen, Helen herself is also condemned as a willing participant. This kind of tension—of episodes that are both parallel and contrasting—is one of the important structuring mechanisms of the poem, and the differentiation in the characters' thoughts and motives gives moments of striking insight and interiority. Asides in the narrative include Paris's judgement in the beauty contest between Juno, Minerva, and Venus, and lengthy descriptions of the heroes on each side.

A sense of fatality hangs over the narrative, as from the outset both poet and audience know what the final outcome will be. *Inventio*, to a medieval poet, lies not in creating material out of whole cloth but instead in how one handles that material. The known and

---

[6] Geoffrey Chaucer, *The House of Fame*, in Larry D. Benson (ed.), *The Riverside Chaucer*, 3rd edn. (Boston, MA, 1987).
[7] Rigg, *History*, 99.

expected end of the story, then, becomes part of Joseph's display of his own abilities. At the beginning of the second book, he muses on Priam's happy state:

> Iam floret Priamus populoso pignore felix,
> Felix coniugio, felix natalibus arvis,
> Si superi, si fata sinant, si stare beatis
> Permissum.[8] (2.1–4)

> Now Priam, blessed with ample progeny, is well,
> Blessed in his wife and blessed in his ancestral lands—
> If gods and fates allow, if happy folk are left
> To thrive.[9]

Felix (happy) consists, in the Latin metrical system, of two heavy syllables, so that each time the word is repeated it attracts considerable weight. This fact is particularly striking at the end of the first line as it means the line potentially ends in the stronger spondee, rather than the weaker trochee often found at the end of a hexameter. The word is repeated twice more in the next line, in first and middle position, thus combining the rhetorical figures of *traductio* (the movement of a word through various positions in a line) and *anaphora* (repetition of the same word at the beginning of successive clauses), the latter in the case of the second line of the example. The repetition of *si* is also important here. The reason Priam's happiness will not last is fate, and that word sits at mid-line, surrounded by the repetitive stressed *si*, 'if', and linked to *felix* through alliteration on f (*fata*). Both *fata* and the final occurrence of *felix* sit at the caesura, creating a metrical parallelism buttressed by the sound repetition. In these lines, then, the uncertainty surrounding Troy's future is walled around with metrical emphasis.

Throughout the poem, Joseph betrays a keen awareness of poetic practice and of its limitations and difficulties. Two standard methods recommended by classical and medieval rhetorical manuals for making poetic material one's own are *amplificatio* (expansion) and *abbreviatio* (contraction). Early in the poem, Joseph wrestles with how he should relate the joy at the return of the Argonauts with the golden fleece: 'Si parcus meminisse velim, vel nolle fateri / Vel seriem non nosse putent; si prodigus, auris / Fastidita neget faciles ad singula nutus' (1. 204–6) ('If I were brief, I might be thought unwilling to / Relate them all, or ignorant; if overlong, / The tired ear would give no credence to each case'). The desire to balance the modes indicates a more than mechanical appreciation of rhetorical tools. Joseph also signals an awareness of the differing resources of different forms of art. For example, in Book 4, he describes the leaders of the armies, considering the differences between written and painted portraits: 'Sic olim positos populis mirantibus offert / Elinguis pictura viros, sic culta profatur / Carta duces, oculis hec blandior, auribus illa' (4. 40–3) '(As, to the gaze of crowds, a wordless picture shows / Those buried long ago, so written page portrays / The lords: one speaks to eyes, the other to the ears'). Later in the same book he provides an ecphrasis of the tomb of Teuthras, concluding it by recounting the couplet engraved on the tomb, in one passage simultaneously illustrating both amplification and abbreviation. These passages, then, both enact and query standard rhetorical devices, and cycle through other ways of communicating story—through painted pictures, through sculpted ones.

---

[8] Joseph of Exeter in Ludwig Gompf (ed.), *Joseph Iscanus: Werke und Briefe* (Leiden, 1970).
[9] A. G. Rigg (trans.), *Joseph of Exeter: Iliad* (Toronto, 2005), https://medieval.utoronto.ca/ylias.

92 MEDIEVAL POETRY: 1100–1400

The narrative voice intrudes from time to time with apostrophes on fate and fortune. The style is dense, with a rich and varied vocabulary, and a full display of rhetorical ornament. To pluck one example from many, consider the apostrophe on the fall of Troy:

> Nox fera, nox vere nox noxia, turbida, tristis,
> Insidiosa, ferox, tragicis ululanda conturnis
> Aut satira rodenda gravi, tu sola triumphas
> Tantorum nisus steriles lucrata dierum!
> Si michi Carpacias linguis equare figuras
> Detur et innumero crescant michi pectora Phebo,
> Non tamen expediam cedes, incendia, luctus,
> Quos Frigiis nox una parit. (4. 760–7)

> O cruel night (so truly named), confused and grim,
> Night, fierce, treacherous, a theme for tragic style
> Or satire's biting pen, for you alone can boast
> A profit from so many days of futile strife.
> If I had just as many tongues as Proteus
> Has shapes, and Phoebus filled my breast with countless songs,
> I could not tell the slaughters, burnings, or the griefs
> That one night brought to Troy.

The repetition, consonance, and alliteration in the first two lines of the apostrophe, combined with the relentless forward movement created by the lack of conjunctions (*asyndeton*), create a sense of urgency. It is a double urgency, of the actors in the poetic drama whose fates are about to be sealed, and of the epic poet, whose claimed inability to portray the horrors of the final battle is performed in the Silver Latin style of classical epic.[10] The highly rhetorical assertion of rhetorical inadequacy is a common tactic of medieval poets, whether Latin or vernacular. This kind of modesty *topos* is often read as display and self-aggrandisement. It can certainly be that, but, as I will suggest at the end of this chapter, poets who are highly aware of what we might think of as the tricks of the trade are also often uneasily conscious of the fact that their trade is tricky. Anxiety about what it means to occupy the poetic space is a trait shared by many of the writers dealt with here, and by their vernacular counterparts and inheritors.

There were once about eleven manuscripts of Joseph's poem, though only five now survive.[11] One of these is Cambridge, Corpus Christi College, MS 406, an early-thirteenth-century manuscript whose contents also include the earliest English copy of the A recension of Seneca's tragedies; the *Architrenius* of Jean de Hauteville; the *Anticlaudianus* of Alain de Lille; the first part of Bernardus Silvestris's *Cosmographia*; the *Poetria Nova* of Geoffrey of Vinsauf; and, following immediately after Joseph's *Ylias*, the *Alexandreis* of Walter of Châtillon. Walter's poem, if we are to judge from its manuscript circulation, was much more popular than Joseph's, surviving in some 200 manuscripts. But it is important that the *Ylias* and the *Alexandreis* both appear in a manuscript like Corpus 406, a compendium of

---

[10] Edoardo D'Angelo argues that Joseph's preference for dactyls in his deployment of hexameter is an Ovidian (as distinct from Virgilian) feature that marks him as a classicising poet; 'The Outer Metric in Joseph of Exeter's *Ylias* and Odo of Magdeburg's *Ernestus*', *The Journal of Medieval Latin*, 3 (1993), 113–34.

[11] Rigg, *History*, 349 n. 116. Rigg notes that while the number of manuscripts suggests 'modest' popularity, the appearance of passages in florilegia indicates it was widely read.

the kinds of texts that formed part of the mental furniture of university-educated monastic and clerical writers. Some of its contents are examples of high style, whether classical or contemporary. It also contains, in Geoffrey of Vinsauf's *Poetria Nova*, an introductory rhetorical text. Some of the works reflect philosophical and cosmological preoccupations. The *Anticlaudianus*, for example, is a twelfth-century allegorical poem imbued with the Platonic philosophy of the school of Chartres. It details Nature's search for understanding about humanity, guided by reason and the Seven Liberal Arts. Its French author, Alain de Lille, also wrote *De Planctu Naturae* (the complaint of Nature), which works through the place of the goddess Nature in the Christian understanding of the world, lamenting the fallenness of man. Nature, derived from Alain's work as well as from French sources that depended on Alain, is a central figure for both Chaucer and Gower.[12] Nature is also a figure in Bernard's *Cosomographia*, another twelfth-century allegorical work, in both poetry and verse, that reflects the thinking of Chartrian teachers and theologians. We can often assess medieval understanding of a text by the manuscript company it keeps, and Corpus 406 tells us several things about Joseph and about our next author, Walter of Châtillon. Apart from Seneca and Joseph himself, the authors of the texts in this collection are French (and Joseph spent time in France, and might well have been educated there). Many of the medieval texts in Corpus 406 are written in high style, and are influenced both by the philosophical ideas of their day and by the sometimes heavy weight of the inherited classical tradition. The *Alexandreis* is, like Joseph's *Ylias*, a remarkable example of a medieval Latin poet seizing classical ground.

Walter was probably born sometime around 1135, and we know that the *Alexandreis* must have been finished before 1184, because John de Hauteville's *Architrenius* refers to the work and can be dated to that year. Like Joseph, Walter had a prose Latin source, in his case the *Historiae Alexandri Magni* by Curtius Quintus Rufus, a first-century Roman historian. The *Alexandreis* retells the story of Alexander the Great's life in ten books of hexameter verse. In many manuscripts, the poem is accompanied by extensive glossing; it was, as David Townsend points out, 'studied intensively as a standard text of the literary curriculum'.[13] Alexander's glory and his ultimate fate run parallel throughout the work, with much foreshadowing of the hero's decline from virtue. Many medieval writers struggled with the balance between fate and personal responsibility in retelling the stories of fallen conquerors (Arthur is a common example in the vernacular tradition). In the early books, young Alexander is educated to be a good king, and while he is a fierce warrior, he tends to treat defeated opponents fairly. From the start, however, we know that he will be partly corrupted by Babylonian luxury; that overweening desire for conquest will lead him to anger the gods; and that he will die as a result of treachery. The poem lavishes both praise and reproof on its protagonist, and is laced with references to Fortune and to fate. In Book 2, Fortune is given a voice, and speaks with irritation at the blame Alexander's soldiers are hurling at her:

> ... si quando retraxero rebus
> Imperiosa manum, rea criminis arguor ac si

---

[12] See George D. Economou, *The Goddess Natura in Medieval Literature*, 2nd edn. (Notre Dame, IN, 2002). Many scholars have commented on the importance of Alain de Lille for Middle English poets; for example, James Simpson, *Sciences and the Self in Medieval Poetry: Alan of Lille's* Anticlaudianus *and John Gower's* Confessio Amantis (Cambridge, 2005); Ann W. Astell, *Chaucer and the Universe of Learning* (Ithaca, NY, 1996); and Hugh White, *Nature, Sex, and Goodness in a Medieval Literary Tradition* (Oxford, 2000).

[13] David Townsend (trans.), *The Alexandreis: A Twelfth-Century Epic* (Peterborough, ON, 2007), 11.

94   MEDIEVAL POETRY: 1100–1400

> Naturae stabilis sub conditione teneri
> Possem. si semper apud omnes una manerem
> Aut eadem, iam non merito Fortuna uocarer.
> Lex michi naturae posita est sine lege moueri,
> Solaque mobilitas stabilem facit.[14] (2.194–200)

> ... As soon as I withdraw
> my sovereign hand, I'm treated as a criminal—
> as though a stable nature could contain me.
> If I remained one and the same toward all,
> I'd scarcely have the proper name of Fortune.
> My nature's fixed law lies in lawless motion,
> and only movement makes me stable. (58)

Paradox, a popular rhetorical figure in Latin and vernacular love poetry, is here deployed to convey Fortune's contradictory nature. The last two lines of this example are particularly rich. *Lex ... sine lege* (law ... without law/lawlessness) is an example of *polyptoton*, the repetition of a word in a different grammatical form. *Mobilitas* (movement) and *stabilem* (stable) flank the caesura. In other words, in these two lines, careful distribution of the elements draws rhetorical attention to Fortune's paradoxical nature.

There are several ecphrases in the *Alexandreis*, and these attract considerable attention from annotators. The description of the tomb of Darius's wife in Book 4 is the most annotated section of the poem, and in some manuscripts one sees a few lines of verse entirely surrounded by dense prose glossing.[15] In Book 7, Darius's tomb is described in terms that suggest a medieval *mappa mundi*.[16] The description of the tomb lists what each country is known for (the section on Britain mentions King Arthur). Part of the appeal of the text for readers seems to lie in its descriptions of the lands through which Alexander travels, and a few manuscripts include diagrams or maps. Alexander's final successful campaign is in India. After that conquest he decides to seek out the Antipodes, which means, in the medieval understanding of the world, that he seeks Eden. This decision provokes the goddess Nature to oppose him, and he dies by poison. The account of Alexander's death is marked out by the poetic voice's impassioned apostrophes to cruel Fortune, and laments for the wretched state of mortals. In a final turn, however, Walter's envoy uses the language of gaming to set his subject aside: 'Iam satis est lusum, iam ludum incidere prestat' (10.457) ('Now is it all played out, now comes the time to end the game'). *Lusus* and *ludum* both mean game, play, or amusement, but their use here does not mean Walter considers his work to be inconsequential. References to play can be found in the works of many Latin writers, and reflect in part the intellectual milieu in which these texts were produced and consumed. If poetry is a game, it is one with high stakes, and as the poets in this chapter understand, even obeying its rules will not necessarily guarantee the outcome.

---

[14] Marvin L. Colker (ed.), *Galteri de Castellione: Alexandreis* (Padova, 1978).
[15] Townsend, 94 n. 1.
[16] Christine Ratkowitsch, *Descriptio picturae: Die literarische Funktion der Beschreibung von Kunstwerken in der lateinischen Grossdichtung des 12. Jahrhunderts* (Vienna, 1991), 164–73.

Satire: Nigel Whiteacre

Vt vetus ipse suam curtam Burnellus inepte
Caudam longari de nouitate cupit ...

As old Burnellus foolishly once wished
To stretch his tiny tail and make it long ...[17] (201–2)

In the opening of Gower's *Vox clamantis*, the appalled speaker describes the crowd marching on London in the 1381 Peasants' Revolt. He compares the peasants and their demands to asses seeking the accoutrements of horses, and dismisses their ambitions by referring to the story of 'old Burnellus'. This is Burnellus the ass, the protagonist of the *Speculum Stultorum* (*Mirror for Fools*) by Nigel Whiteacre (*c* 1135–*c* 1200). The *Speculum* is a satirical poem that traces Burnellus's doomed efforts to lengthen his tail to match his ears, a desire that takes him from his home in Cremona to Salerno in search of medical solutions, and then to Paris, where after seven years of study he can say only 'hee haw' (which he could say before entering the university). His next plan is to enter religious life and become a bishop, a dream that launches a catalogue of the monastic orders (Nigel was a monk of Christ Church Canterbury). But he is captured by his old master, who cuts off his ears. Because a previous accident had already docked Burnellus's tail, he now has the symmetry he sought, though none of the glory. He disappears from the poem, which concludes with another beast story, this one comparing the reactions of three beasts and one man rescued from a pit (the beasts are grateful, the man is not).

Nigel's poem, then, has aspects of both beast epic and beast fable, but it has other affinities as well. Anti-clerical satire is a staple of Anglo-Latin poetry, both in this period and later, as for example in the early-fourteenth-century Goliardic poem 'Sedens super flumina', where a speaker complains at length about the deceptions and failing of the fraternal orders. Furthermore, the *Speculum* also has some points of contact with the highly wrought, philosophically minded poems considered thus far. These are not affinities of style. The *Speculum* is written in elegiac couplets (a dactylic hexameter followed by a dactylic pentameter) rather than the straight hexameters considered suitable for epic verse. There is little of the ornamentation found in the epic poems considered above. Nigel says that he writes 'arata stylo' (in a simple style).[18] However, he also insists on the importance of his poetic project. In a letter to William de Longchamp, he urges William to look beyond the surface of the work:

> I have recently sent you a book, the title and subject of which will seem amusing to its readers and to those who lack understanding. But if you will carefully examine each part and give your attention to the writer's aim and purpose, though the style may be no less crude than the subject matter, you will perhaps be able to gain some instruction from it. That those things, moreover, which are veiled in obscure language, may be clear to you, I consider it proper to explain briefly a few of my hidden meanings.[19]

---

[17] David R. Carlson (ed.) and A. G. Rigg (trans.), *John Gower, Poems on Contemporary Events: The Visio Anglie (1381) and Cronica tripertita (1400)* (Toronto, 2011). The *Visio Anglie* is the name often given to the first book of Gower's *Vox*. I cite the Carlson/Rigg edition here because the translation is drawn from it.

[18] John H. Mozley and Robert R. Raymo (eds), *Nigel de Longchamps Speculum Stultorum* (Berkeley, CA, 1960), 2; Graydon W. Regenos (trans.), *The Book of Daun Burnel the Ass: Nigellus Wireker's Speculum stultorum* (Austin, TX, 1959), 29. One could also translate the phrase as 'rustic pen', as *stylo* can mean pen, and *arata* comes from the verb *aro*, to plough or till.

[19] Regenos, 23.

The idea of hidden meaning, accessible only to those who are properly instructed, was commonplace among medieval writers of Latin and vernacular texts. One sees a reflex of this form of reading when Chaucer's Nun's Priest concludes his own beast story by urging his listeners to 'Taketh the fruyt, and lat the chaf be stille' (VII.3443).[20] The fruit in Nigel's story includes ideas about education that are curiously double-edged. On the one hand, the ass Burnellus fails at education because he is, well, an ass, singularly unsuited to the rigours of education in the liberal arts. Like the ass-peasants in the opening of Gower's *Vox*, Burnellus has ambitions above his station: a Latin education is for people like Joseph of Exeter or Walter of Châtillon, not for donkeys from Cremona. But the apparently simple lesson of Burnellus's fate—an elite argument for holding to one's own social state—is complicated when the poem makes Burnellus the unwitting voice of satire, as his catalogue of religious orders cycles through the familiar tropes of anti-clerical writing, and his criticism of Rome, kings, and bishops hits many of the common notes of estates satire. There is also a tension, perhaps only latent, in suggesting that the ass is uneducable despite seven years with the finest teachers in the world. In the intellectual milieu of the twelfth century, when Latin literature is dominated by university-educated clerics, the total system failure represented by Burnellus has the potential, particularly in a satirical work, to lead to uncomfortable questions about that intellectual milieu.

The *Speculum* was a popular work, quoted by many medieval poets and appearing often in excerpted form in manuscript collections. The headnote to this section from Gower's *Vox* is no accident: Gower borrowed freely from the *Speculum* for his own savage complaint satire,[21] and Chaucer also drew on the tale. Beast literature was a popular genre, and the *Speculum* is easy and enjoyable to read, full of pithy maxims, and often very funny. It is not simply entertainment, however, as Nigel's letter and remarks throughout the poem itself make clear.

Religious Writing: Reginald of Canterbury and John of Garland

Nigel's other poetry includes a series of Miracles of the Virgin. Religious verse was a prominent feature of the Latin poetic landscape in Britain up until the Reformation. There were lyrics, often anonymous. There were lives of saints by such notable figures as Henry of Avranches, who has been called 'one of the first truly professional Latin poets of the Middle Ages' because we know he was paid for his poetry by Henry III from 1243 to 1260.[22] And there was an enormous amount of poetry connected to the Virgin Mary, including hymns, prayers, panegyrics, and collections of miracle stories. Both hagiography in general, and Marian poetry in particular, had a persistent influence on vernacular literature. In this section we consider a saint's life by Reginald of Canterbury, and the Marian poetry of John of Garland.

Reginald was a French monk, from Faye-la-Vineuse, who moved to the Benedictine Abbey of St Augustine's in Canterbury sometime before 1100. Rigg suggests that there was some 'culture shock' in Reginald's move to England, pointing to a line in one of his

---

[20] Jill Mann studies the connections between Chaucer and Nigel in 'The *Speculum Stultorum* and the *Nun's Priest's Tale*', *The Chaucer Review*, 9 (1975), 262–82; and more recently in *From Aesop to Reynard: Beast Literature in Medieval Britain* (Oxford, 2009).

[21] See Robert R. Raymo, 'Gower's *Vox Clamantis* and the *Speculum Stultorum*', *Modern Language Notes*, 70 (1955), 315–20.

[22] Rigg, *History*, 179.

minor poems: 'Vitis Francigenam docet, Anglia discit avenam' ('The vine instructs the Gallic muse, but England's barley-taught').[23] Still, Reginald wrote most of his work in England at St Augustine's. His most significant poem is his *Vita Malchi*, an epic retelling, in six books of rhyming hexameter verse, of the life of Malchus, a fourth-century saint from Syria. Reginald's source was a short prose life by St Jerome. The story is a simple one, in which Malchus, the son of farmers, becomes a monk rather than marry as his parents wish. He leaves his monastery when he hears of his father's death, and is captured on his way home by Saracens and made a slave. His master orders him to marry another slave, a widow; Malchus resists because he wishes to remain celibate. Fortunately, the woman wishes to stay chaste, so she suggests that they live together platonically, while pretending to be married. They eventually escape captivity, and return to monastic life.

Reginald expands the story in ways that look ahead to the genre of hagiographic romance that was to become popular in the vernacular. While Malchus is not a warrior hero, the tale has many exciting incidents. Jerome's version already contained such elements as a daring escape down a river on goat-skin bladders; pursuit through the desert; and an encounter with a lioness. In Reginald's hands added detail and dialogue further enliven these features. The male–female relationship is also expanded. The female slave, unnamed in Jerome's version, becomes Malcha, and is given a substantial role in the narrative. The hero preserves his chastity, while also entering into a life-long relationship with a female companion.

In Reginald's own accounting, the difference between his version and Jerome's lies in its novelty and in its literariness, and in this respect he can be linked with many of the other Anglo-Latin poets considered thus far. In the preludium to the poem he urges his muse to sing 'new songs' (*nova carmina*, 29) about Malchus, and at the opening of book I he compares his approach to Jerome's: 'Ille quidem prosa, metri nos arte iocosa / Scribimus et iuste servit nova Musa vetuste' (1.4–5) ('For that was in prose. Our art is jocose; / And so a new Muse gives the ancients their dues'). The translation here is my own and not literal, but rather attempts to convey Reginald's form. The *Vita Malchi* is in rhymed verse, primarily Leonine hexameters, a popular medieval form that relied on internal rhyme. It can create considerable momentum and also has the potential to be quite funny. An example of the latter effect can be seen in the description of Ocean's home in book 4 and in the translation of the passage by Sylvia Parsons: 'Promere gestio cerula mansio cum sit aquosa, / Quam sit amabilis et recitabilis et numerosa' (4.255–8) ('I'm longing to tell / How delightful, how well / Proportioned, this blue / Mansion was, how fit / To be mentioned (though it / Might be dampish, it's true').[24]

To be clear, Reginald's poem is not a joke, but neither is it an epic. A reader who has ploughed through such features as Malchus lamenting his fate in more than sixty lines, each of which begins with 'Ante', or the lengthy description of the decoration of Cynthia's cloak, is painfully aware of Reginald's stylistic ambitions. Nevertheless, as Rigg points out, Reginald invokes 'Thalia, muse of comedy, as his inspiration ... His recasting of the original tale and his expansions ... are all directed to making it a more entertaining and diverting story'.[25]

Reginald was a French transplant to England. John of Garland (*c* 1195–*c* 1258) was an Englishman who spent the bulk of his life, after a stint at Oxford, in France, mostly in Paris.

---

[23] Rigg, *History*, 11.

[24] Sylvia Parsons, 'A Verse Translation of Book 4 of Reginald of Canterbury's *Vita Sancti Malchi*', in Siân Echard and Gernot Wieland (eds), *Anglo-Latin and Its Heritage: Essays in Honour of A. G. Rigg on His 64th Birthday* (Turnhout, 2001), 78.

[25] Rigg, *History*, 27.

98 MEDIEVAL POETRY: 1100–1400

Much of his work arises from the teaching milieu, and includes a dictionary, a Latin grammatical treatise (in hexameters), and his most famous rhetorical text, the *Parisiana poetria*. This work offers instruction in the writing of prose, letters, and poetry, and many of the examples John uses are his own. He also wrote a great deal of free-standing verse, including two substantial Marian works. The *Epithalamium beatae Mariae Virginis* is an allegorical epic of the sort that would be familiar to writers like Alain de Lille, with the life of the Virgin as its subject. Its ten books range through philosophical and theological subjects.[26] The *Epithalamium*, then, belongs to the highest register of Anglo-Latin writing, but John of Garland's other Marian poem, the *Stella maris*, is an example of the middle register. Rather than being a philosophical epic, this is a collection of the type of popular story known as Miracles of the Virgin. It consists of 192 rhyming stanzas in the Victorine form popular in Latin hymns. One can illustrate both the anti-Semitic cast of much of this genre of Marian literature and the formal features of the Victorine sequence through John's version of a story Chaucer's Prioress would tell as the 'little clergeoun':

> De Maria quicquid scivit
> Puer cantans, enutrivit
> Maternam inopiam.
> Hunc Iudeus nequam stravit
> Domo sua quem humavit
> Diram per invidiam.
>
> Mater querens hunc vocavit,
> Hic in terra recantavit
> Solita preconia.[27] (634–42)

> A little boy, in poverty
> Raised up, yet sang so merrily
> Of Mary, all he knew.
> A vengeful beast cut the boy down
> And buried him outside of town—
> A hateful wicked Jew.
>
> When his mother vainly sought him
> He sang of Mary as she taught him
> Out from earth his voice flew.

Each stanza consists of two eight-syllable lines followed by a seven-syllable one, rhyming *aabccb*. The translation, while not entirely literal, captures the sing-song effect of the metre (particularly uncomfortable for modern readers when paired with the anti-Semitic nature of the subject). Other notable writers of Marian poetry of various types include the thirteenth-century friar Walter of Wimborne (*Ave Virgo* and the *Maria Carmina*); his contemporary John of Howden (who also wrote poetry on the life of Christ); and John Pecham, the Franciscan archbishop of Canterbury from 1279 to 1292. The poetic anthologies typical of the twelfth and thirteenth centuries also often contain devotional verse.

---

[26] The connection between Mary and learning for medieval rhetoricians has been explored by Georgiana Donavin in *Scribit Mater: Mary and the Language Arts in the Literature of Medieval England* (Washington, DC, 2012).

[27] Evelyn Faye Wilson (ed.), *The Stella Maris of John of Garland* (Cambridge, MA, 1946).

Writing in Place: Henry of Huntingdon and Lawrence of Durham

Many of the Anglo-Latin writers discussed thus far reveal their relationship to England from time to time. The 'little clergeoun' miracle in the *Stella Maris* culminates in the expulsion of the Jews from England. In an episode of the *Vita Malchi*, Reginald notes how the ants Malchus is observing favour wheat but leave barley alone when they raid the fields, an echo of his remarks unfavourably comparing English beer to French wine. The political poetry of the fourteenth century includes poems concentrating on the northern wars between the English and the Scots, often naming both significant figures and significant places; examples include poems on the Battle of Neville's Cross and the Battle of Otterburn. There are praise-poems for particular places, such as Oxford or Norfolk. The attention to place—physical place, but also what we might think of as interior or psychic space—is particularly marked in some of the work of Henry of Huntingdon (*c* 1088–*c* 1157) and Lawrence of Durham (*c* 1110–54).

Henry is known today primarily for his historical work, the *Historia anglorum* (*History of the English*), but he was also a prolific poet. In fact, the *Historia* is interspersed with poems marking significant moments in the narrative. Some of these use hexameters and elegiacs; others, as Rigg notes, are attempts 'unique in post-Conquest literature' to 'reproduce the rhythms of Old English verse'.[28] Most striking is his entry for 937, when he translates the Old English poem on the Battle of Brunanburh. He explains the significance of his approach:

> The English writers on this great battle, expressing themselves in a kind of song with strange words and expressions, should be rendered faithfully, so that by interpreting their speech almost word for word we may learn from the solemnity of their words the solemnity of the deeds and spirits of that race.[29]

It is unusual for Latin authors to speak approvingly of the vernacular, so while Henry finds Old English 'strange', it is nevertheless important that he insists on faithful translation, and seeks to convey form as well as content. We can compare his efforts to the opening of the poem in Old English:

> Rex Adelstan   decus ducum,
>
> nobilibus torquium dator   et frater eius
>
> Edmundus longa stirpis   series splendentes
>
> percusserunt in bello   acie gladii
>
> apud Brunebirih.
>
> Her æþelstan cyning,   eorla dryhten,
>
> beorna beahgifa,   and his broþor eac,
>
> Eadmund æþeling,   ealdorlangne tir
>
> geslogon æt sæcce   sweorda ecgum
>
> ymbe Brunanburh.[30]

[28] Rigg, *History*, 37.

[29] Diana Greenway (ed.), *Henry, Archdeacon of Huntingdon: Historia Anglorum (History of the English People)* (Oxford, 1996), 310. Greenway also provides translations in her edition, but in this case I have used Rigg's, *History*, 37.

[30] Michael Livingston (ed.), *The Battle of Brunanburh: A Casebook* (Exeter, 2011). The translation is Greenway's, 311.

100   MEDIEVAL POETRY: 1100–1400

(King Æthelstan, flower of commanders, ring-giver to nobles, and Edmund his brother, the splendid products of a long unbroken lineage, struck with the sword's edge in battle at Brunanburh.)

As Rigg points out, Henry tries to convey the formal qualities, as well as the sense, of the verse.[31] Here he uses alliteration and metrical stresses that sometimes approximate the Old English. Henry's half-lines sometimes match Old English stress patterns, and he strives for alliterative units which, while they do not match the patterns of the Old English poem, nevertheless create similar links between units of verse. Through this experiment, Henry links himself to the *Anglici scriptores* (English writers) whose work he is conveying in his own English history.

Henry also wrote free-standing verse, including his *Epigrams* and the *Anglicanus ortus*. The latter is a versified herbal in which plants and their properties are described in 169 poems in six books, drawing on the usual sources for medical-herbal texts as well as on classical poets.[32] Some of the content is original, but even when it is not, Henry's treatment of it marks it as his own. The speaker takes the listener through a carefully imagined square garden, with a theatre in its centre. Occasionally other figures interact with the speaker, as when a cook mocks him for not having said anything about leeks, onions, and cabbages, and temporarily takes over the poem to provide the content the main voice will not. The cook represents an intrusion of the everyday world into the poetic and intellectual imagined space of the verse garden. Henry also nods to his own English poetic formation in his description of Baldmoney: 'Compatriota tibi dat, baldemonia, laudes: / Anglia te speciem, me reddidit Anglia uatem, / Tam renitens herbis quam non obscura poetis' (1.5, 1–3) ('Your countryman, Baldmoney, sings your praises, / for England made you a spice, and me into a poet, / England, as splendid in herbs as she is not unknown for bards') (87).

The *Anglicanus ortus*, as Winston Black points out, shows affinities with some of the natural philosophical works already mentioned in this chapter, such as Bernard Silvestris's *Cosmographia* or Alain de Lille's *De planctu naturae*. These saw the exploration of the natural world as a way of understanding God's design.[33] At the same time, Henry used his material to demonstrate his poetic virtuosity. While the pragmatically minded cook calls him 'uates paupercule' (5.2.6, 'poor little poetling', 295), the performance is confident and assertive. Henry presents himself as the 'people's poet', transmitting what his audience needs to know: 'uulgo uulgarem ferre poetam / Vota decet' ('It is fitting that a people's poet fulfil / the wishes of the people' (6.Interlude, 9–10; 317). Doing so allows him to display his learning, and the poetic skill that marks him as one of the poets England is known for producing.

Lawrence of Durham (c 1110–54) also locates himself squarely in England, and more specifically in Durham, where he eventually became the prior of the monastery. He is best known for the *Hypognosticon*, a poetic account of the redemption of mankind, but his most localised work is the *Dialogi*, which recounts conversations between Lawrence, another monk called Philip, and their Breton friend Peter over four days. The first two are in the spring of 1143, and the friends meet outside the city of Durham. The next two conversations

---

[31] A. G. Rigg, 'Henry of Huntingdon's Metrical Experiments', *The Journal of Medieval Latin*, 1 (1991), 65–6.

[32] Winston Black (ed. and trans.), *Henry of Huntingdon: Anglicanus ortus. A Verse Herbal of the Twelfth Century* (Toronto, 2012) reconstructs the text. Black cites Virgil, Ovid, Horace, Martial, and Statius as Henry's stylistic models, and says that his medical sources were Macer Floridus's *De viribus herbarum*, Walahfrid Strabo's *Hortulus*, the herbal of Pseudo-Apuleius, and perhaps also a medieval florilegium (3, 27).

[33] Black, *Henry of Huntingdon*, 53.

take place inside Durham in 1144. The historical backdrop is the Anarchy, the civil war between Stephen of Blois and the Empress Matilda. In 1141, William Cumin seized the bishopric of Durham against the wishes of many but with the support of King David of Scotland, a supporter of Matilda's. Some of the monks were forced into exile, and Lawrence presents himself as one of these. Cumin eventually gave up his claim, and his opponents were able to return. In the first two books, set in the period of exile, Lawrence laments the fallen state of England:

> ... nec sine re videor mihi, Petre, tacere,
> Causa subest patriae multa ruina meae.
> Anglia, terra ferax, praecellens insula, regnum
> Rege sub Henrico nobile, lapsa gemit.
> Terrarum jam terra gemit: sed et insula felix
> Exulat. Hoc regnum rege ruente ruit. (53–8)

> ... My silence, Peter, has its cause—
> The widespread ruin of my native land.
> The fertile isle of England, once a realm
> In Henry's days supreme, lies sad and groans.
> This land of lands laments. This blessed isle's
> An exile now: when Henry fell, she fell.[34]

Right before these lines, Peter had teased Lawrence about being tongue-tied. Lawrence's lament makes it clear that he is anything but. In the elegiacs above, poetic tricks abound, with repetition, alliteration, and stress all serving to link the ideas of *regnum* (kingdom), *rex* (king), *ruo* (to fall down), and *ruina* (ruin). In response to Peter's urging, Lawrence then provides a long description of the city and its beauties, a paean of praise and a lament for what has been lost. On the second day, the bumptious Peter continues to urge his friend to poetise, and this time Lawrence's response includes a description of Cumin brimming with the same kinds of paradoxes that Gower would later favour in his own politically focused complaint satire:

> Nam subit huic pro cive latro, pro matre noverca,
> Pro pastore lupus, pro patre tortor atrox.
> Jus pessum civile datur; lex utraque languet:
> Plebis scita vacant: mos abit: ordo perit.
> Nil dicunt edicta boni: responsa quiescunt:
> Virtus, plaga, quies, aret, abundat, abest. (41–6)

> For mother, father, shepherd, citizen,
> We have stepmother, torturer, wolf, thief.
> For civil justice dies, both laws are sick,
> And people's rights, their customs, order, fail.
> Good men proclaim no laws, replies are dumb,
> Good withers, harm abounds, and peace has gone. (60)

---

[34] James Raine (ed.), *Dialogi Laurentii Dunelmensis Monachi ac Prioris* (Edinburgh, 1880). The translation is A. G. Rigg, 'Lawrence of Durham: Dialogues and Easter Poem—A Verse Translation', *The Journal of Medieval Latin*, 7 (1997), 46.

102 MEDIEVAL POETRY: 1100–1400

The final line offers a sequence of three nouns, and then their three corresponding verbs. This unusual syntax has elements of *hyperbaton* (the inversion of normal word order) and *tricolon* (three parallel elements occurring in series), but what is most striking is the arrangement of each sequence so that the negative element—*plaga* (harm) and *abundant* (abounds)—intrudes between the nouns and verbs associated with the previous idyllic state. It is a remarkably balanced line about civil and emotional disorder.

One of the most engaging things about the *Dialogi* is the clear delineation of the characters of the three speakers—the quiet, loyal Philip; the philosophical, sometimes anguished, sometimes lyrical Lawrence; and the effervescent and often irritating Peter. The dialogue structure contains and makes space for a range of poetic movements, from complaint and praise, to the autobiographical introspection of the last two books. Lawrence dwells at length on death in the final book, wrestling with the inadequacy of his learning:

> Versus ille suos seno pede currere cogit,
> Ipsius ista duos huic vetat ire pedes.
> Edocet illa loqui; jubet, ut libet, ista sileri;
> Mors ubi, Petre, jubet, littera multa silet.
> Hoc ego mente videns plus arbitror utile nobis
> Scire mori, quam sit scire vel arte loqui. (4.41–6)

> Where metre's verses run in six-foot lengths,
> The law of death forbids a two-step walk.
> One teaches speech, the other says 'Be still';
> When death commands, then literature is hushed.
> So seeing this, I think to learn to die
> Does far more good than learning skilful speech. (89)

Yet even this conclusion is couched in poetic speech, drawing a punning parallelism between poetic and human feet, with an elegance that suggests while the latter may be faltering, the former never do.

Anxiety and Performance

I have suggested that Lawrence's performance, even as he advocates 'learning to die' rather than learning skilful speech, is confident and polished. Nevertheless, he does express doubt about his abilities, not only in the face of his own death but also in terms of addressing the highest of subjects. In the fourth book, Peter and Philip ask Lawrence, who has been telling them about heaven, to continue his description, and suddenly he asserts the limits of art:

> Pulvis de caelo, de summis infimus, aeger
> De solido, fatuus de sapiente loquor.
> Deque Deo caro, vermis, homo; de sole superno
> Nox in valle loquor; numquid et apta loquor? (4.373–6)

> Do I, mere dust, dare speak of heaven's heights,
> Does the sick of whole, does fool of one who's wise?
> Does flesh, worm, man, dare speak of God? Does night
> In valley speak of sun? Are my words apt
> Or fit? But who is good enough for that? (98)

A profound awareness of the limits of poetic speech binds the writers in this chapter together. Some of the tension derives, as it does for Lawrence, from a suspicion that highly wrought speech is not always aligned with good living. Here, for example, is Joseph of Exeter, rejecting the very classical sources with which he expands his project: 'Desine Cicropii funesta licentia pagi / Incestos generare deos! Non fabula celum, / Sed virtus non ficta dabit' (3.454–6) ('Cease, deadly licence of antiquity! Invent / No more immoral gods, for heaven's won by real / Good life, not lying tales'). But more often it seems that those whose entire training and practice has focused upon the skilled manipulation of words carry a keen suspicion that even the best words can fail. Readers are sometimes at fault. In Joseph's *Ylias*, for example, Priam rejects Helenus's inspired, prophetic voice: 'audit et audet / Dux falli fatisque favet, cum fata recuset' (3.1–8–9) ('he hears, / Yet dares to be deceived. By spurning fate, he aids / Its course'). Nigel Whiteacre's final exhortation urges the reader to seek out the sense of words: 'Non quod verba sonant sed quicquid mystici signant, / Scrutetor lector caute quid ipsa velint' (3882–3) ('The reader should carefully search out, not the sounds of the words, / But their mystical sense, those things they want to signify'). But this appeal comes at the end of a poem which has illustrated, through the uneducable Burnellus, that at least some readers will never learn to read properly. The wilful cook in Henry of Huntingdon's *Anglicana ortus* is another example: he wants to hear about cabbages, and he takes over the poem when he does not get his way. Medieval English poets, whatever their language, often express fears about their audience. Both Joseph of Exeter and Chaucer send off their Trojan poems with envoys that express hope and anxiety about the reception of their work. But as I have already suggested through the example of Lawrence of Durham, perhaps the most profound fear comes from a nagging sense that even the best words are not always enough to assure one's future. The classical past is still present to medieval poets, and seen from one angle offers a profound assurance of survival. Yet it can also represent competition for poetic space and authority. Before entering Fame's house and seeing the hall of poets, the dreamer sees a hill of ice, upon which are written the names of famous people, many of them no longer legible. Posterity is not guaranteed—and that is true for writers in Latin as well as in English.

7

The Poetic Field, III

Anglo-French

Keith Busby

Consideration of the importance of French poetry in medieval England and its relationship with literature in the principal, non-Celtic, vernacular of the island must begin with a recap of the general linguistic and cultural consequences of the Conquest as laid out in more detail in Chapter 2. In this chapter, I look in particular at topics such as the position of French in Britain after the Conquest, the relative precocity of insular literature in French, the types of text and manuscripts produced, verse forms, and authorship.

Language

Late Old English (Anglo-Saxon) or early Middle English did not die out to be replaced by Norman French, and the majority population continued to speak their native language.[1] The encroachment and dispersal of the language of the conquerors was more immediate and widespread in the higher social milieux in which native speakers of English were supplanted by Francophones as government and administration of country and Church changed hands. Even in the case of open conquest and colonisation, language and culture did not change overnight, if at all, among administrators and the lower clergy. After Hastings, native Anglophones continued in their functions for a transitional period and, in many cases, beyond. Crucially, however, for the development of literature, the wherewithal to commission and consume, to create communities of readers and listeners, passed in a large degree to speakers of the *langue d'oïl*. It is tempting here to consider the immediate post-Conquest output of literature in English as a reaction to the increasing production in French, but that may be falling prey to a scholarly inclination to impose discrete categories on less than discrete local situations. In any event, production of literature in the *langue d'oïl* (i.e., the language of northern France) seems to manifest itself earlier in Britain and the western domains of the Continent than in the rest of France. It is by no means clear whether or not the *Peterborough Chronicle* (1122–54) or the *Ormulum* (1150–60), for example, constitute a conscious English-language response to the idiom of the conquerors, for they are exceptional and were both composed in relatively privileged and protected monastic spaces where English maintained a hold. Laȝamon's *Brut* (*c* 1220), an early adaptation of Wace's adaptation (*c* 1155) of Geoffrey of Monmouth's *Historia regum Britanniae* (*c* 1135), however, is a clear attempt to bring material that had hitherto been transmitted in Latin and French to an Anglophone audience; as a Worcestershire priest, Laȝamon is likely to have been in close contact with speakers of English. By his own admission, he draws

---

[1] The best introduction to the position of French in England after the Conquest is the introduction to Ian Short, *Manual of Anglo-Norman*, 2nd edn. (Oxford, 2013), 17–44.

Keith Busby, *The Poetic Field, III*. In: *The Oxford History of Poetry in English*. Edited by Helen Cooper and Robert R. Edwards, Oxford University Press. © Keith Busby (2023). DOI: 10.1093/oso/9780198827429.003.0007

on sources in England's three languages: English (a translation of Bede), Latin (Albinus, Abbot of Canterbury and collaborator of Bede, and St Augustine), and French (the Jersey poet Wace), and although he may appear isolated in a provincial Anglophone location, Laȝamon is actually paradigmatic of the multilingual situation of the time. It is quite possible that Laȝamon is taking up a fictional position of authorship here (neither the English Bede nor Albinus's Latin text survive), but even then the multilingual context is clear. Recent scholarship has also shown that the demise of English after 1066 has been much exaggerated by scholarship. Texts continue to be written and manuscripts copied in considerable numbers in England and in English during what has traditionally been regarded as a period of almost exclusive Anglo-Norman dominance (say, before 1220); pre-Conquest manuscripts also continue to circulate and be used.[2]

There is a fundamental terminological issue that warrants brief discussion here, even if resolution is by definition not fully achievable. It concerns the expression used to denote the kinds of French used by the conquerors and the forms the language took in the islands in the decades and centuries after 1066. Traditionally, philologists and historians have used the term 'Anglo-Norman', thereby indicating the provenance of the particular French idiom in Normandy and its first new context in England; the term also allows for the eventual English influence on Norman French during the insular development of the language of the conquerors. While it is true that some forms of the French spoken and written in the British Isles gradually moved away linguistically from early Norman French, the latter remained its point of departure, and attempts to call it 'the French of England' seem to me too restrictive, if only geographically. It fails to acknowledge the origins of the language in Normandy and seems to exclude Wales, Scotland, and Ireland as regions of medieval Francophonia. 'Insular French' or 'the French of Britain' might be understood as covering both large islands as well as varieties of the idiom, but it then fails to retain an indication of provenance; 'Anglo-French' is another possibility. Strictly speaking in the interests of accuracy and coverage, it might be best to speak of 'Anglo-Norman', 'Scoto-Norman', 'Cambro-Norman', and 'Hiberno-Norman', cumbersome as this would be. The latter three are in current use by historians as designators of cultures and cultural groups, and 'Hiberno-Norman' is also used by the few scholars who have looked at the situation of French language and literature in Ireland. 'Old English' is a strictly chronological term, while 'Anglo-Saxon', like 'Anglo-Norman', is reflective of the provenance of Saxon immigrants whose language and culture had a profound influence on that of England.[3]

The vast bulk of French from Britain and Ireland is certainly from England, and the survivals from Scotland, Wales, and Ireland do not provide linguists with sufficient data with which to distinguish regional variants. This does not mean that the insular language which evolved from the conquerors is monolithic in its phonetic, morphological, and syntactical features. On the contrary, the language shows considerable variation in form from period

---

[2] See, for example, Thomas O'Donnell, 'Talking to the Neighbours', in Jocelyn Wogan-Browne and Elizabeth M. Tyler (eds), *High Medieval: Literary Cultures in England* (Oxford, forthcoming). Cf. also Orietta Da Rold, 'Cultural Contexts of English Manuscripts 1060 to 1220' on the useful website The Production and Use of English Manuscripts 1060 to 1220 at https://www.le.ac.uk/english/em1060to1220/culturalcontexts/intro.htm.

[3] See discussions on https://frenchofengland.ace.fordham.edu. See also Jocelyn Wogan-Browne, 'General Introduction: What's in a Name—The "French" of England', in Jocelyn Wogan-Browne (ed.), with Carolyn Collette, Maryanne Kowaleski, Linne Mooney, Ad Putter, and David Trotter, *Language and Culture in Medieval Britain: The French of England c. 1100–c.1500* (Woodbridge, 2009), 1–13; and the important considerations of Ardis Butterfield in the opening chapters to *The Familiar Enemy: Chaucer, Language, and Nation in the Hundred Years War* (Oxford, 2009), 3–101. On Ireland, see Keith Busby, *French in Medieval Ireland, Ireland in Medieval French: The Paradox of Two Worlds* (Turnhout, 2017).

106 MEDIEVAL POETRY: 1100–1400

to period, place to place, and context to context before the end of the fifteenth century. At the end of the twelfth century the degree of dialectal distinction between insular and Continental French varied from text to text, with some English authors showing little divergence from the Continental 'norms' of 'Standardised Medieval French' (SMF). The loss of Normandy in 1204 has often been taken as the date at which Anglo-Norman began to diverge from Continental idioms, but this is in some respects an exaggeration as insular texts are copied and circulate on the Continent, just as Continental texts are disseminated on the other side of the Channel. This suggests easy transmission and circulation in the insular and Continental regions of medieval Francophonia.[4] In one sense, insular Frenches are but other variations of the medieval *langue d'oïl*, just like the French of Paris, Burgundy, and Picardy. These were recognised as regional idioms, not always mutually comprehensible without effort, in the Middle Ages.[5] There are, of course, also regional features of literary production which can be discerned; but for much of the Middle Ages in some circles, there is a body of literature which transcends geographical barriers and borders. Particular note should be taken of the kind of French current in the highest aristocratic and royal milieux in the later Middle Ages, where the language is essentially what Serge Lusignan has called 'la langue des rois'.[6] In the rest of this chapter, I shall be eclectic, using whatever term seems to me appropriate in the context. 'Anglo-French' is used for the subtitle of this chapter to encompass the long insular developments of the Norman idiom after Hastings, as well as the general impact of French poetry on English. I eschew here the debates, medieval and modern, on Anglo-Norman as 'good' or 'bad' French, although the matter is of some importance to medieval insular authors themselves and relates to the role played by language in the awareness of identity and community.[7]

French in the medieval British Isles was therefore neither uniform nor universal nor restricted to the milieux of the conquerors and their descendants. Many nobles continued to hold lands on both sides of the Channel, considering the lands across the Channel a natural extension of their territory. From this perspective, much literature was not directly related to the Conquest, which expanded its potential audience westwards into England, Scotland, Wales, and Ireland. Some works, however, did reflect colonial ambitions or made use of native English subject matter, while others were susceptible to being interpreted in a colonial light, acquiring renewed significance in the course of time. The languages used in the islands after the Conquest, whether in daily life, administration, the Church, the law, and literature, did not exist in isolation from one another. All contexts were in some degree multilingual, and it should be constantly borne in mind that literature in French co-existed, rather than competed, with that in Latin, English, and the Celtic languages. It has been argued convincingly by Ian Short that within a century or so after Hastings, the descendants of the Normans used English on a daily basis for practical purposes, but that French was used in other contexts, including literature, as a means of consolidating and

---

[4] See 'England and French', in Jocelyn Wogan-Browne, Thelma Fenster, and Delbert Russell (eds), *Vernacular Literary Theory from the French of Medieval England: Texts and Translations* (Cambridge, 2016), 401–13.

[5] For example, Giraldus distinguished between insular and Parisian French in the *Speculum duorum* (c 1208); see Yves Lefèvre and R. B. C. Huygens (eds) and Brian Dawson (trans.), *Speculum Duorum, or a Mirror of Two Men* (Cardiff, 1974), 56–7. Some sixty years later, regional idioms are mentioned by Roger Bacon in his *Compendium studii philosophiae* (chs 6 and 8) and *Opus Tertium* (ch. 25) in J. S. Brewer (ed.), *Opera quaedam hactenus inedita*, I, Rolls Series, 15 (London, 1859), 438–9 and 467; and in his *Opus maius* (Pars Tertia: 'De Utilitate Grammaticae), in John Henry Bridges (ed.), *The Opus Majus of Roger Bacon, Volume I* (London, 1900), 66–7. See also Ian Short, 'On Bilingualism in Anglo-Norman England', *Romance Philology*, 33 (1979–80), 467–79.

[6] Serge Lusignan, *La Langue des rois au Moyen Âge: Le français en France et en Angleterre* (Paris, 2004).

[7] See Ian Short, 'Another Look at "le faus franceis"', *Nottingham Medieval Studies*, 54 (2010), 35–55.

restating their cultural origins on the Continent.[8] Some members of the target audiences of vernacular literature may also have been more Latin-literate than scholars have generally supposed. Most vernacular authors translated or drew on Latin sources and models in one way or another, and while the move to French may well reflect a decrease in Latin literacy broadly speaking, it does not imply conversely that those competent in Latin did not enjoy vernacular literature.

If the production of literature in Old English may appear to be largely stymied after 1066, there is a kind of continuity insofar as its use in, say, psalters or some scientific-didactic texts may have provided models for early French examples produced in England. Indeed, twelfth-century Anglo-Norman psalters are among the very earliest insular works in the *langue d'oïl* and preserved in some of the very earliest insular manuscripts, the *mise en page* of which is closely related to Old English examples. Anglo-Norman scribes also occasionally use Old English letters, suggesting not only that they were trained in England but also that they may have copied both vernaculars, in addition to Latin. Anglo-Norman may take over the role of Old English in rendering accessible Latin learning and doctrine to a vernacular audience. In this sense, the transition from Old English to Anglo-Norman can be seen in the very early post-Conquest period as a linguistic one which develops differently in different contexts as the culture of the colonists continues to impose itself while absorbing native traditions in England. It is worth noting here that much of Gaimar's *Estoire des Engleis* (written *c* 1136 for Constance fitz Gilbert of Lincolnshire) is based directly on the *Anglo-Saxon Chronicle* and shows continuity rather than disruption in an attempt to relate the provincial Anglo-Norman aristocracy to English historical culture, albeit in their own language. Traditions of prose and poetry in Old English are closely related and much prose shares the rhythms of poetry; something similar may be said of literature in Anglo-Norman. Patronage is also a crucial factor in the early rise of Anglo-Norman literature if the examples of Constance and Adeliza of Louvain (see later) are any indication. Thomas O'Donnell has argued that the visible respect for Old English models in very early Anglo-Norman changes gradually into a tendency not to reject but to 'improve' them in the course of the twelfth century. This is also visible in the innovative *mise en page* of some early Anglo-Norman manuscripts, where verse is written out as prose, casting the new in the guise of the old.[9]

Poetry and Prose

I have thus far used the word 'literature' in the broadest sense rather than 'poetry' in this sketch of the situation of French in the British Isles because distinctions between verse and prose are rarely absolute. In particular, prose is sometimes transformed into verse (and vice versa) during the adaptation from one language into another and even in intralingual adaptation. In general, Latin prose is turned into French verse more frequently than into prose, but the distinction between verse as fiction and prose as non-fiction is far from absolute. Early scientific works in Anglo-Norman and the first historiographical texts, for example, are composed in verse. I will now turn to literature in verse in a discussion of what has long been called the 'precocity' of Anglo-Norman literature.[10] This so-called 'precocity'—that is,

---

[8] Ian Short, *Manual of Anglo-Norman*, 31–3, and Short, 'Patrons and Polyglots: French Literature in 12th-Century England', *Anglo-Norman Studies*, 14 (1992), 229–49.

[9] O'Donnell, 'Talking to the Neighbours...'.

[10] See the classic article of M. Dominica Legge, 'La précocité de la littérature anglo-normande', *Cahiers de Civilisation Médiévale*, 8 (1965), 327–49.

the high percentage of Anglo-Norman texts in the earliest period of literature in the *langue d'oïl* (say, before 1150)—is heavy with implications. It necessitates a redrawing of the literary and linguistic maps of both France and England, calling up ghosts of nationalisms past and present, and questioning scholarly assumptions regarding heritage and *patrimoine*. In one sense, the precocity of literature in Anglo-Norman is also the precocity of literature from the western part of the Angevin-Plantagenet domains and not a specifically insular phenomenon, but what is somewhat disorienting for those used to the modern map is the paucity of very early production in the centre of France. Taken together with the intensity of poetic activity in the *langue d'oc* in the eleventh and twelfth centuries, the centre appears peripheral.

The reduced production of English-language poetry by the partial elimination of Anglophone audiences within and without the monasteries after 1066 and its replacement by that in French was not, however, a matter of language alone. Anglo-Saxon poetry is largely heroic, hagiographical, and biblical, although the so-called 'wisdom poems' may at a stretch be considered lyrical, and the translation of Boethius and *The Phoenix* maintain a tenuous connection with classical antiquity. One of the most radical innovations in Anglo-Norman verse narrative of the early period (say, within a century and a half of Hastings) is the introduction and exploitation of subject matter beyond that found in Old English. Saints' lives, biblical paraphrases, and scientific and didactic works are among the first insular French texts (perhaps maintaining a continuity with traditions in English), but verse soon also becomes the medium in which to articulate the *chanson de geste*, the *romans antiques*, Arthurian romance, and religious and didactic subject matters and forms. At first glance, the scarcity of lyric poetry in early Anglo-Norman appears somewhat surprising, but two factors may explain it. First of all, it has been argued that the troubadour lyric in Occitan circulated in courtly circles in England, and secondly, there is the issue (relevant generally) that an absolute distinction between Continental and insular Frenches is something of a red herring insofar as the circulation and reception of poetry on both sides of the Channel are concerned. The northern French *trouvères* were likely known in England as well as France. From a codicological standpoint, the apparent coherence of the northern French and Occitan lyric is assured by their transmission in *chansonniers*, unknown in Middle English before Charles d'Orléans, imprisoned in England after his capture at Agincourt in 1415. Charles taught himself English during his incarceration and even translated some of his own work from one language into the other with no apparent crisis of identity. For the early period, then, the French poetry written in England may best be seen as part of the wider poetic corpus in the *langue d'oïl* whose insular traits do little to lessen its intertextual links with the whole.[11]

The resurgence of English as a literary language is generally seen as a development of the second half of the thirteenth century, and as early as the end of the twelfth, examples of many poetic genres abound in French to provide models for authors ready to capitalise on the rise of a renewed Anglophone audience a few decades later. In addition to Gaimar's *Estoire*, Wace's *Rou* (1169–70), and Benoît de Sainte-Maure's *Chronique des ducs de Normandie* (the continuation of the *Rou*, *c* 1170) are early insular examples of the chronicle, mainly written in octosyllabic rhyming couplets. Benedeit's *Voyage de saint Brendan* (1121, written for Adeliza of Louvain), the first *Vie de saint Alexis*, and Adgar's *Gracial* are among many hagiographical and semi-hagiographical texts written in England before the

---

[11] On the Middle English Lyric, see the various contributions in Thomas Gibson Duncan (ed.), *A Companion to the Middle English Lyric* (Cambridge, 2005).

end of the twelfth century. The Becket life by Guernes de Pont-Sainte-Maixence was written and much copied in England, although Guernes's own idiom is largely Continental. The *Tristan* romance of Thomas, the two *Folie Tristan* texts, Thomas of Kent's *Roman de toute chevalerie, Horn, Haveloc*, the romances of Hue de Rotelande, and the *Lais* of Marie de France are all Anglo-Norman and pre-1200. Béroul's *Tristan* is from Continental Normandy, and Chrétien de Troyes's romances and all three *romans antiques* are known to have circulated early in England, perhaps even written partly with an English audience in mind. Other romances which may have originated on the Continent were copied early in England. The earliest manuscript of the poem espoused enthusiastically by the French as their national epic, *La chanson de Roland*, is English, while *La chanson d'Aspremont, Gormont et Isembart*, and *La chanson de Guillaume* are all early insular *chansons de geste*; two versions of the 'Distichs of Cato' by Everart (mid-twelfth century) and Elie of Winchester (end of the twelfth century), the *Comput* and *Bestiaire* of Philippe de Thaon (1113 and 1120–35, respectively), and several lapidaries (including one attributed to Philippe), as well as collections of homilies and homiletic texts, are Anglo-Norman. All of these, and more besides, attest to the vitality of literature in French composed and circulating in England. From 1200 onwards, the growth is even more spectacular and the dominance of French poetry (and prose) all the more pronounced as Continental works circulate and are copied in England. The corpus of French verse texts which circulated in the British Isles by the end of the Middle Ages is unprecedented in its extent and diversity, offering a practically limitless range of models for Middle English authors.[12] The dominant verse form is the octosyllabic rhyming couplet, while Philippe de Thaon favours hexasyllables, and the *chansons de geste*, of course, are written in assonating sequences (*laisses*) of varying length; strophic poetry in various forms is not uncommon. French became one of the native vernaculars of the islands after Hastings, and French-language texts enjoyed a privileged position as direct and indirect source material for Middle English works, but it is as well to remind ourselves that other literatures (such as Middle High German, Middle Dutch, Old Norse, and Italian) were also radically transformed by the circulation of French literature in their regions or by the travel of their authors.

The introduction of French poetry into Britain had considerable consequences for the evolution of English versification. Like that in other Germanic languages, Old English poetry generally used an alliterative line with an irregular number of syllables but a regular number of stresses; the line is divided into hemistichs at the caesura, and the basis of the ornament is alliteration, not rhyme. Medieval French poetry does exhibit alliteration simply by virtue of the phonology of the language (and this can contribute to the overall effect of a line of verse), but with one important exception, most French poems derive their regularity from a fixed syllable count and rhyme. This is characteristic of poetry written in Romance vernaculars. Forms vary from the hexasyllabic and (dominant) octosyllabic couplet in narrative verse through the basic *abab* quatrain to quite complex stanza forms with lines of varying length and rhyming patterns. The important exception is the decasyllabic or duodecasyllabic assonanced line of the *chanson de geste* in which the regularity is constituted by the identity (or near-identity) of the final stressed vowel and the division of the line at the caesura; the two hemistichs are not necessarily of equal length. Assonanced lines are grouped into long sequences known as *laisses*. Rhyming poetry of various Latin traditions

---

[12] Details of all known Anglo-Norman texts and manuscripts are to be found in Ruth Dean, with the collaboration of Maureen B. M. Boulton, *Anglo-Norman Literature: A Guide to Texts and Manuscripts* (London, 1999).

110   MEDIEVAL POETRY: 1100–1400

was known in England before the Conquest, but seems to have had little influence on Old English. The so-called 'Alliterative Revival' of the mid-fourteenth century may represent an attempt to reassert the native verse tradition, of which there is little trace after Laȝamon's *Brut*.

Rhyming couplets and tail-rhyme stanzas soon became the standard verse forms for Middle English narrative poetry, but the assonanced *laisse* was not appropriated, even though assonance can play a part in English rhyme. Much Middle English versification of the pre-Chaucerian period does not show the kind of strict syllable count required in French. This is often due to the lack of an unstressed syllable at the beginning of a line or the addition of one elsewhere (which may lead to hypo- or hypermetric lines). It is important to point out here that Anglo-Norman versification has been one of the thornier issues of scholarship, especially when viewed from the Continent. Anglo-Norman metre does not conform strictly to the norms of Continental Old French, and frequently shows the same kind of syllabic features as the Middle English line mentioned earlier. Taken together with the more frequent use of alliteration in Anglo-Norman verse than in Continental French, a good case can be made for the influence of English on the insular French idiom.[13] These, of course, are generalisations, and meticulous syllable counters can be found in both early Middle English and Anglo-Norman. Scribal procedures and tendencies also contribute to the ways in which lines of verse ultimately appear on the manuscript page and are mediated to readers or listeners of both languages. Poetry of the later Middle English period is much more regular in form.[14]

Manuscripts

The production of manuscripts in general reflects that of literature itself, although the frequent loss of first-generation copies creates an impression of lag between the date of a text and the manuscripts in which it is transmitted. If the loss of early manuscripts is frustrating, it is also instructive since it shows clearly that texts have a life and an afterlife far beyond the immediate reception in the years after their composition. According to Ian Short, two thirds of the surviving French-language manuscripts (of prose and verse) datable to before 1200 are of insular origin.[15] Many are fragments, many are bilingual, and many contain vernacular additions or glosses to Latin books. The Latin context is both important and consistent, and in some cases the same hand has copied both French and Latin. Oxford, Bodleian Library, MS Digby 23, the earliest manuscript of *La chanson de Roland*, is a *unicum* as a single-text French-language book, difficult to date, but probably the second quarter of the eleventh

---

[13] On Anglo-Norman versification, see David L. Jeffrey and Brian J. Levy (eds), *The Anglo-Norman Lyric: An Anthology* (Toronto, 1990), 17–27. There is an excellent and detailed recent treatment of Anglo-Norman versification in 'Poetry and Prose in the French of England', in Wogan-Brown, Fenster, and Russell, *Vernacular Literary Theory*, 414–29.

[14] The most recent scholarship on Middle English versification has been conducted in the context of the project, 'The Verse Forms of Middle English Romance', directed by Ad Putter. Details are on the project website, https://gtr.ukri.org/projects?ref=AH%2FH00839X%2F1. I am grateful to Ad Putter for his advice on this subject. On the influence of French versification on Middle English, see Martin J. Duffel, 'Syllable and Foot: The Influence of French Metrics on English Verse', in Dominique Billy and Ann Buckley (eds), *Etudes de langue et de littérature médiévales offertes à Peter T. Ricketts à l'occasion de son 70ème anniversaire* (Turnhout, 2005), 571–83.

[15] Short, 'Vernacular Manuscripts I: Britain and France', in Erik Kwakkel and Rodney M. Thompson (eds), *The European Book in the Twelfth Century* (Cambridge, 2018), 311–26, at 316.

century. I mention it here simply as the most evident case of a text whose language and materiality stand in contrast with its position in the canon of Old French literature. Short, Careri, and Ruby list all twelfth-century insular manuscripts containing French verse, classified by genre, and point out characteristic codicological and palaeographical features, including a system of accented vowels to help with reading aloud.[16] Unlike Continental manuscripts, abbreviation and punctuation are sparse, differences which persist through the thirteenth and fourteenth centuries. Short concludes: 'Social conditions in Britain, its multinational aristocracy, its pluri-culturalism and its pluri-lingualism must obviously have been determining factors in making Anglo-Norman vernacular culture so innovative by comparison with its less centralised and unified Continental equivalent.'[17]

What literary history often likes to see as clearly delineated corpora of poetry in Latin, Anglo-Norman, and Middle English are in reality linked not only by intertextuality in its broadest sense but also through manuscript transmission. While most poems are transmitted in monolingual books, a number of important bi- and multilingual manuscripts can be seen as paradigmatic of the linguistic situation beginning in the second half of the thirteenth century: Oxford, Bodleian Library, MS Digby 86 (1272–82); Oxford, Jesus College 29 (second half of the thirteenth century); London, British Library, MS Harley 2253 (1330–40); London, British Library, MS Harley 913 (c 1330); London, British Library, MS Additional 46,919 (first half of the fourteenth century). Confirming the general pattern of vernacular manuscript production, such books suggest strongly that as late as the mid-fourteenth century French was still a principal language of poetry in Britain and Ireland; monolingual Anglo-Norman codices continue to be copied into the fifteenth century. Although most of the French works contained in these multilingual 'miscellanies' were written well before the production of the manuscripts themselves, their continued codicological existence reflects the successful persistence of the *langue d'oïl* in the British Isles. From a reception standpoint, the potential inherent in the transitions from one language to another is considerable and constitutes a form of codicological code-switching in which perceptions of idiom and genre are crucial to reading texts individually or in sequence. The co-existence of three languages within a single book is witness to their complementarity rather than competition between them. Anglo-Norman and Middle English complement and support each other as vernacular poetic idioms. Anglo-Norman poetry is as English as it is French, English by virtue of its point of origin and sometimes by its subject matter, and French by virtue of its linguistic relation to the broader culture of its underlying base.[18]

These manuscripts are all *sui generis*, and each is a product of a particular social and cultural context. Digby 86 is a Worcestershire book which may have been copied in stages by its first owner, while Harley 2253 is the product of a journeyman Ludlow scribe whose hand is visible in other manuscripts and non-literary documents. Both of these were copied in what appear to be informal circumstances far from London bookshops and contain a wide

---

[16] Maria Careri, Christine Ruby, and Ian Short, *Livres et écritures en français et en occitan au XIIe siècle: catalogue illustré* (Rome: Viella, 2011), xlvii–lv. See also Maria Careri and Marcella Lacanale, 'Accents et syllabes dans les manuscrits anglo-normands', in Oreste Floquet and Gabriele Giannini (eds), *Anglo-Français: philologie et linguistique* (Paris, 2015), 35–44.

[17] Ian Short, 'Vernacular Manuscripts I', 323.

[18] On multilingual manuscripts, see John Scahill, 'Trilingualism in Early Middle English Miscellanies: Language and Literature', *Yearbook of English Studies*, 33 (2003), 18–32; Keith Busby, 'Multilingualism, the Harley Scribe, and Johannes Jacobi', in Margaret Connolly and Raluca Radulescu (eds), *Insular Books: Vernacular Manuscripts in Late Medieval Britain* (Oxford, 2015), 49–60; and Ad Putter, 'The Organisation of Multilingual Miscellanies: The Contrasting Fortunes of Middle English Lyrics and Romances', in Connolly and Radulescu, *Insular Books*, 81–100.

112 MEDIEVAL POETRY: 1100–1400

variety of poetry and prose; some of the French texts are standard works from the Continental French canon which can therefore be shown to have circulated in rural England.[19] How the scribes of these and other manuscripts accessed such works is unclear, but there must have been networks of scribes and others involved in the production of books, formal and informal. Additional 46,919 belonged to, and was partly copied by, the Franciscan William Herebert of Hereford; its contents are more noticeably a mixture of the sacred, didactic, and the secular, including an Anglo-Norman 'demande d'amour', a Christian poem on the *Ordene de chevalerie*, works related to aristocratic pastimes such as hunting, a treatise on the monastic life, French poems by Simon de Fresne and Nicholas Bozon, and the Middle English poems of Herebert himself. Jesus 29 is dominated by Middle English didactic poems but also contains *La vie de Tobie* by the Continental poet Guillaume de Normandie, and three poems by the Anglo-Norman Chardri (*Le petit plet*, *La vie des set dormanz*, and *La vie de seint Josaphaz*); its most obviously secular pieces are *The Owl and the Nightingale* and a copy of the *Doctrinal Sauvage*, a Continental treatise on courtly virtues and manners. There appear to be no essential distinctions in Jesus 29 between poems in French and English. *The Owl and the Nightingale* and *Le petit plet* (also both found in London, British Library, MS Cotton Caligula A. ix) have often been considered as related to the school tradition of *disputatio*. Harley 913 is Irish (probably Waterford) and has been called a 'Franciscan' manuscript, although that is only one perspective in which it can be viewed; its contents are primarily religious, in Latin and Middle Hiberno-English, but it contains the entirely secular Hiberno-Norman *Walling of New Ross*, an occasional urban piece which nevertheless shows knowledge of courtly traditions.[20]

If multilingual manuscripts reflect the linguistic perspective in a book-size format, macaronic poetry works on the level of individual poems, usually lyric. There is not a huge corpus of macaronic verse from medieval England, but its very presence is significant as it presupposes an underlying sensibility on the part of readers and listeners to the significance of code-switching.[21] For example, a proverb in French may appear at the end of stanzas in Middle English, or the two languages may simply alternate, as in the well-known poem 'Mayden moder milde':

> Mayden moder milde,
>   Oiez cel oreysoun*;   *hear this prayer*
> From shome thou me shilde
>   E de ly malfeloun*;   *and from evildoers*
> For love of thine childe
>   Me menez de tresoun*.   *lead me from treason*
> Ich wes wod and wilde,
>   Ore su en prisoun*.[22]   *now I am in prison*

---

[19] See discussion in Chapter 3 of this volume.

[20] A good deal of work has been done on these manuscripts, but see especially Susanna Fein (ed.), *Interpreting MS Digby 86: A Trilingual Book from Thirteenth-Century Worcestershire* (Woodbridge, 2019); Susanna Fein (ed.), *Studies in the Harley Manuscript: The Scribes, Contents, and Social Contexts of British Library MS Harley 2253* (Kalamazoo, MI, 2000); Susanna Fein, David Raybin, and Jan Ziolkowski (eds and trans.), *The Complete Harley 2253 Manuscript*, 3 vols. (Kalamazoo, MI, 2014–15); Neil Cartlidge, 'The Composition and Social Context of MSS Jesus College Oxford 29 (II) and BL Cotton Caligula A ix', *Medium Ævum*, 66 (1997), 250–69; Deborah L. Moore, *Medieval Anglo-Irish Troubles: A Cultural Study of BL MS Harley 913* (Turnhout, 2016); Busby, *French in Medieval Ireland*, pp. 107–27; and Ingrid Nelson, *Lyric Tactics: Poetry, Genre, and Practice in Later Medieval England* (Philadelphia, PA, 2017), 60–6 and 76–87(on Additional 46,919).

[21] Little work has been done on macaronic verse in England, but see Carol Harvey, 'Macaronic Techniques in Anglo-Norman Verse', *L'Esprit créateur*, 18 (1978), 70–81.

[22] In I. S. T. Aspin, *Anglo-Norman Political Songs* (Oxford, 1953), no. VI. Other examples are quoted by Harvey.

Here, the alternating lines rhyme *abababab* (*a* English *and b* French). Both theme and syntax are uninterrupted by the language-switching, but the semantic associations of the two languages remain distinct. A second example will illustrate trilingual macaronicity, where the interplay between two amorous idioms is significantly introduced in the language of clerical learning:

> Scripsi hec carmina in tabulis;   *I wrote this song on a (wax) tablet*
> Mon ostel est en mi la vile de Paris;   *my home is in the city of Paris*
> May y sugge namore, so wel me is;
> yef hi deye for love of hire, duel hyt is.[23]

Here, the rhymes in all three languages are in *-is*. The most recent critical attention in this area has been paid to macaronic sermons.[24] The inclusion in a Middle English (or any vernacular, for that matter) poem of Latin words, phrases, and lines of verse (often as a refrain) is widespread and unsurprising, but the presence in Britain of Anglo-Norman as a major language of literature and a significant proportion of the population-at-large provides both poets and the compilers of manuscripts with the opportunity to create supplementary depth and texture in their work. The enormous influence of Anglo-Norman on Middle English lexis is itself a form of macaronicity to which many readers and listeners would have been sensitive. Such language- and code-switching is also evident in narrative contexts, mainly historiographical, in both Anglo-Norman and Middle English poems which often depict dialogue and intralingual (mis)communication. Some of these instances afford insight into real linguistic difficulties in medieval Britain, but interpretation is not always straightforward.

In essence, and bearing in mind that the above outline is necessarily reductionist in nature, this is the situation in England and, to a lesser degree, in other parts of the islands at the moment Middle English once again becomes a significant medium for poetry. Two centuries of French poetic traditions from both sides of the Channel have circulated freely among communities of readers and listeners accustomed to the notion that vernacular literature is a French- (or Celtic-)language phenomenon. The acculturation of French speakers in England gradually expands beyond the realms of the quotidian to literature, creating demand for poetry in English at the same time as French continues as both a spoken and literary language. The audience for literature in English is composed both of descendants of the Francophone colonists and native Anglophones with a new social and economic mobility. French poetry thus provides models and examples when the majority vernacular resumes its role alongside French as a transmitter of verse. I use the term 'model' here not simply in the sense of an object for emulation but also as an element of a corpus which gradually expands by embracing poetry in Middle English.

---

[23] G. L. Brook (ed.), *The Harley Lyrics: The Middle English Lyrics of Ms. Harley 2253* (Manchester, 1948), 55.

[24] See Helena Halman and Timothy Regetz, 'Language Switching and Alliteration in Oxford, MS Bodley 649', in Albrecht Classen (ed.), *Multilingualism in the Middle Ages and Early Modern Age: Communication and Miscommunication in the Premodern World* (Berlin, 2016), 313–28; Herbert Schendl, 'Code-Switching in Late Medieval Macaronic Sermons', in Ad Putter and Judith Jefferson (eds), *Multilingualism in Medieval Britain (c. 1066–1520): Sources and Analysis* (Turnhout, 2012), 153–69; Alan Fletcher, 'Written versus Spoken Macaronic Discourse in Late Medieval England: The View from a Pulpit', in Putter and Jefferson (eds), *Multilingualism in Medieval Britain*, 137–51.

114   MEDIEVAL POETRY: 1100–1400

Adaptatio, Translatio, Imitatio

The most evident manifestation of the importance of French verse for the development of Middle English lies in the act and processes of adaptation. To be sure, Anglo-Saxon had long shown that verse was a suitable medium for narrative, but the disruption in the native tradition had all but erased the potential of English. And when narrative verse comes to be written again, it does not for the most part deal with insular traditions, but rather those already treated in both Anglo-Norman and Continental French. Even narratives of 'the Matter of England', such as the tales of Horn and Haveloc, are based on Anglo-Norman models as the conquerors assimilated native lore; the history of Waldef was never apparently adapted into English.[25] The absence of Anglo-Norman manuscripts of texts adapted into Middle English, even when loss by historical accident is taken into account, is significant insofar as it suggests that Continental copies were available by one means or another to insular authors, either by virtue of being already present in England or because they were sought out for the purpose of adaptation. The pre-Chaucerian period in England is one of transition during which adaptations from the French continue to be written alongside an increasing number of Middle English original works (such as *The Owl and the Nightingale* [as early as 1189 or as late as the later thirteenth century, depending on whether the King Henry mentioned is Henry II or Henry III], the *Cursor Mundi*, the *South English Legendary*, the *Northern Homily Cycle*, and the *Chronicle* of Robert of Gloucester). These latter, of course, both draw directly on Latin sources rather than on French ones, although *The Owl and the Nightingale* may owe something to the tradition of French allegorical debate poetry as well as the *disputatio* of the schools. Robert Mannyng of Brunne's *Handlyng Synne* (1303) adapts William of Waddington's Anglo-Norman *Manuel des pechiés* (c 1260).

Middle English adaptations from both Continental and insular French originals have not wanted for attention in recent decades, and scholars have long abandoned the view that narrative texts such as *Ywain and Gawain*, *Lybeaus desconus*, and the versions of *Ipomedon* (to name but a few) are pale imitations of their models unworthy of critical attention. What defines these English re-castings is their nature as *translatio*, generally retaining the central adventures, but often radically modifying the sense to conform better to the values and expectations of a new audience or readership. The modifications may relate to matters such as chivalry, love, religion, politics, and ethics generally. In essence, the *translatio* moves the text from a Francophone audience with a long tradition of vernacular romance to an Anglophone community without the same background and interests. The move is also now seen by scholars as a social one, from courtly to non-courtly (merchant-class or bourgeois), although this is no doubt too categorical a view. Just as the French bourgeoisie read courtly romances (there is a good deal of evidence in booklists and post-mortem inventories), the higher aristocracy in English surely read Middle English courtly texts. For example, Humphrey, earl of Hereford, commissioned a translation of *Guillaume de Palerne* for his household c 1350.[26] At some point there must have been contact between the various communities of readers and listeners, a conduit whereby the Anglophone audience became acquainted with the kinds of works popular in the Francophone world. This is more than a

---

[25] See Susan Crane, *Insular Romance: Politics, Faith, and Culture in Anglo-Norman and Middle English Literature* (Berkeley, CA, 1986); and more recently, Rosalind Field, 'Children of Anarchy: Anglo-Norman Romance in the Twelfth Century', in Ruth Kennedy and Simon Meecham-Jones (eds), *Writers of the Reign of Henry II: Twelve Essays* (Basingstoke, 2006), 249–62.

[26] Text in G. H. V. Bunt (ed.), *William of Palerne: An Alliterative Romance* (Groningen, 1985). See discussion in Chapter 19 of this volume.

simple desire to ape those who were perceived as social superiors—rather, it is an attempt to mobilise French genres as a means of expressing the values of a different community.[27] That said, we should not discount the certain existence of bilingual readers and listeners capable of appreciating poetry in both French and English. Scholars have generally fallen prey all too readily to the temptation of dividing and ruling Francophone and Anglophone communities in medieval Britain. Literary history as a rule has English running behind French chronologically with regard to the treatment of particular subject matters and genres, and this is surely so; but the prevalence of multilingualism after the Conquest, and for most of the Middle Ages, requires us to nuance the received view.

Alongside adaptation, the influence of French poetry on Middle English can be seen in what are works not directly based on a specific French text but visibly prompted by a desire to produce something comparable in English and to show that the recovering native vernacular was just as capable as French of generating worthwhile poetry. While most types of French poetry (narrative, didactic, religious) begin to find their expression in Middle English without direct reliance on a particular model, lyric poetry will serve here to illustrate the kind of 'emulation' I have in mind. Although the religious lyric in Middle English has antecedents in French, by which it was probably influenced, the most instructive example is in the secular field, in particular the love lyric. The so-called 'Harley Lyrics' are generally acknowledged as some of the most accomplished in Middle English, and they are, not by chance, found in one of the great multilingual manuscripts mentioned earlier, namely Harley 2253. Thoroughly informed by and imbued with the tradition of the Old French courtly lyric, these poems are equally English in their nature and expression, building not only on the *grand chant courtois* but also on a well-developed stylistic and lexical arsenal in the native vernacular, some of which may be popular rather than courtly in origin. The semantics of the affective lexis do overlap in the two languages, but it is worth noting that even though the French *pastourelle*, for example, is said to have popular origins, its vocabulary is largely courtly (*pace* the occasional obscenity); the Harley poems in particular are characterised by a high measure of Anglo-Saxon lexemes. They may also to a degree be ironic and parodic takes on the French courtly tradition. These poems, and others, are also susceptible to analysis in terms of genre (*pastourelle*, *jeu-parti*, *reverdie*, etc.) which forms an organising criterion of some French *chansonniers*.[28] What we see in the evolution of lyric poetry is a form of what Paul Zumthor famously termed *mouvance*, here both inter- and intralingual, in which the transposition of forms, themes, and motifs offers almost infinite possibilities for mutation.[29] The fabliau of *Dame Sirith* and the aesopic fable of *The Fox and the Wolf* from Digby 86 may be seen in a similar light; that is, as attempts to give these genres the *entrée* into Middle English.[30]

---

[27] Still useful as an overview is W. R. J. Barron, *Medieval English Romance* (London, 1987). More recently, see the various contributions in Roberta L. Krueger (ed.), *The Cambridge Companion to Medieval Romance* (Cambridge, 2000); and Corinne Saunders (ed.), *A Companion to Romance: From Classical to Contemporary* (Oxford, 2004).

[28] The texts from Harley 2253 have been edited by Brook (above, n. 23), and Fein, Raybin, and Ziolkowski (n. 20). For studies, see Daniel J. Ransom, *Poets at Play: Irony and Parody in the Harley Lyrics* (Norman, OK, 1985); Thomas G. Duncan (ed.), *A Companion to the Middle English Lyric* (Woodbridge, 2005); and Ingrid Nelson, *Lyric Tactics*, 31–58.

[29] First formulated in ch. 2 of *Essai de poétique médiévale* (Paris, 1972).

[30] See Keith Busby, 'Conspicuous by Its Absence: The English Fabliau', *Dutch Quarterly Review*, 12 (1982), 30–41.

Authorship

Although poetry in French is written in the islands throughout the Middle Ages, there is a point somewhere early in the fourteenth century when Middle English, for various reasons, becomes the general, albeit not exclusive, language of choice. This responds not only to the changing nature and linguistic predilections and capabilities of audiences but also to the development of a more acute sense of authorship and authorial identity, linked to an equally acute awareness of the importance of the vernacular as a bearer of cultural aspirations. It is no coincidence that this is precisely the period in which poetry gradually loses its anonymity and in which authorial personality and presence begin to dominate. The early development of patronage in French-language areas, along with clerical training in the schools, may in part be responsible for a greater awareness of the craft of writing which manifests itself in Old French poetry before the fourteenth century. In the fourteenth and fifteenth centuries, formally or informally, poets such as Dante, Boccaccio and Petrarch, Machaut, Deschamps and Froissart, Chaucer, Lydgate, and Gower, for example, appear as communities of authors with a common resolve. There is, of course, precedent in the close-knit fellowships of troubadours and *Minnesinger*, and medieval manifestations of intertextuality in general suggest a more pronounced shared sense of purpose and aesthetic among poets than is evident at first sight, but the self-awareness and sense of profession across languages and borders becomes particularly pronounced at this time. The cohesion of poets writing in French and English in the second half of the fourteenth century and early fifteenth is also visible in the common use of fixed forms such as the *ballade* by authors such as Machaut, Deschamps, Chaucer, and Gower.[31] It is during this later period that the variety of Frenches in the British Isles becomes increasingly apparent. Although the composition and copying of a recognisable and distinct Anglo-Norman continues well into the fifteenth century, the French of trilingual Gower barely differs from that of the Continent, suggesting that his acquisition of the literary idiom was not 'natural' in the sense that it was a 'mother-tongue' to him.[32] Ardis Butterfield has also reminded us that in addition to Froissart, several poets, such as Jehan de le Mote, Gace de le Buigne, Othon de Grandson, and Jean de Garancières, are known to have written in Continental French in England.[33] All of these poets, writing in English or French, drew on a shared cumulative body of imagery, themes, forms, modes, and devices to the extent that 'originality' in the traditional sense has little meaning. This poetic arsenal, however, is essentially French, reaching back to the *trouvères* through the enormously influential *Roman de la rose* (of which Chaucer translated part) to the above-mentioned group of French poets.

Context, as we have seen, is everything, and each piece of French poetry composed in England or which circulated there, irrespective of its genre, is defined by its context. By context, I mean here the sum of social, cultural, spiritual, linguistic, and literary forces, authorship and audiences, which together determine the nature of the text. These contexts may be characterised approximately as monastic/ecclesiastical, clerical, courtly-chivalric,

---

[31] On Chaucer and the French poets, see Ardis Butterfield, 'Chaucer's French Inheritance', in Piero Boitani and Jill Mann (eds), *The Cambridge Companion to Chaucer* (Cambridge, 2004), 20–35; James I. Wimsatt, *Chaucer and His French Contemporaries: Natural Music in the Fourteenth Century* (Toronto, 1991); and the earlier classic study by Charles Muscatine, *Chaucer and the French Tradition* (Berkeley, CA, 1957).

[32] But see Richard Ingham, 'John Gower, poète anglo-normand: perspectives linguistiques sur *Le Myrour de l'Omme*', in Floquet and Giannini (eds), *Anglo-Français* (Paris, 2015), 91–100.

[33] Butterfield, *The Familiar Enemy*, 281–2.

or popular. They cannot be discretely defined as there is a good deal of overlap, particularly over time and with the increasing complexities of manuscript transmission, but they are useful in that they provide perspectives with which to approach French poetry and its relationship with that in English. Equally crucial are the networks which enable communication between poets, patrons, readers, scribes, and artisans of the book. It may be self-evident to state that hagiography and biblical texts in Anglo-Norman, for example, emerge from a desire on the part of Church and monastery to transmit sacred material to a vernacular audience; it is less self-evident perhaps that scientific and didactic works in the language originate in learned and clerical contexts. Despite any mythical, legendary, or (pseudo-)historical sources, romance is clearly a courtly phenomenon, as is lyric poetry with its seeming 'folk' elements. Yet even here, caution is *de rigueur* as most authors of romance, for example, clearly had clerical training which informs their works at all levels; the popular elements in lyric poetry nevertheless colour an essentially contrived and formal courtly genre. The collection and organisation of different types of poetry in manuscripts, sometimes in the multilingual ones discussed earlier and often long after the dates of composition of individual items, points to the blurring of generic lines and the establishment of a varied canon of sorts.

The co-existence of French alongside English and Latin in the British Isles after 1066 was transformative in its effects on the English language and its literature. It is difficult to imagine the lexis of English without the Romance elements it absorbed from the idiom of the conquerors. In the field of poetry alone, French in all its varieties provided new subjects, models for emulation, an arsenal of stylistic and rhetorical devices, and a renewed, open confidence in the authority of the vernacular. Traditional views of the total supplanting of English by French after Hastings and before Chaucer stand in need of revision. Although there were certainly divides between linguistic communities, often defined by social status, economic circumstances, and cultural conditions, the audiences and readerships of poetry in the islands had more in common than otherwise. Multilingualism and multiculturalism ensured that poetry in medieval Latin, Middle English, and insular French was all to a degree 'English'. But for the landings at Pevensey on 28 September 1066, and the Norman success at Hastings seventeen days later, the Englishness of English poetry would look very different indeed.

8

The Poetic Field, IV

Welsh

Victoria Flood

This chapter explores the interaction between English and Welsh poetry following the Edwardian conquest of Wales in 1282–3, offering an overview of the Welsh poetic field as it intersects with the English.[1] It begins with an assessment of the putative influence of Welsh themes and verse forms on Middle English alliterative verse as it appears in the lyrics contained in London, British Library, Harley MS 2253 (early fourteenth century), and suggests that if we are to look for Welsh influences, we find these most obviously in a limited number of Welsh loan words and names, utilised with a mind to the demands of the English alliterative line. Following a brief overview of the relationship between English and Welsh Arthurian content, and the mediating role played by French and Latin romances and histories, the chapter then returns to the question of the lyric as a site germane to cross-linguistic enquiry. It explores the possible influence of English lyrics on depictions of love and the natural world in the work of Chaucer's near-contemporary, Dafydd ap Gwilym (*c* 1315–50)—suggesting that English song presents a plausible influence on Welsh poetry, although certainly this is one among many. Finally, the chapter considers English-language literary innovations in Wales: the self-conscious integration of English loan words, the composition of English and Welsh macaronic dialogues, and experiments in English poetry written in Welsh orthography. In these examples, we see the integration of English-language elements and even the composition of English-language poetry in *cynghanedd* ('harmony')—the combination of consonantal correspondence and internal rhyme which forms the underlying principles of Welsh strict metre poetry.

Welsh Influence on English Verse: The Harley Lyrics

The customary starting point for discussion of the relationship between Middle English and Welsh poetry is the long-lived argument concerning the influence of Welsh strict metre poetry on English alliterative verse. The fullest case for this has been made in relation to the Middle English lyrics in Harley 2253, a trilingual (English, French, and Latin) manuscript compiled in Ludlow *c* 1340, in the March between England and Wales.[2] The Harley lyrics represent a significant combining of the Continental popular lyric with native English allusions, frames of reference, and poetic strategies. Given the regional context of the manuscript, a case has been made for Welsh influence also, and the author of certain

---

[1] The Edwardian Conquest is conventionally understood as marking a new period in Welsh literary history, as we find, for example, in the organisation of the *Guide to Welsh Literature* volumes (Cardiff, 2000–).

[2] For the most recent scholarship concerning dating and provenance, see Susanna Fein (ed.), *Studies in the Harley Manuscript: The Scribes, Contents, and Social Contexts of British Library MS Harley 2253* (Kalamazoo, MI, 2000).

Victoria Flood, *The Poetic Field, IV*. In: *The Oxford History of Poetry in English*. Edited by Helen Cooper and Robert R. Edwards, Oxford University Press. © Victoria Flood (2023). DOI: 10.1093/oso/9780198827429.003.0008

of the Harley lyrics was once even held to be 'a Welsh-speaking Welshman'—although this claim is certainly a difficult one to substantiate.[3] Most notably, A. T. E. Matonis has suggested that the consonantal alliteration within and across lines, and linking stanzas, in a number of the lyrics might be understood as an English re-imagining of *cynghanedd*.[4] However, as Helen Fulton has observed, the organising principles employed in the English lyrics are at odds with consonantal correspondence as we find it in *cynghanedd*, which works systematically on a unit of one line, divided into two or three sections, rather than across a number of lines.[5] Further, as Fulton observes, a parallel to the alliterative stanza-linking in the Harley lyrics is found in Middle English romance, where alliteration and word repetition are used to sustain the narrative thread across stanzas.[6] The innovation would appear to be most feasibly English.

Rooted in the Welsh language (and its distinctive phonology), *cynghanedd* is not an easy point of application to English-language content. Later examples of *cynghanedd* in English, written by Welsh authors, have little in common with the Harley lyrics, and rest on the sustained application of Welsh orthography. Welsh influence on the lyrics appears most obviously not in verse form but in vocabulary. We might note the word 'wolc' ('hawk') in 'Annot and John' ('Ichot a burde in a bour ase beryl so bryht') (no. 3), where we read of 'Þe wilde laueroc ant wolc ant þe wodwale' (24). This form is recorded nowhere else in Middle English, and is most feasibly a borrowing from the Welsh *gwalch*. Similarly, there is the use of *miles* ('animals') in 'Spring' ('Lenten ys come wiþ loue to toune') (no. 11), which adds the English plural form (-*es*) to the Welsh singular *mil* ('animal'), and again is nowhere else attested in Middle English: 'Wowes þis wilde drakes; / Miles murgeþ [make merry with] huere makes' (19–20).[7] The demands of Middle English alliterative verse were facilitated by a vocabulary expanded by cross-linguistic influence typical of the Marcher region.[8] Middle English poets of the Welsh March also appear to have drawn on an expanded store of available legendary content, with Welsh affinities. In the final stanza of 'Annot and John', the beloved Annot is compared to a number of legendary heroes and heroines:

> Trewe ase Tegeu in tour, ase Wyrwein in wede,
> Baldore þen Byrne þat oft þe bor bede;
> As Wylcadoun he is wys, dohty of dede,
> Ffeyrore þen Floryes folkes to fede,
> Cud ase Cradoc in court carf þe brede,
> Hendore þen Hilde þat haueþ me to hede. (43–8)

---

[3] Saunders Lewis, 'Dafydd ap Gwilym', in A. R. Jones and Gwyn Thomas (eds), *Presenting Saunders Lewis* (Cardiff, 1973), 159–63, at 161.

[4] A. T. E. Matonis, 'An Investigation of Celtic Influences on MS Harley 2253', *Modern Philology*, 70 (1972), 91–103, at 99–101.

[5] Helen Fulton, 'The Theory of Celtic Influence on the Harley Lyrics', *Modern Philology*, 82 (1985), 239–52, at 245.

[6] Fulton, 'Theory of Celtic Influence', 241.

[7] All quotations from the Harley lyrics are from G. L. Brook (ed.), *The Harley Lyrics: The Middle English Lyrics of MS Harley 2253* (Manchester, 1978). For notice of these loan words, see Carleton Brown (ed.), *English Lyrics of the XIIIth Century* (Oxford, 1932), 225; Matonis, 'Investigation of Celtic Influence', 6; Fulton, 'Theory of Celtic Influence', 248. This is not unprecedented in Middle English from this region: Welsh loan words appear in early Middle English prose from the west Midlands in the Katherine group. See E. J. Dobson, *The Origins of Ancrene Wisse* (Oxford, 1976), 115–16.

[8] For discussion of the relationship between English and Welsh during this period, see Llinos Beverley Smith, 'The Welsh Language before 1536', in Geraint H. Jenkins (ed.), *The Welsh Language before the Industrial Revolution* (Cardiff, 1997), 15–44; Llinos Beverley Smith, 'The Welsh and English Languages in Late-Medieval Wales', in D. A. Trotter (ed.), *Multilingualism in Later Medieval Britain* (Cambridge, 2000), 8–21.

120   MEDIEVAL POETRY: 1100–1400

Among this roll call of mixed-gender names, which also includes French and German figures, there are two recognisable Welsh names, the Arthurian hero Caradoc (as he appears in French romance), Tegau, and a third, Wyrwein, who may represent Garwen, daughter of Henen Hen.[9] Tegau's epithet 'eurfron' ('golden-breasted'), as it appears in a Welsh context, connects her with Caradoc, and although she does not appear in the French romances that feature the hero, it is possible that a lost Welsh version identified her as his wife or mistress. Rachel Bromwich has suggested that the poet may have known a Welsh version of the tale involving her successful completion of a chastity test.[10] Notably, the spelling the 'Annot and John'-poet uses ('Tegeu' rather than 'Tegau') is an older Welsh form, which may suggest an acquaintance with a Welsh written, rather than oral, source, or at the very least familiarity with Middle Welsh orthography.[11] However, how fully the 'Annot and John'-poet understood the dimensions of his references to Caradoc and Tegau remains uncertain, including the extent to which he took the two to belong to the same legendary context—there is no suggestion of an overt awareness of this in the lines quoted above. Interestingly, Tegau features without Caradoc in near-contemporary Welsh love poetry, where she appears as a standard of beauty, nobility, and virtue, and we might wonder whether the English poet used her similarly.[12] At the very least, the allusion suggests the integration of Welsh personal names in Middle English verse, although potentially only partially understood, feasibly (although not necessarily) situated in relation to Old French Arthurian romance.

Welsh Influence on English Verse: Arthurian Romance

The question of any direct relationship between English and Welsh Arthurian content is complicated by the integration of Welsh (alongside Breton and Cornish) personal names in Old French Arthurian romance, from which a good deal of English Arthurian romance takes its cue. The precise nature of background content lifted from Welsh into French contexts remains uncertain, as do lines of transmission, both oral and/or literary, and Breton and/or Welsh.[13] Scholarship has increasingly focused on the reception of French romance in Wales, as opposed to questions of early source identification, which remain not only unresolved but in many respects irresolvable. For example, we might note the three Welsh Arthurian prose tales, *Owain* (or *Chwedl Iarlles y Ffynnon*), *Peredur*, and *Geraint*, which contain material in common with the late-twelfth-century romances of Chrétien de Troyes. Although once posited as independent poetry responses to shared narratives, or even indications of Chrétien's source content, the three are now generally regarded as adaptive translations, suggestive of early interests in French romance in Wales.[14] Similarly, scholars have turned their attention to the role played by Latin intermediary texts in the transmission of Welsh Arthurian

---

[9] Brown, *English Lyrics*, 226–7; Matonis, 'Investigation of Celtic Influence', 6–8; Fulton, 'Theory of Celtic Influence', 249.

[10] Rachel Bromwich (ed.), *Trioedd Ynys Prydein: The Triads of the Island of Britain* (Cardiff, 2014), 504–5.

[11] I am indebted to Helen Fulton for this suggestion.

[12] Helen Fulton, *Dafydd ap Gwilym and the European Context* (Cardiff, 1989), 149–50. Fulton suggests that Tegau might be understood as a Welsh folk heroine who was later absorbed into Welsh Arthurian contexts.

[13] Patrick Sims-Williams, 'Did Itinerant Breton "Conteurs" Transmit the Matière de Bretagne?', *Romania*, 116 (1998), 72–111.

[14] Ceridwen Lloyd-Morgan and Erich Poppe, 'The First Adaptations from French: History and Context of a Debate', in Ceridwen Lloyd-Morgan and Erich Poppe (eds), *Arthur in the Celtic Languages: The Arthurian Legend in Celtic Literatures and Traditions* (Cardiff, 2019), 10–16. There are a number of non-Arthurian Welsh prose translations from French or Anglo-Norman, including romances mediated via England, such as *Bevis of Hampton*. See Erich Poppe and Regina Reck, 'Rewriting Bevis in Wales and Ireland', in Jennifer Fellows and Ivana Djordjević (eds), *Sir Bevis of Hampton in Literary Tradition* (Cambridge, 2008), 37–50.

content to England and France—including (although by no means limited to) Geoffrey of Monmouth's *Historia regum Britanniae* (*c* 1138).[15] Geoffrey's *Historia* was significant in its reworking of Welsh legendary-historical and prophetic content for an audience in England and the Continent, alongside a sizeable measure of the author's own invention. It is largely through Geoffrey that English and French authors of Arthurian romance and history acquired their sense of early insular history in the Welsh tradition: from the fall of Troy and the foundation of Britain to the coming of the Saxons.

Chief among the works of Middle English Arthurian poetry once taken to be obliquely suggestive of Welsh legendary background content is *Sir Gawain and the Green Knight*. As has long been noted, the *Gawain*-poet's beheading game finds a close analogue in a narrative associated with another Welsh hero, Caradoc, in continuations of the Old French *Percival*.[16] However, even if we can assume the acquaintance of the Old French author with earlier Welsh (or Breton) traditions concerning Caradoc, the earliest-known Arthurian use of the motif appears in the French, and the *Gawain*-poet's acquaintance with French content is far more feasible than a common affinity of the two to now-lost Welsh (or Breton) background traditions. This is not least because there remains as yet no compelling evidence that the *Gawain*-poet was acquainted with any aspect of Welsh language or literature, beyond names and concepts found in Old French Arthurian romance and Geoffrey's *Historia*.[17] We might note, for example, his use of the word 'Logres' for England in the description of Gawain's journey from Camelot to Hautdesert (line 691, and a brief later allusion in line 1055), a Welsh loan ('Lloegr') mediated in the first instance through Geoffrey's *Historia*, which constructs an etymological association between Locrinus, first son of Brutus, and the land over which he ruled, Loegria (England).[18] This might be understood in the context of the uses of the *Brut* in miniature which frame the opening of *Sir Gawain and the Green Knight*, and certainly the poem's Britishness is more obviously Galfridian than Welsh.

English Influence on Welsh Verse: Dafydd ap Gwilym

If we are to look for sites of interchange between English and Welsh poetic traditions of the thirteenth and fourteenth centuries, we find a possibility of this in the love lyric. It has been suggested that Middle English lyrics, such as those found in Harley 2253, may have had some influence on the poetry of the *cywyddwyr* (poets of the nobility, *c* 1300–1600, who pioneered composition in *cywydd* form), intersecting with pre-existing Welsh traditions of writing love and nature alongside earlier and continuous French-language influences in Wales. In particular, we might note the *cywyddau serch* (love poems) of Dafydd ap Gwilym, which share with the Harley lyrics the invocation of love in a rustic setting and the influence

---

[15] Sims-Williams, 'Itinerant Breton "Conteurs", 111. See also Siân Echard, *Arthurian Narrative in the Latin Tradition* (Cambridge, 1998).

[16] Elisabeth Brewer (ed.), *Sir Gawain and the Green Knight: Sources and Analogues* (Cambridge, 1973), 24–32.

[17] An argument has been made for the possible influence of Welsh poetic features on the *Gawain*-poet on the basis of perceived correspondence between the bob of the English poem and *gair cyrch*, additional syllables added as a tail to a poetic line. See Ordelle G. Hill, *Looking Westward: Poetry, Landscape, and Politics in Sir Gawain and the Green Knight* (Newark, DE, 2009), 30–1. However, as we find it in *Sir Gawain and the Green Knight*, this is more obviously an adaptation from the use of bob and wheel in Latin and Middle English narrative song.

[18] J. R. R. Tolkien and E. V. Gordon (eds), *Sir Gawain and the Green Knight* (Oxford, 1967), 98. 'Logres' is the French form of Geoffrey's 'Loegria', which suggests the *Gawain*-poet's awareness of French Arthurian material, such as the prose *Lancelot*. See Ad Putter and Myra Stokes (eds), *The Works of the Gawain Poet* (London, 2014), 657.

of French popular modes such as the *reverdie*.[19] Dafydd is perhaps best known to scholars of English poetry as a near-contemporary of Chaucer, to whom he presents a familiar standard of comparison. Like Chaucer, Dafydd was one of the most significant poetic innovators of his time: he was one of the first poets to use the formerly colloquial *cywydd* (seven-syllable couplet form) as a vehicle for elite poetry, alongside the formal structures of the *awdl* (long-line unirhyme verse) and *englyn* (short-syllable-count stanzas).[20] Similarly, like Chaucer, Dafydd is customarily recognised as a European poet, innovating in his native vernacular, combining new influences with pre-existing native poetic traditions, original applications, and even pastiche.[21]

Specific affinities have been noted between Dafydd's poetry and the Harley lyrics. For example, we find a particular correspondence in Dafydd's use of the wind as a *llatai* (love messenger) in 'Y Gwynt' ('The Wind'). The *llatai* is conventionally a bird in Welsh love poetry, and although the motif may have arisen independently in both contexts, it is also possible that Dafydd's use of the wind bears the influence of an English lyric such as 'Blow, Northerne Wynd' (Harley lyric no. 14)—although, equally, we may see an engagement with common French source traditions.[22] Yet what the Welsh and English popular lyrics, and related more formal poetic compositions, may owe to each other remains uncertain, and we might even follow Rachel Bromwich in positing underlying affinities between features of French, English, and Welsh popular verse suggestive of multiple, cross-linguistic influences on the sub-literary level, beyond reconstruction.[23] In terms of possible Welsh influences on English popular verse, Bromwich has suggested that the extended descriptions of the natural world as they appear in the Harley lyrics may even 'be a transposition of the craft of *dyfalu* ["comparison"—a developed series of metaphors describing a single person or object], as practiced by Dafydd [ap Gwilym] and his contemporaries.'[24] Yet all remains conjectural, and indeed this is precisely Bromwich's point: possible lines of influence are multiple, and cross-linguistic commonalities are in many respects great even as these are drawn in line with continuing independent traditions.

As with the occurrence of Welsh loan words in the Harley lyrics, if we are to look for evidence of cross-linguistic influence, we find this most obviously in the inclusion of English loan words in Dafydd's poetry. In this respect, we might detect in his work a possible acquaintance with English popular song of a type with the thirteenth-century 'Sumer is i-cumen in' (or similar source content), with its refrain modelled on the cuckoo's song, 'cucu'.[25] Although 'Sumer is i-cumen in' has been associated putatively with Welsh folk songs, a case equally might be made for the later influence of English songs of this type on Welsh poetry.[26] In 'Talu Dyled' ('Paying a Debt'), a *cywydd* to his lover Morfudd, Dafydd

---

[19] Fulton, 'Theory of Celtic Influence', 250–4; Fulton, *Dafydd ap Gwilym,* 180–1, 192.

[20] Stephen Knight, 'Chaucer's British Rival', *Leeds Studies in English,* n.s. 20 (1989), 87–98; Stephen Knight, '"Love's Altar is the Forest Glade": Chaucer in the Light of Dafydd ap Gwilym', *Nottingham Medieval Studies,* 63 (1999), 172–88.

[21] Rachel Bromwich, *Aspects of the Poetry of Dafydd ap Gwilym* (Cardiff, 1974); Fulton, *Dafydd ap Gwilym and the European Context;* Huw M. Edwards, *Dafydd ap Gwilym: Influences and Analogues* (Oxford, 1996).

[22] Fulton, 'Celtic Influence', 250.

[23] Bromwich, *Aspects of the Poetry of Dafydd ap Gwilym,* 89–104.

[24] Bromwich, *Aspects of the Poetry of Dafydd ap Gwilym,* 99.

[25] Brown, *English Lyrics,* xxxix.

[26] Brown, *English Lyrics,* xv. Although Brown's comments here are often interpreted as a suggestion of a Welsh source for the lyric, his point rather seems to relate to commonalities in popular song between England and Wales, as noted by Gerald of Wales. Cf. Edmund Reiss, *The Art of the Middle English Lyric: Essays in Criticism* (Athens, GA, 1972), 9.

compares his single-minded praise of his beloved to the repeated and limited song of the cuckoo. The poem begins with the poet-narrator's contention that as a lover of song (and a lover and a poet), he writes a *cywydd* for Morfudd, and the implication is that, like the cuckoo, the success of his venture collapses, and he sings for his absent lover in a tuneless refrain until he is hoarse. The cuckoo is described through a detailed metaphor, executed in microscopic detail, in line with *dyfalu*:

> Unllais wyf yn lle y safai
> Â'r gog, morwyn gyflog Mai.
> Honno ni feidr o'i hannwyd
> Eithr un llais â'i thoryn llwyd.
> Ni thau y gog â'i chogor,
> Crygu mae rhwng craig a môr.
> Ni chân gywydd, lonydd lw,
> Nac acen onid 'Gwcw!'

> (I have the same voice, where she stood
> As the cuckoo, maidservant of May,
> Who by her nature [has] no metre,
> But one word and her grey mantle.
> The cuckoo is never silent with her prattle,
> She grows hoarse between rock and sea.
> She does not sing cywydd, happy oath,
> Nor any song [or accent] but 'Cuckoo!') (29–36)[27]

Aspects of commonality between Welsh and broader European love conventions complicate easy source analysis: the cuckoo is a common figure in the European love lyric (including as a figure of unrequited or frustrated love), and appears as a *llatai* elsewhere in Dafydd's poetry.[28] Yet particularly notable are the terms in which the frustration of the love missal is here constructed, which are potentially suggestive of English influence on the Welsh. The poem marks the first attested appearance of 'cwcw' in Welsh literature, and, while it might be understood as a common apprehension of the bird's song, it is feasibly an English loan word, of which there are a great number across Dafydd's works, as throughout Welsh poetry written after the Edwardian conquest.[29] Although, as Dafydd Johnston cautions, in an aural context such as medieval Welsh poetry we must be wary regarding assertions of the obvious foreignness of loan words beyond those moments of their obvious clustering; this English loan potentially carries cultural weight associated with the uses of the cuckoo not in Welsh

---

[27] Dafydd ap Gwilym, 'Talu Dyled', in Dafydd Johnston, Huw Meirion Edwards, Dylan Foster Evans, A. Cynfael Lake, Elisa Moras, and Sara Elin Roberts (eds), *Cerddi Dafydd ap Gwilym* (Cardiff, 2010), 400–3. My English translation is based on the volume's modern Welsh. For parallel Modern English translations of a selection of Dafydd's poetry, see Dafydd ap Gwilym.net (Swansea University), http://www.dafyddapgwilym.net/eng/3win.htm.

[28] For a reading of aspects of the cuckoo's presentation in the poem in line with Welsh legendary content, the full extent of which remains obscure to us, see Edwards, *Dafydd ap Gwilym*, 123–5. Conversely, Fulton notes the affinity of the cuckoo's refrain with the repetitions of the *pater noster*, drawn on as a point of comparison earlier in the poem: the *pater noster* is 'pater noster annistaw' ('a noisy pater noster') (19). For discussion of this and the place of the cuckoo in Continental love poetry, see Fulton, *Dafydd ap Gwilym*, 119–21.

[29] 'Cwcw', in *Geiriadur Prifysgol Cymru: A Dictionary of the Welsh Language* (University of Wales, 2020), http://geiriadur.ac.uk/gpc/gpc.html.

124   MEDIEVAL POETRY: 1100–1400

but in English song.[30] Importantly, 'cwkw' appears only once in Dafydd's poem, which is itself a successfully executed *cywydd* without the refrain of the English song. In the essentials of his own poetic practice (unlike the figure of the lover-narrator), Dafydd does not grow hoarse, and we might wonder whether his skill is thrown into relief by comparison to an English precedent understood to be aesthetically inferior.

English in Welsh Verse: Loan Words and Macaronic Verse

While there is little sustained evidence that late-medieval English poets innovated using Welsh poetic forms, during the same period Welsh poets experimented with the full or partial incorporation of English-language content into Welsh poetic systems. We find this experimentation to greater and lesser degrees in poetry of the fourteenth and fifteenth centuries, during the long period in which English gradually displaced French as an administrative language, and eventually a literary one, in the multilingual contexts of the Marcher lordships, and the English-controlled towns in Wales which developed after 1282. In the broader context of commercial trade in the English towns in Wales, we find, with varying degrees of self-consciousness, the incorporation of English loan words and personal names into Welsh poetry, rendered in Welsh orthography.[31] For example, Dafydd ap Gwilym borrows from the language of English officialdom in his description of the cock thrush, a *llatai*, in his love poem of the same name, as a 'iustus' ('justice') (11) and 'ystiwart' ('steward') (12)—terms which might be borrowed from either English or French, and correspond to the types of roles that might have been performed by his *uchelwyr* patrons (members of the Welsh nobility, who occupied significant administrative roles after the settlement of 1282–3).[32] Interestingly, like a member of this class, Dafydd's cock thrush is 'ieithydd ar frig planwydd plas' ('a linguist atop the planted trees of a mansion') (14), and the multilingual *uchelwyr* household provides a component of Dafydd's *dyfalu*.

Less neutrally, we might note Dafydd's use of English personal names in 'Traffern Mewn Tafarn' ('Trouble in a Tavern'), which recounts the travails of a noble poet-narrator who, in his attempt to keep his nocturnal assignation with a barmaid, disturbs three sleeping English guests, who fear the Welsh are robbing them:

> Drisais mewn gwely drewsawr
> Yn trafferth am eu triphac,
> Hicin a Siencin a Siac.
>
> (Three Englishmen in a smelly bed,
> worrying about their three packs,
> Hickin and Jenkin, and Jack) (52–4)[33]

[30] Dafydd Johnston, '"Ceidwaid yr hen iaith?" Beirdd yr Uchelwyr a'r Iaith Saesneg', *Y Traethodydd* (2000), 16–24, at 18. See also Diana Luft, 'Genre and Diction in the Poetry of Dafydd ap Gwilym: The Revelation of Cultural Tension', *Proceedings of the Harvard Celtic Colloquium*, 18/19 (1998/9), 278–97, at 293–4.

[31] Helen Fulton, 'Class and Nation: Defining the English in Late-Medieval Welsh Poetry', in Ruth Kennedy and Simon Meecham-Jones (eds), *Authority and Subjugation in Writings of Medieval Wales* (New York, 2008), 191–212. See further Glyn Roberts, 'Wales and England: Antipathy and Sympathy 1282–1485', *Welsh History Review*, 1 (1960–3), 375–96.

[32] Dafydd ap Gwilym, 'Y Ceiliog Bronfraith', in Johnston et al., *Cerddi Dafydd ap Gwilym*, 202–5. For notice of further Romance loan words associated with weaponry, currency, and law and official administration, see Bromwich, *Aspects of the Poetry of Dafydd ap Gwilym*, 83–5.

[33] Dafydd ap Gwilym, 'Trafferth mewn Tafarn', in Johnston et al., *Cerddi Dafydd ap Gwilym*, 300–5. The English translation is based on the modern Welsh. Discussed in Fulton, 'Class and Nation', 195.

The Welsh reworking of the English names is part of Dafydd's joke: the churlish Englishmen are ridiculously misplaced, not least in terms of their interruption of their noble narrator's amorous design. Differences of language are shot through with differences of class, down to the 'soeg enau' ('beery mouth') (55) with which one of the men whispers his anxieties about Welsh treachery to his companions. The phrase implies a thickness of speech that Stephen Knight has convincingly associated with Dafydd's perception of a lack of English linguistic dexterity, and even the ugliness of the English tongue (an aesthetic judgement we might read in line with his possible distaste for the English popular lyric).[34] Yet by their presence in the poem, the Englishmen's place, and that of their names and language, in a Welsh tavern is nothing if not normalised.

Similarly situated in a context of economic and linguistic exchange is one of the earliest English and Welsh macaronic poems: Tudur Penllyn's dialogue between a Welshman and an English woman (c 1470). The poem appears to have been intended for a bilingual *uchelwyr* audience, very likely in north Wales: the English woman swears by St Asaph, associating her with the Vale of Clwyd, making her Tudur's relatively near neighbour (the poet lived in Caer Gai, in Merionethshire).[35] Although for the greater part of the poem the incomprehension between the pair is mutual, the joke is very much on the woman, and in the final lines of the poem the poet names the Welshman after himself, Tudur—who of course *can* understand English, as the very act of composition demonstrates.[36] The poem's humour rests on Welsh bilingualism and English monolingualism. Indeed, the poem is a display of Tudur's poetic competence across two languages. Just as the English names given in Dafydd ap Gwilym's 'Traffern Mewn Tafarn' are for the most part concordant with the alliterative and stress pattern of the line, the woman's English is given in *cynghanedd*:

> 'Gad i'r llaw dan godi'r llen
> Dy glywed, ddyn deg lawen.'

> *'I am nit Wels, thow Welsman,*
> *for byde the, lete me alone.'*

> ('Let my hand lift up your skirt
> and feel you, fair merry girl.'

> *'I don't speak Welsh, you Welshman,*
> *stop it, leave me alone.')* (9–12)[37]

As we find in macaronic dialogues more widely, much of the two speakers' communication is gestural and relates to acts (such as the lifting of a skirt) familiar to its intended recipient, even if the speaker's language is not. As Patricia A. Malone has noted, the poem is defined by imperfect communication on the level of its prosody. *Cynghanedd* is less fluently executed in the English than the Welsh—a feature which, Malone has argued, may be suggestive of the frustrated communications of the English woman, although we might also read it as

---

[34] Knight, "'Love's Altar is the Forest Glade'", 182.

[35] Patricia A. Malone, "'What saist mon?'": Dialogism and Disdain in Tudur Penllyn's "Conversation between a Welshman and an Englishwoman"', *Studia Celtica*, 46 (2012), 123–36, at 128.

[36] Dafydd Johnston assumes an audience who would 'have derived considerable amusement, and even erotic frisson, from hearing indecent propositions being made to a woman who could not understand a word'. Dafydd Johnston, 'Erotica and Satire in Medieval Welsh Poetry', in Jan M. Ziolkowski (ed.), *Obscenity: Social Control and Artistic Creations in the European Middle Ages* (Leiden, 1998), 60–72, at 72. See also Johnston, 'Ceidwaid yr Hen Iaith', 21–2.

[37] Tudur Penllyn, 'Ymddiddan Rhwyng Cymro a Saesnes', in Dafydd Johnston (ed. and trans.), *Canu Maswedd yr Oesoedd Canol: Medieval Welsh Erotic Poetry* (Pen-y-bont ar Ogwr, 1998), 70–3.

126   MEDIEVAL POETRY: 1100–1400

symptomatic of the limitations of English within Welsh poetic systems, at least as utilised by Tudur.[38]

English in Welsh Verse: An English-Language *Awdl*

Beyond its function as a point of linguistic-social commentary, the incorporation of English in Welsh verse forms was a display of poetic skill. We find one of the most striking examples of this in an English-language *awdl* to the Virgin Mary composed by Ieuan ap Hywel Swrdwal (son of the poet Hywel Swrdwal) at Oxford in 1470, which survives in a large number of later manuscript copies. The poem has been understood as a moment of origin for Welsh writings in English: it is the earliest-known attempt to systematically reproduce *cynghanedd* in English, and as Geraint Evans has observed, it is significant in its address to an audience comprising both Welsh and non-Welsh speakers, although even as it presupposes a cross-linguistic audience the poem also embodies points of cultural and linguistic difference.[39] The Welsh incipit to the poem in the late sixteenth-century London, British Library, MS Additional 14866 details the circumstances of its composition in response to an Englishman who claimed that there was neither metre ('mesur') nor harmony ('cynghanedd') in Welsh:

> Yntau ai attebodd i gwnai ef gerdd o Saesneg ar fesur a chynghanedd Kymraeg fal na fedreur Sais nag yr un oi gyfeillion wneythur moi math yn i hiaith i hunein ac i canodd ef val i canlyn ond am fy mod in scrivennu r llyfr hwn oll ag orthographie Kymbraeg e gaiff hyn o Saesneg ganlyn yn llwybr ni: darllenwch ef val Kymbraeg.

> (He [Ieuan] answered him and said that he would write an English poem in *cynghanedd*, the like of which the Englishman nor any of his friends could not write in his own language, and he sang it as follows, but because I am writing this book in Welsh orthography, this much of English shall follow our path; read it like Welsh.)[40]

The English student has claimed that there is no harmony in Welsh poetry, but of course *cynghanedd* means 'harmony', and is the foundational principle of Welsh strict metre poetry—which Ieuan sets out to demonstrate. I quote the first stanza, which exemplifies Ieuan's poetic practice:

> O michti ladi, owr leding/tw haf
> at hefn owr abeiding:
> yntw ddy ffest eferlasting
> i set a braents ws tw bring.

> (Oh mighty lady, you have our leading
> into heaven, our abiding,
> unto the feast everlasting,
> set a branch [for] us to bring.) (1–4)[41]

---

[38] Malone, '"What saist mon?"', 135–6.

[39] Geraint Evans, 'Tudor London and the Origins of Welsh Writing in English', in Geraint Evans and Helen Fulton (eds), *Cambridge History of Welsh Literature* (Cambridge, 2019), 212–31, at 213–14.

[40] For the incipit, see O. T. Williams, 'Another Welsh Phonetic Copy of the Early English Hymn to the Virgin from a British Museum MS No. 14866', *Anglia*, 32 (1909), 295–300, at 295.

[41] Ieuan ap Hywel Swrdwal, 'Llyma owdyl arall', in Raymond Garlick and Roland Mathias (eds), *Anglo-Welsh Poetry, 1480–1980* (Bridgend, 1984), 45–8 (my translation).

The poem is an ostentatious display of the complexity of Welsh poetry to an English-language audience. The beginning of the Welsh incipit identifies it as 'owdyl arall i dduw ac i fair' ('another *awdl* to God and to Mary'), which it is, and yet is not. The religious allusions were clearly intended to be familiar to Ieuan's Oxford contemporaries. In terms of its Marian content, the poem is decidedly conventional—the lines quoted above conclude with a reference to the tree of Jesse. However, given the cross-linguistic rubric of the activity, this is certainly not just another *awdl*. Ieuan simultaneously dares his English colleagues to attempt such a feat, and implies its impossibility within the confines of English unmediated by Welsh. Indeed, given the use of Welsh orthography in the recording of the poem (positioned in the incipit as an originally oral production), English comprehension of the poem depends not on reading but performance. Certainly, the broader conceit behind the *awdl* suggests awareness of a limited capacity for practical poetic application of the principles of Welsh poetry among writers of English who are not also writers of Welsh.

Conclusion

There is significantly greater evidence for late-medieval English influence on Welsh authors rather than vice versa—although this influence is primarily linguistic rather than on the level of poetics. This is in many respects a product of the colonial situation after 1282–3, which rendered English functionally useful in Wales in a way that Welsh was not in England. Indeed, there would appear to be some truth to the linguistic situation presented in the imagined cultural encounter of Tudur Penllyn: Anglo-Welsh bilingualism was largely monodirectional. While in Wales there is relatively sizeable evidence of engagement with English among Welsh poets and their patrons, among English poets in the March we find only moments of selective cultural reception of Welsh content. Although absence of evidence is not evidence of absence, English acquaintance with Welsh poetry does not appear to have been especially developed. Meanwhile, Welsh poets drew on the English language as a site of subversion, commenting on aesthetic and socio-political difference; and writing across the porous linguistic divide of which macaronic poetry made use, one poet made a clear claim for the beauty of *cynghanedd* to an English audience in an audacious *awdl*, all the while alert to the difficulty of its English application unless mediated by Welsh orthography.

9

Verse Forms

Ad Putter

Anyone interested in poetic form must listen out for patterns generated by repetition of sound, rhythm, and number. Repetitions of sounds give us rhyme and alliteration; repetitions of rhythmical patterns and beats create the metre and pulse of verse; and the repetition of number is the basis for minutiae such as the syllable count and for larger arrangements such as numerological designs. Generalisations about the configuration of these patterns or the degree of regularity that Middle English poets sought to achieve are pointless. In every generation, there existed poets who composed tightly regulated verse and others who did not. So instead of generalising, I aim to illustrate the range and interest of various Middle English verse forms, strict and loose, in a series of close encounters with early and late medieval poets, focusing first on metre, then on rhyme, and finally on alliteration.

Early Middle English Metres: From *Ormulum* to *Horn*

Two contrasting poems, *Ormulum* (*c* 1150–80) and *King Horn* (*c* 1225), show the divergence of metrical practice in early Middle English. The poet of *Ormulum*, who named himself Orm, was a compulsive systematiser. His verse paraphrases of and homilies on Gospel readings are incomplete, but over 10,000 long lines survive, each obeying the same strict constraints. Below is an extract from the poem:

> I þa þatt swelltenn winddweþþ Crist & clennseþþ here his whæte .
> A33 whanne itt cumeþþ to þatt he till hellepine demeþþ .
> Þatt mann þatt unnderr Crisstenndom & unnderr læfe o Criste .
> Wel cwemmde defell wiþþ hiss lif & wiþþ hiss lifess ende.[1]
>
> (Ormulum, 10526–34)

(In those who die, Christ winnows, and always when this happens he cleanses his wheat, condemning to hell-pain that man who under Christendom and under the Christian faith pleased the devil with his life and life's end.)

Our struggles with medieval verse forms begin with the question of *mise en page*. Until the thirteenth century, verse was usually written as continuous prose.[2] This is true for *Ormulum*: only the punctuation in the autograph manuscript (Oxford, Bodleian Library, MS Junius 1) marks the text graphically as poetry. By a convention that continued into the

---

[1] Orm, *Ormulum*, in Robert Holt and R. M. White (eds), *The Ormulum*, 2 vols. (Oxford, 1878), with minor corrections and adjustments to lay-out, punctuation, and abbreviation marks. The line references are based on Holt's edition, which counts each half-line as a single verse.

[2] See M. B. Parkes, *Pause and Effect: An Introduction to the History of Punctuation in the West* (Berkeley, CA, 1993), 97–114.

Ad Putter, *Verse Forms*. In: *The Oxford History of Poetry in English*. Edited by Helen Cooper and Robert R. Edwards, Oxford University Press. © Ad Putter (2023). DOI: 10.1093/oso/9780198827429.003.0009

later Middle Ages,[3] Orm tends to use the *punctus elevatus* (a kind of inverted semi-colon used for a medial pause) or the punctus to indicate the end of the a-verse (the first half-line). The *punctus* is also commonly used to mark the end of the b-verse. Variations in this pattern are also found.[4] In the standard edition, a-verses and b-verses are set out (and numbered) as separate verses. The presentation adopted here probably represents Orm's metrical intentions more faithfully.

The peculiarities of Orm's quasi-phonetic spelling system need not detain us here, except insofar as they affect the syllable count. Final -e in *Ormulum* should be pronounced if (and only if) present in spelling (e.g., hellëpinë), except in the usual eliding contexts (before vowels and unstressed *h-*, as in 'herę his'). Orm was as particular about the syllable count as he was about spelling. Every line has exactly fifteen syllables. The rhythm is overwhelmingly iambic, with four iambic feet in the a-verse and three in the b-verse. Finally, while the syllable before the caesura is always stressed, the one at line end is always unstressed. Whether that is how Orm read his final syllables is another matter. 'Good King Wenceslas looked out / on the feast of Stephen' scans, rather like the lines of *Ormulum*, as a four-beat verse followed by a three-beat one, but anyone who has sung it knows that they are in duple rhythm of equal duration,[5] something singers manage by making both syllables of 'Ste-phen' twice as long as the preceding ones in the b-verse. The rhythm of Orm can be equalised in the same way; and there is some linguistic evidence that Orm gave compensatory weight to his line endings.[6]

The proper term for Orm's metre is the iambic septenary. This had a long pre-history and a long future after Orm. In classical Latin poetry, which was quantitative (based not on word stress but on vowel duration), the iambic septenary was the *versus comicus* of the stage.[7] When medieval Latin and French poets reanalysed the iambic septenary on accentual principles, the resulting form is the one we see in *Ormulum*.[8] The Anglo-Norman song *Venez Dames, Venez Avant* (*c* 1200), in rhymed *aaaa* stanzas, is in this metre:

> La mere fet sun Fiz suant soule la dreite veie.
> Alum, alum, alum avant: Amurs i funt la voie!
> Sun duz Fiz veit en croiz morir, a grant dolur, sanz joye.
> Alum en croyz od Deu morir: Amurs i funt la voie![9] (17–24)

(The mother goes following her Son, on the one true path. Let's go, let's go, let's go ahead: Love leads the way. Her sweet son goes to die on the cross, in deep sorrow, bereft of joy: let's go to the cross with God to die: Love leads the way.)

---

[3] Elizabeth Solopova, 'Layout, Punctuation, and Stanza Patterns in the English Verse', in Susanna Fein (ed.), *Studies in the Harley Manuscript: The Scribes, Contents, and Social Contexts of British Library MS Harley 2253* (Kalamazoo, MI, 2000), 377–89.

[4] The pattern (by no means systematic) can be seen in plate 1 (reproducing folio 24[r]) in R. D. Fulk, *An Introduction to Middle English* (Toronto, 2012), 152. See the digital facsimile of this passage (folio 80[r]) at https://digital.bodleian.ox.ac.uk/objects/90a06f70-880a-4b5b-bd30-798710afff11/surfaces/73738bf9-155d-43dc-81b8-98c58c5309f7/. A more precise description of Orm's metrical pointing must await the forthcoming EETS edition of *The Ormulum* by Nils-Lennart Johannesson and Andrew Cooper, which will reproduce Orm's punctuation.

[5] See Fulk, *Introduction*, 131.

[6] As Fulk noticed, the penultimate syllable of *Ormulum* is always heavy: 'Consonant Doubling and Open Syllable Lengthening in the *Ormulum*', *Anglia*, 114 (1996), 481–513.

[7] Jacqueline Dangel (ed.), *Le poète architecte: arts métriques et art poétique latins* (Louvain, 2001), 200.

[8] See Elizabeth Solopova, 'The Metre of the *Ormulum*', in M. J. Toswell and E. M. Tyler (eds), *Studies in English Language and Literature: 'Doubt Wisely'—Papers in Honour of E. G. Stanley* (London, 1996), 423–39.

[9] In David L. Jeffrey and Brian J. Levy (eds), *The Anglo-Norman Lyric: An Anthology* (Toronto, 1990), 83–9. I have adjusted the layout and punctuation and provided my own translation.

130   MEDIEVAL POETRY: 1100–1400

In English, rhymed iambic septenaries are used in *Poema Morale* (*c* 1170), where the syllable count is much laxer: a-verses can be a syllable shorter (by omission of the first off-beat) or longer (by addition of a final unstressed syllable), and the opening unstressed syllable of the b-verse can also be suppressed.[10] The same flexibility typifies later English poems in septenaries, such as the saints' lives of the *South English Legendary* and the passion narrative of *Cursor Mundi*, where the septenaries are grouped into *aaaa* stanzas, as in *Venez Dames*.

When septenaries rhyme, we see more easily how they provide a blueprint for the ballad stanza. The earliest song that shows all the hallmarks of the ballad—the alternation between four and three beats, the repetitions, the abrupt movement across scenes and into dialogue, and the dramatic focus on family relations—is *Judas* (*c* 1300),[11] which recasts the betrayal committed by Judas as the tragic consequence of the betrayal he himself suffers at the hands of his wicked sister:

> 'Judas, þou most to Jurselem, our mete for to bugge*;   *to buy our food*
> Þritti platen of seluer þou bere upo þi rugge*.   *back*
> 'Þou comest fer i þe brode stret, fer i þe brode strete,
> Summe of þine cunesmen* þer þou meist imete*.'[12]   *kinsmen; may meet* (3–6)

What mattered to this poet was the number of beats, not syllables.

Orm is thus a forerunner of the English septenary tradition. Being the first known English poet to use septenaries, he counted syllables as a French or Latin poet might, and, as in the Anglo-Norman *Venez Dames*, the alternation between masculine and feminine endings is systematic. His pursuit of regularity has not pleased modern readers, who complain about the monotony of his metre,[13] but two things should be said in his defence. First, he shows admirable dexterity in overcoming his self-imposed constrains. *Ormulum* is a treasure trove of syllabic 'minimal pairs', synonyms or variants of the same word with similar meanings but different syllable counts. Thus Orm had two forms, monosyllabic *her* and disyllabic *here*, for the adverb 'here'; if he needed the monosyllable, he switched to *her* or made sure that his normal *here* was followed by a word beginning with a vowel so that -e would elide. Similarly, he varied between 'sannt' and 'sannte', as in 'Sannte Peter' (16,066) but 'Sannt Johan' (19,977) (both nominative). Both spellings make linguistic sense, the former reflecting Old French *seint* and the latter probably reflecting Latin *sanctus*.[14] His choices between different -*ly* suffixes (-*liȝ* and -*like* in *Ormulum*), between adverbial *upp* and *uppe*, *twa* or *tweȝen* ('two'), and so on,[15] were likewise guided by metre. This resourcefulness, combined with the reliability of his spelling, make Orm the ideal guide to the lexical stratagems available to other Middle English poets who cared about syllable count. The poets of the Alliterative

---

[10] See Donka Minkova, 'Prosody-Meter Correspondences in Old English and *Poema Morale*', in Leonard Neidorf, Rafael J. Pascual, and Thomas A. Shippey (eds), *Essays in Old English Philology: Studies in Honour of R. D. Fulk* (Cambridge, 2016), 122–43.

[11] J. C. Hirsh, 'The Earliest Known English Ballad: A New Reading of *Judas*', *Modern Language Review*, 103 (2008), 931–9.

[12] In Kenneth Sisam (ed.), *Fourteenth-Century Verse and Prose* (Oxford, 1990), 168–9.

[13] A more sympathetic reading (with an account of earlier criticism) is given by Christopher Cannon, *The Grounds of English Literature* (Oxford, 2004), 82–110.

[14] E. Talbot Donaldson, 'Middle English *seint*, *seinte*', *Studia Neophilologica*, 21 (1948), 222–30.

[15] For examples of other purposeful alternations, see R. W. Burchfield, 'The Language and Orthography of the Ormulum MS', *Transactions of the Philological Society*, 55 (1956), 56–97; and Richard Dance, '*Ealde Æ, Niwe Laȝe*: Two Words for "Law" in the Twelfth Century', *New Medieval Literatures*, 13 (2011), 149–82. Some instances are inadvertently included in a list of variants which Cannon claims 'Orm never even noticed': see Cannon, *Grounds*, 106.

Revival, who also worried about syllables, made use of many of the same 'minimal pairs',[16] as did Chaucer, who switched between *heer* and *here*, *-ly* and *-lyche*, and *seint* and *seinte* in Orm-like fashion.[17] The second point in Orm's defence is that his syllabic regularity was not pointless box-ticking. Its rationale is that, without end-rhyme, the differences in syllabic structure—eight syllables in the a-verse (masculine), seven in the b-verse (feminine)—are essential to maintaining the asymmetry between the half-lines. This asymmetry matters because it allows listeners to perceive the half-lines as constituent parts of a larger unit.

Noticing the care that Orm took in alternating masculine and feminine endings can awaken us to the prosody of other Middle English poems which alternate systematically between stressed and unstressed line endings. The loss of final -e has made this harder to hear, but we can rediscover it by listening like Orm. The Harley lyric 'I syke when I singe' (*c* 1300) shows the same alternation. Below is the first stanza, marked up with diereses to show pronounced final vowels and with accents to show beats:

I sýkë* whén Y síngë	*sigh*
For sórewë thát Y sé,	
Whén Y, wíth wypíngë,	
Bihólde upón the tré	
Ant sé Jesú the suétë*:	*sweet*
Is hértë blód forlétë*	*losing his heart's blood*
Fór the lóve of mé;	
Ys* wóundes wáxen wétë;	*His*
Thei wépen, stílle ant métë*.	*fittingly*
Maríë, réweth thé*.[18]	*it grieves you*

The three-beat lines, in alternating rhythm, are arranged in six stanzas rhyming *ababc-cbccb*. G. L. Brook in his discussion of the metre of the Harley lyrics commented on the 'marked preponderance of feminine endings' in three-stress lines,[19] but the music of this lyric depends on the counterpoint provided by the masculine lines (indented). The pattern is consistent throughout the poem.

The regularity of 'I syke when I singe' is no doubt related to the fact that its metre was designed to fit a specific melody. Unfortunately, the music of this and other Harley lyrics was not recorded, but the few Middle English poems that do survive with music remind us that the performance context of medieval poetry is crucial to an appreciation of its metre. Trochaic verse is a case in point. The received wisdom is that there was no such thing in English poetry until the Renaissance,[20] but since many medieval Latin hymns are in trochaic metre,[21] medieval English ears must have been attuned to its falling rhythms,

---

[16] See Ad Putter, Judith Jefferson, and Myra Stokes, *Studies in the Metre of Alliterative Verse* (Oxford, 2007), especially 35–48.

[17] Josef Bihl, *Die Wirkungen des Rhythmus in der Sprache von Chaucer und Gower* (Heidelberg, 1916) and, on the specific case of 'seint', Eric Weiskott, '"Seinte Loy": A Metrical Non-Problem in Chaucer's *General Prologue*', *Notes and Queries*, 63 (2019), 361–3, missing the precedent in Orm.

[18] In G. L. Brook (ed.), *The Harley Lyrics* (Manchester, 1956), 59–60. It should be noted that in the Harley manuscript the first four lines are set out as two long lines. See Solopova, 'Layout', 385; and Eric Stanley, 'What Six Unalike Lyrics in British Library MS Harley 2253 Have Alike in Manuscript Layout', in Simon Horobin and Linne R. Mooney (eds), *Middle English Texts in Transition: A Festschrift Dedicated to Toshiyuki Takamiya on His 70th Birthday* (Cambridge, 2014), 125–33.

[19] Brook (ed.), *Harley Lyrics*, 18.

[20] See, for example, Jakob Schipper, *A History of English Versification* (New York, 1971), 242.

[21] See Dag Norberg, *An Introduction to the Study of Medieval Latin Versification* (Washington, DC, 2004), 121–2.

132 MEDIEVAL POETRY: 1100–1400

and competent poets had no difficulty transposing these rhythms into the vernacular. As Susanna Fein points out in her chapter on secular lyrics (see Chapter 18), the famous round 'Sumer is icumen in', which survives with music in an early-thirteenth-century manuscript from Reading Abbey (now British Library, MS Harley 978), is in trochaic metre. The Latin song on which it is based opens 'Pérspicé Christícolá / qué dignácíó' ('Behold, worshipper of Christ, what graciousness'). The Middle English poet changed mood and sense completely, but stuck to the beat exactly: 'Súmer ís icúmen ín / lhúde síng cucú'.[22] A short lyric from thirteenth-century Cheshire, rhyming *abab*, begins 'Fáste ifúndë, fér on fóldë, Fródë-frýth is féirë fré' ('Firmly established, and stretching wide, Frode's forest is splendidly lush') and continues as before, in perfect trochaic tetrameter with alliteration on every stressed syllable.[23]

The metrical regularity of Orm and 'Faste ifunde, fer on folde' illustrates one end of the range of rhythmical possibilities in early Middle English verse. At the other end stands *King Horn*, which has no syllabic regularity to speak of. A few lines from the poem will illustrate its flexibility:

> Hit was vpon a someres day,
> Also ich ʒou telle may,
> Murri þe gode king,
> Rod vpon his pleing*   *for his amusement*
> Bi þe se side,
> Ase he was woned* ride.   *wont to*
> With him riden two—
> Al to fewe were hi þo*![24]   *they at that time (29–36)*

The syllable count in this passage ranges from eight (line 29) to five (line 33). Scanning the entire poem, we can expand the range further. Marina Tarliskaja calculated that just under 3 per cent of lines have four syllables and 1 per cent has nine.[25] Such variation makes it difficult to scan the poem for regular metre. Walter French tried and concluded that *Horn* was composed in iambic trimeter.[26] However, while some lines can certainly be scanned as such ('Ase hé was wóned ríde'), others cannot, and it is implausible to dismiss all these as scribal. A quarter of all lines have only five syllables and two beats. In our extract, 'Bi þe sé síde' is a case in point. The reading is confirmed by all three manuscripts—Cambridge, University Library, MS Gg. 4. 27 (2), *c* 1260; Oxford, Bodleian Library, MS Laud Misc. 108, *c* 1300; London, British Library, MS Harley 2253, *c* 1340—and by repetitions of the formula ('Bi þe se side', 137, 'Fram þe se side', 209), where again the manuscripts are in complete agreement. In short, the authenticity of these lines is beyond question.[27]

What *is* open to question is the layout of these lines. In Laud Misc. 108, as in most modern editions, the short lines are set out as separate lines, with end-rhyme. However, in

---

[22] Both the Latin and the Middle English poem are cited from the edition (with transcription of the music) by Helen Deeming (ed.), *Songs in British Sources, c. 1150–1300*, Musica Britannica 45 (London, 2013), 5a and 85b. The interpretation given here, that the English is a *contrafactum* based on the Latin, follows that of E. J. Dobson and F. Ll. Harrison (eds), *Medieval English Songs* (London, 1979), 143–4.

[23] Oliver Pickering, 'Newly Discovered Secular Lyrics from Late Thirteenth-Century Cheshire', *Review of English Studies*, 43 (1992), 160–79 at 164. The interpretation of 'Frode's forest' as a toponym is Pickering's.

[24] *King Horn*, ed. Rosamund Allen (New York, 1984).

[25] See Marina Tarlinskaja, *English Verse: Theory and History* (The Hague, 1976), 256.

[26] Walter French, *Essays on King Horn* (Ithaca, NY, 1940), 51.

[27] See the parallel-text edition of all three manuscript versions by Joseph Hall (ed.), *King Horn: A Middle-English Romance* (Oxford, 1901).

Harley 2253 each short line is set out as a hemistich of a long line. And while the scribe of the earliest manuscript, Cambridge Gg. 4. 27, writes them out as short lines, he so frequently lapses into the long-line arrangement (e.g., lines 33–4, 37–8, 39–40) that he must have been working from an exemplar in long lines. The long-line layout encourages a different interpretation of the metre, proposed by Jakob Schipper, who argued that *Horn*'s metre is a descendant of the Germanic alliterative strong-stress line. This metre was heteromorphic rather than homomorphic; that is, it is based not on the recurrence of the same rhythmical scheme but on the repetition of four chief beats, two in each half-line, surrounded by shifting patterns of unstressed syllables.[28] The scansion, then, is as follows:

> Hit was vpon a sómeres dáy, also ich you télle máy,
> Múrri, þe gode Kíng, ród vpon his pleíng
> Bi þe sé síde, ase he was wóned ríde.

The obvious difference between *Horn* and Old English metre is that half-lines are linked by rhyme rather than alliteration, though it is worth noting that alliteration is in fact frequently used in *Horn*. For example:

> Þo gunne þe húndes góne aȝeines Hórn al-óne   *Then the dogs all went*
>   *towards Horn* (617–18)
> He slóȝ* þer on háste on húndred bi þe láste*   *killed; at least* (621–2)

The wide variation in the syllable count in *Horn* is the symptom of a metre that hinges on the regularity of beats rather than the regular alternation of stressed and unstressed syllables.

Later Medieval Metres: Gower, Chaucer, and Beyond

Where *Ormulum* epitomises syllabic precision for the earlier period, John Gower and to a lesser extent Geoffrey Chaucer do so for the later period. By the fourteenth century, four-beat couplets in alternating rhythm had become established as the main medium for story and history. Unlike the syllabically regular French octosyllable, the English four-beat couplet before Chaucer and Gower was usually a rough and ready form, with frequent double off-beats, clashing stresses, and headless lines. When Gower turned his hand to English poetry (*c* 1386), however, he smoothed the metre and counted syllables. His earlier syllable-counted compositions in Latin and French, including the long *Mirour de l'Omme* in octosyllables, had shaped his habits.

The template of Gower's short line is x/x/x/x/(x), where x represents an off-beat, / a beat, and (x) an optional final off-beat. Headless lines (/x/x/x/(x)) are outlawed, and trochaic inversion (resulting in /xx/ rather than x/x/, with a double off-beat) is rare. This regularity may look like a recipe for metronomic tedium, but this is not fair to Gower. Metrical stress and linguistic stress are not the same thing, and the corridor of uncertainty between the two gives Gower's regular metre its flexibility. Lines where linguistic and metrical stress coincide (e.g., 'A newe forme and leve hir olde', 1.2692) are normative, but this norm permits Gower to coax regular metre out of lines where the two are at odds, as in

> And foundeden the grete Rome   (5.904)
> For in good feith this wolde I rede*   *advise* (1.78)

---

[28] Schipper, *History of English Versification*, 83.

134 MEDIEVAL POETRY: 1100–1400

Chaucer was less strict than Gower, but even in his rougher earlier work, written in the four-beat couplet which he later abandoned for the pentameter, he was a great regulariser. A comparison of the syllable counts of Chaucer's *Book of the Duchess* with those of the earlier *Floris and Blanchefleur* shows this very clearly. Whereas *The Book of the Duchess* has eight syllables in 84 per cent of the lines, and a small minority of lines with seven (11 per cent) and nine (5 per cent), *Floris* has eight syllables in just 40 per cent of the lines, with the remaining 60 per cent ranging from five syllables to twelve.[29] Thus only Chaucer can be said to have aimed for octosyllables, with a little overspill on either side. The seven-syllable line is the headless line (/x/x/x/) which Gower shunned. Lines of ten syllables or more in *Floris* point to gratuitous double off-beats (not ones caused by trochaic inversion), which Chaucer avoided.

Chaucer's reading in and translations from French poetry in decasyllables and Italian poetry in hendecasyllables led him to the iambic pentameter.[30] In the longer format, too, he wrote headless lines, but many fewer (under 2 per cent).[31] He thus became stricter about the syllable count in the longer line—though more relaxed with regard to strict alternating rhythm. The four-beat line has a more insistent dipodic rhythm than the pentameter,[32] and allowed Chaucer little scope for trochaic inversion. It was the pentameter that freed Chaucer to make ample use of it, and in so doing to absorb into his metre some of the tricks of natural prosody.

An analysis of Chaucer's deviations from the metrical norm of the iambic pentameter shows his sensitivity to living speech. Inversion of the first foot is around four times more common in Chaucer's long line than in his tetrameter, but it remains, at 8 per cent, the exception rather than the rule. This makes it all the more noticeable when inversion does occur in that position: for instance, to emphasise imperative verbs.[33] Below are some examples from the dialogue between Pandarus and Criseyde in *Troilus and Criseyde*:

> *Cache* it anon, lest aventure slake (2.291)

> *Tel* me, for I the bet me shal purveye (2.504)

Mid-line, trochaic inversion inevitably results in clashing stress and is therefore much rarer, but where Chaucer uses it one notices the same pattern:

> And with some frendly lok *gladeth* me, swete (1.538)
> ... and when ye may goodly

> Your tyme se, *taketh* of hem youre leeve (2.1720–1)

In spoken English we give prominence to commands by using a higher pitch, and in writing present-day authors can indicate this by using an exclamation mark or italics. Chaucer had neither option, but creates the illusion of natural-sounding speech by deviating from metrical norms.

Although Chaucer's metre was freer than Gower's, most poets who followed in his footsteps make him look strict. The so-called 'broken-backed line', x/x/x//x/(x), is so rare in

---

[29] Tarlinskaja, *English Verse*, 253.

[30] See Martin J. Duffell, '"The craft so long to lerne": Chaucer's Invention of the Iambic Pentameter', *Chaucer Review*, 39 (2000), 269–88; and also his Chaucer's *Verse Art in Its European Context* (Tempe, AZ, 2018), 135–55.

[31] See Ad Putter, 'In Appreciation of Metrical Abnormality: Headless Lines and Initial Inversion in Chaucer', *Critical Survey*, 29 (2017), 65–85.

[32] See Derek Attridge, *The Rhythms of English Poetry* (London, 1982), 211.

[33] For this and other uses, see Putter, 'In Appreciation of Metrical Abnormality'.

Chaucer that its authenticity seems doubtful;[34] but Chaucer's scribes produced them, and John Lydgate did not baulk at writing them, sometimes to dramatic effect.[35] At the extreme end of syllabic irregularity is Lydgate's contemporary John Metham, whose romance *Amoryus and Cleopes* superficially belongs in the same formal tradition as Chaucer's *Troilus*, being mostly written in the rhyme royal stanza (rhyming *ababbcc*) that Chaucer pioneered for narrative purposes. Rhyme royal had earlier been a lyric stanza form, closely associated with lovers' complaints.[36] But while Metham was clearly capable of writing regular iambic pentameter, this was only one of many metrical possibilities: he also wrote verses with four, six, and seven beats. With his cornucopia of metrical possibilities, Metham sought to push the boundaries of accepted taste,[37] and recognised that it was Chaucer who had defined these boundaries for later generations.

Rhyme in Middle English Verse

Both in early and late Middle English poetry, there was no uniform standard of syllabic regularity. The same was true for rhyme, which was used for every conceivable purpose, including medical treatises and tips for laundresses on stain-removal.[38] So foundational was rhyme for writings of any kind that one might have expected scholarship to have come to grips with it, but it is not so. In Old English, rhyme was ornamental rather than structural. For instance, for the eighth-century poet Cynewulf alliteration was a condition of metricality: it links all of his half-lines. Rhyme he resorted to only in patches, as in the following rhapsodic lines from *Elene*, which thank God for the gift of poetry:

> Ic wæs weorcum fah,
> synnum asæled, sorgum gewæled,
> bitrum gebunden, bisgum beþrungen,
> ær me lare onlag þurh leohtne had
> gamelum to geoce, gife unscynd
> mægencyning amæt ond on gemynd begeat,
> torht ontynde, tidum gerymde,

---

[34] In the first 500 lines of the Riverside Chaucer edition of *Troilus and Criseyde*, based on Cambridge, Corpus Christi College, MS 61, I find only one broken-backed line: 'Ne semed it that she of hym roughte' (I.496). The editor, Stephen Barney, admits such lines as regular, and defends line I.496 in *Studies in Troilus: Chaucer's Text, Meter, and Diction* (East Lansing, MI, 1993): 'It might be argued that lingering stress is thrown expressively on "she"' (61). More sense can be made of the variant manuscript reading ('as that' for 'as').

[35] See Maura Nolan, 'Performing Lydgate's Broken-Backed Metre', in Susan F. Yager and Elise E. Morse-Gagné (eds), *Interpretation and Performance: Essays for Alan Gaylord* (Provo, UT, 2013), 141–59.

[36] Chaucer himself used it in this context in his *Complaint unto Pity*, and would have encountered it in French *ballades*, where this stanza form was well established. See Helen Louise Cohen, *The Ballade* (New York, 1915), 31, 60, 66, 215. On the use of the stanza in Middle English literature more generally, see Martin Stevens, 'The Rhyme Royal Stanza in Early English Literature', *PMLA*, 94 (1979), 62–76 and Elizabeth Robertson, 'Rhyme Royal and Romance', in Ad Putter and Judith A. Jefferson (eds), *The Transmission of Medieval Romance: Metres, Manuscripts and Early Prints* (Cambridge, 2018), 50–68.

[37] Nicolas Myklebust, 'The Problem of John Metham's Prosody', in Putter and Jefferson (eds), *Transmission of Medieval Romance*, 149–69.

[38] I have in mind Lydgate's *Tretise for Lauandres*, in Henry N. MacCracken (ed.), *John Lydgate: The Minor Poems, Vol. II—Secular Poems*, EETS o.s. 192 (Oxford, 1934), 723. Maura Nolan's attempt to find hidden meanings in it ('Lydgate's Worst Poem', in Lisa H. Cooper and Andrew Denny-Brown [eds], *Lydgate Matters: Poetry and Material Culture in the Fifteenth Century* [New York, 2013], 71–87) succeeds only in revealing the difference between medieval and modern conceptions of what poetry was for.

136 MEDIEVAL POETRY: 1100–1400

> bancofan onband,   breostlocan onwand
> leoðucræft onleac.   Þæs ic lustum breac ...[39] (1242–50)

(I was soiled by my deeds, shackled by my sins, harassed by cares, and bound and oppressed by bitter worries before the mighty King granted me knowledge in lucid form as solace to an old man, meted out his flawless grace and instilled it in my mind, revealed its radiance, at times augmented it, unshackled my body, laid open the heart—and unlocked the art of poesy, which I have used joyously ...)[40]

In quite a few lines the rhymes are perfect (*asæled: gewæled; onband: onwand; onleac: breac*), but sometimes we are dealing with 'slant rhyme', when the consonant rhymes while the vowel does not (*amæt: begeat*), and more frequently the vowels are identical but not the consonants (*gebunden: beþrungen; ontynde: gerymde*).

Eric Stanley called these rhymes 'assonances' and argued that such loose rhyming became the norm in Middle English: 'To the extent to which early Middle English rhyming is based on Old English practice, early Middle English poets too need not have striven to provide true rhymes only, and modern philologists have little reason to look for purity in rhyming'.[41] This is true up to a point, but Anglo-Saxon poetry was not necessarily the model for early Middle English poets. They were also influenced by verse in other languages they knew, particularly Latin and French, where traditions of perfect (and imperfect) rhyme were well established.[42] Anyone looking for early Middle English poems that rhyme perfectly will therefore find plenty of them. *Poema Morale* (*c* 1170) is one of the earliest Middle English rhyming poems, surviving in seven manuscript witnesses and much quoted and admired by other writers.[43] All its septenaries rhyme perfectly, usually in single couplets, but occasionally across four lines and even six (see lines 75–80). Of course, one can find instances where rhyme breaks down in individual manuscripts, but comparison with other manuscripts invariably shows such cases to be scribal.[44]

A wittily exact rhymester is the anonymous poet of *Dame Sirith*, from the last quarter of the thirteenth century. The poem mixes dialogue with narrative and employs a variety of verse forms. The default mode is a tail-rhyme stanza rhyming *aabccb*, as in the following stanza, which also offers us in its placenames a clue to the poet's original East Midland dialect:

> 'ȝurstenday Ich herde saie,
> As ich wende bi þe waie,
>   Of oure sire:
> Me tolde* þat he was gon   *They said*
> To þe feire of Botolfston*   *fair of Boston*
>   In Lincolneshire'.[45] (73–8)

---

[39] In Albert S. Cook (ed.), *The Old English Elene, Phoenix and Physiologus* (London, 1919), 3–46.

[40] The translation is by S. A. J. Bradley (trans.), *Anglo-Saxon Poetry* (London, 1982), 195.

[41] Eric Stanley, 'Rhymes in English Medieval Verse: From Old English to Middle English', in Edward Donald Kennedy, Ronald Waldron, and Joseph S. Wittig (eds), *Medieval English Studies Presented to George Kane* (Cambridge, 1988), 19–54.

[42] See Norberg, *Introduction*, ch. 3; and John Vising, 'Anglo-Norman Versification', in his *Anglo-Norman Language and Literature* (London, 1923), 79–88.

[43] Betty Hill, 'The Twelfth-Century *Conduct of Life*, Formerly the *Poema Morale* or *A Moral Ode*', *Leeds Studies in English*, n.s. 9 (1977), 97–144; and Claudio Cataldi, 'A Reassessment of *Poema Morale* and Its Influence on *Penitence for a Wasted Life*', in Letizia Vezzosi (ed.), *Current Issues in Medieval England* (Berlin, 2021), 15-32.

[44] The apparatus in the critical edition by Hans Marcus (ed.), *Das Frühmittelenglische Poema Morale* (Leipzig, 1934) records all substantive variation, including rhymes evidently corrupted by scribes (e.g., lines 8 and 41).

[45] In J. A. W. Bennett and G. V. Smithers (eds), *Early Middle English Verse and Prose* (Oxford, 1968).

Shifts between speakers, and between direct and indirect speech, are often accompanied (and signalled) by changes of verse form, from tail-rhyme to four-beat couplets or from one variety of tail-rhyme (with a two-beat tail) to another (with a three-beat tail).[46] The poet probably drew inspiration from semi-dramatic poems in French and Anglo-Norman, such as *Piramus et Tisbé*, which similarly mixes couplets with tail-rhyme stanzas (used for the lovers' laments).[47]

The single surviving manuscript of the poem, Oxford, Bodleian, Digby 86, was copied in Worcestershire,[48] and unfortunately some of the original rhymes were lost in translation. A standard feature of the scribe's West Midland dialect was the rounding of *a* before nasals, and because he imposed his own dialect on the original, the mono-rhymed tirade beginning at line 195 now appears as:

'Louerd*, for his suete nome*,	*Lord; sweet name*
Lete þe þerfore hauen no schome*.	*Shame*
Þou seruest affter Godes grome*	*deserve God's anger*
Wen þou seist on me silk* blame.	*Such*
For ich am old, and sek, and lame.	
Seknesse haueþ maked me ful tame.' (195–200)	

What the poet wrote was six lines rhyming on the same sound (*name: schame: grame: blame: lame: tame*). As we have seen in *Poema Morale*, poets writing in couplets could swell end-rhyme by keeping the same rhyme going in multiple couplets.[49]

The poet carefully guarded the integrity of the rhyme scheme of the tail-rhyme stanzas, *aabccb*, though it sometimes depends on fine distinctions involving final -*e*. The tail-rhyme stanza at 433, for instance, rhymes *Noen* (none): *iboen* (bound): *saie: fai* (faith): *awai: plaie*. Here the *cc-* rhymes are almost, but not quite, identical with the *b*-rhymes. Such finer points mattered to the poet. Even more playful is the ninth stanza:

Þou mait saien al þine wille,	
And I schal herknen and sitten stille	
Þat þou haue told.	
And if þat þou me tellest skil*,	*what is reasonable*
I shal don after þi wil –	
Þat be þou bold*.	*be sure of that* (49–54)

The similarity between the a-rhymes (*wille: stille*) and the c-rhymes (*skil: wil*) almost throws the rhyme scheme into confusion, but the poet's 'skill' comes to the rescue. If he had repeated the word 'will' in arbitrarily different spellings, this would be lame auto-rhyme, but early English had two distinct words for 'will', one with final vowel (< OE *willa*), and one without (< OE *gewill*), and the poet made clever use of the doublet.

Unfortunately, the work of careful poets is often encountered in copies by careless scribes. The second stanza in the manuscript reads:

---

[46] On the varieties of tail-rhyme in Middle English, see Rhiannon Purdie, *Anglicising Romance: Tail-Rhyme and Genre in Medieval English Literature* (Cambridge, 2008), with discussion of *Dame Sirith* at 61–3.

[47] See Bennett and Smithers (eds), *Early Middle English Verse and Prose*, 78–9 and Purdie, *Anglicising Romance*, 24.

[48] On the manuscript and its poetry, see Susanna Fein (ed.), *Interpreting MS Digby 86: A Trilingual Book from Thirteenth-Century Worcestershire* (Cambridge, 2019).

[49] See also *Dame Sirith*, lines 207–12.

138   MEDIEVAL POETRY: 1100–1400

> To louien he begon
> On wedded wimmon;
> > Þereof he heued* wrong!   *had*
> His herte hire wes al on
> Þat reste neuede he non* –   *he had no rest*
> > Þe loue wes so strong. (7–12)

J. A. W. Bennett and G. V. Smithers gloss 'on' (line 9) as the preposition 'on' ('His heart was set on hir'). The stanza then looks like a different tail-rhyme form with an anomalous rhyme scheme (*aabaab*). But this is an illusion, created in part by the West Midland scribe who has struck again and imposed his rounded vowels on the poet's *began* and *wimman*. Discriminating between the dialects of the poet and scribe and paying attention to the poet's regular tail-rhyme scheme (*aabccb*) can help us to put this right, and can also help us to disambiguate the meaning of 'His herte hire wes al on', which must mean 'His heart was hers alone'. Middle English *ōn* ('one') and *nōn* (none) rhyme; the preposition *on* and *nōn* do not.

The tradition of 'impure' rhyming that Stanley regarded as normative led a parallel existence alongside the strict rhyming of poems such as *Poema Morale* and *Dame Sirith*. The most interesting thing about this parallel tradition is that its rhymes are not as loose as they may appear. We have got used to calling them 'assonances', but the term does not do them justice. Assonance is vowel rhyme. It was a feature of the early Continental and Anglo-Norman *chansons de geste*, in which lines of verse, typically decasyllables or alexandrines, ended with the same vowel sound, regardless of the final consonant.[50] In linguistic terms, what mattered in assonating *chansons de geste* was the nucleus of the rhyming syllable, not the coda. The 'impure rhymes' of Middle English poetry work differently. As most of the so-called 'assonances' in the passage from Cynewulf's *Elene* show—*gebunden: beþrungen*; *ontynde: gerymde*—the final consonants usually do participate in the rhyme on the basis of partial phonological overlap. In *gebunden: beþrungen*, the rhyme involves a nasal followed by a voiced plosive (<ng> was pronounced [ŋg] in Old and Middle English); and in *ontynde: gerymde* he rhymes nasals.

An examination of early Middle English poems with 'impure' rhymes confirms this pattern. A representative example is the *Passion of Our Lord*, extant in Oxford, Jesus College, MS 29(2), which also contains a copy of *Poema Morale* and *The Owl and the Nightingale*. The poem is in septenaries, and many rhymes look like assonances; for instance, *hete: speke* (31); *sune: inume* (37); *drof: wroth* (75), *forbed: fet* (581). The key to appreciating this verse craft is that the consonants in rhyme share phonological features. In speech perception, we distinguish consonants by (1) place of articulation—for example [d] and [t] are dentals; (2) manner of articulation—for example, [θ] (voiceless 'th') and [f] are fricatives, while [p] and [t] are plosives; and (3) voicing—for example, [t] and [p] are both voiceless. In perfect rhyme, consonants match in all three dimensions; in the rhymes of *Passion of Our Lord*, they match in two of three. Since the consonants are integral to the rhyme, the linguistic term 'feature rhyme' is better than 'assonance'.[51] Other conventional practices in the tradition of looser rhyme is the rhyming on only one of the consonants in a consonant cluster, 'auto-rhyme' (rhyming on the same word in the same sense), and subsequence rhyme, where one

---

[50] Georges Lote, *Histoire du vers français*, 9 vols. (Aix-en-Provence, 1951–96), 2:69–72.
[51] Arnold Zwicky, '"Well, This Rock and Roll Has Got to Stop. Junior's Head Is Hard as a Rock"', in Salikoko S. Mufwene, Carol A. Walker, and Sanford B Steever (eds), *Papers from the Twelfth Regional Meeting of the Chicago Linguistic Society* (Chicago, IL, 1976), 676–97.

of the rhyme words has a final sound or syllable that is absent in the other.[52] Subsequence rhyme also occurs in conjunction with feature rhyme.

Both traditions of rhyme, strict and loose, continued into the later medieval period. The carol 'Doll thi ale' shows the vigorous tradition of feature rhyme. The defining characteristic of the carol is that it has a burden that was sung in chorus at the end of all stanzas, which were sung by a solo singer. The most common stanza form of the carol, a quatrain rhyming *aaab*, signposted this musical arrangement well. The switch to a new rhyme (*b*), typically picking up the final rhyme sound of the burden, alerted the listeners to the fact that the communal singing was about to begin. The last line of the stanza is also often shorter, sometimes no more than a 'bob' (a one-beat verse), as in 'Doll thi ale', which begins:

> *Doll* thi ale, doll thi ale, dole;* *mull*
> *Ale mak many a man to have doty poll*.* *confused head*
> Ale mak many a mane to styk at a brere* *get into trouble*
> Ale make many a mane to ly in the myere,
> And ale mak many a mane to slep by the fyere
>   With doll*.[53]   *grief*

The italicised lines are the burden. The short fourth line of every stanza of this carol, the bob, is the verse that cues the communal singing of the repeated burden. In the manuscript (Oxford, Bodleian, MS Eng. poet. e. 1, ff. 51r, 52v), the bob is made to stand out by being set to the right of the longer triplets.[54] It breaks with the preceding lines not only visually and rhythmically but also by setting a new rhyme sound, which cannot be fulfilled unless the burden is repeated. Conrad Laforte in his study of traditional song calls such a cuing verse a *vers signal*.[55] The apparent moral of the stanzas, that ale causes all kinds of misery (*doll/dole*), is mischievously undermined by the burden, urging the drinkers to mull (*doll*) the ale. The consonants in the imperfect rhymes of this carol—*stone: hom* (stanza 2); *stretes: chekes* (stanza 3)—differ with respect to place of articulation but agree in manner of articulation and voicing.

Poets who rhymed strictly were well aware of poets who did not, and their repudiation of licences taken by other poets was meant to be noticed. When poets' rhyming intentions depend on as fine a margin as final -e, as in *Dame Sirith* (*wille: stille*, but *skil: wil*), they are telling us that subsequence rhyme is not good enough for them. Chaucer was that kind of poet. Nowhere does he rhyme French-derived words with final -e (*grace, face*, etc.) with words without final -e, except in his parody of 'rym dogerel', 'The Tale of Sir Thopas'.[56] Autorhyme, acceptable in 'loose' Middle English poetry,[57] finds its antithesis in *rime equivoque* in 'strict poetry'. This type of rhyme involved homophones or identical words used in different senses or in different grammatical functions. The device is occasionally found in *Dame Sirith* and Chaucer:

---

[52] Judith A. Jefferson, Donka Minkova, and Ad Putter, 'Perfect and Imperfect Rhyme: Romances in the *abab* Tradition', *Studies in Philology*, 111 (2014), 631–51.

[53] In Richard Leighton Greene (ed.), *The Early English Carols* (Oxford, 1977), 255–6.

[54] This is the traditional layout of bobs in carols. See Daniel Wakelin, 'The Carol in Writing: Three Anthologies from Fifteenth-Century Norfolk', *Journal of the Early Book Society*, 9 (2006), 25–49.

[55] Conrad Laforte, *Survivances médiévales dans la chanson folklorique: poétique de la chanson folklorique* (Quebec, 1983), 67.

[56] See M. Masui, *The Structure of Chaucer's Rhyme Words* (Tokyo, 1964), 13, and the notes to VII.712 and 781 in *The Riverside Chaucer*.

[57] For example, an endearingly amateurish love-letter rhymes 'as long as I lif' (2) with 'whiles þat I lif' (4): 'To His Mistress H.', in Rossell Hope Robbins (ed.), *Secular Lyrics of the Fourteenth and Fifteenth Century* (Oxford, 1952), 194–5.

140   MEDIEVAL POETRY: 1100–1400

> He wente him to þen *inne**   *the inn*
> Þer hoe wonede *inne**   *she lived in*
>   (*Dame Sirith*, 19–20)

> The holy blisful martir for to seke,
> That hem hath holpen* what that they were seeke*.   *helped; ill*
>   (*Canterbury Tales* I.17–18)

The true showman of this art, however, is John Gower, who revelled in *rimes équivoques*.[58] In one passage of *Confessio Amantis*, they keep coming:

> And in this wise, taketh *kepe**,   *pay attention*
> If I hire hadde, I wolde hire *kepe*,
> And yit no friday wolde I *faste*,
> Thogh I hire kepte and hielde *faste*.
> Fy on the bagges in the *kiste**!   *money bags in the chest*
> I hadde ynogh if I hiere *kiste*. (5.79–84)

And so on for another six lines. The difficulty of finding such rhymes is one reason why they were much admired; the other reason is that they conferred social distinction: poets who used them, and readers who appreciated them, knew themselves to be beyond auto-rhyme.

Alliterative Poetry: From Laȝamon to *Sir Gawain*

While we know much about the normal practices of poets of the so-called 'Alliterative Revival' of the fourteenth century, it is difficult to know what Middle English poets thought normal alliterative poetry should look like. In Old English there were clear constraints: the long line consisted of two half-lines linked by alliteration; each half-line had two lifts (beats) and two dips (sequences of one or more unstressed syllables), occurring in set patterns.[59] When Laȝamon (*c* 1200) wrote his *Brut*, an 'alliterative' history of England, however, he produced something very different that is perhaps best understood as a hybrid of the Old English line and the verse form of his main source, Wace's *Brut* (in rhymed octosyllabic couplets).[60] Below is the passage where Hengist explains the migration of the Germanic tribes. I have marked alliteration with underlining and beats with accents. Lines without alliteration in this passage are linked by rhyme.

> For þer is fólc swiðe múchel   mǽre þene heo wálden.
> Þa wíf fareð mid chílde   swa þe déor wílde.
> Æueralche ȝére   heo bereð chíld þére,
> Þat béoð an us féole   þat we fǽren scolden.
> Ne míhte we bilǽue   for líue ne for dǽðe.
> Ne for náuer nane þínge   for þan fólc-kínge.

---

[58] See R. F. Yeager, *John Gower's Poetic: The Search for a New Arion* (Cambridge, 1990), 43 and Charles Owen, 'Notes on Gower's Prosody', *Chaucer Review*, 28 (1994), 405–13.

[59] Jun Terasawa, *Old English Metre: An Introduction* (Toronto, 2011).

[60] The bibliography on Laȝamon's verse form is vast. Important studies include Herbert Pilch, *Layamon's Brut: eine literarische Studie* (Heidelberg, 1960), 132–55; Thomas E. Bredehoft, *Early English Metre* (Toronto, 1992), 99–120; Eric Weiskott, *English Alliterative Verse: Poetic Tradition and Literary History* (Cambridge, 2016), 71–92; and Ian Cornelius, *Reconstructing Alliterative Metre: The Pursuit of a Medieval Meter* (Cambridge, 2017), 79–92.

Þus we uérden þére   and forþi béoð nu hére,
To séchen vnder lúfte   lónd & godne láuerd.[61] (6921–8)

(For there are many people there, many more than is desirable. The woman is with child as often as the wild deer. Every year she is pregnant, and there are so many of us that we have to go away. We could not stay in the presence of our ruler for life or death or anything. So we journeyed there and so we have come here to look somewhere for land and a good lord.)

Some of Laȝamon's lines show neither rhyme nor alliteration, and he clearly had an elastic notion of what rhyme was. Feature rhyme (e.g., *bufen: cumen*, 816; *sune: cume*, 866) is common, and line 6925 combines this (*bilǽue: dǽðe*) with alliteration. A further characteristic of his rhyming practice is a fondness for 'slant rhyme', where the consonant rather than the vowel rhymes, as in *wenden: londen* (835), *Penda: londa* (820), and *wende: londe* (847). This type of rhyme was so well liked by Old Icelandic poets that they had a term for it: *skothending*.[62] Other early Middle English alliterative poems, such as *The Proverbs of Alfred*, also use it.

The poetry of the Alliterative Revival is a far cry from Laȝamon's *Brut*. The finest formal achievement is *Sir Gawain and the Green Knight*, which combines unrhymed alliterative long lines, in the strict metre developed by poets in this tradition, with a bob and wheel (shorter rhyming lines at the end of the stanza) in iambic metre. Below are the last lines from the third stanza of fit two:

Alle þis cómpayny of cóurt cóm þe kyng nérre	
For to cóunseyl þe knýȝt, with cáre at her hért.	
Þere watz much dérue dóel* dríuen in þe sále*	*fierce sorrow; hall*
Þat so wórthe as Wáwan* schulde wénde on þat érnde*,	*Gawain; mission*
To dryȝe a délful dýnt*, and déle no móre	*endure a grievous blow*
wyth brónde*.	*sword*
Þe knýȝt mad áy god chére,	
And sáyde, 'Quat schúld I wónde*?	*hesitate*
Of déstinés dérf and dére*	*hard and grievous*
What máy mon dó bot fónde*?'[63]	*make trial of* (556–65)

The alliterative long lines have four beats and alliterate in a pattern that became normative across a substantial corpus of unrhymed alliterative poems: *aa/ax*.[64] Compared with rhymed verse, alliterative poetry is much harder to write. The constraint of end-rhyme affects the last word of the line; alliteration constrains three. But as if to show the ease with which he can meet these constraints, the *Gawain*-poet not infrequently crams another alliterating content word into his verses, as in 'To dryȝe a délful dýnt' (560a) and 'cóm þe kyng

---

[61] G. L. Brook and R. F. Leslie (eds), *Laȝamon: Brut*, 2 vols., EETS o.s. 250, 257 (London, 1963–78).

[62] Kristján Árnason, 'On the Principles of Nordic Rhyme and Alliteration', *Arkiv for nordisk filologi*, 122 (2007), 79–116.

[63] J. R. R. Tolkien and E. V. Gordon (eds). *Sir Gawain and the Green Knight*, 2nd edn., rev. Norman Davis (Oxford, 1967).

[64] See Thorlac Turville-Petre, 'Emendation on the Grounds of Alliteration in *The Wars of Alexander*', *English Studies*, 61 (1980), 302–17; and Hoyt N. Duggan, 'Alliterative Patterning as a Basis for Emendation in Alliterative Poetry', *Studies in the Age of Chaucer*, 8 (1986), 73–105.

142   MEDIEVAL POETRY: 1100–1400

nérre' (556b).[65] To help them in their task, alliterative poets had at their disposal an extensive word-hoard that was especially rich in synonyms for 'man' and verbs of motion. They also made ingenious use of alliterative minimal pairs. For example, because the poet alliterates on /w/, he names the protagonist 'Wawan' at 559 (cf. 343), but when he alliterates on /g/ the name is 'Gawan' or 'Gawayn', which in rhyme can also be stressed on the second syllable (1044, 1619). No 'cheating' is involved: second-syllable stress reflects the French origin of the name (Gauvain), and because French /g/ had two reflexes in English, /w/ and /g/ (giving us doublets such as 'guarantee' and 'warranty'), both forms of the name are legitimate.

As far as the metre of the long line is concerned, there seems at first glance to be no pattern in the distribution of stressed and unstressed syllables, but recent research has revealed various rhythmical constraints. One of these affects the line ending, where most alliterative poets, like Orm, wanted only one unstressed syllable. The manuscripts of alliterative poems do not always reflect this (note *Gawain*, 557b, 'with care at her hert'), but since at line ending the poet only wrote nouns with historically justified final -e, this is a scribal matter, and emendation (to 'herte' at 557) is a sensible solution. Mid-line, too, alliterative poets obeyed rhythmical constrains. They invariably wrote b-verses with one and only one 'long dip' (a sequence of two or more unstressed syllables).[66] The constraints governing the a-verse remain matters for debate, but metrists agree that poets carefully safeguarded the metrical asymmetry between the two half-lines by putting things in the a-verse that were outlawed in the b-verse, such as two long dips, or a stressed syllable/multiple unstressed syllables at verse end. The upshot is a metre that is radically heteromorphic. The recurrence of the same rhythmical patterns (such as iambic feet) is outlawed, yielding a metre that is irregular 'by rule'.

The transition in *Gawain* from the alliterative long lines into the smoothly homomorphic metre of the wheel (in iambic trimeter) is signalled by the single-beat bob, which in the manuscript (London, British Library, Cotton Nero A.x) is written to the right of the last or penultimate alliterative long line of the stanza. The wonderful thing about the bob in *Gawain* is that it always comes as a surprise,[67] not only because the number of alliterative long lines per stanza fluctuates wildly—meaning that the end of a stanza is always unpredictable—but also because all alliterative long lines are complete sense units. If the bob affects the grammar of the preceding line, it is by an unexpected twist. The lines 'To dryʒe a délful dýnt, and déle no móre / Wyth brónde' illustrate the point. Before the bob's arrival, 'dele' poses as a transitive verb ('To endure a grievous blow and deal no further ones'), but the bob ('Wyth bronde') pushes the verb towards the sense it usually had in intransitive constructions, 'to fight no more with sword'.[68]

The bob, then, can alter our grammatical understanding of what has gone before (cf. 226–7, 2019–20), even as its chief function is to alert us to what is coming. As a *vers signal*, it bans the recurrence of any further long lines and announces the arrival of the closing lines, the last of which rhymes with the bob. Bob-and-wheel stanzas had become fashionable

---

[65] Many critics scan such verses as three-beat verses. For discussion and for an explanation of the principles underlying my own scansion, see Putter, Jefferson, and Stokes, *Studies*, 145–216; and Ad Putter, 'A Prototype Theory of Metrical Stress: Lexical Category and Ictus in Langland, the *Gawain* Poet and Other Alliterative Poets', in Richard Dance and Laura Wright (eds), *The Use and Development of Middle English* (Bern, 2013), 281–99.

[66] See Hoyt N. Duggan, 'The Shape of the B-Verse in Middle English Alliterative Poetry', *Speculum*, 61 (1986), 564–92; and Thomas Cable, *The English Alliterative Tradition* (Philadelphia, PA, 1991), 85–113.

[67] See Howell D. Chickering, 'Stanzaic Closure and Linkage in *Sir Gawain and the Green Knight*', *Chaucer Review*, 32 (1997), 1–31; and Ad Putter, 'Adventures in the Bob-and-Wheel Tradition', in Nicholas Perkins (ed.), *Medieval Romance and Material Culture* (Cambridge, 2015), 147–64.

[68] See *MED* delen 7(b).

in rhymed alliterative poems, which flourished in the same regions as did unrhymed alliterative poems: the West, North Midlands, and North. An example is *The Pistel of Susan* (*c* 1380), which is in the popular thirteen-line stanza: eight alliterative long lines rhyming *abababab* plus a five-line cauda.[69] In *The Pistel of Susan* the first line of the cauda is also a bob:

So fre*.   *gracious*
Seþþe* þou maiȝt* not be sene   *Because; may*
Wiþ no fleshiliche eyene*,   *fleshly eyes*
Þou wost* wel I am clene*.   *know; chaste*
Haue merci of me.[70] (269–73)

As in *Gawain*, the bob is a one-beat verse that introduces a new rhyme which is completed in the last rhyme of the wheel (rhyming *cdddc*).

These newly fashionable rhymed alliterative poems may well have provided a model for the *Gawain*-poet's stanza form,[71] but if so he changed the metre of the bob and wheel fundamentally. In rhymed alliterative poems with wheels, the metre of the wheel lines is usually alliterative.[72] As the extract from *The Pistel of Susan* shows, they are metrically a-verses except for the last line, which is in b-verse metre. In *Sir Gawain*, on the other hand, the heteromorphic metre of the long lines is resolved in the iambic rhythm of the wheel. The change of music is used brilliantly by the poet to shift narrative gear. Sometimes it facilitates changes of mood and focalisation (in the extract above, from the courtiers and their grief to Gawain and his stoic bravery) and/or shifts from direct speech to indirect speech (see also 896–900, 1745–9) or vice versa (1257–62, 1041–5). At other times it accompanies transitions from intra- to extradiegetic discourse (585–90, 1765–9).

The poet's formal control is all the more impressive since it operates, in one respect, below our level of consciousness. Like *Pearl*, the *Gawain*-poet's other masterpiece, *Gawain* has a numerological design. In *Pearl* the design is above the radar: this poem is written in regular twelve-line stanzas of rhymed tetrameter; the total number of stanzas is 101, giving a total line count of 1,212. Since the last line repeats the first, the poem comes full circle. Because the number twelve is also explicitly associated with heaven (where everything comes in twelves or multiples of twelve), the numerological construction of the poem is both meaningful and explicit.[73]

The poet's numerological interest was not widely shared by other vernacular English poets,[74] though there are a few other examples. When the poet of the alliterative *Pater Noster* (sometimes attributed to John Audelay) composed a poem about the Lord's Prayer, with its seven petitions ('seuen poyntis', 5),[75] he naturally wrote the poem in seven stanzas. He also made the stanzas eleven lines long to produce a total line count of seventy-seven.[76] The

---

[69] Thorlac Turville-Petre, '*Summer Sunday, De Tribus Regibus Mortuis*, and *The Awntyrs off Arthure*: Three Poems in the 13-Line Stanza', *Review of English Studies*, 25 (1974), 1–13; and Susanna Fein, 'The Early Thirteen-Line Stanza: Style and Metrics Reconsidered', *Parergon*, 18 (2000), 97–126.

[70] In Thorlac Turville-Petre (ed.), *Alliterative Poetry of the Middle Ages: An Anthology* (London, 1989).

[71] Turville-Petre (ed.), *Alliterative Poetry*, 7.

[72] See Ralph Hanna (ed.), *The Awntyrs off Arthure at the Terne Wathelyn* (Manchester, 1974), 14–15.

[73] See Barbara Newman, 'The Artifice of Eternity: Speaking of Heaven in Three Medieval Poems', in Ad Putter and Carolyn Muessig (eds), *Envisaging Heaven in the Middle Ages* (London, 2007), 185–207.

[74] Derek Brewer, 'Arithmetic and the Mentality of Chaucer', in Piero Botani and Anna Torti (eds), *Literature in Fourteenth-Century England* (Tübingen, 1983), 155–64.

[75] E. K. Whiting (ed.), *The Poems of John Audelay*, EETS o.s. 184 (London, 1931).

[76] See Ad Putter, 'The Language and Metre of *Pater Noster* and *Three Dead Kings*', *Review of English Studies*, 55 (2004), 498–526.

144 MEDIEVAL POETRY: 1100–1400

numerological principles familiar from Latin verse, such as the fondness for round numbers and the understanding that Marian poems deserve five stanzas (given her five joys, the five letters of 'Maria', and so on), were also carried over into some English poems.[77] A forgotten gem is the poem *Hayl mari!/I am sori*, in five ten-line stanzas, each having only two rhyming sounds, with systematic concatenation (stanza-linking) and circularity (as in *Pearl*). The two last words of a stanza are repeated as the first two words of the following stanza, and though the last line of the poem does not repeat the first, it asks us to return to the beginning and start all over again:

> wan we þenke hu we sal far
> wan he sal dem us alle,
> we sal haf ned þare
> a-pan mari to calle &c.[78] (47–50)

As the '& c.' indicates, the words we shall want to repeat at our hour of need are the first two words of line 1, 'Hail Mary'; and so the poet has us going round in concatenating circles. In private devotion, the Ave Maria was repeated in multiples of fifty, and the poem itself honours that number since it contains precisely fifty lines.

In *Gawain*, the number five (and, more precisely, five times five) is again the key number. It is encoded in the pentangle on Gawain's shield, with its five points, each standing for a constellation of five virtues. Like *Pearl*, the poem has 101 stanzas, and the first alliterative long line is repeated in the last, at exactly line 2525. Yet in contrast with *Pearl*, where it is possible to keep track of the line count as the poem unfolds, in regular twelve-line stanzas, the numerological shape of *Gawain* emerges, entirely unpredictably, from stanzas with apparently random line counts. Since Middle English poems did not come with line numbers, the poet cannot have expected his audience to notice this. What did matter to him is that order should arise out of chaos. Chance ('aventure') and destiny ('destinés derf and dere') and the relationship between the two are what this romance is all about. In the unique form of the poem, its 'irregular' alliterative long lines yielding to orderly iambics, the 'random' stanzaic line counts to numerical design, the poet found a formula that replicates the mysterious connection between the unpredictable and the ordained at the level of literary form.

Sir Gawain is formally *sui generis*, and my reason for ending with it is to dampen expectations of a general conclusion. The verse forms of Middle English poems are as diverse as its themes, and describing them in a single chapter is an exercise in simplification. By overlooking differences of kind, and differences of critical opinion, it becomes possible to describe alliterative long lines, tail-rhyme stanzas, iambic pentameters, and so on. The identification of common 'types' is in any case less important than engagement with the linguistic and cognitive foundations of our typologies: rhyme, rhythm, and the dynamic relationship between parts (e.g., the burden and the stanza in the carol) in the perception and performance of the whole. Questions of taxonomy—what are 'bobs', 'tail-rhyme stanzas', and 'iambic tetrameters'?—matter, but if I have answered them, I hope to have done so in the context of some of the bigger questions that need to be asked. How do we know a stanza is ending? What did medieval poets think rhyme was? How did they coax regular metre out of recalcitrant language?

---

[77] See Ernst Robert Curtius, 'Numerical Composition', in his *European Literature and the Latin Middle Ages*, trans. Willard R. Trask (New York, 1953), 501–9; and Alastair Fowler (ed.), *Silent Poetry: Essays in Numerological Analysis* (London, 1970). On the number five in Marian lyrics, see Vincent J. Crowne, 'Middle English Poems on the Joys and on the Compassion of the Blessed Virgin Mary', *Catholic University Bulletin*, 8 (1902), 304–16.

[78] In Carleton Brown (ed.), *English Lyrics of the XIIIth Century* (Oxford, 1965), 124–5.

10

Poetic and Literary Theory

Andrew Galloway

Teaching has its legendary figures. Although the English lawyer, canon, and diplomat John of Salisbury had probably never met Bernard of Chartres, in the late 1150s John enshrined Bernard's grammar school at Chartres (where John had certainly journeyed to learn from Bernard's student, William of Conches) as an example of how crucial literary study was to a span of the more official disciplines, of grammar, rhetoric, logic, and especially ethics:

> Of all the branches of learning, that which confers the greatest beauty is Ethics, the most excellent part of philosophy, without which the latter would not even deserve its name. Carefully examine the works of Vergil or Lucan, and no matter what your philosophy, you will find therein its seed or seasoning ... Bernard of Chartres, the greatest font of literary learning in Gaul in recent times, used to teach grammar in the following way. He would point out, in reading of the authors, what was simple and according to rule. On the other hand, he would explain grammatical figures, rhetorical embellishment, and sophistical quibbling, as well as the relation of given passages to other studies ... He would dispense his instruction to his hearers gradually, in a manner commensurate with their powers of assimilation. And since diction is lustrous either because the words are well chosen, and the adjectives and verbs admirably suited to the nouns with which they are used, or because of the employment of metaphors, whereby speech is transferred to some beyond-the-ordinary meaning for sufficient reason, Bernard used to inculcate this in the minds of his hearers ... Bernard would bend every effort to bring his students to imitate what they were hearing. In some cases he would rely on exhortation, in others he would resort to punishments, such as flogging. Each student was daily required to recite part of what he had heard on the previous day.[1]

The large remit for classical literary studies that Bernard of Chartres adopted in his grammar schoolroom, which John unfolded as part of his rebuttal of what he claimed were dangerous modern tendencies to skip over the language arts, is a glimpse of only one of many medieval domains of poetic and literary theory (our terms, not theirs). Even merely in clerical, learned, academic, and Latin contexts, such theory can be divided, as it often sharply is in modern scholarship, into two kinds, although both ultimately sprang from the early or at least grammatical study of the sort John nostalgically imagines. One remained close to the tradition of grammar and rhetoric, grounded in written letters ('for the Greeks call letters *grammata*', Isidore's influential sixth-century *Etymologies* observes), proceeding through 'syllables, feet, accent, punctuation, critical signs, spelling, analogy, etymology,

---

[1] Daniel D. McGarry (trans.), *The Metalogicon of John of Salisbury: A Twelfth-Century Defense of the Verbal and Logical Arts of the Trivium* (Berkeley, CA, 1955), 1.24 (pp. 67–8). For John's career, see Christopher Brooke, 'John of Salisbury and His World', in Michael Wilks (ed.), *The World of John of Salisbury*, Studies in Church History Subsidia 3 (Oxford, 1984), 1–20.

Andrew Galloway, *Poetic and Literary Theory*. In: *The Oxford History of Poetry in English*. Edited by Helen Cooper and Robert R. Edwards, Oxford University Press. © Andrew Galloway (2023). DOI: 10.1093/oso/9780198827429.003.0010

glosses, differentiation, barbarisms, solecisms, faults, metaplasms, schemes, tropes, prose, and meter' to 'tales (*fabulae*) and histories (*historiae*)',[2] an attention that developed by the early thirteenth century across England and Europe into a robust tradition of Latin manuals in prose and verse designed for writing more Latin prose and verse, quantities of which emerged in the same settings and readerships as the manuals. These 'arts of poetry' had only limited influence on English poetry, and vernacular versions of such guides appeared only sparsely, and late, in medieval culture;[3] yet the broader grammatical and rhetorical tradition made important contributions to a general set of emphases in both Latin and English poetry, and some important English poetic uses of it appear in the late fourteenth century, at the end of the period considered here.

Although long the main kind of medieval focus on poetics, this body of materials has often been dismissed as narrowly practical, reductive and inconsistent in its claims about genre, and uninterested in fundamental questions of literary meaning, during the centuries when, it has been declared, 'the best minds were otherwise engaged ... in Scriptural commentary'.[4] Indeed, a second kind of literary theory in the commentary and exegetical traditions has gradually gained attention, propounding what we might call 'high theory', focused on the principles of interpretation, narrative production, and authorship and based on more philosophically abstract properties, engines, and purposes of sacred language and narrative. Although this appeared in the commentaries and exegeses of schools of theology, it demonstrably spread into secular, non-academic culture as well. Both traditions, in fact, occupied major roles in literary and intellectual culture, in one way or another influencing all the vernacular literatures of Europe, however alien both such modes of 'theory' might be to humanist and post-medieval philology and literary criticism in general. English poetry was never, however, simply parasitical on these Latin materials, whose intellectual impact might be viewed as a range of possibilities that English poetry sometimes directly but often more remotely registered, and occasionally daringly extended or challenged. Even when lines can be drawn directly back to the academic theories and materials, it is clear that throughout this span English poetry had its own implicit theories of literary production, forms, purposes, and authorship.

The 'Arts' Tradition in Latin

Basic Latin education in England was pursued longer and by older students than on the Continent, so we should not assume that grammar-school or other pre- or para-university Latin texts were strictly to be read by the very young.[5] This is a crucial point for appreciating the significance and influence of the Latin grammatical and rhetorical materials, whose uses and elaborations should not be viewed only under the sepia of nostalgic memories of boyhood, as John of Salisbury's own return to study 'grammar' and philosophy at Chartres

---

[2] Isidore of Seville, in W. M. Lindsay (ed.), *Etymologiae* (Oxford, 1911), 1.5; Stephen A. Barney, W. J. Lewis, J. A. Beach, and Oliver Berghof (trans.), *The Etymologies of Isidore of Seville* (Cambridge, 2006), 42.

[3] See Douglas Kelly, *The Arts of Poetry and Prose*, Typologie des Sources du Moyen Âge Occidental 59 (Turnhout, 1991), 146–79. The judgement is entirely my own.

[4] Alastair Fowler, *Kinds of Literature: An Introduction to the Theory of Genres and Modes* (Oxford, 1982), 146. Similar but even harsher views are in W. K. Wimsatt and Cleanth Brooks, *Literary Criticism: A Short History* (New York, 1957, 1975), 154, and even O. B. Hardison, Jr., 'Towards a History of Medieval Literary Criticism', *Medievalia et Humanistica*, 7 (1976), 1–12.

[5] See Marjorie Curry Woods, *Classroom Commentaries: Teaching the Poetria Nova across Medieval and Renaissance Europe* (Columbus, OH, 2010), 231.

shows.[6] So, too, the rhetorical guides often found copied or bound with materials associated with grammar schooling were fashioned for 'those who prepared students for the university's Arts course or for clerical careers beyond Oxford'.[7] One consequence of this range in uses was that Latin poetry, especially before and during the rise of the manuals on poetic arts, often includes its own guidance, glossing itself in ways that advertise utility not only for basic Latin literacy but also interpretative methods at more consequential levels. Such materials conveyed literary theory along with literary models. The twelfth-century collection of Latin beast-fables attributed to Walter of England and based on Aesop, a text for beginning readers, appropriates (aggressively) Horace's idea of mixing 'sweetness with utility' to invite readers of all levels to enjoy both tenor and vehicle:

> Ut iuuet et prosit conatur pagina presens.
> Dulcius arrident seria picta iocis.
> Ortulus ille parit fructum cum flore. Fauorem
> Flos et fructus emunt. Hic sapit, ille nitet.
> Si fructus plus flore sapit, fructum lege; si flos
> Plus fructu, florem. Si duo, carpe duo.

(The present page strives to be both pleasing and profitable. Serious portrayals amuse more sweetly with jests. This grove bears both fruit and flower: the flower and the fruit give off flavour, the latter in taste, the former in beauty. If the fruit is more pleasing than the flower, choose the fruit; if the flower more than the fruit, then the flower. If both, take both.)[8]

A fifteenth-century manuscript of Walter's fables glosses 'fruit' here as *moralitas* and 'flower' as *fabula*,[9] a technically accurate gloss on the genre of the Aesopian work according to Isidore of Seville's definition (fables 'are presented with the intention that the conversation of imaginary dumb animals among themselves may be recognized as a certain image of the life of humans').[10] The idea that proper interpretation of a beast fable, or any narrative, dourly required readers to take 'the fruyt, and lat the chaf be stille', or to avoid altogether 'fables and swich wrecchednesse', is a secular writer's straw-man portrayal of the clerical world.[11] It is a short step from Walter of England's multiple kinds of narrative profit and pleasure to the self-explicating personifications presented by one of the masters of medieval allegory: the twelfth-century poet and theologian Alan of Lille, whose widely influential poems, *The Plaint of Nature* and *Anticlaudianus*, are often found copied in formats designed for schoolroom use, leaving wide marginal spaces for glosses as is also typical for copies of

---

[6] See generally Christopher Cannon, *From Literacy to Literature: England, 1300–1400* (Oxford, 2016). Cannon insists, however, on the narrow purposes of early childhood grammar schooling for all ownership and use of such materials; for some wider contexts of some eccentric items often included in those materials, see Andrew Galloway, 'The Rhetoric of Riddling in Late-Medieval England: The "Oxford" Riddles, the *Secretum philosophorum* and the Riddles in *Piers Plowman*', *Speculum*, 70 (1995), 68–105, with the stipulation (pp. 72, 78) that 'Oxford' does not mean formal university study but refers to a wide range of settings, from grammar schooling to various religious and administrative settings, a number of which happen to have connections with Oxford.

[7] See Martin Camargo (ed. and trans.), *Tria Sunt: An Art of Poetry and Prose* (Cambridge, MA, 2019), xvii.

[8] Aaron E. Wright (ed.), *The Fables of 'Walter of England'* (Toronto, 1997), 19 (my translation). For Horace, see *Ars Poetica*, 343–4 in Niall Rudd (ed.), *Horace: Epistles Book II and Epistle to the Pisones ('Ars Poetica')* (Cambridge, 1989). In Horace this has no connection to the idea of a moral allegory or metaphor.

[9] *Fables of 'Walter of England'*, 19.

[10] Isidore 1.40.1–2 (trans. Barney, 1:66).

[11] Geoffrey Chaucer, 'The Nun's Priest's Tale', 3443; 'The Parson's Prologue', 34. Citations of Chaucer are from Larry D. Benson (ed.), *The Riverside Chaucer*, 3rd edn. (Boston, MA, 1987).

148   MEDIEVAL POETRY: 1100–1400

ancient texts in the period.[12] The *Anticlaudianus* introduces the seven 'sisters' of the liberal arts to assist Prudence, and the other principles and faculties associated with ethics and theology marshalled by Nature to construct the 'perfect man'; it begins with a prologue describing the poem's value for students at all ages and levels of understanding:

> Let none dare to scorn this work who are still squalling in the nurse's cradle, still being suckled at the breasts of the lesser arts. Let none attempt to discredit this work who have committed themselves to the combat of higher learning. Let not even those who assail heaven from the lofty peaks of philosophy presume to dismiss this work. For in this work the sweetness of the literal sense will give pleasure to a youthful audience; moral doctrine will lend itself to the developing mind; the keener subtlety of allegory will sharpen the proficient intellect.[13]

This emphasis on the link between different responses to the poem's multiple modes of poetic and allegorical signification is not simply an introductory advertisement; self-consciousness of multiple capabilities pervades Alan's personification allegories themselves. These do not simply passively display their multiple meanings but demonstrate the powers that their realms of knowledge and expression exert on those using them at any level. Music's face is a mirror in which readers may see themselves: this may be a way not simply to describe harmonic relationships but to shape and create those, between the text and the reader, in whatever state of being the reader finds himself (and few women would have been trained to read such a work, in spite of its bounty of feminine allegorical figures). Music holds a lyre; 'with such a song the Thracian bard caused rocks to soften, trees to run, rivers to stay their flow, wild beasts to grow gentle, wars to cease' (3.399–402). This emphasis on doing things with the liberal arts is evident in all Alan's personifications. In particular, Rhetoric's robe displays, 'as if in a book, the aim of rhetoric, its inventors, its kinds and their functions, its means, its procedures, what the art of rhetoric comprises, its power, and how, at one moment importunate, it resounds with threats, at the next shines with brilliant language, now pours forth prayers, now fills the ear with praise ... to what goal it moves as it weighs advantage, delivers justice, supports the cause of good, explains what is honourable' (*iustum/iudicet, affirmet rectum, demonstret honestum*; 3.170–7).

Alan's self-glossing and efficacious personae and poems demonstrate how symbolic representations not only speak differently to different audiences but also constitute society and the universe. Such an emphasis is, perhaps, a grammarian's utopia, but it also hints at the growing power of legal and diplomatic powers in the administrative and legalistic world emerging in the twelfth century, in which contracts and interpretations might be consequential in political as well as pedagogic arenas, up to the many clashes between royal and papal power. This was the world of ecclesiastical and secular law, in which the rise of episcopal, royal, and other kinds of chanceries proliferated administrative roles for the university-trained clerical caste. Their tastes and needs fostered the many Latin handbooks in prose and verse for composing poetry, prose, sermons, and, especially, letters that began appearing in the late twelfth century and in numbers during the thirteenth.

---

[12] For an excellent selection and partial reediting of Alan's works, see Alan of Lille, in Winthrop Wetherbee (ed. and trans.), *Literary Works* (Cambridge, MA, 2013). For investigation of medieval English copies of Alan's *Anticlaudianus,* see Margaret Gibson, Danuta Shanzer, and Nigel Palmer, 'Manuscripts of Alan of Lille, *Anticlaudianus* in the British Isles', *Studi medievali*, 28 (1987), 905–1001.

[13] Alan of Lille, *Literary Works*, 223.

POETIC AND LITERARY THEORY   149

Treatises on rhetoric and poetics are a genre from antiquity, instances of which contin-ued to be widely known and used, especially Cicero's incomplete *De Inventione*, the closely related *Rhetorica ad Herennium* ascribed to Cicero, and Horace's *Ars Poetica*; a few other rhetorical treatises by Cicero, such as the *Topica* and *De Oratore*, were known but less often used, while Aristotle's *Rhetoric* and *Poetics* were not generally available except in partial and, in the case of the *Poetics*, fundamentally altered form (as noted below). There were major differences, however, between these ancient works and the medieval treatises' generic and modal concerns. Whereas the Ciceronian prose works stressed the principles and methods of legal and political public oratory, whose institutional contexts defined Roman culture, and Horace's *Ars Poetica* deals with the genres and development of Greek and Roman drama in forms that had become (as some glosses on Horace's poem show) incomprehensibly alien to the Christian Middle Ages, the medieval rhetorical guides present more ecclesiastically and administratively orientated genres. They introduced, for example, a new focus on letter writing, beginning with Alberic of Monte Cassino's *Flores rhetorici* in the late eleventh cen-tury, with rules not only for epistolary structure and tropes but also for shades of deference or superiority to the addressee. Other medieval treatises treat the construction of sermons as elaborate compositions exploiting the multiple sense of words in Scripture, beginning with a tract by Guibert of Nogent in the twelfth century, through others by Robert of Basevorn and Ranulph Higden in the fourteenth, among others. These were supported by the sup-plementary genres of concordances and indexes to Scripture and, especially, alphabetical *distinctiones* that listed key words susceptible to multiple interpretations, engendering a style of preaching that could dazzle with its leaps of association.[14] Arriving in London in the 1170s, the Augustinian canon Peter of Cornwall gushed about a sermon by Gilbert Foliot, bishop of London (1163–88), that was so 'varied by certain *distinctiones*, adorned with flowers of words and sentences and supported by a copious array of authorities, run-ning backward and forward on its path from its beginning back to the same beginning point, as if plowing the seedbeds of a field by many tracts of rivulets', that 'you would have thought him beyond human, who could so superabundantly use so great a copiousness of authorities through every single *distinctio* of his sermon'.[15]

The ancient treatises define and in varying depth treat three kinds of oratory: 'demon-strative' (or epideictic), 'deliberative' (or dialectical debate), and 'judicial' (or argument before others who will judge); such treaties, however, have relatively little to say about the first, the praise and blame of epideictic (*De Inventione* provides only two final paragraphs). In contrast, the medieval guides to rhetoric and poetics emphasise epideixis beyond all other modes. Matthew of Vendôme's *Ars Versificatoria* (*c* 1175), the earliest of the arts of rhetoric, is framed as a counter-attack on a loathsome antagonist (as is John of Salis-bury's *Metalogicon*). Matthew's treatise offers many models of tropes to be used for blame, as well as some for praise.[16] Such works often demonstrate how potent their rules are by

---

[14] See the selection in Joseph M. Miller, Michael H. Prosser, and Thomas W. Benson (eds), *Readings in Medieval Rhetoric* (Bloomington, IN, 1973); also Margaret Jennings (ed.), *The Ars Componendi Sermones of Ranulph Higden, O.S.B.* (Leiden, 1991). For a tenth-century glossator mystified by the ancient drama Horace discusses, including an assertion that each act of ancient drama should have a different set of type-characters, see Joseph Zechmeister (ed.), *Scholia Vindobonensia ad Horatii Artem Poeticam* (Vienna, 1977), 21–2 (glossing *Ars Poetica*, 189–90). Consideration of indexes, concordances, and *distinctiones* are in Richard H. Rouse and Mary A. Rouse, *Preachers, Florilegia, and Sermons: Studies in the Manipulus Florum of Thomas of Ireland* (Toronto, 1979), and, still useful, W. A. Pantin, *The English Church in the Fourteenth Century* (Cambridge, 1955), 189–243.
[15] See R. W. Hunt, 'English Learning in the Late Twelfth Century', *Transactions of the Royal Historical Society*, 4th series, 19 (1936), 38–42 (at 41; my translation).
[16] Matthew of Vendôme, *Ars versificatoria*, in Franco Munari (ed.), *Opera*, vol. 3 (Rome, 1988); Aubrey E. Galyon (trans.), *The Art of Versification* (Ames, IA, 1980).

150 MEDIEVAL POETRY: 1100–1400

showing how they shape their own presentation. Matthew's model poem praising Ulysses, the archetypally shrewd arguer, uses the tropes and poetic elements Matthew discusses (zeugma, hypozeuxis, metaphor, epithet, etc.) but also itself praises Ulysses as a rhetorician embodying the principles Matthew explains. Poetry here is shaped by and reflects back the power of his own instruction, a case of figural discourse creating and mirroring itself:

> Ulysses delights in a pleasing tongue. This man from Ithaca
> Ranks first in genius; strong in mind, prudent in word,
> Mighty in cunning, he is ever mindful of honesty ...
> His genius sows, his zeal cultivates, his ability tends,
> His reason weeds; as servants to these his tongue sounds forth.[17]

The praise of Ulysses elaborates the wide-ranging topos of 'the plowshare of the tongue', which is sometimes granted full agricultural development in exegetical allegories and later emerged into English poetry with *Piers Plowman*. That it is Ulysses' 'genius' who sows (*seminat ingenium*) might be elaborating Alan of Lille's *De planctu Naturae* in which Ingenium (Genius) is Nature's scribe and lover as well as priest, which in turn was directly followed in the thirteenth century by Genius's sexual sowing, as Nature's minion, in the French *Roman de la rose*. Like rhetoricians, poets were drawn to indicate the natural energy and creative force behind their language.[18]

Poetry of praise and blame, so fundamental a feature of medieval poetics,[19] is a basic instance of instrumental language: speech that serves as a weapon or tool, that does things to human friends or antagonists. The guidebooks are intent also on showing how figural topics, like all topics, are conveyed by malleable rhetoric, their tenors expressed by their own vehicles. The influential *tour de force* of this is Geoffrey of Vinsauf's (or Geoffrey the Englishman's) verse *Poetria Nova* (*c* 1201, rev. *c* 1213), which was designed to replace the 'old' poetics of Horace. In popularity at least it succeeded: over 200 medieval copies survive, spanning outward from Geoffrey's Northampton to all parts of Europe, often in heavily glossed form. We may glimpse some of the reasons for the pre-humanist interest in the *Poetria Nova* in its witty instances of demonstrating while defining the rhetorical tropes and features it presents ('apostrophe' is summoned with an apostrophe, 'Come forth, Apostrophe ...', while Geoffrey's categories of tropes that produce 'amplification' and those that create 'compression' are offered with comic mimicry of the things defined: *amplificatio* is lengthily instanced, *compressio* tersely presented). The demonstration of how figural language takes control of contexts is also extended more boldly. Geoffrey's opening dedication to Pope Innocent III observes that his name scans more readily with his head removed; this makes *Innocens* into the frightening *Nocens*, 'harmful one', a trick straight from the Latin tradition of riddles in which words are treated as things or bodies with 'heads' and 'tails', made to signify as the graphic forms themselves, or again as the things to which they refer, providing a toolkit for how language might enable ethics, satire, and social commentary.[20]

As limiting as Geoffrey of Vinsauf's focus on eloquence and ornament may seem, the thousands of glosses and dozens of introductions to it suggest an interest in figural and

---

[17] Matthew of Vendôme, *Art of Versification*, 1.52, lines 4–16.
[18] See Stephen A. Barney, 'The Plowshare of the Tongue: The Process of a Symbol from the Bible to *Piers Plowman*', *Mediaeval Studies*, 35 (1973), 261–93; Winthrop Wetherbee, *Platonism and Poetry in the Twelfth Century: The Literary Influence of the School of Chartres* (Princeton, NJ, 1972), 202–11, 264–6.
[19] See J. A. Burrow, *The Poetry of Praise* (Cambridge, 2008).
[20] Galloway, 'The Rhetoric of Riddling'.

tropological power to which we should closely attend. In early *trecento* Italy, Geoffrey's work was extolled by one commentator as presenting 'the art of poetry' as such, explicitly not just 'eloquence or rhetoric'; the commentator then defines *poetria* in a lengthy range of assertions and quotations that are drawn from Herman the German's Latin translation in 1256 of Averroes's Arabic commentary on Aristotle's Greek *Poetics*—virtually the only version of Aristotle's *Poetics* known to the medieval West, although reshaping Aristotle's treatise to present poetry entirely in terms of tropes for conveying praise or blame.[21] For the Italian commentator on the *Poetria Nova*, these elements prove that poetry is 'innate' in human beings because of 'the delight man naturally takes in meter and harmony', while presenting a form of 'pleading, with a flowing sweetness of words, what has actually happened or not, observing certain rules and properties'.[22] Even in thirteenth-century England, a commentary on the *Poetria Nova* takes the opportunity to define *poetria* as the art of 'devising a theme, arranging what has been devised, adorning what has been arranged, memorizing what has been adorned, delivering aloud what has been memorized'. It praises Geoffrey for teaching low and middle styles, whereas Horace instructs only in grand style.[23] These responses show poetics developing into a recognisable intellectual domain, even before fifteenth- and sixteenth-century humanists abandoned the medieval guides and turned more exclusively to Cicero, Horace, and Aristotle, although often fusing the latter two into yet other novel combinations.[24]

Vernacular Responses to the 'Arts'

The precept tradition's focus on syntactic structures, rhetorical ornaments, and figural features did not often translate well to English poetry, which usually took its rhetorical structures from less bookish traditions. Similes are common ground for all poetics, sustained within vernacular songs, sermons, and no doubt everyday language. Sometimes uses in English were evidently drawn from Latin models: the elaborate, 'epic' similes in Laȝamon's *Brut* may be derived from Latin epics such as the twelfth-century *Alexandreis* by Walter of Châtillon or Vergil's *Aeneid*.[25] Other poetic figures were too inkhorn to flourish in English before the late fourteenth century. Apostrophe, presented by Geoffrey of Vinsauf as a potent mode of 'amplification', and considered by some modern theorists as key to 'the literary' as such (since apostrophe epitomises poetry's capabilities for summoning into existence something that does not exist), seems virtually non-existent in secular Middle English poetry before Chaucer and Gower.[26] Religious English verse, to be sure, often features appeals to Mary, Jesus, and saints, or Jesus's reproaches to his people, based on the

---

[21] Translation in O. B. Hardison, Jr., Alex Preminger, Kevin Kerrane, and Leon Golden (eds), *Medieval Literary Criticism: Translations and Interpretations* (New York, 1974), 81–122.

[22] Woods, *Classroom Commentaries*, 113.

[23] Woods, *Classroom Commentaries*, 31.

[24] See Bernard Weinberg, *A History of Literary Criticism in the Italian Renaissance*, 2 vols. (Chicago, IL, 1961), 1:111–55.

[25] Elizabeth Salter with D. Pearsall and N. Zeeman (eds), *English and International: Studies in the Literature, Art and Patronage of Medieval England* (Cambridge, 1988), 62; Jacqueline M. Burek, '(Not) Like Aeneas: Allusions to the Aeneid in Laȝamon's *Brut*', *Review of English Studies*, 71 (2020), 229–50.

[26] See Edmond Faral (ed.), *Les Arts Poétiques du xiie et du xiiie Siècle: Recherches et Documents sur la Technique Littéraire du Moyen Âge* (Paris, 1962), lines 276–8; Margaret F. Nims (trans.), *Poetria Nova of Geoffrey of Vinsauf* (Toronto, 1967), 26; Jonathan Culler, 'Apostrophe', in *The Pursuit of Signs: Semiotics, Literature, Deconstruction* (Ithaca, NY, 1981), 135–54; Jonathan Culler, *Theory of the Lyric* (Cambridge, MA, 2015), 190, 229, 350, 352. For Gower's uses of apostrophe, see below. Chaucer's uses of this and other rhetorical tropes are plentiful and long studied; see the opening salvo in J. M. Manly, 'Chaucer and the Rhetoricians', *Proceedings of the British Academy*,

152   MEDIEVAL POETRY: 1100-1400

improperia of Good Friday liturgy, but the connection of these addresses to liturgy, prayer, and at least potentially listening heavenly audiences makes these a special case, distinct from the self-consciously fictional apostrophes to a muse or an empty purse found in Chaucer. At the same time, the abundance and variety of addresses to sacred figures in a few late-fourteenth-century collections of religious verse, especially the lyrics in the commonplace book of Friar John of Grimestone (*c* 1372), raise suspicion that poetic power as such is on display at least as much as piety. One lyric by Grimestone addresses a tear from the 'sorful eyʒe' of Mary.[27]

Broad features from Latin rhetorical theory certainly could and sometimes did have effects on Middle English poetry. The wryly comic debate of the anonymous *Owl and the Nightingale*, whose prayer by the Nightingale for the soul of a 'King Henri', either Henry II or III, places it only sometime between the late twelfth and late thirteenth centuries, is a 'fable' in the Isidorean sense of treating matters of human concern through the mouths of animals, and its arguments and characterisations of the two debating birds have stimulated various suggestions for particular referents, though none seems probable. The poem's uses of various devices from the rhetorical tradition have often been noted.[28] Indeed, since the poem is far from a 'fable' in the sense of cloaking a discernible 'moral' under its narrative, it might be better seen as a witty guide to vernacular rhetoric itself: a demonstration of the features, principles, and powers of public speaking in the vernacular, situating that in the tradition of the *Ad Herennium* or Cicero's *De Inventione*. The 'epideictic', 'deliberative', and 'judicial' kinds of discourse treated in those are granted glorious demonstration in the two birds' mutual character-assassination and dialectic ('deliberative') argument; the whole debate is poised to be recast as a judicial discourse since they will, they agree, rehearse it all over again before Nicholas of Guildford (either the poet himself or the poem's addressee) who will make a final judgement. The birds' 'plaiding' (12) centres on no one crime by either bird and leads to no one moral, but ponders the nature, circumstances, associations, and effects of singing that the two birds typically emit. It is debate about debate, an oration about the art of oratory of the kinds that people regardless of academic or clerical connection would experience:

'Þu aishest me'*, þe Hule sede,	*ask me*
'wi ich a winter singe & grede.*	*cry out*
Hit is gode monne iwone,*	*with good people customary*
An was from þe worlde frome,*	*world's beginning*
Þat ech god man his frond icnowe;*	*acknowledges his friends*
An blisse mid hom sume þrowe,*	*celebrates with them on some occasions*
In his huse,* at his borde,*	*house; table*

---

12 (1926), 95–113; and below. An overview of criticism discussing Chaucer and rhetorical traditions with new information is in Martin Camargo, 'Chaucer and the Oxford Renaissance of Anglo-Latin Rhetoric', *Studies in the Age of Chaucer*, 34 (2012), 173–207. However, the persistently alien nature of the trope of apostrophe in medieval English poetic production is indicated by how even Chaucer's fifteenth-century scribes flag apostrophe as simply 'auctor' (i.e., a speech-act originating and aimed outside the narrator's): see Andrew Galloway, 'Authority', in Peter Brown (ed.), *A Companion to Chaucer* (Oxford, 2002), 28. Pre-Conquest secular English poetry has a few, rare instances of this trope, e.g., *Beowulf*, 2441–751, perhaps revealing more firmly clerical venues of English poetry before the Norman Conquest in tandem with more securely monastic venues of grammatical guides themselves in that period.

[27] 'Lovely Tear from Lovely Eye', in Carleton Brown (ed.), *Religious Lyrics of the XIVth Century*, 2nd edn., rev. G. V. Smithers (Oxford, 1957), 87 (no. 69).

[28] See Neil Cartlidge (ed. and trans.), *The Owl and the Nightingale: Text and Translation* (Exeter, 2001), xvi–xxvii.

> Mid faire speche & faire worde—
> & hure & hure* to Cristesmasse,   *particularly*
> Wane riche & poure, more & lasse,
> Singeþ cundut* niȝt & dai.   *Sing carols*
> Ich hom helpe what ich mai ...'   (473–84)

Owl's claim that her winter hooting is not shrieking but a harmonising with Christmas singing invokes 'condut', *conductus*, the term for non-liturgical sacred song in several voices, necessarily in Latin. This confirms the sprawling Latin world of song and argument with which this whimsical poem engages while emphasising the social effects of all such speech-acts, even simply the holiday communion of rich and poor, to which vernacular rhetoric adds a voice as unexpected in tone and articulation as a talking bird's.

Only in the later fourteenth century do Latin rhetorical and grammatical theory, tropological models, and figural ornament fully intervene in English poetry. The sometimes lyrical, sometimes vehemently argumentative late-fourteenth-century satirical allegory *Piers Plowman* is the first vernacular English poem that displays the fully 'academic' awareness of personification allegory found in Alan of Lille, most likely by way of the French allegorical and satirical tradition.[29] *Piers Plowman*'s reworking and reimaging of single words (such as 'meed', 'truth', 'kind'), as well as elaborating whole personifications and scenes on the basis of underlying passages from Scripture and other clerical genres, bespeak the tradition of guides to preaching, plus surely much direct preaching experience by the author. But unlike anything in the guides, the poem allows imagery and meanings to proliferate beyond single ethical or allegorical messages, using images to explain ideas rather the reverse, and even at a micro level glossing one image with another, as when Holy Church describes Truth's teaching:

> For Truthe telleth that love is triacle* of hevene ...   *healing remedy*
> And also the plante of pees, moost precious of vertues*:   *powers*
> For hevene myghte nat holden it, so was it hevy of hymselve,
> Til it hadde of the erthe eten* his fille.   *eaten*
> And whan it hadde of this fold* flessh and blood taken,   *earth*
> Was nevere leef upon lynde* lighter therafter,   *leaf on linden-tree*
> And portatif and persaunt* as the point of a nedle,   *portable and piercing*
> That myghte noon armure it lette* ne none heighe walles.[30]   *stop*

Here the *distinctio* tradition from Latin sermon guides is clearly operative, but reconceived along purely imagistic lines. While broadly outlining the Incarnation by means of a full palette of syntactic and figural elements, this passage allows images and meter to determine the logic of sacred history, rather than the reverse. 'Love' is identified at the outset, but using the unmarked 'it' thereafter retains an openness to rapid and mysterious transformation, allowing each image to develop further what 'love' is. We cannot summarise Truth's teaching more succinctly.

By the late fourteenth century, other English poets more densely adapted but reshaped elements from the precept tradition, often emphasising rhetoric's powers beyond what the

---

[29] See J. A. Burrow, *Langland's Fictions* (Oxford, 1993), 113–18; Andrew Galloway, 'Madame Meed: Fauvel, Isabella, and the French Circumstances of *Piers Plowman*', *The Yearbook of Langland Studies*, 30 (2016), 227–52 (citing other works and studies).

[30] A. V. C. Schmidt (ed.), *William Langland: The Vision of Piers Plowman—A Critical Edition of the B-Text Based on Trinity College Cambridge MS B.15.17*, 2nd edn. (London, 1995), 1.147–58.

154 MEDIEVAL POETRY: 1100–1400

Latin or indeed French materials declare. Gower ingeniously used apostrophe, for example, in his adaptation of Ovid's address to dawn in *Amores* 1.13: in Ovid's poem, the narrator begs Aurora to delay while he is with his lover—and suggests she would delay if she had her beloved young Cephalus in her bed instead of old Tithonus. Refiguring this hypothetical as one of the 'exempla' of the sins of love in his *Confessio Amantis* ('confession of a lover'), Gower adapted Ovid's apostrophe to have Cephalus himself appeal to the sun-god to slow his course. This grants reality to Ovid's hypothetical figure but builds onto that further hypothetical conjuring.[31] And when describing Rhetoric as such—for the first time in English—Gower altered his source, Brunetto Latini's French *Trésor*, to state that Rhetoric is not merely equal to grammar and logic but their governing principle:

> In Ston and gras vertu ther is,
> Bot yit the bokes tellen this,
> That word above alle erthli thinges
> Is vertuous in his doinges,
> Wher so it be to evele or goode.[32]

Late-fourteenth-century learned lay professionals like Gower, and still more his contemporary Geoffrey Chaucer (*c* 1342–1400), contributed to a trend of amplifying the powers of 'word' as extolled in the Latin tradition. Those poets' rhetorical learning was not simply nostalgic vestiges of boyhood; they ransacked Latin and French materials for new purposes throughout their lives. Chaucer's late 'Nun's Priest's Tale' most clearly shows the extravagances of rhetorical features from Geoffrey of Vinsauf such as apostrophe (including, capping this textbook performance, an apostrophe to Geoffrey of Vinsauf himself); this correlates, as it happens, to a late-fourteenth-century revival in rhetorical training and rhetorical guides at Oxford.[33]

Chaucer's uses of generic set-pieces extend throughout his poetic oeuvre, often disposed as if to examine the question of what such poetic forms contribute to larger actions. Lyrics and complaints, for instance, are found from the inset *forme fixes* laments of the Black Knight, contrasted to the blunt naiveté of the narrator in the *Book of the Duchess*; through the many lyrics (including one from Petrarch) and the successively emptier epistolary exchanges scattered through *Troilus and Criseyde*; through the self-indulgent complaints and examples of suicides recited by Dorigen as she wanders by the rocky cliffs awaiting her husband's return in 'The Franklin's Tale', 'as doon thise noble wyves when hem liketh' (V.818), until her discourse slips from fictive hyperbole into a fatally binding promise, albeit offered 'in pley' (988), to grant sexual intimacies to the lowly squire Aurelius if he can make the rocks disappear. Sometimes Chaucer's uses of literary genres, especially those defined by explicit rules, seem as though they were experiments in what particular combinations do, a curiosity about form that is clearest when not successful. How many variations can the formulaic constraints of brief 'tragedies' allow? How might the epic mode of Statius, 'Stace', be grafted to a metrically elaborate love complaint after the model of 'Corinne', spokesperson for Ovid's letters by forlorn women in the *Heroides*? How tightly might verbosely clichéd

---

[31] See Andrew Galloway, 'Gower's Ovids', in Rita Copeland (ed.), *The Oxford History of Classical Reception in English Literature, 800–1558*, Volume I (Oxford, 2016), 435–64, at 456.

[32] *Confessio Amantis*, 7.1545–9, cited from G. C. Macaulay (ed.), *The English Works of John Gower*, EETS e.s. 81–2 (Oxford, 1900–1).

[33] Camargo, 'Chaucer and the Oxford Renaissance of Anglo-Latin Rhetoric'.

romance, 'rime doggerel', be condensed—driven, as if under the constraints of lyric, into successively halved 'fitts'?[34]

This laboratory approach to the properties and effects of forms and genres is consistent with some of the anatomies of poetics in the arts manuals, but also with a wider intellectual world than the courtly French or strictly rhetorical tradition. The world of mysterious Breton scholars and magicians to which Aurelius has recourse in 'The Franklin's Tale' to satisfy Dorigen's impossible stipulation offers a faerie version of vernacular literature's journeys into the more arcane and intellectually ambitious worlds of Latin academic and para-academic inquiry. Aurelius remembers a certain clerk he knew when he studied at Orléans, among the 'yonge clerkes that been lykerous / To reden artes that been curious' (1110–20); at the outskirts of the university, he encounters another such youthful adept, who can perform the tricks Aurelius needs. No French lyric tradition or Latin rhetorical instruction can achieve Aurelius's goal of making Dorigen's words fully performative. The shadowy university margins he enters border a different realm of study, where dubious clerks studying 'artes that been curious' are mingled with theologians pursuing ultimate but sometimes obscure meanings and properties of the Bible or other nearly as authoritative texts, pondering the most serious performative language in Christendom.

High Theory

Good students have their archetypes as well as great teachers. In the Benedictine abbey of Hirsau in the Black Forest, one Brother Conrad wrote a dialogue between Master and Student that features a model student from *c* 1100, not long before John of Salisbury entered the grammar school where he would encounter Bernard of Chartres:

> *Pupil.* I want you (O teacher) to explain briefly and in summary form what we must look for in each of the school authors who are used in training the blossoming minds of beginners, namely, who the author is, what he has written, the scale of his work, when he has written it, and how, that is whether it is in prose or verse, with what subject-matter or intention each has begun his work, what end the composition has in view. I also want to find out about the introduction page: what is the difference between a title, a preface, a proem, and a prologue; between a poet, a writer of history, and a writer of discourses, between poesy and poetry, between explanation and exposition and detailed study and transference of meaning; between allegory, tropology, and anagogy. I wish to have the meaning of 'book' defined, and to find out the nature of prose, verse, fable, the figures which are called tropes, and any other question that must be asked concerning ecclesiastical or pagan authors. A brief answer to all these questions seems to me to constitute a way in to the understanding of authors important and unimportant alike.[35]

Conrad's eager *discipulus* seeks to understand not only basic formal features of texts but also a host of more general definitions, mechanisms, and purposes. Although earlier than the fuller set of translations of Aristotle that were made or discovered in the later twelfth and

---

[34] Respectively: 'The Monk's Tale', *Anelida and Arcite*, 'The Tale of Sir Thopas'.
[35] Conrad of Hirsau, *Dialogue on the Authors*, extracts in A. J. Minnis and A. B. Scott, with the assistance of David Wallace (eds), *Medieval Literary Theory and Criticism, c. 1100–c. 1375* (Oxford, 1988, 1991), 40–1.

156   MEDIEVAL POETRY: 1100–1400

thirteenth centuries, and before the stable establishment of the universities, all the interests in the systematic study of language, literary form, and authorship were soon enough developed in higher educational realms, including the schools of theology, thence trickling back down to lower grammatical and out to wider vernacular levels.

Allegorical exegesis of the Bible was long developed, a mode grounded in Paul's letters (Romans and 1 Corinthians especially) and Augustine's fifth-century *De Doctrina Christiana*; this continued to provide options both in and outside university for allegorising other kinds of narrative in the same intricate theological vein, such as the mid-fourteenth-century *Ovide moralisé* which presents a complete French verse translation of Ovid's *Metamorphoses* followed by elaborate theological allegoreses.[36] At university, this interpretative mode had been supplemented and to some degree displaced by more historical enquiry into the Bible, on the one hand, and more logically precise attention to the meanings and powers of language as such, on the other. A theology student would normally follow a three-year arts degree (unless he was a monk or mendicant thus exempted from the arts degree) by at least four more years of study of the Bible and Peter Lombard's *Sentences*, the capacious textbook compendium of theology and doctrine finished *c* 1150. The candidate would then lecture on the *Sentences* for several years before becoming eligible for inception as a master or doctor of theology, which obligated him to more years as regent lecturer on the Bible.[37]

The length and focus of these studies generated their intensity and detail, along with the ever-present efforts from the late twelfth-century on to integrate Aristotle's works into these Christian analyses. Old-fashioned allegorical and typological interpretation and theory of 'signs' carried over from Augustine and others expanded into enquiries into the powers of language and kinds of agency that propelled it. As the *Sentences* noted, in baptism, you need words and water, as well as an intention; take away the words and you have only water. Adults to be baptised require faith; priests require an intention to baptise for the words to be efficacious. But a priest using bad Latin could still convey a sacrament. Baptism carried out in jest by a mime was a different matter.[38] University 'readers' (doctoral lecturers) in the *Sentences* pursued these issues variously. The phrases used for the sacraments were not exactly as in the Bible, yet the formulae mattered. How could this be explained? Intention matters to any speech-act. But how rigorously must intention be maintained? In the late thirteenth century, Duns Scotus, with his typically fine scrutiny, proposed that a perfectly steady intention could never be guaranteed behind any utterance, thus a priest need only have a 'habitual' intention as he rehearsed sacramental statements.[39]

These topics parallel some modern considerations of the complexities of performative language, including the question of how speech-acts behave outside of direct or serious use and settings, as in literature.[40] Such topics carried more weight and risks especially but not only in the academic theologians' settings. In the thirteenth century, Henry of Ghent considered whether truth is literally present in the Bible's every statement. It would seem not, since untruths, contradictions, and sinful claims often appear, even in Jesus's restatements of

---

[36] C. De Boer (ed.), *Ovide moralisé: Poème du commencement du quatorzième siècle*, 5 vols. (Amsterdam, 1915–38).

[37] For the steps to a theology degree in fourteenth-century Oxford, see William Courtenay, *Schools and Scholars in Fourteenth-Century England* (Princeton, NJ, 1987), 41–2.

[38] *Sententiarum Libri Quattor*, 192:42–52, in the *Patrologia Latina Database*, based on J. P. Migne (ed.), *Patrologiae Cursus Completus* (Paris, 1841–65).

[39] Irène Rosier-Catach, *La Parole Efficace: Signe, Rituel, Sacré* (Paris, 2004), 276–82.

[40] See Jonathan Culler, *Literary Theory: A Very Short Introduction* (Oxford, 2011), 94–107.

others' words. Yet Holy Scripture must present eternal truth in every sense. Henry's solution was to declare that any statement that was either doctrinally or factually false possessed no literal sense at all; in such cases the immediate speaker, the human author, or the ultimate divine author meant those words only figurally.[41] While showing the scholastic preoccupation with distinguishing between quoted statements, narrative statements, and authorial intentions, such proposals indicate the problem of knowing where to anchor meaning to one or another of these levels, while then denying that any of the other levels of signification possessed any meaning of its own.

Such debates might seem hair-splitting, but any challenges to the bases for interpreting the Bible provoked grave concern. The idea of unbounded interpretation of every word's literal meaning in every context, regardless of any plausible authorial intention, was considered interpretation *de virtute verborum*, 'by the force of words', and this mode was deemed so scandalous that the University of Paris passed a statute in 1340 forbidding all arguments based on that principle. For if this guided interpretation, it would show that Scripture was full of lies.[42] Differentiating authorial intention from characters' statements or their own use of quoted statements is a topic that eventually moved out from biblical controversy to other matters, such as the bitter early-fifteenth-century debates in France between the laywoman Christine de Pizan and the Col brothers, concerning just how lecherous and misogynist, or how pious, Jean de Meun's underlying intentions were, that is, how separate from his allegorical characters'.[43] Dante's text had already received commentary in Italy, but Christine de Pizan's attention to the problem of authorial intention of the *Roman de la rose* brought the idea of vernacular literary criticism closer to England. It has been proposed that Thomas Hoccleve's sly reframing of Christine's *Epistle de Cupid* in 1402 takes the argument further.[44]

No medieval English poet openly deconstructed sacramental language or the Bible's truth. But suspicion of institutional power was rampant in vernacular culture, and this often settled on textual interpretation, who could authorise it and how it might be given potency. Late-fourteenth-century Lollards, followers of the anticlerical academic John Wyclif, spurned prayers to the saints, confessions to priests, and any oath 'vppon a boke' as all forms of idolatry;[45] the Wycliffite satire *Pierce the Ploughman's Crede* (*c* 1393–*c* 1400), rendering into blunt weaponry the subtler and often dialogic anticlerical arguments of *Piers Plowman*, presents a narrator demanding from various orders of friars that they teach him the Creed. Each condemns another order for 'leesinges' (lies), but none knows the Creed's simple declaration of faith. Only the humble, illiterate Pierce can teach him.[46]

Chaucer's 'Friar's Tale' dwells on the question of how intention determines the efficacy of curses: a horse driver's impatient curse of his horse leads to nothing; a widow's steadily affirmed curse of a corrupt summoner, and the summoner's shameless acknowledgement, produces a very different outcome. The seeds (or later précis) of this investigation of the topic of sacramental speech-acts are the doubts about the validity of an archdeacon's excommunicating 'curse' satirically raised in the portrait of the Summoner himself in the 'General

---

[41] Minnis and Scott, *Medieval Literary Theory and Criticism*, 264.

[42] William Courtenay, 'Force of Words and Figures of Speech: The Crisis over *virtus sermonis* in the Fourteenth Century', *Franciscan Studies*, 44 (1984), 107–28.

[43] Joseph L. Baird and John R. Kane (eds and trans.), *La Querelle de la Rose: Letters and Documents* (Chapel Hill, NC, 1978).

[44] John V. Fleming, 'Hoccleve's "Letter of Cupid" and the "Quarrel" over the *Roman de la Rose*', *Medium Ævum*, 40 (1971), 21–40.

[45] Anne Hudson, *The Premature Reformation: Wycliffite Texts and Lollard History* (Oxford, 1988), 310–13, 371–4.

[46] *Pierce the Ploughman's Crede*, in Helen Barr (ed.), *The Piers Plowman Tradition* (London, 1993), 59–98.

158   MEDIEVAL POETRY: 1100–1400

Prologue' (658–72). Yet the issue tunnels throughout Chaucer's poetry, informing some of his experiments in genres and forms. The ignorant but unwittingly effective narrator of the *Book of the Duchess* asks the Black Knight for all the circumstantial details of his loss that would be required for a confession, 'telle me hooly / In what wyse, how, why, and wherfore' (846–7); but confession turns out to be a failed genre for grasping the heart of the problem, as the narrator recognises midway when he scolds the knight for spending so much time simply praising his beloved, with no sign of penance for whatever he has done: 'Me thynketh ye have such a chaunce / As shryfte wythoute repentaunce' (1113–14). The *Canterbury Tales* ends its tale-telling by confronting readers of the 'The Manciple's Tale' with the horrific consequences of a talking crow bluntly telling a god of his wife's infidelity, followed by instructions on confession in the 'Parson's Tale', followed in turn by the narrator's (or the poet's) response to the call for confession in the form of the *Retraction*, which manages to list all the poems Chaucer wrote. Is this last a failed sacrament, 'as shryfte wythoute repentaunce', or a successful authorial signature of the book we have been reading, noting many others to which we might next turn?

If these forays tested the power of words in theological and philosophical terrain in ways that only vernacular poetry might manage, they also implicitly granted such poetry significant importance in a topic crucial to wider Christian culture. So too English poetry's absorption of but oblique responses to academic ideas of authorship. As scholars since the late twentieth century have shown, exegetical and commentary materials provided fourteenth-century English poets with a surprisingly usable range of theories of authorship.[47] In some ways those can be seen influencing medieval English poetry because of the dearth of prestigious alternatives in post-Conquest England. Indistinguishable or overlapping kinds of textual agency seem inevitable in vernacular poetry. Even setting aside modern narratological claims that no medieval narrative ever has a narrator unless one is explicitly identified,[48] it is clear that post-Conquest English poets were generally more servile translators, compilers, performers, priests, or scribes, than were either French or Latin poets; when they proclaim their literary role, it is often mainly to combine and translate works to those who 'þe Latyn no Frankys con'.[49] They certainly had few reasons to make claims about their poetic accomplishments like ancient poets such as Horace, who proclaims 'Exegi monumentum aere perennius' ('I have made a monument more lasting than bronze'; *Odes* 3.30), or Statius, who addresses his finished poem, 'O ... Thebai ... vive, precor; nec tu divinam Aeneida tempta, / Sed longe sequere et vestigia semper adora' ('O *Thebaid*, live on, I pray! Nor rival the divine *Aeneid*, but follow afar and ever venerate its footsteps'; *Thebaid* 12.811–17).

Yet it is one of the remarkable turns in literary history that some medieval English poets by the later fourteenth century gained the temerity to make claims not too far from those,

---

[47] See Judson B. Allen, *The Ethical Poetic of the Later Middle Ages: A Decorum of Convenient Distinction* (Toronto, 1982); Alastair J. Minnis, *Medieval Theory of Authorship: Scholastic Literary Attitudes in the Later Middle Ages*, 2nd edn. (Philadelphia, PA, 2010); Minnis and Scott, *Medieval Literary Theory and Criticism*; Alastair J. Minnis and Ian Johnson (eds), *The Cambridge History of Literary Criticism, Vol. 2, The Middle Ages* (Cambridge, 2005); Andrew Kraebel, *Biblical Commentary and Translation in Later Medieval England: Experiments in Interpretation* (Cambridge, 2019).

[48] See A. C. Spearing, *Textual Subjectivity: The Encoding of Subjectivity in Medieval Narratives and Lyrics* (Oxford, 2005).

[49] Robert Mannyng of Brunne, in Idelle Sullens (ed.), *Robert Mannyng: The Chronicle* (Binghamton, NY, 1996), part 1, line 8. See generally Matthew Fisher, *Scribal Authorship and the Writing of History in Medieval England* (Columbus, OH, 2012).

as shown by Chaucer's restatement of Statius's self-praise at the end of *Troilus and Criseyde*, a reprise confirmed by the concluding mention of Statius's name:

> Go, litel bok, go, litel myn tragedye ...
> But, litel book, no makyng thow n'envie,
> But subgit be to alle poesye;
> And kis the steppes where as thow seest pace
> Virgile, Ovide, Omer, Lucan, and Stace. (5.1786–92)

How did this happen? As Chaucer's careful distinction between 'poesye' for ancient writers (except for Petrarch and Dante) and 'makyng' for modern poetry including his own suggests, both Horace and Statius were common school-authors, thus founders of ideas of lauded authorship who belong among Chaucer's row of authors standing on metal pillars and muscularly holding up their 'fame' in the *House of Fame* (1419–1512). Versions of those ideals permeated basic schooling; by the thirteenth century, ancient and biblical authors were routinely named and situated at the outset of their work in brief Latin introductions or *accessus*: placards holding up their fame indeed.[50] These features of basic literary study might seem a long way from theological analysis. But exegetical analyses of authorship were built on similar foundations, even when treating much less distant founding figures. Thus the Franciscan scholar Bonaventure, in his mid-thirteenth-century commentary on Peter Lombard's *Sentences*, pauses to define the nature of authorship in general in very elevated terms, placing an *auctor* (who happens to be a near-contemporary academic writer) second only to God in primal creativity:

> The man who presents and reveals the knowledge which he has in his soul in word or writing is doing something quite different from the One who imprints the condition (*habitus*) of knowledge [on men's souls]. Each is called a teacher and author, but God is the more principal one. The same is true of the book [i.e., the *Sentences*] set before us.[51]

Peter Lombard here serves as a model of nearly primary, unmediated producer of teaching and writing, indebted only to God's 'more principal' imposition of the innate ability to gain the knowledge Peter displays. This focus on the author as a producer, though a primary one, places him within the Aristotelean 'efficient cause', as is traditional for authorship in academic contexts. But Bonaventure goes on to specify this cause in more administrative detail than usual, down to the most mechanical members of literary and intellectual production. There is the scribe, who writes out the words of others without adding or changing anything; the compiler, who writes others' words, putting together material, but not adding his own; the commentator, who writes others' words and his own, 'but with those of other men comprising the principal part while his own are annexed merely to make clear the argument'; and finally the *auctor*, who writes others' words and his own but 'with his own forming the principal part and those of others being annexed merely by way of confirmation'.[52] Each textual labourer has increasing degrees of their own words, up to the author, whose originality of labour is the most 'principal', short only of God's.

---

[50] Minnis and Scott, *Medieval Literary Theory and Criticism*, 12–36.
[51] Minnis and Scott, *Medieval Literary Theory and Criticism*, 230.
[52] Minnis and Scott, *Medieval Literary Theory and Criticism*, 229.

160 MEDIEVAL POETRY: 1100–1400

Medieval vernacular poets' analogous or direct reception of such theory shows they proceeded under different social and economic conditions, with less prestige and fewer rewards for the originality of their labour. Before Chaucer and Gower, no English poet seems to raise the issue of scribes' ancillary contributions to their productions. Such industrial-scale distinctions in the 'efficient cause' were not worth making, although textual labour is sometimes implied, as when the narrator of the *Owl and the Nightingale* overhears the loud debate between the birds ending with the birds themselves proposing to restate their entire debate before Nicholas of Guildford, a promise that seems to stand in for the poet sending to Nicholas a copy of the completed poem (of which only two survive). In the early thirteenth century, the south-western poet Laȝamon relates his composition of the *Brut*, a vivid history of the Saxon and 'Englisca' peoples including the first English Arthurian narrative, as a mingled process of source-seeking, translation, compilation, and scribal labour, offering the English equivalent of an *accessus* to his own poem but in terms of multiple roles:

> An preost wes on leoden . Laȝamon wes ihoten ...
>
> hit com him on mode . & on his mern þonke.
>
> þet he wolde of Engle . þe æðelæn tellen ...
>
> Laȝamon gon liðen . wide ȝond þas leode.
>
> & bi-won þa æðela boc . þa he to bisne nom ...
>
> He nom þa Englisca boc . þa makede Seint Beda.
>
> An-oþer he nom on Latin . þa makede Seinte Albin ...
>
> Boc he mon þe thridde . leide þer amidden.
>
> þa makede a Frenchis clerc.
>
> Wace was ihoten, þe wel couþe writen ...
>
> Laȝamon leide þeos boc . & þa leaf wende.
>
> he heom leofliche bi-heold . liþe him beo Drihten.
>
> Feþeren he nom mid fingren . & fiede on boc-felle.
>
> & þa soþere word . sette to-gadere.
>
> & þa þre boc . þrumde to are.

(There was a priest among the people, called Laȝamon ... it came to his mind, and it seemed glorious, that he would tell about England's noble people ... Laȝamon went travelling across this land and found the noble book that he took as exemplar ... He took the English book that St Bede wrote; another, in Latin he took that St Alban [?] wrote ... a third book he took and placed between them, which a French clerk had written, called Wace, who really knew how to write ... Laȝamon laid out these books and turned their leaves; he gazed at them lovingly—the Lord help him! He took pens in his fingers and combined them on the parchment, and assembled the truer words, compressing those three into one.)[53]

Laȝamon aligns himself with seemingly every kind of textual agency *except* author. Yet his poem proceeds with remarkable freedom from his sources; and no reader doubts his

[53] G. L. Brook and R. F. Leslie (eds), *Laȝamon: Brut*, 2 vols., EETS o.s. 250, 277 (London, 1966, 1978), lines 1–28; my translation.

originality. Even this prologue presents something new. It is an *accessus* not of an *auctor* but of a researcher/translator/book-collector/compiler/truth-seeker. Perhaps to grant this *impressio* role its proper grandeur, Laȝamon goes well beyond factual accuracy. Instead of a trilingual range of sources collected from journeys through the land, as he claims, the *Brut* in fact translates and expands only Wace, a French translation of Geoffrey of Monmouth's Latin Arthurian history that was widely available, adding details and many expansions. In his prologue, however, a compiler's and scribe's and translator's role becomes momentous, re-originating. The poet's unification of a bookish trinity into a unity is nearly priestly, using the poet's professional religious identity as a kind of unifying shell for his many actions as textual worker. It is hard not to imagine that Laȝamon consciously filled in the notion of an 'efficient cause' with this one-man cluster of functions. This shows even humble textual labours can be nearly sacramental.

Even before Chaucer and Gower, scholastic theories of authorship seeped into parts of vernacular culture. Claims on authorial prestige much closer than Laȝamon's to what the scholastics presented can be found in England in the same period, by a French poet. In 1267 one Pierre d'Abernon de Fetcham, chaplain to a Surrey family who had attended Oxford, produced an encyclopaedic poem on sin, the sacraments, and the forms of confession, called the *Lumere as Lais* (*Light for Lay People*), which applies the Aristotelean causes to his own text:

> Cinc choses sount em ja enquere
> Au comencement en livere fere:
> Ki fust autur, e l'entitlement,
> E la matire e la furme ensement,
> E la fin, ceo est par queu reisun
> Fu fest la composiciun.

(There are five things in this to seek at the start of making a book: who the author was, what the title is, and the matter and the form as well, and what its end is; that is, for what purpose the composition was made.)[54]

The poet identifies himself as the book's maker ('Peire qi cest livere fist' [20]), but later remarks that God was its 'principal' author ('De cest livere si est autur / Princeipaument nostre Seignur' [537–8]). Compared to Laȝamon, Pierre's opening more learnedly and conventionally follows both the procedures of *accessus* and the double authorial inscription described in Bonaventure's elaboration of the authorship of the *Sentences*. Bonaventure's commentary, from the early 1250s, might even have been one of Pierre's sources; moreover, Pierre's choice of a work based on the dialogic encyclopaedia the *Elucidarium* offers a scope of theological knowledge at least analogous to the *Sentences*, although offering material of a simpler kind as befits a work explicitly made *as Lais* ('for the laity'). At any rate, the proximity of Pierre's work to academic postures and genres indicates the different sphere occupied by the other main vernacular in England, thus the range of variations in their relations to high theory.

No medieval poet writing in English made claims like Pierre d'Abernon's. By the late fourteenth century, however, English poets in royal administrative and courtly roles were

---

[54] Glynn Hesketh (ed.), *La Lumere as Lais by Pierre d'Abernon of Fetcham*, 3 vols., ANTS 54–8 (London, 1996–2000), lines 531–6(my translation); see E. J. Arnould, 'On Two Anglo-Norman Prologues', *Modern Language Review*, 34 (1939), 248–51.

162   MEDIEVAL POETRY: 1100–1400

likely to claim for themselves the identity of 'maker' (which Laȝamon does not), and even imply that of 'author'. One way they did this was by emphasising that they, as authors, were assisted by scribes, a banal truth they sometimes fashioned into a meaningful feature of their poetry. The diplomat and civil servant Chaucer wrote a small poem scolding 'Adam Scriveyn' (Adam the scribe) for all the errors he leaves in his copies of 'my makyng' (line 4); whatever we might say about the scribe Adam, this posture enforces Chaucer's own authorial supervision.[55] As already noted, Chaucer's *Retraction* to *The Canterbury Tales* lists his most important works in a careful résumé. This is followed, in the Ellesmere manuscript, with the rubric, 'Heere is ended the book of the tales of Caunterbury, compiled by Geffrey Chaucer, of whos soule Jhesu Crist have mercy'. This is a scribal invocation of the modest role of compiler; but there is textual evidence that the rubrics and many of the persistent glosses in manuscripts of *The Canterbury Tales* reach back early in the work's history, and may well have been created by Chaucer himself.[56] If so, those show his own construction of a scribal world framing and purveying the author's work, just as does the narrator's worried mentions of those who may 'mismetre' his poem *Troilus and Criseyde* (5.1795–6).

Chaucer's contemporary and associate Gower, an affluent landowner who was likely a lawyer, went further in using the academic theoretical apparatus of authorship. Gower added prose Latin glosses to the *Confessio Amantis*, including one gloss introducing the *auctor* as fashioning himself in the *persona* of a lover ('quasi in persona aliorum quos amor alligat, fingens se auctor esse Amantem').[57] Like the Latin colophons completing Gower's main manuscripts of his poems and summarising his oeuvre, this implies a team of academic and clerical glossators, elevating Gower as *auctor* by supplying academic summarisers and explicators. Gower uses not only the structures of contemporary clerical glosses of ancient texts but also the contents: just as his English verse sometimes draws on the *Ovide moralisé*, so his Latin glosses to his English versions of Ovid's tales often use the mid-fourteenth-century moral and allegorical commentary on the *Metamorphoses* by the monk Pierre Bersuire. Gower implies his own work's eligibility for authority, as a work to be studied and glossed, transferring the words of an actual contemporary glossator on Ovid to his English poem.[58]

Subtle as they were, these developments were bold for medieval English poets, bespeaking a degree of confidence that could emerge only among such well-connected London and courtly secular poets, whose local fame was prominent enough that one scribe of Gower's *Confessio Amantis* could insert in a visual portrait of the Lover the face of an aged John Gower. Chaucer's portrait, which appears as early as the Ellesmere manuscript, *c* 1407, led to an even longer series of uses of Chaucer's face in the fifteenth century.[59] Yet even at the height of Gower's and Chaucer's invocations or implications of authorial prestige, they did not claim to mount the pedestals of textual authority indicated by so many medieval

---

[55] Adam is identified as Adam Pinkhurst by Linne R. Mooney, 'Chaucer's Scribe', *Speculum*, 81 (2006), 97–138. The identification has not been universally recognised; see, for instance, Jane Roberts, 'On Giving Scribe B a Name and a Clutch of London Manuscripts from *c*. 1400', *Medium Ævum*, 80 (2011), 247–70 and Lawrence Warner, *Chaucer's Scribes: London Textual Production, 1384–1432* (Cambridge, 2018).

[56] See Stephen Partridge, '"The Makere of this Boke": Chaucer's Retraction and the Author as Scribe and Compiler', in Stephen Partridge and Erik Kwakkel (eds), *Author, Reader, Book: Medieval Authorship in Theory and Practice* (Toronto, 2012), 106–53.

[57] *Confessio Amantis*, 1.61 margin; see Robert R. Edwards, *Invention and Authorship in Medieval England* (Columbus, OH, 2017), 94–8.

[58] Galloway, 'Gower's Ovids', 450–6.

[59] For these examples, see Andrew Galloway, 'Fame's Penitent: Deconstructive Chaucer Among the Lancastrians', in Isabel David and Catherine Nall (eds), *Chaucer and Fame: Reputation and Reception* (Woodbridge, 2015), 103–26.

Latin teachers, scholars, and poets, and even some French ones. Nor, perhaps, would their poetry be as wryly complex if they had. The cagey encroachments by post-Conquest English poets on academic rhetorical instruction and scholastic authority required more complex strategies of self-authorising than direct claims would have done, yielding deeper questioning of the uses and structures of poetics and authority as such. This is surely partly why Chaucer's and Gower's works engaged so many followers. They were preceded by a distinguished span of poets who struggled harder, and sometimes no less adroitly, to occupy some corner of the territory of *poetria* that was increasingly visible around them.

PART III
'MATERE'

11

Poetry and National History

Caroline D. Eckhardt

The several versions of the prose *Anglo-Saxon Chronicle*, which since the late ninth century had been recording national history in the English language, gradually fell silent after the Norman Conquest. Nevertheless, the rupture in English historiography was neither lengthy nor complete. Entries in the manuscript of the *Chronicle* kept at Peterborough were extended until 1154, nearly a century after the Conquest, and the story of England continued to be written in Latin as part of the immense production of medieval historical writing in many forms.[1] Further, shortly before the last entry in the Peterborough chronicle there appeared the first verse chronicle of England's story in Anglo-French,[2] Geoffrei Gaimar's *Estoire des Engleis* (*History of the English*, perhaps as early as 1135), based in part on the *Anglo-Saxon Chronicle*. It was soon to be followed by Wace's *Brut* (1155), translated into French verse from Geoffrey of Monmouth's Latin prose *Historia Regum Britanniae* (*c* 1137). English-language historical writing returned as well, now also in verse, with Laȝamon's *Brut* (*c* 1189–1236), after which the extant record of verse chronicles in English shows a gap until the late thirteenth or early fourteenth century. Within less than another century, however, prose again functioned as the predominant medium for disseminating national history in English, especially in John Trevisa's widely circulated prose translation of Ranulph Higden's Latin *Polychronicon* and in the great plenitude of copies of the anonymous English prose *Brut*-chronicle.[3]

The handful of surviving texts from what appears to have been a brief flourishing of English verse historiography constitutes a small corpus, though one work, *Castleford's Chronicle*, is extremely long.[4] These verse chronicles share characteristics such as coverage of an extended timespan, an insistent genealogical sequencing, and, despite occasional episodes that defy credulity, a posture of historicity achieved through a controlled focus on the kings, wars, and politics of Britain/England, along with occasional descriptive passages, disturbances of nature such as storms or famines, or other major events—ostensibly, the *res verae quae factae sunt*, 'the true things that were done', in Isidore of Seville's terms (*Etymologiae* 1.44.5). Some chroniclers are more prone than others to provide a preamble, interject comments, or embellish a good story. Their dialects of origin (subsequent dissemination aside) indicate that the production of verse histories was not concentrated in one or

---

[1] Fundamental resources for historical writing in England include Edward Donald Kennedy, *Chronicles and Other Historical Writing*, volume 8 (1989) of Albert E. Hartung (ed.), *A Manual of the Writings in Middle English 1050–1500*, 11 vols. (New Haven, CT, 1967–2005); Chris Given-Wilson, *Chronicles: The Writing of History in Medieval England* (London, 2004); and Jennifer Jahner, Emily Steiner, and Elizabeth M. Tyler (eds), *Medieval Historical Writing: Britain and Ireland, 500–1500* (Cambridge, 2019).

[2] See Chapter 7 in this volume.

[3] Many versions and some 250 manuscripts of the interrelated Anglo-French, Latin, and English prose *Brut*-chronicles survive; Lister M. Matheson, *The Prose Brut: The Development of a Middle English Chronicle* (Tempe, AZ, 1998) and Julia Marvin, *The Oldest Anglo-Norman Prose Brut Chronicle: An Edition and Translation* (Woodbridge, 2006).

[4] At 39,439 lines, it is among the longest of Middle English poems; Caroline D. Eckhardt (ed.), *Castleford's Chronicle or The Boke of Brut*, 2 vols., EETS, o.s. 305, 306 (Oxford, 1996).

Caroline D. Eckhardt, *Poetry and National History*. In: *The Oxford History of Poetry in English*. Edited by Helen Cooper and Robert R. Edwards, Oxford University Press. © Caroline D. Eckhardt (2023). DOI: 10.1093/oso/9780198827429.003.0011

168   MEDIEVAL POETRY: 1100–1400

two centres of activity.[5] They do not represent a singular or isolated narrative lineage, but were always engaged with multiple related texts, including historical narratives in prose, Latin, or Anglo-French and kindred genres such as romance, genealogy, hagiography, and prophecy. One of the aims of this chapter will be to suggest the generic porosity and stylistic variation that these English verse chronicles embodied. Another aim is to point out that they contributed to the circulation of poetry in English not only at the time of their known or estimated origin but also later, when the manuscript evidence shows that they continued to have an active 'working life' because someone was reading and copying them.

What did these chroniclers envision as English national history—whose nation, and whose history? It is almost invariably the history of those who held power and their immediate communities, with other interlocutors, social networks, and segments of the population only occasionally visible and rarely audible. As suggested by Robert of Gloucester's remark, 'Brutons was þe verste folc. þat to engelonde com' ('Britons were the first people who came to England'),[6] which slides from the one 'folc' to the other, the nation is sometimes Britain, conceived in geospatial terms as the island at the far edge of the world or in ethnic terms as the land of the Britons; or the nation is England, the land of the Angles or the English kin, a concept also both spatial and ethnic; or it is a layered entity embodied in the insular story of successive peoples—Britons, Romans, Saxons, later Danes, 'English', Normans—all arrivals from elsewhere, yet all linked into a temporal continuity reaching back to ancient Troy.

The new (or renewed) production of English-language historiography that began with Laȝamon's *Brut* differed from its Old English predecessors not only by its medium of verse rather than prose but also by its focus on earlier eras and different antecedents. The wellspring of vernacular retellings of the new 'British history' was Geoffrey of Monmouth's *Historia Regum Britanniae*, which offered the first highly crafted narrative of Britain's ancient populations and long-lost kingdoms.[7] In filling the interstitial gaps in the national past, Geoffrey's work performed what the earlier Latin chronicler known as Nennius had described as healing the 'wound' of absent historical memory.[8] With a narrative arc that recalls the migratory trajectories and *translatio imperii* theme of the *Aeneid*, the *Historia* anchors the story in Troy, providing a glimpse of Aeneas's flight from the doomed city and rise to power in Italy, and then recounts the career of Brutus, Aeneas's great-grandson, who is expelled from Italy, wanders in Mediterranean and Atlantic regions, and eventually leads his group of Trojan survivors to a faraway island inhabited only by giants. Brutus calls the island Britain in perpetuation of his name, his companions become Britons, they drive away or kill the giants and build the city of New Troy (later London), and their language gradually transitions from Trojan to British. This foundation-story of arrival, expulsion of indigenous dwellers, and naming and claiming of the land is followed by conflicts, invasions, and other episodes wrapped into stories of figures such as Lear, Gorboduc, Caesar, the Saxons Hengist, Horsa, and Rowena, Merlin, Arthur, and many others along the way. The narrative concludes shortly after the death of the last British king, Cadwallader, and

---

[5] Kennedy's suggestions (*Manual* entries) encompass the central West Midlands, West Midlands, South-west Midlands, North-east Midlands, and Yorkshire.

[6] William Aldis Wright (ed.), *The Metrical Chronicle of Robert of Gloucester*, 2 vols., Rolls Series 86.1–2 (London, 1887), 57.

[7] Geoffrey's history is traditionally titled *Historia Regum Britannie* (*History of the Kings of Britain*); the title *De Gestis Britonum* (*On the Deeds of the Britons*) is preferred by Georgia Henley and Joshua Byron Smith (eds), *A Companion to Geoffrey of Monmouth* (Leiden, 2020).

[8] *Historia Brittonum* (*History of the Britons*) attributed to Nennius, in J. A. Giles (ed. and trans.), *Six Old English Chronicles* (London, 1848), 383.

the consolidation of Saxon rule under Adelstan, events situated nearly 500 years before Geoffrey's own Norman-ruled time.

This creative retrospect upon Britain's past not only populated the immense silences in Britain's ancient history; it also attributed shape and meaning to that past. The design of the *Historia* presented the founder and colonist Brutus and the empire-builder and civiliser Arthur as its two dominating figures within a matrix of more than a hundred other leaders. With its open-ended paratactic structure and its incorporation of recent Crusade-era rhetoric, Geoffrey's widely disseminated 'British history' attracted translations, continuations, and adaptations for several centuries.[9] The English verse chroniclers drew upon it directly or indirectly, often blending multiple sources. Their narratives were also shaped by other formative elements that now resist identification, such as the preferences of patrons, the chroniclers' authorial positions and access to archives, unrecorded oral tales, the practicalities of dissemination, the decisions of medieval editors, and the habits and expertise of scribes. As a body of English poetry, these national histories are very much the products of shared traditions and collaborative labour.

We will consider where, in all this material, the poetry resides. Much of the verse in these chronicles is no more than pedestrian (Laʒamon is the major exception). The aesthetic tensions between poetry and history have been well described by Thorlac Turville-Petre, among others: 'Poetic chronicle is a form which we have difficulty in coming to terms with. ... As a poem it ought to have form and shape, some perceivable pattern, but as chronicle it must remain faithful to its source, recording events not because of their significance to a pattern but just because they took place'.[10] Post-medieval aesthetic judgements have often been lukewarm at best, and a nineteenth-century editor of Robert of Gloucester's *Metrical Chronicle* famously chastised its style for being 'as worthless as twelve thousand lines of verse without one spark of poetry can be'[11]—but, as I hope to show, that harsh assessment does not tell the whole story.

Though the corpus is small, many scholarly controversies about dates, authorship, titles, versions, versification, and sometimes even line numbers underlie the summary list given here.[12]

(1) Laʒamon, *Brut*. Composed *c* 1189–1236; extant in two versions, Caligula (16,095 long lines) and Otho (nearly 20 per cent shorter); predominantly alliterative verse. From the fall of Troy to the death of Cadwallader, the last British king, in 689 CE.[13]

(2) *Metrical Chronicle* attributed to Robert of Gloucester. Composed in the late thirteenth or early fourteenth century; extant in two versions (*c* 12,000 lines, Long Version; *c* 10,000 lines, Short Version); septenary couplets. From Brutus to the year 1270 or to 1272; after 1135 (the death of Henry I) the two continuations diverge.[14]

(3) *The Short Metrical Chronicle*. Composed in the early fourteenth century, with later continuations; extant in five versions (1014 to 2361 lines long) and three

---

[9] J. C. Crick, *The Historia regum Britannie of Geoffrey of Monmouth, IV. Dissemination and Reception in the Later Middle Ages* (Cambridge, 1991); Lawrence Warner, 'Geoffrey of Monmouth and the De-Judaized Crusade', *Parergon*, 21.1 (2004), 19–37.

[10] Thorlac Turville-Petre, *The Alliterative Revival* (Cambridge, 1977), 94–5.

[11] W. Wright (ed), *Metrical Chronicle*, 1.40.

[12] This summary draws primarily upon Kennedy, *Manual*, and the editions noted.

[13] G. L. Brook and R. F. Leslie (eds), *Laʒamon: Brut*, 2 vols., EETS o.s. 250, 277 (London, 1963, 1978); Kennedy, *Manual*, 2611–17. 'Caligula' is London, British Library, MS Cotton Caligula A.ix; 'Otho' is London, British Library, MS Cotton Otho C. xiii. On the different lengths, see Elizabeth J. Bryan, *Collaborative Meaning in Medieval Scribal Culture: The Otho Laʒamon* (Ann Arbor, MI, 1999), 48.

[14] W. Wright (ed.), *Metrical Chronicle*; Kennedy, *Manual*, 2617–22, 2642, including fifteenth-century redactions. Though 'Robert (of Gloucester)' may not have written the entire chronicle, I follow previous practice in associating the whole work with this name.

170   MEDIEVAL POETRY: 1100–1400

brief fragments; four-stress couplets. From Brutus to the accession of Edward II in 1307 or later; one verse continuation ends in 1430. The Auchinleck manuscript's version begins with a counter-narrative origin tale (recalling Hypermnestra) in which the first human arrivals on the island are Albina and her many sisters, expelled from their Greek homeland for plotting to kill their husbands; their matings with the devil produce the race of giants later encountered by Brutus and his companions.[15]

(4) *Castleford's Chronicle, or, the Boke of Brut.* Perhaps completed in 1327; extant in one manuscript (39,439 lines); four-stress couplets. From Albina and her sisters to the deposition and imprisonment of Edward II in 1327.[16]

(5) Robert Mannyng of Brunne, *Chronicle.* Completed in 1338; extant in two parts: Part I (16,638 lines in four-stress couplets) moves from Noah's flood and a quick summary of the Troy tale to the death of Cadwallader; Part II (8,387 lines in five- or six-stress couplets) continues to 1307.[17]

None of these chronicles is a copy or direct derivative of any other. Nevertheless, there may have been multiple interrelations in their textual histories. For example, it has been proposed that Robert of Gloucester and the *Short Metrical Chronicle* used Laȝamon; and that the *Short Metrical Chronicle* used Robert of Gloucester's *Metrical Chronicle*, or, the reverse, that a later recension of Robert of Gloucester's work used an early version of the *Short Metrical Chronicle.* A confluence of some sort in the readership of those two works is indicated by the presence of both, copied by the same scribe, in London, British Library, MS Additional 19,677 (*c* 1390–1400), as well as by the insertion of one leaf of the *Short Metrical Chronicle* into the Cotton MS of Robert of Gloucester's *Metrical Chronicle.*[18] It is sometimes assumed that these English *Brut*-chronicles all had French (or Anglo-French) sources, but given that Latin sources too were available, and multiple little-studied *Brut*-narratives survive, many textual affiliations may still be unidentified.[19]

Variations within the Chronicle Corpus

The representation of episodes that these English chronicles share can suggest their nuances and differences. One such episode, discussed below, occurs at the end of the Arthurian section, when Arthur, at the height of his European conquests, must hastily return home to

---

[15] Ewald Zettl (ed.), *An Anonymous Short English Metrical Chronicle* (London, 1935) (all MSS except 'M199'); Una O'Farrell-Tate (ed.), *The Abridged English Metrical Brut Edited from London, British Library MS Royal 12 c. xii* (Heidelberg, 2002) (MS 'R'); David Burnley and Alison Wiggins (eds), *The Auchinleck Manuscript*, auchinleck.nls.uk, 5 July 2003, accessed 27 February 2021 (MS 'A', Edinburgh, National Library of Scotland Advocates' MS 19.2.1); Peter Grund, 'A Previously Unrecorded Fragment of the Middle English Short Metrical Chronicle in Bibliotheca Philosophica Hermetica M199', *English Studies*, 87.3 (2006), 277–93 (MS 'M199'). This chronicle has been given some nine titles (O'Farrell-Tate, *Abridged*, 14).

[16] Eckhardt (ed.), *Castleford's Chronicle.* Though the attribution to Thomas Castleford is weak (based on a marginal annotation in the MS, Göttingen, Niedersächsische Staats- und Universitätsbibliothek, MS 2° hist. 740 Cim. I follow previous practice in associating the work with this name; Kennedy's title (2624–5) is *Thomas Bek of Castleford's Chronicle of England.* A digitisation of the MS (in 2018) is available on the library's website.

[17] Idelle Sullens (ed.), Robert Mannyng of Brunne, *The Chronicle* (Binghamton, NY, 1996); Kennedy's title (2625–8) is *The Story of England.*

[18] O'Farrell-Tate, *Abridged*, 35–46; Zettl, *Anonymous*, xi–xiii; and, on the leaf in Robert of Gloucester's *Chronicle*, Zettl, *Anonymous*, xxviii–xxxi, and W. Wright, *Metrical Chronicle*, xl–xli.

[19] Françoise le Saux, 'Geoffrey of Monmouth's *De gestis Britonum* and Twelfth-Century Romance', in Henley and Smith (eds), *Companion*, 235–56, especially 250–5. The assumption that the verse chroniclers knew Geoffrey's Latin *Historia* (only) in prose should stop short of certainty, as the *Historia* was also turned into Latin verse; Neil Wright (ed. and trans.), *The Historia Regum Britannie of Geoffrey of Monmouth, V, Gesta Regum Britannie* (Cambridge, 1991). Cf. n. 88, Barbieri, below.

reclaim Britain from the usurper Mordred. In this culminating conflict Arthur is variously said to die, or to be borne away mortally wounded, or, in one account, to survive the battle and live for another ten years. Aside from the Arthurian passages, two of the chronicles will be discussed more fully, as they are of special literary importance: Laȝamon's *Brut* is fundamental for the development of Middle English alliterative poetry; and the *Short Metrical Chronicle* gains significance from its inclusion in the Auchinleck manuscript, where the promulgation of 'Englishness' has been extensively debated.

The greatest poet among the English verse chroniclers is undeniably the first. In his remarkable prologue (1–38), Laȝamon creates an individualised identity (he is a priest, the son of Leouenaþ) and establishes his authority as a trustworthy historian by recounting his process of literary composition, beginning with the idea that he would tell the story of 'wat heo ihoten weoren & wonene heo comen / þa Englene londe ærest ahten' ('what they were called, and whence they came / who first owned England', 8–9). In travelling the length of the land in search of sources, he found three wonderful books, which he laid out in front of him; then he performed the physical act of writing, holding his quill pen, composing on parchment, recording the more truthful words, and thus—marvellous term—he 'þrumde' (compressed; 28) his three volumes into one. The three sources show his trilingual reach: 'þa Englisca boc. þa makede Seint Beda', presumably the Old English translation of Bede's *History of the English Church and People*; a book in Latin by 'Seinte Albin' and 'þe feire Austin', not clearly identified; and a book by 'a Frenchis clerc / Wace wes ihoten [named]'; that is, Wace's *Brut*, which is in fact the main source (Caligula 28, 16–18, 20–1). After requesting prayers, Laȝamon launches into his tale, starting, as Wace did, with the fall of Troy; the first actors named are Menelaus, Helen, Paris, and Aeneas who flees with his followers and his son to the sea. In this prologue, Laȝamon has said more than most medieval poets do about the practice of authorship, though not much about the resultant poetry itself. Since the publication of Frederick Madden's edition in 1847, scholars have discussed the nature of Laȝamon's verse, which achieves a resonating, vigorous, occasionally brutal, and evocative quality that has often been associated with 'archaic dignity' or 'a move back to a more heroic age',[20] even if it does not fully yield to analysis.

Much recent scholarship on the *Brut* has focused on relations between its two manuscripts, Caligula and Otho. After an earlier critical tradition of regarding Caligula as older and more reliable, with Otho as its less important revision, both are now dated to the second half (Caligula) or last third (Otho) of the thirteenth century. Thus, their probable dates overlap, neither was written close to Laȝamon's own time, and, as Elizabeth Bryan, Christopher Cannon, Erik Kooper, and others have argued, we should not always privilege Caligula, Otho is not necessarily Caligula's revision, and there are important variations within as well as between them.[21] Where the two differ, Caligula is closer to Old English in ways that may already have been antiquarian, while Otho is closer to the newer genre of romance.[22] A related issue concerns Laȝamon's position within the development of alliterative poetry, as neither manuscript fully follows the conventions of Old English alliterative style. Many lines do not alliterate in the traditional patterns, rhyme becomes more frequent, and Laȝamon's 'efforts to archaize his style fall short in the well-known features of

---

[20] *Lawman: Brut*, trans. Rosamund Allen (London, 1992), xxv; Kennedy, *Manual*, 2616.

[21] Bryan, *Collaborative Meaning*, 47–50; Erik Kooper, 'Laȝamon's Prosody: Caligula and Otho—Metres Apart', in Rosamund Allen, Jane Roberts, and Carole Weinberg (eds), *Laȝamon's Brut: Approaches and Explorations* (Amsterdam, 2013), 419–41; Christopher Cannon, 'The Style and Authorship of the Otho Revision of Laȝamon's *Brut*', *Medium Ævum*, 62.2 (1993), 187–209.

[22] Cannon, 'The Style and Authorship', quoting E. G. Stanley and others on 'archaic', 'antiquarian', etc., 192; on Otho and the style of romance, 194.

172 MEDIEVAL POETRY: 1100–1400

apposition, enjambment, understatement, convoluted syntax, kennings'.[23] Given characteristics such as these, his work has been associated with oral poetry now lost, with the Old English rhythmic prose of Ælfric and Wulfstan, or with poems such as the *Proverbs of Alfred* and the *Soul's Address to the Body,* which exemplify a post-Conquest 'loose' alliterative style.[24]

Laȝamon provides the first known Arthurian story in English. His remarkable final Arthurian scene differs significantly from that of Wace, whom he usually follows, and thus presents Laȝamon's practice when he is not known to be translating. After the last battle, in which Mordred is slain, the wounded king bequeaths his kingdom to Constantine, son of Cador of Cornwall, explains that he himself will voyage to Avalon, where the elf-queen Argante will heal his wounds, and declares that he will return again: 'And seoðe ich cumen wulle · to mine kineriche. / and wunien mid Brutten · mid muchelere wunne' ('And afterwards I will come [back] to my kingdom and dwell with [the] Britons with much joy', Caligula 14,281–2).[25] When he has finished speaking,

> Æfne þan worden þer com of se wenden.
> þat wes an sceort bat liðen sceouen mid vðen.
> and twa wimmen þer-inne wunderliche idihte.
> and heo nomen Arður anan and aneouste hine uereden.
> and softe hine adun leiden and forð gunnen liðen.
> Þa wes hit iwurðen þat Merlin seide whilen.
> þat weore uni-mete care of Arðures forð-fare.
> Bruttes ileueð ȝete þat he bon on liue.
> and wunnien in Aualun mid fairest alre aluen.
> and lokieð euere Bruttes ȝete whan Arður cumen liðe.
> Nis nauer þe mon iboren of nauer nane burde icoren.
> þe cunne of þan soðe of Arðure sugen mare.
> Bute while wes an witeȝe Mærlin ihate.
> he bodede mid worde his quiðes weoren soðe.
> þat an Arður sculde ȝete cum Anglen to fulste. (Caligula 14,283–97)

(After these words there came gliding from the sea / What seemed a short boat, moving, propelled along by the tide, / And in it were two women in remarkable attire, / Who took Arthur up at once and immediately carried him / And gently laid him down and began to move off. / And so it had happened, as Merlin said before: / That the grief would be incalculable at the passing of King Arthur. / The Britons even now believe that he is alive / And living in Avalon with the fairest of the elf-folk, / And the Britons are still always looking for when Arthur comes returning. / The man has not been born of any favored lady, / Who knows how to say more about the truth concerning Arthur. / Yet once there was a prophet and his name was Merlin: / He

---

[23] Daniel Donoghue, 'Laȝamon's Ambivalence', *Speculum*, 65 (1990), 537–63, at 554.

[24] Norman. F. Blake, 'Rhythmical Alliteration', *Modern Philology*, 67 (1969), 118–24; Kooper, 'Laȝamon's Prosody', 427, 434–9; S. K. Brehe, 'Rhyme and the Alliterative Standard in Laȝamon's Brut', *Parergon*, 18.1 (2000), 11–25.

[25] The 'Breton hope', or expectation that Arthur will return to rule again, appears in, but antedates, Geoffrey of Monmouth and Wace; on early mentions, see Daniel Helbert, '"an Arður sculde ȝete cum": The Prophetic Hope in Twelfth-Century Britain', *Arthuriana*, 26.1 (2016), 77–107.

spoke his predictions, and his sayings were the truth, / Of how an Arthur once again
would come to aid the English. (Trans. R. Allen, 365.[26])

In this memorable and evocative passage, Laȝamon brings together the king's public role
as warrior, ruler, and leader of his people with the Celtic realm of the uncanny associated
with romance—the folkloric boat that moves along without apparent guide, the unidentified women in strange garments, the uncertain but anticipated return of the hero. Laȝamon's
tendency to avoid words of French derivation (especially in Caligula, less so in Otho) has
often been remarked upon,[27] but the two manuscripts show other variations in diction too.
Corresponding to Caligula's line 14,296, quoted above, Otho reads 'he saide mid wordes. his
saȝes were soþe'; where the lines differ, the words 'bodede' and 'quiðes' (Caligula) and 'saide'
and 'saȝes' (Otho) all derive from Old English, but the Otho line alliterates on s-. Further, the
way in which Caligula and Otho position this passage differently as national history is strikingly evident in just one word. In Caligula (14,297, cited above), Arthur's pledge to return
to live among the British is followed by Merlin's prophecy that an Arthur will come to aid
Anglen (the English), perhaps gesturing towards a convergent national paradigm in which
former enemies can share a leader. However, in Otho (also 14,297), instead of *Anglen* Merlin's prophecy reads *Bruttes* (the British), preserving Arthur's traditional role as defender
of the British people and allowing the ethnic contrast between them and the English who
displaced them to stand.

Many critics have pointed out Laȝamon's intricate management of the 'passage of domin-
ion' theme inherent in Geoffrey of Monmouth's legendary history, with its transformation
of Trojans into Britons and its subsequent waves of migration, warfare, and imperial
ambition, which by Laȝamon's time included not only the Norman Conquest but also participation in the would-be conquests of the Crusades. Laȝamon's position has been identified
with conflicting political alignments, perhaps reflecting a fundamental tension between 'the
desire for permanence and the inevitability of change'.[28] If *Anglen* in Caligula's Arthurian
passage is not simply a mistake (as has been suggested), Daniel Donoghue remarks that
Laȝamon 'remains caught between the old and the new, the Anglo-Saxon and the Anglo-
Norman, in an age of competing allegiances', and notes that Merlin's prophecy, which would
'extend Arthur's promise to the English as well as the British', defers such a unifying outcome
to 'the dim and indefinite future'.[29] In a detailed analysis of Laȝamon's 'loose alliterative
metre', S. K. Brehe defends the reading *Anglen*, pointing out that 'unlike the Otho line, it
alliterates, and it does so on the key words "Arþur" and "Anglen"'.[30] In both manuscripts,
though to different degrees, Laȝamon's poem allows for lines that alliterate, lines that rhyme,
lines that both alliterate and rhyme, and occasional lines that neither alliterate nor rhyme,
in what Brehe describes as 'a metric of uncertainty: like human events, like a dying man
carried off in a boat, headed for who knows where, it all turns out quite other than what we
would expect'.[31]

The *Short Metrical Chronicle*, with its eight manuscripts, has a complicated enough textual history that Matthew Fisher sees it not as one chronicle but 'a set of distinct and yet

---

[26] I quote Rosamund Allen's excellent translation: *Lawman: Brut* (London, 1992).
[27] Laȝamon uses 'only about 150 words of Romance origin in his whole work [Caligula]'; Kennedy, *Manual*,
2613. Otho 'has much higher usage of French-derived words'; Bryan, *Collaborative Meaning*, 48.
[28] Donoghue, 'Laȝamon's Ambivalence', 562.
[29] Madden, Laȝamon's first editor, suggested in 1847 that *Anglen* is an error for *Brutten*; qtd. in Donoghue,
'Laȝamon's Ambivalence', 563.
[30] Brehe, 'Rhyme and the Alliterative Standard', 23.
[31] Behre, 'Rhyme and the Alliterative Standard', 24–5.

174 MEDIEVAL POETRY: 1100–1400

interrelated texts'.[32] Although sometimes dismissed as having little or no poetic value—versions were characterised by Turville-Petre as a 'wretched little work' and by Eric Stanley as 'educational pap'[33]—the *Short Metrical Chronicle* holds a special position in the production and readership of medieval English poetry not only on its own literary grounds, but also for the company it kept. In addition to its inclusion in the Auchinleck manuscript, it also appears in London, British Library, MS Royal 12. C. xii, in the hand of the 'Harley Scribe' or 'Ludlow Scribe' who also copied the poems known as the Harley Lyrics in London, British Library, MS Harley 2253.[34] With its very compressed format, the *Short Metrical Chronicle* perhaps functioned 'to teach the main facts to the uneducated through recitation or memorization'.[35] Somewhat resembling royal genealogies, this chronicle may have been known to an anonymous contemporary of Lydgate who wrote a brief political verse chronicle similar to Lydgate's 'Verses on the Kings of England'.[36]

The Auchinleck version of the *Short Metrical Chronicle* gestures towards England's fourteenth-century linguistic diversities in the seven lines of French (1306–12) spoken by the maiden Inge, who brings her companions from 'Speyne' (1275) to Britain in time of famine, and from whom the name of England is said to derive.[37] The British king welcomes her, '& sche answerd in hir language / "Trauaile somes par mere sauage"' ('"We have struggled / travelled on the wild sea"') and requests food and rest: '"En vostre reume auer repos"' ('"in your realm to have repose"') (1305–6, 1312). Inge's first line in French is linked to the previous line in English by a bilingual rhyme ('language/sauage') or, more accurately, it draws upon the lexicon where usage is shared in what Thea Summerfield calls 'semi-French'.[38]

Though language mixing is not unusual in English chronicles,[39] Inge's speech adds crucial nuance to this version's function as national history. The Auchinleck manuscript has sometimes been regarded as a 'handbook of the nation', in Turville-Petre's phrase,[40] with its unusual 'Englishness' evident in works selected or altered to enhance English characteristics, as in *Sir Orfeo*, which situates Orfeo not in Greece but Winchester.[41] Similarly, the *Short Metrical Chronicle* has been seen as supporting an agenda of distinctive Englishness, with its synoptic style and swift brevity tending to merge ethnic and racial groups into one shared story of what became England. Fisher, for example, comments that

[32] Matthew Fisher, *Scribal Authorship and the Writing of History in Medieval England* (Columbus, OH, 2012), 117; Fisher states an earlier date, 1280, for the oldest version.

[33] Thorlac Turville-Petre, *England the Nation* (Oxford, 1996), 109; Eric G. Stanley, rev. of O'Farrell-Tate's edition, *Notes & Queries*, 50 (2003), 229–31.

[34] Fisher, *Scribal Authorship*, 100–6; O'Farrell-Tate, *The Abridged English Metrical Brut*, 17–19 and 46–54.

[35] Kennedy, *Manual*, 2622.

[36] Linne R. Mooney, 'Lydgate's "Kings of England" and Another Verse Chronicle of the Kings', *Viator*, 20 (1989), 255–89; cf. Zettl (ed.), *Anonymous*, cxxxiv–cxxxv, and Kennedy, *Manual*, 2624.

[37] Thea Summerfield, '"And she answered in hir language": Aspects of Multilingualism in the Auchinleck Manuscript', in Judith A. Jefferson and Ad Putter (eds), *Multilingualism in Medieval Britain (c. 1066–1520)* (Turnout, 2013), 241–58, especially 245–57. Mannyng declares that the tale of Inge is a lie (*Chronicle* I.14, 217–18). See also Zettl (ed.), *Anonymous*, lxviii–lxxiii and Fisher, *Scribal Authorship*, 133–9. In other MSS Inge comes from Saxony; the French prose version in MS G reads 'Saxayne en Espaigne'; Inge's speech may recall that of Spanish refugees (Zettl, ed., lxx–lxxii).

[38] Summerfield, '"And she answered"', 245–9; and Thea Summerfield, '"Fi a debles," quath the king': Language Mixing in England's Vernacular Historical Narratives, c. 1290-1340', in Jocelyn Wogan-Browne (ed.), *Language and Culture in Medieval Britain: The French of England c. 1100–c. 1500* (York, 2009), 68–80.

[39] *Castleford's Chronicle* is an exception as it 'does not introduce any French or Latin at all' and even the MS rubrics are in English (Summerfield, '"Fi a debles"', 71).

[40] Turville-Petre, *England the Nation*, 112.

[41] Rhiannon Purdie, *Anglicising Romance: Tail-Rhyme and Genre in Medieval English Literature* (Woodbridge, 2008), 96–102.

in contrast to the ruptures that mark transfers of power in other chronicles, the 'relentless continuity in the *Short Chronicle* manufactures a false sense of the continuity of political power, and obscures all moments of political discontinuity' in order to present 'a seamless narrative'.[42] However, the linguistic and cultural complexity of Auchinleck's construction of Englishness has recently been revisited to also recognise 'how deeply French and Latinate substrates inform every effort at establishing an English identity'.[43] As Anne Laskaya puts it, 'Aside from its overt literary indebtedness to French and Anglo-Norman materials, a number of other features in the Auchinleck suggest we have a manuscript best understood to rest on a fulcrum between Norman (or Anglo-Norman) and English foundations'.[44]

Thus, Inge's direct speech in French makes ethnic and linguistic difference fully visible (or audible). Inge is not an admirable character,[45] for she deceives the gullible king by requesting a bull's-hide-worth of land and then cuts the hide into a thin strip that encompasses enough land for a castle, thus appropriating the trick that the traditional 'British history' (replicating Dido's ruse) otherwise attributes to Hengist. In a second speech, after the castle is built and the king and his companions are invited to a feast, she momentarily speaks Saxon as well, commanding her followers to kill their guests at dinner when she gives the signal '"wessayl"' and herself kills the king (1332–8).[46] That Inge speaks French in her decorous plea for assistance and Saxon in her shout to unleash mass murder marks not only her difference but also her cleverness, power, and success, acknowledging the complicated identities that she represents. In this chronicle, where the very name of England is attributed, perhaps somewhat confusingly, to the smart, deceptive, French-and-Saxon-speaking maiden Inge from Spain, the presence of multiple languages is often close to the English surface.

The couplets of the *Short Metrical Chronicle* show many variations within and between versions. Focusing on MS R (London, British Library, MS Royal 12.C.xii), the poem's most recent editor, Una O'Farrell-Tate, identifies a 'norm of four stresses and seven to nine syllables' per line, along with 'two main forms of irregularity': lines that are notably shorter or longer and lines that are difficult to scan and may not always have four stresses.[47] In MS R's Arthurian passage, cited below, the lines 'Þat Moddred hys cosyn / Englond wolde bynymen him' (291–2) show some metrical uncertainty (does the first line have three stresses?) and imperfect rhyme. There are occasional uses of alliteration (e.g., 'Þat he louede so ys lyf', 296) and of repetition, as in the couplet that closes Arthur's life, 'After þon he liuede ten ȝer, / To Glastingbury me him ber' (303–4), which reprises the couplet that closed the life of his father Uther, 'He reignede þritti ȝer / To Glastinbury me him ber' (259–60), linking the generations while bringing conventional closure to each reign.[48]

In the different versions of the *Short Metrical Chronicle*, the account of Arthur's passing, if it appears at all, is extremely compressed. MS R presents the entire Arthurian story

---

[42] Fisher, *Scribal Authorship*, 136. Fisher finds, however, that MS R recovers some of 'the *translatio imperii* from the British to the Saxons', 137, 139.

[43] Susanna Fein, 'Introduction', in Susanna Fein (ed.), *The Auchinleck Manuscript: New Perspectives* (York, 2016), 7.

[44] Anne Laskaya, 'Graftings, Reweavings and Interpretation: The Auchinleck Middle English Breton Lays in Manuscript and Edition', *Etudes Epistémè*, 25 (Spring 2014), http://journals.openedition.org/episteme/203.

[45] Summerfield, '"Fi a debles"', provides other examples of the 'use of French in negative portrayals' (75).

[46] A second Saxon word, 'drinkheyl' (1264), is attributed to Inge and her followers, but not represented in direct speech.

[47] O'Farrell-Tate, *Abridged*, 56–8 on meter; citation 57.

[48] O'Farrell-Tate, *Abridged*, identifies other uses of repetition, 61–2.

176 MEDIEVAL POETRY: 1100–1400

in forty-seven lines (261–306).[49] Towards the end, after Arthur has defeated the Roman emperor's armies in France, the chronicler says, news arrives:

Þat Moddred hys cosyn	
Englond wolde bynymen* him,	take away from
Ant hede yleye* by þe quene,	lain
Geneure, þat wes bryth* [and] schene*,	bright, fair; beautiful, fair
Þat wes king Arthures wyf	
Þat he louede so ys lyf.	
Ase sone ase Arthur þe king	
Hede herd þis tiding,	
To Englelond he turned aȝein	
Boþe wiþ knyth [and] wiþ sueyn	
And Englond haþ ynome* ywys	taken, captured
Ant halt* hit ase rith* ys.	holds, rules; right
After þon he liuede ten ȝer,	
To Glastingbury me him ber. (291–304)	

Although Mordred and Guenevere momentarily come to the fore, there is no room here for a confrontation between Arthur and his betrayer, no concern about the succession, no uncertainty about the king's death. The bare narrative of events flattens the end of the Arthurian story into similitude with many other events that the chronicler also briefly recounts. Earlier in the Arthurian passage, the king is praised in superlative (and alliterative) terms, for 'Þer nes neuer such king bifore, / Ne no[n] ne byht* þer neuermore' (will be; 269–70); his reign is also distinguished for its chivalry, for 'Whyl king Arthur wes alyue / In Bretaigne wes chyualerie' (271–2). However, the diction is general and the king is not shown in action. The report that after Mordred's rebellion Arthur lived (and presumably) reigned in Britain for another ten years is of course contrary to the many tales of his death or departure to Avalon after the last battle; if audiences were anticipating what came to be accepted as the canonical ending, the outcome so blandly stated here would have constituted a notable surprise. Yet accounts of Arthur that fit him into national histories may have varied far more than is now recognised, and this ten-year extension is far from being the strangest chronicle adaptation of his reign. The nearly contemporary Anglo-French prose *Petit Bruit* (1309), also a very highly compressed retelling of the 'British history', reports that Arthur had three sons (Adeluf, Morgan, and Patrick), and was grandfather to King Alfred.[50]

Let us turn back chronologically to more briefly consider the remaining three chronicles. The *Metrical Chronicle* attributed to Robert of Gloucester is the first English verse history to extend almost to the chronicler's own times, providing a main narrative (to 1135) followed by continuations, Long (to 1270) and Short (to 1272). The author is mentioned once, in authenticating a report of the frightening darkness ('derk weder') that occurred at Evesham in 1265—'this isei [saw] roberd / that verst [first] this boc made · & was wel sore aferd' (11,742, 11,748–9). There has been much debate over who 'Robert' was, whether he wrote the entire chronicle, and what role he had in the *South English Legendary*, a contemporary collection of saints' lives and other tales.[51] The *Metrical Chronicle* and the *Legendary*, both

---

[49] This Arthurian passage occurs only in MS R. MS A (Auchinleck) has no confrontation with Mordred; after reigning for twenty-two years, Arthur dies and is buried at Glastonbury. MS B compresses the Arthurian reign into six bland lines (243–8).

[50] Rauf de Boun, in Diana B. Tyson (ed.), *Le Petit Bruit*, ANTS (London, 1987), 12–13.

[51] See Chapter 15 in this volume.

written in septenary couplets, share hundreds of lines and other similarities that might represent common authorship, borrowing, or imitation. Oliver Pickering and Philip A. Shaw have identified the stylistic traits of a proposed 'outspoken poet' at work in both poems: the use of direct speech, dialogue, couplet enjambment, and interjected comments that are sarcastic, ironic, or gently mocking.[52] In the chronicle this style is unevenly distributed, with 'few obvious examples before the period surrounding the Norman Conquest'.[53]

The end of the Arthurian section in the *Metrical Chronicle* displays some partial overlap with the postulated 'outspoken' style, along with using the newly naturalised diction of chivalry and nobility. The narrator praises Arthur as 'þe beste kniȝt' who has completed his 'last chiualerye' and done 'nobliche', remaining unconquered despite his mortal wounds:

Ac ouercome nas* he noȝt. þei* is wounden dedlich were.	*was not; though*
Þo he adde is last chiualerye*. þus nobliche ydo* þere.	*act of chivalry; done*
He ȝef þe croune of þis lond. þe noble constantin.	
Þe erl cadoures sone of cornwayle. þat was is cosin.	
& he let him lede in to an yle. vor to hele is wounde.	
& deide as þe beste kniȝt. þat me wuste* euere yfounde.	*knew*
& naþeles the brutons. & þe cornwalisse of is kunde*.	*kindred, people, nation*
Weneþ he be aliue ȝut. & abbeþ* him in munde*.	*have; mind, memory*
Þat he be to comene ȝut. to winne aȝen this lond.	
& naþeles at glastinbury. his bones suþþe me fond.	
& þere at uore* þe heye* weued*. amydde þe quer* ywis.	*before; high; altar; choir*
As is bones liggeþ*. is toumbe wel vair* is.	*lie; fair*
In þe vif hundred ȝer of grace. & vourty & tuo.	
In þis manere in cornwaile. to deþe he was ydo. (4583–96)	

Although the British and Cornish believe that Arthur will return, to the chronicler there is no question of his survival, for his fine tomb where his bones lie can be seen at Glastonbury. The specification of the tomb's location in front of the high altar, in the midst of the choir, suggests a desire to reinforce credibility about the burial, but there is little focus on the still-living Arthur, who does not speak to Constantine although the 'outspoken' style might have included direct speech here. This relatively low-key account is preceded, however, by a vigorous though brief battle scene in which Arthur declares that if he slays the traitor it will be 'gret ioye & honour' to die (4572) and then kills Mordred with an almost anti-climactic simile: 'He smot of is heued as liȝtliche [lightly] · as it were a scouple' (4578; stubble, stalk of grain; other MSS read 'stouple'). These details of decapitation and stubble may have come from Henry of Huntingdon's *Historia Anglorum*.[54] Though the simile implies ease, Henry does not state that the deed was done lightly, easily; in Robert's version that observation creates a more emphatic moment of grim humour.

The characteristic of enjambment and fluidity in managing couplets, attributed to the 'outspoken' poet's style, is evident in the Arthurian passage above (but not to an

---

[52] Oliver S. Pickering, 'Outspoken Style in the *South English Legendary* and Robert of Gloucester', in Heather Blurton and Jocelyn Wogan-Browne (eds), *Rethinking the South English Legendaries* (Manchester, 2011), 106–45, at 139; Philip A. Shaw, 'The Composition of the Metrical Chronicle Attributed to Robert of Gloucester', *English Manuscript Studies 1100–1700*, 17 (2012), 140–54.

[53] Pickering, 'Outspoken Style', 133.

[54] Henry of Huntingdon, in Diana Greenway (ed. and trans.), *Henry, Archdeacon of Huntingdon: Historia Anglorum (The History of the English People)* (Oxford, 1996), 580–1: Arthur cuts through Mordred's neck 'uelut stipulam', as if it were a 'a head of corn' (581) or a bundle of stalks of grain.

178 MEDIEVAL POETRY: 1100–1400

extraordinary extent). For example, enjambment or a very light pause seems natural at the end of line 4589, with continuation from the cesura in 4590 to the end of 4591. There is occasional alliteration, as in Arthur's leaving the crown to 'þe erl cadoures sone of cornwayle. þat was is cosin' (4586), along with the structural principles of metre and rhyme.

As with the chronicle attributed to Robert of Gloucester, authorship of the long work in four-stress couplets known as *Castleford's Chronicle* remains unclear. The name in the chronicle's received title, based on a notation in the manuscript, does not furnish a definite identity, although an association with Castleford in Yorkshire is appropriate for the dialect and Yorkshire details are sometimes featured, as in the anecdote of the collapse of a bridge at York, in which, because of the archbishop's appeals to God, nobody on the bridge or in the water died (33,554–601).[55] After a prologue about Albina, Castleford follows Geoffrey's *Historia*, probably in Latin, and then uses an array of sources, not all yet identified.

In Book VII in the Arthurian section, after the fight against Mordred the narrator contrasts the king's imperial reputation and former fearsome power over 'alle landes' with his wounded condition on the battlefield:

And Arthur selfe—þe noble kyng,	
Of erdelike* kynges maste of louing*,	*earthly; glory, praise*
For qwam alle landes trembled and quok*—	*quaked*
Þat daie in felde dede wondes he tok.	
Fra þeþen* he went, alls for a quile,	*thence*
To duel in Auolones hile,	
Þarin for to warisse* his wondes,	*cure*
Bot, certes, he lifede bot schort stondes*.	*time* (23,956–63)

The couplets are managed with some flexibility, as the first sentence with its embedded clauses flows over four lines, and there is occasional alliteration, as in 'warisse his wondes' above.

Book VII ends with ten more lines on Constantine's succession. Eliminating any doubt about Arthur's death, the opening passage of Book VIII partially repeats and then completes the story:

Wondede was Arthur in bataile,	
Nan medicines might help ne waile*.	*avail*
Dede wondes he hade, so fele* and grefe*,	*many; grievous*
He diede wiჳ schorte quile and brefe—	
He diede wiჳin brefe tim and schorte,	
Alle Britaine to gret descomforte.	
He diede in þe hile of Auolon.	
His pople, wiჳ grete compunccion*,	*regret*
His cors into Britaine þai broght ...	
To Glaskenbir his cors þai bare,	
And wiჳ honour þai delfe* it þar.	*buried* (23,976–84, 23,988–9)

This passage demonstrates two characteristics that contribute to the often leisurely pace of *Castleford's Chronicle*: the stylistic penchant for unelaborated repetition (Arthur's wounds are reported four times in the lines above, but without much advance upon the statement of their severity); and the fondness for chiasmus ('schorte ... and brefe' / 'brefe ... and schorte',

---

[55] Kennedy notes that Camden's *Britannia* (1586) cites this episode, perhaps from *Castleford's Chronicle* (*Manual*, 2624); however, Camden may have found it elsewhere.

23,979–80), a rhetorical figure that similarly dwells upon a moment by reiteration rather than expansion. Except for the Albina prequel, which is demarcated at the juncture ('Here endys þe Prolog Olbyon ... Nowe her begynnys þe Boke of Brut', 227, 229), the earlier parts of this chronicle often follow Geoffrey's *Historia* closely, including translating the entirety of its *Prophetia Merlini* (Prophecies of Merlin) section.[56] Like Robert of Gloucester, this author may have drawn directly upon the Latin *Historia* in prose, rather than, or in addition to, a French intermediary already in verse. Diction does not always differentiate between a Latin or French source; in the passage above, the unusual word 'compunccion' (23,983) could reflect an etymon in either language.

The opening section of Robert Mannyng's *Chronicle* includes a fifty-six-line 'prosody passage'[57] where Mannyng explains that he writes 'not for þe lerid [learned] bot for þe lewed [uneducated]', for those without Latin or French, so they can have 'solace & gamen / in felawschip when þai sitt samen' (I.6, 9–10)—a communal audience, listening in English, sitting together in fellowship. Having stated his scope, from Noah through the deeds of the Britons and the English, and having identified Wace and Langtoft as sources, Mannyng circles back to his claim of simplicity of style to suit a 'symple' audience:

I mad noght for no disours*,	*storytellers, minstrels*
Ne for no seggers*, no harpours*,	*reciters, performers; harpists*
Bot for þe luf of symple men	
þat strange Inglis can not ken. ...	
If it were made in ryme couwee*,	*tail-rhyme*
or in strangere* or enterlace*,	*obscure; intertwined (rhyme)*
þat rede Inglis it ere* inowe	*there are; enough*
þat couthe not haf coppled* a kowe*;	*linked; a tail (rhyme)*
þat outhere* in couwee or in baston*,	*either; stanzaic form*
som suld haf ben fordon*,	*undone, defeated*
so þat fele* men þat it herde	*many*
suld not witte howe þat it ferde*.	*fared* (I.75–8, 85–92)

After using *Sir Tristrem* as an example of a poem whose complicated stanzas become mangled in performance ('Non þam says as þai þam wroght', I.95), Mannyng returns yet again to the claim of simplicity, adding requests from others and a lack of skill to his reasons for choosing 'light ryme':

and my witte was oure thynne,	
so strange speche to trauayle* in. ...	*work, labour*
And men besoght me many a tyme	
to turne it bot in light ryme ...	
And þerfore for þe comonalte	*common people, community*
þat blythely wild* listen to me,	*would*
On light lange* I it began	*language, speech*
For luf of þe lewed man ... (I.113–14, 117–18, 123–6)	

---

[56] *Castleford's Chronicle* apparently provides the only full English translation of Geoffrey's prophecies (which other chroniclers mostly omit) until the seventeenth century; Caroline D. Eckhardt, 'The First English Translations of the *Prophetia Merlini*', *The Library*, Series 6.4 (March 1982), 25–34.

[57] Joyce Coleman, 'Strange Rhyme: Prosody and Nationhood in Robert Mannyng's Story of England', *Speculum*, 78 (2003), 1214–38, at 1216.

180   MEDIEVAL POETRY: 1100–1400

Mannyng's insistent justifications of the plain style have sometimes been taken as a straight-forward self-representation, yet the lerid/lewed dichotomy and modesty-topos are conventional.[58] As Helen Phillips notes, '[s]uch topoi derive from classical literature ... are ubiquitous in texts of the period in all languages, and can never be taken at face value'[59]. The Latin apparatus of the *Chronicle*'s manuscripts,[60] while not authorial, implies use beyond 'lewed' listeners, and, more important, Mannyng's poetry itself is not always simple. Joyce Coleman demonstrates that Mannyng engages 'progressively in a series of stylistic experiments' and either employs or admires all the formal characteristics (*rime couwee* [tail-rhyme], *enterlace*, *baston*, *strangere*) rejected in the prologue.[61] In addition to using short couplets in Part I, longer couplets in Part II, and monorhyme at several points, Mannyng adds mid-line rhyme in Part II,[62] preserves the tail-rhyme form of Langtoft's political songs, and supplies twenty-six lines of new tail-rhyme himself.[63] Thus, the poetry of the chronicle repeatedly undoes the plain-style posture of its prologue.[64]

Mannyng's final Arthurian episode displays little of the agilities of versification mentioned above, though the rhyming couplets show some variability in metre around the four-stress norm, with enjambment across the boundaries of the couplet ('... did him lede / into þe ilde of Aualoun', 13,708–9), and there is a homonymic repetition of the rhyme drede/lede ('lede' as verb at 13,708, as noun at 13,720). Distancing himself slightly with 'Men sais', as Wace did with 'si la geste ne mente' (if the *geste* does not lie),[65] the narrator comments on Arthur after Mordred, his men, and the flower of the Round Table are all slain:

> & Arthur himself þore*,   *there*
> Men sais, he wonded sore;
> for his wondes wer to drede*,   *dread*
> þerfor þei did him lede
> into þe ilde* of Aualoun;   *isle*
> & þus sais ilk a* Bretoun   *every*
> þat o lyue þer he es ...
> Merlyn sais full meruailous
> þat Arthur dede was doutous;
> þerfor þe Bretons drede
> & sais he lyues in lede*;   *land*

---

[58] On Mannying's more extreme modesty-claim, 'my spech ... is bot skitte' [trash, excrement] (15,930), see Coleman, 'Strange Rhyme', 1224, and Nicole Nyffenegger, *Authorising History: Gestures of Authorship in Fourteenth-Century English Historiography* (Cambridge, 2013), 57–8.

[59] Helen Phillips, 'Robert Mannyng, *Chronicle*: Prologue', in Jocelyn Wogan-Browne, Nicholas Watson, Andrew Taylor, and Ruth Evans (eds), *The Idea of the Vernacular: An Anthology of Middle English Literary Theory 1280–1520* (University Park, PA, 1999), 19–24, at 19.

[60] Sullens (ed.), 34, 36–7, 44.

[61] Coleman, 'Strange Rhyme', 1218–21, 1224, 1234–5. Richard Rolle too claims to 'seke no strange Inglis, bot lightest and comunest' (Coleman, 1217).

[62] Thea Summerfield, *The Matter of Kings' Lives: The Design of Past and Present in the Early Fourteenth-Century Verse Chronicles by Pierre de Langtoft and Robert Mannyng* (Amsterdam, 1998), 151–3.

[63] Thea Summerfield, 'The Political Songs in the *Chronicles* of Pierre de Langtoft and Robert Mannyng', in Evelyn Mullally and John Thompson (eds), *The Court and Cultural Diversity* (Woodbridge, 1997), 139–48. Mannyng might have encountered tail-rhyme in Latin hymnody and French poems; Purdie, *Anglicising Romance*, 26–31.

[64] Cf. Lesley Johnson, 'Robert Mannyng's History of Arthurian Literature', in Ian Wood and G. A. Loud (eds), *Church and Chronicle in the Middle Ages: Essays Presented to John Taylor* (London, 1991), 129–47, especially 137.

[65] Wace, *Brut*, 13,275; Judith Weiss (ed. and trans.), *Wace's Roman de Brut: A History of the British* (Exeter, 1999), 332.

> bot I sai þei trowe* wrong,   *believe*
> if he life, his life is long.
> Bot þe Bretons loude lie;
> He was so wonded þat him burd* die.   *must* (13,705–11, 13,717–24)

This rejection of belief in the wounded king's survival is followed by lists of 'lords of renoun' killed on each side and a statement that Arthur left the kingdom in Constantine's keeping 'vntille he com', until his own return (13,744). The passage as a whole thus ends with an Arthurian anticipation of return that the narrator has already discounted. The 'I sai' intervention, with the wry comment that if Arthur is alive, he has lived (extremely) long, contributes to the directness of Mannyng's voice, supporting the plain-style persona at this point even if other characteristics of the chronicle may not.

As this brief comparison of final Arthurian episodes shows, in the English verse chronicle tradition there is no single version of the passing of Arthur. A specifically 'Inglis' identity for Arthur can be asserted, occluded, or something in between. In one chronicle the king has a ten-year reign after what is elsewhere the last battle. The three chroniclers who report his burial at Glastonbury may have known that in 1191, bones alleged to be Arthur's and Guinevere's were exhumed there, an event politically convenient for dismissing the 'Breton hope'; the others allow for indeterminateness about his physical body. Chroniclers can omit the scene of Arthur's departure to Avalon, give it a brief glance, or make the mind's eye linger on this moment. None of the other presentations of the final Arthurian scene resembles Laȝamon's, with its strange boat and caregiving women and concept of the king as living still among the fairest of the elf-people in Avalon.

There is also no clear norm for verse form. Though the four-stress rhyming couplet (often with variations) is most frequent, it constitutes the narrative medium only in the *Short Metrical Chronicle*, *Castleford's Chronicle*, and Part I of Mannyng's *Chronicle*. The exact metre of Laȝamon's *Brut* and its affiliations with other alliterative poetry (or with rhythmical prose) are still disputed. In Mannyng's *Chronicle*, the midway shift from four-stress to five- or six-stress couplets may represent only the change of French source from Wace's octosyllabic couplets to Langtoft's *laisses*. However, the Latin explicit and incipit in the P manuscript of Mannyng's *Chronicle* align this change of source and form with the British/English ethnic distinction: ('Explicit historia britannie ... Incipiunt Gesta Anglorum', 'Here ends the History of Britain ... here begin the Deeds of the English', I.15,901–4). Mannyng also experiments briefly with monorhyme and tail-rhyme, as noted, and Robert of Gloucester's septenaries show formal resemblances to those of the *South English Legendary* and other works. Questions of versification are sometimes complicated by differences between scribal practice and modern editorial judgement. Laȝamon's *Brut*, written across the page like prose in both its manuscripts, was first printed by Madden in short (half-)lines but is now regularly printed in long lines;[66] Robert of Gloucester's verse form can be interpreted as septenary couplets or stanzas of alternating three- and four-stress lines.[67] For medieval audiences who heard rather than saw the text, the *mise en page* may not have been significant in any case. Further, although the chronological sequence among these five works evidently begins with Laȝamon's alliterative verse and ends with the rhyming couplets of the later versions of the *Short Metrical Chronicle*, these few data-points within a small corpus could represent a significant trend within English historical poetry, or just the chance results of survival.

---

[66] Laȝamon, in Sir Frederic Madden (ed.), *Laȝamons Brut, or Chronicle of England; A Poetical Semi-Saxon Paraphrase of The Brut of Wace*, 3 vols. (London, 1847).
[67] Kennedy, *Manual*, 2617.

182 MEDIEVAL POETRY: 1100–1400

Despite their differences, the five verse chronicles discussed here all belong to the *Brut* tradition, which means that they share a broadly recognised, highly durable, multilingual, and transnational construction of the insular past. This taxonomic category is documented in the medieval word itself, for a '*Brut*' came to mean a narrative presenting this formulation of British history.[68] However, as will be discussed below, the grouping of these texts together represents only part of their extended genealogical family, for they are also linked to the genre of romance and to works in other literary forms.

Permeable Taxonomies in Verse and Prose

Let us return to the question of what it means to recount the national history in English poetry—whose English? What nation, or which perspectives on its history? To slightly stretch the geographical and political parameters of the corpus above, we might include, as Kennedy does, historical verse written in 'southern Scots (northern English)'—in particular, John Barbour's *Bruce*, *c* 1375–7 (13,684 lines in mostly four-stress rhyming couplets).[69] The *Bruce* is not a national history in the sense of recounting the course of a nation over a long timespan; instead, it is a poem of war and chivalry focused on Robert I (Bruce), king of Scotland 1306–29, and especially on his struggles against England. However, it complements the chronicles discussed above in re-framing and amplifying events that they report more briefly. Since Geoffrey's *Historia*, the 'British history' had promulgated a distinctly England-centric narrative about Scotland; for example, Geoffrey's genealogy made Scotland subsidiary to England and the traitorous Scots are said to fight for Mordred against Arthur.[70] The Scottish perspective provided by Barbour's *Bruce*, though on a very limited segment of this contested history, is consistently expressed and is grounded in a breadth of literary associations, including invocations of Fortune, who alternately smiles and attacks, for 'In na tym stable can scho stand' (13.639). Theo van Heijnsbergen has pointed out 'the rhetorical and generic (*accessus*) context' of Book I, as well as Barbour's use of 'carefully weighted couplets of complementary or oppositional concepts and qualities' to anticipate themes to be addressed later, such as 'chewalry / cowardy', 'discord / accord', 'king / offspryng', and 'thrillage / parage', with this last rhyme pointing towards the central issue of thraldom and freedom.[71] Indeed the poem's best-known passage is probably the 16-line declaration that begins:

> A! Fredome is a noble thing
> Fredome mays man to haiff liking*.   *to have pleasure*
> Fredome all solace to man giffis,
> He levys at es* that frely levys.   *ease* (I.225–8)[72]

---

[68] '*Brut*' is used in this sense in the Auchinleck *Short Metrical Chronicle* (4), Castleford (229), Mannyng (I.65), and (see *MED*) the Auchinleck 'Arthur and Merlin'.

[69] Kennedy, *Manual*, 2681; John Barbour, in A. A. M. Duncan (ed. and trans.), *The Bruce* (Edinburgh, 1997).

[70] Geoffrey's *Historia* gave England primacy over Scotland: Brutus's eldest son, Locrinus, receives England (Loegria); his second son, Kamber, Wales (Cambria); Albanactus, the youngest, Scotland (Albany).

[71] Theo van Heijnsbegen, 'Scripting the National Past: A Textual Community of the Realm', in Steve Boardman and Susan Foran (eds), *Barbour's Bruce and Its Cultural Contexts: Politics, Chivalry, and Literature in Late Medieval Scotland* (Cambridge, 2015), 75–99, at 83, 91–3.

[72] The *Brut* tradition also shares a freedom theme, beginning with Brutus's declaration in Geoffrey's *Historia* that his Trojans would prefer the life of wild animals in freedom to luxuries in servitude; e.g., Laʒamon, 235–7; *Castleford*, 581–634; Mannyng, I.953–7.

Anaphora launches this passage with almost the effect of a chant or a shout. The *Bruce* has been associated with historiography, life-writing, epic, the academic preface or *accessus* (in its preamble), and 'genres such as prophecy, legend, allegory or even sacred writing', but especially with romance.[73] Barbour himself called his work a 'romanys' (1.446), though he integrated multiple narrative and lyric models. A. A. M. Duncan indicates that although the *Bruce* includes 'over a thousand alliterative lines', reflecting Barbour's knowledge of English alliterative poetry, nevertheless 'the vocabulary is shot through with words borrowed from French'.[74] For example, in a spring-topos passage where the birds are 'Melland [mingling] thar notis with seymly soune / For softnes of the swet sesoun' (16.65–6), Rhiannon Purdie finds that 'Barbour is demonstrating his skill at a very English (and Scots) kind of rhymed-alliterative verse', yet here his 'primary inspiration' lies in the French *romans antiques*.[75]

The parameters of the national history corpus could be further stretched if questions such as 'whose nation?' and 'whose perspective?' were to encompass not only the *Bruce*'s view from Scotland, but also the longstanding cultural insistence on the Britons' Trojan ethnicity. Gaimar's narrative, now partially lost, reportedly reached from Jason and the Golden Fleece through William II;[76] similarly, Mannyng's *Chronicle* launches 'alle þe story of Inglande' (1.3) with a glance at Noah's flood and then brief versions of Jason and the Golden Fleece and the story of Troy: in such accounts the Trojan story is integral as well as ancestral to what became English national history. To some extent Troy haunts all the narratives of the *Brut* tradition, for the Virgilian model that underlies the historical visions of Geoffrey of Monmouth and his followers inevitably memorialises the old Troy as well as the new.

In this long view, another English verse narrative with some chronicle characteristics might be welcomed into the margins of an extended corpus of England's national history: John Clerk's *Gest Hystoriale of the Destruction of Troy* (c ?1350–1400), an alliterative translation (14,044 lines) of Guido delle Colonne's *Historia Destructionis Troiae*.[77] Although this work is appropriately categorised as romance, 'the tone and manner are those of a rapidly moving chronicle presenting historical truth'.[78] To blend the 'matter of Britain' with the ancient world's 'matter of Rome' in this way would conflate two of Jean Bodel's famous three 'matters', but Bodel's taxonomy, though often cited, did not actually sever these narratives from each other, as the poet of *Sir Gawain and the Green Knight* demonstrated by framing Arthur within Troy.

What difference to our assessment of the Middle English poetry of national history would it make to include works at the margins, such as Barbour's *Bruce* and Clerk's *Gest Hystoriale*? One difference is that the apparent chronological development of verse forms mentioned above, from alliteration to rhyme, would be invalidated, since the *Bruce* and the *Gest* both belong to the latter part of the fourteenth century and one uses primarily rhyming couplets, the other alliterative lines. In other words, there is no trend from one form to the other; they coexist. Further, these two works together can exemplify the temporal elasticity of the poetry of national history, which can reach back into the great frame of ancient time (the *Gest* amplifies Mannyng's brevity in this regard) or dilate time to expand on one

---

[73] Van Heijnsbergen, 'Scripting the National Past', 79, 98.

[74] Duncan (ed.), John Barbour, *The Bruce*, 4.

[75] Rhiannon Purdie, 'Medieval Romance and the Generic Frictions of Barbour's *Bruce*', in Boardman and Foran (eds), *Barbour's* Bruce, 51–74, at 65.

[76] Ian Short, 'Gaimar's Epilogue and Geoffrey of Monmouth's *Liber vetustissimus*', *Speculum*, 69 (1994), 323–43.

[77] See Chapter 20 in this volume.

[78] R. M. Lumiansky, 'Legends of Troy', in J. Burke Severs (ed.), *A Manual of the Writings in Middle English 1050–1500*, 11 vols. (New Haven, CT, 1967), 1:116.

184   MEDIEVAL POETRY: 1100–1400

ruler (the *Bruce* offers a more fully developed hero-tale than Laȝamon's long section on Arthur provides). And if the *Bruce* can be sketched into the edge of an extended family tree that connects poetry and national history, perhaps so might be the *Alliterative Morte Arthure*, which, as Thorlac Turville-Petre remarks, 'associates itself with both "cronycle" and "romance", unsettling and in the end evading genre classifications'.[79]

Beyond the possibility of opening the temporal or 'national' boundaries of the corpus itself, resemblances of the English verse chronicles to other genres, especially romance, have long been recognised.[80] Aside from shared verse forms, which of course other genres use too, there are shared terrains of subject matter. The Arthurian legend, central to *Brut*-chronicles and well represented in romances, offers many examples, including a remarkable passage on Lancelot and Guinevere in the Auchinleck *Short Metrical Chronicle*.[81] Guy of Warwick, Bevis of Hampton, and Tristan (all subjects of romances in the Auchinleck manuscript) make cameo appearances in *Castleford's Chronicle*, as does a figure who is arguably Havelok, best known through the romance *Havelok the Dane*.[82] Mannyng too refers to Havelok's story, and one manuscript of his *Chronicle* inserts an eighty-two-line summary; similarly, a fifteenth-century redaction of Robert of Gloucester's *Metrical Chronicle* inserts the romance *Richard Coeur de Lion* at the reign of Richard I.[83]

A further type of kinship relationship is the display within a verse chronicle of diction shared with romance, as in the *Short Metrical Chronicle*: in MS A (Auchinleck), Albina's sisters are 'briȝt & schene' (44); in MS R, Guinevere is 'bryth [and] schene' (294); in several MSS, the wily maid Inge is 'bryȝt & schene' (278); and in the romance of *King Horn*, this formulaic description is applied to the young hero: 'Horn þu art ... bryht of hewe & schene' (97–8).[84] A more elaborate chronicle passage that resonates with romance occurs in *Castleford's Chronicle*, where Locrine, king of Britain, falls in love with the captive princess Astrild as soon as he beholds her:

> Þose days was non, þe soth to dyme*   *deem (judge)
> Þat myght vnto hyr fayrhed seme.
> So qwyt and cler it was hyr flech
> As snawe þat falles fro heven so freich,
> Ne lylye floures, ne eburs* bone,   *ivory
> Qwytter to se it myght be none—
> Eburs bone, ne lilies flour,
> Past noght hyr fayrhed in colour,
> Ne hyr qwytnese no fallyn snawe
> Was noght to pase, in syght to knawe. (2669–78)

This stylised passage exhibits widespread European romance (and lyric) conventions in its elements of love-at-first-sight and cultural stipulations of female beauty: nobody else is

---

[79] Thorlac Turville-Petre, *Description and Narrative in Middle English Alliterative Poetry* (Liverpool, 2018), 57–8. One might also add the poem 'Arthur', in rhyming couplets (Kennedy, *Manual*, 2599).

[80] Resonances could also be demonstrated with hagiography, genealogy, *lai*, 'tale', and other storytelling forms.

[81] Helen Cooper, 'Lancelot, Roger Mortimer, and the Date of the Auchinleck Manuscript', in A. M. D'Arcy and A. J. Fletcher (eds), *Studies in Late Medieval and Early Renaissance Texts in Honour of John Scattergood* (Dublin, 2005), 91–9.

[82] Caroline D. Eckhardt and Bryan A. Meer, 'Constructing a Medieval Genealogy: Roland the Father of Tristan in "Castleford's Chronicle"', *MLN*, 115.5 (2000), 1085–1111; Caroline D. Eckhardt, 'Havelok the Dane in *Castleford's Chronicle*', *Studies in Philology*, 98 (2001), 1–17; Chapter 23 in this volume.

[83] Sullens (500–2) provides the Havelok summary. On *Richard Coeur de Lion*, see Chapter 22 in this volume.

[84] Joseph Hall (ed.), *King Horn: A Middle-English Romance* (Oxford, 1901); Harley 2253 version.

as fair as Astrild, and, in particular, her beauty is associated with whiteness. Her flesh is as white and clear as the snow, as lily flowers, and as ivory. As if Locrine's eyes were dwelling upon her, the chiasmic structure of the verse then repeats those terms in opposite order: ivory, lily, and snow.[85]

In addition to kinship with other genres, at the margins there are interrelations of medium and form. The medieval concept of a *Brut*, mentioned above, embraced both verse and prose, yet the question remains of why (despite the continuing life of some of these verse histories), this form of remembrance of things past apparently receded after the fourteenth century in favour of prose. Actually, the question might be not why the predominance of verse chronicles ceased, but why it occurred at all. When La3amon took up his quill to write truer words on parchment, Wace's *Brut*, on which he profoundly relied, provided a precedent for verse, but why had the French chroniclers themselves, beginning with Gaimar and Wace, versified their prose sources? Neil Wright, editing a Latin hexameter versification of Geoffrey's *Historia*, aptly points to 'a long tradition of verse paraphrases of prose texts which ... reaches back to Antiquity',[86] yet a more precise explanation would be welcome.

The preferences of patrons must have been a factor, though now these are often unknowable. Chronology disturbs any assumption that Gaimar and Wace chose verse in order to build upon a pre-existing popularity of verse romances, for their work seems to have just preceded (Gaimar) or roughly paralleled (Wace) the rise of the French verse romances.[87] However, Gaimar and Wace may have found productive analogues, if not actual models, in other genres of the new French literary culture, which already included a wide range of poetic works from Anglo-Norman England, such as Philippe de Thaun's calendar treatise *Comput* (1113) and his *Bestiary* (1121–39), and Benedeit's *Voyage of St Brendan* (1118–21); by La3amon's time, if not Wace's, there were also multiple versifications of Geoffrey's *Historia*.[88] Yet the richness of the new verse culture in French is not a full explanation, for prose remained as a model too. Similarly, performance for a community of listeners provides a partial explanation for this turn to verse, given the advantages of verse for memorisation, yet prose too can be read aloud. Medieval theoretical statements comparing the domains of prose and verse do not necessarily align with writers' (or readers') actual practices,[89] and of course not all verse is the same. Despite Mannyng's observation that nobody performs stanzaic verse such as that of *Sir Tristrem* correctly, it has been suggested that tail-rhyme may have been easier to memorise than hundreds or thousands of individual small units formed by couplets,[90] yet none of these chronicles is definitely stanzaic. Perhaps the chroniclers' references to written sources, spurious or not, are a signal that memorial transmission or performance without book was not expected, in which case any distinction in ease of memorisation between prose and verse, or types of verse, should not matter in determining form. Further, the distinction itself between prose and verse, though often obvious, was not always absolute.[91] Finally, perhaps sometimes aesthetic criteria tilted the balance in favour of verse.

---

[85] In Geoffrey's *Historia* (the probable source) the sequence of ivory, snow, lilies is stated once.
[86] N. Wright (ed.), *The Historia Regum Britannie*, xv.
[87] The first French verse romances (*Thèbes, Enéas, Troie*) are usually dated *c* 1150–65.
[88] For twelve French verse translations of Geoffrey's *Historia*, all plausibly *c* 1150–1200, see Beatrice Barbieri (ed.), *Geste des Bretuns en alexandrins ou Harley Brut* (Paris, 2015), 21–2, 66–7.
[89] Given-Wilson, *Chronicles*, 143–7, collects chroniclers' comments on verse vs. prose.
[90] Purdie, *Anglicising Romance*, 90–2.
[91] Anne Savage, 'Old and Middle English, Poetry and Prose', *Studies in the Age of Chaucer*, 23 (2001), 503–11; Oliver S. Pickering, 'Verse to Prose or Prose to Verse? A Problematic Text of *The Nine Points Best Pleasing to God*', in Margaret Connolly and Raluca Radulescu (eds), *Editing and Interpretation of Middle English Texts* (Turnhout, 2018), 191–210, especially 193, 204.

186   MEDIEVAL POETRY: 1100–1400

To use Barbour's formulation, which draws upon familiar tropes and classical precedent, stories bring pleasure, yet a double pleasure derives from truthful stories well told:

> Storys to rede ar delatibill
> Suppos that* thai be nocht bot fabill,   *even if*
> Than suld storys that suthfast wer
> And that war said on gud maner
> Have doubill pleasance in heryng (I.1–5)

Perhaps to tell the story 'on gud maner' suggests the art and craft of verse, as Barbour himself exemplifies. Many reasons, probably none of them likely to satisfy in full, may have contributed to the observed oscillation, in which prose as in Geoffrey's *Historia*, verse in these chronicles, and prose again in the French and English prose *Brut*-narratives, predominated in turn among the national histories.

In what might be odd accidents of survival, the *Short Metrical Chronicle*, with its recently reported sixteenth- or seventeenth-century fragment, and Robert of Gloucester's *Metrical Chronicle*, with seventeenth- and eighteenth-century transcripts, seem to have had the longest manuscript 'working lives' among these chronicles that memorialised their perceptions of the national past.[92] It is tempting to speculate that other verse histories were among the lost books whose traces remain in library inventories, wills, or other written sources, and that more survivors will still be found.[93] Even within the small known corpus, however, the many thousands of lines in these poems demonstrate the vigour and variety of historical storytelling at the times when they were composed, as well as the durability of their work for at least the generations that immediately followed, and in some cases for subsequent audiences as well.[94]

---

[92] Kennedy, *Manual*, 2620; Grund, 'Previously Unreported Fragment'.

[93] R. M. Wilson, *The Lost Literature of Medieval England*, 2nd rev. edn. (London, 1952, 1970), 24–59, especially 25; on *Brut*-chronicles in wills, see Elizabeth Bryan, 'The English Reception of Geoffrey of Monmouth', in Henley and Smith (eds), *Companion*, 449–53, especially 449.

[94] The MSS—one each of Castleford and the *Gest Historiale*, two of Laȝamon and Barbour, three of Mannyng, eight of the *Short Metrical Chronicle*, and 'some fifteen' (Fisher, *Scribal Authorship*, 94) of Robert of Gloucester—confirm that all were being copied at least a generation or two after their probable origin; all but Laȝamon were still being copied during the era when prose chronicles of national history predominated.

12

Poetry in Its Age

Satire and Complaint

Craig E. Bertolet

Satires and complaints are poems of grievance. According to Wendy Scase, the 'complaint' specifically originates in the legal term *pleinte*, which is 'the expression of a grievance as a means of initiating litigation.'[1] The poems of satire and complaint selected for inclusion in this chapter form a rough representative sample of surviving texts, which falls into two groups of grievances. One group (poems attributed to Laurence Minot, some lyrics from London, British Library, MS Harley 2253, and the anonymous *Richard the Redeless*) condemns political actors, casting blame on their actions rather than arguing for reform. The other group condemns socioeconomic practices but argues for their reform. These poems (*Song of the Husbandman, Satire on the Consistory Courts, The Simonye, Wynnere and Wastoure*, and *Piers the Ploughmans Crede*) react to a changing political economy that comes to base worthiness on material possessions instead of on traditional land ownership. The poems emphasise money's inherent corrupting power, especially to Church governance and practices.

All these poems tend to respond to sociopolitical events, especially the tensions between the English and French kings over feudal rights to lands in France. English kings had possessed territory on the Continent since the Norman Conquest of 1066, but by holding these lands they were vassals of the French king. Edward III (r. 1327–77) changed the dynamics of this relationship by directly claiming the French throne, thereby igniting the Hundred Years' War. Ardis Butterfield has called the result of his decision 'a civil war between two contrasting models of exercising power'—insular independence for the English and centralising state power for the French.[2] Poets responding to the Anglo-French struggle and its proxy wars in Scotland and Flanders increasingly adopt the English language as a vehicle for creative expression. In their subject matter, these poets tend to define what English people are by what they are not, such as not French, not Scottish, or not Flemish.

Poems surveyed in this chapter also respond to socioeconomic changes. The cultural upheavals resulting from the mid-fourteenth-century visitation of the Black Death led to greater migrations from the manors to the towns, an increase in money-based wages, and a reactionary backlash that sought to retain the power and interests of lords by regulating the labour and purchasing abilities of the common people. Compounding the social unrest these changes were causing was the increase in the need for the crown, the Church, the manor, and the towns to create a bureaucratic culture to preserve records and administer their often competing jurisdictions. Much complaint poetry of this period indicts the bureaucratic specialisation in the manorial economy and the growing power

---

[1] Wendy Scase, *Literature and Complaint in England, 1272–1553* (Oxford, 2007), 1–2.

[2] Ardis Butterfield, *The Familiar Enemy: Chaucer, Language, and Nation in the Hundred Years War* (Oxford, 2009), 20.

Craig E. Bertolet, *Poetry in Its Age*. In: *The Oxford History of Poetry in English*. Edited by Helen Cooper and Robert R. Edwards, Oxford University Press. © Craig E. Bertolet (2023). DOI: 10.1093/oso/9780198827429.003.0012

188   MEDIEVAL POETRY: 1100–1400

of money-based trading systems originating in the towns that were making avarice (rather than pride) the most contagious sin in English society. Some of these poems also represent the rich tradition of ecclesiastical satire, which was directed at the avarice and acquisitiveness of the Church. As a historical record, these poems react to or provide impressions of the individuals and practices seen to be influencing their author's world.

Political Invective

John of Garland writes in his thirteenth-century poem, *Morale Scolarium*, 'here is the law of satire: to mock vice, move suddenly, change behaviour, and expose hidden ugliness' ('Hec est lex satire: vitiis ridere, salire / Mores excire, que feda latent aperire') (423–4).[3] As a genre, satire is polemical with its writers inclining 'toward self-promotion as judges of morals and manners, of behavior and thought'.[4] Some of the surviving Middle English poems identified by modern editors as satire do mock their subjects but are probably better classified as invective. The difference between satire and invective is, according to the *Princeton Encyclopedia of Poetry and Poetics*, that invective is 'personal, motivated by malice, and unjust'.[5] In other words, the scorn that the writer directs at the subjects of the poetic invective must not be altogether deserving of it despite the writer's intention to make them so, while the subject of the satire presumably deserves the attack.

Poetic invective appears in Old and Middle English in a form known as *flyting*, when characters exchange insults with each other. Although sixteenth-century Scottish poets engaged in poetic *flyting* matches, the most famous early example of a *flyting* in English poetry is Unferth's scolding Beowulf for his foolish contest with Breca. Beowulf counters Unferth's insult with a tale proving that he is both strong and brave, clearly implying that Unferth is neither. Some satiric Middle English poems insult groups or individuals not with the hope for the redemption of that group or individual, but to taunt them in their folly. The speaker wants to create a relationship with the audience as a sort of 'us versus them' dichotomy, with the insulted 'them' often dehumanised to explain away any empathy for 'them', and 'we' deriving cruel pleasure from it. To construct this relationship, the poet uses artistic devices to attack the subject of the poem, such as exaggeration, insults, and metaphors based in scatology, animalistic behaviour, or ugliness. Characters in the poems are ridiculed because of a clear moral or intellectual failing that the poet can see, but they cannot. The poems below invite their audiences to jeer with their speakers at the object of the speaker's scorn, thereby creating a bond of good will (and dark pleasure in being party to the abuse) with the audience against those whom the poem attacks.

For instance, the early-fourteenth-century poem that begins 'Of rybauds y ryme' ('Of ribalds I rhyme') is a scathing invective against the grooms who take care of the horses of the nobility and the royal family.[6] It is written in ten quatrains of alliterative long lines, each quatrain having a single rhyme. Scase comments that the poem shows 'the private profiteering so often imputed to royal officials'.[7] While the poem argues that these men are a drain on

---

[3] John of Garland, in Louis John Paetow (ed.), *Morale Scolarium of John of Garland* (Berkeley, CA, 1927).
[4] Alex Preminger and T. V. F. Brogan (eds), *The New Princeton Encyclopedia of Poetry and Poetics* (Princeton, NJ, 1993), 1114.
[5] *Princeton Encyclopedia of Poetry and Poetics*, 627.
[6] Susanna Fein (ed.), *The Complete Harley 2253 Manuscript*, 3 vols. (Kalamazoo, MI, 2014–15), 3:218–21; Julia Boffey and A. S. G. Edwards (eds), *A New Index of Middle English Verse* (London, 2005), 2649. Citations for this text will be indicated as *NIMEV* with the poem's index number.
[7] Scase, *Literature and Complaint*, 34–5.

the rural communities forced to provision them whenever the king or his nobles and their entourage visited, the focus of the poem is to describe the grooms as irredeemable wasters. Inside each line, at least one of the alliterating sounds is an insult. The speaker says in the third stanza, 'The Shuppare that huem shupte, to shome he huem shadde, / To fles ant to fleye, to tyke ant to tadde' ('The Shaper that made them, he shamefully spawned them from fleas and flies, from dogs and toads', 9–10). The second of the two lines shows the richness of poetic variation with pairs of alliterating insults modifying the grooms' shameful births and distancing them from the rest of humanity which God, the Shaper, created separately. It also shows the poet's consistent deviation from the *aa/ax* alliteration pattern. Some lines do have three stressed alliterating sounds, but in the two lines above, the poet writes one line with four alliterating sounds and the second with two different alliterating pairs. This pattern of variation appears in many of the poems of invective showing the flexibility of the alliterative line and its capacity to mimic at a formal level the rhetorical strategy of excess and exaggeration.

A great deal of the poetry of political invective in this period is in verse celebrating military victories that jeers at the defeated foe. For instance, the thirteenth-century English lyric *The Song of Lewes*, in London, British Library, MS Harley 2253 (itself from the mid-fourteenth century),[8] praises Simon de Montfort (1208–65) but mostly condemns those whom he defeated at the Battle of Lewes, fought on 14 May 1264.[9] The poem is in eight eight-line stanzas rhyming *aaaabccb*, the last three lines serving as a refrain that is repeated with slight variation throughout the poem. The first stanza ends: 'Ant so he dude more. / Richard / Thah thou be ever trichard, / Triccen shalt thou nevermore!' ('And so, he did more, Richard, though you will be a traitor forever, you will no longer betray!', 5–8). 'Richard' here is Richard of Cornwall, Emperor of Germany (1209–72), brother to Henry III (r. 1216–72). Apart from this first and the last stanza (where the rhyming word is 'lore', 63), the leading rhyme in the refrain is 'Wyndesore' ('Windsor'), a metonymy for King Henry. Each stanza is a specific complaint against both brothers with the refrain repeating the conclusion that Richard's treason against England is the reason for him losing the battle.

While de Montfort is praised in the two stanzas dedicated to him, *The Song of Lewes* mostly consists of insulting Richard. The poet condemns Richard's wrongly placed pride in his own leadership (27). He claims that Richard 'saisede the mulne for a castel' in the delusion that the sails of this windmill were a 'mangonel' or catapult (18–20), an allusion to Richard's having hidden in a windmill after the battle until he was captured. Saying that he seized it exaggerates his military incompetence for comic effect. A mill would not have been defended, and it would not have been able to serve as a fortress. The poet appears to assume his audience would recognise Richard's decision as folly and share the poet's scorn for him because of it.

In the fourteenth century, the role of the scorned foe in English verse is mostly played by the Scots or the French. The general grievance of English poets against the Scots is that they are traitors against English kings, because Edward I (r. 1272–1307) maintained that he was the overlord of Scotland and its king was merely Edward's vassal. For instance, a 233-line

---

[8] Harley MS 2253 contains some of the earliest surviving political lyric poetry in English, as well as in Latin and French, compiled by a scribe working in Ludlow in the West of England. It is the only source for many of the texts contained in it. See Susanna Fein, 'Compilation and Purpose in MS Harley 2253', in Wendy Scase (ed.), *Essays in Manuscript Geography: Vernacular Manuscripts of the English West Midlands from the Conquest to the Sixteenth Century* (Turnhout, 2007), 67–94.

[9] Fein, *Complete Harley 2253*, 2:86–9; *NIMEV*, 3155.

190 MEDIEVAL POETRY: 1100–1400

poem in Harley MS 2253 beginning 'Lystneth, lordynges' and describing the execution of
the Scottish knight, Sir Simon Fraser, in September 1306 explains that the speaker will tell
about 'the traytours of Scotlond that take beth wyth gynne' ('the traitors of Scotland, taken
by guile', 2).[10] In contrast, the general grievance against the French is their arrogance, and
poets tend to present any military triumph over them as a fitting punishment for their pride.
As an example, a seventeen-stanza poem beginning 'Lustneth, lordynges, bothe yonge ant
olde' is also found in Harley MS 2253. It describes the Flemish insurrection against the
French that began on 18 May 1302, addressing the fall of the 'proude ant bolde' ('proud
and arrogant', 2) French who lose not to an army of knights but to 'webbes' and 'fullaris'
('weavers' and 'fullers', 17), townspeople not trained in the art of warfare.[11] As such, the
poem echoes the Old Testament proverb in which humiliation follows the proud and glory
should uphold the humble in spirit (Proverbs 29.23). The poem's form is in a variant of
the tail-rhymed stanza. This stanza usually consists of '6 or 12 lines (or multiples) in which
a rhyming couplet is followed by a tail line, the rhyme of which unites the stanza'.[12] The
tail line is usually shorter than the other lines in the stanza. Tail-rhymed stanzas are often
found in the Middle English romance. The poem on the Flemish insurrection is in an eight-
line, rather than a six-line, stanza which rhymes *aaaBcccB*. The B-lines are the tail. The tail
succinctly anchors the rhetorical point made in the A-lines much as the couplet does an
English sonnet.

Political grievances were not always against foreigners. The poem beginning 'Ther is a
busch that is forgrowe' ('There is an overgrown bush') from the end of the fourteenth century has been read as a political allegory that shows the harm that corrupt royal counsellors
do to the political order of England. At the same time, it dehumanises some of these counsellors with insults that are extended puns based on their names. The three men specifically
condemned in this poem are the most notorious counsellors of Richard II (r. 1377–99):
Sir John Bussy ('Bushy', d. 1399), William Bagot (d. 1407), and Sir Henry Green (d. 1399).
The poem is written in fifteen six-line tail-rhymed stanzas, and it appears in the MS Bagot
D(W) 1721/3/186, now held in the Staffordshire Record Office. It was probably written
between September 1398 and July 1399 when Henry Bolingbroke, the future Henry IV
(r. 1399–1413), returned from exile. Bussy is the bush that the speaker argues must be
cropped well 'or elles hit wolle be wilde' ('or else it will be wild', 3).[13] Green is the grass
that 'most be mowe, and raked clene; / For-growen hit hath the fellde' ('must be mown and
raked clean; it has overgrown the field', 5–6). Bagot is a rotten bag that is falling apart so
that its bottom is nearly out and cannot be repaired (7–12). The *Middle English Dictionary*
(*MED*) also cites as a definition of 'bagge' a cyst or growth. This additional meaning may
harmonise with the poet's image of the bush and the grass that can only be controlled by
violence and must be cut: a bag-like cyst should be cut as well. Cutting them would be necessary for good governance. Later in the poem, the grass rots (73–8) and the bush goes bare
(67–72), so they are useful to no one. As a result, the kingdom has become full of 'lene bestes'
(77). Lean beasts, of course, are features of Old Testament prophecy. Pharaoh's dream of the
seven years of plenty and the seven years of dearth in Genesis 41 symbolises them as fat and
lean beasts, and Joseph warns him to prepare for the years of dearth so as not to have Egypt
full of lean beasts. In Ezekiel 34, God warns the prophet that He will judge among the fat

---

[10] Fein, *Complete Harley 2253*, 98–109; *NIMEV*, 1889.
[11] Fein, *Complete Harley 2253*, 214–21; *NIMEV*, 1894.
[12] *Princeton Encyclopedia of Poetry and Poetics*, 1264.
[13] James Dean (ed.), *Medieval English Political Writings* (Kalamazoo, MI, 1996), 150–2; *NIMEV*, 3529.

and lean cattle, meaning those righteous and those steeped in sin. Consequently, the lean beast is a thematically resonant image of what a king should prepare for and avoid.

None of these images describe an individual who is necessary or whose presence brings pleasure to anyone. In contrast with these images, the Lords Appellant (five members of the aristocracy who, in 1388–9, engineered a brief coup against Richard) are identified by animals deriving from their heraldic emblems. Thomas of Woodstock, duke of Gloucester (1355–99), is called a swan that has been slain (13): he was murdered in Calais on 8 September 1399. Richard FitzAlan, earl of Arundel (1346–97), executed at Westminster on 21 September 1397, is a steed (20). Thomas Beauchamp, earl of Warwick (1338–1401), is referred to as the 'bereward' ('bearward', 25) because of his emblem of a bear. Bolingbroke is referred to as the heron (just one of his badges), noting that he 'toke his flyt' (43), referring to his exile at the time of the poem's composition. The poet probably chose Bolingbroke's heron badge to represent Henry because he describes the Commons in Parliament as geese (49) and the nobles as peacocks (52). The contrast of the animals with the bag, grass, and bush underscores the natural order that the poet suggests has been set aside when control of the kingdom reverts to figures of sterility and decay instead of vigorous action.

A longer poetic invective from the end of the century is the anonymous fragment known as *Richard the Redeless* (*Richard the Ill-Counselled*). It exists in a single manuscript (Cambridge, Cambridge University Library, MS Ll.4.14) dating from the second quarter of the fifteenth century, but was probably written in the first few years of Henry IV's reign as a poem of advice to princes. The poem is in alliterative verse and divided into four parts or *passūs*. *Richard* is clearly an imitation of Langland's *Piers Plowman*, but with its focus on criticising the king and his practices. As such, it is like another alliterative poem, *Mum and the Sothsegger*, written slightly later and discussed in the next volume. *Richard* tends to follow a regular *aa/ax* pattern of three alliterating syllables per line. It also addresses, as did the previous poem, the adverse influence that Bussy, Bagot, and Green had on Richard. Often, a grievance that the poet makes against the king takes the form of alliterating pairs, such as 'myssecheff and the mysserule' ('mischief and misrule', 1:22), or that Richard ruled in 'wyles and wronge' ('wiles and wrong', 90), through 'willffull werkis' ('willful deeds', 92), or his days 'Weren wikkid thoru youre cursid conceill; youre karis weren newed' ('were wicked because of your evil counsellors; your cares were renewed', 94).[14] The speaker explains that pity moves him to advise the king 'to written him a writte to wissen him better' ('to write him a document to advise him better', 31) and advises him 'not to grucchen a grott ageine godis sonde' ('not to grumble a bit against God's commands', 35). Any amendment Richard makes is ostensibly for his soul's redemption since he is no longer king. The blame for that change in his fortunes entirely falls on Richard.

The poet also criticises male fashions of the period as a sign of the royal court's excess (3:124–96). Sleeves are too long (152–5). The cloth is dagged, or cut in jagged patterns (163–9), and this fashion raises the price of the clothing for no reason (168–9). The poet exaggerates this style of dress by commenting that 'seuen goode sowers sixe wekes after / Moun not sett the seemes ne sewe hem ayeyn' ('seven good sewers could not set the seams again even after six weeks', 165–6). The tone here is similar in its bluntness to the comments made of the king. It is a denunciation that ties sartorial decadence to royal misrule. Fashion is going to be a reflection of the moral failure of the king. The poet's condemnation

---

[14] *Richard the Redeless*, in Helen Barr (ed.), *The Piers Plowman Tradition* (London, 1993), 101–33.

192 MEDIEVAL POETRY: 1100–1400

originates from the belief that one should dress modestly rather than ostentatiously, a condemnation taken up about the same time by many moralising works including Chaucer's 'Parson's Tale' in *The Canterbury Tales* and Thomas Hoccleve's *Regement of Princes*. The 'I' of the poem adopts the same instructional role in his condemnations as John Gower in his poetry or the Old Testament prophets. His condemnations ostensibly focus on Richard but use that focus as a way to condemn the faults of others, all of which are symptomatic of a kingdom in need of reform.

A last example of political invective is a body of eleven poems that have been attributed to a writer named in two of them as Laurence Minot. These poems concern a sequence of events dating from 1333 to 1352. They survive together in a single fifteenth-century manuscript, London, British Library, MS Cotton Galba E.ix, a miscellany that also includes other texts, such as *Ywain and Gawain*, the *Prick of Conscience*, a version of the *Gospel of Nicodemus*, and some shorter poems. Manuscript rubrics connect the stanzas as if they were, according to one of Minot's modern editors, Richard H. Osberg, a continuous narrative 'romance'.[15] A. S. G. Edwards has questioned whether Minot indeed wrote all of them, since only two of the eleven poems mention him by name; but this fact would not disqualify him from having written any of the other nine.[16] The poems appear in different verse forms, line lengths, and with varied techniques which, while not collectively discounting a single author, would seem to sow a reasonable amount of doubt.

Much of the scholarly work on Minot focuses on his evident pride in the achievements of the English. What has not been commented upon is that this 'national pride' is really the corollary of invective against enemies. Minot is consistent in his praise of the English because he is consistent also in mocking those whom the English defeat. Those who lose the battles he describes, such as David II of Scotland (r. 1329–71), some Castilian pirates, and the hapless Philip VI of France (r. 1328–50), do so because the English prove superior to them in ability or cunning. For instance, Poems 1 and 2 serve as companion arguments for recounting the details of the Battle of Halidon Hill (19 July 1333): these explain a bit tortuously how the victorious English action is a corrective to the military blunders committed a generation earlier at the Battle of Bannockburn (23/24 June 1314) where the Scots under Robert the Bruce (1274–1329) soundly defeated the English under Edward III's father Edward II (r. 1307–27). But the French endure more invectives in these poems than do the Scots. Poem 5, a stanzaic poem with a four-stress line, having both rhyme and alliteration, records that Edward 'blinned thaire boste' ('countered their boast', 87) of the Normans, who 'made mekill din' ('made a lot of noise', 84), when he defeated them in the Battle of Sluys (24 June 1340). The alliterating terms are repeated from line 86 where 'boste blin' makes the rhyme, repeating the emptiness of French arrogance.

Throughout these poems, while Edward and many of his nobles are praised for their heroism or cleverness, their victories often come due to the miscalculation, unreliability, or the inept character of the French. Philip VI in these poems is primarily cowardly, arriving too late to a battle or fleeing it before it concludes. In Poem 6, another stanzaic poem but with a three-stress rather than four-stress line, the poet reports that Edward takes the city of Tournai (July–September 1340) because Philip arrived too late to defend it. As a result, the speaker says to the townspeople, 'With hert ye may him hate' (52). In Poem 7, a stanzaic

---

[15] Laurence Minot, in Richard H. Osberg (ed.), *The Poems of Laurence Minot, 1333–1352* (Kalamazoo, MI, 1996), 1.

[16] A. S. G. Edwards, 'The Authorship of the Poems of Laurence Minot: A Reconsideration', *Florilegium*, 23 (2006), 145–53.

poem with a bob-and-wheel structure, the speaker says that Philip fled following his defeat at the Battle of Crécy (26 August 1346), showing that 'Unkind he was and uncurtayse' (145). This poem also castigates his son John, the future John II (r. 1350–64), who likewise arrived too late to the battle at Caen (26 July 1346) for which the people 'misliked' (60) him. This language of hate, cursing, and ruin forms a consistent pattern of abuse throughout all the poems.

If this language is consistent, the variation of poetic forms allows the poet different ways of presenting these insults. As an example, in Poem 9 Philip promises aid to David of Scotland if David would raid Northern England but fails to deliver on his promise. This stanzaic poem uses a fairly rigid rhyme scheme of *aaaabb* with stanzas 1, 4, and 7 having eight lines rhyming *aaaabbbb*. Repetitions in the poem, often because of the need of the rhyme, emphasise the unreliability of the French and David's recognition that he has a 'fals' ally. Stanza 8 has David speak a scornful invective against his betrayal by Philip and John, blaming his imprisonment in the Tower of London on them. It is the only speech by any character in all the poems. At no point in any of the poems are Philip or John called kings, the poet referring to them consistently as knights. In contrast, the poet identifies Edward as the 'Trew king that sittes in trone' in the first line of Poem 1 and as a king throughout.

Each of these poems presents its arguments for the supremacy of the English and the failures of the French in different complicated verse structures. If the poems were written by a single poet whom we could for convenience call Laurence Minot, they show diverse experimentation in different lyric forms, expanding on the rules of alliterative verse and showing various rhyme schemes. If they are the product of different poets, the collection itself is indeed remarkable in providing examples of the flexibility of the lyric form in the generation before Chaucer. While their different forms make each poem unique in its structure within the sequence, what joins the group together is their mocking the failures of England's opponents (their ill-founded pride, inability to coordinate movements, flight after a battlefield loss) as much as it is the praise of the English. They fit a pattern of political poetry of this period with others that invite readers to share with the poet in celebrating the deserved fall of the proud and the ridiculing of the foolish.

Socioeconomic Complaint

In contrast to the poems discussed above, the following poems couch their grievances against systems rather than individuals, and do so in order either to point out where they should be reformed or demonstrate how their practices materially harm the political, social, and even economic order. For instance, the poem in Harley 2253 known as the *Song of the Husbandman*, an item in six stanzas of twelve alliterating lines that also follow a rhyme scheme of *abababababcdcd* from Harley MS 2253, is an early-fourteenth-century critique of the rural economic system that victimises the peasantry at the expense of England's growing manorial bureaucracy.[17] The poem's speaker complains that he is being taxed into

---

[17] Fein, *Complete Harley 2253*, 128–31; *NIMEV*, 1320.5. Richard Newhauser mentions that various dates have been proposed for this poem's composition, ranging from 1294 to *c* 1315–17 to 1340; he concludes that the complaints raised in the poem were common throughout the late thirteenth and early to mid-fourteenth centuries and that the real point of the poem is the list of oppressions of the poor, which cannot be tied down to a dateable specific historical moment. See Richard Newhauser, 'Historicity and Complaint in *Song of the Husbandman*', in Susanna Fein (ed.), *Studies in the Harley Manuscript: The Scribes, Contents, and Social Contexts of British Library MS Harley 2253* (Kalamazoo, MI, 2000), 210–12. The second and third date of composition proposed

194   MEDIEVAL POETRY: 1100–1400

poverty because of greedy officials.[18] These grievances result from specific fiscal demands. The speaker complains that the king gets 'euer the furthe peni' ('every fourth penny'; 8) of all his produce collected by the king's 'budeles' ('beadles' or tax collectors). In addition, he needs to pay the hayward, bailiff, and woodward. The tasks that these three officers supervise are necessary for the orderly running of the manor: the bailiff, among other things, collects rents for the lord of the manor, the principal income for nobles and gentry in the feudal economy; the hayward is responsible for fences and enclosures in the parish, ensuring that cattle do not run free and cause damage; the woodward (a less usual target of complaint poetry) is in charge of managing the local timber.[19] The speaker charges each one with a grievance alliterating with their title: the bailiff 'bockneth us bale' ('summons us to misery'); the hayward 'heteth us harm' ('promises us harm'); the woodward 'waiteth us wo' ('brings us woe') (15–17). The speaker associates each of these members of the rural bureaucracy not with any productive role in it, but with the distress they do collectively to 'us', by which he includes the reader in sharing the misery.

A medieval poem's audience is usually difficult to know, especially when the date of composition is uncertain. For a poem in a compilation, such as the MS Harley 2253, the question is why the anonymous scribe or his patron wanted a copy of a poem possibly written long before the period when he was compiling his manuscript. Carter Revard has speculated that other poems in this manuscript, specifically one known as *Against the King's Taxes*, respond to the financial demands that Edward III had on the kingdom to pay for his war with France.[20] Edward's taxes took a particular toll in the Ludlow area where the manuscript was probably composed and where local landowners and merchants were deeply engaged in the lucrative wool trade. Edward's demand for a 'ninth part of every lamb, fleece, and sheaf' in 1339–40 'proved impossible to collect, partly because the weather, which had made for excellent harvests in 1337 and 1338, turned very bad in 1338–9, just when a desperate shortage of money among his people, and a desperate effort to gouge taxes out of them, were driving formerly prosperous people to the wall'.[21] The fiscal demands of the officers in the poem could have resonated with the scribe or his patron. For instance, the king in the poem demands every fourth penny; Edward III wants every ninth, not as much as the poem's king but still a significant amount. These taxes and fees lamented by the poem's speaker are so great that he must sell his livestock and his grain while it is still green to pay them, thereby reducing further his livelihood (65, 46). The poem shows the irony of the manorial bureaucracy worsening the lives of the people who support it.

The late thirteenth century saw population increases that caused manors and freeholds to be divided into much smaller parcels in order to satisfy surviving heirs until many estates were just barely sustainable. At the same time, to serve this growing population tasks that had been apportioned to members of the peasant community became sanctioned as offices, each requiring monetary support to maintain them. The speaker describes his problems

---

would show the growing imposition of the coin-based economy, since these years fall firmly within the period of frequent bad weather, famine, and livestock plagues noted in chronicles and other documents. A composition date of 1294 falls slightly before this period; however, Edward I's changes to the Exchequer in 1290 resulted in much greater supervision of taxation and could have influenced the poem's composition. See Michael Prestwich, *Edward I* (New Haven, CT, 1997), 342–4.

[18] The poem is often read as a peasant protest. Scase argues that it has the language of a judicial complaint that the speaker 'carpeth for the kyng' ('complains before the king', 9) with his plea against all those who are impoverishing the people of England with their fiscal demands (*Literature and Complaint*, 36–8).

[19] Newhauser, 'Historicity and Complaint', 215.

[20] Fein, *Complete Harley 2253*, 3:290–9.

[21] Carter Revard, 'Political Poems in MS Harley 2253 and the English National Crisis of 1339–41', *Chaucer Review*, 53 (2018), 69.

beginning when he had to keep accounts and 'to seche selver to the kyng' ('to find silver for the king', 62–3). The need for money rather than goods or labour to pay these financial obligations caused a burden on a rural economy where physical coins were probably not as plentiful. Additionally, an increase of bad weather and plagues on livestock lasting roughly from the 1280s to 1330s strained an already stressed rural economy.[22] A landowner facing similar bad weather, high taxes, and a rapacious king may have found the poem speaking directly to his own grievances at his situation.

Many complaint poems attack the greed of the Church and fit into the broad category of ecclesiastical satire that directly indicts Church officials and the bureaucracy they served without necessarily condemning specific named individuals. As an example, the poem usually referred to as the *Satire on the Consistory Courts* details the costs the poem's speaker incurs from his experience appearing in one of the courts run by the Church. The poem is in five eighteen-line alliterating stanzas with twelve lines rhyming *aabccbddbeebb* and a six-line wheel rhyming *ffgggf*. It was probably composed in the first quarter of the fourteenth century. It is written from the perspective of a 'lewed' ('illiterate') man who 'on molde mote with a mai' ('happened to lie on the ground with a maiden', 4) and shows how he suffers for it.[23] The woman accuses him of fornication in the Church court and demands that he marry her; the court agrees. Unlike the labourer in the previous poem, the speaker of this dramatic monologue has brought his fiscal hardship on himself; but he fails to recognise that he has sinned and is outraged to learn that his punishment will be against his reputation (since he will be publicly shamed) and against his purse (since he is forced now to marry and maintain the woman).

The poem criticises the members of the court for a system based on material profit and one with a perverse interest in sex crimes. For instance, the speaker comments that there is a curiously large number of individuals (more than forty!) present at his trial, drawn possibly by the potentially lurid nature of the testimony (23). The tone of the speaker is caustic towards everyone involved. He calls the summoners who would have hauled him into the court 'mysmotinde men alle' ('false accusers all', 38) because they believe the woman and not him. The speaker is disgusted by the willingness of the members of the court to believe a woman who 'monie byswyketh' ('deceives many', 68). But despite the inventiveness of his insults, he is angry and bewildered by what is happening to him, complaining finally that 'ase dogge Y am dryue' ('I'm driven like a dog', 82) through the market until he is finally married to the woman at the church. Throughout the poem, his status moves from being in control (he had sex with this woman) to being driven through a public space where everyone can see his shame. He loses his freedom in a marriage with a woman whom he must now financially support as well as any children that she might bear.

A fuller grievance directed at widespread greed is in the poem known as *The Simonye* which, though its editorial name would indicate a Church focus, also addresses the desire for money throughout society. It survives in three different manuscripts: Edinburgh, National Library of Scotland, Advocates' MS 19.2.1 (the Auchinleck MS); Cambridge, Cambridge University Library, MS Peterhouse 104; and Oxford, Bodleian Library, MS 48. The Auchinleck MS, dating from around 1330, is the earliest surviving witness. The poem was probably written around 1320. James Dean calls it one of the 'chief documents in the Middle English

---

[22] Bruce M. S. Campbell, *The Great Transition: Climate, Disease and Society in the Late-Medieval World* (Cambridge, 2016), 253–61.

[23] Fein, *Complete Harley 2253*, 188–93; *NIMEV*, 2287.

196 MEDIEVAL POETRY: 1100–1400

Abuse of Money tradition.[24] It opens by posing the questions of why there is war, hunger, and dearth, all of which the speaker claims to answer in an extended indictment of pride, but whereas the indictments in the political invective surveyed earlier are largely directed at the pride of a poem's speaker's opponents, this poem and the others following show instead that avarice, not pride, is the principal sin affecting the stability of society.[25] The poet exhibits a keen understanding of how the presence of money is transforming and specifically harming his society. The speaker identifies much of the deviant behaviour he catalogues in the poem as 'shrewdness', that is 'wickedness'. That archdeacons take bribes to allow priests to break their vows of celibacy (51–2) and priests take from their benefices and buy goods for themselves rather than for the benefit of the parish (67–78) are both described as 'shrewedelichest worche' (50, 68) condemnable in clerics. He also condemns it in laypeople. For example, a man who wants to divorce his wife can come to the priest with 'tweye false' ('two liars', 201), pay silver, and then be separated from her so that he can live now 'a shrewede lyf' (204). Office-holders show shrewishness because they cheat the king (331–3). These are all transactions that cause 'shrewedom' ('villainy', 373) to reign in the land. The poem argues that 'shrewedom', the wickedness that is ruining the kingdom, comes then from using money for satisfying individual appetites instead of for any greater or 'common profyt' or more succinctly, 'shrewedom' is the equivalent to simony.

The practices of getting and spending are also the subject of another anonymous poem, *Wynnere and Wastoure*, written probably in the 1350s, after the first visitation of the Black Death in England. The poem survives in a single manuscript, London, British Library, MS Additional 31,042, compiled around 1450.[26] It comprises 503 alliterative long lines and is divided into three fits plus a prologue. In the prologue, a speaker describes a woodland setting where he lies down and immediately has a dream that the rest of the poem recounts. The dream consists of a debate between the leaders of two armies, Wynnere and Wastoure, in front of the king. The descriptions of the armies allow the poet to exploit the alliterative structure for rich variation in the material trappings of the members of his army, such as the banners they carry. For instance, the Franciscan 'banere one bent es of blee whitte, / With sexe galegs, I see, of sable withinn, / And iche one has a brown brase with bokels twayne' ('banner has a field of bright white, with six sandals, I see, of black and each one has a brown strap and two buckles', 156–8).[27] This description uses the heraldic language of the field, specific colours (white and black), but the devices, the sandals, refer to the Franciscans, who would have no need of a military banner. Heraldic emblems, frequently found in romances, were associated with knights to identify their own family and property; Franciscans, however, should own no property beyond their basic clothing. Here, the poet plays with generic expectations to emphasise the material associations of his subjects so that the emblem of a nonmilitary group that should own nothing is the one thing that they can own: their shoes.

---

[24] Dean, *Medieval English Political Writings*, 180.

[25] Dan Embree and Elizabeth Urquhart have recognised that the poet's perspective 'is socially below and physically distant from the centres of power. Despite his [the speaker's] claims, he simply does not know as much about the evils of the court as about the evils of the town'. Dan Embree and Elizabeth Urquhart (eds), *The Simonie: A Parallel-Text Edition* (Heidelberg, 1991), 41. Citations, unless otherwise indicated, are from the A-text from this edition.

[26] See John Scattergood's discussion on the dating problem of the poem. Scattergood, 'Winner and Waster and the Mid-Fourteenth-Century Economy', in Tom Dunne (ed.), *The Writer as Witness: Literature as Historical Evidence* (Cork, 1987), 40–2. He assigns the poem's composition to 1352–3.

[27] Stephanie Trigg (ed.), *Wynnere and Wastoure*, EETS o.s. 297 (Oxford, 1990).

Scholarly work on this poem has addressed its rhetorical structure or how it addresses questions of the economic landscape, from the household upward.[28] The poem alludes to the Statute of Labourers (1351), the Statute on Treasons (1351), and the sumptuary laws (1363), all passed by parliaments intending to enforce a status quo that could no longer be easily defended or sustained. Rising wages resulting from a dramatic drop in a labouring population allowed more people to acquire money and material property in excess of what they would need to live.[29] The poem interrogates the practice of gathering versus spending money as a function of status in the post-pandemic world when possession of land was no longer the only way to gain status in medieval society. The inventiveness of the poem comes from subverting the generic expectations of debate or dream poetry: beyond those, it is an extended complaint.

The prologue begins, as in *Sir Gawain and the Green Knight*, with Britain's founding by Brutus, but then affirms that 'witt and wyles' (5) are now how contemporaries deal with one another: 'Wyse wordes and slee, and icheon wryeth othere' ('Wise and subtle words obscure each other's meaning', 6). Treason in both action and language have disrupted the world and specifically England, the successor to Brutus's empire. As a result, the dreamer finds himself in a landscape that seems less conventionally pleasant than the ideal places other dreamers in medieval poetry tend to encounter. The birds he hears and the stream by which he lies down do not provide him the peaceful setting to distract him from the problem bothering him; they just annoy him (31–69). Similarly, the social order no longer follows its traditional models of the three estates: those who fight, those who pray, and those who labour. They instead seem concerned with money.

Even the pavilion in the dream where the king receives the two debaters and their armies has as its principal decorations 'Ynglysse besantes full brighte, betyn of golde' ('Very bright English besants of beaten gold', 61). The besant was a gold coin originating from Byzantium. Medieval England did not mint a gold coin until Edward III had the noble struck in the mid-1340s. As the passage indicates, the design of the besant was also used in the decorative art of the period. In this poem, the besant is both ornamental and, because of its material and the topic of the debate, specifically evocative of a coin. Therefore, the image of the pavilion is that it is luxurious and figuratively covered in money. The banner that flies over it bears the words, 'Hethyng haue the hathell þat any harmes thynkes' ('Evil to him who evil thinks'), which is the English translation of the Anglo-Norman motto of the Order of the Garter, 'Honi soit qui mal y pense' (68). This banner and Edward's coat of arms (74–80) blend the chivalric ideal on which the Order was alleged to be founded with the reality that power in the realm is based on money. Wastoure spends; Wynnere hoards. Each complains that the other practises extreme behaviour. While the point is property, the measuring commodity for the two debaters is money. Money is either spent or hoarded, with neither disputant accepting that moderating spending is the wisest course. John Scattergood identifies each as the 'traditional misusers of money: Winner is the "avarus" who exceeds in acquisition and is deficient in giving, Waster is the "prodigus" who exceeds in spending

---

[28] For examples of analyses of its rhetorical structure, see Thomas H. Bestul, *Satire and Allegory in Wynnere and Wastoure* (Lincoln, NE, 1974); Cara Hersh, '"Wyse words within": Private Property and Public Knowledge in *Wynnere and Wastoure*', *Modern Philology*, 107 (2010), 507–27. For analyses concerning household management in the poem, see D. Vance Smith, *Arts of Possession: The Middle English Household Imaginary* (Minneapolis, MN, 2003), 76–7; Kellie Robertson, *The Laborer's Two Bodies: Labor and the 'Work' of the Text in Medieval Britain, 1350–1500* (New York, 2006), 40–1.

[29] The poem mentions William Shareshull, who served as Chief Justice from 1350 to 1361, which helps to date the poem. He helped promulgate the statutes. Richard Kaeuper calls him a 'tireless collector of sizable amounts of revenue through judicial fines' (*Oxford Dictionary of National Biography*).

198   MEDIEVAL POETRY: 1100–1400

but is deficient in getting'. Wynnere will appear as an 'acquisitive merchant' and Wastoure 'a prodigal landowner'.[30] The poem shows how two contrary arguments on political economy potentially motivate the king's policy action. It is also one of the first attempts in poetic form to examine economic activity in English.

Another anonymous alliterative complaint about the material interests of the English Church, particularly among the orders of friars, is the poem known as *Piers the Ploughmans Crede*. It survives in no complete copy before the Tudor period, but its allusion to John Wyclif (1330–84) and Walter Brut, a West Country Lollard who was tried for heresy in 1393, indicate that the poem was composed sometime near the end of the fourteenth century. Like *Richard the Redeless* and *Mum and the Sothsegger*, it also shows significant influence from Langland's *Piers Plowman*. The poem contrasts the materialistic friars, who express their greatest concern not for the education of the laity, but in competition for the coins of the faithful with other fraternal orders and against the honest labour and poverty of Piers Ploughman. The condemnations of the friars in the poem follow the standard criticisms of anti-fraternal tradition. For the author of the poem, friars devote their ministry to the rich and to the supremacy of their own orders. They see the other fraternal orders as rivals rather than partners. The speaker is dismayed to hear a friar 'blamen his brother, and bacbyten him foule' ('blame his brother and maliciously slander him', 139).[31] As we have seen in other poems, the grievance is expressed in alliterating pairs. Even the poor person who gives half of his own livelihood for the friars' enrichment is not helping others with it— hence the consequence of these practices is the Dominican friar whom the speaker meets with 'a face as fat as a full bledder' ('a face as fat as a full bladder', 222). As a full bladder ends a satisfying meal, the fat friar is a figure of material contentment from rewards obtained without doing any labour to achieve them. He is unwilling to teach the speaker his creed, despite the Dominican order having as its purpose to preach and teach.

In contrast, the speaker describes Piers Ploughman ploughing his fields in his tattered rags, accompanied by his weary wife and crying children. Piers labours out of necessity so that his family does not starve. In a poignant passage, the poet describes Piers's mittens 'maad all of cloutes; / The fyngers weren for-werd and ful of fen honged' ('made all of rags, the fingers of which were worn out and hanging', 428–9). The *Crede*'s grievance against the materialism of an English Church, which needs to be expressed in monetary comparisons for full comprehension, is spoken by Piers: 'But there as wynnynge lijth, he loketh none other' ('But they only look to where they can gain profit and look nowhere else', 471). Piers's sermon at the end of the poem condemns the Church for offering loans just 'as burgeses vsithe' ('just as townspeople practise', 716). The purpose is as much to refocus the reader to the spiritual contemplation of the needs of the soul as it is to condemn the material expenses of the Church.[32]

These poems on economic grievance indict systems that were perhaps well intentioned when they began but have become corrupted in their practices. Much of what has caused the corruption, the poems argue, is the need for money. The poems focus on images of money and the things it can buy as markets have become more diverse and as individuals who in decades past could not afford these goods can now purchase them. The alliterative line is a useful vehicle for this kind of poetry because of its ability to use repetition to underscore

---

[30] Scattergood, '*Winner and Waster*', 50.

[31] *Pierce the Ploughman's Crede*, in Helen Barr (ed.), *The Piers Plowman Tradition*, 61–97.

[32] Although the poem cites Wycliff, much of the theology, according to Barr, may not be entirely orthodox, but also not entirely heretical either: for instance, the poem does not deny transubstantiation or the sacrament of penance. Barr, *Piers Plowman Tradition*, 12.

the immediacy or the pervasiveness of the problems the poems explore. This small sample can serve only as a portion of the many rich poetic commentaries on the changing socioeconomic conditions of the fourteenth century. Their writers were not so much providing a chronicle record of their times as an impression of what they believed was going wrong and how much it was costing them all, socially as well as financially.

13

Doctrine and Learning

Stephen M. Yeager

One of the more strikingly elliptical statements in Chaucer's ambiguous Retraction to *The Canterbury Tales* is his comment: 'For our book seith, "All that is writen is writen for oure doctrine", and that is myn entente' (X.1083). As Manish Sharma has compellingly argued, Chaucer's quotation from Matthew 15.4 in this passage nicely expresses the undecidable contradiction that shapes Chaucer's self-representation as an author in all of his work.[1] If the Bible stipulates that all writing necessarily accords with doctrine, whether the writer intends it to or not, then why does Chaucer bother to tell us what his 'entente' was? To whom, and in what way, does authorial intention matter in poetry written 'for our doctrine'?

The title of this chapter uses two words, 'doctrine' and 'learning', to divide Chaucer's singular 'doctrine' into two distinct modern concepts as a way of framing this chapter's consideration of the Middle English poems that engage with these vexed questions. 'Doctrine' here will refer specifically to the faith-based, culturally determined, and so frequently ritualised and social knowledge of (especially religious) orthodoxy, which may be distinguished from the more experience-based, materially determined, and so frequently technical and practical forms of scientific and historical 'learning'. These two categories of knowledge were deeply intertwined in the medieval period, and their interrelationship is best imagined as a fluid negotiation between the more abstract and philosophical knowledge of official, regulated doctrine—which defined, for example, the nature of God and hence of existence—and the more pragmatic and instrumental knowledge of medical and natural 'lore'. Chaucer's ambiguous claim to write his poetry 'for our doctrine' is only one instance in the corpus where we see the didacticism of Middle English verse both occasioning and shaping poetic forms and narratives for the purposes of knowledge production. This chapter will survey several other examples.

In medieval England as today, formal tensions between the various modes of information storage commonly reflected the political tensions between the religious and secular institutions that collected, authorised, codified, and disseminated both doctrine and learning to both specialist and popular audiences. Such tensions are particularly manifest in the English language poetry that takes doctrine and learning as its primary subject, as these works by their very nature tended to be adapted to the emergent needs of new and evolving audiences.[2] As a result, few of the works cited here are the official products of ecclesiastical or secular authorities, and seem on the contrary to be acts of artistic expression that repurpose official knowledge to enact novel forms of representation and cultural critique.

In the first section of this chapter, I will briefly survey the enormous variety of medieval mnemonic verse to ground this general claim, identifying a few examples of Middle English

---

[1] Manish Sharma, 'Hylomorphic Recursion and Non-Decisional Poetics in the *Canterbury Tales*', *Chaucer Review*, 52 (2017), 253–72. See also Larry Scanlon, 'The Authority of the Fable: Allegory and Irony in the *Nun's Priest's Tale*', *Exemplaria*, 1 (1989), 43–68 and Alastair Minnis, *Medieval Theory of Authorship: Scholastic Literary Attitudes in the Later Middle Ages*, 2nd edn. (Philadelphia, PA, 2010), 190–210.

[2] Siegfried Wenzel, *Preachers, Poets, and the Early English Lyric* (Princeton, NJ, 1986).

Stephen M. Yeager, *Doctrine and Learning*. In: *The Oxford History of Poetry in English*. Edited by Helen Cooper and Robert R. Edwards, Oxford University Press. © Stephen M. Yeager (2023). DOI: 10.1093/oso/9780198827429.003.0013

poetry where the need to authorise knowledge occasioned structural and formal innovations. In the second, I will focus on the history of versified maxims and proverbs, before I turn in the third and final section to the closely related genre of debate poetry. In this final dialogic form, we see most clearly how the subjects of doctrine and learning can lead poets to engage directly with questions of poetic and narrative form itself.

As James J. Morey noted in an earlier survey of didactic English literature, 'one could level the field at a single stroke and claim that nearly all Middle English literature was written with instruction as its primary aim.'[3] The present chapter will aim to situate this ubiquitous didacticism of Middle English poetry in relation to its appropriations of and innovations in existing poetic genres and forms. Though it may seem counterintuitive to modern readers, who tend to associate formal inventiveness with the expression of individual creative visions, it is often the case that the pressure to conform with established doctrine and to convey complex learning exerted a pressure on Middle English poetic form. Not only Chaucer's poetry but also the versions of *Piers Plowman* and the works of the Pearl poet all demonstrate how the subject matter of doctrine and learning is commonly correlated to Middle English poetry's most breath-taking flights of formal inventiveness.[4] In my selections below, I will highlight instances where the efforts by poets to use didactic verse to store and disseminate facts and protocols contributed directly to the broader trend whereby Middle English poets developed complex, hybridised, or otherwise innovative forms of poetic expression.

Verse and Didacticism

As we might expect, uses of verse to store and disseminate culturally important information is not a specifically English or even European phenomenon, and in fact poetic forms have long had a related pragmatic function in cultures around the world. This common use of poetic metre seems related to the so-called 'rhyme-as-reason effect' observed by recent research on the reception of aphorisms, as has been summarised in the witticism that 'if it rhymes it must be true.'[5] But whatever the cause of the phenomenon, it is nonetheless clear that poetic forms have long served to literally encode cultural authority in the contexts of their use, and so they became markers of that authority that functioned irrespective of their content. In making this claim, I do not deny the obvious importance of prose formats to knowledge storage, attested not only in Middle English but back to the very beginning of the historical record. On the contrary, Middle English prose is a highly sophisticated form, well suited to the task of storing and disseminating complex information in a manner that is both intelligible and pleasing to its intended audience. Indeed, the common presumption that didactic verse forms were chosen for their Chaucerian 'solaas' hardly accounts for the historical fact that even despite the constrained affordances of writing technology—which attached considerable cost both to the space on the page and the time of the scribe—neutral, telegraphic Middle English prose did not replace the metrical forms and conventions used by earlier oral cultures to help them memorise information.[6] The very fact that didactic

---

[3] James J. Morey, 'Didactic Literature', in David Johnson and Elaine Treharne (eds), *Readings in Medieval Texts: Interpreting Old and Middle English Literature* (Oxford, 2005), 183–97, 183.

[4] A. V. C. Schmidt, *Clerkly Maker: Langland's Poetic Art* (Woodbridge, 1987).

[5] Matthew S. McGlone and Jessica Tofighbakhsh, 'Birds of a Feather Flock Conjointly(?): Rhyme as Reason in Aphorisms', *Psychological Science*, 11 (2000), 424–8.

[6] See, for example, the case of Old English legal prose, which becomes more 'poetic' and alliterative as written law becomes more important: Dorothy Loomis Bethurum, 'Stylistic Features of the Old English Laws', *Modern Language Review*, 27 (1932), 263–79, at 269–70.

202   MEDIEVAL POETRY: 1100–1400

Middle English poetry exists in such abundance therefore suggests that there is more at play in these formal choices than strictly utilitarian concerns.

Here, I will presume that didactic verse genres persisted in Middle English poetry because the inherited authority of oral traditional knowledge made (and makes) poetic statements *sound true*, whatever the content of the statements themselves. This true-sounding quality of verse may serve to memorialise culturally received wisdom about complex philosophical or moral conditions, as in the commonly quoted iambic tetrameters of Andrew Marvell's 'To His Coy Mistress' ('But at my back I always hear / Time's winged chariot hurrying near'). It may also help one to remember useful facts, as in the internally rhyming trochaic tetrameters taught to children in the American southwest about the distinct coloration patterns of the poisonous coral snake ('red and yellow kills a fellow') and the harmless scarlet king snake ('red and black is friend to Jack'). These verses are both memorable because of the metrical forms used to shape them and their compelling reminders of the ways mortality can drive human action serve to reinscribe the cultural authority of verse forms generally.

This pragmatic function of verse helps to explain this rhyme-as-reason effect. As cultures evolve in response to emergent historical circumstances, so also are innovations introduced to the encoding techniques that record and disseminate received authority. And as literary texts have been written down over centuries, the fact of this evolution has become legible to authorities and so a source of anxiety for both authorities and authors. The line from Chaucer's (prose) Retraction with which I began, which contrasts suggestively with the oft-quoted passage from the 'General Prologue' where Chaucer speaks of his duty to record exactly even the most impious and offensive words of his fellow pilgrims (I.725–47), is only one particularly noteworthy instance in the corpus where we see a Middle English author vexed by the relationship between the correctness of authorising form and the truth of authoritative content. And though the poems of doctrine and learning surveyed below each represent the tension between form and information in varying ways, the tension itself is widely attested in the poetry of this period.

One of the earliest examples of how this pressure is manifest in Middle English doctrinal poetry is the *Ormulum*.[7] This 20,000-line translation of the entire year's missal readings into English verse is most commonly remembered for its innovative use of phonetic standardised spelling, which has led some readers to speculate that it was produced for preachers who did not speak English but who served an Anglophone constituency.[8] Just as important to this apparent purpose is the strict syllabic regularity of the collection's septenary verse form, highly unusual in Middle English poetry, which indeed would be a helpful aid to a preacher with no natural feel for Middle English patterns of linguistic stress. Hence the *Ormulum* is representative of the broader trend, whereby emergent pragmatic difficulties facing those charged with disseminating correct doctrine to a popular audience can drive major innovations in the structure and deployment of metrical forms in Middle English verse.

---

[7] Robert Holt and R. M. White (eds), *The Ormulum*, 2 vols. (Oxford, 1878); Carla María Thomas, 'Orm's Vernacular Latinity', *SELIM*, 20 (2013), 167–98. On the manuscript, see also M. B. Parkes, 'On the Presumed Date and Possible of the Manuscript Orrmulum: Oxford, Bodleian Library, MS Junius 1', in E. G. Stanley and Douglas Gray (eds), *Five Hundred Years of Words and Sounds: A Festschrift for Eric Dobson* (London, 1978), 115–27.

[8] Barbara Strang, *A History of English* (London, 1970), 242 and passim; Meg Worley, 'Using the Ormulum to Redefine Vernacularity', in Fiona Somerset and Nicholas Watson (eds), *The Vulgar Tongue: Medieval and Postmedieval Vernacularity* (University Park, PA, 2003), 19–30.

The Ormulum is also an example of a Middle English text where we see evidence of continuity in writing across the Norman Conquest, for instance in its use of lists. From the catalogue of ships in Homer's *Iliad* to the series of tragic downfalls in Lydgate's *Fall of Princes*, poetic lists have long served the dual function of both storing and disseminating culturally important information and of marking the poem that contains the list as itself culturally important. There are many examples of such lists in Middle English poetry, especially of information related to penance and reflection. One of the most important and popular examples of listed information in verse is the text called *The Prick of Conscience*, surviving in some 130 manuscripts and attributed (falsely) to the innovative author and poet Richard Rolle.[9] The various sections of this text's various recensions do not so much advance arguments about the procedures of repentance and restitution that structure its narrative as they use each subject as an occasion for listing related facts, which cover not only religious and devotional subjects (such as the orders of angels and the fifteen signs of Final Judgment) but also scientific and historical ones (such as the eyesight of the lynx and the orbits of the planets).[10] *The Prick of Conscience* can therefore be imagined as an intermediate point between the sort of wisdom-encoding list-poem one would expect to find in the Exeter book or the Norse Edda and the entries of the modern encyclopaedia, whose existence demonstrates just how long verse continued to be useful for the collection and dissemination of useful information. Though *The Prick of Conscience* may be considerably longer, more comprehensive, and structured according to a more transparent logic than an Old English poem such as *Maxims*, it not only retains the basic structural form as a poem but also successfully and influentially renovates that form.

A similar text of doctrine and learning from the early fourteenth century, attributed to the Gilbertine canon Robert Mannyng of Brunne, is the 11,000-line handbook *Handlyng Synne*.[11] This popular treatise survives in nine manuscripts, including the celebrated Vernon and Simeon collections (Oxford, Bodleian Library MS English Poetry a.1 and London, British Library, MS Additional 22,283 respectively). The text is based on the Anglo-Norman *Manuel de Pechiez* attributed to William of Waddington, which in turn is only one of many penitential compendia written for lay instruction in this period. *Handlyng Synne* is organised as a list of commandments, deadly sins, sacraments, and the elements of confession, all of which are illustrated through exemplary narratives that are in many cases expansions of the Anglo-Norman original. As Elizabeth Allen has written, the 'poetics of exemplarity' instantiated by *Handlyng Synne* transforms the exempla into 'a principal site for sophisticated inquiry into the educational methods of poetic narrative, highlighting the limits of authorial control, the importance of narrative as inspiration or seduction, and the possibilities of imaginative freedom'.[12] The poem's introduction states that it was written for 'lewed men' (43) and in particular those who 'talys and rymys wyl bleþly here' ('will happily listen to tales and rhymes') (46), to ensure that such people do not follow immoral entertainments into 'velanye, / To dedly synne, or outher folye' ('villainy, deadly sin, or other folly') (49–50),

---

[9] Ralph Hanna and Sarah Wood (eds), *Richard Morris's Prick of Conscience: A Corrected and Amplified Reading Text*, EETS o.s. 342 (Oxford, 2013).

[10] On the fifteen signs of judgement and their depiction in stained glass, see Vincent Gillespie, 'Medieval Hypertext: Image and Text from York Minster', in P. R. Robinson and Rivkah Zim (eds), *Of the Making of Books: Medieval Manuscripts, Their Scribes and Readers—Essays presented to M.B. Parkes* (Aldershot, 1997), 206–29.

[11] Robert Mannyng of Brunne, in Idelle Sullens (ed.), *Robert Mannyng of Brunne: Handlyng Synne* (Binghamton, NY, 1983).

[12] Elizabeth Allen, *False Fables and Exemplary Truth in Later Middle English Literature* (Basingstoke, 2005), 2.

204 MEDIEVAL POETRY: 1100–1400

but rather 'weyl dyspende here tyme' ('spend their time well') (52). In other words, the poem promises to benefit both the unlearned audience, who might otherwise waste time by listening to inappropriate poems, and the Middle English poets who might otherwise waste rhythmical, metrical 'time' by writing such poems.[13] It is clear from this passage that *Handlyng Synne* aimed not only to promote moral behaviour but also to intervene specifically in the practices of consuming and producing poetic narratives that might otherwise impede this promotion.

The Prick of Conscience and *Handlyng Synne* are only two of the many Middle English manuals that were useful not only to preachers, as their Latin predecessors and sources had been, but also to an unlearned readership who received spiritual instruction from the text directly. Nor was penitential doctrine the only form of knowledge promoted in this manner by Middle English texts; medical knowledge, law, and natural history received similar treatments. Particularly interesting to modern scholars have been the various texts and genres emerging from the *Physiologus*, which used allegorical reading to describe observed or legendary phenomena in the animal kingdom to exemplify the close connection between religious doctrine and scientific learning in this period. Originally a Greek text dated to the second or third century CE, the *Physiologus* circulated in several Latin versions which in turn were translated as both Old and Middle English poems.[14] Particularly important to the current discussion is the thirteenth-century Middle English translation, titled *The Bestiary* by its Victorian editor, which appears in alliterative verse in the same manuscript as two other alliterative poems in a later hand titled 'The Chorister's Complaint' and 'Satire on the Blacksmiths'.[15]

As Jill Mann has documented, the *Physiologus* tradition lay at the root of a number of key medieval genres, not least of which is the 'beast fable' exemplified by Chaucer's 'Nun's Priest's Tale'.[16] Particularly famous in English letters is its typological description of the whale, appearing in the first epic simile in Milton's *Paradise Lost* (1.194–208). In the Middle English *Bestiary*, the sailors who mistake the whale for an island build a fire to 'warmen hem wel and heten and drinken' ('to warm them well and eat and drink') (537), which causes the whale to dive and drown them. The poem then goes on to explain that the whale's behaviour makes it a type for the devil, who 'doð men hungren and hauen ðrist, / and mani oðer sinful list' ('makes men hunger, thirst, and have other sinful desires') (543–4). That this poem's description of an animal's behaviour is used to drive home a doctrinal point about the relation between appetite and sin exemplifies the interrelationship between 'doctrine' and 'learning' in this period.

As the medieval period progressed, prose began increasingly to serve as the preferred vehicle for transmitting knowledge, at the same time that poetry began increasingly to serve the more purely expressive ends it would serve in the modern period. Be that as it

---

[13] For another Middle English occurrence of the phrase *dispenden time* with this double meaning, see *Canterbury Tales* VII.931.

[14] Jill Mann, *From Aesop to Reynard: Beast Literature in Medieval Britain* (Oxford, 2009), 23–4, citing Nikolaus Henkel, *Studien zum Physiologus im Mittelalter* (Tubingen, 1976); Florence McColloch, *Medieval Latin and French Bestiaries* (Chapel Hill, NC, 1960); Debra Hassig, *Medieval Bestiaries: Text, Image, Ideology* (Cambridge, 1995).

[15] Richard Morris, *The Early English Bestiary*, EETS o.s. 49 (Oxford, 1872);see also Hanneke Wirtjes (ed.), *The Middle English Physiologus*, EETS o.s. 299 (Oxford, 1991). The manuscript is London, British Library, MS Arundel 292. See Edwin Duncan, 'The Middle English Bestiary: Missing Link in the Evolution of the Alliterative Long Line?', *Studia Neophilologica*, 64 (1992), 25–33; Weiskott, *English Alliterative Verse: Poetic Tradition and Literary History* (Cambridge, 2016), 84–5.

[16] Mann, *From Aesop to Reynard*, 2–27.

may, the basic parallel between verse and other formal structures of language—that both are deployed to authorise facts—led to the emergence of hybrid forms. Among the most remarkable of these are the poems that take the shape of legal documents, including, for example, *The Charter of Christ* and *The Charter of the Abbey of the Holy Ghost*.[17] Such hybrid forms were not limited to devotional works like these, and they also included poems that attempted to formalise real political relationships or that were even passed off as forgeries, albeit not especially convincing ones. An example of the former is the inscription of a brief Middle English rhyming poem on the side of Cooling castle, depicted as a charter with the image of a seal carved beneath it, affirming that the castle was built to help the people.[18] An example of the latter is a Middle English charter-poem in rhyming couplets, attributed to King Athelstan (*c* 894–939) and surviving in two late-medieval copies, one of which is a single-sheet charter.[19] Poetic documents like these anticipate the sorts of negotiations between forms of knowledge and forms of literature that would emerge in the modern period, after the explosion in the production of both types of forms. The key aspect of these Middle English hybrid works is that when they span distinct formalisms, they are not so much joining together disparate modes as they are exposing and playing off of the original uses of formal patterns to encode language. The common feature shared by penitential doctrine, beast lore, and legal claims is that they each represented a kind of information that the participants in English identity wished to record and disseminate. Middle English poetry was clearly considered to be a particularly useful tool towards these ends.

Sententiousness and Form: The Proverb Collection

Proverbs, aphorisms, maxims, and other such sententious statements are the building blocks of doctrine and learning, discrete and modular units that can be used to construct and support a wide variety of arguments applied by both specialist and lay audiences.[20] In *A Theory of the Aphorism*, Andrew Hui has posited that 'aphorisms are before, against, and after philosophy', and that 'the history of aphorisms can be narrated as an animadversion, a turning away from grand systems through the construction of literary fragments'.[21] I have argued elsewhere that an individuated *sentence*—which is to say, an expression of wisdom in a form encompassing not only aphorisms and proverbs but also gnomes, maxims, and other related statements—is the primordial form of recorded data, whose descendants include not only didactic poems but also law codes and other authoritative modes of data

---

[17] On *The Charter of Christ*, see Emily Steiner, *Documentary Culture and the Making of Medieval English Literature* (Cambridge, 2003), 193–228. On *The Charter of the Abbey of the Holy Ghost*, see Julia Boffey, 'The Charter of the Abbey of the Holy Ghost and its Role in Manuscript Anthologies', *Yearbook of English Studies*, 33 (2003), 120–30.

[18] C. M. Cervone, 'John de Cobham and Cooling Castle's Charter Poem', *Speculum*, 83 (2008), 884–916; on John de Cobham, see also Sebastian Sobecki, 'A Southwark Tale: Gower, the 1381 Poll Tax, and Chaucer's *The Canterbury Tales*', *Speculum*, 92 (2017), 630–60.

[19] This charter poem is S 451 and *IMEV* 3300 / *DIMEV* 4183: *Digital Index of Middle English Verse*, http://www.dimev.net. Printed in J. R. Whitty, 'The Rhyming Charter of Beverley', *Transactions of the Yorkshire Dialect Society*, 22 (1921), 36–44; see also D. A. Woodman, 'The Forging of the Anglo-Saxon Past in Fourteenth-Century Beverley', *English Manuscript Studies*, 17 (2012), 26–42. The medieval manuscripts of this text are London, British Library, Cotton Charter IV 18 and Add MS 61,901.

[20] Lori Ann Garner, 'The Role of Proverbs in Middle English Narrative', in Mark C. Amodio (ed.), *New Directions in Oral Theory* (Tempe, AZ, 2005), 255–77; Cameron Louis, 'Authority in Middle English Proverb Literature', *Florilegium*, 15 (1998), 85–123. For a useful survey of the categories of sententious statement, see Paul Cavill, *Maxims in Old English Poetry* (Cambridge, 1999), 41–59.

[21] Andrew Hui, *A Theory of the Aphorism from Confucius to Twitter* (Princeton, NJ, 2019), 2.

206   MEDIEVAL POETRY: 1100–1400

storage.[22] Hence Middle English proverbs and proverb collections are highly telling about the changes and continuities in English culture over the course of the later Middle Ages.

In her influential analysis of Old English sententious poetry, Elaine Tuttle Hansen has observed that these are 'texts "about language", in a distinctly structuralist sense of the phrase'.[23] This observation applies to many Middle English poems of doctrine and learning, as these commonly use poetic forms and push against their limits to represent as transparently but memorably as possible the facts they aim to record. More to the point, the fact that such pressure commonly originates in both popular and institutional efforts to preserve dominant ideologies is starkly witnessed by the explicitly misogynistic statements about the untrustworthiness of women that are a feature of virtually every medieval proverb collection (e.g., *The Proverbs of Alfred* 225–360). Counterintuitive though it may seem, formal innovation is at least as important to maintaining cultural traditions as it is to challenging them, as custom thrives especially when it looks like evolution and progress.

In the specific case of Middle English proverbs, Susan Deskis has observed that their tendency to alliterate may well be an aftereffect of earlier English alliterative verse traditions, in what we might call an 'alliteration-as-reason effect' that reflects not only the mnemonic utility of alliteration but also its prominence in the forms of earlier English prose and verse.[24] This feature of Middle English proverbs is not only witnessed in the individual proverbs that appear in collections like the *Proverbs of Hendyng*,[25] but also in the alliterative poem *The Proverbs of Alfred*, which is moreover a key attestation of alliterative metre dated between the Norman Conquest and the great flowering of Middle English manuscript production that began *c* 1350.[26] Alliteration in proverbs likely speaks to the continued importance of alliterative sound-patterning in both English verse and prose throughout the medieval period.[27] It also reinforces the basic point that even centuries before the rhyme-as-reason effect was subjected to scientific enquiry, there was a fairly solid evidentiary basis for arguing that many proverbs may be imagined as miniature poems, which may not be as specific in their advice as the coral snake mnemonic cited above but which are nonetheless similarly intended to stick in the minds of listeners and help to shape their future actions.

The Proverbs of Alfred appeared during a lull in the production of new English proverb collections and an apparent surge in French texts, presumably to help preachers and train lawyers.[28] The attribution of the proverbs to Alfred is only one indication that the collection may have had the latter purpose. The poem follows the same basic structure as an Old English law code, as it purports to record the pronouncements of a king made before a collection of wise counsellors or *witan*. In this case, the pronouncements are not literally laws, but simply statements of wisdom pertinent to a good life. Not least important are the several proverbs asserting the importance of literacy. Alfred asserts that that no king may be 'ryhtwis' unless 'he beo / In boke ilered; / And he his wyttes / Swiþþe wel kunne'

---

[22] Stephen M. Yeager, *From Lawmen to Plowmen: Anglo-Saxon Legal Tradition and the School of Langland* (Toronto, 2014), 39–45.

[23] Elaine Tuttle Hansen, *The Solomon Complex: Reading Wisdom in Old English Poetry* (Toronto, 1988), 8.

[24] Susan E. Deskis, *Alliterative Proverbs in Medieval England: Language Choice and Literary Meaning* (Columbus, OH, 2016).

[25] Deskis, *Alliterative Proverbs*, 76–7, citing Samuel Singer, 'Die Sprichwörter Hendings', *Studia Neophilologica*, 14 (1941/2), 31–52; Cameron Louis, 'Manuscript Contexts of Middle English Proverb Literature', *Mediaeval Studies*, 60 (1998), 219–38; Facsimile of Oxford, Bodleian Library, MS Digby 86: https://medieval.bodleian.ox.ac.uk/catalog/manuscript_4426.

[26] Olof Arngart (ed.), *The Proverbs of Alfred: An Emended Text*, 2 vols. (Lund, 1978). See Yeager, *From Lawmen to Plowmen*, 114–20; Deskis, *Alliterative Proverbs*, 79.

[27] Weiskott, *English Alliterative Verse*.

[28] J. Morawski, 'Les recueils d'anciens proverbes français analysés et classés', *Romania*, 48 (1922), 481–558.

('he be learned in books and masters his wits very well') (63–6). For all that it is staged as an oral pronouncement, *The Proverbs of Alfred* is ultimately a literary text, which deploys the self-evident truth of its collected proverbs to literally inscribe the authority of written poetry.

Debate Poetry and Poetic Form

The Middle English debate poem is related to, but ultimately distinct from, both the learned genres of the debate or dialogue and the traditional genres of so-called *flyting* and 'sounding'.[29] The common attribute of these seemingly disparate texts is their use of narrative conflict to collect and disseminate wisdom, whether this wisdom is considered to be the 'content' of proverbs, mythology, history, riddles, or other forms of knowledge (as it tends to be, for example, in Old Norse eddic poems), or the 'form' of reasoned argumentation (as it tends to be in the many medieval dialogues based on Boethius's *De Consolatio Philosophiae*). As the title of Thomas Reed's classic study *Middle English Debate Poetry and the Aesthetics of Irresolution* signifies, debate poems from this period rarely result in a clear victor, and there is considerable grounding for Reed's view that these poems 'often seem less interested in settling on a winner than in the apprehension or appreciation (in the multiple senses of the words) of the differences that give rise to the debate'.[30] This appreciation and representation of difference, and in particular its potential irresolvability, marks these poems as particularly concerned with the implicit problem of form and its relation to authority that faces all poems of doctrine and learning. It is no wonder, then, that these poems are among the most formally inventive and unusual of all of the poetry dated to this period.

One of the most intriguing analogues for our present purposes are the various poems recording debates between King Solomon and a Persian interlocutor, often named Saturn, which frames the contest as one between Jewish and non-Jewish, 'heathen' culture.[31] Of particular note to scholars of English literature are the riddling debates between these figures in the Old English poems *Solomon and Saturn I* and *II*, the latter of which supplied the memorable 'time' riddle to the 'Riddles in the Dark' chapter of Tolkien's novel *The Hobbit*.[32] The legacy of this tradition continues in texts like the late-thirteenth-century *Proverbes of Hendyng,* a text witnessing proverbs attested in *The Proverbs of Alfred* which is attributed to Hendyng the son of 'Marcolf', who in turn appears in both German poems and late-Middle English prose texts from the *Solomon and Saturn* tradition.[33] The apparent connections between Middle English debates with these Old English and German poems, the learned tradition of Latin *Enigmata* compiled by St Boniface and Aldhelm, and the many debates, contests, and recitations of traditional wisdom in the Old Icelandic edda indicate how widespread is the three-way conjunction of riddles, debate poems, and proverb collections in the literature of English and its closest linguistic relations.

But while proverbs do appear frequently in Middle English debate poems, they do so as only one set of pieces on a vast chessboard of weaponised knowledge, alongside a wide range

---

[29] Ward Parks, 'Flyting, Sounding, Debate: Three Verbal Contest Genres', *Poetics Today*, 7 (1986), 439–58; Thomas Reed, *Middle English Debate Poetry and the Aesthetics of Irresolution* (Columbia, MO, 1990), 97–152.
[30] Reed, *Middle English Debate Poetry*, 2.
[31] Reed, *Middle English Debate Poetry*, 101–2. See especially the Old English version, Daniel Anlezark (ed. and trans.), *The Old English Dialogues of Solomon and Saturn* (Cambridge, 2009).
[32] Thomas Shippey, *J. R. R. Tolkien: Author of the Century* (Boston, MA, 2014), 24–5.
[33] Deskis, *Alliterative Proverbs*, 76–9; Nancy Mason Bradbury and Scott Bradbury (eds), *The Dialogue of Solomon and Marcolf: A Dual-Language Edition from Latin and Middle English Printed Editions* (Kalamazoo, MI, 2012).

208 MEDIEVAL POETRY: 1100–1400

of doctrinal, scientific, and sapiential authorities. In this the poems recall the forms of both scholastic dialectic and of Boethius's *De Consolatione Philosophiae*. This text represents a 'debate' that is far less contentious than those listed above: philosophy frequently refers to herself as the prisoner's physician, and her 'debate' with the prisoner is a didactic method for bringing him peace of mind. The original Latin text of *De Consolatione* is a prosimetrum, and it remained an important model for this form in (especially early) medieval European literature.[34] And though it is not necessarily proof of direct influence, it is helpful nonetheless to note that the text is seemingly unfinished and so its inconclusive debate is a possible model for the unresolved endings of Middle English debate poems.

The Middle English texts that are arguably the most consistent with earlier analogues are the various debates between the body and the soul. These poems are instances of what Reed calls 'an inexhaustibly popular medieval subgenre', attested in a wide variety of languages and traditions that extend back to the ancient world.[35] As Masha Raskolnikov has argued, the poems in this genre 'produce and express an immanent psychological theory', whose allegorical mode 'enables a kind of flexible theorizing of the self that formal treatises cannot offer'.[36] These poems are famously fixated, for example, on the material processes of decomposition, for example the way rotting flesh swells as it is consumed by worms (e.g., *DIMEV* 605, lines 14–15).[37] This grisly imagery does not express any specific point of doctrine, but rather elicits an affect of disgust at the body's abjection as a way of driving home the key doctrinal points. The vexed and irresolvable contradiction of the body and the soul is emblematic of the sorts of contradictions that occasioned the popularity of this narrative form in poems of doctrine and learning generally. The debates are not purely intellectual contests between opposing ideas as much as they are vacillations between embodied, personified poles whose contrast enables audiences to find their own coherent identities. In psychological as in theological terms, the contradiction between the body's material abjection and the soul's intellectual abstraction is precisely the substance of human experience. Hence doctrines that aim to explain that experience in terms of a theological system are well represented by expressions of that contradiction. The same goes for the other contradictory identities that are the subjects of Middle English debate poems.

Perhaps the most famous of the Middle English debate poems is also one of the earliest, titled *The Owl and the Nightingale* and attributed internally to a Nicholas of Guildford.[38] It is noteworthy that the poem is not written in *scripta continua* like much alliterative verse (for example, the copy of Laȝamon's Middle English *Brut* with which it shares a manuscript) but in keeping with its form of tetrameter couplets, recently imported into English poetry from French, is lineated in double columns, a mode of presentation that is consistent with its early effort to write English poetry in imitation of the Continental courtly tradition. At the same time, the poem represents itself as a *plaiding* (12) or lawsuit, and so as a document transcribing oral testimony in a legal conflict.[39] Again, this tension between poetic and legal

---

[34] A. G. Rigg, *A History of Anglo-Latin Literature 1066–1422* (Cambridge, 1992), 14–15.

[35] Reed, *Middle English Debate Poetry*, 1, citing Francis Lee Utley, 'Dialogues, Debates, and Catechisms', in J. E. Wells (ed.), *A Manual of Writings in Middle English*, rev. J. Burke Severs and Albert E. Hartung, 11 vols. (New Haven, CT, 1967–2005), 3:691.

[36] Masha Raskolnikov, *Body Against Soul: Gender and Sowlehele in Middle English Allegory* (Columbus, OH, 2004), 5.

[37] Oliver F. Emerson, *A Middle English Reader* (London, 1905), 47–64.

[38] N. R. Ker (ed.), *The Owl and the Nightingale: Reproduced in Facsimile from the Surviving Manuscripts, Jesus College, Oxford 29, and British Museum*, Cotton Caligula A.ix, EETS o.s. 251 (London, 1963; rpt. 1993); see also the more recent edition of Neil Cartlidge, *The Owl and the Nightingale* (Exeter, 2001); and Neil Cartlidge, 'Nicholas of Guildford and "The Owl and the Nightingale"', *Medium Ævum*, 79 (2010), 14–24.

[39] Wendy Matlock, 'Law and Violence in *The Owl and the Nightingale*', *Journal of English and Germanic Philology*, 109 (2010), 446–67.

forms is not an unusual one, in either legal or literary texts, and its presence here speaks to the text's self-conscious engagement with questions of form and authority. As Jill Mann observes, 'the plurality of literary contexts invoked by the poem—love-poetry, religious verse, Goliardic, parody, debate ... beast literature—is indeed one of its most noteworthy features, and the primary source of its sophisticated wit'.[40] To these might be added the fusion of its couplet form with an almost exclusively Old English-derived vocabulary. Perhaps the clearest sign that the plurality and instability of generic forms themselves is a major thematic concern of poem is suggested by the frequency with which the argument between the Owl and the Nightingale addresses their respective manners of singing and expressing themselves. The argument begins because the Nightingale dislikes the Owl's song (33–40), while the Owl in contrast compares the Nightingale to the chattering of an Irish priest (322). Indeed, the Owl echoes a proverb of Alfred from the poem above in the course of criticising the Nightingale's excessive singing: 'Evrich þing mai losen his godhede / Mid unmeþe and mid overdede' (350–1). This parallel and the many explicit citations of Alfred that surround it are especially noteworthy because of the fact that one of its two manuscripts, Oxford, Jesus College 29, also witnesses *The Proverbs of Alfred*.

One other moment where we see an attention to form in the dialogue between these two birds occurs in a speech by the Nightingale, in a passage beginning in line 1149. The Nightingale offers a long list of the terrible events that the Owl's call predicts, in an anaphoric list extending eight lines where each line begins 'Oþer'. A few lines later, the Nightingale uses a repetitive alliterative doublet ('totorveþ and tobuneþ', line 1166) followed by a list of tools used to perform this action of beating ('mid stave, and stoone, and turf, and clute', 1167). As I have stated above, repetitive listing is a traditional method for performing poetic authority, which had a history of deployment in early English legal and homiletic texts.[41] The relevance of this context for the passage is suggested by the Owl's response to the Nightingale's statement, in which she interprets the Nightingale's final statement that any bearer of bad news should be cursed as a literal attempt to excommunicate her (1169–74), and responds by pointing out that the Nightingale is not a priest and so her performance is illegitimate (1175–82).[42]

In brief, the Nightingale's statement of principle—to the effect that the Owl's ability to foretell disaster is morally suspect—elicits a response from the Owl that responds not to the substance of the statement but its form. The apparent echoes of religious-legal rhetoric cited above make it seem that the Nightingale is claiming an authority she does not and cannot have. In this way, the passage is a helpful illustration of the irresolution that informs Middle English debate poetry as a genre. The interlocutors switch back and forth between challenging each other's authoritative statements and challenging the formal techniques whereby those statements are authorised, and they do so because the forms derive their authority from the truth of the statements they encode at the same time that the encoded statements are marked as true by their formal attributes. So, too, is the authority of the doctrine and learning on display in the poem contingent on the use of proper forms in articulating their contents, in addition to the veracity of the contents themselves. Authoritative

---

[40] Jill Mann, *From Aesop*, 150. See also Kathryn Hume, *The Owl and the Nightingale: The Poem and Its Critics* (Toronto, 1975); Ivana Djordjevic, 'The "Owl and the Nightingale" and the Perils of Criticism', *Neuphilologische Mitteilungen*, 96 (1995), 367–80.

[41] Yeager, *From Lawmen to Plowmen*, 69–72.

[42] On ecclesiastical jurisdiction in the poem, see Bruce Holsinger, 'Vernacular Legality: The English Jurisdictions of The Owl and the Nightingale', in Emily Steiner and Candace Barrington (eds), *The Letter of the Law: Legal Practice and Literary Production in Medieval England* (Ithaca, NY, 2002), 154–84.

210 MEDIEVAL POETRY: 1100–1400

form and authoritative content each derive their authority from the other, and so each may be undermined by a challenge to the other.

Another Middle English debate poem where we see this interplay is 'Winnere and Wastour'. In striking contrast to the tetrameter couplets of *The Owl and the Nightingale*, later medieval Middle English debate poems tend to be alliterative, even long after Continental verse forms become ubiquitous in the corpus. 'Winnere and Wastour' is among the more influential of these alliterative debates, and it may have even predated or inspired the similar *Piers Plowman*.[43] This poem depicts a debate between the two titular characters— representative of collectors and consumers of resources respectively—in front of a king who is often believed to be Edward III.[44] A further alliterative debate poem appearing alongside 'Winnere and Wastour' in Robert Thornton's manuscript (London, British Library, MS Additional 31,042) is *The Parlement of Thre Ages*.[45] This text deploys what is arguably one of the least predictable narrative structures in Middle English poetry, in the service of what is arguably a more or less conventional articulation of the *memento mori* motif. The poem begins with a naturalistic description of a hunter waiting for his opportunity to kill a deer, in a hunting scene of a sort with several analogues in alliterative poetry.[46] Only after the narrator has described in detail both the hunt and the process of cleaning his quarry does he reveal that he is a poacher.[47] Once the hunt is finished, the narrator goes to sleep and has a dream with no obvious connection to this frame narrative, about a three-way argument between Youth, Middle Age, and Old Age, the last of whom seems at first to be the arbiter of the debate but ends up taking it over. Old Age delivers a long sermon on the Nine Worthies, after which he lists several famously wise men and also several famous lovers. The poem then ends abruptly, the narrator awakens, and he goes into town. It is no wonder, then, that A. C. Spearing should criticise the Nine Worthies section especially for its 'shoddy formalism': for all the brilliance of its best set-pieces, the overarching logic of the poem reads as almost perversely bewildering to most of its modern readers.[48]

One clue revealing the conventions that lay beneath the poem's unconventional narrative appears near its end, when Elde quotes 'Ecclesiastes the clerke' (638) to state: 'alle es vayne and vanytes and vanyte es alle' (640).[49] The progression through the three allegorical figures matches the autobiographical passages of Ecclesiastes 2. The biblical speaker of Ecclesiastes begins in 2:1 with an account of how he used to enjoy good things, as Youth does, before then turning in 2:2–14 to describe how he accumulated the material wealth and status that is the primary focus of Middle Elde. Then in Ecclesiastes 2:15 and for the remainder of the book, the speaker tells us about his realisation in old age that all of these pursuits were, in the biblical phrase, 'vanity of vanities'. Given, then, that this narrative matches the dream

---

[43] Stephanie Trigg (ed.), *Wynnere and Wastoure*, EETS o.s. 297 (London, 1990); Reed, *Middle English Debate Poetry*, 259–93. On the relationship to *Piers Plowman*, see Weiskott, *English Alliterative Verse*, 111; J. A. Burrow, 'The Audience of Piers Plowman', *Anglia*, 75 (1957), 373–84.

[44] Reed, *Middle English Debate Poetry*, 263.

[45] In the manuscript's fifth booklet, fols. 169–81. See Susanna Fein, 'The Contents of Robert Thornton's Manuscripts', in Susanna Fein and Michael Johnston (eds), *Robert Thornton and His Books: Essays on the Lincoln and London Thornton Manuscripts* (York, 2014), 13–66, 60; and Reed, *Middle English Debate Poetry*, 213–18. Text in Warren Ginsberg (ed.), *Wynnere and Wastoure and The Parlement of the Thre Ages* (Kalamazoo, MI, 1992).

[46] Russell A. Peck, 'The Careful Hunter in *The Parlement of the Thre Ages*', *ELH*, 39 (1972), 333–41.

[47] Randy P. Schiff, 'The Loneness of the Stalker: Poaching and Subjectivity in *The Parlement of the Thre Ages*', *Texas Studies in Literature and Language*, 51 (2009), 263–93.

[48] A. C. Spearing, *Medieval Dream-Poetry* (Cambridge, 1976), 136, cited by Reed, *Middle English Debate Poetry*, 215.

[49] This comparison builds on Turville-Petre's broader survey of the three ages as a conventional motif: Thorlac Turville-Petre, 'The Ages of Man in "The Parlement of the Thre Ages"', *Medium Ævum*, 46 (1977), 66–76.

portion of *The Parlement of the Thre Ages* and that Ecclesiastes is quoted directly at the very end of this section, it seems likely that the parallels between the texts are intentional.

It is particularly noteworthy that both Youth and Middle Elde express the concepts they allegorise in part through their deployments of and allusions to literary forms, both of which anticipate Elde's own speech and so position it as a sort of synthesis of their arguments. Middle Elde deploys an anaphoric list of the sort cited above, which anticipates the repetitive listing of Elde's speech and also happens to include a use of the legal doublet 'park and plow' in reference to territorial rights.[50] Meanwhile, Elde's speech is also anticipated by Youth, who includes among the pleasures of the court 'Riche romance to rede and rekken the sothe / of kempes and of conquerours, of kynges full noblee' (250–1)—precisely the subject matter of the Nine Worthies. In this way, it seems that Elde in the poem is taking the relatively novel formats used recreationally by Youth (i.e., romance) and pragmatically by Middle Elde (i.e., property management) and returning to their original, implicit purpose of moral instruction. Ultimately the fact of human mortality is the most important lesson we can learn, and all other forms of information must be positioned subordinate to it. Hence while it is certainly concerned with doctrine and learning, *The Parlement of the Thre Ages* is ultimately less concerned with moral truth per se than it is with the problem of expressing moral truths in a manner that an audience will hear. The poem exposes in this way a set of uncomfortable contradictions that are indeed present in all of the poetry concerned with doctrine and learning in this period.

Historically, the poems surveyed by this chapter have been marginalised by literary scholars, except for when they have been mined for examples of orthodox or otherwise typical medieval English views that may then be contrasted with the nominally greater nuance or subtlety of named (or, in the case of the Pearl poet, conjectured) authors. In this chapter I have endeavoured to show that these poems are misunderstood when they are treated as merely transparent representations of received cultural values. Indeed, their appearance as such to modern readers is precisely the proof of the extraordinary literary craft brought to bear in their production, as in fact these poems both represent and contain complex negotiations between received wisdom and authorial intent, abstract information and embodied self-expression, inherited forms and emergent needs. We have only begun the task of understanding how these poems reflect the circumstances of their composition and their influence on the poetry of later periods. This chapter's survey of doctrine and learning in Middle English poetry is offered as a prelude to such investigations.

---

[50] Yeager, *From Lawmen to Plowmen*, 166–7.

14
Poetry and the Bible

Jacqueline Tasioulas

The Lollard desire for access to the Bible in English does not emerge from a dearth of vernacular biblical texts in the Middle Ages. In fact, the opposite is the case, for what John Wycliff and his followers encountered was, from their point of view, an over-abundance of English material: a world in which holy writ had not simply been translated, but one in which the text had been expanded, commented upon, and embellished. Worse, it had been versified: taken from 'þe fowrme þat Crist ȝaf it', by those who would 'tateren it bi þer rimes'.[1] The unadorned prose translation of later centuries was only one of the possibilities that the Middle Ages embraced, the extent and variety of biblical literature revealing a culture intent on salvation by any textual means possible. In effect, this means the adoption of the Bible as essentially a base text that is then enhanced by moralisation, commentary, and amplification. It is not the case that the intention was wilfully to 'add' to the scriptures but rather that the need to understand led inevitably to 'unpacking' and a great spreading out of what had been tightly contained. The Lollard insistence on the 'form' of the biblical text is not, therefore, a major preoccupation of most of those engaging with the Bible before the fifteenth century. The Word can, not surprisingly, be served by other words, and the way is, therefore, open not just for translation but for any literary enterprise that might lead to salvation. Among these, poetry in the vernacular ranked highly. The author of the mid-thirteenth-century *Genesis and Exodus* takes the time to explain its appeal to his own audience as a delighted response to enlightenment:

> Man og to luuen ðat rimes-ren
> Ðe wisseð wel ðe logede men
> Hu man may him wel loken
> Ðog he be lered on no boken ...
> Ut of latin ðis song is dragen
> On engleis speche on soðe-sagen;
> Cristene men ogen ben so fagen
> So fueles arn quan he it sen dagen,
> Ðan man hem telleð soðe tale
> Wið londes speche and wordes smale. (1–18)[2]

(One ought to love that run of rhymes that teaches lewd men well how a man may look after himself, even though he is not learned in terms of books ... This song is drawn out of Latin into English speech as a true rendering. Christian men ought to be as delighted as the birds are when they see the dawn, when they are told a true tale in their native speech and in plain words.)

---

[1] John Wyclif, in Thomas Arnold (ed.), *Select English Works of John Wyclif*, 3 vols. (Oxford, 1869–71), 3:180.
[2] Text in Olof Arngart (ed.), *The Middle English Genesis and Exodus* (Lund, 1968), 1–18.

Jacqueline Tasioulas, *Poetry and the Bible*. In: *The Oxford History of Poetry in English*. Edited by Helen Cooper and Robert R. Edwards, Oxford University Press. © Jacqueline Tasioulas (2023). DOI: 10.1093/oso/9780198827429.003.0014

The poet here gathers the key concerns of every medieval composer of English biblical verse: salvation of the unlearned through the beauty and simplicity of poetry in their native tongue. How these concerns manifest themselves varies—and works in the period range from relatively close biblical paraphrase to metrical creations based on the apocrypha—but it is nevertheless a variety that keeps at its heart the salvation through verse of the English people by use of the English language. Biblical translation, far from being a source of anxiety, is a source of joy, and love of language itself is a recurring theme.

To begin with the *Ormulum,* then, is to start at the conservative end of biblical verse translation. Composed *c* 1200, it was intended as a gospel paraphrase. It is, nevertheless, a very unusual text, its unique manuscript telling us a great deal even before a word of it is read. It is a fascinating artefact in itself: a book created from scraps of vellum and the discarded remnants of regular manuscript pages, gathered up and cherished in order to present the life of Christ as vernacular poetry. If we take the word 'poetry' back to its original Greek meaning of 'creation', then nowhere is that creative process seen more clearly than in the stitched together, assertive, autograph text that is the *Ormulum.* We know its name because this is what it is named by its author: 'forrþi þatt Orrm itt wrohhte' ('because Orm composed it').[3] As for Orm himself, he appears to have been an Augustinian canon in the Abbey of Bourne in Lincolnshire in the final quarter of the twelfth century, and if the *Ormulum* cannot necessarily be claimed to be his life's work, it is nevertheless clear that it bears all the signs of many years' composition and prolonged revision and correction.[4] Correction is key. Other medieval authors will, as we shall see, blend Bible with the apocrypha, with legend, and with popular tales; but Orm's agenda is one of careful translation, careful explanation, and careful delivery. As he explains it in his prologue, his intention was to gather together the gospels used in the liturgy throughout the year, provide a close English translation of each, and accompany each one with detailed exegesis in order to help priests bring the meaning of the gospels to their English flock:

> Icc hafe sammnedd o þiss boc   Þa Goddspelless neh alle,
> Þatt sinndenn o þe messeboc   Inn all þe ʒer att messe.
> & aʒʒ affterr þe Goddspell stannt   Þatt tatt te Goddspell meneþþ,
> Þatt mann birrþ spellenn to þe follc   Off þeʒʒre sawle nede;
> & ʒët tær tekenn mare inoh   Þu shallt tær onne findenn.
> Off þatt tatt Cristess hallʒe þed   Birrþ trowwenn wel & follʒenn. (29–40)

(I have brought together in this book nearly all the gospels that are in the missal throughout the year for mass. And always after the gospel comes what the gospel means, what someone should preach to the people for the good of their souls; and in addition to that much more will be found in it, concerning that which Christ's holy people should firmly believe and follow.)

---

[3] Orm, in Robert Holt and R. M. White (eds), *The Ormulum,* 2 vols. (Oxford, 1878), 8. This edition presents the text as half-lines. The current chapter reinstates the manuscript's full septenary line form. See further discussion of *Ormulum* in Chapters 2, 5, and 9 in this volume.

[4] For dating and provenance, see M. B. Parkes, 'On the Presumed Date and Possible Origin of the Manuscript of the "Orrmulum": Oxford, Bodleian Library, MS Junius I', in E. G. Stanley and Douglas Gray (eds), *Five Hundred Years of Words and Sounds: A Festschrift for Eric Dobson* (Cambridge, 1983), 115–27. For details of the layers of revision undertaken by Orm, see J. E. Turville-Petre, 'Studies in the *Ormulum* MS', *Journal of English and Germanic Philology,* 46 (1947), 1–27.

214 MEDIEVAL POETRY: 1100–1400

It is an ambitious plan, even if the original scheme of 242 gospel lections is reduced in the end to 32. These in themselves result in 20,000 completely regular lines of text, Orm having chosen the classical septenary form (seven feet, with fifteen syllables, the caesura coming after the eighth syllable) to present the orderly truth of the gospels.

Traditionally, it is said to be in the *Ormulum* that we first encounter in English the French loan word 'rime':

> Icc hafe sett her o þiss boc   Amang Goddspelles wordess
> All þurrh me sellfenn maniʒ word   Þe rime swa to fillenn. (41–4)

(I have set down here in this book, among the words of the Gospel, many words all by myself, in order to fulfil the 'rime'.)

That 'rime' should here mean 'metre' has been challenged, a much broader claim for overall 'reckoning' being more likely.[5] Similarly, 'fillenn' goes beyond the sense of 'filling up' the lines and reaches instead towards the much loftier aim of fulfilling the promise of the biblical text.[6] In the end, it is a claim not for counting syllables but for the fulfilment of a narrative, the truth of which is reflected in the orderliness of the verse form.

What is perhaps surprising is that Orm should have chosen verse as his medium at all, given that it necessarily imposes a greater distance from the original prose. He is, however, wholly faithful to the words and forms of the evangelists, creating a translation that mirrors the biblical text in style and construction as much as possible. In addition, the septenary form imposes order, and order is what Orm craves here as he attempts to construct a life of Christ from the gospel narratives. That he should have felt the need to do so is revealing in terms of popular engagement with Scripture. The Bible tended not to be viewed as a single book, worked through in chronological order, but was instead encountered as fragments and episodes. These in turn were often set beside other fragments and episodes, the rationale being not a chronological understanding but rather a spiritual and moral understanding based on typology. By this method of reading, the place of the attempted sacrifice of Isaac by his father Abraham is next to the sacrifice of Christ on the Cross, which in turn relates to Moses and the brazen serpent. It is a highly selective form of interpretation, gathering episodes from all parts of the Bible and placing them side by side.[7] One passage of the Bible can easily be replaced by another because the pattern is one of recurring truth. The selection of the Sunday gospel works on the same principle: the actual chronology of events in the life of Christ not being the important factor.

For Orm, however, chronology clearly is important and his work is a peculiar working backwards from the liturgical order to reassemble the parts as a chronological sequence, as found in the works of the evangelists themselves.[8] An ordinary collection of homilies—and Orm must have been familiar with many—would have retained the order of events as they occurred in the mass readings in the course of the church year; but, in spite of his fidelity to the division of episodes as dictated by the liturgy, Orm abandons the liturgical sequence

---

[5] See Nils-Lennart Johannesson, 'The Etymology of Rime in the *Ormulum*', *Nordic Journal of English Studies*, 3 (2019), 61–75.

[6] For the importance of the concept of fulfilment, see Christopher Cannon, *The Grounds of English Literature* (Oxford, 2007), 98–102.

[7] For the classic exposition of this technique of *figura*, see Erich Auerbach, 'Figura', in *Scenes from the Drama of European Literature* (Minneapolis, MN, 1984), 11–78.

[8] For the *Ormulum* as the first homiletic life of Christ in English, see Elizabeth Salter, 'Nicholas Love's "Myrrour of the Blessed Lyf of Jesu Christ"', *Analecta Cartusiana*, 10 (1974), 78–81.

and asserts instead an earthly chronology.[9] In so doing, he recovers the order of events in the gospels, while retaining the episodic structure as sanctioned by the Church. What he produces is arguably the first homiletic life of Christ, but, that accomplished, the *Ormulum* adheres to established order, and digs itself in to withstand further change.

This includes preservation at all costs of the highly idiosyncratic system of orthography that has come to define Orm's text. It should be noted, however, that it is truly a system, the nature of which has been discerned to be both phonetically and etymologically consistent.[10] The aim is to ensure that all lay people are in a position 'tunnderrstanndenn' ('to understand'), the irony of the difficult formulation not being lost on the critics (48). Nevertheless, the ultimate recipients of the text are not readers, but listeners: those who, 'wiþþ aere [ears] shollde listen itt' (133). The spelling system devised by Orm is designed to aid performance: to differentiate short vowels (marked by succeeding double consonants) from long vowels, for the benefit of the speaker.[11] This is not the case of Scripture being forced into a 'barbarous tongue' by a diligent missionary, but rather the conduit that is language being kept clear for Scripture.[12] To that end, the changes that the manuscript undergoes—most of them in Orm's own hand as he scrapes out letter forms and replaces them with consistently revised forms—is testimony to the desire for clarity that explicitly motivates his text.

There is then a gap of a hundred years or so to the next surviving verse sermon cycle in English. There are numerous Latin examples, but nothing extant in English until the *Northern Homily Cycle* in the early fourteenth century. In all likelihood it was originally composed by another Austin canon attempting to provide for the needs of a lay congregation, but unlike Orm's solitary text, it flourished and survives in three versions, the first expansion datable to the late fourteenth century and the second to the fifteenth century.[13] As for the unexpanded version, it alone runs to around 20,000 lines of octosyllabic couplets.

The unknown poet does not have Orm's agenda of reconstructing the narrative of Christ's life from the Sunday gospels. Instead, he adheres to the liturgical order, tagging the reading for the day with the first few words of the Vulgate, before providing his paraphrase, then proceeding to his exegesis of the text, and finishing off with a popular story of some kind (an exemplum). That there was some expectation that the text would be read to a lay congregation can be seen in the entry for the second Sunday in Advent. The gospel is from Luke ('Today Sain Louk telles us') and is an account of the Day of Judgement, accompanied by the 'fiften / Ferli takeninges ('fifteen marvellous signs', lines 103–4), a list of horrors thought to signal the end of the world.[14] A summary version is provided in English in which the oceans boil and rise, whales and dolphins will scream, trees and plants will seem to bleed, and the bones of men will rise and stand up in their graves. The Latin text (as always, in the Middle

---

[9] See Stephen Morrison, 'Sources for the *Ormulum*: A Re-examination', *Neuphilologische Mitteilungen*, 84 (1983), 419–36. Old English influences are developed in Stephen Morrison, 'A Reminiscence of Wulfstan in the Twelfth Century', *Neuphilologische Mitteilungen*, 96 (1995), 229–34.

[10] See R. W. Burchfield, 'The Language and Orthography of the *Ormulum* MS', *Transactions of the Philological Society*, 55 (1956), 56–87. For the argument for etymological consistency, see Roger Lass, 'Phonology and Morphology', in Norman Blake (ed.), *The Cambridge History of the English Language*, 6 vols. (Cambridge, 1994), 2:31–2.

[11] For the argument that Orm is attempting to improve the pronunciation of Francophone preachers engaging with the English laity, see Kenneth Sisam, *Studies in the History of Old English Literature* (New York, 1953), 193–5. More recently, Meg Worley engages with the same premise: 'Forr þeȝȝre sawle need: The *Ormulum*, Vernacular Theology and a Tradition of Translation in Early England', *English Studies*, 95 (2014), 256–77.

[12] The claim was made by Geoffrey Shepherd in W. F. Bolton (ed.), *The Middle Ages* (London, 1970), 115.

[13] See Thomas J. Heffernan, 'The Authorship of the *Northern Homily Cycle*: The Liturgical Affiliation of the Sunday Gospel Pericopes as a Test', *Traditio*, 41 (1985), 289–309. For dates and versions, see the discussion in Saara Nevanlinna, *The Northern Homily Cycle: The Expanded Version in MSS Harley 4196 and Cotton Tiberius E vii* (Helsinki, 1972).

[14] See Anne B. Thompson (ed.), *The Northern Homily Cycle* (Kalamazoo, MI, 2008), 30.

216   MEDIEVAL POETRY: 1100–1400

Ages, erroneously attributed to St Jerome) is provided, together with a Latin instruction: 'Isti versus omittantur a lectore quando legit Anglicam coram laycis' ('These verses may be omitted by the reader when he reads in English before the laity').[15]

That the language of the text is at the forefront of the author's mind is clear from the same Sunday's gospel paraphrase, ending, as it does, with an appeal to the 'strenthe of our Godspel, / Als man wit Inglis tung may tel' (lines 39–40). The 'als' is potentially a disclaimer, a self-effacing 'as good as', or 'to the extent that'.[16] However, the preceding 'our' does its work. This is a self-consciously English gospel, belonging in common to the author and to his English-speaking congregation. It is 'our Godspel', a text that is far from self-effacing, and is sufficient to carry the 'strenthe' of the word of God, a choice of term that manages to appropriate both meaning and power for the translation. To that end, the paraphrases tend to adhere very closely to the biblical text, preserving the indirect speech, and ensuring that the nouns of the gospels are accounted for in translation. The author is not, however, above a little adaptation of the text. The order of the evangelists' lines can be rearranged for ease, and less familiar phrases adapted. Luke's apocalyptic fig trees, for example, which he employs memorably as natural signs of high summer, become less exotic 'froit ("fruit")' trees in the English text (line 26).[17]

The entertaining tales of miracles, and of sin indulged or averted, that constitute the *exempla* were justifiably popular, and some later manuscripts see the shortening or disappearance of the gospel paraphrases in favour of the short stories with which they conclude.[18] Nevertheless, the lively octosyllabic couplets carry forward even the most sombre sections of the Bible. Here we encounter 'leprousnes' inventively paired in a couplet with 'Moyses', and the water-into-wine miracle of the Wedding at Canaa acquires a judge named Architricline, whose name rhymes handily with 'wyne'.[19] The links between the sermons and medieval mystery cycles are readily apparent, as the dramatic rendering of events such as the Massacre of the Innocents shows:

> Sum wemen þe knightes light
> And ful frekly with þam fight,
> For þam war leuer ded to be
> Þan þat sorow on þaire suns to se.
> And oft bitid so in þaire tene
> Þat childer war slane þam bitwene ...
> Also sum moders in þat tyde
> Vnto þe knightes karefully cried:
> 'Whi rauyss þou fro me with force
> Þe fruit þat es cumen of my corse?'[20]

(Some women struck the knights and fiercely fought with them, for they would rather have died than see that sorrow befall their sons. In their rage, too, it often happened that children were slain between them ... Also, some mothers cried out sorrowfully to the knights at that time: 'Why do you take from me with force the fruit that has come from my body?')

---

[15] Thompson, *Northern Homily Cycle*, 32.

[16] *MED*, s.v. 'als' (conj.): 9. as good as; to the extent that.

[17] Thompson, *Northern Homily Cycle*, 29.

[18] See James H. Morey, *A Guide to Middle English Biblical Literature* (Urbana, IL, 2000), 324, n. 5.

[19] Thompson, *Northern Homily Cycle*, 182, lines 131–2; Nevanlinna, *Northern Homily Cycle*, lines 4999–5000.

[20] Nevanlinna, *Northern Homily Cycle*, lines 3379–90.

This is the horror of the massacre brought to life, the voices of the mothers not present in the Bible, but here given full expression.

The same might be said of the stanzaic *Gospel of Nicodemus*. Revered as almost a fifth gospel in the Old English period, the apocryphal work was widespread in medieval Europe, existing in both prose and metrical versions. The first poetic version in Middle English dates to the fourteenth century and appears to have been the inspiration for several of the plays in the York mystery cycle. There are many similarities in terms both of the content of the plays and the unusual scheme of twelve-line stanzas. While the verse is not completely regular, the standard pattern is of eight lines that alternate four stresses and three, followed by four lines with three stresses.[21] The work begins with Christ's appearance before Pilate, but was best known for its account of the non-biblical Harrowing of Hell in which the crucified Christ descended into the darkness to battle with the devil and overcome death, before rising again on the third day. The dramatic arrival of the light of the world to redeem all souls in hell is met with terror by the demons and joy on the part of the patriarchs, the structure of the stanza separating the panic in hell from the lines of promise fulfilled delivered by David:

> A voyce spak þan full hydusly,
> Als it war thonours blast:
> 'Vndo yhour yhates bilyue, byd I,
> Þai may no langer last,
> Þe king of blys comes in yhow by.'
> Þan hell a voyce vpkast:
> 'What es he þat þai say in hy?
> He sall be set ful fast.'
> Þan said dauid: 'ʒe ne wate
> How þat I said þus right,
> "He es lord of grete state,
> In batayle mekill of might..."' (1381–92)[22]

(Then a hideous voice spoke like thunder: 'Open your gates at once, I tell you, for they will not stand much longer, as the king of bliss will enter'. Then a voice rose up from hell: 'Who is he that they announce so quickly? He shall be set upon at once'. Then David said: 'Do you not remember that I prophesied this, "He is the lord of greatness, of great power in battle..."').

The Harrowing of Hell also features in the vast early-fourteenth-century *Cursor Mundi*, though here it is only a minor part of an extensive work that aims to give a full account of the history of the world. Its title is derived from its author's own suggestion: 'Cursur o werld man aght it call, / For almast it ouer-rennes all' (lines 267–8).[23] Derived from the Latin 'to run', the *Cursor Mundi* does indeed 'course' through biblical history, from Creation to Judgement Day, but while 'coursing' and 'cursory' share the same root, the work is too animatedly detailed to have any such criticism levelled against it. Thirty-thousand lines makes for a hefty volume, though is still not a great deal to cover the whole of the history of mankind's salvation; but it is the lively detail and the poet's ability to pick out key moments

---

[21] See William Henry Hulme (ed.), *The Middle English Harrowing of Hell and Gospel of Nicodemus* (London, 1907), xvii–xix.

[22] Text in Hulme, *Middle English Harrowing of Hell*, 110.

[23] Text in Richard Morris (ed.), *The Cursor Mundi*, 7 vols. (London, 1874–93).

that captures his audience's attention and prevents the work from racing away into a cat-alogue of successive events. The poem opens, for example, not with a merely serviceable account of the creation of the world but with an account that takes it upon itself to explain the very nature of the Creator, exploring the three-persons-in-one-God that is the mystery of the Trinity by reference to the heat and light of the sun:

> In þe sune þat schines clere
> Es a thing a[nd] thre things sere;
> A bodi rond, and hete and light,
> Þir thre we find al at a sight;
> Þis things thre wit nankins art
> Mai man nan fra oþer part. (291–6)

(In the sun that shines brightly is both one thing and three things together; a round physical form, and heat and light, we discover these three things whenever we observe the sun; man cannot part these three things with any kind of art.)

The metaphor is not original, but it is nevertheless the example of a poet-teacher: keen to take what he knows from Latin texts, French texts, and his own observation, and place his knowledge at the disposal of those who better understand what is presented to them in English.[24]

At the same time, he understands the lure of the popular French verse romances. The very first lines of this immense text are a statement of that fact: 'Man yhernes rimes for to here, / And romans red on maneres sere' (lines 1–2). It is a 'longing' that he intends to divert from Arthur and his Round Table and focus on the Bible instead, by means of a prologue that is part advertisement and part careful suggestion. Courtly romance tastes are not overtly condemned. Instead, it is delicately stated that our tastes reveal a great deal about our moral character as the poet reveals that his own courtly 'paramour' is the Virgin Mary (line 69). He extols her as the worthy recipient of literary attention, a more than fitting subject for 'rimes':

> Off suilk an suld ʒe [mater] take,
> Crafty þat can rimes make;
> Of hir to mak bath rim and sang ...
> Þof rimes fele of hir be made,
> Qua-sa will of hy[r] fa[y]rnes spell,
> Find he sal inogh to tell. (85–96)

(You should take such a one as your subject, the craftsman who can compose verse; compose both verses and songs about her ... Although many poems have been com-posed in her honour, whoever wishes to spell out her fairness shall find plenty to say.)

Following Mary as courtly lady, it is easy to characterise the Old and New Testaments as heroic 'gestes', among which the author mentions the Massacre of the Innocents, the miracle

---

[24] For the Latin and French sources and analogues of the poem, see John J. Thompson, *Cursor Mundi: Poem, Texts and Contexts* (Oxford, 1998).

of the loaves and fishes, and the account of the 'spouse-brek' (adulterous) woman, saved from stoning. These are all legitimate biblical episodes, but the poet also declares that the audience will hear about Mary's parents, Joachim and St Anne, and about the childhood adventures of Christ.[25]

It becomes clear at this point that the *Cursor*-poet is going to go well beyond biblical paraphrase and will extend his repertoire to include legend, apocryphal material, and general bits and pieces of history. Like the author of *Genesis and Exodus* quoted earlier, he takes as his main source the vast and influential *Historia Scholastica* of Petrus Comestor ('the Devourer'), who, as his name suggests, omnivorously digested all that came his way in his desire to put together a providential history of the world.[26] Comestor's own plan for salvation involves gathering texts, piecing together as many answers as possible, and filling in the blanks. There is no sense in his work, or of others of the period, that the Bible was expected to stand alone and inviolable. It was to be supported and explained by other texts and, in this, his own work becomes of crucial importance.

Other poets tease out their exact relationship to Comestor in a way that reveals a confident distillation process from the Bible through salvation history to the essence of their own text. The so-called *Middle English Metrical Paraphrase of the Old Testament* makes explicit its own sense of the vastness of the Bible being mined for its key episodes by, among others, Comestor as 'maystur of storyse', and then further condensed by the poet's own hand:

> This buke is of grett degre,
> Os all wettys that ben wyse,
> Ffor of the bybyll sall yt be
> The poyntes that ar mad most in price,
> Als maysters of dyuinite
> And on, the maystur of storyse,
> Ffor sympyll men soyn forto se,
> Settes yt þus in this schort assyse;
> And in moyr schort maner
> Is my mynd forto make yt,
> That men may lightly leyre
> To tell and vnder take yt. (13–24)[27]

(This book is of great merit, as everyone knows who is wise, for its main topics are taken from the Bible by masters of divinity and by one, the master of stories, who have arranged it in this short form, for unlearned men to understand at once; and it is my intention to present it in even shorter form, so that people can easily learn to speak of it and understand it.)

In so doing, he hopes that those not learned in Latin will 'lightly' learn and disseminate what they find. It could be a manifesto for all those combining paraphrase with the material gleaned from the *Historia Scholastica* and the popular holy legends.

---

[25] Morris, *Cursor*, lines 161–2 and lines 181–2; lines 185–6; lines 153–4; lines 165–6.
[26] For the influence of Comestor on the *Cursor*-poet and more widely, see James H. Morey, 'Peter Comestor, Biblical Paraphrase, and the Medieval Popular Bible', *Speculum*, 68 (1993), 6–35.
[27] Text in Herbert Kalén (ed.), *A Middle English Metrical Paraphrase of the Old Testament* (Göteborg, 1923). See also Morey, 'Comestor' for analysis of these lines.

220   MEDIEVAL POETRY: 1100–1400

Certainly, the *Cursor*-poet emulates the Latin work to produce his own account, arranged into the seven ages of salvation—the Old Testament, the birth and childhood of Christ, his public life and crucifixion, the Harrowing of Hell, the Resurrection and Ascension, the Finding of the True Cross, and the Day of Judgement—and he is clearly as interested in what the Bible does not say, as what it does. To that end, he expounds on how Adam came to be called Adam, delivers an account of King David's encounter with the mystical rods of Moses, and recounts the dragon-taming adventures of the holy family (lines 585–616, 7973–8262, and 11,595–628) Indeed, the poet includes a substantial amount of material on the childhood exploits of Christ, including three infant homicides, brought about for the wrecking of divinely constructed mud pies (among other offences), and derived ultimately from the apocryphal gospels. The verse skips through a homely account of outraged relatives, worried parents, and a step-father who very much wants his wife to speak to their son:

> His freindes þan bigan to cri
> Agains ioseph and mari;
> 'Yur sun þat wantun, and þat wild,
> Wit his banning has slan vr child'.
> Quen þai war þus don to resun,
> Maria and ioseph dred tresun
> O þe freinds o þis barn.
> Iesus wel blethli wald þai warn;
> þan spak ioseph to marie,
> 'Speke þou wit him al priueli,
> And ask him qui he þus-gat gers
> Vs hatted be for his afers,
> Vr neghburs mai þam on vs wreke?
> Sai þou; i der noght til him speke'. (11951–64)

(His relatives then began to cry out against Joseph and Mary, 'Your son, that ill-disciplined and wild [one], has killed our child with his curses'. As they were inclined to argue in this way, Mary and Joseph feared trouble from the friends of this child, who very much wanted to admonish Jesus; then Joseph said to Mary, 'Speak with him quietly and ask him why he has caused us to be hated on account of his behaviour, to the point that our neighbours may avenge themselves upon us? Go speak to him; I dare not speak to him myself'.)

Less domestic scenes are delivered in not just the metre, but also the tone, of the average medieval romance, as the account of the Old Testament's King David and the woman Bathsheba shows:

> He had a dughti knight o fam,
> His wijf had bersabe to name,
> Allas, sco was sa fair and bright,
> þe king kest ans on hir his sight,
> He askes, quat was þat leuedi?
> 'Yur knyghtes wijf', þai said, 'vri'. (7883–8)

(He had a renowned, doughty knight, whose wife was named Bathsheba. Alas, she was so fair and beautiful that, as soon as the king saw her, he asked, 'Who is that lady?'. 'Sir, your knight's wife,' they said.)

We encounter the typical romance rhyming correlation of 'doughty knight' with 'fair and bright' lady. Ultimately, though, the taste of the 'commun' for verse romances is redirected to material fit for the salvation of the soul. The Bible is called upon to pick up its pace and is enhanced with all the little details that holy Scripture had omitted, but which popular legend was only too happy to provide. If the poet occasionally laments that Hebrew names are 'lath ... for to lig in rim' (line 9240) and so disrupt the regularity of his verse, he nevertheless manages to shape a whole history of salvation into almost perfect rhyming couplets.[28] It is, therefore, no surprise that the Fairfax Manuscript should contain the verdict of one of its medieval readers at the top of its first page: the straightforward endorsement that 'þis is þe best boke of alle'.[29]

A rival for that title would, however, be anything in the *Vita Adae* tradition: the immensely popular apocryphal material that speculated as to what happened to Adam and Eve once they had been ejected from paradise. If the *Cursor Mundi* had combined biblical and non-biblical text in happy coexistence, the Adamic material is weighted heavily towards legend in all the versions that circulated in the vernaculars of western Europe and beyond.[30] Pre-Reformation interest in the Bible was such that there was a simple accretion of information surrounding its literal interpretation, and ultimately a vast accumulation of material, the purpose of which was to explain, fill the gaps, and interpret. Such apocryphal material fell foul of the Reformation, of course, and its associated art and literature met its end. Of the two surviving metrical lives of Adam and Eve in English, one found itself ignominiously used for the covers of notebooks in St Andrews in the eighteenth century. Reclaimed as the *Life of Adam*, it is still incomplete, the beginning having been lost, and parts existing in fragments. However, it is clear that it began its life as part of the celebrated Auchinleck manuscript, an important miscellany of romance and popular religious literature.[31] The other metrical text, the *Canticum de Creatione*, declares its own date to be 1375, the year when, 'þis rym y telle ʒow / Were turned into Englisch' (1184–5).[32]

Brought together as the only surviving metrical examples of the apocryphal Adam and Eve material in English, the two poems are nevertheless different. The Auchinleck text is, of course, incomplete, but it is clear that its source is not the same as that of the *Canticum*. What the poems have in common, however, is a fascination with the lives of the first human pair, cast out in their fallen state into a world that was not intended for them. The *Life of Adam* returns repeatedly to the notion of evil, foregrounding the material on the fall of Lucifer as 'Liʒtbern' refuses to honour God's latest creation: man. The original temptation of Eve is quickly passed over, the poet preferring to focus on the second temptation, as the first pair try to adapt to their new surroundings. As with most of the *Vita Adae* material, the focus is on the confusion that Adam and Eve feel in a world that no longer provides them with abundant food, that subjects them to cold, and that will ultimately introduce

---

[28] See J. J. Lamberts, 'The 'Proloug' to *Cursor Mundi*, VV 1–270', *Neophilologus*, 68 (1984), 292–316.

[29] See Lamberts, 'Proloug', 316.

[30] For the widespread circulation of the *Vita Adae* material, see Brian Murdoch, *Adam's Grace: Fall and Redemption in Medieval Literature* (Cambridge, 2000).

[31] See Derek Pearsall and I. C. Cunningham (eds), *The Auchinleck Manuscript. National Library of Scotland Advocates' MS 19.2.1* (London, 1977).

[32] Text in Brian Murdoch and J. A. Tasioulas (eds), *The Apocryphal Lives of Adam and Eve* (Exeter, 2002).

222 MEDIEVAL POETRY: 1100–1400

them to pain and death. Death, in particular, needs further heavenly guidance, for while God declares to Adam that he will die, the poet makes it clear that this can be no more than a word to a man who has no concept of death, a fact of which God seems very much aware, telling Adam not to forget this new word:

> And he seyʒe me wiþ his eyʒe,
> And seyd: 'Adam, þou scalt dye—
> Hold þat word in þi þouʒt,
> And loke þou forʒete it nouʒt!'
> Þus seyd God almiʒti to me. (353–7)

The word is not forgotten, but the concept of mortality needs to be learned by the first mortal man, closely followed by his wife as Eve faces her own death. Having seen one death already, her own concern is not mortality, but that what she has learned should not be forgotten, and that her son Seth should write the words that will keep the pair forever in memory. This is the preoccupation of the final quarter of the poem: the carving of the lives of the first pair in stone, the preservation through fire and flood, the survival of the account down through the generations. While the poet's appeals to written authority in the form of 'the good book' vacillate between what are clearly references to the Bible and those which are, in fact, references to the *Vita Adae* tradition, the poem's final reference to 'the boke' is one in which all the sources merge:

> SeÞ anon riʒt bigan
> Of Adam, þat was þe forme man,
> Al-togider he wrot his liif,
> As Eue hade beden, Adames wiif.
> As telleþ þe boke, þat wele wot,
> In ston alle þe letters he wrot. (673–8)

Fascinatingly, the poet is declaring that the words that Seth carves in stone must be both the Genesis account and the apocryphal material, for, needing an eyewitness, neither account would otherwise survive the death of Eve. The biblical text therefore becomes inextricably joined to its poetic vehicle. The traditional urgency of transmission of the poets, their use of rhyme and the vernacular to preserve truth, their gathering of extraneous material, is all given a parallel in the urgency of Eve and the work of Seth, that preserved the account of the life of Adam and Eve in what was not yet, but would become, the Bible.

The slightly later *Canticum de Creatione* has a similar view of itself as an intrinsic part of biblical history, claiming to have been translated from Hebrew into Latin, and finally into English (lines 1189–91).[33] It even writes itself into the great account of the age of the world that begins with the very moment of the divine creation of paradise and ends with the creation of the poem:

> ʒif þow wilt wite what tyme it is,
> Fro tyme þat God made paradys
> And man þerynne to dwelle,

---

[33] Text in Murdoch and Tasioulas, *The Apocryphal Lives.*

Til þat Nowelis flod were
Two þousand two hundred and twelf ȝere ...

And fro Abraham to Moysen ...
And from Moyses to Dauid kynge ...

And fro þe incarnacioun of Ihesu,
Til þis rym y telle ȝow
Were turned in to Englisch:
A þousand þre hundred and seuenty
And fyue ȝere witterly.
Þus in bok founden it is. (1162–88)

In stanzas of supreme confidence, the translation into English of the poem is situated directly next to the translation into flesh of Christ himself, and the poem takes its place in the line of succession that runs through Noah, Abraham, Moses, and King David. Indeed, it is the end point: the reference to the 'bok' gathering the full force of Bible, apocrypha, salvation history, and legend.

In spite of the illustrious metrical company it had kept in the Auchinleck manuscript, the *Life of Adam* is a poem in straightforwardly steady rhyming couplets. The *Canticum*, on the other hand, is in tail-rhyme stanzas of an *aabccb* variety. As such, it of course aligns itself with a great English romance tradition.[34] It is not directly referenced by the poet, but he nevertheless delivers one of the liveliest renderings of the Adam and Eve material, retaining all the vestiges of a more wondrous world. It is one in which Eve can appeal to the sun and moon to deliver messages on her behalf, and where Adam can appeal to the River Jordan to join him in his lament, not as the poetic fallacy of the later post-lapsarian world, but as a literal act of natural sympathy with the first pair:

Þo alle þe fisches in þe flode
Gaderen him aboute,
And þe flod noȝt ne ran,
Bote stod stille þat tyme þan,
Sertis wiþouten doute. (164–8)

The birth of Cain is equally wondrous, in spite of the directive of Genesis that Eve should bring forth children in pain. Twelve angels attend the first mother, but the birth is accomplished in a single line, the baby instantly jumping to his feet ('wiþoute lesyng', says the poet) in order to gather flowers for his mother (lines 425–44).

It is not Cain, however, but the apocryphal Seth who undertakes the quest for the Oil of Mercy in an attempt to cure the dying Adam. Having gathered his thirty additional sons and his thirty-two daughters, Adam declares his 'siknesse', at which point the narrative voice comments on the first family's likely unfamiliarity with the concept:

Anon þeȝ alle, as y gesse,
For to wyten what was siknesse,
Faste on him gonne craue. (532–4)

---

[34] For English tail-rhyme romances, including those in the Auchinleck manuscript, see Rhiannon Purdie, *Anglicising Romance: Tail-Rhyme and Genre in Medieval English Literature* (Woodbridge, 2008).

224   MEDIEVAL POETRY: 1100-1400

Once again, the poet-translator privileges the interest in words, interweaving his own desire to offer explanations with humankind's first need for definitions. It is an explicit imaginative projection, the poet seeing the same needs in Adam's kin as he sees in the audience for his own poem: the things that matter must be unpacked and translated, if souls are going to be saved. The death of the post-lapsarian Adam cannot, of course, be prevented; but, armed with the knowledge of sickness and death, Seth's quest for the Oil of Mercy will at least bring with it the promise of future redemption. It is a poetic narrative of vivid moments: of footprints of withered grass leading away from paradise, of animals in mute sympathy with the exiled pair, of the diabolic serpent biting the face of Seth (lines 620–4, 172–4, 637–40).[35] The final adventures of Seth draw heavily on the traditional Holy Rood material, and we learn of the three seeds placed in the mouth of the dead Adam that would eventually produce the tree for the crucifixion. It is the supreme example of the medieval need to join the dots. Providential order would indicate that all the details have been taken care of: all the poets are required to do is make the connections.[36]

More than connections are made in the brief *Jacob and Joseph* and *The Pistil of Swete Susan*, both of which are inventive in terms of what they add to the Old Testament. Parts of *Jacob and Joseph* are still close enough to the Genesis account of Joseph and his brothers to be thought of as paraphrase, but there are significant additions and re-orderings. Dating from the second half of the thirteenth century, the poem is addressed not to a clerical audience but to what is clearly expected to be an uproarious crowd in the tavern. The tavern sin of gluttony is at the forefront of the poet's mind, accompanied by the striking image of bloated corpses, having 'drunk their fill' in Noah's flood: 'Þo hi miȝten drinke þat hi weren fulle' (line 17).[37] Having secured his audience's attention, he moves away from Noah and announces his intention to tell instead the tale of Jacob and his son Joseph. Dating from the second half of the thirteenth century, the poem employs the septenary form like the *Ormulum* poet but mixes this with six-stressed alexandrine lines, and arranges everything in rhyming couplets. The emphasis in this case is not order, but lively performance, and it is no surprise after the strong presence of the minstrel in the opening lines that what is added to the biblical narrative here is a strong interest in the power and beauty of words.[38]

The adventures of Joseph—for even in the Bible his life is very much an adventure story—make for a lively narrative, as he is set upon by his brothers and then sold into slavery in Egypt. The slave traders, a couple of 'chapmen', are made more familiarly northern with their donkeys laden with hides and fur, as opposed to the camels of Genesis (lines 112–16). Nevertheless, the poet is clearly interested in the exotic land of Egypt, or at least what it means to be suddenly alone in a foreign land, and he greatly expands the section describing Joseph's arrival. It is, however, not recognisably Egyptian, but rather a medieval 'burȝ', with castles and broad streets, and lords and ladies keen to see the beautiful prisoner:

> Castles heie & proute, stretes wide & long,
> Mani feir halle & mani feir bour,
> Whit so eni lilie, briȝt so eni flour ...

---

[35] For explanation of the mistranslation that led to the account of Seth being bitten on the face, see Murdoch and Tasioulas, *The Apocryphal Lives*, 120–1, n. 635–52.

[36] For examples of such inventiveness in the *Cursor Mundi*, most of which are derived from the *Historia Scholastica*, see David C. Fowler, *The Bible in Early English Literature* (London, 1977), 129–32.

[37] Text in Arthur S. Napier (ed.), *Iacob and Iosep: A Middle English Poem of the Thirteenth Century* (Oxford, 1916).

[38] For the poem's reliance upon repetition and the shadow of the alliterative long line, see Fowler, *Bible*, 134, and 138–9.

Þider comen kniȝtes & burgeis ful bolde,
Hi comen into þe street Iosep to biholde.
Leuedis of boure & maidenes fre
Comen into þe street Iosep to ise. (146–53)

In the midst of this, Joseph weeps, but not on account of his captivity, or any kind of fear, but rather because 'of Egipitene speche couþe he no þing' (line 143). Once again, we encounter the poet's privileging of language in these narratives, for what troubles the exiled Joseph is only his inability to understand and communicate in this new, Egyptian, tongue. Years later, when his brothers come begging for help from famine, not knowing that the rich man they have approached is their brother Joseph, he feasts them and entertains them, but what he wants most is to hear them sing in Hebrew, his native language (line 395). It is a poet's account of a biblical episode, where pain is centred on the inability to use words, and where longing focuses on the language of home. There is even a minstrel, with his harp on his back, appearing in the narrative at just the right moment in order to show the brothers the way to Joseph's 'castel' (lines 360–8).

The Pistel of Swete Susan is much later in terms of composition, but similar to *Jacob and Joseph* in that it gives a medieval cast to the biblical account. The allegedly Babylonian home of Susannah and her husband has the well-tended orchards, shrubberies, and garden paths of a fourteenth-century aristocratic household, together with a deep moat to enclose it all. The effect is to present Susannah as the biblical enclosed garden, the inviolate woman, while also familiarising her—lily-white, gracious, and lovely as she is—in the medieval style (lines 16–17).[39] There is no prologue, but the importance of words is brought to the fore in the form of Susannah herself, who is notably learned in Hebrew:

Þei lerned hire lettrure of þat langage,
Þe Maundement of Moises þei marked to þat may,
To þe Mount of Synai þat went in Message
Þat þe Trinite bi-tok of tables a peire
To Rede. (18–22)

(They taught her the letters of that language, they instructed that maid in the commandments of Moses, who went as a messenger to Mount Sinai, and who took a pair of tablets from the Trinity as guidance.)

The literate Susannah is connected, therefore, via the letters on the stone tablets of Moses, to the Trinity itself, with the verse form allowing the emphasis to fall on 'rede'.

The verse itself is an elaborate construction of thirteen-line stanzas, with the first eight lines in an *ababababab* rhyme scheme, followed by a bob-and-wheel rhyming *cdddc*. While the ghosts of alliterative long-lines were occasionally glimpsed in *Jacob and Joseph*, *The Pistel of Swete Susan* gives itself over to full alliterative verse. The poet favours the customary three alliterating stresses in a line, but sometimes squeezes in a fourth, for example in the non-biblical account of the teeming abundance of the garden:

Þe costardes comeliche in cuþþes þei cayre,
Þe Britouns, þe Blaunderers, Braunches þe bewe,

---

[39] Text in Carl Horstmann and Frederick J. Furnivall (eds), *The Minor Poems of the Vernon MS*, 2 vols., EETS o.s. 98, 117 (London, 1892, 1901).

226   MEDIEVAL POETRY: 1100–1400

> Fele floures and fruit, frelich of flayre,
> With wardins winlich, and walshenotes newe,
> Þey waled. (96–100)

(The lovely apples were to be found in clusters, those from Brittany and the white apples too, weighing down the branches; so many flowers and fruits, beautifully scented, with fine pears and fresh walnuts for them to choose.)

Even an earthly Eden, however, must have its snakes, and the poet returns to the biblical narrative for the arrival of the two judges who will attempt to blackmail Susannah. As she undressed to bathe in her garden, we are told that many wonders befell her around noon, a traditional fairy hour in the romance narratives, and she is addressed politely as 'ladi' as the would-be rapists phrase their coercion using the romantic terms of 'loue' and 'lemmone' (lines 129–30 and 135–6). The choice between being raped or being put to death for adultery (for the judges say they will have her falsely condemned, as in the biblical account) is briefly considered by Susannah, before she heaves forth a great scream which all the household servants answer at a run. What follows is then her condemnation to death until the prophet Daniel intervenes in a dramatic piece of courtroom cross-examination of the two corrupt elders. The tension is greatly heightened from the biblical account, and the poet adds some touching details, such as the removal of the fetters from Susannah's feet by her husband. The Old Testament model of chastity and patience becomes a golden-haired heroine of medieval verse, still chaste and patient, but with the added virtue of an educated, reasoning mind.

Such heroines are the stuff that biblical poetry is ultimately made of. The noble aim of ensuring that the word of God could be understood by all in the vernacular tongue is brought together in verse with other desires: for the creation of what is more easily remembered and is also persuasive and beautiful. The prologues of the gospel paraphrases move beyond a mere claim for accessibility and invoke verse for reasons as varied as imposing discipline on what would otherwise be a vast welter of material, to moving their audiences to engagement through the familiar verse forms of medieval popular romance. In the spirit of fair exchange, the debt also sometimes goes the other way, medieval poets finding in the Bible a ready source of adventurous tales, heroes, and villains. Among the myriad details that are unpacked by the poets from the biblical texts, we find the writer's interest in words themselves, whether it is in the first-naming of unknown concepts in a post-lapsarian world, the longing of the exile to hear songs in his native tongue, or even the very invention of writing itself, becoming part of the life story of our first parents. With the lines between holy writ, apocrypha, legend, and salvation history blurred, the medieval experience of the Bible is of a vast body of material, spooling out in many directions at once. What unites the English metrical versions is a faith in the native tongue and its capacities, to ensure that there were no closed books.

15

Saints' Lives and Sacred Biography

Karen A. Winstead

Literature about the saints, or hagiography, was one of the earliest, most popular, and most enduring medieval genres.[1] The earliest hagiographies were eyewitness accounts of the trials and executions of early Christian martyrs such as Polycarp of Smyrna (d. 155) and Perpetua of Carthage (d. *c* 203). Following the Edict of Milan (313), which legalised Christianity within the Roman empire, lives of non-martyred saints, or confessors, proliferated. Such lives featured early theologians known as Church fathers—for example, the bishops Ambrose of Milan (d. 397) and Augustine of Hippo (d. 430)—and so-called 'desert' fathers and mothers, such as Anthony of Egypt (d. 356) and Paula of Rome (d. 404), who fled civilisation to lead ascetic lives in the wilderness. The corpus of hagiography was further swelled by lives of those pursuing religious vocations—abbots and abbesses, monks and nuns, recluses and anchorites—and even of the occasional layperson.

Though many subjects of hagiography were historical persons, many others, perhaps most, were wholly invented. Sometimes a life story would be built on nothing more than the martyr's name in a document or an inscription on an ancient monument.[2] Others were written to provide a back story for bones said to belong to a holy man or woman that were treasured possessions of a shrine or church.[3] Still others were fabricated out of thin air to edify, entertain, and inspire the faithful. Most authors of these fictive lives did not think of themselves as perpetrators of fraud but rather as teachers of morality and purveyors of spiritual truths far superior to biographical fact. The stories of these invented saints—holy transvestites, virgin martyrs, reformed prostitutes, and knights like George the dragon slayer—figure prominently in the corpus of medieval literature.

In the West, most hagiography was originally composed in Latin by professional religious and fell into two broad categories: lives (*vitae*) of confessors, passions (*passiones*) of the martyrs. During the early Middle Ages, these religious assembled accounts of the lives and posthumous miracles of the saints into enormous collections, or legendaries, to be read during church services or at meals.[4] Some religious also wrote freestanding lives of saints, in prose, in verse, or occasionally in a hybrid of prose and verse known as an *opus geminatum* (twinned work). Old English saints' lives survive abundantly in both prose and verse. Middle English saints' lives composed during the thirteenth and fourteenth centuries, by contrast, were overwhelmingly poetic. Indeed, the only Middle English lives dating from then that today's scholars agree are prose were formerly considered poetic by at least

---

[1] Thomas Head's anthology, *Medieval Hagiography* (New York, 2000),provides an excellent introduction to the genre, representing its major forms and classic texts. See also Thomas J. Heffernan, *Sacred Biography: Saints and Their Biographers in the Middle Ages* (New York, 1988).

[2] The classic study of the invention (in every sense of the term) of saints is Hippolyte Delehaye, *The Legends of the Saints: An Introduction to Hagiography*, trans. V. M. Crawford (Notre Dame, IN, 1961). See also René Aigrain, *L'hagiographie: ses sources, ses méthodes, son histoire* (Mayenne, 1953).

[3] Patrick Geary, *Furta Sacra: Thefts of Relics in the Central Middle Ages* (Princeton, NJ, 1990).

[4] 'Legend' and 'legendary' derive from Latin *legenda*, things that ought to be read.

Karen A. Winstead, *Saints' Lives and Sacred Biography*. In: *The Oxford History of Poetry in English*. Edited by Helen Cooper and Robert R. Edwards, Oxford University Press. © Karen A. Winstead (2023). DOI: 10.1093/oso/9780198827429.003.0015

228 MEDIEVAL POETRY: 1100–1400

some scholars. These ambiguous lives are our earliest Middle English saints' lives, those of the virgin martyrs Margaret, Juliana, and Katherine, collectively known as the Katherine Group.

Middle English Hagiography in Poetry and 'Prose'

The Katherine Group lives were composed in the west Midlands c 1200 in an alliterative style reminiscent of Old English poetry. Thus some early scholars considered them poems and edited them as such; however, others argued that there were too many 'imperfections' in the works' alliterative patterns and noted that their system of punctuation is found in no other poetry.[5] The current consensus is that the Katherine Group's form more nearly resembles the 'rhythmic prose' of Ælfric and Wulfstan than the alliterative poetry of Cynewulf. Norman Blake proposed in 1969 that the Katherine Group lives, along with the writings of Ælfric and Wulfstan, represent 'an intermediary form between verse and prose' that he termed 'rhythmical alliteration'.[6] Similarly, Derek Pearsall considered them instances of 'transitional "prose"', which combines 'emphatic rhythm and heavy alliteration, often exuberantly prolonged on a single letter … with controlling rhetorical devices of balance, repetition and repetition-with-variation'.[7] For our purposes it is not necessary to take a position on the poetry versus prose question, only to recognise the poetic qualities that characterise these early-thirteenth-century lives. I will elaborate upon those qualities below. Within the Katherine Group lives we do also find a few lines in rhyming couplets.[8] These couplets are not part of the narrative but rather comprise the prayers that conclude the lives of Margaret and Juliana as well as a bit of the devil's lecture to Margaret.

The Katherine Group remained exceptional for most of the thirteenth century, as saints' lives written in England were mostly composed in either Latin or French.[9] Indeed, the paucity of Middle English saints' lives prior to the fourteenth century contrasts with the abundance of French lives. Most of the lives composed in the French of England were verse works by poets whose names are known to us, including Clemence and Marie of Barking, Guillaume de Berneville, Simund de Freine, Simon de Walsingham, and Guillaume Le Clerc de Normandie.[10] By contrast, we know the names of only two hagiographers writing in English prior to the fifteenth century: William Paris and Geoffrey Chaucer. French poets tended to write their hagiographies in the octosyllabic verse favoured by French poets of courtly romance.[11] By contrast, only one Middle English hagiography employs tail-rhyme,

[5] See, for example, the introductions to the following editions of *Saint Katherine*, both of which render the text as verse: Morton James (ed.), *The Legend of St. Katherine of Alexandria*, (London, 1841) and Eugen Einenkel (ed.), *The Life of Saint Katherine*, EETS o.s. 80 (London, 1884). Einenkel argues at length (xxi–xxxix) that the Katherine-Group hagiographies should be considered poems, despite the 'imperfections' and apparent 'corruptions'. S. R. T. O. D'Ardenne summarises the debate in introducing *The Liflade ant te Passiun of Seinte Iuliene*, EETS o.s. 248 (London, 1961), xxviii–xxix. See also Bella Millet, 'The *Ancrene Wisse* Group', in A. S. G. Edwards (ed.), *A Companion to Middle English Prose* (Woodbridge, 2004), 1–17; 'Introduction', in Emily Rebekah Huber and Elizabeth Robertson (eds), *The Katherine Group MS Bodley 34* (Kalamazoo, MI, 2016).

[6] N. F. Blake, 'Rhythmical Alliteration', *Modern Philology*, 67 (1969), 118–24.

[7] Derek Pearsall, *Old English and Middle English Poetry* (London, 1977), 81, 83.

[8] *Seinte Margarete*, 44, 5–6 and 75, 1–5; and *Seinte Iuliene* 76, 1–2 in Huber and Robertson (eds), *The Katherine Group*.

[9] The most comprehensive study of saints' lives in the French of England is Jocelyn Wogan-Browne, *Saints' Lives and Women's Literary Culture, c. 1150-1300: Virginity and Its Authorizations* (Oxford, 2001).

[10] Delbert W. Russell has translated several of these French lives in *Verse Saints' Lives Written in the French of England* (Tempe, AZ, 2012).

[11] Brigitte Cazelles, *The Lady as Saint: A Collection of French Hagiographic Romances of the Thirteenth Century* (Philadelphia, PA, 1991), 3.

the form most closely associated with pre-1400 Middle English romance, though the thematic affinities between romance and hagiography were as strong in English as they were in French.[12] It is perhaps no coincidence the only pre-1400 tail-rhyme saint's life in Middle English is 'Saint Eustace', whose plot, of all the hagiographies written in Middle English, most nearly resembles a romance.[13] Perhaps most hagiographers felt that the jingly rhythm of the tail-rhyme stanza, which Chaucer parodied in 'Sir Thopas', was inappropriate to sacred biography. 'Eustace' *does* jingle, even in its most sombre moments, as when Eustace mourns his abducted family:

> God almiȝen, þou hit wost,
> Fader and sone and holi gost!
> To þe ich mene mi mone,
> Of mi spouse þat was so trewe,
> Fayr and hende and briȝt of hewe—
> Welle wo is me al-one! (175–80)[14]

Though, as we will see, some Middle English writers of saints' lives showed a penchant for levity, they may have felt, as Chaucer apparently did, that tail-rhyme was a bit much.

Around 1270, a major collection of Middle English saints' lives known as the *South English Legendary* (*SEL*) took shape. This would remain the most comprehensive and widely circulated collection of Middle English saints' lives until prose translations of the principal Latin anthology, the *Legenda Aurea* (*Golden Legend*), were undertaken during the fifteenth century. The *SEL* is unquestionably poetic: the dominant form is septenary couplets; that is, rhyming pairs of lines with each line having seven stresses.

The *South English Legendary* should really be called the *South English Legendaries*, for the core text compiled in the late thirteenth century changed substantially as it was copied and circulated. Legends were omitted or altered, sometimes radically, and new legends were added.[15] The study of this polymorphous collection is still in its infancy. We have complete editions based on only three of its fifty-one extant manuscripts, as well as a smattering of legends edited from other manuscripts.[16] The saints' lives found in the various *SEL* manuscripts have been listed and compared,[17] but nobody has yet systematically investigated how the tellings of the lives vary from manuscript to manuscript. The comparisons that have been made, however, suggest that the narratives were often reworked and may differ from each other substantially in content. Nonetheless, revisors generally retain the septenary couplet form.[18]

---

[12] Rhiannon Purdie, *Anglicizing Romance: Tail-Rhyme and Genre in Medieval English Literature* (Woodbridge, 2008), 58–9.

[13] On *Eustace*'s romance qualities, particularly its affinity with the romance *Sir Isumbras*, see Laurel Braswell, 'Sir Isumbras and the Legend of Saint Eustace', *Mediaeval Studies*, 27 (1965), 128–51 and Anne B. Thompson, 'Jaussian Expectation and the Production of Medieval Narrative: The Case of "Saint Eustace" and Sir Isumbras', *Exemplaria*, 5 (1993), 387–407.

[14] Carl Horstmann (ed.), *Altenglische Legenden: Neue Folge* (1881; reprint, Hildesheim, 1969), 211–19.

[15] Heather Blurton and Jocelyn Wogan-Browne (eds), *Rethinking the South English Legendaries* (Manchester, 2011).

[16] Carl Horstmann (ed.), *The Early South-English Legendary*, EETS o.s. 87 (Oxford, 1887)and Charlotte D'Evelyn and Anna J. Mill (eds), *The South English Legendary*, 3 vols., EETS o.s. 235, 236, 244 (London, 1956, 1959).

[17] Manfred Görlach, *The Textual Tradition of the South English Legendary* (Ilkley, 1974).

[18] Compare, for example, the two very different tellings of 'Saint George' in E. Gordon Whatley, Anne B. Thompson, and Robert K. Upchurch (eds), *Saints' Lives in Middle English Collections* (Kalamazoo, MI, 2004), 71–102, as well as the two very different versions of 'Saint Frideswide' in Sherry L. Reames (ed.), *Middle English*

230 MEDIEVAL POETRY: 1100–1400

The *SEL* was by far the most popular, but not the only, hagiographical text in English during the late thirteenth and fourteenth centuries. Interestingly, three other legendaries eschew its septenary couplets for tetrameter couplets: the *North English Legendary*, a smaller collection that took shape in the late fourteenth century and comprises thirty-four items, mostly saints' lives; the so-called *Vernon Golden Legend*, a translation of eight items from the *Legenda Aurea* and a ninth from the *Vitae Patrum* (*Lives of the Fathers*); and the *Scottish Legendary*, a collection of fifty legends, mostly from the *Legenda Aurea*, translated during the last quarter of the fourteenth century.[19] A 'Mary Magdalene' included in the Auchinleck manuscript, a large miscellany produced in London during the 1330s, likewise employs tetrameter couplets, but other freestanding saints' lives incorporated in thirteenth- and fourteenth-century miscellanies are stanzaic.[20] I have already mentioned the tail-rhyme 'Saint Eustace', relayed in six-line stanzas with the rhyme scheme *aabccb*, the *a* and *c* lines typically possessing four stresses, the *b* lines three. The 'Katherine' and 'Margaret' of the Auchinleck manuscript employ eight-line stanzas with a rhyme scheme of *abcbdbeb*. The lines of 'Katherine' typically contain four stresses each. 'Margaret', however, includes many three-stress lines, often in its *b*-rhyme lines; therefore, although the manuscript presents the poem as eight-line stanzas, many of those stanzas read much like septenary quartets (and indeed, Carl Horstmann arranged 'Margaret' as septenary quartets in his edition).[21]

Middle English Poetic Margaret Legends

The formal range of poetic hagiography during the thirteenth and fourteenth centuries can be seen by comparing treatments of a single incident from the life of one of the most popular saints of the Middle Ages, the virgin martyr Margaret of Antioch.[22] Margaret's story was wholly fabricated; though she is said to have died during the persecutions of the late third century, the earliest surviving references to her date from the eighth century. Her cult grew quickly, and evidence of its popularity is variously registered in churches dedicated to her, women named after her, images made of her, and lives written of her. Juliana Dresvina catalogues forty-one distinct versions of Margaret's legend (in Latin, French, or English) that originated or circulated in medieval England.[23] One reason for Margaret's popularity is the fame she gained as the patroness of birthing mothers and their children. Margaret's own escape from the belly of a dragon symbolises safe delivery, and the legend ends with Margaret's explicit prayer that God aid mothers in labour who call upon her.[24] Margaret's encounter with the dragon is the legend's most sensational and controversial episode and

---

Legends of Women Saints (Kalamazoo, MI, 2003), 23–50. Allison Adair Alberts discusses formal and thematic variations among the Margaret legends in 'Spiritual Suffering and Physical Protection in Childbirth in the *South English Legendary* Lives of Saint Margaret', *Journal of Medieval and Early Modern Studies*, 46 (2016), 289–314.

[19] For an overview of these legendaries and a list of manuscripts and editions, see Charlotte D'Evelyn and Frances A. Foster, 'Saints' Legends', in J. Burke Severs (ed.), *A Manual of the Writings in Middle English, 1050–1500*, 11 vols. (Hamden, CT, 1970), 2:410–46, 556–635. For the *North English Legendary*, see Horstmann (ed.), *Altenglische Legenden*, 3–173. For the *Vernon Golden Legend*, see C. Horstmann (ed.), *Sammlung Altenglischer Legenden* (Heilbronn, 1878).

[20] David Burnley and Alison Wiggins (eds), *The Auchinleck Manuscript Project*, https://auchinleck.nls.uk (launched 2003) includes a transcription of the manuscript, a digital facsimile, and background information.

[21] Horstmann (ed.), *Altenglische Legenden*, 225–35.

[22] On Margaret's cult in England, see Julia Dresvina's invaluable *A Maid with a Dragon: The Cult of St Margaret of Antioch in Medieval England* (Oxford, 2016).

[23] *A Maid with a Dragon*, 207–25.

[24] See Alberts, 'Spiritual Suffering'; Jocelyn Wogan-Browne, 'The Apple's Message: Some Post-Conquest Hagiographic Accounts of Textual Transmission', in A. J. Minnis (ed.), *Late-Medieval Religious Texts and Their Transmission: Essays in Honour of A. I. Doyle* (Cambridge, 1994), 39–53; and Wendy R. Larson, 'Who Is the Master

the scene most frequently represented in art, and its sensationalism doubtless enhanced the appeal of her legend. Yet even some of the earliest tellers of Margaret's legend found it hard to credit. Middle English poets, as we might expect, took very different approaches to rendering the attack on and delivery of the saint.

Most vernacular lives of Margaret were based, directly or indirectly, on some version of the ninth-century Latin *Passio Sancte Margaretae Martyris* (*Passion of the Martyr Saint Margaret*). Here is a translation of the dragon episode from a copy of that *vita* produced in early medieval England and preserved in Paris, Bibliothèque Nationale, Lat. 5574 (I have elided the long prayer, which does not occur in most of the Middle English lives I will be discussing):

> Behold, suddenly a dreadful dragon came out from the corner of the prison, all adorned with different colours in its coat and with a gold-coloured beard. Its teeth seemed like the sharpest iron. Its eyes shone like the flame of fire, and from its nostrils issued fire and smoke; its tongue hung out panting over its neck, and a two-edged sword could be seen in its hand. It was fearsome and it caused a stench in the prison from that fire which issued from the mouth of the dragon. The blessed Margaret became as pale as grass and the fear of death came upon her, and all her bones were shattered ...
>
> While the blessed Margaret was saying this the dragon opened its mouth and placed it over the head of the blessed Margaret and extended its tongue as far as her heel and swallowed her into its stomach. But the cross of Christ, which the blessed Margaret had made for herself, grew in the mouth of the dragon and split it into two parts. The blessed Margaret emerged from the stomach of the dragon without any injury.[25]

The Katherine Group's *Seinte Margarete* begins the same scene as follows:

> Ant com ut of an hurne hihendliche towart hire an unwiht of helle on ane drakes liche, se grislich thet ham gras with thet sehen thet unselhthe glistinde as thah he al overguld were. (4) His lockes ant his longe berd blikeden al of golde, ant his grisliche teth semden of swart irn. (5) His twa ehnen | steareden steappre then the steoren ant ten gimstanes, brade ase bascins in his ihurnde heaved on either half on his heh hokede nease. (6) Of his speatewile muth sperclede fur ut, ant of his nease-thurles threste smorthrinde smoke, smecche forcuthest. (7) Ant lahte ut his tunge, se long thet he swong hire abuten his swire, ant semde as thah a scharp sweord of his muth scheate, the glistnede ase gleam deth ant leitede al o leie. (8) Ant al warth thet stude ful of strong ant of stearc stench, ant of thes schucke schadewe schimmede ant schan al. (9) He strahte him ant sturede toward tis meoke meiden, ant geapede with his genow upon hire ungeinliche, ant bigon to crahien ant crenge with swire, as the the hire walde forswolhe mid alle.

> (And there came quickly out of a corner towards her a demon of hell like a dragon, so frightening that they were horrified when they saw that evil thing glistening as though he were all gilded over. (4) His locks and his long beard gleamed all with gold, and his grisly teeth seemed made of blackened iron. (5) His two eyes, broad as basins in his horned head on either side of his hooked nose, stared brighter than the

---

of This Narrative? Maternal Patronage of the Cult of St. Margaret', in Mary C. Erler and Maryanne Kowaleski (eds), *Gendering the Master Narrative: Women and Power in the Middle Ages* (Ithaca, NY, 2003), 94–104.

[25] Mary Clayton and Hugh Magennis (eds), *The Old English Lives of St Margaret* (Cambridge, 1994), 205, 207.

232 MEDIEVAL POETRY: 1100–1400

stars and gemstones. (6) From his disgusting mouth fire sparkled out, and from his nostrils smouldering smoke pressed out, most hateful of stinks. (7) And he darted out his tongue, so long that he flung it about his neck, and it seemed as though a sharp sword, which glistened like a beam of light does and burned all in flame, shot out of his mouth. (8) And everything in that place was full of a strong and a foul stench, and everything shimmered and shone from the reflection of this demon. (9) He moved and made his way towards this meek maiden, and gaped with his mouth over her threateningly, and began to stretch and arch his neck, as though he would swallow her completely.)[26]

The hagiographer has not only kept the vivid details of the Latin—the dragon's golden locks, teeth like iron, flaming eyes, smoking nostrils, long sword-like tongue, and stench—but also embellished them: its teeth were like *blackened* iron, its eyes were like basins and shone like stars, its head was horned and its nose hooked; its sword-like tongue was like a flaming light beam. The environment, too, is rendered more vivid, not only infused with stench but glowing. The visual power of the scene is reinforced with heavy alliteration that accents the most spectacular ingredients: the dragon's 'lockes and his longe beard blikeden al of gold', 'His twa ehnen | steareden steappre then the steoren'.

This passage illustrates the hybridity of the Katherine Group's *Seinte Margarete*. The rhythmic alliteration within this passage is unmistakable, but so is its irregularity: we cannot divide the passage into lines with anything even approximating the regular patterning we can discern in Old English poetic hagiography or in the Middle English *Saint Erkenwald* (which I will be discussing later). The alliteration, as Bella Millett and Jocelyn Wogan-Brown put it, 'is more decorative than structural, and its pattern varies throughout the text'.[27]

Whereas *Seinte Margarete* revels in physical detail, the Auchinleck 'Margaret' eliminates almost all of it. Its tight metre and jingly rhyme quicken the pace and accent the tension:

⁊ Maiden Mergrete þo	
loked hir biside	
& seiȝe a loþlich dragoun	
out of an hirn* glide;	*corner*
His eiȝen wer ful griseliche,	
his mouþe ȝened* wide.	*gaped*
& Mergrete miȝt nowhar fle,	
Þer sche most abide.	
⁊ Maiden Mergrete	
stod stille so ani ston.	
& þat loþliche worm	
to hirward gan gon.	
He toke hir in his foule mouþe	
& swalled hir flesche & bon.	
Anon he tobrast	
—damage no hadde sche non. (202–17)[28]	

---

[26] Huber and Robertson (eds), *The Katherine Group MS Bodley 34*, 31.
[27] Bella Millet and Jocelyn Wogan-Browne (eds), *Medieval English Prose for Women* (Oxford, 1990), xxxv.
[28] *The Auchinleck Manuscript Project*, https://auchinleck.nls.uk.

The short lines convey a gripping scene, made more suspenseful because each line conveys just one detail: Margaret/glancing beside her/seeing a hideous dragon/gliding from a corner/with fearsome eyes/and gaping mouth/Margaret is trapped/she can't escape. The terror is enhanced by the iteration of the same shocking realisation in the last lines of the first stanza: no way out. Instead of conjuring up a distinct image, adjectives such as 'loþlich' and 'griseliche' leave an impression of horror as they encourage the reader to hurry on. In short, we experience the dragon more or less as Margaret would have. The second stanza continues this breathless narration, conveying one detail per line: Margaret/freezes/the hideous dragon/advances/seizes her/swallows her/bursts/she's unharmed.

Where the Auchinleck 'Margaret' gives us only a terrifying blur, the 'Margaret' of the *Scottish Legendary* conjures up a fire-spewing monster with scales and hard bristles:

> Þane rase scho fra hyr oracione
> & lukit by hyre vpe & downe:
> & saw a dragone nere hyr by,
> Sa mykil, sa gret & sa vgly
> Þat of wit scho wes wel nere,
> Of þat best for þe fellone bere;
> Þa scayland schalis set vp rath,
> With vryss ful lang & ful hard bath,
> & tung & techt brymnand as fyre;
> & schot one hyre in gret ire
> & tuk hyr in his mouth hale
> To suely hyr in mekil bale.
> But, as scho enterand was to pas
> Þe throt of þat ful Sathanas,
> Þe takine of þe croice scho mad
> One hyre: & þe best but bad
> Brast-in-twa, & scho but hurt
> Eschapid wele or ony sturt. (407–24)[29]

(Then she arose from her prayer and looked up and down beside her and saw a dragon near her, so big and great and ugly that she was nearly out of her mind from the foul clamour of the beast, covered with scales, with its long, hard bristles, with tongue and teeth burning like fire; and [it] struck at her in great anger and took her in its mouth to swallow her whole with great suffering. But as she passed through that Satan's throat she made the sign of the cross and the beast immediately burst in two, and she escaped unharmed without any trouble.)

The Scottish hagiographer packs more detail into each line, thus slowing the pace and offering an image terrifying in its specificity.[30] Margaret's mental state is mentioned only in passing—and not pinned down; she could be 'of wit ... wel nere' from the deafening din as much as from terror. The poet seems most concerned with eliciting wonder from the *reader.*

---

[29] Carl Horstmann (ed.), *Barbour's des Schottischen Nationaldichters Legendensammlung* (Heilbronn, 1881).
[30] See also Eva von Contzen's discussion of this scene in *The Scottish Legendary: Towards a Poetics of Hagiographic Narration* (Manchester, 2016), 130–32.

234 MEDIEVAL POETRY: 1100–1400

The English version of the scene in the *SEL*, relayed in its standard septenary couplets, is the blandest and most cerebral:

> Me telþ þat þe deuel   com to þis maide swie
> In þe forme of a dragon   ac inot weþer me lie
> He ʒonede and gan is ouer cheke   ouer hure heued do
> And is neþer cheke and is tonge   bineþe at hure ho
> And forswolwyde so in þis maide   he ʒonede er wel wide
> He[o] wende into a sori wombe   ac he[o] wolde lite abide
> For þe signe he[o] made of þe crois   þe deuel barst anon
> And þis maide hol and sond   out of þis worm gang on. (157–64)[31]

(They say that the devil came to this maiden in the form of a dragon, but I don't know whether that is a lie. He opened his mouth and put his upper jaw over her head and his lower jaw and his tongue underneath her and swallowed this maiden; he gaped widely. She went into a dismal belly but she would not stay there long. Because she made the sign of the cross, the devil burst and this maiden went whole and sound out of the dragon.)

The poet says nothing of the dragon's appearance. Three of the eight lines belabour the obvious: that to swallow Margaret, the dragon would have had to take her between his jaws. Thus relayed, Margaret's swallowing seems to take place in slow motion. The poet does not even try to generate horror—the only adjectives are 'ouer', 'neþer', and 'sori'. Given the poet's stated scepticism, it is perhaps not surprising that the episode is recounted without sensationalism and apparently without enthusiasm, but the fact that it is included at all suggests that readers considered it an essential part of Margaret's legend.

Though the verse 'Margarets' take different approaches to rendering the same passage from the Latin *passio*, they illustrate a key feature of Middle English hagiography prior to the fifteenth century: its emphasis on action.[32] The saint and her adversary dominate the scene. The deity is all but absent, indicated only in the bursting of the dragon. The lengthy prayers that punctuate the Latin description of this scene and that are reproduced in the Katherine Group's *Seinte Margarete* are gone. End-stopped lines accentuate the rhymes and quicken the pace.

Though the form of the Middle English lives complements their emphasis on action, short lines of end-stopped rhyming couplets could also produce a more decorous rendering of the scene, as we see in the translation of the dragon scene into Anglo-French by the Franciscan friar, Nicholas Bozon:

> Lors aparut en la prison
> Un trop hidus e fiers dragon.
> De sa bouche issit tel feu
> Ke la ou lumer avant ne fu
> Chescun angle de la meyson
> Ele pout vere cel dragon.

---

[31] *South English Legendary*, 1:297.
[32] Karen A. Winstead, *Virgin Martyrs: Legend of Sainthood in Late Medieval England* (Ithaca, NY, 1997), 64–111.

Lors fit ele signe de la croice,
El pria Dieu de haute voice
K'il la sauvast de l'enmi.
E le dragoun se mist a li,
Overt la bouche, la transgluta,
Mes par la croice le dragon creva.
Seyne e heytee ele se leva
E Jhesu Crist mult mercia. (125–38)[33]

(Then a very hideous and fierce dragon appeared in the prison. Such fire issued from its mouth that where there was formerly no light, in every corner of the house, she could see the dragon. Then she made the sign of the cross, she prayed to God in a loud voice that he save her from the enemy. And the dragon approached her, opened its mouth, swallowed her, but by the cross the dragon burst. She emerged safe and healthy and thanked Jesus Christ greatly.)

This rendering of the scene is no longer than the Middle English versions discussed above, but Bozon accents its devotional components rather than the action. The appearance of the dragon is less important than the fact of Margaret's *seeing* him, and the dragon's physical characteristics are conveyed with the same generality that characterises the 'Margaret' of the Auchinleck manuscript. But Bozon's object is not to generate terror, suspense, or even empathy for Margaret, but rather to convey enlightenment: the dragon's fiery breath illuminates the entire cell. The emphasis on light and sight in the first six lines of the passage connects the dragon directly with Margaret's prayer to *see* (*vere*) her enemy. The remainder of the passage foregrounds her devotion: her prayer for safety, her act of crossing herself, her prayer of thanksgiving. Readers are not left to infer that Margaret's devotion caused her delivery; Bozon specifies that dragon burst 'par la croice'.

Literary Hagiographies of the Late Fourteenth Century

I now turn to three extraordinary hagiographies of the late fourteenth century, each *sui generis*, which demonstrate that the generic experimentation associated with Ricardian romance and dream visions was also occurring in hagiography. All three are extraordinary in their content as well as in their form. Two are also remarkable for being the only saints' lives known to have been written by laypeople: Geoffrey Chaucer's 'Cecilia', ascribed in the *Canterbury Tales* to the Second Nun; and William Paris's 'Christine'. The third is the anonymous *Saint Erkenwald*, a miracle story rather than a saint's life and the only surviving Middle English hagiography that everybody agrees is an alliterative poem.

Chaucer is well known for transforming the Middle English saint's life into a self-consciously 'literary' genre. His 'Cecilia' is more formally and rhetorically elaborate than any prior Middle English hagiography. Chaucer introduces his account of the saint's life with an extended prologue that casts his writing of that life as an attempt to avoid sinful 'ydelnesse' through 'leveful bisynesse' (2, 5).[34] He composes it using his signature rhyme royal stanza, seven lines of iambic pentameter following the rhyme scheme *ababbcc*. Rhyme royal was Chaucer's choice for many of what we might call his more sententious

---

[33] M. Amlia Klenke (ed. and trans.), *Three Saints' Lives by Nicholas Bozon*, (New York, 1947), 34.
[34] In Larry D. Benson (gen. ed.), *The Riverside Chaucer*, 3rd edn. (Boston, MA, 1987).

236 MEDIEVAL POETRY: 1100–1400

works, including *Troilus and Criseyde*, his miracle story ('The Prioress's Tale'), and his hagiographical romances ('The Clerk's Tale' and 'The Man of Law's Tale'). Though fifteenth-century hagiographers, as I have argued elsewhere, were to celebrate ideals of sainthood quite different from Chaucer's, several of them—John Lydgate and John Capgrave, for instance—nonetheless would adopt his rhyme royal stanzas to tell their own saints' lives.[35]

'Cecilia' differs from earlier Middle English hagiography not only in Chaucer's use of rhyme royal but also in his liberal use of caesuras and enjambment: that is, Chaucer makes a habit of withholding pauses at the ends of lines and of inserting them within lines. Enjambments occur in practically every stanza, as the first few stanzas illustrate: Cecilia was 'from hir cradel up fostred in the faith / Of Crist' (VIII.122–3); 'And whan this mayden sholde unto a man / Ywedded be' (VIII.127–8); 'my soule and eek my body gye / Unwemmed' (VIII.136–7); 'The nyght cam, and to bedde moste she gon / With hire housbonde' (VIII.141–2). The combination of enjambments and caesuras makes Chaucer's dialogues sizzle with tension, as we see in the following stanza, which captures a heated exchange between Cecilia and her judge Almachius:

> Almachius seyde, 'Ne takestow noon heede
> Of my power?' And she answered hym this:
> 'Youre myght', quod she, 'ful litel is to dreede,
> For every mortal mannes power nys
> But lyk a bladder ful of wynd, ywys.
> For with a nedles point, whan it is blowe,
> May al the boost of it be leyd full lowe'. (VIII.435–41)

The enjambment and rhyme of 'nys/ywys' nicely reproduces at a formal level Cecilia's denial ('nys') of Almachius's assertion of power ('ywys'). The concluding rhyme serves as a kind of exclamation mark, underscoring Cecilia's rhetorical thrust with the concluding rhyme of 'blowe' and 'lowe'.

Similar strategies are evident in the life of Christine composed by Chaucer's contemporary William Paris, who may or may not have known Chaucer's poetry. 'Christine', like 'Cecilia', is more than just the life of the saint. Where Chaucer prefaces 'Cecilia' with a meditative prologue, Paris concludes 'Christine' with an autobiographical epilogue, wherein he identifies himself as the squire of Thomas Beauchamp, Earl of Warwick, who has accompanied Beauchamp in his imprisonment on the Isle of Man following Beauchamp's conviction for treason in 1397.[36] For Paris, as for Chaucer, writing a saint's life was a way to stay productively busy.

Paris's is the most polished of the five verse renderings of Christine's life extant in Middle English.[37] He writes in eight-line stanzas with the rhyme scheme *ababbcbc*, as Chaucer did in several works ('The Monk's Tale', 'An ABC', 'To Rosemounde', and 'The Former Life'); Paris's lines, however, contain only four stresses to Chaucer's five, and they generate an energy and levity wholly absent in those works of Chaucer. Glee is perhaps the dominant

---

[35] Winstead, *Virgin Martyrs*.

[36] Mary-Ann Stouck, 'A Poet in the Household of the Beauchamp Earls of Warwick, c. 1393–1427', *Warwickshire History*, 9 (1994), 113–17.

[37] Including Paris's, we have seven Middle English lives of Christine: the verse lives included in the *South English Legendary*, the *North English Legendary*, and the *Scottish Legendary*, the verse life by Osbern Bokenham, and the prose lives of the 1438 *Gilte Legende* and Caxton's *Golden Legend*.

theme of Paris's 'Christine', as Paris recounts his heroine's effortless triumphs over a succession of dim-witted persecutors. In the following passage, the first such persecutor, her father Urban, throws a fit when he discovers that she has shattered the household idols she was supposed to be worshipping:

> 'Do feche hir forth!' said Urban.
> 'Befor the barre that she were ibrouth,
> And I shall assay if I can
> To make her turne hir wikked thought.
> She said my doughter was she noghte.
> Thus coppid* the kene,* on me began;   *argued; disobedient (one)*
> She braste my godes so richely wrouth—
> What wondur if I were wrothe than?'[38] (VIII.201–8)

Natural pauses at the end of most of the lines accentuate the rhyme scheme; the mostly iambic tetrameter complements Urban's quick temper with a quick tempo. Alliteration accents his fury: feche/forth, befor/barre/ibrouth, coppid/kene. The off-rhyme of doughter/noghte echoes the thought/noght rhyme, and the 'wrothe' alliterating with 'wondur' in the final line echoes the 'wrouth' of the penultimate line. Strategic alliteration occurs elsewhere in the poem. Paris uses it to heighten Christine's triumph as spits her tongue at her persecutor's eye: 'For she hym hit softely smylid she' (468). Paris is the only one of Christine's Middle English hagiographers to exploit the alliterative potential inherent in Jesus's baptism of her: 'Christe cristynd Cristyne' (273).

Though Paris is happy to accentuate rhyme and metre to lighten the pace of his narrative, he also uses caesuras and enjambments for dramatic effect, as Chaucer does in 'Cecilia'. Paris frequently employs these devices to convey the natural rhythms of speech, as we saw Chaucer do in Cecilia's exchange with Almachius. For example, when Christine's father demands of her companions how she dared destroy the gods she was supposed to worship, they reply testily: 'She auntred hir, as ye may see; / Now are thei all in peces dyght. / Sir, make them hole! Lat se, can ye?' (150–2). To convey the effect of 'ordinary speech', enjambment often muffles a stanza's rhymes, as when Urban declares: 'Do have hir up anon in hye / In depe prison' and 'Hir hed shall of full sekerly / tomororne'. Paris similarly muffles the rhyme through enjambment to obtain a more sombre tone, as when he describes Christine's conversion to Christianity: 'But soddenly ther com socour / Fro God' (45–6); 'And he [the Holy Ghost] hath tawghte hir to forsake / Hir fals goddess ilkone' (50–1), 'And full of purpose now will she take / to drede no ded [death]'; 'Thus God can of uncrysten make / Right holy martirs' (55–6).

Paris's 'Christine' evinces a more liberal and varied use of enjambment and caesura than does Chaucer's 'Cecilia'. For example, Paris frequently uses these devices to reinforce through form the actions he is describing. Thus, when Christine's mother falls to her knees before her daughter in prison, Paris conveys her fall through enjambment: 'Whan she se Cristyn, she felle downe / Anon to hir doughter fete' (175–6). This 'falling' from one line into the next, which parallels the falling of Christine's mother to her knees, is particularly effective because it concludes a stanza whose other lines all end with natural pauses. Paris similarly renders movement through enjambment when he 'enjambs' the lines in which Christine commands a pair of serpents to slither off into the desert: 'She bade the serpens voyde awaye / Into deserte' (435–6) and when she throws gold and silver 'oute away hir

---

[38] I am using the edition in Reames (ed.), *Middle English Legends of Women Saints*.

238   MEDIEVAL POETRY: 1100–1400

froo / To pore Goddes men' (136–7). He does likewise with the line describing Christine's flesh 'scraped of by the bon / with hokyd nayles' (228–9) and the order 'lede that wyght / To Apolyn' (349–50).

An analogous alignment of form and content occurs as caesuras cut the lines that report, respectively, the cutting of Christine's hair and breasts: 'Than Dyon: "Kytt of hir tresse!"' (345); 'They kitte them of—the more dole is' (443). Paris breaks and rends the lines comprising the stanza that describes the breaking of Christine's limbs and the rending of her flesh:

> Urban commanded than anon
> Hir flesch, that was so white and shene,
> It shuld be scraped of bi the bon
> With hokyd nayles, sharpe and kene.
> He bad that all hir lymmes bedene
> They shuld be brokyn, on be on.
> It was gret pete, wo had it seen,
> Of such a mayde, be Seinte John! (225–32)

And when Urban ducks to avoid the morsel of flesh Christine flings at him, Paris introduces a blip in the regular alternation of stressed and unstressed syllables: 'And he had not blenchyd, she had hym hitte' (236).

Both Paris and Chaucer evince a more strategic use of form than any prior Middle English hagiographers. An analogous experimentation is evident in the anonymous Middle English poem, *Saint Erkenwald*, which is the only hagiographical work surviving from the literary movement that arose during the last quarter of the fourteenth century known as the Alliterative Revival.[39] Poems of the Alliterative Revival are characterised by long alliterating lines reminiscent of Old English poetry, though there is no evidence that the poets were influenced either by direct acquaintance with Old English poetry or by the survival of its techniques in oral tradition. Some make use of rhyme (for example, the so-called 'bob and wheel' that ends each stanza in *Sir Gawain and the Green Knight*), but most rely exclusively on patterns of alliteration to produce their rhythm. Though an innovation of the late fourteenth century, long alliterative lines convey an air of antiquity well suited to the preoccupation with the deep past that informs most poetry of the Alliterative Revival.[40] *Saint Erkenwald*, appropriately, is more invested in that deep past than are most hagiographies, which, though often *set* in the past, do not reflect upon it.

A miracle story rather than a saint's life, *Saint Erkenwald* recounts in 352 lines a single wonder from the life of Erkenwald, a seventh-century bishop of London. The poem relates that, as builders are laying the foundations for what would become St Paul's Cathedral, they

---

[39] On the complicated features of this phenomenon, which most scholars today are reluctant to call a 'movement', see Christine Chism, *Alliterative Revivals* (Philadelphia, PA, 2002). Scholars continue to debate whether a single author wrote *Saint Erkenwald* and the narrative ascribed to the '*Gawain*-poet' (also known as the '*Pearl*-poet'). On this issue and others, see Marie Boroff's translation of *Saint Erkenwald*. Boroff does a splendid job of preserving the alliteration of the original Middle English poem. Her apparatus includes, among other things, a particularly useful discussion of *Saint Erkenwald*'s alliterative form. She also provides an illuminating discussion of the debate surrounding the poem's date and authorship. Boroff, *The Gawain Poet: Complete Works* (New York, 2011). In the following discussion, I am citing Boroff's translation.

[40] Eric Weiskott, *English Alliterative Verse: Poetic Tradition and Literary History* (Cambridge, 2016), especially 127–47.

discover an ancient tomb containing a splendidly dressed, uncorrupt corpse. Bishop Erkenwald is forthwith summoned. The bishop, proving that his reputation for saintliness is richly deserved, compels the corpse to speak. The dead man identifies himself as a denizen of pre-Christian Britain, a judge so renowned for his goodness that his mourners buried him like a prince. God endorsed their high opinion by allowing the body and its garments to remain as fresh as the day they were entombed. The judge laments that his ignorance of Christianity has excluded him from salvation. Moved, the bishop weeps, and the judge exclaims that Erkenwald's tear has baptised him and allowed him entry into heaven. Thereupon the body blackens and turns to rot.

A miracle such as this would typically occur within the birth-to-death *vita* of a confessor. Indeed, the chapter devoted to Erkenwald in the 1438 *Gilte Legende* consists largely of numerous miracles God performed on behalf of the bishop both during his life and following his death.[41] Individual miracle stories were sometimes anthologised as discrete narratives within collections of moral tales, or *exempla*, prepared for preachers. *Saint Erkenwald* is, to my knowledge, the first miracle story in Middle English that occurs neither as part of a saint's life nor as part of a preacher's handbook.

Saint Erkenwald is composed in the signature long lines of the Alliterative Revival. These lines consist of two half-lines, each with at least two heavily stressed syllables. The two heavily stressed syllables of the first half-line typically alliterate with each other and with the first heavily stressed syllable of the second half-line. In addition, the poet will sometimes add a third alliterating sound in a less stressed syllable in the first half-line. The following passage, describing Londoners rushing to see the wondrous tomb, illustrates the pattern:

> Quen tithynges token to þe ton of þe toumbe-wonder,
> Mony hundred hende men highide þider sone;
> Burgeys boghit þer to, bedels ande othire,
> & mony a mesters-mon of maners dyuerse.
> Laddes laften hor werke & lepen þiderwardes,
> Ronnen radly is route with ryngande noyce ... (57–62)

> (When the word of the wonder spread wide in the town,
> Many hundred men in haste thronged eagerly about,
> Burgesses bustled in, beadles and others,
> Magistrates and merchants, men of all trades;
> Lads left their work and ran like the wind,
> Raced along in rivalry with ringing shouts.)

Sometimes, as we see in lines 57, 61, and 62, the alliteration is denser. More frequent alliteration often marks moments of particular significance, thematically, visually, or dramatically. For example, the discovery of the judge's tomb is relayed thus: 'Þei founden fourmyt on a flore a ferly faire toumbe' which 'Was metely made of þe marbre & menskefully planede' ('they found on the floor a wondrous fair tomb', with 'a matching slab of marble, made suitably smooth' [46, 50]). The corpse appears 'as he in sounde sodanly were slippide opon slepe' ('as if he suddenly had swooned or slipped into sleep' [92]). It was 'cladden for þe curtest þat courte couthe þen holde' ('Clad ... as the most courteous who convened ever a court' [249]) and 'coronyd' as 'þe kidde kynge of kene iustises' ('crowned' as 'king of all

---

[41] Richard Hamer and Vida Russell (eds), *Supplementary Lives in Some Manuscripts of the Gilte Legende*, EETS o.s. 315 (Oxford, 2000), 47–72.

240 MEDIEVAL POETRY: 1100–1400

judges' [254]). The repetition of 'b' sounds to convey Erkenwald's bold address to the body carries over into the next line: 'Be þou bone to his bode, I bydde in his behalue / As he was bende on a beme, quen he his blode schedde' ('Be obedient to His bidding, I beg on his behalf / As He spilt and spent His blood, outspread on the cross' [181–2]). The alliterating 'b' is resumed as the corpse obeys: 'Þe bryȝt body in þe burynes bray[þ]ed a litelle' ('The fair body in the box bestirred itself a little' [190]) and later when Erkenwald persists in his questioning: 'The bishop bides þat body, "biknowe þe cause ..."' ('The bishop bids the body, "Let the cause be known ..."' [221]).

Lines of four alliterating syllables are used most dramatically and poignantly to convey the tragedy of the judge's damnation and the joy of his redemption. Alliteration accents the despair of a man whose garments and corpse are preserved but whose soul is lost:

> [He] gefe a gronynge ful grete, & to Godde sayde:—
> 'Maȝty maker of men, thi myghtes are grete,
> How myȝt þi mercy to me amounte any tyme?' (282–4)

> [He] gave a great groan, and grieving he spoke:
> 'O you Maker of man, Your might is great!
> How could any part of Your mercy ever have been mine?'

Unsurprisingly, a line of four alliterating syllables marks the miracle, as the corpse exclaims: 'Þen sayd he with a sadde soun, "Oure Sauyoure be louyd!"' ('[He] said in a sober voice, "Our Savior be praised!"' [324]). And with lines of four alliterating syllables the judge describes the migration of his soul to heaven—'Liȝtly lasshit þer a leme loghe in þe abyme, / Þat spakly sprent my spyrit with vnsparid murthe' ('A flame flashed suddenly far in the abyss, / That sped my spirit in space with unspeakable joy' [3334–5])—and gives thanks to Erkenwald, who 'Fro bale has broȝt us to blis, blessed þou worthe!' ('Who have changed our bale to bliss—blessings upon you!' [340]). A line of four alliterating syllables stresses the surprisingly mixed feelings that attend the miracle: 'Meche mournynge & myrthe was mellyd to-geder' ('Much mourning and gladness were mingled together' [350]); joy at the salvation of the soul, mourning at the decay of the body.

Saint Erkenwald is an unusual narrative in that it focuses not on action but rather on spectacle and, later, on speech.[42] The miraculous baptism happens, as many have pointed out, by accident rather than design. The signs are all wrong for hagiography: the incorrupt body, which conventionally signals exceptional holiness, here signals damnation, while its decay signals salvation. Also unusual for a miracle are the tricky theological issues raised by God's apparent willingness to damn a man who did not—*could* not—have known Christ.[43] These unusual features may explain why the story of Erkenwald's baptism of the pagan judge does not appear among the miracles ascribed to Erkenwald either in Erkenwald's Latin *vita* or in the Middle English prose life found in the 1438 *Gilte Legende*.

Middle English poetic hagiography continued to be written into the fifteenth century and beyond. John Lydgate and Osbern Bokenham, vocal admirers of Chaucer, continued his

---

[42] On the various anomalies of this hagiography, see Anne Schuurman, 'Materials of Wonder: Miraculous Objects and Poetic Form in Saint Erkenwald', *Studies in the Age of Chaucer*, 39 (2017), 275–96.

[43] E. Gordon Whatley. 'Heathens and Saints: *Saint Erkenwald* in Its Legendary Context', *Speculum*, 61 (1986), 330–63. Whatley notes parallels between Erkenwald's miracle and that of Pope Gregory, whose tears bring salvation to the just pagan emperor, Trajan. Whatley, 'The Uses of Hagiography: The Legend of Pope Gregory and the Emperor Trajan in the Middle Ages', *Viator*, 15 (1984), 25–64, traces the development of the Gregory/Trajan miracle story and discusses the versions of it found in *Piers Plowman* and in Dante's *Commedia*.

'literary' approach to the saint's legend, and Chaucer's influence, though unacknowledged, is evident in John Capgrave's rhyme royal *Life of Saint Katherine.*[44] Though no alliterative hagiography survives from the fifteenth century, the focus of Lydgate's 'Saint Austin' on a single miraculous event from the life of a saint is reminiscent of *Saint Erkenwald.*[45] Though we have no evidence that Paris's 'Christine' influenced any fifteenth-century hagiographers, the autobiographical elements present in 'Christine' become increasingly common in the writings of fifteenth-century hagiographers.[46]

Against these continuities, there were also significant changes in the later writing of Middle English hagiography. Lydgate and Bokenham may have imitated Chaucer's poetic form, but their own saints' lives are more focused on exemplarity and devotion than on plot and spectacle. Moreover, beginning in the fifteenth century, poetry ceased to be the dominant mode of writing saints' lives.[47] Lives of British saints from the *South English Legendary* were 'updated' for inclusion in the 1438 *Gilte Legende* not only by translating them into 'modern' Middle English but also by converting their verse to prose.[48] Prose hagiography would remain predominant up to and beyond the Reformation.

---

[44] Karen A. Winstead, 'John Capgrave and the Chaucer Tradition', *Chaucer Review*, 30 (1996), 389–400.

[45] John Lydgate, 'The Legend of Saint Austin at Compton', in Henry Noble MacCracken (ed.), *The Minor Poems of John Lydgate*, 2 vols., EETS e.s. 107 and 192 (London, 1911, 1934), 1:193–206.

[46] Karen A. Winstead, *The Oxford History of Life-Writing, Vol. 1: The Middle Ages* (Oxford, 2018), 128–31.

[47] For an overview of Middle English prose hagiography, see O. S. Pickering, 'Saints' Lives', in Edwards (ed.), *Companion to Middle English Prose*, 249–70.

[48] These prose 'translations' can be found in Hamer and Russell (eds), *Supplementary Lives.*

PART IV
GENRE POETICS

16

Narrative on the Margins

Tales and Fabliaux

Christopher Cannon

The tale, fable, or short narrative in the variety of metrical and prose forms in which it is found in the Middle Ages is the oldest inheritance of English poetry. *Beowulf* begins as if it is repeating a well-known tale ('Yes, we have heard of the glory of the Spear-Danes, kings in the old days'),[1] and many of the fables told in the Middle Ages were older still, traced back by Jacob and Wilhelm Grimm to 'ancient solar, stellar, and crepuscular myths born among the Indo-European people before their division into Slavic, German, Latin, Celtic, Iranian and Indian groups'.[2] A deep past so conceived is also one of the reasons tales and fables used to sit on the margins of most literary histories, for their very age seemed to philologists like the Brothers Grimm to suggest their inevitable 'degradation' from these ancient myths: in this view, time has attenuated a richer content and stripped away stylistic virtues so that 'a pre-historic mythos' has declined into legend, and then, 'under the pressure of Christianity' become all too simple.[3] The results, according to another nineteenth-century philologist, Max Müller, were 'in their literal meaning ... absurd and irrational' and 'frequently opposed to the principles of thought, religion and morality which guided the Greeks as soon as they appear to us.'[4]

Short narratives have continued to sit on the margins of English literary history for the more prosaic reason that there are only four surviving poems in English prior to the late fourteenth century that can easily be described as 'fables': *The Fox and the Wolf* (c 1300), *Dame Sirith* (c 1275), the *Land of Cockaygne* (c 1300), and *A Penniworth of Wit* (c 1330).[5] This number increases many times when we take into account the short narratives absorbed to sermons and penitential literature as exempla. Still, if the fable becomes central to Middle English poetry by the end of this period—as I will argue in what follows—that achievement had an unpropitious start.

This dearth derived in the main from the oldest marginalising attitude of all, the suspicion ancient and medieval readers and writers had of any writing that declared itself or was known to be untrue. Such distrust of fiction was part and parcel of the morality of the Greeks Müller is thinking of, for, as is well known, Plato banished poets from his republic

---

[1] E. Talbot Donaldson (trans.), *Beowulf: A New Prose Translation* (New York, 1966).
[2] R. Howard Bloch, *The Scandal of the Fabliaux* (Chicago, IL, 1986), 2.
[3] Bloch, *Scandal of the Fabliaux*, 2.
[4] Max Müller, in A. Smythe Palmer (ed.), *Comparative Mythology: An Essay* (London, 1909), 13.
[5] The *Interludium de Clerico et Puella* shares a subject with *Dame Sirith* but consists entirely of marked speeches and so is usually understood as a 'play'. See J. A. W. Bennett and G. V. Smithers (eds), *Early Middle English Verse and Prose*, 2nd edn. (Oxford, 1968), 196 (for the designation) and 197–200 (for the text). There is also the interesting case of 'The Wenche that Loved a King' in the Auchinleck MS (Edinburgh, National Library of Scotland, Advocates' MS 19.2.1) which shows all the tendencies of a fabliau in the few lines that can be read, but also seems to have been censored at some stage since the beginning of the text has been largely scraped away and the following folio has been cut out. See Melissa Furrow, '"The Wench", the Fabliau, and the Auchinleck Manuscript', *Notes and Queries*, n.s. 41, 239 (1994), 440–3.

Christopher Cannon, *Narrative on the Margins*. In: *The Oxford History of Poetry in English*. Edited by Helen Cooper and Robert R. Edwards, Oxford University Press. © Christopher Cannon (2023). DOI: 10.1093/oso/9780198827429.003.0016

246   MEDIEVAL POETRY: 1100–1400

because of their mendacity.[6] Cicero was equally critical in the *De Inventione* when he distinguished 'fabula', which described 'things that are not true nor similar to truth' (nec verae nec veri similis res), from 'historia', which were accounts 'of actual occurrences' (gesta res).[7] His memorable example of such untruth, neatly compressed into one line of verse, was:

> Angues ingentes alites iuncti iugo ...
>
> (Huge winged dragons yoked to a car.)[8]

As Isidore traced its origins by his own etymological system the fable's untruth was inherent in its mode of production, not so much distinct from real-life event as an occurrence of a particular kind: 'poets named "fables" (fabulas) from "speaking" (a fando)', he said, 'because they are not things that were actually done but only what had been created in the telling' ('quia non sunt res factae, sed tantum loquendo fictae').[9] But even if the fable could be said to be an instance of what we would now call a speech act, its similarity to an everyday utterance did not change the fact that, as Aquinas insisted, 'poets lie' ('poëtae ... mentiuntur').[10]

Fables were also marginal in the Middle Ages because, as Macrobius argued in his commentary on Cicero's *Dream of Scipio*, they were childish:

> Hoc totum fabularum genus, quod solas aurium delicias profitetur, e sacrario suo in nutricum cunas sapientiae tractatus eliminat.
>
> (This entire category of fables, which only provide delight to the ear, are sent away from the respected province of philosophical treatises to children's nurseries.)[11]

This was not just an opinion about the status of fiction but a historical observation about the habits of ancient and medieval literacy training where fables were usually the first forms of poetry a medieval reader met in school. The most common of such texts were the *Fables* of Avianus, which not unsurprisingly begin with a defence of the fable, crowing in an introductory epistle about how a 'falsehood' (falsitas) can become suitable 'if gracefully conceived' (deceat), while also understanding such grace as the consequence of not being 'oppressed by the necessity of adhering to the truth' (non incumbat necessitas veritatis) (681).[12] And it is certainly the case that the first of Avianus's fables is graceful (the whole narrative is unfolded in eight heroic couplets), 'childish' in its subject (it is 'about a nurse and her child' [De nutrice et infante]), demonstrably false (the child is told by the nurse he will be thrown to the wolves if he does not behave; the foolish wolf waits outside for this figure of speech to

---

[6] 'Then the mimetic art is far removed from truth, and this, it seems, is the reason why it can produce everything, because it touches or lays hold of only a small part of the object and that a phantom', Plato, *Republic* (10.598b) in Edith Hamilton and Huntington Cairns (eds), *The Collected Dialogues of Plato* (New York, 1961), 893.

[7] Cicero, *De Inventione* (1.19.27), in H. M. Hubbell (ed. and trans.), *On Invention; Best Kind of Orator; Topics* (Cambridge, MA, 2014).

[8] *De Inventione*, 1.19.27. The line is a quotation from the Roman poet Pacuvius; see E. H. Warmington (ed. and trans.), *Remains of Old Latin: Livius Andronicus, Naevius, Pacuvius, Accius* (Cambridge, MA, 1936), 242, 254–5.

[9] Isidore of Seville, in W. M. Lindsay (ed.), *Etymologiarum sive originum libri XX*, 2 vols. (Oxford, 1911), xl.

[10] Thomas Aquinas, in M. R Cathala and R. M. Spiazzi (eds), *Duodecim Libros Metaphysicorum Aristotelis Expositio*, 2nd edn. (Rome, 1950),I.63 (19), cited in Peter Dronke, *Fabula: Explorations Into the Use of Myth in Medieval Platonism* (Leiden, 1985), 3 n. 1.

[11] Macrobius, *Commentarii in Somnium Scipionis*, in vol. 2 of James Willis (ed.), *Macrobius* (Leipzig, 1963), Book I 2.8.

[12] *The Fables of Avianus*, 669–749 in J. Wight Duff and Arnold M. Duff (eds), *Minor Latin Poets* (Cambridge, MA, 1934, 1961), Epistula [Dedicatory Letter], lines 4–5.

come true; in the end, he must return home to his mate empty-handed), and it concludes with a moral that, in its unnecessary misogyny, seems hardly oppressed by the need even to make sense ('Let anyone who believes in a woman's sincerity reflect that to him these words are spoken and that it is he whom this lesson censures' ['haec sibi dicta putet seque hac sciat arte notari, / femineam quis quis credidit esse fidem']).[13] Even ancient fables themselves insisted on their marginality by a generic commitment to triviality.

Medieval fables remain on the margins in the literary histories we write now by means of a paradox whereby the very scholarly attitudes and methods that take them the most seriously look right through them.[14] This is particularly true of the subspecies of fable usually called 'fabliaux', 'des contes à rire en vers' ('funny stories in verse'), as Joseph Bédier described them, where the tendency among readers has been to identify humour with realism[15]— 'evidence of the history of culture', as Charles Muscatine put it, fictional events, involving characters who never lived, that are nevertheless accurate records of the social world in which these events and characters were situated.[16] Not many of these fabliaux survive: in addition to the one English example, there are only seven surviving tales in French that seem to have been written in England (there are, in fact, no more than 150 French fabliaux written on the Continent). And yet it is inherent to the modern view that these texts' untruth gives them a 'representative power'; they are, in that understanding, records of past life and practice.[17]

There are ways, however, that the fable was more significant to Middle English poetry than even the most favourable views of such texts, medieval or modern, have been able to credit, and it is how the fable did (and does) matter, even at the margins, that I want to explore in the remainder of this chapter. It is Chaucer who provides a particularly helpful guide here, not least because he is the Middle English poet who, in the end, made the most of the ancient and medieval fable's potential. And so, at the conclusion of the elaborate fable we call 'The Nun's Priest's Tale', Chaucer directly addresses the doubts his contemporaries had about such a form:

> But ye that holden this tale a folie
> As of a fox, or of a cok and hen,
> Taketh the moralitee, goode men.
> For Seint Paul seith that al that writen is,
> To oure doctrine it is ywrite*, ywis;   *written*
> Taketh the fruyt, and lat* the chaf be stille.[18]   *let*

The claim that Chaucer here derives from St Paul's letter to the Romans (15.4) uses scriptural warrant to insist that fables, *even if* untrue, have value. Macrobius advanced a similar view in his commentary on the *Dream of Scipio*, arguing that 'truth' may be 'expressed by way

---

[13] Duff and Duff (eds), *Fables of Avianus*, I.15–16.

[14] See Bloch, *Scandal of the Fabliaux*, 5.

[15] This phrase is often quoted from Joseph Bédier, *Les Fabliaux: Etudes de littérature populaire et d'histoire littéraire du moyen âge*, 5th edn. (Paris, 1925).

[16] Charles Muscatine, *The Old French Fabliaux* (New Haven, CT, 1986), 45–6.

[17] Ardis Butterfield, 'English, French and Anglo-French: Language and Nation in the Fabliau', in C. Young, T. Reuvekamp-Felber, and M. Chinca (eds), 'Novellistik im Europäischen Mittelalter', special number of *Zeitschrift für deutsche Philologie* (2005), 238–59, at 239. On the number of fabliaux as well as the difficulty in firmly delimiting the category, see Butterfield, 'English, French and Anglo-French', 238–9 and Muscatine, *Old French Fabliaux*, 4 and 171 n. 3.

[18] Geoffrey Chaucer in Larry D. Benson (gen ed.), *The Riverside Chaucer*, 3rd edn. (Boston, MA, 1987), VII.3438–43. Hereafter I will cite Chaucer from this edition by line (and, in the case of the *Canterbury Tales*, fragment) number in my text.

248   MEDIEVAL POETRY: 1100–1400

of fictional devices' ('veritas per quaedam composita et ficta profertur').[19] Such valuations do not rest on ancient opinions about fables, but, rather, a classical understanding of their shaping substrate, what we would call 'plot': as Quintilian put it, 'an action done or deemed to be done' ('rei factae aut ut factae') could be 'designed' in order to be 'persuasive' ('utilis ad persuadendum').[20] When Geoffrey of Vinsauf says in the *Poetria Nova* (c 1200) that in 'comic stories' ('res comica') 'it is sometimes a colour to avoid colours' ('est quandoque color vitare colores'), he even seems to be claiming that story itself is a 'colour' akin to a figure of rhetoric.[21] It is this view in particular that I would like to explore in what follows, for, while Chaucer tended to go to Geoffrey of Vinsauf for the kinds of verbal ornamentation we usually associate with such figures, what he also seemed to understand was what we might call the power of plot: the extent to which a fable's narrative is not only the foundation around which all its other figures turn, but a figure itself capable of producing a fable's most potent effects.[22]

The Power of Plot

Such a view did not lead directly to the writing of fables, but it meant that they played significant roles in larger texts in Middle English because they were valued highly *for* their plots. One particularly rich use of fables in this instrumental way was Robert Mannyng's *Handlyng Synne* (1303), a treatise on the sins and the proper forms of confession (translated from William of Waddington's *Manuel de Péchiez* [c 1250–70]) that often illustrated its points with short tales.[23] A useful instance of such illustration is Mannyng's treatment of the 'Tale of the Hermits and the Thieves', which can also be found in a collection of fables by the English cleric Odo of Cheriton (1180–1246):

> Quidam heremita pecuniam sibi datam ad capud lecti reposuit. Quadam nocte uenerunt fures ut pecuniam sibi auferrent; quo cognito accepit pecuniam heremita et proiecit latronibus dicens: Accipite tremorem capitis mei.
>
> (A hermit used some money that had been given to him as a pillow for his head. That night some thieves came in order to take it from him. Realising this, the hermit took the money and threw it at the thieves saying: Take this trembling from my head.)[24]

What Mannyng saw in this spare series of events is a vivid lesson in the ways that possessions can themselves be a caution against covetousness. In his expansion the hermit has gathered the money because he has 'nede'; when he has a full purse, he lies down on it to keep it safe, but can't sleep 'so moche on hyt was hys thoght' (6126). When the thieves arrive

---

[19] Macrobius, *Commentarii* in Willis (ed.), Book I 2.9. Cited in Dronke, *Fabula*, 21.

[20] Quintilian in Donald A. Russell (ed. and trans.), *The Orator's Education*, 4 vols. (Cambridge, MA, 1920), 4.2.31 (2:234–5). Emphasis mine.

[21] Geoffrey of Vinsauf, *Poetria Nova*, in Edmond Faral (ed.), *Les Arts Poétiques du XIIᵉ et du XIIIᵉ Siècle: Recherches et Documents sur la Technique Littéraire du Moyen Âge* (Paris, 1962), 194–262, at line 1883. Cited in Muscatine, *Old French Fabliaux*, 58. Chaucer refers to Geoffrey as his 'deere maister soverayn' (VII.3346) and briefly parodies here (VII.3347–52) Geoffrey's elegy for Richard I (*Poetria Nova*, lines 368–430).

[22] Geoffrey of Vinsauf, *Poetria Nova*, line 1885.

[23] Robert Mannyng, in Idelle Sullens (ed.), *Robert Mannyng: Handlyng Synne* (Binghamton, NY, 1983). *Handlyng Synne* will be cited from this edition by line number in my text. Sullens counts sixty-six distinct and embedded tales as well as sources and analogues in an appendix (381–7).

[24] Odo of Cheriton, *Parabolae*, in Léopold Hervieux (ed.), *Les fabulistes latins depuis le siècle d'Auguste jusqu'à la fin du Moyen Age*, 5 vols. (Paris, 1893–9), 4:283–343, at 271.

the hermit also throws his money at them, but as he does so, he spells out the cause of the 'trembling' Odo only mentions:

He parseyued weyl* whydyrward they cam	*well*
And swythe* after hys purs he ran	*quickly*
And kaste hyt to hem euerydeyl*	*entirely*
And seyde, 'haueth & brouketh* hyt weyl,	*enjoy*
For myn herte was neure yn reste	
Syn y had hem a nyghtes geste*.	*as an overnight visitor*
For shal y neure after thys day,	
Purse, pens, yf that y may'. (6143–50)	

In the elaborations that give this plot its striking 'colour' the money is transformed from an object to a house guest, not only an unwelcome possession but something akin to a character capable of dangerous action. Sermons also used fables in this colourful way as preachers' manuals often recommended.[25] Most of these sermons were in Latin, but the tales did not themselves need to be, and one manual recommends using another fable collected by Odo, the 'Tale of the Priest and the Dead Girl', as a compelling way to describe the dangers of a belated confession. The manual then translates the gripping cry of the girl who has left her confession too late from Latin into English:

Alas, alas that I was born
Both lyf and sowle y am for-lorn![26]

The fable's plot reveals its rhetorical force as it is distilled into a couplet itself made the more powerful because presented as if overheard (in the very form in which it was uttered). In this way, both story and couplet transform the emotional content of this narrative into an instrument of pastoral care.

The power of plot to determine both the form and function of poems is most clearly on view in English literary history in the four free-standing fables that I mentioned at the start of this chapter, and the most accomplished of these is probably *The Fox and the Wolf*. True to fable form, it is beguilingly simple in its manner (it is in roughly octosyllabic four-stress lines) as well as in its plot, in which a fox, thwarted in his attempt to raid a hen house, falls into a well but then tricks a wolf into helping him get out. Such a story teaches no obvious lesson and its humour derives almost entirely from a reader's pleasure in the caricatured misfortune of another. But there is also great wit in the way its poet turns a simple phrase, as when the fox seeks to reassure the suspicious rooster, Chauntecleer, by insisting that he has been helpful to sick chickens in the past:

I nabbe* don her nout* bote goed	*have; nothing*
I have leten* thine hennen* blod	*drawn; hens'*
Hy* weren seke ounder the ribe	*they*
That hy ne mightte non lengour libe.*[27]	*live*

[25] Siegfried Wenzel, *Verses in Sermons:* Fasciculus morum *and Its Middle English Poems* (Cambridge, MA, 1978), 187–8.

[26] Wenzel, *Verses in Sermons*, 187. The narrative 'De Quodam Sacerdote et Puella Defuncta et Damnata' as Hervieux collects it and the cry in the Latin text is 'Ve mihi, ve mihi!! quod unquam fui nata; tam corpus quam anima utraque sunt dampnata' (see *Fabulistes Latins*, 4:315).

[27] 'The Fox and the Wolf', in Bennett and Smithers (eds), *Early Middle English Verse and Prose*, 65–76, at lines 39–42. Hereafter I will quote from this edition by line number in the text.

250 MEDIEVAL POETRY: 1100–1400

The joke expands the common claim that a cure can be far worse than the disease into the proposition that a cure may itself be deadly. When the fox ends up at the bottom of a well the pleasure is not only in seeing the malevolent trickster tricked but in seeing this plot condensed into a single, summative image. The fox does not understand the necessary physics ('he ne hounderstod nout of the ginne [mechanics]') (77) so he climbs into the empty bucket at the top of a pulley whereupon his own weight ensures that he will be unable to lift himself up again:

Tho he wes in the ginne* ibrout	*trap*
Inou he gon him bithenche*	*was aware*
Ac hit ne halp mid none wrenche*:	*device*
Adoun he most, he was therinne	
Ikaut he wes mid swikele ginne*.	*a great trick* (82–6)

The meaning of this image is in turn condensed in the single word 'ginne', which names both the instrument in the well as well as the manner in which the fox has been caught just as it is also a word for the kind of trick the fox has just tried to perpetrate on Chauntecleer and his hens, and that he will in turn successfully perpetrate on the wolf when he persuades him to climb into the bucket at the top of the well, thus drawing him back up:

The wolf gon sinke*, the vox arise—	*sank*
Tho gon the wolf sore agrise*	*very much afraid*
Tho he com amide* the putte,	*halfway down*
The wolf thene vox opward* mette.	*on the way up* (239–42)

The defining brilliance of the poem is the way that it underscores the rhetorical force of its plot in a single constituent action with wolf sinking just as his fortunes do and the fox rising just as his fortune finally looks up. The moment when the two pass in the middle provides a physical correlative for the recognition that the reader shares with the fox and the wolf of a trick well played, and, to the very extent that it has been so perfectly rendered as a sight gag.

We might compare such an achievement to *Dame Sirith* and see a greater coarseness in its telling mirrored throughout in a verse form that is both less elegant (much of it in 'tail-rhyme' in which, here, a short four-stress couplet is followed by a third line with three stresses—the tail—that then rhymes with the line after the next couplet) and awkward (since, for no apparent reason, this form shifts to couplets before returning to tail-rhyme). But this narrative of another simple trick (in which Dame Sirith helps a clerk named Wilekin to deceive a married woman by persuading her that she will be turned into a dog if she does not assent to his advances) is forceful by means of its minimalism. Letters that seem to mark speakers of particular lines in the margin of the one copy we have of the text may indicate that it was performed (C for 'clericus', 'V' for 'uxor', F for 'femina'), and these markings are necessary because the narrative itself does not always indicate transitions from speaker to speaker. At the very moment when Dame Sirith describes the method she will use to deceive the wife (in the seventh line below), there is an unacknowledged change in the direction of her address:

So Ich euere brouke* hous other flet*,	*enjoy; room*
Neren* neuer pones* beter biset	*were; pounds*
Then thes shulen ben!	
For I shal don a iuperti*	*play a trick*

And a ferli* maistri,   *marvellous; feat*
That thou shalt ful wel sen.
Pepir nou shalt thou eten;
This mustart shal ben thi mete*,   *food*
And gar thin eien to rene.[28]

Here is an instance of narrative 'colour' consisting of a shedding of every possible other resource of rhetoric, since the significant action whereby the turning of Dame Sirith's head (from the man who is paying her to the dog she is going to use for her trick) is signalled only in the content of what she says (making the dog eat pepper and mustard so that it will 'weep'). The subterfuge itself is described in the space of only two couplets (when Dame Sirith says that her dog—which she has also said is her daughter—is crying because she would not assent to a clerk's advances):

He ne mightte his wille haue,
For nothing he mightte craue.
Thenne bigon the clerc to wiche*,   *use sorcery*
And shop* mi douter til* a biche.   *transformed; into* (351–4)

And this austerity of narration extends to the actions that constitute the rest of the plot, for the wife never pauses even to doubt that Dame Sirith's implausible story is anything but true, and so her volte-face is instantaneous:

Louerd Crist, that me is wo,
That the clarc me hede* fro   *went*
Ar* he me heuede biwonne!   *until*
Me were leuere* then ani fe*   *I would rather; wealth*
That he heuede enes* leien bi me,   *once*
And efftsones* bigunne.   *immediately* (379–84)

It is the very simplicity of the sequence of spare actions in this poem that makes visible what Muscatine called the 'fabliau ethos'; in this case, the way that even the most defining aspects of class and station (celibacy for clerks, fidelity for wives, dotage for old women) could be dismantled by guile.[29] Such narratives, if fictional, were therefore still consequential. As Robert Darnton has put it, they were 'good to think with', evoking just enough of the 'booming, buzzing confusion' of the everyday world to show those in that world how to better navigate it.[30]

Part of that demonstration derived from the way that both fabliau and beast fable fostered a disposition towards happy or at least tidy endings and humorous or at least satisfying outcomes, and it is largely because it makes humorous outcomes to action so inevitable that the *Land of Cockaygne* must be included in any discussion of Middle English fable. This poem is, in the main, a lengthy description of a world of concrete things so delightfully beneficent that geese fly to the table already roasted on a spit and rivers run with oil, milk, honey, and wine.[31] These things are arranged according to the social and physical orientations of

---

[28] 'Dame Sirith', in Bennett and Smithers (eds), *Early Middle English Verse and Prose*, 77–95, at lines 273–81. Hereafter I will quote from this edition by line number in the text.

[29] Muscatine, *Old French Fabliaux*, 73–104.

[30] Robert Darnton, *The Great Cat Massacre: And Other Episodes in French Cultural History* (New York, 1984), 62 ('moral' and 'ironic') and 64 ('piece').

[31] 'The Land of Cockaygne', in Bennett and Smithers (eds), *Early Middle English Verse and Prose*, 136–44, at lines 45–6 (for description of the rivers) and 102–6 (for description of the geese). Hereafter I will quote from this edition by line number in the text.

252 MEDIEVAL POETRY: 1100–1400

a fabliau plot: 'there is a wel fair abbei / of white monkes and grey' (51–2) as well as 'a gret fair nunnerie' (147) where 'the yung nunnes ... makith ham nakid forto plei' (152–6) and, when the abbot calls the monks to evensong, his method is violent but sexually suggestive:

> He taketh maidin of the route*   *company*
> And turnith up hir white toute*,   *bottom*
> And betith the taburs* with is hond   *drums*
> To make is monkes light* to lond.   *alight* (135–8)

Cokaygne is a 'Paradis ... miri and bright' (7) and, in that sense, both the energy and pleasure of this text derive from the rhetorical ornament that, I have been suggesting, fable customarily eschews: this is a poetry of lists, lexical variety, and extravagant imagery. And yet, once the libidinous monks and naked nuns have been so humorously described, there is nothing for the description to do but condense itself into a revealing action:

> [The yung monkes] commith to the nunnes anon,
> And euch monke him taketh on*,   *one*
> And snellich* berith forth har prei* *quickly; prey*
> To the mochil grei* abbei.   *large grey* (161–4)

For such an event to occur requires a penance akin to wading for seven years through pig 'dritte' ('dung'), the poem insists but to convert such action into a moral is to invert it in exactly the way the poem's descriptions invert Christian morality from the start: the reward for penance turns out to be exactly the kind of thing a Christian ought to do penance for.

Literary historians sometimes try to differentiate fabliau from fable by insisting that the latter must end with a moral, but *A Penniworth of Wit* confounds this distinction by embedding a fable-like moral in a fabliau shape.[32] Certainly its plot is fabliau-like since it begins by describing a merchant's devotion to his mistress at his wife's expense. In focusing on the products of his trade, both in the riches he bestows on his mistress and the neat reversal inherent in the wife's recommendation that he buy some 'wit' (or wisdom) with the penny she gives him—a reversal that finally brings all the mistress's riches to her instead—this is also, like a fabliau, a poem of concrete things. And like *Dame Sirith* and other fabliaux, its realism is 'good to think with'. After the penny is paid to an old man who recommends that the merchant test his mistress's real affections by pretending that he has lost all his goods and is now a criminal, having accidentally killed a man, and the merchant's mistress in turn rejects him when she realises he can no longer enrich her, the merchant's response is muted but thoughtful:

> Stille he stode answerd he nought
> As man that is in gret thought
> He thought ferther for to gon
> For help no fond* he ther right non   *found*
> Sum better solauce for to finde
> For ther was comfort al bihinde.[33]

---

[32] Marie Nelson and Richard Thomson, 'The Fabliau', in Laura Cooner Lambdin and Robert Thomas Lambdin (eds), *A Companion to Old and Middle English Literature* (Westport, CT, 2002), 255–76, at 257.

[33] *A Penniworth of Wit*, in David Laing (ed.), *A Penni Worth of Witte: Florice and Blauncheflour—And Other Pieces of Ancient English Poetry* (Edinburgh, 1857), 1–14, at lines 235–40. Hereafter I will quote from this edition by line number in the text.

The poem is so spare that its plot can be hard to follow: transitions between speakers are here also unmarked, and its 400 lines of tetrameter verse unfold in the plainest of statements. But after the merchant recovers his wealth from his mistress and returns to his wife and lays all these riches before her, his simple summary of this transaction reveals that this fabliau-like series of tricks and reverses does not so much arrive at a moral as it has one coiled within it:

> Lo dame, he seyd, by mi chaffare* *by means of my trading*
> Ichaue ybrought thi Peni worth ware * *your penny's worth of goods* (387–8)

Both this couplet's and the poem's point is that to be even a little wise is to have all the riches one needs, and this conflation—itself represented in a single image (of the 'value' of wit)—means that this implicit moral also condenses the achievement of all fables in English up until this point. Individually and collectively they show how an idea can be made coextensive with a set of the unfolding actions that constitute a plot.

The Well-Turned Tale

Some effort has gone into discovering why there are not only so few fables in Middle English but also (given the number of such texts surviving in French) why there are so few fabliaux in general. To be sure, the genre flourished only for a limited period of time in France (the last identifiable author of a fabliau died in 1346). Muscatine thought the form died out quickly because it was an 'expression of a subculture' and was therefore only made possible by the circumstances that gave rise to that subculture.[34] Another possibility is that the genre of fabliau 'exist[ed] in a sort of adversarial relationship to romance', and since English romances were, on the whole, more coarse in their characters and plots than their French counterparts, thereby inhabiting the 'lower mimetic ground that fabliau normally covers', those romances simply did not 'provoke a reaction in the form of fabliaux'.[35] It may also be that fabliau never took hold in England because the poems that were written were not compelling enough to inspire other writers (*Dame Sirith* is, in that sense, a failed experiment).[36]

As I have been observing throughout this chapter, however, fabliau is only one species of fable, so it is only to tell a very small part of the story of the form to emphasise this dearth or to focus on the triumph of Chaucer's perfection of its possibilities (though I will turn to those below). In fact, if we want to take the measure of the culminating importance of the master category of which fabliau is only a part, we could do no better than to turn to the B-text of *Piers Plowman* (*c* 1378) where William Langland tells the fable of the rat and the cat. The narrative is added to the B-text and so it seems Langland turned to it as a way of elaborating the denunciation of the upper reaches of society (corrupt bishops and archbishops in particular) he had begun in the A-text. In the version of this fable told by

---

[34] Muscatine, *Old French Fabliaux*, 4 and 155.

[35] Melissa Furrow, 'Middle English Fabliaux and Modern Myth', *ELH*, 56 (1989), 7 ('adversarial') and 11 ('lower' and 'provoke'). Keith Busby makes a similar point in 'Conspicuous By Its Absence: The English *Fabliau*', *The Dutch Quarterly Review of Anglo-American Letters*, 12 (1982), 30–41 (esp. 41).

[36] Busby notes that *The Vox and the Wolf* and *Dame Sirith* both occur in only Oxford, Bodleian Library, MS Digby 86 and proposes that 'the compiler of Digby 86 made an attempt, unsuccessful in the long run, to promote Middle English as a medium for two genres, fabliau and animal tale', 'Conspicuous by Its Absence', 38.

254 MEDIEVAL POETRY: 1100–1400

Odo of Cheriton no rat is willing to bell the cat or 'oppose the bishop' ('opponit se contra episcopum') and it therefore demonstrates how it is 'the lesser [who] allow the elevated to live and rule' ('minores permittunt maiores vivere et preesse').[37] If Langland also uses this fable because he appreciates the power of a narrative to make a point (it was known to have been preached in at least one contemporaneous sermon),[38] he also alters that point by changing the narrative's plot. In his version, a mouse enters the parliament of rats and offers two reasons why no one *should* bell the cat:

> 'Though we hadde ykilled the cat, yet sholde ther come another
> To cracchen* us and al our kynde, though we cropen* under benches.   *Snatch; creep*
> Forthi I counseille al the commune to late the cat worthe*   *be*
> And be we neuere so bolde the belle hym to shewe.
>
> ...
>
> For many mannes malt* we mees* wolde destruye,   *grain; mice*
> And also ye route of ratons rende mennes clothes,
> Nere* the cat of the court that that kan yow ouerlepe*;   *were it not for;*
>   *overcome*
> For hadde ye rattes youre wille, ye kouthe* noght rule yowselue.[39]   *could*

This use of fable is exemplary because Langland so fully absorbs the point he wants to make to the shape of the tale he wants to tell. If a fable could be an instrument capable of elaborating a larger poetic purpose, as it was in Mannyng's *Handlyng Synne* or a sermon, Langland shows that, where a fable's plot was shaped to be particularly appropriate to its circumstances, it could be—like any rhetorical figure—particularly well turned.

The end of the fourteenth century is a moment when this realisation of the power of poetic fable could be said to culminate in three distinct ways. The first is allied with Langland's use but mobilises a fable's narrative, not only as a constituent part of a poem, but in effect to generate it, and Chaucer's *Book of the Duchess* (*c* 1369) is a key example here. When the narrator of this poem opens his 'book' of 'fables' (52) what he lights on is not a story from the *Fables* of Avianus but something very similar, an episode from Ovid's *Metamorphoses* (8 CE), another common school text.[40] Once again the immediate value of this fable also lies in its plot in which Seys travels 'over see' (67) and his wife, Alcyone, sick with worry during his absence, dies of her grief when she learns he has died. The plot of this inset fable throws a deep shadow over all that follows and also, fully anticipates the larger poem's climactic moment when another passionate lover has to recognise that a loved one 'ys ded' (1309). Such a fable is a 'colour' in exactly sense that Geoffrey of Vinsauf described other colours, an ornament to another plot even though it is a plot itself, marginal to all

---

[37] Odo of Cheriton, *Fabulae*, 4:173–255 in *Les fabulistes latins*, ed. Hervieux, 4:226.

[38] On the use of the fable in a sermon of Thomas Brunton, Bishop of Rochester, and its recording in a volume that survives as London, British Library, MS Harley 3760, see Eleanor H. Kellogg, 'Bishop Brunton and the Fable of the Rats', *PMLA*, 50 (1935), 57–68 and Matthew Giancarlo, *Parliament and Literature in Late Medieval England* (Cambridge, 2010), 182.

[39] William Langland, in A. V. C. Schmidt (ed.), *The Vision of Piers Plowman: A Critical Edition of the B-Text* (London, 1995), prologue, 185–8, 198–201.

[40] Chaucer is thought to have been inspired by the passage in Machaut's *Livre de la fonteinne amoureuse* in which the lover uses the story of Ceyx and Alcyone to illustrate 'the sorrow' (la dolour) love can bring, but its events are narrated there and in no way marked off as a tale or fable: Guillaume de Machaut, *Livre de la fonteinne amourese*, 89–239 in R. Barton Palmer (ed. and trans.), *The Fountain of Love (La Fonteinne Amoureuse) and Two Other Love Vision Poems* (New York, 1993), 89–239, at lines 543–698 and line 556 (for the term I quote).

that follows because it is introductory, but also central because, by adumbrating the poem's most important affective qualities, it intensifies them.

The same could be said of the second way in which late-fourteenth-century English writers made significant use of fables, embedding a *series* of them in larger plots which then seem to have generated them. Such use is different from the instrumental fable we find in Mannyng or in sermons because the larger end they advanced was, in effect, another fable. It was Gower's *Confessio Amantis* that embraced this amalgamated form most comprehensively, embedding 133 narratives in a poem that also frames them in the form of a lover's confession to a priest (the context in which they are told) and also classifies them (since the poem is divided into eight books, the first six of which focus on one of the deadly sins, the seventh on the lover's education, and the eighth on incest). For the priest, Genius, the purpose of each fable is exemplary, as he makes clear when he introduces the tale of Acteon as an illustration of the importance of governing the five senses and the perils of sight:

Mi Sone, herkne* now forthi	*listen to*
A tale, to be war* therby	*made aware*
Thin yhe* forto kepe and warde,	*eye*
So that it passe noght his warde*.	*safekeeping*
Ovide telleth in his bok	
Ensample touchende of mislok*,	*sinful looking*
And seith hou whilom* ther was on,	*once*
A worthi lord, which Acteon,	
Was hote*...[41]	*called*

The tales in the *Confessio* can be as short as the fable of the rat and cat in *Piers Plowman* or the tale of Ceyx and Alcyone in *The Book of the Duchess*, no more than fifty lines, or they can occupy the bulk of a book, as the nearly 2,000 lines of the tale of 'Apollonius of Tyre' does in Book 8, although, whatever their size, Gower insists on their importance by summarising them in elaborate Latin intertexts and glosses.

Plot also functions as a form of rhetorical colour in the four fabliaux in the *Canterbury Tales*—'The Miller's Tale', 'The Reeve's Tale', 'The Summoner's Tale', 'The Merchant's Tale', and 'The Shipman's Tale'—and it could also be said that these tales represent culminations of this technique because Chaucer not only embeds much of what he wants to say in each tale in its plot, but he also uses a variety of techniques to render this formal fact unusually visible. In 'The Miller's Tale', for example, Chaucer unfolds not one plot but two—a ruse about an imminent flood and a bedroom farce that concludes with a scalding—and so fully entwines them that the one plot resolves the other. A similar visibility is achieved for the plot of 'The Shipman's Tale' by a deft use of language, for the events in this poem activate a series of puns in which the word 'pay' refers to money (VII.11, 180, 291, 331, 414) as well as sex (as in the marriage 'debt') in VII.417, 424. Those puns activate a second meaning in the word 'taille', which is both 'tally' or sum but also genitals ('score it upon my taille' [VII.416]).

But Chaucer's most important achievement in the writing of fable—and the third way fable became uniquely valuable to English poetry at the end of the fourteenth century (alongside its ability to generate the subject of a whole poem or to generate a larger, framing narrative)—was to pull the fable from the margins to the very centre of two important tales

---

[41] John Gower in Russell A. Peck, *Confessio Amantis*, 3 vols. (Kalamazoo, MI, 2006–13), 1.329–37. Hereafter I will quote from this edition by book and line number in the text.

256 MEDIEVAL POETRY: 1100–1400

and, in the process, the centre of the *Canterbury Tales* as a whole. As a collection, *The Canterbury Tales* accomplishes this very simply by means of a plot that should only advance by tale-telling (even if it is sometimes also defined by deviations from that purpose) and it is the Parson who notes how this makes the *Tales* a sequence of 'fable[s]' (X.31). Although the history of the fable in Middle English that I have related here was almost certainly not on Chaucer's mind when he wrote 'The Nun's Priest's Tale' and 'The Manciple's Tale', a beast fable and an Ovidian 'tale', respectively, in so doing he firmly set all other forms of poetic ornament over against plot in these pivotal narratives, and he thereby uses them to declare that a set of events not only can be but *are* as powerfully meaningful as any poetic figure. In the first half of the 'Nun's Priest's Tale' plot is shown to be equivalent to rhetoric because of the arabesques of argument between Chauntecleer and Pertelote, his wife; in the dramatic actions that constitute the poem's second half (in which Chauntecleer is seized by a fox and nearly eaten) rhetoric *becomes* plot when Chauntecleer persuades the fox to open his mouth to speak ('if that I were as ye / Yet shoulde I seyn' [VII.3407-8]). But it is 'the Manciple's Tale' that makes Chaucer's crucial point (and insight) most forcefully insofar as it demonstrates the perils of telling tales by characterising the 'tongue' as a 'swerd' (it 'forkutteth and forkerveth' [IX.340]) and thereby showing plots to be powerful enough to kill. In his mobilising of the power of plot in such extended fables, Chaucer shows how central this form could be to any poet's techniques and purpose by making them central to his own.

17

Religious and Didactic Lyrics

Denis Renevey

In her introduction to *The English Religious Lyric in the Middle Ages* published in 1968, Rosemary Woolf addresses the still ongoing problem of defining the term 'lyric' and the application of this term to medieval religious poetry more specifically:

> It now suggests a poem short, delightful, and melodious, and with a sweetness and light-heartedness that distinguish it from more serious and reflective poems. This description does not fit the religious lyrics. Many of these are long, few were set to music, and all of them are devotionally and didactically serious.[1]

As a sub-category of the lyric genre, the religious lyric does not necessarily fit with the characteristics of the secular lyric, some of which derived from the French secular lyric influenced by the troubadour and trouvères traditions.[2] Some of the religious and didactic lyrics are, as suggested by Woolf, quite long, although some others are surprisingly short. The poetic features and formal devices of an eight-line lyric like *Sainte Marye, Virgine*, by St Godric of Finchale (d. 1170), work quite differently from a long lyric, such as the 172-line *On god ureisun of ure lefdi*, which is part of the thirteenth-century Wooing Group Prayers. However much the length of these works affects the way in which poetic features are used, religious and didactic lyrics are all characterised by their lack of narrative intent. They may occasionally have recourse to events extracted from the Passion narrative or the life of Christ more generally, but they do so in order to generate feeling or convey a point of doctrine, usually with the use of a first-person discourse which the reader will be invited to perform internally. Several religious and didactic lyrics are para-liturgical. Their poetic form and thematic concerns are inspired by liturgical pieces and events, and in that sense these lyrics function as complementary devices to the Latin liturgical pieces whose content they translate and transform for consumption in the Middle English vernacular. As such, these lyrics participate importantly in the making of the large body of affective devotional writing in verse form.

Although there is no figure for the period 1150 to 1400 showing the proportion between religious and secular lyrics, the balance tips strongly in favour of the religious ones.[3] They explore a large number of affective and spiritual states, such as mourning, fear, joy,

---

[1] See Rosemary Woolf, *The English Religious Lyric in the Middle Ages* (Oxford, 1968), 1.

[2] There is no consensus about the definition of the 'medieval English lyric'. Boffey and Whitehead equate Middle English lyrics to short poems, concurring with the New Critical approach which characterised them as 'short, concise, ambiguous, intense and rich in meaning'; see Julia Boffey and Christiania Whitehead (eds), *Middle English Lyrics: New Readings of Short Poems* (Cambridge, 2018) and Ardis Butterfield, 'Why Medieval Lyric', *ELH* (2015), 325.

[3] Boffey and Whitehead, based on Robbins, offer the approximate number of 2,000 lyrics between 1066 and 1500. This chapter is greatly indebted to the introduction in Boffey and Whitehead. For an anthology presenting lyrics from 1200 to 1400, see Thomas G. Duncan (ed.), *Medieval English Lyrics 1200–1400* (New York, 1995).

Denis Renevey, *Religious and Didactic Lyrics*. In: *The Oxford History of Poetry in English*. Edited by Helen Cooper and Robert R. Edwards, Oxford University Press. © Denis Renevey (2023). DOI: 10.1093/oso/9780198827429.003.0017

258 MEDIEVAL POETRY: 1100–1400

celebration, compassion, praise, and ecstasy.[4] These specific states emerge from the exploration by vernacular authors of public interiorities—that is, pieces of language in the form of texts or speeches that lyric writers, and subsequently their readers, redeploy, revoice, and to which therefore they give a new resonance.[5] The way in which lyrics reinvent, literally revoice, these public interiorities found in the liturgy and affective devotional literature, by means of formal devices such as prosody, verse form, diction, and imagery, is one of the main concerns of this chapter. Thus, the revoicing of public interiorities and its attribution to the speaker of the poem, which can be appropriated by the reader, differentiate medieval (religious) lyrics from the modern later ones in which individuation predominates.

Modern editions highlight the significance of manuscript context and the way it affected the reading or singing of some of the lyrics. Some recent scholarship has gone one step further in producing editions of lyrics from specific manuscripts, or even editing the whole manuscript.[6] Together with the digitalisation of medieval manuscripts containing lyrics, both religious and secular, such editorial enterprises have made possible an understanding of the manuscript context for a much larger readership. This in turn has led scholars and readers in general to become much more sensitive to the notion of lyric sequence and to take that aspect into consideration when assessing the way in which lyrics invent their subject matter according to formal devices.[7] Combining assessment of poetic form within a broader manuscript context yields new understandings about the role of the medieval lyric, to the point of interrogating the categories in which we have neatly placed them. For instance, does a reading of a sequence of lyrics such as found in London, British Library, MS Harley 2253, support the traditional division of lyrics into secular and religious?[8] And how does one negotiate lyric voice and public interiority in a sequence of lyrics that moves from Latin to the French and English vernaculars, from secular to political to devotional? And how does poetic form impact within a manuscript that contains both prose and verse texts in relatively equal measure? These ways of interrogating Middle English lyrics need therefore to be taken into consideration when looking at the poetic features of the religious and didactic lyrics that span the period from 1150 to 1400.

Early Northern Middle English Lyrics

London, British Library, MS Royal 5 F. vii points to scribal interest in arranging early Middle English lyrics as a sequence. The three hymns attributed to Godric but recorded in his Latin *vita* written by Reginald of Durham in the following decade, are among the first examples

---

[4] John Hirsh (ed.), *Medieval Lyric: Middle English Lyrics, Ballads, and Carols* (Oxford, 2005), covers some of these themes.

[5] See David Lawton, *Voice in Later Medieval English Literature: Public Interiorities* (Oxford, 2017), 8.

[6] See, for instance, Susanna Greer Fein, David Raybin, and Jan Ziolkowski (eds and trans.), *The Complete Harley 2253 Manuscript*, 3 vols. (Kalamazoo, MI, 2014–15).

[7] Although beyond the scope of the period defined for this volume, the sequence of lyrics as found in Oxford, Bodleian Library, MS Digby 102, as well as the sequence of short poems found in London, British Library, MS Harley 682 (Charles d'Orléans's *Fortune Stabilnes*), offer fascinating material for the development of our understanding of 'short poem sequences' in the late medieval period; see Helen Barr (ed.), *The Digby Poems: A New Edition of the Lyrics* (Exeter, 2009) and Mary-Jo Arn (ed.), *Fortunes Stabilnes: Charles of Orleans's English Book of Love: A Critical Edition* (Binghamton, NY, 1994).

[8] Boffey and Whitehead convey in their introduction the suggestion by the editors of MS Harley 2253 for us to get rid of categories such as 'political lyric, courtly love lyric, and so on'; see Boffey and Whitehead, *Middle English Lyrics*, 9; and David Fuller, 'Lyrics, Sacred and Secular', in Corinne Saunders (ed.), *A Companion to Medieval Poetry* (Oxford, 2010), 258–76.

RELIGIOUS AND DIDACTIC LYRICS   259

of early Middle English lyric poetry written in a Northern dialect.[9] Here is one of the three lyrics, the original four-line Marian lyric attributed to Godric:

Sainte Marye, Virgine,
Moder Jesu Cristes Nazarene,
Onfo*, schild*, help þin Godric,   *receive; shield*
Onfang*, bring heȝilich* wið þe in Godes ric*. *and received; honourably; kingdom* (1–4)

This brief poem, made up originally of one four-line stanza, is the earliest extant Middle English Marian lyric. Rather than following an alliterative pattern derived from the Old English tradition, the stanza, with irregular lines rhyming *aabb* and with the off rhyme '-ine'/'-ene', offers in its first two lines, following the invocation of 'Sainte Marye', a sequence of qualifiers in praise of the Virgin. The sequence delays the expression of agency that the main verb defines for the Virgin. However, once the suspension of expectation is released, the poem defines the speaker as imploring her to welcome, protect, and help him. The delay in grammatically resolving the first couplet is compensated by the offering of these three verbs, 'onfo, schild, help', as a sequence, with no direct object disrupting it. Such construction registers a strong sense of the need for the speaker to receive the attention of the Virgin. The pun falling on the last two lines, with 'Godric' rhyming with 'Godes ric', allows for the lyric to affirm the ambitious goal that the speaker wishes to attain with the support of the Virgin. The lyric ends here in most versions, but the version found in MS Royal 5 F. vii adds a second stanza, which formally mirrors the first one:[10]

Sainte Marye, Cristes bur*,   *bower*
Maidenes clenhad*, moderes flur*,   *purity; blossom*
Dilie* mine sinne, rixe* in min mod*,   *blot out; reign; mind*
Bring me to winne* wið þe self* God.   *bliss; self-same* (5–8)

The stanza begins with the same invocation, followed by a set of qualifiers that develop further the Virgin's miraculous motherhood. They are followed in the third line by three main verbs, therefore structurally imitating the construction of the first stanza. However, in this stanza, each verb is immediately followed by its complement and the reference to the speaker in the form of personal pronouns, who stands for Godric or possibly the reader that could appropriate the lyric for his/her own use.[11] The rhyme of the last two verses, on 'mod' and 'God', echoes the penultimate syllable of the final rhyme of the preceding stanza, thus successfully contributing to the coherence of the hymn. The gloss to the hymn to St Mary as found in the *vita* insists on the role played by the Virgin in teaching Godric the lines, thus attributing Marian agency for the composition of the hymn.[12] The addition of the second stanza in MS Royal 5 F. vii attests to the way formal features of the source text participate

---

[9] See Elaine Treharne (ed.), *Old and Middle English: An Anthology* (Oxford, 2000), 272; references are to this edition, given by line numbers.

[10] See Helen Deeming, 'The Songs of St Godric: A Neglected Context', *Music and Letters*, 86 (2005), 176.

[11] The Latin version that follows the Middle English one in Cambridge, Cambridge University Library, MS Mm.4.28 has replaced the name Godric with 'N', therefore inviting speakers to have their name instead, and thus participating in the reward promised to anyone invoking the Virgin. It is interesting that the process of substitution is made where the pun 'Godric'/'Godrices' is absent in the Latin version; see Deeming, 'The Songs of St Godric', 174.

[12] I am grateful to Whitehead who made her unpublished paper, 'The Marian Voice: Female Pedagogy and Laudation in the Early Vernacular Hymns of Godric of Finchale and the *Meditaciones* of the Monk of Farne', available to me. The *vita* by Reginald of Durham contains only the first stanza. The second stanza may be a later addition.

260 MEDIEVAL POETRY: 1100–1400

in the reinvention of the subject matter, with the hymn rejigged from a prayer for salvation to Godric to an invocation to the Virgin available to the reader.

The two-line hymn that precedes this short Marian lyric in MS Royal 5 F. vii complicates further the way female agency partakes in the composition of these early Middle English lyrics: 'Crist and Sainte Marie swa on scamel [crutch] me iledde [carried] / Þat Ic on þis erðe ne silde [had to] wið mine bare fote itredie [tread]' (1–2).[13] By claiming that Godric is only reporting words that were sung by the spirit of Godric's sister Burgwine, during a vision reassuring him of her being saved, the two-line lyric stands as a composition that was transmitted to him by his sister's spirit, which Godric memorised and wrote down or transmitted orally to a scribe. Composed of two long irregular verses with imperfect rhymes ('iledde' and 'itredie'), the first line reinvents Psalm 98.5: 'Exaltate Dominum Deum nostrum / Et adorate scabellum pedum eius / Quoniam sanctum est' ('Exalt ye the Lord our God / And adore his footstool; / for it is holy'). Where the Psalm ends by claiming the sanctity of His altar, the hymn instead redirects the content of the verse to showcase Burgwine's personal spiritual achievement. Although not of Marian origin, the lyric purports to render a female voice in the English vernacular reinventing the Latin liturgical tradition. The hymns of MS Royal 5 F. vii may very well have been sung by northern Cistercian monks at Rievaulx or Fountains in the thirteenth century, at a moment when the cult of the Virgin and report of her miracles were flourishing in the Cistercian milieu. They blend elements of eremitic, Benedictine, and Cistercian spiritual culture, allowing the emergence of female lyrical voices ventriloquised by Godric and all subsequent performers of the hymns. They posit the significance of female lyrical voice in the history of religious poetry in English, which is further complicated by its male impersonation in this specific case.

The role played by the Virgin and Burgwine for the composition of these two hymns demonstrates the way in which the hymns transform a devotion to Godric into an invocation of the Virgin for the former and reinvent public interiorities based on Psalm 98.5 for the latter. The additional stanza that is added to the original hymn to the Virgin in MS Royal 5 F. vii refashions it by mimicking the formal characteristics of the original stanza. It attests to the multifaceted compositional invention that characterises religious lyrics, more particularly devotional lyrics. Their form calls for transformation, invention, and even contestation of the genre in which they are couched. Besides a rhyme scheme rather than the alliterative pattern characteristic of Old English poetry, the two hymns also form a mini-sequence on folio 85 recto of the manuscript, which includes musical annotation for each of them.[14] The folio, added later, now forms a cover page to the fourth and final booklet, which probably dates from the first quarter of the thirteenth century. The hymns preface the first section of this fourth booklet, from folio 85 recto to folio 118 verso, which is made up of the *Vita S. Godrici* and the *Letter to Godric*.[15] It is not impossible that the early northern Middle English may have proved difficult to read for a later readership; indeed, an interlinear Latin translation of the first stanza of the hymn to St Mary in a fourteenth-century hand seems to

---

[13] The lyrics in London, British Library, MS Royal 5.F.vii are taken out of their initial hagiographicnarrative context. The relationship between 'crutch' and the psalm's 'footstool' is presumably a reference to those little stool-shaped hand-held props held by a crawling cripple.

[14] See Treharne, *Old and Middle English*, 272; London, British Library, MS Royal 5.F.vii, folio 85r is available at the following address: https://www.bl.uk/catalogues/illuminatedmanuscripts/record. asp?MSID=6026&CollID=16&NStart=50607 (last accessed 14.12.2019).

[15] For a discussion of the hymns, see Deeming, 'The Songs of St Godric', 169–85; for a discussion of London, British Library, MS Royal 5.F.vii, fol. 85r, see 176–8.

point to this possibility.[16] The content of the manuscript as a whole bears the influence of Cistercian spirituality, with its first three parts containing works by Bernard of Clairvaux or attributed to him in the medieval period. The final section, from folio 119 recto to 138 verso, is devoted to the legend of the miraculous image of the Virgin at Sardenay. At whatever stage the parts of the manuscripts were put together, the Marian connection between the second hymn by Godric and the Sardenay legend is worth noting. Both emphasise the special relationship between the eremitic life and the Virgin Mary. The Sardenay legend features a noble lady living in a hermitage near Damascus who asks a monk from Constantinople to bring her back from Jerusalem an image of the Virgin. After several adventures involving forgetfulness and the appropriation of the miraculous image by the monk for his community, the image intervenes so that the monk has no other choice but to bring it to the female hermit, its original sponsor.[17] The hymn to St Mary equally invests the hermit Godric with a special relationship to the Virgin, who, accompanied by Mary Magdalene, teaches him the hymn. This episode, leading to the recording of the first hymn in the three different versions of Godric's *vita*, stands on a folio that complements the life in the Royal manuscript, rather than being part of the narrative.[18] Also, the order of the hymns on the folio does not correspond to the chronology of the episodes as found in the *vita*, which have the episode leading to the composition of the hymn to the Virgin first in the chronology of the events. Several indicators point to an independent circulation of the hymns from the *vita* at an early stage of their existence, which could account for the chronological disruption in MS Royal 5 F. vii.

Whether the result of serendipity or rather careful reconsideration of the best possible order for the lyrics based on thematic and/or spiritual content, the display in MS Royal 5 F. vii stands as attractive evidence of an early mini-sequence with musical annotation. The arrangement highlights Godric's spiritual interactions with female figures, with the hymn of Burgwine sung by her in a vision to him opening the sequence, followed by the hymn to the Virgin. The sequence ends with a hymn to St Nicholas sung by the saint to Godric in the course of a vision of the saint. In this arrangement the Marian hymn becomes literally and thematically the centrepiece of the sequence. It fills the centre of the folio, thus giving the theme of Marian intercessory devotion strong emphasis.

Lyrical Meditations: The Wooing Group

The Wooing Group provides interesting information in the assessment of the parameters that define religious lyrics.[19] *Þe wohunge of ure lauerd, On wel swuðe god ureisun of God almithti, Þe oreisun of seinte Marie, On lofsong of ure louerde,* and *On god ureisun of ure lefdi* circulate in different groupings in four manuscripts dating from the first half of the

---

[16] London, British Library, MS Royal 5.F.vii, fol. 85r, https://www.bl.uk/catalogues/illuminatedmanuscripts/record.asp?MSID=6026&CollID=16&NStart=50607 (last accessed 14.12.2019).

[17] See Hans Belting, *Likeness and Presence: A History of the Image before the Era of Art*, trans. Edmund Jephcott (Chicago, IL, 1996), 310.

[18] For more details about the hymns in the other extant manuscripts, see Deeming, 'The Song of St Godric', 172–80; for a discussion of the French version of the *vita*, see Alexandra Barratt, 'The Lyrics of St Godric: A New Manuscript', *Notes and Queries*, n.s. 32, 230 (1985), 439–45.

[19] See Catherine Innes-Parker (ed.), *The Wooing of our Lord and The Wooing Group Prayers* (Peterborough, ON, 2015). References to the texts of the Wooing Group are to this edition and are given by line numbers. However, rather than following Innes-Parker's practice of punctuation, which aims to reproduce medieval pointing, I have modernised it when necessary; see also W. Meredith Thompson (ed.), *Þe Wohunge of Ure Lauerd*, EETS o.s. 241 (Oxford, 1958).

262   MEDIEVAL POETRY: 1100–1400

thirteenth century.[20] With the exception of the last meditation, they are written with a female performer in mind, and have been associated with the kind of anchoritic readership for whom *Ancrene Wisse* was written, and with which some of the lyrical pieces keep manuscript company. These lyrical meditations, with the exception of *On gud ureisun of ure lefdi*, are usually considered as prose. And yet they share so many features with poetic texts that they complicate further the questions of lyric as a poetic genre and generic change.[21] The Wooing Group pieces have many affinities with the Anselmian tradition and more particularly with Anselm's own prayers and meditations. These continuities, formal, thematic and expressive, whose prayers and meditations are couched in complex rhymed prose, illuminate the situatedness of the Wooing Group as a literary production blurring the lines between prose and poetry.[22] *Þe wohunge of ure lauerd* is a good case in point:

> Ihesu swete ihesu,
> mi druð*,   *dearest*
> mi derling,
> mi drihtin*,   *lord*
> mi healend*,   *saviour*
> mi huniter*,   *my honey drop*
> mi haliwei*,   *my healing balm*
> Swetter is munegunge* of þe   *memory; nectar*
> þen mildeu* o muðe.
> Hwane mei luue þi luueli leor*?   *face* (1–9)

Anaphora characterises this piece, as demonstrated with this brief extract which emphasises the personal affective relationship of the speaker (repetition of 'mi') with Jesus. Alliteration is prevailing as well in this passage, even if used more loosely in some other parts of the meditation. As stated in the epilogue, the reader/performer is invited to perform the lyrical meditation thoughtfully, 'on eise', giving each word the right kind of attention so that meaning can be sifted from some of its metaphorical utterances derived from the tradition of the Song of Songs.[23] The author of *Þe Wohunge* means to offer a piece that is rhetorically powerful. For that he uses poetic devices and metaphorical language without necessarily intending to formally compose poetry.[24]

On god ureisun of ure lefdi stands as an exception as part of the Wooing Group: it is undoubtedly poetry. However, because of its rhymed and metred couplets, its imagery, poetic style, and male monastic narrative voice, it is excluded by Thompson from the group.[25] Indeed, unlike the other Wooing Group pieces which use alliteration, *On god ureisun of ure Lefdi* is written in unalliterated rhymed couplets of uneven lengths. The lyric,

---

[20] See Innes-Parker (ed.), *The Wooing*, 19–20.

[21] For a general discussion about lyric as genre, see Jonathan Culler, *Theory of the Lyric* (Cambridge, MA, 2015), 39–90.

[22] See Anselm, in Benedicta Ward (trans.), *The Prayers and Meditations of Saint Anselm: With the Proslogion* (London, 1988), 19–20. I explore thematic continuities in my 'Enclosed Desires: A Study of the Wooing Group', in William F. Pollard and Robert Boenig (eds), *Mysticism and Spirituality in Medieval England* (Cambridge, 1997), 39–62.

[23] See Innes-Parker (ed.), *The Wooing*, 112 n. 3.

[24] See Thompson (ed.), *Þe Wohunge*, xxv, who offers evidence in favour of prose. Innes-Parker, n. 3, instead decides to translate the Wooing Group texts as poetry rather than alliterative prose.

[25] See Thompson (ed.), *Þe Wohunge*, xiv n. 1, who excludes it from the group because of its rhymed and metred couplets, and its overall difference. I reinstated it as part of the Wooing Group in, 'Enclosed Desires', 39–62. It is also sometimes excluded altogether from lyric discussion because of its unusual length, as is the case for instance in Donavin's history of Marian Middle English lyric: see Georgiana Donavin, *Scribit Mater: Mary and the Language Arts in the Literature of Medieval England* (Washington, DC, 2012), 221–49.

by highlighting devotion to the Virgin Mary as intercessor and model, contributes to the tradition of devotion to the Virgin already initiated by Godric in his hymn. It partakes of that tradition while adopting stylistic and thematic features borrowed from the French courtly tradition, mediated via Latin and French lyrics and hymns devoted to the Virgin Mary but having its roots in the *grand chant courtois* of the *trouvères*. The following lines express powerfully the complete state of devotion of the speaker to his lady, a feature that is mirrored in secular lyrics:[26]

> Mi leoue lif urom þine luue ne schal me no þing to dealen,
> Vor oðe is al ilong mi lif ant eke min heale.
> Vor þine luue i swinke ant sike wel ilome,
> Vor þine luue ich ham ibrought in to þeoudome,
> Vor þine luue ich uorsoc al þet me leof was,
> And ȝef ðe al mi suluen; looue lif, iþench þu þes:
> Þet ich ðe wreðede sume siðe hit me reoweð sore. (95–101)

> (Nothing will part me from your love, love of my life,
> For all my life and my salvation depend on you.
> I labour and often sigh for your love.
> I forsook all that was dear to me for your love,
> And gave you all myself; love's life, consider this.
> That I sometimes angered you, I sorely regret.)

The use of anaphora ('Vor þine luue i' and 'mi'), combined with alliteration on 'luue', 'lif', and 'leof', highlights the affective bond that the speaker expresses towards the lady. 'Þeoudome' mimics the state of service characteristic of the male speaker towards a secular lady. While one should not exclude the influence of the bridal imagery of the Song of Songs tradition, secular motifs shine through as if unmediated by the religious context.[27] Of course, physical characteristics, which are part of the panegyric of the lady, make way for a praise of the lady's spiritual beauty, but the effusive way in which the narrative voice expresses its complete admiration, love, and service to the lady matches that of many *grand chants courtois* in their complete fixation on the service one should devote to the lady:

Þu ert briht* ant blisful* ouer alle wummen,	*bright; blessed*
And god ðu ert, ant gode leof* ouer alle wepmen*.	*well-beloved; men*
Alle meidene were wurðeð* þe one*	*honoured; for you alone*
Vor þu ert hore* blostme* biuoren godes trone.	*their; blossom*
Nis no wummon iboren þet ðe beo iliche*,	*similar to*
Ne non þer nis þin efning* wið inne heoueriche*.	*equal; heaven's kingdom*
Heih is þi kinestol*, onuppe* cherubine,	*throne; above*
Biuoren ðine leoue* sune, wiðinnen seraphine.	*dear*
Murie dreameð* engles biuoren þin onsene*,	*rejoice; presence*
Pleieð ant sweieð* ant singeð bitweonen.	*make melody*
Swuðe wel ham likeð biuoren þe to beonne,	
Vor heo neuer ne beoð sead* þi ueir* to iseonne*.	*weary; beauty; see* (19–30)

[26] See Paul Zumthor, *Essai de poétique médiévale* (Paris, 1972).
[27] The Song of Songs tradition is, however, more immediately recognisable in some other Wooing Group pieces, such as *Þis is on wel swuðe god ureisun of God almihti* and *Þe wohunge of ure lauerd*.

264   MEDIEVAL POETRY: 1100–1400

Angels contribute to the praise of the Virgin with music and song, while other 'cristene men' are invited to join in such worship. The splendour of the Virgin, her beauty, and her superiority over all other women, are obviously generic and spiritual. As can be expected in a poem that makes constant recourse to superlatives, ineffability expressed by means of negative statements serves to describe the generosity of the heavenly queen:

Nei mei non heorte þenchen, ne nowiht arechen*,	*explain*
Ne no muð imelen*, ne no tunge tegen*,	*utter; ordain*
Hu muchel god ðu ȝeirkest* wið inne paradise	*prepare*
Ham þet swinkeð* dei ant niht i ðine seriuse.	*toil*
Al þin hird* is ischrud* mid hwite ciclatune*	*retinue; dressed; silk and gold*
And alle heo beoð ikruned mid guldene* krune.	*golden*
Heo beoð so read* so rose, so hwit so þe lilie,	*red*
And euer more heo beoð gled ant singeð þuruhut* murie*.	*most; merrily* (47–54)

The rhyming pattern on the words 'paradise' and 'seruise', 'ciclatune' and 'krune' heightens the use of secular courtly imagery for a heavenly setting. Although the lyric does not celebrate the coronation of the Virgin directly, which gained in popularity in the twelfth century, the imaginary textual representations suggest such a setting (see, for instance, the reference to 'holi heouene kwene' ['heaven's holy queen']) and were very possibly influenced by the emergence of visual representations of her coronation, which constituted the fifth of the five joys of the Virgin in western Europe.[28] The Virgin's intercessory function is limited to a few passages that shift attention away from the Virgin's current heavenly location to her physical position at the foot of the cross during the crucifixion. So, the Virgin is not the mediating figure that may bring the narrative voice closer to her son, nor is she the model that the performer of the lyric could emulate. She is the object of attention of a persona that wants to develop a special loving relationship with the Virgin, with very little emphasis on her motherhood but great attention to her regal figure, beauty, and power. The sinner is the undeserving lover of the courtly tradition, whose hopeless service to a taxing lady is echoed by the protagonist's sinful sense of inferiority in this piece. And yet, in a moment of seemingly uncontrolled boldness, the protagonist establishes a possessive reciprocity with the Virgin, stated anaphorically as: 'Mi lif is þin mi luue is þin mine heorte blod is þin / And ȝif ich der seggen mi leoue [beloved] leafdi þu ert min' (157–8). The shift from 'mi/þin', repeated twice, to 'mi/þu/min' triggers an audacious move on the part of the speaker who concludes his transaction by cautiously claiming ownership of the Virgin.

This lyric is indeed quite distinct from the other Wooing Group texts, with their alliterative system and protagonists whose love for Christ can easily be associated with female narrators expressing their love from a perspective of enclosure. Here instead the narrator unambiguously reveals his monastic status in his call that the Virgin bring him to her blessedness. A few lines earlier he makes reference to his 'ureondmen' (167), which I would translate as 'male friends', peculiarly translated by Innes-Parker as 'brothers and sisters' in view of the feminine audience of the other Wooing Group texts. But the male monastic protagonist of this lyrical sequence, possibly a Cistercian in view of the order's early interest in the devotion to the Virgin, and the reference to his male brotherhood, together with the

---

[28] See Innes-Parker (ed.), *The Wooing*, 156–7; see also Annie Sutherland's excellent close reading of this lyric in 'The Unlikely Landscapes of *On God Ureisun of Ure Lefdi*', in Boffey and Whitehead (eds), *Middle English Lyrics*, 73–86.

difference in poetic style from the other Wooing Group texts, should not lead us to exclude the poem from it, but rather redefine the group as a more composite, possibly less strictly anchoritic group of lyrics, which both echoes the earlier tradition of devotion to the Virgin exposed by St Godric and, in the case of *On god ureisun of ure lefdi*, loosely imitates the French secular continental tradition. The 'I-voice' emphasises further the lyrical tradition to which this piece belongs by calling it an English lay and stressing twice in the last five lines that the piece, as it reaches completion, has been sung for the attention of the narrator's beloved lady. Although the use of the term 'lai' (168) easily prompts reference to the well-known tradition of the lais as written by Marie de France, the textual dynamics engendered by the tension between the lady and the lover support a meaning of 'lai' as song or lyric.[29] *On god ureisun of ure lefdi* stands as an accomplished English transposition of the psychology of secular love exchanges between lover and beloved to a religious context. The accommodation of these strategies to the English religious context broadens the extent to which the notion of service to the lady expressed by the speaker can be performed by readers practising the religious life in various forms, either individually or as part of a religious community. Its inclusive characteristics make it suitable as part of a group of lyrical meditations for a female readership. No doubt female performers of the Wooing Group texts would unproblematically pass over references to the male voice and the monastic brotherhood for which the poem was originally written. But the adjective 'englissce' (168), combined with 'lai', highlights an awareness by the author of inventing a panegyric of the Virgin Mary in the English language, in contrast to the Latin and French (including Anglo-Norman) traditions.[30] The poet seems to be cognisant of these traditions and conscious of contributing a significant and innovative literary piece to the emerging English vernacular devotion to the Virgin Mary in the early thirteenth century.

The Whole Book Approach and Lyrical Form: MS Harley 2253

MS Harley 2253 has long been known as the manuscript containing more than half of Middle English secular lyrics from before the end of the fourteenth century.[31] More recently, its multilingual characteristics, the arrangements of some of its lyrics into sequences, and the 'whole book' approach to textual scholarship, allow new interpretations of the religious and penitential lyrics within the manuscript.[32] The latter consists of seven booklets, copied by three scribes, but with the second scribe responsible for most of the manuscript, from booklet three (fol. 49r) to the end of the last booklet with a Latin prose text as the last item (fol. 140v). The second scribe is at ease with the three languages spoken on English soil in the early fourteenth century—that is Latin, French, and English. Indeed, booklet four, entirely copied by this scribe, contains verse in those three languages. The 'whole book' approach shows the manuscript to be thematically eclectic, with a broad range of topics

---

[29] Innes-Parker (ed.), *The Wooing*, 161 n. 1, emphasises too much the context of the Breton lais of Marie de France as an influence *On god ureisun of ure lefdi*.

[30] Sutherland, 'The Unlikely Landscapes', 85, emphasises the combination of continental tradition with innovativeness of form and language; see also her interesting discussion of the possible pun on 'englene londe' in the following paragraphs.

[31] G. L. Brook (ed.), *The Harley Lyrics: The Middle English Lyrics of MS. Harley 2253* (Manchester, 1978), xiii.

[32] See Boffey and Whitehead, *Middle English Lyrics*, 8–9; see also Rory G. Critten, 'The Multilingual English Household in a European Perspective: London, British Library MS Harley 2253 and the Traffic of Texts', in Glenn D. Burger and Rory G. Critten (eds), *Household Knowledges in Late-Medieval England and France* (Manchester, 2019), 219–43.

266   MEDIEVAL POETRY: 1100–1400

intended to entertain and educate a household. But even a cursory look at the contents of the manuscript reveals its strong religious focus, with several saints' lives, moral and religious epistles, masses, prayers, and religious lyrics.[33] The composite nature of the manuscript suggests a household audience interested in different spheres of knowledge, including scientific and technical texts, such as the seven recipes for the making of paints used for book illuminators. But such a broad-based perspective attempting the satisfaction of the different tastes and needs of individuals constituting a household shows as well in the selection of religious lyrics offered in the manuscript. As the arrangement of the religious lyrics in MS Harley 2253 is not programmatic, it suggests rather a collection from which each reader would pick, read, and perform the lyrics according to his/her specific spiritual need and maturity at a particular moment.

The penitential tone of *Heye Louerd, thou here my bone* does not as such limit its recipients to a secular audience.[34] The lyric is made up of six stanzas related to tail-rhyme in form, five of seventeen alliterating lines, structured either as four—or three-stress lines, combined to a complex five-rhyme scheme, and ending with a five-line stanza. The persona, an old man, reflects on his early life led among the wealthy and the powerful but marked by sinful activities. The first stanza omits reference to any religious form of life, and the nostalgic glance at the past with the moral comment 'Fol [fool] Ich wes, in folies fayn [pleased]' (7) suggests an old man no longer favourably welcomed in wealthy secular households. The joylessness of the persona, the loss of social marker and hence of power, recall the situation of exile as described in Old English elegiac literature, as in *The Wanderer*. Here, though, exile is not experienced by spatial displacement, but by mocking disempowerment: 'Ne semy [suited] nout ther Y am set: / Ther me calleth me "fulle-flet" [floor-filler] / Ant "waynoun-wayteglede" [good for nothing fire-gazer]!' (15–17). It is literally *in situ* that psychological exile and disempowerment take place. Nostalgic reflections on deprivation and loss are pursued further with reference to horsemanship: not only is the persona no longer able to ride lofty horses, but he has to use a staff while going about hesitatingly in the hall. The persona is now deprived of performing other empowering gestures or activities such as finger clasping, surely a reference to an amorous gesture towards someone else, which is mentioned twice, once in the second stanza, 'Nou Y may no fynger folde [clasp]' (21), and repeated in the third, with 'Ant mey no fynger felde' (40). The speaker's inability to clasp his fingers emphasises his diminishing physical strength, his failure in closing his fingers around objects or people.

The loss of pleasures and power is imputed to old age up to the end of the third stanza, with no reference to moral weakness bearing responsibility for the deterioration of the life situation of the persona. Moral and religious concerns appear only in the last two lines of the third stanza, with the 'why' question addressed to God, expressing ultimate sorrow and sadness and concluding the 'Ubi sunt' motif of this first half of the lyric. The tone of the poem shifts from the expression of loss of material pleasure, wealth, and power to a morally depraved life led through subservience to the seven deadly sins. If the abrupt shift from old age and its disadvantages to an infamous life is anomalous, the continuity in the use of household imagery from one part to the other allays it significantly. Each sin is personified as one of the persona's companions: gluttony is his minstrel, pride his playmate, lechery his

---

[33] See Fein, Raybin, and Ziolkowski (eds), *The Complete Harley 2253 Manuscript*: https://d.lib.rochester.edu/teams/text/fein-harley2253-volume-2-appendix (last accessed 08.11.2019). References to the lyrics of the Harley Manuscript are to this edition and are given by line numbers.

[34] See Vincent Gillespie, 'Moral and Penitential Lyrics', in Thomas G. Duncan (ed.), *A Companion to the Middle English Lyric* (Cambridge, 2005), 68–95; Gillespie, 76–7 has a brief discussion of *Heye Louerd, thou here my bone*.

laundress, covetousness his porter, envy and anger his companions, liar his interpreter, sloth and sleep his bedfellows. Such personifications would be familiar to a secular reader, more particularly to a wealthy householder whose familiarity with these roles would resonate with his day-to-day existence.

Apart from its complex rhyme scheme with alliteration and concatenation, the lyric offers a fascinating account of a persona's ongoing struggle with the lure of sinful activity. It consists in part in the honest account of the persona's difficulties giving up the pleasures of the life of a late medieval retainer:

Sunnes bueth unsete*!	*unattractive*
Godes heste* ne huld* Y noht,	*command; uphold*
Bote ever ageyn is* wille Y wroht*;	*his; acted*
Mon lereth* me to lete*!	*teaches; too late*
Such serewe* hath myn sides thurhsoht*	*sorrow; pierced through*
That al Y weolewe* away to noht,	*wither*
When Y shal murthes* mete*.	*pleasure; encounter*
To mete murthes Ich wes wel fous*,	*eager*
Ant comely* mon to calle	*fine*
(Y sugge* by other ase bi* ous*),	*speak; as well as; me*
Alse ys hirmon* halt* in hous,	*retainer; regarded*
Ase heued* hount* in halle.	*chief; huntsman* (74–85)

Sins are in fact attractive, and this chief huntsman has been fighting against their appeal up to his old age. Is the desire for death the result of a serious and honest self-examination that shows him to have succeeded in renouncing worldly pleasures, or is it rather the dissatisfaction of not being able to enjoy them any longer, due to a body that is letting him down ('I falewe [wither] as flour ylet forthfare [left to die]') (90)? The persona hesitatingly, and perhaps *faute de mieux*, envisions the religious dimension in preparation for his death and for the afterlife. This moving account encompasses a psychological state that could be performed and revoiced by readers. It bears similarities with another item in MS Harley 2253, *Herkne to my ron*, a 275-line long poem offering an old man's perspective on life.[35] Other collections of penitential and moral lyrics, such as the Vernon manuscript and its companion volume, the Simeon manuscript (London, British Library, MS Additional 22,283), offer another version of *Herkne to my ron*.[36] The Old Man's Lament is therefore a staple penitential theme that underwent minimal transformation from the Anglo-Saxon period to the early modern period.[37] It asks questions about our broad categorisation in terms of secular or religious, as well as more thematic divisions. Indeed, the old man's lament type of lyric easily crosses these boundaries, as it can opt to emphasise its secular dimension by highlighting the physical weakening of the body and the loss of social status into old age, or refashion itself by adding a moral dimension coloured by reference to the lure of the seven deadly sins, as is the case in the second part of *Heye Louerd, thou here my bone*.

---

[35] It is influenced by the tradition of the *Elegies* attributed to Maximianus, a poet thought to have lived in the sixth century and to have been a friend of Boethius; see Fein, Raybin, and Ziolkowski (eds), *The Complete Harley 2253 Manuscript*, and Woolf, *The English Religious Lyric*, 105.

[36] For information on the Vernon manuscript, see Derek Pearsall (ed.), *Studies in the Vernon Manuscript* (Cambridge, 1990).

[37] For a history of the lament genre and different types of lament, see Anne L. Klinck, 'Singing a Song of Sorrow: Tropes of Lament', in Jane Tolmie and M. Jane Toswell (eds), *Laments for the Lost in Medieval Literature* (Turnhout, 2010), 1–20.

268 MEDIEVAL POETRY: 1100–1400

The eclecticism of MS Harley 2253 is notable as a whole, but also by the variety of its lyrics and lyrical poems, with secular and religious themes, as well as its multilingual dimension. The Anglo-Norman song *Ferroy chaunsoun* combines its three-stanza secular topic of love for the absent lover with a prayer to God and St Thomas, which stands for the refrain and offers forgiveness to the female character.[38] The following lyric, *Dum ludis floribus*, blends Latin and Anglo-Norman to offer a macaronic lyric full of linguistic playfulness expressing ribald thoughts about the desire for the beloved: 'Dieu la moi doint sua misericordia, / Beyser e fere que secuntur alia' ('May God grant her to me by his mercy, / To kiss and to do the other things that follow' [15–16]).[39] Yet, a previous lyric, *Charnel amour est folie*, warns its Anglo-Norman and English readership about the brief pleasure experienced by lechery, in contrast to eternal torment. Some of the lyrics of MS Harley 2253 seem to mediate the transference of focus from secular to religious love. These lyrics, in English, Anglo-Norman, or in a bilingual form, may be normative in the way they make possible psychological shifts from secular to religious concerns. Another 176-line-long lyrical poem, *Quant fu en ma juvente*, equally positioned in the manuscript to facilitate psychological transformation, reflects from the standpoint of an experienced persona on the delusion of worldly pleasures before moving on to a presentation of Jesus as a true lover.[40] A small group of lyrics from *Quant fu en ma juvente* onwards explores devotional poses linked to the life of Christ, his mother, and the devotion to his name.[41]

For instance, the lyric *Jesu, suete is the love of the*, also headed *Dulcis Jesu memoria*, whose Latin title provided by the scribe is borrowed from the lyric attributed to Bernard of Clairvaux but most likely written by a Cistercian monk on English soil, is part of the large body of material devoted to the Name of Jesus.[42] Harley 2253 offers several lyrics inspired by the devotion to the Name and hence contributes to its circulation in the early fourteenth century.[43] The lyric precedes an Anglo-Norman Marian lyric and is fully integrated into the devotional group that focuses on the humanity of Jesus. Unlike some other Name of Jesus lyrics that exclusively explore the linguistic potential of the Name, *Jesu, suete is the love of the*, although beginning each of its forty-eight and a half stanzas with 'Jesu', focuses on the Name of Jesus and his humanity rather than exclusively focusing on the former. The first two stanzas make use of the name Jesus:

> Jesu, suete is the love of the.
> Nothing so suete may be:
> Al that may with eyen se
> Haveth no suetnesse ageynes* the!   *beside*

[38] See Fein, Raybin, and Ziolkowski (eds), *The Complete Harley 2253 Manuscript*: https://d.lib.rochester.edu/camelot/text/fein-harley2253-volume-2-article-54 (last accessed 30.11.19).
[39] See Fein, Raybin, and Ziolkowski, (eds), *The Complete Harley 2253 Manuscript*: https://d.lib.rochester.edu/camelot/text/fein-harley2253-volume-2-article-55 (last accessed 01.12.19).
[40] See Fein. Raybin, and Ziolkowski (eds), *The Complete Harley 2253 Manuscript*: https://d.lib.rochester.edu/camelot/text/fein-harley2253-volume-2-article-56 (last accessed 01.12.19).
[41] For a recent study of the devotion to the Name of Jesus, see Denis Renevey, *Devotion to the Name of Jesus in Medieval English Literature, c. 1100–c. 1530* (Oxford, 2022).
[42] For a discussion of the Latin *Dulcis Iesu memoria*, see Helen Deeming, 'Music and Contemplation in the Twelfth-Century *Dulcis Jesu Memoria*', *Journal of the Royal Musical Association*, 139 (2014), 1–39 and Denis Renevey, 'Anglo-Norman and Middle-English Translations and Adaptations of the Hymn *Dulcis Iesu Memoria*', in R. Ellis and R. Tixier (eds), *The Medieval Translator*, 5 (Turnhout, 1996), 264–83.
[43] See, for instance, the lyric *Sweet Jesus, King of Bliss* (item 50) and *Jesus Christ, Heaven's King* (item 51).

> Jesu, nothing may be suettere,
> Ne noht in eorthe blysfulere*,   *more blissful*
> Noht may be feled lykerusere*   *more sensuous*
> Then thou, so suete a luviere.   (1–8)

The lyric does not offer a reflection on the power that the repetition of the name 'Jesu' may have. It does not consciously predicate the devotion to the Name. In fact, the iteration of the name 'Jesu' is more an integral part of the devotion to the humanity of Jesus, which the lyric emphasises with the reference to the crucifixion in its third stanza. Apart from its contribution to the emerging devotion to the Name, this lyric also deepens our understanding of the malleability of lyrical form: stanzas from this lyric and several other lyrics devoted to the Name are easily subtracted, expanded, and merged with stanzas originally composed separately from this particular version.[44]

However thematically compact this small group of lyrics, neither MS Harley 2253 nor its booklets provide a tool-kit for progressive spiritual development.[45] Indeed, following *Nou skrinketh rose ant lylie-flour*, which makes subtle use of the lexical field of medicine to portray the salvific role of the Virgin Mary, the next lyric offers in dialogic form an exchange between a cleric and a girl, with the former begging the female protagonist to give in to his request for pity and therefore fulfil all his sexual desires.[46] MS Harley 2253, however, expects its readers to be able to negotiate from one language to another, and to select according to their own personal desires and agenda the most useful reading material that it offers. The design of MS Harley 2253 encourages tolerant and selective reading by a large readership with wide-scale interests.[47]

William Herebert's Commonplace Book

The commonplace book of the Franciscan William Herebert (1270?–1333?), London, British Library, MS Additional 46919, also contributes to the evidence for multilingual communities in early fourteenth-century England. The content of the manuscript is eclectic, with a large number of Anglo-Norman texts, including treatises on venery and falconry, as well as religious lyrics, some of them written by the Franciscan friar Nicholas Bozon.[48] The authorial manuscript is copied in about thirteen different hands, collated by Herebert himself. It contains all the extant writings in Latin and English attributed to him. These include six Latin sermons and nineteen religious lyrics, found at the end of the manuscript, and four additional poems found in the margins of other texts. Most of the Middle English lyrics are relatively close translations of Latin hymns and antiphons.[49] If the rationale behind the arrangement of some of the items found in Herebert's commonplace book is difficult to

---

[44] See Daniel McCann, 'Blood and Chocolate: Affective Layering in *Swete Ihesu, now wil I synge*', in Boffey and Whitehead (eds), *Middle English Lyrics*, 45–56.

[45] Unlike London, British Library, MS Additional 37790, which provides an example of a purpose-built spiritual anthology; see Marleen Cré, *Vernacular Mysticism in the Charterhouse: A Study of London, British Library, MS Additional 37790* (Turnhout, 2006).

[46] See Fein, Raybin, and Ziolkowski (eds), *The Complete Harley 2253 Manuscript*: https://d.lib.rochester.edu/camelot/text/fein-harley2253-volume-2-article-64.

[47] For a discussion of the lyrics of MS Harley 2253, see Nancy Vine Durling, 'British Library MS Harley 2253: A New Reading of the Passion Lyrics in Their Manuscript Context', *Viator*, 40 (2009), 271–307.

[48] For a list of the contents of the manuscript, see Stephen R. Reimer (ed.), *The Works of William Herebert, OFM* (Toronto, 1987), 8–9; references to the lyrics of Herebert are to this edition and are given by line numbers.

[49] See Whitehead, 'Middle English Religious Lyrics', in Duncan (ed.), *A Companion to the Middle English Lyric*, 97.

270   MEDIEVAL POETRY: 1100–1400

understand, the religious lyrics seem to confirm the role they could have played in the dissemination of significant theological lessons offered in sermon form. Equally, in the case of Herebert and possibly other friars, the religious lyrics could have been copied down for private use. The brief four-line poem found at the bottom margin of the first sermon by Herebert has no known source, but it seems to be influenced by sermon fifteen on the Song of Songs by Bernard of Clairvaux, thus contributing to the early circulation of the association of the verse 'oleum effusum nomen tuum' (Canticle 1.4) with the Name of Jesus in Middle English:

Þis nome ys also on honikomb* þat ȝyfþ ous sauour and swetnesse,	*honeycomb*
Ant hyt ys a seollich* nome þat maketh ous wondren hys héynesse,	*remarkable*
Ant hyt ys on holsom* nome þat bryngh ous bóte* of wykkenesse,	*healing; remedy*
Ant hyt ys a nome of lyf þat bryngþ ous ioie and gladsomnesse*.	*happiness* (1–4)

This short lyric is remarkable for its ingenious simplicity, with the end rhyme on 'esse' (*aaaa*) and its simple syntax for each line, with the main clause and relative clause in each line grammatically similar to one another, and with anaphora ('Ant hyt ys') in lines two to four. Such poetic features use syntactic repetition to convey the meditative disposition one should find oneself in in order to practice devotion to the Name of Jesus. This lyric, found in the margin of Herebert's first sermon, could possibly be linked to the role played by the Franciscans who advocated greater reverence and devotion to the Name of Jesus at the Second Council of Lyon in 1274 and who subsequently spread the devotion to the Name of Jesus within their order and beyond.[50]

Some of the lyrics devoted to the Virgin Mary attributed to Herebert are translations of Latin hymns. *Hayl, Leuedy, se-stærre bryht*, for instance, translates the well-known medieval *Ave maris stella*. Another lyric, *Com Shuppere, Holy Gost, ofsech oure þouhtes* is a translation of the Pentecost hymn *Veni creator spiritus*, attributed to Rabanus Maurus (776–856). These examples remind us of the close relationship vernacular lyrics maintain with liturgical performances.[51] There is no known source for the tail-rhyme nine-stanza lyric, *Þou wommon boute uére* [equal], which forms one of the most extensive lyrics from Herebert's collection. The lyric first explores the wonder of the Virgin's conception. To be giving birth to the second person of the Trinity following conception by the Holy Spirit brings about a complete reassessment of the motherly characteristics of the Virgin Mary. The Virgin is mother to the son, but she is also mother to her father, and mother to her brother, as developed by the first stanza. That statement does not lead to further theological discussions, but instead it leads the 'I-voice' to emphasise the strengthening of bonds between it and this tightly knit family unit, which serves to reinforce the Virgin's role as mediatrix between the speaker and Jesus on doomsday. The toning down of the element of fear linked to the Last Judgement is negotiated by the construction of close family relationships between the speaker and Jesus, who has become the 'I-voice's' brother before taking on his role of judge:

[50] See Denis Renevey, 'The Name Poured Out: Margins, Illuminations and Miniatures as Evidence for the Practice of Devotions to the Name of Jesus in Late Medieval England', in James Hogg (ed.), *The Mystical Tradition and the Carthusians*, vol. 9 (Salzburg, 1996), 127–47, especially 129; see also Renevey, *Devotion to the Name of Jesus*, pp. 62–91.
[51] For a study of the close relationship between lyrics and the liturgy, see Katherine Zieman, *Singing the New Song: Literacy, Liturgy, and Literature in Late Medieval England* (Philadelphia, PA, 2008).

Þou my suster and moder,
And þy sone my broþer;
Who shulde þœnne dréde?
Who hauet þe kyng to broder
And ek þe quéne to moder
Wel auhte uor to spéde*. *be successful*

Dame, suster and moder,
Say þy sone, my broþer,
Þat ys domes mon*, *judge*
Þat uor þe þat hym bere
To me bœ debonere*; *that he be gracious to me*
My robe he haueth opon*. *wears (7–18)*

The poem combines assonance and rhyme on the vowel sounds 'suster', 'moder', 'broþer' in the second and third stanzas to highlight the *mater et filia* paradox. 'Dame', repeated three times (lines 13, 32, 37), translates the appreciation of her dignified status by the speaker, who uses it in the last occurrence to call for her help.

The lyrics composed and collated by Herebert at the end of his commonplace book may have served several different functions. Some, such as *Hayl, Leuedy, se-stoerre bryht* or *Com, Shuppere, Holy Gost, ofsech oure þouhtes*, are revoicings of popular hymns.[52] The translation of virginity and the notion of the Virgin as the gateway to heaven from the Latin original in *Hayl, Leuedy* are rendered in a rather heavy-handed way, with the metaphorical expression 'Mayden euer vurst and late, / Of heueneriche sely ʒáte' (3–4). Used as accompaniments and complements to their Latin originals in the context of liturgical performances, aesthetic features and poetic invention may not have been central to the process of composition. Other lyrics, such as *Þis nome ys also on honikomb* and *Þou wommon boute uére*, may have served as complements to liturgical moments, offering para-liturgical pieces that would emotionally strengthen some of the theological points touched upon in the liturgy. The complex reflections on the Trinitarian God and the role played by the Virgin Mary are expressed in paradoxical language that reflects the meditative use this lyric could serve. Equally, these same pieces could have been used for more personal observance, in the household, at a moment when the reader would be inclined to shift his focus from secular (hawking, venery, sewing, household management, etc.) to more spiritual concerns.

Poetic Form and Prose: Richard Rolle, Epistolary Writings, and Lyrics

Rolle's process of composition of lyrics or songs helps in the creation of performative pieces that readers can revoice. Poetic form takes precedence over new content, performance over composition, as is evidenced in the Middle English epistles written towards the end of Rolle's writing career, which make use of earlier texts composed in Latin or Middle English. *Ego Dormio*, *The Commandment*, and *The Form of Living* were written for the attention of a female readership eager to emulate the spiritual accomplishments of Rolle. Of the three epistles, *The Commandment* is the only one not to include songs to be performed by the recipients.

---

[52] See Reimer (ed.), *The Works of William Herebert*, 120–2.

272   MEDIEVAL POETRY: 1100–1400

The Middle English epistles and the *Emendatio vitae* clearly support the contention that Rolle had, by the end of his career, fashioned a system that combines practical advice and tools with highly ambitious spiritual concerns. For instance, *Ego Dormio*, written for a nun of Yedingham Priory in Yorkshire, as the *explicit* indicates, includes lyrics to be performed, as they will help the reader reach the level of spiritual development described in the three degrees of love (insuperable, inseparable, and singular). As such *Ego Dormio* is a very practical tool-kit for the contemplative life, in which the lyrics play a significant role. The third part of *Ego Dormio* describes the third degree of love, called the contemplative life, and ends with what a scribal hand has called the *Cantus Amoris*, which the reader will have 'delyte in when þou ert lufand [loving] Jhesu Criste'.[53] That comment presupposes spiritual preparation for the performative reading of the lyric so that it can bring the reader to the degree described by Rolle. Interestingly but not surprisingly, the invocation of the name 'Jhesu' shows the importance of the devotion as part of his system:

Jhesu, þi lufe es fest*, and me to lufe thynk best.	*fastened*
My hert, when may it brest* to come to þe, my rest?	*burst*
Jhesu, Jhesu, Jhesu, til þe it es þat I morne	
For my lyfe and my lyvyng. When may I hethen* torne?	*hence*
Jhesu, my dere and my drewry*, delyte ert þou to syng.	*sweetheart*
Jhesu, my myrth and melody, when will þou com, my keyng?	
Jhesu, my hele and my hony, my whart* and my comfortyng,	*joy*
Jhesu, I covayte for to dy when it es þi payng.*[54]	*pleasure* (337–44)

The presence of a lyric using the name 'Jhesu' to facilitate the experience of the third degree of love as described in *Ego Dormio* shows the importance of the devotion in Rolle's spiritual system. The lyric ends by situating lyrical performance at the heart of the heavenly activities that the 'I-voice' imagines once it will be reunited with Jesus: 'And I þi lufe sal syng thorow syght of þi schynyng [shining light] / In heven withowten endyng' (362–3). Lyrics in this spiritual system fulfil an essential function in bringing individuals to the highest contemplative state possible. The contrast between the function of prose and poetry is most telling in this piece. While the prose, which makes up the core of the epistle, provides explanatory information about the state implied by the three degrees of love and the spiritual work required to reach them, the poetic features of the lyric partake in affectively uplifting the performer to an ecstatic state. Poetic craftsmanship is impressive in this piece. The lyric, or song, as Rolle calls it, consists of ten stanzas of uneven length, with the iambic hexameter line prevailing. The caesura is clearly apparent, as it is marked by internal rhyme in several lines. Each line of the short four-line seventh stanza begins with 'Ihesu'. The name 'Ihesu' is structurally additional to the otherwise regular iambic hexameter lines of this stanza. This anomaly within the otherwise fairly regular poetic form of the lyric suggests a performance that would be marked by the voicing of 'Ihesu' on its own, marked by a momentary pause and followed by the regular verse. Such performance highlighting the devotion to the name 'Jhesu' would fit with the devotion that the poem tries to emulate.

From this exploration into the period 1150–1400, the following may help in investigating further the medieval lyric. Manuscript studies in general and the 'whole book' approach in

---

[53] See Hope Emily Allen (ed.), *English Writings of Richard Rolle* (Gloucester, 1988), p. 70; references to the lyrics of Richard Rolle are to this edition and are given by line numbers.
[54] See Allen (ed.), *English Writings of Richard Rolle*, 71.

particular provide a new perspective on the different functions assigned to religious lyrics in late medieval England. As in later collections, such as the lyrics of Oxford, Bodleian Library, MS Digby 102, with their hands-on approach to religious and political questions, the division between secular and religious lyrics can sometimes prevent a broader and more encompassing perspective on what lyrics or collections of lyric try to do.[55] Some of the poems in MS Harley 2253 may defy thematic categorisation in a similar way, as do some of the lyrics found in preachers' manuals or in codices designed for the consumption of a small secular unit forming a household community. These collections of lyrics and their possible arrangement within sequences may generate new insights into their function, as individual pieces or as a sequence. A portion of the medieval English readership was linguistically highly competent, enjoying the linguistic move back and forth from Latin to Anglo-Norman or continental French to English, taking the subtleties of each language into account in its making meaning of groups of lyrics or other texts, which were contained in their household copies or which were available from the hands of itinerant Franciscan friars. Public interiority is thus revoiced in multiple languages, and the lyric, itself a flexible poetic genre, is embodied under different linguistic attires. Also, the composition of lyrics must be attended to closely, with special attention paid to the ways in which translation and compilation activity play a significant role in the making of the large corpus of lyrics extant today. The medieval lyric scholarly landscape is changing rapidly with emerging interests in the form and function of the lyrics, their manuscript contexts, their possible multilingual audience, and the kind of theology they purport to convey, to be performed communally or individually.

---

[55] See, for instance, the lyric *The Declaryng of religioun*, in Barr (ed.), *The Digby Poems*, 254–63.

18

Secular Lyrics

Susanna Fein

What defines the Middle English secular lyric is its subject. The word *secular*, from Latin *saeculum*, has a two-dimensional valence: what is material ('of or belonging to the world') and what is temporal ('existing in time').[1] Both dimensions privilege the sensations of day-to-day existence. In essence, the secular lyric records moments in the life of the body—corporeal and utilitarian acts as well as emotional states. Inherently, too, the secular lyric is defined by what it is *not*: it is not the religious lyric, a ubiquitous verse genre that affirms Christian worship and devotion, the life of the spirit.

The well-known *Earth upon Earth*, a lyric that surfaces in many forms across centuries, distils the concerns of the medieval English secular lyric with stark simplicity:

Erthe toc* of erthe erthe wyth woh*;	*took from; woe*
Erthe other* erthe to the erthe droh*;	*another; drew*
Erthe leyde erthe in erthene throh*:	*earthly grave*
Tho hevede* erthe of erthe erthe ynoh*.[2]	*had; enough*

These lines in London, British Library, MS Harley 2253 preserve the lyric formula in its briefest, earliest rendition (*c* 1307).[3] Riddling on the word *erthe*, these enigmatic lines convey a minimalist paradigm of existence. By a plausible decoding, it denotes mortal life as no more than matter. Line 1: a creature enters life (partakes of matter), becoming a mortal doomed to sorrow. Line 2: on the ground, the grown mortal mates with another. Line 3: into the ground, others bury the now-deceased mortal. Line 4: the mortal body returns to dust, 'for dust thou art, and into dust thou shalt return' (Genesis 3.19).[4] A pattern of inception, growth, death, decay is shared by all, to be repeated again and again. Each line advances the process temporally, and, in each, key actions happen prone, that is, grounded ('earthed'). The riddle bleakly paints the sorrowful birth-to-death, dust-to-dust cycle of each person. It also includes the social, as 'erthes' mate with and bury other 'erthes'.[5] The riddle begins in taking and ends in relinquishing.

---

[1] *MED*, s.v. *seculere*, adj., senses 1, 3. Compare Charlton T. Lewis and Charles Short, *A Latin Dictionary*, s.v. *saeculum*, senses B ('the utmost lifetime of a man'), C ('the world, worldliness') (Perseus Digital Library, http://www.perseus.tufts.edu/hopper/text?doc=Perseus%3Atext%3A1999.04.0059%3Aentry%3Dsaeculum).

[2] Susanna Fein (ed. and trans.), with David Raybin and Jan Ziolkowski. *The Complete Harley 2253 Manuscript*, 3 vols. (Kalamazoo, MI, 2014–15), 2:96–7, 387–8 (art. 24b).

[3] Hilda M. R. Murray (ed.), *The Middle English Poem, Erthe upon Erthe, Printed from Twenty-Four Manuscripts*, EETS o.s. 141 (1911; repr. Oxford, 1964); and Nancy P. Pope, '"Erthe upon Erthe" Revisited', *Journal of the Early Book Society*, 21 (2018), 53–95.

[4] Perhaps alluding to the liturgy for Ash Wednesday: 'Remember, O man, that thou art ashes, and unto ashes shalt thou return' ('*Memento homo quod cinis es et in cinerem reverteris*'). See Frederick E. Warren (trans.), *The Sarum Missal in English, Part 1* (London, 1911), 147; and Murray (ed.), *The Middle English Poem, Erthe upon Erthe*, xxxii, 6, 8, 12–13.

[5] Critics have offered a range of interpretations of *Earth*. For example, Rosemary Woolf deflects the sexual valence of line 2: 'Man, whose body is made of earth, is born in sin; in his lifetime he accumulates riches for himself' (*The English Religious Lyric in the Middle Ages* [Oxford, 1968], 85). Russell A. Peck provides a fourfold interpretation, secular and religious: 'Public Dreams and Private Myths: Perspective in Middle English Literature', *PMLA*, 90 (1975), 461–8, at 465–6.

Susanna Fein, *Secular Lyrics*. In: *The Oxford History of Poetry in English*. Edited by Helen Cooper and Robert R. Edwards, Oxford University Press. © Susanna Fein (2023). DOI: 10.1093/oso/9780198827429.003.0018

In the secular lyric, the imaginative resources of poetry are mustered to celebrate or lament the experiences of the body in the world. Taken collectively, these lyrics relay a human's emotional and corporeal, sensory perceptivity of material things. Thus, insofar as poems dwell in the physical and the worldly, they are secular. In the genre of short, non-narrative verse—that is, lyric—the subjects embraced are birth, growth, love, sex, death, decay; good and bad fortune, health, wealth, illness, poverty; natural seasons, quotidian affairs; dancing, drinking, eating, loving, marrying, aging, surviving; and the range of emotions associated with these events and actions: joy, grief, desire, regret, hope, despair. The substance of all lyrics classed as 'secular' concerns the body—its senses and pleasures, also its losses and deprivations, and even its extinction, as in signs-of-death lyrics (*c* 1250):

Hwenne thin heou bloketh*,	*hue grows pale*
And thi strengthe woketh*,	*weakens*
And thi neose coldeth,	
And thi tunge voldeth,	
And the byleveth* thi breth,	*leaves you*
And thi lif the atgeth*,	*departs from you*
Me nymeth the nuthe*, wrecche;	*They take you now*
On flore me the streccheth,	
And leyth the on bere*,	*bier*
And bipreoneth* the on here*,	*sew; hairshirt*
And doth the ine putte wurmes ivere*—	*pit with worms*
Theonne bith hit sone of the al so* thu never nere.[6]	*as if*

Lyrics such as these are bound in the time and space of a mortal consciousness: feel *this*, your dying moment, awareness snuffed out, bit by bit, until *it is as if you never were*. The secular lyric occludes the immortal aspirations of the spirit.

Critical Approaches

Categorising the varieties of Middle English secular lyric and charting its continuous history are complex endeavours because the corpus of non-religious verse is multivalent in type, purpose, outlook, and circumstance of survival. In comparison to the religious lyric, the corpus is also scarcer in preservation and more ragged in contour. Rossell Hope Robbins lamented that 'the continuity of the secular lyric must be inferred from fragments and hints'.[7] In his 1955 anthology *Secular Lyrics of the XIVth and XVth Centuries*, items are sorted by category and sub-category: Popular Songs (minstrel rhymes, drinking songs, love songs), Practical Verse (charms, the almanack, the body, gnomic tags); Occasional Verse (book plates, presentation verses, the craft of writing); and Courtly Love Lyrics (a great variety of types). For Robbins, 'The most significant feature of the Middle English secular lyric is its subordinate position in relation to the religious. For every secular lyric there are three or four religious'.[8] Many survive only as singular, random bits—scribbled in margins,

---

[6] Oxford, Jesus College MS 29 (II), fol. 189r; Susanna Fein (ed. and trans.), *The Owl and the Nightingale and the Poems of Oxford, Jesus College, MS 29 (II)* (Kalamazoo, MI, 2022), 260–1, 389 (art. 22). Like *Earth*, this lyric (*NIMEV* 4047, *DIMEV* 6462) belongs to a widespread corpus of affiliated lyrics.

[7] Rossell Hope Robbins (ed.), *Secular Lyrics of the XIVth and XVth Centuries*, 2nd edn. (Oxford, 1955), xxi.

[8] Robbins (ed.), *Secular Lyrics*, xvii.

276   MEDIEVAL POETRY: 1100–1400

on flyleaves, on inserted scraps of parchment—or as off-hand accidents, as when a preacher recites a profane song only to condemn or reframe it. We are left with an array of secular utterances voiced from the margin, a hodgepodge, at times studied, at times casual, intruding into the culture of sanctioned texts given prominence in manuscripts. As Robbins's categories show, these voices range from the pragmatic and the technical to what is our interest here: the poetic and the imaginative. And the critical situation has changed relatively little since Robbins's anthology: a recent writer concedes that, compared to the corpus of religious lyric, 'secular lyrics have not attained the status of a confidently achieved category'.[9]

Early critics of the religious lyric—most influentially Rosemary Woolf and Douglas Gray—wrote magisterially of the genre's themes and images, grounded in meditative piety, sacred liturgy, and pastoral theology.[10] In the same era (mid-twentieth century), studies of the secular lyric also emerged, but their impact was less felt because their evaluation of items in Robbins's imaginative categories (popular songs, courtly lyrics) tended to be subjective in ways that now seem dated and unhelpful, with comments such as 'cliché is endemic in such poems'.[11] More recently, a distinction between popular verse and courtly verse has come to shape secular lyric studies. The former category isolates a body of poetry supposedly sprung, directly or indirectly, from folk tradition, oral song, dancing games, and other spirited types said to be natively vernacular, spontaneous, commonly shared, malleable, and broadly anonymous. Seen as later in development, the courtly lyric is, generally speaking, thought of as more learned, sophisticated, and textually fixed; cognisant of Latin and European models; and often the product of named authors like Geoffrey Chaucer, Charles d'Orléans, and William Dunbar. Consequently, in the study of pre-1380 secular lyrics, recent decades have witnessed a turn towards 'popular literature' as a chief framework. Such an approach is taken up in Karin Boklund-Lagopoulou's 'I have a yong suster': Popular Song and the Middle English Lyric (2005), and, most astutely, in Douglas Gray's Simple Forms: Essays on Medieval English Popular Literature (2015).[12] Their focus on the popular—as a point of origin, sprung from oral culture—leads these writers to adopt a lens wider than the secular lyric per se, as when Boklund-Lagopoulos scrutinises the popular ballad form of Judas, a religious lyric, or when Gray scours numerous narrative forms: myth, epic, heroic lay, folk tale, animal fable. By Gray's expansive perspective, the corpus of secular 'popular' lyric grows substantially:

> in spite of all the uncertainties and all the losses, the corpus of the Middle English popular lyric is an impressively extensive one, with many fascinating byways to be investigated. It gives us precious glimpses of a large lost body of oral song, and many examples of how this material could be taken into the written tradition by poets who in different degrees imitated, adapted, re-created, and polished it in a varied popular style.[13]

---

[9] Bernard O'Donoghue, '"Cuius Contrarium": Middle English Popular Lyrics', in Thomas G. Duncan (ed.), A Companion to Middle English Lyric (Cambridge, 2005), 210–26, at 212.

[10] Woolf, The English Religious Lyric; and Douglas Gray, Themes and Images in the Medieval English Religious Lyric (London, 1972).

[11] Arthur K. Moore, The Secular Lyric in Middle English (Lexington, KY, 1951); and Raymond Oliver, Poems Without Names: The English Lyric, 1200–1500 (Berkeley, CA, 1970). See the discussion by O'Donoghue, who cites the quote from Oliver ('"Cuius Contrarium"', 213).

[12] Karin Boklund-Lagopoulou, 'I have a yong suster': Popular Song and the Middle English Lyric (Dublin, 2002) and Douglas Gray, Simple Forms: Essays on Medieval English Popular Literature (Oxford, 2015). On the courtly lyric, see Julia Boffey, Manuscripts of English Courtly Love Lyrics in the Later Middle Ages (Woodbridge, 1985).

[13] Gray, Simple Forms, 230–1.

For Gray, the boundary between 'popular' and 'courtly' is less than distinct: 'the connection between popular literature and the more obviously learned, or courtly, literature is a close and dynamic one, with constant interchange and symbiosis'. He emphasises that the relation of popular to courtly, and of secular to religious, should be regarded as more 'a continuous spectrum' than a strict division.[14]

Configurations of the corpus have also devolved from modern anthologies. Some classic examples, such as those by R. T. Davies (1963) and Robert Stevick (1964), have helped to familiarise students with the poetry and create a canon of best specimens.[15] Davies and Stevick do not, however, isolate secular lyrics as a category. Each presents a range of medieval English lyric verse in roughly chronological order and sprinkles secular poems among religious ones. Taking a different approach, the Norton *Middle English Lyrics* (1974) groups poems into ten thematic categories, five of which represent secular content: 'Worldes bliss' (nature), 'All for love' (love), 'I have a gentil cok' (bawdy), 'Thirty dayes hath November' (useful lore), and 'When the turuf is thy tour' (death).[16] In *Medieval English Lyrics and Carols* (2013), Thomas Duncan divides the corpus by era (early, c 1200–1400, and late, c 1400–1530) and within sections separates secular from religious content: the early secular units are 'love lyrics' and 'miscellaneous lyrics', the late ones 'courtly lyrics' and 'popular and miscellaneous lyrics'.[17] Appearing more recently is the freshly conceived, capacious *Make We Merry More and Less: An Anthology of Medieval English Popular Literature* (2019), with sections aligned to the chapters of Gray's *Simple Forms*.[18] Here secular lyrics dominate categories called 'Voices from the Past', 'Proverbs and Riddles', 'Satire', and 'Songs', while narrative works dominate other sections. In comparison to all the other post-Robbins anthologies, *Make We Merry* is exceptional for aligning secular lyric not with religious lyric but instead with secular narrative.

Meanwhile, there is now a new breed of anthology studies that has turned deliberately towards representing how lyrics survive in whole manuscripts. A critical document for secular lyric studies is the fascinating manuscript that preserves the version of *Earth upon Earth* cited above. MS Harley 2253 is a treasure-trove in three language (French, English, and Latin), filled with verse and prose, secular and religious, in many genres (lyrics, saints lives, romance, fabliau, debate, and more), compiled c 1340–9 by a literary scribe with legal and clerical training, in or around the town of Ludlow near the Welsh border in west England.[19] Its eclectic contents instantly assumed a central spot in Middle English lyric studies when thirty-two of its English poems (some secular, some religious) were published in 1948 by editor G. L. Brook as *The Harley Lyrics*.[20] What Brook did propelled Harley 2253 into prominence as a medieval collection of high literary value. Today no collection of medieval English verse is complete without a sampling of Harley lyrics. Viewed in terms of whole-manuscript studies, however, Brook's edition is marred by its method of modern extraction. Although the collection is named for the manuscript, Brook's selectivity removed the scribe's

---

[14] Gray, *Simple Forms*, 239.

[15] R. T. Davies (ed.), *Medieval English Lyrics: A Critical Anthology* (London, 1963) and Robert D. Stevick (ed.), *One Hundred Middle English Lyrics*, 2nd edn. (Urbana, IL, 1994) (1st edn., 1964).

[16] Maxwell S. Luria and Richard L. Hoffman (eds), *Middle English Lyrics* (New York, 1974).

[17] Thomas G. Duncan (ed.), *Medieval English Lyrics and Carols* (Cambridge, 2013).

[18] Douglas Gray and Jane Bliss (eds), *Make We Merry More and Less: An Anthology of Medieval English Popular Literature* (2019), https://www.openbookpublishers.com/product/981.

[19] Susanna Fein, 'Literary Scribes: The Harley Scribe and Robert Thornton as Case Studies', in Margaret Connolly and Raluca Radulescu (eds), *Insular Books: Vernacular Manuscripts in Late Medieval Britain* (London, 2015), 61–80, at 64–70.

[20] G. L. Brook (ed.), *The Harley Lyrics: The Middle English Lyrics of Ms. Harley 2253*, 4th edn. (Manchester, 1968) (1st edn., 1948).

own arrangements from view, thus blunting additional meanings to be discovered in the scribe's layouts, juxtapositions, and linkages by verbal resonance. Indeed, the Harley scribe displays strong anthologising tendencies that add interesting nuance to individual lyrics in the collection.[21] Thus, in the instance of Harley 2253, context matters greatly. In a climate of secular verse so often surviving only by haphazard accident, we should attend all the more closely to rare instances of authentic medieval collecting, wherein a compiler has grouped poems for literary effect. Such anthologies provide keen aids for grasping the appeal of secular lyrics to original readers or listeners. What is now coming into better focus, as whole-manuscript studies grow, is how internationally connected are some of the chief trilingual pre-1350 collections, particularly in terms of their pan-European francophone contents.[22] Such findings reveal that many fine lyrics are preserved in settings not evidently of popular folk origin, but instead, explicitly, of considerable sophistication.

Other developments in the analysis of secular lyrics introduce new theoretical or cultural paradigms by which to read them. Although few limit themselves to the purely secular category, each does forge a new direction. Narrowing in on the Harley lyrics—religious and secular, English and French—Ingrid Nelson finds combined written and performing voices, aimed at achieving 'tactical' forms of authority; her theorising draws our thinking on secular verse away from tropes of popular, oral song towards formal poetic deliberation and rhetorical performance.[23] Seeta Chaganti forges pioneering work on the intersection of medieval song and dance: detecting dance movement as an influential element is clearly appropriate for lyrics with popular refrains or burdens, such as carols, or with *danse macabre* imagery.[24] Other recent critical moves pursue the socially constructed meanings of lyrics. Carissa M. Harris interrogates secular lyrics for their ethics in schooling youth on love and sex, pleasure and regret, thus imparting advice (in which the bodily, the corporeal, dominates over the moral) specifically within their own gender groups.[25] Noting how secular lyrics may openly mock and parody religious phrases, Bernard O'Donoghue queries the notion that the 'popular' is always the older, simpler form; such lyrics suggest a world of profuse vernacular comedy that surely nurtured Chaucer's art.[26] Taking an historical approach, Andrew Taylor documents the career and oeuvre of a Tudor minstrel, thereby adding insight on possible avenues for the composition and performance of secular verse in earlier centuries.[27] One of the most fruitful of the new approaches is both aesthetic and pragmatic. Looking at medieval lyric broadly, Ardis Butterfield describes how an individual lyric might develop laterally into a 'literary corpus that goes beyond any one author's control: it is a public corpus, a cluster of verbal and musical materials that is (in part) common intellectual property', revealing 'the nuances of human connection'. The two clusters she selects for study, *Worldes Blis* and *Byrd on Brere*, demonstrate how 'a poem that has several distinct realizations' might

---

[21] Seth Lerer, 'Medieval English Literature and the Idea of the Anthology', *PMLA*, 118 (2003), 1251–67. See also Susanna Fein, 'Compilation and Purpose in MS Harley 2253', in Wendy Scase (ed.), *Essays in Manuscript Geography: Vernacular Manuscripts of the English West Midlands from the Conquest to the Sixteenth Century* (Turnhout, 2007), 67–94.

[22] Keith Busby, 'Multilingualism, the Harley Scribe, and Johannes Jacobi', in Connolly and Radulescu (eds), *Insular Books*, 49–60; and Rory G. Critten, 'The Multilingual English Household in a European Perspective: London, British Library MS Harley 2253 and the Traffic of Texts', in Glenn D. Burger and Rory G. Critten (eds), *Household Knowledges in Late-Medieval England and France* (Manchester, 2019), 219–43.

[23] Ingrid Nelson, *Poetry, Genre, and Practice in Later Medieval England* (Philadelphia, PA, 2017), 31–58.

[24] Seeta Chaganti, *Strange Footing: Poetic Form and Dance in the Late Middle Ages* (Chicago, IL, 2018).

[25] Carissa M. Harris, *Obscene Pedagogies: Transgressive Talk and Sexual Education in Late Medieval Britain* (Ithaca, NY, 2018), 103–85.

[26] O'Donoghue, '"Cuius Contrarium"', 221–6. On Chaucer and popular poetry, see also E. T. Donaldson, 'The Idiom of Popular Poetry in the Miller's Tale', in E. T. Donaldson, *Speaking of Chaucer* (New York, 1970), 13–29.

[27] Andrew Taylor, *The Songs and Travels of a Tudor Minstrel: Richard Sheale of Tamworth* (Woodbridge, 2012).

as readily devolve from secular as from religious material.[28] By introducing the term 'public corpus', Butterfield helpfully provides a new category for understanding lyric.

One may now see, for example, how the many permutations of *Earth upon Earth* constitute, over its centuries-long lifespan, a 'public corpus'. Each instance may be also read, furthermore, as adapted to its setting. In Harley 2253 (its earliest known formulation), *Earth* exists as one third of a trilingual cluster that also includes two aphorisms—one in Latin, one in French—on worldly transience. The next earliest version delivers it as a bilingual event, the English poem juxtaposed with a Latin translation of it.[29] Many anonymous poems that I will treat in this chapter could easily be featured in a discussion of 'popular song'—indeed, many have been. Yet it cannot be safely inferred that any originated outside of learned models and influences. Caution is therefore in order: the idea of the 'popular' is a slippery notion to attach to verse preserved in demonstrably erudite settings, like a monastic Latin songbook, such as London, British Library, MS Harley 978 (*Sumer is icumen in*), or a trilingual miscellany that anthologises secular and religious poetry, such as Harley 2253 (*Earth upon Earth*). Each of the three modes that I will highlight in the following sections—*reverdie* (spring song), love verse, proverb—are amply represented in the precedent literatures of Latin and French, not to mention Provençal, Welsh, and more. All individual poems have, moreover, some tangible history of survival—however slim—and many have decipherable manuscript contexts that may provide further insights. Hints of a rationale for a lyric's inclusion may be detectible: it may be paired with another item or two, or made part of a sequence or section. Instead of addressing lyric in terms of its ultimately unknowable origins or even its unknowable intended destinations, that is, instead of presuming that it stems from popular 'simple forms' or, conversely, was aimed at an audience of 'simple' layfolk, I will adhere here to a content-driven definition of the secular lyric (its conveyance of secular, non-religious meaning) further refined by metrical form—its existence as a *written* artefact in verse, with other potential aesthetic dimensions (music, dance, performance) being now intangible, though no less important.

Secular or Religious?

Our records of secular song in medieval England rely greatly on the frequently religious contexts that mediate them. A cautionary tale told by Gerald of Wales exemplifies how we may learn of a lost song—even hear a line of it—only because it was thought to be scandalous. Disturbed all night by revellers dancing in the churchyard, a parish priest erred in his sacred duties the next morning: instead of intoning the benediction, he sang out a phrase ringing in his head, 'Swete lemmen, thin ore' ('Sweet lover, your mercy'), to the shock of his bishop.[30] Stories like this one tell of diocesan opposition to secular love songs, yet they also show the pull that catchy songs will have over people in general, even that priest.

---

[28] Ardis Butterfield, 'Why Medieval Lyric?', *English Literary History*, 82 (2015), 319–43, at 330.

[29] On the trilingual setting in Harley, see Fein (ed.), *The Complete Harley 2253 Manuscript*, 2:96–7, 387–8 (arts. 24a, 24a*, 24b). On the longer, bilingual version in the Kildare manuscript, see Marjorie Harrington, 'Of Earth You Were Made: Constructing the Bilingual Poem "Erþ" in BL MS Harley 913', *Florilegium*, 31 (2014), 105–37.

[30] John Scattergood, 'The Love Lyric before Chaucer', in Duncan (ed.), *A Companion*, 39–67 (44–5). Gray, too, cautions that 'what references we have to the beliefs, practices, or literature of the "unlearned" come to us in texts written by the "learned"' (*Simple Forms*, 4). On condemnations, yet professional uses made, of secular songs by churchmen, see also Michael Swanton, *English Literature before Chaucer* (Essex, 1987), 245; Davies (ed.), *Medieval English Lyrics*, 24; Ardis Butterfield, 'Lyric', in Larry Scanlon (ed.), *The Cambridge Companion to Medieval English Literature 1100–1500* (Cambridge, 2009), 95–109, at 101–2, 107; Ardis Butterfield, 'Poems without Form? *Maiden in the mor lay* Revisited', in Cristina Maria Cervone and D. Vance Smith (eds), *Readings in Medieval Textuality: Essays in Honour of A. C. Spearing* (Cambridge, 2016), 169–94, at 182–3; and Gray, *Simple Forms*, 215–20.

280 MEDIEVAL POETRY: 1100–1400

The high ratio of religious compared to secular lyrics reflects the identities of those who controlled most book production: generally speaking, clerics and monks. When a lyric pair is created by direct borrowing, one from another, the poems are called *contrafacta*. In vocal music, *contrafactum* is the substitution of one text for another without substantial change to the music. The order of composition for such a pair is typically thought to be secular to religious, by a widespread practice of popular song being appropriated for pious instruction.[31] An exceptional but little-recognised *contrafacta* pair occurs in the two thirteenth-century manuscripts that hold the great avian debate poem *The Owl and the Nightingale*: London, British Library, MS Cotton Caligula A.ix and Oxford, Jesus College MS 29 (II).[32] Right after *Owl* in Cotton, and likewise in Jesus but with a few poems intervening, appears a pair of songs on opposing topics, *Death's Wither-Clench* and *An Orison to Our Lady*, each in ten-line stanzas and probably sung to the same tune.[33] In *Death's Wither-Clench*, listeners are told to prepare for Death's inauspicious coming. In four ways in four stanzas, personified Death stealthily intrudes: he offers a potion, strikes a violent blow, lurks in a shoe, and tosses one down from a height. *An Orison to Our Lady* changes the subject but retains intimations of death, which strike an odd note in a Marian lyric. Even in praise of Mary, the speaker's mind dwells on death and eternal punishment; he prays for Mary's remedy and begs her to strike him with remorse before Death has a chance to seize him. Detecting the pair as *contrafacta*, advertised as such by the scribes who juxtaposed them, allows one to infer that *Death's Wither-Clench* enjoyed a degree of prior, popular currency because it—the secular one—prompted the making of the religious one.

Interestingly, in the Cotton manuscript, these *contrafacta* immediately follow *Owl*, which may suggest that the scribe wanted the songs to complement the long debate wherein avian foes defend opposite musical styles and outlooks on life. The Owl's solemn notes are said to be portents of death; the Nightingale's melodic song offers, she claims, a foretaste of heaven's joys. If an original audience understood the two successive songs as *contrafacta*—the same tune rendered for different meanings—then their placement as a musical afternote to *Owl* seems apt and creative.[34] Of the notoriously hard-to-pin-down message of *Owl* itself, Derek Brewer has observed that it has 'an emotional bias towards the secular and perhaps an intellectual bias towards the religious'.[35] This idea might well be applied and extended outward to the sometimes blurred divide between what is 'secular' and what is 'religious' in the Middle English verse record. The polarised debate, for example, over the mysterious meaning of *Maiden in the mor lay*—is the maiden a woman, a fairy, or Mary?—shows the sort of quandaries raised if neither language nor context provides clear signs.[36]

In actual collections compiled by medieval scribes, subjects that are predominantly worldly often nestle untroubled beside others that are sacred, suggesting that divisions were less compartmentalised for medieval readers than we tend to make them. Subjects

---

[31] Scholars generally accept this order of composition and borrowing. See, for example, Gray: 'the fact that they are selected and quoted probably indicates that the religious writers are consciously appealing to the common knowledge of their lay folk' (*Simple Forms*, 215).

[32] MS Cotton Caligula A.ix, fol. 246r–v, and Jesus MS 29, fols. 179v–180v; Fein (ed.), *The Owl and the Nightingale*, 204–11, 355–59 (arts. 7–8).

[33] E. J. Dobson and F. Ll. Harrison (eds), *Medieval English Songs* (Cambridge, 1979), 122–36, 242–3, 298–9. Music survives for *Death's Wither-Clench* ('Mon may longe lyves wene'; *NIMEV* 2070, *DIMEV* 3370); Dobson and Harrison argue that their pairing indicates the same tune for *Orison* ('On hire is al my lif ilong'; *NIMEV* 2687, *DIMEV* 4270).

[34] The sequence in Jesus MS 29 is longer. Three poems—*The Saws of Saint Bede*, *The Woman of Samaria*, and *Weal*—appear immediately after *Owl* and before the *contrafacta*.

[35] Derek Brewer, *English Gothic Literature* (New York, 1983), 35.

[36] On the range of ways scholars now read *Maiden in the mor lay*, see especially J. A. Burrow, 'Poems without Context', *Essays in Criticism*, 29 (1979), 6–32, at 21–5; Gray, *Simple Forms*, 224–29; Butterfield, 'Poems without Form?', 169–71; and Chaganti, *Strange Footing*, 257–76. Excerpts of the secular-versus-religious debate, c 1951–66, appear in Luria and Hoffman (eds), *Middle English Lyrics*, 321–5.

instead alternate and modulate, and, in doing so, express contrarieties and complementarities of body and spirit. In *Owl*'s manuscripts, the bird-debate serves as lead item for a series of largely religious verse wherein scribes include the *contrafacta* just discussed, plus (in the Jesus manuscript) the comic-religious *Little Sooth Sermon* and the worldly-mystic *Love Rune* (both *sui generis* hybrids of secular and sacred tropes), the worldly *Proverbs of Alfred*, and many verse aphorisms on manipulating life's challenges.[37] During the same era, in the important trilingual miscellany Oxford, Bodleian Library, MS Digby 86 (*c* 1280), each section of English poetry begins in religion and drifts towards secular matter: the first begins with *The Harrowing of Hell* and ends with *Maximian, The Thrush and the Nightingale, The Fox and the Wolf*, and *Hending* (fols. 113–48); the second begins with *On the Vanity of This World* and ends with *Dame Sirith* and *The Names of the Hare* (fols. 157–68); and the third begins with *The Debate between the Body and the Soul* and ends with *What Love Is Like* (fols. 193–200).[38] Both Digby and the spectacular Harley 2253 look like volumes meant for social and recreational functions: games, debates, fabliaux, and entertainments mix without fanfare with religious items, and items are often set side by side to elicit discussion and conversations. Thorlac Turville-Petre observes how the Harley scribe's initial French items—the *ABC of Women* and *The Debate between Winter and Summer*—alert listeners that what is to come is 'poetry as polemic'.[39] The latter piece, a debate with no resolution, asks the audience, and especially all maidens who love deeply, to judge the winner:

> Seigneurs e dames, ore emparlez
> Que nos paroles oy avez
>   Apertement.
> E vous puceles que tant amez,
> Je vous requer que vous rendez
>   Le jugement.[40] (272–7)

> (Lords and ladies, deliberate now,
> You who've heard our words
>   Spoken aloud.
> And you maidens who love so much,
> I ask you to pronounce
>   The verdict.)

Summer's Mirth and Walking with Sorrow

In Harley's lively debate poem, the joys of summer are expressed in lilting tail-rhyme stanzas (as shown above), contrasted with weightier-sounding octosyllabic couplets uttered by winter. The quick flow of summer's speeches reflects the strains of *reverdie*, the lyric form for

---

[37] On *Little Sooth Sermon*, see Susanna Fein, 'All Adam's Children: The Early Middle English Lyric Sequence in Oxford, Jesus College, MS 29 (II)', in Julia Boffey and Christiania Whitehead (eds), *Middle English Lyrics: New Readings of Short Poems* (Cambridge, 2019), 224–6. On secular love tropes in *Love Rune*, see Swanton, *English Literature*, 246–9.

[38] Susanna Fein, 'The Middle English Poetry of MS Digby 86', in Susanna Fein (ed.), *Interpreting MS Digby 86: A Trilingual Book from Thirteenth-Century Worcestershire* (Woodbridge, 2019), 162–97.

[39] Thorlac Turville-Petre, *England the Nation: Language, Literature, and National Identity, 1290–1340* (Oxford, 1996), 211–12.

[40] Fein (ed.), *The Complete Harley 2253 Manuscript*, 2:34–47, 372–3 (46–7) (art. 9).

282 MEDIEVAL POETRY: 1100–1400

celebrating the advent of warm weather and renewed animal spirits in spring and summer. It is an ancient motif, found across languages, to mark humanity's relief from the deprivations of winter. Spring songs describe the landscape's burgeoning growth awakened by the season, along with the sheer joy of sensate existence. Creation bursts with energy; youthful vigour flourishes; the plenitude of nature shines forth. The often anthologised *Sumer is icumen in* provides a sparkling early example (*c* 1125), employing trochaic verse derived from its Latin companion 'Perspice christicola':

> Svmer is icumen in,
> Lhude* sing cuccu*!   *Loud; cuckoo*
> Groweþ sed and bloweþ med*   *meadow*
> and springþ þe wde* nu.   *woods*
> Sing cuccu!
>
> Awe* bleteþ after lomb,   *Ewe*
> Ihouþ* after calue cu*;   *Lows; cow*
> Bulluc sterteþ, bucke uerteþ*.   *farts*
> Murie sing cuccu!
> Cuccu, cuccu,
> Wel singes þu cuccu.
> ne swik* þu nauer nu*!   *cease; never now*
>
> > Sing cuccu nu, Sing cuccu!
> > Sing cuccu, Sing cuccu nu![41]

Like many of the later English *reverdies*, this lyric survives with music, in this case, set in a Latin songbook copied at Reading Abbey. Interlineated with a Latin hymn, this song, which seems so exquisite in its pure secularity, is in fact a part-song joined to a Christian song set to the same music. It is, as Andrew Taylor notes, 'a bilingual cultural artifact', sung in a religious setting, and owing its very survival to that setting: 'only if the monk copies it can the cuckoo's song be preserved'.[42] The presence of music, and also the potential for its being performed as a round with its Latin counterpart, are integral to its character and basic aesthetics. The Latin part praises God as 'celestial husbandman' ('celicus agricola') and honours 'that son who will give life to the half-alive captives', while the English has four voices singing 'cuccu' as virtual devotees of the natural bird. Its celebratory words honour the bird as awakener of nature. As it sings aloud, seeds grow, breezes blow, woods quicken to life. Animals instinctively chime in, adding orchestral depth to the bird's two merry notes: ewes bleat for lambs (high notes), cows low for calves (low notes), bulls kick and bucks fart (percussion).

As a *reverdie*, *Sumer is icumen in* performs merriment and youth as if the present moment never ends: 'ne swik þu nauer nu!'. Bliss is preternaturally eternal, and dark reflection does not exist. The song goes on, ceasing 'nauer nu' (never now). Later instances of the secular

---

[41] Carleton Brown (ed.), *English Lyrics of the XIIIth Century* (Oxford, 1932), 13, 168–9 (no. 6).

[42] Andrew Taylor, *Textual Situations: Three Medieval Manuscripts and Their Readers* (Philadelphia, PA, 2002), 76–84 (79, 83). See also Butterfield, 'Lyric', 98–9; Dobson and Harrison (eds), *Medieval English Songs*, 143–5; and Julia Boffey, 'Middle English Lyrics and Manuscripts', in Duncan (ed.), *A Companion*, 1–18 (6). The lyric survives uniquely in the songbook section of London, British Library, MS Harley 978, fol. 11v (reproduced in Taylor, 80), a book in Latin and French (except for this English half-song), which also contains the *Lais* and *Fables* of Marie de France.

English *reverdie* rarely permit the same totality of mental and physical respite. Another specimen (*c* 1225) typifies how contrary notes may not be suppressed:

> Mirie it is whil sumer ilast
> wiþ fugheles* song;   *birds'*
> oc nu necheþ* windes blast   *but now draws near*
> and weder* strong.   *weather*
> Ej! ej! what þis nicht* is long,   *night*
> and ich* wid wel michel* wrong   *I; very great*
> soregh* and murne and fast.[43]   *sorrow*

This song, for which music also survives, evokes summer's mirth only to name it a transient pleasure. Merriment exists 'whil sumer ilast', but the end is nigh, winds blast, rough weather approaches. The present-tense *is* of line 1 and the adverb *nu* of line 3 set two seasons at odds, and winter seems wholly arrived by lines 5–7. *Reverdie* leads to internal reflection about what is sure to come, the joyful moment yielding to its contrary. Cuckoo song is replaced by mournful lament—'Ej! ej!'—over lengthening nights, advancing sorrow, deprivation. Despite the lyric's secular air, the speaker aligns the earth's season with his spiritual state, and winter especially with a 'michel wrong' that brings him mental anguish.

A perception of nature's spontaneous burgeoning—to which a speaker responds, his senses heightened—set in counterpoint with inner turmoil marks the introspective turn taken in other medieval English *reverdies*. The well-known *Foweles in þe frith*, another lyric with accompanying music (*c* 1270), raises similar thoughts, albeit cryptically:

> Foweles* in þe frith*,   *Birds; field*
> Þe fisses* in þe flod*,   *fish; river*
> And i mon waxe wod*.   *mad*
> Mulch sorw I walke with
> for beste of bon and blod.[44]

Birds of field and fish of river constitute, in brilliant shorthand, the springtime setting: natural life carrying on, chirping, flitting, swimming, with a human narrator who is both sensorily in tune with it (as another creature) and wretchedly divorced from it (as a conscious mind). The lyric packs dense meaning into line 3: *mon* is an extraordinary pun upon 'must' (he is fated to 'waxe wod') and 'man' (neither bird nor fish, he is inherently different). Like the narrator of *Mirie it is*, the speaker walks with sorrow amid living nature. Here he explains why: 'For beste of bon and blod'. The final line has allowed many to read the poem as a love lyric: the speaker pines for the best creature of bone and blood, perhaps a beautiful but inaccessible woman. But it also suggests an alternative, spiritual, inward sense, built from the pun in line 3: the speaker pines that he too is a corporeal 'beast', the 'best' of God's making, yet cursed by mortal sins that separate him from nature's spontaneity.

The *reverdie*'s vegetative woodland trope appears in classic form in *Sumer is icumen in*: the woods are animate with growth ('spryngþ þe wde nu'). In *Foweles*, the topos shifts into a man waxing *wod*, stimulated environmentally to feel part of, yet also out of sorts with, nature. While birds and fish carry on instinctively, it is the speaker who *waxes*—burgeons,

---

[43] Brown (ed.), *English Lyrics of the XIIIth Century*, 14, 169 (no. 7) (wen printed here as *w*); Oxford, Bodleian Library, MS Rawlinson MS G.221, fol. 1v (with music).

[44] Brown (ed.), *English Lyrics of the XIIIth Century*, 14, 169 (no. 8); Oxford, Bodleian Library, MS Douce 139, fol. 5r (with music). For useful discussions, see Nelson, *Poetry*, 15–18; Scattergood, 'The Love Lyric', 54–5; Swanton, *English Literature*, 238–41 (music reproduced, 239); and excerpted criticism in Luria and Hoffman (eds), *Middle English Lyrics*, 263–4 (Peter Dronke), 278–9 (Stephen Manning), 319–21 (Edmund Reiss).

284   MEDIEVAL POETRY: 1100–1400

grows, changes—and his going *wod* punningly suggests a third landscape element: frith, flood, 'wood'. Again, in the richly compressed language of *Foweles*, the speaker feels akin to nature (being *of* the woods) while also distressingly contrary to it (mad).

The confluence of wild nature and compulsory human madness reaches fever pitch in the most notable *reverdie* in Middle English, the Harley lyric *Spring* (*c* 1320), which opens in floral splendour and a lush array of birdsong:

Lenten ys come with love to toune,	
With blosmen ant with briddes roune*,	*song*
That al this blisse bryngeth.	
Dayeseyes in this dales,	
Notes suete of nyhtegales—	
Uch foul* song singeth!	*Each bird*
The threstelcoc* him threteth* oo;	*song thrush; chides*
Away is huere wynter wo,	
When woderove* springeth.	*woodruff*
This foules singeth, ferly fele*,	*amazingly many*
Ant wlyteth* on huere wynne wele*,	*warble; wealth of joys*
That al the wode ryngeth!⁴⁵ (1–12)	

The poet's adroit blend of alliteration and rhyme causes this first stanza to excite through sound. The second of its three stanzas continues to dazzle the senses with exuberant, verdant sights: the rich-hued rose, the moonlit woods waxing leafy with desire ('waxen al with wille', line 15), the gorgeous lily, the fennel and chervil, and animals happily wooing and mating: 'Wowes this wilde drakes; / Miles murgeth huere makes, / Ase strem that striketh stille' ('In wooing go these wild drakes; animals make merry with their mates, like a stream that flows contentedly') (lines 19–21). The ensuing scene of intense activity is likened to a smooth rivulet because all nature awakens spontaneously with the season, flowing exactly as it ought to.

Again, it is the lyric speaker who finds himself worrisomely at odds: 'Mody meneth, so doh mo— / Ichot, Ych am on of tho— / For love that likes ille' ('Moody ones complain, and yet do more—I know, for I am one of those—of love that hardly pleases') (lines 22–4). But despite this discordant human note, the third stanza resumes the alliterative buzz of celebratory nature: beaming moon, brilliant sun, boisterous birdsong, glistening dew, contented beasts. The final twist in mood comes in the last half-stanza, when the speaker introduces a bizarre, suggestive image of worms also wooing below ground:

Wormes woweth* under cloude*,	*woo; ground*
Wymmen waxeth wounder proude,	
So wel it wol hem seme*.	*Just as suits them*

---

⁴⁵ Fein (ed.), *The Complete Harley 2253 Manuscript*, 2:194–7, 423–4. There is no music, but a lyric in the same metre, *Advice to Women*, is copied next to *Spring* in Harley 2253, fols. 71v–72r. The conjunction probably indicates the same tune for both, and that tune may also have been the musical setting for the earlier bird-debate *Thrush and the Nightingale*, from which *Spring* borrows its opening line. See Susanna Fein, 'The Fillers of the Auchinleck Manuscript and the Literary Culture of the West Midlands', in Carol M. Meale and Derek Pearsall (eds), *Makers and Users of Medieval Books: Essays in Honour of A. S. G. Edwards* (Woodbridge, 2014), 60–77 at 70–1. See also Anne Marie D'Arcy, 'The Middle English Lyrics', in David Johnson and Elaine Treharne (eds), *Readings in Medieval Texts: Interpreting Old and Middle English Literature* (Oxford, 2005), 306–22, at 314–16; Scattergood, 'The Love Lyric', 55–6, 65; and Swanton, *English Literature*, 241–3.

Yef me shal wonte wille of on*	*If I must lack assent of one*
This wunne weole Y wole forgon*	*wealth of joys I must forgo*
Ant wyht in wode be fleme*.	*quickly in woods be exiled* (31–6)

Wooing worms turn the imagery towards a standard topos for medieval death lyrics: worms that invade a corpse—here rendered poetically as a kind of macabre sexuality. The women of the next line, too proud to accept suitors' carnal proposals, will ironically find themselves 'waxing' as food for worms—which, says the speaker ruefully, will *greatly* flatter their looks. Frustrated in love, the speaker finds himself a desolate outsider in the arena of nature's fertility, all because he cannot turn the 'wille of on' towards his physical desire. The last line caps his condition, and it may be read in two complementary ways: either he will quickly ('wyht') flee to the woods in exile, or he will become a banished madman ('wyht in wode').[46] The *reverdie*'s ever-latent pun on the enveloping *wode*—woodland, wilderness, madness, distress caused by thwarted desire, as well as the burden of earthly woe that human mortals walk with—becomes the bursting climax in this fine and powerful lyric.

Love's Yearning, Love's Madness

The gradation of difference between the spring lyric and the love lyric is reflected in the move from *Earth upon Earth*'s line 1 to line 2. Spring lyrics are about nature's renewal and the urges it raises in the human creature, most particularly in male lyric speakers. The world is young, the man's discontent is newly arisen, and he thus embodies 'erthe with woe'; that is, he walks in sorrow surrounded by verdant vegetation and birdsong. In contrast, the body of lyrics on secular love might be thought of as having advanced to *Earth*'s line 2, which is more specifically about the satisfactions and dissatisfactions of enacted love, normally presented (again) from a male point of view and with a specific, if imagined, woman in mind. A cache of lyrics, stretching from the thirteenth to the fifteenth centuries and stemming from latinate traditions, define 'what love is'. Perhaps unsurprisingly, love is first and foremost *wodenesse*, a madness of the mind ('mentis insania', 'une pensee enragee') as in an early trilingual rendering (*c* 1300):

Loue is selkud wodenesse*	*a peculiar madness*
Þat þe idel* mon ledeth by wildernesse*,	*worthless; to wantonness*
Þat þurstes of wilfulscipe* and drinket sorwenesse	*thirsts for wilfulness*
And with lomful* sorwes menget* his blithnesse*.[47]	*frequent; taints; happiness*

This first stanza is followed by a Latin one and then a French one, each metrically identical and each a pithy, direct rendering of the same sentiment. The source text is likely to be the Latin one, and it is fascinating to see how the poet repeats the terms classic to the English *reverdie* tradition.[48] The English stanza on 'what love is' might easily stand as a gloss on

---

[46] On this ending on exile, juridically a form of civil death, see *MED, fleme* n.(1) & adj., and *fleme* v.(1). One might compare another poem in Harley 2253: *Trailbaston*, an Anglo-Norman lyric lament uttered by an outlaw who dwells exiled in the forest (Fein [ed.], *The Complete Harley 2253 Manuscript*, 3:144–9 [art. 80]).

[47] Brown (ed.), *English Lyrics of the XIIIth Century*, 14–15, 169–70 (no. 9); MS Douce 139, fol. 157r.

[48] Thomas C. Moser, Jr., traces an ancillary translational tradition derived from John of Garland, Alan de Lille, and Richard Fournivall ('Love and Disorder: A Fifteenth-Century Definition of Love and Some Literary Antecedents', in James M. Dean and Christian K. Zacher (eds), *The Idea of Medieval Literature: New Essays on Chaucer and Medieval Culture in Honor of Donald R. Howard* [Newark, DE, 1992], 234–64, especially 246–7).

286   MEDIEVAL POETRY: 1100–1400

Foweles's waxing 'wod' and walking with 'mulch sorw', for love here betokens a peculiar madness, a wandering wildly and wilfully astray, and a burdensome multitude of sorrows.

A lyric in Digby 86 offers another English definition of love. *What Love Is Like* (*c* 1280) consists of twenty-eight lines in monorhyming stanzas of different lengths. The poem chimes the word *loue* like an incantation:

Loue is sofft, loue is swet, loue is goed sware*.	*proper speech*
Loue is muche tene*, loue is muchel kare.	*trouble*
Loue is blissene mest*, loue is bot ȝare*.	*most blissful; brief*
Loue is wondred* and wo, wiþ for to fare*.	*misery; to deal with*
Loue is hap, wo* hit haveþ; loue is god hele*.	*fortune, [for he] who; health*
Loue is lecher and les*, and lef for to tele*.	*false; eager to betray*
Loue is douti* in þe world, wiþ for to dele.	*bold*
Loue makeþ in þe lond moni hounlele*.[49]	*unfaithful*

Loue accrues here a head-spinning array of definitions. Clearly, secular love embraces everything good and, also, every less-good contrary. The lyric is notable for its attention to female feelings, when the poet states that 'Loue is loueliche a þing to wommone nede' and 'Loue makeþ moni mai wiþ teres to wede [rage]' (lines 10, 12). Women's perspective ends the poem, too, where the poet claims to quote a popular love song: 'Hit is I-said in an song, soþ is I-sene [truly seen], / Loue comseþ wiþ kare and hendeþ wiþ tene [ends with trouble], / Mid leuedi, mid wiue, mid maide, mid quene' (lines 26–8). In Digby 86, this English lyric precedes a religious song in French, *Chaunçoun de Noustre Seingnour*, which opens 'Couuard est ki amer ne ose ki ne veut amer' ('Faint-hearted is he who dares not love or does not want to love'). The scribe has deliberately paired the English secular definition beside a French opposite: contrarious earthly love beside stable divine love.[50]

Indeed, in surveying the theme of love in another manuscript context, Harley 2253, where different languages and outlooks also form a sociable mix, one might readily conclude that a much-discussed subject was, precisely, 'what love is'. The *Way of Love* lyrics (*c* 1335), a *contrafacta* pair on folio 128, tellingly propound the secular/religious contrast, with *Lutel wot hit any mon hou loue hym haueþ ybounde* heading the page, and *Lutel wot hit any mon hou derne loue may stonde* set below it.[51] The first lyric is on Christ's love, the second on woman's disloyal love. The earlier song is evidently the secular one, now reformulated in an identical metre (with exact phrasing borrowed for the refrain) to offer praise of Christ's constancy.[52] The religious song is copied above the secular one, however, perhaps to set it hierarchically above its worldly model. Yet it has also been noted that, by this arrangement, the secular speaker asserts the last word: 'The anguished voice of the lover is never silenced'.[53] In these English poems, the manuscript's final love poems, the Harley scribe lays before a reader two starkly differing definitions of 'what love is'.

---

[49] Brown (ed.), *English Lyrics of the XIIIth Century*, 107–8, 208–9 (listing more lyric definitions of love) (no. 53, lines 1–8); MS Digby 86, fol. 200v. See Scattergood, 'The Love Lyric', 39–40.

[50] Fein, 'The Middle English Poetry of MS Digby 86', 166–7, 175.

[51] Fein (ed.), *The Complete Harley 2253 Manuscript*, 3:240–3, 338–40 (arts. 92–3).

[52] There are two fragmentary analogues of the religious song, suggesting that there may have been formal competitions to remake secular lyric. See Richard Firth Green, 'The Two "Litel Wot Hit Any Mon" Lyrics in Harley 2253', *Mediaeval Studies*, 51 (1989), 304–12.

[53] Turville-Petre, *England the Nation*, 211.

Like the *Way of Love contrafacta*, many other love lyrics occur uniquely in Harley 2253. Their variety, quantity, and quality, plus the scribe's moves to group them creatively, suggest that an ample range of now-lost poetry was available to him. Thus, in the record of secular medieval verse, this manuscript is an extraordinary event, entirely unlike the typically chance recordings of single poems in incongruous places. Harley 2253 allows us to capture something close to a contemporary performance setting. Additional definitions of love arise through the many lyric voices emergent in Booklet 5 (fols. 63–105; *c* 1335), the Harley scribe's major spot for gathering lyrics. Its opening leaf compactly groups three poems specifically to spotlight the highs and lows of worldly love. They play out 'what love is' in three registers, and the layout reveals the scribe's keen intent to cluster them.[54] When he began to run out of space for the third one, *The Lover's Complaint*, he copied it as prose so as to fit it with the others on the same folio. In *Annot and John*, the first male speaker, wildly in love with Annot, infectiously compares her beauty to an array of gems, flowers, birds, and spices. In Annot's returned affection, John finds joy and corporeal health. The male lover in *Alysoun* likewise exudes a giddy infatuation with brown-haired Alysoun. She is out of his reach, so he suffers on, exhausted but happy, in a never-ending state of lovestruck longing, devotion, and blissful hope:

> Betere is tholien whyle* sore   *to feel pain awhile*
> Then mournen evermore.
> Geynest under gore*,   *Most kind under skirt*
> Herkne to my roun*!   *song*
>   *An hendi hap Ichabbe yhent*!*   *happy fate I have found*
>   *Ichot* from hevene it is me sent;*   *I know*
>   *From alle wymmen mi love is lent*
>   *Ant lyht on Alysoun.* (41–8)

The speaker in *The Lover's Complaint*, whose passion is utterly unrequited, endures an agony much like death:

> With longyng Y am lad;
> On molde* Y waxe mad;   *earth*
>   A maide marreth* me.   *injures*
>   Y grede*, Y grone*, unglad,   *wail; groan*
> For selden Y am sad*   *satisfied*
>   That semly* forte se.   *seemly one*
>   Levedi, thou rewe* me!   *pity*
>   To routhe thou havest me rad*!   *brought me to grief*
> Be bote* of that Y bad*:   *cure; prayed*
>   My lyf is long* on the!   *depends* (1–10)

He castigates the lady as the cruel agent of suffering, his only hope for relief. Three extreme states of secular love are enacted here. Three male speakers wax mad to varying degrees.

The secular love lyrics of Harley 2253 typically set the male gaze directly on a woman's body, and, as he proceeds in praise of her attractive features, he eventually dwells on the part to which sexual desire drives him. Annot is 'Coynte ase columbine, such her cunde is. / Glad under gore, in gro ant in grys' ('Pretty as columbine, such is her nature [with *cunde* punning on *cunt* in a flattering way], / Merry under skirt, with gray and rich furs',

---

[54] Fein (ed.), *The Complete Harley 2253 Manuscript*, 2:120–9, 397–401 (arts. 28–30).

288   MEDIEVAL POETRY: 1100–1400

lines 15–16). Alysoun is similarly 'geynest under gore'. And at the conclusion of *The Lover's Complaint*, the lady is praised as 'Brihtest under bis [linen]', with the plaintiff declaring that 'Hevene Y tolde [I'd count] al his / That o nyht were hire gest' (lines 38–40). Many other lyrics end in this overtly sexual manner: the natural final gesture for the male-centred love poem is the imagined coital act, his desired 'bliss' resting in the lady's 'curtel'.[55] Whether attainable or not, the desired female is imagined in tangible terms, and she is often named, corporeally recreated in rhyme, specifically wooed, and even implicitly shared, voyeuristically, with other men, as in *The Fair Maid of Ribblesdale* and *Annot and John*. When the lyrics allow for a feminine subjectivity, as in *The Meeting in the Wood* (a pastourelle) and *The Clerk and the Girl* (a night-time meeting at a window), they deflect an openly sexual ending in favour of demonstrating a girl's steady persuasion towards assent.[56]

Love is thus defined and redefined in Harley 2253 by means of different metres, voices, stances, and settings. The compiler's arrangements sometimes exceed the purely English or purely secular to engage this grand theme in hybrid ways. A trilingual display on folio 76r has long delighted scholars: it holds a trio of poems, each dissimilar from the next, yet always about love: on top, an English love song to Jesus; in the middle, a French love song with a rollicking, irreverent refrain ('I pray to God and Saint Thomas / That they forgive her her trespass, / And very truly will I give it / Should she "mercy" beg me!'); at the base, a macaronic Latin-French-English love lament by a clerk studying in Paris, who in the final two lines yearns for his girlfriend in English: 'May I sugge [say] namore, so wel me is; / Yet Hi [If I] deye for love of hire, duel [sad] hit is!' (lines 19–20).[57] Like the French lover of the second poem, this Anglophone clerk directs his most devout prayer towards achieving his carnal desire: 'Dieu la moi doint sua misericordia, / Beyser e fere que secuntur alia' ('May God grant her to me with his mercy, to kiss and do the other things that follow') (lines 15–16).

These two secular lyrics are bookended by the religious one above them, *A Spring Song on the Passion*, and another that follows after them (fols. 76v–77r). In the first, an English lyric, the speaker is a devout meditant who cannot match the depth of Jesus' loving sacrifice: 'Alas, that Y ne con [cannot] / Turn to him my thoht, / And cheosen him to lemman [as lover]!' (lines 31–3). In the poem that follows the two secular ones, the French *Song of Jesus' Precious Blood*, the speaker, deciding to abandon worldly amusements and very foolish love ('trop fol amour', line 16), listens instead to a song about true love.[58] It leads him on a spiritual journey into Jesus' heart-wound, an enticing place of comfort as Jesus hangs on the cross. From inside there, he peers out, sees weeping Mary and the apostle John, and takes shelter from the devil. The sequence on love thus fluctuates in language from English, to French,

---

[55] See, for example, the refrain of *A Beauty White as Whale's Bone* ('Ich wolde ich were a thretelcok [throstlecock], / ... / Bituene hir curtel [gown] and hire smoke [smock] / I wolde ben hyd!'); and discussions in Susanna Fein, 'A Saint "Geynest under Gore": Marina and the Love Lyrics of the Seventh Quire', in Susanna Fein (ed.), *Studies in the Harley Manuscript: The Scribes, Contents, and Social Contexts of British Library MS Harley 2253* (Kalamazoo, MI, 2000), 351–76, at 354–61; Turville-Petre, *England the Nation*, 204–9; and Scattergood, 'The Love Lyric', 56–9.

[56] See John Scattergood, 'The Language of Persuasion: *De Clerico et Puella* from London, British Library MS Harley 2253 and Related Texts', in John Scattergood, *The Lost Tradition: Essays on Middle English Alliterative Poetry* (Dublin, 2000), 43–62.

[57] *A Spring Song on the Passion* ('When Y se blosmes springe'), *I Pray to God and Saint Thomas* ('Ferroy chaunsoun que bien doit estre oyé'), and *While You Play in Flowers* ('Dum ludis floribus'). On fol. 76r, see Turville-Petre: 'The reader is forced by the readjustment ... to assess the respective values of earthly and heavenly love' (*England the Nation*, 212); Lerer, 'Medieval English Literature', 1251–67; and Critten, 'The Multilingual English Household', 232–4.

[58] On this poem, see also Nelson, *Poetry*, 46–50, who remarks that it 'is as much about lyric transmission as it is about conversion' (48).

to trilingual, and then back to French, as the love object shifts from divine, to worldly and worldly, and finally back to divine.

As we examine the medieval verse anthology that is Harley's Booklet 5—its core collection of secular and religious lyrics, holding forty-odd works and over thirty short English poems—it is crucial to see how a medieval scribe felt it was natural and most effective to present some in monolingual groups and mix others multilingually. And it is equally crucial to detect how the scribe sometimes blended, sometime opposed, secular with pious. The poems before fol. 76 (fols. 63–75) are mainly secular; those after it (fols. 77–105) are mainly religious. The scribe created here a nuanced transition point by subtly countering the secular perspective, showing how the carnal drive for repose in a woman might instead aim for spiritual shelter in Christ.

Manoeuvring Life by Aphorism and Proverb

Aphoristic lyrics and poetic proverbs offer prudent advice for manoeuvring successfully in the here and now. They are pithy, folksy truths, honed by lived experience and bequeathed to the present generation by ancestors. By being *of* the world, they are quite distinct from a preacher's spiritual lore. And yet, as Siegfried Wenzel notes, preachers loved to use them, because of 'their recognized value as proof texts'.[59] The best of them offer wry, pragmatic observations about human nature and life's experiences made witty and memorable in one's native tongue, as in *Earth upon Earth*. Aphoristic lyrics were frequently attached to the name of a renowned sage. For example, a popular saying on marriage (directed at men) is attributed to both King Alfred and Hending:

> Moni mon syngeth
> When he hom bringeth
>   Is* yonge wyf.   *His*
> Wyste wot* he brohte   *If he knew what*
> Wepen he mohte*   *must*
>   Er syth* his lyf.[60]   *For the rest of*

Similarly, a sentiment found in *The Proverbs of Alfred* appears often by itself as a simple mnemonic with many variations, known generally as Three Sorrowful Tidings:

> Uyche* day me cumeth tydinges* threo,   *Each; musings*
> For wel swithe sore beoth heo*:   *And they're of great sorrow*
> The on is that ich schal heonne*;   *go from hence*
> That other, that ich noth* hwenne;   *don't know*
> The thridde is my meste kare—
> That ich not hwider* ich scal fare.[61]   *whither*

---

[59] Siegfried Wenzel, *Verses in Sermons: Fasciculus Morum and Its Middle English Poems* (Cambridge, MA, 1978), 96. On proverbs and riddles as popular forms, see also Gray, *Simple Forms*, 162–92.

[60] *Hending*, in Fein (ed.), *The Complete Harley 2253 Manuscript*, 3:220–37, 334–7 (art. 89, lines 148–53). Compare *The Proverbs of Alfred*: 'Mony mon singeth / That wif hom bryngeth; / Wiste he hwat he brouhte, / Wepen he myhte' (Jesus MS 29, fol. 190v; Fein (ed.), *The Owl and the Nightingale*, 272, 274 (lines 168–71)).

[61] Jesus MS 29, fol. 189r; Fein (ed.), *The Owl and the Nightingale*, 262–63, 390 (art. 23). Compare *The Proverbs of Alfred*: 'Not no mon thene tyme hwanne he schal heonne turne. / Ne no mon thene ende hwenne he schal heonne wende. / Dryhten hit one wot, dowethes Louerd [Only God knows, Lord of hosts], / Hwanne ure lif leten schule' (Jesus MS 29, fol. 190r). See also the Harley lyric *A Winter Song*, an inverted *reverdie*, where the speaker

290 MEDIEVAL POETRY: 1100–1400

The speaker ponders death's certainty beside the fearful uncertainty of not knowing one's time or eternal fate. Worldly life betokens death but leaves one ignorant of the rest. The sentiment is secular because it speaks of experience in the world, not of faith-filled expectations regarding spiritual realms.

The Jesus manuscript of *Owl* holds a remarkable set of lyrics that follow the bird-debate, and while the sequence is often thought to be mainly about religion, a discriminating look shows how allied are many poems to *Owl*, and especially those that pose aphorisms on life. Here, as in Harley 2253, we have an invaluable medieval anthology of secular and religious poetry, this one witnessed in two manuscripts because the Cotton manuscript holds an abridged set of the same poems in the same order.[62] In this case, we can ascertain that an established sequence of poems circulated in the West Midlands, *c* 1250, lending context to a select group of secular poems. Besides *Owl*, the aphoristic verse contents of Jesus are *The Proverbs of Alfred* (important because the birds regularly spout King Alfred's sayings), *Signs of Death* and *Three Sorrowful Tidings* (as previously quoted), and *Ten Abuses*, *Will and Wit*, and *Weal*.

The most charming of these is *Will and Wit*, a clever, tongue-twisting saw that imagines how two sides of the human psyche vie for control:

> Hwenne-so Wil Wit oferstieth, thenne is Wil and Wit forlore;
> Hwenne-so Wil his hete hieth, ther nis nowiht Wit icore.
> Ofte Wil to seorhe sieth bute yif Wit him wite tofore,
> Ac hwenne-so Wil to wene wrieth, the ofo of Wisdom is totore.[63]

> (Whenever Will overcomes Wit, then are Will and Wit lost;
> Whenever Will pursues his ardour, then there's no Wit chosen at all.
> Often Will comes upon sorrow unless Wit warns him beforehand,
> But whenever Will turns to speculation, Wisdom's cap is torn to pieces.)

It is a reconceived debate between Body and Soul, here enacted not after death, when remedies are out of reach, but during life, when wisdom may instruct present actions. The contest is therefore comic: Wit struggles with Will, yet all is not lost. The poem's humour anticipates the later *Piers Plowman*: Will's earnest attempts to understand and Do-wel. The speaker explains how Wit needs to keep Will in line, but the effort is never-ending, for if Will overcomes Wit, both will falter. Will is prone to chase wild passions and encounter trouble unless Wit warns him beforehand. And whenever Will foolishly attempts independent thought, then poor Wit's cap is destroyed! Another aphorism in the sequence, *Weal*, is a clear-eyed address to personified Wealth:

> Weole, thu art a waried thing; unevene constu dele.
> Thu yevest a wrecche weole ynouh, noht thurh his hele.
> Wyth freomen thu art ferly feid with sauhte, and make heom sele.
> The poure i londe naveth no lot with riche for to mele.[64]

---

walks in woe and muses on the Three Sorrowful Tidings; Fein (ed.), *The Complete Harley 2253 Manuscript*, 3:228–31, 432–3 (art. 52).

[62] On the manuscripts' shared contents, see Fein, 'All Adam's Children', 218–19.

[63] MS Cotton Caligula A.ix, fol. 246v; Fein (ed.), *The Owl and the Nightingale*, 212–13, 359 (art. 9). Jesus MS 29 lacks the lyric because a folio is missing; it is virtually certain that the item was copied there.

[64] Jesus MS 29, fol. 179v; Fein (ed.), *The Owl and the Nightingale*, 202–03, 355 (art. 6).

(Wealth, you're a cursed thing; unjustly do you deal.
You give a wretch wealth enough, but nothing for his well-being.
With free men you're curiously joined in peace, and give them joy.
The poor of the land get no portion by which to mingle with the rich.)

The speaker blames Wealth for the world's unfair distribution of goods. The lyric's grim outlook is inherently political: poor wretches survive but receive nothing by which to secure their health. Wealth favours the *freomen* (nobles and gentry) and deals them peace and joy, while the poor enjoy none of the rich men's goods. Economic disparity determines social status and consigns poor men to lasting poverty.

When short lyrics catch on, they may circulate in an expanding public corpus not only as new variations (enlarged or reduced) but also as embedded bits in longer poems. The creation of a secular lullaby lyric from proverbial tags, as well as its later uses and adaptations, shows the flux and movement of popular lyric strands. Two English lullabies survive in different manuscripts separated by half a century, but they are nonetheless related as *contrafacta*—that is, the religious one derives from the secular one, both set to a common tune (the music now lost). The first one, *Whi wepistou so sore*, survives only in London, British Library, MS Harley 913 (*c* 1320–30), opening thus:

Lollai, lollai, litil child, whi wepistou* so sore?	*why do you weep*
nedis mostou wepe, hit was iȝarkid þe ȝore*	*prepared for you long ago*
euer to lib* in sorow, and sich* and mourne euer,	*live; sigh*
as þin eldren* did er* þis, whil hi aliues were.	*elders; before*
Lollai, lollai, litil child, child lollai, lullow,	
In-to vncuþ* world icommen so ertow*![65]	*rude; have you come*

The later *Child reste þe a þrowe* appears solely in John Grimestone's commonplace book (1372):

Lullay, lullay litel child, child reste þe a þrowe*,	*rest yourself awhile*
Fro heyȝe hider* art þu sent with us to wone lowe*;	*high above; dwell below*
Pore & litel art þu mad, vnkut* & vnknowe*,	*strange; unknown*
Pine* an wo to suffren her for þing þat was þin owe*.	*Pain; your own*
Lullay, lullay litel child, sorwe mauth* þu make;	*must*
Þu art sent in-to þis werd, as tu* were for-sake.[66]	*world, as if you*

Of all Middle English lullaby lyrics, *Whi wepistou so sore* is the earliest in date and also the only one sung by an ordinary mother rather than Mary. Moreover, of such poems, only these two match metrically, sharing the refrain form *aaaaBB*, which is similar to that of the *Way of Love* poems in Harley 2253. Perhaps one tune was used for all four.

While many have detected that the two lullabies are intimately related, no one has specifically labelled them *contrafacta*. Yet that is evidently what they are. Carleton Brown classes both as religious.[67] Woolf, on the other hand, rightly names the earlier lyric a 'secular lullaby' with 'themes of death ... skilfully adapted'. In her estimation, it ingeniously recasts the defeatist mood of death lyrics, 'for the content is not delivered as a well-merited warning

---

[65] Carleton Brown (ed.), *Religious Lyrics of the XIVth Century*, 35–6, 255 (no. 28, lines 1–6); MS Harley 913, fol. 32r–v.

[66] Brown (ed.), *Religious Lyrics of the XIVth Century*, 83–4, 266 (no. 65, lines 1–6); John Grimestone's *Commonplace Book* (Edinburgh, National Library of Scotland, Advocates' MS 18.7.21), fol. 120r–v.

[67] By inclusion in his anthology of religious poems; see Brown, *Religious Lyrics of the XIVth Century*, 255.

292 MEDIEVAL POETRY: 1100–1400

to the sinner, but as a sad statement to the child of man's condition in the world', mingling 'grim warning with melancholy'.[68] Wenzel documents *Whi wepistou so sore*'s long afterlife, observing that 'whatever the background of this lullaby may have been, it was certainly used in preaching'.[69] It surfaces not only as the basis for *Child reste þe a þrowe* in Grimestone's book, but also in a later sermon when a fifteenth-century preacher quotes it and cites its former popularity: 'there used to be a popular song as follows' ('De cuius dibilitate cantabatur vulgariter sic').[70]

As a secular lyric, *Whi wepistou so sore* is quite fascinatingly knit from proverbial scraps, becoming a pastiche of wisdoms passed to newborns via mothers who introduce them at once to their native tongue, inheritance of lore, and corporeal trials in the world. To construct a cradle-song from proverbs overtly denotes the secular state of existence. A baby born into new consciousness is schooled in the sorrow that awaits it. The child destined to die will always carry the uncertainty of Three Sorrowful Tidings. In the poem's third stanza, the poet borrows directly from the proverb:

> Child, if be-tidiþ* þat þou ssalt þriue and þe*,   *if it happens; thrive*
> Þench* þou wer ifostred vp þi moder kne;   *Be mindful*
> euer hab mund in þi hert of *þos þinges þre*,
> *Whan þou commist*, whan þou art, and what ssal com of þe.*   *From whence you came*
> > Lollai, lollai, litil child, child lollai, lollai;
> > Wiþ sorow þou com into þis world, wiþ sorow ssalt wend awai.
>
> > > > (13–18; my emphasis)

The mother reminds the infant that its weeping is an age-old condition, repeating what 'þin eldren did er þis, whil hi aliues were'. Holding onto proverbs will be the child's best means to 'þriue', for old saws are survival tips in an unstable world. Here exists no hint of the redemption foretold in the later lullaby—where sorrow and death face the one born to be Saviour and redeem humankind.

Whi wepistou so sore is therefore not just a reworked death lyric; it is also generic cousin to *Hending* and *The Proverbs of Alfred*. It also incorporates the language of *Foweles in þe frith*:

> bestis, and þos foules, þe fisses in þe flode,
> *And euch schef aliues*, imakid of bone and blode,*   *living creature*
> Whan hi* commiþ to þe world, hi doþ ham silf* sum gode–   *they; themselves*
> All bot þe wrech brol* þat is of adam-is blode.   *wretched child*
> > > > (7–10; my emphasis)

These echoes of *Foweles*, clearly not coincidental, gloss the enigma of that earlier speaker's sorrow: as a mortal son of Adam, he walks in sin, at odds with other creatures ('euch shef alives'). *Foweles*'s notion of constant sorrow informs the ensuing refrain: 'Lollai, lollai, litil child, to kar ertou bemette [you are joined to woe], / Þou nost noȝt þis world-is wild [do not know this world's wildness/madness] bifor þe is isette' (lines 11–12).

---

[68] Woolf, *The English Religious Lyric*, 155.
[69] Siegfried Wenzel, *Preachers, Poets, and the Early English Lyric* (Princeton, NJ, 1986), 164–6 (165).
[70] Wenzel, *Preachers*, 166.

Beyond these two instances, a third commonplace of received wisdom resides in the lullaby's fourth stanza—the much-circulated lyric *Fortune* (*c* 1325), quoted here in its entirety:

Þe leuedi* fortune is boþe frend and fo,	*lady*
Of pore che* makit riche, of riche pore also*,	*she; as well*
Che turneʒ wo* al into wele*, and wele al into wo,	*woe; weal*
No triste* no man to þis wele*, þe whel it turnet so.[71]	*trust; wheel*

In *Fortune*'s expansive public corpus, it surfaces in a Latin sermon in *Fasciculus morum*, where it is introduced as a proverb ('antiquum proverbium').[72] Elsewhere it is copied as half of a translation pair, its mate composed in French.[73] The lyric's base language is clearly English, however, because the 'wele'/'wele' pun (good fortune/Fortune's Wheel) is quintessentially so, as is the alliterating *weal*/*woe* opposition. Here is how *Fortune* is knit into *Whi wepistou so sore*:

Ne tristou* to þis world: it is þy ful vo*,	*Do not trust; your very foe*
Þe rich he makiþ pouer, þe pore rich al so;	
Hit turneþ wo to wel and ek wel to wo—	
Ne trist no man to þis world, whil hit turniþ so. (19–22; my emphasis)	

An audience would have instantly recognised the saying before hearing it folded into the refrain: 'Lollai, lollai, litil child, þe fote is in þe whele; / Þou nost whoder [know not whether it will] turne to wo oþer [or] wele' (lines 23–4).

The popularity of clever sayings is in evidence whenever they accrue a 'public corpus', an ongoing afterlife of use and reuse: as tags in sermons, as halves of translation-pairs, as entries in proverb collections, or as items situated in verse anthologies. The poet of *Whi wepistou so sore* wove together powerful little lyrics to form its texture; then it, in turn, inspired a religious song. Sorrow-filled wisdoms from elders are conveyed to a barely comprehending newborn by the maternal matter (*erthe*) that formed him. Her words are then converted— co-opted—as a cleric's message of sanctioned spiritual doctrine.

Butterfield notes that the medieval English lyrics that most garner our attention tend to meet modern criteria for what makes a good poem: 'short, concise, ambiguous, intense and rich in meaning' and 'tightly constructed'. When we critically celebrate such poems, she adds, we 'blot out large swathes of verse that do not so conform'.[74] Yet it is not so much the ordinary medical charm or book plate in verse that dilutes the category of secular poem. It is, instead, the frequent intercourse of such poems with spiritual sensibilities, as in *Whi wepistou so sore*. Secular poets themselves do not ever seem to wholly disagree with the practices of scribes or preachers, who are just as attached to the worldly when they express a need to counter it, or partner it, with its spiritual opposite. The riddling, proverbial *Earth* concludes that 'Tho hevede erthe of erthe erthe ynoh'. The content and contexts of medieval secular poetry seem to concede and profess that eventually everyone will have had 'ynoh' of earth, and will desire something beyond it.

---

[71] Brown (ed.), *Religious Lyrics of the XIVth Century*, 56, 260 (no. 42); Cambridge, University Library, MS Oo.7.32.

[72] Siegfried Wenzel (ed. and trans.), *Fasciculus Morum: A Fourteenth-Century Preacher's Handbook* (University Park, PA, 1989), 330–3 (330). See also Wenzel, *Verses in Sermons*, 103–4, 173–5.

[73] Brown (ed.), *Religious Lyrics of the XIVth Century*, 260.

[74] Butterfield, 'Why Medieval Lyric?', 325; see also Woolf, *The English Religious Lyric*, 1.

19
Non-Cyclic Romances of Love

Rhiannon Purdie

Romance is often thought of in terms of the great 'matters'—that is, of France, Britain, antiquity, and latterly of England—and the present volume contains separate chapters on all of these. Roughly a third of Middle English romances do not fall readily into any of these categories, however. This chapter will look at those non-'matter' romances that are united by a genre-signalling focus on passionate love, and how this is reconciled with romance's broader concerns with social order and the kinds of personal bonds that either reinforce or threaten it.[1] Because romances are often concerned with finding a legitimate place in society for powerful, potentially anarchic emotions (certainly those romances covered in this chapter), they are designed to evoke emotional, as well as intellectual, responses in their readers. While this hardly makes them unique among the genres of medieval literature, it is a key source of their popularity and one of their defining features. In metrical romances, this primarily emotional response may be amplified by the poetic form, whose readily graspable patterns and well-signalled resolutions mimic the wider narrative arc of their texts.

Cyclic and Non-Cyclic Romance

It is worth considering at the outset what independence from the larger established 'matters' of romance may mean for a text. A romance that is not joined to a known cycle or 'matter' cannot rely on any pre-existing knowledge of, or liking for, its characters or situation in order to attract an audience. Not partaking of an established cycle may nevertheless offer romancers some advantages: they are less restricted by audience's expectations of how the story must go, a character should behave, or what significance the various components of the tale are meant to carry. Setting aside the general expectations of the romance genre, this can leave a poet freer to explore a different kind of love—the intense male friendship of *Amis and Amiloun*, for example—or to adopt a new perspective, as when love and marriage are viewed entirely from the heroine's standpoint in *Emaré* or *Le Bone Florence of Rome*.

Nevertheless, the gravitational pull of the great romance cycles is undeniable and can be seen in the way that some originally independent tales get drawn into them. Most famously, the Celtic legend of Tristan and Isolde gradually became attached to the juggernaut of Arthurian legend. The early-fourteenth-century Middle English *Sir Tristrem* is still independent of it, but a century and a half later, 'The Tale of Sir Tristram' has been absorbed into Malory's *Morte Darthur*. Some Continental versions of the *Amis and Amiloun* story (although not the Middle English version discussed below) extend a hopeful tendril towards

---

[1] Cf. Richard Kaeuper's remarks on European chivalric writing (including fictional romance) more generally: 'the direction of much of this writing points us towards the fundamental issue of securing order in society. In other words, if most chivalric literature involves criticism, debate, and reform, much of it was written in the shadow of fears for public order'. See Kaeuper, *Chivalry and Violence in Medieval Europe* (Oxford, 1999), 35.

Rhiannon Purdie, *Non-Cyclic Romances of Love*. In: *The Oxford History of Poetry in English*. Edited by Helen Cooper and Robert R. Edwards, Oxford University Press. © Rhiannon Purdie (2023). DOI: 10.1093/oso/9780198827429.003.0019

the matter of France by making its heroes serve at the court of Charlemagne, and one hero the lover of Charlemagne's daughter.[2]

An even more fleeting attempt to attach independent material to one of the great cycles can be seen in the Middle English tail-rhyme romance *Sir Degrevant*. This Northern or North Midland text dates from the turn of the fourteenth and fifteenth centuries and has no known direct source, although its plot is suggestively similar to that of the *Erle of Tolous*.[3] It is an amalgam of romance commonplaces, or what is sometimes termed a 'composite romance' (although this term could really be applied to any romance).[4] There is a hero in love with a lady above his social station; a father who is vehemently opposed to him (in *The Erle of Tolous*, the opposition comes rather more understandably from the lady's husband); trysts in gardens; three-day tournaments; treacherous stewards; faithful squires and maidservants, and a happy outcome with marriage and children, all packaged up with loving descriptions of rich clothing (e.g., Melidor's dress, 641–72), heraldry (1045–56), luxurious meals (1397–1432), and beautiful chambers (1441–1520)). The decorative extravagance is echoed by the verse-form itself, a sixteen-line extended form of tail-rhyme stanza which stitches three-stress triplets (rather than the usual four-stress couplets) together with rhymed two-stress tail-lines. In the second stanza, the poet attempts to attach it to the Arthurian cycle:

> With kyng Arthure, I wene,
> And Dame Gaynore þe quene,
> He was knawen for kene*, *valour*
>   Þis commly knyghte;
> In Haythynnes* and in Spayne, *Muslim lands*
> In France and in Bretayne,
> With Perceuelle and Gawayne,
>   For hardy and wyghte.
>
>   ...
>
> For-thi þay named [him] þat stownde* *at that time*
> Knyghte of þe Table Rownde,
> As it es made in mappamonde*, *the world*
>   In story full ryghte. (Lincoln MS, 17–24, 29–32)[5]

But the only other point at which anything remotely Arthurian appears is in a passage towards the end of the poem in which the luxurious fittings of the lady Melidor's chamber are described. These include carvings or statues of the Nine Worthies in little gables around the walls, among whom is King Arthur. The poet appears to have completely forgotten that

---

[2] For useful summaries of the different versions, see Françoise Le Saux (ed.), *Amys and Amylion* (Exeter, 1993), 105–12. Perhaps significantly, the Charlemagne connection is also absent from the Anglo-Norman version, itself closest to the Middle English romance: see Hideka Fukui (ed.), *Amys et Amillyoun* ANTS Plain Texts Series 7 (London, 1990).

[3] For date and provenance, see Rhiannon Purdie, *Anglicising Romance: Tail-Rhyme and Genre in Medieval English Literature* (Cambridge, 2008), 174–5 (*Degrevant*) and 182–5 (*Erle*). The ME *Erle of Tolous* is of sufficiently similar date to *Degrevant* that its influence on the latter is not assured. Continental analogues suggest that the *Degrevant*-poet could have come across the story independently: see Laura A. Hibbard, *Mediaeval Romance in England* (New York, 1960), 37–40 and the introduction to *The Erle of Tolous* in Anne Laskaya and Eve Salisbury (eds), *The Middle English Breton Lays* (Kalamazoo, MI, 1995).

[4] See W. A. Davenport, 'Sir Degrevant and Composite Romance', in J. Weiss, J. Fellows, and M. Dickson (eds), *Medieval Insular Romance: Translation and Innovation* (Cambridge, 2000), 111–31. *A Manual of the Writings in Middle English*, gen. ed. J. Burke Severs, vol. 1: Romances (New Haven, CT, 1967), categorises romances by traditional 'matter' as far as possible, but lists *Degrevant* among 'Composites of Courtly Romance', itself a subset of 'Miscellaneous Romances'.

[5] Text in L. F. Casson (ed.), *Sir Degrevant*, EETS o.s. 221 (London, 1949).

296   MEDIEVAL POETRY: 1100–1400

Degrevant is supposed to be a member of Arthur's Round Table himself, and Arthur should therefore not be appearing before him immortalised in statue-form as a long-dead representative of chivalry's golden past. To *Degrevant*'s careless Arthurian setting may be added the possibility that its relatively challenging (if awkwardly executed) extended tail-rhyme stanza was inspired by the genuine Arthurian romance of *Sir Percyvell of Gales*, a somewhat earlier composition, similarly Northern, whose greater technical ambition is illustrated by the concatenation linking almost every stanza. (*The Erle of Tolous*, which may have influenced *Degrevant*'s plot, uses instead the standard twelve-line tail-rhyme stanza). Although *Percyvell* survives uniquely in a single fifteenth-century manuscript copy, Lincoln, Dean and Chapter Library MS 91, which also contains a copy of *Degrevant*, it was cited by Chaucer in his 'Tale of Sir Thopas', so was presumably available to the *Degrevant*-poet as a model of style even if he did not (or perhaps could not) follow it completely.[6]

Eglamour, Emaré, and the Prosody of Emotion

The emotional impact on readers and listeners of even the simplest of metrical romances—those with entirely predictable plots enacted by stock characters—is nonetheless enhanced by the medium of verse. Since Middle English popular romances have been so frequently derided for the limited prosodic ambition that many seem to display,[7] it is important to point out that even the kinds of 'rym dogerel' pilloried by Chaucer in his 'Tale of Sir Thopas' can still enhance an audience's emotional response.[8] For example, the sparsely recounted scene in which Sir Eglamour and his beloved Christabelle get together (and as we later learn, conceive a child) could never serve as an example of sophisticated prosody. The syntax is straightforward—mostly paratactic—and the language plain to the point of being pedestrian. But this only serves to highlight the rhythm and mounting repetition of the couplet-plus-tail-line units, giving this passage a momentum and a satisfying sense of inevitability and (therefore) rightness which would be hard to replicate in prose.

> Aftir sopir gan he fare
> To Cristabelle chambir, whare scho ware,
>   Þare torchis brynnes bryghte.
> The lady was of mekill pryde,
> And sett hym on hir beddis syde,
>   And said, 'Welecom, sir knyghte!'
> 'Dameselle', he sayd, 'So hafe I spede,
> Thorow þe grace of God I schall þe wedd!'
>   And þare þay trouthes plyghte.

[6] 'Sir Thopas', lines 915–16, in Larry D. Benson (ed.), *The Riverside Chaucer*, 3rd edn. (Boston, MA, 1987), where the peculiar statement 'Hymself drank water of the well' is a deliberate echo of *Percyvell*'s 'He dranke water of þe welle' (7); text in Maldwyn Mills (ed.), *Ywain and Gawain, Sir Percyvell of Gales, The Anturs of Arther* (London, 1992). The only other romance to use the sixteen-line tail-rhyme stanza, *The Avowing of King Arthur*, is roughly contemporary with *Degrevant*: it is likewise both Northern and Arthurian, and frequently shows the *Percyvell*-like concatenation and heavy alliteration that *Degrevant* lacks. For further discussion of the range of forms within tail-rhyme, see Chapter 20 in this volume.

[7] In a 2011 essay, Derek Pearsall upbraids his younger self for sneering at the poetic skills of Middle English romances: see 'The Pleasure of Popular Romance: A Prefatory Essay', in R. Purdie and M. Cichon (eds), *Medieval Romance, Medieval Contexts* (Cambridge, 2011), 9–18, referring to 'The Development of Middle English Romance', *Mediaeval Studies*, 27 (1965), 91–116.

[8] 'Thopas', line 925. Cf. J. A. Burrow, 'Sir Thopas: An Agony in Three Fitts', *Review of English Studies*, n.s. 22 (1971), 54–8 and Alan T. Gaylord, 'Chaucer's Dainty "Dogerel": The "Elvyssh" Prosody of *Sir Thopas*', *Studies in the Age of Chaucer*, 1 (1979), 83–104.

> So gracyously he gun hir telle
>
> Of dedis of armys þat hym byfelle
>
> > Þat þare he duellid all nyghte. (Lincoln MS, 673–84)

At least one psychological study has found that the aesthetic properties of rhyme tend, against all logic, to enhance an audience's impression of the 'truth' of a statement, as does simple repetition.[9] Repetition is a key structural feature of Middle English romances at all levels, from their strongly formulaic diction to their highly patterned plots built up of comfortingly familiar episodes or tropes, or what Helen Cooper has called 'memes'.[10] Thus, the very elements that can make them appear simplistic are also those that contribute most directly to an audience's sense that they contain satisfyingly fundamental human truths. Might this partly explain why prose romance was slow to catch on in Middle English literature? Prose romances were composed in French from the beginning of the thirteenth century, but there are no surviving Middle English examples from before the fifteenth.[11]

An interesting example of high levels of repetition in both plot and diction is offered by *Emaré*. This is one of several Middle English romances composed towards the end of the fourteenth century which feature noble women threatened with ravishment and/or unjustly accused before being banished, often in a rudderless boat. In romances such as *Sir Triamour,* both versions of *Octavian* (tail-rhyme and stanzaic), *The Erle of Tolous, Eglamour of Artois* and the early fifteenth-century *Torrent of Portyngale,* the heroine's honour is eventually restored by the eponymous hero of the romance, whether lover or son, and he therefore remains the main focus of the romance's attention, but in *Emaré* and *Le Bone Florence of Rome,* the heroines are the genuine stars of the show. These last two romances look at the traditional preoccupation with love and dynasty from the other end of the telescope, as it were: the peripheral men serve as foils to the heroine's superlative endurance, wisdom, and virtue. Each woman operates within her tale as a kind of living philosopher's stone, gradually transforming the misdirected lust, hatred, or envy of those around her into virtuous love (providing the evil-doers survive the experience). The popularity of this type of tale is attested to by Chaucer and Gower, both of whom tell the tale of the twice-exiled Constance; Chaucer includes another variation on this theme with the 'Clerk's Tale' of patient Griselda.[12] None of the Middle English romances in this group are particularly long—they range from the brisk 1035 lines of *Emaré* to the 2671 lines of *Torrent*—and all are in tail-rhyme stanzas, perhaps the most distinctively English form of romance.[13]

---

[9] Matthew S. McGlone and Jessica Tofighbakhsh, 'Birds of a Feather Flock Conjointly (?): Rhyme as Reason in Aphorisms', *Psychological Science*, 11 (2000), 424–8. On the effects of repetition, see I. M. Begg, A. Anas, and S. Farinacci, 'Dissociation of Processes in Belief: Source Recollection, Statement Familiarity, and the Illusion of Truth', *Journal of Experimental Psychology: General*, 121 (1992), 446–58.

[10] On formulaic diction, see the classic studies by Albert C. Baugh: 'Improvisation in the Middle English Romance', *Proceedings of the American Philosophical Society*, 103 (1959), 418–54; 'The Middle English Romance: Some Questions of Creation, Presentation, and Preservation', *Speculum*, 42 (1967), 1–31; 'Convention and Individuality in Middle English Romance', in J. Mandel and B. Rosenberg (eds) *Medieval Literature and Folklore Studies* (New Brunswick, NJ, 1970), 122–46; also Susan Wittig, *Stylistic and Narrative Structures in the Middle English Romances* (Austin, TX, 1978). On romance 'memes', see Helen Cooper, *The English Romance in Time: Transforming Motifs from Geoffrey of Monmouth to the Death of Shakespeare* (Oxford, 2004), 3–7 and 15–22.

[11] The Prose *Siege of Troy* and *Siege of Thebes, c* 1450 or earlier, seem to be redactions of Lydgate's verse *Troy Book* and *Siege of Thebes*, respectively. The other fifteenth-century ME prose romances are of *Alexander, Merlin,* and *The Lyfe of Joseph of Aramathy*: all of these deal with supposedly historical matter, suggesting that prose retained some of its associations with learned or academic material. It might be added that there are no prose romances at all in the parallel tradition of Older Scots literature.

[12] Chaucer, 'Man of Law's Tale'; John Gower, in R. A. Peck (ed.), *Confessio Amantis*, 3 vols. (Kalamazoo, MI, 2006), lines 587–1612.

[13] See most recently Purdie, *Anglicising Romance.*

298   MEDIEVAL POETRY: 1100–1400

The eponymous heroine of *Emaré* is the daughter of the widowed emperor Artyrus (emperor of where, we never learn), who falls in love with her and obtains papal permission for an incestuous marriage. When Emaré reacts with horror, he has her cast away in a boat 'wythowte anker or ore' (275), wearing a robe which he had had made for his intended daughter-bride from an extraordinary cloth embroidered with, among other things, images of famous lovers.[14] The robe amazes all who see it and it has been the focus of modern critical attention too, interpreted variously as representing sexual allure, inner virtue, divine grace, or even the poem itself.[15] The wind blows Emaré's boat to the shores of 'Galys' (Wales? Galicia? It is not clear and does not matter) where she changes her name to 'Egaré' ('the lost one') and is taken in. In a variation of the initial scene with her father, the king of Galys is dazzled by her beauty and determines to marry her. Although there is no moral impediment to marriage this time, inappropriate parental love still lurks, albeit at one remove, in the form of the murderously possessive mother of the king. This jealous mother-in-law eventually succeeds in sending Emaré/Egaré into her second exile-by-boat—the parallel enhanced by the fact that lines 325–36 are repeated almost verbatim at 673–84—except that Emaré now has her infant son with her. This time her boat lands near Rome, where the married merchant who finds them is by now predictably dazzled by the beauty of her and her robe. As Ad Putter points out, the obvious parallels between this and the previous episodes with father and husband episodes, both culminating in exile at sea, make disaster at the hands of a third dazzled man seem inevitable.[16] It is thus a delightful surprise when the merchant Jurdan manages to avoid either falling in love with her or attempting to ravish her. Lee Ramsay had labelled *Emaré* an 'anti-love romance',[17] but Putter argues rather that the entire plot stems from two basic activities, 'loving' (or its negative, hating) and 'travelling' (whether away from or towards), and this is what the formal repetitions help to emphasise.[18] This third time around, Emaré's steadfast virtue is at last rewarded by love of an entirely positive kind from both Jurdan and his wife. The wrongs committed against her and the love that was misdirected (in her father's case) or thwarted (in her husband's case) is finally righted as both men come to Rome on pilgrimages of repentance for their part in her supposed death, only to discover that she and her son are alive and well. The story is not complex, and the extreme repetitiveness of its diction maddened its early editor Edith Rickert,[19] but, as noted above, the very repetitiveness of its patterning may have been part of its original appeal.

Emaré concludes by identifying itself as a specific type of romance known as a Breton lay (1031). These were brief, supernaturally charged verse romances dealing with love that were popularised in French literature at the end of the twelfth century by Marie de

---

[14] Text in Maldwyn Mills (ed.), *Six Middle English Romances* (London, 1973).

[15] Space does not permit a list of all studies of the cloak: for useful critical summaries, see R. G. Arthur, 'Emaré's Cloak and Audience Response', in J. N. Wasserman and L. Roney (eds), *Sign, Sentence, Discourse: Language in Medieval Thought and Literature* (Syracuse, NY, 1989), 80–92; and Amanda Hopkins, 'Veiling the Text: The True Role of the Cloth in *Emaré*', in Weiss, Fellows, and Dickson (eds), *Medieval Insular Romance*, 71–82. On robe-as-poem, see Elizabeth Scala, 'The Texture of *Emaré*', *Philological Quarterly*, 85 (2006), 223–46. Ad Putter dispenses with all of these interpretations to argue that the cloak is a chiefly a mnemonic device to help performers distinguish Emaré's tale from the many other suffering-heroine plot-lines: 'The Narrative Logic of *Emaré*', in A. Putter and J. Gilbert (eds), *The Spirit of Medieval English Popular Romance* (Harlow, 2000), 157–80 (175–6).

[16] Putter, 'Narrative Logic', 166–7.

[17] Lee C. Ramsey, *Chivalric Romances: Popular Literature in Medieval England* (Bloomington, IN, 1983), 184.

[18] Putter, 'Narrative Logic', 160–1, adapting the grammatical metaphor from Tzvetan Todorov, *Grammaire du Décaméron* (The Hague, 1969).

[19] Rickert estimated that 16.5 per cent of the poem consists of repeated lines, because 'whenever the idea recurs the phrase, line, sentence, stanza or even group of stanzas, is repeated, with only slight necessary changes': see Edith Rickert (ed.), *The Romance of Emaré*, EETS e.s. 99 (London, 1906), xxvi.

France, who developed the form, so she tells us, from ancient tales set to music by the Bretons.[20] The brevity and focus of Marie's Old French *lais* (nearly all under 1,000 lines, and some under 100) contrasted markedly with the languorous expanse of other Old French romances, but this distinction is less meaningful in the world of Middle English romance, where brevity is the norm. Nevertheless, the earliest Middle English lays—recorded in the Auchinleck manuscript of *c* 1330–40 (Edinburgh, NLS, Advocates' MS 19.2.1)—are short even by English standards: *Lay le Freine* (based on Marie's original) is under 400 lines, and *Sir Orfeo* is *c* 600 lines. On the other hand, the Auchinleck copy of the 'lay' of *Sir Degare* runs to 1,065 lines, which is within the 1–2,000-line norm for Middle English romances, and *Emaré* itself is 1,035 lines. *Lay le Freine*'s assertion about Breton lays that 'mest o love for sothe thai beth' seems to be the main justification for the claims of many later romances to be 'a lay of Bretayne', but the 'lay' of *Sir Gowther*, with its demon-turned-saint protagonist, seems to draw instead on the term's associations with brief stories of the supernatural (*Gowther* comes in at under 660 lines).[21]

Evaluating Love in *Sir Orfeo, Floris and Blauncheflur,* and *Amis and Amiloun*

Of all the non-cyclic Middle English romances, the lay of *Sir Orfeo* is the one that has attracted the most modern critical attention.[22] In *Orfeo*'s reworking of the classical myth of Orpheus and Eurydice, 'Heurodis' does not die from a snake-bite but is kidnapped by the king of Fairy. The grief-stricken Orfeo goes into despairing self-exile in the forest for ten years until he happens across a fairy hunting-party in which he recognises Heurodis, which galvanises him to seek her. In the fairy otherworld, Orfeo charms its king with his extraordinary harping, much as his classical counterpart did to win Eurydice, but there is no fatal backward glance. Instead, Orfeo and Heurodis return to their kingdom to be received by their people with joy, and the faithful steward who has been regent all this time is rewarded by being declared Orfeo's official heir. *Orfeo* thus manages to focus on romantic love within a royal marriage while side-stepping the question of dynastic continuity, or at least prioritising social stability over the continuation of a family line.

No French source survives for *Orfeo*, but it seems likely that one existed since there are scattered references to a *lai d'Orphey* in older French works, and a tale with striking similarities to *Orfeo* is told by Walter Map in his twelfth-century *De nugis curialium*.[23] Both the classical myth and the romance reworking have Orfeo's/Orpheus's great love for his wife at their core, but where the overpowering nature of this love is denigrated in medieval Christian allegorical readings of the classical myth, it is unashamedly celebrated in *Sir Orfeo*. It is nevertheless the overtones of those Christian allegorical readings that give *Orfeo* much of its power, because for at least some members of its medieval audience (and all modern

---

[20] 'Les contes ... / Dunt li Bretun unt fait les lais' ('the tales from which the Bretons created their *lais*', *Guigemar*, 19–20) and see also her prologue, 33–42 in J. Rychner (ed.), *Les lais de Marie de France* (Paris, 1983).

[21] For self-identification as Breton lays, see *Lay le Freine* 12; *Erle of Tolous* 1214; *Emaré* 1030–2; *Gowther* 28–30, in Laskaya and Salisbury (eds), *The Middle English Breton Lays*. Chaucer's 'Franklin's Tale', lines 709–15, also claims to be one.

[22] The earliest witness is the Auchinleck manuscript of *c* 1330–40; the latest Oxford, Bodleian Library MS Ashmole 61 from the end of the fifteenth century. The condensed text in London, British Library, MS Harley 3810 (only 509 lines to Ashmole's 604) dates from the early fifteenth century.

[23] See A. J. Bliss (ed.), *Sir Orfeo*, 2nd edn. (Oxford, 1966), xxxi–xxxiii, and Walter Map, in M. R. James (ed.), *De nugis curialium* (Oxford, 1914), Dist. 2, Cap. 13 and Dist. 4, Cap. 8.

300   MEDIEVAL POETRY: 1100–1400

critics) it is impossible not to be reminded of them.[24] The vivid descriptions of the fairy kingdom echo both Paradise, with its sparkling castle of gems and gold and its eternal light (A355–76), and Hell, as Orfeo takes in the horrifying sight of 'folk þat were þider ybrouȝt, / & þouȝt dede, & nare nouȝt' (A389–90), among whom he finds his wife under her 'ympetre'. Does this turn Orfeo into something of a Christ-figure, harrowing Hell?[25] For some it is Orfeo's status as a harper that holds the key: is the poem about the redemptive power of art?[26] *Orfeo*'s continued appeal lies in its ability to suggest several kinds of reading simultaneously. But interpretations of the classical myth which denigrate the value of Orpheus's love for Eurydice cannot in the end be transferred successfully to *Orfeo* with its triumphant recovery of Heurodis. Boethius laments, 'Who can give lovers laws? Love is a greater law unto itself', as he describes Orpheus's fatal glance back, offering the tale as a warning to those who cannot tear themselves away from the false happiness of earthly delights.[27] But *Sir Orfeo* celebrates exactly that, portraying such romantic love as an unalloyed virtue.

The focus on love to the exclusion of that other great mainstay of medieval romance, chivalry, is also shared by the late-thirteenth-century *Floris and Blauncheflur*. This is the English representative of a story widely disseminated on the Continent in France, Italy (including, most famously, Boccaccio's *Il Filocolo*), Germany, the Netherlands, Scandinavia and elsewhere.[28] Its immediate source is the Old French *Floire et Blanchflor*, which must be consulted to supply the beginning of the Middle English poem since it has been lost from all four of its surviving manuscripts.[29] Set in an imagined Eastern world of Muslim Spain and Babylon, it tells of the tragic separation and triumphant reunion of childhood sweethearts Floris, son of the Muslim King of Spain, and Blauncheflur, daughter of the captured Christian woman who nurses Floris. The children grow up adoring each other, but unlike any other English romance in which the protagonists meet in childhood, they *remain* children virtually until the end of the narrative. In a very unusual move for a medieval romance, this effectively uncouples romantic love from chivalry, for Floris is only knighted at the very end of the tale and he never performs any deeds of chivalry at all. They are seven years old when Floris tearfully insists that Blauncheflur should be schooled with him (E15–25); they are still only twelve when the king realises with alarm that Floris's love for Blauncheflur may stop him from marrying anyone else (E31–40). Their passion for each other is as all-consuming as that of any other famous pair of lovers, and described in the usual hyperbolic terms:

> Yf eny man to him [*i.e., Floris*] speke
> Loue is on his hert steke*.   *fixed*
> Loue is at his hert roote

---

[24] See, for example, Patrizia Grimaldi, '*Sir Orfeo* as Celtic Folk-Hero, Christian Pilgrim, and Medieval King', in M. Bloomfield (ed.) *Allegory, Myth and Symbol* (Cambridge, MA, 1981), 147–61. On the difficulties of allegorical reading in this text, see Jeff Rider, 'Receiving Orpheus in the Middle Ages: Allegorization, Remythification and *Sir Orfeo*', *Papers on Language and Literature*, 24 (1988), 343–66.

[25] See especially Penelope Doob, *Nebuchadnezzar's Children: Conventions of Madness in Middle English Literature* (New Haven, CT, 1974), 158–207 and J. B. Friedman, 'Eurydice, Heurodis, and the Noon-Day Demon', *Speculum*, 41 (1966), 22–9.

[26] E.g., Seth Lerer, 'Artifice and Artistry in *Sir Orfeo*', *Speculum*, 60 (1985), 92–109.

[27] 'Quis legem det amantibus? Maior lex amor est sibi' (3.m12.47–8); text and translation in Boethius, 'Consolation of Philosophy', in H. F. Stewart, E. K. Rand, and S. J. Tester (eds and trans.), *The Theological Tractates: The Consolation of Philosophy* (Cambridge, MA, 1973).

[28] See F. C. De Vries (ed.), *Floris and Blauncheflur* (Groningen, 1966), 54–60.

[29] In approximate order of date, these are: the fragmentary London, British Library, MS Cotton Vitellius D.iii (V); Cambridge, University Library, MS Gg.4.27 part 2 (C); the Auchinleck manuscript (A); and British Library, MS Egerton 2862 (E).

þat noþing is so soote:
Galyngale* ne lycorys   [a spice]
Is not so soote as hur loue is,
Ne nothing ne non other [flour] ... (C115–21)

But the tale's insistent reminders of the couple's youth—they are referred to throughout as 'children'—works to distinguish this passion from a morally ambiguous sexual obsession.[30] Oddly, its innocence is only emphasised further by the hints that their relationship *will* become sexual very soon: when Floris's parents build a false tomb for the secretly exiled Blauncheflur, they have it inscribed: 'Here lyth swete Blauncheflour,/Þat Florys louyd *par amoure*' (E265–6, italics mine). Later, Floris is smuggled into the harem in a huge basket of flowers, comically inverting the *Roman de la Rose* trope of the virgin as flower ready to be plucked by a male lover: 'Knowestu oȝt ȝete þis flur?' (C518) Clarice quips to Blauncheflur when Floris emerges, apparently understanding what is going on far better than either protagonist. This will clearly be the end of their sexual innocence: Clarice leads them to a bed, promising that they will be healed of their 'drury' ('love-service', V294, E820) and the narrator coyly observes that 'If þer was aȝt bute custe / Swete Blaucheflur hit wiste' (i.e., 'If anything other than kissing happened there, sweet Blauncheflur would know', C 551–2).[31] Yet when they are later discovered asleep in bed together, the emir still cannot decide whether the beautiful, beardless creature with Blauncheflur is male or female until he has the covers pulled down and sees that only one of them has breasts.

Floris and Blauncheflur is a romance that tests boundaries on several levels: between male and female, Muslim and Christian, child and adult. The catalyst that dissolves all difficulties raised by such boundaries is the purity of Floris and Blauncheflur's love for each other. Floris's parents resign themselves to having a Christian daughter-in-law when they realise the strength of his attachment to her; the emir lifts his death-sentence upon them when he sees how the 'children' try so desperately to save each other's lives at the expense of their own; the Auchinleck version also has the emir convert to Christianity. More than perhaps any other romance, the message of *Floris and Blauncheflur* is that love alone may conquer all.

A more ambiguous illustration of love conquering all is provided by the tail-rhyme romance of *Amis and Amiloun*, which centres on the extraordinary bond of friendship and loyalty between the two heroes. Like *Floris and Blauncheflur*, this was a popular tale with many Continental analogues. The Middle English version is closest to the Anglo-Norman *Amys e Amillyoun*, but is almost twice the length, and some details (such as the name of the love-interest, Belisaunt) correspond instead to the *chanson de geste* of *Ami et Amile* and some Latin versions of the story.[32] The four surviving copies of the Middle English text—from the c 1330–40 Auchinleck manuscript to the later fifteenth-century Oxford, Bodleian Library MS Douce 326—demonstrate its popularity in medieval England. Amis and Amiloun are born on the same night to neighbouring baronial families of Lombardy. Like Floris and

---

[30] ME 'child' had a wider range of meaning than in Modern English—it could be used for an adolescent of either sex, or a young nobleman who has not yet inherited his estate—but its primary sense was still that of a young child below the age of puberty (see *MED child* n., senses 1–5).

[31] The damaged early V also retains a fragment of this at 299–300, although A has a more innocent 'þo bigan þai to clippe and kisse, / & made ioie and mochele blisse' (530–1).

[32] See Hideka Fukui (ed.), *Amys e Amillyoun*. For a summary of sources, see Françoise Le Saux (ed.), *Amys and Amylion*, 1–4 and appendixes 1–4; MacEdward Leach (ed.), *Amis and Amiloun*, EETS o.s. 203 (London, 1937), ix–xxxii. Quotations from Leach.

302 MEDIEVAL POETRY: 1100–1400

Blauncheflur, they grow up together the best of friends; their physical resemblance is much remarked upon and mirrored—once again like Floris and Blauncheflur—by the similarity of their names. They are taken into the household of the Duke of Lombardy where their bond continues to strengthen—'Bitvix hem tvai, of blod & bon / Trewer loue nas neuer non' (142–3)—until they swear a formal oath of allegiance to each other. They will:

> hold to-gider at eueri nede,
> In word, in werk, in wille, in dede
> ...
> Fro þat day forward neuer mo
> Failen oþer for wele no wo. (151–5)

When Amiloun is called away by the death of his parents, he is distraught at leaving Amis and has two identical golden cups made. Giving one to Amis, he says:

> Lete neuer þis coupe fro þe
> Bot loke her-on & þenk on me,
> It tokneþ our parting. (322–4)

The world of medieval romance may be resolutely heterosexual, but the gift or exchange of a precious token between separated lovers is such a widespread romance motif that one begins to wonder if a parallel is being implied here. Shortly after this (and after Amiloun has acquired a nameless wife in the space of three lines), there is another extended scene in which the envious steward of the Lombard court attempts to replace Amiloun in Amis's affections. 'Y schal þe be a better frende/Þan euer зete was he', he wheedles (359–60); he suggests that he and Amis swear brotherhood '& pliзt we our trewþes to' (364). Amis's staunch avowal of loyalty to Amiloun would not be out of place in the mouth of any besieged heroine of romance. He declares that he has plighted his troth once and forever to 'þe gentil kniзt' and 'þat hende', and 'Y no schal neuer by niзt no day / Chaunge him for no newe' (383–4). It is not the powerful loyalty to a sworn brother itself that strikes an off-note, for there is ample support for such within the broader ideals of chivalry, but the immediate context in which this poet has placed it. The tearful exchange of 'forget-me-not' gifts has been reinforced by a second well-worn motif of romance—the jealous steward who tries to seduce the hero(ine) in the absence of the hero.

Amis and Amiloun is full of things that ought to be wrong but are not, or that ought to be right but are made to feel wrong. The duke's daughter Belisaunt manages to trick Amis into an affair with her by threatening to cry rape, only for the steward—the same whom Amis had spurned—to betray them to her father. Amis offers to defend their innocence in a judicial duel, but of course he is guilty as charged and can expect to be struck down by God. Taking advantage of their physical resemblance, he and Amiloun exchange places. Amis pretends to be Amiloun to the latter's own wife for a fortnight (baffling her by placing a sword between them each night), while Amiloun-as-Amis kills the steward in the judicial duel. Before doing so, he receives a heavenly warning that he will be stricken with leprosy and cast out by his own family if he goes ahead with it: Amiloun is torn, but concludes that 'To hold mi treuþe schal y nouзt spare, / Lete god don alle his wille' (1283–4). It is true that the heavenly voice does not actually forbid him to fight—it merely outlines the dire consequences if he does—but the phrasing of his conclusion is still disconcerting in appearing to prioritise Amis even above God. As with the misdirected romance motifs described earlier, it adds to the impression that there may be something problematic about the intense bond between Amis and Amiloun.

This unease comes to a head when the now-unrecognisable leper Amiloun pitches up at the castle of Amis, tended only by a self-sacrificingly loyal nephew. Amis has by this point married Belisaunt (apparently undisturbed by her attempts to blackmail him), inherited the dukedom and fathered two children on her. In a romance of 'Sir Amis', this would be the happy ending of love requited and the dynasty secured. As it is, the nephew's complete devotion to the leper (he refuses an offer of service with another knight) attracts the admiration of Amis. Their matching golden cups—the only thing Amiloun has retained of his former life—lead to an emotional reunion and, after a year of Amis tenderly nursing Amiloun, a second message comes from Heaven. Amis dreams that he could cure Amiloun's leprosy if he were to murder his own two children and bathe Amiloun in their blood. As a test of faith it recalls that of the Biblical Abraham and Isaac, yet it is framed, not as a test of Amis's faith in God, but of how much *more* important Amiloun is to him than anyone or anything else. He murders his children; Amiloun is cured by their blood; the children are then miraculously restored to life. As for Amis and Amiloun themselves, once they have imprisoned Amiloun's disappointing wife and left the loyal nephew in charge of his lands, they appear to live happily ever after. Amis's wife and children are never mentioned again, but of Amis and Amiloun themselves we are told:

> In much ioy with-out stryf
> To-geder ladde þey her lyf,
> Tel god after hem dide sende. (2494–6)

In another romance, these lines might summarise the married life of hero and heroine. As it is, the two friends die as they were born, upon a single day, and are buried in a single grave (2503–5).

If, as I. A. Richards once wrote, a book is 'a machine to think with',[33] what is the romance of *Amis and Amiloun* prompting us to think about, exactly? The loyalty and devotion of the heroes are admirable characteristics in themselves, yet some of the consequences of this devotion are distinctly less so. The way in which this text misdirects common romance tropes or displaces the standard romance ending provokes questions—about the nature of passionate human attachments and their place in society—which the text ultimately declines to answer. The self-absorption of Amis and Amiloun's love for each other is as great as that of Lancelot and Guinevere, but whereas a medieval moralist could condemn the latter on a number of conventional charges (adultery, treason), the audience of *Amis and Amiloun* is forced to evaluate the self-absorption of passionate attachment directly, without any such convenient distractions. *Amis and Amiloun* is often seen as straddling the genres of romance and hagiography, but its disquietingly intense focus on the heroes' love for each other, rather than on their Christian faith, draws it firmly back towards romance.[34]

---

[33] I. A. Richards, *Principles of Literary Criticism* (New York, 1924), 1.

[34] See Ojars Kratins, 'The Middle English *Amis and Amiloun*: Chivalric Romance or Secular Hagiography?', *PMLA*, 81 (1966), 347–54 and Kathryn Hume, 'Structure and Perspective: Romance and Hagiographic Features in the Amicus and Amelius Story', *Journal of English and Germanic Philology*, 69 (1970), 89–107. John Finlayson rejects it as a romance altogether, re-labelling it an *exemplum*: 'Definitions of Middle English Romance', *The Chaucer Review*, 15 (1980), 168–81 (175–7). But Andrea Hopkins re-admits it to the genre on the grounds that 'the particular aspect of the heroic character under scrutiny is the quality of friendship, the love and loyalty between knights—a legitimate subject for a romance'; see *The Sinful Knights: A Study of Middle English Penitential Romance* (Oxford, 1990), 17.

William of Palerne

No such questions of generic affiliation hang over the mid-fourteenth-century *William of Palerne*, which contains all that one might expect of a medieval romance and more: lost inheritances (all eventually regained); disguises; love-longing; flight and danger; spectacular displays of chivalric prowess on the part of the hero; comically improbable coincidences, and an array of happy marriages to conclude. The 'more' element is a friendly werewolf who, for modern readers, tends to overshadow the more conventional hero William, confirming W. C. Fields's famous dictum that one should never work with children or animals. *William of Palerne* is unusual for other reasons too. It translates its Old French source *Guillaume de Palerne* with surprising fidelity, including substantial monologues of love-longing of a kind more often stripped out by English translators. It is therefore long for a Middle English romance, originally running to *c* 5,828 lines against the 9,663 lines of the French.[35] Its use of the alliterative long line puts it in a small subset of English romances.[36] While there seems to have been an intermittent tradition of translating the *laisses* of French *chansons de geste* into unrhymed Middle English alliterative verse,[37] *Guillaume de Palerne* is in octosyllabic couplets and it would surely have been easier to have retained them, or at most performed minor surgery to produce the ubiquitous English tail-rhyme stanzas. As it is, the alliterative long lines give the romance an unaccustomed gravity, here deployed not to amplify the glory of battle, but to further its unabashed emphasis on sentimental, romantic love. *William of Palerne* is, finally, unique among fourteenth-century Middle English romances in having a named noble patron, Humphrey IX de Bohun, earl of Hereford (d. 1361), who apparently desired it 'for hem þat knowe no Frensche' (5533).[38]

The central pillar of the plot is the love between William, son of the king of Apulia and Sicily, and Melior, daughter of the emperor of Rome, but the interwoven tale of William and the werewolf is almost as important. For most of the story, no one knows who William is— not even William—apart from this kindly werewolf, who had abducted him as a four-year-old to save him from a murderous uncle intent on claiming the throne for himself. Although the werewolf's own name, Alphouns, is not revealed until the end of the romance when his enchantment is broken, we are told almost as soon as he is introduced that 'werwolf was he non wox of kinde' ('he had not become a werewolf naturally', 109), and he was in fact the first-born son of the king of Spain, magically transformed by his stepmother to ensure the succession of her own son instead. A parallel between the disinherited man-beast and William is thus immediately established, and will be made more explicit when the teenaged William takes a werewolf as his battlefield emblem (3215–20). The Spanish king

---

[35] The extant text of 5,540 lines survives only in Cambridge, King's College MS 13, which is now missing four folios containing *c* 288 lines: see G. H. V. Bunt (ed.), *William of Palerne: An Alliterative Romance* (Groningen, 1985), 3. For the French text, see Alexandre Micha (ed.), *Guillaume de Palerne: roman du XIIIᵉ siècle* (Geneva, 1990).

[36] Roughly 40 per cent of Middle English verse romances from before 1500 are in tail-rhyme stanzas, with almost the same percentage in rhyming couplets. Alliterative long lines account for only 12 per cent of the total, with the remainder of romances (less than 10 per cent) in stanzas of some kind: statistics derived from the romances as listed in Severs' *Manual*, excluding Older Scots works and the tales of Chaucer and Gower.

[37] On the links between *laisses* and the alliterative line, and the martial and epic or historical concerns that normally characterise alliterative romance, see Rosalind Field, 'The Anglo-Norman Background to Alliterative Romance', in D. A. Lawton (ed.) *Middle English Alliterative Poetry and Its Literary Background* (Cambridge, 1982), 54–69.

[38] On Humphrey, see Bunt (ed.), *William of Palerne*, 14–15 and R. F. Green, 'Humphrey and the Werewolf', in J. A. Burrow and H. N. Duggan (eds), *Medieval Alliterative Poetry: Essays in Honour of Thorlac Turville-Petre* (Dublin, 2010), 107–24 (108–12).

does not meet his werewolf-son until he has been defeated by the latter's human stand-in William, now also nick-named 'þe werwolf' (3911): the fact that the genuine werewolf is still unnamed at this point further conflates the two disinherited protagonists.

Animal transformations also enhance the love-story of William and Melior directly: when Melior is due to be married off to the son of the Greek emperor, her resourceful confidante Alisaundrine arranges for her and William to escape together wearing white bearskins. The 'bears' (who still wear human clothes beneath their disguises) are cared for by the werewolf until word of the ruse spreads, whereupon he helps them to exchange their bearskins for those of a hart and hind. This time spent as 'animals' in the forest may symbolise the lack of place in society for such unmarried, unsanctioned young lovers, but the English translator draws extra attention to the improbability of their disguise. After reaching Sicilian shores by stowing away in a barge, the werewolf helps them to sneak ashore by luring the sailors away, at great risk to himself (*Guillaume* 4602–10). The English translator here adds a vignette in which a 'barlegged bold boie' spots the 'deer' emerging from the hatches and strikes at the 'hind'. He later reports in amazement that he saw the 'hart' scoop up the injured 'hind', 'wiþ so comely contenaunce clippend in armes, / and ferden ferst on foure fet, and seþþe up tweyne' ('embracing in its arms in such a lovely way, and moving first upon four feet, then upon two', 2808–9). Elsewhere, both French and English versions blur the human/animal boundary still more comically when the Sicilian queen, alerted by a dream to the human natures of the two new deer in her park, approaches them at night herself stitched into a deerskin, as if it were impossible otherwise to communicate across even this false human/animal border: 'I am swiche a best as ȝe ben' (3133), she reassures the startled couple before persuading them into the castle and out of their ripe deerskins for a much-needed bath. These metamorphoses are memorable for their quirkiness, but it is also notable how positive they are, as if the irrationality associated with beasts—normally viewed as a negative trait—here serves to highlight the purity of the protagonists' love.

One of the other distinguishing features of this romance is its portrayal of the paralysing bashfulness of young love. In this it is reminiscent of *Floris and Blauncheflur*, and is the reason that both stories are sometimes classified as 'idyllic romances',[39] although William differs from Floris in being allowed to shine on the battlefield as well. *William of Palerne* not only retains much of the anguished self-examination of the soliloquies in its French source, but even expands upon them at times, displaying an interest in the psychology of love that is rarely seen in Middle English romance. Melior's first sleepless night over Guillaume takes up 121 lines, but the English Melior agonises for 137 lines, and even this is incomplete thanks to a missing folio.[40] Her speech is full of the usual oxymorons of love and the paralysis of indecision they induce. She resolves to be his forever, only to fall back into imagining his reaction if she were to confess her love to him: how awful, she agonises, if William were to respond with a mortifyingly distant 'Serteinly, swete damisele, þat me sore rewes'! (562: this additional detail of psychological realism is not in the French).

Cooper has argued for what she dubs a 'feminine poetics' of love in the speeches and internal debates of such heroines, which often—as here—precede and overshadow the expression of love-longing on the part of the hero, redressing the balance of 'the whole male-centred courtly love phenomenon of the disdainful lady as the object of the poetry

---

[39] E.g., William Calin, *The French Tradition and the Literature of Medieval England* (Toronto, 1994), 479.
[40] ME 433–570, beginning after the lost fol. 10; OF 829–949.

of desire'.[41] The foregrounding of Lavine's love-agonies in the mid-twelfth-century *Roman d'Eneas*, memorably represented by her stutter over Eneas's name as she confesses her love to a confidante, highlight the differing emphases of epic and the emerging genre of romance. In Virgil's *Aeneid*, the affair with Dido was a distraction and marriage to Lavinia a practical necessity, but in the *Roman d'Eneas*, the foundation of his marriage to Lavine upon love becomes the point. Lavine's famous stutter is imitated directly by the heroine of the later twelfth-century Anglo-Norman *Ipomédon*, and this scene is retained in the most faithful of its three Middle English translations, the 8,890-line tail-rhyme *Ipomadon* which, throughout, proves to be more sympathetic to its female characters than its more sardonic Anglo-Norman source.[42] It is probably no accident that the poet renders the Anglo-Norman heroine's nick-name 'la Fiere' ('the Proud One') as the more ambiguous (or deliberately punning?) 'Fere', which *can* mean 'proud' but more readily translates as 'companion, equal', and was often misread by scribes as the even more flattering 'fair'.[43] But the Middle English *Ipomadon* nevertheless retains its source's primary focus on the hero's *Scarlet Pimpernel*-like determination to hide his prowess beneath a series of increasingly comical disguises while building up sufficient honour to become worthy of his beloved 'Fere', whereas the Middle English *William of Palerne* seems deliberately to rebalance his entire romance in favour of the emotional and social development of the protagonists, male and female. Accounts of William's chivalric exploits (against the Duke of Saxony outside Rome and the Spanish in Sicily) are shortened, while scenes of emotional interplay are expanded, thus making up a far greater proportion of the English translation. These include love soliloquies of course, but also scenes which heighten the emotional impact of the romance more subtly, such as what is now the opening scene in the acephalous English text. Where the French tells, in 39 lines, how a cowherd with his hound discovers Guillaume alone in the forest, soothes his fear of the dog, and brings him home to his wife (187–226), the English translator expands this into a seventy-five-line pastoral idyll now set 'in þe Mey sesoun', with 'buschys þat were blowed grene / and leved ful lovely, that lent grete schade' (21–2 and 24). The beauty of the surroundings tempts the little child to emerge from the werewolf's den 'faire floures to fecche þat he bifore him seye/and to gadere of þe grases þat grene were and fayre' (21–7). The cowherd's attempts to soothe the child's terror of the hound who sniffs him out are likewise carefully elaborated. He

... to þe barn* talked,	*child*
and foded* it wiþ floures and wiþ faire byhest*,	*enticed; promises*
and hiȝt* it hastely* to have what it wold* ȝerne,	*promised; soon; desire*
apeles and all þinges þat childern after wilnen. (55–9)	

It is difficult to quantify the impact of the fresh optimism of the spring described here, or these tiny details of human interaction, but they underpin the English romance's enhanced emotional focus.

This in turn highlights the extreme emphasis of *William of Palerne* on repentance, forgiveness and reconciliation. The plot may require the king of Spain and his son to stop making war on Sicily so that the werewolf Alphouns may be reunited with his father and a rash of marriages, including William and Melior's, may ensue, but there is no narrative

---

[41] Helen Cooper, 'Passionate, Eloquent and Determined: Heroines' Tales and Feminine Poetics', *Journal of the British Academy*, 4 (2016), 221–44, at 237.

[42] Hue de Rotelande, in A. J. Holden (ed.), *Ipomédon* (Paris, 1979), lines 1499–1517; R. Purdie (ed.), *Ipomadon*, EETS o.s. 316 (Oxford, 2001), lines 1439–71.

[43] See *MED fer* adj.[2] and *fere* n.[1]; and Purdie (ed.), *Ipomadon*, notes to 99, 106–8, and 7315.

necessity for the earnest speeches of repentance by the Spaniards for attacking in the first place (3981-4006). More surprising is the treatment of the evil stepmother Braunde: although William assures a mistrustful Alphouns that she will be killed if she refuses to reverse her enchantment of him, when she tearfully repents and restores Alphouns as required, she too is forgiven by all and suffers no further punishment (4386ff.). Even the Greek emperor and his son, disappointed suitor of Melior, are grudgingly reconciled to William and Melior's marriage. Once again, this recalls the pacifying effects of Floris and Blauncheflur's devoted love upon those around them. It is tempting to speculate that this extraordinary emphasis on forgiveness and reconciliation is one of the things that may have attracted the translator's patron Humphrey de Bohun. Humphrey's father had taken part in the failed marcher lords' rebellion against Edward II, and the family's lands and goods were forfeited after his death in battle against Royalist forces in 1322, at which point the teenaged Humphrey and his brothers were also imprisoned. But the de Bohuns were forgiven and restored to their earldoms five years later by Edward III, a spectacular fall and revival.[44]

One of the greatest compliments that has been paid to the skill of this poet is George Kane's speculation (recently revived by Lawrence Warner) that it might be an unrecognised early work by William Langland.[45] Although the notion was effectively dismissed by its most recent editor Gerrit Bunt (who demonstrated that four clear aspects of Langland's alliterative practice which Michael Samuels had used to localise *Piers Plowman* to southwest Worcestershire are *not* shared by *William of Palerne*),[46] it is a testament to this poet's skill that one of *Piers Plowman*'s most dedicated editors was prepared to even entertain the possibility. Kane's admiration is not universal: W. R. J. Barron describes its lines as being 'bloated by alliterative grandiloquence', while Thomas Honegger complains that it employs the alliterative form 'without either exploiting its rhetorical or formal potential'.[47] But either way, we are some distance from the 'rym dogerel' which many modern critics, following Chaucer's disingenuous lead in his 'Tale of Sir Thopas', feel characterises the prosody of Middle English romances.

Middle English metrical romances are sometimes treated as if their status as poems were little more than incidental, but this last should caution readers against dismissing their poetic qualities so readily. We are so used to evaluating poetry on the grounds of complexity and originality that its other potential aims are often ignored. This is not to say that Middle English romances are never complex or original, but that neither of these features— whether in narrative design or prosodic detail—are the sources of their strength or their lasting appeal. Many of the romances discussed in this chapter exploit the mesmerising regularity of their patterning—the more obvious the better—to heighten the emotional impact on their readers in poems which themselves take a powerful emotion as their subject. The concerns of romance with social order mean that love is often paired with dynasty, with a drive towards marriage, the consolidation of power, and the birth of legitimate heirs to ensure the safe transfer of inheritance. But several of the romances discussed in this

---

[44] Although Green's biographical reading ('Humphrey and the werewolf') does not suggest this emphasis as a reason for Humphrey's interest in the text, he does explore Humphrey's status as orphan, lack of military career, and evidence for an interest in magic.

[45] George Kane, *Chaucer and Langland: Historical and Textual Approaches* (London, 1989), 282 n. 4; Lawrence Warner, *The Myth of Piers Plowman* (Cambridge, 2014), 22–36.

[46] Gerrit H. V. Bunt, 'Localizing *William of Palerne*', in Jacek Fisiak (ed.), *Historical Linguistics and Philology* (Berlin, 1990), 73–86, at 80–1.

[47] W. R. J. Barron, *English Medieval Romance* (London, 1987), 197; Thomas Honegger, 'Romancing the Form: Alliterative Metre and *William of Palerne*', in W. Rudulf, T. Honegger, and A. J. Johnston (eds), *Clerks, Wives and Historians: Essays on Medieval English Language and Literature* (Frankfurt/Main, 2007), 117–24, at 122.

308   MEDIEVAL POETRY: 1100–1400

chapter demonstrate that the romancers' interests extended to the mysterious nature of love itself—even, in cases like *Amis and Amiloun* or *Sir Orfeo*, to the exclusion of concerns about dynastic stability. The fact that these romances are not part of an established 'matter' perhaps allowed their authors that little bit more freedom to explore the emotion that was so fundamentally associated with the genre of romance that 'love' and 'romance' have become almost interchangeable in modern usage.

20
Romances of the Ancient World

Wolfram R. Keller

In Geoffrey Chaucer's *The House of Fame*, the narrator Geffrey travels upwards in the claws of an eagle to visit Fama's palace, where he sees several pillared statues representing different historiographical traditions: Homer, Dares, Dictys, Lollius, Guido delle Colonne, and one 'Englyssh Gaufride'. They are all 'besy for to bere up Troye', a dauting task, since 'to bere hyt was no game' (1464–74).[1] This list of authorities, later supplemented by Virgil and Ovid (1481–9), represents Trojan historiography as it would have been known to late-fourteenth-century insular poets. These are also the authorities Chaucer has to grapple with, perhaps at the same time, in penning his own Troy story, *Troilus and Criseyde*.[2] Geffrey's encounter with Trojan history betokens the belatedness of a late-medieval author in engaging with antecedent poetic traditions, captured, for instance, in Chaucer's self-conscious authorial reference in the prologue to the *Legend of Good Women*: 'And I come after, glenyng here and there, / And am ful glad yf I may fynden an ere / Of any goodly word that ye han left' (75–7). As poems, however, Chaucer's Troy stories benefit *aesthetically* from what one could anachronistically call 'historiographical relativism'. After all, there is disagreement between the historians he mentions; Geffrey notices 'a litil envye' between them (1476). The focus falls specifically on Homer for his supposed Greek bias. Therefore, at the interstices of multiple and subjective, frequently contradictory accounts of Troy, authorial invention becomes not only possible but necessary. What Geffrey's encounter with Trojan historiography dramatises is the authorial confrontation of *multiple* antiquities, which prompts a sustained reflection upon the craft of poetry, upon models of literary authorship driven by invention.[3] And Chaucer is not the only late-medieval poet whose interest in classical antiquity is concomitantly an interest in poetics. In fact, most late-medieval romances of the ancient world are pivotally concerned with vernacular poetics and literary authorship.

In histories of English literature, romances of the ancient world are usually discussed under the rubric of 'the matter of Rome', the widely adopted, albeit problematic classification of 'matters' going back to Jehan Bodel's distinction between the matters of France, Brittany, and Rome in his twelfth-century *Song of Saxons*, to which scholars later added the 'matter of England'.[4] The matter of Rome was popular in Continental literature of the twelfth and thirteenth centuries, as evinced by a plethora of texts retelling the siege of Thebes, the lives and deeds of Alexander and Aeneas, and the Trojan War. Middle English poetry before the fifteenth century, however, is concerned primarily with Troy and Alexander rather than

---

[1] Geoffrey Chaucer, in Larry D. Benson (gen. ed.), *The Riverside Chaucer*, 3rd edn. (Boston, MA, 1987).

[2] Helen Cooper, 'Chaucerian Poetics', in Robert G. Benson and Susan J. Ridyard (eds), *New Readings of Chaucer's Poetry* (Cambridge, 2003), 31–50.

[3] For recent work on medieval literary authorship, see especially Robert R. Edwards, *Invention and Authorship in Medieval England* (Columbus, OH, 2017).

[4] Jehan Bodel, in Annette Brasseur (ed.), *La chanson de Saisnes*, Textes littéraires français, 2 vols. (Geneva, 1989), 1:7. For problems with the matters-classification, see Dieter Mehl, *The Middle English Romances of the Thirteenth and Fourteenth Centuries* (London, 1968), 30–8.

Wolfram R. Keller, *Romances of the Ancient World*. In: *The Oxford History of Poetry in English*. Edited by Helen Cooper and Robert R. Edwards, Oxford University Press. © Wolfram R. Keller (2023). DOI: 10.1093/oso/9780198827429.003.0020

310 MEDIEVAL POETRY: 1100–1400

Thebes or Aeneas.[5] The reasons for the insular interest particularly in Troy and Alexander were most likely topical. While these romances treated the past, 'the uses to which it is put serve the exigencies of a new and particular historical moment'.[6] For English audiences, the Troy story was notably not concerned with a remote culture, but with the beginnings of English history itself. In courtly and political contexts, Troy was thus an important reference point for historicising contemporary courtly practices and legitimising dynastic claims. Furthermore, the popularity of vernacular accounts of the Trojan War coincided with the Hundred Years' War, the former potentially providing important political lessons for the latter. At a first glance, the case is different with Alexander romances, which seem unconcerned with insular politics. Yet, Alexander's rise to power and his impressive conquests as much as his tragic downfall caused by foolhardiness and treason were instructive for English audiences with a view to the government of self and the community. Moreover, Alexander's exploration and conquest of the East not only furnished marvellous stories but resonated also with the fascination with—and fear of—Otherness in the context of the Crusades. And for poets, I would add, the 'Englishing' of Alexander entailed an engagement with complex textual histories that simultaneously offered ample opportunity to reflect upon *textual* sovereignty and poetics.

Middle English romances of the ancient world have generally not found much favour with later audiences, philological studies concerned with dating, manuscript contexts, and sources notwithstanding. The romances under discussion here were largely seen as uninspired 'translations' of French or Latin sources,[7] their scholarly neglect being based precisely on what is the topic of this chapter: their poetry. Recently, the romances of the ancient world have attracted greater scholarly interest because of their ideological investments. What is often sidestepped in such accounts are the aesthetic concerns of Middle English Troy and Alexander poems, especially the way in which they reflect about their status as poems. To be sure, romances treating the matters of France, Brittany, or England are not any less concerned with poetry.[8] However, in their belated encounters with Troy and Alexander, late-medieval insular poets faced layers of often contradictory versions of their material, frequently in different languages as well as genres. This forced authors to make choices that are inevitably also *poetic* choices, provoking questions about the role of the poet in the mediation of texts and the re-*making* of classical antiquity to address contemporary concerns. In this chapter, I provide a short overview of the extant Middle English Troy and Alexander romances, followed by discussion of the poetic choices made by the authors of the *Destruction of Troy* and *Kyng Alisaunder* in their specific reworkings of antecedent traditions and their concomitant advancements of a poetics suitable to the rewriting of antiquity. Reading romances of the ancient world thus means uncovering a meta-poetic repository, as multiple antiquities become a laboratory for writers to explore new forms and themes as well as ideas of literary authorship.

Rebuilding Troy

When Chaucer's Geffrey calls Homer a liar, he voices a widespread view of a poet whose works were not known directly in the Middle Ages. Consequently, the medieval Troy

---

[5] See Albert C. Baugh, 'The Middle English Period (1100–1500)', in Kemp Malone and Albert C. Baugh, *The Middle Ages*, 2nd edn. (London, 1967), 181.

[6] Helen Cooper, 'Romance after 1400', in David Wallace (ed.), *The Cambridge History of Medieval English Literature* (Cambridge, 1999), 690.

[7] See, e.g., Dorothy Everett, 'The Alliterative Revival', in Patricia Kean (ed.), *Essays on Middle English Literature* (Oxford, 1955), 58, and below.

[8] For the problems with Orientalist readings of medieval romances, see Chapter 22 in this volume.

story differed from the account offered in Homer's *Iliad* and *Odyssey*. The Troy story was nonetheless the most widely disseminated secular narrative in the European Middle Ages. It came to England by way of different textual traditions, which James Simpson distinguishes as 'Galfridian', 'elegiac', and 'tragic'—all alluded to in Chaucer's *Fame*.[9] As Helen Cooper suggests, Chaucer's reference to one 'Englyssh Gaufride' most likely refers to Chaucer and his *Troilus* rather than to Geoffrey of Monmouth and his *Historia Regum Britanniae* (1136).[10] And yet, contemporary audiences may well have enjoyed the ambiguity. Geoffrey's *Historia* is not a Troy story as such but opens with the exiled Trojan Brutus and his odyssey across Europe, ending with the conquest of Britain and the founding of a New Troy (London).[11] It conceptualises for an insular audience what made the Troy story so attractive for the European aristocracy, which habitually traced its lineages to Troy: the destruction of Troy was the birth of Rome (Aeneas), of France (Francus), of Britain (Brutus), a westward transfer of power and empire (*translatio imperii*). Quickly available in the French and English vernaculars, Geoffrey's *Historia* popularised the Trojan origins of Britain and was used to legitimate dynastic claims.[12] With the 'elegiac' tradition, Simpson refers to Ovid's treatments of Trojan material, which offered a counterpoint to Virgil's imperial *Aeneid*. Especially influential are Ovid's *Heroides*, the collection of epistolary laments by women abandoned in the course of male empire-making, detailing its emotional costs—a narrative strategy adopted by Chaucer in representing Dido or Criseyde.[13]

The other Trojan authorities mentioned by Geffrey (Dares, Dictys, Guido) are part of the 'tragic' tradition, which is essentially a 'Guido tradition'. Guido delle Colonne's *Historia Destructionis Troiae* (1287), extant in over 150 manuscripts, was a veritable bestseller and the most influential medieval Troy story throughout Europe.[14] In this Latin prose chronicle, Guido claims to be following only the most reliable sources instead of the fictions of poets like Homer, Virgil, and Ovid. Supposedly following Dares and Dictys, presumed eyewitnesses of the Trojan War, Guido actually 'translates' and redacts Benoît de Sainte-Maure's *Roman de Troie* (*c* 1160), a vernacular romance *not* mentioned in the *Historia* at all. Benoît's *Troie* combines Dares and Dictys, adding courtly flourish, especially expanding the love stories and inventing that of Troilus and Briseis/Criseyde. By way of turning Benoît's lively vernacular romance into a sober Latin chronicle, Guido removes most references to courtly culture and abridges the love stories, while retaining the narrative arc from Jason's quest for the Golden Fleece and the first destruction of Troy via the siege at Troy to the eventual deaths of the Greek victors.

Guido's *Historia* was translated into Middle English in the anonymous *Laud Troy Book*, John Clerk of Whalley's *Destruction of Troy*, and John Lydgate's *Troy Book* (1420).[15]

---

[9] James Simpson, 'Anti-Virgilianism in Late Medieval Troy Narratives', *Troianalexandrina*, 19 (2019), 293–312.

[10] Cooper, 'Chaucerian Poetics', 48–50.

[11] For London as the New Troy, see Sylvia Federico, *New Troy: Fantasies of Empire in the Late Middle Ages* (Minneapolis, MN, 2003), 1–28.

[12] See Francis Ingledew, 'The Book of Troy and the Genealogical Construction of History: The Case of Geoffrey of Monmouth's *Historia regum Britanniae*', *Speculum*, 69 (1994), 665–704; Simpson, *Reform and Cultural Revolution* (Oxford, 2002), 69–70.

[13] See Marilynn Desmond, *Reading Dido: Gender, Textuality, and the Medieval 'Aeneid'* (Minneapolis, MN, 1994).

[14] Guido delle Colonne, in Nathaniel Edward Griffin (ed.), *Historia destructionis Troiae* (Cambridge, MA, 1936). For biography, transmission, and reception, see Mary Elizabeth Meek (trans.), *Historia destructionis Troiae* (Bloomington, IN, 1974).

[15] For the reception of Guido in medieval England, see C. David Benson, *The History of Troy in Middle English Literature: Guido delle Colonne's 'Historia destructionis Troiae' in Medieval England* (Woodbridge, 1980); James Simpson, *Reform*; Wolfram R. Keller, *Selves and Nations: The Troy Story from Sicily to England in the Middle Ages* (Heidelberg, 2008); Władysław Witalisz, *The Trojan Mirror: Middle English Narratives of Troy as Books of Princely Advice* (Frankfurt/Main, 2011); Alex Mueller, *Translating Troy: Provincial Politics in Alliterative Romance* (Columbus, OH, 2013).

312   MEDIEVAL POETRY: 1100–1400

Moreover, the Troy story also served as a framing device in poems such as *Sir Gawain and the Green Knight* and *Wynnere and Wastoure*. In the late thirteenth or early fourteenth century—at the beginning of the insular 'Trojan craze'—the anonymous *Seege or Batayle of Troye* likewise retells the whole story of the Trojan War. The poet mentions Dares as his source, but the poem is based on the Latin *Excidium Troiae*, Benoît's *Troie*, and the *Compendium Historiae Troianae-Romanae*, and it omits the destinies of the Greeks.[16] The *Seege* represents an admirable effort in narrative economy as it relays the history of the war in only 2,067 lines of short, four-stressed couplets of—what critics see as—questionable quality. Given some mythological misconceptions on the poet's part, he has been seen as 'crude, unlearned', although J. A. W. Bennett allows that the poem contains 'some fine vivid and dramatic scenes'.[17] The poet re-organises the material to fit in with other popular romances treating ancient matter. He incorporates 'folktale patterns' and, while he claims to be interested in the battle—'ffor such a bataile as hit was on / y wis me nuste neuer non' (Lincoln's Inn, 9–10)—he shifts the focus towards specific individuals, Paris in the first part, Achilles in the second.[18]

A similar emphasis on the destiny of individuals is characteristic of the *Laud Troy Book*, which, with its 18,644 lines, is nine times longer than the *Seege*. The *Laud* is extant in one manuscript (Oxford, Bodleian Library, MS Laud Misc. 595), appears to originate in the Northwest Midlands, and was composed between 1343 and the early fifteenth century; most likely, it is the first translation of Guido's *Historia*.[19] Early on, Robert Root set the tone for discussions of the poem, which he deemed 'quite untouched by any breath of true poesy'. Still, scholars have noted the care with which the poet preserves the historical account. Bennett believes it is 'the most interesting' of the Trojan romances; C. David Benson argues that it is the 'freest translation of the *Historia*'.[20] With its four-stress couplets and the poet's frequent address of the audience, an atmosphere of oral performance is generated, however fictional that may be.[21] Like the *Seege*, the *Laud* appears to be interested particularly in individuals, especially Hector, wherefore the poem has been referred to as a 'Hector-romance'.[22] The poet likens the *Laud* to other romances dealing with individual (English) heroes, which he lists in the prologue: Bevis, Gawain, Richard, Havelok, Horn, etc. (15–21). What is missing is a romance concerned with the 'worthiest wyght in wede / That euere by-strod any stede' and with the war that marks the beginnings of knighthood, 'There alle prowes of knyghtes began' (27–8, 32). As a poem, the *Laud* is characterised by those features distinctive of the Middle English romances alluded to in the prologue: direct address of the audience; emotional and lively narration; reported speech rendered as dialogue. The poet also employs (unconventional) figurative language—for instance, when knights fight

---

[16] Mary Elizabeth Barnicle (ed.), *The Seege or Batayle of Troye: A Middle English Metrical Romance*, EETS, o.s. 172 (1927; New York, 1971), xxx–xxxiii, lvi–lxxiv.

[17] Benson, *History*, 134; J. A. W. Bennett, in Douglas Gray (ed.), *Middle English Literature 1100–1400* (Oxford, 1986), 194. See further Nancy Mason Bradbury, *Writing Aloud: Storytelling in Late Medieval England* (Urbana, IL, 1998), 106–10.

[18] For the diptych structure, dominated by Paris and Achilles, respectively, see Nicola McDonald, 'The Seege of Troye: "ffor wham was wakened al this wo"', in Ad Putter and Jane Gilbert (eds), *The Spirit of Medieval English Popular Romance* (Harlow, 2000), 183–4, 193–4.

[19] J. Ernst Wülfing (ed.), *The Laud Troy Book*, 2 vols., EETS o.s. 121, 122 (London, 1902, 1903). See further Dorothy Kempe, 'A Middle English Tale of Troy', *Englische Studien*, 29 (1901), 5–6; Wülfing, 'Das Laud-Troybook: Hs. Bodl. Laud 595 (früher K. 76)', *Englische Studien*, 29 (1901), 376–7.

[20] Robert K. Root, rev. of *The Laud Troy Book, a Romance of about 1400 A.D.*, edited by J. Ernst Wülfing, *Journal of English and Germanic Philology*, 5 (1905), 367; Bennett, *Middle English*, 194; Benson, *History*, 67.

[21] Thorlac Turville-Petre, *The Alliterative Revival* (Cambridge, 1977), 37–8. Paul Strohm, 'Storie, Spelle, Gest, Romaunce, Tragedie: Generic Distinction in the Middle English Troy Narratives', *Speculum*, 46 (1971), 354.

[22] See especially Benson, *History*, 82–8; Strohm, 'Storie', 354.

as rats and cats (6787–8)—and he uses vague passages in the *Historia* to invent the necessary details (e.g., 7445–52). Here and elsewhere the poet dresses antiquity in contemporary garb, transposing the Trojan War into fourteenth-century English contexts. Moreover, his acts of invention also show his familiarity with the rhetorical and poetical conventions of his day, including alliterative poetry.[23] One such lapse into alliteration occurs when the poet tells of the Greek departure to besiege Troy:

> In this talkyng may ʒe here telle
> Off ferly fyght, ffele and felle,
> Of comely kynges corouned and kene,
> That Troye distroyed alle be-dene,
> And brende her houses on a blase;
> And how that strong knyghtes here lyff lase.
> Ther was the worthiest wyght In wede
> That euer by-strode palfray or stede ... (3247–54)

Opening a new movement of the narrative, marked by the repetition of the prologue's characterisation of Hector as the 'worthiest wyght In wede', the poet's sudden use of alliteration gestures towards a different tradition and a different mode of poetic representation the poet chooses not to use consistently, as is the case in Clerk's translation of Guido's *Historia*.

Clerk's *Destruction of Troy* boasts 14,000 unrhymed, regular lines of alliterative verse, written in the North-West Midland dialect. Surviving in only one manuscript (Glasgow, University Library, Hunterian MS V.2.8), the *Destruction* probably dates to the end of the fourteenth century and originates in a climate of Lancastrian nationalism.[24] Clerk's translation is often seen as a rather uninspired, faithful rendering of his source, although scholars have noticed that the poet introduces some changes to Guido's structure: Guido's thirty-six books, for instance, become thirty-five in the *Destruction*. Clerk also shortens or omits Guido's moral outbursts and mythological ramblings, which has been seen as evidence for his lack of learning.[25] Like the *Laud* poet, Clerk enlivens Guido's prose by occasionally switching from an omniscient narrator's to a character's point of view and rendering reported speech dialogically.[26] Noting that Clerk highlights the importance of individual choice rather than blaming fickle Fortune, Alex Mueller has argued that the *Destruction* is a 'raw expression of human freewill', a finding contextualised within the ideological dynamics of other alliterative poems that bespeak a 'deep-seated skepticism about the possibility of an English nation' and a strong anti-aristocratic bias, the latter generally seen as characteristic of the Guido tradition.[27] Scholarship interested in Clerk's poetry has hitherto mainly

---

[23] See especially Bennett, *Middle English*, 195–8.

[24] Hiroyuki Matsumoto (ed.), *The Destruction of Troy: A Critical Edition; Hunterian MS v.2.8 in Glasgow University Library* (Okayama, 2010), xiv–xv; see also Mueller, *Translating Troy*, 40 n. 1, 46 n. 13. In-text quotations are from G. A. Panton and D. Donaldson (eds), *The 'Gest Hystoriale' of the Destruction of Troy*, 2 vols., EETS o.s. 39, 56 (London, 1869, 1874). For Clerk's authorship, see Thorlac Turville-Petre, 'The Author of *The Destruction of Troy*', *Medium Ævum* 57 (1988), 264–9.

[25] Nicolas Jacobs, 'Alliterative Storms: A Topos in Middle English', *Speculum*, 47 (1972), 695–719; D. A. Lawton, 'The Destruction of Troy as Translation from Latin Prose: Aspects of Form and Style', *Studia Neophilologica*, 52 (1980), 259–70; John Finlayson, 'Guido de Columnis' *Historia destructionis Troiae*, The 'Gest Hystorial' of the Destruction of Troy, and Lydgate's Troy Book: Translation and the Design of History', *Anglia*, 113 (1995), 141–62. For the rearrangement of the plot and the omission of moralisation and mythologising, see Benson, *History*, 47–9; Finlayson, 'Guido', 152–3.

[26] Benson, *History*, 62–6.

[27] Mueller, *Translating Troy*, 63, 66; quotation at 4; see also Simpson, *Reform*, 85–6.

314 MEDIEVAL POETRY: 1100–1400

commented upon the repetitiveness of his verse, especially in the battle descriptions, while emphasising, more generously, the poet's ability to 'vivify the often dull facts of Guido's eye-witness style', and the poet's skill in describing 'violent action—battles and storms at sea in particular'.[28] The use of alliterative verse is a conscious choice that is, I believe, also reflected in Clerk's advancement of a model of translation that clears historiographical space for the poet to emerge as a literary author.

Clerk's neglect of Guido's moral and mythological digressions is integral to his poetics. What seems like the poet's lack of learning or interest is a poetic strategy diverting attention away from potentially troubling questions regarding poetical and historiographical authority. For example, Clerk cuts Guido's history of Achilles's Myrmidons: 'More of thies Myrmydons mell I not now' (109). Similarly, he abruptly cuts short Guido's (confusing) description of Delos in Book 10 of the *Historia*, which includes a reference to Isidore's *Etymologies*: 'Of þis mater nomore but meue to our tale' (4278).[29] When pointing out, following Guido, that Homer is a liar, Clerk flags his familiarity with Homer, while simultaneously dismissing him: 'Of his trifuls to telle I haue no tome nowe' (43). The cumulative effect of such passages is that the authority of Clerk's sources is sidelined, lending gravitas to the poet's poetic enterprise of transforming chronicle into alliterative romance.

The transposition of the ancient world into contemporary insular poetic contexts in the *Destruction* develops by analogy to the rebuilding of Troy. Clerk conceptualises the rebuilding of Troy *and* his poem as *werke*, both of which presuppose mental planning or *inventio*: 'Now, god, of þi grace graunt me þi helpe, / And wysshe me with wyt þis werke for to end!' (3–4). As Clerk rehearses Priam's rebuilding of Troy into English, his invention and craft restructure Books 4 and 5 of the *Historia*. The fourth book of the *Destruction* closes with the genealogical outline of Priam's offspring, so that the fifth book begins with the rebuilding of Troy, marking 'the beginning of a new movement in the story'.[30] Moreover, this modification spotlights generational-genealogical as well as architectural rupture and repair. In translating Guido, Clerk shows himself to be particularly interested in households and domestic spaces, for instance, by noting that the Trojans are 'Hurlet out of houses', their possessions being taken away from their 'priuey chambur[s]' (1365, 1371). Also, for Priam the destruction of Troy is epitomised by the demolished houses, 'the buyldynges brent & beton to ground' (1519). As in the *Historia*, Priam assembles skilled craftsmen of all kinds for the rebuilding of the city, 'Wise wrightis to wale werkys to caste' (1530). However, *werke* appears to not only refer to the rebuilding of Troy. When Priam, his cheeks wet from excessive crying, discusses the debris and rubble, the destruction of Troy emerges also as *werke*—'Soche wo for þat werke þan þe wegh thowlit, / Þat all his wongys were wete for weping of teres, / Thre dayes þroly …' (1520–2). Clerk goes on to speak of Troy as a *werke* in describing the city's towers: 'Mony toures vp tild þe toune to defende, / Wroght vp with the walle as þe werke rose, / One negh to Anoþer nobly deuyset …' (1551–3). Moreover, the 'inventiveness' of design is repeatedly highlighted as, for instance, in the arcades that protect pedestrians from the rain—'By the sydes for sothe of sotell deuyse, / Was archet full Abilly for aylyng of shoures …' (1576–7)—or in the splendour of Priam's palace—'fful worthely wroght & by

---

[28] Benson, *History*, 57; Everett, 'Alliterative Revival', 58; both with a view to lines 12,467–74, 1983–2011; but cf. John Finlayson, 'Alliterative Narrative Poetry: The Control of the Medium', *Traditio*, 44 (1988), 423–9.

[29] At this point, Benson (*History*, 49) surmises the poet realised that 'he had made a muddle of things'.

[30] Finlayson, 'Guido', 150. Clerk also re-organises Guido's 21st Book, linking the demise of Hector to the eventual deaths of the Greek heroes, underscoring Clerk's commitment to the possibility of 'open-process' in view of the inevitable (153–4).

wit caste' (1632). Finally, Clerk asserts, the whole city was built as a product of imagination: 'As Priam hade purpost all with pure wit' (1690). This recalls Geoffrey of Vinsauf's observation that architecture, just like poetry, first has to be *imagined* and *invented*.[31] The result of Priam's architectural imagination is an exemplary city, compared to Rome by both Guido and Clerk. Only in the *Destruction*, however, does Troy become the model for Rome: 'In Ensample of this Cite, sothely to telle, / Rome on a River rially was set, / ... / Tild vpon Tiber after Troy like' (1610–13).

The poetic rebuilding of the Troy story—which, by means of the narrative rearrangements and attendant ideological reassessments, is already a rebuilding with a difference—is, in fact, more deeply embedded within the poetic structure of the poem. As both Benson and Mueller have noted regarding the prologue, Clerk could hardly have seconded Guido's condemnation of poets as makers of fictions. Instead, Clerk 'distinguishes true from false poets'.[32] Importantly, Clerk's reflection regarding the translation of ancient matter into 'modern' form becomes a reflection on the *poetic* vicissitudes of such a project. True stories of the deeds of one's noble ancestors ('aunstris nobill') and the great battles of the most valiant knights and wisest of men, Clerk observes, are struck from memory, are swallowed up by the passing of years: 'Sothe stories ben stoken vp, & straught out of mind, / And swolowet into swym by swiftenes of yeres ...' (11–12). Old stories are superseded by new works, often written for other purposes (e.g., the emboldening of hearts), pleasant to peruse and accomplished through chance and changeability, some trustworthy, some not:

> Ffor new þat ben now, next at our hond,
> Breuyt into bokes for boldyng of hertes;
> On lusti to loke with lightnes of wille,
> Cheuyt throughe chaunce & chaungyng of peopull;
> Sum tru for to traist, triet in þe ende,
> Sum fenyit o fere & ay false vnder. (13–18)

Subsequently, Clerk turns to the deeds of the 'ancients', recorded by those who actually witnessed them and wrote them down for succeeding generations, to know exactly how the case fell by means of acts of transmission: 'Be writyng of wees þat wist it in dede, / With sight for to serche, of hom þat suet after, / To ken all the crafte how þe case felle, / By lokyng of letturs þat lefte were of olde' (23–6). This prologue is, indeed, a 'poetic manifesto',[33] albeit not a straightforward one: even if people delight in the deeds of the ancients as recorded by eyewitnesses, the latter are inevitably also part of a process of transmission, the 'lokyng of letturs', a phrase that has been interpreted variously: as referring to the Old English alliterative tradition; as combining Dares and Dictys; as 'linking' 'Trojan and British history' in a 'work of sober history that privileges truth over entertainment'.[34] Problematically, given the prologue's emphasis on textual *and* generational changeability, the 'lokyng of letturs'

---

[31] In his *Poetria nova*, Geoffrey of Vinsauf compares poetic invention to the construction of a house: 'Mentis in arcano cum rem digesserit ordo, / Materiam verbis veniat vestire poesis' ('when due order has arranged the material in the hidden chamber of the mind, let poetic art come forward to clothe the matter with words'). See *Poetria nova*, in Edmond Faral (ed.), *Les arts poétiques du XIIe e du XIIIe siècle*, (1924; Paris, 1958) 1.60–1; I use Margaret F. Nim (trans.), *Poetria Nova of Geoffrey of Vinsauf* (Toronto, 1967), 17.

[32] Benson, *History*, 37. See further Mueller, *Translating Troy*, 53–4.

[33] Finlayson, 'Guido', 144.

[34] Mueller, *Translating Troy*, 55–60, quotations at 56, 59, argues against the former, offering the two latter options, echoing Benson, *History*, 47. Christine Chism, *Alliterative Revivals* (Philadelphia, PA, 2002), 36, reads the 'locking of letters' in *Sir Gawain and the Green Knight* (30–6) as an 'anchoring process by suggesting the antiquity of the meter as a native tradition. The poem wants it both ways, claims both types of poetic legitimacy:

of Clerk's *werke* is also affected by the mutability and changeability inherent in any kind of rebuilding whether of towns or poems *about* towns. In this respect, poetic genealogy is no different from a Trojan genealogy, which, as Simpson observes in a different context, 'guarantees very little indeed'.[35] Appropriately, then, the 'lokyng of letturs' becomes the aesthetic correlative of the rebuilding of cities and poems, which are not—and can never be—identical, a point emblematised in Clerk's choice of the alliterative line (*aa/ax*), which ultimately propels phonetic familiarity and similarity forwards into something unfamiliar and different.

The forward-moving lines of alliterative verse and their progressive defamiliarisation and changeability as an aesthetic correlative for the translation of antiquity into fourteenth-century insular poetic context also has a temporal dimension. This temporal dimension becomes manifest and poetically important in the jarring of temporalities within medieval English Alexander romances. For example, the different poetic forms used by the *Kyng Alisaunder* poet to represent diverse experiences of time, different temporalities (teleological, cyclical, static) which can be read as self-conscious reflections of the poet's poetics.

Time and Poetry in the Alexander Romances

Stories about Alexander circulated already in Anglo-Saxon England, gaining popularity again in the late thirteenth century,[36] as evinced not only by the Alexander romances under discussion here, but by frequent allusions to Alexander, for instance, in Chaucer's 'Monk's Tale', Gower's *Confessio Amantis*, in (vernacular) historiography, or in accounts of the Nine Worthies.[37] In relaying the rise to power and tragic death of the greatest conqueror of all times, Middle English writers variously admire or critique Alexander's imperial ambitions, while marvelling at his conquests and his exploration of the East. Generally, Alexander texts can be subdivided into two different traditions, a Latin 'historical' tradition, believed to be more critical of Alexander, and a Greek 'romance' tradition, believed to offer a more positive assessment.[38] The 'historical' tradition is constituted by Quintus Curtius Rufus's *Res Gestae Alexandri Magni*, the chief source of Walter of Châtillon's *Alexandreis* and Pompeius Trogus's *Historicae Philippicae*, a world history redacted by M. Julianus Justinus (Justin's *Epitome*), which, in turn, is the source for Orosius's *Historiae Adversus Paganos*. A more 'fantastic' account of Alexander can be found in the Greek Alexander romance. Much like the Troy stories of Dares and Dictys, the Greek Alexander romance was erroneously believed to be an eyewitness account provided by one Callisthenes, allegedly a nephew of Aristotle travelling with Alexander. Pseudo-Callisthenes exists in numerous recensions, including the Julius Valerius *Epitome* (also *Zacher Epitome*), which is the main source for the Anglo-Norman *Roman de toute chevalerie*, the source for the Middle English *Kyng Alisaunder*. Pseudo-Callisthenes was available also through the various recensions of the *Historia de*

---

speaking tongue and written letter, comparative metrical flexibility and rigidity, "toun" and "londe," eye and ear, innovation and tradition'.

[35] Simpson, *Reform*, 98.

[36] For Old English Alexander texts, see David Ashurst, 'Alexander Literature in English and Scots', in David Zuwiyya (ed.), *A Companion to Alexander Literature in the Middle Ages* (Leiden, 2011), 257–63; Gerrit H. V. Bunt, *Alexander the Great in the Literature of Medieval Britain* (Groningen, 1994), 14–18.

[37] Bunt, *Alexander*, 35–60; David Ashurst, 'Alexander the Great', in Neil Cartlidge (ed.), *Heroes and Anti-Heroes in Medieval Romance* (Cambridge, 2012), 27–42.

[38] For the transmission of the Alexander material in the Middle Ages, see George Cary, *The Medieval Alexander*, ed. D. J. A. Ross (Cambridge, 1956); Zuwiyya (ed.), *Alexander Literature*. See further Bunt, *Alexander*, 1–13; Ashurst' 'Alexander Literature', 255–90.

Preliis Alexandri Magni, often interpolated with the *Fuerre de Gadres* (relaying the siege of Tyre, entry into Jerusalem, and the overpowering of Darius), and reworked in the *Roman d'Alexandre* by Alexander of Paris. The Greek Alexander romance recounts the birth and upbringing of Alexander, the son of Neptanabus, an Egyptian emperor, soothsayer, and magician. Fleeing from Egypt on account of a Persian attack, Neptanabus seeks refuge in Macedonia, where he seduces Olympias, the wife of king Philip, and impregnates her disguised as the god Ammon, begetting Alexander. Alexander grows up as Philip's son, unwittingly kills his father Neptanabus, is crowned by Philip, rescues his mother Olympias from slander and imprisonment, and, eventually, begins his conquest of the world. The second part of the narrative is focused on the long conflict with the Persian Darius. A third part of the narrative continues with Alexander's Eastern campaign, which conveys much detailed information about the Wonders of the East, while the last part of the narrative relates the prophecy of the trees of the Sun and the Moon, foretelling the conqueror's death by poison. The romance ends with the posthumous distribution of Alexander's wealth.

Like the Troy romances, Middle English Alexander romances are extant in alliterative and non-alliterative form, all of which have suffered critical neglect and are aesthetically underappreciated.[39] Two alliterative Middle English Alexander romances can be dated with certainty to the fourteenth century. *Alexander A* and *Alexander B* (also called *Alexander and Dindimus*) are both fragments based on the Latin version of the Pseudo-Callisthenes known as the I^2 recension of the *Historia de Preliis*. A third alliterative romance, *The Wars of Alexander* (*Alexander C*), probably dates to the late fourteenth century or early fifteenth century and is based on the I^3 recension of the *Historia de Preliis. Alexander A* is included in an early seventeenth-century school notebook (Oxford, Bodleian Library, MS Greaves 60), appears to originate in the South-West Midlands, and was probably written in the first half of the fourteenth century. The 1,247 alliterative long lines relate Alexander's birth and early life, supplemented with details of Philip's conquests not contained in Orosius's *Historiae*.[40] While the poem does include an original portrait of Olympias, which points to the poet's interest in poetic embellishments, critics have dismissed *Alexander A* as 'mechanical and uninspired'.[41] *Alexander B* (included in Oxford, Bodleian Library, MS Bodley 264) most likely dates to the mid fourteenth century. In 1,139 long lines, the poet represents Alexander's encounter with the Gymnosophists, especially Alexander's epistolary conversation with the Brahmin king Dindimus. Scholars have been largely unimpressed by the poem's aesthetic quality, especially since the poet appears to follow his source rather closely.[42] Karl Heinz Göller, however, observed several modifications offering a more arrogant image of Alexander, who nonetheless has to eventually acknowledge that he, too, is a mere mortal.[43]

---

[39] Occasionally, Alexander and Troy texts appear in the same manuscript contexts; London, Lincoln's Inn MS 150, for instance, includes *Seege* and *Kyng Alisaunder*. For the medieval English reception of the Alexander material, see especially Bunt, *Alexander*. For (lack of) critical appreciation, see D. A. Lawton, 'The Middle English Alliterative *Alexander A* and C: Form and Style in Translation from Latin Prose', *Studia Neophilologica*, 53 (1981), 259–68; Karl Heinz Göller, 'Alexander und Dindimus: West-östlicher Disput über Mensch und Welt', in Willi Erzgräber (ed.), *Kontinuität und Transformation der Antike im Mittelalter* (Sigmaringen, 1989), 105–19, at 105–6. Rosalind Field observes that the 'story of Alexander never lost its bookish nature and did not lend itself to free adaptation and abbreviation'. See her 'Romance in England, 1066–1400', in David Wallace (ed.), *The Cambridge History of Medieval English Literature* (Cambridge, 1999), 172–3.

[40] Francis Peabody Magoun, Jr., (ed.), *The Gests of King Alexander of Macedon: Two Middle English Alliterative Fragments, 'Alexander A' and 'Alexander B'* (Cambridge, MA., 1929), 3–8; Bunt, *Alexander*, 27; Ashurst, 'Alexander the Great', 31.

[41] See, e.g., Bunt, *Alexander*, 28.

[42] Bunt, *Alexander*, 29; Bennett, *Middle English*, 192–3; Everett, 'Alliterative Revival', 56.

[43] Göller, 'Alexander', 112.

318   MEDIEVAL POETRY: 1100-1400

The almost 6,000 alliterative long lines of *The Wars of Alexander* recount Alexander's story up to his conquest of Babylon and the death of his horse Bucephalus, at which point the poem breaks off. The *Wars* survives in two manuscripts (Oxford, Bodleian Library, MS Ashmole 44; Dublin, Trinity College, MS 213) and originates in the north-west Midlands.[44] The poet offers a much longer account of Alexander's life, and he does so in narrative sections or *passūs*. The poem is subdivided, like the non-alliterative *Kyng Alisaunder*, into two parts: birth, early life, and Alexander's Darius campaign as well as the Wonders of the East and Alexander's death. While the poem's literary achievement has occasionally come into view,[45] scholarship has hitherto mainly studied the depiction of Alexander's Eastern campaigns and aristocratic contexts of reception, in keeping with the focus of recent Alexander scholarship more generally. Thus, for instance, Christine Chism argues that the Alexander represented in the *Wars of Alexander* offers a model of chivalry going back much further than Arthur and Rome, ultimately enabling audiences to imagine 'the possibility of victory over the whole eastern world', while offering, through Alexander's ambiguous hybrid East-Western origins, a model of 'self-analysis and critique for a culture still desperately invested in oriental conquest but gradually forced to realize the futility of its dreams'.[46] Here, the scholarly focus on baronial culture overlaps with Orientalist concerns, manifest also in (scholarship concerned with) *Kyng Alisaunder* and its source, the Anglo-Norman *Roman de toute chevalerie* (1180s).[47]

Since the two other Alexander romances that can be securely dated to the fourteenth century are only fragments, *Kyng Alisaunder* affords the best opportunity to study the fourteenth-century English Alexander tradition's concern with poetics. *Kyng Alisaunder*, written most likely in London, boasts 8,000 rhymed, largely octosyllabic lines and is dated to the end of the thirteenth or beginning of the fourteenth century. On account of stylistic similarities and contexts of transmission, *Arthour and Merlin* and *Richard Coeur de Lion*, which are included with *Kyng Alisaunder* in the Auchinleck MS, are often seen as composed by the same poet. The text is extant, more completely, in two further manuscripts (Oxford, Bodleian Library, MS Laud Misc. 622 [B]; London, Lincoln's Inn, MS 150).[48] The Middle English poet's concern with poetics, especially with the multiplicity of sources for the history of Alexander, is certainly not as pronounced and condensed as Geffrey's encounter with Troy authorities in Chaucer's *House of Fame*. However, the *Kyng Alisaunder* poet's bookishness and self-conscious literary performance have been noted in scholarship. In a recent study that highlights the poem's transcultural dynamics (rather than its exploration

---

[44] Hoyt N. Duggan and Thorlac Turville-Petre (eds), *The Wars of Alexander*, EETS s.s. 10 (Oxford, 1989).

[45] Peter Dronke, for instance, draws attention to the poet's use of ekphrasis to increase the audience's fascination with the unfamiliar. Dronke, 'Poetic Originality in *The Wars of Alexander*', in Helen Cooper and Sally Mapstone (eds), *The Long Fifteenth Century: Essays for Douglas Gray* (Oxford, 1997), 123–39.

[46] Chism, *Alliterative Revivals*, 130. Studies concerned with aristocratic ideologies and cultural Otherness in the medieval English and European Alexander traditions further include Christine Chism, 'Too Close for Comfort: Dis-Orienting Chivalry in the *Wars of Alexander*', in Sylvia Tomasch and Sealy Gilles (eds), *Text and Territory: Geographical Imagination in the European Middle Ages* (Philadelphia, PA, 1998), 116–42; Suzanne Conklin Akbari, *Idols in the East: European Representations of Islam and the Orient, 1100–1450* (Ithaca, NY, 2009), 67–111; Markus Stock (ed.), *Alexander the Great in the Middle Ages: Transcultural Perspectives* (Toronto, 2016); and Su Fang Ng (ed.), *Alexander the Great from Britain to South-East Asia: Peripheral Empires in the Global Renaissance* (Oxford, 2019).

[47] For these, see especially Akbari, *Idols*, 102. For an extended discussion of the differences between the Anglo-Norman poem and *Kyng Alisaunder*, see Theodor Hildebrand, *Die altfranzösische Alexanderdichtung 'Le Roman de toute chevalerie' des Thomas von Kent und die mittelenglische Romanze 'Kyng Alisaunder' in ihrem Verhältnis zu einander* (Amorbach, 1911). See further Charles Russell Stone, *The 'Roman de toute Chevalerie': Reading Alexander Romance in Late Medieval England* (Toronto, 2019).

[48] G. V. Smithers (ed.), *Kyng Alisaunder*, 2 vols., EETS o.s. 227, 237 (London, 1952, 1957), 2:1–64.

of more narrowly English local identities or English exclusivity), Venetia Bridges stresses the poet's 'conscious intellectualization of Alexander sources'.[49] With an early reference to the 'colours of rhetoric', for instance, the poet explicitly contrasts different sources by means of referencing their language: 'Þis bataile distincted is / Jn the Freinsshe, wel jwis. / þerefore [J] habbe [hit] to coloure / Borowed of Latyn a nature ...' (B 2195–8), the Latin referring to the *Alexandreis*, which is part of the historical tradition.[50] Moreover, in prefacing Alexander's conquest of the East, the poet provides a much longer list than his source, including Aristotle, Solomon, Isidore, 'Eustroge', Saint Jerome, Megasthenes, Dionysius, Pompeius, and 'þe lijf of Alisaunder' (i.e., the *Alexandreis*) (B 4763–88). The poet's treatment of Alexander's siege of Thebes testifies to his familiarity with the *Roman de Thèbes*. And when Alexander is able to easily pick an unremovable sword from the ground, betokening the future conquest of the world, the poet alludes to *Arthour and Merlin* and the Arthurian tradition (B 2622–34).[51] The poet's self-consciousness in view of the multiplicity of sources is further underscored on the plot level, aligning Alexander's military with the poet's *poetic* sovereignty.

Frequently, the poet emphasises Alexander's hermeneutic and rhetorical skills, his ability in world-reading and fiction-making (lying, disguise), qualities intricately related to Alexander's rise and fall. In the recounting of Alexander's birth, for instance, illusions are frequently fabricated and signs need to be read: Neptanabus poses as Ammon in order to sleep with Olympias, which is forecast to her in a dream (B 346–56, 384–92); Neptanabus sends a dream to her husband king Philip, which allegorically presages the birth of Alexander (B 483–516, 543–604). Furthermore, in relaying Alexander's campaign against Darius, the English poet highlights Alexander's hermeneutic superiority: after Alexander's refusal to pay tribute to him, Darius sends messengers with a letter and three gifts to Alexander. In the *Roman*, the gifts are reins made from grey silk, a golden ball, and two purses containing golden coins; in *Kyng Alisaunder*, Darius sends 'A scourge [whip] and a toppe [spinning top] of nobleys, / And ful of gold an haumd[u]deys [purse]' (B 1705–6). In the *Roman*, Darius explicates at length the relevance of these gifts, noting that Darius's messengers are the best orators of Persia: 'Toz les mielz parlanz del regné de Persie' (1368).[52] Omitting the reference to the messengers' oratorical talents, the Middle English poet emphasises instead his own rhetorical skills. And while Darius explicates the (symbolic) significance of each of the gifts in the *Roman*—'Trois dons t'envoy icy, [e] par figure mant / Iceo qe demostre chescun en son semblant' (1401–2)—the Middle English poet merely mentions that the gifts are suitable for a boy. By means of these (and other) small changes, in *Kyng Alisaunder*, it is only Alexander who interprets the presents as betokening his conquest of the world (B 1751–64), linking Alexander's hermeneutic superiority and military conquest. Increasingly, though, Alexander's success at fiction-making fails him: frequently, others see through his disguise, notably towards the end of the poem, when queen Candace, Alexander's lover, immediately

---

[49] Venetia Bridges, *Medieval Narratives of Alexander the Great: Transnational Texts in England and France* (Cambridge, 2018), especially 206. See further Bradbury, *Writing*, 133–74; Christine Chism, 'Winning Women in Two Middle English Alexander Poems', in Sara S. Poor and Jana K. Schulman (eds), *Women and Medieval Epic: Gender, Genre, and the Limits of Epic Masculinity* (New York, 2007), 18.

[50] The *Alexandreis* was mined for decorative details (Smithers, *Kyng Alisaunder*, 2:15, 22, 98n) as well as 'thematic emphasis' (Bridges, *Medieval Narratives*, 210–11). For the author's general familiarity with various Alexander traditions and the reference to the colours of rhetoric, see further Bennett, *Middle English*, 188–9; Bradbury, *Writing*, 173; Bridges, *Narratives*, 207.

[51] Smithers, *Kyng Alisaunder*, 2:24, 103n.

[52] Brian Foster and Ian Short (eds), *The Anglo-Norman 'Alexander' (Le Roman de toute chevalerie) by Thomas of Kent*, 2 vols., ANTS (London, 1976–7).

320   MEDIEVAL POETRY: 1100–1400

identifies him (he poses as Alexander's messenger) because of a bust she has had made of him, which he later marvels at in her bedroom. Hermeneutic authority transfers to Candace at this point, which is underscored by the poet by means of emphasising her 'poetic' knowledge—the passage opens with a reference to the *Aeneid*, which is expanded in the English poem by inclusion of a brief ekphrastic reference to Trojan imagery in her halls (B 7656–7).[53] Besides highlighting his literary craftsmanship by way of referencing the multiplicity of available sources and emphasising the power of rhetoric, the poet also adds small lyrical passages, the headpieces, which bring into play different experiences of time. While Alexander's fall and death are part of an inevitably teleological narrative, the poet operates on a different temporal and poetic plane. And it is the temporal jarring between Alexandrian teleology and lyrical circularity that empowers the poet as a literary author.

Unlike the up-and-down-arc of *de casibus* tragedy in Alexander's life, the poem's much-discussed headpieces by and large represent the cyclical recurrence of the seasons. Moreover, these lyrical vignettes in mono-rhymed lines also list related aspects of courtly love and aristocratic life as well as moral maxims. The majority of the headpieces is focused on the times of the day or seasons of the year. A vast array of narrative and visual traditions have been offered as sources for the headpieces, from epic poetry (especially Statius and Virgil) via *chansons de gestes* to Latin lyrics.[54] And they have been seen as serving variegated narrative functions: granting a short break from the storytelling; providing a gloss on the plot and/or a moral frame of reference; or placing the poem in what John Scattergood calls a 'deftly articulated high-life context'.[55] Given both the multitude of literary sources and their multiple narrative functions, the headpieces are poetic emblems.[56] As such, I believe, they are the cornerstones of the poet's poetic programme for the translation of conflicting poetical accounts of antiquity into Middle English poetry. They represent, to adapt Robert Frost's famous phrase, a momentary stay against the confusing confluence of different traditions. In their rootedness in various poetic traditions and flagging different temporalities, the headpieces' mixing of traditions and temporalities literally write the poet out of time,[57] enabling a Middle English remaking of Greek, Latin, and Old French versions of Alexandrian antiquity.

That the headpieces are important poetic moments for the poet to reflect about poetry is indicated already in the prologue. In a passage original to *Kyng Alisaunder*, the poet first introduces the subject of his poem with an emphasis on the benefit of studying other people's lives, even though listeners may prefer 'ribaudye' (B 21). The poem then follows— while self-referentially modifying—the *Roman's* explanation of the division of the world and the subdivision of the year into months. The Anglo-Norman poet groups the months by

[53] For the bust of Alexander, see also Chism, 'Winning', 35.

[54] Summary regarding the sources of the headpieces in Smithers, *Kyng Alisaunder*, 2:35–9; Bridges, *Medieval Narratives*, especially 211–13: see further Bennett, *Middle English*, 190; for their quality of manuscript illuminations and their sources in Calendars, see especially Derek Pearsall and Elizabeth Salter, *Landscapes and Seasons of the Medieval World* (London, 1973), 136–8, 168–70. For the 'Englishness' of the headpieces, see Hildebrand, 'Alexanderdichtung', 44; for their minstrel quality, see Bradbury, *Writing*, 151–7.

[55] John Scattergood, 'Validating the High Life in *Of Arthour and Merlin* and *Kyng Alisaunder*', *Essays in Criticism*, 54 (2004), 323–50, at 324; see further Louise M. Haywood, 'Spring Song and Narrative Organization in the Medieval Alexander Legend', *Troianalexandrina*, 4 (2004), 101; G. H. V. Bunt, 'Alexander's Last Days in the Middle English *Kyng Alisaunder*', in W. J. Aerts, Jos. M. M. Hermans, and Elizabeth Visser (eds), *Alexander the Great in the Middle Ages* (Nijmegen, 1978), 208.

[56] In his 'Poetic Emblems in Medieval Narrative Texts', in Lois Ebin (ed.), *Vernacular Poetics in the Middle Ages* (Kalamazoo, MI, 1984), 1–32, Robert W. Hanning defines a poetic emblem as a 'symbolic artifact or character within a narrative that transcends its role as an element of the fiction in which it appears and becomes a powerful comment on the artistic enterprise of its creator' (1).

[57] But cf. Mehl, *Romances*, 238–9, who sees the headpieces as reminders of the transitoriness and inconstancy of life.

means of their specific characteristics: March, April, and May, for instance, are the 'purest' months; in November and December, Sagittarius is at work with his slingshot (37–44). Whoever would like to know more about the months, the poet concludes, should look elsewhere for answers: 'Qui de ceo pus querant, querge qui ly l'esponde' (45). In *Kyng Alisaunder*, the months are listed chronologically, starting with March, before specifying that by means of the months, people know when to sow, when to irrigate, when to harvest corn and wine: 'By hem men han þe seysyne / To londe, to watre, to corne, to wyne ...' (B 61–2). Additionally, at the end of the passage, the poet draws attention to his learning: whoever would like to know more should turn to Ptolemy: 'Who-so wil þe nature ysee, / Hij moten yheren Tholome ...' (B 65–6). Emphasising his learning and alluding to his exact knowledge of relevant source texts, the poet's modification of the prologue foregrounds issues of time—the chronology of the months of the year as marking the circularity of rural life—which are taken up in the headpieces, which, in their emphasis on temporal circularity and/or stasis, are likewise framed by poetic self-reference, underscoring the poet's learning and his poetic skills.[58]

Allusions to cyclical recurrence are one of the most obvious characteristics of the head-pieces. Six headpieces actually refer to specific months explicitly, beginning with the first headpiece's reference to April (following on the prologue's March) with which the poet introduces the first narrative section concerned with Neptanabus's seduction of Olympias and the birth and upbringing of Alexander (B 139–44). Then follow headpieces mentioning June (at the beginning of Alexander's campaign against Darius, B 1843–7), May (B 2049–56, 2543–6, 5201–6), and April (B 6988–94), opening the last section of the poem. With Alexander's death in March, this (non-chronological) calendrical structure has come full circle. Interspersed across the narrative are headpieces concerned more generally with the seasons without explicit references to months; in relaying the upbringing of Alexander around the first two headpieces (April and June), two headpieces refer to autumn, one to spring (B 457–64, 795–800, 911–19), another headpiece comments more generally on the passing of the day, which is true of most of the headpieces included in the report of the Darius campaign (B 2517–18, 2897–902, 4056–61, 4101–4, 4283–6), two of which indicate summer and autumn (B 2567–73, 3289–94). Thus, the headpieces continually keep alive in the audience's minds the cyclical recurrence of the seasons, frequently combined with brief expositions of the attendant, (in)appropriate courtly and/or agricultural practices. In a way, the cyclic recurrence is thereby arrested in time. That is, the headpieces bring into a play the constant recurrence of the same, a temporal paradox. This is encapsulated in the time-lessness generated by the lyricism of the headpieces and is underscored by the poet's use of the present tense. The following headpiece, included in the narration of one of Alexander's many battles with Darius, is exemplary:

> In tyme of Maij þe niȝttyngale
> Jn wood makeþ mery gale.
> So don þe foules, grete and smale,
> Summe on hylles and summe in dale.
> Þe day daweþ, þe kyng awakeþ;
> He and hise men her armes takeþ.

---

[58] Most of the headpieces are framed by poetic self-reference (145, 240, 455–6, 1572, 1576, 2047–8, 2892–4, 3287–8, 3438, 4100, 4282, 4313–6, 4321, 4745–8, 5206, 5456, 5759, 6982–7, 7351). Additionally, in the meta-poetically charged reflection about the differences between the French and Latin traditions, a reference to the weather alludes to the headpieces: 'Now telleþ þis gest, saunz faile, / So on þe shyngel liþe þe haile / Every kniȝth so liþ on oþer' (B 2205–7).

322 MEDIEVAL POETRY: 1100–1400

> Hij wendeþ to þe batailes stede,
> And fyndeþ nouȝth bot bodies dede.
> Ȝonge and elde fele hii fonde—
> Kniȝttes dede of Grece londe. (B 2543–52)

The headpiece shifts the focus away from the battlefield to reflect about things that are typical of May—the singing nightingale, the chirping birds. Noteworthy in temporal terms, the lyricism of the headnotes is associated with a cyclical recurrence of activities and a temporal simultaneity—different activities ensue at the same time—that are not characteristic at all of the story of Alexander's conquest, in which one thing chronologically leads to another. The poet then continues with a description of what ensues at daybreak, not any daybreak accompanied by birdsong, though, but a very particular daybreak: Alexander readies himself for battle, first of all inspecting (transitioning into past tense) the body-strewn battlefield. The shift from the May scene to the battlefield is underscored also by a shift from mono-rhyme to rhymed couplets, the latter in keeping with the inevitable progress of Alexander's conquest, the former literally halting the changing rhymes of the couplets, staying teleological-imperial progress, however momentarily. In other headpieces, this effect is further intensified by the length of the mono-rhymed passage and/or its enumerative quality (anaphora, assonance) as, for example, in the next headpiece within the poem, which continues with the May setting:

> Mery is þe blast of þe styuoure*   *bagpipe player*
> Mery is þe touchyng of þe harpoure.
> Swete is þe smellyng of þe floure;
> Swete it is in maydens boure.
> Appel swete bereþ fair coloure;
> Of trewe loue is swe[te] amoure. (B 2567–72)

The poetic effect of the headpieces in *Kyng Alisaunder* is to frame and contain the teleology of Alexander's epic life—ambiguous birth, military conquest and rule of the world, death by treason and loss of empire—by means of lyrical intermissions that blend a multiplicity of foregoing poetic traditions. In this manner, the headpieces are literally places of invention and represent the poetic program advanced by the *Kyng Alisaunder* poet. From the perspective of the recurrence of an aristocratic timelessness, the poet's headpieces distance and discover as poetic material a teleological narrative of military conquest and, ultimately, defeat.[59] Like the *Destrucion of Troy*, then, *Kyng Alisaunder* self-consciously considers the appropriate poetic medium to remake the life of Alexander in Middle English poetry. By means of condensing and replicating the problem of a multiplicity of foregoing Alexander traditions within the headpieces, the poet juxtaposes their cyclical lyricism with the imperial teleological narrative they frame and ultimately contain. The poem's opposition of Alexandrian teleology and a cyclical lyrical temporality enables and legitimates authorial invention—and represents yet another way in which romances of antiquity, their seemingly slavish reliance on foregoing traditions notwithstanding, become prominent places for the negotiation of literary poetics.

---

[59] For an account of how medieval texts self-referentially reflect and construct their own temporality, see Andrew James Johnston, *Performing the Middle Ages from 'Beowulf' to 'Othello'* (Turnhout, 2008). The metapoetic temporal distancing accomplished primarily by the headpieces finds an analogue on the plot level by way of Alexander's lack of direct (emotional) engagement with the marvels he encounters. The latter is a characteristic feature of the Middle English text, which Akbari reads as underscoring that Alexander 'remains fundamentally the same man he was before' (*Idols*, 104).

21

The Matter of Britain

Elizabeth Archibald

English Arthurian romance writers had a wide range of sources and themes to draw on. Many stories must have been circulating orally in post-Conquest England, emerging from both Welsh and Breton traditions. The 'twelfth-century Renaissance' brought an increasing flow of texts in Latin and French, some written in England or for Anglo-Norman rulers and aristocrats. The appearance in 1135 of the best-selling *History of the Kings of Britain* of Geoffrey of Monmouth changed everything.[1] It included a birth-to-death account of Arthur, presenting him as a bold warrior and wise ruler who first subdued the other British kings and the Saxon invaders, and then took his Continental war successfully to the gates of Rome before returning to confront the treacherous Mordred. Two major streams of stories about Arthur and his knights developed from Geoffrey's influential Latin prose pseudo-history, which was rapidly translated into French and then English.[2] The chronicle tradition focused on the king himself and on war and national politics, including the Roman campaign; the romance tradition, beginning in the later twelfth century, tended to put a single knight centre-stage during peacetime. The earliest known Arthurian romances were composed in French by Chrétien de Troyes, long and sophisticated poems in rhyming couplets in which individual knights have fantastic adventures when they ride out from Arthur's court; usually (though not always) they return to tell their tales and win the all-important honour and respect accorded by the court, and the love of their chosen ladies. Love and chivalry are intertwined, not always positively, and prowess and morality are tested by both human and supernatural encounters.

Lancelot first appears as the lover of the queen in Chrétien's *Chevalier de la Charrete* (*The Knight of the Cart*), and the Grail makes an enigmatic first appearance in his *Perceval* or *Conte du Graal*.[3] French poets introduced a number of important innovations into the legend of King Arthur, whom they often presented as a rather feeble, passive figure, a *roi fainéant*, very different from Geoffrey's heroic warrior. From the early thirteenth century extended French prose cycles of Arthurian stories were also produced and were widely read and adapted across western Europe: the Vulgate Cycle, the post-Vulgate Cycle, and the Prose *Tristan*.[4] The main protagonists in these texts are Lancelot and Tristan, rather

---

[1] Geoffrey of Monmouth, in Michael Reeve (ed.) and Neil Wright (trans.), *The History of the Kings of Britain: An Edition and Translation of the* De gestis Britonum (Woodbridge, 2007).

[2] For overviews of the Latin, French, and English traditions, with discussion of individual texts, see Siân Echard (ed.), *The Arthur of Medieval Latin Literature: The Development and Dissemination of the Arthurian Legend in Medieval Latin* (Cardiff, 2011); Glyn Burgess and Karen Pratt (eds), *The Arthur of the French: The Arthurian Legend in Medieval French and Occitan Literature* (Cardiff, 2006); and W. R. J. Barron (ed.), *The Arthur of the English: The Arthurian Legend in Medieval English Life and Literature* (Cardiff, 1999).

[3] Chrétien's romances are available in numerous editions, including the Classiques Français du Moyen Age series; for translations, see Chrétien de Troyes, in William W. Kibler (trans.), *Arthurian Romances* (London, 1991).

[4] For summaries and bibliography, see Burgess and Pratt (eds), *The Arthur of the French*.

Elizabeth Archibald, *The Matter of Britain*. In: *The Oxford History of Poetry in English*. Edited by Helen Cooper and Robert R. Edwards, Oxford University Press. © Elizabeth Archibald (2023). DOI: 10.1093/oso/9780198827429.003.0021

than Arthur; the quest for the Holy Grail changes and challenges the nature of chivalric adventure, and the criteria for success. English romance writers in the thirteenth and fourteenth centuries knew and drew on these French works, but adapted and added to them in distinctive ways, writing in verse rather than prose. Some English poets follow a French source fairly closely, but not exactly; others stitch together episodes from various French (and perhaps also Celtic) narratives in innovative ways, often using familiar motifs such as the testing of the hero, the arrival of a stranger at court, or claims of unjust treatment by Arthur (the king is not immune from criticism in English romances). Lancelot rarely features in English poems of this period, nor does the Grail; Arthur's nephew Gawain is the Top Knight, with a series of adventures that do not always have direct (known) analogues in French. Some poems focus on important phases in Arthur's life, his birth and parentage, or his death and the collapse of Camelot; there is no birth-to-death English cycle until Malory's prose *Morte Darthur* in the late fifteenth century. Today much the best known of the Middle English Arthurian verse romances is *Sir Gawain and the Green Knight*;[5] the rest are usually relegated to second-class status and are less frequently studied, but they contain much of interest in both content and style.

Considered as a group, the English romances (Arthurian and non-Arthurian) are remarkable for the variety of poetic forms in which they are written. Ad Putter comments that 'The metres of the French and Anglo-Norman sources and analogues seem restricted and predictable by comparison'.[6] The French romances are either in octosyllabic rhyming couplets, or in *laisses* of varying length with ten- or twelve-syllable lines and a single rhyme. English poets did not use the *laisse*, but drawing on Anglo-Saxon tradition as well as French sources created a range of options: rhyming tetrameter couplets, alternating rhyme, tailrhyme, tail-rhyme plus wheel and sometimes bob too, full alliteration with and without rhyme, and occasional alliteration. Chaucer indicates in the Prologue to his 'Parson's Tale' that alliteration was considered to be northern, and by implication rather provincial: when asked to tell a tale, the Parson says indignantly 'I am a Southren man; / I kan nat geeste "rum, ram, ruf" by lettre'.[7] Many of the surviving Arthurian romances do seem to have been produced in the north of England, and some are set there. Alliteration had a long history in England (including *Beowulf*), and was coming back into fashion in various genres in the fourteenth century.[8] It is frequently used in Arthurian poems, whether they derive from the chronicle or the romance tradition: *Sir Gawain and the Green Knight* is pure romance, whereas the Alliterative *Morte Arthur* is closer in content and tone to a chronicle, or an epic. Alliterative writing requires a complex vocabulary of many synonyms, including unusual words often found only in these texts; and there are many local variations in the form of the bob and wheel, and the stanza structure.

It is not easy to generalise about reasons for the choice of verse form; rhyming couplets, so common in French lays and romances, are less frequently used for English Arthurian ones. One early example is *Of Arthur and of Merlin*, a rather free adaptation of the French prose *Estoire de Merlin*, which covers Arthur's conception, birth, and ascent to the throne,

---

[5] Discussed in Chapter 25 in this volume.

[6] Ad Putter, 'The Metres and Stanza Forms of Popular Romance', in Raluca Radulescu and Cory Rushton (eds), *A Companion to Medieval Popular Romance* (Cambridge, 2009), 111–31 at 31.

[7] Chaucer, *The Canterbury Tales*, X. 42–3, in Larry D. Benson (ed.), *The Riverside Chaucer*, 3rd edn. (Boston, MA, 1987). All references to Chaucer are to this edition.

[8] See, for instance, Thorlac Turville-Petre, *The Alliterative Revival* (Cambridge, 1976).

including the sword in the stone episode (the first appearance of this scene in English).[9] The author gives a very clear explanation of why it is written in English:

Mani noble ich haue yseiȝe*	*seen*
Þat no Freynsche couþe seye,*	*could speak*
Biginne ichil* for her loue	*I shall*
Bi Ihesus leue þat sitt aboue	
On Inglische tel mi tale—	
God ous sende soule hale.*	*save our souls*

The narrative is focused on Merlin's magic and on Arthur's early reign, rather than the adventures of his knights, and is thus closer to the chronicle tradition. The poet uses rhyming couplets such as he would have encountered in other French romances; this form would not have been an obvious choice to accommodate his target audience, specified as nobles who know no French. *Of Arthour and of Merlin* is preserved in the Auchinleck Manuscript (*c* 1330) with numerous other romances including *Sir Tristrem*.[10] Originally a separate legend, the Tristan story was gradually drawn into the Arthurian sphere, not least because of the parallels between the love triangles of king, queen, and favourite knight at the courts of King Arthur and King Mark (but Arthur and his knights do not appear in the English poem). The English *Tristrem* is firmly part of the romance tradition, and is written in a complex and unusual form, eight lines of alternating rhyme followed by a bob and two-line wheel, with occasional alliteration. This passage is taken from the scene where the lovers drink the fatal love potion:

The coupe was richeli wrought:	
Of gold it was, the pin.*	*peg, marker*
In al the warld nas nought	
Swiche drink as ther was in.	
Brengwain was wrong bithought.*	*ill-advised*
To that drink sche gan win*	*went*
And swete Ysonde it bitaught.*	*gave*
Sche bad Tristrem bigin,	
To say.	*indeed*
Her* love might no man tuin*	*their; separate*
Til her ending day.	(1662–72)

The bob and wheel at the end of a stanza is often used to emphasise important speeches or details, and here the change of rhyme adds extra stress; the spotlight is on the power of the potion which bound the lovers 'til her ending day'.[11]

---

[9] Text in O. D. Macrae-Gibson (ed.), *Of Arthur and of Merlin*, 2 vols., EETS o.s. 268, 279 (London, 1973, 1979), 1:5 (Auchinleck MS, lines 25–30). Glosses for verse quotations are taken from the editions cited, unless otherwise noted. In some cases I have slightly altered them.

[10] Edinburgh, National Library of Scotland, Advocates' MS 19.2.1. References are to *Sir Tristrem*, in Alan Lupack (ed.), *Lancelot of the Laik and Sir Tristrem* (Kalamazoo, MI, 1994), 143–277. The source is Thomas's Anglo-Norman *Tristan* poem (in rhyming couplets). See also Susanna Fein (ed.), *The Auchinleck Manuscript: New Perspectives* (Woodbridge, 2018). Ad Putter discusses the poem and its metrical analogues (including lyrics and carols in both English and French) in 'The Singing of Middle English Romance: Stanza Forms and Contrafacta', in Ad Putter and Judith A. Jefferson (eds), *The Transmission of Medieval Romance: Metres, Manuscripts and Early Prints* (Cambridge, 2018), 69–90.

[11] The *Gawain*-poet uses the bob and wheel with particular sophistication in *Sir Gawain and the Green Knight*; see Helen Cooper's comments in Chapter 25 in this volume.

326   MEDIEVAL POETRY: 1100–1400

Another romance in couplets is *Ywain and Gawain*, based on Chrétien's *Yvain* (also known as *Le Chevalier au lion*); this is the only close adaptation in English of a Chrétien romance.[12] It was probably written in the north of England in the late fourteenth century, and broadly follows the plot of the French poem, though with less emphasis on the psychology of the protagonists, and less irony. Chrétien ends his poem with a reference to the 'roman du chevalier au lion', thus giving the romance its alternative title, but the English poet gives Ywain and Gawain equal billing in the opening lines:

> Almyghti God þat made mankyn,
> He schilde* His servandes out of* syn   *may he protect; from*
> And mayntene þam with myght and mayne
> Þat herkens* Ywayne and Gawayne;   *who listen to*
> Þai war knightes of the Tabyl Rownde,
> Þarfore listens a lytel stownde.*   *little while* (1–6)

This foregrounding of Gawain is an indication of his high status in English romance, even though his role here, as in Chrétien's version, is to disrupt Ywain's marriage early on by luring him away to the tournament circuit, and to act as a foil to the protagonist.

The English *Lybeaus Desconus*, a Fair Unknown story about Gawain's son Guinglain, is in tail-rhyme, whereas its nearest analogue, the late twelfth-century French romance *Le Bel Inconnu* by Renaut de Bâgé, is in couplets.[13] The same is true of *Sir Launfal*, Thomas Chestre's rewriting of Marie de France's *lai* 'Lanval';[14] here Arthur's court is presented negatively—the king is unjust to the outsider Launfal and the queen accuses him of rape after failing to seduce him—and as in the French source, the protagonist leaves the court at the end with his fairy lover, never to return.

> Thus Launfal, wythouten fable,*   *without doubt*
> That noble knyght of the Rounde Table,
>   Was take ynto Fayrye;
> Seththe* saw hym yn thys lond noman,*   *since then; this land; no one*
> Ne no more of hym telle y ne can,
>   For sothe*, wythoute lye.   *truth*
> Thomas Chestre made thys tale
> Of the noble knyghte Syr Launfale,
>   Good of chyvalrye.
> Jhesus, that ys hevene kyng,
> Yeve* us alle Hys blessyng,   *give*
>   And Hys moder Marye!   (1033–44)

The widespread popularity of tail-rhyme, and its possible failings (such as the padding evident in this final stanza), are highlighted in Chaucer's parodic 'Sir Thopas', the first attempt at a tale by the pilgrim Chaucer.[15]

---

[12] References are to Mary Flowers Braswell (ed.), *Sir Perceval of Galles and Ywain and Gawain* (Kalamazoo, MI, 1995), 77–202.

[13] Text in Eve Salisbury and James Weldon (eds), *Lybeaus Desconus* (Kalamazoo, MI, 2013).

[14] Thomas Chestre, *Sir Launfal*, in Anne Laskaya and Eve Salisbury (eds), *The Middle English Breton Lays* (Kalamazoo, MI, 1995), 201–62.

[15] *Canterbury Tales* VIII.712–918. See the section on 'Sir Thopas' in Robert Correale and Mary Hamel (eds), *Sources and Analogues of the* Canterbury Tales, 2 vols. (Cambridge, 2003–5), 2:649–714.

The poet Chaucer had clearly read a lot of tail-rhyme romances (possibly in the Auchinleck Manuscript); he mocks both their style and their content in this ridiculous account of the bourgeois hero who decides to take an elf queen as his mistress before ever meeting one, and on encountering a giant has to go home to get his armour. The unheroic protagonist is explicitly compared to Sir Perceval, though for a very trivial reason: 'Hymself drank water of the well, / As dide the knyght sire Percyvell, / So worly under wede [worthy under his clothes]' (VII.915–17). This is an allusion to the opening lines of *Sir Percyvell of Galys*, which Chaucer clearly considered irrelevant padding and clumsy rhyming:[16]

Lef,* lythes* to me	*friend; listen*
Two wordes or thre,	
Of one that was faire and fre*	*noble*
And felle* in his fighte.	*fierce*
His righte name was Percyvell,	
He was fosterde in the felle,*	*hill country*
He dranke water of the welle,*	*spring*
And yitt* was he wyghte.*	*yet; powerful* (1–8)

The detail about drinking from a spring is unimportant in both poems, and Chaucer's tale is rapidly going nowhere when it is interrupted in mid-sentence by the Host, who declares that he cannot stand any more 'drasty [crude] ryming' (VII.930). Chaucer the pilgrim is given a second chance, and retreats to prose for a serious moral tale. A. C. Spearing has argued that Chaucer shows 'a contempt for romance of all kinds', and he certainly seems to subvert the genre in his own tale, as well as elsewhere in the *Canterbury Tales*.[17] But tail-rhyme romances can be both witty and moving, and *Sir Percyvell* should not be dismissed because of Chaucer's mockery.

This is the only English romance dedicated to the hero made popular by Chrétien's *Conte du Graal*; it is an unusual version of the Perceval story in that the Grail and the Grail Quest are entirely omitted, though the transformation of the hero from a naïve and boorish boy to a capable and compassionate knight is retained.[18] Gawain, who is so important in Chrétien's poem as a foil to Perceval, only makes a brief appearance. Instead new adventures are inserted, including a marriage, but the happy ending revolves round the protagonist's reunion with his mother (in most of the French sources she dies early on, and Perceval is blamed for this). The English poem was probably composed in the early fourteenth century, though it survives in a fifteenth-century manuscript. The poet may have known a version of Chrétien's text, but if so clearly felt no need to follow it closely; other French versions had been produced by this time.[19] He (or she) also opted for a challenging sixteen-line stanza form with five different rhymes, and frequent concatenation between stanzas.

---

[16] All references are to Mary Flowers Braswell (ed.), *Sir Perceval of Galles and Ywain and Gawain*, 1–76, but I use the more familiar spelling 'Percyvell of Galys' in my discussion.

[17] A. C. Spearing, *Medieval to Renaissance in English Poetry* (Cambridge, 1985), 36.

[18] References to *Perceval* in William Roach (ed.), *Perceval ou Le Conte du Graal* (Geneva, 1959); translations are my own, based on Kibler's version (which uses a different edition with some variant wording).

[19] It is possible that the English poet knew the idiosyncratic French prose *Perlesvaus*, in which many new adventures are added, and the mother also survives until the end. For summaries of this and the various Continuations of Chrétien, see Burgess and Pratt (eds), *The Arthur of the French*. For a detailed comparison with Chrétien's poem, see Ad Putter, 'Story Line and Story Shape in *Sir Percyvell of Gales* and Chrétien de Troyes' *Conte du Graal*', in Nicola McDonald (ed.), *Pulp Fictions of Medieval England: Essays in Popular Romance* (Manchester, 2004), 171–96. See also his comments in 'Arthurian Romance in Popular Tradition: *Sir Percyvell of Gales*, *Sir Cleges*, and *Sir Launfal*', in Helen Fulton (ed.), *A Companion to Arthurian Literature* (Oxford, 2009), 235–51.

328   MEDIEVAL POETRY: 1100–1400

One of the innovations in the English version is that Percyvell is Arthur's nephew, son of his sister Acheflour; the poem begins with his parents' wedding, but then his father is killed by the Red Knight, and his mother keeps him in seclusion from the chivalric world, as in earlier versions, until the naïve boy encounters some knights and insists on leaving home for Arthur's court. The emphasis on the hero's ignorance and uncouthness is less promi-nent in *Sir Percyvell* than in Chrétien's version, but elements of the original remain and are presented in new ways. The French Perceval encounters several uncles, including the Fisher King, and is given much good advice by the elderly knight Gornemont with whom he lodges. The English Percyvell is befriended by an old knight who is his uncle (though this is not explicitly stated); the Red Knight had killed his brother long ago, he reports, and a little later the narrator comments that Percyvell had now met 'his emes [uncles] twoo' (1050—the other is Arthur), but neither offers any chivalric instruction.

Percyvell succeeds in killing the Red Knight, and also his witch mother, and burns both bodies; the witch mother and the burning are additions to the French tradition (the English poet seems particularly interested in mother-son relationships).[20] The long central section of *Sir Percyvell* describes his battle against the Sultan who is besieging the lady Lufamour; Percyvell kills him, watched by Arthur and Gawain and the court, and marries Lufamour. After a happy year of marriage, he remembers his mother, and sets out to find her:

'Blythe* sall I never be	*happy*
Or*I may my modir see,	*before*
And wete* how scho fare*'.	*find out; is* (1790–2)

The ensuing adventure is the climax of the romance; it centres on a ring which his mother gave him on his departure from home as a recognition token. He leaves it with a sleeping maiden he finds in a tent, in exchange for the ring he takes from her finger; later she is pun-ished for supposed infidelity by her lover, the Black Knight. The tent maiden episode and its unhappy consequences are in Chrétien's version, but the English poet gives them a new twist through this exchange of rings. When Percyvell meets the maiden again and explains, he offers to swap the ring he took for his mother's, but the Black Knight says that he gave Per-cyvell's ring to his own overlord, a giant who turns out to be the Sultan's brother. Percyvell fights and kills the giant, and then asks the porter about his lost ring. The porter curses the ring, and reports that the giant offered it to a neighbouring lady he was courting, who recog-nised it as her son's; she assumed the giant had killed him, and is now wandering mad in the forest. Percyvell finds his mother, restores her to health, and takes her home. Only after this does he set out for the Holy Land, in the final stanza, and dies fighting there. Nothing in the poem has prepared the ground for this crusade; the Grail is never mentioned, nor any kind of religious conversion. The happy ending focuses on Percyvell's reunion with his mother rather than his wife, and there is no reference at the end to Arthur; the focus seems to be entirely on individual domestic and chivalric virtues. Although Percyvell starts as a naïve boy like his French counterpart, his education is rapid and relatively painless; he is not blamed by others for mistakes of which he could not have been aware at the time, as in Chrétien's poem.

There is little complexity in the style of *Sir Percyvell*. In contrast to the flowing syntax of French octosyllabic verse, the line is the principal unit of sense. The concatenation linking

---

[20] See Elizabeth Archibald, 'The Importance of Being an Arthurian Mother', in Larissa Tracy and Geert Claassens (eds), *Medieval English and Dutch Literatures: The European Context, Essays in Honour of David F. Johnson* (Cambridge, 2022), 329–50.

most of the stanzas can sometimes seem mechanical, a way of allowing the minstrel to catch his breath and think of the next lines (perhaps a sign of oral composition as well as oral performance):

> Hys swerde owt he get.

> By then hys swerde out he get,
> Strykes the geant withowtten lett* ...   *delay* (2063–5)

But the technique can also be deployed to greater effect. When Percyvell resolves to rescue his mother, who has gone mad in the forest in the belief that her son is dead, his reasoning is touchingly explained in his own words:

> 'Me aught to bring her of wa*:   *I ought to deliver her from woe*
> I laye in hir syde'*.   *Womb*

> He sayse, 'I laye in hir syde;
> I sall never one horse ryde
> Till I hafe sene hir in tyd*:   *(one) time*
> Spede if I may* ...'   *have better luck* (2175–80)

The concatenation here conveys Percyvell's sense of a powerful debt to the mother who bore him. The poem contains a lot of alliteration, though it is not consistently used, and stock phrases are common: 'so stiffe in stour [strong in battle]' (1565), 'holtis hare [gray woods]' (300, 1779). Kay is described as 'the kene knyghte' (1392); Percyvell is often referred to as 'the fole one the filde [country bumpkin]' (289, 505). Sometimes the alliteration extends over two lines: 'The mayden mengede his mode [raised his spirits] / With myrthes at the mete' (1327–8); 'Of that fare was he fayne [glad], / In felde there they fighte' (1495–6). Compared with the alliterative romances, the choice of vocabulary seems quite pedestrian, designed to do its narrative job efficiently, rather than to impress. There are no elaborate descriptions of feasts or weddings, clothes or physical appearance; hunting and battles are reported to take place, but with very little detail. Percyvell finds the sleeping maiden in a chamber within a 'haulle' which is not described at all (434), whereas in Chrétien she is in a brilliantly coloured pavilion (641–4). When Percyvell first sees knights in the forest, we are told only that 'In riche robes thay ryde' (265) and they are 'clothede al in grene' (277); more lines are devoted to the boy's outfit of goat-skins (268–74). In the equivalent scene in the *Conte du Graal*, Perceval sees their shining armour and weapons, and the bright colours they wear glitter in the sun (129–35). This is described at some length, in a sentence which flows over many lines rather than being endstopped, as the Middle English often is:

> Et vit les haubers fremïans
> Et les elmes clers et luisans,
> Et vit le blanc et le vermeil
> Reluire contre le soleil,
> Et l'or et l'azur et l'argent ...

(he saw the glittering hauberks and the bright, gleaming helmets, and he saw the white and the scarlet shining in the sun, and the gold and azure and silver ...)

Conversations are mainly functional and brisk. The lengthy account of family history by the mother at the beginning of Chrétien's poem is greatly reduced in *Sir Percyvell*, as is her

330 MEDIEVAL POETRY: 1100–1400

advice to her naïve son. Acheflour says nothing about religion, or about gallantry to women, but does offer one very specific detail of etiquette, that he should doff his cap to any knight he meets. When he asks how to recognise a knight, she gives him a practical demonstration:

Scho schewede hym the menevaire*—	*fur lining (for helmet)*
Scho had robes in payre.*	*in sets*
'Sone, ther* thou sees this fare	*where*
In thaire hodes* lye'.	*hoods* (409–12)

Percyvell puts this practical advice to use early in his adventures, after killing the Red Knight:

... Till he was warre of* a knyghte,	*perceived*
And of the menevaire* he had syght;	*fur*
He put up his umbrere* on hight,	*visor*
And said, 'Sir, God luke* thee!'	*protect* (881–4)

It is the ermine which confirms the status of the stranger, and so he raises his visor. In view of this attention to details of chivalric clothing, it is striking that when Percyvell goes to the forest to find his deranged mother, he leaves his armour behind and dresses in goat-skins (2196–7). No explanation is given; he apparently chooses to regress to the simple child he was on leaving home, presumably so that she will recognise him and not be alarmed, a detail which adds to the circularity of the poem's structure. Putter has noted how the final phase of the plot reverses the opening sequence: having left home on Christmas Day, Percyvell leaves his wife on the same day years later to find his mother, and re-encounters the tent maiden on his journey.[21] Putter also notes that Percyvell's last words in the poem, 'My modir full dere / Wele byde [await] ye me!' (2223–4), echo her promise early on to wait for him when he leaves home (428).[22]

There is plenty of direct speech in the poem, but no inner monologues or agonising between the calls of love and duty, or sly comments by the narrator, such as are found in Chrétien. The protagonist faces few moral dilemmas, and says little to suggest that he has changed significantly in the course of his adventures. Direct speech is sometimes used to show his naivety, as when he urges the Red Knight, who is already dead, to remount and keep fighting:

'I hafe broghte to the thi mere*	*mare*
And mekill of thyn other gere;	
Lepe on hir, as thou was ere,*	*before*
And* thou will more fighte!'	*if*
The knyghte lay still in the stede*:	*in that place*
What sulde* he say, when he was dede*?–	*should; dead*
The childe couthe* no better rede*	*knew; advice*
Bot down gun he lyghte*.	*dismounted* (733–40)

The chosen stanza form falls naturally into four-line sections, each introducing new rhyme words; this structure helps to create contrasts, as in this quotation between Percyvell's lack of understanding and the narrator's ironic comment. Percyvell is described throughout

---

[21] Putter, 'Story Line and Story Shape', 183–8. Professor Helen Cooper has pointed out to me that there may also be a penitential element, though he is not explicitly blamed for her plight.

[22] Putter, 'Story Line and Story Shape', 192; he notes that this echo is for the benefit of the reader/listener, not the deranged woman.

as 'childe', a term with a range of meanings including an immature youth, an apprentice, an aspiring knight and an actual knight.[23] It is used without irony of the heroes of other romances such as Horn Child, a dispossessed prince seeking to regain his rightful throne, but here is surely intended to imply both immaturity and warrior potential. Chaucer refers to 'child Thopas' (830), again playing on the double meaning.

The rescue of Percyvell's future bride is the central event of the poem, but little attention is paid to their romance. Lufamour first sees Percyvell sleeping exhausted on the battlefield; she invites him into her castle, and hopes that he will win her in battle (1241–1312); but we hear nothing of his response to her. The poet is more interested in the battles, and so is Percyvell. Lufamour is amazed that 'He was so styffe in stour [strong in battle] / And couthe so littill of nurtour [and knew so little of courtesy]' (1566–7). After killing the Sultan, Percyvell marries Lufamour, but we are never told anything about his feelings for her. Their relationship is overshadowed by the final adventure, when he finds and rehabilitates his mother. When Percyvell has taken his mother home and revived her, he goes on crusade and dies:

> Grete lordes and the Qwene
> Welcome hym al bydene*;   *altogether*
> When thay hym one lyfe* sene;   *alive*
>   Than blythe myghte thay bee.
> Sythen he went into the Holy Londe,
> Wanne many cités ful stronge,
> And there was he slayne, I undirstonde;
>   Thusgatis* endis hee.   *in this way* (2277-84)

No insight is given into Percyvell's motivation for abandoning his wife and home; no account is given of his battles in the Holy Land; no mention is made of Arthur. Percyvell is detached from the Grail tradition, yet the poem does have an unexpectedly pious finale. There is a rather perfunctory feeling to this hasty ending, not unlike that of *Sir Gawain and the Green Knight*.

Sir Percyvell is preserved in the Thornton Manuscript, where the following text is the early-fifteenth-century *Awntyrs of Arthur*.[24] This alliterative poem exemplifies the tendency of English Arthurian romance writers to use elements of both the romance and the chronicle traditions, and often to include a moralising aspect. The stanzas consist of nine four-stress alliterative lines with alternating rhyme followed by a four-line wheel. The first three lines of the wheel have a single rhyme, and the final line returns to the rhyme of the ninth line, as a way of neatly finishing off the stanza:

> In the tyme of Arthur an auntur bytydde*,   *happened*
> By the Turne* Wathelan, as the boke telles,   *Lake (Tarn)*
> Whan he to Carlele was comen, that conquerour kydde*, *famous*
> With dukes and dussiperes* that with the dere* dwelles, *companions; i.e., Arthur*
> To hunte at the herdes that longe had ben hydde*,   *hidden (in the wild)*

---

[23] *MED, s.v. child.*

[24] References are to the edition and glosses in Thomas Hahn (ed.), *Sir Gawain: Eleven Romance and Tales* (Kalamazoo, MI, 1995), 169–226. I have also consulted Ralph Hanna III (ed.), *The Awntyrs off Arthure at the Terne Wathelyn* (Manchester, 1974), which includes detailed commentary on the vocabulary; and Maldwyn Mills (ed.), *Ywain and Gawain, Sir Percyvell of Galles, The Anturs of Arther* (London, 1992), 161–82. There are four manuscripts, so readings can vary considerably between editions.

On a day thei hem dight* to the depe delles*;	*went off; valleys*
To fall* of the femailes* in forest were frydde*	*kill; does; enclosed*
Fayre by the fermesones in frithes and felles.*	*thriving because of the close season in the woods and hills*
Thus to wode arn thei went, the wlonkest in wedes,*	*splendidly dressed*
Bothe the Kyng and the Quene,	
And al the doughti bydene.*	*brave ones together*
Sir Gawayn, gayest* on grene,	*best attired*
Dame Gaynour* he ledes.	*Guinevere* (1–13)

The final lines of the wheel contain significant information, as so often with this form; here they introduce the protagonists of the tale, Gawain and Guinevere. The manuscript title is derived from the opening line, but Arthur is not in fact the protagonist; the two adventures recounted take place at his court, and Gawain, his eldest nephew and the Top Knight in the English tradition, is central to both.

Gawain and Guinevere are spectators at Arthur's deer hunt around the Tarn Wadling, a lake near Carlisle which features in several northern Arthurian romances. The ghost of the queen's mother rises from the lake, in shockingly grisly form: she asks her daughter to arrange masses for her soul, and urges her not to be proud and to be charitable to the poor. Then she warns Gawain that Arthur's aggressive ambitions to conquer more lands will lead to disaster. At supper that night Sir Galeron of Galloway appears at court, led by a lady, and demands a duel with Gawain, who has received some of Galeron's lands which had been unjustly taken over by Arthur. The knights prove to be evenly matched, so the queen stops the fight; Arthur gives Galeron back his lands, and grants others to Gawain in compensation. Galeron marries the lady who brought him to court, and Guinevere has masses said for her mother's soul.

There has been much critical debate about the unity of the poem: is it really two separate works, possibly by different poets, unsatisfactorily linked, or a carefully constructed diptych with common themes relating to chivalric values?[25]

The first part of the poem draws on devotional material and the widespread motif of the warning vision, most notably the *Trental of Saint Gregory*, a popular legend in which the Pope's mother appears to him as a ghost suffering the torments of hell, and is redeemed by the masses he has said for her. The ghost of the queen's mother is described using the full potential of alliteration for both visual and aural impact; Gawain calls it 'the grisselist goost that ever herd I grede [moan]' (99). The body is naked but 'Al biclagged in clay uncomly cladde [clotted with clay foully covered]' (106), weighed down by the earth from the grave. A toad with hollow glowing eyes bites the head—this is recounted in the wheel, as the shocking culmination of the stanza (115); and serpents and innumerable toads encircle the body (120). At first the ghost is painfully unable to speak:

Hit stemered*, hit stonayde*, hit stode as a stone:	*stammered; was stunned*
Hit marred, hit memered, hit mused for madde.*	*it grieved, it muttered, it grumbled madly* (109–10)

[25] For discussion of the unity question, see A. C. Spearing, 'The Awntyrs off Arthure', in Bernard S. Levy and Paul E. Szarmach (eds), *The Alliterative Tradition in the Fourteenth Century* (Kent, OH, 1981), 183–202. Hanna prints the poem as two separate parts, A and B; Putter also thinks it is probably an amalgamation of two separate poems (personal communication).

But then she becomes very articulate, insisting on her past beauty and power and her fall from that life to the torments of hell. Her last word to her daughter in this speech is succinctly placed at the end of the wheel: 'Be war be my wo [be warned by my woe]' (195). The repetition and assonance suggest a fading voice.

Concatenation is a feature of this text too: the next stanza begins '"Wo is me for thi wo [I grieve for your woe]", quod Waynour' (196). The woe is transferred from the mother's torments to the daughter's compassion; such links are deftly and consistently inserted throughout. Proper names can be sonorously accumulated: when the ghost first appears, Gawain complains that he has been abandoned by the other knights out hunting, 'Sir Cadour, Sir Clegis, Sir Costardyne, Sir Cay' (96). Although the rules of alliteration do not require a fourth instance in each line, this poet tends to include one. Place names also appear quite frequently, anchoring the plot in a familiar geography; the ghost prophesies that Mordred will be crowned at Carlisle, that the news of his treachery will reach the king in 'Tuskan' (Tuscany, during the Roman campaign), and that the bravest Round Table knights will die in 'Dorsetshire', including Gawain himself, 'The boldest of Bretayne' (288, 291, 295, 297; Britain appears several times as a rhyme for Gawain). Landscape and weather are important to the creation of atmosphere: when the ghost appears, it has turned so dark that that Gawain tells the queen it must be 'the clippes [eclipse] of the son' (94), a surprisingly sophisticated explanation (attributed to a clerk). The hunting party takes refuge in the forest 'For the sneterand snawe snartly hem snelles [driving snow that hurt them keenly]' (82); very similar phrasing is used in *Sir Gawain and the Green Knight* when during Gawain's search for the Green Chapel 'The snawe snitered ful snart' (2003).[26]

When the scene shifts to the banquet at court that evening, in the second half of the diptych, the descriptions are equally elaborate; but instead of dwelling on the horror of the ghost's appearance, the poet elaborates on the costumes of the strange knight and the lady who leads him into the hall. The lady is described in terms of her clothes and jewellery, rather than her own beauty; the description is quite similar to that of the queen at the beginning of the poem, as if to set them against one another, though it could be argued that more impressive detail is given about the strange lady. Many of the technical terms here are of French origin, and some are not attested elsewhere. Her 'contrefelet', apparently a sort of headdress (370; a *hapax*), seems to be interlaced with a 'perré' (a jewelled comb); with them she also wears a 'kelle' (370; a headdress) and a 'belle' (367; a cloak), both Old English terms. Two stanzas are then dedicated to the knight. At his entrance we are told that 'He was the soveraynest [lordliest] of al sitting in sete / That ever segge [man] had sen with his eye sight' (358–9); the repetition of the alliterating letter over two lines here emphasises his magnificence. The various colours he wears are listed in consecutive lines: gold, milk-white, silver, black (381–5), as if to insist on the contrasts, or the richness, or both. The bling and the colourfulness continue with his armour, encrusted with jewels:

> In stele* he was stuffed, that stourne upon stede,*   *armour; mounted warrior*
> Al of sternes* of golde, that stanseld was one straye;*   *stars; scattered randomly*

---

[26] The verb *sniter* is derived from Old Norse and is used of snow only in these two instances; see the note on line 2003 in Ad Putter and Myra Stokes (eds), *The Works of the Gawain Poet: Sir Gawain and the Green Knight, Pearl, Cleanness, Patience* (London, 2014). Snow features in some Scots poems, too; it is less common in French romance, though it does appear in Chrétien's *Conte du Graal*, when Percival is reminded of Blancheflor by seeing drops of blood on snow (4161ff.).

334 MEDIEVAL POETRY: 1100–1400

His gloves, his gamesons* glowed as a glede*	*outer coat; ember*
With graynes of rebé* that graithed ben gay*.	*beads of ruby; graciously fashioned*
And his schene schynbaudes*, that sharp wer to shrede* ...	*bright greaves; sharp for slashing* (391–5)

Such descriptions occur in other verse romances, and in prose too, in both French and English; but the alliteration adds enormously to the sense of splendour here. Most of the terms for armour come from French, but 'schynbaudes' (395) is of English origin, as are the accompanying adjectives 'schene' and 'sharp'.[27] These three alliterating words follow one another without any interruption, and this with the final 'shrede' again adds emphasis.

The knight declares his name, Galeron, and his quarrel with Arthur, listing the lands that the king has taken from him and given to Gawain:

'Mi name is Sir Galaron withouten eny gile*,	*guile*
The grettest of Galwey of greves and gyllis,*	*thickets and ravines*
Of Connok, of Conyngham, and also Kyle,	
Of Lomond, of Losex, of Loyan hilles'.	(417–20)

Here again the poet enjoys geographical lists which anchor the poem in a very specific region, the Scottish borders. It is agreed that Galeron and Gawain will fight next day, and the guest is conducted to a splendid pavilion:

Pight* was it prodly with purpour* and palle*,	*decorated; purple; fine cloth*
Birdes brauden* above, in brend* golde bright.	*birds embroidered; burnished*
Inwith was a chapell, a chambour, a halle,	
A chymné with charcole to chaufe* the knight.	*warm* (443–6)

The court may be away from home on a hunting trip, but they are living comfortably; it is the equivalent of modern glamping.

When the battle between Gawain and Galeron begins, the combination of French and Old English vocabulary is striking:

Shaftes in schide wode* thei shindre in shides,*	*split wood; splinter in shards*
So jolilé* thes gentil* justed on were*!	*spiritedly; nobles; in combat*
Shaftes thei shindre* in sheldes so shene ...	*splinter upon; bright* (501–3)

The romance words 'jolilé' and 'gentil' in line 502 seem dainty and almost inappropriate when sandwiched between so much vocabulary derived from Old English, particularly the two forceful lines of alliteration on 'sh' which are onomatopoeic in their evocation of clashing weapons and splintering shields. The knights are equal in skill, and equally exhausted; Galeron's lady begs the queen to stop the fight, and Gaynour takes off her crown and kneels before the king:

---

[27] Hanna notes that many of these words are rare in Middle English.

'The grones of Sir Gawayn dos my hert grille*.   *torment*
The grones of Sir Gawayne greven* me sare*.   *grieve*
Wodest thou leve,* Lorde,   *if you please*
Make thes knightes accorde,
Hit were a grete conforde*   *comfort*
For all that here ware'. (632–7)

Again the extension of the alliteration on one letter over two consecutive lines at 632–3 is emphatic, and the effect is increased by the repetition of 'the grones of Sir Gawayn'. Arthur restores the disputed lands to Galeron, and gives Gawain new holdings in Wales and else-where. They return to court; the knights' wounds are attended to, and Galeron joins the Round Table.

But the poet has not forgotten the first part of the poem. The final stanza, which is not linked to the previous one by any form of concatenation, describes the queen establishing a million masses (perhaps intended to convey a non-specific but large number) across Eng-land, though there is no explicit reference to the ghost's warnings either to her daughter or to Gawain. The final lines, 'In the tyme of Arthore / This anter betide', echo the opening line, 'In the tyme of Arthur an aunter bytydde'; this circular technique is a feature of the poems attributed to the *Gawain* poet. It is possible that the *Awntyrs* poet knew *Sir Gawain and the Green Knight*, but there is no doubt about the influence of the Alliterative *Morte Arthure*, which recounts Arthur's Roman war, civil war against Mordred, and death. Hanna calls the borrowings in the *Awntyrs* 'abundant and unmistakable'.[28] His evidence includes references in both poems to the Wheel of Fortune, Arthur's conquests in France, Tuscany, the site of Gawain's death, and Mordred's coat of arms which features a Scottish saltire. He also notes that in the *Morte* Arthur links the names of Gawain and Galeran.[29] The poet clearly knew a range of Arthurian narratives, and probably a number of other alliterative texts too. The emphasis on local place names—Inglewood Forest, the Tarn Wadling—indicates that the story was written for a north-western audience; a number of northern Gawain romances are set in this region.[30]

Most English Arthurian romances of this period focus on specific heroes and adventures; only two describe the collapse of Camelot and the deaths of the main characters, the Allit-erative *Morte Arthure* and the Stanzaic *Morte Arthur*, both late fourteenth-century.[31] The Alliterative *Morte Arthure* is very much in the chronicle tradition; it starts with the arrival of Roman envoys demanding tribute, and focuses on Arthur's battles across Europe till he is summoned back to deal with Mordred's usurpation, ending with the king's burial at Glas-tonbury in the presence of clergy and aristocracy. Malory follows this poem closely in his 'Tale of King Arthur and the Emperor Lucius', the second section of his *Morte Darthur*; he preserves much of the phrasing and alliteration in his prose, though the tale comes so early

---

[28] See the discussion in Hanna's introduction, 38ff.

[29] Alliterative *Morte Arthur*, 4182 and 3636, in L. D. Benson (ed.), *King Arthur's Death* (Exeter, 1986; rpt. Kalamazoo, MI, 1994). It is also striking that Mordred is described by the ghost in *Awntyrs* as a child playing in Arthur's hall (309–12); in the Alliterative *Morte* Arthur seems to imply that Mordred has been raised at court, addressing him as 'my nurree of old' and 'a child of my chamber' (689–90). This detail does not occur in any other medieval romance, to my knowledge.

[30] See Thomas Hahn, 'Gawain and Popular Chivalric Romance in Britain', in Roberta L. Krueger (ed.), *The Cambridge Companion to Romance* (Cambridge, 2006), 218–34; his introduction to Thomas Hahn (ed.), *Sir Gawain: Eleven Romances and Tales* (Kalamazoo, MI, 1995); and Roger Dalrymple, 'Sir Gawain in Middle English Romance', in Helen Fulton (ed.), *A Companion to Arthurian Literature* (Oxford, 2009), 265–77.

[31] The two texts are edited together by Benson as *King Arthur's Death* (see note 29 above); all references are to this edition.

336 MEDIEVAL POETRY: 1100–1400

in his cycle that he allows Arthur to conquer Rome and rule for many more years.[32] The alliterative verse here is uncomplicated by rhyme and uninterrupted by any bob or wheel; this has the effect of driving the story relentlessly onward to the tragic ending, where there is no uncertainty about Arthur's death:

> He said '*In manus*'* with main*   on molde* where he ligges,   *[Into (your) hands]; strength; ground*
>
> And thus passes his spirit   and spekes he no more!
> The baronage of Bretain then,   bishoppes and other,
> Graithes them* to Glashenbury   with glopinand* hertes   *Take themselves; dismayed*
>
> To bury there the bold king   and bring to the erthe
> With all worship* and welth   that any wye sholde.*   *honour; man should have* (4326–31)

The Stanzaic *Morte Arthur* is interested in relationships as much as battles, and keeps Arthur's end mysterious. It is closely based on the French prose *Mort Artu* of the Vulgate Cycle and thus has to deal with the various loves and betrayals and clashes of loyalties that bring about the fall of Camelot. It is unique among the pre-Malory romances in giving a central role to the Lancelot–Guinevere affair. It covers the Poisoned Apple episode, when the queen is falsely accused of murder and has to be defended in a judicial duel by Lancelot; the Fair Maid of Astolat, when a young girl dies of unrequited love for Lancelot; the outing of the lovers by Mordred and Agravain; the war between Arthur and Lancelot; Mordred's usurpation and the civil war in England; and the deaths of all the main characters. Malory drew heavily on it for his final two tales. Although the plot moves along at pace, there is also room for many dialogues, and for much expression of emotion. Here the form is eight-line stanzas with four stresses and the simple rhyme scheme *abababab*, with some alliteration.

The romance opens, most unusually, with Arthur and Guinevere in bed. The Grail Quest is over, and adventures are in short supply:

> Til on a time that it befell
>   The king in bed lay by the queen;
> Of aunters* they began to tell,   *adventures*
>   Many that in that land had beene.
> 'Sir, yif that it were your will,
>   Of a wonder thing I wolde you mene*,   *tell*
> How that your court beginneth to spill*   *become empty*
>   Of doughty knightes all bydene* ...'   *completely* (17–24)

This is a strikingly intimate scene, and it is also surprising to see the queen worrying about the reputation of the court; she goes on to advise the king to hold a tournament. The references to Lancelot that follow clearly imply that the audience/readers will know about the affair, though they would have had to read about it in French romances, as it is rarely

---

[32] In the first printed edition of the *Morte*, Malory's version is shortened and the language modernised, whether by Caxton or another. C. S. Lewis described Malory's alliterative prose as 'a noisy rumble', and in his view 'Caxton wisely abridged the whole dreary business'; quoted by Eugene Vinaver (ed.), *The Works of Sir Thomas Malory*, rev. P. J. C. Field, 3 vols. (Oxford, 1990), 3:1367.

mentioned in Middle English ones.[33] It is also noticeable that the dialogue begins without explicit naming of the speaker, a technique often described as ballad-like. Such shifts from indirect to direct speech occur frequently and indicate extreme emotion bursting out, often at the climax of a scene, and often in mid-stanza. Sometimes it is hard to know who is speaking, or indeed if a comment is made by a character or by the narrator, but the effect is to shine a spotlight on the feelings, and often the motivations, of the characters in a zoom lens close-up, adding emotional intensity to the story.[34] When Gawain comes to Astolat in search of Lancelot, the naïve Fair Maid reveals her love for the knight she has nursed:

> Sir Gawain gan that maiden take
> > And sat him by that sweete wight,
> And spake of Launcelot du Lake,
> > In all the world nas such a knight.
> The maiden there of Launcelot spake,
> > Said all her love was on him lighte:
> 'For his leman he hath me take;
> > His armour I you shewe might'. (576–83)

We do not need to hear Gawain's praise of Lancelot in detail; what is important is the Maid's claim to be his 'leman', which will cause trouble when reported to the queen, and we hear that from her own lips.

The relative sparsity of dialogue in the poem makes the few extended passages particularly powerful. The most obvious example is the parting of Lancelot and Guinevere in the convent where she has become a nun, almost one hundred lines of dialogue and strong emotion, with the queen determined to blame their love for the deaths of Arthur and his knights and her own possible damnation.[35] Their intense conversation continues completely uninterrupted from 3638 to 3693; and in the following twenty-seven lines the only interruption is an occasional 'the queen gan say' or 'then said Launcelot du Lake'. Rejected as a lover, Lancelot swears to follow Guenevere into religious life:

> 'A, wilt thou so,' the queen gan say,
> > Fulfill this forward that thou hast ment?'
> Launcelot said: 'Yif I said nay,
> > I were well worthy to be brent*.   *burnt
> 'Brent to ben worthy I were,
> > Yif I wolde take none such a life,
> To bide in penaunce, as ye do here,
> > And suffer for God sorrow and strife.' (3694–3702)

The concatenation between the stanzas (used only in this section of the poem) compels complete attention to their words; it underlines both the cause-and-effect principle that Guinevere is laying out in terms of their guilt and Lancelot's lasting devotion which makes

---

[33] See Elizabeth Archibald, 'Lancelot as Lover in the English Tradition before Malory', in Bonnie Wheeler (ed.), *Arthurian Studies in Honour of P. J. C. Field* (Cambridge, 2006), 199–216.

[34] See Elizabeth Archibald, 'Some Uses of Direct Speech in the Stanzaic *Morte Arthur* and Malory', *Arthuriana*, 28.3 (2018), 66–85; this special issue of the journal is devoted to the poem.

[35] This scene has no source or analogue in earlier tradition apart from a more sentimental account in one variant manuscript of the Vulgate *Mort Artu*; see Archibald, 'Some Uses of Direct Speech', 78–80.

338   MEDIEVAL POETRY: 1100–1400

him accept 'That same destainy that you is dight' (3687), the penitential life of a hermit. But there is no concatenation when Lancelot asks for a last kiss, and the queen refuses:

> The sorrow that the tone to the tother gan make
> > Might none erthely man see it.
> 'Madame', then said Launcelot du Lake,
> > 'Kiss me, and I shall wend as-tite*.'   *go quickly away*
>
> 'Nay', said the queen, 'that will I not;
> > Launcelot, think on that no more.' (3710–15)

At this point the queen is anxious to separate herself for ever from Lancelot, and the stanza structure reflects this. It is a shattering scene; no wonder Malory used it almost word for word, turning the original verse into equally poignant prose.[36] In its deceptively simple style, the poem offers links too with the spare narratives of the ballad tradition.

Jane Gilbert offers a useful series of characterisations of Arthurian romance and Arthurian ethics.[37] She comments in relation to Chrétien's *Perceval* that 'the sense of discovering a new world and the play with expectations are essential elements of any twelfth-century Arthurian romance'; she sees works of this period as ironic, paradoxical, ethically open. Thirteenth-century works, she argues, are less playful and more didactic, specially the French prose cycles with their 'tragic paradoxes, dramatic ironies and pessimism'. Knights are presented as morally flawed; they can redeem themselves up to a point, but failure to live up to the highest ideals is inevitable: 'Early Arthurian romances did not speak the same moral language as did the late medieval centuries'.[38] English Arthurian romances belong to this second phase and can seem fairly straightforward in comparison with French analogues such as Chrétien's poems; few could be described as ironic, paradoxical, ethically open. But they are more succinct and direct than most thirteenth- and fourteenth-century French romances; and their directness can create moments of comedy, as in *Sir Percyvell*, and of great poignancy, as in the Stanzaic *Morte Arthur*. The use of alliteration allows for the display of a rich and varied vocabulary which can create powerful visual effects, terrifying or glamorous; both can be seen in *The Awntyrs of Arthure*. The flexibility of English verse forms allowed poets to vary stanza lengths and formats, manipulating rhyme schemes and line lengths to create dramatic effects, for instance with the bob and wheel. Dramatic is the right word, for romances were performed as well as read; Putter has made a strong case that they were not only recited but also sung.[39] The intricacies of metre and rhyme devised by English poets allow them to translate, adapt, and invent romances in the equivalent of complex musical forms, making their versions quite distinct from their French sources. They offer some ingenious twists on earlier plots and on characterisations of familiar Arthurian figures, and some powerful and original narratives of their own.

---

[36] Malory, in Vinaver (ed.), *Works of Sir Thomas Malory*, 3: 1252–3.

[37] Jane Gilbert, 'Arthurian Ethics', in Elizabeth Archibald and Ad Putter (eds), *The Cambridge Companion to the Arthurian Legend* (Cambridge, 2009), 154–70.

[38] Gilbert, 'Arthurian Ethics', 160.

[39] Putter, 'The Singing of Middle English Romance'.

22

Crusade Romances and the Matter of France

Marcel Elias

In recent years, the Middle English crusade romance has emerged as a major literary category in the field of late-medieval literary studies, subsuming texts that previous scholarship had generally assigned to other subgroups, including the homiletic or pious romance, the alliterative romance, the historical romance, and the romance of nation or empire. While the large number of romances exhibiting crusade-related concerns has led scholars to differ widely in their understandings of what qualifies as a crusade romance, basing our conception of the subgenre on historical evidence of contemporary identification with the crusading movement puts us on solid ground. The nine verse romances of the Matter of France or 'Charlemagne romances' occupy a central position in this corpus because references to the Carolingian king and his peers as protocrusaders permeate high and late-medieval writings on the crusades. The siege of Jerusalem in 70 CE by the Roman generals Titus and Vespasian, poetically retold in the alliterative *Siege of Jerusalem*, was conflated with the conquest of the city in 1099 during the First Crusade in various chronicles and treatises. And *Richard Coeur de Lion* is a semi-historical, semi-fantastical account of the Third Crusade (1189–92).[1]

The subject of crusade may tempt an Orientalist approach to these romances; however, the later Middle Ages were a period in which West-East power relations were different from those brought about by the rise of modern colonialism. If the crusader conquest of Jerusalem (1099) and its environs was conducive to a nascent sense of European colonial authority manifested in Orientalist stereotypes prefiguring those described by Edward Said for the post-Napoleonic era,[2] these representational tendencies came to be increasingly complicated by the crusading reversals that followed: the recapture of Jerusalem in 1187 by Ṣalāḥ al-Dīn, who pushed the crusaders back to a thin strip of land on the Palestinian coast; the defeats suffered by Louis IX of France during the thirteenth century; the Mamlūk campaigns culminating in the fall of Acre in 1291 and what came to be known in Europe as the loss of the Holy Land; and the victories of the rising Ottoman empire at Nicopolis in 1396 and Varna in 1444, to name only a few. As I have argued elsewhere, the military and geopolitical circumstances of the eastern Mediterranean from the late twelfth through fifteenth centuries destabilised binary, oppositional understandings of religious and racial identity in European writings on Muslims and Islam produced across various genres and traditions.[3]

---

[1] I discuss the historical evidence in my monograph, *English Literature and the Crusades: Anxieties of Holy War, 1291–1453* (Cambridge, forthcoming). For an overview of previous scholarly definitions of the crusade romance, see Siobhain Bly Calkin, 'Crusades Romance', in Siân Echard and Robert Rouse (eds), *The Encyclopedia of British Medieval Literature* (Chichester, 2017), 583–9.

[2] Edward W. Said, *Orientalism* (London, 1978, 1995). While tracing the origins of Orientalism to ancient Greece via medieval Europe, Said focused the bulk of his analysis on the late eighteenth through mid-twentieth centuries.

[3] See Marcel Elias, 'Unsettling Orientalism: Toward a New History of European Representations of Muslims and Islam, c. 1200–1450' (forthcoming). On conceptions of race in medieval Europe, see further, for two different

Marcel Elias, *Crusade Romances and the Matter of France*. In: *The Oxford History of Poetry in English*. Edited by Helen Cooper and Robert R. Edwards, Oxford University Press. © Marcel Elias (2023). DOI: 10.1093/oso/9780198827429.003.0022

340   MEDIEVAL POETRY: 1100–1400

At the time in which the Middle English crusade romances were being composed, long-established beliefs that God punishes the sinful with defeat and rewards the worthy with victory fostered increasing attention in Europe to similarities between Islam and Christianity. This was in part strategic: taking an analogical, rather than oppositional, approach to Islam enabled writers to use their descriptions of Muslim piety and 'good works' to show up the failures of Christians, invite emulation, and encourage reform. A key tension animates works by such authors as John Bromyard, Riccoldo da Monte di Croce, Roger Stanegrave, Honorat Bovet, and Johann Schiltberger: between conviction that Islam is a false religion and concession that adherence to its tenets may result in behaviour of the highest moral standards.

Though focusing on the fictional, legendary, or historically grounded adventures of protocrusading and crusading figures of the past, poets of fourteenth-century English crusade romances engaged their audiences' responses and reflections on a broad range of contemporary preoccupations, with a particular interest in tackling the points of conflict and tension raised by the disappointments and failures of the enterprise. They did so by creatively refashioning their sources, in most cases *chansons de geste* in Old French or Anglo-Norman, taking a highly dynamic approach to translation, experimenting with the stylistic and poetic possibilities afforded by the English language and the verse forms they chose, and engaging innovatively with, or deviating from, the well-established conventions of the French epic. The appreciative account of the poetic qualities and aesthetic effects of the insular romances of the Matter of France that I offer here contributes to a wider 'rehabilitation' of these texts, which were for a long time dismissed by literary critics as derivative and flawed renditions of the stories of the French tradition.[4] Over the past few decades, these romances have received increasing scholarly attention as repositories of valuable information on contemporary approaches to the crusades, Islam and the 'Orient', issues of gender, race, and nationhood—but also, though to a lesser extent, as accomplished literary works subject to *mouvance* or *variance*: to the creative innovations of authors or adaptors who conceived of translation as a poetic act of topical interpretation.[5] However, their position within the genre of Middle English romance remains ambiguous and contested. In an article published in 1980, John Finlayson argued that, given their direct descendance from the epic tradition, the Middle English Charlemagne texts should be altogether stripped of the designation of romance, while much more recently, Melissa Furrow challenged the very existence of a distinction between the two genres, claiming that *chanson de geste* became a subset of the capacious category of romance in late-medieval England.[6] Yet the permeability of generic boundaries that was characteristic of medieval literary culture does not prevent us

---

approaches, Geraldine Heng, *The Invention of Race in the European Middle Ages* (Cambridge, 2018) and Victoria Turner, *Theorizing Medieval Race: Saracen Representations in Old French Literature* (Cambridge, 2019).

[4] See, e.g., H. M. Smyser, 'Charlemagne Legends', in J. B. Severs (ed.), *A Manual of the Writings in Middle English, 1050–1500*, 11 vols. (New Haven, CT, 1967–2005), 1:80; W. R. J. Barron, *English Medieval Romance* (London, 1987), 98.

[5] See, e.g., Suzanne Conklin Akbari, *Idols in the East: European Representations of Islam and the Orient, 1100–1450* (Ithaca, NY, 2009); Siobhain Bly Calkin, *Saracens and the Making of English Identity: The Auchinleck Manuscript* (New York, 2009). The full-length study is Marianne Ailes and Philippa Hardman, *The Legend of Charlemagne in Medieval England: The Matter of France in Middle English and Anglo-Norman Literature* (Cambridge, 2017), which offers a detailed examination of various changes undergone by these stories in the course of their translation and dissemination, and a comprehensive coverage of the relationship between the different manuscripts. I borrow the terms *mouvance* and *variance* from Paul Zumthor's seminal *Essai de poétique médiévale* (Paris, 1972); and Bernard Cerquiglini's insightful sequel *Éloge de la variante: histoire critique de la philologie* (Paris, 1989).

[6] John Finlayson, 'Definitions of Middle English Romance', *The Chaucer Review*, 15 (1980), 169–70; Melissa Furrow, *Expectations of Romance: The Reception of a Genre in Medieval England* (Woodbridge, 2009), 95–116.

(and did not prevent medieval audiences) from 'recognizing romance', as Helen Cooper notes, through a series of 'common features that cumulatively indicate family resemblance'.[7] In the case of the crusade romances, what ties them to the broader corpus of fourteenth-century Middle English popular romances can only be adequately understood in relation to a series of cultural anxieties engendered by the failures of the crusades: God's will and support to the enterprise; the mutual obligations between human and divine; Christendom's military vulnerability and beleaguered state; the corruptness of the chivalric classes; the moral and providential status of Muslims; questions of poor leadership, domestic politics, and chivalric motivation; notions of shared humanity across the religious divide; and the morality of violence.[8]

Middle English romance became the vehicle of choice for the expression, negotiation, and wide dissemination of these complex crusade-related anxieties across late-medieval English society not only because of its historical consciousness, textual malleability, and broad social reach, but also because this is specifically the type of cultural work that came to be expected of the genre. Modern scholarship no longer predominantly sees medieval popular romance as a genre of easy stereotypes, simplistic value systems, and starkly delineated oppositions, but rather as deriving its character from the ambivalence and admiration it sustains towards protagonists and antagonists alike, the tensions it exposes between ideals and experiential realities, its combination of conventional and transgressive elements, and its commitment to provoking discussion and debate through historically or culturally evocative fictional narratives.[9] These tendencies are as important to our understanding of the genre as the more specific thematic interests and formal features that demarcate romance from *chanson de geste*: an enhanced focus on love, courtliness, and the supernatural; a heightened concern with the emotions, thoughts, and achievements of individual characters; a general preference for fast-moving, shorter narratives; and an openness to metrical variety and formal experimentation.[10] A close investigation of the changes undergone by the Middle English crusade romances in the course of their translation or adaptation bears out these claims. These romances emerged out the *chanson de geste* and are thus inevitably suffused with its themes, including 'Saracens' or Muslims as polytheistic idolaters who abuse their 'gods' (accusations of polytheism and idolatry were commonplace during the crusades, on the part of both Christians and Muslims), religious warfare as an act of compassionate vengeance, and conversion of the Muslim hero after a duel with a Christian champion. However, these themes receive innovative treatment, often involving a loosening or troubling of boundaries: Christians, as well as Muslims, express divinely addressed accusations; Muslims, as well as Christians, take on the role of righteous avengers of wrongful injuries; and conversion becomes the site of sustained tensions between entrenched beliefs in the falsity of Islam and hopes that converted Muslims will bring with them qualities lacking in Christians. In making both fine and more substantial adjustments to their sources, authors of insular crusade romances were often more interested in unsettling and deconstructing binary oppositions—such as Christian–Muslim, ally–enemy, virtuous–sinful, loyal–treacherous,

---

[7] Helen Cooper, *The English Romance in Time: Transforming Motifs from Geoffrey of Monmouth to the Death of Shakespeare* (Oxford, 2004), 9–10.

[8] On the historical and cultural contexts grounding these romances, see further Elias, *English Literature and the Crusades*.

[9] See, e.g., Nicola McDonald, 'A Polemical Introduction', in *Pulp Fictions of Medieval England: Essays in Popular Romance* (Manchester, 2004), 1–21; Neil Cartlidge (ed.), *Heroes and Anti-Heroes in Medieval Romance* (Cambridge, 2012); Christine Chism, 'Romance', in Larry Scanlon (ed.), *The Cambridge Companion to Medieval English Literature 1100–1500* (Cambridge, 2009), 57–69.

[10] Cooper, *The English Romance*, 10; Ailes and Hardman, *Legend*, 85–6.

342 MEDIEVAL POETRY: 1100–1400

righteous–unrighteous, even saved–damned—than in upholding or reifying them. Within this subgenre, religious and racial identities are notably malleable and fluid.[11] Poets opted for different verse forms according to the themes they wished to develop, frequently infusing their sources with courtly, amorous, and supernatural elements in the depiction of both Christians and Muslims. The resulting poems feature a striking range of tensions and contradictions: they elicit sympathy and judgement towards both Christian and Muslim characters, make Christian victory contingent on the infusion of Muslim strength and virtue, assert the righteousness of the Christian cause but question its human implications, disparage Muhammad yet also at times admit to his greatness, condemn Muslims to damnation while positing the salvation of a select few, and call into question foundational beliefs in God's supernatural support through moments of religious doubt. Their openness to contradictory currents and clashing modes is what made their public performance or reading such a startling and thought-provoking experience for late-medieval audiences.

In identifying 'trois materes' (three subject matters)—the Matters of Britain, Rome, and France—Jehan Bodel (c 1165–c 1210) deemed the latter most historical and topical: it is both 'true' and evident every day (*chascun jour aparant*).[12] To a certain degree, this view that the principal interest of the Charlemagne texts (whether in *chanson de geste* or romance form) lies in their politically and culturally engaged nature has also prevailed in modern scholarship, from Erich Auerbach's mid-twentieth century claim that courtly romance lacks the 'politico-historical context' of the *chanson de geste* to twenty-first-century studies of the insular Matter of France romances for the ideas they express about chivalric culture, crusading, national identity, religion, and race.[13] But these ideas are expressed dramatically and poetically, with authors taking a thoughtful and serious approach to the relationship between form and content, and to the artistic contributions they were making to the shared poetics of a genre in the making.

The Fantasy of Conversion

The corpus of Middle English verse romances of the Matter of France to have survived consists of nine texts showcasing a wide range of formal variation: nearly half are in tail-rhyme stanzas, while the rest are in couplets, quatrains, septenaries, alexandrines, and alliterative verse. This formal variety seems to have been as much the result of ongoing engagement on the part of English poets with the challenge of finding an appropriate substitute for the *laisses* (strophes of various length in which lines, typically of ten or twelve syllables, are linked by assonance or rhyme) of their Old French or Anglo-Norman sources as the result of more specific aesthetic and narrative agendas: as I discuss below, translational or adaptive decisions related to form were often inseparable from those related to content.[14] As

---

[11] In this respect, these romances can be viewed as prefiguring Renaissance theatre; see Daniel J. Vitkus, *Turning Turk: English Theater and the Multicultural Mediterranean, 1570–1630* (New York, 2003), 23–4.

[12] See Jehan Bodel, in Annette Brasseur (ed.), *La Chanson des Saisnes*, 2 vols. (Geneva, 1989), 6–15. For a discussion of Jehan's classification focusing on the relation between romance and history, see Jon Whitman, 'Romance and History: Designing the Times', in *Romance and History: Imagining Time from the Medieval to the Early Modern Period* (Cambridge, 2015), 3–20.

[13] Erich Auerbach, *Mimesis: The Representation of Reality in Western Literature*, Willard R. Trask (trans.) (Princeton, NJ, 1968); Whitman, 'Romance and History', 3, 6.

[14] Ailes and Hardman, *Legend*, 86–9; Ad Putter, 'The Metres and Stanza Forms of Popular Romance', in Raluca L. Radulescu and Cory James Rushton (eds), *A Companion to Medieval Popular Romance* (Cambridge, 2009), 111–31 (at 131).

Marianne Ailes and Philippa Hardman have observed, because English writers tended to employ poetic forms involving much more frequent rhyme changes and to opt for an abbreviated narration of events, the English romances are generally shorter and more fast-paced than the *chansons de geste* they derive from.[15] Their formal heterogeneity contrasts with their relative homogeneity of subject matter: all are concerned with religious warfare, and six centre on a Muslim character who, after demanding the surrender of Christian lands and challenging Charlemagne's most valorous peers to meet him in combat, relinquishes his faith and fights for the defence and expansion of Christianity. During the thirteenth and fourteenth centuries, anxieties about the loss of Christian-held territories to non-Christian enemies were rife, with the westward conquests of the Mongols, the recovery of the last crusader strongholds in the Levant by the Mamlūks, and Ottoman encroachment into eastern Europe endowing the figure of the hostile Muslim who converts to Christianity with unprecedented cultural resonance. The fantasy of incorporating the strength and prowess of a powerful non-Christian adversary captured the imagination of English romance poets, who reworked their sources with a remarkable degree of creative independence. In the case of *Otuel* (before 1330), *Otuel and Roland* (c 1330), *Duke Roland and Sir Otuel of Spain* (c 1400), and *Sir Ferumbras* (c 1380), the alterations made to the *chansons de geste* of *Otinel* and *Fierabras* have two principal effects: a heightened sense of peril, vulnerability, and disunity in the face Muslim power; and an amplification of the eponymous characters' military and moral contributions to the Christian army after they convert.[16]

Comparing the literary strategies used to achieve these effects in *Otuel*, composed in rhyming couplets, and *Duke Roland and Sir Otuel of Spain* (hereafter *Roland and Otuel*), written in tail-rhyme stanzas, is illuminating, not least because most extant Middle English romances fall into these two formal categories.[17] Several decades ago, Derek Pearsall argued that the rhyming couplet was the preferred poetic medium for 'epic romances', tales that are 'more prosaic, realistic, historical, and martial', whereas tail-rhyme was the form of choice for 'lyric romances', stories that are 'more concerned with love, faith, constancy, and the marvellous'.[18] While the limitations of such an approach are readily apparent in the numerous romances that cut across the two categories, Pearsall's classification is perhaps best understood not in terms of a strict division between 'epic' and 'lyric' stories, but as outlining some of the principal narrative ends to which these metres were particularly well suited to be used. *Otuel* and *Roland and Otuel* are different versions of the same

---

[15] Marianne Ailes and Philippa Hardman, 'How English Are the English Charlemagne Romances?', in Neil Cartlidge (ed.), *Boundaries in Medieval Romance* (Woodbridge, 2008), 43–55 (at 47–9).

[16] References are to the following editions: Mary Isabelle O'Sullivan (ed.), *Firumbras and Otuel and Roland*, EETS o.s. 198 (London, 1935); Sidney J. H. Herrtage (ed.), *Sir Ferumbras*, EETS e.s. 34 (London, 1879, 1903, 1966); Sidney J. H. Herrtage (ed.), *The Sege off Melayne and The Romance of Duke Rowland and Sir Otuell of Spayne*, EETS e.s. 35 (London, 1880, 1931); *The Tale of Rauf Coilyear with the Fragments of Roland and Vernagu and Otuel*, in Sidney J. H. Herrtage (ed.), *The English Charlemagne Romance, Part VI: The Taill of Rauf Coilyear*, EETS e.s. 39 (London, 1882, rpt. 1931, 1969). For all editions of the crusade romances, citation to line numbers will be given parenthetically in the text.

[17] *Otuel* is believed to derive from a lost Middle English source very close to the Anglo-Norman version of *Otinel* preserved in Cologny-Geneva, Bodmer Library MS 168, fols. 210v–221r. *Duke Roland and Sir Otuel of Spain* is thought to be an independent adaptation, containing points in common with both the Anglo-Norman text and the Old French version edited by François Guessard and Henri Victor Michelant in *Les anciens poètes de la France*, 10 vols. (Paris, 1858–70), 1.1–92. I am grateful to Diane Speed for sharing her transcription of the Anglo-Norman text preserved in the Bodmer Library. Both versions have been consulted as a basis for comparison with the Middle English romances. On the relationship between the different versions, see Paul Aebischer, *Etudes sur Otinel: de la chanson de geste à la saga norroise et aux origines de la légende* (Bern, 1960), 96–104.

[18] Derek Pearsall, 'The Development of Middle English Romance', *Mediaeval Studies*, 27 (1965), 91–116.

344   MEDIEVAL POETRY: 1100–1400

epic poem, yet they invoke broadly distinguishable narrative registers when altering their sources, the former playing upon the conventions of *chanson de geste* in its distinctive treatment of public honour, reciprocal duty, and homosocial loyalty, and the latter tending more towards the 'lyric' with its augmented emphasis on faith, prayer, and heterosexual love. In *Otuel*, the short rhyming couplet lends itself well to the fast-moving action and dialogues of the initial scenes, which narrate the Christians' unsuccessful attempt to kill Otuel in contravention of their king's orders that he be granted the protection befitting a royal envoy (insistently reiterated in this version, see 141–3, 193–6, 205–8, 329–32, 355–8), and the fierce duel opposing Roland and the eponymous Muslim character, drawing special attention to their courtesy and mutual respect. The poet supplements the emotional repertoire of the *chanson de geste* of *Otinel*, using rhyme words such as 'tene' and 'kene' (149–50), 'agramed' and 'aschamed' (169–70, 277–8), and 'afriȝt' and 'kniȝt' (557–8), to describe the alarm, disunity, and humiliation caused by Otuel's menacing presence and martial prowess. An atmosphere of imminent peril is maintained throughout the duel, and only gives way to newfound confidence and communal strength when Otuel, on the point of defeating Roland, is struck by an epiphany and decides to embrace Christianity. In an expanded scene of reconciliation, Otuel's incorporation into the Christian fellowship is couched in terms of love and brotherhood: 'Bote clippe & kusse eyþer oþer / As eiþer hedde been oþeres broþer' (605–6).[19] Throughout the rest of the narrative, the poet consistently heightens the title character's commitment to the 'epic' values of community and mutual solidarity: he surpasses Charlemagne's most valorous knights in strength and prowess, condemns their 'envie' and selfishness (in a passage unique to this version),[20] and is repeatedly described as acting out of 'loue' for Charlemagne (652, 1028), serving the interests of his king and peers before his own, thus ultimately leading the Christians to victory.

The later tail-rhyme romance of *Roland and Otuel* also creatively engages with the anxieties and tensions inherent in this 'dream of conversion', but in a way that conforms to a different aesthetic and speaks to different thematic interests. The threat of imminent defeat during the episode of combat between Otuel and Roland finds dramatic expression in Charlemagne's repeated appeals to God for help, which are augmented in number and length, are made more impactful through the conversion of indirect into direct speech, and are supplemented with descriptions of the king's emotional states (fear, sorrow, and love of God) and physical gestures (kneeling or upholding his hands to heaven) (487–92, 506–16, 568–76). The longest of these prayers is amplified for a sense of greater urgency with an interpolated plea to save Roland 'fro schame' (510) and an elaboration on why Otuel's conversion is so desirable—he is 'hardy', 'wighte' [brave; valiant], 'ferse in armes', 'doghtey',

---

[19] Cf. Guessard and Michelant, 594–95.

[20] The passage in question presents Roland sneaking away from camp, accompanied only by Oliver and Ogier, in search of adventures to reassert his wounded chivalric honour. Upon learning of the peers' absence, Otuel rebukes them for their envious response to his recent chivalric success, and provides a clear counter-example to their self-serving, immoderate behaviour:

> Beþ went for envie of me,
> To loke wher þei miȝten spede
> To don any douȝti deede
>
> ...
>
> þouȝ þei habben envie to me,
> Ich wille for þe loue of þe [Charlemagne],
> Fonden whoþer i miȝte comen,
> To helpen hem ar þei weren inomen. (1020–2, 1027–30)

'gentill', and 'of mekill myghte' (511–16).[21] Otuel, a Muslim warrior, embodies knightly ideals to which Roland, medieval Europe's paragon of chivalry, can only aspire: when Otuel, clearly presented as having the upper hand, finally consents to become Christian after a dove 'fro the holy gaste' (578) settles on his helmet, in a statement that finds no counterpart in the French texts, Roland admits to having 'foghten with þe beste knyghte, / In alle this werlde es none so wighte' (595–6) before announcing the good news to Charlemagne, who falls upon his knees and worships God (601–3). If Otuel's martial energy and moral integrity are unrivalled, both as a Muslim and as a Christian, so too is his religious zeal: 'there es no god bot one / þat euer made ne blode ne bone / Nowe sone it schall be sene' (1294–6) is the assertion, unique to the present version, that he makes before defeating the Muslim champion Clarel through force of arms alone, unassisted by divine supernatural interference, thus succeeding where Roland had failed. While Otuel's incorporation into the politico-religious folds of Christendom is accompanied by the offer of marriage to Charlemagne's daughter Belisent in all versions of the story, *Roland and Otuel* turns this marital 'contract' into a more sentimental amorous relationship grounded in shared religious duty. The poet infuses the narrative with notes of lyricism and courtliness in added or expanded depictions of the couple's amatory interactions—as when Otuel, after being introduced to this 'louelyeste' of women (616) and asking for her consent to marry him, solemnly vows that he has 'chosen' his ('my') 'lady, / þat es so mylde of mode' (644–5); or when Belisent kisses him full-heartedly after he is absolved of his sins by Bishop Turpin: 'Scho kiste hym thryse with herte full fyne, / Bytaughte hym vn to dere dryghtyne, / þat Mayden faire to fande' (1282–4). The space for elaboration afforded by the tail-line, following the 'action' typically contained in the couplet, enables the poet to embellish the narrative with added details of Belisent's beauty and virtues (618, 645, 1284), and to describe her emotions (1305, 1344). The love they immediately share is inseparable from Otuel's dedication to the Christian cause, with this version departing from the French *chanson de geste* in making their wedding contingent on his final capture of Emperor Garcy (658–60).[22] In characteristic Middle English romance fashion, the dual goal of military victory and marital love is established in the course of the narration and achieved in the final scenes, which see Otuel (rather than Roland and the other peers, as in the French texts) capture Garcy (1573–5) and return to Paris, where he marries Belisent and is made lord of Lombardy:

> And than þay helde a Mangery*   *a feast*
> With alle þe noble cheualry,
> þat seemly* was to see.   *pleasing*
> þay made hym lorde of lumbardy
> to hafe it alle in his Bayly,
> þat contre faire & free.
> And thus he duellys & es a pere*,   *peer*
> Rowlande felawe, and Olyuere,
> A gud Cristyn man was hee.
> And Iesus Criste þat boghte vs dere,
> Brynge vs to thi Blisses sere!
> Amen, par charite! (1585–96)

---

[21] The Anglo-Norman and Old French versions omit the laudatory material; see Guessard and Michelant, 503.

[22] This detail is also noted by Ailes and Hardman, *Legend*, 380–1.

346   MEDIEVAL POETRY: 1100–1400

In soothingly formulaic style, this final stanza presents a picture of marital bliss, worldly prosperity, and fellowship in the Christian faith. Yet the central question posed by the romance to a contemporary audience well aware of Christendom's crusading failures in the Levant and eastern Europe (most recently at Nicopolis against the Ottomans in 1396) is anything but soothing and reassuring: was Christian victory possible without the intervention of a strong, morally principled non-Christian ally? This tension between the pleasure afforded by conventional formulae, courtly tropes, and happy endings, and the challenging questions provoked in the course of the narration, is one of the most fascinating features of Middle English romance.[23]

In reworking the *chanson de geste* of *Fierabras*, *Sir Ferumbras* exhibits a broadly similar authorial agenda to the *Otuel* romances: the eponymous character benefits from interpolated qualifiers of praise, stressing his greatness and fearlessness (121–3, 437); and, in a considerably lengthened statement following his defeat by Oliver, he asserts his intentions to become Christian, to persecute those who 'bileueþ on Mahounde' both 'niȝt & day', and to make 'peynymes cristned be' (759–69).[24] Yet after the 'trial by combat' scene that unites the *Otinel* and *Fierabras* traditions, Ferumbras's role in the narrative is eclipsed by that of his sister Floripas, who converts to Christianity for love of Guy of Burgundy, and is provided with various opportunities for female agency. When Charlemagne's best knights are imprisoned by Emir Balam, both *Sir Ferumbras* and the fragmentary *Firumbras* (1375–1400) enhance the part Floripas plays in helping them escape and avoid death, notably by emphasising her resourcefulness, spirit of initiative, and piety at crucial points in the narrative. In *Firumbras*, for instance, after Floripas frees the Christian knights from the dungeon, killing their jailer and enabling them to attack Balam and barricade themselves in his castle, she comes up with the ingenious idea (unparalleled in the French *chanson de geste*) of turning the Greek fire deployed by the Muslim besiegers against them: 'y schall turne the fyr and the flames that ben lyȝt / Aȝen on the sarisins to brenne well bright, / thorow crafte that ȝe couthe and queyntyse of gynne [ingenious means]' (799–801). The 'gynne' [ingenuity, cleverness] with which she responds to the Muslims' 'gynnes' [war engines] (789) represents a triumph of intellect over force, while also suggesting an effective alternative to martial prowess.[25] Equally relevant are the poet's gestures towards parallelism in depicting Floripas's religious devoutness, and commitment to encouraging devoutness in others, both before and after she decides to convert. Two episodes in particular are refashioned for further structural and verbal symmetry. The first presents Floripas fetching the statues of her 'gods' and (unsuccessfully) enjoining the Christian knights to 'cometh forth hyder in gode dyuocyoun, / And kneleth & cryeth to my lord mahoun' (261–2) before making a sally against the Muslim forces; and the second sees her bring the relics of the Passion to the peers 'in good deuocyoun' in the lead-up to another sortie: 'here hys the croune of goddys passyoun / Lo, here ys the spere and the nayles also / That longes [Longinus] pyt in hys hert, the blod ran there-fo' (593–6). Invoking the language of 'deuocyoun' in relation to

---

[23] Christine Chism reaches a similar conclusion in her discussion of *Amis and Amiloun*: see Chism, 'Romance', in *The Cambridge Companion to Medieval English Literature*, 63.

[24] Of the three Middle English versions of the *Fierabras* story, *Sir Ferumbras* is the closest to the original Old French *chanson de geste*, the 'Vulgate', composed at the end of the twelfth century, and most recently edited by Marc Le Person as *Fierabras: chanson de geste du XIIᵉ siècle* (Paris, 2003).

[25] In my analysis of this passage, I am indebted to Ailes and Hardman, *Legend*, 291–3; and Robert W. Hanning, 'Engin in Twelfth-Century Romance: An Examination of the *Roman d'Enéas* and Hue de Rotelande's *Ipomedon*', *Yale French Studies*, 51 (1974), 82–101. Here, the term 'gynne' functions much like the Old French word 'engin' discussed by Hanning.

both 'mahoun' and 'goddys passyoun', the poet highlights the direct transferral of Floripas's unwavering trust in the power of devotional objects from one religion to the other. When assimilated to Christianity, her reverent attitude represents a considerable asset, with this version uniquely having her present, 'with wel god entent' (592), not just the Crown of Thorns, but also the Holy Lance and Holy Nails to the peers, who fall 'to grounde' (597) in prayer for protection, which they are subsequently granted.[26] The eponymous heroes of the *Otuel* and *Ferumbras* romances prove invaluable not because conversion to Christianity changes them but specifically because it does not: they were already brave, fierce, courteous, resourceful, and religiously devout as Muslims, and these are the attributes which they carry into their 'new' Christian lives, contributing crucially to the survival of an otherwise vulnerable, enfeebled, and divided Christian camp.

Similarity in Difference

It has sometimes been suggested that Muslim characters in *chansons de geste* and romances are only portrayed as noble and courteous to presage their future conversion to Christianity.[27] Yet some of the most admirable displays of militaristic honour are ascribed to Muslim figures who remain true to their faith. In the *Siege of Milan* (*c* 1400), for instance, the Muslim King of Macedonia refuses to slay the unhorsed Bishop Turpin, and loses his hand while attempting to ward off a blow aimed at the latter's head (1115–26).[28] The non-converted Muslim Clarel of the *Otuel* romances honours the favour of freedom he was previously granted by offering his wounded Christian enemy Ogier protection and medical assistance, and promptly cutting off the head of a fellow coreligionist who opposes his decision. In *Roland and Otuel*, a romance which not only refers to the Prophet as 'grete Mahoun' (176, 425, 545, 776, 970) but introduces altogether new Muslim characters famed for their 'noble' and chivalrous behaviour (1069–74, 1093–5),[29] Clarel is in fact given the ultimate reward of salvation, despite his previous rejection of Christianity. When Otuel kills Clarel, this 'noble kyng' of 'hert fre' (1309, 944), rather than making him curse Muhammad in his final breath of life as the French texts do ('Et Mahomet son seignor maudisant'), the romance describes his 'saule' going up 'vn-to Mahoun' (1340).[30] Remarkable as it is, this poet's concern with the fate of non-converted Muslims after death is not unique within the genre of Middle English romance. *The Sultan of Babylon* (*c* 1400) features a Muslim soldier whose soul is brought 'to his blis', which the adaptor explains by asserting 'He [Mahoun] loved him wel and al his kyn' (447–9).[31] Similarly, if some versions of the romance of *Bevis of Hampton* do

---

[26] That Floripas uniquely presents the whole set of relics in this version is also noted by Ailes and Hardman, *Legend*, 297.

[27] See, e.g., Jerold C. Frakes, *Vernacular and Latin Literary Discourses of the Muslim Other in Medieval Germany* (New York, 2011), 35–6.

[28] *The Siege of Milan* is the only Middle English Charlemagne verse romance for which there is no extant source material. References are to Stephen H. A. Shepherd (ed.), *Middle English Romances* (New York, 1995).

[29] See further my discussion in 'Rewriting Chivalric Encounters: Cultural Anxieties and Social Critique in the Fourteenth Century', in Elizabeth Archibald, Megan G. Leitch, and Corinne Saunders (eds), *Romance Rewritten: The Evolution of Middle English Romance—A Tribute to Helen Cooper* (Cambridge, 2018), 49–66 (at 53–4).

[30] Cf. Guessard and Michelant's edition, 1525, which is almost identical in the Anglo-Norman manuscript.

[31] References are to Alan Lupack (ed.), *Three Middle English Charlemagne Romances* (Kalamazoo, MI, 1990). *The Sultan of Babylon* stems from the Anglo-Norman texts edited by Louis Brandin as 'La Destruction de Rome et Fierabras, MS Egerton 3028, Musée Britannique', *Romania*, 64 (1938), 18–100. The Muslim character's salvation features in the Anglo-Norman version, but the quoted line is unique to *The Sultan of Babylon*: see Brandin, 595.

348   MEDIEVAL POETRY: 1100–1400

not comment on the final destination of the soul of Ermin, the Muslim king who raises the title character as his own son, others convey enthusiastic support: 'to hevene mote his saule wende!'[32] Thus, poets of romance engaged in intertextual dialogue and debate on whether or not 'righteous' Muslims were deserving of salvation, using fictional characters to invite their large, heterogeneous audiences to ponder a controversial theological doctrine of the later Middle Ages: that by doing 'what lies within themselves' (the *facere quod in se est* formula) virtuous non-Christians, though lacking the Christian faith, may nevertheless obtain God's grace. While authors writing about salvational questions in the vernacular typically focused on righteous pagans (such as Trajan in *Piers Plowman* and *St Erkenwald*) 'born too early or too far away' to know about Christ, the fact that poets of romance reworked their sources to posit the salvation of Muslim figures (such as Clarel) who are not only fully aware of Christianity but vehemently reject it and strive to kill its followers is a compelling testimony to the bold cultural work performed by the genre.[33]

The fascinating habit of Middle English crusade romances to manipulate their audiences' expectation and provoke reflection by casting Muslims in roles otherwise typically ascribed to Christians, and vice versa, is well illustrated by *The Sultan of Babylon*, which transforms the archetypal villain Balam (named Laban, here) of *La Destruction de Rome* and *Fierabras* into a worthy conqueror whose soldiers, like so many Christians of *chanson de geste* and romance, are wrongfully attacked and left in 'sorwe and care' (79), in this case by Christian Romans. Composed in cross-rhymed quatrains, where most other rhyming romances are in couplets or tail-rhyme, and imbued with a degree of liveliness and vigour unparalleled by the other *Fierabras* romances, *The Sultan of Babylon* sets the tone for an ambitious reimagining of the received tradition with an interpolated prologue foretelling Rome's fall from 'grace' on account of its 'offences to God' (12–13). Yet after the 'worthy Sowdon' (29) Laban claims legitimate vengeance and destroys Rome, the initial framework of sin and punishment is complicated by Charlemagne's introduction into the story as a mirror image of his Muslim counterpart: a 'worthy kinge' (583) intent on avenging the 'grete sorowe' (574) of his coreligionists, the Romans. However, any assumption that Charlemagne will surpass Laban in moral and political virtue is rapidly dispelled. Rather, we witness a double movement towards negative and positive parallelism, with new episodes uniting Laban and Charlemagne as indiscriminate killers of 'childe, wyfe, man', mercilessly ordering their men to 'brenne, slo and distroye alle' (note the similar language used at 413–18 and 783–6), and as noble, courtly kings. Far from being presented as incongruous, the Sultan's non-Christian identity and repeatedly asserted worthiness are harmoniously reconciled, a connection further enhanced through intertextual allusion to the 'virtuous pagan' tradition. A long interpolation containing echoes of Chaucer's 'Knight's Tale'—with its elaborate springtime landscapes, refined discourse of love, and 'worthy' pagan duke who swears by 'myghty Mars the rede' (*Canterbury Tales*, I.1742, 1747)—presents Laban dramatically invoking 'rede Mars armypotente' (939), a god rarely included in the Muslim

---

[32] Citation at line 4016 of Edinburgh, National Library of Scotland, Advocates' MS 19.2.1, fols. 176r–201r, in Ronald B. Herzman, Graham Drake, and Eve Salisbury (eds), *Four Romances of England* (Kalamazoo, MI, 1999). See also line 4380 of Naples, Biblioteca Nazionale, MS XIII.B.29, fols. 23–79, in Jennifer Fellows (ed.), *Sir Bevis of Hampton*, 2 vols. EETS o.s. 349, 350 (Oxford, 2017).

[33] Citation from Amilcare Iannucci, 'Limbo: The Emptiness of Time', *Studi Danteschi*, 52 (1979–80), 69–118 (77). On the vernacular virtuous pagan tradition in England, see Frank Grady, *Representing Righteous Heathens in Late-Medieval England* (New York, 2005).

'pantheon', and follows this up with an account of the Sultan's commitment to the pursuit of love, worthiness, and honour, prefaced by a lyric celebration of spring:[34]

> In the semely seson of the yere,
> Of softenesse of the sonne,
> In the prymsauns* of grene vere*,   *beginning; spring*
> Whan floures spryngyn and bygynne,
> And alle the floures in the frith*   *forest*
> Freshly shews here kynde*,   *nature*
> Than it is semely therwyth
> That manhode be in mynde;
> For corage* wole a man to kith*,   *spirit; proclaim*
> If he of menske* have mynde,   *honour*
> And of love to lystyn and lithe*,   *hearken*
> And to seke honure for that ende.
> For he was nevere gode werryoure
> That cowde not love aryght;
> For love hath made many a conqueroure
> And many a worthy knighte.
> This worthy Sowdan, though he hethen were,
> He was a worthy conqueroure;
> Many a contrey with shelde and spere
> He conquerede wyth grete honoure. (963–82)

In line with the poem's concern with symmetry in the depiction of the two kings, the Mars and spring passages are preceded by new material describing Charlemagne's dedication to 'Almyghty God' (915) and to fostering 'worthynesse' (923) and 'knighthode' (925) in his peers; but the comparison here and elsewhere is clearly to the advantage of Laban, rather than the other way around. A sense of aristocratic value and courtly refinement is conferred upon this 'worthy conqueroure', whose military achievements, like those of so many heroes of romance, are ascribed to love's fruitful inspiration. His worthiness is underpinned by a strong conviction that his cause is just, as reflected in his quasi-juridical assessment of the Christians' actions: they 'have done me distruccion / And grete disherytaunce / And eke slayn my men with wronge' (959–61). But while Laban's non-Christian beliefs do not prevent him from living up to the highest standards of militaristic honour, they do preclude ultimate victory over the Christians. Unlike Charlemagne, who loses his temper against his peers, Laban places a great deal of trust in his counsellors, but is constantly let down by his 'gods', who thus become the targets of repeated emotional tantrums. Whereas Christian pleas to 'Lord God in Trinite' are answered through the intervention of angels or through direct proof that 'might is right', Sultan Laban wrathfully castigates his gods and threatens to abandon his faith when learning of the rout of his forces.

Scholars have tended to interpret the ubiquitous motif of the 'raging Sultan' who abuses his gods as serving to uphold a Christian/Muslim binary.[35] However, there exists a vast body of neglected historical evidence showing that, in the decades preceding the emergence of

---

[34] On this interpolation and its relation to the 'Knight's Tale', see further H. M. Smyser, 'The Sowdon of Babylon and Its Author', *Harvard Studies and Notes in Philology and Literature*, 13 (1931), 185–218, at 205–6. Smyser also discerns echoes of Langland's *Piers Plowman*.

[35] See, especially, Akbari, *Idols in the East*, 200–21.

350 MEDIEVAL POETRY: 1100–1400

these romances, Christians, not Muslims, were the ones who accused heaven of injustice and expressed impulses towards religious apostasy in response to military defeats in north Africa and the eastern Mediterranean.[36] Given prevailing beliefs in the mutual rights and responsibilities between the supernatural and natural worlds, God, Christ, and the Virgin Mary were themselves blamed for failing to give victory to those who fought wars in their names.[37] This context is indispensable to our understanding of the coherent intertextual trajectory of this motif within the genre of Middle English romance: scenes of divinely directed rebuke were interpolated in the adaptation of *The Sultan of Babylon*, *Otuel and Roland*, and *Guy of Warwick*, and they feature prominently in other romances, such as *The King of Tars* and *Richard Coeur de Lion*, that have no extant French or Anglo-Norman counterpart.[38] These episodes were so popular because they fulfilled the projective needs of a European society profoundly affected by the failures of crusade and conquest, and harbouring deep collective anxieties about divine will and support. Yet the genre's capacity for self-interrogation also enabled an assimilation of these providential anxieties to the Christian 'self'. In *Firumbras*, Charlemagne himself dramatically vows to beat holy images to the ground and 'neuer worschyp god' (1122) again if his men are overcome. It comes to be up to the newly converted Firumbras, fantasised as an agent of Christian regeneration, to reason with the king: 'Syr, let þe þese words' (1124). But perhaps the most striking of these heavenly addressed rebukes is voiced by Bishop Turpin in *The Siege of Milan*, which tells of the invasion of Lombardy by Muslim forces, the slaughter of Roland's army, and Charlemagne's reluctant military intervention, employing the tail-rhyme stanza to memorable effect. Ad Putter has drawn attention to the early use of the tail-rhyme form in Anglo-Norman saints' lives to explain its strongly pious associations, illustrating how tail-lines in romance are often the locus for expressions of Christian sentiment.[39] The poet of *The Siege of Milan*, by contrast, reappropriates the conventionally pious tail-line to intensify Turpin's accusatory stance, bordering on blasphemy, towards the Virgin Mary for allowing the death of 40,000 'wighte' and 'gud' Christian men:

A! Mary mylde, whare was thi myght	
That thou lete thi men thus to dede* be dighte*	*death; consigned*
That wighte* and worthy were?	*brave*
Art thou noghte halden of myghtis moste,	
Full conceyvede of the Holy Goste?	
Me ferlys of thy fare*.	*Your behaviour astonishes me*
Had thou noghte, Marye, yitt bene borne,	
Ne had noghte oure gud men thus bene lorne*—	*lost*
The wyte is all in the*!	*The blame is all with you*

---

[36] See Elias, *English Literature and the Crusades*. These accusations bear affinity with medieval Christian rituals of humiliation of the saints: see Patrick Geary, 'Humiliation of Saints', in Stephen Wilson (ed.), *Saints and Their Cults: Studies in Religious Sociology, Folklore and History* (Cambridge, 1983), 123–40.

[37] This body of evidence, consisting of poems, letters, and chronicles, is discussed in Elias, *English Literature and the Crusades*. For a selection, see Ricaut Bonomel, 'Ir'e dolors s'es dins mon cor asseza', in Antoine de Bastard (ed.), 'La colère et la douleur d'un templier en Terre Sainte', *Revue des langues Romanes*, 81 (1974), 333–73; Matthew Paris, *Chronicles of Matthew Paris*, in Richard Vaughan (ed. and trans.), *Chronicles of Matthew Paris: Monastic Life in the Thirteenth Century* (Gloucester, 1984), 256; Salimbene di Adam, *The Chronicle of Salimbene de Adam*, in Joseph L. Baird, Giuseppe Baglivi, and John Robert Kane (eds and trans.), *The Chronicle of Salimbene de Adam* (Binghamton, NY, 1986), 453; Riccold de Monte Croce, in René Kappler (ed. and trans.), *Pérégrination en Terre Sainte et au Proche Orient: Lettres sur la chute de Saint Jean d'Acre* (Paris, 1997), 210–52.

[38] On this, see further Elias, *English Literature and the Crusades*.

[39] Putter, 'Metres and Stanza Forms', 121–6.

> Thay faughte holly in thy ryghte,
> That thus with dole* to dede es dyghte—   *Who thus so grievously*
> A Marie, how may this bee? (548–59)

This tirade is representative of the role played by Turpin in the poem as a whole: like the eponymous Muslim-turned-Christian of the *Otuel* romances, the zealous bishop carries the Christians towards victory, not so much through his martial prowess (though far from insignificant) as by bullying no less than the Virgin Mary and King Charlemagne into supporting the cause of crusade, castigating the former for failing her followers and threatening the latter with excommunication (698–705). The dual problem of royal and heavenly dereliction of duty re-emerges powerfully and finds resolution when, after Charlemagne is challenged to a duel and offered lands and possessions as incentive to embrace Islam, Turpin again dramatically questions the king's commitment—'A, Charles, thynk appon Marie brighte / To whayme oure luffe es lentt! [love is given]' (1041–2)—and aggressively calls upon the Virgin Mary to show her power on earth (note the use of the tail-line for further emphasis on the question of her power): 'And if ever that thou hade any myghte, / Latt it nowe be sene in syghte / What pousté [power] that thou hase' (1043–5). Divine 'myghte' is thereafter 'sene in syghte' when Charlemagne refuses to forsake his 'lay' (1056) and slays his 'nobill' and 'chevallrouse' (996) Muslim adversary. Throughout, the poem relies for its powerful effect on the transgressions to Christian collective identity that it dramatically stages and ultimately resolves.

Violence and Its Consequences

The tendency of many of the later Middle English crusade romances to assert their independence from the dominant conventions of *chanson de geste*, for instance by incorporating tropes of love and courtliness in the case of *Roland and Otuel* and *The Sultan of Babylon*, is brought to a whole new level in the composite romance of *Richard Coeur de Lion*, extant in several Middle English versions but believed to derive from a lost Anglo-Norman original. In the course of the romance's manuscript history, the more 'historical' core text, which charts the main events of the Third Crusade in 'epic' mode, was supplemented with a number of late-fourteenth-century 'romance'-like interpolations: approximately 1,200 lines grafted to the beginning of the romance, recounting Richard's demonic heritage, the tournament in which he contends disguised, and his captivity, love affair, and related chivalric adventures in Germany; and around 350 lines of non-historical material added to the crusading campaign, including the two infamous episodes in which he consumes the flesh of Muslim enemies.[40] Invoking myth, legend, and a cultural legacy of crusader cannibalism going back to the siege of Ma'arra during the First Crusade, these romantic accretions reconfigure the heroic image of Richard presented in the epic 'base text' by stressing ambivalent features of his character and background.[41] He is made the grandson of King Corbaryng of Antioch—a name which the poem appropriates from the Muslim leader of the *Chanson d'Antioche*, whose conversion to Christianity is recounted by the *Chrétienté*

---

[40] References are to Peter Larkin (ed.), *Richard Coer de Lyon* (Kalamazoo, MI, 2015). On the complex manuscript history of the romance, see Marcel Elias, 'Violence, Excess, and the Composite Emotional Rhetoric of *Richard Coeur de Lion*', *Studies in Philology*, 114 (2017), 1–38.

[41] On crusader cannibalism, see, to start, Geraldine Heng, *Empire of Magic: Medieval Romance and the Politics of Cultural Fantasy* (New York, 2003), 21–61; Jay Rubenstein, 'Cannibals and Crusaders', *French Historical Studies*, 31 (2008), 525–52.

352   MEDIEVAL POETRY: 1100–1400

Corboran[42]—and the son of Cassodorien, a demonic princess characterised by her inability to witness the Eucharist. Conflated with Muslim ancestry, Richard's subhuman identity is manifested in unchivalrous, uncourtly, and immoderately violent behaviour, which consistently gives rise to accusations of devilishness (500, 529–30, 574, 1112, 3657, 3664).[43] One of the strongest signs of the ambivalence of the interpolations towards Richard's acts of unbridled violence resides in the amount of narrative space given to the suffering and complaints of his victims and their families. The attribution of compassion-arousing grief to injured or bereaved antagonists, both Christian and Muslim, evinces a new concern, unparalleled in *chanson de geste*, with the universality of human experience, posing probing ethical questions about the practical implications of chivalric prowess. These scenes of lament stand out vividly, interrupting the forward thrust of the narrative and showing ample evidence of literary sophistication.[44] Throughout the interpolations, Richard's martial achievements are placed under close moral scrutiny through a consistent mode of narration: they are first recounted by the narrator, and then again by members of the injured parties. After telling of how Richard unchivalrously breaks the established terms of an exchange of blows with the German King Modard's son Ardour by wrapping his fist in wax, killing this 'curtese' (773) and 'trewe man' (786) on the spot, the poem solicits further evaluation of the eponymous hero's culpable immoderateness by dwelling at length, and with distinct sympathy, on the dispossessed parents' distress. Upon being informed of the death of his son, Modard exclaims 'Allas … now have I non!' (802), a conventional formula used in medieval laments for the dead to elicit compassion, but is unable to say more and falls to the ground 'As man that was in woo ibounde' (804). Fuller exploitation of the dramatic potential of the situation occurs with the arrival of Modard's wife:

> 'Allas!' sche sayde, 'Hou may this bene?
> Why is this sorwe and this fare*?   *behaviour*
> Who has brought yow alle in care*?'   *sorrow*
> 'Dame', he sayde, 'wost thou nought*   *don't you know*
> Thy fayre sone to dethe is brought!
> Syththen* that I was born to man,   *Since*
> Swylke sorwe hadde I nevere nan*!   *Never had I experienced such sorrow*
> Alle my joye is turnyd to woo,
> For sorwe I wole myselven sloo*!'   *slay*
> Whenne the qwene undyrstood,
> For sorwe, sertys, sche wax nygh wood*.   *nearly became mad*
> Her kerchers* she drewe* and heer also,   *scarves; tore*
> 'Alas', she sayd, 'what shall I do?'
> Sche qahchyd* here self in the vysage*,   *scratched; face*

---

[42] See Suzanne Conklin Akbari, 'The Hunger for National Identity in *Richard Coeur de Lion*', in Robert M. Stein and Sandra Pierson Prior (eds), *Reading Medieval Culture: Essays in Honor of Robert W. Hanning* (Notre Dame, IN, 2005), 198–227 (at 201).

[43] Richard's fiendish heritage, Muslim ancestry, and unchivalrous behaviour conjure both the stock figure of the demonic Muslim giant and other diabolical romance heroes, notably the protagonist of *Sir Gowther*. The Muslim giant Amoraunt of *Guy of Warwick*, for instance, is described as both unchivalrous and, like Richard, as 'no mannes sone: / It is a deuel fram helle come'. See *Guy of Warwick*, in Julius Zupitza (ed.), *The Romance of Guy of Warwick*, EETS e.s. 42, 49, and 59 (London, 1966; 1st edition as three volumes in 1883, 1887, 1891), citation at 95:10–11; *Sir Gowther*, in Anne Laskaya and Eve Salisbury (eds), *Three Middle English Breton Lays* (Kalamazoo, MI, 1995).

[44] On the medieval literary tradition of laments for the dead, the full-length study is Velma Bourgeois Richmond, *Laments for the Dead in Medieval Narrative* (Pittsburgh, PA, 1966).

As a wymman that was in a rage.
The fase fomyd al on* blood,   *gushed with*
Sche rente* the robe that sche in stood,   *tore*
Wrong here handes that sche was born:
'In what manere is my sone ilorn*?'   *lost* (816–34)

The unity and rhetorical effectiveness of the passage are achieved through intensification of the verbal and somatic manifestations of grief (from swooning and threats of suicide to self-laceration), dramatic interplay between husband and wife, repetition of the conventional 'Alas', parallel phrases (such as 'As man that was in woo ibounde' and 'As a wymman that was in a rage'), and sibilance, enhancing the tone of frenzy and despair. Parental sorrow gives grounds for corrective action, which the romance's audience can only construe as legitimate in view of Richard's immoral deeds—his 'dedes that aren unwrest', as put by Modard (874). After three days of juridical deliberation, a fierce lion is released upon Richard, who manages to tear the beast's heart out, carries it into the royal hall, seasons it with salt, and eats it in front of the horrified King Modard, earning his famous epithet Coeur de Lion. Drawing upon a recognisable register of militaristic black humour, this episode demonstrates the effectiveness of Richard's crude brutality, establishing his reputation as a hero of unrivalled might. Yet the poetry of suffering and lament, here as elsewhere in the interpolations, precludes readings of the depicted violence as normatively meritorious, inviting reflection on the lengths to which Richard's martial energy takes him and the human costs involved.

The late-fourteenth-century alliterative *Siege of Jerusalem*, one of the most emphatically violent and artistically accomplished Middle English romances to have survived, presents us with similar dilemmas of rhetorically charged dualism.[45] Invoking a long tradition of armed and unarmed pilgrimage as medicine for body and soul, the romance literalises the regenerative power of crusading by framing the physical restoration of its leading protagonists through emotional and physical violence: the Roman generals Titus and Vespasian are miraculously cured (from cancer and leprosy) upon lamenting Christ's death and swearing revenge on the Jews of Jerusalem; they are reborn as crusaders 'þat for Crist werred' (194 and 954). *The Siege* thus grounds its narrative in a logic of curative, salvific crusade, underpinned both morally and rhetorically by the compassion the protagonists and readers are invited to partake of for Christ's Passion. Yet despite the carefully crafted moral, ideological, and diegetic underpinnings set up to exalt the 'necessities' of Christian religious violence, the poem takes an unforeseen trajectory in its ambivalent rendering of the dire realities of war, exploiting the inherent suitability of alliterative verse for dealing with violence and switching between contrasting registers—horror and beauty, pleasure and discomfort, unsettling brutality and poignant distress. Dextrously interweaving and reworking his or her sources—the principal of which are the apocryphal *Vindicta Salvatoris*, Jacobus de Voragine's *Legenda Aurea*, Roger of Argenteuil's *Bible en François*, Ranulph Higden's *Polychronicon*, John of Tynemouth's *Historia Aurea*, and Josephus's *De Bello Iudaico*—the *Siege*-poet almost consistently heightens the unbridled passions at play in the enactment of divine vengeance on the battlefield.[46] As noted by Elisa Narin van Court, the poem proceeds to a key inversion: it is no longer the Jews who are spurred by immoderate rage, but instead Vespasian who is depicted as 'neuer ... so wroþe' (375), 'Wode we[ll]ande wroþ' (385),

---

[45] References are to Ralph Hanna and David Lawton (eds), *The Siege of Jerusalem*, EETS o.s. 320 (Oxford, 2003). This and the next paragraph derive from my discussion in *Questioning the Crusades*.

[46] On the romance's sources, see Hanna and Lawton's introduction, xxxvii–lv.

354 MEDIEVAL POETRY: 1100–1400

and 'wroþ as a wode bore' (785), repeatedly cursing his enemies to the Devil.[47] The Jews, on the other hand, come to be described in key episodes as brave, valiant, and noble (621, 625, 867).

The audience of *The Siege of Jerusalem* is invited both to partake in the vindictive crusading impetus framed as an act of sorrowful solidarity for Christ *and* to decry the lamentable human consequences involved. This notion that the horrors inherent even in the most doctrinally sanctioned type of warfare should be deplored with *animi dolore*, anguish of the soul, stems back to the very origins of just war theory, with Augustine's *De Civitate Dei* (19.8): 'Haec itaque mala tam magna, tam horrenda, tam saeua quisquis cum dolore considerat, miseriam fateatur' ('Let everyone, therefore, who reflects with pain upon such great evils, upon such horror and cruelty, acknowledge that this is misery').[48] What is particularly striking when comparing *The Siege of Jerusalem* with other historical and literary narratives adopting ambivalent or critical stances towards the deployment of excessive force is the interjection of empathic authorial pronouncements, such as 'was deil [sorrow] to byholde' (645), 'was pite to byholde' (1247), 'þat deil was to hure' (1101), 'were [tore] [difficult] forto telle' (1069), or 'Bot alle was boteles bale [hopeless agony]' (1145), when evoking the fate of the Jewish victims. These interjections crop up in particular around the romance's infamous episode of infanticide and cannibalism, contributing to its exposure of the appalling afflictions of war. This scene directly follows one in which Titus, lapsed into sickness again, is healed through 'hate' of an unnamed Jewish man, thus offering an immediate counterpoint to the poem's stark endorsement of 'curative' violence. The force of the cure-through-hate metaphor is juxtaposed with equally potent imagery invoked to highlight the physical and emotional distress of the besieged. In the *Siege*-poet's version, the troubles of the town become '[tore] forto telle' (1069), as the besieged are afflicted with sorrow (1079), having neither food to eat nor water to drink, except for the tears they weep (1074). In line with the poem's more general concern with the suffering of Jewish women, Mary's act of maternal cannibalism is no longer decried as horrid, unnatural, and spurred by fury as in the romance's sources (here, Higden's *Polychronicon* and Josephus's *De Bello Iudaico*),[49] but is transformed into one of piteous grief, performed in utter despair by a 'myld' and 'worþi' mother (1081 and 1093):

> Rostyþ rigge* and rib with rewful* wordes,   *spine; piteous*
> Sayþ, 'sone, vpon eche side our sorow is alofte:
> Batail about þe borwe* our bodies to quelle*;   *around the town; kill*
> Withyn h[u]nger so hote þat neȝ our herte brestyþ*'.   *our hearts almost burst*
> (1083–6)

The poet juxtaposes the crusaders' unbridled rage with Mary's extreme, poignant distress, appealing to a long historiographical tradition of infanticide and other acts of self-sacrifice performed in despair and framed to deplore the cruelty of the conditions that provoked

---

[47] Elisa Narin van Court, '*The Siege of Jerusalem* and Augustinian Historians: Writing about Jews in Fourteenth-Century England', *The Chaucer Review*, 29 (1995), 227–48 (at 234).

[48] Augustine, in R. W. Dyson (ed. and trans.), *The City of God against the Pagans* (Cambridge, 1998), 929.

[49] See Josephus in Gaalya Cornfeld (ed. and trans.), *The Jewish War* (Grand Rapids, MI, 1982), 416–17; Ranulph Higden, *Polychronicon*, in Joseph Rawson Lumby (ed.), *Polychronicon Ranulphi Higden Monachi Cestrensis; Together with the English Translation of John Trevisa and of an Unknown Writer of the Fifteenth Century*, 9 vols. Rolls Series 41. (London, 1865–86), 4:444–7.

them. The empathic potential of the scene is exploited to the full in the narration of the townspeople's response:

> [Forþ] þey went for wo wep[ande sore*]   *weeping in agony*
> And sayn, 'alas in þis lif how longe schul we dwelle?
> 3it beter were at o brayde in batail to deye*   *one blow in battle to die*
> þan þus in langur to lyue* and lengþen our fyne*'.   *languish to live; end*
>
>   (1097–1100)

In the cognate passages of the *Siege*-poet's sources, the Jewish onlookers' stupefaction and horror convey explicit condemnation of an unspeakable crime, branded as heinous and abhorrent. Here, by contrast, their sorrow and the act itself operate in an altogether different register, commenting instead on the direness of their collective fate at the hands of the Christian Romans. This reconfiguration thus creates a shift in scope and meaning: Mary's infanticide is no longer the object of moral scrutiny as such, but instead serves as a vehicle for ambivalent evaluation of the circumstances and individuals that prompted it. The *Siege*-poet does not so much challenge the premise of the crusaders' righteous vengeance on the enemies of the faith as question its range of application. The poem transcends concerns over the justness or unjustness of the conflict, registering more fundamental anxieties about the harms of unbridled violence and war's inherent capacity for horror. The competing impulses animating the romance partake in a broader tension, characteristic of late-medieval attitudes to crusading, between the transcendent ideal of the enterprise and the complications inherent in its human performance.

The poetic art of the Middle English crusade romances is characterised by provocative instabilities, blurred boundaries, clashing modes, and striking contradictions that engage the audience's reflections on a wide range of topical concerns. These poems yield unique insight into the realities of thinking and feeling of a late-medieval English society deeply conflicted in its approach to crusading, preserving the ideals of the enterprise, yet with deep anxieties concerning their possible success, their enactment, their providential underpinnings, and even their justification. Romance poets sought to carve out a territory distinct from the *chanson de geste* by creatively reconfiguring, or deliberately moving away from, its conventions. The boundaries of romance vis-à-vis *chanson de geste* are porous but nevertheless discernible, manifested in further destabilisation of polarised characterisations across religious and racial divides; fuller exploration of tensions or outright gaps between ideology and experience; sustained experimentation with how different verse forms shape expression; and (often) incorporation or development of typically 'romance' motifs. These features are crucial to our understanding of the formative phases and constitutive elements of Middle English romance.

23

The 'Matter of England'

Andrew James Johnston

For English literary history, and, especially, for the history of English poetry, the 'Matter of England' poses something of a problem. The term 'Matter of England' refers to a comparatively small subgenre of Middle English romance, and it is not entirely clear whether the group of texts in question really does merit the designation of a subgenre in the strictest sense.[1] What is clear, however, is that the Matter of England constitutes the very beginning of Middle English fictional narrative and that it has been the target of what one might call the first act of literary criticism in English. The two earliest Middle English romances known to us, *Havelok* and *King Horn*, both happen to be Matter of England-romances. And of the six romances Geoffrey Chaucer directly refers to in 'Sir Thopas', a parody of the romance genre told by his fictional *alter ego* in the *Canterbury Tales*, three are Matter of England-romances: 'Horn child' (*King Horn*), 'Beves' (*Bevis of Hamptoun*), and 'sir Gy' (*Guy of Warwick*).

> Men speken of romances of prys,
> Of Horn child and of Ypotys,
> Of Beves and sir Gy,
> Of sir Lybeux and Pleyndamour—
> But sir Thopas, he bereth the flour
> Of roial chivalry![2]

Chaucer's parody foreshadowed much of the criticism to come. For a long time, the Matter of England-romances were seen as the most unsophisticated specimens of a genre marked by its pervasive lack of aesthetic and intellectual lustre. Middle English romance could certainly achieve such lustre, as is shown by *Sir Gawain and the Green Knight*—though, admittedly, a 'matter of Britain'-romance with a distinctively English setting. Recent decades have witnessed a considerable change both in the evaluation of Middle English romance in general and in that of the Matter of England in particular.[3] Yet the Matter of England-romances have primarily been studied for their role in the development of a medieval sense of 'Englishness' or for their contribution to constructing an idea of the body politic or for other thematic concerns. Attempts to address them in terms of their poetics have been less frequent.[4]

---

[1] Rosalind Field, 'The Curious History of the Matter of England', in Neil Cartlidge (ed.), *Boundaries in Medieval Romance* (Cambridge, 2008), 29–42.

[2] Geoffrey Chaucer, *The Canterbury Tales*, in Larry D. Benson (ed.), *The Riverside Chaucer*, 3rd edn. (Boston, MA, 1987), Fragment VII, ll. 897–902. For all editions, initial citation will be given in full in the notes but thereafter included parenthetically in the text.

[3] Helen Cooper's magisterial study of romance may in many ways be seen as the apex of this development: *The English Romance in Time: Transforming Motifs from Geoffrey of Monmouth to William Shakespeare* (Oxford, 2004).

[4] It may be seen as indicative of the lingering low appreciation of the Matter of England-romances that one of the most audacious studies of the politics of Middle English romance to have been published in recent decades

---

Andrew James Johnston, *The 'Matter of England'*. In: *The Oxford History of Poetry in English*. Edited by Helen Cooper and Robert R. Edwards, Oxford University Press. © Andrew James Johnston (2023). DOI: 10.1093/oso/9780198827429.003.0023

Especially when judged by admittedly anachronistic post-Romantic aesthetic standards, the Matter of England-romances do, at first glance, appear to be placed at the roughest end of the Middle English romance spectrum. George Kane's dismissive assessment of *Bevis of Hamtoun* concisely expresses what long remained the dominant view:

[Bevis] has a better effect than its component material would seem to warrant, for this almost formless story, with its miracles and marvels, ranting Saracens and dragons, is told without any polish or skill in a style generously padded and tagged, with little sense of poetic or narrative art, and still the romance is more than merely readable. As with *Horn* and *Havelok* we tolerate its artistic crudity for the sake of the company of the hero and heroine, Beues and Iosiane, who reflect the warm humanity of the imagination that created them.[5]

In Kane's view, the poems' only saving graces are an undefined readability and a 'warm humanity of the imagination', an oddly timeless and non-aesthetic value that puts a somewhat child-like gloss on them, attributing to them a charming immaturity that chimes well with Chaucer's parody.[6] The stories of Bevis and Guy, however, went on to enjoy many centuries of popularity in England, and not only there. The Anglo-Norman *Boeve* went on to inspire versions in a range of languages from Welsh, to Yiddish and Russian, including an Italian opera, *Buovo d'Antona* by Tommaso Traetta (1758). As late as 1881, a Romanian version appeared.[7] Guy was known of in Spain, was upgraded to courtly status in Elizabethan England, and appears too in America, where a considerably abridged and redacted version of Samuel Rowland's *The Famous History of Guy, Earl of Warwick* from 1609 is included 'in a short verse chapbook printed in Vermont and Massachusetts in 1792–93'.[8]

This chapter is less interested in proving the high aesthetic quality of these romances than in showing that their much-maligned poetic and narrative structures are capable of producing an aesthetic meaning of their own, one easily overlooked if viewed only in terms of lack or deficiency. First, it seems appropriate to establish a general notion of the Matter of England. This will be followed by a brief discussion of three typical examples—*Horn*, *Havelok*, and the stanzaic *Guy of Warwick*—and, finally, special attention will be paid to the specifically aesthetic problems these romances raise. The focus will be on *Havelok*, in particular, not least because some of the more important studies of the aesthetic structures of the Matter of England have centred on *Havelok*.

The supposed lack of sophistication displayed by *King Horn* or *Havelok* has been explained among other things in terms of the early dates of their composition. According to this style of criticism, the (early) Matter of England-romances were produced at a

---

virtually ignores them: Geraldine Heng, *Empire of Magic: Medieval Romance and the Politics of Cultural Fantasy* (New York, 2003).

[5] George Kane, *Middle English Literature: A Critical Study of the Romances, the Religious Lyrics,* Piers Plowman (London, 1970), 50.

[6] Interestingly, Lee Patterson perceived 'Sir Thopas' not so much in parodic but rather in child-like terms: Lee Patterson, '"What Man Artow?": Authorial Self-Definition in the Tale of Sir Thopas and the Tale of Melibee', in Lee Patterson, *Temporal Circumstances: Form and History in the Canterbury Tales* (Basingstoke, 2006), 97–128, at 103–5.

[7] Jennifer Fellows, 'Introduction', in Jennifer Fellows (ed.), *Sir Bevis of Hampton: Edited from Naples, Bibliotheca Nazionale, MS XIII.B.29 and Cambridge, University Library, MS Ff.2.38,* 2 vols., EETS o.s. 349–50 (Oxford, 2017), 1:xv–xvi.

[8] Helen Cooper, 'Guy as Early Modern English Hero', in Alison Wiggins and Rosalind Field (eds), *Guy of Warwick: Icon and Ancestor* (Cambridge, 2007), 198.

358 MEDIEVAL POETRY: 1100–1400

time when English poets did not yet fully grasp the conventions and complexities of French chivalric romance. Another line of argument, by no means mutually exclusive with the first, runs along sociological, if not snobbish lines. This critical perspective attributes the supposedly primitive style and narrative structures of the Matter of England-romances to their supposedly catering for a middle-class audience deficient in poetic refinement.[9] By contrast, the defence of these romances' supposed weaknesses is often based on vaguely historicising arguments stressing their alterity, while by and large bracketing their aesthetic characteristics: according to this mode of thinking, the various texts' perceived shortcomings testify to their particularly medieval nature and to the altogether different aesthetic standards obtaining in the Middle Ages. But as romances such as *Sir Gawain and the Green Knight* prove, aesthetic alterity as such does not preclude sophistication, nor does a text's poetic alterity require it to stand in *absolute* opposition to modern standards and understanding. The aesthetic structures of a poem like *Sir Gawain and the Green Knight* are unmistakably medieval, yet they produce a compelling and intriguing effect on modern audiences nevertheless.

This brief sketch of the lenses through which the Matter of England-romances have been viewed helps us garner an impression of the principal obstacles one is up against when seeking to explore, in the context of a history of English *poetry* rather than in the more inclusive context of English *literature*, the particular aesthetic nature of the Matter of England-romances. After all, none of the above-mentioned positions attempts to attribute what one might call a particular 'aesthetic' meaning to the instances of a genre that, from a modern perspective, has been perceived in primarily negative terms.

Besides, all three of these major types of argument possess a degree of plausibility: as early vernacular texts, the (early) Matter of England-romances—*Havelok* and *King Horn*, especially—do, at first glance, appear to display a distinct lack of familiarity with some courtly romance conventions and with the sense of genre that seems to pervade later Middle English romances in general, despite their extensive reliance on earlier Anglo-French versions. Yet that supposed lack of understanding need not be seen as a weakness but could instead be perceived as a different focus, one that is determined by aesthetic concerns of its own.

This is a view Chaucer may have shared, since his irreverent lampoon of Middle English romance turns out to be more complex than meets the eye. Beneath the 'drasty riming' of *Sir Thopas*'s surface is an underlying cosmic scheme.[10] The tale's division into three fits echoes the cosmic harmonies, as the fits diminish in length according to the ratio of 2: 1. In Pythagorean thought this ratio is termed 'diapason' and constitutes the mathematical principle according to which the planetary spheres are arranged. The musical equivalent of the diapason is the octave, the mathematical basis for the music of the spheres.[11] Thus Chaucer imbues 'Sir Thopas'—and by extension the early romances—with a hidden sense of cosmic dignity, thereby honouring what would have constituted, from his historical point of view, the origins of the secular, fictional native tradition he was able to draw on. It is as

---

[9] The notion that Middle English romances primarily catered to a middle-class audience was most cogently advanced by Gisela Guddat-Figge, *Catalogue of Manuscripts Containing Middle English Romances* (Munich, 1976), 42–52; rpt. as 'The Audience of the Romances', in Stephen H. A. Shepherd (ed.), *Middle English Romances: Authoritative Texts, Sources and Backgrounds, Criticism* (New York, 1995), 498–506.

[10] As Harry Bailly declares after interrupting and thereby bringing to an end Geoffrey's Tale: 'Thy drasty ryming is nat worth a toord!', Fragment VII, 930.

[11] For the mathematical/cosmic/musical structures underlying 'Sir Thopas', see John Burrow, '*Sir Thopas*: An Agony in Three Fits', *The Review of English Studies*, n.s. 22 (1971), 54–8; see also E. A. Jones, '"Lo Lordes Myne, Here is a Fit!": The Structure of Chaucer's *Sir Thopas*', *The Review of English Studies*, 51 (2000), 248–52.

though Chaucer were suggesting that the romances' apparent naiveté was veiling a poetic logic that demands both to be detected and respected.

The term 'Matter of England' was coined in the modern age as an extension of Jean Bodel's late-twelfth-century division of romance into the 'Matter of Rome', the 'Matter of Britain', and the 'Matter of France'. Bodel's tripartite model implies a hierarchy in quality and purpose: the Matter of France was considered to be 'true', that of Rome 'wise', and that of Britain frivolous and entertaining. The division of romance into three distinct *matières* was driven, among other things, by the political requirements of Bodel's day.[12] Because of this hierarchy, Bodel's model has proved surprisingly durable and shapes scholarly discussions to this very day; but he was describing French romance as he knew it, and the categories do not sit altogether easily with Middle English. Besides, as Robert R. Edwards has reminded us, medieval literary taxonomies are rarely consistent or systematic. They have a tendency to conflate issues of genre with those of generic form.[13] Moreover, the rhetorical terminology that constitutes the backbone of what one might call medieval literary criticism by no means exhausts the aesthetic complexities medieval poetic forms are capable of producing. And as Helen Cooper points out, from a modern point of view what matters more than the Middle Ages' own generic definitions is the fact that there appears to have been a clear understanding among vernacular writers of romance that they were working within a set of traditions from which they drew in a manner best described in terms of a 'family resemblance'. While not all romances share each and every one of the characteristics to be found in medieval romance, they do share a sufficient number of typical features to be recognisable as such.[14]

The term 'Matter of England', well entrenched though it has become, is marked by a palpable unease. Indeed, Rosalind Field has cautioned against taking the designation too seriously, not only because the Matter of England-romances are extremely diverse but also because the main thematic concerns attributed to them—such as nationhood and national identity—are burdened with an anachronistic 'ideological weight in ... [their] assumptions about national literature and language'.[15]

It is by no means clear what criteria exactly characterise the genre, nor do critics agree which texts count as Matter of England-romances, though one might claim with some accuracy that in addition to those already mentioned *Athelston* tends to be included as a fifth in the majority of Matter of England-lists.

While a considerable number of Matter of England-romances seem to have been lost—especially those dealing with historical and legendary characters, often outlaws, from the aftermath of the Norman Conquest[16]—the extant ones share a number of characteristics, most of them typical of Middle English romance in general rather than specific to a particular 'matter'. They are diverse in topic and content, which is why it is not entirely helpful to pigeon-hole them thematically in the way their modern designation suggests. Some, like *King Horn*, *Bevis of Hamtoun*, and *Guy of Warwick*, clearly possess chivalric elements. But it is doubtful whether this can be said of *Havelok*, where the hero demonstrates his prowess in a style more akin to the *chansons de geste* and sometimes even, as in the carnivalesque violence he uses to overcome his competitors for a job in the earl of Lincoln's kitchen, in

[12] Field, 'Curious History', 30.
[13] Robert R. Edwards, *Ratio and Invention: A Study of Medieval Lyric and Narrative* (Nashville, TN, 1989), xiii–xviii.
[14] Cooper, *English Romance in Time*, 8–9.
[15] Field, 'Curious History', 39.
[16] R. M. Wilson, *The Lost Literature of Medieval England* (London, 1952), 112; Hereward (extant in Latin) and Fouke Fitzwaryn (extant in French) are prime examples.

360   MEDIEVAL POETRY: 1100–1400

a fashion more familiar from the so-called 'popular romances'.[17] And at least one of the Matter of England-romances, *Guy of Warwick*, could easily be grouped with the homiletic romances, as its hero, for all his many chivalric actions, spends most of his life as a pilgrim knight and is shown to be interested primarily in shedding all worldly vanities.

As Robert Rouse has suggested, what most of the surviving Matter of England-romances do have in common is a certain fascination with an imaginary pre-Conquest England— whence they derive their name.[18] To varying degrees, this is true of *Havelok, King Horn, Guy of Warwick, Bevis of Hamtoun*, and *Athelston*. Yet in some of these poems, the idea of pre-Conquest England, instead of being brought to the forefront as a major issue, is evoked more as a vague background, as in *King Horn*. One way in which these romances often highlight their (pre-Conquest) Englishness is through personal names or references to individual place names, such as Grimsby in *Havelok* where the story is concerned with establishing an etymology for the name of the town. The same is true of *Bevis of Hamtoun* where the town Arundel in West Sussex is said to have been named after the protagonist's ultraloyal horse, Arondel. In one of the more doubtful cases, *Gamelyn*—sometimes referred to as a Matter of England-romance, too—it is by no means clear that the text is set in a pre-conquest historical environment at all, which is why Robert Hanning, drawing on R. M. Wilson, made a point of referring to the Matter of England as dealing with both pre- *and* post-conquest England.[19]

The notion of a fictional world preceding William the Conqueror's invasion is probably strongest in *Havelok* and *Athelston*. The latter's very title harks back to pre-Conquest English rulers, while the former features an idealised early medieval English setting embodied by the good King Athelwold's reign. That period of political bliss comes to an end when treacherous nobles take advantage of the minority of the princess Goldborw, heiress to the throne. *Havelok* fleshes out, in addition to the poem's pre-Conquest English setting, a recognisably Danish context in remarkable, but anachronistic, historical detail. Most importantly, there is the character called 'Birkabeyn', whose name derives from the ultimately victorious rebel party in the civil war period of Norwegian history which lasted from around 1130 to 1240. Though not a true reference to Danish history at all, this allusion does imply a desire for establishing a clear affinity with Scandinavia. *Havelok* thus evokes, in a general sense, a geographical imaginary akin to the one that already shaped *Beowulf*. What is perhaps most remarkable about the fictional world depicted is the way that the downfall of an ideal pre-Norman past, the just reign of King Athelwold, provides the motivation for much of the action that follows. Already within the romance itself, that nostalgic early English order is under threat and, *mise-en-abyme*-like, seems to foretell the destiny of pre-Conquest England in historical reality.

The plausibility of the term 'Matter of England' becomes even more problematic when we remember that quite a few of these romances derive from well-attested Anglo-Norman sources. Cooper suggests that there may even have been earlier English versions to some of these. Indirect evidence for these may, for instance, be found in the name of *King Horn*'s eponymous protagonist, which is involved in some punning for which French phonology is rather ill-equipped. But likely though the previous existence of such English versions may be, no evidence of them survives.[20]

---

[17] Ad Putter and Jane Gilbert, 'Introduction', in Ad Putter and Jane Gilbert (eds), *The Spirit of Medieval Popular Romance* (Harlow, 2000), 1–38.

[18] Robert Rouse, *The Idea of Anglo-Saxon England in Middle English Romance* (Cambridge, 2005), 52.

[19] Robert W. Hanning, '*Havelok the Dane*: Structure, Symbols, Meaning', *Studies in Philology*, 64 (1967), 586–605, at 605.

[20] Cooper, *English Romance in Time*, 29.

In some respects, it is easier to identify commonalities between the texts on the basis of what they all lack rather than what they share. For instance, while authors active in the received medieval *matières* were in a position to engender the ambience of their fictional worlds with a mere sprinkling of generic hints, such as references to King Arthur or to ancient Troy—that is, references that would immediately have triggered a particular set of generic, aesthetic and even affective expectations on the part of the audience—Matter of England-writers have to begin from scratch, creating a fictional world of their own, the terms of which, one might assume, would have been by no means clear to the readers or listeners encountering them for the first time.[21]

King Horn is the earliest Matter of England-romance. The English version was composed early in the thirteenth century and survives in three manuscripts. The Anglo-Norman original it is based on is generally assumed to have been written late in the twelfth century. There is a faint element of the *Bildungsroman* to the narrative. When Horn is fifteen years old, his father, King Murry of Suddene, is killed by Saracens (probably meant to represent the pagan Vikings). Instead of flaying Horn, the Saracen ruler, impressed with the boy's beauty, sets him adrift in a boat together with several other boys. The company of boys has two prominent members, Horn's closest friends, Athulf—a name with obvious Old English resonances—and Fikenild. The first proves loyal to Horn, the second turns out to be a traitor. They arrive in Westernesse where Horn distinguishes himself through martial deeds against the Saracens. Rymenild, the king's daughter, falls in love with Horn. She actively pursues him and finds that he reciprocates her feelings. They become secretly betrothed. Having discovered their secret, the jealous Fikenild accuses Horn of wanting to steal the throne. Horn flees to Ireland where he once again proves himself a worthy warrior. He refuses the offer of the King's daughter's hand in marriage. She is named Reynild, which produces an echoing effect with the hero's betrothed, Rymenild. Horn spends seven years in Ireland before he receives news that Rymenild is about to be married to King Mody. Horn attends Rymenild's wedding feast in a beggar's disguise, makes puns on horns and recalls the fishing net that had featured in a dream Rymenild had told him about before he left. Rymenild eventually recognises him when he places a ring she had given him in her cup. Horn kills the bridegroom but does not marry Rymenild immediately, deciding, instead, to return to the kingdom of his origin with the aim of regaining it. After an extended sequence of fighting and treacherous deeds, the narrative comes to an end with Horn slaying Fikenild and saving Rymenild in the process.

The fast-paced narrative is composed in short, irregular couplets that suggest a formal tightness at the metrical level which is matched by the supposedly repetitive nature of the plot. What may, to a modern reader, appear as tedious repetition can just as well be seen in terms of a strong emphasis on order and symmetry. The importance of this symmetry is stressed, for instance, by the almost identical repetition of the line which describes Horn's first putting to sea when, after he has successfully saved his beloved Rymenild from the hands of treacherous Fikenhild, Horn and Rymenhild can finally return home at the end of the romance.

> The se bigan to flowe,
> And Horn child to rowe ... (121–2)
>
> The se bigan to flowe,
> And Horn gan to rowe.   (1517–18)

---

[21] Field, 'Curious History', 35.

362   MEDIEVAL POETRY: 1100–1400

The repetition of this line underscores the way in which Horn, in the second half of the plot, succeeds in righting all the wrongs done in the first half.

The exile-and-return theme is entangled but not entirely congruent with the love-plot. One might even argue that there are two exile-and-return themes set into each other like Russian Dolls; the first concerns the orphaned prince's relations to his own kingdom, the second that pertaining to his relationship with Rymenild. Only when the logic of both these plots has been served is Horn permitted to marry Rymenild. The point at which the two exile-and-return-plots begin to converge, instead of merely existing side by side, is when Horn kills King Mody. This convergence of the two plots is artfully marked by the theme of disguise and recognition, with its sequence of puns and symbolic actions that increase not only the suspense of the disguise theme but translates that theme onto a semiotic level with fabliau-like overtones. The idea of a ring being put into a cup can be read as a doubly reinforced form of sexual symbolism. The result is an underlying sense of excess: the twofold exile-and-return theme is shown to be interlocking in a scene that reaches its climax in the doubly sexual symbolism of putting a ring into a cup. As Corinne Saunders remarks with regard to the text's general aesthetic structures: 'King Horn plays on repetitions and patternings'.[22] And this is a feature typical of the Matter of England-romances in general.

One of *King Horn*'s more interesting characteristics is the emotional and sexual freedom it grants Rymenild. While the lovers do not have sex before marriage, Rymenild takes the initiative in attracting Horn's attention and her love for him is expressed in strongly passionate words: 'Heo luvede so Horn child / That negh heo gan wexe wild'.[23]

Havelok dates to the end of the thirteenth century and suggests an origin in Lincolnshire. As a small child, Havelok, the King of Denmark's son, is taken to England by Grim, whom the usurper-king Godard had originally ordered to kill the prince. Despite the poverty the hero grows up in with Grim's family, he develops considerable physical power, which he proves, among other things, in the decidedly uncourtly activity of stone-throwing. His rugged strength forms the basis of a career that begins in the earl of Lincoln's kitchen and takes him through marrying a princess to revenge on his enemies and, ultimately, his accession to the thrones of England and of Denmark. The early stages of his tale run parallel to those of his future spouse, the English princess Goldborw, who finds herself similarly dispossessed by an evil usurper called Godrich, a name that reinforces the relative symmetry of the plotlines set in England and Denmark, respectively.

There is a naïve and even clownish element to the protagonist's early development that emphasises the folktale motif of the chosen child unaware of his innate claims to royalty, claims supported by physical features such as a birthmark on his shoulder and rays of light emitting from his mouth during sleep. Here the miraculous merges with the comfortably domestic, since Havelok himself is not aware of his nocturnal illuminations and readers only learn of this when Goldborw spots this phenomenon in bed with a husband obviously sleeping with his mouth open. The scene betrays a sense of dramatic irony because Goldborw's momentous discovery is immediately preceded by her indignantly contemplating the shame of being married to a man of low birth, of her having been 'yeven unkyndelike' (1251). Marriage contributes to Havelok's gaining in maturity and acquiring the characteristics necessary for assuming the royal status he is destined for. Close to the end, we witness

---

[22] Corinne Saunders, 'The Romance Genre', in Robert DeMaria, Jr., Heesok Chang, and Samantha Zacher (eds), *A Companion to British Literature: Volume I—Medieval Literature 700–1450* (Oxford, 2014), 161–79.

[23] King Horn, in Ronald B. Herzman, Graham Drake, and Eve Salisbury (eds), *Four Romances of England: King Horn, Havelok the Dane, Bevis of Hampton, Athelston* (Kalamazoo, MI, 1999), ll. 255–6.

a grand feast lasting forty days. The catalogue-like description of the feast concentrates on the materiality of aristocratic largesse, detailing the food and wine on offer. But the feast also provides the occasion for a moment of literary or even generic self-consciousness when it mentions 'romanz reding on the bok' (2327) and people listening to 'the gestes' being sung (2328) as part of the entertainments provided.

As we have seen, politically, the romance ends in a dynastic union of England and Denmark, thereby envisioning a geo-political alternative to the Angevin Empire that, at the time of the poem's composition, had recently been ingloriously diminished. The romance's emphasis on the restoration of English law betrays an acutely native sense of social and political order, though by the time the poem was written this was already a well-established political cliché.[24]

The Anglo-Norman original that the Middle English *Guy of Warwick* is based on was composed around 1240. The earliest surviving version of the English text is to be found in the Auchinleck manuscript (*c* 1320). Set in England, the impressively long narrative— more than 12,000 lines—concerns Guy, the son of an earl's steward. Compared with the earlier two romances, both of which feature heroes of royal blood, the protagonist's social position is especially interesting, as it addresses the issue of social advancement. Guy falls in love with Felice, the earl's daughter—spurning the attention of thirty other maidens who have fallen for him—who proves fully aware of her suitor's social inferiority. Guy must now prove himself in a series of adventures including fighting Saracens, a giant, and a dragon. In one episode Guy befriends a lion, a theme reminiscent of the Lion in Chrétien's *Yvain*. He returns and marries Felice, but after fifteen days of amorous bliss, he experiences a religious conversion and embarks on a chivalric pilgrimage, leaving behind his pregnant wife; she will give birth to their son Reynbroun who will grow up and have chivalric adventures of his own within the narrative.

Guy's spiritual development is possibly modelled on the life of St Alexis, whose religious revelation actually happens on his wedding night, who embarks on a holy life in the East and, on his return, lives in his father's house as a beggar.[25] Guy's conversion itself is quite remarkable. Returning from hunting, the hero climbs a tower from the top of which he sees 'that firmament, / That thicke with steres stode'.[26] This visual impression of the magnificence of God's creation motivates him to contemplate 'On Jhesu omnipotent / That alle his honour hadde him lent' (244–5). Understanding that he owes everything he has achieved to Christ alone, he becomes aware of never having done anything to repay the Saviour for his generosity. Saunders notes the 'affective realism in the work's portrayal of Guy's interior shift of perspective'.[27] What she refers to as 'affective realism' might also be conceived of as translating religious experience into aesthetic experience and vice versa. As an extended metaphor of transcendence, the notion of climbing a tower and witnessing the beauty of the universe in an unimpeded panorama of the night sky is remarkably powerful.

While in purely structural terms, Guy's series of episodic adventures on his chivalric pilgrimage is very similar to the ones he experienced while asserting his suitability as a noble husband, we now become more aware of the constant presence of religious themes even though these have been there from the very beginning. Especially when fighting Saracens and giants, Guy is depicted within a binary structure of good versus evil. There is something

---

[24] Rouse, *The Idea of Anglo-Saxon England in Middle English Romance*, 97.

[25] Saunders, 'Romance Genre', 169–70.

[26] *Stanzaic Guy of Warwick*, in Alison Wiggins (ed.), *Stanzaic Guy of Warwick* (Kalamazoo, MI, 2004), ll. 242–3.

[27] Saunders, 'Romance Genre', 170.

364 MEDIEVAL POETRY: 1100–1400

devilish about the giants he encounters, while the supernatural aspects of his own powers have decidedly Christian overtones and he is described in almost angelic terms. Prior to Guy's confronting the African giant Colbrond, an ally of the invading Danes, King Athelstan of England and his followers support their champion not only through prayers but through a three-day fast. The hagiographic nature of the narrative reaches its crescendo shortly before the end, when the archangel Michael himself informs Guy that he is soon to die and will be followed by Felice not long after. She does, indeed, pass away forty days later. While 1,007 angels gather to take his soul to heaven to the accompaniment of 'gret molodi' (3515), the transport of his body, emitting a pleasing fragrance, requires more than a hundred men. Hence, one cannot entirely agree with Derek Brewer that the 'essence of the story is pure chivalric folktale'.[28] The hagiographic aspects of the romance inextricably merge with its pre-Conquest epic characteristics. As Saunders observes: 'Exile and return are rewritten as penitence and redemption, and the affect of secular love is replaced by that of the divine'.[29] One might argue that things are even more complex than that because human love becomes intertwined with divine love, rather than merely being supplanted by it. In the face of death, Guy sends Felice a ring she once gave to him, so that husband and wife can be reunited before he expires. The material token of their secular love is permitted to enter into the final hagiographical tableau. And it is in this final hagiographical tableau that the issue of Guy's social inferiority is finally and absolutely decided in his favour. As a saint-like figure he proves more than worthy of Felice's hand and assumes a position of unassailable superiority over his wife.

In the stanzaic *Guy of Warwick* the legitimacy of the term Matter of England is warranted among other things by direct expressions of a patriotic nature. King Athelston asks Guy to fight against the Danes to 'save ous the right of Inglond' (2951), with the patriotic sentiment being expressed in close to legal, or even constitutional, terms. Patriotism is again linked to the issue of religion that is so dominant a feature of the narrative when, only a few lines later, Guy declares that he fights for 'God in Trinité / And for to make Inglond fre' (2968–9). Precisely because it is so all-pervasive, Christianity can be coupled with patriotic sentiment just as religion proves capable of entering into an alliance with heterosexual love.

As even these brief discussions of three Matter of England-romances show, all the texts in question make use of distinctly poetic strategies that highlight their complex literariness. To recount only a few examples: there are the pervasive principles of symmetry and repetition that infuse order into what might otherwise appear to be overly episodic plots. We encounter word-play—in *Bevis of Hamtoun* there is a nicely ironic pun on the double meaning of the English word 'crown': 'At the laste a threw Yvour doun / And al to-brak the kinges kroun' (1521–2)—and even implicit punning, as when Horn returns to Rymenild in disguise and makes use of a drinking horn to allude to his own name. There are instances of dramatic irony, as when Goldborw complains about her enforced mésalliance only to discover Havelok's near-miraculous sign of royal descent. In *Guy of Warwick*, we even witness a powerfully religious moment of affective and aesthetic experience founded on an almost lyrical appreciation of God's creation. It is worthwhile, therefore, to take a closer look at the more particular poetic structures and devices in the Matter of England-romances, at issues such as rhyme and metre and especially at stylistic, rhetorical, and other formal features. Before embarking on this overview, a caveat is in order. None of the following observations

---

[28] Derek Brewer, 'The Popular English Metrical Romances', in Corrine Saunders (ed.), *A Companion to Romance from Classical to Contemporary* (Oxford, 2004), 45–64.

[29] Saunders, 'Romance Genre', 170.

are in any way exclusive to the Matter of England-romances: all the stylistic, rhetorical and the more narrowly poetic characteristics listed here are shared, in one way or another, by the vast majority of Middle English romances in general.

In metrical terms, most of the Matter of England-poems consist of rhyming couplets with lines being made up of several stresses, usually four-stress lines. There are, however, alternatives. As far as verse form is concerned, the most sophisticated pattern to be found in the Matter of England-romances is the intricate rhyme scheme of the stanzaic *Guy of Warwick*, which consists of twelve-line stanzas of tail-rhyme verse with a rhyme scheme of *aabccbd-dbeeb*.[30] In tail-rhyme a set of rhymed lines, most often couplets or triplets, is succeeded by a different, usually shorter line, 'the tail'. The tail rhymes not with the preceding set of lines but with other tails, as does the '*b*' in the rhyme scheme referred to above. Such a complex verse form requires a high number of rhymes and thus encourages the use of stock epithets. Depending on the individual poet's competence, the effect of tail-rhyme can be repetitive, but it may also have a distinctly haunting quality. In his 'Tale of Sir Thopas', Chaucer stresses the former effect.

In addition to rhyme, the Matter of England-romances express their literariness through a wide range of rhetorical strategies revealing the degree to which these texts, like their direct Anglo-Norman sources, are indebted to the medieval epic tradition as embodied in the *chansons de geste*.[31] One typically epic feature we find in the Matter of England-poems is the epic catalogue. In *Havelok* there is more than one example, with perhaps the most impressive instance—owing to its long and varied list of items—also being the most unexpected in relation to the device's epic nature: the catalogue of fish that Grim catches after having relocated to England with his family and his newly acquired foster child Havelok:

Grim was fishere swithe* god,	*very*
And mikel couthe* on the flod—	*was very skilled*
Mani god fish therinne he tok,	
Bothe with neth and with hok.	
He tok the sturgiun and the qual*,	*whale*
And the turbut and lax* withal;	*salmon*
He tok the sele* and the hwel*—	*seal; eel*
He spedde* ofte swithe wel.	*succeeded*
Keling* he tok and tumberel*,	*cod; porpoise*
Hering and the makerel,	
The butte*, the schulle*, the thornebake*.	*flounder; plaice; skate*
Gode paniers* dede he make,	*baskets*
On til him and other thrinne*	*One for him and three for the others*
Til hise sones to beren fishe inne,	
Up o londe to selle and fonge*—	*collect money*
Forbar* he neyther tun* ne gronge*	*Neglected; toun; farm*
That he ne to yede* with his ware.	*went (750–67)*

Within a romance context, this comprehensive list of marine species rather than knights, weapons, or courtly entertainments must, at first glance, appear out of place—all the more

---

[30] For the switching of the rhyme scheme in the Auchinleck *Guy*, see Julie Burton, 'Narrative Patterning and *Guy of Warwick*', *The Yearbook of English Studies*, 22 (1992), 105–16.

[31] For a comprehensive analysis of *Havelok*'s style with a special focus on the ancient and medieval Latin rhetorical tradition, see G. V. Smithers, 'The Style of "Hauelok"', *Medium Ævum*, 57 (1988), 190–218.

366   MEDIEVAL POETRY: 1100–1400

so because it concludes by stressing the commercial nature of Grim's piscatorial venture. Yet within the text's particular narrative arc, which takes its protagonist from complete loss of status to social and political resurrection, such a less-than-chivalric catalogue makes perfect sense, as this insistent focus on the profession of Havelok's low-born foster-father reinforces the protagonist's utter social abasement. At the same time, because of its ironic overtones, this particular epic catalogue betrays a self-consciously literary function as it draws attention to the poet's familiarity with the concepts and conventions of epic narrative.

Both the number and the sophistication of the rhetorical devices employed in *Havelok* are remarkable. As we have already seen, one formal feature that recurs constantly is repetition. We witness it at various levels. Repetition may happen to whole couplets. Thus, throughout the poem, the couplet 'He was the wicteste man at nede / Þat þurte riden on ani stede' (9–10) is repeated four times. There are also instances where all the individual words contained in a single line are repeated in another line, but in a different order and with minimal grammatical changes, providing, thereby, a different rhyme: 'Hwo mithe so mani stonde ageyn?' (2025)—'Hwo mouthe ageyn so mani stonde' (2031). Here the variation in the word order of a line repeated so soon produces an echoing effect. Such echoing can also provide the basis for a 'resumptive device', as when a new development in the action is embarked on and the import of the concluding words of the previous passage is immediately repeated in the opening line of the next passage:

> Her that* he the speche leyde*,   *at the moment when; laid aside*
> To Jesu Crist began to calle
> And deyde biforn his heymen* alle.   *noblemen*
> Than* he was ded, there micte* men se   *When; could*
> The meste sorwe that micte* be.   *could* (229–33)

As G. V. Smithers points out, this device is highly unusual in Middle English romance in general, whereas in *Havelok* it appears with surprising frequency. In the manuscript, the temporal conjunctions that belong to this device are often highlighted by an illuminated large initial, as though the manuscript were intent on drawing attention to a feature that, at first glance, may appear 'bizarrely primitive'.[32]

Another form of repetition typical of *Havelok* and the Matter of England-romances is periphrasis, a procedure Smithers calls 'arrestingly calculated and artificial', whereby a certain statement is reformulated in immediate succession, without any new idea being added, a device frequently mentioned in the rhetorical handbooks from classical antiquity:

> And seyde, 'Wether she sholde be
> Quen and levedi over me?
> Hwether sho sholde al Engelond
> And me and mine haven in hir hond?' (292–5)

Further rhetorical devices to be found in *Havelok* are apostrophes and exclamations. Sometimes the narrator addresses the characters directly as though he were personally participating in the action. The curse 'Datheit (who) the recke!' occurs more than once in *Havelok*; we come across it in dialogue, but also three times in narratorial interjections addressed at the characters (1914, 2511, 2757). Virgil often uses this device in the *Aeneid*,

---

[32] Smithers, 'Style', 194.

THE 'MATTER OF ENGLAND' 367

evoking not only a sense of pathos but also one of foreshadowing, a narrative technique typical also of medieval epic.[33]

Similes abound in the Matter of England-romances and are overwhelmingly employed to describe forceful actions in combat. Especially frequent in the epic tradition are animal similes and vocational similes. In *Havelok* these animal similes tend to derive from hunting, as in the case of a dog chasing a hare (1994)—though there is also an example from the slightly less chivalric activity of bear-baiting (1838–40)—but some clearly originate in agricultural or economic contexts, such as the beast of burden's fear of the goad (278–9) or a horse's fear of the spur (2568–9). Vocational similes feature less prominently in *Havelok*, but are literally striking when they occur, to quote one example: 'And beten on him so doth the smith / With the hamer on the stith' (1876–7). Hyperbole is another rhetorical device frequently to be found, whereas the *descriptio* is fairly rare in the Matter of England-romances. Perhaps the closest that *Havelok* comes to a rhetorical description is when the narrator discusses the close-to-ideal King Athelwold. Here, however, we do not get the top-to-toe description of a person or a list of their impressive moral characteristics, but rather the standard praise, the *encomium*, of a perfect ruler.

In *Havelok* one also notices a preference for listing things in a chain-like succession of smaller clusters; that is, combinations of several items one after the other, making up a larger whole, such as society:

> Erl and barun, dreng and thayn,
> Knict, bondeman, and swain,
> Wydues, maydnes, prestes and clerkes ...   (31–3)

or:

> And alle that in Denemark wone—
> Em and brother, fader and sone,
> Erl and baroun, dreng and thayn,
> Knightes and burgeys and sweyn—   (1326–9)

Like the devices already mentioned, this one, too, contributes to the poem's powerfully formulaic style, as do the many tags which put emphasis on a statement, but which, due to their frequent occurrence, acquire a rather clichéd character. Typical examples are 'I wene', 'withuten ley', and 'withuten faile'.[34]

A further rhetorical device well attested in the Matter of England-romances, as well as in Middle English romances in general, is the practice of deliberately referring to an oral performance situation at the very beginning of the text. In *Bevis* the first three stanzas serve this function:

> Lordinges, herkneth to me tale!
> Is merier than the nightingale,
>   That I schel singe;
> Of a knight ich wile yow roune,
> Beves a highte of Hamtoune,
>   Withouten lesing*.   *lie*
>
> Ich wile yow tellen al togadre

---

[33] Smithers, 'Style', 203.
[34] Smithers, 'Style', 211.

368 MEDIEVAL POETRY: 1100–1400

> Of that knight and of is fadre,
>   Sire Gii.
> Of Hamtoun he was sire
> And of al that ilche schire,
>   To wardi.
>
> Lordinges, this, of whan I telle,
> Never man of flesch ne felle
>   Nas so strong.
> And so he was in ech strive.
> And ever he levede withouten wive,
>   Al to late and long. (1–18)

These narrative stagings of the apparently oral performance of the text—like the formulaic nature of the romances—have often been taken as direct evidence of the oral origins of these early texts or else as evidence of their having been orally performed. The fraught questions of orality and literacy in medieval literature would obviously deserve an in-depth discussion of their own. They must be mentioned here briefly, however, for the ways in which the supposed orality or oral style of the Matter of England-romances has been adduced as evidence of their comparatively primitive character, and, by implication, of their defective literary quality.

There have, however, been dissenting voices. Carol Fewster, for instance, has offered an important assessment of the formulaic style of Middle English romance—an assessment drawing heavily on evidence from *Guy of Warwick*—that locates a sophisticated sense of self-conscious literariness in those very characteristics that made so many scholars recoil from the Matter of England-romances:

> Far from being a naive style, limited by its evolution through oral transmission, romance style develops its own literary language in which continual references to its transmission are a part of this romance style's emphasis on its own history. Middle English romance is a sophisticated genre which uses a single set of intertextual markers to create meaning in different ways.[35]

The picture Fewster draws is a paradoxical one. It is the romances' very limitations, determined, as they are, by the texts' oral transmission, that enable them to develop their own form of intertextuality, a style that elevates its traditionality to the level of a self-conscious aesthetic traditionalism and that results in an historically sensitive generic self-referentiality. Fewster's perspective is important because it analytically acknowledges the genre's poetic potency in the very features which had long served to give it a bad name. Yet where Fewster's perspective coincides with positions frequently held by the detractors of the Matter of England is in the primarily negative and, ultimately, naïvely mimetic light she casts on orality. After all, Fewster regards orality primarily as a negative force, a historical condition shaping the evolution of romance through limitation. In an important contribution to the debate, Ananya Jahanara Kabir has attempted to recast the oral aspects of the Matter of England-romances by seeing orality less as an historical mould shaping the genre than as an aesthetic device, self-consciously deployed in the process of poetic meaning-making. For Kabir, the oral or oral-derived characteristics of the Matter of England-romances constitute

---

[35] Carol Fewster, *Intertextuality and Genre in Middle English Romance* (Cambridge, 1987), 150–1.

a consciously contrived effect, such as can only be possible in socio-cultural conditions of an advanced literacy. Kabir draws attention to the curious mismatch between the poems' tendency to stress their status as oral performance, on the one hand, and what she refers to as 'a narratorial voice that resonates with our understanding of the fictionality of medieval literature as a consequence of its increasing writtenness', on the other. Hence, with special reference to *Havelok*, she invites us to 'reassess the formulaic style, thematic concerns, and realism [...] as manifestations of a feigned orality'.[36] According to Kabir, in *Havelok*—and we can extend this view to the other Matter of England-romances—this feigned orality is part of a larger aesthetic constellation. *Havelok* does not engender its non-courtly outlook because it caters to a non-courtly audience, but rather because its specific brand of non-courtliness actually appeals to an aristocratic audience; that is, an elite audience capable of self-consciously enjoying moments of literary non-courtliness.[37] Within a specifically medieval context, such a situation is by no means unheard of. The fabliaux may constitute a typical example of a seemingly non-courtly genre produced for a courtly audience. In the fabliaux a decidedly bourgeois or even lower-class *dramatis personae* engages in non-courtly activities for the delectation of aristocratic readers or listeners.

The evidence Kabir marshals in support of her theory is compelling. A comparison of *Havelok* with its Anglo-Norman sources, for instance, reveals the degree to which additional 'oral' and folktale elements have been introduced into the English narrative so as to increase its non-courtly effect. To name only a few examples: neither Gaimar's *Estoire des Engleis*, which also tells the story, nor the *Lai d'Havelok* is remotely so obsessed with establishing parallels between Havelok's early years and those of Goldborw—parallels that are, as we have seen, emphasised also by the conspicuous naming of the two principal villains, Godrich and Godard. In both Old French sources, the equivalent to Godrich is called Edelsi, and neither features a character comparable to Godard. The reason Havelok has to flee Denmark in the Old French narratives is that his father was killed during King Arthur's conquest of Denmark.[38]

The most cited instance of *Havelok*'s feigned orality happens when the narrator introduces the narrative by addressing the audience with stereotypical references to an oral performance.

Herkneth* to me, gode men—	*Listen*
Wives, maydnes, and alle men—	
Of a tale that ich wile you telle,	
Whoso it wile here and therto* dwelle*.	*for that purpose; stay*
The tale is of Havelok imaked:	
Whil he was litel, he yede* ful naked.	*went*
Havelok was a ful god gome*—	*guy*
He was ful god in everi trome*;	*company*
He was the wicteste* man at need*	*bravest; in time of need*
That thurte riden* on ani stede.	*might ride*
That ye mowen* now yhere*,	*may; hear*
And the tale you mowen ylere*,	*may learn*

---

[36] Ananya Jahanara Kabir, 'Forging an Oral Style: *Havelok* and the Fiction of Orality?', *Studies in Philology*, 98 (2001), 18–48, at 20.

[37] Kabir, 'Forging an Oral Style', 20.

[38] Kabir, 'Forging an Oral Style', 21–2.

370 MEDIEVAL POETRY: 1100–1400

> At the beginning of oure tale,
> Fil me a cup of ful god ale;
> And wile drinken, her I spelle*,   *tell a story*
> That Crist us shilde* alle fro helle.   *shield*
> Krist late* us hevere* so for to do   *let; ever*
> That we moten* comen Him to;   *may*
> And, witthat* it mote* ben so,   *in order that; might*
> *Benedicamus Domino!*
> Here I shal beginnen a rym*;   *rhyme*
> Krist us yeve* wel god fyn*!   *give; end*
> The rym is maked of Havelok—
> A stalworthi man in a flok*.   *group*
> He was the stalwortheste man at nede
> That may riden on any stede. (1–26)

These introductory verses seem to offer an almost excessive image of the oral performer. What is especially significant about this written performance of orality is the demand for a cup of ale. This demand draws attention to the performer and his situation in a way that can easily be undercut in the moment of performance—let alone during the experience of silent reading—simply because the mere absence or unavailability of a cup of ale would automatically highlight, as theorists of medieval fictionality have established for this kind of device, the fictional nature of the text being spoken, the distinction between the text and the outside world. The evocation of the minstrel scene draws attention to the fictional character of the poem's orality even as the subsequent narrative itself does its best to create as perfect an image of traditional orality as possible. When it comes to the poem's conclusion, however, the romance presents the opposite image of itself by stressing its very writtenness. It does so through not only evoking the many sleepless nights during which the text had been composed but also by suggesting, implicitly, that it was not composed by the person producing the oral performance, but by someone else, the actual author, present only in writing, and by no means identical to the performer.

> Forthi ich wolde biseken you
> That haven herd the rim nu,
> That ilke of you, with gode wille,
> Seye a Pater Noster stille
> For him that haveth the rym maked,
> And ther-fore fele* nihtes waked,   *for that purpose many*
> That Jesu Crist his soule bringe
> Biforn his Fader at his endinge. (2994–3001)

After all, as the text itself has mentioned not long before, *one* of the typical ways in which an audience enjoys a narrative poem like *Havelok* is through 'romanz reding on the bok' (2327). Even as the audience potentially witnesses this oral performance, it is simultaneously made to understand that the performer, the narrator, and even the empirical author are not the same person. The real-life production of the text, its narrative presentation and its performative rendition, are thus prised apart epistemologically.

How does this affect our aesthetic assessment of the Matter of England-romances? These poems betray a considerable degree of literary self-consciousness. This is expressed, among other things, in their strategic highlighting of their own fictionality through an elaborate scheme of imitating supposedly oral poetic forms and a narrative traditionality that they want their audience to understand as being skilfully constructed. While this may not be true of all Matter of England-romances to the same degree, it is clearly an aesthetic option. These romances betray, therefore, a thoroughly medieval poetics, but one that is intent on situating its sense of its fictionality and, hence, its literariness squarely within the rhetorical and narrative traditions of pre-modernity and within the media-contexts of its time—viz., the large capitals that the *Havelok*-manuscript employs to stress its supposedly oral features. The Matter of England-romances' poetic alterity is thus not to be sought in some kind of primitive simplicity rooted in an archaic orality, or in the medieval bourgeoisie's lack of taste, but in the poems' impressive awareness of the traditionality of their repertoire of poetic devices and, hence, in the poems'—sometimes even audacious—willingness to self-consciously exploit that traditionality.

PART V

THE RICARDIAN POETS

24

Piers Plowman

Nicolette Zeeman

In memory of Mary Clemente Davlin, O.P.,
a most wise and kind scholar of Piers Plowman

Poet and Poem

Perhaps deliberately, the poet of *Piers Plowman* left few traces of himself apart from his poem, a long, alliterative political and religious allegory that exists in at least three versions: the unfinished 'A-text', the much longer 'B-text', and the 'C-text', a comprehensive reworking of B, bar the minimally revised last two sections, described as *passūs* ('steps') along the poem's narrative 'journey'.[1] Scholarship on the C-text suggests that the revision of B into C was complicated and not necessarily sequential; whether or not the poet stopped writing before he was able to revise the last two *passūs*, it seems fairly clear that, in its (at least) three versions, the poem was a kind of life work.[2]

Until very recently, the bulk of our information about its poet, whom we tend to call William Langland, came from the poem and its manuscripts, and in particular the early fifteenth-century manuscript of the C-text, Dublin, Trinity College, MS 212 (D.4.1). Here he is described as 'Willielm[us] de Langlond', son of Stacy de Rokayle, and identified as the one who composed the book called 'Perys Ploughman'. The comment has been taken as a confirmation of one dimension of the identity of the narrator, who is in parts of the poem named 'Wil', a term that also personifies him as some version of the psychological powers of desire or volition.[3] More recently, the Rokayle connection has been explored in some depth, leading to the new hypothesis that the poet was a member of a minor gentry family and even a former priest.[4] Our lack of historical information about the poet might just be due to poor historical transmission. But it is also true that writing anonymously or referring to oneself only obliquely or emblematically is not uncommon among poets of the period. Anne Middleton has explored the ethical and political implications of the poet's anagrammatic and partial representation of himself in the poem as a man who defines his life's work in

---

[1] The poem was widely disseminated in all three versions (including amalgams of the A-text 'completed' with C, and several manuscripts that have been claimed to represent interim texts and an early version of the A-text); we still have over fifty manuscripts of the poem. There is no evidence of any other writing attributed to the poet. See Ralph Hanna, 'The Versions and Revisions of *Piers Plowman*', in Andrew Cole and Andrew Galloway (eds), *The Cambridge Companion to* Piers Plowman (Cambridge, 2014), 33–49; Simon Horobin, 'Manuscripts and Readers of *Piers Plowman*', in Cole and Galloway (eds), *Cambridge Companion*, 179–97.

[2] On the poem as a 'life work', see note 5.

[3] For a summary of the biographical data available from the poem and its manuscripts, see Ralph Hanna, *William Langland*, Authors of the Middle Ages 3 (Aldershot, 1993), citing the Dublin manuscript, 2. On the narrator as 'Wil' and the consequences of this for reading the poem, see Joseph S. Wittig, '*Piers Plowman* B, Passus IX–XII: Elements in the Design of the Inward Journey', *Traditio*, 28 (1972), 211–80; Nicolette Zeeman, *Piers Plowman and the Medieval Discourse of Desire* (Cambridge, 2006).

[4] See Robert Adams, *Langland and the Rokele Family: The Gentry Background to* Piers Plowman (Dublin, 2013); this trail is probably not yet exhausted, and, for a summary of the most recent developments, see Andrew Galloway, 'Parallel Lives: William Rokele and the Satirical Literacies of *Piers Plowman*', *Studies in the Age of Chaucer*, 40 (2018), 43–111, at 44, n. 2.

Nicolette Zeeman, *Piers Plowman*. In: *The Oxford History of Poetry in English*. Edited by Helen Cooper and Robert R. Edwards, Oxford University Press. © Nicolette Zeeman (2023). DOI: 10.1093/oso/9780198827429.003.0024

376   MEDIEVAL POETRY: 1100–1400

counterpoint to other more institutional or devotional versions of the working or good life ('I have lyved in londe … my name is Longe Wille').[5] Nevertheless, the obliquity of these self-representations may also suggest that the poet did not wish to foreground his local and historical identity. This tension between the critical and conceptual ambition of the poem and the little we know of the poet remains provoking: it could have been because he feared that his political and ecclesiastical radicalism had put him at risk; but he may simply have regarded his identity as a diversion from the world-transforming spiritual project on which he was engaged.

Piers Plowman is an uncompromisingly moral and spiritual text whose religious outlook shapes a sustained and searching engagement with the social world and its institutions: parliament, the monarchy, the law courts, the organisation of labour and food production, but above all the church and its educational, pastoral, and conversionary mission. It articulates a distinctively conflicted, but also highly critical, view of its historical moment.[6] Although it has proved difficult to map the religious politics of the poem onto any one of the various reformist political or spiritual movements of the period, including that of Wycliffitism/Lollardy, the poem's expressed discontent with the contemporary Church means that it shares much with them; the poem was also printed in 1550 and by the Reformation seems to have been read as a proto-Reformation text.[7] But Langland's writing and thought are also very much his own. His decision to write serious politics and theology in the vernacular suggests a desire to address a wide audience directly, and is surely connected to his concern for the good functioning of society and its institutions, food production, and the care of the poor. The poem is preoccupied with both the corruption of the contemporary Church and the mechanics of pastoral care. It insists, for instance, on the need for the clergy to weave a path between pastoral severity and gentleness, oscillating between intense penitentialism and a highly inclusive, Christological soteriology: in its climactic *passūs* (B.16–18) the poem emphasises the loving, redemptive work of Christ. The poet's formal psychology is broadly oriented towards the affective powers and the will, but at the same time the poet remains highly preoccupied with the forms of spiritual understanding, as we will see below. His larger vision of human nature and its endemic proneness towards failure and sin, towards corruption and self-deception, is dark and in many ways pessimistic; yet the poem is also punctuated with instances of startling spiritual poetry and moments when protagonists seem to experience sudden affective and cognitive illumination.[8] The not-fully-explicable

---

[5] William Langland, *Piers Plowman. A Parallel-Text Edition of the A, B, C and Z Versions*, ed. A. V. C. Schmidt, 2 vols., 2nd edn. (Kalamazoo, MI, 2011), B.15.152. I shall be citing from this edition throughout, mostly using the B-text, replacing medieval 'þ' and 'ȝ' and regularising 'i' and 'j' according to modern usage. On the poem not just as a 'life's work' but also as a work organised around the experience of the lived historical life, see Anne Middleton, 'William Langland's "Kynde Name": Authorial Signature and Social Identity in Late Fourteenth-Century England', in Lee Patterson (ed.), *Literary Practice and Social Change in Britain, 1380–1530* (Berkeley, CA, 1990), 15–82; 'Acts of Vagrancy: The C Version "Autobiography" and the Statute of 1388', in Steven Justice and Kathryn Kerby-Fulton (eds), *Written Work: Langland, Labor and Authorship* (Philadelphia, PA, 1997), 208–317.

[6] Work on the poem's relation to its historical moment and its politics continues to flourish, with David Aers still attributing to the poet some of the most radically critical views: see David Aers, *Community, Gender and Individual Identity: English Writing 1360–1430* (London, 1988) and *Beyond Reformation? An Essay on William Langland's* Piers Plowman *and the End of Constantinian Christianity* (Notre Dame, IN, 2015). See also Middleton, 'Acts of Vagrancy'; Andrew Galloway, *The Penn Commentary on* Piers Plowman *1* (Philadelphia, PA, 2006).

[7] See Wendy Scase, Piers Plowman *and the New Anticlericalism* (Cambridge, 1989); Anne Hudson, 'Langland and Lollardy?', *Yearbook of Langland Studies*, 17 (2003), 91–105; Kathryn Kerby-Fulton, *Books under Suspicion: Censorship and Tolerance of Revelatory Writing in Late Medieval England* (Notre Dame, IN, 2006); on the later influence of *Piers Plowman*, see Anne Hudson, 'Epilogue: The Legacy of *Piers Plowman*', in John A. Alford (ed.), *A Companion to* Piers Plowman (Berkeley, CA, 1988), 251–66.

[8] See Robert Adams, 'Langland's Theology', in Alford (ed.), *A Companion*, 87–114; Nicholas Watson, 'Piers Plowman, Pastoral Theology, and Spiritual Perfectionism: Hawkyn's Cloak and Patience's *Pater noster*', *Yearbook of Langland Studies*, 21 (2007), 83–118; David Aers, *Sanctifying Signs: Making Christian Tradition in Late Medieval England* (Notre Dame, IN, 2004), 29–51, 99–156; Aers, *Salvation and Sin: Augustine, Langland*

nature of such visionary moments seems to point to the hidden workings of grace in the spiritual life: when the narrator is rebuked by the personification Scripture, for instance, he tells us: 'wepte I for wo and wrathe of hir speche / And in a wynkynge worth [began to drowse] til I was aslepe. / A merveillous metels [dream] mette me [I dreamed] thanne ...'; or later, when a long absent protagonist is mentioned, '"Piers the Plowman!" quod I tho, and al for pure joye / That I herde nempne [speak] his name anoon I swowned after' (B.11.4–6; B.16.18–19).

As lines such as these suggest, although the issues that concern Langland are issues that concern the scholastic theologians of the day, the poet formulates them in what are on the whole very un-scholastic terms.[9] The poem's primary modes of procedure are narratival, scriptural, debaterly, satirical, visionary, figural, and poetic. However, whatever the generic perspective from which the poem is viewed, *Piers Plowman* remains idiosyncratic.

The poem is written in a loose alliterative metre, for example, but most of the time it avoids the characteristic vocabulary and style of other fourteenth-century alliterative poets, with their exploitation of the vivid and verbally encrusted effects of alliteration. Langland's alliterative verse is instead a flexible and hospitable vehicle for the poem's conceptual and formal diversity. His lines tend to be longer than those of other alliterative poems, with semantically and metrically weightier second line halves; sometimes his stress-carrying words alliterate only partially, or not at all, and alliteration may occur on unstressed words or syllables (see B.11.5; B.16.19, cited above). Hoyt Duggan describes Langland's alliterative lines as 'through composed', as always co-opted for larger purposes. But these lines are also always strongly rhythmical; relations between the line halves and across multiple lines are dynamic, and Latin insertions are often wittily folded into the alliterative and echoic patterning of the English:[10]

> Thanne Scripture scorned me and a skile* tolde,   *saying*
> And lakked* me in Latyn and light by me she sette,   *disparaged*
> And seide, '*Multi multa sciunt et seipsos nesciunt*'.[11]

A crucially distinctive feature of *Piers Plowman* is the diversity of the conceptual frameworks and textual genres that are gathered within it. The poem draws on a range of materials that includes scripture, pastoralia, devotional writing, debate, satire, allegorical narrative, even romance; the poem's diegesis is multi-layered, prismatic, and startlingly metamorphic.[12] *Piers Plowman* is also full of dialogues and conversations, and its deep structures have been recognised to be dialectical, even 'negating'.[13] This formal multiplicity is exemplified

---

and Fourteenth-Century Theology (Notre Dame, IN, 2009), 83–131; Aers, *Beyond Reformation?*; Zeeman, *Piers Plowman*; Zeeman, *The Arts of Disruption: Allegory and* Piers Plowman (Oxford, 2020), 160–84, 323–81.

[9] On the poem's formal patterning, and even the possibility that its recurring narrative structures might constitute a kind of narrative 'self-theorisation', see Zeeman, *Piers Plowman*; Zeeman, 'Piers Plowman in Theory', in Cole and Galloway (eds), *Cambridge Companion*, 214–29, at 227–9.

[10] Hoyt N. Duggan, 'Notes on the Metre of *Piers Plowman*: Twenty Years On', in Judith Jefferson and Ad Putter (eds), *Approaches to the Metres of Alliterative Verse* (Leeds, 2009), 159–85, at 184; also Elizabeth Salter, *Piers Plowman: An Introduction* (Oxford, 1963), 12–24; A. V. C. Schmidt, *The Clerkly Maker: Langland's Poetic Art* (Cambridge, 1987), 21–80.

[11] B.11.1–3; 'Many people know many things and do not know themselves'.

[12] Readers who have stressed the poem's multi-genericism include Steven Justice, 'The Genres of Piers Plowman', *Viator*, 19 (1988), 291–306; Zeeman, *Arts of Disruption*.

[13] On the dialectical nature of the poem, see Aers, *Beyond Reformation?*, 98; D. Vance Smith, 'Negative Langland', *Yearbook of Langland Studies*, 23 (2009), 33–59; on its ferocious dialogues, see Anne Middleton, 'Narration and the Invention of Experience: Episodic Form in *Piers Plowman*', in Larry Benson and Siegfried Wenzel (eds), *The Wisdom of Poetry: Essays in Honor of Morton Bloomfield* (Kalamazoo, MI, 1982), 91–122; Zeeman, *Arts of Disruption*, 121–3, 160–88, 243–61.

378   MEDIEVAL POETRY: 1100–1400

by the poem's protagonists—so often seen in lively debate with each other. Many of these protagonists are fully fledged, elaborated personifications, though the poem's ingrainedly 'personificatory' modes of thought are also manifest in the plethora of short-lived personifications that emerge from the local texture of the poem and vanish almost immediately ('sith charite hath ben chapman ...', 'Waryn Wisdom wynked upon Mede / And seide, "Madame, I am youre man ..."', B.prol.64, B.4.154–5). But Langland also mingles personifications with other protagonists of a more exemplary, historical or scriptural sort (a king, 'a maister', 'a lewed vicory', Trajan, Abrahame). Elsewhere he explicitly identifies some of his actants as both exemplary and personificatory (Wil/the narrator, Actyf/Haukyn, Faith/Abrahame, Hope/Moyses, [Love]/'the Samaritan'). Multiple or overlaid identities also characterise a protagonist such as Anima (the soul, but also attributed with many other names that relate to its different functions), as well as figures such as Piers Plowman (discussed below) and even Christ ('semblable to the Samaritan' and wearing 'Piers armes ... his helm and ... his haubergeon, *humana natura*', B.18.10, 22–3). With these last examples, Langland is also drawing on typology, the mode of thought whereby spiritual protagonists anticipate and echo each other across Christian history.[14] Langland's allegory also has a pervasive satirical, critical, and deflationary aspect, which can be seen when he allows his protagonists to turn into lesser or corrupt versions of themselves (Conscience accused by Mede, Studie as author of bad sciences, Clergie offering to read intellectual riddles, Wil going astray). These are versions of what I have elsewhere described as the poem's pervasive trope of *paradiastole*, the vice that looks like a virtue or the 'hypocritical figure'.[15] Although we might be more inclined to describe as 'allegorical' the poem's more immediately graspable or readable personifications, exemplars, and 'types', these shifting and deflationary figures are in respect of their multi-dimensionality in fact just as characteristic of allegorical narrative.

The discursive multiplicity illustrated by these protagonists is also fundamental to the poem's allegory.[16] All allegory is after all put together through the juxtaposition and interplay of shifting, contrasting, and even conflicting discourses. Because of this, it is not in my view helpful to divide the text up into discursive levels, such as 'narrative' or 'image' versus 'explication' or 'gloss';[17] more useful is Angus Fletcher's description of allegory's tendency to polarise into dynamic oppositions and 'symbolic power struggles'.[18] If this is a feature of all allegorical narrative, however, it is particularly marked in *Piers Plowman*, as the poem zigzags between different and often contrary emphases—among them, repeating patterns of ethical instruction, moral slippage, outright corruption, chastisement, insight, and fresh spiritual departure. Versions of this oppositional or dialectical work also appear in the way that the poem performs much of its pastoral and theological work in the sharp-tongued, but also often question-begging, modes of debate. If some of its dialogues seem to lead to

[14] Elizabeth Salter, *Piers Plowman*, 65–105; Mann, 'Allegory and *Piers Plowman*', in Cole and Galloway (eds), *Cambridge Companion*, 65-83, at 66–7.

[15] Many readers have noted the reiterative occurrences of moral slippage and sin in the poem; in *Piers Plowman* I claimed that many of the poem's scenes of failure were also sites for new departure and renewal. On *paradiastole* and the hypocritical figure, see Aers, *Beyond Reformation?*, 85–7; Zeeman, *Arts of Disruption*, 37–117.

[16] On the poem's allegory, see Elizabeth Salter, '*Piers Plowman*: an Introduction', in her *English and International: Studies in the Literature, Art and Patronage of Medieval England*, with Derek Pearsall and Nicolette Zeeman (eds) (Cambridge, 1988), 111–57; David Aers, *Piers Plowman and Christian Allegory* (London, 1975); Maureen Quilligan, *The Language of Allegory: Defining the Genre* (Ithaca, NY, 1979); Jill Mann, *Langland and Allegory*, Morton W. Bloomfield Lectures on Medieval Literature 2 (Kalamazoo, MI, 1992); Mann, 'Allegory and *Piers Plowman*'; Zeeman, *Arts of Disruption*.

[17] See Quilligan, *Language of Allegory*, 53; Mann, 'Langland and Allegory'.

[18] Angus Fletcher, *Allegory: The Theory of a Symbolic Mode*, with a new afterword (Princeton, NJ, 2012), 23.

discursive disruption and aporia,[19] others use the dynamic incrementalism of conversation to open up new possibilities. The poem's dialogues pose spiritual challenges and invitations, both for their protagonists and the poem's reader.

Langland's citations, textual allusions, and satirical or theological word play are the small-scale counterparts to these larger allegorical structures. Much work has been done on the identification and interpretation of the poem's many Latin (and occasionally French) quotations and insertions,[20] as well as on the decipherment of its theological, scriptural and poetic word clusters, its enigmatic sayings and riddles.[21] Langland's word play has long been recognised as one of the most memorable aspects of the poem. Often it involves the provocative juxtaposition of contrasting languages and perspectives, as when the attraction of lying is signalled by a euphemistic description of pardoners 'taking pity' on Lyere (Liar) as if he were a street child: 'Til pardoners hadde pite, and pulled hym into house, / They wesshen hym and wiped hym and wounden hym in cloutes [rags]' (B.2.220–1); or when the spiritual life that has been described as a moral journey in the material world turns out to end in the heart with a vision of Truthe in a 'chain' of love:

> And if Grace graunte thee to go in in this wise,
> Thow shalt see in thiselve Truthe sitte in thyn herte
> In a cheyne of charite, as thow a child were. (B.5.605–7)

As we can see here, Langland's word play ranges from sharp satire and the simulation of moral dubiety to audacious forms of spiritual figuration; sometimes he allows terms to move down the semantic register, turning into depleted versions of themselves, and sometimes he reworks them so that they move up the semantic register in an aspirational way.[22] So, when in B.5 Repentaunce exhorts the people to ask for God's mercy and 'A thousand of men ... Cride upward to Crist ... To have grace to go to Truthe' (B.5.510–12), the poem invokes a vision of spiritual pilgrimage to Truthe. But immediately after this vision is deflated and materialised, partly because the people discover that they do not know the way (they 'blustreden [strayed] forth as beestes over baches [valleys] and hilles'), and partly because of the appearance of a pilgrim, a man accoutred with the marks of his own diminished spirituality—material pilgrim badges, 'An hundred of ampulles ... And many a crouch [cross] on his cloke, and keyes of Rome, / And the vernycle before, for men sholde ... se bi his signes whom he sought hadde (B.5.514, 520–4). The notion of pilgrimage is then definitively undermined when the people ask the pilgrim if he knows how to seek Truthe (now revealingly described as a material *corseint*, a 'saint's body/shrine'), and he says no—he has never known a pilgrim seek after him (B.5.532-6). However, in the lines that follow Piers Plowman arrives, claiming that he does indeed know Truthe. Piers now entirely respiritualises the notion of pilgrimage by offering a 'roadmap' for the journey to Truthe; this is

---

[19] As shown so influentially by Middleton in 'Narration'.

[20] See John A. Alford, Piers Plowman: *A Guide to the Quotations* (Binghamton, NY, 1992); on the 'grammatical' wit with which Langland uses non-English citation, see Christopher Cannon, *From Literacy to Literature, England 1300–1400* (Oxford: 2016), 125–58.

[21] For a recent study of enigma in *Piers Plowman*, see Curtis A. Gruenler, Piers Plowman *and the Poetics of Enigma: Riddles, Rhetoric and Theology* (Notre Dame, IN, 2017); see references here to the work of R. E. Kaske, Edward C. Schweitzer, Anne Middleton, Raymond St.-Jacques, and Andrew Galloway.

[22] See Mary Clemente Davlin, *A Game of Heuene: Word Play and the Meaning of* Piers Plowman B (Cambridge, 1989); Jill Mann, 'Eating and Drinking in *Piers Plowman*', *Essays and Studies*, 32 (1979), 26–43; James Simpson, *Piers Plowman: An Introduction*, 2nd edn. (Exeter, 2007), 135–9; Cristina Maria Cervone, *Poetics of the Incarnation: Middle English Writing and the Leap of Love* (Philadelphia, PA, 2012), 26–31, 66–72, 105–17, 126–38.

380   MEDIEVAL POETRY: 1100–1400

the passage mentioned above, which ends up with the paradoxical vision of Truthe sitting 'in thyn herte / In a cheyne of charite'. But Langland goes further. Although Piers suggests that once he has completed his ploughing he will join the people on pilgrimage, he in fact never sets out; as the ploughing progresses, it turns out that true pilgrimage is no ordinary, material journey, but rather the good working life enacted in the spirit of pilgrimage. Piers is already in all the important senses a pilgrim. 'I wol worshipe therwith Truthe by my lyve, / And ben his pilgrym atte plow ...' (B.6.100–1).[23] Langland's point is not just that work and pilgrimage might ultimately be the same thing; it is rather that both must be enacted in the spirit of the other. Word play of this sort demands constant vigilance. If Langland unnervingly exploits the reader's possibly complacent misapprehensions of words, he also requires us to stay alert to the 'poetry' of the poem's deep spiritual thought.

In B.11 Langland famously reflects on the nature of his poem. Here, he stages an interrogation of the narrator-as-poet, in which the personification Ymaginatif disparagingly suggests that he is just 'meddling' with *makynge* ('vernacular verse', B.12.16). However, despite the fact that elsewhere the poem also makes a number of disparaging references to 'japeris [jesters] and jogelours and jangleris of gestes [tales]',[24] it seems clear that Langland does not despise vernacular imaginative writing. His poem is, after all, full of allusions to traditions of non-Latin narrative, debate, vision and romance. And yet the language of genre does not provide the terms in which he justifies the writing of *Piers Plowman* itself. This poem is something altogether more challengingly spiritual, but also more risky and hard to define. In response to Ymaginatif's critique, the narrator initially offers the rather feeble defence of the need for relaxation. But then, without warning, he switches to a much more ambitious claim altogether—this poem will teach things that no other text has:

> Ac if ther were any wight that wolde me telle
> What were Dowel* and Dobet and Dobest at the laste,   *'do well'*
> Wolde I nevere do werk, but wende to holi chirche
> And there bidde my bedes* ...   *prayers* (B.12.25–8)

In these lines, Langland refuses to situate the poem in terms of any recognisable authority, tradition or genre, describing it rather as a spiritual search of the most strenuous, patient and open-ended sort. Something of this is echoed in the rather different passage that seems to replace it in the C-text, the 'apologia' that concludes by describing the poet's work as a mysterious combination of perseverance, chance, and grace. Here the narrator admits that he is like one who has many times traded and lost, 'and at the laste hym happed [chanced] / A bouhte [he acquired] suche a bargayn he was the bet evere ... Suche a wynnyng hym warth thorw wordes of grace'.[25]

The Shape of the Poem

Piers Plowman is unusual among medieval dream poems in that its narrator dreams several dreams over the poem. If this narrator has long been recognised as a figure for the poem's author, he has also been seen as a recipient of the poem's teaching, even as a version of

---

[23] J. A. Burrow, 'The Action of Langland's Second Vision', *Essays in Criticism*, 15 (1965), 247–68.
[24] B.10.31; see also B.prol.33–9; B.5.395–7; B.13.222–35.
[25] C.5.92–8. On the B-text passage, see Middleton, 'Narration', 110–22 (where Middleton also claims that Langland appropriates the notion of 'meddling' with *makynge* to describe how his poem 'interposes' a life's work between authorities and genres); Simpson, *Piers Plowman*, 121–2.

the poem's reader.[26] Equally important for either of these readings is the fact that this narrator is a hermeneutic challenge, a troubled 'pastoral case' who oscillates between a range of responses—eager enthusiasm, misinterpretation, exclamations, ripostes, disagreement, apparent non-sequiturs, questions, and silences. The poem requires that the poem's reader, like a pastoral carer, scrutinise his words for clues as to his imagined inner spiritual state and its implications for what is going on in the text.

The first section of the poem (B.prol.-7) is social and political in orientation. Here the narrator witnesses various institutions of government, the law, and social hierarchy, attempting, partly succeeding, but in the end failing, to make people do well. This preoccupation is illustrated in a wry political fable in the Prologue, where the commons, imagined as a crowd of rats and mice, plan to control the cat who terrorises them by placing a bell round its neck; the plan comes to nothing because everyone is too frightened to attach the bell. But the whole idea is then thrown into question by a mouse who observes that, if there were no cat to control them, both the rats and the mice would run amok. By the end of the fable it is unclear where moral authority lies at all. In the visions that follow, we see various protagonists using different medieval institutions to organise society for the better—Conscience arguing against Mede ('reward', 'bribe') before the King's bench, Repentaunce urging confession, Piers Plowman organising labour on the land and obtaining a 'pardon' for those who do well. But throughout these sections, too, the poem illustrates the difficulty of finding and holding onto moral positions, along with the constantly vivacious ingenuity of hypocritical ill-doers, who repeatedly evade their enforcers and reappear in new forms, equipped with new justifications for their actions. Langland's interest in the recursive manifestations of human moral failure is typified by the B.5 sequence in which he imagines the personified sins confessing, but unable to emancipate themselves from the sins that make them the personifications they are. This part of the poem concludes with an argument over the meaning of Piers' redemptive pardon, which turns out to contain the seemingly un-pardonlike words of the Athanasian crede, Englished as: "'Do wel and have wel, and God shal have thi soule", / And "Do yvel and have yvel, and hope thow noon oother / That after thi deeth day the devel shal have thi soule"' (B.7.112–14). The interpretative conflict over this pardon within the poem, reflected by critical debates ever since, produces a crisis—in the B-text Piers Plowman tears up the pardon—that catapults the poem into a third dream.

This next section, often known as the 'inward psychological journey', is instigated by the recognition that *Dowel* cannot be coerced but must come from within. Here the narrative turns away from political and social institutions, though not from the ethical issues that underlie them, as the narrator engages with representations of the powers and processes by which the soul acquires understanding (distinctively formulated by the poet in the terminology of *thought, wit, studie, ymaginatif*) and the sources of its understanding (*clergie* and *kynde*, revealed and natural understanding and experience); the sequence raises questions about both the use, and the abuse, of understanding.[27] Here, the narrator, now called 'Wil', tussels eagerly and discontentedly with his interlocutors; his troubled encounters dramatise how 'doing well' involves both understanding and desire, failures and fresh starts, works and penance—as well as long endurance, the gifts of grace and sudden moments of illumination. These pastoral themes continue to play a central role in the *passūs* that follow,

---

[26] For the narrator 'as reader', see James Simpson, 'Desire and the Scriptural Text: Will as Reader in *Piers Plowman*', in Rita Copeland (ed.), *Criticism and Dissent in the Middle Ages* (Cambridge, 1996), 215–43.

[27] On this sequence, see Wittig, '*Piers Plowman* B'; Mary Clemente Davlin, '*Kynde Knowyng* as a Major Theme in *Piers Plowman* B', *Review of English Studies*, n.s. 22 (1971), 1–19; Zeeman, *Piers Plowman*.

382   MEDIEVAL POETRY: 1100–1400

where a figure named Haukyn, who represents the active life, enters into dialogue with the personifications Patience and Conscience about how to live spiritually within the world.

We are arguably still in a version of the inward psychological journey in B.15–16 when the narrator finds himself in conversation with Anima (the soul). At the beginning of B.16, the narrator asks what *charite* ('love') is and is told that it is a beautiful tree that grows in the human heart, tended by free will, on land leased from Piers Plowman. At the name of the poem's titular protagonist, the narrator swoons into a visionary dream within a dream, in which he sees the tree and asks to taste the *savour* of 'the fruyt Charite', the apples of human good lives that hang on it (B.16.1–17, 73–4; citation line 9). However, confusingly this apparently good desire leads to a replay of the Fall, as the apples are shaken from the tree and carried off by the devil to hell; like the pardon, the meaning of the tree depends on bringing together apparently opposed forms of understanding. To simplify greatly, just as the B.7 pardon scene brings together a number of seemingly contradictory formulations of pardon to show that God both 'pardons' and yet still requires human effort in the world, so the tree of *charite* scene shows that human and divine *charite* can perhaps only, paradoxically, be seen or 'tasted' through the experience of sin and the Fall, and their consequences in Christ's loving, redemptive work. In both cases, ideas about divine pardon and Christian love are formulated in terms that foreground their apparent contradictions and the mystery of their reconcilement: these are matters that can only ever be partially understood—and the strange and enigmatic forms of the poem reflect this.

Over the next two *passūs* (B.17–18) the complexities and paradoxes of the redemption are dramatically debated and played out. An inventive narrative reworking of the parable of the Good Samaritan imagines figures from the Old Testament on the road to Jerusalem (instead of Jericho), unable to help the wounded man of fallen humanity by the roadside. As they rush along behind a Christ-like Samaritan, the scene seems to show the whole Old Testament world racing to the moment when Christ will 'joust' for humanity at the crucifixion—the heroic work of suffering that will cure wounded humanity. When Christ is crucified, he passes into the underworld to conquer hell; here, the 'four daughters of God' (four personified virtues representing aspects of God himself) stand before hell in confusion, trying to work out what is going on. The narrative culminates in Christ's extraordinary speech repudiating sin in the form of the devil, the 'doctour of deeth', and describing Christ's desire for his natural human *bretheren* as a kind of loving, semi-human thirst for humanity ('me thursteth yet, for mannes soule sake').[28] In many ways, this triumphant sequence is the one exception to the poem's disturbing and disorienting narratives of recursive human failure and sin.

In the last dream of the poem Langland narrates the establishment of the church, imagined as a barn of *unite*, for the gathering in of the 'harvest' of human souls. But, in a highly characteristic move, he does not leave the poem on this optimistic note. Instead he provides a desperate and apocalyptic version of the corrupt society that we saw at the beginning of the poem, as the barn is gradually infiltrated by paradiastolic hypocrites until it has become the empty shell of itself. The poem ends shockingly, with the personification Conscience leaving the barn of the church once more to seek 'Piers the Plowman'.[29]

Piers Plowman is present surprisingly rarely in the poem and is for much of its narrative both a mysterious teacher and an absent object of desire.[30] We meet him for the first time

---

[28]   B.18.328–404. See Mann, 'Eating and Drinking', 41–3.
[29]   B.20.386; for the most stimulating recent reading of the poem's ending, see Aers, *Beyond Reformation?*
[30]   See Middleton, 'Narration', 108–9; also on Piers Plowman, see Salter, *Piers Plowman*, 83–105; Zeeman, *Arts of Disruption*, 350–69.

five *passūs* into the poem, when he arrives with the dramatic exclamation 'Peter!' to guide the crowd of penitents to Truth; after the tearing of the pardon in B.7, he disappears again. Mentioned in B.13, he does not actually return till the vision of the tree of *charite* in B.16. He is present for the last time at the founding of the barn of *unite* (B.19), but by the end of the poem he has once more vanished. He is one of the poem's most prismatic allegorical figures. He is a version of the good working layman whose vernacular Anglo-French name 'Piers' is nevertheless also an allusion to St Peter, the rock on whom Christ founded the church, and the first pope. He seems to represent the human end of the spectrum of the 'divine in the human' that is represented in its fullest form by Christ: it is Piers who oversees the tending of the tree of *charite* that grows in the human heart, and when Christ comes to Jerusalem to be crucified, he wears 'Piers armes' of 'human nature' (B.16.17; 18.22–3). But Piers is also part of a troubled world that is struggling to turn towards God; however good they seem, all his projects are compromised by human failure. And yet, wherever he turns up in the poem, Piers seems to be ahead of those around him; if we look at him in light of the poem's endless 'questing', he is a kind of seeker, but also a seeker 'sought' by other seekers. This seems to be more than ever the case when, after the disintegration of the barn of *unite*, Conscience once again departs, calling after grace and Piers the Plowman.

Asking and Listening

In the second part of this chapter, I will be looking at Langland's exploration of 'asking' and 'listening', two crucial elements in the process of learning, as they occur in *Piers Plowman*. Langland's focus on asking and listening may have something to show us about the kinds of spiritual understanding that the poem proposes; it may also, however, have something to tell us about the kinds of reading that the poem demands. Previously I have looked at some of the passages that I will discuss here in terms of their pastoral teaching and spiritual psychology;[31] now I will revisit them to see what they can tell us about how Langland asks us to read his poem.

Piers Plowman has often been said to advocate an Augustinian and 'sapiential' ('wisdom'-like) version of understanding. This is an understanding that is never merely intellectual, but rather embedded in the forms of experience, whether within the soul or out in the phenomenal world; it is motivated by the desire to do well and infused with spiritual love.[32] This understanding is as much a way of being as it is a form of knowledge. At the same time, Langland is also very interested in the many contingent forms of understanding available to the Christian subject—as the poem's criss-crossing discourses, conflicting figures, punning word play, dialectical thought, negations and aporias (its allegory) reveal. Langland is also interested in the risks and temptations associated with understanding. The poem's discursive multiplicity seems to be both a response to the inadequacy of any one individual formulation and a recognition that all formulations, however good, can be misunderstood and abused—as when knowledge becomes an object of desire in its own right, an excuse for complacency, a pretence of spirituality or just something that looks like 'the answer'. This is what Augustine called *curiositas*.[33] A version of *curiositas* that particularly preoccupies Langland is the desire to know everything; this is no doubt partly because the desire lays

[31] Zeeman, *Piers Plowman*, 100–8, 119–31, 201–58.
[32] See Wittig, '*Piers Plowman* B'; Davlin, '*Kynde Knowyng*'; Simpson, *Piers Plowman*; Zeeman, *Piers Plowman*.
[33] See William Watts (trans.), *Augustine: Confessions*, 2 vols. (Cambridge, MA, 1988), 10.35.

384 MEDIEVAL POETRY: 1100–1400

claim to a divine omniscience, but also because it encourages the illusion that there is an answer. The personification Ymaginatif (himself a very provisional psychological power[34]) describes the Fall in terms of Adam's pursuit of full knowledge: when Adam 'mamelede [chattered] aboute mete and entremeted [insisted] to knowe / The wisedom and the wit of God, he was put fram blisse' (B.11.416–17). The same problem is at stake in B.15 when the irrepressible narrator asks to know about Anima's many names, plus 'Alle the sciences under sonne and alle the sotile craftes ... kyndely [naturally/fully] in myn herte', earning the rebuke: 'Thanne artow inparfit ... and oon of Prides knyghtes!' As Anima explains, echoing the narrator's word *kyndely*, but using it in a different and deeper sense, 'It were ayeins kynde ... and alle kynnes reson / That any creature sholde konne al, except Crist one' (B.15.40–53).

Countering this dangerous desire to know must be one reason for the purposeful difficulty, slippery language and labile poetic figuration of *Piers Plowman*. Curtis Gruenler has described Langland's use of enigma in similar terms, as the refusal of closed and possessive forms of understanding: enigma is 'open ... infinite, mysterious, and unpossessable', describing 'mysteries to be lived into by faith rather than open revelations possessed'.[35] This is also why in the inward psychological journey the narrator never receives a conclusive answer to his question, 'what is Dowel?' When in B.13 Conscience himself finally asks the question of Clergie, the personification conjures up a mysterious and aporetic little scene involving a castle, a legal or chivalric disputation, and the absent Piers Plowman; gently, he places the 'seven sones' of the liberal arts, 'alle sciences', under erasure:

> 'I have seven sones', he seide, 'serven in a castel
> Ther the lorde of lif wonyeth*, to leren him what is Dowel.   *lives*
> Til I se tho seven and myself accorden,
> I am unhardy', quod he, 'to any wight to preven it.
> For oon Piers the Plowman hath impugned us alle,
> And set alle sciences at a sop save love one ...'   (B.13.120–5)

This scene exemplifies how *Piers Plowman* keeps revisiting and reformulating its own previous thought. In the five preceding *passūs* the poet has analysed the various forms of moral and spiritual understanding available to the Christian subject, all the while also signalling their partiality and contingency; now Clergie's figural gesture affirms this, but in terms that are, if anything, even more emphatically provisional. Clergie suggests that the only possible response to the question 'what is Dowel?' must involve love, but also thinking—asking, but also listening.

Over the course of *Piers Plowman*, Langland also revisits and gradually reconceives what it means to ask and to listen. From early in the poem, he presents the formulation of questions and the receiving of answers as the basis of a Christian spiritual education, showing how they might work, or not work, and how they might be used to balance, reform, and spiritualise each other. However, as the poem progresses, Langland begins to think about asking and listening in new ways, using them to represent transformed conceptions of understanding. Asking and listening come to stand for modes of apprehension that involve the eagerness of the one who asks and the patience of the one who listens; together, they seem to connote a distinctively desirous but open-hearted form of engagement. Once again

---

[34] The best discussion of Ymaginatif remains Alastair J. Minnis, 'Langland's Ymaginatyf and Late-Medieval Theories of Imagination', *Comparative Criticism: A Yearbook*, 3 (1981), 71–103; also Zeeman, *Piers Plowman*, 79–84, 245–57.

[35] Gruenler, *Piers Plowman*, 220, 239.

in the poem, we see two terms working in tandem. And, as the poet explores what it might be truly to ask and listen, he also tells us how he hopes that we will read his poem.[36]

Langland first formulates terms for thinking about asking and listening in the narrator's B.1 dialogue with Holi Chirche. This begins with a sequence of questions and acts of hearing that illustrates the pastoral conversation functioning as it should. When Holi Chirche asks, 'Sone, slepestow? Sestow this peple, / How busie they ben aboute the maze?', the narrator replies, 'Mercy, madame, what may this be to mene?' More pastoral questions and answers ensue, culminating in his request, 'Teche me to no tresor, but tel me this ilke— / How I may save my soule', a question that is answered by Holi Chirche with a famous spiritual and poetic celebration of the treasure of *truthe*. The narrator listens quietly (B.1.5–6, 11, 83–137). The narrator then asks another question that seems, on the surface of it, to indicate proper eagerness to learn: '"Yet have I no kynde [natural/innate/full] knowynge", quod I, "yet mote ye kenne me bettre / Be what craft in my cors [body] it comseth, and where"'. But Holi Chirche responds in a surprising manner:

> 'Thow doted daffe!' quod she, 'dulle are thi wittes.
> To litel Latyn thow lernedest, leode*, in thi youthe: *man*
> *Heu michi quod sterilem duxi vitam juvenilem!*'[37]

The usual reading of Holi Chirche's comically aggressive response is that the narrator has asked one too many questions—evidence that his *wil* is focused on the pursuit of knowledge rather than on internalising and enacting it. He has slipped from the desire for spiritual understanding praised by Augustine as 'studium sapientiae' ('the desire for wisdom') in the direction of the adjacent vice of *curiositas*. The fact that the reader would probably not even have noticed anything wrong if it had not been for Holi Chirche's words means that this is just one of the many points in the poem where we find ourselves in the realm of the scrutiny of souls, trying to work out what must be going on in the imagined head of the narrator. If it is hard to be sure, that is precisely the point about the difficult business of pastoral care and the vices that masquerade as virtues. Nevertheless, his words do offer clues. With their emphasis on natural understanding ('kynde knowynge') and their 'philosophical' insistence on knowing what innate cognitive powers are involved in this understanding, they seem to emphasise the lure of knowledge: if he asks enough questions, perhaps eventually he will have the full answer.

This interpretation may, paradoxically, be supported by the startling non-sequitur of Holi Chirche's response, as she resorts to an insult ('Thow doted daffe!') and attacks the narrator's poor Latin and stupidity. One reading of Holi Chirche's words is that she is engaging the narrator's emotional and volitional powers by shocking and upsetting him.[38] But it may also be important that her words do not really make sense in relation to his question about the powers of his soul: by failing to answer him, she disrupts any possible assumption on the part of the narrator (or reader) that what we need is more knowledge. With a graphic and comic gesture, Holi Chirche puts a halt to the seeming coherence of the language of knowledge; implicitly, she demands that he think harder, ask better, but also listen more carefully.

As so often in *Piers Plowman*, this is not the end of the process. It is entirely characteristic of the poem's unwavering pastoral impetus that Holi Chirche then goes on to clarify matters by using a more accommodating language—albeit one that is also shot through with

---

[36] In thinking about these materials I have much benefited from conversations about patience with Conor McKee.

[37] B.1.138–41a, 'Alas, what a useless life I led my youth'.

[38] See Zeeman, *Piers Plowman*, 125–6.

386   MEDIEVAL POETRY: 1100–1400

transformative poetic figures, puns, and word play. As the narrator now listens quietly, she appropriates his phrase 'kynde knowynge' but uses it in a newly rich sense to describe the 'natural' action of love, the greatest virtue, in the human heart:

> 'It is a kynde knowynge that kenneth in thyn herte
> For to loven thi Lord levere* than thiselve.   *more dearly*
> No dedly synne to do, deye theigh thow sholdest ...'   (B.1.142–4)

The phrase 'kynde knowynge' now refers to sapiential forms of understanding; this is not knowledge as answer, but an understanding in the heart, a mode of being that naturally involves love of the creator and recognises that all understanding is incomplete without it.[39] Holi Chirche now engages in some of the most extraordinary poetic and theological word play of the poem, gliding swiftly from a description of *truthe* as loving your God better than yourself to the claim that love is the 'triacle [medicine] of hevene', and a series of exotic medical images (*spice*, the 'plante of pees') that recall the idea of Christ as 'spiritual doctor'. To all this, the narrator now listens quietly. At the end of her speech, Holi Chirche again signals the provisionality of what she has to say by announcing she must go; but before she does, he asks one more question, now formulated in modest and open-ended terms:

> Yet I courbed* on my knees and cried hire of grace,   *bowed down*
> And seide, 'Mercie, madame, for Marie love of hevene ...
> Kenne* me by som craft to knowe the false'.   *teach* (B.2.1–2, 4)

In response Holi Chirche willingly fulfils her pastoral remit by answering him.

In this scene, then, Langland explores how asking relates to knowledge and its risks; Holi Chirche subverts a question that seemed to imply these risks were indeed present, and by means of comic aggression and an epistemological non-sequitur imposes more attentive forms of listening; once these risks have been countered, the right kind of asking can begin again.

My next example is the scene between the narrator and the personification Wit. This time the narrator does not seem to have asked one too many questions, but is instead listening quietly, when out of the blue Dame Studie arrives with a tirade of abuse:

> She was wonderly wroth that Wit me thus taught,
> And al starynge Dame Studie sterneliche seide.
>   'Wel artow wis*', quod she to Wit, 'any wisdomes to telle   *clever*
> To flatereres or to fooles that frenetike ben of wittes!'—
> And blamed hym and banned* hym and bad hym be stille—   *reproached*
> 'With swiche wise wordes to wissen* any sottes!'   *teach* (B.10.3–8)

In the long and colourful speech that follows, Studie silences Wit, implies that the narrator is unworthy to be taught, critiques the abuse of learning and attacks over-subtle intellectualism, concluding with a jibe at people who want to know it all:

> 'And tho that useth thise havylons* to ablende* mennes wittes   *tricks; blind*
> What is Dowel fro Dobet, now deef mote he worthe*—   *become*
> Siththe he wilneth to wite whiche thei ben alle—
> But if he live in the lif that longeth to Dowel!'   (B.10.131–4)

---

[39] Davlin, 'Kynde Knowyng', 11–12.

What do we make of this, given that this time the narrator has not said anything at all? Once again we find ourselves at the difficult-to-read scene of pastoral care. What Studie's words seem to introduce this time is the spectre of a different hidden vice: lazy listening masquerading as dutiful attention, a new version of the assumption that knowledge is the answer.

Like Holi Chirche, Studie startles Wit and the narrator with some entirely counter-intuitive words. The shock, rudeness and bizarre humour of her speech introduce what we can now see is the crucial element of epistemological rupture into the pastoral scene, forcing the narrator to think again, to listen harder—but also to ask better. Wit backs Studie up by refusing to speak further, signalling that the narrator should now ask Studie, but in the right way, that is, desirously, but also humbly, unprescriptively, and non-possessively:

> ... al laughynge he louted* and loked upon Studie   *bowed*
> In signe that I sholde bisechen hire of grace.
>   And whan I was war of his wille, to his wif gan I loute,
> And seide, 'Mercy, madame; youre man shal I worthe*   *become*
>   ... for to werche youre wille the while my lif dureth,
> With that ye kenne me kyndely to knowe what is Dowel'.   (B.10.142–5, 147–8)

In response to this question, formulated in the reformed mode of the eager and open-hearted listener, Studie answers willingly: '"For thi mekenesse, man", quod she ...'.

The later part of the poem continues to explore what it might mean to pursue understanding in the mode of the eager asker and the patient listener. In B.13–18 *Piers Plowman* is increasingly marked by emotive, experiential, typological, and even seemingly grace-given visionary forms.[40] Something of this is reflected in the changing forms of asking and listening that we now see, which seem to be both newly inspirational and receptive. Interestingly, several of the narrator's responses (both his questions and his reactions to what he has heard) now also have the quality of a non-sequitur. Above, I noted how the poem's teachers use the non-sequitur to refuse the forms of coherence that characterise knowledge; but now, as the responses of those being taught also take on this quality, Langland again points to the sorts of understanding that derive not from the coherence of knowledge, but from the less easily accessible workings of the mind, perhaps from grace itself.

My first example relates to the second term of my pair, listening. At the end of B.11, the narrator wakes out of a series of encounters with the sources of revealed and natural understanding, Clergie, Scripture, and the visions of Kynde. As he thinks, mentally talking to himself ('thanne seide I to myself'), he has exactly the kind of unexpected insight that suggests the obscure workings of the mind:

> And thanne seide I to myself, and chydde that tyme*,   *chided myself*
> 'Now I woot what Dowel is', quod I, 'by deere God, as me thynketh!'
> And as I caste up myne eighen, oon loked on me and asked
> Of me, what thyng it were? 'Ywis*, sire', I seyde;   *for sure*
> 'To se muche and suffre moore, certes', quod I, 'is Dowel'.   (B.11.406–10)

It is probably no coincidence that, as the narrator articulates this thought about the necessarily tentative nature of listening, his interlocutor is the very provisional power Ymaginatif. The narrator's words here, 'To se muche and suffre moore', are one endpoint of a set of ideas about nature as the site of experience but also suffering that Langland has been developing

---

[40] See Simpson, *Piers Plowman*, 152; Zeeman, *Piers Plowman*, 264; Gruenler, *Piers Plowman*, 285.

388 MEDIEVAL POETRY: 1100–1400

in the previous *passūs*. In his collocation of 'seeing and suffering', the verb 'to se' seems to denote not just visual perception but also natural experience more generally, while the verb '[to] suffre' denotes to 'allow' or 'undergo', but also to 'be patient' and to 'be silent'.[41] Both here and in the long speech about the relative value of the teachings of *clergie* and *kynde* that follows, moreover, Ymaginatif makes clear that the collocation 'seeing and suffering' includes the act of listening:

> 'Haddestow* suffred', he seide, 'slepyng tho thow were,   *if you had*
> Thow sholdest have knowen that Clergie kan* and conceyved   *knows*
>   moore thorugh Reson'.   (B.11.411–12)

Also a mode of listening, then, 'seeing and suffering' is a form of attention that is neither completist nor possessive—one that is keen but also patient, open to nature but also to grace. When Ymaginatif concludes, the narrator is again left deep in thought ('I lay doun longe in this thoght', B.13.21).

This, I suggest, is the 'thinkerly', open-hearted listening that is the necessary counterpart to asking in the poem. It is, in fact, similar to a spiritual attitude that is repeatedly illustrated in the later climactic visions of the poem, especially at the crucifixion and the harrowing of hell. As the light that is Christ approaches across the landscape of hell, for example, the 'four daughters of God' (Truthe, Mercy, Rightwisnesse and Pees) stand arguing and questioning each other about what is happening; finally Truthe tells the others, 'Suffre we! ... I here and see bothe / A spirit speketh to helle ...' (B.18.260–1). This is the 'allowing' kind of seeing and listening that the poem demands of its protagonists and that Langland asks of his reader.

And what about the evolving forms of asking in this later part of the poem? Asking comes to the fore in two echoic passages in B.14–15; although one of these passages does not involve the narrator, their similarity shows Langland returning to structures that may be important to him. In each case Langland simulates the scene of hidden thought and the possibility of grace: it appears that the speaker has been listening, and that an insight about something that he cannot fully comprehend has suddenly formed in his mind. In each case, however, this insight takes the form of a startling non-sequitur and is articulated as a question.

The first passage occurs in the dialogue between Conscience, Patience, and Haukyn, the 'active man'. Patience has been discoursing on penance, contrition, confession, and satisfaction, when suddenly Haukyn interjects:

> 'Where wonyeth Charite? ... I wiste nevere in my lyve
> Man that with hym spak, as wide as I have passed'. (B.14.97–8)

It is of course a Pauline commonplace that human actions (including penance) mean nothing if not motivated by love (1 Corinthians 13.1–3). What makes this moment extraordinary is the way that, even though Patience has not actually mentioned love, Haukyn suddenly apprehends its relevance.[42] Equally extraordinary is the fact that Haukyn's apprehension takes the form of a question, simultaneously suggesting eagerness, openness, and deferral. These effects are reinforced as Haukyn goes on to speak of his uncertainty and wonder about

---

[41] See Zeeman, *Piers Plowman*, 157–200, 267–83; also *Middle English Dictionary*, 'sufferen' v 4–7.

[42] On the 'dramatic value' of related, albeit different, lines in the C-text, see William Langland, in Derek Pearsall (ed.), *Piers Plowman: A New Annotated Edition of the C-text* (Exeter, 2008), note to C.15.272.]

what *charite* is or where it might be: 'I wiste nevere in my lyve / Man that with hym spak'. There are some forms of understanding that are best articulated in the mode of asking. As Patience obligingly replies, 'Ther parfit truthe and poore herte is, and pacience of tonge ...' (see 1 Corinthians 13.4–7), it transpires that Patience and Haukyn are between them 'speaking Corinthians'. Langland has turned Paul's sermon into a dialogue, or antiphon,[43] of discovery.

If there were any doubt about the work of the question here, it is confirmed in the following *passūs*. This time Anima is talking about clerical corruption, the abuse of goods and alms giving; almost by chance, it seems, he pauses on a reference to 'parfit charite', at which point the narrator now suddenly exclaims, 'What is charite?' Once again, these words reveal understanding, but understanding marked as having the quality of a question. Anima replies by alluding to Christ's words on coming as a child to the kingdom of heaven (Matthew 18.3), which then stimulates the narrator both to another question and to a statement of wonder that could also have been a question:

> ... 'A childissh thyng', he seide—
> '*Nisi efficiamini sicut parvuli, non intrabitis in regnum celorum*—
> Withouten fauntelte* or folie a fre* liberal wille'.   *childishness; generous*
>   'Where sholde men fynde swich a frend with so fre an herte?
> I have lyved in londe', quod I, 'my name is Longe Wille—
> And fond I nevere ful charite, bifore ne bihynde'.[44]

Although the narrator has never fully seen *charite*, and is not sure what it is or where it might be, like Haukyn, he has read the signs and begins to grasp something of it. His use of the language of asking and thinking signals desire, humility, but also a kind of deferral. In the following lines of this famous passage, the narrator internalises Anima's description of the soul as 'a fre liberal wille', naming himself 'Longe Wille', in what has been interpreted as a historically and theologically punning reference to the poet's own name.[45] But once again, he and Anima are also 'talking Paul' in the forms of question and answer, and the narrator is now contributing as much as Anima. Referencing 'charite that Poul preiseth best and moost plesaunt to Oure Saveour', the narrator replays a version of 1 Corinthians 13.12 as he speaks of looking into himself and seeing, however obscurely, Christ:

> Clerkes kenne me that Crist is in alle places;
> Ac I seigh hym nevere soothly but as myself in a mirour:
> *Hic in enigmate, tunc facie ad faciem.*[46]

Although this reference to the Pauline 'enigma' does not actually take the form of a question, its meditative, half-seeing form means that, implicitly, it acts as one. We begin to see how close wondering and asking are to listening, seeing and suffering. Of course, they are not the

---

[43] I thank Graham Caie for this suggestion.

[44] B.15.149–53; Matthew 18.3, 'Unless you are converted and become as little children, you shall not enter the kingdom of heaven'.

[45] See Middleton, 'William Langland's "Kynde Name"'.

[46] B.15.161–2a, 'We see now through a glass in a dark manner [in an enigma], but then face to face'. On this passage, see James Simpson, '"Et vidit deus cogitationes eorum": A Parallel Instance and Possible Source for Langland's Use of a Biblical Formula at *Piers Plowman* B.XV.200a', *Notes & Queries*, n.s. 31, 231 (1986), 9–13; on this and the equivalent (but changed) C-text passage, Cervone, *Poetics of the Incarnation*, 26–31; Gruenler, *Piers Plowman*, 286–95.

390   MEDIEVAL POETRY: 1100–1400

same; but Langland's 'dialectical' point may at the very least be that each has to be performed in the spirit of the other.

At the Tree

In conclusion I return to the tree of *charite*. One of the most visionary sequences of the poem, this is another scene cast in the transforming modes of asking and listening. In its opening lines, the narrator once again addresses uncertain and question-like words to Anima, recalling his earlier 'What is charite?': 'Ac yit I am in a weer what charite is to mene' (B.16.3). As ever in *Piers Plowman*, we are in the pastoral scene, so Anima obliges by explaining about a figural tree on which the 'apples' of *charite* grow; the dreamer then expresses a desire to see the tree and taste its fruit, asking another question:

> 'I wolde travaille', quod I, 'this tree to se, twenty hundred myle,
> And to have my fulle of that fruyt forsake al other saulee*.   *food*
> Lord!' quod I, 'if any wight wite whiderout it groweth?'   (B.16.10–12)

In response, Anima explains more, concluding with the observation that care of the tree is overseen by Piers Plowman. To this, the narrator responds with the kind of unadorned exclamation that in *Piers Plowman* is a signal of hidden thought, dawning insight and the possibility of grace:

> 'Piers the Plowman!' quod I tho, and al for pure joye
> That I herde nempne* his name anoon I swowned after,   *speak*
> And lay longe in a love-dreem; and at the laste me thoughte
> That Piers the Plowman al the place me shewed,
> And bad me toten* on the tree ...   *look* (B.16.18–22)

This swoon has always been taken as an expression of intense desire, but it is also an extreme version of 'seeing and suffering'. The narrator then 'lies long' without speaking and in a state of desirous alertness, until Piers Plowman appears to show him the tree.[47]

At this point, asking begins again. The narrator requests that Piers tell him about the trinitarian piles that sustain the tree, and Piers explains at some length; unsatisfied, the narrator asks for more details in a language that once again sounds suspiciously preoccupied with knowing: 'Ac I have thoughtes a threve [bundle] of thise thre piles— / In what wode thei woxen, and where that thei growed ...' (B.16.55–6). Piers's response is measured, but he also makes clear the distinction between useful pastoral teaching and knowledge pursued for its own sake, quietening the narrator with a sharp look:[48]

> 'That is sooth', seide Piers, 'so it may befalle.
> I shal telle thee as tid* what this tree highte*.   *at once; is called*
> The ground ther it growth, goodnesse it hatte;
> And I have tolde thee what highte the tree: the Trinite it meneth'—
> And egreliche* he loked on me, and therfore I spared   *sharply*
> To asken hym any moore therof ...   (B.16.60–6)

---

[47] On this scene, see Salter, *Piers Plowman*, 73–6; Aers, *Piers Plowman*, 89–109; Ralph Hanna, 'The Tree of Charity—Again', in John A. Burrow and Hoyt Duggan (eds), *Medieval Alliterative Poetry: Essays in Honour of Thorlac Turville-Petre* (Dublin, 2010), 125–39.

[48] It is no coincidence that the exchange pivots on the difficult theology of the Trinity, which priests were discouraged from discussing in detail with parishioners (see Zeeman, *Piers Plowman*, 203–4).

In response to Piers's firm gesture, the narrator now asks about tree's fruit and, once more, Piers replies.

Finally the narrator makes a surprising request:

> I preide Piers to pulle adoun an appul, and* he wolde,   *if*
> And suffre me to assaien what savour it hadde.   (B.16.74–5)

It is a request that repeats the narrator's earlier expression of his desire 'this tree to se ... And to have my fulle of that fruyt'; it almost certainly represents another version of the desire to 'see and suffer', that allowing and receptive form of encounter that is for Langland the necessary companion to eager asking. Although these words report a request for knowledge (and are thus a version of the question), they are also formulated in transforming figural terms. The words have long been recognised as an allusion to Augustinian sapiential understanding, due to the etymology whereby the Latin term *sapientia* ('wisdom') was understood to allude to the Latin verb *sapere* ('to taste'), making *sapientia* a 'tasted'—that is, internalised and loving—form of understanding.[49] But whereas elsewhere the narrator's pursuit of *sapientia* has been formulated in recognisably epistemological terms, here the physical and experiential figures of 'eating' and 'tasting' have become the dominant mode of diegesis (anticipating Christ's loving 'thirst' for experience and humanity at the crucifixion). This recasting of the pursuit of understanding in terms of ingestion reformulates the pursuit of understanding metaphorically, placing the usual notions of knowledge under erasure; it also describes that pursuit less as an act of conceptual grasping than as a desire for experience undergone and internalised.

The fact that at a narrative level the request to taste the apples is not fulfilled (the narrator never tastes an apple) means that it is just one more of the poem's many askings without answers. At another level, of course, the request is answered by the narrative that follows, but in transformed terms. In this respect what happens here is analogous to the way that in B.5 Piers Plowman's description of the journey to Truthe ended with Truthe 'sitt[ing] in thyn herte', or the way that in B.6 Piers' plans for pilgrimage turned out to be already taking place with Piers as a 'pilgrym atte plow' on the half acre (see above, pp. 379–80). Here at the tree of *charite*, in response to the narrator's request to taste the apples, Piers shakes the tree and the apples fall to the ground; the devil picks them up and carries them off to his 'hoord *in Limbo Inferni*'; Piers throws the 'pile' of the second person of the Trinity after him. The narrator's desire to know *charite*, in other words, has resulted in a replay of the Fall, but also in the first intimations of Christ's coming. Like many such passages in *Piers Plowman*, these are answers whose surprising formulations and mysterious matter always beg more questions. The only response must be to ask, but also to listen, which is what the poet demands of his reader.

---

[49] See Davlin, '*Kynde Knowyng*'; Zeeman, *Piers Plowman*, 2.

25

The *Gawain*-Poet

Helen Cooper

The *Gawain*-poet was a latecomer to the hall of fame of Middle English poets. To the fifteenth and sixteenth centuries, the triumvirate of Chaucer, Gower, and Lydgate were the poets who mattered, and of those, the monk Lydgate largely dropped out after the Reformation. Langland's *Piers Plowman* was printed at around the same time as Lydgate was disappearing, but it never achieved the fame or the popularity of the others. The *Gawain*-poet, by contrast, remained unknown until he was rediscovered in the nineteenth century, and it was the mid-twentieth before a full critical appreciation of his work began. His current high status, with a place assigned to him on almost every Middle English syllabus and a plethora of translations of *Gawain* itself, has emerged only since the mid-twentieth century, and it has transformed our sense of the map of fourteenth-century literature and what it could achieve.[1]

There are good reasons for his long obscurity. The four poems ascribed to him, *Sir Gawain and the Green Knight*, *Pearl*, *Patience*, and *Cleanness*, are preserved in a single manuscript, London, British Library, MS Cotton Nero A.x, and were neither recopied (so far as we know) nor printed. The titles are all editorial: in the manuscript, the texts simply start with the first line. They are written in a north-west Midlands dialect significantly different from the east Midland/London dialect of Chaucer, Gower, and Lydgate that was the direct ancestor of modern English. The poet drew on a wide vocabulary that was non-standard even for his own dialect area, but whereas Chaucer often provides the first usage in English of words that have become commonplace elements of the language, the *Gawain*-poet is likely to offer the last or near-last appearance of words that were already passing out of use, often because they belonged to a lexis associated with forms of poetry that were fast disappearing.[2] And whereas Chaucer wrote in the poetic forms deriving from French and Anglo-Norman, forms that rhymed and scanned in ways that became the norm for later poets, the *Gawain*-poet's choice of alliterative verse became rare in England over the fifteenth century (it survived longer in Scotland). An appreciation of his remarkable poetic skill, in other words, had to fight the combined effects of inaccessibility, linguistic obscurity, and formal unfamiliarity before it could be recognised.

---

[1] The edition used here is that by Ad Putter and Myra Stokes (eds), *The Works of the Gawain Poet: Pearl, Cleanness, Patience, Sir Gawain and the Green Knight* (London, 2014); this modernises the thorns and yoghs and a number of the spellings preserved in many editions, both for ease of comprehension and for metrical reasons. It also provides a comprehensive commentary, including generous information on sources and linguistic and metrical features. My thanks to Ad Putter for his comments on this chapter.

[2] See Thorlac Turville-Petre, *The Alliterative Revival* (Cambridge, 1977), 70–80.

Helen Cooper, *The Gawain-Poet*. In: *The Oxford History of Poetry in English*. Edited by Helen Cooper and Robert R. Edwards, Oxford University Press. © Helen Cooper (2023). DOI: 10.1093/oso/9780198827429.003.0025

The Poet and the Poems

Nothing is known about the *Gawain*-poet beyond what can be inferred from his work. It is not even certain that the four poems uniquely contained in the Cotton manuscript were all written by a single poet, or that he did not write other work as well.[3] Manuscripts most often contained the work of multiple authors, but the presence together of these poems nonetheless signals some kind of association, as does their common dialect, their high poetic quality, and a number of shared interests across the three religious poems as well as *Sir Gawain*.[4] On the evidence of such details as dress (especially in *Pearl*) and armour (in *Gawain*) they all also seem likely to have been written around the same time, towards the end of the fourteenth century. These details are found not only in the texts themselves, but in the full-page (and rather crude) illustrations that accompany them:[5] an unusual feature of anglophone manuscripts, where decoration is normally limited to some elaborate penwork or on occasion small individual pictures at the start of a text (the Ellesmere manuscript of the *Canterbury Tales* would be the best known example; the Auchinleck manuscript also once contained a number, now largely destroyed; the programme of illustration for the Corpus Christi manuscript of *Troilus and Criseyde* never got beyond the frontispiece). There are twelve of these illustrations in the *Gawain* manuscript, appearing at the beginning or end of each text: four each for *Pearl* and *Gawain*, two for *Cleanness*, and two (one of them of half a page) for *Patience*.

There is general agreement that the language of the poems is rooted in south-east Cheshire, near the Staffordshire border, though the dialect of the scribe of the manuscript may not exactly match the poet's own. He had a good knowledge of the Bible, which is generously on display in the three religious poems and shows he had some Latin education (which would confirm that he was indeed male), whether through a monastic or cathedral school or conceivably a university. He also had an acquaintance with a number of French works including the *Roman de la Rose*, part of the prose *Lancelot*, and the *Travels* of Sir John Mandeville, itself composed not long before the Cotton Nero poems and claiming to have been written by an Englishman. In addition, *Gawain* shows a broad general acquaintance with French Arthurian romance, including a number of analogues, possibly sources, for elements of its plot.[6] These texts were available in England, but the detailed lists of ships' tackle in *Cleanness* and *Patience*, which go well beyond the mast, rudder, sail, and oar recurrent in other texts, might suggest that he had travelled at least across the Channel. The poems encompass both religious and courtly material—or, in *Pearl* and *Cleanness*, an inextricable mixture of the two; but on the basis of his account of *listening* to sermons at the opening of *Patience*, he seems not to have been ordained himself. If *Pearl* is indeed an elegy on the death of his infant daughter, that too would militate against the idea that he was in religious orders. Latin education beyond the most basic provided some training in formal rhetoric, but that is barely identifiable: his vivid portraits of the Pearl maiden and the Green Knight fail to follow the Latin rules prescribed for *effictio*, formal description, whether or

---

[3] *St Erkenwald*, another high-quality alliterative poem of comparable date and dialect area, preserved in London, British Library, MS Harley 2250, is the main contender. This recounts a legend concerning the discovery of an uncorrupted pagan corpse during the building of St Paul's Cathedral.

[4] See further A. C. Spearing, *The Gawain-Poet: A Critical Study* (Cambridge, 1970), 32–40; and Chapter 9 in this volume.

[5] Digital reproductions are available on the British Library website. An informative website is under construction at http://gawain.ucalgary.ca.

[6] See Ad Putter, *Sir Gawain and the Green Knight and French Arthurian Romance* (Oxford, 1995).

394 MEDIEVAL POETRY: 1100–1400

not he knew about them. The ability to move inside different minds was valued in Latin, as witnessed by the indications of voicing in some manuscripts for reading aloud Dido's lament in the *Aeneid*, and by the school requirement to practise composition written from such subject positions;[7] but even when *Gawain* deploys omniscient narration, as in many of the landscape descriptions, they carry the cinematographic immediacy of a subjective eye behind the camera, conveying a strong sense of spatial awareness from wide-angle to close-up.[8] Beyond that, as Sarah Stanbury notes, 'description becomes a powerful narrative tool for dramatizing the limitations of human experience'[9]—a technique that goes well beyond formal rhetorical training. More suggestive for the poet's educational background is the interest in the number of lines and stanzas expressed in *Pearl* and *Gawain*. This kind of numbering gets no mention in the *artes poeticae*, the ideas of harmony and proportion they encode being of importance rather in arithmetic and music.[10] Such numbers were therefore tangential to rhetoric, though their use could suggest a degree of sophistication and learning in both poet and patron, or at least in some of the audience, that the bare numbers might not now indicate. Education, however, can only go so far in explaining the poet's exceptional skills, however much it may have helped to hone them. These derive more from an acute linguistic sense; an ear for sound and stress; an alertness to narratological possibilities, not least chiastic mirror structures and focalisation; and a deep understanding of the best qualities in other alliterative poems.

A number of possible identities have been suggested for the poet, though none has moved up from the possible to the probable.[11] Similarly, although various patrons have been proposed, nothing can be proved.[12] It may be more illuminating for understanding the poet's work to think about the contemporary intellectual and literary context provided by the area around Cheshire. The region had a vibrant literary culture, with strong links to the royal court and a steady procession of military personnel into the English-dominated areas of France: it was not a provincial backwater. A diocesan, baronial, or cultured gentry household could have provided a congenial milieu for both his religious and secular poetry. In the previous generation, though probably overlapping into the *Gawain*-poet's lifetime, a monk of the monastery of St Werburgh's in Chester, Ranulph Higden (d. 1364), composed the widely disseminated chronicle the *Polychronicon*. Nearer contemporaries of the poet, of the kind who might have acted as occasional patrons or indeed employed the poet in their households, included men such as Richard Scrope, a Yorkshireman from a baronial family active in the royal service. He became, first, bishop of Lichfield, the diocese that included Staffordshire and Cheshire, and where lavish celebrations were held for Richard II when

---

[7] Most fully explored by Marjorie Curry Woods, *Weeping for Dido: The Classics in the Medieval Classroom* (Princeton, NJ, 2019).

[8] The comparison, first made by Alan Renoir, has been universally noted since; see in particular Sarah Stanbury, *Seeing the Gawain-Poet: Description and the Act of Perception* (Philadelphia, PA, 1991), 99, 104–7.

[9] Stanbury, *Seeing the Gawain-Poet*, 4.

[10] Although number symbolism was of key importance for biblical interpretation and was explicated in the commentaries, and units larger than the line might be both numbered and significant (most famously in the *Divine Comedy*), numbers of lines are not mentioned as a principle in any of the handbooks of poetics. A few Latin poets did count their lines (see E. R. Curtius, *European Literature and the Latin Middle Ages*, trans. Willard R. Trask [London, 1953], 506–9), but vernacular evidence is much harder to come by. Proportion, rather than counting, was central to Boethius's treatise on arithmetic, widely disseminated as a textbook: see Michael Masi, *Boethian Number Theory* (Amsterdam, 1983). My thanks to Mary Carruthers for guidance.

[11] See the survey by Malcolm Andrew, 'Theories of Authorship', in Derek Brewer and Jonathan Gibson (eds), *A Companion to the Gawain-Poet* (Cambridge, 1997), 23–33; hypotheses have not moved on much since then.

[12] Michael J. Bennett gives a wide survey of possible patrons in 'The Historical Background', in Brewer and Gibson (eds), *Companion*, 71–90. John M. Bowers argues for a context in the royal court in *The Politics of Pearl: Court Poetry in the Age of Richard II* (Cambridge, 2001).

he stayed at the bishop's palace for Christmas and New Year in 1397–8 and 1398–9; and then archbishop of York. He was involved in diplomatic missions to Scotland and Rome before his participation in the Northern Rising of 1405 led to his execution, carried out at his request with five blows of the axe in honour of the five wounds of Christ—one of the fives memorialised in Gawain's pentangle (*Gawain* 642–3).[13] The poet makes mention at one point of the inconvenience for a servant to have to travel to Rome at the bidding of 'my lege lord' (*Patience* 51), a comment that would fit with an ecclesiastical master, though the remark is not framed as autobiographical. From the lay world, Sir John Stanley (d. 1414) was a leading Cheshireman who achieved high office under Henry IV, including as royal steward and as master forester of three of the great forests of the region. He was made a Knight of the Garter, a fact that could connect with the motto of the Order, 'Honi soit qui mal [y] pense', 'Shame be to him who thinks ill [of it]', appended to the end of *Gawain*. He might have been an early owner, since the motto was added after the rest of the poem was copied; and it is in any case appropriate as an ending for the poem (on which more below). Stanley was a man around whom legends accreted: his father-in-law had supposedly been rescued as a baby from an eagle's nest, and later family tradition asserted that Sir John himself had had an affair with the daughter of the Grand Turk and left her pregnant. He was also reputed to have been killed by the venom of an Irish lampoon while serving as deputy governor of Ireland.[14] Later members of the family were the subjects, perhaps the patrons, of the group of historical Stanley poems: they became, if they were not so already, a family with strong poetic connections.

The Craft of *Pearl*

The *Gawain*-poet's craftsmanship is most comprehensively on display in *Pearl*, where he creates a structure and verse form unique in its demands. The poem is a dream vision in the sense that it starts with the first-person dreamer/speaker falling asleep, and ends with him waking. It follows the pattern of other dream poems in not claiming literal truth for the fact of the dream; but as it progresses, it increasingly takes on the qualities of religious vision, as its account of the New Jerusalem draws directly on the account in Revelation and therefore on a superior biblical truth.

The dream concerns an encounter between the dreamer and a maiden he sees across a river; she is dressed entirely in white, and wears a pearl on her breast. We are given to understand—it is never quite explicit, but it is strongly hinted and makes much the best sense of the poem—that the girl represents the dreamer's infant daughter, who had died before the age of two: it is a premise of all other dream poetry that the first-person speaker is not altogether different from the poet himself. The dreamer is not, however—and again,

---

[13] S.v. Scrope, Richard (c 1350–1405), archbishop of York, in the *Oxford Dictionary of National Biography*, https://www.oxforddnb.com, article by Peter McNiven (2004); on the frequency of Richard's stays at Lichfield, see Nigel Saul, *Richard II* (London, 1997), and Bennett, 'Historical Background', 87, though the especially lavish visit of 1398–9 happened under Scrope's successor. On Lichfield Cathedral as a major centre for the copying of vernacular manuscripts, see Chapter 3 in this volume. Another ecclesiastical figure who is good to think with is the Lancashire Robert Hallum, bishop of Salisbury (d. 1417), who co-commissioned a Latin translation of the *Divine Comedy* at the Council of Constance (*ODNB*, article by R. N. Swanson (2004, updated 2009); he is discussed by Cecilia A. Hatt, *God and the Gawain Poet* (Cambridge, 2015), 228–31, though she concludes that 'it is tempting but probably unwise to speculate' that he was the poet's actual patron.

[14] S.v. Stanley, Sir John (c 1350–1414), *ODNB*, article by Michael J. Bennett (2004), and 'The Stanley Poem' of c 1562, in James Orchard Halliwell (ed.), *The Palatine Anthology* (London, 1850), 208–71. See also Helen Cooper's introduction to Keith Harrison's translation of *Sir Gawain and the Green Knight* (Oxford, 1998), xii–xvii.

396 MEDIEVAL POETRY: 1100–1400

this is a general principle of dream poetry—exactly the same as the poet. The poet is writing with a strategy beyond anything that his speaker sees, and especially after he has entered into the dream—it being part of the experience of dreaming that one does not have a fully rational grasp of its content. It is a crucial element of a dream poem, furthermore, that the dream constitutes a learning process for the dreamer, and through him for the audience. The poet will therefore be implicitly addressing his audience over the head of his dreamer, who as a consequence will necessarily be a less impressive or knowledgeable figure than the poet—whose spokesperson within the poem is therefore typically, as here, not the first-person dreamer but the work's authority figure. Here, it is the maiden who expresses the message the poet wants to get across; but the restriction to the dreamer's point of view means that the audience learns with him, or only slightly ahead.[15] By the end of the dream, the initially earthbound dreamer has absorbed enough of the maiden's teaching for him to be allowed a vision of the New Jerusalem. When he wakes, the naïve dreamer, the narrating voice recounting the dream, and the poet have come closer together—perhaps even amalgamated—in a process foreshadowed only in a single line at the start, on the comfort offered by the 'kynde of Cryst' (55).

This is all carried through in a *tour de force* of poetics unparalleled in the rest of the manuscript. The work is written in twelve-line stanzas, each with just three rhymes, *ababababbcbc*, which the poet further complicates by grouping the stanzas into sets of five with a slightly varying refrain line but using the identical c-rhyme across each set. Twelve, representing totality or the perfect number, takes on key importance later in the poem as the basis of the New Jerusalem; that there is an extra stanza in one set gives a total of 1,212 lines in 101 stanzas. The stanzas are copied continuously and without numbers for either the groups or the lines, but the first line of each new section is given a slightly larger initial. Each refrain line, furthermore, is linked to the first line of the next stanza in a process of concatenation (from Latin *catena*, chain) though often with a shift in the meaning of the words. The first verse will illustrate the process, as the key word 'spot' in the refrain line is given a different meaning in the following first-line repetition, from 'spot' as mark or blemish to 'spot' as place:

Perle, plesaunte to prynces pay*	*pleasure*
To clanly clos* in golde so clere—	*purely set*
Out of orient, I hardily say,	
Ne proved* I never her precios pere:*	*met with; equal*
So rounde, so reken* in uch aray,	*fair*
So smal,* so smothe her sides were,	*slender*
Wheresoever I jugged gemmes gay,	
I set her sengeley* in synglere.*	*apart; as unique*
Alas, I lest hyr in an erbere;*	*garden*
Thurgh gresse to grounde hit fro me yot*.	*went*
I dewyne,* fordolked* of luf-daungere	*waste away; badly wounded*
Of that privy* perle withouten spot.	*my own/hidden*
Syn in that spot hit fro me sprang ...	(1–13)

That complexity of rhyme is further elaborated by complexity of alliteration. The poem is not in alliterative metre—it is in four-stress approximately iambic lines, though with the

---

[15] Stanbury's *Seeing the Gawain-Poet* gives a comprehensive analysis of focalisation.

kind of freedom of exactly where the stresses are placed of the sort found throughout the history of poetry in English—but it none the less deploys alliteration generously: here, the very first line alliterates on all four of its stressed syllables, the next five lines on three (h- words, as in the third line, alliterating with all vowels), others on just two. While the basic groups of stanzas provide the structure, the alliteration is not itself structural in the way that it is in the poems in alliterative metre. It functions here rather as decorative elaboration, though it is far from being merely ornamental. The whole poem has an emblematic form as well as a prosodic one, set by its twelves and by the key word 'pearl'. In its primary meaning, the pearl is a jewel, and the jewelled quality of the verse, given substance in the landscapes of the poem, is designed to enhance and embody that. The roundness of the pearl that is stressed in this first stanza is also carried through to the very last, which ends by linking back to the first line:

> And precious perles unto His pay. (1212)

The concatenation is not finally just sequential, but binds the ending back to the start in a circular movement—though the sense of the words has changed so much along the way that it becomes quite hard, in reading this final stanza, to remember their original more limited meaning.

That circularity of emblematic structure is echoed in the chiastic symmetry of its content. The groups of five stanzas can themselves be paired up with each other from each end of the poem. The first and last sections present the dreamer awake; the three within those (II–IV, XVII–XIX) contain the descriptions of the paradisal landscape and the New Jerusalem; and the central twelve recount the debate between the dreamer and the maiden. There is more going on than circularity alone, however, for despite the similarities of the beginning and end of the poem, there has been a transformation in the course of it, measured by the changing meanings of 'pearl' across the poem. In the first few lines it appears to be a jewel, though the terms in which it is described, together with the feminine associations of the vocabulary—'So smal, so smothe her sydes were'—are already suggesting that the gem is a metaphor for a girl or young woman. 'Luf-daungere' too is a term borrowed in from secular love—specifically, courtly secular love, in so far as the French term 'daunger', hostile control, was used in erotic contexts in the sense of disdain, but here, as is revealed only later, for death. This meaning begins to emerge towards the end of this first section, as the loss of the pearl in the earth in turn redefines the mound on which the speaker falls asleep as her grave. Increasingly through the work, such transformations are focused through the refrain lines, where the pressure of repetition finally breaks through from an earthly to a spiritual meaning in a kind of transcendental code-switching (the shift from Jerusalem as an earthly city to the New Jerusalem is an especially clear example). So too the pearl is refigured across the poem to move it away from its material meaning towards the heavenly. The gem of the opening becomes the soul of the maiden herself (253); by way of the parable of the pearl of great price that is worth all a merchant's earthly goods (Matthew 13.45–6), the pearl on her breast comes to symbolise the purity of the saved soul, cleansed in the blood of a thoroughly metaphorical lamb, and ultimately the kingdom of heaven. In parallel with that movement, the earthly prince of the poem's first line is transformed by the end into Christ, the prince of heaven.

Initially, the dreamer does not understand the transformations that the language and imagery undergo, but the process of the poem shows a parallel transformation in his own comprehension. The garden in which he falls asleep is an earthly one, filled with appeals

398   MEDIEVAL POETRY: 1100–1400

to the lower, physical senses, smell in the odour of its flowers and taste through its spices, contrasting with touch in the 'colde' of his grief; but it is also subject to time and mortality— the poem is set not in the dream season of spring of the *Roman de la rose*, but at harvest, 'when corne is corven with crokes kene' (40). The paradisal landscape of his dream offers wider vistas with cliffs and a river, paralleling his release from the misery that had tied him to the 'spot' of the garden. It is moreover outside any earthly seasonal and organic change; the birds are flame-coloured, the trunks of the trees are blue and the leaves of polished silver. The appeal here is to the higher, more spiritual, senses of sight and hearing. The dominant verbal figure for conveying the wonder of this is what one might call the *dis*simile, what things are *not* like: tapestries come nowhere near its richness, the sunbeams are dark by comparison with the intensity of the light, the joy of the birdsong is beyond imagination, and the dreamer's mood accordingly shifts to one of joy and bliss (126–8).

The dreamer has to be educated in this new imagery and language by the maiden he sees on the other side of the river. Initially, the gulf between them is at its greatest. He recognises her as the pearl he has lost, but she rebukes him for his belief that what he is seeing is in any material sense actually there (295–302): he only imagines that he is really seeing her, her earthly form was mortal, and she now belongs to Christ. He is devastated, described in idiomatically simple lines that capture in miniature his shock and bewilderment:

> When we departed, we were at one;
> God forbede we be now wrothe,
> We meten so selden by stok or stone. (378–80)

He has to learn some tough lessons across the course of the dream: that earthly love is inadequate; that an infant (a female one at that) can become his teacher; that her brief life can give her a right to salvation that no length of life, however well lived, can match; and that his ideas of what is fair have to be completely rethought in this new divine world, a paradoxical point made through her exposition of the parable of the labourers in the vineyard who are all paid the same no matter how many hours they have worked. It takes the long debate between them—a debate in which she increasingly takes the larger part as he learns to stay quiet and listen—before he can begin even to understand what she is saying. To start with, they are speaking different languages: his, earthly and largely literal; hers, the language of God as given in the Bible, where spiritual and figurative senses dominate. So the Lamb is not a lamb, a queen carries no sense of earthly hierarchy, courtesy (like 'daungere', a word borrowed into English from the courtly register of French) is a matter of mutual love without distinction of rank, and the pearl is something radically other than a pearl. Even the 'more' and 'less' of earthly comparison are absorbed into the overwhelming greatness of the grace of God—an idea again given emblematic form as it is the section with the refrain phrase 'never the less' (XV) that contains six stanzas rather than the usual five.

This process presents something of a dilemma for ending the poem. It has moved away so decisively in many respects from its earthly grounding as to risk leaving the mortal first-person and his readers with no point of contact. The emotional human point of view has kept clashing with the spiritual, in the dreamer's initial bewilderment or the resentment of the workers in the vineyard in being cheated, as they see it, out of their proper wages; but the human is allowed to return at the end, and without that level of condemnation. When the dreamer sees his 'little quene', laden ('laste and lade') with life and having fun ('mirthe') among her companions in the procession in the heavenly Jerusalem (1146–50), he is so carried away with delight and 'luf-longing' that he attempts to jump into the river—and wakes up. It is very easy to condemn him, and many readers do—indeed he recognises that it was against God's will; but quite apart from its being a brilliantly conceived way to wake, it also makes the point that there comes a moment when the human mind can take no more: 'My manes mynde to madding malt' (1154), melted into madness. The combination of the child and the Lamb together are too much for him; but that does not therefore mean that he is simply wrong. Fallibility is inseparable from being human:

> Aye wolde man of hap* more hent*   *happiness; seize*
> Then myght by right upon hem clyven.*   *belong to* (1195–6)

Back in the waking world, he is still grieving, but for the loss of that sight of the Lamb rather than just for the death of his child. Humankind, moreover—and the poem's shift to the plural 'us' is important, as the work extends out for the first time from the 'I' of the dreamer to all of its audience, potentially all of the Christian world—has the consolation of seeing Christ every day in the transubstantiation of the Host in the Mass. It ends with a prayer that 'we' too may become Christ's 'homly hyne', household labourers, in a Germanic-derived phrase far from the courtly register of heaven, but which also opens out into the transformation of those servants into saved souls, precious pearls.

Homiletic Style: *Cleanness* and *Patience*

Pearl is followed in the manuscript by the two homiletic poems *Cleanness* and *Patience*. These form a pair: both are written in standard alliterative lines without stanza division, though the syntax and the placing of the larger capitals that mark significant shifts in the narrative (and possibly also small marks in the manuscript) apparently indicate a grouping of the lines into fours, and some editions print them accordingly. Both poems present themselves as an exposition of one or more of the Beatitudes (Matthew 5.3–12). *Patience* concentrates on two, 'Blessed are the poor in spirit' and 'Blessed are they that suffer persecution [*patiuntur*] for justice's sake',[16] though the Latin word is developed across the poem in its broader sense of suffering, and therefore of having to put up with whatever your earthly or divine lord sends you. The narrating voice—and again, the lines carry an assumption, but no proof, of autobiographical experience—claims that he has to embrace the exemplary ladies Dame Poverty and Dame Patience, and suffer in silence. *Cleanness* selects a single Beatitude, 'Blessed are the clean of heart [the Authorised Version reads "pure of heart"], for they shall see God':

> The hathel* clene of his hert   hapenes ful fayre,*   *man; is blessed*
> For he schal loke on our Lord   with a love-chere. (27–8)

Both poems then expound their chosen virtues through negative biblical examples: on the need for patience in the face of suffering, by retelling the story of Jonah; and on God's requirement for purity, spiritual and ritual as well as physical, principally through the stories of Noah and the Flood, Sodom and Gomorrah, and Belshazzar's feast. Each of these comes with a clearly expressed moral based on what is present in the Hebrew Bible, but without the theological allegories attached to them in medieval biblical commentaries and

---

[16] Translations here and throughout are from the Douai-Rheims version of the Vulgate (repr. Rockford, IL, 1989).

400   MEDIEVAL POETRY: 1100–1400

elsewhere: Jonah's sojourn in the whale's belly, for instance, is not offered as an allegory of Christ's descent into hell, nor the ark represented as a figure for the Church. They are concerned primarily with *quid agas*, how one should act, rather than with doctrine, *quid credas*.

In keeping with the homiletic emphasis, the poems display much less of the rhetorical fireworks found in *Pearl* and *Sir Gawain*. The use of a plain style for teaching had been advised by St Augustine:

> He, then, shall be eloquent, who can say little things in a subdued style, in order to give instruction, moderate things in a temperate style, in order to give pleasure, and great things in a majestic style, in order to sway the mind.[17]

The plain style itself was thus a recognised form of verbal skill. The plainness here shows itself not only in the simpler verse form, based on the line rather than the stanza, but in the choice of words. The poet makes less use of the higher-style French-derived vocabulary associated with the court than in the other poems, and sparer use too of the specialised alliterative poetic diction that marks out *Gawain*: both are present, but they are much less noticeable, and the homiletic poems will run for many lines at a time with scarcely a romance-derived word intruding. When the poet offers greater elaboration, such as in the description of Belshazzar's feast, the shift in language is designed to sway the mind against approval. The king himself is a model of sinful pride:

> Thus in pryde and olipraunce*   his empire he holdes,   *pomp*
> In lust and in lecherye.   (*Cleanness* 1349–50)

And the feast itself, with its guest-list of barons and concubines, its many courses brought in on horseback on richly enamelled silver dishes, and its thirty-seven-line account of the splendour of the vessels looted from the temple in Jerusalem (1452–88), offers a chilling sense by contrast of what moral and ritual pollution looks like. A number of the details, such as the serving of the courses to the accompaniment of trumpets, are replicated in the New Year's celebrations at Arthur's court in *Gawain*, but there the feast is appropriate to the occasion and in keeping with the Christian ritual year; here, it is an act of blasphemy. Elsewhere, in the account of the writing on the wall, the very lack of detail can invoke the uncanny:

> In contrary of the candelstik,   that clerest it schined,
> There apered a paume,*   with poyntel* in fyngres,   *palm; stylus*
> That was grysly and gret,   and grymly he wrytes—
> None other forme bot a fyste,   faylande* the wryste.   *lacking* (*Cleanness* 1532–5)

In the Noah episode, a thick list of all the essential tackle of a ship (mast-step, bowline, capstan, tiller and so on) *not* present in the ark makes the point that God alone is its pilot (417–24). On the sea, Noah and his family have to cede control to Him, while the unclean are drowned.

The sinners of the story are not, however, presented in a way that invites condemnation by the reader. Whatever God may think of them, the poet concentrates not on their vices

---

[17] St Augustine (citing Cicero), *On Christian Doctrine* 4.17, 19, in Philip Schaff (ed.), *Nicene and Post-Nicene Fathers of the Christian Church*, vol. 2, 1st series (repr. Grand Rapids, MI, 1979).

but on what we would now call their humanity. Far from trying to save themselves at others' expense or cursing God, they 'cryed for care' to Him, mothers try to carry their babies to safety, friends agree to die together, and loved ones take leave of each other (378–9, 393, 399–402). When there is outright condemnation of a sin, as happens with the Sodomites when they want Lot to hand over his male guests (actually angels), God's account of their 'fautes the worste'—a description almost inevitable given the cultural context, taken over in the Middle Ages from the Bible—is balanced by His further speech in which He praises faithful heterosexual activity without any of the usual caveats about the superiority of virginity or the obligation to restrict the purposes of sex to procreation, and only the broad ethical term 'honest' to suggest that even marriage might be a good thing:

The play of paramores I portrayed* myselven,—	*devised*
And made therto a maner meriest of other:	
When two true togeder had tyed hemselven,	
Bitwene a male and his make* such mirthe schuld come,	*sexual partner*
Wel negh pure* Paradise myght preve no better,	*i.e., itself*
Elles* thay myght honestly ayther other welde:*	*provided that; act with*
At a stille stollen steven* unstered with* sighte,	*secret time; secreted from*
Luf-lowe* hem bitwene lasched* so hote	*flame of love; burned*
That all the meschefes on mold myght hit not sleke. (700–8)	

To find love 'paramores'—a French term very much not associated with marriage—described in this way in the Middle Ages is unusual; to put the words into the mouth of God, even as a counterbalance to homosexuality, may be unique for the period.

If the God of *Cleanness* takes a hard line on human weakness, *Patience* treats its very imperfect protagonist much more sympathetically.[18] It opens with an apparently autobiographical passage on the narrator's determination to 'play' with poverty and patience, turning them into exemplary friends rather than enemies. After this introduction, the work is divided by larger capitals into four parts, approximating loosely to the four chapters of the Book of Jonah. The first (corresponding to chapter 1) recounts God's command to Jonah to go to Nineveh to preach repentance, his attempt to escape by ship, and the fierce storm that leads the mariners to throw him overboard. The second, with no biblical equivalent, describes what it was like for him to be swallowed by the whale. The third (the biblical chapter 2) contains the canticle he sings to God from within its stomach, and (chapter 3) his preaching to the Ninevites and their repentance. The fourth (chapter 4) tells how he retreats to a hill above the city to watch what happens, and attempts to shade himself with a scrawny shelter of grass; overnight, God sends a woodbine to make him a better arbour, but the next night destroys it, to Jonah's great resentment. He needs God to point out the greater value of the Ninevites whom He has spared over the woodbine He has destroyed.

The poet makes the most stylistically of the various subjects and moods of the narrative. As in *Cleanness*, the more homiletic passages are in plain style, the vocabulary is predominantly Germanic in etymology, and specialised alliterative vocabulary is used without ostentation. There are no rich descriptive French-dominated passages to parallel Belshazzar's feast, but the twenty-eight lines describing the storm (137–64) more than make up for

---

[18] Cathy Hume gives a sympathetic and informative account of the poem, including its sources beyond the Book of Jonah and its similarities to and differences from other Middle English biblical narratives, in her *Middle English Biblical Poetry: Romance, Audience and Tradition* (Cambridge, 2021), 119–45.

402   MEDIEVAL POETRY: 1100–1400

that. Storms at sea are something of a speciality of alliterative poetry;[19] the *Gawain*-poet writes brilliantly on foul weather (in contrast to the usual medieval emphasis on spring), not least here where he makes the most of the heavy stresses basic to alliterative verse:

> Anon out of the north-est   the noyse begins
> When bothe brethes* con blowe   upon blo* wateres;   *contrary winds; dark*
> Rogh rakkes* ther ros   with rudnyng* anunder;   *storm clouds; ruddy*
> The see soughed ful sore,   gret selly* to here.   *wonder* (137–40)

The tackle of the ship on which Jonah travels is described with all the technical detail that is listed as absent from Noah's ark (*Patience* 101–7, 149–53): that is, where the ark lacks all a ship's usual accoutrements since God guides it, Jonah's ship possesses them all but in the storm they prove worse than useless, as the sail is lost, the mast breaks, and the rigging has to be cut loose and cast overboard. In contrast to that, we next have a description of the stink and revoltingness of the whale's guts (274, 279–80). Then, in a transformation of register to the liturgical power of the Vulgate, Jonah's canticle is given as a close translation of Jonah 2.2–10, opening:

> 'Lord, to thee have I cleped   in cares ful stronge.
> Out of the hole thou me herde   of hellene wombe;
> I calde, and thou knew   myn uncler steven.
> Thou diptes me of the depe see   into the dymme herte.
> The gret flem of thy flod   folded me umbe'. (305–9)

'I cried out of my affliction to the Lord, and he heard me: I cried out of the belly of hell, and thou hast heard my voice. And thou hast cast me forth into the deep into the heart of the sea, and a flood hath compassed me'. (Vulgate, Jonah 2.3–4)

Any hint of an allegory of Christ's sojourn in hell has to come from the reader, not the poet, and certainly not from Jonah: an absence that is underlined a few lines later when the prophet's presence in its belly makes the whale feel sick, 'to wamel at his herte' (300).

It is worth pausing on that phrase as illustrating two stylistic features. One is a general one about alliterative poetry: that the structural, and therefore compulsory, element of alliteration makes it hard to identify the intentional use of onomatopoeia or phonic mimesis. 'Wamel' is a wonderfully evocative word, which was perhaps already on its way down into local dialect; but it is hard—just as it is hard in the poet's descriptions of fierce weather, or the sliminess of filth (that Jonah's clothes become 'sluchchede' inside the whale, for instance, 341)—to believe he was not fully aware of the mimetic effects his choice of words could provide. The second feature concerns his handling of point of view. Here, he gives a momentary insight into the whale's own feelings, in a line without precedent in the biblical text. In *Pearl*, the primary opposition of points of view is between the unenlightened dreamer and the maiden, though hers is presented objectively, as is appropriate when her thought processes are those of God. With the exception of the canticle—and that represents a state of mind, and a register, that stands in isolation from the rest of the poem—Jonah occupies a position akin to the dreamer's in *Pearl*, of a man who does not fully understand what is going on. The narrating voice here is that of the homilist, who is looking over Jonah's shoulder and speaking with a voice close to God's, but who is prepared to enter into the prophet's

---

[19] For a survey and analysis, see Nicolas Jacobs, 'Alliterative Storms: A Topos in Middle English', *Speculum*, 47 (1972), 695–719. The centrality of the sea to *Patience* is further discussed in Sebastian Sobecki, *The Sea and Medieval English Literature* (Cambridge, 2008), 119–34.

mind—as happens most comprehensively when Jonah retreats from Nineveh and tries to build himself his shelter. His fury with God when the Ninevites repent, his misery beneath his inadequate booth, his childlike delight in the woodbine that grows up to shade him, and his devastation when it withers are conveyed through his own perceptions and his own voice. He is 'glad of his gay loge', 'so blythe of his wodbynde', that he forgets to be hungry (457–60), and he is correspondingly furious with God for depriving him of 'my wodbynde so wlonk [splendid]' (487)—the possessive pronouns are of course significant. When God responds that the matter is trivial, Jonah is even more cross: 'Hit is not little', but against all justice. God's final message of mercy to sinners is accompanied by His injunction to Jonah, 'Be noght so gryndel' (524), don't get so worked up: in contrast to the *Pearl* dreamer's having to learn God's language, here God speaks in humankind's. The work closes with God's voice and the homilist's delivering a single message, of patience, to Jonah and his audience alike, in a repetition of the opening line: 'That pacience is a noble poynt, thagh hit displese ofte'.

Sir Gawain: Poetic Structures

Sir Gawain shares many of its remarkable poetic skills with the other poems in the Cotton manuscript, but it develops those further, and adds new ones. Its basic prosody is of the *aa/ax* form of the alliterative line, but the poet also divides the lines into irregular stanzas with a five-line bob and wheel (one two-syllable line followed by four three-stress lines rhyming *ababa*), which often summarises the preceding action, utters warnings of what is about to happen, or provides a pause for reflection.[20] The work is further divided by larger capitals into four 'fitts', though they are neither headed nor numbered in the manuscript, and a number of smaller capitals suggest the possibility of further subdivision. Its 101 stanzas and the lines themselves, in common with all manuscript Middle English poetry, are likewise unnumbered, by scribes or readers: the idea of linking the work's repeated stress on fives with its 2,525 lines—in fact, 2,530, if the final bob and wheel is included—is offered more obviously to modern readers familiar with arabic notation than to medieval audiences who were still writing it as MMDXXV. Quite apart from the necessity for early readers or listeners to keep a count on their fingers in such a text (for which sophisticated processes were available), it presents much more of a challenge than the 101 twelve-line stanzas of *Pearl* and their largely regular groupings. In *Gawain*, the pattern is there for the finding, but it is not pushed to the forefront; it needs the analogy of *Pearl* to bring the harmonies underlying it to prominence, and a highly educated patron or readers to appreciate it, or indeed to have it pointed out to them.

The attraction of *Gawain* derives from its handling of prosody and language alongside its subtlety of plot and implication. Its layers of meaning are conveyed not by the transcendental code-switching of *Pearl*, but by a process of increasing comprehension of what is happening. In so far as there is a significant use of code-switching, it is to highlight Gawain's subjunctive-rich courtly language with its polite 'you' forms ('Wolde ye …', 343, 1218) against his forceful imperative as he *thous* the Green Knight ('Thresch on, thou thro [fierce] man', 2300), or in the contrast of the ambiguous verbal sparring between him and the lady against the noise and energy of the hunts. As in the other poems of the manuscript,

---

[20] See also the summary in Chapter 9 in this volume, on metrical forms, and the more detailed discussion in Putter and Stokes, *The Works of the Gawain Poet*, xxi–viii. A bob and wheel is also used to follow eight rhyming alliterative lines in contemporary poems of thirteen-line stanzas such as *The Pistil of Swete Susan*; see Susanna Fein, 'The Early Thirteen-Line Stanza: Style and Metrics Reconsidered', *Parergon*, 18 (2000), 97–126.

404 MEDIEVAL POETRY: 1100–1400

the vocabulary is predominantly Germanic in etymology, but the poet deploys the higher-style register of French in particular to endorse passages describing luxury, armour, clothes, and furnishings. The virtuoso mix of vocabulary makes itself clear from the opening lines, the first with its alliteration derived from romance roots as befits its Classical reference, the second line on the brutality of war (a recurrent topic elsewhere in alliterative poetry) from Germanic, the third mixing Old Norse ('tulk') with French:

> Sithen the sege and the assaut   was sesed at Troye,
> The burgh brittened* and brent   to brondes and askes*,   *destroyed; ashes*
> The tulk* that the trammes*   of tresoun there wroghte ...   *man; stratagems* (1–3)

A considerable proportion of the poem's vocabulary belongs to a specialised alliterative register, or was passing into obsolescence. Both choices indicate a degree of stylistic ambition, but the *Gawain*-poet's reaching for archaic or exotic words compounds the difficulties offered by his dialect even while their richness contributes so much to the texture of the poem. That range of vocabulary is more marked than in many other works of the Alliterative Revival, but the need for three alliterating stressed syllables in every line makes the form more intensively demanding than end-of-line rhyme, and encourages the use of a wide range of synonyms. *Gawain*'s range is aided by its Norse-derived elements: in part a marker of its dialect area, but the poet pushes beyond the norms for the region.[21] The poet has a particular need for words he requires frequently, such as 'man', for which in addition to proper names (where the French dialect g/w variation is picked up in Gawain/Wawain) he has close on one synonym for every alliterating letter: burne, freke, gome, hathel (which also alliterates with all vowels), lede, renk, schalk, segge, tulk, and wye—all Old English except for the Norse 'tulk'.[22] In contrast to the commonplace 'man' and 'knight', which can appear anywhere in the line, these are used only when they are required for alliteration, so that their quality as poetic diction is highlighted not only by their comparative unfamiliarity but by their metrical stress in the cadence of the lines.

This is not the kind of thing that can be taught in the monolingual Latin *artes poeticae*, but it does show very clearly the poet's deliberate artistry in his own alliterative medium. He makes the most of the muscular energy stored within stress-based alliteration, such as he gives too to the storm in *Patience*. He is particularly good on weather, and he is perhaps unique in Middle English for his interest in clouds.[23] His excursus on the changing weather over the year before Gawain sets out (516–31) is a virtuoso piece. It opens with winter and its transition to spring and summer, with birds singing and a name-check of the Classical Zephyrus, but it rapidly moves on to the winds of autumn: 'Wroth wynd of the welkin (sky) wrasteles with the sunne' (525). The technique used here of an extra alliterating syllable (aaa/ax) appears a number of times in the poem's weather descriptions, not least the account of the depths of winter on the morning on which Gawain has to set out on his final journey to the Green Chapel, where quadruple alliteration extends over several lines (e.g., 1998–2003). Onomatopoeic effects are here unmistakeable:

> Brokes boyled and breke   by bonkes aboute,
> Schyre schaterande* on schores   there thay doun schowved.*   *breaking up;*
>   *rushed* (2082–3)

---

[21] See further Richard Dance, *Words Derived from Old Norse in Sir Gawain and the Green Knight: An Etymological Survey*, 2 vols. (Oxford, 2019). The glossary to the edition by J. R. R. Tolkien and E. V. Gordon (Oxford, 1967) notes the etymological origin of all the words in the poem.

[22] For an extended discussion, see Marie Borroff, *Sir Gawain and the Green Knight: A Stylistic and Metrical Study* (New Haven, CT, 1962).

[23] See *Gawain* 505, 727–8, 1695–6, 2001, 2079–81; *Cleanness* 414, 951–2; *Patience* 139.

Even the silence of frozen stasis can be evoked phonically: 'Thay clomben by clyffes there clenges the colde' (2078). And if the whale's queasiness is given a thought in *Patience*, in this poem the same happens for the wretchedness of the 'unblythe' birds piping 'for pine of the colde' on bare twigs (746–7), in a symmetrical counterpoint to the description of their spring songs among the leaves.

The larger structures of the narrative are thematically crucial as well as aesthetically satisfying. The poem operates, like *Pearl*, on a chiastic mirror symmetry, but here that encompasses both whole episodes and many smaller details (such as those birds), to give them exceptional weight. If there is a single symbol for this, it is the pentangle, the five-pointed star that can be drawn in a single interlocking unbroken line, and which the poet spends some fifty lines expounding (619–65). It brings together the five qualities by which Gawain lives: his five wits, his five fingers or manual strength, the five wounds of Christ (an object of veneration here as for Archbishop Scrope), the five joys of Mary, and his five virtues—generosity and nobility of mind ('fraunchis'), friendship ('felawschyp'), chastity ('clannesse': not the same, as *Cleanness* has shown, as celibacy, and in this secular context more like 'sexual restraint'), courtesy, and 'pyty', akin to modern 'compassion'. The most important thing about the pentangle, however, is the one stated first, that brings all these together: that it is a 'bytoknyng of trauthe' (626), a symbol of truthfulness. 'Trauthe' is a word closely allied to ideas of God; in relation to humankind, the closest modern equivalent would be integrity, as an ethical and contractual ideal. That is the ideal Gawain sets himself; but at the end, he bears the girdle as his new heraldic symbol, which he acknowledges as a 'token of untrauthe' (2509).[24] A quest romance, such as *Gawain* is, will usually include the knight's return to his starting point; but here, every event of the poem, including those opposing definitions of the pentangle, is balanced around the central scenes of the exchange of winnings from the lady's three sexual pursuits of Gawain in his chamber and Bertilak's simultaneous pursuits of different prey. 'In both cases it is a hunt to the death',[25] but that these bedroom scenes, and not the return blow, are the climax of the plot passes unnoticed by both Gawain and the first-time reader. *Gawain*, like *Patience*, ends with a final line that repeats its opening; but here, the final lines run time backwards, from Arthur's court to the arrival of Brutus to the siege of Troy, to distance the whole story back to the far past.

Within that historical frame, the paralleling of episodes is thematically crucial, as their mirror symmetry compels a fresh interpretation of what has happened before. The opening court scene contains Gawain's reference to Arthur as his uncle, with the king's blood in his body being the only praiseworthy thing about him:

> For as much as ye are myn em*   I am only to prayse;   *uncle*
> No bounte* bot your blod   I in my body knowe.   *excellence* (356–7)

And immediately before his return to court, he is given the revelation that the old lady of Bertilak's household stands in an exactly parallel blood relationship to him as Arthur. Morgan le Faye is 'even thyn aunt, Arthures half-sister' (2464), whose morally equivocal reputation threatens to cancel out the 'bounte' he has claimed for himself through the king. Inside those episodes come the Green Knight's challenge to receive a blow in return for another, at the start; and at the end, what happens when it is returned. Inside those are the scenes of Gawain's arming, initially with its emphasis on the 'endeles knotte' (630) of the pentangle as his heraldic badge; the second, corresponding, scene shows him taking care to

---

[24] On the symbolism of these, and of the wound to Gawain's neck, see further Ross G. Arthur, *Medieval Sign Theory and Sir Gawain and the Green Knight* (Toronto, 1987).

[25] Spearing, *The Gawain-Poet*, 217.

tie the girdle, that 'token of untrauthe', over the pentangle that he carries on his surcoat as on his shield. His transition from truth to untruth is demonstrated in the central scenes in which he finally fails to keep his word, his 'trauthe', to hand over his winnings, despite Bertilak's warning (1637–8, 1679–80). The narrative structure, in other words, enacts a thorough dismantling of the claims of excellence made for him at the start, and his scrupulously polite denial of virtue before Arthur is replaced by his comprehensive humiliation when he realises what he has done. Or not quite comprehensive: he may return to court in a state of deep self-abasement, but his companions' response is to laugh. This is even harder to interpret than the question of just what he has done wrong; but in that mirroring of events across the poem, they had wept when he set out, so a response of laughter—which can indicate delight or happiness just as readily as mockery or frivolity—may be entirely appropriate. Humankind, even as represented by the best of Arthur's knights who has set his aim on perfection, will ultimately be fallible. Nor does this amount to a condemnation of chivalric ideals. The Green Knight describes Gawain as like a pearl beside white peas (2364); it is his determination to live out those ideals that enables him to reach so far.

The story is unusual in the degree of surprise that it generates. It is possible to predict roughly what is going to happen in most narratives down to the nineteenth century and beyond; it is very rare for the audience to be kept in the dark until the final revelation. The revelation in *Gawain*, however, that the Green Knight and Sir Bertilak are one and the same, requires a re-evaluation of the entire plot for the listener or reader as for Gawain, so that reading the poem for a second time is a markedly different experience from a first encounter. The poet's holding back what is 'really' going on is made possible by the restriction of its focus. From the moment Gawain rides out of Camelot, the action is limited to what he sees (even, on occasion, from inside his eyelids, 1201, 2007) and understands. Even when the narration appears neutral, that restriction has the effect of making the knight the fallible narrator of his own story. The poet gives only the briefest of glimpses into the minds of other characters: a half-line each to the suggestion that the lady might have other things in mind than she is letting on (1550); and with far greater consequences, the Green Knight's pleasure that Gawain has come through his testing so well (2335). Otherwise, the focalisation through Gawain is so consistent that the reader is very unlikely to be a step ahead of him, in marked contrast to Jonah or the dreamer of *Pearl*. The consequent disagreement about just what Gawain does wrong has led to a wide divergence of critical responses, in ways that come close to putting the work into generic association with debate poetry as much as romance. The possible infringements of the various virtues of the pentangle (or all of them) are often discussed; but the issue of 'trauthe', which encompasses the whole set, is what is most emphasised at the end. Gawain's own sense of failure begins only when the Green Knight treats his aggression after his receipt of the non-blow with a kind of patronising amusement: 'Be not so gryndel' (2338). That this is what God says to Jonah may be a warning against condemning Gawain too harshly.

The only thing that the audience knows and that Gawain does not—and it is crucial that he should lack that privileged knowledge—is that he has to survive somehow, since he lives to fight on in all the other Arthurian romances. For those in the audience familiar with earlier French romances, however, following the ethical trajectory of the work is complicated by its mixture of romance traditions. In all English romance before Malory, Gawain is the best knight of the Round Table and a model of courtesy, as here, and until he breaks his word to the host he always maintains that courtesy. The French Gawain has a much less moral interpretation of courtesy, and the pentangle's chastity was not one of his qualities; few in the audience would need to have been told that he had the reputation for 'luf-talkyng' that those in the castle, including the lady, ascribe to him. Likewise, English medieval romances before Malory give minimal space to adultery. If they allow a couple sex before their marriage—and even that is unusual—they insist on its grounding in faithfulness. French romance takes a much more casual attitude to marriage, and the better acquainted the *Gawain* audience was with that, the more they might have been misled into thinking that it was after all the French Gawain they were presented with, with all the consequent adjustments of understanding that the English poem required. If they knew only the English Gawain, they might well have missed the ethical climax by sharing the knight's own long belief that he had done nothing wrong.

The moral qualities of much Middle English romance have often been remarked on, but they are rarely taken so seriously as in *Gawain*. The work is not overtly homiletic in the manner of the other Cotton poems: it puts far more emphasis on making the audience work out its ethics for themselves. It invites debate from its readers (and notably continues to do so), not as explicitly as Chaucer's direct posing of questions in the Knight's or Franklin's Tales,[26] but by the number of puzzles the work leaves us with. Some of these are matters of plot: is the host's primary form as Bertilak or the Green Knight?—just as we think we know, at the end, he rides off 'whidersoever he wolde', and still green. Is Gawain's life preserved by his taking of the supposedly magic girdle, as the lady claims, or is its lack of magic reflected in his injury, as the Green Knight tells him? How far does Morgan control the plot, given that the Green Knight insists that the tempting of Gawain was his own idea (2361)?—her schemes to damage the court and scare Guinevere to death are after all completely unsuccessful. What exactly does the Virgin do, if anything? These are unresolvable, since the poet does not tell us, and there is no 'real fact' to appeal to behind what we are told in the story.

The more significant puzzles concern interpretation rather than plot alone. In *Pearl*, the audience is allowed to be a small step ahead of the dreamer and has to learn more alongside him, with God as the ultimate standard of measurement; in the homiletic poems, it is made clear through direct statement from the poet/storyteller what the moral principles are that are being transgressed. *Gawain* is never so clear, even at the end. The layering there of praise and blame contains no overt indication of how we should choose between them. The court's approval of Gawain's achievement, however, is indicated less by their ambiguous laughter than by their decision to copy his wearing of the green girdle, in what amounts to the creation of a new order of chivalry. That was recognised by the author of the one later work that shows an unequivocal knowledge of the poem (or at least of its story), the rather unimpressive tail-rhyme *Greene Knight*, where a white lace is substituted for the girdle and explicitly linked to the Order of the Bath.[27] The end of *Gawain* recalls the highly prestigious Order of the Garter, a connection made by that early reader who added the motto of the Order at the end, 'Hony soyt qui mal pence', 'shame on him who thinks evil'. The implication is that it is the discourteous, the less chivalrous, who will read the worst into human

---

[26] See *Canterbury Tales* I.1347–53, V.1493–8, 1621–3, in Larry D. Benson (ed.), *The Riverside Chaucer*, 3rd edn. (Boston, MA, 1987; Oxford, 1988).

[27] Surviving in the Percy Folio, London, British Library, MS Add. 27879; text in Thomas Hahn (ed.), *Sir Gawain: Eleven Romances and Tales* (Kalamazoo, MI, 1995), 309–35.

action: more shame may accrue to his detractors, those who think evil, than to Gawain. The invocation of the crown of thorns in the closing prayer recasts a symbol of shame still more decisively.

The combination of all these qualities—a wide ethical sense, awareness of the poetic possibilities within the English language and alliterative form, play with structure and point of view, human sympathy, a genius for storytelling—makes the *Gawain*-poet stand comparison not only with his great contemporaries but also in the larger canon of English literature. The chance survival of a single manuscript alters our sense of that whole canon.

26

Chaucer's Courtly Poetry

David Lawton

Chaucer wrote courtly poetry throughout his career. In the beginning, *The Book of the Duchess* (*c* 1368) was an eclectic and original reworking of the fourteenth-century French *dits amoureux* to commemorate the death of Blanche, Duchess of Lancaster, and there may well have been earlier poems, perhaps some in Anglo-French, using *formes fixes* (*ballade*, *rondeau*, and *virelai*—the forms, as with the *carole*, are derived from the patterns of courtly dance). Chaucer had a reputation in his own day for writing, as he puts it, 'many an ympne' for Love's 'halidayes' (*Legend of Good Women* F 423); in the Retraction it becomes 'many a song and many a lecherous laye'.[1] It is perhaps an index of the occasional or coterie nature of such lyrics that few securely attributed to Chaucer have survived, though it may also show a lack of interest in collecting them on Chaucer's part, or even in being particularly prolific in *formes fixes*; for whatever reason, there is nothing like the number for Chaucer of the *Cinkante Ballades* written by Gower, still less the thousand or more *ballades* by Deschamps. As I suggest below, his interest may have lain in the use and adaptation of the *ballade* metre, not the writing of free-standing *ballades*. Chaucer's work as, in Gower's phrase, Venus's 'owne clerk'[2] continues late in his career in *The Legend of Good Women*; and what was probably the last poem Chaucer wrote, the 'Complaint to his Purse', is a *ballade* (three stanzas, here of seven lines rhyming *ababbcc* with one stanza of envoy; this is therefore a *ballade* in form, employing the seven-line rhyme royal stanza that had become a Chaucerian speciality).

Dream Poems

Chaucer's life, like his poetry, was shaped by the courtly. He entered court service in late boyhood, and served as soldier and diplomat as well as public servant and holder of various offices under the crown. His wife (the sister of John of Gaunt's lover and eventual wife) was a lady-in-waiting to Edward III's queen, Philippa of Hainault; his family benefitted from Gaunt's patronage; and he himself lived in a grace-and-favour residence above Aldgate from 1374 to 1386. Such connections gave him social as well as textual access to an international courtly culture, multilingual (Latinate and mainly Francophone). He travelled in Europe, often on the king's behalf, and—formatively—to Italy, where he encountered the work of Boccaccio before it became widely known in England. At the English court itself, or in coteries close by, he probably made the acquaintance of major Francophone poets: the Savoyard Oton de Grandson, several of whose *ballades* he adapted for

---

[1] All Chaucer text is quoted from Larry D. Benson (ed.), *The Riverside Chaucer*, 3rd edn. with new foreword by Christopher Cannon (Oxford, 2008), *Canterbury Tales* X.1086, at 328. Hereafter I provide citational information from this edition in the body of the text.

[2] John Gower, *Confessio Amantis*, 8.*2954, in G. C. Macaulay (ed.), *The English Works of John Gower*, EETS e.s. 81–2 (London, 1901), 466.

David Lawton, *Chaucer's Courtly Poetry*. In: *The Oxford History of Poetry in English*. Edited by Helen Cooper and Robert R. Edwards, Oxford University Press. © David Lawton (2023). DOI: 10.1093/oso/9780198827429.003.0026

The Complaint of Venus; Jean Froissart, the opening of whose Paradys d'amours ('Je sui de moi en grant mervelle') prompted Chaucer's use of the first person at the start of The Book of the Duchess ('I have gret wonder, by this lyght / How that I lyve'—both uses invoke the poet-persona of Le Roman de la Rose); and the younger poet Eustache Deschamps, who was to pay hyperbolic homage to Chaucer in a ballade, probably in the 1380s.

From being Venus's 'owne clerk', Chaucer is promoted by Deschamps to being the god of Love himself, if only by right of translation in England ('Tu es d'amors mondiaus diex en Albie'); and his poem fixes Chaucer's fame on his having transplanted 'la Rose' into English.[3] For the Roman de la Rose (in both its parts, by Guillaume de Lorris and by Jean de Meun) is the indispensable ground of subsequent courtly poetry, which exists in its slipstream even as it seeks to differentiate itself. The Roman's range of subjects is so capacious as to appear all-encompassing. The French humanist Laurent de Premierfait wrote that Dante found in it 'un vraye mappemounde' ('a true map of the world'),[4] and later courtly writers read it as a vast anthology of modes, genres, and tones—a self-sufficient ars poetica of the courtly. It is a poetic of contraries, collocating lyric and narrative, Ovid and the poetry of troubadours and trouvères, love and jealousy, classicism and modernity, beauty and satire, idealism and irony, life and death, joy and pain, heaven and hell. Formally, the supple octosyllabic couplet of the Roman serves Chaucer and others as a model, but is supplemented by the influence of the other thirteenth-century Roman de la Rose, that of Jean Renart, which sets lyric into its narrative in a range of poetic forms, pioneering a practice of intercalated lyrics that is all but standard in the courtly poetry of fourteenth- and fifteenth-century French poets, to the point that it is sometimes difficult to be sure of the boundaries of individual poems or know whether a work is one or many (a question that for Chaucer culminates in The Canterbury Tales).

Chaucer's relation to courtly poetry is the subject of the Prologue to The Legend of Good Women. There is no hint in this text of Deschamps's archly flattering identification of Chaucer with the god of Love; Chaucer rather depicts himself as the defender of the Rose and therefore—if, as the narrator argues, inappropriately (F 468–70)—Love's target. The Prologue opens with the strong narratorial 'I' that is by now a feature of Chaucer's poetry, much indebted to both the Roman and the dits amoureux, and foregrounds the way

---

[3] Eustache Deschamps, in A. H. S. de Queux de Saint-Hilaire and G. Raynaud (eds), Œuvres Complètes de Eustache Deschamps, 10 vols. (Paris, 1878–1903), 2:138–40. For an important new reading of the ballade in terms of the 'diachronic translation of antiquity', see Elizaveta Strakhov, 'Tending to One's Garden: Deschamps's "Ballade to Chaucer" Reconsidered', Medium Ævum, 85 (2016), 236–58, at 237. For a positive reading of this tribute, see Laura Kendrick, 'Deschamps' Ballade Praising Chaucer and Its Impact', Cahiers de Recherches Médiévales et Humanistes, 29 (2015), 215–33. A sceptical reading is that of David Wallace, Premodern Places: From Calais to Surinam, Chaucer to Aphra Behn (Oxford, 2016), 54–6. A more negative reading is that of Ardis Butterfield, The Familiar Enemy: Chaucer, Language and the Nation in the Hundred Years War (Oxford, 2009), 153. Butterfield's work on Chaucer's French context is of prime importance. See especially her 'Chaucerian Vernaculars', Studies in the Age of Chaucer, 31 (2009), 25–51; 'The Book of the Duchess, Guillaume de Machaut, and the Image of the Archive', in Jamie Fumo (ed.), Chaucer's Book of the Duchess Reopened: Context and Exchange (Woodbridge, 2018), 199–212; 'Chaucer's French Inheritance', in Piero Boitani and Jill Mann (eds), Cambridge Companion to Chaucer (Cambridge, 2004), 20–35; and 'The Dream of Language: Chaucer "en son Latin"', Studies in the Age of Chaucer, 41 (2019), 3–29. Important recent studies are by Jenni Nuttall, '"Many a Lay and Many a thing": Chaucer's Technical Terms', in Thomas A. Prendergast and Jessica Rosenfeld (eds), Chaucer and the Subversion of Form (Cambridge, 2018), 21–37 and Stephanie A. Viereck Gibbs Kamath, 'The French Context', in Ian Johnson (ed.), Geoffrey Chaucer in Context (Cambridge, 2019), 117–25. For poetry in France, see Adrian Armstrong and Sarah Kay (eds), Knowing Poetry: Verse in Medieval France from the Rose to the Rhétoriqueurs (Ithaca, NY, 2011).

[4] Quoted by John V. Fleming, The Roman de la Rose: A Study in Allegory and Iconography (Princeton, NJ, 1969), 62, 129.

in which that voice as it reaches Chaucer is already echoic, linking the individual experience with cultural memory:

> A thousand tymes have I herd men telle
> That ther is joy in hevene and peyne in helle,
> And I acorde wel that it ys so. (1–3)

In the Prologue's dream he is arraigned before the court of Love for the *Troilus*, but also his role in translating the *Rose* itself, which given this change in subject position can freely be cited as 'heresye' against Love's 'lawe' (330). A plea in mitigation is entered by Love's queen, Alceste, featuring a *catalogue raisonée* of Chaucer's own works, and the penalty imposed, which is to be the writing of the legends themselves. But the dream itself does not occur in the Prologue for more than 200 lines; it is preceded by Chaucer's meditation on 'olde bokes' as the key of remembrance (25–6), by an extended libretto for birdsong, echoing or anticipating both *The Parliament of Fowls* and the 'General Prologue' (166–73), and by the long and haunting account of his devotion to the daisy, the flower into which Alcestis is transformed.

The whole poem is redolent of courtly observances and forms: ceremonies for May morning or Valentine's Day (first celebrated in English poetry by Chaucer himself, for a date in spring), involving music and procession; the ludic contest between leaf and flower, in which Chaucer sets his adoration of the daisy; protocols such as the mediation of the queen on behalf of an accused, such as Chaucer depicted elsewhere in the 'Wife of Bath's Tale' and, according to Froissart, queen Philippa enacted in life before the gates of Calais in 1347. It evokes a gilded world, such as that of the *Troilus* frontispiece in Cambridge, Corpus Christ College, MS 61, the foreground of which could as easily show Chaucer on trial before the court of Love as the subject sometimes construed, Chaucer reading—or, in the absence of a book, reciting—to the royal court.[5] For courtly poetry invites our historical gaze, and tempts modern readers, as in a very different way the 'General Prologue' will tempt us, to identify its characters in life. The problem with this arises partly because modern readers lack the knowledge of occasions and codes medieval audiences would have had, but the impulse is not a modern one: John Shirley sought to provide historical contexts for some of Chaucer's shorter poems, and Lydgate was the first to identify Alceste in the Prologue to the *Legend* as Richard II's queen, Anne of Bohemia. Yet the courtly exists in performance: if Love 'is' Richard and Anne 'is' Alceste, Richard and Anne are nevertheless called upon not *in propria persona* but to perform Love and Alceste, roles imagined for them by Chaucer. And if courtly performance rests on consensual make-believe, what is to prevent the representation of that performance from itself being a pretence? In her fine recent biography of Chaucer, Marion Turner appears in no doubt: this is a courtly audience, Chaucer is performing at court, and the Prologue and subsequent legends enact his growing resistance to the tyranny of royal patronage. Here is a Chaucer who desires to get out of the garden, even Love's garden, onto the open road of the *Canterbury Tales*.[6] Such a reading fits the narrative arc of a biography,

---

[5] Elizabeth Salter and Derek Pearsall suggested that the background depicted the exchange of Criseyde for Antenor; see Elizabeth Salter, 'The Troilus Frontispiece', in M. B. Parkes and Elizabeth Salter (eds), *A Facsimile of Corpus Christi College Cambridge MS 61* (Cambridge, 1978), 15–23; Elizabeth Salter and Derek Pearsall, 'Pictorial Illustration of Late Medieval Poetic Texts: The Role of the Frontispiece or Prefatory Picture', in Flemming G. Andersen et al. (eds), *Medieval Iconography and Narrative: A Symposium* (Odense, 1980), 100–23.

[6] Marion Turner, *Chaucer: A European Life* (Princeton, NJ, 2019), 353, 359–62. Turner's discussion of the garden of Love is important and perceptive.

412   MEDIEVAL POETRY: 1100–1400

a teleological perspective in which all roads lead to Canterbury. It is encouraged by Love's instruction to the fictive Chaucer to bring the book of his legends to Eltham or Sheen; but such claims of royal patronage, as in the two prologues to Gower's *Confessio Amantis*, may be little more than the literary equivalent of putting 'By Royal Appointment' on a jar of marmalade. Given the political instability of the mid-1380s, and Chaucer's quitting both his Customs post and his Aldgate apartment, it seems unlikely that he would have felt at ease in the royal court just then; and if so we should look for a different audience, perhaps across the Thames in Southwark.[7]

Courtliness is a culture, not a place. It is also two-faced, and the two faces both belong to the *Roman de la Rose*: the one is the courtly lover in an idealised garden as imagined by Guillaume de Lorris, channelling troubadour and Italian lyric and, indirectly, the influence of Arabic poetry; and the other is the clerkly, blasphemous and scatological wit that reaches its extreme point in Jean de Meun's conclusion as the lover finally impregnates the rose (Chaucer imitates Jean's mock apology to women for his rudeness at the climax of the Merchant's Tale). The Prologue to the *Legend* has more to do with Chaucer's relation to the *Roman* than with the royal court or the reception of *Troilus*. That is the tyranny, if any, that Chaucer seeks to resist, for his subjection to it is his whole reputation—or so Deschamps suggests in his *ballade*. Though Chaucer would surely have taken the Rose's side had he lived to see the *querelle* of the *Roman de la Rose*, his work shows an awareness that among the myriad poetic gifts conferred by the *Roman* is an essential misogyny, since the work and the tradition rely on the universalised objectification of women. This is the issue he addresses in the Prologue to the *Legend*, and so he proposes an alternative to the rose: the daisy, in its role as Alcestis.

The fact that Alcestis is already mentioned at the end of *Troilus* (5.1772–8)—in the appeal to 'every lady bright of hewe / And every gentil womman' not to judge him too harshly for writing about Criseyde's untruth—might prompt a suspicion that Chaucer was already working on the *Legend* as he finished *Troilus*, and did not so much require as imagine the spur of a hostile response from an actual audience. The lines in *Troilus* set the programme for the *Legend*, and are echoed in his queasy joke—trust no man but me—at the end of the legend of Phyllis (2559–61). Alcestis is not a familiar figure in medieval literature, unlike Love from *Roman de la Rose* or almost all the women in the *Legend* themselves, who are to be found in Ovid's *Metamorphoses* or *Heroides*; part of the pleasure of the legends is in seeing what Chaucer does *not* say, how in his professed desire following Love's orders to present each woman as good he stops short, as in the cases of Medea or Philomela, of acts of murder.[8] Alcestis, by contrast, is a mystery character, with a presence in Latin literature much less prominent and from Greek sources. Chaucer most likely found her in Boccaccio's Latin *De Claris Mulieribus* (*c* 1362), which may well have acted as a provocation to Chaucer's invention of his own 'good women'. Chaucer is the first author to bring Alcestis into English, and she does not appear in his French sources; the link to the daisy is his alone, and he draws on Boccaccio again, but this time on the prologue to *Il Filostrato*, for his most moving and serious passage in the daisy's praise as 'the clernesse and the verray light / That in this derke world me wint and ledeth' (84–5).[9] His description of Alcestis reworks that of Froissart's poem on the daisy, 'La Dittie de la flour de la Margherite', switching the

---

[7] See Sebastian Sobecki, 'A Southwark Tale: Gower, the 1381 Poll Tax, and Chaucer's *Canterbury Tales*', *Speculum*, 92 (2017), 630–60.

[8] Most recently, see Lucy M. Allen-Goss, *Female Desire in Chaucer's* Legend of Good Women *and Middle English Romance* (Woodbridge, 2020)

[9] J. L. Lowes, 'The Prologue to the *Legend of Good Women* as Related to the French *Marguerite* Poems, and the *Filostrato*', *PMLA*, 19 (1904), 593–683, 618–26. For the emotion in the poem, see Anne Schuurman, 'Pity and Poetics in Chaucer's *Legend of Good Women*', *PMLA*, 130 (2015), 1302–17.

woman's but retaining the *margarite* as the 'o perle fin oriental' from which the crown of Alcestis is fashioned (221), and twice calling the crown's filigree spikes *florouns*, Froissart's word for the daisy's petals. The daisy is Alcestis because it has two lives, opening and closing by night and by day; Alcestis is the daisy because she died and returned to life. It is a brilliant and moving conceit; one might compare Chaucer's *Complaint unto Pity*, which invokes Proserpina to similar effect.

There is a familiar gap here between author and dreamer. As in the *Book of the Duchess*, the dreamer is slow to recognise the human reality of death and transformation; even though Alcestis has already named herself (432), he asks 'That I may knowe soothly what ye be' (460), allowing Love to summarize her story. As the sun draws to the west, Love says he must go home 'To Paradis', leaving the poet with an assurance that also identifies the women of 'al this companye' (564):

> But er I go, thus muche I wol the telle,
> Ne shal no trewe lover come in helle.
> Thise other ladies sitting here arowe
> Been in thy balade, if thou canst hem knowe,
> And in thy bookes alle thou shalt hem finde. (552–6)

The scene becomes uncanny after the fact. The poet has been surrounded by the women of his ballade, the very women about whom it will be his job to write: Cleopatra, Ariadne, Philomela, and the rest. Though it seems discourteous to say so, they are dead women, brought back to life in the moment of the text. What Chaucer as dreamer has seen is not unlike the appearance of Helen of Troy in *Doctor Faustus*, though Marlowe's emphasis is on mortality and Chaucer's on mutability. We should not fail to see how spectral this scene has become as it raises the veil of the long-ago past; yet the ability to fuse temporalities is very much in the repertoire of courtly dream poems. So in *The Book of the Duchess*, the narrator reads Ovid and then in his dream steps into Ovid's world, a time in which Augustus Caesar is hunting in the forest, and from which he is to be recalled by the ringing within that same dream landscape of John of Gaunt's castle bell. Such an impossible temporal mix is what happens when books act as the key of remembrance: they resurrect the dead, and readers meet them. In this way reading too is an act of love both communal and solitary, like the adoration of the daisy.

Thus Chaucer's courtly poetry achieves original effects under cover of its own tradition— its classical sources, medieval models, and the modern authors it emulates. The longest modern shadow over the dream poetry is cast by Machaut, from whom Chaucer takes many narrative and discursive elements, not least the fitfully ironic promotion of his own celebrity; it is a thoroughly Machaudian scheme to set up a mock trial that enables detailed advertisement of his own works by name. As a weak courtly counterweight on behalf of humility, the fiction stresses that he works to order. 'Make the metres of hem as the leste', says Love, and immediately qualifies even the freedom this implies: do not amplify your sources, but keep it short, giving only 'the grete' (574). Yet it is only the dreamer, not the author, whom Love commands, and these instructions explicitly signal important literary innovations on Chaucer's part; it is a decorum of courtly poetry that they should be represented as a form of duress. The interplay of agency and duress offers a model of poetic craft—'new science' from 'olde feldes', in the words of *The Parliament of Fowls* (22–5)—as both inherited and original.

Chaucer's dream poems are all poetic manifestoes, and one of their central concerns is the making of poems in general, be it from an initial state of apathy in *The Book of the Duchess* or the discovery of 'tidinges' in *The House of Fame*. In all but *The House of Fame* they are also poems that contain other poems set apart by their metres from the surrounding poetic narrative. In *The Book of the Duchess,* this separation cues the initial song of the man in Black speaking of his bereavement (475–86). The textual transmission of this seems to have been imperfect; William Thynne's edition of 1532 supplies an extra line (480), without which it would look like a single stanza of eleven lines, *aabbaccdccd* (the length but not the usual rhyme scheme of a stanza of the French *chant royal*). This song is glossed as a 'complainte' (487); understanding its content determines the subsequent dialogue between the man in Black and the dreamer. *The Parliament of Fowls* concludes with the song of the small birds, glossed as a 'roundel' (675), one of the three *formes fixes*—again, there is considerable textual uncertainty, but the great Victorian editor W. W. Skeat reconstructed it in fourteen lines with the rhyme scheme (including refrain) *abbababbabbabb*.[10] In both these cases, the surrounding narrative could be seen as framing the short poem that is anthologised. In the *Legend of Good Women* Prologue, the inset poem is marked, glossed as a 'song' (F 248) and (correctly) as a 'balade' (F 270) in three stanzas of seven lines each, on three rhymes only and with the identical rhyme scheme *ababbcc* (again, identical with rhyme royal). All these are virtuoso performances; all might have existed separately from the narrative in which they are placed and from which they are metrically distinct. Each is made integral to the narrative poem in which it is placed, in the case of the Prologue because it lists the virtuous women of the work's programme—themselves imagined as present in the audience of the ballade, and in the case of the G manuscript as actually singing it—except for Alcestis, whose omission becomes a further reason for Love's rebuke of the poet (F 537–50). As with the 'complainte' of *The Book of the Duchess,* the ballade becomes the engine of the narrative poem around it. In both these poems, that narrative is in the non-stanzaic form of continuous rhyming couplets (in *The Parliament of Fowls* it is in rhyme royal, itself a form of *ballade* metre, to be considered below). In *The Book of the Duchess,* as in the *Rose* and most *dits amoureux,* the couplets are in tetrameter; but in *The Legend of Good Women* they are in the decasyllabic line that Chaucer employs in *The Canterbury Tales.* Models for the decasyllabic line were freely available to him in Latin, French, and Italian poetry; and Gower uses a similar metre in his poem *In Praise of Peace* (1399/1400), whether independently or not. Chaucer is generally taken to be following Italian usage in allowing an extra syllable, in Italian for so-called 'feminine' rhyme and in Chaucer's prosody to enable metrically helpful sounding of final *-e* where phonologically allowable.[11] This flexibility enables Chaucer to follow a largely iambic pattern for these longer lines, and in this he pioneers the staple line of most English poetry from the fifteenth century to the twentieth, even though fifteenth-century scribes were unable to follow his use of final *-e* (which had become obsolete), and the use of the line to enable the flow of narrative was consolidated in the sixteenth century in blank verse rather than couplets. This formal innovation (or importation) is important to Chaucer's reputation as a forerunner, or as 'father' of subsequent poetry. The longer line also allowed for a denser semantic texture (polysyllabic words, for example, and a greater use of adjectives and adverbs); combined with courtly subject matter and his deft versification, this helped form a high style for courtly English poetry that was quickly utilised by the next generation of poets, especially Hoccleve and Lydgate.

---

[10] W. W. Skeat (ed.), *Complete Works of Geoffrey Chaucer,* 7 vols. (Oxford, 1894), 7:359.

[11] On Chaucer's pentameter, see Eric Weiskott, *Meter and Modernity in English Verse 1350–1650* (Philadelphia, PA, 2021), 164–9 and Martin J. Duffell, *A New History of English Metre* (London, 2008), 85–7.

Complaint Poetry

The core of *The Book of the Duchess* is a specimen of modern suffering placed in apposition to Froissart's rendering of Ovid's account of Ceyx and Alcyon and dealing with the question of poetic inspiration through pain that Chaucer, following Froissart, associates with the figure of Orpheus.[12] The genealogy of poetry in pain leads Chaucer, in the traces of his French precursors and contemporaries, to the genre of complaint; and throughout his career Chaucer is the author of quite remarkable poems of complaint, some with complaint in their scribal or editorial titles (the *Complaint unto Pity*, the *Complaint of Mars* and the *Complaint of Venus*). Perhaps the most majestic complaint Chaucer ever wrote is in a woman's voice, that given to Anelida, queen of Armenia, in his *Anelida and Arcite*. This occurs singly in some manuscripts, but in most it is prefaced by a lengthy narrative frame (in rhyme royal, and based on Boccaccio) concerning the siege of Thebes, Arcite's lovemaking and infidelity, and the devastating effect on Anelida; in most manuscripts, the poem ends after Anelida's letter of complaint to the unfaithful Arcite, with its sublime reflections on pain and memory, 'vois memorial' (18). The letter is a virtuoso and innovative performance in both metre and form, marrying Italian and French influence: instead of rhyme royal, it employs a distinctive nine-line stanza on only two rhymes (*aabaabbab*), mainly of pentameter lines, but both its strophe and antistrophe end with two stanzas of mainly tetrameter with a final line of pentameter (256–71, 317–32), followed by one stanza with end rhyme and two internal rhymes: 'Ne never mo myne eyen two be drie, / And to your routhe and to your trouthe I crie' (336–7)—this last line draws into the climax of Anelida's appeal the rhyme of 'routhe' and 'trouthe' that is a hallmark of Chaucer's poetry about love (culminating in *Troilus* 5.1098–9). While in both power and theme it demands to be set alongside *Troilus*, as a poetic performance it is altogether exceptional.[13]

The fact that the poem then ends clearly puzzled some scribes; some manuscripts add an unconvincing extra stanza promising a resumption of the narrative. This is hard to credit: Anelida's complaint is beautifully crafted and complete, ending with a line that picks up its first, 'So thirleth with the poynt of remembraunce / The swerd of sorowe' (211, cf. 350), and one can hear an elegant merging of poet's and speaker's voice in its concluding stanza: 'Then ende I thus, sith I may do no more. / I yeve it up, for now and evermore' (342–3). The reader has a choice of response ranging from admiration of the poem's metrical mastery all the way to empathetic identification with Anelida's eloquent anguish, seeing in the work what Ardis Butterfield has described as 'a free-floating assemblage of memorial elements with the capacity to find temporary formal realization on the page'.[14] Yet memory in this poem is not elusive or fugitive; it is the sword of sorrow, the sharpness of what Simone Weil calls 'extreme affliction ... whose point is applied at the very centre of the soul'.[15] Remembrance

---

[12] For this reading, see David Lawton (ed.), *The Norton Chaucer* (New York, 2019), 947–8; and David Lawton, *Voice in Later Medieval English Literature: Public Interiorities* (Oxford, 2017), 46–57.

[13] See Turner, *Chaucer*, 168; Helen Cooper, 'Chaucerian Poetics', in Robert G. Benson and Susan Ridyard (ed.), *New Readings of Chaucer's Poetry* (Cambridge, 2003), 31–50, 37. The textual complications are ably set out by A. S. G. Edwards, 'The Unity and Authenticity of *Anelida and Arcite*: The Evidence of the Manuscripts', *Studies in Bibliography*, 41 (1988), 177–88, though most subsequent commentary has resisted his conclusion that the complaint may not be by Chaucer.

[14] Ardis Butterfield, 'The Construction of Textual Form: Cross-Lingual Citation in Some Medieval Lyrics', in Yolanda Plumley (ed.), *Citation, Intertextuality and Memory in the Middle Ages and Renaissance* (Exeter, 2011), 41–57, at 57. For a focus on Anelida's complaint as exploring female distrust of masculine rhetoric of fin'amors, see Kara Doyle, '"Je maviseray": Chaucer's Anelida, Shirley's Chaucer, Shirley's Readers', *Studies in the Age of Chaucer*, 38 (2016), 275–85.

[15] Simone Weil, *Waiting for God*, trans. Emma Craufurd (New York, 1951), 119–22.

416 MEDIEVAL POETRY: 1100–1400

here is bitter and static; it is the inability to forget, the doom of living in a state of constancy to one who has been unfaithful and moved on: 'Arcite hath born awey the keye / Of al my world' (323–4). The subject of the poem is Anelida's contrasting inability to move beyond complaint—it is, she says, her 'destinee' (243)—even while recognising that it is both futile and a trap: 'I wil ben ay ther I was ones bounde; / That I have seid, be seid for evermore' (245–6). 'Evermore', here and in line 343, is the duration of sorrow and complaint.

This is therefore the point at which story stops; for all the wind of narrative in a reader's or poet's sails, you reach a complaint—and that becomes the destination. It is strikingly similar to what happens to the 'Squire's Tale', left in suspension with Canace's falcon, and not so dissimilar to what happens in the *Book of the Duchess* if one reads the ending as I am inclined to do, with the man in Black singing with 'vois memorial in the shade' while the Emperor Octavian returns to his castle and the dreamer leaves to write his poem. To look for narrative development is beside the point; what matters is the virtuoso expression of human loss, of which these poems are anthologies. It is intriguing how often, as in *Anelida* or indeed *Troilus*, as in Ovid's *Heroides*, the complaint takes the form of writing, such as a letter, reinforcing the idea that it forms part of a vast, ever incomplete anthology of multiple texts in the field of remembrance. Narrative is neither the *telos* nor the engine of such work. The poem moves toward a moment of suffering that unfolds its own history; it does not sweep up that moment into a larger narrative unfolding. The point is not movement but arrest: the work moves toward and culminates in the perfect indwelling of a scene of feeling. The reader is left like Theseus's victim Ariadne, stranded on an island of grief and grievance. One can see Chaucer attempting to solve this resistance of complaint to narrative in his late work: in the *Legend* largely by focusing on the narrative context and underplaying any formal expectation of a set piece complaint; in the 'Franklin's Tale', most intriguingly, devising a tale in which Dorigen's two big complaints do not in fact cut off the arc or eventually alter the story. Until then, however, in the framing of complaint and in the early dream poetry the reader, and the narrator, advance step by step, exploring the ground, uncertain of what will follow—until they reach another's 'state of mind or affect', as expressed in the individual poem, and cannot go further. Seen in this context the narrative advances to a poetic act and cannot go past it even if it seeks to gloss it: Anelida's recrimination, the man in Black's bereavement, more positively—leaving the pain of the raptors behind—the lower birds' roundel. This becomes almost a poetic habit, and persists into the *Canterbury Tales* with the 'Squire's Tale'.

Marion Turner sees deference in this diffidence—a petitionary voice that implies intimacy with a defined circle of readers; but its premise is not knowing, not seeing beyond what the narrator or dreamer can see, taking one step at a time. Turner argues that the major change in Commons procedure in the 1370s—and the election of the first Speaker—enabled Chaucer to develop a more public voice that allowed more readily for mediation and mobility of genre. It is a reading indebted to the work of Paul Strohm on 'social Chaucer', and she uses it to argue against the notion of a narrow male coterie audience for *The Canterbury Tales*.[16] I would agree, but I also want to argue that the *Tales* sidesteps a real coterie by creating a virtual one. In the *Tales* Chaucer extends his public by speaking to his readers with a medley of voices *as if* the discourse was private, intimate, conversational, and

---

[16] Turner, *Chaucer*, 402; Paul Strohm, *Social Chaucer* (Cambridge, MA, 1994), and *The Poet's Tale* (London, 2016), 227–30. Turner argues against the view of Derek Pearsall, 'The *Canterbury Tales* and London Club Culture', in Ardis Butterfield (ed.), *Chaucer and the City* (Cambridge, 2006), 95–108, and shares the contrary view of Helen Cooper, 'London and Southwark Poetic Companies: "Si tost c'amis" and the *Canterbury Tales*', in *Chaucer and the City*, 109–26. See also Sobecki, 'A Southwark Tale'.

grounded in a shared foreknowledge. This is another, more potent version of complicity, different from that of *Book of the Duchess* or *Anelida and Arcite*. Here, in the *Canterbury Tales*, the narrator knows everything, and ensures that the reader does too. In rhetorical terms, this is irony at the level of structure. In almost all cases, the reader of the *Tales* shares with its narratorial voices knowledge that the characters lack: Saturn will not let Arcite win Emily even if he wins the tournament; unknown to Nicholas, Absolon has a red-hot poker in his hand; the cock will escape from the fox through their mutual garrulity; and so on. It is what makes it so difficult in the 'Clerk's Tale'—the Tale that above all others problematises courtliness—to sympathise fully with Griselda: not only does she not get a complaint that would evoke such sympathy, since she is sworn to remain mute, but readers also know what she does not, that all (bar her pain) will be well. In keeping with Boccaccio's original version of the tale (*Decameron* 10.10), we have for the most part, however uncomfortably, a Walter's eye view of her dilemma. The anti-courtly genre of comic tales is central to Chaucer's new poetics, which it both prompts and enables: fabliaux absolutely depend upon knowing who is being duped by whom and how, on the readers' being in on the plot at the expense of the characters; and their narration therefore acts out a late Chaucerian poetics of complicity. Complicity between readers and narrator, effectively between reader and text, is a principle of the narrative poetics of the *Canterbury Tales*, and it contrasts with what might be called the prior poetics of complaint.

Troilus and Criseyde

This shift can be seen as the pivot of Chaucer's poetic career, and it is worked out in detail and at length in *Troilus and Criseyde*. This must have astonished its first readers for its scope and scale; a massive and finished work in five books and 8,239 lines, it is by far the longest single courtly narrative poem written in English in or before its day, and it wastes no time in stating its ambition, to bring together the modes of classical epic (the Trojan War) and elegy (verses that weep as the poet writes them: 1.7) in recounting Troilus's double sorrow, his love and loss of Criseyde. It is the fulfilment of two principles that motivate Chaucer's courtly work: translation and formal experimentation. This is no longer a question of writing in multiple metres but of crafting a single poetic form, the rhyme royal stanza of seven decasyllabic lines, that serves all the needs of the poem—narrative, lyric, and even didactic. This seven-line stanza is a rare variant of the French *ballade*, which usually has eight lines; it is Chaucer's standard form for the *ballade*, but its use in *Troilus* and in *The Parliament of Fowls* (and in the narrative frame for *Anelida and Arcite*) shows him thoroughly retooling it for narrative purposes. In all these cases, the choice of metre is linked to his use of a source by Boccaccio, and it would seem that Chaucer regarded it as a perfect English counterpart to Boccaccio's *ottava rima*. It responds well to a diversity of narrative needs from high poetic invocation through idiomatic, sometimes comic exchange (especially involving Pandarus) to the careful account of a particular action or, as here, the setting of the work's scene through summary narrative:

> Yt is wel wist how that the Grekes stronge
> In armes with a thousand shipes wente
> To Troiewardes, and the cite longe
> Assegeden—neigh ten yer er they stente—
> And in diverse wise and oon entente:

418   MEDIEVAL POETRY: 1100–1400

> The ravysshyng to wreken of Eleyne,
> By Paris don, they wroughten al hir peyne. (1.57–63)

As usual in *Troilus*, the stanza is a self-contained syntactic unit, forming a period that is self-sufficient without suggesting narrative completion; the regularity and recurrence of ending and beginning sets the rhythm of both narrative and poem. This stanza turns midway on the polysyllabic 'assegeden', coming like a kind of whiplash after 'longe'. The rhyme words underscore the importance of key ideas that reverberate beyond their immediate context (the fact that Greeks are 'stronge'—Criseyde is overwhelmed by Diomede's stress on this in Book 5; the force of their 'oon entente', which looks forward as well as back; the association of Helen and pain). Yet the rhyme does not routinely end-stop the line, and its force is often muted to give the second of the two couplets its full effect, sometimes the last word, as in the stanza preceding:

> For now wol I gon streght to my matere,
> In which ye may the double sorwes here
> Of Troilus in lovynge of Criseyde,
> And how that she forsook hym er she deyde. (1.53–6)

Chaucer tests the versatility of his medium in ways that go well beyond the diegetic demands of narrative or his immediate source. His lengthy translation in Book 4 of a passage from Boethius 5, pr. 3 has been the occasion of critical puzzlement—is it significant that the translation breaks off before Philosophy replies to the prisoner's questioning?—but the decision to attempt a verse translation of a key passage in Boethius here is in any case audacious, probably relevant to Chaucer's intellectual circle (including 'moral Gower' and 'philosophical Strode', 5.1856–7), and inventively warranted by the subject of the poem: foreknowledge. What is the point of a long poem of which the outcome is already known? The point must lie in the telling; the telling must depend on the perception of the reader; and this is all it takes to activate Boethius's contribution to the debate about free will and necessity. It runs as follows: the idea that God either does not foreknow or does so imperfectly is a denial of God. But if God always foreknows, what becomes of human free will? God only foreknows because he already knows what we will choose. But if God already knows that, we are not in fact free to choose as we think we are—and so on, *ad infinitum*. This question is perhaps moot in a debating society or a university, but it cannot be avoided if you are a Prince of Troy caught up in the Trojan War. So Chaucer allows Troilus to ask it after the Trojan Parliament has decreed his separation from Criseyde, and he takes the opportunity to translate into poetry a passage he may already have translated, or was simultaneously translating, as prose. The comparison it enables us to make is a unique one, and it shows the extent to which rhyme royal organizes and enables his syntax and his expression. Critical judgments have not been kind—I pick up the passage just after a line R. K. Root called 'probably the least poetical line that Chaucer ever wrote'[17] ('And further over now ayenward yit' 4.1027), though there are others just as occupied with the difficult business of getting to the next rhyme. Boethius posits the example of how we are to understand a person sitting down.

---

[17] Geoffrey Chaucer, in R. K. Root (ed.), *The Book of Troilus and Criseyde* (Princeton, NJ, 1926). The line also signals the point at which Chaucer has Troilus reverse the direction of Boethius's argument, investing in the question rather than Lady Philosophy's answer.

Does the necessity of his sitting down consist in our perceiving him to sit, or does our perception depend on the necessity that he is sitting? I give Chaucer's prose translation (which includes Jean de Meun's gloss), his version in *Troilus* 4.1037–43, and a rough translation of that into modern prose, the latter just to keep track of the argument:

> But therfore ne sitteth nat a wyght for that the opynioun of the sittynge is soth, but the opinioun is rather soth for that a wyght sitteth byforn. And thus, althoughe that the cause of the soth cometh of that other side (as who seith, that althoughe the cause of soth cometh of the sittynge, and nat of the trewe opinioun), algatis yit is there comune necessite in that oon and in that othir. (5, pr. 3, 63–71)

> > But thow mayst seyn, the man sit nat therefore
> > That thyn opynyoun of his sittynge soth is,
> > But rather, for the man sit ther byfore,
> > Therfore is thyn opynyoun soth, ywis.
> > And, I seye, though the cause of soth of this
> > Comth of his sittyng, yet necessite
> > Is entrechaunged, both in hym and the. (4.1037–43)

> (You may say that a man does not sit by virtue of the fact that your opinion that he is sitting is true, but rather that your opinion is true by virtue of the fact that he is already sitting. And I say, though the real cause of this comes from his sitting, that both (his sitting and your opinion) are necessarily true.)

There is no fallacy in the reasoning here, but there is a little too much punning on necessity; in Boethius, Lady Philosophy picks up on it and answers it, well or not. That Chaucer makes Troilus deviate from her counsel is an index of the Trojan's dilemma, not necessarily of his folly. The verse translation, albeit not without sign of strain ('ywis'), is more cogent than the prose, and the rhyme helps both brevity and clarity; it also does just enough to make Boethian language work in Troilus's mouth—instead of a scholastic working through propositions, Troilus turns the opposing argument into an adversarial 'thow', and allows himself to speak up in his internal colloquy as he had failed to do in the parliament. And at that point Chaucer lets the rhyme royal stanza organize his thoughts; his verse line finds the polysyllabic word not obviously prompted by Boethius's text that turns the stanza into an insight into Troilus' loss, 'entrechaunged'. The verb echoes the use of 'chaunge' at this point in the poem to mean exchange but also to hint at more that Troilus does not know ('So sore him sat the chaunging of Criseyde', 4.231). Just as Shakespeare's poetry allows characters to speak a truth of which they are quite unaware (like Theseus when he ridicules 'the poet's eye'), so Troilus, using Boethius's concept, speaks beyond himself—poetically, not philosophically—what is a perfect summary of his position vis-à-vis Criseyde and his as yet unidentified adversary, Diomede: 'necessite / Is entrechaunged, both in hym and the'.

Chaucer's turn to Boethius in *Troilus* can, I think, be placed in a larger context already apparent in its opening lines: he does not want to let his translation of Boccaccio's tale set in Troy become an entirely modern-dress production. Boccaccio, like Chaucer, is a child of the *Rose*; and the two temporalities of courtly poetry are in play in both works. For all both writers' careful contextualising of the classical, both texts run some danger of turning into modern courtly narratives with a period flavour. Troilus may turn up at the temple in

420   MEDIEVAL POETRY: 1100–1400

Book 1 to honour the Palladion, but his scorning of Love is straight out of the *Roman*, and Criseyde's simple black dress is medieval mourning garb. Both poems are pleasing miscellanies of courtly life, with dances, dinner parties, songs, ladies-in-waiting, back stairs, and go-betweens; the Trojan War itself becomes the stuff of chivalry (with a princely lover who kills by day and languishes by night). In the next century, Henryson will more or less forget about the war in his vindictive desire to clear up Chaucer's loose ends. Less confident than Boccaccio, Chaucer makes courtly poetry his guide in wishing to emphasise the mediation in his work of old books. So many scribes place the full Latin argument of Statius's *Thebaid* beside Cassandra's exposition of Troilus's dream in Book 5 that it appears the placement must be authorial. At this late moment of the text its effect is to turn the love triangle of Troilus-Criseyde-Diomede, and the outcome of the Trojan War, into the revenge of Greek warriors who fell at Thebes. It is in this light that we should reconsider Chaucer's ascription of his source to a spurious classical author, Lollius, rather than to Boccaccio.[18] Chaucer's failure ever to make due attribution to Boccaccio has been widely, and rightly, noted, sometimes with the excuse that Boccaccio's name was hardly known in England in the 1380s, joined with an acknowledgement that Chaucer might not have felt the same need to conceal his true source had he worked a generation later when Boccaccio's Latin works were gaining him status as an authority. But it is also that Boccaccio is no use to him insofar as he wishes to place his text in the cultural context of what Strakhov calls 'the diachronic translation of antiquity'.[19] Indeed, Chaucer does not use the Lollius fiction to conceal features of Boccaccio's text, but rather invokes it, disingenuously, at points where he turns away from that source either to another (such as Petrarch at 1.393–420) or to his own invention. The desire for classical gravity fulfils Chaucer's programme as translator, moving across both languages and temporalities. So the court of Love can have as its king the *Roman*'s modernised version of Love, but it must also have a classical queen, Alceste. Since Chaucer is normally specific about his classical sources, he cannot simply cite Virgil or Ovid or any easily verifiable later author; the only solution is a plausible-sounding reference apparently based on a Horatian ode. This does not make it any less of a fiction, but it places that fiction in Chaucer's understanding of classicising courtly poetry.

When Chaucer cites his source in the telling of the poem, it is also always to emphasise what has or has not already been told: all that can be retold is foreknown. This foreknowledge is not absolute, because like Boethius's text it allows for some contingencies, what Boethius calls conditional necessity—not what will happen, but how exactly it may come to pass. It is played out by the movement of planets and stars, and Chaucer's extensive knowledge of astrological matters forms a high-style descant to the narrative. Not only is foreknowledge the stance of the narrator; it is also that of Criseyde's father, Calkas. It is shared with readers from the opening summary of the story (quoted above). It is not the same as the often more detailed complicity of *The Canterbury Tales*, but it creates the conditions for it—character and comedy. The gap between what a character says or does and what the reader knows is the field of characterisation. It barely exists in complaint, where the pathos generally arises from the speaker's all too bitter knowledge; and attempts find it in the dream poems have proved elusive, as the reader depends, albeit at times ironically,

---

[18] To complicate matters, Lollius (or 'myn auctour') is most often invoked as source when Chaucer has departed from Boccaccio's text, either to draw on another source (Petrarch in 1.393–420) or to work freely without one.

[19] Strakhov, 'Tending to One's Garden', 237.

on the narrator's unfolding eyewitness. In *Troilus*, however, we know what is in Troilus's mind; we see him teased, aided, and manipulated by Pandarus; and we understand him throughout, even in touchingly comic moments, as a tragic figure, doomed without knowing it. Criseyde is both his love and his doom. Though she is a strong character, and greatly developed by Chaucer in Book 2, as the poem progresses we are not so consistently given access to her thoughts; we cannot always see past what Troilus sees, and the narrator is left registering his lack of key pieces of information (whether she had children, how old she was, and so on: 5.826). Readers know whatever the writer shares with us at the characters' expense, through overt narratorial commentary or by much subtler means. The rhyme royal stanza proves to be a potent instrument for dialogue, for human interplay, for the sharing of a joke or the passage of a thought, for a sudden change or undercutting that occurs in the final couplet; however high the narrative, the last line of the stanza tends to be plainly spoken ('And she to soper cam, when it was eve', 3.595; 'As time hem hurt, a time doth hem cure', 5.350).

Characterisation flourishes in the idiomatic potential of the poetic medium. Pandarus is the poem's low mimetic parody of foreknowledge, the character who knows more than other characters (in Book 1 he believes that Criseyde can be seduced, and in Book 5 he does not expect her to return from the Greek camp) and whose plots concerning those characters occupy the greater part of Books 2 and 3. He functions fully in a courtly milieu, apparently operates in the knowledge of high-style astrological occasion, yet is uniquely able to express himself in low style ('thow wrecched mouses herte', 3.736), and his character's capacity to span contradictions ('Thus often wyse men ben war by fooles', 1.635) opens the door to comedy of manners and of style—a door that leads to the comic *Canterbury Tales*. Even in quiet moments, Pandarus brings into the poem an extraordinary mobility of tone. In a single stanza of Book 5, for example, he expresses somewhat non-committal agreement ('It may be wel enough', 5.1170) to Troilus's assertion that Criseyde will return that night, but the rhyme two lines later is on what he thought in his heart 'and softe lough' (5.1173); and what he refrains from saying aloud spans literary worlds, from pastoral byplay ('joly Robyn')—'from haselwode' here means never, but for Pandarus it seems also to have a sexual connotation (he uses it in exclamations elsewhere in 3.890 and 5.505)—to a mixture of proverb and elegaic song:

> 'From haselwode, ther joly Robyn pleyde,
> Shal com al that thow abydest heere!
> Ye, fare wel al the snow of ferne yere!' (5.1174–6)

For all its massive narrative architecture, *Troilus and Criseyde* is still a thing of parts, an anthology of forms. Whereas Boccaccio's original had a proem and nine parts, Chaucer divides his poem into five books, perhaps as homage to Boethius's *Consolation*, and all but Book 5 has a proem calling for classical inspiration appropriate to the book (the Fury Tisiphone in Book 1 and all three Furies in 4, the muse Cleo in 2, Venus and Calliope in 3); these serve as framing lyrics and recall the looser structure of courtly dream poetry. Within the narrative, there is Antigone's song in Book 2 and five major inset pieces that are often scribally marked: three called *Canticus Troili* in 1.400–20, 3.1744–71 and 5.638–44; and the letters of Book 5, that of Troilus (1317–1421) and Criseyde's much briefer response (1590–1631)—these recall their earlier acts of letter writing in Books 1 and 2. Unlike

422 MEDIEVAL POETRY: 1100–1400

Chaucer's practice in the dream poems or Complaints, all these are rendered in the poem's single metre, rhyme royal. Book 1's *Canticus Troili* is the first translation of a Petrarchan sonnet in English, but does not attempt to imitate the form, producing a version in three rhyme royal stanzas that nevertheless adheres closely but inventively to the Italian: Chaucer's noun *quantite* (412), for example is prompted by Petrarch's adverb *tanto* (and is therefore not, as the Riverside edition claims, a mistranslation):

> O quike deth, O swete harm so queynte,
> How may of the in me such quantite
> But if that I consente that it be? (1.411–13)

> O viva morte, O dilettoso male,
> come puoi tanto in me s'io nol consento?[20]

Complaint too is a regular feature in this poem: Criseyde's, generally against Fortune or false accusation, and Troilus's, against Fortune and eventually, in the *Litera Troili* of Book 5, against Criseyde herself: this is the second most sustained complaint Chaucer wrote, surpassed in length only by Anelida's, but in total contrast to the latter by its adherence to the whole poem's single poetic form. That adherence marks the successful integration of complaint into a larger narrative, even as this final complaint by Troilus portends its end.

The final poetic form in *Troilus* might have been more distinct in a courtly work of looser structure—the Envoy: 'Go, litel bok, go litel myn tragedye' (5.1786–end). This is a most intricately constructed poem in its own right, in which the twelve stanzas echo and reflect one another chiastically. The first and last begin and end with Dante's *Paradiso*, from which comes the reference to tragedy and comedy and (very closely translated) the final soaring prayer to the Trinity, 'Uncircumscript, and al maist circumscrive' (1865). The seventh and tenth are anaphoric, modelled on Boccaccio, and exclaim both on the nobility of the pagan past and its 'corsed olde rites' (1849). In between them occurs the address in stanzas eight and nine to a living audience ('O yonge, fresshe folkes, he or she', 1835), appealing to them to give up concerns of 'This world, that passeth soone as floures faire' and think of Christ ('For he nyl falsen no wight, dar I seye'). These two stanzas are a response to the Envoy's return to Boccaccian narrative to speak of Troilus's posthumous reward for love after his death (that reward being his temporary ascent to the eighth sphere)—in the Envoy, not the main narrative, because this is the place where Chaucer has interpolated the passage originally concerning Arcite from the *Teseida*. The added narrative, part of the Envoy, not the main text, allows a final mention of the Trojan War, with its disconcerting reprise of the opening of the *Iliad* ('The wrath', 5.1800), which looks back to the list of the classical writers whom the book is bidden to greet: 'Virgile, Ovide, Omer, Lucan, and Stace' (5.1792). This is Chaucer's audacious use of what David Wallace identifies as the 'sixth of six *topos*', in which he implicitly places himself, as author of the 'litel boke', as the sixth in company of the five classical *auctores*.[21] Their names stand right beside the author's concern for the textual

---

[20] Francesco Petrarca, 'S'amor non è', in Robert M. Durling (ed. and trans.), *Petrarch's Lyric Poems* (Cambridge, MA, 1976), 270–1.

[21] David Wallace, *Chaucer and the Early Writings of Boccaccio* (Woodbridge, 1985), 50–3; and *Chaucerian Polity: Absolutist Lineages and Associational Forms in England and Italy* (Stanford, CA, 1997), 80–2. The precedent is Dante, in *Inferno* 4.82–96. On Chaucer's possible use of this for the statue of 'Englyssh Gaufride' in *House of Fame* (1470), see Helen Cooper, 'The Four Last Things in Dante and Chaucer: Ugolino in the House of Rumour', *New Medieval Literatures*, 3 (1999), 39–66, especially 58–60. On Deschamps's use of the motif to link himself and Chaucer, see Strakhov, 'Tending to One's Garden', 246: 'For Deschamps, the use of classical allusion is no longer

transmission of his brand-new book; conversely, the concern for 'yonge, fresshe folkes' will give way, even in a stanza censuring pagan practices, to a last insistence on the classical pedigree of the text:

> Lo here, the forme of olde clerkis speche
> In poetrie, if ye hir bokes seche. (5.1854–5)

Poetry is not a word Chaucer uses of his own writing, but of classical writing (and, in the 'Clerk's Prologue', of Petrarch). It is conferred upon his own poetry by Deschamps in his ballade about Chaucer, and first in English by Lydgate at the origin of what Christopher Cannon has called the Chaucer myth.[22] This Envoy certainly makes claims for Chaucer's own poem, both anxiously and with pride, but it does so by summoning up all the contradictions that we have seen as characteristic of courtly poetry in the tradition of the *Rose*: classical and modern, old books and new; attraction and repulsion, especially positive and negative views of love, often simultaneous; heaven and hell; pagan and Christian; young and old.

There is no resolving such contradictions within courtly poetry: they are formative, one might say generic. The Envoy ends with two more stanzas of address: to 'moral Gower and philosophical Strode', modern dedicatees who might offer further tuition, and to Christ and the Trinity in the magnificent final stanza, whose rhetorical display comes to rest more simply, as so often with the last line of Chaucer's rhyme royal, in the plainer and more homely mention of the Virgin Mary. That the poem ends in prayer should remind us of Chaucer's investment and strength as a religious poet, especially perhaps of his 'Prier a Nostre Dame', the *ABC*, in twenty-three stanzas of eight lines, which alone among the translations of Deguileville's text (a poem inset into his *Pèlerinage de la vie humaine*) takes the trouble to retain the abecedary sequence of the French stanzas. The desire for perfection articulated in such poetry is also a technical concern, the desire for perfection in poetry itself.

What materials a perfect poem might be made from is the subject of *The House of Fame*. Rather than where most editions put it, beside *The Book of the Duchess*, it may be useful to consider this alongside *Troilus* and the *Legend*. Its sympathy for Dido puts it in similar territory to the *Legend*, and the explicit focus on Virgil speaks to the whole tension between Trojan destiny and sexual love. It is probably the first of his works to feature Chaucer by name (Geoffrey), and is explicitly occupied with what kind of poetry he might write, called here 'tydynges'. Tellingly, it also makes free use of Boethius, which would argue for a date in the mid-1380s rather than the commonly suggested *c* 1378, unduly influenced by the poem's tetrameter; the example of French poets or of Gower does not suggest that poets stop writing in one metre because they get good at another.[23] Whatever the date, the poem is an extraordinary, multifold and novel fusion of the preoccupations of courtly poetry throughout Chaucer's career. Everything is here. His allegiance to a tradition of complaint is registered in his preference for Ovid (Ovid's version of Dido, Ovid's Rumor) rather than Virgil, but what this allegiance really does, especially when linked with Boethius, is declare a different and covert allegiance: to Jean de Meun, the *Rose*, and the thrills of modern versions of the classical. The narrator's quitting of the palace of Fame and his entry into the House

---

simply about where one is in francophone Europe, but where one stands in the literary pantheon of great poets stretching from antiquity to the present day'.

[22] Christopher Cannon, *The Making of Chaucer's English: A Study of Words* (Cambridge, 1998), 214–17.

[23] On the date, see Cooper, 'The Four Last Things', 59, 63–4. This redating is strongly supported by Turner, *Chaucer*, 356–9.

of Rumor are all but universally taken to foreshadow *The Canterbury Tales* (2121–30) and to figure a rejection of the courtly world of Fame; but the real news is that it does the one but not the other. All poetic subjects remain 'love-tydynges' (2143). For the purpose of his poem, Chaucer, uniquely, gives different names, Fame and Rumor, to what in Virgil and Ovid are not two but one, *Fama*. To move courtly poetry into the world of pardoners and pilgrims is not to reject it but to expand it. And this—in the steps of Boccaccio but also of Jean de Meun before them both—is what Chaucer does.

27

The Canterbury Tales

Barry Windeatt

Chaucer's last and most ambitious project, *The Canterbury Tales* (*c* 1388–1400), presents itself as the twenty-four tales told by a chance group of pilgrims during their pilgrimage to Canterbury. The tales read as if reported by a Geoffrey Chaucer who inserts a version of himself into the fiction as their companion, sketches in the pen-portraits of his 'General Prologue' the pilgrims' characteristics, dress, and professional histories, and records their vivid interactions in the link-passages that interconnect most but not all of the tales. But is the *Canterbury Tales* therefore one work or twenty-four? In effect it functions as both, a sequence of interlinked stories where in practice individual tales were always likely to be enjoyed separately. However, the meta-narrative of the pilgrimage—a story-telling competition among a socially diverse group embodying various professional, class, and gender rivalries—implies more distinction between the tellers' tales in poetic practice than Chaucer always pursues. Pilgrims very different in class and culture express themselves in the same strikingly homogenous versification, deploying equally learned allusions and symbolism across their tales. No drunken oaf of a miller could tell the 'Miller's Tale': it is a 'cherles tale' (I.3169) in its ribald plot and rebel spirit, not in its exuberant artfulness and faultless versification.[1] Yet so strong has been the critical imperative to interpret tales as the personal expression of pilgrims' individual characters and professional identity that this risks underestimating what is common to the poetry of the *Tales*.[2] The *Canterbury Tales* certainly attempts stylisations of different voices for different kinds of tales, but there is also a foundational Chaucerian poetic with defining features consistent across the *Tales*. This is the poetry of the *Canterbury Tales* that is this chapter's focus.[3]

Despite Chaucer's evident fascination with the craft of versification, modern evaluation remains curiously blank to how most of his works are written in verse, are poems. By the time Chaucer turned to the *Canterbury Tales* he had invented and mastered his own verse forms in English. In *The Parliament of Fowls* and *Troilus* Chaucer had not only created stanzaic narrative verse in rhyme royal but, in crafting ten-syllabled lines with a broadly alternating stress-pattern, he had founded the tradition of what becomes the English iambic pentameter. The sheer ambition of Chaucer's pioneering innovations in English poetic form is astonishing, but this was already behind him. What is distinctive about how Chaucer takes these personal metrical innovations forwards into the *Canterbury Tales* is the way verse forms are matched with new themes and contexts, both in the four tales in rhyme royal

---

[1] All reference is to Larry D. Benson (general ed.), *The Riverside Chaucer* 3rd edn. (Boston, MA, 1987; Oxford, 1988).

[2] See C. David Benson, *Chaucer's Drama of Style: Poetic Variety and Contrast in 'The Canterbury Tales'* (Chapel Hill, NC, 1986).

[3] For helpful studies, see especially: Robert O. Payne, *The Key of Remembrance: A Study of Chaucer's Poetics* (New Haven, CT, 1963); Derek Brewer, 'Towards a Chaucerian Poetic', *Proceedings of the British Academy*, 60 (1974), 219–52; Joerg O. Fichte, *Chaucer's 'Art Poetical': A Study in Chaucerian Poetics* (Tübingen, 1980); Robert M. Jordan, *Chaucer's Poetics and the Modern Reader* (Berkeley, CA, 1987); Amanda Holton, *The Sources of Chaucer's Poetics* (Aldershot, 2008).

Barry Windeatt, *The Canterbury Tales*. In: *The Oxford History of Poetry in English*. Edited by Helen Cooper and Robert R. Edwards, Oxford University Press. © Barry Windeatt (2023). DOI: 10.1093/oso/9780198827429.003.0027

426   MEDIEVAL POETRY: 1100–1400

and in the sixteen tales that, despite all their thematic and stylistic diversity, are uniformly in decasyllabic lines rhymed in couplets. There are pointedly few exceptions: the six-line-stanza envoy to the 'Clerk's Tale', the deadly spoof in 'Sir Thopas' of the tail-rhyme stanza of popular metrical romances, and the eight-line-stanza of the 'Monk's Tale' (probably written before the *Tales*).

In the Prologue to the *Legend of Good Women* (*c* 1386) Chaucer lists as already written two works—'the lyf ... of Seynt Cecile' and 'al the love of Palamon and Arcite' (F 426, 420)—that were presumably repackaged into the *Canterbury Tales* as the 'Second Nun's Tale' and the 'Knight's Tale' (with whatever revision, now unknowable). In these two distinctly different verse narratives, Chaucer's practice in versification and as a translator-poet can help focus some characteristic features of his poetry across the *Canterbury Tales*. The 'Second Nun's Tale' shows Chaucer following his sources' Latin closely. Fittingly for the life of St Cecilia, patron saint of music, Chaucer's creativity as a translator here lies in something analogous to setting a text to music, giving the sources' Latin prose a stanzaic format that realises meaning in it. In *Troilus* Chaucer had reworked an Italian stanzaic narrative into an English one, but in the tales of the Second Nun, Clerk and Man of Law he undertakes a more fundamental versificatory invention, translating the content of Latin or French prose sources into English narratives in stanzaic verse. These major transformations by means of versification may appear effortless, but they stem from countless decisions about how the original's prose content is disposed into stanza-length units, decisions involving word-order within lines, syntax across lines and rhyme patterns. Stanza opening lines can exploit the energy of new beginnings—'But ther is bettre lif in oother place ...' ('Second Nun's Tale', VIII.323)—while the close of stanzas may exploit mini-climaxes to shape the action:

> He kitte his throte, and in a pit hym caste ('Prioress's Tale', VII.571)

> He *Alma redemptoris* gan to synge
> So loude that al the place gan to rynge ('Prioress's Tale', VI.612–13);

> 'This with o voys we trowen, thogh we sterve!'
>   ('Second Nun's Tale', VIII.420)

A powerful sense of forwards impetus, in which the stanza breaks are no more than a form of punctuation, coexists with the opposite, in which the space between stanzas allows new stanzas to open up new angles, so that the narrative gains a multi-perspectival dimension. While the prose of *The Golden Legend* and Petrarch's *Epistolae Seniles* is versified into English distinctly respectfully in the 'Second Nun's Tale' and the 'Clerk's Tale', Chaucer shapes his stanzaic 'Man of Law's Tale' with bold adaptation out of Trevet's Anglo-Norman chronicle, the stanzaic form allowing for easy interpolation of new material.[4] Such decisive intervention in both content and poetic form also characterises the difference between Chaucer's accounts of the garden of Venus in the *Parliament* (183–294) and the temple of Venus in the 'Knight's Tale' (I.1918–66), both derived from the same stanzas of Boccaccio's *Teseida*. For whereas the *Parliament*'s stanzas match the descriptive fullness of Boccaccio's stanzas, the 'Knight's Tale' briskly compacts *Teseida*'s leisurely catalogue into an edgy summary of lovers' sufferings ('The broken slepes ... The firy strokes of the desirynge', I.1920, 1922) together with lists of abstractions ('Charmes and Force, Lesynges, Flaterye ...' 1927), yet then pushes beyond Boccaccio by including allusions to the *Roman de la Rose* and the mythographical tradition of Venus. The effect is at once to quicken, to enliven, and to intensify allusiveness, but all within a confidently regular poetic form. If 'al the love

---

[4] Robert M. Correale and Mary Hamel (eds), *Sources and Analogues of* The Canterbury Tales, 2 vols. (Cambridge, 2002, 2007), hereafter *SA*. For Trevet's chronicle, see 2:296–329.

of Palamon and Arcite' preceded the *Legend*, it was Chaucer's prototype for tales in ten-syllabled lines rhyming in couplets. While the technical accomplishment of the 'Second Nun's Tale' represents achieved mastery of poetic practice, the 'Knight's Tale' signals new possibilities ahead.

If Chaucer had already invented his metrical resources before the *Canterbury Tales*, he was apparently in a hurry to apply them. The verse narratives of the *Canterbury Tales* are strikingly shorter than Chaucer's earlier works. Thirteen tales—the tales, minus any prologues—are even briefer than the *Parliament* (699 lines). *The Book of the Duchess* (1,334 lines) is considerably longer than any verse tale except the 'Knight's Tale' (2,449 lines), but even that tale, despite being twice as long as any other, is less than a hundred lines longer than *The House of Fame* (2,158 lines), and is distilled from a source—Boccaccio's *Teseida*—which is almost 10,000 lines. Tales as accomplished in their genres as those of the Reeve, Shipman, Wife, or Second Nun are little more than 400 lines long. The 'Friar's Tale' and the 'Manciple's Tale' are briefer still, and the 'Prioress's Tale' achieves perfection in its kind in just over 200 rhyme-royal lines. Chaucer's response to very different sources is to rewrite them in the *Tales* into a more dynamic sequence of scenes and moments of intensified drama. Distracting sub-plots, secondary characters, flabby connecting passages, repetitions, and digressions are decisively excised. Chaucer's preference for such concise narratives represents a particular understanding of the apparently unstoppable impetus of happenings and events, so that form embodies an interpretation of the world. This defining concision is significant in determining the distinctive fusion of theme and style in the poetry of the *Tales*, yet works in conjunction with all kinds of amplification within tales. 'What nedeth gretter dilatacioun?' asks the 'Man of Law's Tale' (II.232), highlighting at the line-end a rather rare Latinate word for that amplifying expansion that Chaucer's texts may deny but usually exemplify. Complementing the drive to concision in narrative is Chaucer's impetus to dilate his tales with many new kinds of materials, transforming how characters and events are understood, adding new thematic dimensions along with ambitious formal and stylistic innovations. Characters are introduced with eye-opening descriptive detail, and most characters are known through their own words in direct speech. Events are rewritten so as to happen more by chance than in the sources and analogues, and this allows for reflections on providence, destiny, and free will. Within narratives the significance of time is highlighted, and often marked by passages of extraordinary poetic beauty inflected with astrological references to the heavens. The coherence of tales around informing images is tautened into poetic unities of symbol and theme. Interpretative possibilities are offered within stories in the shape of non-narrative passages of reflection, apostrophe, and stories within stories, set into a mode of commentary on the action. Tales collected together in the *Canterbury Tales* include various genres—romance, fabliau, saint's life, miracle-story, beast-fable, exemplum—but more intense interplay between genres occurs inside tales, where genres are hybridised in challenging reconfigurations. Mixtures and juxtapositions of styles are also key to the *Tales'* poetry, effective through more complex shadings than mere binary stylistic contrasts of high and low, official and unofficial, or conventional and naturalistic.[5] The prologues that newly contextualise many of the *Canterbury Tales* are only one aspect of a concern to intensify and deepen old stories with new materials, implications and dimensions within Chaucer's newly crafted poetic forms. A process of such dilating upon a subject in diction, style, and theme is key to Chaucer's poetry in the *Canterbury Tales*.

---

[5] For paradigms of courtly and bourgeois, conventional and realistic, and Chaucer's mixed style, see Charles Muscatine, *Chaucer and the French Tradition: A Study in Style and Meaning* (Berkeley, CA, 1957). For stylistic commentary on each tale, see the 'Style' sections in Helen Cooper, *The Oxford Guides to Chaucer: 'The Canterbury Tales'* (Oxford, 1989).

428 MEDIEVAL POETRY: 1100–1400

Beginnings, Speaking, Feeling

To begin at beginnings is to notice how Chaucer customarily dilates at the start on a figure or two, closely observing in concretely detailed poetry their appearance, circumstances, and characteristics. Nicholas and Alison are introduced early in the 'Miller's Tale' so vividly that the rest of the tale develops the implications of how their sensuality is evoked ('Of deerne love he koude and of solas' ... 'And sikerly she hadde a likerous ye', I. 3200, 3244). In the analogues to the 'Reeve's Tale' the miller is just a miller, and it is Chaucer who opens with his vividly observed portrayal of the miller and his family (I.3925–76). The poetry pulses with the barely-contained truculence of this swaggering bully, armed to the teeth, while his pushy wife absurdly pretends to social status, rather than disgrace, from being a priest's bastard ('And eek, for she was somdel smoterlich [besmirched in reputation], / She was as digne [haughty] as water in a dich', I.3963–4). How a tale's characters are introduced may represent Chaucer's radical re-conceptualising. In the *Roman de Renart*, the main analogue for the 'Nun's Priest's Tale', the chickens belong to a rich male peasant (*SA*, 1.456–7), which Chaucer reverses into his account of a poor widow, whose frugal lifestyle ('Ful sooty was hir bour and eek hir halle', VII.2831) contrasts pointedly with her cockerel ('Thus roial, as a prince is in his halle', 3184). So characteristic is Chaucer's way of beginning with an individual described that the 'Friar's Tale' opens with a portrait of an Archdeacon that bristles with technical terms ('Of diffamacioun, and avowtrye, / Of chirche reves and testamentz', III.1306–7)—and so introduces the rackety practices of his employee, the summoner—even though the Archdeacon makes no further appearance in the tale. Such introductory character portraits can furnish themed beginnings that Chaucer's sources do not provide, as in Chaucer's opening accounts of Virginia in the 'Physician's Tale' (VI.5–71, 105–16) or Phoebus in the 'Manciple's Tale' (IX.105–29). Each such portrayal works by claiming the individual as extraordinary or distinctive in some way, expressed through a poetry of superlatives that sets up expectations against which the rest of the tale develops.

Chaucer also rethinks new prequels to tales where, in other versions, those narratives start further along in the story with a pre-existing situation. One analogue for the 'Shipman's Tale' in Boccaccio's *Decameron* begins with a soldier, already accustomed to borrowing money from merchants, and desiring to sleep with a merchant's wife (*SA*, 2.570–1). Instead, Chaucer first establishes, in poetry of acutely observed detail, the characters and relationship of a merchant, his wife and a monk (VII.1–88). The 'Franklin's Tale' represents a more elaborate case where Chaucer invents a prequel missing from other versions. Both the Boccaccio analogues start with a happily married lady who already has an unwanted admirer (*SA*, 1.220–1, 238–9), but the 'Franklin's Tale' opens further back in the story, with Arveragus's chivalrous courtship of Dorigen and their exceptional understanding of reciprocal forbearance in marriage ('Thus hath she take hir servant and hir lord', V.791–2). This allows their mutual devotion, established through some of Chaucer's most eloquent poetry of love and marriage, to furnish a thematic prelude to the tale ('Love is a thyng as any spirit free', 767), that posits a value-system against which all that follows may be gauged.[6] Chaucer's beginnings mean that tales open with multiple implications.

---

[6] The extent of critical debate over the nature and value of the marriage imagined in the 'Franklin's Tale' registers the multiple implications of Chaucer's beginnings. For concise discussion of twentieth-century critical debates over each tale—which is beyond the scope of this chapter—see the 'Themes' sections in Cooper, *Oxford Guides*, and Derek Pearsall, *The Canterbury Tales* (London, 1985).

Chaucer's characters are known through their own words, and Chaucer has an unerring ear for pithy colloquial idiom: 'Stynt thy clappe!' (I.3144), as the Reeve tells the Miller. Tolerating broad language testifies to the *Tales* being an uncensored record, 'Al speke he nevere so rudeliche and large' (I.734). Chaucer's comic tales are shaped by their direct speech, unlike the sparse use of direct speech in French fabliaux. Analogues for the 'Reeve's Tale' do not include the clerks' initial dialogue with the Miller (I.4022–56; cf. *SA*, 1.30–3, 44–7), nor the exchanges that occupy much of the tale's second half. The 'Friar's Tale'—unlike the brief Latin exempla that are its nearest analogues—develops through extended dialogue between summoner and devil ('"Artow thanne a bailly?" "Ye", quod he', III.1392). This tale could easily make a short radio play, as might the 'Summoner's Tale', which unfolds largely through the friar's utterance. The 'Shipman's Tale', after initial scene-setting, proceeds through direct-speech exchanges, unlike the spare reportage of the Italian analogues. The tale explores through speech the doubleness of language, and something comparable happens in tales—like the 'Canon's Yeoman's Tale' and the second part of the 'Squire's Tale'—that are structured as an encounter followed by self-revelation. That 'The wordes moote be cosyn to the dede' (I.742), and how often they are not, is a pervasive concern of the *Tales*' poetry.

A dynamic feature of the poetry of the *Tales* is Chaucer's dramatic dilations of direct speech expressing vehement emotion. Feeling—in both characters and readers—is intensified by voicing it, but so too is questioning. The chronicle source for the 'Man of Law's Tale' includes almost no direct speech: Custance's parting speech to her parents (II.274–87), her prayers when twice set adrift (449–62, 826–63) or unjustly accused (638–44) are instances of Chaucer's added voicings of plangent feeling for the heroine, but her husband's feelings are also recorded in the first person (757–67, 1037–43). Inner lives of the protagonists are vividly revealed in their own words by such inclusions, but exchanges between a humble messenger and Donegild (732–42), or the constable's reflections on the wickedness of the world (810–19), are also provided in direct speech. Across the *Tales* Chaucer invents speeches voicing emotional responses, such as Griselda's parting blessing to her baby daughter in the 'Clerk's Tale' (IV.555–60) and her overwhelming emotions when rediscovering her children (1088–98). Aurelius's declaration of love to Dorigen ('Franklin's Tale', V.967–78) and his later announcement that 'the rokkes been aweye' (1311–38) are without equivalent in the analogues and allow a voicing of desperate feeling, as do Virginia's frantic pleas to her father ('Physician's Tale', VI.231–50), or Palamon and Arcite's vehement quarrel as soon as they both see Emelye (I.423–86), and their later dispute in the grove (1580–1620). In other cases, potentates voice feeling more formally in public contexts, reflecting the speaker's status and political purposes: only Chaucer's Sultan in the 'Man of Law's Tale' summons his privy council to announce his passion for Custance (II.225–31), and his mother summons her own council to voice her outrage at her son's apostasy (330–57), while the lengthy reflective monologues that Chaucer expands for his Theseus play a key role in the thematic development of the 'Knight's Tale' (I.1785–1825, 2987–3089).

Characteristic of Chaucer's dilations on direct speech are questioning soliloquies of complaint by his characters, such as the female falcon's complaint about her false lover ('Squire's Tale', V.479–629), the mirroring complaints by Palamon and Arcite lamenting continued imprisonment, or release (I.1223–1333), Arcite's complaint in the grove (I.1542–71), Dorigen's complaint on the existence of the rocks (V.865–93), and her later lengthy complaint (a ninth of the 'Franklin's Tale') when they have disappeared (1355–1456). As speech goes, such complaint is formal, matching its themes and circumstances, while including the passionate and immediate, and this disposition to complaint reflects a pervasive world-view

430 MEDIEVAL POETRY: 1100–1400

in the *Tales*' poetry. Complaint is evidently valued but usually resembles an observance performed for its own sake, accepted to have an indeterminate effect in a world of helpless suffering. Dorigen is spurred to her rash promise to Aurelius 'Syn I yow se so pitously complayne' (V.991), but Chaucer's 'ugly sergeant' reminds Griselda that while lords' wills 'mowe wel been biwailled or complayned' (IV.530), they must be obeyed nonetheless.

Chance, Time, Astrology

Misfortune and chance are themes informing Chaucer's poetry in the *Tales*, as if inseparable from Chaucer's realisations of narrative plots: in the 'Knight's Tale' it 'so bifel, by aventure or cas' (I.1074) that Palamon's glance first fell upon Emelye; Arcite is warned by a god in a dream to return to Athens (1384–92), whereas Boccaccio's Arcita decides for himself (*Teseida*, 4.37); Palamon and Arcite coincide in the grove by chance (1488–90, 1516–27), whereas Boccaccio's Palamone goes there on purpose seeking out Arcita (5.33); and Theseus chances on the lovers duelling (1663–72), but in the *Teseida* Emilia has Teseo called to the spot (5.81). In each case Chaucer opts for a more edgily coincidental sequence, and a similar emphasis on unexpected encounters occurs in the 'Franklin's Tale'. In Boccaccio's analogous versions the lady, already aware of her admirer, calculates on thwarting him by setting an impossible task as the price of winning her, but Chaucer's Dorigen is taken so unawares by Aurelius's unexpected declaration that she is flustered into a rash promise. When her husband tells Dorigen to keep that promise, Aurelius happens to meet her in the street on her way to visit him. The chance encounter and his amazement at her errand greatly intensify the denouement's drama (V.1499–1524). This greater incidence of chance lends occurrences more mysterious force and invites reflections on possible patterns in events. Hauntingly beautiful references to how humanity's fate 'in the sterres, clerer than is glas, / Is writen' are among Chaucer's additions to his source in the 'Man of Law's Tale':

> Paraventure in thilke large book
> Which that men clepe the hevene ywriten was
> With sterres, whan that he his birthe took,
> That he for love sholde han his deeth, allas! (II.190–3)

The very precocity in English of Chaucer's astrological-cum-astronomical poetic makes it avidly imitated by post-1400 poets. Chaucer habitually notices times and dates, introducing precise time-schemes into his borrowed plots, and this shapes poetic style in the *Canterbury Tales*. In the 'Shipman's Tale' the monk whips out his portable sundial to tell the time (VII.206), and the date on which the wife's debt is due determines the tale's time-scheme (180, 307). Palamon, Emelye, and Arcite go to pray at the hours astrologically propitious for the gods they petition (I.2209–20, 2271–4, 2367–70). Palamon's escape from prison, and Chaunteclere's narrow escape from the fox, are both dated to 3 May (I.1462–3; VII.3189–90), a traditionally portentous date, while other added dates increase precision and actuality. Aurelius makes his declaration to Dorigen on 6 May (V.906) and visits the magician in December (1244). The Squire dates Cambyuskan's feast to 15 March (V.47). The pear-tree incident in the 'Merchant's Tale' is dated to the first week in June (IV.2222–4). Such chroniclings of time determine style in the *Tales* by importing technical astrological diction that makes poetry out of definitions of planetary motion in time:

> Parfourned hath the sonne his ark diurne;
> No lenger may the body of hym sojurne
> On th'orisonte, as in that latitude. (IV.1795–97)

With Chaucer's alertness to the heavens comes a style with all the exhilaration of glittering light in his astrologically-informed poetry of dawn and morning. Chaucer is a poet of sunlight: 'Bright was the sonne as in that someres daye', notes the 'Man of Law's Tale' (II.554), where Chaucer's source does not mention the weather (*SA*, 2.304–5). Palamon—newly escaped after years in a lightless prison—discovers Arcite in a grove next morning:

> The bisy larke, messager of day,
> Salueth in hir song the morwe gray,
> And firy Phebus riseth up so bright
> That al the orient laugheth of the light,
> And with his stremes dryeth in the greves
> The silver dropes hangynge on the leves. (I.1491–6)

Sheer energy of poetic language here shimmers with renewal at dawn, and the day when January glimpses May and Damian in the pear-tree is comparably flooded with brilliant sunlight, carefully dated through astrological calibration ('Bright was the day, and blew the firmament; / Phebus hath of gold his stremes doun ysent', IV.2219–20). By contrast, mid-winter is defined by the fading of such glorious light, in Chaucer's poetic evocation of sunlight's wintry withdrawal:

> Phebus wax old, and hewed lyk laton* *brass alloy*
> That in his hoote declynacion
> Shoon as the burned gold with stremes brighte;
> But now in Capricorn adoun he lighte,
> Where as he shoon ful pale, I dar wel seyn. (V.1245–9)

Chaucer's poetry about sunlight typically involves astrological definition of time and season, and with the implication that a whole cast of unlikely characters supposedly share in Chaucer's astrological knowledgeableness, from Harry Bailey who 'saugh wel that the brighte sonne / The ark of his artificial day hath ronne' (II.1–2) to the Franklin and the Man of Law, the Squire ('Phebus the sonne ful joly was and cleer, /For he was neigh his exaltacioun / In Martes face ...' V.48–50), and even Chaunteclere, the cockerel: 'By nature he knew ech ascencioun / Of the equynoxial in thilke toun' (VII.2855–6). The Franklin may jest at astrological language ('For th'orisonte hath reft the sonne his lyght— / This is as muche to seye as it was nyght', V.1016–18) but, in the Franklin's account of how the clerk magics away the sight of the rocks, Chaucer thinks nothing of making poetry out of impenetrable calculations ('As been his centris and his argumentz / And his proporcioneles convenientz', 1277–8). When the 'Man of Law's Tale' anguishes over the stars at Custance's departure for Syria ('Infortunat ascendent tortuous ...' II.302) Chaucer sees no difficulty in making poetry out of abstruse astrological allusions, in order to frame commentary on the action.

Commentary, Example, Allusion

Across very different tales Chaucer deploys a comparable technique, introducing significant interpolations of non-narrative material, many in direct speech, set into a form of thematic commentary on the narrative. Such dilations—typically dominating the first half of a tale—are a determining feature of the *Tales*' structure and idiom.[7] In the 'Pardoner's Tale',

---

[7] See Barry Windeatt, 'Literary Structures in Chaucer', in Piero Boitani and Jill Mann (eds), *The Cambridge Companion to Chaucer*, 2nd edn. (Cambridge, 2003), 214–32.

432 MEDIEVAL POETRY: 1100–1400

which he volunteers as an instance of his preaching for personal gain, once the revellers and their lifestyle have been introduced briefly, the Pardoner expatiates on lengthy examples of his preaching against drunkenness, gluttony, gambling, and swearing (VI.483–659), only returning to the story itself ('... now wol I telle forth my tale', 660) nearly halfway through his tale. Several longer tales exhibit a comparable technique. In the 'Merchant's Tale', after twenty lines introducing January's belated determination to marry, an ambivalent excursus dilates upon marriage's delights (IV.1267–1393), as if voiced by a sardonic clerical speaker, soon followed by a direct-speech rehearsal of clashing opinions by Placebo and Justinus (1478–1565), and discussion of January's fear 'that I shal have myn hevene in erthe heere' (1634–85). These reflections occupy a quarter of the whole tale before the plot proceeds. A comparable ratio between story and commentary figures in the 'Nun's Priest's Tale', where over a third of the tale's total lines (235 out of 625) are devoted to the chickens' debate about the validity of dreams (VII.2921–3156), providing a form of thematic preface to the narrative. In briefer tales the proportion of commentary may be even greater. In the 'Physician's Tale' almost the first half of the total dilates on Nature's satisfaction with her creation of Virginia, the narrator's account of Virginia's virtues, and an address to governesses and parents on their responsibilities (VI.9–117), before the story proper—based on a brief episode from Roman history mediated through the *Roman de la Rose*—gets underway. Similarly, in the 'Manciple's Tale', Ovid's story of metamorphosis (when a crow is not thanked for telling the god Apollo that he is a cuckold) has been restructured with an excursus on natural instinct (IX.159–95) and another on language (207–37) before the denouement, followed by a final commentary on discretion (309–61). Comparable dilations commenting on the action include the hag's wedding-night speech in the 'Wife of Bath's Tale' (III.1109–1227) and the dispute between Pluto and Proserpina ('Merchant's Tale', IV.2237–2319). In all such tales, passages of interpolated commentary—often appearing out of scale—shape poetic idiom through unsettling transitions and juxtapositions of material, style, and tone, with disruptions of illusion and contradictions of perspective reminiscent of form and composition in contemporary medieval painting and structures.

One particular rhetorical form of commentary dilating on narrative action—and a feature of Chaucer's poetry in the *Tales*—is apostrophe, which, with its exclamatory urgency of reflection, invites yet tests reader-response. In Christian invocations apostrophe seems wholly fitting (VII.467, 3050), as too where the narrator comments sympathetically on a character's misfortune ('O nedelees was she tempted in assay!', 'Clerk's Tale', IV.621), or even interrogates a character in the tale ('Merchant's Tale', IV.1869–70). The 'Man of Law's Tale' is interspersed with frequent apostrophes, all interpolated by Chaucer into his source, which punctuate the narrative with commentary on wicked characters (II.358–67, 771–84), morally instructive incidents ('O foule lust of luxurie, lo, thyn ende!' 925), or invitations to compassion (654). Here, apostrophe as the tale's defining mode may distil proportionate commentary on earthly uncertainties, but elsewhere apostrophe trembles on the verge of comic excess. There is delicious bathos in the Nun's Priest's apostrophes on happenings in the farmyard when the fox seizes Chaunteclere in its jaws ('O destinee, that mayst nat been eschewed!' VII.3338; cf. 3230–1). More ambivalent are apostrophes in the 'Merchant's Tale' where language and register are elevated, although the misfortune is notably domesticated ('O perilous fyr, that in the bedstraw bredeth!' IV.1783). Even more overheated is the Pardoner's horrified apostrophising of the belly: 'O wombe! O bely! O stynkyng cod [bag] ...!' (VI.534), here drawing, as Chaucer's apostrophes often do, on the poetic power of lists

('O traytous homycide, O wikkednesse! / O glotenye, luxurie and hasardrye!' 896–7),
a power that Chaucer's poetry deploys throughout the *Tales*.[8]

When the 'Man of Law's Tale' apostrophises the Sultaness, likening her to an infamous
Babylonian queen ('Virago, thou Semyrame the secounde!' II.359), this exemplifies a recurrent feature texturing Chaucer's poetry in the *Tales*: the deployment of thumbnail allusions
to exemplary figures and lives, biblical or classical, legendary or historical. There is a poetry
in these clusters of resonant names that characterise the rhetoric of such ecclesiastics as the
Pardoner, Summoner, or Nun's Priest. The Pardoner summarises the stories of Lot, Herod,
and Attila the Hun to illustrate his arguments against drunkenness (VI.485–91, 579–81),
cites Adam and Eve to exemplify gluttony (505–11), and summons classical examples to
warn against gambling (603–26). The Summoner's friar cites to old Thomas the examples of Moses and Aaron on abstinence (III.1885–1901) and tells anecdotes against anger
citing the Persian kings Cambyses and Cyrus (2017–82). Although this device figures in
Chaucer's earlier poems, such a mode of argument by means of named figures is applied
intensively across the *Tales*. The effect is that exemplary instances, usually summarised
in a nutshell, are nested, stories within stories, inside the *Canterbury Tales*, so that other
examples are constantly being read against each other, enabling new meanings by means
of comparison. Such an allusive poetic style might seem suited to a cleric like the Nun's
Priest, but when his extended exemplary stories about prophetic dreams (VII.2984–3121)
and his catalogue of biblical and classical instances—Daniel, Joseph, Croesus, Andromache
(3127–50)—are voiced by a cockerel, this puts style under pressure of comic mismatch with
content and context. Another possible stylistic mismatch occurs in the 'Merchant's Tale'
where the narrator—perhaps originally intended to be an ecclesiastic—summarises the stories of Jacob, Judith, and Abigail (1362–73), associates both the blind classical guardian
Argus and Pyramus and Thisbe with January's garden (IV.2111–13, 2125–31), and recalls
the story of Pluto and Proserpina ('In Claudyan ye may the stories rede, / How in his grisely
carte he hire fette', 2230–3). As with the 'Miller's Tale' that no miller could tell, here is a most
unusual merchant, whose erudite reading equals Chaucer's. Even more exceptional is the
deployment of this name-checking style by a woman. In her Prologue the Wife of Bath cites
for herself Solomon's many wives (III.35–6) but also reproduces at length her fifth husband's style of expounding to her biblical and classical instances of 'wicked' wives (642–9,
721–85), and interrupts her tale to repeat a classical story by way of example ('Witnesse
on Myda—wol ye heere the tale?', 951). This citational style spills over into the 'Wife's Tale',
where the elderly bride recommends 'Reedeth Senek, and redeth eek Boece', and cites Dante,
Valerius Maximus (1165–6), and Juvenal's example of a happy pauper (1192–4). Another
wife's attempt, in Dorigen's soliloquy, to argue by means of exemplary stories recalled in
nutshell form struggles with an uneasy fit between content, style, and context, implying the
strains in her predicament (V.1355–1456).

Comparisons between characters or episodes in the *Canterbury Tales* and classical or
biblical figures or events prompt questions about the appropriateness of the match, producing an ambivalently allusive poetic style. Disproportionate comparisons may prompt
ironical interpretations, as when the fox in the 'Nun's Priest's Tale' is likened to those infamous betrayers, Judas Iscariot, Ganelon, and Sinon who betrayed Troy (VII.3227–9). But
when the lamenting falcon in the 'Squire's Tale' compares her faithless lover to Jason, Paris,

---

[8] E.g., I.1925–8, 2920–3; III.285–9, 869–71, 1746–53; VIII.788–818.

434   MEDIEVAL POETRY: 1100–1400

and Lameth, the first biblical bigamist (V.548–54), her rhetorical style matches allusion with feeling not disproportionately for a female plaintiff (although possibly so for a female bird). In the 'Merchant's Tale' there is an uneasy mismatch in comparisons between May and the meekness and beauty of the biblical Esther, or between January's lovemaking and Paris and Helen of Troy (IV.1744–5, 1756). Music at their wedding feast is claimed to surpass legendary classical and biblical musicians, in lines so resonant that they sit uncomfortably with the morally dubious occasion (IV.1715–37). Yet likening the magnificence of Custance's reception in Syria (II.400–3) to a famous classical triumph can work as an accurate comparison. The Nun's Priest's learnedly referenced claim that Chauntecleres's singing surpassed that of mermaids ('For Phisiologus seith sikerly / How that they syngen wel and myrily', VII.3271–2) reads like ironic excess, whereas the Wife of Bath's dry aside that her fourth husband was not buried as richly as King Darius's celebrated tomb by a legendary sculptor ('... the sepulcre of hym Daryus / Which that Appelles wroghte subtilly', III.498–9) reminds us that such dilations upon exemplary instances characterise a Chaucerian poetic style across the *Tales*, and not always what each speaker is realistically likely to know (unless, in this case, recalled by dint of Jankin's book). The Nun's Priest's assertion that the hens' distress at Chauntecleres's abduction *exceeds* the lamentations heard at the falls of Troy and Carthage, or at Nero's persecutions, seems gloriously disproportionate ('But sovereynly dame Pertelote shrighte [shrieked], / *Ful louder than* did Hasdrubales wyf', VII.3355–72; my italics). Yet the very comparable avowals that the grief when Custance leaves Rome for Syria exceeded the weeping at the falls of Troy, Thebes, and Carthage (II.288–94) are evidently not designed to seem equally disproportionate to feeling. Context determines.

Genres, Styles, Symbols

One determining context must be story-type, although both Chaucer's romances and comic tales in the *Canterbury Tales* represent more fluid 'mixed' versions than other examples of those genres.[9] Chaucer's generic hybrids distinguish themselves from each other by how they deploy poetic style to represent understandings of material reality and the quiddities of the worlds they describe in objects, spaces, and bodies, or in social observance. Different story-types encode different understandings of the world's experience. In this, Chaucer's poetry of food proves an illuminating case-study, since distinct approaches to food serve to differentiate the varying interpretations of materiality in the poetry of Chaucer's diverse tales. The frugal widow, Chauntecleres's owner, provides one benchmark, subsisting on 'Milk and broun breed, in which she foond no lak, / Seynd [broiled] bacoun, and somtyme an ey or tweye' (VII.2844–5). While an unmarried peasant, Griselda subsists on cabbage and greens (I.226), but her diet once a lady goes unmentioned. By contrast, the comic tales describe abundant food with relish: as a dinner-guest, the monk in the 'Shipman's Tale' brings 'a jubbe [large jug] of malvesye [malmsey], / And eek another ful of fyn vernage [Italian white wine], / And volatyl [game fowl] ...' (VII.70–2). In the 'Summoner's Tale' the friar orders a gourmet's menu while pretending to a meagre appetite:

> 'Have I nat of a capon but the lyvere,
> And of youre softe breed but a shyvere,
> And after that a rosted pigges heed ...' (III.1839–41)

---

[9] See Susan Crane, *Gender and Romance in Chaucer's 'Canterbury Tales'* (Princeton, NJ, 1994), and the 'Genre' sections in Cooper, *Oxford Guides*.

In the 'Miller's Tale' Absolom woos Alison with presents of sweet wines and piping-hot cakes and calls her a honeycomb and sweet cinnamon (I.3378–9, 3698–9), while in the 'Reeve's Tale' the miller provides the clerks with a supper of roast goose, ale, and bread (I.4137). Of a feast in the Squire's romance, by contrast, we only hear 'I wol nat tellen of hir strange sewes [broths], / Ne of hir swannes, ne of hire heronsewes [young herons]' (V.67–8). Food is rarely consumed in Chaucer's romances: years pass without mention of meals taken, while a quasi-saint like Custance almost does without food for years on end or is miraculously sustained (II.466, 498–9, 869–72). It is therefore not promising that in 'Sir Thopas' the romance hero's face is as pale as a fine white loaf (VII.725), and positively queasy that January insists on a teenage bride because 'bet than old boef is the tendre veel' (IV.1417, 1420). Although the Franklin can sustain munificent hospitality ('It snewed in his hous of mete and drynke', I.343), his intent interest in that food ('Wo was his cook but if his sauce / Were poynaunt and sharp ...' 351–2) may not quite fit with a romance world, and is unaffordable for such as the Nun's Priest's poor widow ('Of poynaunt sauce hir neded never a deel', VII.2834). Food helps define genre, and whereas Alison's mouth—sweet as mead 'Or hoord of apples leyd in hey or heeth' (I.3262)—suggests that unstaled wholesomeness through which she complicates fabliau stereotypes, the Cook's breath is foul (IX.39). His re-heated dishes and poor hygiene give his customers food-poisoning rather than nourishment ('For in thy shoppe is many a flye loos', I.4352), and his ulcerated shin is mentioned rather too close to his excellent chicken stew (I.385–7). The Pardoner's repulsed characterisation of cooking as food pulverised, strained, and ground for ease of passing through the gullet and stinking belly conveys his tortured sense of flesh corrupted (VI.537–48). In his *Tale* two members of a criminal trinity murder the third member but subsequently die by the bread and wine that he has already poisoned for them (VI.879–88). Petrarch may remark that the celebrations at Griselda's reinstatement were more joyful than her wedding, but the 'Clerk's Tale'—more uneasily mixed in tone than Petrarch's tale—observes concretely that 'This feste was ... gretter of costage' (IV.1126; cf. *SA*, 1.128–9, 164–5).

Chaucer's poetry across different genres is also differentiated by how it includes or avoids material realities of bodily existence. The pitilessly observed decrepitude of the slack skin shaking on January's elderly neck and his croaky voice (IV.1849–50) distances the 'Merchant's Tale' from youth-centred romances. Unblenchingly, Chaucer's poetry is invigorated by bodiliness, but in some tales bodies have little place. Chaucer catches in words how the Cook has a cold, speaking nasally and sneezing (IX.61–2), and the miller in the 'Reeve's Tale' belches and sounds as hoarse as if he has a cold after overindulging (I.4151–2). No one in Chaucer's romances belches or sneezes. Once everyone retires for the night in the 'Reeve's Tale' the air is filled with unconscious emissions of snoring, farting, and snorting in one's sleep (4163–7), but anal-retentive Absolom in the 'Miller's Tale' is tellingly 'somdeel squaymous / Of fartyng' (I.3337–8). In the 'Summoner's Tale' the over-ingenuity in dividing a fart wryly shows intellectuality controlling bodiliness, where the squire's problem-solving is a surrogate for Chaucer's ingenuity in making something thought-provoking from what might otherwise be coarse bodily jest. Once such polite discourse breaks down, the Host instead voices gendered threats of bodily violence against the sexually ambivalent Pardoner's genitalia ('Lat kutte hem of ... / They shul be shryned in an hogges toord!', VI.952–3). Body is identity, or the clothes that mask it. So seedy is the Canon who shows up in the Canon's Yeoman's Prologue that an inquisitive Host comments

436 MEDIEVAL POETRY: 1100–1400

to the Yeoman on the mismatch between his employer's grubby and tattered clothes and his claims to be a successful alchemist:

> 'Why is thy lord so sluttish*, I the preye,   *slovenly*
> And is of power bettre clooth to beye,
> If that his dede accorde with thy speche?' (VIII.636–8)

This mismatch between appearance and reality is often the question implicit in descriptions of looks, dress and comportment across the *Tales*.

Such poetry of body and appearance is further galvanised by Chaucer's genius for realising bodies in motion, in a kinetic poetry of gesture and movement. When the student Alan in the 'Reeve's Tale' mistakenly gets into bed with the miller and boasts to him that he has 'thries in this shorte nyght / Swyved the milleres doghter bolt upright [flat on her back]' (I.4265–6), a fight promptly ensues: 'And in the floor, with nose and mouth tobroke, / They walwe as doon two pigges in a poke' (4277–8). The quickfire succession of intended and accidental movements conveys to the mind's eye a wholly convincing sequence of bodies in motion. Even more telling, because it includes an unpredictable resolution, is the Wife's recollection of how—exasperated by her younger husband's endless reading to her in bed from his book about wicked wives—she tore three leaves out of his detested book and cuffed him. Chaucer translates the ensuing flurry of blows, trips, and falls into a highly kinetic poetry, ending in magical stillness when the Wife improvises her faux deathbed forgiveness scene, triumphantly manipulating men to the last (III.788–810). Modern readers—spoiled by the fight or chase sequences in films—risk not giving enough credit for Chaucer's skill in making such sequences a reality in poetry. The chase in the 'Nun's Priest's Tale', after the fox makes off with Chaunteclere, shows Chaucer's brilliant mastery of this poetry of and about movement. The whole farmyard joins in the chase ('Ran cow and calf, and eek the verray hogges', VII.3385), and the din from hotly pursuing people and animals is stupendous ('They yolleden as feendes doon in helle', 3389). Chaucer's camera-eye keeps moving between reporting pell-mell motion and immense cacophony: now a whole hiveful of bees join the chase (3392); now trumpets and horns are blaring, with people shrieking and whooping (3398–3401). Into this *tour de force* of kinetic poetry Chaucer drily drops a comparison with the screams of a mob's racist violence against Flemish immigrants during the Peasants' Revolt—

> Certes, he Jack Straw [a peasant leader] and his meynee
> Ne made nevere shoutes half so shrille
> Whan that they wolden any Flemyng kille (3394–6)

—one of what are probably wisely infrequent allusions to contemporary events by a poet who lived through the politics of increasingly unsafe and uncertain times.

The essence of Chaucer's poetry in the *Canterbury Tales* is its sheer bravura, animated by a pent-up energy of language that goes along with a kind of exhilarated perceptiveness. When the Canon and his Yeoman have ridden hard to overtake the pilgrims the narrator exclaims 'But it was joye for to seen hym swete!' (VIII.579), as if even the sight of perspiring exertion prompts excited delight. Chaucer has a knack for distilling into words the vitality and brio of life: Placebo assures January 'Your herte hangeth on a joly pyn!' (IV.1516), and the Wife of Bath, looking back 'Upon my yowthe, and on my jolitee' remarks with satisfaction 'It tikleth me aboute myn herte roote ... That I have had my world as in my tyme' (III.470–3). January's pleasure may be less savoury, but Chaucer's poetry catches his friskiness:

> He was al coltish*, ful of ragerye*,   *like a colt; wantonness*
> And ful of jargon* as a flekked pye*.   *chatter; varicoloured magpie* (IV.1847–8)

Comparisons with the characteristics of animals, and especially birds, are ingrained in Chaucer's poetic language ('As any pecok he was proud and gay', I.3926). Such comparisons are particularly good at conveying a spark of joy, as with the carefree young London apprentice in the 'Cook's Tale' ('Gaillard [merry] he was as goldfynch in the shawe [wood]', I.4367), or the merchant after clinching a deal in the 'Shipman's Tale' ('And hoom he gooth, murie as a papejay [parrot]', VII.369). In this, Chaucer's poetic idiom is one with his imaginative world, which is marked by the same restless energy across diverse story-types, whether it is the seizing of advantage in the comic tales, otherworldly aspirations in the religious tales, or the open-ended strivings demanded of lovers in romance ('For May wole have no slogardie [sluggishness] anyght', I.1042).

What also informs the poetry of the *Canterbury Tales* is the imagistic and symbolic unity that Chaucer gives his tales. Comparison with sources and analogues reveals how Chaucer integrates plot and image more tautly into thematic unities. In the 'Shipman's Tale' of sexual and financial exchange, Chaucer tightens the interconnection between sex and money by setting the tale in a world where merchants profit by complex loan agreements:

> That nedes moste he make a chevyssaunce*   *raise a loan*
> For he was bounden in a reconyssaunce*.   *repayment pledge; bond*(VII.329–30)

Chaucer has no problem with making the technicalities of how business transactions are financed the subject of poetry. In the 'Reeve's Tale' Chaucer also makes poetry out of describing the mill as a mechanism of moving parts (I.4036–9), while the clerks' parodied northern accents highlight how Chaucer's poetry tests its London-centred sophistication to explore provincial exclusion. Chaucer makes more than any French analogue of how the clerks' stolen sexual pleasure is vengeful exchange for their stolen property, emphasising parallels between the clerks' lovemaking and the very material process of grinding corn. As in the tales of the Squire and Summoner, technology and gadgetry are part of the *Tales'* symbolic unity as poems, as are the construction of ambitious symbolic architecture in the 'Knight's Tale', the commissioning of a private pleasure garden in the 'Merchant's Tale', or thematic settings of sea-shore and garden in the 'Franklin's Tale'. In the analogues for the latter, the task that the lady sets her unwanted admirer is something impossible in nature—a garden blooming in mid-winter—but this garden possesses no larger thematic significance for the plot. Instead, Chaucer's Dorigen sets Aurelius the task of removing the rocks. Her dismay at the danger they pose to her returning husband is the measure of her marital devotion, yet the task comments on Dorigen's ill-considered rebellion against a divine dispensation that necessarily includes risks. Her unwanted lover's removal of one danger to her husband will bring their marriage into another peril. Chaucer's change to the impossible task is a masterstroke in re-drawing the symbolic and poetic unity of his version of the story.

How, after so much 'dilatacioun', could poems be brought to a resolution? Two thirds of tales that conclude without interruption end with some form of prayer, however perfunctory or unconventional: the Wife prays for husbands 'fressh abedde' and the power to

438   MEDIEVAL POETRY: 1100–1400

control them (III.1258–64). This makes all the more exceptional the distinctly unprayerful envoy to the 'Clerk's Tale', Chaucer's sole use of six-line stanzas in the *Tales* and headed 'Lenvoy de Chaucer' in manuscripts—as if scribes disbelieved that the Clerk would end patient Griselda's story with this incitement to turn the tables on men. It is a double ballade with only three rhymes (*-ence, -aille, -inde*), and in its exuberant rhetoric and rhyme it exemplifies Chaucer's audacious poetic when ending both lines and poems. Modern criticism undervalues Chaucer as a poet who achieves significant effects through rhyme. Yet Chaucer's masterly rhyming is key to his poetry's style and effect. His successors recognised this in attempting to imitate flourishes like Chaucer's strikingly unusual Latin polysyllables at line-ends, such as 'Ther stood the temple of Mars armypotente [powerful in arms]' in the 'Knight's Tale' (I.1982). Clerical speakers in the *Tales* deploy such Latinate diction in rhymes: the Friar has his summoner quiz the devil, 'Han ye a figure thanne determinat / In helle …?' (1459–60), and in the 'Merchant's Tale', whose teller often sounds clerical, Proserpina spurns her husband's citation of Solomon's authority all the more resoundingly with the help of two Latinate rhymes:

> 'Pardee, as faire as ye his name emplastre*,   *gloss over; stick a plaster on*
> He was a lecchour and an ydolastre*.'   *idolator* (IV.2297–8)

Yet supposedly uneducated and non-clerical tellers also deploy such words in rhyme. Owner of many books, it is unremarkable for the Monk to describe how Deianira 'envenymed' [poisoned] Hercules' shirt (VII.2124), but it is more remarkable for the Wife of Bath to deploy the verb in a moment of poignant regret:

> 'But age, alas, that al wole envenyme,
> Hath me biraft my beautee and my pith*.'   *vigour* (III.474–5)

Even more noticeable are Latinate rhyme-words from humble speakers, as when the 'Cook's Tale' declares 'For thefte and riot [riotous behaviour], they been convertible [interchangeable]' (I.4395). Between discovering that his daughter has just been deflowered, and assaulting her deflowerer, the miller in the 'Reeve's Tale' exclaims, 'Who dorste be so boold to disparage / My doghter, that is come of swich lynage?' (I.4271–2). Ludicrous social climbing is exposed by his unlikely rhyme-words. The 'Miller's Tale' is even more given to such rhymes, remarking 'An housbonde shal nat been inquisityf' (I.3163), grandly observing of the Oxford carpenter 'He knew nat Catoun, for his wit was rude, / That bad man sholde wedde his simylitude' (3227), and rhyming 'rubible' with 'quynyble' (3332–3), terms for a fiddle and a treble, when describing Nicholas's musicianship. Chaucer's evident delight in such rhymes imports words unrecorded outside his works, as when the Friar's summoner visits the widow: '"Com out", quod he, "thou old virytrate [hag?]"' (III.1581–2). Chaucer's excitement with words in verse, whether Latinate or Germanic, crystallises meaning with music through rhyme across the *Tales*.

Such relish for rhyme informs the 'Clerk's Tale' envoy in its clarion call for women's power, through language, to control men and the world ('Ne dreed hem nat; doth hem no reverence', IV.1201), exultantly imagining a husband in armour yet defenceless because

> The arwes of thy crabbed eloquence
> Shal perce his brest and eek his aventaille*,   *neck-armour* (IV.1203–4)

or so manipulated by jealousy that 'thou shalt make hym couche [cower] as doth a quaille' (1206). Disparities in physical strength can be overcome by nagging and answering back ('But evere answereth at the countretaille'). Lack of beauty can be circumvented by spending money to buy friends and influence. The envoy's manifesto for a joyous world on women's terms ('Be ay of chiere as lyght as leef on lynde', 1211) is a distillation of what typifies Chaucer's poetry in the *Tales*: technically perfect poetic form, inseparable from the bravura of a comic, compassionate observation of humanity. Yet in their ambiguity these stanzas also exemplify the iridescence that characterises Chaucer's poetic across the *Canterbury Tales*. For whose voice is actually speaking through the stanzas, and how seriously is that voice questioning, or jesting, or both?

28

John Gower

R. F. Yeager

John Gower (d. 1408) is unique in the English poetic canon. He remains the only English poet of any age to have written major poetry in three languages—in his case, French, Middle English, and Latin. That it seemingly never occurred to any of his contemporaries, all living as he did in the same trilingual culture, to attempt this feat underscores the purposive individuality inherent in Gower's achievement. For it is quite clear that, at least in the latter years of his life, Gower's poetic ambition had at its centre a vision of himself as a poet of three languages, and that this sense of a poetic self took Virgil's example for its inspiration. Evidence of several kinds points towards this conclusion, but the case can be made well enough by citing two examples.

One is a short poem in Latin hexameter couplets beginning 'Eneidos, Bucolis, que *Georgica* metra perhennis / Virgilio laudis serta dedere scolis' ('The metres of the *Aeneid*, *Bucolics*, and *Georgics*, woven together by Virgil have found perpetual praise in the schools'). Copies appear in five manuscripts of Gower's works.[1] Purportedly written by an unnamed 'philosopher' to 'commemorate the completion of his three books', the verses are rather more likely the work of Gower himself. The poem is an encomium, comparing Gower favourably to Virgil, and who, the 'philosopher' notes, also composed a *cursus* of three great poems, albeit 'only in the Latin tongue' just for his 'Italian' countrymen. Moreover, Virgil expended his talent on 'vanities' ('vanis') that won him fame in Rome, but consequently—the 'philosopher' implies—are of passing value. Gower, on the other hand, excels because his *cursus* is in three languages for the 'broader schooling' ('scola lata') of all men, and will win 'heavenly praise' ('celicolis laus') for addressing Christians on subjects more pleasing to God. The second example, Gower's tomb in what is now Southwark Cathedral, makes the same point in stone. Undoubtedly designed by Gower himself, the tomb features a three-quarter life-size effigy of the poet, his head recumbent upon three great tomes, each bearing the Latin title of one of his three major poems: *Speculum Meditantis* (for the *Mirour de l'Omme*), *Vox Clamantis*, Gower's salient Latin work, and the *Confessio Amantis*, his primary composition in Middle English. Like 'Eneidos, bucolis', the tomb is thus a purposive exercise in poetic self-fashioning, with an eye cocked steadily towards posterity.

Both poem and tomb thus offer the useful insight that, to a significant degree, Gower understood himself and his craft in comparative, often competitive, relation to other poets. Some, like Virgil, he knew by reputation (for little evidence exists that Gower read Virgil directly, or in depth); others, including Guillaume de Lorris, Jean de Meun, Machaut, Deschamps, Froissart, of course Chaucer, and pre-eminently Ovid, he had studied thoroughly, learning from all of them while in his own way seeking to match or outdo them. Such an attitude has obvious implications for his poetics. Among other things it helps to explain

---

[1] Oxford, All Souls College, MS 98; Oxford, Bodleian Library, MS Fairfax 3; London, British Library, MS Cotton Tiberius A. iv; London, British Library, MS Harley 6291; Glasgow, University Library, Hunterian MS T.2.17.

R. F. Yeager, *John Gower*. In: *The Oxford History of Poetry in English*. Edited by Helen Cooper and Robert R. Edwards, Oxford University Press. © R. F. Yeager (2023). DOI: 10.1093/oso/9780198827429.003.0028

not only his decision to write extensively—and continually—in French, Latin, and Middle English, but also the effects of the broad strain of experimentalism that runs throughout his work in all three. Clearly there was overlap: discoveries made writing verse in one language at times carried over influentially into his work in the others. Hence it is essential, while recognising Gower's Englishness—for he wrote for Englishmen about issues pointedly of English import, no matter in which language—to approach his English poetics neither in isolation nor as if the *Confessio Amantis* and 'In Praise of Peace' were in his view the aesthetic apex of his career.

Tracing the development of that aesthetic is complicated, however, particularly if the intention is to identify how one formal discovery influences another. The basic problem is a lack of precision about when, and in what order, Gower produced various works. Few of the surviving manuscripts can be dated to Gower's lifetime, and those that can seem to have been copied not many years before his death. Internal references to datable events are the most reliable guide, although some of the more significant, particularly in the *Mirour de l'Omme* and *Vox Clamantis*, appear to have been post-facto additions. Variation in copies of the *Confessio Amantis* led G.C. Macaulay, Gower's best editor, to posit three successive versions, or (as he termed them) 'recensions'.[2] While recently this notion by broad agreement has been simplified to two versions—the earlier dedicated to Richard II and the later to Henry IV (hence 'Ricardian' and 'Henrician' versions)—in certain manuscripts one or two of the exemplary tales appear to have been later additions. Nonetheless, a general arc of Gower's *oeuvre* is discernible, and largely sufficient for sketching some assumptions about his poetic development.

French Connections

The earliest of Gower's known poems, written in the 1370s or somewhat earlier, seems to be the *Mirour de l'Omme*, found in a single manuscript, Cambridge, University Library, MS Additional 3035. The manuscript lacks four leaves at the start, seven others variously throughout, and an indeterminable number at the end. Even so, the poem amounts to 28,603 lines—an ambitious enterprise, particularly if it was indeed Gower's initial poetic project. From the viewpoint of poetics the *Mirour* is several ways interesting, beginning with its stanza: twelve lines following the pattern *aab aab bba bba* throughout. Gower's direct model is Hélinand de Froidmont's *Vers de la Mort* (*c* 1195). Gower cites both 'Mestre Helemauns' and 'Lez Vers du Mort' in the *Mirour*, and quotes three lines:

> Houstez voz troeffes et voz gas,
> Car tiel me couve soubz ses dras
> Q'assetz quide estre fortz et seins. (*Mirour* 11407–9)

(Quit your jesting and boasting, because I'm hiding already under the cloak of many who think themselves strong and healthy.)

The choice of stanza, no less than the direct citation, is noteworthy. In England manuscripts of the *Vers de la Mort* are extremely rare. Although Hélinand's stanza had some currency in thirteenth-century France in 'Congiés' (a type of moral verse written by Rutebeuf among

---

[2] G. C. Macaulay (ed.), *The Complete Works of John Gower*, 4 vols. (Oxford, 1899–1902). All references to the work of Gower are to this edition.

442 MEDIEVAL POETRY: 1100–1400

others), the form was moribund even on the Continent by 1300. Indeed, the anonymous romance *Perceforest* (*c* 1340), which includes some verses inset in the prose, and the *Mirour* are the only known examples, French or English, of the stanza put to use so late.[3]

The rationale for employing a relatively intricate stanza instead of simple couplets—the structure, say, of the *Roman de la Rose*, which stands behind the *Mirour* and the *Confessio Amantis* as both inspiration and antithetical target—cannot be retrieved.[4] The important implication for Gower's writing, however, is clear from so ambitious a beginning: even as (we must assume) a novice, the poet challenged himself by following a difficult formal path. The twelve-line stanza of the *Mirour* repeated over such an expanse—even in the damaged manuscript there are 2,384-plus of them—obviously was intended to establish Gower from the onset as a significant poetic presence. Doubtless too the effort involved helped prepare him for the sustained demands of composing very long poems like the *Vox Clamantis* and the even lengthier *Confessio Amantis*. In the case of the latter, because four pairs of rhymes in the 'Hélinand' stanza are essentially couplets and the line in the *Mirour* and the *Confessio* is octosyllabic, such practice had all the more specific application.

The *Mirour* predicts Gower's future poetics in other ways too. Notable is the regularity of the metre, a characteristic common to all of Gower's poetry, whether in French, Latin, or English, that sets him apart from the writing of his near-contemporaries. That Gower was willing to subordinate both syntax and grammar in the *Mirour* in order to achieve strictly regular metre is an early indication of the significant place of smoothly flowing verse among his poetic priorities. Some of the oddities familiar to readers of the *Confessio*, such as the moveable placement of conjunctions to regularise the metre—for example, 'With al his herte and most it hateth' (*CA* I.2454)—originate when writing the *Mirour*.[5] Similarly, it is worth remarking that, although in the *Mirour* the verse is formally syllabic in the French manner, Gower's 'Englishness' nonetheless comes through rhythmically in the steady alternation of accent on even and odd syllables. His approach is visible if one compares the borrowed lines from the *Vers de la Mort* as they appear in the *Mirour* (above) with Hélinand's original:

> Teus me cueve desoz ses dras
> Qui cuide estre haitiez et seins.[6]

Finally, by way of leaving discussion of the *Mirour*, a word should be said about the originality of its contents. Although the poem bears some superficial resemblance to estates satire and to works of moral instruction such as the *Somme le Roi* and the *Manuel des Pechiez*, another case can be made, based upon the 'Life of the Virgin' and the first-person introspection in the concluding section, for centring the *Mirour* in the inward turn noticeable in later fourteenth-century literature towards contemplation and private moral reform—an element the title of the poem as it appears on the tomb, *Speculum Meditantis*, picks up.[7]

---

[3] See R. F. Yeager, 'The "*Strophe d'Hélinand*" and John Gower' in Silvère Menegaldo (ed.), *Une forme médiévale à succès: La strophe d'Hélinand*, *Cahiers de recherches médiévales et humanistes*, 36 (2019), 115–33. On Perceforest, see Levante Seláf, 'La strophe d'Hélinand dans Perceforest' in the same volume, 135–52.

[4] On Gower's response to the *Roman*, see R. F. Yeager, *John Gower's Poetic: The Search for a New Arion* (Cambridge, 1990).

[5] For a fuller discussion of Gower's syntactic and grammatical adjustments, see Macaulay, *Complete Works*, 1:xl–xli.

[6] Text quoted from the now-standard edition, Friedrich Wulff and Emile Walberg (eds), *Les Vers de la Mort par Hélinant, Moine de Froidmont*, SATF (Paris, 1905), XV.11–12, an edition collated from 'tous les manuscrits connus'. Based on its idiom, Gower's source was probably Anglo-Norman.

[7] See Thomas H. Bestul, 'Gower's *Mirour de l'Omme* and the Meditative Tradition', *Mediaevalia*, 16 (1993), 307–28.

Nonetheless, the combination of elements, moving from allegory to social commentary to intense self-scrutiny, is altogether unprecedented in late medieval literature, and represents Gower's own vision. This willingness to strike out independently into territory unknown, discernible early in the *Mirour*, carries throughout Gower's oeuvre. One result bearing directly on his poetics has been intermittent criticism of the *Confessio* in particular for not conforming to established types or genres. Gower's formal iconoclasm is better recognised, however, as of a piece with precedent set for his subsequent poetics at the beginning by the *Mirour*.

Gower's two other major works in French, the *Cinkante Balades* and the *Traitié selonc les auctours pour essampler les amantz marietz*, are similarly ground-breaking, each in its own way. Both offer important lessons for what subsequently would become Gower's English poetry. As with the *Mirour*, it is difficult to date their composition exactly, but while the *Cinkante Balades* is best considered a product of the early 1390s, the *Traitié* may be considerably earlier. The *Traitié* balades, without envoys, seem constructed following the older model of Machaut, while those of the *Cinkante Balades*, with envoys, may better align with the ideal of 'natural music' (i.e., without musical scoring) promoted by Deschamps in his *L'art de Dictier* (1392).[8] Of the *Traitié* there are thirteen known copies in manuscript, all found in combination with other poems: nine with the *Confessio*, two with the *Vox Clamantis* and the *Cronica Tripertita*, one with the *Cinkante Balades* and 'In Praise of Peace', and one fragment.[9] (There is also a translation into fifteenth-century Yorkshire dialect, providing additional evidence, along with the number and nature of the copies, that the *Traitié* had a significant readership.[10]) Possibly, given the preponderance of copies of the *Traitié* conjoined to the *Confessio Amantis*, and several similarities between the balades and the Middle English poem, the *Traitié* and the *Confessio* were composed in proximity.[11] The implications of this for the poetic structure of the *Confessio*, and vice versa, are worth considering.

The *Traitié* consists of eighteen balades conceived as a unity. Unlike the *Cinkante Balades*, which properly may be called a sequence in the manner of Petrarch's *Rime*, the *Traitié* is instead precisely what the word implies—a treatise, in which an argument of some complexity is unfolded, one balade at a time. In this regard it is an entirely original conception, apparently unique to Gower: the only instance from the period in which the balade form is used to proffer a case and present supportive evidence. The over-arching theme of the *Traitié* is the importance of marital loyalty. Nonetheless, it is unlikely that Gower's marriage in 1398 served as inspiration, as once was thought. Its composition was earlier, and the learned theological positions taken in defence of conjugal relations of man and wife seem unsuited for a bride who may or may not have been literate, particularly in French.[12]

---

[8] See R. F. Yeager, 'John Gower's Audience: The Ballads', *Chaucer Review*, 46 (2005), 81–105.

[9] Oxford, Bodleian Library, MS Fairfax 3; Oxford, All Souls College, MS 98; Oxford, Bodleian Library, MS Bodley 294; Oxford, Wadham College, MS 13; London, British Library, MS Additional 59495; London, British Library, MS Harley 3869; London, British Library, MS Arundel 364 (fragmentary); Cambridge, Trinity College, MS R.3.2; Geneva, Fondation Bodmer, MS 178; Nottingham, University Library, Wollaton Library Collection, MS WLC LM 8; New Haven, Yale University, Beinecke Library, Osborn Collection, MS fa.1; Princeton, Princeton University, Firestone Library, Robert H. Taylor Collection, MS Taylor 5.

[10] London, British Library, MS Stowe 951.

[11] The *Traitié* in most manuscripts is linked to the *Confessio* with a heading in French (here quoted from MS Fairfax 3; translation mine): 'Because the preceding poem in English [i.e., the *Confessio Amantis*] was by way of example of the foolishness of those in particular who love in a courtly manner, now the subsequent treatise will be in French, for all the world generally, following the authorities, as an example for married lovers, in order that they might be able to protect the promise of their sacred spousal through perfect loyalty, and truly hold fast to the honour of God'. Of these manuscripts, however, only Fairfax was copied during Gower's lifetime, rendering the heading of uncertain worth as evidence of Gower's intentions.

[12] For differing views on the date, see Yeager, 'Ballads'; and Cathy Hume, 'Why Did Gower Write the *Traitié*?', in Elisabeth Dutton with John Hines and R. F. Yeager (eds), *John Gower, Trilingual Poet: Language, Translation,*

The *Traitié* shares two important features with the *Confessio Amantis*: fifteen tales of adulterers, and attached their Latin glosses. Such coincidence points towards either simultaneous composition or subsequent revision. Both do suggest that in the *Traitié* and the *Confessio* Gower was exploring, albeit in somewhat different forms, dialogic argument as a means to examine ideas. The enterprise in both works, in light of each other's example, was evidently structural: the exchanges of Genius and Amans come easily to mind, of course, but so, less obviously, does the interaction of the glosses with the fictive narration; and more subtly still, the poet's own voice in the Prologue and denouement of the *Confessio*, as played against the exemplary tales and the confessional frame. In the *Traitié*, the same dialogic effect is sought after through a similar reciprocity between the balades offered as exempla and those in which an unidentified, supra-narrative 'voice' resembling that present at the beginning and conclusion of the *Confessio* sets out the theological rationale for the poet's eventual claim, put in the *Traitié*'s final balade, that he speaks truth to a universal audience. (And here, as in the *Confessio*, he names himself 'John Gower'.)

Those are the similarities. There are also anomalies that speak in favour of revision rather than co-terminal composition of the *Traitié* and the *Confessio*. All manuscripts containing both post-date Gower's death, except Bodley Fairfax 3, and this was heavily corrected after the fact. In voice and tone, the *Traitié* glosses differ radically from those in the *Confessio*, almost as if the work of another sensibility. There are two forms of heading conjoining the two poems, both likely scribal, not authorial, additions. That conclusion gains support from two versions of the Latin prose *Quia unusquisque*, describing Gower's trilingual *oeuvre* and found in all manuscripts with the *Traitié*. In all the later manuscripts, *Quia* refers to Gower as dead; only in the two earliest, Fairfax and Glasgow Hunterian 59 (T.2.17), does he seem alive during copying.[13] Thus, dating the *Traitié* based on the *Confessio* hangs on slender threads. Gower might, in fact, have written the *Traitié* much earlier.

If he did, and depending on how much earlier, the implications are interesting. By Gower's time, Anglo-Norman it is thought had adopted English stress patterns. That would render, for example, 'Nectanabus, qui vint en Macedoine' from *Tr* VI, a perfect iambic pentameter line. Indeed, unlike the *Cinkante Balades*, which seem modelled on French *vers de dix* with approximate English stress, this metre is consistent throughout the *Traitié*. Gower, rather than Chaucer, may have invented iambic pentameter—albeit in French.[14]

In the *Cinkante Balades* Gower is no less original than in the *Traitié*, although differently, and for different purposes. The poems are known from one manuscript, London, British Library, MS Additional 59495 (*olim* Trentham), which also contains a copy of the *Traitié* and 'In Praise of Peace'. The manuscript may exhibit additions made in his own hand. From dedicatory verses, some fragmentary, praising Henry IV, that precede the *Cinkante Balades* proper, it appears that the poems were assembled as a gift for Henry, although this manuscript never reached him. While more elaborate than an author's working copy,

---

and Tradition (Cambridge, 2010), 263–75; and further R. F. Yeager, 'Twenty-First Century Gower: The Theology of Marriage in John Gower's *Traitié* and the Turn toward French', in Thelma Fenster and Carolyn Collette (eds), *Essays on the French of England in Honour of Jocelyn Wogan-Browne*, (Cambridge, 2016), 257–71.

[13] For full discussion, see Malcolm Parkes, 'Patterns of Scribal Activity and Revisions in the Text of Early Copies of Works by John Gower', in Richard Beadle and A. J. Piper (eds), *New Science Out of Old Books: Essays in Honour of A.I. Doyle* (London, 1995), 81–121.

[14] See Martin J. Duffell, 'Chaucer, Gower, and the History of the Hendecasyllable', in C. B. McCully and J. J. Jefferson (eds), *English Historical Metrics* (Cambridge, 1996), 210–18; and more recently Eric Weiskott, *Meter and Modernity in English Verse, 1350–1650* (Philadelphia, PA, 2021), 153–96.

it nevertheless falls short aesthetically as a gift for a new monarch—and in any event seems still to have been in Gower's possession at the time of his death.[15]

Precisely when Gower composed the *Cinkante Balades* is not certain. Unlike the linked argument of the *Traitié*, many of the *Cinkante Balades* may have been separately written, possibly over years, and assembled into the version we now have when Gower saw a purpose.[16] That purpose is, however, easier to date: The appearance of *Le Livre de Cent Ballades*. Begun by Jean de Saint-Pierre, seneschal d'Eu, in the late 1380s but with eventual contribution from other French chevaliers, the collection grew to a hundred balades. The *Cent Ballades* were in high vogue by 1390 when they came to English attention during the tournament at St-Inglevert, at which Henry IV, then earl of Derby, took part.[17] Evidently the jousting spirit, for national as well as individual honours, inspired responses to the *Livre* as the *au courant* poetic work. The Savoyard knight Oton de Graunson, friend of Chaucer (and possibly Gower), occasional member of the retinue of John of Gaunt, *c* 1391 linked a group of his own balades to the *Cent Ballades*; by 1402 Christine de Pizan had produced her *Cent Ballades d'Amant et de Dame*, an *homage* to the *Livre*.[18] That Gower's *Cinkante Balades* represent an Englishman's riposte to the French knights' challenge—written in French, very probably, with that competition directly in mind—seems hardly in doubt. That it earned him Henry of Derby's admiration in 1393 and an honorific neck chain is less certain, but possible.

It is true, however, that the *Cinkante Balades* represents highly polished poetry, comparable without qualification to the best of its type written in the period. Nothing produced by an English poet, certainly, matched it until Sidney two hundred years into the future. Like *Astrophil and Stella*, the *Cinkante Balades* is a true sequence, each poem building upon the next to supply information about events, and particularly character, both of the male lover and the lady he addresses. The skill evinced in narrative development, plotting the course of a love affair extending over two-plus years by means of seasonal references, announcements of travel by the lover, and other quotidian details mostly in the epistolary voice of the ultimately disappointed male lover—but with vehement replies by the lady—is extraordinary. Had Gower elected to write the *Cinkante Balades* in English, his subsequent reputation would have been very different.

Nevertheless, any assumption that the *Cinkante Balades* lacked influence on Gower's work in English would be mistaken. Like the *Traitié*, perhaps, the *Cinkante Balades* in some form seems to have been occupying his attention as the *Confessio Amantis* neared completion. There are at least three observable ways in which one mirrors the other, and vice versa. Foremost, perhaps, is the character of Amans, who resembles the disappointed lover of the *Cinkante Balades*. For both, Gower follows the same method, crafting each accretively: the image of neither lover is presented 'in the round', but rather each emerges from a pastiche of partial views—in Amans's case via evolving interchanges with others, in the

---

[15] See Sebastian Sobecki, '"Ecce patet tensus": The Trentham Manuscript, "In Praise of Peace", and John Gower's Autograph Hand', *Speculum*, 90 (2015), 925–59.

[16] Some indication of separate composition is suggested by occasionally less-than-seamless cohesion of voices and chronology. Whether the lady takes another lover or welcomes back her original has, for example, been a subject of debate. See Holly Barbaccia, 'The Woman's Response in John Gower's *Cinkante Balades*', in Dutton, Hines, and Yeager (eds), *John Gower, Trilingual Poet*, 230–8.

[17] On the tournament and Henry's participation, see Chris Given-Wilson, *Henry IV* (New Haven, CT, 2016), 61–3.

[18] Charity Canon Willard suggests that Christine began her *Cent Ballades* in 1393–4, although she released them later: see *Christine de Pizan: Her Life and Works* (New York, 1984), 43–4.

446 MEDIEVAL POETRY: 1100–1400

Cinkante Balades by epistolary revelation. Both lovers, too, share an erroneous sense of self-deserving throughout the two works.

Another similarity is vocabulary. Gower's fluent trilingualism was an asset in the flux of late-fourteenth-century English, to the benefit of some of the *Confessio Amantis*'s moments of high poetry. One strong example of apparent overlap between the *Cinkante Balades* and the *Confessio* must suffice by way of illustration here. Many years ago C. S. Lewis called attention to the 'poetical' choice of 'faye' ('faerie') to describe the ghostly ladies in the 'Tale of Rosiphelee' in *CA* 4.1321: 'The beaute faye upon her face'.[19] The word appears to have been a last-minute change. It occurs only in a few Henrician manuscripts—most others have 'faire' ('fair')—and pointedly it is present in Bodleian MS Fairfax 3 and Huntington MS HM 150, the two manuscripts of the *Confessio* most likely to have been seen by Gower. 'Faye' or 'faie' is French in origin, and Gower uses it five times in the *Confessio*—but only twice in his French poetry, just in the *Cinkante Balades* (24.22, 27.22).[20]

The third and perhaps most important resonances of the *Cinkante Balades* are detectable in Gower's English prosody. This will be discussed further on, as part of a detailed examination of the *Confessio*.

Latinitas

Gower held his Latin writing, if anything, in higher regard than his French, or so one could judge by his turn towards that language almost exclusively in the final decade of his life. Most of it, in consequence, including the *Cronica Tripertita*, occurred too late to have impacted directly any of his English work save 'In Praise of Peace', and so will not be discussed here. The *Vox Clamantis*, however, is another case entirely. A poem of maximally 10,265 lines distributed among seven Books in nine copies, it exists also in one copy of six Books, and one fragmentary copy.[21] Many of these manuscripts were produced at the end of the fourteenth century or the dawn of the fifteenth—that is, during Gower's lifetime—and exhibit multiple changes, some of them seemingly made under authorial direction. Gower was a frequent reviser of his work to account for shifts in the social and /or political winds—a practice that complicates dating. Nonetheless, internal evidence suggests that a first version of the *Vox* was complete, in six Books, about 1377.[22] The upheaval of 1381 prompted Gower to attach a new first Book of 2,150 lines describing in allegorical form his experience of the Revolt. Essentially a stand-alone poem, the *Visio Anglie* (as it is known) opens with a typical dream-vision landscape of springtime verdure and birdsong, but quickly transforms into a harrowing nightmare unmatched in English literature save only, perhaps, by the 'Nighttown' section of James Joyce's *Ulysses*.[23] As Gower's first experiment with

---

[19] C. S. Lewis, *The Allegory of Love: A Study in Medieval Tradition* (Oxford, 1936), 204. See most recently Richard Firth Green, 'A Poet at Work: John Gower's Revisions to the "Tale of Rosiphilee"', in Susannah Mary Chewning (ed.), *Studies in the Age of Gower: A Festschrift in Honour of R.F. Yeager* (Cambridge, 2020), 217–26.

[20] I.e., 1.2317, 2.1019, 5.3769, 4105, and the example above.

[21] Seven-Book copies: Dublin, Trinity College, MS D.4.6 (214); Glasgow, University Library, Hunterian MS T.2.17; Hertfordshire, Hatfield House MS (Marquess of Salisbury); Lincoln, Cathedral Library, MS A.72; London, British Library, MS Cotton Tiberius A.iv; British Library, MS Harley 6291; Oxford, All Souls College, MS 98; Oxford, Bodleian Library, MS Digby 138; San Marino, Huntington Library, MS HM 150 (*olim* Ecton Hall). Six-Book copy: Oxford, Bodleian Library, MS Laud (Misc.) 719 lacks the *Visio Anglie*, as the first Book is known in most manuscripts. London, British Library, MS Cotton Titus A.xiii contains only Prologue-3.116.

[22] See David R. Carlson, 'A Rhyme Distribution Chronology of John Gower's Latin Poetry', *Studies in Philology*, 104 (2007), 15–55.

[23] 'Visio Anglie' is Maria Wickert's term: see *Studien zu John Gower* (Köln, 1953); Robert J. Meindl, (trans.), *Studies in John Gower*, 2nd edn. (Tempe, AZ, 2016).

dream-vision form, the *Visio* offers some slight precedent for the *Confessio Amantis*; but the bulk of the *Vox* proper is social critique in the manner of estates satire, and so more closely resembles the *Mirour*.

Yet the influence of the *Vox Clamantis* on Gower's English writing is nonetheless notable. The *Vox* seems the venue where he developed the idea of following a stylistic 'middel weie' (*CA* Pro.17)—a matter-of-fact voice variously described as 'the first [example] of the plain style in [English] poetry', 'the perfection of a common language', and a *locus standi* of 'public poetry'.[24] Unlike Gower's late Latin poems, including the *Cronica Tripertita*, which are more typically scholastic in their recourse to dactylic Leonine hexameters and ornate rhyme, the *Vox* is composed almost classically, in unrhymed elegiac distichs. The relative simplicity of statement this permits—albeit for those sufficiently trained, for whom the straightforward style must also have appeared surprising—had little contemporary precedent in England.[25] One imagines that Gower's decision to write social satire to benefit a public audience, even if only of the Latin literate, lay behind his simpler poetics. This seems the main point embedded in the otherwise-typical humility topos that opens Book 2 (28–9); for example, 'Sint licit hii versus modice virtutis ad extra, / Interior virtus ordine maior erit' ('Although outwardly these verses may be of only moderate worth, the inner worth in turn will be the greater').[26]

The *Vox* thus in a way puts Gower on a similar footing with Langland (whose poem he may have known by 1377), in his concern to craft a 'plain style' able to ensure being read and understood by a discernible audience, many of whom would have been Langland's readership as well.[27] No less, and to his mind probably of greater importance, in the *Vox* Gower positioned himself with Virgil and Ovid, at least to the degree that by eschewing rhyme and maintaining strictly regular metre his work, if measured against then-current standards of highly artificial scholastic verse, was 'classical': the form of Ovid's epistles, after all, was also elegiac couplets. With allowance made for the non-accentual nature of Latin scansion, the metrical discipline practiced in the *Vox* doubtless contributed to the high value placed upon that quality in his English poetry. Certainly, the notable regularity already present in Gower's syllabic French poetry would have been reinforced by the demands of composing the lengthy *Vox* when he came to write the *Confessio*. Moreover, the view of himself as free to remould classical sources, particularly Ovid, has direct relevance for assessing both the *Vox Clamantis* and the poetics of Gower's oeuvre overall.

This remoulding has been much discussed, and described very differently, as, on the one hand, 'schoolboy plagiarism', a 'mosaic', and on the other consciously centonic.[28] Not

---

[24] Lewis, *Allegory of Love*, 201; Donald Davie, *Purity of Diction in English* Verse (London, 1992), 59; Anne Middleton, 'The Idea of Public Poetry in the Reign of Richard II', *Speculum*, 53 (1978), 94–114.

[25] A. G. Rigg, *A History of Anglo-Latin Literature 1066–1422* (Cambridge, 1992), 287, has called the *Vox Clamantis* 'the first substantial Anglo-Latin work in unrhymed elegiac couplets since Henry of Avranches' (d. *c* 1260); Walter of Peterborough also used the metre for a 102-line prologue to his *Victoria Belli in Hispania* (*c* 1367), on which see David R. Carlson, *John Gower: Poetry and Propaganda in Fourteenth-Century England* (Cambridge, 2012), 68–92.

[26] Translation in Eric W. Stockton, *The Major Latin Works of John Gower* (Seattle, WA, 1962).

[27] For a slightly later example of such a reader, see A. G. Rigg, 'Anglo-Latin in the Ricardian Age', in A. J. Minnis, Charlotte C. Morse, and Thorlac Turville-Petre (eds), *Essays on Ricardian Literature in Honour of J.A. Burrow* (Oxford, 1997), 121–41, at 121. The anonymous author of a Life of Edward the Confessor dedicated to Henry VI, complaining at the fallen state of Latin, notes 'Quod vulgi plus sermo placet, quem dicat arator / Vulgari lingua, quam mellica musa Maronis' ('What the ploughman says in vulgar tongue / Has more appeal than Virgil's honeyed muse'; translation Rigg). Two others are Richard Maidstone and Richard Rolle.

[28] See respectively Macaulay, *Complete Works*, I:xxxii; Paul E. Beichner, 'Gower's Use of *Aurora* in *Vox Clamantis*', *Speculum*, 30 (1955), 582–95; and R. F. Yeager, 'Did Gower Write Cento?', in R. F. Yeager (ed.), *John Gower: Recent Readings* (Kalamazoo, MI, 1989), 113–32.

448   MEDIEVAL POETRY: 1100–1400

incidentally, the technique is most visible in the *Visio* portion of the *Vox*, where *mutatis mutandis* Gower transposes 327 single lines and entire passages from Ovid (247) and other sources: the *Aurora* of Peter Riga (37), Nigel Whiteacre's *Speculum Stultorum* (26), and Godfrey of Viterbo's *Pantheon* (17).[29] The infrequency of such borrowing in the remaining six Books of the *Vox* suggests two things: first, the probability that the six-Book Laud manuscript preserves the original state of the poem, and second, that several years after completing the *Vox* proper Gower had advanced his thinking (and perhaps his confidence) so that—without abandoning his ideological commitment to 'plain style'—he could attempt something new poetically in the added *Visio* besides contorting the dream-vision model into unprecedented nightmare.

The evidence for this is his handling of the borrowed lines. In their new context the excerpts acquire fresh meaning altogether. For example:

> Qui prius attulerat *verum michi semper amorem*
> Tunc *tamen adverso tempore* cessat *amor*:
> *Querebam fratres* tunc fidos, non tamen ipsos
> *Quas suus optaret non genuisse pater.*[30]   (*Vox Clamantis* 1.1501–4)
>
> (The love which up to then had always brought
> True love departed when the times turned bad.
> I sought for trusty brothers, but not such
> As fathers would have wished they had not sired.)

The italicised portions above are taken from Ovid. In the first two, from *Ex Ponto*, 4.6.23–4, they are part of a letter to one 'Brutus', who stood by Ovid in adversity (as, in contrast, no one does by Gower's narrator); in the second, from *Tristia*, 3.1.65–6, the 'brothers' are not human beings, as Gower has it, but Ovid's books (and he the father), those that brought about his exile.[31] Precisely what to call this procedure is less important than understanding what Gower was probably up to. Rather than an attempt to pad out his verse in 'schoolboy' fashion, Gower's borrowing seems instead to be an intentional engagement with predecessors of all kinds, including the classical master Ovid, on their own poetic turf. As such, it is viewable as competition of a certain order—the later poet selectively culling earlier writers' poems for useful elements to subsume in his own, taking possession and transforming them via contextual adjustment. No less than the 'plain style' that Gower essentially re-introduces to Latin poetry in England near the end of the fourteenth century his device of remoulding his Latin sources should be assessed positively, as thoughtful, innovative poetics. And like those of the *Mirour* and the balades, these ideas, tested in the *Vox Clamantis*. are replicated in Gower's Middle English work, if in somewhat different garb.

'For Engelondes Sake'

The third book under the head of Gower's tomb effigy is the *Confessio Amantis*. His most popular work from the beginning, it survives today in forty-nine complete manuscripts, five

---

[29] See John H. Fisher, *John Gower: Moral Philosopher and Friend of Chaucer* (New York, 1964), 150.
[30] David R. Carlson (ed.) and A. G. Rigg (trans.), *Poems on Contemporary Events: The Visio Anglie (1381) and Cronica Tripertita (1400)* (Toronto, 2011).
[31] Fuller discussion in Yeager, *John Gower's Poetic: The Search for a New Arion*, 45–60.

others in fragmentary condition, and ten containing excerpts.[32] William Caxton printed a black-letter *Confessio* in 1483, and Thomas Berthelette followed with two editions, in 1532 and 1554.[33] As with all of Gower's major works, the chronology of the *Confessio* is difficult, the more so because it exists in two versions, the earlier with a dedication to Richard II, that opens with a meeting of the king and Gower in the royal barge on the Thames, during which Richard requests he write 'som newe thing ... / That he himself it mihte loke' (*CA* Pro. 51*–52*). This scene is missing from the later Henrician version, where in place of 'A boke for king Richardes sake' (*CA* Pro. 24*) and any mention of Richard, Gower promises to write 'A bok for Engelondes sake' (*CA* Pro. 24).[34] Later (*CA* Pro. 83–7) he explains 'This bok, upon amendment / ... I sende unto myn oghne lord, / Which of Lancastre is Henri named'. Most of the manuscripts containing the new dedication also delete a passage greeting Chaucer in Book 8 (2941*–57*), which led some early scholars erroneously to suspect a quarrel between the two poets.[35] Gower's habits as a tinkerer further complicate matters. Most manuscripts closely resemble each other, dedications excepted, but a few nevertheless contain variations extending to entire tales. In the face of these and other complications, it is probably safest to adopt a chronological range for the poem in both versions of 1380–98, and a workable length of roughly 33,000 lines of Middle English.

The *Confessio* is not a monolingual text, however. Gower envisioned it as a work in two languages, English and Latin. The latter takes two forms: prose passages, placed in some manuscripts in the margins, in others intruded into the Middle English, and seventy stanzas in elegiac couplets, varying in length between ten lines and two. The prose passages resemble those in the *Traitié*, where, as here, they function on one level somewhat like glosses in learned or religious texts. Indeed, such glossed texts may have provided Gower's inspiration. As suggested above, however, the interaction of the Latin prose commentary with the vernacular poetry in both the *Traitié* and the *Confessio* is more complex than the simpler explanatory function of glosses. The interrelationship of the Latin prose and the vernacular verse is integral to Gower's poetic sensibility, and to the operative design of the *Confessio Amantis* and the *Traitié*. He breaks new poetic ground not only by 'glossing' his own texts (for the prose passages do, in many cases, explain or summarise the poetry), but also more capaciously by incorporating bilingual polyvocality as a means of realising the dialogic potential of a Latin-English (or French) exchange. The result offers Gower an alternative 'voice', unidentifiably sourced in the text but specifically non-authorial, with which to usher the reader into, and engage with, the vernacular poetry.[36] Nowhere is this put to more significant use than opposite *CA* 1.60, where the unnamed commentator facilitates the metamorphosis of the 'auctor' into the Lover, Amans: 'Hic quasi in persona aliorum ... fingens se auctor esse Amantem' ('Here as if in the persona of another ... the author fashions himself to be Amans').

Gower clearly intended the Latin verses in the *Confessio* to act in the same dialogic manner as the prose, as described above. His evident labour in producing them, however,

---

[32] For a complete listing, see Derek Pearsall and Linne R. Mooney, *A Descriptive Catalogue of the English Manuscripts of John Gower's* Confessio Amantis (Woodbridge, 2021).

[33] On Caxton and Berthelette, see Siân Echard, 'Gower in Print', in Echard (ed.), *A Companion to Gower* (Cambridge, 2004), 115–38.

[34] Macaulay, following Bodleian MS Fairfax 3, prints the Henrician version as his main text, as does Russell A. Peck (ed.), *John Gower: Confessio Amantis*, 3 vols. (Kalamazoo, MI, 2004, 2006, 2013). Both include the Ricardian prologue variation as a parallel text.

[35] An exception is Nottingham, University Library, Middleton Collection, MS Mi LM 8 (*olim* Wollaton Hall), which uniquely contains the Henry dedication and the Chaucer greeting.

[36] See R. F. Yeager, 'English, Latin, and the Text as "Other": The Page as Sign in the Work of John Gower', *Text*, 3 (1987), 251–67.

450   MEDIEVAL POETRY: 1100–1400

suggests additional aesthetic ambition. It is therefore essential to look closely at what he does with the verses, and at how they are made, to gain a fuller view of the *Confessio*'s poetic design. Structurally, most of the Latin verses mark stages in Amans's confession, occurring when Genius takes up a new topic; for example:

> De ypocrisia
> Celsior est Aquila que Leone ferocior ille,
>   Quem tumor elati cordis ad alta mouet.
> Sunt species quinque, quibus esse Superbia ductrix
>   Clamat, et in multis mundus adheret eis.
> Laruando faciem ficto pallore subornat
>   Fraudibus Ypocrisis mellea verba suis.
> Sicque pios animos quamsepe ruit muliebres
>   Ex humili verbo sub latitante dolo.[37]

(Higher than an eagle and more fierce than a lion is that one whom the swelling of a heart, borne upwards, moves to the heights. There are five species over which Pride clamours that she is the leader, and the world clings to those in many ways. By enchanting the face with feigned paleness, Hypocrisy decks out honey-sweet words with his frauds. And thus time and again he overwhelms pious, womanly souls by means of humble speech with deceit hidden underneath.)

But the Latin verses go beyond merely introducing new topics, which after all could be accomplished more simply by—as in this case—a one-term heading: 'Hypocrisy'. Purposefully, Gower takes advantage of the greater verbal compression Latin affords over English to introduce ideas, and also images that will arise in the English often many lines later, but require more lines to articulate. A good example is 'Laruando faciem ficto pallore subornat / Fraudibus Ypocrisis mellea verba suis', taken from the passage above, which becomes, in Genius's words:

> The colour of the reyni* Mone   *watery (pale)*
> With medicine upon his face
> He set, and thane he axeth grace,
> As he which hath sieknesse feigned.
> Whan his visage is so desteigned,
> With yhe upcast on hire he siketh,
> And many a countenance he piketh,
> To bringen hire in to believe
> Of thing which that he wolde achieve,
> Wherof he berth the pale hewe;
> And for he wolde seme trewe,
> He makth him siek, whan he is heil,
> Bot whanne he berth lowest the Seil,
> Thanne is he swiftest to beguile
> The woman, which that ilke while
> Set upon him feith or credence. (*CA* 1.692–707)

---

[37] Verses at *CA* 1.574; translations by Andrew Galloway, in Peck (ed.), *Confessio Amantis*.

Sixteen English lines to unpack an image the Latin renders in two: Gower exploits the linguistic discontinuity for poetic effect, as a means here of limning Genius's character, and on other occasions Amans's. For Gower's anticipated reader, able to follow the Latin alongside the English, the Confessor's prolixity could only be amusing, compared to Latin brevity.

The Latin verses thus allow Gower a form of anonymous remove, whence to view the flow of the Middle English poem with deliberated irony. They do so in a frequently convoluted manner, however, that makes for challenging reading. Often punning is the culprit: Gower seems seldom to have met a paranomasia he didn't like, and Latin was rife with possibilities; for example, this at *CA* 4.1614: 'Quem probat armorum probitas Venus approbat, et quem / Torpor habet reprobum reprobat illa virum' ('Venus approves whom prowess proves in arms, / Reproves the reprobate in Torpor's grip').[38] On other occasions Gower adopts a riddling style in the verses as a device to focus the reader's attention and to seek answers in the Middle English poem. Those at *CA* 2.3110 are illustrative:

> Inuidie stimulus sine causa ledit abortus,
>   Nam sine temptante crimine crimen habet.
> Non est huius opus temptare Cupidinis archum,
> Dumque faces Veneris ethnica flamma vorat.
>   Absque rubore gene, pallor quas fuscus obumbrat,
> Frigida nature cetera membra docent.[39]

(The twisted spur of envy causeless harms, / Is criminal though unprovoked by crime. / He needs not Cupid's bow when Aetna's fire / Consumes the torch that Venus calls her own. / Cheeks not red, but shadowed by dark pallor / Reveal that Nature's parts are weak with cold.)

Gower's general point, in the Middle English also, is the causeless, unnatural essence of Envy, that 'dehumanises' in every sense of the word. It acts like a 'spur' (the equine inference is intentional) to goad desire to volcanic levels which, ironically, 'consumes the (phallic) torch that Venus calls her own'—that is, 'unmans' the envious.[40] In the Middle English Gower puts it obliquely ('Envie hath kinde put aweie ... So mai ther be no kinde plesed', *CA* 2. 3140, 3144), but here in the Latin verse, at least for medieval readers, he's more specific, enriching and thickening the English, albeit in riddling—even Donnean—fashion. Gower's central conceit, grounded in contemporary medical theory, is that the envious are impotent because their dominant humour is choleric—fiery, but replete with black bile (hence the 'dark pallor') which leaves 'Nature's parts' like a burnt-out torch, gone cold. Later, in Book 7 (431, 436–40), describing a 'Colre' man, he reprises the point of the Latin verse in English:

> He hath riht gret besinesse,
> To thenke of love and litel may:
> Though he behote* wel a day,   *promises*
> On nyht what that he wole assaie,
> He may ful evele his dette paie.

---

[38] This and the next example are taken from the introduction to Siân Echard and Claire Fanger (eds), *The Latin Verses in the Confessio Amantis: An Annotated Translation* (East Lansing, MI, 1991), xli. Echard's and Fanger's observations on the Latin verses in the *Confessio* remain the most persuasive to date.

[39] Translation by Echard and Fanger.

[40] The Aetna reference asks the reader to recall the 'Tale of Acis and Galatea', the first Genius tells in Book 2 (98–220), to illustrate Envy for Amans. Discussion in R. F. Yeager, 'John Gower's Images: "The Tale of Constance" and "The Man of Law's Tale"', in R. F. Yeager and Charlotte C. Morse (eds), *Speaking Images: Essays in Honor of V.A. Kolve* (Asheville, NC, 2000), 525–57, especially 530–4.

452   MEDIEVAL POETRY: 1100–1400

What is missing in the English, however, is the playfulness of the Latin. The anonymous remove of the Latin verses opens a space for humour that in general the Middle English avoids. In conjunction with the English, these verses help round out Gower's early promise to write 'Somwhat of lust, somewhat of lore' (*CA* Pro.19), to a degree impossible to appreciate fully, without the Latin.

Such playfulness notwithstanding, one would be mistaken to conclude that Gower's 'middel weie' between 'lust' and 'lore' implies his retreat in the *Confessio* from that powerful wish to communicate publicly the socio-political concerns underlying both the *Mirour de l'Omme* and the *Vox Clamantis*. Both in the *Confessio* Prologue and the opening lines of the first Book, where he writes of taking up a new 'Stile' (*CA* 1. 8), he makes clear that, while his tactics are shifting, the basic strategy and socially ameliorative purpose remain the same in all three major poems. Thus in the Prologue of the Henrician version, he is straightforward about his plan:

> The wyse man mai ben avised,
> For this prologe is so assised*,   *devised*
> That it to wisdom al belongeth ...
> Whan the prologe is so despended,
> This bok schal afterward ben ended
> Of love ...
> And in this wyse I thenke trete
> Towardes hem that now be grete,
> Betwen the vertu and the vice
> Which longeth unto this office.   (*CA* Pro. 65–7; 74–5; 77–80)[41]

Earlier, in both Ricardian and Henrician versions, Gower has stated his reason for the new style: 'Bot for men sein, and soth it is, / That who that al of wisdom writ / It dulleth ofte a mannes wit / To him that schal it aldai rede' (*CA* Pro. 12–15). In short, he wants a medium that bears his message effectively—and more broadly. Hence also his new venture into English: it's because '... fewe men endite / In our oure englissh, I thenke make / A bok for king Richardes sake' (*CA* Pro. 22*–24*). The inspiration to use English may have come initially from Richard, and to that degree have been a gesture to please the king. However, in the later Henrician version, line 24 importantly becomes 'A bok for Engelondes sake', a revision obviously necessitated by the change in regimes, but carrying with it unambiguous expectations of a public readership not present in the Ricardian poem. This readership would have been qualitatively different from that of the *Vox Clamantis*, and certainly, by the 1380s, of the *Mirour de l'Omme* as well. That said, however, we would still do well to remember '*Eneidos, bucolis*': the ambition to surmount the Virgilian *cursus* may have taken shape, and determined the language of the *Confessio*, along with its original draft.

In any case, whatever eye Gower cast on Virgil, and of course Ovid, that so influenced the *Vox Clamantis*, he kept no less open while writing the *Confessio*, wherein much he had learned in his earlier long poems he applied to effect. Viewed superficially, much of this work appears recursive—and French. Certainly, there are many similarities between the *Mirour de l'Omme* and the *Confessio*. As in the *Mirour*, each major sin in the *Confessio* becomes the focal point of a section of the text, and both poems present the sins in the same order. In both, too, each section is further subdivided into the same sub-sins. Nothing

---

[41] In Ricardian manuscripts the description of meeting Richard on the Thames occupies this space.

remains of the *Mirour*'s elaborate allegories in the *Confessio*, however. That cruder technique has given way to the greater sophistication of exemplary tales, which figure more completely within the *Confessio*'s sacramental frame. The main divisions of the *Confessio* are dictated by the conventions of confession, the structure around which the poem's fiction of the Lover, Amans, and Genius, Venus's priest, is built. The conceit works for Gower, incongruous yoking though it initially sounds, because the sins that spot the soul also make for an undesirable lover. Accordingly, each of the seven cardinal sins is allotted a Book, although there are deviations. Incest is exchanged for Luxuria, as the nominal subject of Book 8; Book 7 recounts Aristotle's lessons for Alexander, and combines encyclopaedic elements with advice on how to rule, applicable equally to kings and to the individual's control over the self—a delicate balancing that allows Gower to meld the shrift of a single lover with his consistent themes of national good governance.

What Gower did adapt from his French poetry is his English prosody, especially noticeable in his handling of rhyme and metre. Each merits separate consideration. Of the first, it may be said that the discipline acquired fashioning the *Mirour*'s twelve-line stanzas with just two rhymes in each—however much aided there by French inflections—can be felt stiffening Gower's couplets in the *Confessio*. The uncertainty surrounding the composition date of the *Cinkante Balades* occludes claims of direct influence (indeed, writing the *Confessio* may have sharpened them, instead of vice versa), but the probable simultaneity of his work on the *Traitié* and the *Confessio* almost assures mutual crossover. As in the French poetry, the great majority of his English rhymes are monosyllabic, or simple bi-syllables, counting the final -e (e.g., 'schewe/rewe', 'finde/kinde', 'seie/preie'). When he does rhyme polysyllabic words, he does so oftenest bi-syllabically ('longeth/underfongeth', 'amendeth/entendeth')—in this case, a characteristic more common to the word play in his later Latin Leonines ('confregit/subegit', 'cepit/recepit') than in his French. As like as not the mandate for plain-speaking developed in the *Vox Clamantis* deterred him from some of the more adventurous French patterns. Nothing of Gower's approaches Chaucer's *rime equivoque* 'Morpheus/moo feës thus' (*BD* 267), for example. *Rime riche* did attract him, probably because of its compatibility with monosyllabic rhyme, but—ever ambitious—with few exceptions he eschewed the easy road, very often seeking out noun/verb pairs ('laste/laste', *CA* 5.6957–8; 'reule/reule', *CA* 5.7127*–28*) rather than opting for elementary repetition of the same speech-part.[42] (Intriguingly, however much the style is French, in his English poetry *rime riche* word-pairs are generally of native origin, with roots in Old English, not French.)[43]

Gower also incorporates rhyme royal into the *Confessio*, making him the only poet other than Chaucer to use the form in English in the fourteenth century. Doubtless he adapted the stanza from his own French balades where it is common rather than from Chaucer, pointedly because he was writing the *Traitié* and possibly some of the *Cinkante Balades* in close proximity. Amans's so-called 'Supplication' (*CA* 8. 2217–2300) is a *tour de force*. Its twelve rhyme royal stanzas include thirty-six rhyming pairs with but one repeated, proving that the fancier forms of French versifying were neither beyond him nor less possible in English. The sole departure from octosyllabic couplets in the poem, the 'Supplication' characterises not only Gower's verbal facility but his careful poetics as well. Like each of the *Cinkante*

---

[42] See further Kim Zarins, 'Rich Words: Gower's Rime Riche in Dramatic Action', in Dutton, Hines, and Yeager (eds), *John Gower, Trilingual Poet*, 239–53.

[43] See Masayoshi Ito, 'Gower's Use of *Rime Riche* in *Confessio Amantis*: As Compared with His Practice in *Mirour de L'Omme* and with the Case of Chaucer', *Studies in English Literature*, 46 (1969), 29–44.

454   MEDIEVAL POETRY: 1100–1400

Balades, the 'Supplication' is a letter, in this case from Amans to Venus.[44] No empty flourish, then, the shift in rhyme pattern was calculated, both to replicate this epistolary style, and to provide Amans with a 'voice' in a register fit to address a goddess.

Gower paid close attention to his metrics no less than to his rhyming. The near-absolute regularity of metre in the *Confessio* has no English counterpart; to find his equal, one must look to the French, Machaut and Deschamps in particular, and to Gower's own work in the *Mirour* and his balades. The result in English of his strict adherence to the French manner of counting syllables—eight per line, sometimes elided, or ten when once he shifts from octosyllabics to pentameter, as he does for Amans's 'Supplication'—while also maintaining the accentual pattern of conventional English speech over thousands of lines is a formal control Gower alone achieves.[45] Chaucer seldom matches it; Hoccleve and Lydgate, never. The effect is best appreciated at length; here, however, a brief example must suffice. Note especially how the movement of caesurae and enjambment replicate speech, while remaining strictly iambic:

> Whanne I have sen an other blithe
> Of love, and hadde a goodly chiere,
> Ethna, which brenneth yer by yere,
> Was thanne noght so hot as I
> Of thilke Sor which prively
> Min hertes thought withinne brenneth. (*CA* 2.18–23)

Yet for all he brought from French into the *Confessio Amantis*, the challenge Gower set for himself of maintaining a poetics based on closely observed linguistic standards required a refinement of skills beyond those he had exercised in the *Mirour* or the balades. The translation of those skills into a new language, itself still undergoing refinement of a sort, was the cause. Into a mastery of the octosyllabic couplet acquired from French, he imported a firm sense of what he called 'congruite' of words—grammar, syntax, precise word selection—which he attributes to practice in Latin versification (*CA* 4.2638 ff.). 'Congruite' manifests itself in two ways in Gower's English work: first, in his ability to carry extended thoughts smoothly over many lines, notwithstanding the shortness of the four-beat couplet that renders this task demanding, and second, in his choice of words. Gower's mastery of the verse-paragraph is nonpareil. *Confessio* 5.7225–34 is a good example from among so many, short by Gowerian standards, but sufficiently illustrative:

> King Lamedon, which deide thus,
> He hadde a Sone, on Priamus,
> Which was noght thilke time at hom:
> Bot whan he herde of this, he com,
> And fond hou the Cite was falle,
> Which he began anon to walle
> And made ther a cite newe,
> That thei whiche othre londes knewe
> Tho seiden, that of lym and Ston
> In al the world so fair was non.

---

[44] See Peter Nicholson, 'Writing the *Cinkante Balades*', in Russell A. Peck and R. F. Yeager (eds), *John Gower: Others and the Self* (Cambridge, 2017), 306–28; and most recently Nicholson, 'Gower's Ballades for Women', in Chewning, (ed.), *Studies in the Age of Gower*, 79–97.

[45] See Dominique Billy and Martin J. Duffell, 'Le Décasyllabe de John Gower et le dernier mètre Anglo-Normand', *Revue linguistique romane*, 69 (2005), 75–95.

The passage also captures Gower making poetry in the 'plain style', out of simple words but carefully selected and placed. Consider the choice of 'lym and Ston'. It's a common pairing, meaning 'bricks and mortar'. Substitute 'wood'—a possible reading for 'lym'—instead. Certainly the resonance of 'wood' with 'Ston' and 'so/non' in the following line, where it also alliterates with 'world', creates an attractive music, one to which Gower's ear was always sharply attuned (compare, e.g., the 'water-music' of 'In Temse whan it was flowende', *CA* Pro. 39*). But insert 'wood' and the line, along with the next, become mellifluous to no purpose. To be sure, Gower can do mellifluousness—but for a reason:

> There is growened upon the ground
> Popi, which berth the sed of slep,
> With othre herbes such an hep.
> A stille water for the nones
> Rennende upon the smale stones,
> Which hihte of Lethes the rivere,
> Under that hell in such manere
> Ther is, which yifth gret appetit
> To slepe. (*CA* 4.1306–14)

The subject is Morpheus's Cave, where, gently, Lethe's 'stille water ... / Rennende upon the smale stones' carries us 'to slepe'. Here also the combination of the 'h', 'th', and 's' sounds join with nasals and liquids ('n', 'l', 'r') to incorporate both 'hep' and 'Popi', thereby approximating the trickle and drip of the water over the gravel bed of Lethe. The aural imagery thus conveys the 'feel' of the home of the god of sleep. In the previous example, what makes 'lym and Ston'—'bricks and mortar'—the right choice despite the aural temptation of 'lym/wood' is precisely their paired familiarity, and the synechoche this allows. Gower counts on it, in collaboration with 'to walle' (l. 7230), to conjure the Trojan rampart visually for the reader.

The more one reads Gower, the more such moments materialise, made vivid by precise word choice. Sometimes they come in a single line: 'The beaute faye upon her face', discussed above, is one such. Another is:

> The grete stiedes were assaied
> For joustinge and for tornement,
> And many a perled garnement
> Embroudered was ayein the dai. (*CA* 1.2508–11)

The effect of 'perled', striking amidst generality, is 'exquisite' in its precision and arresting vividness.[46] In the 'Tale of Nebuchadnezzar' comes this example:

> And so thenkende he gan doun bowe,
> And thogh him lacke vois and speche,
> He gan up with his feet areche*,   *reached*
> And wailende in his bestly stevene
> He made his pleignte unto the hevene.
> He kneleth in his wise and braieth,

---

[46] The term is Burrow's: see J. A. Burrow, *Ricardian Poetry: Chaucer, Gower, Langland, and the 'Gawain' Poet* (London, 1971), 76.

456 MEDIEVAL POETRY: 1100–1400

> To seche merci and assaileth
> His god ...[47] (*CA* 1.3022–9)

Here once-proud king Nebuchadnezzar, transformed into an ass for his presumption, at last asks God for forgiveness. But only, in his asinine form, as he can: with his 'feet areche', lacking hands, 'in his bestly stevene' he 'braieth'. The genius of 'braieth', not unlike 'lym', is its entire appropriateness in context and its simultaneous, complete unpredictability. One expects 'prayeth', to point towards God's restoration of Nebuchadnezzar to human shape. The 'brayer' is necessary, however, before forgiveness, and Gower—with a single, well-chosen word, holds the king a beast for a single, extra moment—thus brilliantly underscores that point.

Effects such as these, emerging as they do, suddenly, from the extended narrative progress that is the *Confessio* are the more impressive *because* of that lengthy progress. Gower's greatest gift was for the long poem, as he seems to have known, and particularly so when writing in his two vernaculars, French and English.[48] Hence his various experiments, discussed above, show him pressing to turn shorter poetic forms into longer unities: to this both the *Traitié* and the *Cinkante Balades*, in their argumentative and narrative adaptations of the balade, respectively stand witness. He approaches 'In Praise of Peace', his only other extant work in Middle English, the same way. Known from a single copy in London, British Library, MS Additional 59495, and composed not many years after the Lancastrian usurpation, the poem consists of fifty-five rhyme royal stanzas in English, preceded by another of Latin Leonines, also in rhyme royal. 'In Praise of Peace' thus outdoes Amans's 'Supplication' in terms of length, and with its Latin opening stanza exemplifies Gower's concern to maintain multi-linguality to the end. (Indeed, it has been suggested that the poems in French, Latin, and English collected in MS Add. 59495 represent Gower's attempt to create a second, briefer Virgilian *cursus*.)[49] Like the 'Supplication', the poem is a prayer, to Henry to avoid foreign war save in a crusade; like the *Traitié*, it sets balade stanza in service of complex, rational argument. Most importantly for present purposes, as a brief illustration shows, Gower maintained control over every aspect of his poetics—language, metre, music—and his moral empathy too, even unto the close of his life:

> For vein honour or for the worldes good
> Thei that whilom the stronge werres made,
> Wher be thei now? Bethenk wel in thi mod.
> The day is goon, the nyght is derk and fade,
> Her crualte, which mad hem thanne glade,
> Thei sorwen now, and yit have noght the more;
> The blod is schad, which no man mai restore. (*IPP*, 99–105)

---

[47] See further the discussion of Christopher Ricks, 'Metamorphosis in Other Words', in A. J. Minnis (ed.), *Gower's Confessio Amantis: Responses and Reassessments* (Cambridge, 1983), 25–49.

[48] That 'Gower's is essentially a long-poem style' has been noted by Burrow; see 'Gower's Poetic Styles', in Echard (ed.), *Companion to Gower*, 239–50 at 249.

[49] See Robert R. Edwards, *Invention and Authorship in Medieval England* (Columbus, OH, 2017), 63–104.

29

Reception of the Middle English Poetic Tradition

Julia Boffey

A fifteenth-century reader in England might have been very surprised by John Gower's assertion, made *c* 1400 in the prologue to *Confessio Amantis*, that 'fewe men endite / In oure englisshe' ('few people write poetry in our English language').[1] Written evidence from even the early years of the fifteenth century testifies abundantly to the contrary. The mental libraries of fifteenth-century poets would have included not just the newly influential works of Gower and Chaucer but much English verse of other kinds, from metrical romance to versified biblical paraphrase, and their own poems can be read as products of this variously inflected formation. Instances of allusion, citation, and imitation suggest their continuing connectedness to earlier traditions. The material witness of English manuscripts copied in the early fifteenth century, or in some cases continuing in use from earlier dates of production, confirms that scribes and readers had access to a wide range of English verse writing; the numbers and contents of these manuscripts remain a valuable source of information. Drawing on these different forms of evidence, and especially on the detail of some poems from the first half of the fifteenth century, this chapter will trace some of the continuities and innovations following from fourteenth-century English poetic practice.

Comparison of the tally of surviving poetic manuscripts from the fourteenth and the fifteenth centuries suggests not only that more English verse was copied and preserved after about 1400, but also that more attempts were made to compose it. Verse remained in vogue in the earlier part of the century for a wide range of works, whether for private reading or devotion, performance, or practical instruction; and it took an increasing variety of modes and forms.[2] Alongside poems newly composed or newly translated from French and Latin, some works that had already enjoyed a long life remained available to fifteenth-century readers, possibly still shared in manuscripts passed from person to person on the model recommended in John Mirk's *Instructions to Parish Priests* (compiled *c* 1380–1400):

> ... I pray þe, leue broþer,
> Rede þys ofte, and so lete oþer;
> Huyde hyt not in hodymoke,
> Lete other mo rede þys boke;
> The mo þer-In doth rede & lerne,
> Þe mo to mede hyt schale terne;

---

[1] John Gower, *Confessio Amantis*, in G. C. Macaulay (ed.), *The English Works of John Gower*, 2 vols., EETS e.s. 81–2 (London, 1900–1), 1:2 (lines 22–3).

[2] The later fifteenth century would, however, see a growing taste for prose romances and prose chronicles. Useful anthologies are Eleanor P. Hammond (ed.), *English Verse between Chaucer and Surrey* (Durham, NC, 1927); Derek Pearsall (ed.), *Chaucer to Spenser: An Anthology* (Oxford, 1998); Douglas Gray (ed.), *The Oxford Book of Late Medieval Verse and Prose* (Oxford, 1985). See also Julia Boffey and A. S. G. Edwards (eds), *A Companion to Fifteenth-Century English Poetry* (Cambridge, 2013).

Julia Boffey, *Reception of the Middle English Poetic Tradition*. In: *The Oxford History of Poetry in English*. Edited by Helen Cooper and Robert R. Edwards, Oxford University Press. © Julia Boffey (2023). DOI: 10.1093/oso/9780198827429.003.0029

Hyt ys I-made hem to schowne
Þat haue no bokes of here owne ...[3]

(I pray you, dear brother, read this often, and allow others to do so; don't hide this book away privately, but let others read it. The more people who read it and learn from it, the more it will turn to good. It is made to show to people who have no books of their own.)

But while Mirk's recommendation for sharing books probably retained its force, fifteenth-century developments in manuscript production enabled poetry to circulate in more copies, and in written rather than oral form. The increasing use of paper rather than expensive parchment, the preference for more easily formed cursive scripts, and the refinement of systems of book production made possible the cheaper production of greater numbers of manuscripts, and thus the wider transmission of texts of all kinds. Such developments would necessarily play a part in enhancing awareness of the potential of an English poetic tradition.

Alongside these changes, the political and cultural climate of the early fifteenth century encouraged greater scrutiny of the role of English and its potentialities, and an increasing interest in translations into English from Latin and French.[4] Continuing hostilities with France, in the form of the Hundred Years' War, had the double effect of enhancing interest in English while at the same time exposing greater numbers of English people to the writings of contemporary French poets.[5] In England itself, the Lancastrian regime inaugurated after the deposition of Richard II in 1399 may have seen advantages in cultivating poetry in English in order to legitimate its claims.[6] And anxieties about heresy, brought to the fore in the late fourteenth-century production of an English translation of the Bible, and given focus by the publication of Archbishop Thomas Arundel's anti-Lollard Constitutions in 1409, alerted sensitivities to both English and the transmission of written words more generally.[7] All of these concerns extended in the early fifteenth century to the wider boundaries of Britain, if to varying degrees. In Ireland, the Pale, around Dublin, remained an English-speaking enclave. In Wales, Owain Glyndŵr's attempts to overthrow English rule were suppressed by 1412 and the English presence remained strong. Scotland's tradition of poetic writing in 'Inglis', already well established, would absorb new influences, especially in and following the early decades of the century while its king, James I, was held captive in England between 1406 and 1423/4.[8]

---

[3] Gillis Kristensson (ed.), *John Mirk's Instructions for Parish Priests*, Lund Studies in English, 49 (Lund, 1974), 175 (lines 1917–24).

[4] See Nicholas Watson, 'The Politics of Middle English Writing', in Jocelyn Wogan-Browne, Nicholas Watson, Andrew Taylor, and Ruth Evans (eds), *The Idea of the Vernacular: An Anthology of Middle English Literary Theory 1280–1520* (Exeter, 1999), 331–52 and Roger Ellis (ed.), *The Oxford History of Literary Translation in English: Volume I, to 1550* (Oxford, 2008).

[5] Ardis Butterfield, *The Familiar Enemy: Chaucer, Language and Nation in the Hundred Years War* (Oxford, 2009), 308–49; Catherine Nall, *Reading and War in Fifteenth-Century England, from Lydgate to Malory* (Cambridge, 2012), 1–113.

[6] Paul Strohm, *England's Empty Throne: Usurpation and the Language of Legitimation, 1399–1422* (New Haven, CT, 1998).

[7] Among the relevant essays in Vincent Gillespie and Kantik Ghosh (eds), *After Arundel: Religious Writing in Fifteenth-Century England*, Medieval Church Studies, 21 (Turnhout, 2011), see Vincent Gillespie, 'Chichele's Church: Vernacular Theology in England after Thomas Arundel', 3–42; David Lawton, 'Voice after Arundel', 133–51; and Helen Barr, '"This Holy Tyme": Present Sense in the *Digby Lyrics*', 307–23. See also David Lawton, 'Dullness and the Fifteenth Century', *ELH*, 54 (1987), 761–99.

[8] See Brynley F. Roberts, 'Writing in Wales'; Terence Dolan, 'Writing in Ireland'; R. James Goldstein, 'Writing in Scotland, 1058–1560', all in David Wallace (ed.), *The Cambridge History of Medieval English Literature* (Cambridge, 1999), 182–207, 208–28, 229–54.

Factors of different kinds, including geography, still limited the circulation of some poems very far beyond their place of origin. The early-fourteenth-century English poems of the Franciscan friar William Herebert, for example, copied by him into a collection of Latin sermons and other material, probably in Oxford, do not seem to have found a wider medieval audience at all; *Castleford's Chronicle*, composed in Yorkshire, survives only in one Yorkshire manuscript; John Barbour's verse history of Robert the Bruce in only two fifteenth-century Scottish copies.[9] But local boundaries were sometimes more permeable. In the case of alliterative poetry, traditionally connected with the west and north of England where the taste for verse composition on this model was strong, the movement of texts brought alliterative works to wider audiences. *Piers Plowman* had a significant London circulation, and one of the Lollard responses it provoked, the anonymous late fourteenth-century *Pierce the Ploughman's Crede*, was still available to a London scribe *c* 1460–70.[10] The alliterative poem *Crowned King*, an account of a dream experienced on the eve of Corpus Christi 1415 concerning Henry V's request for a war subsidy, survives only in a London manuscript.[11] *The Siege of Jerusalem*, probably composed in the late fourteenth century in West Yorkshire and surviving in some copies of northern provenance, was available in the fifteenth century to scribes in London.[12] In some cases the travels of poets themselves took regional preferences across local boundaries. The short alliterative poem *A Bird in Bishopswood* was copied in some blank space on an account roll for the Dean and Chapter of St Paul's *c* 1396 by John Tickhill, a collector of rents for the cathedral. Living and working in London, but perhaps from Yorkshire, he chose traditional four-stress, unrhymed alliterative lines for his account of an inconclusive Maytime encounter with 'a bryd ... on a bough, fast me besyde, / Þe fayrest fowyl of fethyr þat I had say beforne'.[13] Also somehow associated with St Paul's, the alliterative *St Erkenwald*, although surviving only in a late copy from the north-west midlands, was clearly the work of a poet with a detailed knowledge of London, and may have had a London readership.[14]

A number of substantial poems from the earlier fourteenth century had a fifteenth-century life. Metrical romances, in particular, retained their appeal—in some cases on into

---

[9] For Herebert's poems (in London, British Library, MS Additional 46919), see Stephen R. Reimer (ed.), *The Works of William Herebert, OFM*, Studies and Texts, 81 (Toronto, 1987). For *Castleford's Chronicle* (in Niedersächsische Staats- und Universitätsbibliothek Göttingen, MS 2° Cod. Hist. 740 Cim.), see Caroline D. Eckhardt (ed.), *Castleford's Chronicle or the Boke of Brut*, 2 vols. EETS o.s. 305–6 (Oxford, 1996), and 'The Manuscript of *Castleford's Chronicle*: Its History and Scribes', in Jaclyn Rajsic, Erik Kooper, and Dominique Hoche (eds), *The Prose Brut and Other Late Medieval Chronicles: Books Have Their Histories—Essays in Honour of Lister M. Matheson* (Cambridge, 2016), 199–217; for Barbour's *Bruce* (in Cambridge, St John's College, MS G. 23 [191] and Edinburgh, National Library of Scotland, Advocates' MS 19. 2. 2), see M. P. McDiarmid and J. A. C. Stevenson (eds), *Barbour's 'Bruce'*, 3 vols., STS, 4th series, 12, 13, 15 (Edinburgh, 1980–5).

[10] For recent discussion of the London circulation of *Piers Plowman*, and relevant bibliography, see Sarah Wood, 'Two Annotated *Piers Plowman* Manuscripts from London and the Early Reception of the B and C Versions', *Chaucer Review*, 43 (2017), 274–97. For *Pierce the Ploughman's Crede* in London, British Library, Harley MS 78, see Helen Barr (ed.), *The Piers Plowman Tradition* (London, 1993), 61–97; and A. I. Doyle, 'An Unrecognised *Piece of Piers the Ploughman's Creed* and Other Work by its Scribe', *Speculum*, 34 (1959), 428–36.

[11] Oxford, Bodleian Library, MS Douce 95; see Barr (ed.), *Piers Plowman Tradition*, 205–10, and Derek Pearsall, '"Crowned King": War and Peace in 1415', in Jenny Stratford (ed.), *The Lancastrian Court*, Harlaxton Medieval Studies, 13 (Donington, 2003), 163–72.

[12] Ralph Hanna and David Lawton (eds), *The Siege of Jerusalem*, EETS o.s. 320 (Oxford, 2003), xiii–xxxvii, lxviii–lxix.

[13] Ruth Kennedy, '"A Bird in Bishopswood": Some Newly Discovered Lines of Alliterative Verse from the Late Fourteenth Century', in Myra Stokes and T. L. Burton (eds), *Medieval Literature and Antiquities: Studies in Honour of Basil Cottle* (Cambridge, 1987), 71–87 (the quotation is from lines 21–2).

[14] Edited from London, British Library, Harley MS 2250 in Thorlac Turville-Petre (ed.), *Alliterative Poetry of the Later Middle Ages: An Anthology* (London, 1989), 101–19; see also John Scattergood, '*St Erkenwald* and the Custody of the Past', in John Scattergood, *The Lost Tradition: Essays on Middle English Alliterative Poetry* (Dublin, 2000), 179–99.

460   MEDIEVAL POETRY: 1100–1400

the seventeenth century.[15] Chronicles also had a long life. Copies of Robert of Gloucester's *Chronicle* (*c* 1300) continued to be made, sometimes amalgamated with newer works.[16]
Although Robert Mannyng's chronicle had a more limited circulation, his *Handlyng Synne*,
begun in 1303, was copied in the fifteenth century both whole and in extracted form.[17]
Copies of the *South English Legendary* and of *The Northern Passion*, both begun in the
late thirteenth century, and of the northern *Cursor Mundi* (*c* 1300), went on being produced.[18] Chief among the earlier long poems to remain in circulation was *The Prick of
Conscience*, composed in the first half of the fourteenth century, surviving in complete
form in around 118 copies (as well as in numerous extracts), many actually produced in
the fifteenth century. The work of an anonymous north Yorkshire cleric, the *Prick* runs to
nearly 10,000 lines, translated into English four-stress couplets in order 'to stirre lewed men
til mekenes' ('to make unlearned people humble').[19] The extent of its life is indicated not
only by partial printed editions from early-sixteenth-century London, but also by records
of ownership: a copy annotated by a monk of Westminster in the late fifteenth century, for
example, and another present in a London parish church in 1472.[20]

The attractions of all these works must have included on the one hand their compre-
hensiveness and on the other their malleability and capacity to be revised or mined for
shorter extracts. As the texts travelled, some were 'translated', with the effect that originally
northern texts (the *Prick* and *Cursor Mundi*, for example) were made available in southern
recensions. Other forms of adaptation could regularise or modernise features of verse form,
even at times subjecting parts of works to processes of *dérimage* or 'unrhyming' as with
extracts from *The Prick of Conscience*.[21] These works lent themselves readily to processes of
excerption, with individual lives from the *South English Legendary* appearing in fifteenth-
century manuscripts, for example, and an exemplum from Mannyng's *Handlyng Synne* put
to use in a fifteenth-century family compilation.[22]

Stories familiar from earlier collections could however appear in new dress. In 1443–7
the Austin friar Osbern Bokenham revisited some of the saints' lives compiled in collections
like the *South English Legendary*, and in tailoring his new versions to the tastes of his local
East Anglian female readers adopted a more self-consciously poetic voice. The *South English*

---

[15] See Helen Cooper, *The English Romance in Time: Transforming Motifs from Geoffrey of Monmouth to the
Death of Shakespeare* (Oxford, 2004), especially 22–40.
[16] Anne Hudson, 'Tradition and Innovation in Some Middle English Manuscripts', *Review of English Studies*,
17 (1966), 359–72.
[17] Idelle Sullens (ed.), *Robert Mannyng: Handlyng Synne* (Binghamton, NY, 1983), and *Robert Mannyng: The
Chronicle* (Binghamton, NY, 1996).
[18] On the manuscripts, see Manfred Görlach, *The Textual Tradition of the South English Legendary* (Leeds,
1974); Frances A. Foster and W. Heuser (eds), *The Northern Passion*, 3 vols., EETS o.s. 145, 147, 183 (London,
1913–30); John J. Thompson, *The Cursor Mundi: Poem, Texts and Contexts* (Oxford, 1998).
[19] Ralph Hanna and Sarah Wood (eds), *Richard Morris's Prick of Conscience: A Corrected and Amplified
Reading Text*, EETS o.s. 342 (Oxford, 2013), 262 (line 9595).
[20] On the manuscripts, see Robert E. Lewis and Angus McIntosh, *A Descriptive Guide to the Manuscripts of
the Prick of Conscience* (Oxford, 1982); and for the specific instances mentioned, Hanna and Wood (eds), *Prick*,
xxxii–xxxiv and Pamela R. Robinson, 'A "Prik of conscience cheyned": The Parish Library of St Margaret's, New
Fish Street, London, 1472', in Takami Matsuda, Richard Linenthal, and John Scahill (eds), *The Medieval Book
and a Modern Collector: Essays in Honour of Toshiyuki Takamiya* (Cambridge, 2004), 209–21.
[21] Sarah Wood, 'A Prose Redaction of The Prick of Conscience Part VI in Bodleian Library MS Laud Misc. 23',
Medium Ævum, 80 (2011), 1–17.
[22] See Görlach, *Textual Tradition*, for extracts from the *South English Legendary*. The Mannyng extract is in
Oxford, Bodleian Library, MS Ashmole 61; see George Shuffelton (ed.), *Codex Ashmole 61: A Compilation of
Popular Middle English Verse* (Kalamazoo, MI, 2008), available at https://d.lib.rochester.edu/teams, item 18.

Legendary version of St Lucy's life, in septenary lines, concludes with a brief summary of the saint's death and translation:

> Wiþ þe laste word heo ȝaf þe gost; as hi amen sede
> Angles al ȝare were; hire soule to heuene lede
> Þer heo is wiþ Iesu Crist; in ioye wiþouten ende
> Nou God for þe loue of hire ous lete þider wende Amen.[23] (171–4)

(with the final word she gave up her spirit, as they said 'amen'. Angels were all ready to lead her soul to Heaven, where she is with Jesus Christ in endless joy. Now, may God, for the love of her, let us go there!)

Bokenham's couplet version is altogether more artful:

> And þan anoon she dede comende
> To god hyr soule, & forth it sende
> To heuene blysse, þourgh goddys grace;
> Whos body was beryid in þe same place,
> And þere-ouyr a cherche made hastyly,
> In whych yt ys shrynyd ful reuerently,
> Abydyng þe day of þe greth assyse;
> In whych, o Lucye, in humble wyse,
> I the beseche that þe translatour
> Of þi legende for hys labour,
> By mene of þe, wych clepyd art lyht
> Aftyr þi name, may haue a syht
> Of þe greth lyht and eek bryhtnesse
> Of hym þat sunne ys of ryhtwysnesse,
> And illumynyth wyth his grace alle men,
> Whom onys to seen ys ioye. AmeN.[24] (9439–54)

(Only then did she commend her soul to God and send it forth to heaven's bliss through God's grace. Her body was buried in the same place and a church built over it, in which it is reverently enshrined, awaiting the great judgement day. On that day, O Lucy, I humbly beg that the translator of your legend may for his labours (by mediation of you who are called 'light' according to your name) have a glimpse of him who is the sun of righteousness and who illumines everyone with his grace. To see him once is joy. Amen.)

He invokes Lucy's shrine and the etymology of her name, addresses her with an apostrophe ('o Lucie … I the biseche'), develops the 'grete light' of heaven with further metaphors, and foregrounds the role of the poet-translator: humble, but nonetheless deserving of his own reward (he can even work the concluding 'Amen' into the rhyme scheme). Words only

---

[23] Charlotte d'Evelyn and Anna J. Mill (eds), *The South English Legendary*, 3 vols., EETS o.s. 235, 236, 244 (London, 1956, 1959), 2:571.

[24] M. S. Serjeantson (ed.), *Osbern Bokenham: Legendys of Hooly Wummen*, EETS o.s. 206 (London, 1938), 256–7. The translation is from Sheila Delany, *A Legend of Holy Women: A Translation of Osbern Bokenham's 'Legends of Holy Women'* (Notre Dame, IN, 1992), 174.

462   MEDIEVAL POETRY: 1100–1400

recently introduced into English help to give this version an air of learnedness and novelty.[25] Nonetheless, the availability of new versions of older saints' lives did not necessarily displace the earlier narratives. As with older metrical romances, their continuing circulation kept in view verse forms like septenary and four-stress couplets; they remained attractive reading and were not entirely obscured by newer forms.

These newer forms were most visible in the verse of the late-fourteenth-century poets Chaucer and Gower, of inestimable importance to fifteenth-century poetic culture. While acknowledging and drawing on existing traditions of English verse writing, both poets introduced into English poetry a range of new topics, new forms, and new ways of conceiving of poetic endeavour. Their knowledge and use of continental verse traditions, and their reflections on English and the crafting of vernacular poetry, were profoundly influential. Their creation of two such large and evidently ambitious poetic oeuvres was in itself a stimulus to the English tradition, whose fourteenth-century exponents had tended to categorise English verse as 'symple speche', matter for the 'lewed', or unlearned, rather than for more sophisticated palates.[26] In addition, Gower and Chaucer had identities, naming themselves, and each other, in their poems, in contrast to the largely anonymous body of their poetic predecessors.[27] Although all of Chaucer's work and much of Gower's was produced before the end of 1400, little documented evidence of their reception survives from before this date. The fifteenth century was the great age for the production of manuscript copies of their works: Chaucer's *Canterbury Tales* survives more or less complete in fifty-seven manuscripts, his *Troilus and Criseyde* in sixteen, and Gower's *Confessio Amantis* in forty-nine complete copies. Excerpts from all of these works were also made for a variety of purposes; and by the mid-fifteenth century Chaucer's shorter poems were making appearances in manuscript anthologies.[28]

Explicit praise of Chaucer and Gower emerged quickly in the decades following their deaths (Chaucer died in 1400, Gower in 1408). In the preface to his translation of Boethius's *De Consolatione Philosophiae* (1410), John Walton invoked both in a modesty topos whose key terms would be repeated by many fifteenth-century poets:[29]

> To Chaucer þat is floure of rethoryk
> In Englisshe tong and excellent poete,
> This wot I wel, no þing may I do like,
> Þogh so þat I of makyng entirmete;

[25] See the *MED* entries for the words 'commend', 'reuerently', 'translatour', and 'illumyneth'. Fifteenth-century and earlier versions of saints' lives can be conveniently compared in Sherry L. Reames (ed.), *Middle English Legends of Women Saints* (Kalamazoo, MI, 2003).

[26] Sullens (ed.), *Robert Mannyng: Chronicle* (lines 35, 8).

[27] On self-naming, see Robert J. Meyer-Lee, *Poets and Power from Chaucer to Wyatt* (Cambridge, 2007), 32–42.

[28] A. S. G. Edwards and Derek Pearsall, 'The Manuscripts of the Major English Poetic Texts', in Jeremy Griffiths and Derek Pearsall (eds), *Book Production and Publishing in Britain, 1375–1475* (Cambridge, 1989), 257–78; Derek Pearsall and Linne R. Mooney, *A Descriptive Catalogue of the English Manuscripts of John Gower's Confessio Amantis* (Woodbridge, 2021). M. C. Seymour, *A Catalogue of Chaucer Manuscripts*, 2 vols. (Aldershot, 1995–7).

[29] Caroline F. E. Spurgeon, *Five Hundred Years of Chaucer Criticism and Allusion, 1357–1900*, 3 vols. (Cambridge, 1925), offers a comprehensive collection of passages relating to Chaucer; on Gower, see Robert R. Edwards, 'Gower 1400–1700', in R. F. Yeager, Brian Gastle, and Ana Sáez-Hidalgo (eds), *Routledge Research Companion to John Gower* (New York, 2017), 197–209. Facets of the early reception of Chaucer and Gower are discussed by A. C. Spearing, *Medieval to Renaissance in English Poetry* (Cambridge, 1985), 59–120; Seth Lerer, *Chaucer and His Readers: Imagining the Author in Late-Medieval England* (Princeton, NJ, 1993), 3–146; Meyer-Lee, *Poets and Power*, 43–125; and Robert R. Edwards, *Invention and Authorship in Medieval England* (Columbus, OH, 2017), 149–96.

And Gower þat so craftily doþ trete
As in hys book[es] of moralite;
Þogh I to þeym in makyng am vnmete,
Ȝit must I schewe it forth þat is in me.[30]

(However much I practise the writing of poetry, I know well that I can do nothing like Chaucer, flower of the craft of rhetoric in English, and an excellent poet; and Gower too, who writes so skilfully in his books about morality. Though I'm not to be compared with them in the writing of poetry, still I must demonstrate what is in me.)

The words used here ('rethoryke', 'craft', 'makyng'), recurring in a number of later eulogies, emphasise a command of poetic language and style that brought something new to the English poetic tradition. For Thomas Hoccleve (*c* 1368–1426), poet and clerk of the Privy Seal at Westminster, who probably knew Chaucer, his poetic 'father' was nothing less than the 'firste fynder of our fare langage' (the first inventor of our fair language).[31] For the Benedictine monk John Lydgate (1371–1449), eulogising at a greater distance, Chaucer was the first English poet 'to reyne / þe gold dewe-dropis of rethorik so fyne / Oure rude langage only tenlwmyne' ('to rain down the gold dew-drops of such fine rhetoric to illuminate our rough language').[32] For later fifteenth-century poets, such praise, frequently extended to include Lydgate, would become a form of reflex.

Early tributes to the work of Chaucer took a number of forms. His short poem 'Gentilesse' was incorporated by his friend Henry Scogan into a 'Moral balade' sent to acquaintances at a dinner held in London round about 1407.[33] Walton's verse translation of Boethius offered an alternative to Chaucer's *Boece*. An anonymous addition to *The Canterbury Tales* from *c* 1420 combines a fabliau-like prologue detailing the pilgrims' overnight activities in Canterbury with a tale about the adventures of a young Roman named Beryn.[34] Lydgate's *Troy Book* (1412–20), an Englishing of Guido delle Colonne's *Historia Destructionis Troiae*, offers an expansive account of the Trojan story as a complement to Chaucer's version in *Troilus and Criseyde*.[35] By 1421–2 he had produced his own version of a Canterbury Tale in the form of *The Siege of Thebes*, an account of the history preceding Chaucer's 'Knight's Tale', introducing it with a prologue describing his own incorporation into Chaucer's group of pilgrims; and his last major work, *The Fall of Princes*, was a massive response to the tragedies compiled in Chaucer's 'Monk's Tale'. Hoccleve, having written admiringly of Chaucer and Gower in the prologue to his *Regement of Princes* (1411), inserted towards the end of his long poem a prayer for Chaucer's soul, and for good measure a portrait ('I haue heere his lyknesse / Do make').[36]

The examples of both Chaucer and Gower showed the fifteenth century new ways of appropriating stories from antiquity, suggesting the potential of these narratives for

---

[30] Mark Science (ed.), *Boethius: De Consolationae Philosophiae, translated by John Walton*, EETS o.s. 170 (London, 1927), 2 (stanza 5).

[31] F. J. Furnivall (ed.), *Hoccleve's Works, III: The Regement of Princes*, EETS e.s. 72 (London, 1897), 179 (line 4978). J. A. Burrow, *Thomas Hoccleve*, Authors of the Middle Ages, 4 (Aldershot, 1994), 10, notes that 'no English poet had previously written in this fashion about an English predecessor'.

[32] Henry Bergen (ed.), *John Lydgate: Troy Book*, 4 vols. EETS e.s. 97, 103, 106, 126 (London, 1906–35), 1:279 (Book 2.4698–9). See further Derek Pearsall, *John Lydgate (1371–1449): A Bio-Bibliography* (Victoria, BC, 1997).

[33] Walter W. Skeat (ed.), *The Complete Works of Geoffrey Chaucer*, 7 vols. (Oxford, 1894–7), 7: xli–xliii and 237–44.

[34] F. J. Furnivall (ed.), *The Tale of Beryn*, EETS e.s. 105 (London, 1909).

[35] Bergen (ed.), *Troy Book*.

[36] Furnivall (ed.), *Regement*, 180 (lines 4995–6; and see also 1867, 1958–81).

464   MEDIEVAL POETRY: 1100–1400

anatomising the operation of human decisions and emotions while offering instruction and commentary on matters of wider political moment.[37] Hoccleve's *Regement* and Lydgate's *Troy Book, Siege of Thebes,* and *Fall of Princes,* substantial poems that would be reproduced in many copies, were an important means of disseminating verse of the broadly Chaucerian tradition to a wider fifteenth-century readership, and of giving the stamp of authority to the new verse forms that Chaucer's long poems had introduced: iambic pentameter couplet and rhyme royal and balade stanzas (Lydgate's preference seems to have been for longer pentameter lines; the two substantial works in octosyllabic couplets with which he is sometimes associated, *Reson and Sensualyte* and a translation of Deguileville's *Pèlerinage de la vie humaine,* are linked with his name only by sixteenth-century annotators).[38] Hoccleve's own London connections, and Lydgate's association with patrons of means who commissioned scribal and decorative work from London artisans, gave a metropolitan visibility to their works that must have further encouraged the replication of copies. Like the long poems of Chaucer and Gower, the longer works of Hoccleve and Lydgate circulated separately but also in extracted form, and on occasion were amalgamated with other materials in manuscript anthologies.

Chaucer and Gower may have achieved the status of all-purpose moral authorities for the fifteenth century, but they also had an important legacy as poets of love. Even though the trajectory of Gower's *Confessio Amantis* reaches a close with the dismissal of the ageing Amans from love's service, its exemplary stories are framed by amorous concerns; and as Venus parts from Gower's narrator she mentions Chaucer as another member of her entourage, a 'clerk' and 'disciple' known for his own dedication to the kind of secular love no longer appropriate to his 'later age'.[39] Love had featured in other forms of fourteenth-century English verse, in romances and lyrics especially, but Gower and Chaucer gave new focus to its centrality to the feeling, creative self. Gower's anatomy of love, in the framework to the *Confessio* and in some of its exemplary narratives, along with Chaucer's *Troilus,* certain of *The Canterbury Tales,* and some of the dream visions and shorter poems, offered templates for love poetry that drew into English some of the concerns treated by fourteenth-century French and Italian poets.

Chaucer's experiments with *dits amoureux* (short narratives about love, on models exemplified in the works of Froissart and Machaut, often autobiographical, and often involving a dream) are reflected in many later courtly narratives. Sir John Clanvowe's *Boke of Cupide* (dating from before 1391) is the earliest surviving response to Chaucer's *dits,* drawing on *The Parliament of Fowls* in its construction of a lovesick poet-narrator's dream (and alluding for good measure to 'The Knight's Tale' and the Prologue to *The Legend of Good Women*).[40] Clanvowe's choice of a five-line stanza form (*aabba*), does not replicate the rhyme royal

---

[37] See James Simpson, *The Oxford English Literary History, Volume 2, 1350–1547: Reform and Cultural Revolution* (Oxford, 2002), 201–29 and Maura Nolan, *John Lydgate and the Making of Public Culture* (Cambridge, 2005).

[38] See Eric Weiskott, 'Before Prosody: Early English Poetics in Practice and Theory', *Modern Language Quarterly,* 77 (2016), 473–98 (who notes, 487, that 'the Chaucer canonization industry was also a pentameter canonization industry'); and Martin Duffell, '"The Craft So Long to Lerne": Chaucer's Invention of the Iambic Pentameter', *Chaucer Review,* 34 (2000), 269–88. For works in octosyllabic couplets that have been associated with Lydgate, see F. J. Furnivall (ed.), *The Pilgrimage of the Life of Man,* 3 vols., EETS e.s. 77, 83, 92 (London, 1899–1904) and E. Sieper (ed.), *Lydgate's Reson and Sensuallyte,* 2 vols., EETS e.s. 84, 89 (London, 1901–3).

[39] Macaulay (ed.), *The English Works of John Gower,* 2:466 (lines 2941*–57*).

[40] V. J. Scattergood (ed.), *The Works of Sir John Clanvowe* (Cambridge, 1975), 35–53. A number of the poems that accompany *The Boke of Cupide* in manuscript anthologies consider problems concerning love or the conduct of lovers; see further Julia Boffey and John J. Thompson, 'Anthologies and Miscellanies: Production and Choice of Texts', in Griffiths and Pearsall (ed.), *Book Production,* 279–315 (especially 280–3).

stanzas of the *Parliament* or those of any other surviving Chaucerian poem, but it has parallels in French verse, and presses home the debt to French that Clanvowe shared with Chaucer. Love is analysed here through the opposing views of a cuckoo and a nightingale, whose debate follows a long tradition attractive to both French and English poets,[41] and takes place within a dream induced by the delights of the natural world. Springtime revival of energy is a familiar topos in medieval verse, especially in lyrics and romance: the action of *Kyng Alisaunder*, for example, is nudged forward at many points with passages of natural description: 'In tyme of Maij the niȝttyngale / Jn wood makeþ mery gale. / So don the foules, grete and smale, / Summe on hylles and summe in dale. / þe day daweþ, þe kyng awakeþ ...' (2543–7).[42] But Clanvowe's external world is constructed as if to inspire the creative imagination of those who find themselves within it or reading about it ('euery trewe, gentil herte fre', 21), promoting an openness to 'felyng' (36), and as a consequence to the exploration of inner concerns that can be given shape in dreams. His own out-of-body experience is brief and not especially illuminating, but some elements of his poem—its structured relationship between outer and inner worlds, its preoccupation with sensibility and discrimination in matters of love—are reflected in fifteenth-century *dits* where varieties of framework enclose dreams within carefully delineated waking worlds.[43]

In some of these works the experience of love serves as a prompt not only for analysis of individual feeling, but also for meditation on social connectedness, and on the creative mental exercise that generates poetry. The harmony of the natural world, one of the preoccupations of *The Book of Cupid*, becomes an important feature, realised in both descriptive detail and in allusions to music and song. Clanvowe makes music part of his poem's sensuous landscape, with 'foules ermonye' sending the narrator to sleep, and references to specific songs puncturing the course of the narrative.[44] The sonic and figurative potential of song is explored still further in *The Kingis Quair* (the 'quire' or book of King James I of Scotland), composed during 1423/4 at the end of the author's period of imprisonment in England. Here, stanzas of song are interpolated at significant moments, birdsong suggests the wider social harmony from which the imprisoned narrator is at first excluded, and special attention is drawn to the poem's form in mellifluous rhyme royal stanzas ('lynis sevin') in a concluding prayer for the souls of Chaucer and Gower.[45]

The varieties of poetic effect to be achieved through invocations of song and, more broadly, through modulations of form in the course of a poem, were explored in a number of contexts: Lydgate, for example, incorporated song in his courtly poem *The Floure of Curtesy*, and foregrounded lyric complaints and petitions in *The Temple of Glass* through modulations of verse form.[46] Even in his longer narratives he explored such variation, whether for emphasis or to counter the possibility that a single form might pall over the course of a long poem. Into the series of rhyme royal narratives that make up *The Fall of Princes* occasional

---

[41] See John W. Conlee (ed.), *Middle English Debate Poetry: A Critical Anthology* (East Lansing, MI, 1991) and Neil Cartlidge (ed.) *The Owl and the Nightingale* (Exeter, 2001).

[42] G. V. Smithers (ed.), *Kyng Alisaunder*, 2 vols., EETS o.s. 227, 237 (London, 1952–7), 1:143.

[43] Judith M. Davidoff, *Beginning Well: Framing Fictions in Late Middle English Poetry* (Cranbury, NJ, 1988).

[44] Scattergood (ed.), *Clanvowe*, 39 (line 83), 51 (line 250), 53 (line 289).

[45] In Julia Boffey (ed.), *Fifteenth-Century English Dream Visions* (Oxford, 2003), 90–157 (see 157, lines 1373–9). Hoccleve's translation of Christine de Pizan's polemical *Epitre de Cupide*, the *Letter of Cupid* (1402) is one of the earliest works in the rhyme royal stanza used extensively by Chaucer and by Gower for 'In Praise of Peace'; see Thelmer S. Fenster and Mary Carpenter Erler (eds), *Poems of Cupid, God of Love* (Leiden, 1990), 158–218.

[46] Henry Noble MacCracken (ed.), *John Lydgate: The Minor Poems*, 2 vols., EETS e.s. 107 and o.s. 192 (London, 1911 and 1934), 2:410–18; Boffey (ed.), *Dream Visions*, 15–89.

466 MEDIEVAL POETRY: 1100–1400

eight-line stanzas are introduced, mostly incorporated in the envoys that conclude individual stories.[47] Walton's translation of Boethius similarly moves at the end of the third book from eight-line balade stanzas into seven-line rhyme royal stanzas, marking the change with a translator's prologue that draws attention to the difficulties of preserving Boethius's 'sentence' in 'metre trewe'.[48]

Chaucer's long narrative poems demonstrated the potential of rhyme royal and balade stanza in English, but the experiments that both he and Gower made with these forms in shorter lyrics were also influential. Their model here was the French *ballade*: a short poem, usually in seven- or eight-line stanzas, often employing repetition in the last line of each stanza to form a refrain, and often brought to a close with an envoy that might be formally distinct, sending the poem on its way to a recipient or dedicatee. Consolidation of the English balade form came by way of French-language experiments such as Gower's *Cinkante ballades* and his ballade sequence, the *Traitié selonc les auctours pour essampler les amantz marietz*, later translated into English by an individual named Quixley, who noted the 'grete studie' expended by Gower in the composition.[49] Chaucer's English lyrics, including balades of seven- and eight-line stanzas as well as some experimental balade-like forms, would be important to his successors. Hoccleve was an early exponent of these short forms, employing them often in poems conceived for social purposes; in his autograph manuscripts his balades often have introductions in French, as if to stress their affiliations.[50] The balade was Lydgate's preferred short form, often extended over many stanzas, with refrains pressing home key phrases or memorable nuggets of advice: 'every thing draweþe to his semblable'; 'that now is hey some tyme was grase'.[51]

The widespread circulation of the verse of Chaucer, and in turn of Hoccleve and Lydgate, gave currency to these stanza forms and demonstrated their flexibility; they could be extended to nine or ten lines, and they could be constituted of octosyllabic or four-stress lines (Lydgate, for example, evidently favoured the shorter lines for love complaints, especially those ventriloquising women's voices).[52] Such variety complemented other English experiments with French *ballade*-stanza forms that had been taking place outside the circles of Chaucer and Gower, notably in the series of refrain lyrics copied into the massive Vernon manuscript, compiled in the west midlands.[53] The shorter, four-stress lines of these lyrics contrive effects rather different from fifteenth-century balades on the Chaucerian model.

---

[47] Henry Bergen (ed.), *Lydgate's Fall of Princes*, 4 vols., EETS e.s. 121–4 (London, 1924–7).

[48] Science (ed.), *Boethius*, 210 (stanza 576).

[49] R. F. Yeager (ed.), *John Gower: The French Balades* (Kalamazoo, MI, 2011) at https://d.lib.rochester.edu/teams; 'A Translation of the *Traitié*', line 5.

[50] Frederick J. Furnivall and I. Gollancz (eds), *Hoccleve's Works: The Minor Poems*, 2 vols., EETS e.s. 61, 73, revised in one volume by Jerome Mitchell and A. I. Doyle (Oxford, 1970), 39–72; J. A. Burrow and A. I. Doyle (intro.), *Thomas Hoccleve: A Facsimile of the Autograph Verse Manuscripts*, EETS s.s. 19 (Oxford, 2002). English experiments with other of the French *formes fixes*, roundel and virelai, were limited: see Jenni Nuttall, 'The Vanishing English Virelai: French *Complainte* in English in the Fifteenth Century', *Medium Ævum*, 85 (2016), 59–76; and '"Many a Lay and Many a Thing": Chaucer's Technical Terms', in Thomas A. Prendergast and Jessica Rosenfeld (eds), *Chaucer and the Subversion of Form* (Cambridge, 2018), 21–37.

[51] MacCracken (ed.), *Minor Poems*, 2:801–13.

[52] See 'A Gentlewoman's Lament', 'My Lady Dere', and 'A Complaint for My Lady of Gloucester and Holland': MacCracken (ed.), *Minor Poems*, 2:418–20, 420–4, 608–13.

[53] Oxford, Bodleian Library, MS Eng. poet. a. 1. Carleton Brown (ed.), *Religious Lyrics of the XIVth Century*, 2nd edn., rev. G. V. Smithers (Oxford, 1952), 125–208 and J. A. Burrow, 'The Shape of the Vernon Refrain Lyrics', in Derek Pearsall (ed.), *Studies in the Vernon Manuscript* (Cambridge, 1990), 187–99. Burrow terms the Vernon lyrics 'pseudo-ballades', noting their adoption of eight-line or twelve-line stanzas with refrains (*ababbcbC* or *ababababbcbC*) and suggesting that they are 'the very first attempts to produce in English something like an extended version of the "balades de moralitez" of Chaucer's French contemporary, Deschamps' (188).

The Vernon poem 'On the death of Edward III' contemplates the accession of the infant king Richard II as follows:

> Þus ben þis lordes I-leid full lowe;
> > Þe stok is of þe same rote;
> An ympe biginnes for to growe,
> > And ʒit I hope schal ben vr bote,
> > To holde his fomen vnder fote,
> And as a lord be sete in sete.
> > Crist leue þat he so mote,
> Þat selden I-seʒe be not forʒete.[54] (81–8)

(Thus are these lords laid low; the stock is from the same root. A shoot begins to grow, and I hope it will bring us relief if he subjugates his enemies and is enthroned as a lord. May Christ allow him to do this. What is seldom seen is not forgotten.)

Some decades later, Hoccleve's ballade on the interment of Richard II's bones in Westminster Abbey uses the same rhyme scheme but longer, pentameter lines:

> What mighten folk of good byleeue seye,
> > If bent were our kynges affecioun
> To the wrong part, who shold help hem purueye?
> > A king set in þat wrong opinioun
> > Mighte of our faith be the subuersioun.
> But eterne god, in persones three,
> > Hath regned dropes of conpassioun,
> And sent vs our good king for our cheertee![55] (25–32)

(What might right-thinking people say, if our king's affection were perverted? Who would help provide for them? But immortal God, in three persons, has rained down drops of compassion, and sent us our good king for our joy!)

The word choices here, including a number of polysyllabic nouns of French derivation little if at all attested in English before the late fourteenth century,[56] account for part of the difference in flavour; the longer lines also accommodate words of varied lengths and relatively complex syntax. These lines may well have sounded 'crafty' and somehow 'golden', to invoke the terms so often used of Chaucer's verse. The strength of the Vernon lyric, in contrast, is precisely its economy of expression, with effects derived from a reliance on monosyllables, the use of alliteration to connect key words, and a refrain line that is a memorable paradox.

Rhyme royal and ballade stanzas were attractive options for writers of short poems in English: they soon became a preferred choice for occasional poems, where modes of complaint, petition, or compliment, for which they were well suited, were appropriate. 'Pseudo-balades' on the model of the Vernon lyrics dominate the collection of 'Digby poems', probably from the 1420s, and probably attributable to just one author, who may have had

---

[54] R. H. Robbins (ed.), *Historical Poems of the XIVth and XVth Centuries* (New York, 1959), 102–6.
[55] *Historical Poems*, ed. Robbins, 106–8.
[56] See the *Middle English Dictionary* entries for the rhyme words 'affecioun', 'opinioun', 'subuersioun', 'compassioun', 'eterne'.

468   MEDIEVAL POETRY: 1100–1400

connections with both the west midlands and London.[57] But the range of stanza and verse forms is much greater in the approximately contemporary manuscript associated with John Audelay, a priest at Haughmond Abbey near Shrewsbury, which includes carols and alliterative verse as well as religious lyrics in many different forms.[58] One context for short poems of these kinds, the substratum of popular poem and song, is hard to excavate from written survivals, but the easy appropriation of demotic modes in the late-fifteenth- and early-sixteenth-century poems of John Skelton testifies to its ongoing life throughout the period.[59]

Although it is tempting to foreground Chaucer and his legacy as the most significant element in the reception of fourteenth-century poetry, what remains most striking is the variety of English verse in circulation after 1400, and the continuing energy expended on different forms of poetic composition. Some of this energy and variety must have been present in dramatic verse which no longer survives: stray survivals like *Pride of Life* have traces of what might have been its vigour, while the intricacy and range of stanza forms used in play-texts copied in the fifteenth century suggest the earlier existence of developed traditions.[60] Forms of rhymed alliterative verse, as used in *The Castle of Perseverance* and in some of the civic play cycles, became more current, especially in Scotland and the north.[61] In the field of metrical romance, early-fifteenth-century works were produced in many shapes and forms, from the alliterative *Morte Arthure* (*c* 1400), to the tail-rhyme of *Torrent of Portyngale* (*c* 1400), and the couplets of Henry Lovelich's *Merlin* and *The Holy Grail* (after *c* 1425).[62] Lovelich's remark that English is not only 'more cler to ʒoure vndirstondyng' but also 'swettere to sowne' than the French from which he translated *The Holy Grail* is a rousing claim.[63] The anonymous translation of the romance of *Partonope of Blois* (*c* 1420), also in couplets, is suffused with Chaucerian echoes, sometimes to curious effect,[64] as when narration of the tournament which will finally reunite Partonope with Melior is held up by the narrator's musings on his own unlikeliness as a lover:

> And I dare sey truly as for me
> I love oon in þe world, where euer she be.
> Bounte, beaute, curtesy, and gentilnesse,
> Estate, fredome, womanhode, and such richesse,

---

[57] For the Digby poems, in Oxford, Bodleian Library, MS Digby 102, see Helen Barr (ed.), *The Digby Poems: A New Edition of the Lyrics* (Exeter, 2009)

[58] See Susanna Fein (ed.), *John the Blind Audelay, Poems and Carols* (Oxford, Bodleian Library MS Douce 302) (Kalamazoo, MI, 2009); Susanna Fein (ed.), *My Wyl and My Wrytyng: Essays on John the Blind Audelay* (Kalamazoo, MI, 2009); E. G. Stanley, 'The Verse Forms of Jon the Blynde Awdelay', in Helen Cooper and Sally Mapstone (eds), *The Long Fifteenth Century: Essays for Douglas Gray* (Oxford, 1997), 99–121.

[59] John Scattergood (ed.), *The Complete English Poems of John Skelton*, rev. edn. (Liverpool, 2015). On popular materials and oral transmission, see Karl Reichl (ed.), *Medieval Oral Literature* (Berlin, 2012), especially Ad Putter, 'Middle English Romances and the Oral Tradition', 335–51, and Karin Boklund-Lagopoulou, 'Popular Song and the Middle English Lyric', 555–80.

[60] David N. Klausner (ed.), *Two Moral Interludes: The Pride of Life and Wisdom* (Kalamazoo, MI, 2008).

[61] See Ralph Hanna, 'Alliterative Poetry', in Wallace (ed.), *Medieval English Literature*, 485–512; Susanna Fein, 'The Early Thirteen-line Stanza: Style and Metrics Reconsidered', *Parergon*, 18 (2000), 97–126; and, on the handling of such verse in romances, Ad Putter, 'Adventures in the Bob-and-Wheel Tradition: Narratives and Manuscripts', in Nicholas Perkins (ed.), *Medieval Romance and Material Culture* (Cambridge, 2015), 147–63.

[62] See Ad Putter, 'The Metres and Stanza Forms of Popular Romance', in Raluca L. Radulescu and Cory James Rushton (eds), *A Companion to Popular Romance* (Cambridge, 2009), 111–31.

[63] F. J. Furnivall and Dorothy Kempe (eds), *The History of the Holy Grail by Herry Lovelich*, 5 vols., EETS e.s. 20, 24, 28, 30, 95 (London, 1874–1905), 4:355 (ch. LVI, lines 527–8).

[64] Barry Windeatt, 'Chaucer and Fifteenth-Century Romance: *Partonope of Blois*', in Ruth Morse and Barry Windeatt (eds), *Chaucer Traditions: Studies in Honour of Derek Brewer* (Cambridge, 1990), 62–80.

God hath departed with hir so habundauntly,
That in þe worlde I dare sey sikerly
Anoþer such one liveþ not as she is.
In hir can I se no þing amysse,
Save oo þing, truly, þat likeþ not me:
In hir herte she can not fynde in noo degre
Me forto love as I hir truly do;
Wherfore ofte she maketh me þinke so
Which wole be cause hastely me to bryng,
There as I shall haue my longe abidyng.
    BE-gonne wele now is þe turnement ...[65] (10909–22)

(And I venture to say truly, for my part, I love someone in the world, somewhere. God has endowed her so abundantly with goodness, beauty, courtesy, nobility, degree, liberality, womanliness, and such wealth, that I dare say truly there is no-one like her living in the world. I can see nothing wrong with her, except for one thing that doesn't please me: she can't find it in her heart in the smallest degree to love me as I truly love her. Because of this she often makes me thoughtful in a way that will soon bring me to the place where I will stay for a long time [i.e., my death]. The tournament has got off to a good start ...)

Fifteenth-century readers knew and evidently appreciated the variety of the English poetic traditions available to them. From our vantage point in the twenty-first century, it is easy to be swayed by the concentration of literary histories on Chaucer and his legacy, by accounts of fifteenth-century poetry as a response to this legacy, further muted by the specifics of changing political dispensations, and to overlook the extent and diversity of the landscape.[66] The assortment of works found together in individual fifteenth-century manuscripts is a reminder of readerly appetites for variety that helped to keep many different traditions alive. Oxford, Bodleian Library, MS Laud 416, for example, brings together *Cursor Mundi*, parts of Mannyng's *Handlyng Synne*, Lydgate's *Siege of Thebes* and Chaucer's *Parliament of Fowls*.[67] And one notable fifteenth-century response to *The Canterbury Tales*, evident in no less than twenty-five manuscript copies, was to include in it the tale of *Gamelyn*, a couplet romance from the middle of the fourteenth century, to constitute the missing 'Cook's Tale'.[68] Such further extension of the poetic range already programmed by Chaucer into *The Canterbury Tales* suggests tastes on the part of fifteenth-century readers that accommodated verse of many kinds.

---

[65] A. Trampe Bödtker (ed.), *The Middle English Versions of Partonope of Blois*, EETS e.s. 109 (London, 1912), 440.

[66] For some revisions of such views, see Andrea Denny-Brown (ed.), 'The Provocative Fifteenth Century', special issue of *Exemplaria*, 29:4 (2017) and 30:1 (2018).

[67] See Thompson, *The Cursor Mundi*, 41–2.

[68] Stephen Knight and Thomas H. Ohlgren (eds), *Robin Hood and Other Outlaw Tales* (Kalamazoo, MI, 1997), at https://d.lib.rochester.edu/teams.

Complete Bibliography

Manuscripts cited:

Aberystwyth, National Library of Wales, MS Peniarth 392D (Hengwrt MS)
Amsterdam, Bibliotheca Philosophica Hermetica (Ritman Library), MS M199
Cambridge, Cambridge University Library, MS Additional 3035
Cambridge, Cambridge University Library, MS Dd.1.17
Cambridge, Cambridge University Library, MS Ff.2.38
Cambridge, Cambridge University Library, MS Gg.1.1
Cambridge, Cambridge University Library, MS Gg.4.27
Cambridge, Cambridge University Library, MS Ll.4.14
Cambridge, Cambridge University Library, MS Mm.4.28
Cambridge, Cambridge University Library, MS Peterhouse 104
Cambridge, Corpus Christi College, MS 61
Cambridge, Corpus Christi College, MS 70
Cambridge, Corpus Christi College, MS 145
Cambridge, Corpus Christi College, MS 406
Cambridge, King's College, MS 13
Cambridge, St John's College, MS G.23
Cambridge, Trinity College, MS B.14.39
Cambridge, Trinity College, MS B.14.52
Cambridge, Trinity College, MS B.15.17
Cambridge, Trinity College, MS R.3.2
Cambridge, Trinity College, MS R.3.8
Cologny-Geneva, Fondation Martin Bodmer, MS 168
Cologny-Geneva, Fondation Martin Bodmer, MS 178
Dublin, Trinity College, MS 212
Dublin, Trinity College, MS 213
Dublin, Trinity College, MS 214
Edinburgh, National Library of Scotland, MS Advocates' 18.2.1
Edinburgh, National Library of Scotland, MS Advocates' 18.7.21
Edinburgh, National Library of Scotland, MS Advocates' 19.2.1 (Auchinleck MS)
Edinburgh, National Library of Scotland, MS Advocates' 19.2.2
Glasgow, University Library, MS Hunter T.2.17
Glasgow, University Library, MS Hunter V.2.8
Göttingen, Niedersächsische Staats- und Universitätsbibliothek, MS 2° Hist. 740 Cim.
Göttingen, Niedersächsische Staats- und Universitätsbibliothek, MS Theol. 107
Hertfordshire, Hatfield House MS (Marquess of Salisbury)
Lichfield, Cathedral Library, MS Lich 50
Lincoln, Cathedral Library, MS A.72
Lincoln, Cathedral Library, MS 91 (Thornton)
London, British Library, MS Additional 19,677
London, British Library, MS Additional 22,283 (Simeon MS)
London, British Library, MS Additional 27,879
London, British Library, MS Additional 31,042
London, British Library, MS Additional 37,787
London, British Library, MS Additional 37,790
London, British Library, MS Additional 46,919

London, British Library, MS Additional 59,495
London, British Library, MS Additional 61,901
London, British Library, MS Arundel 292
London, British Library, MS Arundel 364
London, British Library, MS Cotton Caligula A.ix
London, British Library, MS Cotton Charter IV.18
London, British Library, MS Cotton Galba E.ix
London, British Library, MS Cotton Nero A.x
London, British Library, MS Cotton Otho C.xiii
London, British Library, MS Cotton Tiberius A.iv
London, British Library, MS Cotton Tiberius E.vii
London, British Library, MS Cotton Titus A.xiii
London, British Library, MS Cotton Vespasian A.iii
London, British Library, MS Cotton Vitellius D.iii
London, British Library, MS Egerton 613
London, British Library, MS Egerton 2862
London, British Library, MS Egerton 2891
London, British Library, MS Egerton 3028
London, British Library, MS Harley 78
London, British Library, MS Harley 273
London, British Library, MS Harley 682
London, British Library, MS Harley 913
London, British Library, MS Harley 978
London, British Library, MS Harley 1205
London, British Library, MS Harley 2250
London, British Library, MS Harley 2253
London, British Library, MS Harley 3760
London, British Library, MS Harley 3810
London, British Library, MS Harley 3869
London, British Library, MS Harley 4196
London, British Library, MS Harley 6291
London, British Library, MS Royal 12 C.xii
London, British Library, MS Royal 8 D.xiii
London, British Library, MS Royal 5 F.vii
London, British Library, MS Stowe 951
London, College of Arms, MS Arundel 57
London, Lincoln's Inn, MS 150
Naples, Biblioteca Nazionale, MS XIII.B.29
New Haven, Yale University, Beinecke Library, Osborn Collection, MS fa.1
New Haven, Yale University, Beinecke Library, MS Takamiya 15
New York, Morgan Library & Museum, MS M.817
Nottingham, University Library, Wollaton Library Collection, MS WLC LM 8
Oxford, All Souls College, MS 98
Oxford, Bodleian Library, MS Ashmole 44
Oxford, Bodleian Library, MS Ashmole 61
Oxford, Bodleian Library, MS Bodley 34
Oxford, Bodleian Library, MS Bodley 48
Oxford, Bodleian Library, MS Bodley 257
Oxford, Bodleian Library, MS Bodley 264
Oxford, Bodleian Library, MS Bodley 294
Oxford, Bodleian Library, MS Bodley 343
Oxford, Bodleian Library, MS Bodley 638
Oxford, Bodleian Library, MS Bodley 649
Oxford, Bodleian Library, MS Digby 23

Oxford, Bodleian Library, MS Digby 86
Oxford, Bodleian Library, MS Digby 102
Oxford, Bodleian Library, MS Digby 138
Oxford, Bodleian Library, MS Douce 95
Oxford, Bodleian Library, MS Douce 139
Oxford, Bodleian Library, MS Douce 302
Oxford, Bodleian Library, MS Douce 326
Oxford, Bodleian Library, MS Eng. poet. a.1 (Vernon MS)
Oxford, Bodleian Library, MS Eng. poet. e.1
Oxford, Bodleian Library, MS Fairfax 3
Oxford, Bodleian Library, MS Fairfax 14
Oxford, Bodleian Library, MS Fairfax 16
Oxford, Bodleian Library, MS Greaves 60
Oxford, Bodleian Library, MS Hatton 113
Oxford, Bodleian Library, MS Hatton 114
Oxford, Bodleian Library, MS Junius 1
Oxford, Bodleian Library, MS Laud Misc. 23
Oxford, Bodleian Library, MS Laud Misc. 108
Oxford, Bodleian Library, MS Laud Misc. 416
Oxford, Bodleian Library, MS Laud Misc. 595
Oxford, Bodleian Library, MS Laud Misc. 622
Oxford, Bodleian Library, MS Laud Misc. 719
Oxford, Bodleian Library, MS Rawlinson A.389
Oxford, Bodleian Library, MS Rawlinson G.221
Oxford, Bodleian Library, MS Tanner 346
Oxford, Jesus College, MS 29
Oxford, St John's College, MS 57
Oxford, University College, MS 97
Oxford, Wadham College, MS 13
Paris, Bibliothèque Nationale Française, MS Lat. 5574
Paris, Bibliothèque Nationale Française, MS Lat. 8352
Princeton, Princeton University, Firestone Library, Robert H. Taylor Collection, MS Taylor 5
San Marino, CA, Huntington Library, MS EL 26 C 9 (Ellesmere MS)
San Marino, CA, Huntington Library, MS HM 150
Stafford, Staffordshire Record Office, MS Bagot D(W) 1721/3/186
Vatican City, Biblioteca Apostolica Vaticana, MS Vat. Lat. 2871
Vercelli, Biblioteca Capitolare di Vercelli, MS CXVII
Worcester, Cathedral Library, MS F.174

Adams, Robert. 'Langland's Theology'. In John A. Alford (ed.), *A Companion to* Piers Plowman. Berkeley, CA, 1988. 87–114.

Adams, Robert. *Langland and the Rokele Family: The Gentry Background to* Piers Plowman. Dublin, 2013.

Aebischer, Paul. *Etudes sur Otinel: de la chanson de geste à la saga norroise et aux origines de la légende.* Bern, 1960.

Aers, David. *Piers Plowman and Christian Allegory.* London, 1975.

Aers, David. *Community, Gender and Individual Identity: English Writing 1360–1430.* London, 1988.

Aers, David. *Sanctifying Signs: Making Christian Tradition in Late Medieval England.* Notre Dame, IN, 2004.

Aers, David. *Salvation and Sin: Augustine, Langland and Fourteenth-Century Theology.* Notre Dame, IN, 2009.

Aers, David. *Beyond Reformation? An Essay on William Langland's* Piers Plowman *and the End of Constantinian Christianity.* Notre Dame, IN, 2015.

Aigrain, René. *L'hagiographie: ses sources, ses méthodes, son histoire.* Mayenne, 1953.

Ailes, Marianne and Philippa Hardman. 'How English Are the English Charlemagne Romances?'. In Neil Cartlidge (ed.), *Boundaries in Medieval Romance*. Woodbridge, 2008. 43–55.

Ailes, Marianne and Philippa Hardman. *The Legend of Charlemagne in Medieval England: The Matter of France in Middle English and Anglo-Norman Literature*. Cambridge, 2017.

Akbari, Suzanne Conklin. 'The Hunger for National Identity in *Richard Coeur de Lion*'. In Robert M. Stein and Sandra Pierson Prior (eds), *Reading Medieval Culture: Essays in Honor of Robert W. Hanning*. Notre Dame, IN, 2005. 198–227.

Akbari, Suzanne Conklin. *Idols in the East: European Representations of Islam and the Orient, 1100–1450*. Ithaca, NY, 2009.

Alan of Lille. In Winthrop Wetherbee (ed. and trans.), *Literary Works*. Cambridge, MA, 2013.

Alberts, Allison Adair. 'Spiritual Suffering and Physical Protection in Childbirth in the *South English Legendary* Lives of Saint Margaret'. *Journal of Medieval and Early Modern Studies*, 46 (2016), 289–314.

Alford, John A. Piers Plowman: *A Guide to the Quotations*. Binghamton, NY, 1992.

Allen, Elizabeth. *False Fables and Exemplary Truth in Later Middle English Literature*. Basingstoke, 2005.

Allen, Judson B. *The Ethical Poetic of the Later Middle Ages: A Decorum of Convenient Distinction*. Toronto, 1982.

Alliterative Morte Arthur. In L. D. Benson (ed.), *King Arthur's Death*. Exeter, 1986; rpt. Kalamazoo, MI, 1994. 113–238.

Amis and Amiloun. In MacEdward Leach (ed.), *Amis and Amiloun*. EETS, o.s. 203. London, 1937.

Amys and Amylion. In Françoise Le Saux (ed.), *Amys and Amylion*. Exeter, 1993.

Amys et Amillyoun. In Hideka Fukui (ed.), *Amys et Amillyoun*. ANTS Plain Texts Series 7. London, 1990.

AND: W. Rothwell, L. W. Stone, and T. B. W. Reid (eds). *Anglo-Norman Dictionary*. Publications of the Modern Humanities Research Association 8. London, 1992. www.anglo–norman.net.

Andrew, Malcolm. 'Theories of Authorship'. In Derek Brewer and Jonathan Gibson (eds), *A Companion to the Gawain-Poet*. Cambridge, 1997. 22–33.

Anlezark, Daniel (ed. and trans.). *The Old English Dialogues of Solomon and Saturn*. Cambridge, 2009.

Anselm. In Benedicta Ward (trans.), *The Prayers and Meditations of Saint Anselm: With the Proslogion*. London, 1988.

Aquinas, Thomas. In M. R. Cathala and R. M. Spiazzi (eds), *In Duodecim Libros Metaphysicorum Aristotelis Expositio*. 2nd edn. Rome, 1950.

Archibald, Elizabeth. 'Lancelot as Lover in the English Tradition before Malory'. In Bonnie Wheeler (ed.), *Arthurian Studies in Honour of P. J. C. Field*. Cambridge, 2006. 199–216.

Archibald, Elizabeth. 'Some Uses of Direct Speech in the Stanzaic *Morte Arthur* and Malory'. *Arthuriana*, 28.3 (2018), 66–85.

Archibald, Elizabeth. 'The Importance of Being an Arthurian Mother'. In Larissa Tracy and Geert Claassens (eds), *Cross-Channel Encounters*. Woodbridge, 2021.

Armstrong, Adrian and Sarah Kay (eds). *Knowing Poetry: Verse in Medieval France from the* Rose *to the* Rhétoriqueurs. Ithaca, NY, 2011.

Árnason, Kristján. 'On the Principles of Nordic Rhyme and Alliteration'. *Arkiv for nordisk filologi*, 122 (2007), 79–116.

Arngart, Olof (ed.). *The Middle English Genesis and Exodus*. Lund, 1968.

Arngart, Olof (ed.). *The Proverbs of Alfred: An Emended Text*. 2 vols. Lund, 1978.

Arnold, Thomas (ed.). *Select English Works of John Wyclif*. Oxford, 1871.

Arnould, E. J. 'On Two Anglo-Norman Prologues'. *Modern Language Review*, 34 (1939), 248–51.

Arthur, Ross G. *Medieval Sign Theory and Sir Gawain and the Green Knight*. Toronto, 1987.

Arthur, Ross G. 'Emaré's Cloak and Audience Response'. In J. N. Wasserman and L. Roney (eds), *Sign, Sentence, Discourse: Language in Medieval Thought and Literature*. Syracuse, NY, 1989. 80–92.

Ashe, Laura. *The Oxford English Literary History Vol. 1: 1000–1350. Conquest and Transformation*. Oxford, 2017.

Ashe, Laura. 'The Originality of the *Orrmulum*'. *Early Middle English*, 1 (2019), 35–54.

474   COMPLETE BIBLIOGRAPHY

Ashurst, David. 'Alexander Literature in English and Scots'. In David Zuwiyya (ed.), *A Companion to Alexander Literature in the Middle Ages*. Leiden, 2011. 255–90.

Ashurst, David. 'Alexander the Great'. In Neil Cartlidge (ed.), *Heroes and Anti-Heroes in Medieval Romance*. Cambridge, 2012. 27–42.

Aspin, I. S. T. *Anglo-Norman Political Songs*. Anglo-Norman Text Society Occasional Publication no. 6. Oxford, 1953.

Astell, Ann W. *Chaucer and the Universe of Learning*. Ithaca, NY, 1996.

Attridge, Derek. *The Rhythms of English Poetry*. London, 1982.

Audelay, John. In E. K. Whiting (ed.), *The Poems of John Audelay*, EETS, o.s. 184. London, 1931.

Auerbach, Erich. *Mimesis: The Representation of Reality in Western Literature*, trans. Willard R. Trask. Princeton, NJ, 1968.

Augustine. *On Christian Doctrine*. In Philip Schaff (ed.), *Nicene and Post-Nicene Fathers of the Christian Church*. 1st series, vol. 2. Grand Rapids, MI, 1979.

Augustine. *St Augustine's Confessions*. In William Watts (trans.). 2 vols. Cambridge, MA, 1988.

Augustine. In R. W. Dyson (ed. and trans.), *The City of God against the Pagans*. Cambridge, 1998.

Avianus. *The Fables of Avianus*. In J. Wight Duff and Arnold M. Duff (eds), *Minor Latin Poets*. Cambridge, MA, 1934, 1961. 669–749.

The Awntyrs of Arthur. In Thomas Hahn (ed.), *Sir Gawain: Eleven Romance and Tales*. Kalamazoo, MI, 1995. 169–226.

Bacon, Roger. *Compendium studii philosophiae*. In J. S. Brewer (ed.), *Opera quaedam hactenus inedita*. Vol. 1. London, 1859.

Bacon, Roger. In John Henry Bridges (ed.), *The Opus Majus of Roger Bacon, Volume I*. London, 1900.

Baird, Joseph L. and John R. Kane (eds and trans.). *La Querelle de la Rose: Letters and Documents*. Chapel Hill, NC, 1978.

Baker, Denise N. 'The Priesthood of Genius: A Study of the Medieval Tradition'. *Speculum*, 51 (1976), 277–91.

Bale, Anthony and Sebastian Sobecki (eds). *Medieval English Travel: A Critical Anthology*. Oxford, 2019.

Banchich, Claire. 'Holy Fear and Poetics in John Gower's *Confessio Amantis*, Book I'. In R. F. Yeager (ed.), *John Gower: Essays at the Millennium*. Kalamazoo, MI, 2007. 188–215.

Barbaccia, Holly. 'The Woman's Response in John Gower's Cinkante Balades'. In Elisabeth Dutton with John Hines and R. F. Yeager (eds), *John Gower, Trilingual Poet: Language, Translation, and Tradition*. Cambridge, 2010. 230–8.

Barber, Charles and Nicholas Barber. 'The Versification of the *Canterbury Tales*: A Computer-Based Statistical Study'. *Leeds Studies in English*, 21 (1990), 81–103 and 22 (1991), 57–84.

Barbieri, Beatrice (ed.). *Geste des Bretuns en alexandrins ou Harley Brut*. Paris, 2015.

Barbour, John. In A. A. M. Duncan (ed. and trans.), *The Bruce*. Edinburgh, 1997.

Barbour, John. In M. P. McDiarmid and J. A. C. Stevenson (eds), *Barbour's 'Bruce'*. 3 vols. STS 4th series, 12, 13, 15. Edinburgh, 1980–5.

Barney, Stephen A. 'The Plowshare of the Tongue: The Process of a Symbol from the Bible to *Piers Plowman*'. *Mediaeval Studies*, 35 (1973), 261–93.

Barney, Stephen A. *Studies in Troilus: Chaucer's Text, Meter, and Diction*. East Lansing, MI, 1993.

Barr, Helen (ed.). *The Piers Plowman Tradition*. London, 1993.

Barr, Helen. *Socioliterary Practice in Late Medieval England*. Oxford, 2001.

Barr, Helen (ed.). *The Digby Poems: A New Edition of the Lyrics*. Exeter, 2009.

Barr, Helen. '"This Holy Tyme": Present Sense in the *Digby Lyrics*'. In Vincent Gillespie and Kantik Ghosh (eds), *After Arundel: Religious Writing in Fifteenth-Century England*. Turnhout, 2011. 307–23.

Barratt, Alexandra. 'The Lyrics of St Godric: A New Manuscript'. *Notes & Queries*, n.s. 32, 230 (1985), 439–45.

Barron, W. R. J. *English Medieval Romance*. London, 1987.

Barron, W. R. J. (ed.). *The Arthur of the English: The Arthurian Legend in Medieval English Life and Literature*. Cardiff, 1999.

Barron, W. R. J. and S. C. Weinberg (eds and trans.). *Layamon's Arthur: The Arthurian Section of Layamon's Brut*. Exeter, 2001.

Baswell, Christopher. *Virgil in Medieval England: Figuring the Aeneid from the Twelfth Century to Chaucer*. Cambridge, 1995.

Baugh, Albert C. 'Improvisation in the Middle English Romance'. *Proceedings of the American Philosophical Society*, 103 (1959), 418–54.

Baugh, Albert C. 'The Middle English Period (1100–1500)'. In Kemp Malone and Albert C. Baugh (eds), *A Literary History of England, Vol. 1: The Middle Ages (to 1500)*. 2nd edn. London, 1967. 107–312.

Baugh, Albert C. 'The Middle English Romance: Some Questions of Creation, Presentation and Preservation'. *Speculum*, 42 (1967), 1–31.

Baugh, Albert C. 'Convention and Individuality in Middle English Romance'. In J. Mandel and B. Rosenberg (eds), *Medieval Literature and Folklore Studies*. New Brunswick, NJ, 1970. 122–46.

Baugh, Nita S. (ed.). *A Worcestershire Miscellany, Compiled by John Northwood, c. 1400*. Philadelphia, PA, 1956.

Baum, Paull. *Chaucer's Verse*. Durham, NC, 1961.

Baxter, Stephen. 'Edward the Confessor and the Succession Question'. In Richard Mortimer (ed.), *Edward the Confessor: The Man and the Legend*. Woodbridge, 2009. 77–118.

Beadle, Richard. 'Middle English Texts and their Transmission, 1350–1500: Some Geographical Criteria'. In Margaret Laing and Keith Williamson (eds), *Speaking in Our Tongues*. Cambridge, 1994. 69–81.

Bédier, Joseph. *Les Fabliaux: Etudes de littérature populaire et d'histoire littéraire du moyen âge*. 5th edn. Paris, 1925.

Begg, I. M., A. Anas, and S. Farinacci. 'Dissociation of Processes in Belief: Source Recollection, Statement Familiarity, and the Illusion of Truth'. *Journal of Experimental Psychology: General*, 121 (1992), 446–58.

Beichner, Paul E. 'Gower's Use of *Aurora* in *Vox Clamantis*'. *Speculum*, 30 (1955), 582–95.

Belting, Hans. *Likeness and Presence: A History of the Image Before the Era of Art*, trans. Edmund Jephcott. Chicago, IL, 1996.

Bennett, J. A. W. *Middle English Literature 1100–1400*, ed. Douglas Gray. Oxford, 1986.

Bennett, J. A. W. and G. V. Smithers (eds). *Early Middle English Verse and Prose*. 2nd edn. Oxford, 1968.

Bennett, Michael J. 'The Historical Background'. In Derek Brewer and Jonathan Gibson (eds), *A Companion to the Gawain-Poet*. Cambridge, 1997. 71–90.

Bennett, Michael J. 'Stanley, Sir John (c. 1350–1414)'. *Oxford Dictionary of National Biography*, Oxford University Press, 2004. https://www.oxforddnb.com.

Benson, C. David. *The History of Troy in Medieval English Literature: Guido delle Colonne's 'Historia destructionis Troiae' in Medieval England*. Woodbridge, 1980.

Benson, C. David. *Chaucer's Drama of Style: Poetic Variety and Contrast in the* Canterbury Tales. Chapel Hill, NC, 1986.

Benson, C. David and Elizabeth Robertson (eds). *Chaucer's Religious Tales*. Cambridge, 1990.

Benson, Larry D. and Theodore M. Andersson (eds). *The Literary Context of Chaucers's Fabliaux*. Indianapolis, IN, 1971.

Beowulf. In E. Talbot Donaldson (trans.), *Beowulf: A New Prose Translation*. New York, 1966.

Beryn, Tale of. In F. J. Furnivall (ed.), *The Tale of Beryn*. EETS, e.s. 105. London, 1909.

Bestul, Thomas H. *Satire and Allegory in Wynnere and Wastoure*. Lincoln, NE, 1974.

Bestul, Thomas H. 'Gower's *Mirour de l'Omme* and the Meditative Tradition'. *Mediaevalia*, 16 (1993), 307–28.

Bethurum, Dorothy Loomis. 'Stylistic Features of the Old English Laws'. *Modern Language Review*, 27 (1932), 263–79.

Bevis of Hampton. In Ronald B. Herzman, Graham Drake, and Eve Salisbury (eds), *Four Romances of England: King Horn, Havelok the Dane, Bevis of Hampton, Athelston*. Kalamazoo, MI, 1999.

Bevis of Hampton. In Jennifer Fellows (ed.), *Sir Bevis of Hampton*. 2 vols. EETS, o.s. 349–50. Oxford, 2017.

Bihl, Josef. *Die Wirkungen des Rhythmus in der Sprache von Chaucer und Gower*. Heidelberg, 1916.

476 COMPLETE BIBLIOGRAPHY

Billy, Dominique and Martin J. Duffell. 'From Decasyllable to Pentameter: Gower's Contribution to English Metrics'. *Chaucer Review*, 38 (2004), 383–400.

Bishop, Ian. *The Narrative Art of 'The Canterbury Tales'*. London, 1987.

Blake, Norman F. 'Rhythmical Alliteration'. *Modern Philology*, 67 (1969), 118–24.

Blake, Norman F. 'The Ellesmere Text in Light of the Hengwrt Manuscript'. In Martin Stevens and Daniel Woodward (eds), *The Ellesmere Chaucer: Essays in Interpretation*. San Marino, CA, 1995. 205–24.

Blamires, Alcuin. *Chaucer, Ethics, and Gender*. Oxford, 2006.

Bloch, R. Howard. *The Scandal of the Fabliaux*. Chicago, IL, 1986.

Blurton, Heather. 'The Songs of Godric of Finchale: Vernacular Liturgy and Literary History'. *New Medieval Literatures*, 18 (2018), 75–104.

Blurton, Heather and Jocelyn Wogan-Browne (eds). *Rethinking the South English Legendaries*. Manchester, 2011.

Bly Calkin, Siobhain. *Saracens and the Making of English Identity: The Auchinleck Manuscript*. New York, 2009.

Bly Calkin, Siobhain. 'Crusades Romance'. In Siân Echard and Robert Rouse (eds), *The Encyclopedia of British Medieval Literature*. Chichester, 2017. 583–9.

Bodel, Jehan. In Annette Brasseur (ed.), *La Chanson des Saisnes*. Textes littéraires français. 2 vols. Geneva, 1989.

Boethius. In H. F. Stewart, E. K. Rand, and S. J. Tester (eds and trans.), *The Theological Tractates: The Consolation of Philosophy*. Cambridge, MA, 1973.

Boffey, Julia. *Manuscripts of English Courtly Love Lyrics in the Later Middle Ages*. Woodbridge, 1985.

Boffey, Julia. 'The Charter of the Abbey of the Holy Ghost and Its Role in Manuscript Anthologies'. *Yearbook of English Studies*, 33 (2003), 120–30.

Boffey, Julia (ed.). *Fifteenth-Century English Dream Visions*. Oxford, 2003.

Boffey, Julia. 'Middle English Lyrics and Manuscripts'. In Thomas G. Duncan (ed.), *A Companion to Middle English Lyric*. Cambridge, 2005. 1–18.

Boffey, Julia and A. S. G. Edwards (eds). *A New Index of Middle English Verse*. London, 2005.

Boffey, Julia and A. S. G. Edwards (eds). *A Companion to Fifteenth-Century English Poetry*. Cambridge, 2013.

Boffey, Julia and John J. Thompson. 'Anthologies and Miscellanies: Production and Choice of Texts'. In Jeremy Griffiths and Derek Pearsall (eds), *Book Production and Publishing in Britain, 1375–1475*. Cambridge, 1989. 279–315.

Boffey, Julia and Christiania Whitehead (eds). *Middle English Lyrics: New Readings of Short Poems*. Cambridge, 2018.

Bokenham, Osbern. In M. S. Serjeantson (ed.), *Osbern Bokenham: Legendys of Hooly Wummen*. EETS, o.s. 206. London, 1938.

Bokenham, Osbern. In Sheila Delany (trans.), *A Legend of Holy Women: A Translation of Osbern Bokenham's 'Legends of Holy Women'*. Notre Dame, IN, 1992.

Boklund-Lagopoulou, Karin. *'I have a yong suster': Popular Song and the Middle English Lyric*. Dublin, 2002.

Boklund-Lagopoulou, Karin. 'Popular Song and the Middle English Lyric'. In Karl Reichl (ed.), *Medieval Oral Literature*. Berlin, 2012. 555–80.

Bonomel, Ricaut. 'Ir'e dolors s'es dins mon cor asseza'. In Antoine de Bastard (ed.), 'La colère et la douleur d'un templier en Terre Sainte'. *Revue des langues romanes*, 81 (1974), 333–73.

Boroff, Marie (ed. and trans.). *The Gawain Poet: Complete Works*. New York, 2011.

Borroff, Marie. *Sir Gawain and the Green Knight: A Stylistic and Metrical Study*. New Haven, CT, 1962.

Bowers, John M. *The Politics of Pearl: Court Poetry in the Age of Richard II*. Cambridge, 2001.

Bozon, Nicholas. In M. Amelia Klenke (ed. and trans.), *Three Saints' Lives by Nicholas Bozon*. New York, 1947.

Bradbury, Nancy Mason. *Writing Aloud: Storytelling in Late Medieval England*. Urbana, IL, 1998.

Bradbury, Nancy Mason and Scott Bradbury (eds). *The Dialogue of Solomon and Marcolf: A Dual-Language Edition from Latin and Middle English Printed Editions*. Kalamazoo, MI, 2012.

Bradley, S. A. J. (trans.). *Anglo-Saxon Poetry*. London, 1982.

Braswell, Laurel. '*Sir Isumbras* and the Legend of Saint Eustace'. *Mediaeval Studies*, 27 (1965), 128–51.

Bredehoft, Thomas E. *Early English Metre*. Toronto, 1992.

Brehe, S. K. 'Rhyme and the Alliterative Standard in Laȝamon's Brut'. *Parergon*, 18.2 (2000), 11–25.

Brewer, Derek. 'Towards a Chaucerian Poetic'. *Proceedings of the British Academy*, 60 (1974), 219–52.

Brewer, Derek. 'Arithmetic and the Mentality of Chaucer'. In Piero Botani and Anna Torti (eds), *Literature in Fourteenth-Century England*. Tübingen, 1983. 155–64.

Brewer, Derek. *English Gothic Literature*. New York, 1983.

Brewer, Derek. *Chaucer: The Poet as Storyteller*. London, 1984.

Brewer, Derek. 'The Popular English Metrical Romances'. In Corrine Saunders (ed.), *A Companion to Romance from Classical to Contemporary*. Oxford, 2004. 45–64.

Brewer, Derek and Jonathan Gibson (eds). *A Companion to the Gawain-Poet*. Cambridge, 1997.

Brewer, Elisabeth (ed.). *Sir Gawain and the Green Knight: Sources and Analogues*. Cambridge, 1973.

Bridges, Venetia. *Medieval Narratives of Alexander the Great: Transnational Texts in England and France*. Cambridge, 2018.

Bromwich, Rachel. *Aspects of the Poetry of Dafydd ap Gwilym*. Cardiff, 1974.

Bromwich, Rachel (ed. and trans.). *Trioedd Ynys Prydein: The Triads of the Island of Britain*. Cardiff, 2014.

Brook, G. L. (ed.). *The Harley Lyrics: The Middle English Lyrics of Ms. Harley 2253*. 4th edn. Manchester, 1968.

Brook, G. L. and R. F. Leslie (eds). *Laȝamon: Brut*. 2 vols. EETS, o.s. 250, 277. London, 1963, 1978.

Brooke, Christopher. 'John of Salisbury and his World'. In Michael Wilks (ed.), *The World of John of Salisbury*. Studies in Church History Subsidia 3. Oxford, 1984.

Brown, Carleton (ed.). *English Lyrics of the XIIIth Century*. Oxford, 1932, 1965.

Brown, Carleton (ed.). *Religious Lyrics of the XVth Century*. Oxford, 1939.

Brown, Carleton (ed.). *Religious Lyrics of the XIVth Century*. 2nd edn., rev. G. V. Smithers. Oxford, 1952.

Brown, Carleton and Rossell Hope Robbins (eds). *The Index of Middle English Verse*. New York, 1943.

Brown, Peter. *Chaucer at Work: The Making of the 'Canterbury Tales'*. London, 1994.

Bryan, Elizabeth J. *Collaborative Meaning in Medieval Scribal Culture: The Otho Laȝamon*. Ann Arbor, MI, 1999.

Bryan, Elizabeth J. 'The English Reception of Geoffrey of Monmouth'. In Georgia Henley and Joshua Byron Smith (eds), *A Companion to Geoffrey of Monmouth*. Leiden, 2020. 449–53.

Bryan, Elizabeth J. 'Laȝamon's *Brut* and the Vernacular Text: Widening the Context'. In Rosamund Allen, Jane Roberts, and Carole Weinberg (eds), *Reading Laȝamon's Brut: Approaches and Explorations*. Amsterdam, 2013. 661–89.

Bullón-Fernández, María. *Fathers and Daughters in John Gower's* Confessio Amantis: *Authority, Family, State and Writing*. Cambridge, 2000.

Bunt, G. H. V. 'Alexander's Last Days in the Middle English *Kyng Alisaunder*'. In W. J. Aerts, Jos. M. M. Hermans, and Elizabeth Visser (eds), *Alexander the Great in the Middle Ages*. Nijmegen, 1978. 202–29.

Bunt, G. H. V. (ed.). *William of Palerne: An Alliterative Romance*. Groningen, 1985.

Bunt, G. H. V. 'Localizing *William of Palerne*'. In Jacek Fisiak (ed.), *Historical Linguistics and Philology*. Berlin, 1990. 73–86.

Bunt, G. H. V. *Alexander the Great in the Literature of Medieval Britain*. Groningen, 1994.

Burchfield, R. W. 'The Language and Orthography of the Ormulum MS'. *Transactions of the Philological Society*, 55 (1956), 56–87.

Burek, Jacqueline M. '(Not) Like Aeneas: Allusions to the Aeneid in Laȝamon's *Brut*'. *Review of English Studies*, 71 (2020), 229–50.

Burgess, Glyn and Karen Pratt (eds). *The Arthur of the French: The Arthurian Legend in Medieval French and Occitan Literature*. Cardiff, 2006.

Burke, Linda Barney. 'Women in John Gower's *Confessio Amantis*'. *Mediaevalia*, 3 (1977), 239–59.

Burnley, J. D. 'Chaucer's Literary Terms'. *Anglia*, 114 (1996), 202–35.

Burnley, J. D. and Alison Wiggins (eds). *The Auchinleck Manuscript Project*. https://auchinleck.nls.uk. Launched 2003.

Burrow, J. A. 'The Audience of Piers Plowman'. *Anglia*, 75 (1957), 373–84.

Burrow, J. A. 'The Action of Langland's Second Vision'. *Essays in Criticism*, 15 (1965), 247–68.

Burrow, J. A. *Ricardian Poetry: Chaucer, Gower, Langland, and the 'Gawain' Poet*. London, 1971.

Burrow, J. A. 'Sir Thopas: An Agony in Three Fitts'. *Review of English Studies*, n.s. 22 (1971), 54–8.

Burrow, J. A. 'Poems without Context'. *Essays in Criticism*, 29 (1979), 6–32.

Burrow, J. A. 'The Portrayal of Amans in "Confessio Amantis"'. In A. J. Minnis (ed.), *Gower's Confessio Amantis: Responses and Reassessments*. Cambridge, 1983. 5–24.

Burrow, J. A. 'The Shape of the Vernon Refrain Lyrics'. In Derek Pearsall (ed.), *Studies in the Vernon Manuscript*. Cambridge, 1990. 187–99.

Burrow, J. A. *Langland's Fictions*. Oxford, 1993.

Burrow, J. A. *Thomas Hoccleve*. Authors of the Middle Ages, 4. Aldershot, 1994.

Burrow, J. A. 'Gower's Poetic Styles'. In Siân Echard (ed.), *A Companion to Gower*. Cambridge, 2004. 239–50.

Burrow, J. A. *The Poetry of Praise*. Cambridge, 2008.

Burrow, J. A. and A. I. Doyle (intro.). *Thomas Hoccleve: A Facsimile of the Autograph Verse Manuscripts*. EETS, s.s. 19. Oxford, 2002.

Burrow, J. A. and Thorlac Turville-Petre (eds). *A Book of Middle English*. 3rd edn. Oxford, 2004.

Burton, Julie. 'Narrative Patterning and *Guy of Warwick*'. *The Yearbook of English Studies*, 22 (1992), 105–16.

Busby, Keith. 'Conspicuous by Its Absence: The English Fabliau'. *Dutch Quarterly Review of Anglo-American Letters*, 12 (1982), 30–41.

Busby, Keith. 'Multilingualism, the Harley Scribe, and Johannes Jacobi'. In Margaret Connolly and Raluca Radulescu (eds), *Insular Books: Vernacular Manuscripts in Late Medieval Britain*. Oxford, 2015. 49–60.

Busby, Keith. *French in Medieval Ireland, Ireland in Medieval French: The Paradox of Two Worlds*. Turnhout, 2017.

Butterfield, Ardis. 'Chaucer's French Inheritance'. In Piero Boitani and Jill Mann (eds), *Cambridge Companion to Chaucer*. Cambridge, 2004. 20–35.

Butterfield, Ardis. '*Confessio Amantis* and the French Tradition'. In Siân Echard (ed.), *A Companion to Gower*. Cambridge, 2004. 165–80.

Butterfield, Ardis. 'English, French and Anglo-French: Language and Nation in the Fabliau'. In C. Young, T. Reuvekamp-Felber, and M. Chinca (eds), 'Novellistik im Europäischen Mittelalter', special number of *Zeitschrift für deutsche Philologie* (2005). 238–59.

Butterfield, Ardis. 'Chaucerian Vernaculars'. *Studies in the Age of Chaucer*, 31 (2009), 25–51.

Butterfield, Ardis. *The Familiar Enemy: Chaucer, Language, and Nation in the Hundred Years War*. Oxford, 2009.

Butterfield, Ardis. 'Lyric'. In Larry Scanlon (ed.), *The Cambridge Companion to Medieval English Literature 1100–1500*. Cambridge, 2009. 95–109.

Butterfield, Ardis. 'Why Medieval Lyric'. *ELH*, 82 (2015), 319–43.

Butterfield, Ardis. 'Poems without Form? *Maiden in the mor lay* Revisited'. In Cristina Maria Cervone and D. Vance Smith (eds), *Readings in Medieval Textuality: Essays in Honour of A. C. Spearing*. Cambridge, 2016. 169–94.

Butterfield, Ardis. '*The Book of the Duchess*, Guillaume de Machaut, and the Image of the Archive'. In Jamie Fumo (ed.), *Chaucer's* Book of the Duchess *Reopened: Context and Exchange*. Woodbridge, 2018. 199–212.

Butterfield, Ardis. 'The Dream of Language: Chaucer "en son Latin"'. *Studies in the Age of Chaucer*, 41 (2019), 3–29.

Cable, Thomas. *The English Alliterative Tradition*. Philadelphia, PA, 1991.

Calin, William. 'John Gower's Continuity in the Tradition of Fin' Amor'. *Mediaevalia*, 16 (1993), 91–111.

Calin, William. *The French Tradition and the Literature of Medieval England*. Toronto, 1994.

Camargo, Martin. 'Chaucer and the Oxford Renaissance of Anglo-Latin Rhetoric'. *Studies in the Age of Chaucer*, 34 (2012), 173–207.

Camargo, Martin (ed. and trans.). *Tria Sunt: An Art of Poetry and Prose*. Cambridge, MA, 2019.

Campbell, Bruce M. S. *The Great Transition: Climate, Disease and Society in the Late-Medieval World*. Cambridge, 2016.

Cannon, Christopher. 'The Style and Authorship of the Otho Revision of Laȝamon's *Brut*'. *Medium Ævum*, 62 (1993), 187–209.

Cannon, Christopher. *The Making of Chaucer's English: A Study of Words*. Cambridge, 1998.

Cannon, Christopher. 'Chaucer's Style'. In Piero Boitani and Jill Mann (eds), *The Cambridge Companion to Chaucer*. 2nd edn. Cambridge, 2003. 233–50.

Cannon, Christopher. *The Grounds of English Literature*. Oxford, 2004.

Cannon, Christopher. *From Literacy to Literature: England, 1300–1400*. Oxford, 2016.

Careri, Maria and Marcella Lacanale. 'Accents et syllabes dans les manuscrits anglo-normands'. In Oreste Floquet and Gabriele Giannini (eds), *Anglo-Français: philologie et linguistique*. Paris, 2015. 35–44.

Careri, Maria, Christine Ruby, and Ian Short. *Livres et écritures en français et en occitan au XIIe siècle: catalogue illustré*. Rome, 2011.

Carlson, David R. 'The Invention of Anglo-Latin Public Poetry (circa 1367–1402) and Its Prosody, esp. in Gower'. *Mittellateinische Jahrbuch*, 39 (2004), 389–406.

Carlson, David R. 'A Rhyme Distribution Chronology of John Gower's Latin Poetry'. *Studies in Philology*, 104 (2007), 15–55.

Carlson, David R. 'The Parliamentary Sources of Gower's *Cronica Tripertita* and Incommensurable Styles'. In Elisabeth Dutton with John Hines and R. F. Yeager (eds), *John Gower, Trilingual Poet: Language, Translation and Tradition*. Cambridge, 2010. 98–111.

Carlson, David R. *John Gower: Poetry and Propaganda in Fourteenth-Century England*. Cambridge, 2012.

Carlson, David R. 'Gower's Amans and the Curricular Maximianus'. *Studia Neophilologica*, 89 (2017), 67–80.

Carpenter, David. 'King Henry III's "Statute" against Aliens: July 1263'. *English Historical Review*, 107 (1992), 925–44.

Cartlidge, Neil. 'The Composition and Social Context of Oxford, Jesus College, MS 29(II) and London, British Library, MS Cotton Caligula A.IX'. *Medium Ævum*, 66 (1997), 250–69.

Cartlidge, Neil (ed. and trans.). *The Owl and the Nightingale: Text and Translation*. Exeter, 2001.

Cartlidge, Neil. 'Nicholas of Guildford and "The Owl and the Nightingale"'. *Medium Ævum*, 79 (2010), 14–24.

Cartlidge, Neil (ed.). *Heroes and Anti-Heroes in Medieval Romance*. Cambridge, 2012.

Cartlidge, Neil. 'Debate Poetry'. In Sîan Echard and Robert Rouse (eds), *The Encyclopedia of Medieval British Literature*. Oxford, 2017. 646–9.

Cary, George. *The Medieval Alexander*, ed. D. J. A. Ross. Cambridge, 1956.

Castleford's Chronicle. In Caroline D. Eckhardt (ed.), *Castleford's Chronicle or the Boke of Brut*. 2 vols. EETS, o.s. 305–6. Oxford, 1996.

Cataldi, Claudio. 'A Reassessment of *Poema Morale* and Its Influence on *Penitence for a Wasted Life*'. In Letizia Vezzosi (ed.), *Current Issues in Medieval England*. Berlin, 2021. 15–32.

Cavill, Paul. *Maxims in Old English Poetry*. Cambridge, 1999.

Cazelles, Briggite. *The Lady as Saint: A Collection of French Hagiographic Romances of the Thirteenth Century*. Philadelphia, PA, 1991.

Cerquiglini, Bernard. *Éloge de la variante: histoire critique de la philologie*. Paris, 1989.

Cervone, Cristina Maria. 'John de Cobham and Cooling Castle's Charter Poem'. *Speculum*, 83 (2008), 884–916.

Cervone, Cristina Maria. *Poetics of the Incarnation: Middle English Writing and the Leap of Love*. Philadelphia, PA, 2012.

Chaganti, Seeta. *Strange Footing: Poetic Form and Dance in the Late Middle Ages*. Chicago, IL, 2018.

Chardri. In B. S. Merrilees (ed.), *Le Petit Plet*. Oxford, 1970.

Charles d'Orléans. In Mary-Jo Arn (ed.), *Fortunes Stabilnes: Charles of Orleans's English Book of Love: A Critical Edition*. New York, 1994.

Chaucer, Geoffrey. In W. W. Skeat (ed.), *Complete Works of Geoffrey Chaucer*. 7 vols. Oxford, 1894.

Chaucer, Geoffrey. In R. K. Root (ed.), *The Book of Troilus and Criseyde*. Princeton, NJ, 1926.

Chaucer, Geoffrey. In Larry D. Benson (gen. ed.), *The Riverside Chaucer*. 3rd edn. Boston, MA, 1987.

Chaucer, Geoffrey. In David Lawton (ed.), *The Norton Chaucer*. New York, 2019.

Chestre, Thomas. *Sir Launfal*. In Anne Laskaya and Eve Salisbury (eds), *The Middle English Breton Lays*. Kalamazoo, MI, 1995. 201–62.

Chickering, Howell D. 'Stanzaic Closure and Linkage in *Sir Gawain and the Green Knight*'. *Chaucer Review*, 32 (1997), 1–31.

Chism, Christine. 'Too Close for Comfort: Dis-Orienting Chivalry in the *Wars of Alexander*'. In Sylvia Tomasch and Sealy Gilles (eds), *Text and Territory: Geographical Imagination in the European Middle Ages*. Philadelphia, PA, 1998. 116–42.

Chism, Christine. *Alliterative Revivals*. Philadelphia, PA, 2002.

Chism, Christine. 'Winning Women in Two Middle English Alexander Poems'. In Sara S. Poor and Jana K. Schulman (eds), *Women and Medieval Epic: Gender, Genre, and the Limits of Epic Masculinity*. New York, 2007. 15–39.

Chism, Christine. 'Romance'. In Larry Scanlon (ed.), *The Cambridge Companion to Medieval English Literature 1100–1500*. Cambridge, 2009. 57–69.

Chrétien de Troyes. *Perceval*. In William Roach (ed.), *Perceval ou Le Conte du Graal*. Geneva, 1959.

Chrétien de Troyes. In William W. Kibler (trans.), *Arthurian Romances*. London, 1991.

Cicero, *De inventione*. In H. M. Hubbell (ed. and trans.), *On Invention; Best Kind of Orator; Topics*. Cambridge, MA, 2014. 1–346.

Clanchy, M. T. *From Memory to Written Record: England 1066–1307*. 3rd edn. Chichester, 2013.

Clanvowe, Sir John, *Boke of Cupide*. In V. J. Scattergood (ed.), *The Works of Sir John Clanvowe*. Cambridge, 1975. 35–53.

Clark, Cecily (ed.). *The Peterborough Chronicle 1070–1154*. 2nd edn. Oxford, 1970.

Clayton, Mary and Hugh Magennis (eds). *The Old English Lives of St Margaret*. Cambridge, 1994.

Clerk, John [of Whalley]. In G. A. Panton and D. Donaldson (eds), *The 'Gest Hystoriale' of the Destruction of Troy*. 2 vols. EETS, o.s. 39, 56. London, 1869, 1874.

Cohen, Helen Louise. *The Ballade*. New York, 1915.

Cole, Kristin Lynn. 'Chaucer's Metrical Landscape'. In Clíodhna Carney and Frances McCormack (eds), *Chaucer's Poetry: Words, Authority and Ethics*. Dublin, 2013. 92–106.

Coleman, Joyce. 'Strange Rhyme: Prosody and Nationhood in Robert Mannyng's Story of England'. *Speculum*, 78 (2003), 1214–38.

Comparetti, Domenico. *Vergil in the Middle Ages*, trans. E. F. M. Benecke. Princeton, NJ, 1997.

Conlee, John W. (ed.). *Middle English Debate Poetry: A Critical Anthology*. East Lansing, MI, 1991.

Conrad of Hirsau. *Dialogue on the Authors*. In A. J. Minnis and A. B. Scott, with the assistance of David Wallace (eds), *Medieval Literary Theory and Criticism, c. 1100–c. 1375*. Oxford, 1988, 1991.

Conti, Aidan. 'The Circulation of the Old English Homily in the Twelfth Century: New Evidence from Oxford, Bodleian Library, MS Bodley 343'. In Aaron J. Kleist (ed.), *The Old English Homily: Precedent, Practice, and Appropriation*. Turnhout, 2007. 365–402.

Cook, Albert S. (ed.). *The Old English Elene, Phoenix and Physiologus*. London, 1919.

Cooper, Helen. *The Structure of the 'Canterbury Tales'*. London, 1983.

Cooper, Helen (ed.). *The Oxford Guides to Chaucer: 'The Canterbury Tales'*. Oxford, 1989.

Cooper, Helen. '"Piesed Evene in the Balance": A Thematic and Rhetorical Topos in the *Confessio Amantis*'. *Mediaevalia*, 16 (1993), 113–39.

Cooper, Helen. 'Introduction'. In Keith Harrison (trans.), *Sir Gawain and the Green Knight*. Oxford, 1998.

Cooper, Helen. 'The Four Last Things in Dante and Chaucer: Ugolino in the House of Rumour'. *New Medieval Literatures*, 3 (1999), 39–66.

Cooper, Helen. 'Romance after 1400'. In David Wallace (ed.), *The Cambridge History of Medieval English Literature*. Cambridge, 1999. 690–719.

Cooper, Helen. 'Chaucerian Poetics'. In Robert G. Benson and Susan J. Ridyard (eds), *New Readings of Chaucer's Poetry*. Cambridge, 2003. 31–50.

Cooper, Helen. *The English Romance in Time: Transforming Motifs from Geoffrey of Monmouth to the Death of Shakespeare*. Oxford, 2004.

Cooper, Helen. 'Lancelot, Roger Mortimer, and the Date of the Auchinleck Manuscript'. In A. M. D'Arcy and A. J. Fletcher (eds), *Studies in Late Medieval and Early Renaissance Texts in Honour of John Scattergood*. Dublin, 2005. 91–9.

Cooper, Helen. 'London and Southwark Poetic Companies: "Si tost c'amis" and the *Canterbury Tales*'. In Ardis Butterfield (ed.), *Chaucer and the City*. Cambridge, 2006. 109–26.

Cooper, Helen. 'Guy as Early Modern English Hero'. In Alison Wiggins and Rosalind Field (eds), *Guy of Warwick: Icon and Ancestor*. Cambridge, 2007.

Cooper, Helen. 'Passionate, Eloquent and Determined: Heroines' Tales and Feminine Poetics'. *Journal of the British Academy*, 4 (2016), 221–44.

Copeland, Rita. *Rhetoric, Hermeneutics, and Translation in the Middle Ages*. Cambridge, 1991.

Cornelius, Ian. *Reconstructing Alliterative Verse: The Pursuit of a Medieval Meter*. Cambridge, 2017.

Correale, Robert M. and Mary Hamel (eds). *Sources and Analogues of the* Canterbury Tales. 2 vols. Cambridge, 2002, 2007.

Corrie, Marilyn. 'The Compilation of Oxford, Bodleian Library, MS Digby 86'. *Medium Ævum*, 66 (1997), 236–49.

Corrie, Marilyn. 'Harley 2253, Digby 86, and the Circulation of Literature in Pre-Chaucerian England'. In Fein, Susanna (ed.). *Studies in the Harley Manuscript: The Scribes, Contents, and Social Contexts of British Library MS Harley 2253*. Kalamazoo, MI, 2000. 427–43.

Coss, P. R. 'Aspects of Cultural Diffusion in Medieval England: The Early Romances, Local Society and Robin Hood'. *Past and Present*, 108 (1985), 35–79.

Courtenay, William. 'Force of Words and Figures of Speech: The Crisis over *virtus sermonis* in the Fourteenth Century'. *Franciscan Studies*, 44 (1984), 107–28.

Courtenay, William. *Schools and Scholars in Fourteenth-Century England*. Princeton, NJ, 1987.

Cowen, Janet and George Kane (eds). *Geoffrey Chaucer: 'The Legend of Good Women'*. East Lansing, MI, 1995.

Crane, Susan. *Insular Romance: Politics, Faith, and Culture in Anglo-Norman and Middle English Literature*. Berkeley, CA, 1986.

Crane, Susan. *Gender and Romance in Chaucer's 'Canterbury Tales'*. Princeton, NJ, 1994.

Cré, Marleen. *Vernacular Mysticism in the Charterhouse: A Study of London, British Library, MS Additional 37790*. Turnhout, 2006.

Crick, J. C. *The Historia regum Britannie of Geoffrey of Monmouth, IV: Dissemination and Reception in the Later Middle Ages*. Cambridge, 1991.

Critten, Rory G. 'The Multilingual English Household in a European Perspective: London, British Library MS Harley 2253 and the Traffic of Texts'. In Glenn D. Burger and Rory G. Critten (eds), *Household Knowledges in Late-Medieval England and France*. Manchester, 2019. 219–43.

Crowne, Vincent J. 'Middle English Poems on the Joys and on the Compassion of the Blessed Virgin Mary'. *Catholic University Bulletin*, 8 (1902), 304–16.

Culler, Jonathan. 'Apostrophe'. In *The Pursuit of Signs: Semiotics, Literature, Deconstruction*. Ithaca, NY, 1981.

Culler, Jonathan. *Literary Theory: A Very Short Introduction*. Oxford, 2011.

Culler, Jonathan. *Theory of the Lyric*. Cambridge, MA, 2015.

Curtius, Ernst Robert. 'Numerical Composition'. *European Literature and the Latin Middle Ages*, trans. Willard R. Trask. New York, 1953. 501–9.

D'Angelo, Edoardo. 'The Outer Metric in Joseph of Exeter's *Ylias* and Odo of Magdeburg's *Ernestus*'. *The Journal of Medieval Latin*, 3 (1993), 113–34.

D'Arcy, Anne Marie. 'The Middle English Lyrics'. In David Johnson and Elaine Treharne (eds), *Readings in Medieval Texts: Interpreting Old and Middle English Literature*. Oxford, 2005. 306–22.

D'Ardenne, S. R. T. O. (ed.). *The Liflade ant te Passiun of Seinte Iuliene*. EETS, o.s 248. London, 1961.

D'Evelyn, Charlotte and Frances A. Foster. 'Saints' Legends'. In J. Burke Severs (ed.), *A Manual of the Writings in Middle English, 1050–1500*. 11 vols. Hamden, CT, 1970. 2: 410–46, 556–635.

482   COMPLETE BIBLIOGRAPHY

D'Evelyn, Charlotte and Anna J. Mill (eds). *The South English Legendary*. 3 vols. EETS, o.s. 235, 236, 244. London, 1956, 1959.

Da Rold, Orietta. 'Cultural Contexts of English Manuscripts 1060 to 1220'. *The Production and Use of English Manuscripts 1060 to 1220*. http://www.le.ac.uk/english/em1060to1220/culturalcontexts/2.htm.

Da Rold, Orietta, Takako Kato, Jo Story, Mary Swan, and Elaine Treharne. *The Production and Use of English Manuscripts 1060 to 1220*. Leicester, 2010–13. www.le.ac.uk/english/em1060to1220.

Dafydd ap Gwilym. In Dafydd Johnston, Huw Meirion Edwards, Dylan Foster Evans, A. Cynfael Lake, Elisa Moras, and Sara Elin Roberts (eds and trans.), *Cerddi Dafydd ap Gwilym*. Cardiff, 2010.

Dafydd ap Gwilym.net. Swansea University. http://www.dafyddapgwilym.net/eng/3win.htm.

Dalrymple, Roger. 'Sir Gawain in Middle English Romance'. In Helen Fulton (ed.), *A Companion to Arthurian Literature*. Oxford, 2009. 265–77.

Dance, Richard. 'The Old English Language and the Alliterative Tradition'. In Corinne Saunders (ed.), *A Companion to Medieval Poetry*. Oxford, 2010. 34–50.

Dance, Richard. '*Ealde Æ, Niwe La3e*: Two Words for "Law" in the Twelfth Century'. *New Medieval Literatures*, 13 (2011), 149–82.

Dance, Richard. 'Getting a Word In: Contact, Etymology and English Vocabulary in the Twelfth Century'. *Journal of the British Academy*, 2 (2014), 153–211.

Dance, Richard. *Words Derived from Old Norse in Sir Gawain and the Green Knight: An Etymological Survey*. 2 vols. Chichester, 2019.

Dangel, Jacqueline (ed.). *Le poète architecte: arts métriques et art poétique latins*. Louvain, 2001.

Dareau, Margaret G. and Angus McIntosh. 'A Dialect Word in Some West Midland Manuscripts of the *Prick of Conscience*'. In A. J. Aitken, Angus McIntosh, and Hermann Pálsson (eds), *Edinburgh Studies in English and Scots*. London, 1971. 20–6.

Darnton, Robert. *The Great Cat Massacre: and Other Episodes in French Cultural History*. New York, 1984.

Davenport, W. A. *Chaucer: Complaint and Narrative*. Cambridge, 1988.

Davenport, W. A. '*Sir Degrevant* and Composite Romance'. In J. Weiss, J. Fellows, and M. Dickson (eds), *Medieval Insular Romance: Translation and Innovation*. Cambridge, 2000. 111–31.

Davidoff, Judith M. *Beginning Well: Framing Fictions in Late Middle English Poetry*. Cranbury, NJ, 1988.

Davie, Donald. *Purity of Diction in English Verse*. London, 1992.

Davies, R. T. (ed.). *Medieval English Lyrics: A Critical Anthology*. London, 1963.

Davlin, Mary Clemente. '*Kynde Knowyng* as a Major Theme in *Piers Plowman* B'. *Review of English Studies*, n.s. 22 (1971), 1–19.

Davlin, Mary Clemente. *A Game of Heuene: Word Play and the Meaning of* Piers Plowman B. Cambridge, 1989.

De Boer, C. (ed.). *Ovide moralisé: Poème du commencement du quatorzième siècle*. 5 vols. Amsterdam, 1915–38.

Dean, James M. (ed.). *Medieval English Political Writings*. Kalamazoo, MI, 1996.

Dean, Ruth with the collaboration of Maureen B. M. Boulton. *Anglo-Norman Literature: A Guide to Texts and Manuscripts*. London, 1999.

Deeming, Helen. 'The Songs of St Godric: A Neglected Context'. *Music and Letters*, 86 (2005), 169–85.

Deeming, Helen (ed.). *Songs in British Sources, c. 1150–1300*. Musica Britannica 45. London, 2013.

Deeming, Helen. 'Music and Contemplation in the Twelfth-Century *Dulcis Jesu Memoria*'. *Journal of the Royal Musical Association*, 139 (2014), 1–39.

Delehaye, Hippolyte. *The Legends of the Saints: An Introduction to Hagiography*, trans. V. M. Crawford. Notre Dame, IN, 1961.

Denny-Brown, Andrea (ed.). 'The Provocative Fifteenth Century'. *Exemplaria*, 29 (2017) and 30 (2018).

Deschamps, Eustache. In A. H. S. de Queux de Saint-Hilaire and G. Raynaud (eds), *Œuvres Complètes de Eustache Deschamps*. 10 vols. Paris, 1878–1903.

Deskis, Susan E. *Alliterative Proverbs in Medieval England: Language Choice and Literary Meaning.* Columbus, OH, 2016.

Desmond, Marilynn. *Reading Dido: Gender, Textuality and the Medieval 'Aeneid'.* Minneapolis, MN, 1994.

DIMEV: Digital Index of Middle English Verse. http://www.dimev.net.

Dinshaw, Carolyn. *Chaucer's Sexual Poetics.* Madison, WI, 1989.

Djordjevic, Ivana. 'The "Owl and the Nightingale" and the Perils of Criticism'. *Neuphilologische Mitteilungen*, 96 (1995), 367–80.

Dobson, E. J. *The Origins of Ancrene Wisse.* Oxford, 1976.

Dobson, E. J. and F. Ll. Harrison (eds). *Medieval English Songs.* London, 1979.

DOE: Angus Cameron, Ashley Crandell Amos, Antonette diPaolo Healey et al. (eds). *Dictionary of Old English: A to I online.* Toronto, 2018. http://doe.utoronto.ca/pages/index.html.

DOEWC: Antonette diPaolo Healey with John Price Wilkin and Xin Xiang (eds). *Dictionary of Old English Web Corpus.* Toronto, 2009. tapor.library.utoronto.ca/doecorpus.

Dolan, Terence. 'Writing in Ireland'. In David Wallace (ed.), *The Cambridge History of Medieval English Literature.* Cambridge, 1999. 208–28.

Donaldson, E. Talbot. 'Middle English seint, seinte'. *Studia Neophilologica*, 21 (1948), 222–30.

Donaldson, E. Talbot. 'The Idiom of Popular Poetry in the Miller's Tale'. In *Speaking of Chaucer.* New York, 1970. 13–29.

Donavin, Georgiana. *Scribit Mater: Mary and the Language Arts in the Literature of Medieval England.* Washington, DC, 2012.

Donoghue, Daniel. 'Laȝamon's Ambivalence'. *Speculum*, 65 (1990), 537–63.

Doob, Penelope. *Nebuchadnezzar's Children: Conventions of Madness in Middle English Literature.* New Haven, CT, 1974.

Doyle, A. I. 'An Unrecognised Piece of *Piers the Ploughman's Creed* and Other Work by Its Scribe'. *Speculum*, 34 (1959), 428–36.

Doyle, A. I. 'University College, Oxford, MS. 97 and Its Relationship to the Simeon Manuscript (British Library Add. 22283)'. In Michael Benskin and M. L. Samuels (eds), *So meny people longages and tonges: Philological Essays in Scots and Mediaeval English Presented to Angus McIntosh.* Edinburgh, 1981. 265–82.

Doyle, A. I. 'English Books In and Out of Court from Edward III to Henry VII'. In V. J. Scattergood and J. W. Sherborne (eds), *English Court Culture in the Later Middle Ages.* London, 1983. 163–82.

Doyle, A. I. (ed.), *The Vernon Manuscript: A Facsimile of Bodleian Library, Oxford MS. Eng. poet. a.i.* Cambridge, 1987.

Doyle, A. I. and Malcolm Parkes. 'The Production of Copies of the Canterbury Tales and the *Confessio Amantis* in the Early Fifteenth Century'. In Malcolm Parkes and Andrew G. Watson (eds), *Medieval Scribes, Manuscripts, and Libraries: Essays Presented to N. R. Ker.* London, 1978. 163–210.

Doyle, Kara. '"Je maviseray": Chaucer's Anelida, Shirley's Chaucer, Shirley's Readers'. *Studies in the Age of Chaucer*, 38 (2016), 275–85.

Dresvina, Julia. *A Maid with a Dragon: The Cult of St Margaret of Antioch in Medieval England.* Oxford, 2016.

Dronke, Peter. *Fabula: Explorations into the Use of Myth in Medieval Platonism.* Leiden, 1985.

Dronke, Peter. 'On the Continuity of Medieval English Love-Lyric'. In E. Chaney and P. Mack (eds), *England and the Continental Renaissance: Essays in Honour of J. B. Trapp.* Woodbridge, 1990. 7–21.

Dronke, Peter. *The Medieval Lyric.* 3rd edn. Woodbridge, 1996.

Dronke, Peter. 'Poetic Originality in *The Wars of Alexander*'. In Helen Cooper and Sally Mapstone (eds), *The Long Fifteenth Century: Essays for Douglas Gray.* Oxford, 1997. 123–39.

Duffell, Martin J. 'Chaucer, Gower, and the History of the Hendecasyllable'. In C. B. McCully and J. J. Jefferson (eds), *English Historical Metrics.* Cambridge, 1996. 210–18.

Duffell, Martin J. '"The Craft So Long to Lerne": Chaucer's Invention of the Iambic Pentameter'. *Chaucer Review*, 39 (2000), 269–88.

Duffell, Martin J. 'Syllable and Foot: The Influence of French Metrics on English Verse'. In Dominique Billy and Ann Buckley (eds), *Etudes de langue et de littérature médiévales offertes à Peter T. Ricketts à l'occasion de son 70ème anniversaire.* Turnhout, 2005. 571–83.

Duffell, Martin J. 'Chaucer's Pentameter: Linguistics, Statistics, and History'. *Chaucer Review*, 49 (2014), 135–60.

Duffell, Martin J. *Chaucer's Verse Art in Its European Context*. Tempe, AZ, 2018.

Duggan, Hoyt N. 'Alliterative Patterning as a Basis for Emendation in Alliterative Poetry'. *Studies in the Age of Chaucer*, 8 (1986), 73–105.

Duggan, Hoyt N. 'The Shape of the B-Verse in Middle English Alliterative Poetry'. *Speculum*, 61 (1986), 564–92.

Duggan, Hoyt N. 'Notes on the Metre of *Piers Plowman*: Twenty Years On'. In Judith Jefferson and Ad Putter (eds), *Approaches to the Metres of Alliterative Verse*. Leeds, 2009. 159–85.

Duggan, Hoyt N. and Thorlac Turville-Petre (eds). *The Wars of Alexander*, EETS, s.s. 10. Oxford, 1989.

Duncan, Edwin. 'The Middle English Bestiary: Missing Link in the Evolution of the Alliterative Long Line?'. *Studia Neophilologica*, 64 (1992), 25–33.

Duncan, Thomas G. (ed.). *Medieval English Lyrics 1200–1400*. London, 1995.

Duncan, Thomas G. (ed.). *A Companion to the Middle English Lyric*. Cambridge, 2005.

Duncan, Thomas G. (ed.). *Medieval English Lyrics and Carols*. Cambridge, 2013.

Durkin, Philip. *Borrowed Words: A History of Loanwords in English*. Oxford, 2014.

Durling, Nancy Vine. 'British Library MS Harley 2253: A New Reading of the Passion Lyrics in Their Manuscript Context'. *Viator*, 40 (2009), 271–307.

Echard, Siân. *Arthurian Narrative in the Latin Tradition*. Cambridge, 1998.

Echard, Siân. 'With Carmen's Help: Latin Authorities in the *Confessio Amantis*'. *Studies in Philology*, 95 (1998), 1–40.

Echard, Siân. 'Gower in Print'. In Siân Echard (ed.), *A Companion to Gower*. Cambridge, 2004. 115–38.

Echard, Siân. *The Arthur of Medieval Latin Literature: The Development and Dissemination of the Arthurian Legend in Medieval Latin*. Cardiff, 2011.

Echard, Siân and Claire Fanger (trans.). *The Latin Verses in the* Confessio Amantis: *An Annotated Translation*. East Lansing, MI, 1991.

Echard, Siân and Robert Rouse (eds). *The Encyclopedia of Medieval British Literature*. Oxford, 2017.

Eckhardt, Caroline D. 'The First English Translations of the *Prophetia Merlini*'. *The Library*, Series 6.4 (March 1982), 25–34.

Eckhardt, Caroline D. 'Havelok the Dane in *Castleford's Chronicle*'. *Studies in Philology*, 98 (2001), 1–17.

Eckhardt, Caroline D. 'The Manuscript of *Castleford's Chronicle*: Its History and Scribes'. In Jaclyn Rajsic, Erik Kooper, and Dominique Hoche (eds), *The Prose Brut and Other Late Medieval Chronicles: Books Have Their Histories – Essays in Honour of Lister M. Matheson*. Cambridge, 2016. 199–217.

Eckhardt, Caroline D. and Bryan A. Meer. 'Constructing a Medieval Genealogy: Roland the Father of Tristan in "Castleford's Chronicle"'. *MLN*, 115 (2000), 1085–111.

Economou, George D. *The Goddess Natura in Medieval Literature*. 2nd edn. Notre Dame, IN, 2002.

Edwards, A. S. G. 'The Unity and Authenticity of *Anelida and Arcite*: The Evidence of the Manuscripts'. *Studies in Bibliography*, 41 (1988), 177–88.

Edwards, A. S. G. 'The Manuscript: British Library MS Cotton Nero A.x'. In Derek Brewer and Jonathan Gibson (eds), *A Companion to the Gawain-Poet*. Cambridge, 1998. 197–220.

Edwards, A. S. G. 'The Authorship of the Poems of Laurence Minot: A Reconsideration'. *Florilegium*, 23 (2006), 145–53.

Edwards, A. S. G., and Derek Pearsall. 'The Manuscripts of the Major English Poetic Texts'. In Jeremy Griffiths and Derek Pearsall (eds), *Book Production and Publishing in Britain, 1375–1475*. Cambridge, 1989. 257–78.

Edwards, Huw M. *Dafydd ap Gwilym: Influences and Analogues*. Oxford, 1996.

Edwards, Robert R. *Ratio and Invention: A Study of Medieval Lyric and Narrative*. Nashville, TN, 1989.

Edwards, Robert R. 'Gower 1400–1700'. In R. F. Yeager, Brian Gastle, and Ana Sáez-Hidalgo (eds), *Routledge Research Companion to John Gower*. New York, 2017. 197–209.

Edwards, Robert R. *Invention and Authorship in Medieval England*. Columbus, OH, 2017.

Einenkel, Eugen (ed.). *The Life of Saint Katherine*. EETS, o.s. 80. London, 1884.

Elias, Marcel. 'Violence, Excess, and the Composite Emotional Rhetoric of *Richard Coeur de Lion*'. *Studies in Philology*, 114 (2017), 1–38.

Elias, Marcel. 'Rewriting Chivalric Encounters: Cultural Anxieties and Social Critique in the Fourteenth Century'. In Elizabeth Archibald, Megan G. Leitch, and Corinne Saunders (eds), *Romance Rewritten: The Evolution of Middle English Romance – A Tribute to Helen Cooper*. Cambridge, 2018. 49–66.

Elias, Marcel. *English Literature and the Crusades: Anxieties of Holy War, 1291–1453*. Cambridge, forthcoming.

Elias, Marcel. 'Unsettling Orientalism: Toward a New History of European Representations of Muslims and Islam, c. 1200–1450'. Forthcoming.

Ellis, Roger (ed.). *The Oxford History of Literary Translation in English. Volume I, to 1550*. Oxford, 2008.

Emaré. In Edith Rickert (ed.), *The Romance of Emaré*. EETS, e.s. 99. London, 1906.

Embree, Dan and Elizabeth Urquhart (eds). *The Simonie: A Parallel-Text Edition*. Middle English Texts 24. Heidelberg, 1991.

Emerson, Oliver F. *A Middle English Reader*. London, 1905.

Evans, Geraint. 'Tudor London and the Origins of Welsh Writing in English'. In Geraint Evans and Helen Fulton (eds), *Cambridge History of Welsh Literature*. Cambridge, 2019. 212–31.

Everett, Dorothy. 'The Alliterative Revival'. In Patricia Kean (ed.), *Essays on Middle English Literature*. Oxford, 1955. 46–96.

Faulkner, Mark. 'Oxford, Bodleian Library, Junius 1'. In Orietta Da Rold, Takako Kato, Jo Story, Mary Swan, and Elaine Treharne (eds), *The Production and Use of English Manuscripts 1060 to 1220*. Leicester, 2010. https://www.le.ac.uk/english/em1060to1220.

Faulkner, Mark. 'Archaism, Belatedness and Modernisation: "Old" English in the Twelfth Century'. *Review of English Studies*, 63 (2011), 179–203.

Federico, Sylvia. *New Troy: Fantasies of Empire in the Late Middle Ages*. Minneapolis, MN, 2003.

Fein, Susanna (ed.). *Moral Love Songs and Laments*. Kalamazoo, MI, 1998.

Fein, Susanna. 'The Early Thirteen-Line Stanza: Style and Metrics Reconsidered'. *Parergon*, 18 (2000), 97–126.

Fein, Susanna. 'A Saint "Geynest under Gore": Marina and the Love Lyrics of the Seventh Quire'. In Susanna Fein (ed.), *Studies in the Harley Manuscript: The Scribes, Contents, and Social Contexts of British Library MS Harley 2253*. Kalamazoo, MI, 2000. 351–76.

Fein, Susanna (ed.). *Studies in the Harley Manuscript: The Scribes, Contents, and Social Contexts of British Library MS Harley 2253*. Kalamazoo, MI, 2000.

Fein, Susanna. 'Compilation and Purpose in MS Harley 2253'. In Wendy Scase (ed.), *Essays in Manuscript Geography: Vernacular Manuscripts of the English West Midlands from the Conquest to the Sixteenth Century*. Turnhout, 2007. 67–94.

Fein, Susanna (ed.). *John the Blind Audelay: Poems and Carols (Oxford, Bodleian Library MS Douce 302)*. Kalamazoo, MI, 2009.

Fein, Susanna (ed.). *My Wyl and My Wrytyng: Essays on John the Blind Audelay*. Kalamazoo, MI, 2009.

Fein, Susanna. 'The Contents of Robert Thornton's Manuscripts'. In Susanna Fein and Michael Johnston (eds), *Robert Thornton and His Books: Essays on the Lincoln and London Thornton Manuscripts*. York, 2014. 13–66.

Fein, Susanna. 'The Fillers of the Auchinleck Manuscript and the Literary Culture of the West Midlands'. In Carol M. Meale and Derek Pearsall (eds), *Makers and Users of Medieval Books: Essays in Honour of A. S. G. Edwards*. Woodbridge, 2014. 60–77.

Fein, Susanna. 'Literary Scribes: The Harley Scribe and Robert Thornton as Case Studies'. In Margaret Connolly and Raluca Radulescu (eds), *Insular Books: Vernacular Manuscripts in Late Medieval Britain*. London, 2015. 61–80.

Fein, Susanna (ed.). *The Auchinleck Manuscript: New Perspectives*. York, 2016.

486 COMPLETE BIBLIOGRAPHY

Fein, Susanna. 'All Adam's Children: The Early Middle English Lyric Sequence in Oxford, Jesus College, MS 29 (II)'. In Julia Boffey and Christiania Whitehead (eds), *Middle English Lyrics: New Readings of Short Poems*. Cambridge, 2018. 213–26.

Fein, Susanna (ed.). *Interpreting MS Digby 86: A Trilingual Book from Thirteenth-Century Worcestershire*. Woodbridge, 2019.

Fein, Susanna. 'The Middle English Poetry of MS Digby 86'. In Susanna Fein (ed.), *Interpreting MS Digby 86: A Trilingual Book from Thirteenth-Century Worcestershire*. Woodbridge, 2019. 162–97.

Fein, Susanna (ed. and trans.). *The Owl and the Nightingale and the Poems of Oxford Jesus College MS 29 (II)*. Kalamazoo, MI, 2022.

Fein, Susanna (ed.) with David Raybin and Jan Ziolkowski (trans.). *The Complete Harley 2253 Manuscript*. 3 vols. Kalamazoo, MI, 2015.

Fellows, Jennifer (ed.). *Sir Bevis of Hampton*. 2 vols. EETS o.s. 349, 350. Oxford, 2017.

Fewster, Carol. *Intertextuality and Genre in Middle English Romance*. Cambridge, 1987.

Fichte, Joerg O. *Chaucer's 'Art Poetical': A Study in Chaucerian Poetics*. Tübingen, 1980.

Field, Rosalind. 'The Anglo-Norman Background to Alliterative Romance'. In D. A. Lawton (ed.), *Middle English Alliterative Poetry and Its Literary Background*. Cambridge, 1982. 54–69.

Field, Rosalind. 'Romance in England, 1066–1400'. In David Wallace (ed.), *The Cambridge History of Medieval English Literature*. Cambridge, 1999. 152–76.

Field, Rosalind. 'Children of Anarchy: Anglo-Norman Romance in the Twelfth Century'. In Ruth Kennedy and Simon Meecham-Jones (eds), *Writers of the Reign of Henry II: Twelve Essays*. Basingstoke, 2006. 249–62.

Field, Rosalind. 'The Curious History of the Matter of England'. In Neil Cartlidge (ed.), *Boundaries in Medieval Romance*. Cambridge, 2008. 29–42.

Fierebras. In Marc Le Person (ed.), *Fierabras: chanson de geste du XIIe siècle*. Paris, 2003.

Finlayson, John. 'Definitions of Middle English Romance'. *The Chaucer Review*, 15 (1980), 168–81.

Finlayson, John. 'Alliterative Narrative Poetry: The Control of the Medium'. *Traditio*, 44 (1988), 419–51.

Finlayson, John. 'Guido de Columnis' *Historia destructionis Troiae*, The *'Gest Hystorial' of the Destruction of Troy*, and Lydgate's *Troy Book*: Translation and the Design of History'. *Anglia*, 113 (1995), 141–62.

Firumbras. In Mary Isabelle O'Sullivan (ed.), *'Firumbras' and 'Otuel and Roland'*. EETS, o.s. 198. London, 1935.

Fisher, John H. *John Gower: Moral Philosopher and Friend of Chaucer*. New York, 1964.

Fisher, Matthew. *Scribal Authorship and the Writing of History in Medieval England*. Columbus, OH, 2012.

Fitzgerald, Christina M. '"Ubbe dubbede him to knith": The scansion of *Havelok* and ME *–es, –ed*, and *–ede*'. In Susan M. Fitzmaurice and Donka Minkova (eds), *Studies in the History of the English Language IV: Empirical and Analytical Advances in the Study of English Language Change*. Berlin, 2008. 187–204.

Fleming, John V. *The Roman de la Rose: A Study in Allegory and Iconography*. Princeton, NJ, 1969.

Fleming, John V. 'Hoccleve's "Letter of Cupid" and the "Quarrel" over the *Roman de la Rose*'. *Medium Ævum*, 40 (1971), 21–40.

Fletcher, Alan. 'Written versus Spoken Macaronic Discourse in Late Medieval England: The View from a Pulpit'. In Ad Putter and Judith Jefferson (eds), *Multilingualism in Medieval Britain (c. 1066–1520): Sources and Analysis*. Turnhout, 2012. 137–51.

Fletcher, Angus. *Allegory: The Theory of a Symbolic Mode*. New afterword. Princeton, NJ, 2012.

Floris and Blauncheflur. In F. C. De Vries (ed.), *Floris and Blauncheflur: A Middle English Romance*. Groningen, 1966.

Fowler, Alastair (ed.). *Silent Poetry: Essays in Numerological Analysis*. London, 1970.

Fowler, Alastair. *Kinds of Literature: An Introduction to the Theory of Genres and Modes*. Oxford, 1982.

Fowler, David C. *The Bible in Early English Literature*. London, 1977.

Frakes, Jerold C. *Vernacular and Latin Literary Discourses of the Muslim Other in Medieval Germany*. New York, 2011.

Frankis, John. 'The Social Context of Vernacular Writing in Thirteenth Century England: The Evidence of the Manuscripts'. In P. R. Coss and S. D. Lloyd (eds), *Thirteenth Century England 1: Proceedings of the Newcastle Upon Tyne Conference 1985*. Woodbridge, 1986. 175–84.

Franzen, Christine. *The Tremulous Hand of Worcester: A Study of Old English in the Thirteenth Century*. Oxford, 1991.

French, Walter. *Essays on King Horn*. Ithaca, NY, 1940.

Friedman, J. B. 'Eurydice, Heurodis, and the Noon-Day Demon'. *Speculum*, 41 (1966), 22–29.

Fulk, R. D. 'Consonant Doubling and Open Syllable Lengthening in the *Ormulum*'. *Anglia*, 114 (1996), 481–513.

Fulk, R. D. *An Introduction to Middle English*. Toronto, 2012.

Fulk, R. D., Robert E. Bjork, and John D. Niles (eds). *Klaeber's Beowulf and the Fight at Finnsburg*. 4th edn. Toronto, 2008.

Fuller, David. 'Lyrics, Sacred and Secular'. In Corinne Saunders (ed.), *A Companion to Medieval Poetry*. Oxford, 2010. 258–76.

Fulton, Helen. 'The Theory of Celtic Influence on the Harley Lyrics'. *Modern Philology*, 82 (1985), 239–52.

Fulton, Helen. *Dafydd ap Gwilym and the European Context*. Cardiff, 1989.

Fulton, Helen. 'Class and Nation: Defining the English in Late-Medieval Welsh Poetry'. In Ruth Kennedy and Simon Meecham-Jones (eds), *Authority and Subjugation in Writings of Medieval Wales*. New York, 2008. 191–212.

Furnivall, Frederick J. and Carl Horstmann (eds). *The Minor Poems of the Vernon MS*, 2 vols. EETS, o.s. 98, 117 London, 1892, 1901.

Furrow, Melissa. 'Middle English Fabliaux and Modern Myth'. *ELH*, 56 (1989), 1–18.

Furrow, Melissa. '"The Wench", the Fabliau, and the Auchinleck Manuscript'. *Notes & Queries*, n.s. 41, 239 (1994), 440–3.

Furrow, Melissa. *Expectations of Romance: The Reception of a Genre in Medieval England*. Woodbridge, 2009.

Gaimar, Geffrei. In Ian Short (ed. and trans.), *Estoire des Engleis*. Oxford, 2009.

Galloway, Andrew. 'The Rhetoric of Riddling in Late-Medieval England: The "Oxford" Riddles, the *Secretum philosophorum* and the Riddles in *Piers Plowman*'. *Speculum*, 70 (1995), 68–105.

Galloway, Andrew. 'Authority'. In Peter Brown (ed.), *A Companion to Chaucer*. Oxford, 2002. 23–39.

Galloway, Andrew. *The Penn Commentary on* Piers Plowman *1*. Philadelphia, PA, 2006.

Galloway, Andrew. 'Fame's Penitent: Deconstructive Chaucer among the Lancastrians'. In Isabel David and Catherine Nall (eds), *Chaucer and Fame: Reputation and Reception*. Woodbridge, 2015. 103–26.

Galloway, Andrew. 'Gower's Ovids'. In Rita Copeland (ed.), *The Oxford History of Classical Reception in English Literature, 800–1558, Volume I*. Oxford, 2016. 435–64.

Galloway, Andrew. 'Madame Meed: Fauvel, Isabella, and the French Circumstances of *Piers Plowman*'. *The Yearbook of Langland Studies*, 30 (2016), 227–52.

Galloway, Andrew. 'Gower's Classicizing Vocations'. In Ana Sáez-Hidalgo, Brian Gastle, and R. F. Yeager (eds), *The Routledge Research Companion to John Gower*. New York, 2017. 266–80.

Galloway, Andrew. 'Parallel Lives: William Rokele and the Satirical Literacies of *Piers Plowman*'. *Studies in the Age of Chaucer*, 40 (2018), 43–111.

Gamelyn. In Stephen Knight and Thomas H. Ohlgren (eds), *Robin Hood and Other Outlaw Tales*. Kalamazoo, MI, 1997.

Garlick, Raymond and Roland Mathias (eds). *Anglo-Welsh Poetry, 1480–1980*. Bridgend, 1984.

Garner, Lori Ann. 'The Role of Proverbs in Middle English Narrative'. In Mark C. Amodio (ed.), *New Directions in Oral Theory*. Tempe, AZ, 2005. 255–77.

Gaylord, Alan T. 'Chaucer's Dainty "Dogerel": The "Elvyssh" Prosody of *Sir Thopas*'. *Studies in the Age of Chaucer*, 1 (1979), 83–104.

Geary, Patrick. 'Humiliation of Saints'. In Stephen Wilson (ed.), *Saints and Their Cults: Studies in Religious Sociology, Folklore and History*. Cambridge, 1983. 123–40.

Geary, Patrick. *Furta Sacra: Thefts of Relics in the Central Middle Ages*. Princeton, NJ, 1990.

488 COMPLETE BIBLIOGRAPHY

Geiriadur Prifysgol Cymru: A Dictionary of the Welsh Language. University of Wales, 2020. http://geiriadur.ac.uk/gpc/gpc.html.

Geoffrey of Monmouth. In Michael D. Reeve (ed.) and Neil Wright (trans.), *The History of the Kings of Britain: An Edition and Translation of the* De gestis Britonum [Historia Regum Britanniae]. Woodbridge, 2007.

Geoffrey of Vinsauf. *Poetria Nova*. In Edmond Faral (ed.), *Les Arts Poétiques du xiie et du xiiie Siècle: Recherches et Documents sur la Technique Littéraire du Moyen Âge*. Paris, 1924, 1962. 194–262.

Geoffrey of Vinsauf. *Poetria Nova*. In Margaret F. Nims (trans.), *Poetria Nova of Geoffrey of Vinsauf*. Toronto, 1967.

Gerald of Wales. *Gemma Ecclesiastica*. In J. S. Brewer, James F. Dimock, and George F. Warner (eds), *Giraldi Cambrensis: Opera*. 8 vols. London, 1861–91.

Gerber, Amanda. *Medieval Ovid: Frame Narrative and Political Allegory*. London, 2015.

The Gests of King Alexander of Macedon. In Francis Peabody Magoun (ed.), *The Gests of King Alexander of Macedon: Two Middle-English Alliterative Fragments, 'Alexander A' and 'Alexander B'*. Cambridge, MA, 1929.

Giancarlo, Matthew. *Parliament and Literature in Late Medieval England*. Cambridge, 2010.

Gibson, Margaret, Danuta Shanzer, and Nigel Palmer. 'Manuscripts of Alan of Lille, *Anticlaudianus* in the British Isles'. *Studi medievali*, 28 (1987), 905–1001.

Gilbert, Jane. 'Arthurian Ethics'. In Elizabeth Archibald and Ad Putter (eds), *The Cambridge Companion to the Arthurian Legend*. Cambridge, 2009. 154–70.

Giles, J. A. (ed. and trans.). *Six Old English Chronicles*. London, 1848.

Gillespie, Vincent. 'Medieval Hypertext: Image and Text from York Minster'. In P. R. Robinson and Rivkah Zim (eds), *Of the Making of Books: Medieval Manuscripts, Their Scribes and Readers— Essays Presented to M. B. Parkes*. Aldershot, 1997. 206–29.

Gillespie, Vincent. 'Moral and Penitential Lyrics'. In Thomas G. Duncan (ed.), *A Companion to the Middle English Lyric*. Cambridge, 2005. 68–95.

Gillespie, Vincent. 'Chichele's Church: Vernacular Theology in England after Thomas Arundel'. In Vincent Gillespie and Kantik Ghosh (eds), *After Arundel: Religious Writing in Fifteenth-Century England*. Turnhout, 2011. 3–42.

Gillespie, Vincent and Kantik Ghosh (eds). *After Arundel: Religious Writing in Fifteenth-Century England*. Turnhout, 2011.

Gillingham, John. *Richard I*. New Haven, CT, 1999.

Ginsberg, Warren (ed.). *Wynnere and Wastoure and The Parlement of the Thre Ages*. Kalamazoo, MI, 1992.

Giraldus Cambrensis (Gerald of Wales). In Yves Lefèvre and R. B. C. Huygens (eds), *Speculum duorum, or a Mirror of Two Men*. Cardiff, 1974.

Given-Wilson, Chris. *Chronicles: The Writing of History in Medieval England*. London, 2004.

Given-Wilson, Chris. *Henry IV*. New Haven, CT, 2016.

Goldstein, R. James. 'Writing in Scotland, 1058–1560'. In David Wallace (ed.), *The Cambridge History of Medieval English Literature*. Cambridge, 1999. 229–54.

Göller, Karl Heinz. 'Alexander und Dindimus: West-östlicher Disput über Mensch und Welt'. In Willi Erzgräber (ed.), *Kontinuität und Transformation der Antike im Mittelalter*. Sigmaringen, 1989. 105–19.

Görlach, Manfred. *The Textual Tradition of the South English Legendary*. Leeds, 1974.

Gower, John. In G. C. Macaulay (ed.), *The Complete Works of John Gower*. 4 vols. Oxford, 1899–1902.

Gower, John. *Confessio Amantis*. In G. C. Macaulay (ed.), *The English Works of John Gower*. EETS, e.s. 81–2. Oxford, 1900–1.

Gower, John. *Confessio Amantis*. In Russell Peck (ed.), *Confessio Amantis*. 3 vols. Kalamazoo, MI, 2006.

Gower, John. In David R. Carlson (ed.) and A. G. Rigg (trans.), *John Gower, Poems on Contemporary Events: The Visio Anglie (1381) and Cronica tripertita (1400)*. Toronto, 2011.

Gower, John. In R. F. Yeager (ed.), *John Gower: The French Balades*. Kalamazoo, MI, 2011.

Grady, Frank. *Representing Righteous Heathens in Late-Medieval England*. New York, 2005.

Gray, Douglas. *Themes and Images in the Medieval English Religious Lyric*. London, 1972.

Gray, Douglas (ed.). *The Oxford Book of Late Medieval Verse and Prose*. Oxford, 1985.

Gray, Douglas (ed.). *English Medieval Religious Lyrics*. Exeter, 1992.

Gray, Douglas. *Simple Forms: Essays on Medieval English Popular Literature*. Oxford, 2015.

Gray, Douglas and Jane Bliss (eds). *Make We Merry More and Less: An Anthology of Medieval English Popular Literature*. 2019. https://www.openbookpublishers.com/product/981.

Green, Richard Firth. 'The Two "Litel Wot Hit Any Mon" Lyrics in Harley 2253'. *Mediaeval Studies*, 51 (1989), 304–12.

Green, Richard Firth. 'Humphrey and the Werewolf'. In J. A. Burrow and H. N. Duggan (eds), *Medieval Alliterative Poetry: Essays in Honour of Thorlac Turville-Petre*. Dublin, 2010. 107–24.

Green, Richard Firth. 'A Poet at Work: John Gower's Revisions to the "Tale of Rosiphilee"'. In Susannnah Mary Chewning (ed.), *Studies in the Age of Gower: A Festschrift in Honour of R. F. Yeager*. Cambridge, 2020. 217–26.

Greene, Richard Leighton (ed.). *The Early English Carols*. Oxford, 1977.

Greig, Pamela L. C. 'The "Lay Folks" Catechism: An Edition'. PhD Diss. University of Nottingham, 2018.

Griffiths, Jeremy and Derek Pearsall (eds). *Book Production and Publishing in Britain, 1375–1475*. Cambridge, 1989.

Grimaldi, Patrizia. 'Sir Orfeo as Celtic Folk-Hero, Christian Pilgrim, and Medieval King'. In M. Bloomfield (ed.), *Allegory, Myth and Symbol*. Cambridge, MA, 1981. 147–61.

Gruenler, Curtis A. Piers Plowman *and the Poetics of Enigma: Riddles, Rhetoric and Theology*. Notre Dame, IN, 2017.

Grund, Peter. 'A Previously Unrecorded Fragment of the Middle English Short Metrical Chronicle in Bibliotheca Philosophica Hermetica M199'. *English Studies*, 87 (2006), 277–93.

Guddat-Figge, Gisela. 'The Audience of the Romances'. In Stephen H. A. Shepherd (ed.), *Middle English Romances: Authoritative Texts, Sources and Backgrounds, Criticism*. New York, 1995. 498–506. Reprinted from: Guddat-Figge, Gisela. *Catalogue of Manuscripts Containing Middle English Romances*. Munich, 1976. 42–52.

Guido delle Colonne. In Nathaniel Edward Griffin (ed.), *Historia destructionis Troiae*. Cambridge, MA, 1936.

Guido delle Colonne. In Mary Elizabeth Meek (trans.), *Historia destructionis Troiae*. Bloomington, IN, 1974.

Guillaume de Palerne. In Alexandre Micha (ed.), *Guillaume de Palerne: roman du XIIIe siècle*. Geneva, 1990.

Guy of Warwick. In Julius Zupitza (ed.), *The Romance of Guy of Warwick*. EETS, e.s. 42, 49, and 59. London, 1966. 1st edn. London, 1883, 1887, 1891.

Hahn, Thomas (ed.). *Sir Gawain: Eleven Romances and Tales*. Kalamazoo, MI, 1995.

Hahn, Thomas. 'Gawain and Popular Chivalric Romance in Britain'. In Roberta L. Krueger (ed.), *The Cambridge Companion to Romance*. Cambridge, 2006. 218–34.

Halle, Morris and Samuel Jay Keyser. 'Chaucer and the Study of Prosody'. *College English*, 28 (1966), 187–219.

Halliwell, James Orchard (ed.). *The Palatine Anthology*. London, 1850.

Halman, Helena and Timothy Regetz, 'Language Switching and Alliteration in Oxford, MS Bodley 649'. In Albrecht Classen (ed.), *Multilingualism in the Middle Ages and Early Modern Age: Communication and Miscommunication in the Premodern World*. Berlin, 2016. 313–28.

Hamer, Richard and Vida Russell (eds). *Supplementary Lives in Some Manuscripts of the Gilte Legende*. EETS, o.s. 315. Oxford, 2000.

Hammond, Eleanor P. (ed.). *English Verse between Chaucer and Surrey*. Durham, NC, 1927.

Hanna, Ralph (ed.). *The Awntyrs off Arthure at the Terne Wathelyn*. Manchester, 1974.

Hanna, Ralph. 'Sir Thomas Berkeley and His Patronage', *Speculum*, 64 (1989), 878–916.

Hanna, Ralph. *William Langland*. Authors of the Middle Ages 3. Aldershot, 1993.

Hanna, Ralph. 'Alliterative Poetry'. In David Wallace (ed.), *The Cambridge History of Medieval English Literature*. Cambridge, 1999. 485–512.

Hanna, Ralph. 'Reconsidering the Auchinleck Manuscript'. In Derek Pearsall (ed.), *New Directions in Later Medieval Manuscript Studies: Essays from the 1998 Harvard Conference*. York, 2000. 91–102.

Hanna, Ralph. 'Yorkshire Writers'. *Proceedings of the British Academy*, 121 (2003), 91–109.

Hanna, Ralph (ed.). *Speculum Vitae: A Reading Edition*. EETS, o.s. 331–2. Oxford, 2008.

Hanna, Ralph. 'The Tree of Charity—Again'. In John A. Burrow and Hoyt Duggan (eds), *Medieval Alliterative Poetry: Essays in Honour of Thorlac Turville-Petre*. Dublin, 2010. 125–39.

Hanna, Ralph. 'The Versions and Revisions of *Piers Plowman*'. In Andrew Cole and Andrew Galloway (eds), *The Cambridge Companion to* Piers Plowman. Cambridge, 2014. 33–49.

Hanna, Ralph. 'Lichfield'. In David Wallace (ed.), *Europe: A Literary History, 1348–1418*. 2 vols. Oxford, 2015. 1: 279–84.

Hanna, Ralph. *Patient Reading/Reading Patience: Oxford Essays on Medieval Literature*. Liverpool, 2017.

Hanna, Ralph. 'Cambridge University Library, MS Dd.1.17: Some Historical Notes'. *Transactions of the Cambridge Bibliographical Society*, 16 (2018), 141–60.

Hanna, Ralph and Sarah Wood (eds). *Richard Morris's* Prick of Conscience: *A Corrected and Amplified Reading Text*. EETS, o.s. 342. Oxford, 2013.

Hanning, Robert W. '*Havelok the Dane*: Structure, Symbols, Meaning'. *Studies in Philology*, 64 (1967), 586–605.

Hanning, Robert W. '*Engin* in Twelfth-Century Romance: An Examination of the *Roman d'Enéas* and Hue de Rotelande's *Ipomedon*'. *Yale French Studies*, 51 (1974), 82–101.

Hanning, Robert W. 'Poetic Emblems in Medieval Narrative Texts'. In Lois Ebin (ed.), *Vernacular Poetics in the Middle Ages*. Kalamazoo, MI, 1984. 1–32.

Hansen, Elaine Tuttle. *The Solomon Complex: Reading Wisdom in Old English Poetry*. Toronto, 1988.

Hardison, O. B., Jr. 'Towards a History of Medieval Literary Criticism'. *Medievalia et Humanistica*, 7 (1976), 1–12.

Hardison, O. B., Jr., Alex Preminger, Kevin Kerrane, and Leon Golden (eds). *Medieval Literary Criticism: Translations and Interpretations*. New York, 1974.

Harrington, Marjorie. 'Of Earth You Were Made: Constructing the Bilingual Poem "Erþ" in BL MS Harley 913'. *Florilegium*, 31 (2014), 105–37.

Harris, Carissa M. *Obscene Pedagogies: Transgressive Talk and Sexual Education in Late Medieval Britain*. Ithaca, NY, 2018.

Harvey, Carol. 'Macaronic Techniques in Anglo-Norman Verse'. *L'Esprit créateur*, 18 (1978), 70–81.

Hassig, Debra. *Medieval Bestiaries: Text, Image, Ideology*. Cambridge, 1995.

Hatt, Cecilia A. *God and the Gawain Poet*. Cambridge, 2015.

Haywood, Louise M. 'Spring Song and Narrative Organization in the Medieval Alexander Legend'. *Troianalexandrina*, 4 (2004), 87–105.

Head, Thomas (ed.). *Medieval Hagiography*. New York, 2000.

Heffernan, Thomas J. 'The Authorship of the *Northern Homily Cycle*: The Liturgical Affiliation of the Sunday Gospel Periscopes as a Test'. *Traditio*, 41 (1985), 289–309.

Heffernan, Thomas J. *Sacred Biography: Saints and Their Biographers in the Middle Ages*. New York, 1988.

Helbert, Daniel. '"an Arður sculde ȝete cum": The Prophetic Hope in Twelfth-Century Britain'. *Arthuriana*, 26.1 (2016), 77–107.

Heng, Geraldine. *Empire of Magic: Medieval Romance and the Politics of Cultural Fantasy*. New York, 2003.

Heng, Geraldine. *The Invention of Race in the European Middle Ages*. Cambridge, 2018.

Henkel, Nikolaus. *Studien zum Physiologus im Mittelalter*. Tübingen, 1976.

Henley, Georgia and Joshua Byron Smith (eds). *A Companion to Geoffrey of Monmouth*. Leiden, 2020.

Henry of Huntingdon. In Diana Greenway (ed.), *Henry, Archdeacon of Huntingdon: Historia Anglorum (History of the English People)*. Oxford, 1996.

Henry of Huntingdon. In Winston Black (ed. and trans.), *Henry of Huntingdon: Anglicanus ortus. A Verse Herbal of the Twelfth Century*. Toronto, 2012.

Herebert, William. In Stephen R. Reimer (ed.), *The Works of William Herebert, OFM*. Studies and Texts 81. Toronto, 1987.

Hersh, Cara. '"Wyse words within": Private Property and Public Knowledge in *Wynnere and Wastoure*'. *Modern Philology*, 107 (2010), 507–27.

Herzman, Ronald B., Graham Drake, and Eve Salisbury (eds). *Four Romances of England: King Horn, Havelok the Dane, Bevis of Hampton, Athelston*. Kalamazoo, MI, 1999.

Hesketh, Glynn (ed.). *La Lumere as Lais by Pierre d'Abernon of Fetcham*. 3 vols. ANTS 54–8. London, 1996–2000.

Hibbard, Laura A. *Mediaeval Romance in England*. New York, 1960.

Higden, Ranulph. *Polychronicon*. In Joseph Rawson Lumby (ed.), *Polychronicon Ranulphi Higden Monachi Cestrensis; Together with the English Translation of John Trevisa and of an Unknown Writer of the Fifteenth Century*. 9 vols. Rolls Series 41. London, 1865–86.

Higden, Ranulph. In Margaret Jennings (ed.), *The Ars Componendi Sermones of Ranulph Higden, O.S.B.* Leiden, 1991.

Hildebrand, Theodor. *Die altfranzösische Alexanderdichtung 'Le Roman de toute chevalerie' des Thomas von Kent und die mittelenglische Romanze 'Kyng Alisaunder' in ihrem Verhältnis zu einander*. Amorbach, 1911.

Hill, Betty. 'The Twelfth-Century *Conduct of Life*, Formerly the *Poema morale* or *A Moral Ode*'. *Leeds Studies in English*, n.s. 9 (1977), 97–144.

Hill, Ordelle G. *Looking Westward: Poetry, Landscape, and Politics in Sir Gawain and the Green Knight*. Newark, DE, 2009.

Hines, John. *The Fabliau in English*. London, 1993.

Hines, John. *Voices in the Past: English Literature and Archaeology*. Woodbridge, 2004.

Hines, John, Nathalie Cohen, and Simon Roffey. 'Iohannes Gower, Armiger, Poeta: Records and Memorials of His Life and Death'. In Siân Echard (ed.), *A Companion to Gower*. Cambridge, 2004. 23–41.

Hirsh, John C. (ed.). *Medieval Lyric: Middle English Lyrics, Ballads, and Carols*. Oxford, 2005.

Hirsh, John C. 'The Earliest Known English Ballad: A New Reading of *Judas*'. *Modern Language Review*, 103 (2008), 931–9.

Hoccleve, Thomas. *The Regement of Princes*. In F. J. Furnivall (ed.), *Hoccleve's Works. III, The Regement of Princes*. EETS, e.s. 72. London, 1897.

Hoccleve, Thomas. In Frederick J. Furnivall and I. Gollancz (eds), *Hoccleve's Works: The Minor Poems*. 2 vols. EETS, e.s. 61 and 73, rev. Jerome Mitchell and A. I. Doyle. Oxford, 1970.

Hoccleve, Thomas. *Letter of Cupid*. In Thelmer S. Fenster and Mary Carpenter Erler (eds), *Poems of Cupid, God of Love*. Leiden, 1990.

Hogg, Richard M. 'Phonology and Morphology'. In Richard M. Hogg (ed.), *The Cambridge History of the English Language* I, *The Beginnings to 1066*. Cambridge, 1992. 67–167.

Holden, A. J., S. Gregory, and D. Crouch (ed. and trans.). *History of William Marshal*. 3 vols. London, 2002–6.

Holmes, G. A. *The Estates of the Higher Nobility in Fourteenth-Century England*. Cambridge, 1957.

Holsinger, Bruce. 'Vernacular Legality: The English Jurisdictions of The Owl and the Nightingale'. In Emily Steiner and Candace Barrington (eds), *The Letter of the Law: Legal Practice and Literary Production in Medieval England*. Ithaca, NY, 2002. 154–84.

Holton, Amanda. *The Sources of Chaucer's Poetics*. Aldershot, 2008.

Honegger, Thomas. 'Romancing the Form: Alliterative Metre and *William of Palerne*'. In W. Rudulf, T. Honegger, and A. J. Johnston (eds), *Clerks, Wives, and Historians: Essays on Medieval English Language and Literature*. Frankfurt/Main, 2007. 117–24.

Hopkins, Amanda. 'Veiling the Text: The True Role of the Cloth in *Emaré*'. In J. Weiss, J. Fellows, and M. Dickson (eds), *Medieval Insular Romance: Translation and Innovation*. Cambridge, 2000. 71–82.

Hopkins, Andrea. *The Sinful Knights: A Study of Middle English Penitential Romance*. Oxford, 1990.

Horace. In Niall Rudd (ed.), *Horace: Epistles Book II and Epistle to the Pisones ['Ars Poetica']*. Cambridge, 1989.

Horobin, Simon. '"In London and Opelond": The Dialect and Circulation of the C-Version of *Piers Plowman*'. *Medium Ævum*, 74 (2005), 248–69.

Horobin, Simon. *Chaucer's Language*. Basingstoke, 2007.

Horobin, Simon. 'Adam Pinkhurst, Geoffrey Chaucer and the Hengwrt Manuscript of the *Canterbury Tales*'. *Chaucer Review*, 44 (2010), 351–67.

Horobin, Simon. 'The Scribe of Bodleian Library, MS Digby 102 and Circulation of the C Text of *Piers Plowman*'. *Yearbook of Langland Studies*, 24 (2010), 89–112.

Horobin, Simon. 'Manuscripts and Readers of *Piers Plowman*'. In Andrew Cole and Andrew Galloway (eds), *The Cambridge Companion to* Piers Plowman. Cambridge, 2014. 179–97.

Horobin, Simon and Jeremy J. Smith. 'The Language of the Vernon Manuscript'. In Wendy Scase (ed.), *A Facsimile Edition of the Vernon Manuscript: A Literary Hoard from Medieval England*. Bodleian Digital Texts. Oxford, 2012.

Horrall, Sarah M. (gen. ed.). *The Southern Version of Cursor Mundi*. 5 vols. Ottawa, 1978–2000.

Horrall, Sarah M. 'Thomas of Hales, O.F.M.: His Life and Works'. *Traditio*, 42 (1986), 287–98.

Horrall, Sarah M. '"For the commun at understand": *Cursor Mundi* and Its Background'. In Michael G. Sargent (ed.), *De cella in seculum: Religious and Secular Life and Devotion in Late Medieval England*. Cambridge, 1989. 97–107.

Horrall, Sarah M. '"Man Yhernes Rimes for to Here": A Biblical History from the Middle Ages'. In Carol G. Fisher and Kathleen L. Scott (eds), *Art into Life: Collected Papers from the Kresge Art Museum Medieval Symposia*. East Lansing, MI, 1995. 73–93.

Horstmann, Carl (ed.). *Sammlung Altenglischer Legenden*. Heilbronn, 1878.

Horstmann, Carl (ed.). *Altenglische Legenden: Neue Folge*. Hildesheim, 1881.

Horstmann, Carl (ed.). *Barbour's des Schottischen Nationaldichters Legendensammlung*. Heilbronn, 1881.

Horstmann, Carl (ed.). *The Early South-English Legendary*. EETS, o.s. 87. Oxford, 1887.

Horstmann, Carl and Frederick J. Furnivall (eds). *The Minor Poems of the Vernon MS*. 2 vols. EETS, o.s. 98, 117. London, 1892–1901.

Hudson, Anne. 'Tradition and Innovation in Some Middle English Manuscripts'. *Review of English Studies*, 17 (1966), 359–72.

Hudson, Anne. 'Epilogue: The Legacy of *Piers Plowman*'. In John A. Alford (ed.), *A Companion to* Piers Plowman. Berkeley, CA, 1988. 251–66.

Hudson, Anne. *The Premature Reformation: Wycliffite Texts and Lollard History*. Oxford, 1988.

Hudson, Anne. 'Langland and Lollardy?'. *Yearbook of Langland Studies*, 17 (2003), 91–105.

Hue de Rotelande. *Ipomédon*. In A. J. Holden (ed.), *Ipomédon*. Paris, 1979.

Hue de Rotelande. *Ipomadon*. In Rhiannon Purdie (ed.), *Ipomadon*. EETS, o.s. 316. Oxford, 2001.

Hughes, Jonathan. *Pastors and Visionaries: Religion and Secular Life in Late Medieval Yorkshire*. Woodbridge, 1988.

Hui, Andrew. *A Theory of the Aphorism from Confucius to Twitter*. Princeton, NJ, 2019.

Hulme, William Henry. *The Middle English Harrowing of Hell and Gospel of Nicodemus*. EETS, e.s. 100–1. London, 1907.

Hume, Cathy. 'Why Did Gower Write the *Traitié*?'. In Elisabeth Dutton with John Hines and R. F. Yeager (eds), *John Gower, Trilingual Poet: Language, Translation, and Tradition*. Cambridge, 2010. 263–75.

Hume, Cathy. *Middle English Biblical Poetry and Romance*. Cambridge, 2021.

Hume, Kathryn. 'Structure and Perspective: Romance and Hagiographic Features in the Amicus and Amelius Story'. *Journal of English and Germanic Philology*, 69 (1970), 89–107.

Hume, Kathryn. *The Owl and the Nightingale: The Poem and Its Critics*. Toronto, 1975.

Hunt, R. W. 'English Learning in the Late Twelfth Century'. *Transactions of the Royal Historical Society* 4th series, 19 (1936), 38–42.

Iannucci, Amilcare. 'Limbo: The Emptiness of Time'. *Studi Danteschi*, 52 (1979–80), 69–118.

Imagining History Project, Queen's University Belfast. https://www.manuscriptsonline.org/resources/ih.

Ingham, Richard. 'John Gower, poète anglo-normand: perspectives linguistiques sur *Le Myrour de l'Omme*'. In Oreste Floquet and Gabriele Giannini (eds), *Anglo-Français: philologie et linguistique*. Paris, 2015. 91–100.

Ingledew, Francis. 'The Book of Troy and the Genealogical Construction of History: The Case of Geoffrey of Monmouth's *Historia regum Britanniae*'. *Speculum*, 69 (1994), 665–704.

Innes-Parker, Catherine (ed.). *The Wooing of Our Lord and the Wooing Group Prayers*. Peterborough, ON, 2015.

Ipomadon. In Rhiannon Purdie (ed.), *Ipomadon*. EETS, o.s. 316. Oxford, 2001.

Irvin, Matthew W. *The Poetic Voices of John Gower: Politics and Personae in the* Confessio Amantis. Cambridge, 2014.

Isidore of Seville. In W. M. Lindsay (ed.), *Etymologiarum sive originum libri XX*. 2 vols. Oxford, 1911.

Isidore of Seville. In Stephen A. Barney, W. J. Lewis, J. A. Beach, and Oliver Berghof (trans.), *The Etymologies of Isidore of Seville*. Cambridge, 2006.

Ito, Masayoshi. 'Gower's Use of *Rime Riche* in *Confessio Amantis*: As Compared with His Practice in *Miroir de L'Omme* and with the Case of Chaucer'. *Studies in English Literature*, 46 (1969), 29–44.

Jacobs, Nicholas. 'Alliterative Storms: A Topos in Middle English'. *Speculum*, 47 (1972), 695–719.

Jahner, Jennifer, Emily Steiner, and Elizabeth M. Tyler (eds). *Medieval Historical Writing: Britain and Ireland, 500–1500*. Cambridge, 2019.

Jefferson, Judith A., Donka Minkova, and Ad Putter. 'Perfect and Imperfect Rhyme: Romances in the *abab* Tradition'. *Studies in Philology*, 111 (2014), 631–51.

Jeffrey, David L. and Brian J. Levy (eds). *The Anglo-Norman Lyric: An Anthology*. Toronto, 1990.

Johannesson, Nils-Lennart. 'The Etymology of Rime in the *Ormulum*'. *Nordic Journal of English Studies*, 3 (2019), 61–75.

Johannesson, Nils-Lennart. *The Orrmulum Project*. http://www.orrmulum.net/orrmulum_site. html.

John of Garland. In Louis John Paetow (ed.), *Morale Scolarium of John of Garland*. Berkeley, CA, 1927.

John of Garland. In Evelyn Faye Wilson (ed.), *The Stella Maris of John of Garland*. Cambridge, MA, 1946.

John of Salisbury. In Daniel D. McGarry (trans.), *The Metalogicon of John of Salisbury: A Twelfth-Century Defense of the Verbal and Logical Arts of the Trivium*. Berkeley, CA, 1955.

Johnson, Lesley. 'Robert Mannyng's History of Arthurian Literature'. In Ian Wood and G. A. Loud (eds), *Church and Chronicle in the Middle Ages: Essays Presented to John Taylor*. London, 1991. 129–47.

Johnston, Andrew James. *Performing the Middle Ages from 'Beowulf' to 'Othello'*. Turnhout, 2008.

Johnston, Dafydd (ed. and trans.). *Canu Maswedd yr Oesedd Canol: Medieval Welsh Erotic Poetry*. Pen-y-bont ar Ogwr, 1998.

Johnston, Dafydd. 'Erotica and Satire in Medieval Welsh Poetry'. In Jan M. Ziolkowski (ed.), *Obscenity: Social Control and Artistic Creations in the European Middle Ages*. Leiden, 1998. 60–72.

Johnston, Dafydd. '"Ceidwaid yr hen iaith?" Beirdd yr Uchelwyr a'r Iaith Saesneg'. *Y Traethodydd*, 155 (2000), 16–24.

Jones, E. A. '"Lo Lordes Myne, Here is a Fit!": The Structure of Chaucer's *Sir Thopas*'. *The Review of English Studies*, 51 (2000), 248–52.

Jordan, Robert M. *Chaucer's Poetics and the Modern Reader*. Berkeley, CA, 1987.

Joseph of Exeter. In Ludwig Gompf (ed.), *Joseph Iscanus: Werke und Briefe*. Leiden, 1970.

Josephus. In Gaalya Cornfeld (ed. and trans.), *The Jewish War*. Grand Rapids, MI, 1982.

Jost, Jean E. with Hoyt Greeson (eds). The Pricke of Conscience: *An Annotated Edition of the Southern Recension*. Jefferson, NC, 2020.

Juster, A. M. (ed. and trans.). *The Elegies of Maximianus*. Philadelphia, PA, 2018.

Justice, Steven. 'The Genres of Piers Plowman'. *Viator*, 19 (1988), 291–306.

Kabir, Ananya Jahanara. 'Forging an Oral Style: *Havelok* and the Fiction of Orality?'. *Studies in Philology*, 98 (2001), 18–48.

Kaeuper, Richard. *Chivalry and Violence in Medieval Europe*. Oxford, 1999.

Kaeuper, Richard. 'William Shareshull'. *Oxford Dictionary of National Biography*. Oxford, 2019. oxforddnb.com.

Kalén, Herbert. *A Middle English Metrical Paraphrase of the Old Testament*. Göteborg, 1923.

Kamath, Stephanie A. Viereck Gibbs. 'The French Context'. In Ian Johnson (ed.), *Geoffrey Chaucer in Context*. Cambridge, 2019. 117–25.

Kane, George. *Middle English Literature: A Critical Study of the Romances, the Religious Lyrics*, Piers Plowman. London, 1970.

Kane, George. *Chaucer and Langland: Historical and Textual Approaches*. London, 1989.

Kay, Christian, Jane Roberts, Michael Samuels, and Irené Wotherspoon (eds). *The Historical Thesaurus of the Oxford English Dictionary*. 2 vols. Oxford, 2009. http://historicalthesaurus.arts.gla.ac.uk.

Kean, P. M. *Chaucer and the Making of English Poetry*. 2nd edn. London, 1982.

Keiser, Rolf. *Zur Geographie des mittelenglischen Wortschatzes*. Palaestra 205. Leipzig, 1937.

Keller, Wolfram R. *Selves and Nations: The Troy Story from Sicily to England in the Middle Ages*. Heidelberg, 2008.

Kellogg, Eleanor H. 'Bishop Brunton and the Fable of the Rats'. *PMLA*, 50 (1935), 57–68.

Kelly, Douglas. *The Arts of Poetry and Prose*. Typologie des Sources du Moyen Âge Occidental 59. Turnhout, 1991.

Kempe, Dorothy. 'A Middle English Tale of Troy'. *Englische Studien*, 29 (1901), 1–26.

Kendrick, Laura. 'Deschamps' Ballade Praising Chaucer and Its Impact'. *Cahiers de Recherches Médiévales et Humanistes*, 29 (2015), 215–33.

Kennedy, Edward Donald. *Chronicles and Other Historical Writing*. Volume 8 of Albert E. Hartung (ed.), *A Manual of the Writings in Middle English 1050–1500*. 11 vols. New Haven, CT, 1989.

Kennedy, Ruth. '"A Bird in Bishopswood": Some Newly Discovered Lines of Alliterative Verse from the Late Fourteenth Century'. In Myra Stokes and T. L. Burton (eds), *Medieval Literature and Antiquities: Studies in Honour of Basil Cottle*. Cambridge, 1987. 71–87.

Ker, N. R. (ed.). *The Owl and the Nightingale: Reproduced in Facsimile from the Surviving Manuscripts, Jesus College Oxford 29 and British Museum Cotton Caligula A.ix*. EETS, o.s. 251. London, 1963, 1993.

Ker, N. R. Ker (intro.). *Facsimile of British Museum MS. Harley 2253*. EETS, o.s. 255. London, 1965.

Kerby-Fulton, Kathryn. *Books Under Suspicion: Censorship and Tolerance of Revelatory Writing in Late Medieval England*. Notre Dame, IN, 2006.

King Horn. In Rosamund Allen (ed.), *King Horn*. New York, 1984.

King Horn. In Joseph Hall (ed.), *King Horn: A Middle-English Romance*. Oxford, 1901.

King Horn. In Ronald B. Herzman, Graham Drake, and Eve Salisbury (eds), *Four Romances of England: King Horn, Havelok the Dane, Bevis of Hampton, Athelston*. Kalamazoo, MI, 1999.

Klenke, M. Amlia (ed. and trans.). *Three Saints' Lives by Nicholas Bozon*. New York, 1947.

Klinck, Anne L. 'Editing *Cursor Mundi*: Stemmata and the "Open" Text'. In Siân Echard and Stephen Partridge (eds), *The Book Unbound: Editing and Reading Medieval Manuscripts and Texts*. Toronto, 2004. 3–13.

Klinck, Anne L. 'Singing a Song of Sorrow: Tropes of Lament'. In Jane Tolmie and M. Jane Toswell (eds), *Laments for the Lost in Medieval Literature*. Turnhout, 2010. 1–20.

Knight, Stephen. *Rymyng Craftily: Meaning in Chaucer's Poetry*. Sydney, 1973.

Knight, Stephen. 'Chaucer's British Rival'. *Leeds Studies in English*, n.s. 20 (1989), 87–98.

Knight, Stephen. '"Love's Altar Is the Forest Glade": Chaucer in the Light of Dafydd ap Gwilym'. *Nottingham Medieval Studies*, 63 (1999), 172–88.

Kobayashi, Yoshiko. 'Letters of Old Age: The Advocacy of Peace in the Works of John Gower and Philippe de Mézières'. In Russell A. Peck and R. F. Yeager (eds), *John Gower: Others and the Self*. Cambridge, 2017. 204–22.

Kölbing, Eugen (ed.). *The Romance of Sir Beues of Hamtoun*. EETS, e.s. 46, 48, 65. London, 1885–94.

Kolve, V. A. *Chaucer and the Imagery of Narrative: The First Five 'Canterbury Tales'*. London, 1984.

Kolve, V. A. *Telling Images: Chaucer and the Imagery of Narrative II*. Stanford, CA, 2009.

Kooper, Erik. 'Laʒamon's Prosody: Caligula and Otho—Metres Apart'. In Rosamund Allen, Jane Roberts, and Carole Weinberg (eds), *Laʒamon's Brut: Approaches and Explorations*. Amsterdam, 2013. 419–41.

Kraebal, Andrew. *Biblical Commentary and Translation in Later Medieval England: Experiments in Interpretation*. Cambridge, 2019.

Krapp, George Philip (ed.). *The Vercelli Book*. New York, 1932.

Kratins, Ojars. 'The Middle English *Amis and Amiloun*: Chivalric Romance or Secular Hagiography?' *PMLA*, 81 (1966), 347–54.

Krueger, Roberta L. (ed.). *The Cambridge Companion to Medieval Romance*. Cambridge, 2000.

Kuczynski, Michael P. 'Gower's Virgil'. In R. F. Yeager (ed.), *John Gower: Essays at the Millennium*. Kalamazoo, MI, 2007. 163–87.

Kyng Alisaunder. In G. V. Smithers (ed.), *Kyng Alisaunder*. 2 vols. EETS, o.s. 227, 237. London, 1952, 1957.

La Destruction de Rome and Fierabras. In Louis Brandin (ed.), '*La Destruction de Rome* et *Fierabras*, MS Egerton 3028, Musée Britannique'. *Romania*, 64 (1938), 18–100.

Laforte, Conrad. *Survivances médiévales dans la chanson folklorique: poétique de la chanson folk-lorique*. Quebec, 1983.

Laing, Margaret. 'Notes on Oxford, Bodleian Library, MS Digby 86, *The Names of a Hare in English*'. *Medium Ævum*, 67 (1998), 201–11.

Laing, Margaret. *A Linguistic Atlas of Early Middle English, 1150–1325*, version 3.2 (introduction by Margaret Laing and Roger Lass, webscripts by Keith Williamson, Vasilis Karaiskos, and Sherrylyn Branchaw). Edinburgh, 2013–. http://www.lel.ed.ac.uk/ihd/laeme2/laeme2.html.

Lamberts, J. J. 'The "Proloug" to *Cursor Mundi*, VV 1–270'. *Neophilologus*, 68 (1984), 292–316.

Langland, William. In A. V. C. Schmidt (ed.), *William Langland: The Vision of* Piers Plowman: *A Critical Edition of the B-Text Based on Trinity College Cambridge MS B.15.17*. 2nd edn. London, 1995.

Langland, William. In George Russell and George Kane (eds), Piers Plowman: *The C Version*. London, 1997.

Langland, William. In Derek Pearsall (ed.), Piers Plowman: *A New Annotated Text*. Exeter, 2008.

Langland, William. In A. V. C. Schmidt. Piers Plowman: *A Parallel-Text Edition of the A, B, C and Z Versions*. 2 vols. 2nd edn. Kalamazoo, MI, 2011.

Larson, Wendy R. 'Who Is the Master of This Narrative? Maternal Patronage of the Cult of St. Margaret'. In Mary C. Erler and Maryanne Kowaleski (eds), *Gendering the Master Narrative: Women and Power in the Middle Ages*. Ithaca, NY, 2003. 94–104.

Laskaya, Anne. 'Graftings, Reweavings and Interpretation: The Auchinleck Middle English Breton Lays in Manuscript and Edition'. *Etudes Epistémè*, 25 (Spring 2014), http://journals.openedition.org/episteme/203.

Laskaya, Anne and Eve Salisbury (eds). *The Middle English Breton Lays*. Kalamazoo, MI, 1995.

Lass, Roger. 'Phonology and Morphology'. In Norman Blake (ed.), *The Cambridge History of the English Language* II, *1066–1476*. 6 vols. Cambridge, 1992. 2: 23–155.

Laud Troy Book. In J. Ernst Wülfing (ed.), *The Laud Troy Book*. 2 vols. EETS, o.s. 121–2. London, 1902, 1903.

Laurent, Frère. In Édith Brayer and Anne-Françoise Leurquin-Labie (eds), *La* Somme le roi *par Frère Laurent*. SATF. Abbeville, 2008.

Lawrence of Durham. In James Raine (ed.), *Dialogi Laurentii Dunelmensis Monachi ac Prioris*. Edinburgh, 1880.

Lawton, David. 'Dullness and the Fifteenth Century'. *ELH*, 54 (1987), 761–99.

Lawton, David A. 'The *Destruction of Troy* as Translation from Latin Prose: Aspects of Form and Style'. *Studia Neophilologica*, 52 (1980), 259–70.

Lawton, David A. 'The Middle English Alliterative *Alexander A* and *C*: Form and Style in Translation from Latin Prose'. *Studia Neophilologica*, 53 (1981), 259–68.

Lawton, David A. 'Voice after Arundel'. In Vincent Gillespie and Kantik Ghosh (eds), *After Arundel: Religious Writing in Fifteenth-Century England*. Turnhout, 2011. 133–51.

Lawton, David A. *Voice in Later Medieval English Literature: Public Interiorities*. Oxford, 2017.

Laȝamon. *Brut*. In Sir Frederic Madden (ed.), *Laȝamons Brut, or Chronicle of England; A Poetical Semi-Saxon Paraphrase of The Brut of Wace*. 3 vols. London, 1847.

Laȝamon. *Brut*. In G. L. Brook and R. F. Leslie (eds), *Brut: Edited from British Museum MS. Cotton Caligula A. ix and British Museum MS. Cotton Otho C. XXIII*. 2 vols. Oxford, 1963–78.

Laȝamon. *Brut*. In Rosamund Allen (trans.), *Lawman: Brut*. London, 1992.

Laȝamon. *Brut*. In W. R. J. Barron and S. C. Weinberg (ed. and trans.), *Brut, or Hystoria Brutonum*. Harlow, 1995.

Le Saux, Françoise. 'Geoffrey of Monmouth's *De gestis Britonum* and Twelfth-Century Romance'. In Georgia Henley and Joshua Byron Smith (eds), *A Companion to Geoffrey of Monmouth*. Leiden, 2020. 235–56.

Legge, M. Dominica. 'La précocité de la littérature anglo-normande'. *Cahiers de Civilisation Médiévale*, 8 (1965), 327–49.

Lerer, Seth. 'Artifice and Artistry in *Sir Orfeo*'. *Speculum*, 60 (1985), 92–109.

Lerer, Seth. *Chaucer and His Readers: Imagining the Author in Late-Medieval England*. Princeton, NJ, 1993.

Lerer, Seth. 'Old English and Its Afterlife'. In David Wallace (ed.), *The Cambridge History of Medieval English Literature*. Cambridge, 1999. 7–34.

Lerer, Seth. 'Medieval English Literature and the Idea of the Anthology'. *PMLA*, 118 (2003), 1251–67.

Lewis, Charlton T. and Charles Short. *A Latin Dictionary*. Perseus Digital Library. https://www.perseus.tufts.edu/hopper.

Lewis, C. S. *The Allegory of Love: A Study in the Medieval Tradition*. Oxford, 1936.

Lewis, Robert E. 'The Relationship of the Vernon and Simeon Texts of the *Pricke of Conscience*'. In Michael Benskin and M. L. Samuels (eds), *So meny people longages and tonges: Philological Essays in Scots and Mediaeval English Presented to Angus McIntosh*. Edinburgh, 1981. 251–64.

Lewis, Robert E. and Angus McIntosh. *A Descriptive Guide to the Manuscripts of the* Prick of Conscience. Oxford, 1982.

Lewis, Saunders, 'Dafydd ap Gwilym'. In A. R. Jones and Gwyn Thomas (eds), *Presenting Saunders Lewis*. Cardiff, 1973. 159–63.

Livingston, Michael (ed.). *The Battle of Brunanburh: A Casebook*. Exeter, 2011.

Lloyd-Morgan, Ceridwen and Erich Poppe. 'The First Adaptations from French: History and Context of a Debate'. In Ceridwen Lloyd-Morgan and Erich Poppe (eds), *Arthur in the Celtic Languages*. 110–16.

Lombard, Peter. *Sententiarum Libri Quattor*. In *Latina Database*, based on J. P. Migne (ed.), *Patrologiae Cursus Completus*. 221 vols. Paris, 1841–65.

Loomis, Laura Hibbard. 'The Auchinleck Manuscript and a Possible London Bookshop of 1330–1340'. *PMLA*, 57 (1942), 595–627.

Lote, Georges. *Histoire du vers français*. 9 vols. Aix-en-Provence, 1951–96.

Louis, Cameron. 'Authority in Middle English Proverb Literature'. *Florilegium*, 15 (1998), 85–123.

Louis, Cameron. 'Manuscript Contexts of Middle English Proverb Literature'. *Mediaeval Studies*, 60 (1998), 219–38.

Love, Harold. *Scribal Publication in Seventeenth-Century England*. Oxford, 1993.

Lovelich, Henry. In F. J. Furnivall and Dorothy Kempe (eds), *The History of the Holy Grail by Herry Lovelich*. 5 vols. EETS, e.s. 20, 24, 28, 30, 95. London, 1874–1905.

Luft, Diana. 'Genre and Diction in the Poetry of Dafydd ap Gwilym: The Revelation of Cultural Tension'. *Proceedings of the Harvard Celtic Colloquium*, 18/19 (1998/1999), 278–97.

Lumiansky, R. M. 'Legends of Troy'. In J. Burke Severs (ed.), *A Manual of the Writings in Middle English 1050–1500*, 11 vols. New Haven, CT, 1967. 1: 114–18, 274–7.

Luria, Maxwell S. and Richard L. Hoffman (eds). *Middle English Lyrics*. New York, 1974.

Lusignan, Serge. *La Langue des rois au Moyen Âge. Le français en France et en Angleterre*. Paris, 2004.

Lybeaus Desconus. In Eve Salisbury and James Weldon (eds), *Lybeaus Desconus*. Kalamazoo, MI, 2013.

Lydgate, John. *Pilgrimage of the Life of Man*. In F. J. Furnivall (ed.), *The Pilgrimage of the Life of Man*. 3 vols. EETS, e.s. 77, 83, 92. London, 1899–1904.

Lydgate, John. *Reson and Sensualyte*. In E. Sieper (ed.), *Lydgate's Reson and Sensualyte*. 2 vols. EETS, e.s. 84, 89. London, 1901–3.

Lydgate, John. *Troy Book*. In Henry Bergen (ed.), *John Lydgate: Troy Book*. 4 vols. EETS, e.s. 97, 103, 106, 126. London, 1906–35.

Lydgate, John. In Henry Noble MacCracken (ed.), *John Lydgate: The Minor Poems, Vol. I: Religious Poems*. EETS, e.s. 107. Oxford, 1911.

Lydgate, John. *Fall of Princes*. In Henry Bergen (ed.), *Lydgate's Fall of Princes*. 4 vols. EETS, e.s. 121–4. London, 1924–7.

Lydgate, John. In Henry Noble MacCracken (ed.), *John Lydgate: The Minor Poems, Vol. II: Secular Poems*. EETS, o.s. 192. Oxford, 1934.

Lydgate, John. *Temple of Glass*. In Julia Boffey (ed.), *Fifteenth-Century English Dream Visions*. Oxford, 2003. 15–89.

Lynch, Kathryn L. *The High Medieval Dream Vision: Poetry, Philosophy, and Literary Form*. Palo Alto, CA, 1988.

Machan, Tim William. *English in the Middle Ages*. Oxford, 2003.

Machaut, Guillaume de. *Livre de la fonteinne amourese*. In R. Barton Palmer (ed. and trans.), *The Fountain of Love (La Fonteinne Amoureuse) and Two Other Love Vision Poems*. New York, 1993. 89–239.

Macrobius. In James Willis (ed.), *Commentarii in Somnium Scipionis*. Vol. 2 of *Macrobius: Opera*. 2 vols. Leipzig, 1963.

Maddicott, J. R. 'Responses to the Threat of Invasion, 1085'. *English Historical Review*, 122 (2007), 986–97.

Maddicott, J. R. 'Politics and the People in Thirteenth-Century England'. *Thirteenth-Century Studies*, 14 (2013), 1–13.

Malone, Patricia T. '"What saist mon?": Dialogism and Disdain in Tudur Penllyn's "Conversation between a Welshman and an Englishwoman"'. *Studia Celtica*, 46 (2012), 123–36.

Malory, Sir Thomas. In Eugene Vinaver (ed.), *The Works of Sir Thomas Malory*, rev. P. J. C. Field. 3 vols. Oxford, 1990.

Manly, J. M. 'Chaucer and the Rhetoricians'. *Proceedings of the British Academy*, 12 (1926), 95–113.

Mann, Jill. *Chaucer and Medieval Estates Satire*. Cambridge, 1973.

Mann, Jill. 'The *Speculum Stultorum* and the *Nun's Priest's Tale*'. *The Chaucer Review*, 9 (1975), 262–82.

Mann, Jill. 'Eating and Drinking in *Piers Plowman*'. *Essays and Studies*, 32 (1979), 26–43.

Mann, Jill. *Langland and Allegory*. Morton W. Bloomfield Lectures on Medieval Literature 2. Kalamazoo, MI, 1992.

Mann, Jill. 'Chaucer's Meter and the Myth of the Ellesmere Editor of the *Canterbury Tales*'. *Studies in the Age of Chaucer*, 23 (2001), 71–107.

Mann, Jill. *From Aesop to Reynard: Beast Literature in Medieval Britain*. Oxford, 2009.

Mann, Jill. 'Allegory and *Piers Plowman*'. In Andrew Cole and Andrew Galloway (eds), *Cambridge Companion to* Piers Plowman. Cambridge, 2014. 65–82.

Mannyng, Robert. In Idelle Sullens (ed.), *Robert Mannyng: Handlyng Synne*. Binghamton, NY, 1983.

Mannyng, Robert. In Idelle Sullens (ed.), *Robert Mannyng: The Chronicle*. Binghamton, NY, 1996.

Map, Walter. In M. R. James (ed.), *De nugis curialium*. Oxford, 1914.

Map, Walter. In M. R. James (ed. and trans.), *De nugis curialium; Courters' Trifles*, rev. C. L. N. Brooke and R. A. B. Mynors. Oxford, 1983.

Marie de France. In Jean Rychner (ed.), *Les lais de Marie de France*. Paris, 1983.

Marotti, Arthur. *Manuscript, Print, and the English Renaissance Lyric*. Ithaca, NY, 1995.

Marvin, Julia. *The Oldest Anglo-Norman Prose Brut Chronicle: An Edition and Translation*. Woodbridge, 2006.

Masi, Michael. *Boethian Number Theory*. Amsterdam, 1983.

Masui, M. *The Structure of Chaucer's Rhyme Words*. Tokyo, 1964.

Matheson, Lister M. *The Prose Brut: The Development of a Middle English Chronicle*. Tempe, AZ, 1998.

Matlock, Wendy. 'Law and Violence in The Owl and the Nightingale'. *Journal of English and Germanic Philology*, 109 (2010), 446–67.

Matonis, A. T. E. 'An Investigation of Celtic Influences on MS Harley 2253'. *Modern Philology*, 70 (1972), 91–103.

Matsumoto, Hiroyuki (ed.). *The Destruction of Troy: A Critical Edition; Hunterian MS v.2.8 in Glasgow University Library*. Okayama, 2010.

Matthew of Vendôme. In Aubrey E. Galyon (trans.), *The Art of Versification*. Ames, IA, 1980.

Matthew of Vendôme. *Ars versificatoria*. In Franco Munari (ed.), *Opera*, vol. 3. Rome, 1988.

McCabe, T. Matthew N. *Gower's Vulgar Tongue: Ovid, Lay Religion, and English Poetry in the Confessio Amantis*. Cambridge, 2011.

McCann, Daniel. 'Blood and Chocolate: Affective Layering in *Swete Ihesu, now wil I synge*'. In Julia Boffey and Christiana Whitehead (eds), *Middle English Lyrics: New Readings of Short Poems*. Cambridge, 2018. 45–56.

McColloch, Florence. *Medieval Latin and French Bestiaries*. Chapel Hill, NC, 1960.

McDonald, Nicola. 'The Seege of Troye: "ffor wham was wakened al this wo"'. In Ad Putter and Jane Gilbert (eds), *The Spirit of Medieval English Popular Romance*. Harlow, 2000. 181–99.

McDonald, Nicola (ed.). *Pulp Fictions of Medieval England: Essays in Popular Romance*. Manchester, 2004.

McGlone, Matthew S. and Jessica Tofighbakhsh. 'Birds of a Feather Flock Conjointly(?): Rhyme as Reason in Aphorisms'. *Psychological Science*, 11 (2000), 424–8.

McIntosh, Angus. 'The Textual Transmission of the Alliterative *Morte Arthure*'. In Norman Davis and C. L. Wrenn (eds), *English and Medieval Studies Presented to J. R. R. Tolkien*. London, 1962. 231–40.

McIntosh, Angus. 'The Language of the Extant Versions of *Havelok the Dane*'. *Medium Ævum*, 45 (1976), 36–49.

McIntosh, Angus. 'Two Unnoticed Interpolations in Four Manuscripts of the *Prick of Conscience*'. *Neuphilologische Mitteilungen*, 77 (1976), 63–78.

McIntosh, Angus. 'A Supplementary Note to the Middle English Poem *The Four Foes of Mankind*'. *Neuphilologische Mitteilungen*, 94 (1993), 79–81.

McIntosh, Angus and M. L. Samuels, 'Prologemona to a Study of Medieval Anglo-Irish', *Medium Ævum*, 37 (1968), 1–11.

McIntosh, Angus, M. L. Samuels, and Michael Benskin (eds). *A Linguistic Atlas of Late Medieval English*. 4 vols. Aberdeen, 1986. www.lel.ed.ac.uk/ihd/elalme/elalme_frames.html.

McIntosh, Angus, M. L. Samuels, and Michael Benskin. *An Electronic Version of* A Linguistic Atlas of Late Mediaeval English, with the assistance of Margaret Laing and Keith Williamson, webscripts by Vasilis Karaiskos and Keith Williamson. Edinburgh, 2013. http://www.lel.ed.ac.uk/ihd/elalme/elalme.html.

McNelis III, James I. 'Laȝamon as Auctor'. In Françoise Le Saux (ed.), *The Text and Tradition of Laȝamon's Brut*. Cambridge, 1994. 253–72.

McNiven, Peter. 'Scrope, Richard (c.1350–1405)'. *Oxford Dictionary of National Biography*. Oxford, 2004. oxforddnb.com.

McSparran, Frances. 'The Language of the English Poems: The Harley Scribe and His Exemplars'. In Susanna Fein (ed.), *Studies in the Harley Manuscript: The Scribes, Contents, and Social Contexts of British Library MS Harley 2253*. Kalamazoo, MI, 2000. 391–426.

MED: Sherman M. Kuhn, Hans Kurath, and Robert E. Lewis (eds). *Middle English Dictionary*. 14 vols. Ann Arbor, MI, 1956–. quod.lib.umich.edu/m/middle-english-dictionary.

Mehl, Dieter. *The Middle English Romances of the Thirteenth and Fourteenth Centuries*. London, 1968.

Meyer, Robert (ed.). *Biblia Sacra iuxta vulgatam versionem*. Stuttgart, 1969.

Meyer-Lee, Robert J. *Poets and Power from Chaucer to Wyatt*. Cambridge, 2007.

Middleton, Anne. 'The Idea of Public Poetry in the Reign of Richard II'. *Speculum*, 53 (1978), 94–114.

Middleton, Anne. 'Chaucer's "New Men" and the Good of Literature in the *Canterbury Tales*'. In Edward Said (ed.), *Literature and Society*. English Institute Essays 1978. Baltimore, MD, 1980. 15–56.

Middleton, Anne. 'The Audience and Public of *Piers Plowman*'. In David A. Lawton (ed.), *Middle English Alliterative Poetry and Its Literary Background*. Woodbridge, 1982. 101–23, 147–54.

Middleton, Anne. 'Narration and the Invention of Experience: Episodic Form in *Piers Plowman*'. In Larry Benson and Siegfried Wenzel (eds), *The Wisdom of Poetry: Essays in Honor of Morton Bloomfield*. Kalamazoo, MI, 1982. 91–122.

Middleton, Anne. 'William Langland's "Kynde Name": Authorial Signature and Social Identity in Late Fourteenth-Century England'. In Lee Patterson (ed.), *Literary Practice and Social Change in Britain, 1380–1530*. Berkeley, CA, 1990. 15–82.

Middleton, Anne. 'Acts of Vagrancy: The C-Version "Autobiography" and the Statute of 1388'. In Steven Justice and Kathryn Kerby-Fulton (eds), *Written Work: Langland, Labor, and Authorship*. Philadelphia, PA, 1997. 208–317.

Middleton, Anne. '*Piers Plowman*, the Monsters and the Critics: Some Embarrassments of Literary History' [1998]. In Daniel Donoghue, James Simpson, and Nicholas Watson (eds), *The Morton W. Bloomfield Lectures 1989–2005*. Kalamazoo, MI, 2010. 94–115.

Miller, D. Gary. *External Influences on English, from its Beginnings to the Renaissance*. Oxford, 2012.

Miller, Joseph M., Michael H. Prosser, and Thomas W. Benson (eds), *Readings in Medieval Rhetoric*. Bloomington, IN, 1973.

Millet, Bella. 'The *Ancrene Wisse* Group'. In A. S. G. Edwards (ed.), *A Companion to Middle English Prose*. Woodbridge, 2004. 1–17.

Millet, Bella and Jocelyn Wogan-Browne (eds). *Medieval English Prose for Women*. Oxford, 1990.

Mills, Maldwyn (ed.). *Six Middle English Romances*. London, 1973.

Mills, Maldwyn (ed.). *Ywain and Gawain, Sir Percyvell of Gales, The Anturs of Arther*. London, 1992.

Minkova, Donka. 'Prosody-Meter Correspondences in Old English and *Poema Morale*'. In Leonard Neidorf, Rafael J. Pascual, and Thomas A. Shippey (eds), *Essays in Old English Philology: Studies in Honour of R. D. Fulk*. Cambridge, 2016. 122–43.

Minnis, Alastair J. 'Langland's Ymaginatyf and Late-Medieval Theories of Imagination'. *Comparative Criticism: A Yearbook*, 3 (1981), 71–103.

Minnis, Alastair J. 'De Vulgari Auctoritate: Chaucer, Gower and the Men of Great Authority'. In R. F. Yeager (ed.), *Chaucer and Gower: Difference, Mutuality, Exchange*. Victoria, 1991. 36–74.

Minnis, Alastair J. *Medieval Theory of Authorship: Scholastic Literary Attitudes in the Later Middle Ages*. 2nd edn. Philadelphia, PA, 2010.

Minnis, Alastair J. and Ian Johnson (eds). *The Cambridge History of Literary Criticism, Vol. 2, The Middle Ages*. Cambridge, 2005.

Minnis, Alastair J. and A. B. Scott, with the assistance of David Wallace, (eds), *Medieval Literary Theory and Criticism, c. 1100–c. 1375*. Oxford, 1988, 1991.

Minot, Laurence. In Richard H. Osberg (ed.), *The Poems of Laurence Minot, 1333–1352*. Kalamazoo, MI, 1996.

Mirk, John. *Instructions for Parish Priests*. In Gillis Kristensson (ed.), *John Mirk's Instructions for Parish Priests*. Lund Studies in English, 49. Lund, 1974.

Moffat, Douglas (ed.). *The Soul's Address to the Body: The Worcester Fragments*. East Lansing, MI, 1987.

Moffat, Douglas (ed.). *The Old English Soul and Body*. Woodbridge, 1990.

Mooney, Linne R. 'Lydgate's "Kings of England" and Another Verse Chronicle of the Kings'. *Viator*, 20 (1989), 255–89.

Mooney, Linne R. 'Chaucer's Scribe'. *Speculum*, 81 (2006), 97–138.

Mooney, Linne R. and Estelle Stubbs. *Scribes and the City: London Guildhall Clerks and the Dissemination of Middle English Literature, 1375–1425*. Woodbridge, 2013.

Moore, Arthur K. *The Secular Lyric in Middle English*. Lexington, KY, 1951.

Moore, Deborah L. *Medieval Anglo-Irish Troubles: A Cultural Study of BL MS Harley 913*. Turnhout, 2016.

Morawski, J. 'Les recueils d'anciens proverbes francais analysés et classés'. *Romania*, 48 (1922), 481–558.

Morey, James H. 'Peter Comestor, Biblical Paraphrase, and the Medieval Popular Bible'. *Speculum*, 68 (1993), 6–35.

Morey, James H. *A Guide to Middle English Biblical Literature*. Urbana, IL, 2000.

Morey, James H. 'Middle English Didactic Literature'. In David Johnson and Elaine Treharne (eds), *Readings in Medieval Texts: Interpreting Old and Middle English Literature*. Oxford, 2005. 183–97.

Morris, Richard (ed.). *Old English Homilies of the Twelfth Century from the Unique MS B. 14. 52 in the Library of Trinity College, Cambridge*. EETS, o.s. 53. London, 1873.

Morris, Richard (ed.). *Cursor Mundi (The Cursur o the World): A Northumbrian Poem of the XIVth Century in Four Versions*. 7 vols. EETS, o.s. 57, 59, 62, 66, 68, 99, 101. London, 1874–93.

Morrison, Stephen. 'Sources for the *Ormulum*: A Re-examination'. *Neuphilologische Mitteilungen*, 84 (1983), 419–36.

Morrison, Stephen. 'A Reminiscence of Wulfstan in the Twelfth Century'. *Neuphilologische Mitteilungen*, 96 (1995), 229–34.

Morton, James (ed.). *The Legend of St. Katherine of Alexandria*. London, 1841.

Moser, Thomas C., Jr. 'Love and Disorder: A Fifteenth-Century Definition of Love and Some Literary Antecedents'. In James M. Dean and Christian K. Zacher (eds), *The Idea of Medieval Literature: New Essays on Chaucer and Medieval Culture in Honor of Donald R. Howard*. Newark, DE, 1992. 243–64.

Mosser, Daniel W. *A Digital Catalogue of the Pre-1500 Manuscripts and Incunables of the Canterbury Tales*. 2nd edn. https://www.mossercatalogue.net.

Mueller, Alex. *Translating Troy: Provincial Politics in Alliterative Romance*. Columbus, OH, 2013.

Müller, Max. In A. Smythe Palmer (ed.), *Comparative Mythology: An Essay*. London, 1909.

Murdoch, Brian. *Adam's Grace: Fall and Redemption in Medieval Literature*. Cambridge, 2000.

Murdoch, Brian and J. A. Tasioulas. *The Apocryphal Lives of Adam and Eve*. Exeter, 2002.

Murray, Hilda M. R. (ed.). *The Middle English Poem, Erthe upon Erthe, Printed from Twenty-Four Manuscripts*. EETS, o.s. 141. London, 1911; rpt. Oxford, 1964.

Muscatine, Charles. *Chaucer and the French Tradition: A Study in Style and Meaning*. Berkeley, CA, 1957.

Muscatine, Charles. *The Old French Fabliaux*. New Haven, CT, 1986.

Myklebust, Nicolas. 'The Problem of John Metham's Prosody'. In Ad Putter and Judith A. Jefferson (eds), *The Transmission of Medieval Romance: Metres, Manuscripts and Early Prints*. Cambridge, 2018. 149–69.

Nall, Catherine. *Reading and War in Fifteenth-Century England, from Lydgate to Malory*. Cambridge, 2012.

Napier, Arthur S. *Iacob and Iosep: A Middle English Poem of the Thirteenth Century*. Oxford, 1916.

Nelson, Ingrid. *Lyric Tactics: Poetry, Genre, and Practice in Later Medieval England*. Philadelphia, PA, 2017.

Nelson, Marie and Richard Thomson. 'The Fabliau'. In Laura Cooner Lambdin and Robert Thomas Lambdin (ed.), *A Companion to Old and Middle English Literature*. Westport, CT, 2002. 255–76.

Nevanlinna, Saara. *The Northern Homily Cycle: The Expanded Version in MSS Harley 4196 and Cotton Tiberius E vii*. Helsinki, 1972.

Newhauser, Richard. 'Historicity and Complaint in *Song of the Husbandman*'. In Susanna Fein (ed.), *Studies in the Harley Manuscript: The Scribes, Contents, and Social Contexts of British Library MS Harley 2253*. Kalamazoo, MI, 2000. 203–17.

Newman, Barbara. 'The Artifice of Eternity: Speaking of Heaven in Three Medieval Poems'. In Ad Putter and Carolyn Muessig (eds), *Envisaging Heaven in the Middle Ages*. London, 2007. 185–207.

Ng, Su Fang (ed.). *Alexander the Great from Britain to South-East Asia: Peripheral Empires in the Global Renaissance*. Oxford, 2019.

Nicholson, Peter. *Love and Ethics in Gower's* Confessio Amantis. Ann Arbor, MI, 2005.

Nicholson, Peter. 'Writing the *Cinkante Balades*'. In Russell A. Peck and R. F. Yeager (eds), *John Gower: Others and the Self*. Cambridge, 2017. 306–28.

Nicholson, Peter. 'Gower's Ballades for Women'. In Susannnah Mary Chewning (ed.), *Studies in the Age of Gower: A Festschrift in Honour of R. F. Yeager*. Cambridge, 2020. 79–97.

Nolan, Maura. *John Lydgate and the Making of Public Culture*. Cambridge, 2005.

Nolan, Maura. 'The Poetics of Catastrophe: Ovidian Allusion in Gower's *Vox Clamantis*'. In Christopher Cannon and Maura Nolan (eds), *Medieval Latin and Middle English Literature: Essays in Honour of Jill Mann*. Cambridge, 2011. 113–33.

Nolan, Maura. 'Lydgate's Worst Poem'. In Lisa H. Cooper and Andrew Denny-Brown (eds), *Lydgate Matters: Poetry and Material Culture in the Fifteenth Century*. New York, 2013. 71–87.

Nolan, Maura. 'Performing Lydgate's Broken-Backed Metre'. In Susan F. Yager and Elise E. Morse-Gagné (eds), *Interpretation and Performance: Essays for Alan Gaylord*. Provo, UT, 2013.

Nolan, Maura. 'Sensation and the Plain Style in Gower's *Confessio Amantis*'. In Russell A. Peck and R. F. Yeager (eds), *John Gower: Others and the Self*. Cambridge, 2017. 111–40.

Norberg, Dag. *An Introduction to the Study of Medieval Latin Versification*. Washington DC, 2004.

Northern Passion. In Frances A. Foster and W. Heuser (eds), *The Northern Passion*. 3 vols. EETS, o.s. 145, 147, 183. London, 1913–30.

Nuttall, Jenni. 'The Vanishing English Virelai: French *Complainte* in English in the Fifteenth Century'. *Medium Ævum*, 85 (2016), 59–76.

Nuttall, Jenni. '"Many a Lay and Many a Thing"'. In Thomas A. Prendergast and Jessica Rosenfeld (eds), *Chaucer and the Subversion of Form*. Cambridge, 2018. 21–37.

Nyffenegger, Nicole. *Authorising History: Gestures of Authorship in Fourteenth-Century English Historiography*. Cambridge, 2013.

O'Brien, Bruce. *Reversing Babel: Translation among the English During an Age of Conquests, c. 800 to c. 1200*. Newark, DE, 2011.

ODNB: Oxford Dictionary of National Biography. Oxford, 2019. oxforddnb.com.

Odo of Cheriton. *Parabolae*. In Léopold Hervieux (ed.), *Les fabulistes latins depuis le siècle d'Auguste jusqu'à la fin du Moyen Age*. 5 vols. Paris, 1893–9. 4: 283–343.

O'Donnell, Thomas. 'Talking to the Neighbours'. In Jocelyn Wogan-Browne and Elizabeth M. Tyler (eds), *High Medieval: Literary Cultures in England*. Oxford, forthcoming.

O'Donoghue, Bernard. '"*Cuius Contrarium*": Middle English Popular Lyrics'. In Thomas G. Duncan (ed.), *A Companion to Middle English Lyric*. Cambridge, 2005. 210–26.

OED: 1st edn. James A. H. Murray, Henry Bradley, W. A. Craigie, and C. T. Onions (eds). Oxford, 1888–1928; 2nd edn. J. A. Simpson and E. S. C. Weiner (eds). Oxford, 1989; 3rd online edition in progress. oed.com.

Of Arthur and of Merlin. In O. D. Macrae-Gibson (ed.), *Of Arthur and of Merlin*. 2 vols. EETS, o.s. 268, 279. London, 1973–9.

O'Farrell-Tate, Una (ed.). *The Abridged English Metrical Brut Edited from London, British Library MS Royal 12 c. xii*. Heidelberg, 2002.

Oliver, Raymond. *Poems without Names: The English Lyric, 1200–1500*. Berkeley, CA, 1970.

Olsson, Kurt. 'The Cardinal Virtues and the Structure of Gower's *Speculum Meditantis*'. *Journal of Medieval and Renaissance Studies*, 7 (1977), 113–48.

Olsson, Kurt. *John Gower and the Structures of Conversion: A Reading of the* Confessio Amantis. Cambridge, 1992.

Orm. *Orrmulum*. In Robert Holt and R. M. White (eds), *The Ormulum*. 2 vols. Oxford, 1878.

Orm. 'The Ormulum'. In *The Digital Bodleian*. Oxford, 2011–. https://digital.bodleian.ox.ac.uk/inquire/p/2df386ab–abf6–48d3–9b30–0c6d22586b7d.

Orme, Nicholas. *English Schools in the Middle Ages*. London, 1973.

Orr, John. 'On Homonymics'. In *Studies in French Language and Mediaeval Literature Presented to Professor Mildred K. Pope by Pupils, Colleagues, and Friends*. Manchester, 1939. 253–97.

Otinel. In François Guessard and Henri Victor Michelant (eds), *Les anciens poètes de la France*. Vol. 1. Paris, 1858–70.

Owen, Charles. 'Notes on Gower's Prosody'. *Chaucer Review*, 28 (1994), 405–13.

Owl and the Nightingale. In Neil Cartlidge (ed.), *The Owl and the Nightingale*. Exeter, 2001.

Pantin, W. A. *The English Church in the Fourteenth Century*. Cambridge, 1955.

502 COMPLETE BIBLIOGRAPHY

Paris, Matthew. *Chronicles of Matthew Paris*. In Richard Vaughan (ed. and trans.), *Chronicles of Matthew Paris: Monastic Life in the Thirteenth Century*. Gloucester, 1984.

Parkes, M. B. 'On the Presumed Date and Possible Origin of the Manuscript of the "Orrmulum": Oxford, Bodleian Library, MS Junius 1'. In Eric G. Stanley and Douglas Gray (eds), *Five Hundred Years of Words and Sounds: A Festschrift for Eric Dobson*. Cambridge, 1983. 115–27; rpt. in M. B. Parkes (ed.), *Scribes, Scripts and Readers: Studies in the Communication, Presentation and Dissemination of Medieval Texts*. London, 1991. 187–200.

Parkes, M. B. *Pause and Effect: An Introduction to the History of Punctuation in the West*. Berkeley, CA, 1993.

Parkes, M. B. 'Patterns of Scribal Activity and Revisions in the Text of Early Copies of Works by John Gower'. In Richard Beadle and A. J. Piper (eds), *New Science Out of Old Books: Essays in Honour of A. I. Doyle*. London, 1995. 81–121.

Parkes, M. B. and Judith Tschann (eds). *Facsimile of Oxford, Bodleian Library, MS Digby 86*, EETS, e.s. 16. Oxford, 1996.

Parks, Ward. 'Flyting, Sounding, Debate: Three Verbal Contest Genres'. *Poetics Today*, 7 (1986), 439–58.

Parsons, Sylvia. 'A Verse Translation of Book 4 of Reginald of Canterbury's *Vita Sancti Malchi*'. In Siân Echard and Gernot Wieland (eds), *Anglo-Latin and Its Heritage: Essays in Honour of A. G. Rigg on His 64th Birthday*. Turnhout, 2001. 67–91.

Partonope of Blois. In A. Trampe Bödtker (ed.), *The Middle English Versions of Partonope of Blois*. EETS, e.s. 109. London, 1912.

Partridge, Stephen. '"The Makere of this Boke": Chaucer's Retraction and the Author as Scribe and Compiler'. In Stephen Partridge and Erik Kwakkel (eds), *Author, Reader, Book: Medieval Authorship in Theory and Practice*. Toronto, 2012. 106–53.

Pascual-Argente, Clara. 'Iberian Gower'. In Ana Sáez-Hidalgo, Brian Gastle, and R. F. Yeager (eds), *The Routledge Research Companion to John Gower*. New York, 2017. 210–21.

Patterson, Lee. *Negotiating the Past: The Historical Understanding of Medieval Literature*. Madison, WI, 1987.

Patterson, Lee. '"What Man Artow?": Authorial Self-Definition in the Tale of Sir Thopas and the Tale of Melibee'. In Lee Patterson, *Temporal Circumstances: Form and History in the Canterbury Tales*. Basingstoke, 2006. 97–128.

Payne, Robert O. *The Key of Remembrance: A Study of Chaucer's Poetics*. New Haven, CT, 1963.

Pearsall, Derek. 'The Development of Middle English Romance'. *Mediaeval Studies*, 27 (1965), 91–116.

Pearsall, Derek. *Old English and Middle English Poetry*. The Routledge History of English Poetry, vol. 1. London, 1977.

Pearsall, Derek. *The Canterbury Tales*. London, 1985.

Pearsall, Derek. 'Middle English Romance and Its Audiences'. In Mary-Jo Arn and Hanneke Wirtjes with H. Jansen (eds), *Historical and Editorial Studies in Medieval and Early Modern English for Johan Gerritsen*. Groningen, 1985. 37–48.

Pearsall, Derek (ed.). *Studies in the Vernon Manuscript*. Cambridge, 1990.

Pearsall, Derek. *John Lydgate (1371–1449): A Bio-Bibliography*. Victoria, BC, 1997.

Pearsall, Derek. 'Langland's London'. In Steven Justice and Kathryn Kerby-Fulton (eds), *Written Work: Langland, Labor, and Authorship*. Philadelphia, PA, 1997. 185–207.

Pearsall, Derek (ed.). *Chaucer to Spenser: An Anthology*. Oxford, 1998.

Pearsall, Derek. '"Crowned King": War and Peace in 1415'. In Jenny Stratford (ed.), *The Lancastrian Court*. Harlaxton Medieval Studies, 13. Donington, 2003. 163–72.

Pearsall, Derek. 'The Manuscripts and Illustrations of Gower's Works'. In Siân Echard (ed.), *A Companion to Gower*. Cambridge, 2004. 73–97.

Pearsall, Derek. 'The *Canterbury Tales* and London Club Culture'. In Ardis Butterfield (ed.), *Chaucer and the City*. Cambridge, 2006. 95–108.

Pearsall, Derek. 'The Pleasure of Popular Romance: A Prefatory Essay'. In Rhiannon Purdie and M. Cichon (eds), *Medieval Romance, Medieval Contexts*. Cambridge, 2011. 9–18.

Pearsall, Derek. 'The Auchinleck Manuscript Forty Years On'. In Susanna Fein (ed.), *The Auchinleck Manuscript: New Perspectives* (York, 2016), 11–25.

Pearsall, Derek and I. C. Cunningham. *The Auchinleck Manuscript. National Library of Scotland Advocates' MS 19.2.1.* London, 1977.

Pearsall, Derek and Linne R. Mooney. *A Descriptive Catalogue of the English Manuscripts of John Gower's* Confessio Amantis. Cambridge, 2021.

Pearsall, Derek and Elizabeth Salter. *Landscapes and Seasons of the Medieval World.* London, 1973.

Peck, Russell A. 'The Careful Hunter in *The Parlement of the Thre Ages*'. *ELH*, 39 (1972), 333–41.

Peck, Russell A. 'Public Dreams and Private Myths: Perspective in Middle English Literature'. *PMLA*, 90 (1975), 461–8.

Peck, Russell A. *Kingship and Common Profit in Gower's* Confessio Amantis. Carbondale, IL, 1978.

Peck, Russell A. 'John Gower and the Book of Daniel'. In R. F. Yeager (ed.), *John Gower: Recent Readings.* Kalamazoo, MI, 1989. 159–87.

A Penniworth of Wit. In David Laing (ed.), *A Penni Worth of Witte: Florice and Blauncheflour: and Other Pieces of Ancient English Poetry.* Edinburgh, 1857. 1–14.

Petrarca, Francesco. In Robert M. Durling (ed. and trans.), *Petrarch's Lyric Poems*, rev. edn. Cambridge, MA, 1979.

'Phillipps MS. 8336 …'. Robinson's of Pall Mall catalogue 79. London, 1950.

Phillips, Helen. 'Robert Mannyng, *Chronicle*: Prologue'. In Jocelyn Wogan-Browne, Nicholas Watson, Andrew Taylor, and Ruth Evans (eds), *The Idea of the Vernacular: An Anthology of Middle English Literary Theory 1280–1520.* University Park, PA, 1999. 19–24.

Phillips, Helen. *An Introduction to the Canterbury Tales: Reading, Fiction, Context.* Basingstoke, 2000.

Phillips, Helen. 'Auchinleck and Chaucer'. In Susanna Fein (ed.), *The Auchinleck Manuscript: New Perspectives.* York, 2016. 139–55.

Phillips, Helen and Nick Havely (eds). *Chaucer's Dream Poetry.* London, 1997.

Pickering, Oliver S. 'Newly Discovered Secular Lyrics from Late Thirteenth-Century Cheshire'. *Review of English Studies*, 43 (1992), 160–79.

Pickering, Oliver S. 'Saints' Lives'. In A. S. G. Edwards (ed.), *Companion to Middle English Prose.* Cambridge, 2004. 249–70.

Pickering, Oliver S. 'Outspoken Style in the *South English Legendary* and Robert of Gloucester'. In Heather Blurton and Jocelyn Wogan-Browne (eds), *Rethinking the South English Legendaries.* Manchester, 2011. 106–45.

Pickering, Oliver S. 'Verse to Prose or Prose to Verse? A Problematic Text of *The Nine Points Best Pleasing to God*'. In Margaret Connolly and Raluca Radulescu (eds), *Editing and Interpretation of Middle English Texts.* Turnhout, 2018. 191–210.

Pierce the Ploughman's Crede. In Helen Barr (ed.), *The* Piers Plowman *Tradition.* London, 1993. 59–98.

Pilch, Herbert. *Layamon's Brut: eine literarische Studie.* Heidelberg, 1960.

PL: J. P. Migne (ed.). *Patrologiae cursus completus, Series Latina.* 221 vols. Paris, 1844–64.

Plato. *Republic.* In Edith Hamilton and Huntington Cairns (eds), *The Collected Dialogues of Plato.* New York, 1961. 575–844.

Poema Morale. In Hans Marcus (ed.), *Das Frühmittelenglische Poema Morale.* Leipzig, 1934.

Pons-Sanz, Sara M. *The Lexical Effects of Anglo-Scandinavian Linguistic Contact on Old English.* Turnhout, 2013.

Pons-Sanz, Sara M. *The Language of Early English Literature.* Basingstoke, 2014.

Pons-Sanz, Sara M. 'Norse-Derived Terms in Orm's Lexico-Semantic Field of EMOTION'. *Journal of English and Germanic Philology*, 114 (2015), 552–86.

Pope, Nancy P. '"Erthe upon Erthe" Revisited'. *Journal of the Early Book Society*, 21 (2018), 53–95.

Poppe, Erich and Regina Reck. 'Rewriting Bevis in Wales and Ireland'. In Jennifer Fellows and Ivana Djordjević (eds), *Sir Bevis of Hampton in Literary Tradition.* Cambridge, 2008. 37–50.

Preminger, Alex and T. V. F. Brogan (gen. eds). *The New Princeton Encyclopedia of Poetry and Poetics.* Princeton, NJ, 1993.

Prestwich, Michael. *Edward I.* New Haven, CT, 1997.

504   COMPLETE BIBLIOGRAPHY

Prick of Conscience. In Ralph Hanna and Sarah Wood (eds), *Richard Morris's* Prick of Conscience: *A Corrected and Amplified Reading Text.* EETS, o.s. 342. Oxford, 2013.

Pride of Life. In David N. Klausner (ed.), *Two Moral Interludes: The Pride of Life and Wisdom.* Kalamazoo, MI, 2008.

Purdie, Rhiannon. *Anglicising Romance: Tail-Rhyme and Genre in Medieval English Literature.* Woodbridge, 2008.

Purdie, Rhiannon. 'Medieval Romance and the Generic Frictions of Barbour's *Bruce*'. In Steve Boardman and Susan Foran (eds), *Barbour's Bruce and Its Cultural Contexts: Politics, Chivalry, and Literature in Late Medieval Scotland.* Cambridge, 2015. 51–74.

Putter, Ad. *Sir Gawain and the Green Knight and French Arthurian Romance.* Oxford, 1995.

Putter, Ad. 'The Narrative Logic of *Emaré*'. In A. Putter and J. Gilbert (eds), *The Spirit of Medieval English Popular Romance.* Harlow, 2000. 157–80.

Putter, Ad. 'The Language and Metre of *Pater Noster* and *Three Dead Kings*'. *Review of English Studies,* 55 (2004), 498–526.

Putter, Ad. 'Story Line and Story Shape in *Sir Percvell of Gales* and Chrétien de Troyes' *Conte du Graal*'. In Nicola McDonald (ed.), *Pulp Fictions of Medieval England: Essays in Popular Romance.* Manchester, 2004. 171–96.

Putter, Ad. 'Arthurian Romance in Popular Tradition: *Sir Percyvell of Gales, Sir Cleges*, and *Sir Launfal*'. In Helen Fulton (ed.), *A Companion to Arthurian Literature.* Oxford, 2009. 235–51.

Putter, Ad. 'The Metres and Stanza Forms of Popular Romance'. In Raluca L. Radulescu and Cory James Rushton (eds), *A Companion to Medieval Popular Romance.* Cambridge, 2009, 111–31.

Putter, Ad. 'Middle English Romances and the Oral Tradition'. In Karl Reichl (ed.), *Medieval Oral Literature.* Berlin, 2012. 335–51.

Putter, Ad. 'A Prototype Theory of Metrical Stress: Lexical Category and Ictus in Langland, the *Gawain* Poet and Other Alliterative Poets'. In Richard Dance and Laura Wright (eds), *The Use and Development of Middle English.* Bern, 2013. 281–99.

Putter, Ad. 'Adventures in the Bob-and-Wheel Tradition: Narratives and Manuscripts'. In Nicholas Perkins (ed.), *Medieval Romance and Material Culture.* Cambridge, 2015. 147–63.

Putter, Ad. 'The Organisation of Multilingual Miscellanies: The Contrasting Fortunes of Middle English Lyrics and Romances'. In Margaret Connolly and Raluca Radulescu (eds), *Insular Books: Vernacular Manuscripts in Late Medieval Britain.* Oxford, 2015. 81–100.

Putter, Ad. 'The Linguistic Repertoire of Medieval England, 1100–1500'. In Tim William Machan (ed.), *Imagining Medieval English: Language Structures and Theories, 500–1500.* Cambridge, 2016. 126–44.

Putter, Ad. 'In Appreciation of Metrical Abnormality: Headless Lines and Initial Inversion in Chaucer'. *Critical Survey,* 29 (2017), 65–85.

Putter, Ad. 'The Singing of Middle English Romance: Stanza Forms and Contrafacta'. In Ad Putter and Judith A. Jefferson (eds), *The Transmission of Medieval Romance: Metres, MSS and Early Prints.* Cambridge, 2018. 69–90.

Putter, Ad (dir.). 'The Verse Forms of Middle English Romance'. https://gtr.ukri.org/projects?ref=AH%2FH00839X%2F1.

Putter, Ad and Jane Gilbert. 'Introduction'. In Ad Putter and Jane Gilbert (eds), *The Spirit of Medieval Popular Romance.* Harlow, 2000. 1–38.

Putter, Ad and Judith A. Jefferson (eds). *The Transmission of Medieval Romance: Metres, Manuscripts and Early Prints.* Cambridge, 2018.

Putter, Ad and Myra Stokes. 'The *Linguistic Atlas* and the Dialect of the *Gawain* Poems'. *Journal of English and Germanic Philology,* 106 (2007), 468–91.

Putter, Ad and Myra Stokes (eds). *The Works of the Gawain Poet: Sir Gawain and the Green Knight, Pearl, Cleanness, Patience.* London, 2014.

Putter, Ad, Judith Jefferson, and Myra Stokes. *Studies in the Metre of Alliterative Verse.* Oxford, 2007.

Quilligan, Maureen. *The Language of Allegory: Defining the Genre.* Ithaca, NY, 1979.

Quintilian. In Donald A. Russell (ed. and trans.), *The Orator's Education.* 4 vols. Cambridge, MA, 1920.

Ramsey, Lee C. *Chivalric Romances: Popular Literature in Medieval England*. Bloomington, IN, 1983.

Ransom, Daniel J. *Poets at Play: Irony and Parody in the Harley Lyrics*. Norman, OK, 1985.

Raskolnikov, Masha. *Body Against Soul: Gender and Sowlehele in Middle English Allegory*. Columbus, OH, 2004.

Ratkowitsch, Christine. *Descriptio picturae: Die literarische Funktion der Beschreibung von Kunstwerken in der lateinischen Grossdichtung des 12. Jahrhunderts*. Vienna, 1991.

Rauf de Boun. In Diana B. Tyson (ed.), *Le Petit Bruit*. ANTS. London, 1987.

Raymo, Robert R. 'Gower's *Vox Clamantis* and the *Speculum Stultorum*'. *Modern Language Notes*, 70 (1955), 315–20.

Reames, Sherry L (ed.). *Middle English Legends of Women Saints*. Kalamazoo, MI, 2003.

Reed, Thomas. *Middle English Debate Poetry and the Aesthetics of Irresolution*. Columbia, MO, 1990.

Reichl, Karl. *Religiöse Dichtung im englischen Hochmittelalter: Untersuchung und Edition der Handschrift B.14.39 der Trinity College in Cambridge*. Munich, 1973.

Reichl, Karl (ed.). *Medieval Oral Literature*. Berlin, 2012.

Reimer, Stephen R. (ed.). *The Works of William Herebert, OFM*. Studies and Texts 81. Toronto, 1987.

Reiss, Edmund. *The Art of the Middle English Lyric: Essays in Criticism*. Athens, GA, 1972.

Renevey, Denis. 'Anglo-Norman and Middle-English Translations and Adaptations of the Hymn *Dulcis Iesu Memoria*'. In R. Ellis and R. Tixier (eds), *The Medieval Translator 5*. Turnhout, 1996. 264–83.

Renevey, Denis. '*The Name Poured Out*: Margins, Illuminations and Miniatures as Evidence for the Practice of Devotions to the Name of Jesus in Late Medieval England'. In James Hogg (ed.), *The Mystical Tradition and the Carthusians*, vol. 130, no. 9. Salzburg, 1996. 127–47.

Renevey, Denis. 'Enclosed Desires: A Study of the Wooing Group'. In William F. Pollard and Robert Boenig (eds), *Mysticism and Spirituality in Medieval England*. Cambridge, 1997. 39–62.

Revard, Carter. '*Gilote et Johane*: An Interlude in B.L. MS. Harley 2253'. *Studies in Philology*, 79 (1982), 122–46.

Revard, Carter. 'Scribe and Provenance'. In Susanna Fein (ed.), *Studies in the Harley Manuscript: The Scribes, Contents, and Social Contexts of British Library MS Harley 2 253*. Kalamazoo, MI, 2000. 21–109.

Revard, Carter. 'Political Poems in MS Harley 2253 and the English National Crisis of 1339–41'. *Chaucer Review*, 53 (2018), 60–81.

Riccold de Monte Croce. In René Kappler (ed. and trans.), *Pérégrination en Terre Sainte et au Proche Orient: Lettres sur la chute de Saint Jean d'Acre*. Paris, 1997.

Richard Coer de Lyon. In Peter Larkin (ed.), *Richard Coer de Lyon*. Kalamazoo, MI, 2015.

Richard of Devizes. *The Chronicle of Richard of Devizes*. In Richard Howlett (ed.), *Chronicles of the Reigns of Stephen, Henry II, and Richard I*. 4 vols. London, 1884–9.

Richards, I. A. *Principles of Literary Criticism*. New York, 1924.

Richmond, Velma Bourgeois. *Laments for the Dead in Medieval Narrative*. Pittsburgh, PA, 1966.

Ricks, Christopher. 'Metamorphosis in Other Words'. In A. J. Minnis (ed.), *Gower's* Confessio Amantis: *Responses and Reassessments*. Cambridge, 1983. 25–49.

Rider, Jeff. 'Receiving Orpheus in the Middle Ages: Allegorization, Remythification and *Sir Orfeo*'. *Papers on Language and Literature*, 24 (1988), 343–66.

Rigg, A. G. 'Henry of Huntingdon's Metrical Experiments'. *The Journal of Medieval Latin*, 1 (1991), 60–72.

Rigg, A. G. *A History of Anglo-Latin Literature 1066–1422*. Cambridge, 1992.

Rigg, A. G. 'Anglo-Latin in the Ricardian Age'. In A. J. Minnis, Charlotte C. Morse, and Thorlac Turville-Petre (eds), *Essays on Ricardian Literature in Honour of J. A. Burrow*. Oxford, 1997. 121–41.

Rigg, A. G. 'Lawrence of Durham: Dialogues and Easter Poem—A Verse Translation'. *The Journal of Medieval Latin*, 7 (1997), 42–126.

Rigg, A. G. (trans.). *Joseph of Exeter: Iliad*. Toronto, 2005, https://medieval.utoronto.ca/ylias.

Robbins, Rossell Hope (ed.). *Secular Lyrics of the XIVth and XVth Centuries*. 2nd edn. Oxford, 1955.

Robbins, Rossell Hope (ed.). *Historical Poems of the XIVth and XVth Centuries*. New York, 1959.

506   COMPLETE BIBLIOGRAPHY

Robbins, Rossell Hope and John L. Cutler (eds). *Supplement to the Index of Middle English Verse*. Lexington, KY, 1965.

Roberts, Brynley F. 'Writing in Wales'. In David Wallace (ed.), *The Cambridge History of Medieval English Literature*. Cambridge, 1999. 182–207.

Roberts, Glyn. 'Wales and England: Antipathy and Sympathy 1282–1485'. *Welsh History Review*, 1 (1960–3), 375–96.

Roberts, Jane. 'A Preliminary Note on British Library, Cotton MS Caligula A. ix'. In Françoise Le Saux (ed.), *The Text and Tradition of Laȝamon's Brut*. Cambridge, 1994. 1–14.

Roberts, Jane. 'On Giving Scribe B a Name and a Clutch of London Manuscripts from *c.* 1400'. *Medium Ævum*, 80 (2011), 247–70.

Robertson, Kellie. *The Laborer's Two Bodies: Labor and the 'Work' of the Text in Medieval Britain, 1350–1500*. New York, 2006.

Robinson, Pamela R. 'A Study of Some Aspects of the Transmission of English Verse Texts in Late Medieval Manuscripts'. PhD Diss. University of Oxford, 1972.

Robinson, Pamela R. 'A "Prik of conscience cheyned": The Parish Library of St Margaret's, New Fish Street, London, 1472'. In Takami Matsuda, Richard Linenthal, and John Scahill (eds), *The Medieval Book and a Modern Collector: Essays in Honour of Toshiyuki Takamiya*. Cambridge, 2004. 209–21.

Roger of Howden. In William Stubbs (ed.), *Chronica magistri Rogeri de Houedene*. 4 vols. London, 1868–71.

Roger of Howden (unattrib.). In William Stubbs (ed.), *Gesta regis Henrici Secundi Benedicti abbatis*. 2 vols. London, 1867.

Rolle, Richard. In Hope Emily Allen (ed.), *English Writings of Richard Rolle*. Gloucester, 1988.

Root, Robert K. Rev. of J. Ernst Wülfing (ed.), *The Laud Troy Book, a Romance of about 1400 A.D. Journal of English and Germanic Philology*, 5 (1905), 367–8.

Roscow, G. H. *Syntax and Style in Chaucer's Poetry*. Cambridge, 1981.

Rosier-Catach, Irène. *La Parole Efficace: Signe, Rituel, Sacré*. Paris, 2004.

Rouse, Richard H. and Mary A. Rouse. *Preachers, Florilegia, and Sermons: Studies in the Manipulus Florum of Thomas of Ireland*. Toronto, 1979.

Rouse, Robert. *The Idea of Anglo-Saxon England in Middle English Romance*. Cambridge, 2005.

Rowlands, Eurys. 'Cynghanedd, Metre, Prosody'. In A. O. H. Jarman and Gwilym Rees Hughes (eds) and Dafydd Johnston (rev.), *A Guide to Welsh Literature 1282–c. 1550, Volume II*. Cardiff, 1997. 182–7.

Rubenstein, Jay. 'Cannibals and Crusaders'. *French Historical Studies*, 31 (2008), 525–52.

Ruelle, Pierre (ed.). *Les Dits du Clerc de Vouday*. Brussels, 1969.

Runacres, Charles. 'Art and Ethics in the "Exempla" of 'Confessio Amantis'. In A. J. Minnis (ed.), *Gower's* Confessio Amantis: *Responses and Reassessments*. Cambridge, 1983. 106–34.

Russell, Delbert W. (ed.). *Verse Saints' Lives Written in the French of England*. Tempe, AZ, 2012.

Said, Edward W. *Orientalism*. London, 1978, 1995.

Salimbene di Adam. *The Chronicle of Salimbene de Adam*. In Joseph L. Baird, Giuseppe Baglivi, and John Robert Kane (eds and trans.), *The Chronicle of Salimbene de Adam*. Binghamton, NY, 1986.

Salter, Elizabeth. Piers Plowman: *An Introduction*. Oxford, 1963.

Salter, Elizabeth, 'Nicholas Love's "Myrrour of the Blessed Lyf of Jesu Christ"'. *Analecta Cartusiana*, 10 (1974), 78–81.

Salter, Elizabeth. 'The Troilus Frontispiece'. In M. B. Parkes and Elizabeth Salter (eds), *A Facsimile of Corpus Christi College Cambridge MS 61*. Cambridge, 1978. 15–23.

Salter, Elizabeth. *Fourteenth-Century English Poetry: Contexts and Readings*. Oxford, 1983.

Salter, Elizabeth. 'Piers Plowman: An Introduction'. In Derek Pearsall and Nicolette Zeeman (eds), *English and International: Studies in the Literature, Art and Patronage of Medieval England*. Cambridge, 1988. 111–57.

Salter, Elizabeth and Derek Pearsall. 'Pictorial Illustration of Late Medieval Poetic Texts: The Role of the Frontispiece or Prefatory Picture'. In Flemming G. Andersen et al. (eds), *Medieval Iconography and Narrative: A Symposium*. Odense, 1980. 100–23.

Salter, Elizabeth, with D. Pearsall and N. Zeeman (eds). *English and International: Studies in the Literature, Art and Patronage of Medieval England*. Cambridge, 1988.

Samuels, M. L. 'Langland's Dialect'. *Medium Ævum*, 54 (1985), 232–47; rpt. in J. J. Smith (ed.), *The English of Chaucer and His Contemporaries*. Aberdeen, 1988. 70–85.

Saul, Nigel. *Richard II*. London, 1997.

Saul, Nigel. 'John Gower: Prophet or Turncoat?' In Elisabeth Dutton with John Hines and R. F. Yeager (eds), *John Gower, Trilingual Poet: Language, Translation and Tradition*. Cambridge, 2010. 85–97.

Saunders, Corinne (ed.). *A Companion to Romance: From Classical to Contemporary*. Oxford, 2004.

Saunders, Corinne. 'Chaucer's *The Canterbury Tales*'. In Corinne Saunders (ed.), *A Companion to Medieval Poetry*. Oxford, 2010. 452–75.

Saunders, Corinne. 'The Romance Genre'. In Robert DeMaria, Jr., Heesok Chang, and Samantha Zacher (eds), *A Companion to British Literature: Volume I, Medieval Literature 700–1450*. Oxford, 2014, 161–79.

Savage, Anne. 'Old and Middle English, Poetry and Prose'. *Studies in the Age of Chaucer*, 23 (2001), 503–11.

Scahill, John. 'The Friars' Miscellanies'. PhD Diss. University of Sydney, 1990.

Scahill, John. 'Trilingualism in Early Middle English Miscellanies: Language and Literature'. *Yearbook of English Studies*, 33 (2003), 18–32.

Scala, Elizabeth. 'The Texture of *Emare*'. *Philological Quarterly*, 85 (2006), 223–46.

Scanlon, Larry. 'The Authority of the Fable: Allegory and Irony in the *Nun's Priest's Tale*'. *Exemplaria*, 1 (1989), 43–68.

Scase, Wendy. Piers Plowman *and the New Anticlericalism*. Cambridge, 1989.

Scase, Wendy. *Literature and Complaint in England, 1272–1553*. Oxford, 2007.

Scattergood, John. '*Winner and Waster* and the Mid-Fourteenth-Century Economy'. In Tom Dunne (ed.), *The Writer as Witness: Literature as Historical Evidence*. Cork, 1987. 39–57.

Scattergood, John. 'Authority and Resistance: The Political Verse'. In Susanna Fein (ed.), *Studies in the Harley Manuscript: The Scribes, Contents, and Social Contexts of British Library MS Harley 2253*. Kalamazoo, MI, 2000. 163–201.

Scattergood, John. 'The Language of Persuasion: *De Clerico et Puella* from London, British Library MS Harley 2253 and Related Texts'. In John Scattergood, *The Lost Tradition: Essays on Middle English Alliterative Poetry*. Dublin, 2000. 43–62.

Scattergood, John. '*St Erkenwald* and the Custody of the Past'. In John Scattergood, *The Lost Tradition: Essays on Middle English Alliterative Poetry*. Dublin, 2000. 179–99.

Scattergood, John. 'Validating the High Life in *Of Arthour and of Merlin* and *Kyng Alisaunder*'. *Essays in Criticism*, 54 (2004), 323–50.

Scattergood, John. 'The Love Lyric before Chaucer'. In Thomas G. Duncan (ed.), *A Companion to Middle English Lyric*. Cambridge, 2005. 39–67.

Schaar, Claes. *Some Types of Narrative in Chaucer's Poetry*. Lund, 1954.

Schaar, Claes. *The Golden Mirror: Studies in Chaucer's Descriptive Technique and Its Literary Background*. Lund, 1955.

Schendl, Herbert. 'Code-Switching in Late Medieval Macaronic Sermons'. In Ad Putter and Judith Jefferson (eds), *Multilingualism in Medieval Britain (c. 1066–1520): Sources and Analysis*. Turnhout, 2012. 153–69.

Schiff, Randy P. 'The Loneness of the Stalker: Poaching and Subjectivity in *The Parlement of the Thre Ages*'. *Texas Studies in Literature and Language*, 51 (2009), 263–93.

Schipper, Jakob. *A History of English Versification*. New York, 1971.

Schmidt, A. V. C. *Clerkly Maker: Langland's Poetic Art*. Cambridge, 1987.

Schuurman, Anne. 'Materials of Wonder: Miraculous Objects and Poetic Form in *Saint Erkenwald*'. *Studies in the Age of Chaucer*, 39 (2017), 275–96.

The Seege or Batayle of Troye. In Mary Elizabeth Barnicle (ed.), *The Seege or Batayle of Troye*. EETS, o.s. 172. London, 1926.

508   COMPLETE BIBLIOGRAPHY

Seláf, Levante. 'La strophe d'Hélinand dans *Perceforest*'. In Silvère Menegaldo (ed.), *Une forme médiévale à succès: La strophe d'Hélinand. Cahiers de recherches médiévales et humanistes*, 36 (2019), 135–52.

Severs, J. Burke, Albert E. Hartung, and Peter G. Beidler (eds). *A Manual of the Writings in Middle English, 1050–1500*. 11 vols. New Haven, CT, 1967–2005.

Seymour, M. C. *A Catalogue of Chaucer Manuscripts*. 2 vols. Aldershot, 1995–7.

Sharma, Manish. 'Hylomorphic Recursion and Non-Decisional Poetics in the *Canterbury Tales*'. *Chaucer Review*, 52 (2017), 253–72.

Shaw, Philip A. 'The Composition of the Metrical Chronicle Attributed to Robert of Gloucester'. *English Manuscript Studies 1100–1700*, 17 (2012), 140–54.

Shepherd, Geoffrey T. 'Early Middle English Literature'. In W. F. Bolton (ed.), *The Middle Ages*. London, 1970. 67–106.

Shippey, Thomas. *J. R. R. Tolkien: Author of the Century*. Boston, MA, 2014.

Shonk, T. A. 'A Study of the Auchinleck Manuscript: Bookmen and Bookmaking in the Early Fourteenth Century'. *Speculum*, 60 (1985), 71–91.

Short, Ian. 'On Bilingualism in Anglo-Norman England'. *Romance Philology*, 33 (1980), 467–79.

Short, Ian. 'Patrons and Polyglots: French Literature in Twelfth-Century England'. *Anglo-Norman Studies*, 14 (1992), 229–49.

Short, Ian. 'Gaimar's Epilogue and Geoffrey of Monmouth's *Liber vetustissimus*'. *Speculum*, 69 (1994), 323–43.

Short, Ian. 'Another Look at 'le faus franceis''. *Nottingham Medieval Studies*, 54 (2010), 35–55.

Short, Ian. *Manual of Anglo-Norman*. 2nd edn. Oxford, 2013. 17–44.

Short, Ian. 'Vernacular Manuscripts I: Britain and France'. In Erik Kwakkel and Rodney M. Thompson (eds), *The European Book in the Twelfth Century*. Cambridge, 2018. 311–26.

Shuffelton, George (ed.), *Codex Ashmole 61: A Compilation of Popular Middle English Verse*. Kalamazoo, MI, 2008.

The Siege of Jerusalem. In Ralph Hanna and David Lawton (eds), *The Siege of Jerusalem*. EETS, o.s. 320. Oxford, 2003.

The Siege of Milan. In Sidney J. H. Herrtage (ed.), *The Sege off Melayne and The Romance of Duke Rowland and Sir Otuell of Spayne*. EETS, e.s. 35. London, 1880, 1931.

The Siege of Milan. In Stephen H. A. Shepherd (ed.), *Middle English Romances*. New York, 1995.

Simpson, James. '"Et vidit deus cogitationes eorum": A Parallel Instance and Possible Source for Langland's Use of a Biblical Formula at *Piers Plowman* B.XV.200a'. *Notes & Queries*, n.s. 31, 231 (1986), 9–13.

Simpson, James. 'Desire and the Scriptural Text: Will as Reader in *Piers Plowman*'. In Rita Copeland (ed.), *Criticism and Dissent in the Middle Ages*. Cambridge, 1996. 215–43.

Simpson, James. *The Oxford English Literary History, Volume 2. 1350–1547: Reform and Cultural Revolution*. Oxford, 2002.

Simpson, James. *Sciences and the Self in Medieval Poetry: Alan of Lille's* Anticlaudianus *and John Gower's* Confessio Amantis. Cambridge, 2005.

Simpson, James. Piers Plowman: *An Introduction*. 2nd edn. Exeter, 2007.

Simpson, James. 'Anti-Virgilianism in Late Medieval Troy Narratives'. *Troianalexandrina*, 19 (2019), 293–312.

Sims-Williams, Patrick. 'Did Itinerant Breton "Conteurs" Transmit the Matière de Bretagne?'. *Romania*, 116 (1998), 72–111.

Singer, Samuel. 'Die Sprichwörter Hendings'. *Studia Neophilologica*, 14 (1941/2), 31–52.

Sir Degrevant. In L. F. Casson (ed.), *The Romance of Sir Degrevant*. EETS, o.s. 221. London, 1949.

Sir Ferumbras. In Sidney J. H. Herrtage (ed.), *The English Charlemagne Romance, Volume I: Sir Ferumbras*. EETS, e.s. 34. London, 1879, 1903, 1966.

Sir Gowther. In Anne Laskaya and Eve Salisbury (eds), *The Middle English Breton Lays*. Kalamazoo, MI, 1995.

Sir Orfeo. In A. J. Bliss (ed.), *Sir Orfeo*. 2nd edn. Oxford, 1966.

Sir Perceval. In Mary Flowers Braswell (ed.), *Sir Perceval of Galles and Ywain and Gawain*. Kalamazoo, MI, 1995. 1–76.

COMPLETE BIBLIOGRAPHY   509

Sir Tristrem. In Alan Lupack (ed.), *Lancelot of the Laik and Sir Tristrem*. Kalamazoo, MI, 1994.

Sisam, Kenneth (ed.). *Fourteenth-Century Verse and Prose*. Oxford, 1921.

Sisam, Kenneth. *Studies in the History of Old English Literature*. New York, 1953.

Skelton, John. In John Scattergood (ed.), *The Complete English Poems of John Skelton*. Rev. edn. Liverpool, 2015.

Smith, D. Vance. *Arts of Possession: The Middle English Household Imaginary*. Minneapolis, MN, 2003.

Smith, D. Vance. 'Negative Langland'. *Yearbook of Langland Studies*, 23 (2009), 33–59.

Smith, Llinos Beverley. 'The Welsh Language before 1536'. In Geraint H. Jenkins (ed.), *The Welsh Language before the Industrial Revolution*. Cardiff, 1997. 15–44.

Smith, Llinos Beverley. 'The Welsh and English Languages in Late-Medieval Wales'. In D. A. Trotter (ed.), *Multilingualism in Later Medieval Britain*. Cambridge, 2000. 8–21.

Smithers, G. V. (ed.). *Havelok*. Oxford, 1987.

Smithers, G. V. 'The Style of "Hauelok"'. *Medium Ævum*, 57 (1988), 190–218.

Smyser, H. M. 'The Sowdon of Babylon and Its Author'. *Harvard Studies and Notes in Philology and Literature*, 13 (1931), 185–218.

Smyser, H. M. 'Charlemagne Legends'. In J. B. Severs (ed.), *A Manual of the Writings in Middle English, 1050–1500*. 11 vols. New Haven, CT, 1967. 1:80–100.

Sobecki, Sebastian. *The Sea and Medieval English Literature*. Cambridge, 2008.

Sobecki, Sebastian. '"Ecce patet tensus": The Trentham Manuscript, "In Praise of Peace", and John Gower's Autograph Hand'. *Speculum*, 90 (2015), 925–59.

Sobecki, Sebastian. 'A Southwark Tale: Gower, the 1381 Poll Tax, and Chaucer's *The Canterbury Tales*'. *Speculum*, 92 (2017), 630–60.

Solopova, Elizabeth. 'The Metre of the *Ormulum*'. In M. J. Toswell and E. M. Tyler (eds), *Studies in English Language and Literature: 'Doubt Wisely'—Papers in Honour of E. G. Stanley*. London, 1996. 423–39.

Solopova, Elizabeth. 'Layout, Punctuation, and Stanza Patterns in the English Verse'. In Susanna Fein (ed.), *Studies in the Harley Manuscript: The Scribes, Contents, and Social Contexts of British Library MS Harley 2253*. Kalamazoo, MI, 2000. 377–89.

Solopova, Elizabeth (ed.). *The Wycliffite Bible: Origin, History and Interpretation*, Medieval and Renaissance Authors and Texts, 16. Leiden, 2016.

South English Legendary. In Charlotte d'Evelyn and Anna J. Mill (eds), *The South English Legendary*. 3 vols. EETS, o.s. 235–6. London, 1956.

Spearing, A. C. *The Gawain-Poet: A Critical Study*. Cambridge, 1970.

Spearing, A. C. *Medieval Dream-Poetry*. Cambridge, 1976.

Spearing, A. C. 'The Awntyrs off Arthure'. In Bernard S. Levy and Paul E. Szarmach (eds), *The Alliterative Tradition in the Fourteenth Century*. Kent, OH, 1981. 183–202.

Spearing, A. C. *Medieval to Renaissance in English Poetry*. Cambridge, 1985.

Spearing, A. C. *Textual Subjectivity: The Encoding of Subjectivity in Medieval Narratives and Lyrics*. Oxford, 2005.

Spurgeon, Caroline F. E. *Five Hundred Years of Chaucer Criticism and Allusion, 1357–1900*. 3 vols. Cambridge, 1925.

Stanbury, Sarah. *Seeing the Gawain-Poet: Description and the Act of Perception*. Philadelphia, PA, 1991.

Stanley, E. G. 'The Date of Laȝamon's *Brut*'. *Notes & Queries*, 15 (1968), 85–8.

Stanley, E. G. 'Laȝamon's Antiquarian Sentiments'. *Medium Ævum*, 38 (1969), 23–37.

Stanley, E. G. 'Rhymes in English Medieval Verse: from Old English to Middle English'. In Edward Donald Kennedy, Ronald Waldron, and Joseph S. Wittig (eds), *Medieval English Studies Presented to George Kane*. Cambridge, 1988. 19–54.

Stanley, E. G. 'The Verse Forms of Jon the Blynde Awdelay'. In Helen Cooper and Sally Mapstone (eds), *The Long Fifteenth Century: Essays for Douglas Gray*. Oxford, 1997. 99–121.

Stanley, E. G. Rev. of Una O'Farrell-Tate (ed.), *The Abridged English Metrical Brut Edited from London, British Library MS Royal 12 c. xii. Notes & Queries*, 50 (2003), 229–31.

Stanley, E. G. 'What Six Unalike Lyrics in British Library MS Harley 2253 Have Alike in Manuscript Layout'. In Simon Horobin and Linne R. Mooney (eds), *Middle English Texts in Transition: A Festschrift Dedicated to Toshiyuki Takamiya on His 70th Birthday*. Cambridge, 2014. 125–33.

Stanley, E. G. and Douglas Gray (eds). *Five Hundred Years of Words and Sounds: A Festschrift for Eric Dobson*. Cambridge, 1983.

Steiner, Emily. *Documentary Culture and the Making of Medieval English Literature*. Cambridge, 2003.

Stemmler, Theo. 'Miscellany or Anthology? The Structure of Medieval Manuscripts: MS Harley 2253, for Example'. In Susanna Fein (ed.), *Studies in the Harley Manuscript: The Scribes, Contents, and Social Contexts of British Library MS Harley 2253*. Kalamazoo, MI, 2000. 111–20.

Stenroos, Merja. 'Regional Language and Culture: The Geography of Middle English Linguistic Variation'. In Tim William Machan (ed.), *Imagining Medieval English: Language Structures and Theories, 500–1500*. Cambridge, 2016. 100–25.

Stevens, Martin. 'The Rhyme Royal Stanza in Early English Literature'. *PMLA*, 94 (1979), 62–76.

Stevick, Robert D. (ed.). *One Hundred Middle English Lyrics*. 2nd edn. Urbana, IL, 1994.

Stock, Markus (ed.). *Alexander the Great in the Middle Ages: Transcultural Perspectives*. Toronto, 2016.

Stockton, Eric W (trans.). *The Major Latin Works of John Gower*. Seattle, WA, 1962.

Stone, Charles Russell. *The Roman 'de toute Chevalerie': Reading Alexander Romance in Late Medieval England*. Toronto, 2019.

Stouck, Mary-Ann. 'A Poet in the Household of the Beauchamp Earls of Warwick, c. 1393–1427'. *Warwickshire History*, 9 (1994), 113–17.

Strakhov, Elizaveta. 'Tending to One's Garden: Deschamps's "Ballade to Chaucer" Reconsidered'. *Medium Aevum*, 85 (2016), 236–58.

Strang, Barbara. *A History of English*. London, 1970.

Strohm, Paul. 'Storie, Spelle, Geste, Romaunce, Tragedie: Generic Distinctions in the Middle English Troy Narratives'. *Speculum*, 46 (1971), 348–59.

Strohm, Paul. *Social Chaucer*. Cambridge, MA, 1994.

Strohm, Paul. *England's Empty Throne: Usurpation and the Language of Legitimation, 1399–1422*. New Haven, CT, 1998.

Strohm, Paul. *The Poet's Tale*. London, 2016.

Sullivan, Matthew. 'The Author of the *Manuel des Péchés*'. *Notes & Queries*, 236 (1991), 235–37.

The Sultan of Babylon. In Alan Lupack (ed.), *Three Middle English Charlemagne Romances*. Kalamazoo, MI, 1990.

Summerfield, Thea. 'The Political Songs in the *Chronicles* of Pierre de Langtoft and Robert Mannyng'. In Evelyn Mullaly and John Thompson (eds), *The Court and Cultural Diversity*. Woodbridge, 1997. 139–48.

Summerfield, Thea. *The Matter of Kings' Lives: The Design of Past and Present in the Early Fourteenth-Century Verse Chronicles by Pierre de Langtoft and Robert Mannyng*. Amsterdam, 1998.

Summerfield, Thea. '"Fi a debles", quath the king": Language Mixing in England's Vernacular Historical Narratives, c. 1290–1340'. In Jocelyn Wogan-Browne (ed.), *Language and Culture in Medieval Britain: The French of England c. 1100–c. 1500*.York, 2009. 68–80.

Summerfield, Thea. '"And she answered in hir language": Aspects of Multilingualism in the Auchinleck Manuscript'. In Judith A. Jefferson and Ad Putter (eds), *Multilingualism in Medieval Britain (c. 1066–1520)*. Turnout, 2013. 241–58.

Sutherland, Annie. 'The Unlikely Landscapes of *On God Ureisun of Ure Lefdi*'. In Julia Boffey and Christiana Whitehead (eds), *Middle English Lyrics: New Readings of Short Poems*. Woodbridge, 2018. 73–86.

Swan, Mary. 'Preaching Past the Conquest: Lambeth Palace 487 and Cotton Vespasian A.XXII'. In Aaron J. Kleist (ed.), *The Old English Homily: Precedent, Practice, and Appropriation*. Turnhout, 2007. 403–23.

Swan, Mary and Elaine Treharne (eds). *Rewriting Old English in the Twelfth Century*. Cambridge, 2000.

Swanson, R. N. 'Hallum, Robert, Bishop of Salisbury (d. 1417)'. *Oxford Dictionary of National Biography*. Oxford, 2004. oxforddnb.com.

Swanton, Michael. *English Literature before Chaucer*. Essex, 1987.

Sweet, Henry. 'The History of English Sounds'. *Transactions of the Philological Society*, 15 (1874), 461–623.

The Tale of Rauf Coilyear with the Fragments of Roland and Vernagu and Otuel. In Sidney J. H. Herrtage (ed.), *The English Charlemagne Romance, Volume VI: The Taill of Rauf Coilyear*. EETS, e.s. 39. London, 1882; rpt. 1931, 1969.

Tarlinskaja, Marina. *English Verse: Theory and History*. The Hague, 1976.

Tatlock, J. S. P. 'Milton's Sin and Death'. *Modern Language Notes*, 21 (1906), 239–40.

Taubman, Andrew W. 'New Biographical Notes on Robert Mannyng of Brunne'. *Notes & Queries*, n.s. 56 (2009), 197–201.

Taylor, Andrew. *Textual Situations: Three Medieval Manuscripts and Their Readers*. Philadelphia, PA, 2002.

Taylor, Andrew. *The Songs and Travels of a Tudor Minstrel: Richard Sheale of Tamworth*. Woodbridge, 2012.

Terasawa, Jun. *Old English Metre: An Introduction*. Toronto, 2011.

Thomas, Carla María. 'Orm's Vernacular Latinity'. *Journal of the Spanish Society for Medieval English Language and Literature (SELIM)*, 20 (2013), 167–98.

Thomas, Hugh M. *The English and the Normans: Ethnic Hostility, Assimilation, and Identity 1066–c. 1220*. Oxford, 2003.

Thomas of Kent. In Brian Foster and Ian Short (eds), *The Anglo-Norman 'Alexander' (Le Roman de toute chevalerie) by Thomas of Kent*. Anglo-Norman Texts. 2 vols. London, 1976, 1977.

Thompson, Anne B. 'Jaussian Expectation and the Production of Medieval Narrative: The Case of "Saint Eustace" and Sir Isumbras'. *Exemplaria*, 5 (1993), 387–407.

Thompson, Anne B. (ed.). *The Northern Homily Cycle*. Kalamazoo, MI, 2008.

Thompson, John. 'Textual Instability and the Late Medieval Reputation of Some Middle English Religious Literature'. *TEXT*, 5 (1991), 175–94.

Thompson, John. *The* Cursor Mundi: *Poem, Texts and Contexts*. Oxford, 1998.

Thompson, W. Meredith (ed.). *Þe Wohunge of Ure Lauerd*. EETS, 241. Oxford, 1958.

Todorov, Tzvetan. *Grammaire du Décaméron*. The Hague, 1969.

Tolkien, J. R. R. and E. V. Gordon (eds). *Sir Gawain and the Green Knight*. 2nd edn. rev. Norman Davis. Oxford, 1967.

Townend, Matthew. 'Contextualizing the *Knútsdrápur*: Skaldic Praise-Poetry at the Court of Cnut'. *Anglo-Saxon England*, 30 (2001), 145–79.

Townend, Matthew. *Antiquity of Diction in Old English and Old Norse Poetry*. E. C. Quiggin Memorial Lectures 17. Cambridge, 2015.

Treharne, Elaine (ed.). *Old and Middle English c.890–c.1450: An Anthology*. 3rd edn. Oxford, 2009.

Treharne, Elaine. 'Worcester, Cathedral Library, F. 174'. In Orietta Da Rold, Takako Kato, Jo Story, Mary Swan, and Elaine Treharne, *The Production and Use of English Manuscripts 1060 to 1220*. Leicester, 2010. https://www.le.ac.uk/english/em1060to1220.

Trigg, Stephanie (ed.). *Wynnere and Wastoure*, EETS, o.s. 297. London, 1990.

Tschann, Judith, and M. B. Parkes. *Facsimile of Oxford, Bodleian Library, MS Digby 86*. EETS, s.s. 16. Oxford, 1996.

Turner, Marion. '"Certaynly his noble sayenges can I not amende": Thomas Usk and *Troilus and Criseyde*'. *Chaucer Review*, 37 (2002), 26–39.

Turner, Marion. *Chaucer: A European Life*. Princeton, NJ, 2019.

Turner, Ralph V. 'Coutances, Walter de (d. 1207)'. *Oxford Dictionary of National Biography*. Oxford, 2019. oxforddnb.com.

Turner, Ralph V. 'Longchamp, William de (d. 1197)'. *Oxford Dictionary of National Biography*. Oxford, 2019. oxforddnb.com.

Turner, Victoria. *Theorizing Medieval Race: Saracen Representations in Old French Literature*. Cambridge, 2019.

Turville-Petre, J. E. 'Studies in the *Ormulum* MS'. *Journal of English and Germanic Philology*, 46 (1947), 1–27.

Turville-Petre, Thorlac. '*Summer Sunday, De Tribus Regibus Mortuis*, and *The Awntyrs off Arthure*: Three Poems in the 13-Line Stanza'. *Review of English Studies*, 25 (1974), 1–13.

Turville-Petre, Thorlac. 'The Ages of Man in "The Parlement of the Thre Ages"'. *Medium Ævum*, 46 (1977), 66–76.

Turville-Petre, Thorlac. *The Alliterative Revival*. Cambridge, 1977.

Turville-Petre, Thorlac. 'Emendation on the Grounds of Alliteration in *The Wars of Alexander*'. *English Studies*, 61 (1980), 302–17.

Turville-Petre, Thorlac. 'The Author of *The Destruction of Troy*'. *Medium Ævum*, 57 (1988), 264–9.

Turville-Petre, Thorlac (ed.). *Alliterative Poetry of the Later Middle Ages: An Anthology*. London, 1989.

Turville-Petre, Thorlac. *England the Nation: Language, Literature, and National Identity, 1290–1340*. Oxford, 1996.

Turville-Petre, Thorlac. *Description and Narrative in Middle English Alliterative Poetry*. Liverpool, 2018.

Tyler, Elizabeth M. *Old English Poetics: The Aesthetics of the Familiar in Anglo-Saxon England*. York, 2006.

Tyler, Elizabeth M. *England in Europe: English Royal Women and Literary Patronage, c. 1000–c. 1150*. Toronto, 2017.

Utley, Francis Lee. 'Dialogues, Debates, and Catechisms'. In J. Burke Severs and Albert Hartung (eds), *A Manual of Writings in Middle English*. 11 vols. New Haven, CT, 1972. 3:669–745, 829–902.

Van Court, Elisa Narin. '*The Siege of Jerusalem* and Augustinian Historians: Writing about Jews in Fourteenth-Century England'. *The Chaucer Review*, 29 (1995), 227–48.

Van Dussen, Michael. *From England to Bohemia: Heresy and Communication in the Later Middle Ages*. Cambridge, 2012.

Van Heijnsbegen, Theo. 'Scripting the National Past: A Textual Community of the Realm'. In Steve Boardman and Susan Foran (eds), *Barbour's Bruce and Its Cultural Contexts: Politics, Chivalry, and Literature in Late Medieval Scotland*. Cambridge, 2015. 75–99.

Varnhagen, Hermann. 'VI. Zu dem klageliede Maximian's'. *Anglia*, 3 (1880), 275–85.

Vising, John. *Anglo-Norman Language and Literature*. London, 1923.

Vitkus, Daniel J. *Turning Turk: English Theater and the Multicultural Mediterranean, 1570–1630*. New York, 2003.

Von Contzen, Eva. *The Scottish Legendary: Towards a Poetics of Hagiographic Narration*. Manchester, 2016.

Vulgate (Douai-Rheims). Rockford, IL, 1989.

Wace. *Brut*. In Judith Weiss (ed. and trans.), *Wace's Roman de Brut: A History of the British*. Exeter, 1999; rev. edn. 2002.

Wada, Yoko (ed.). *A Companion to Ancrene Wisse*. Cambridge, 2003.

Wakelin, Daniel. 'The Carol in Writing: Three Anthologies from Fifteenth-Century Norfolk'. *Journal of the Early Book Society*, 9 (2006), 25–49.

Walker, Greg (ed.). *Medieval Drama: An Anthology*. Oxford, 2000.

Wallace, David. *Chaucer and the Early Writings of Boccaccio*. Woodbridge, 1985.

Wallace, David. *Chaucerian Polity: Absolutist Lineages and Associational Forms in England and Italy*. Stanford, CA, 1997.

Wallace, David. *Premodern Places: From Calais to Surinam, Chaucer to Aphra Behn*. Oxford, 2016.

Walter of England. In Aaron E. Wright (ed.), *The Fables of 'Walter of England'*. Toronto, 1997.

Walter of Châtillon. In Marvin L. Colker (ed.), *Galteri de Castellione: Alexandreis*. Padova, 1978.

Walter of Châtillon. In David Townsend (trans.), *The Alexandreis: A Twelfth-Century Epic*. Peterborough, ON, 2007.

Walton, John. *Boethius*. In Mark Science (ed.), *Boethius: De consolationae Philosophiae*, translated by John Walton. EETS, o.s. 170. London, 1927.

Warmington, E. H. (ed. and trans.). *Remains of Old Latin: Livius Andronicus, Naevius, Pacuvius, Accius*. Cambridge, MA, 1936.

Warner, Lawrence. 'Geoffrey of Monmouth and the De-Judaized Crusade'. *Parergon*, 21.1 (2004), 19–37.

Warner, Lawrence. *The Myth of Piers Plowman*. Cambridge, 2014.

Warner, Lawrence. *Chaucer's Scribes: London Textual Production, 1384–1432*. Cambridge, 2018.

Warren, Frederick E. (trans.). *The Sarum Missal in English, Part 1*. London, 1911.

The Wars of Alexander. In Hoyt N. Duggan and Thorlac Turville-Petre (eds), *The Wars of Alexander*. EETS, s.s. 10. 1989.

Watson, Nicholas. 'The Politics of Middle English Writing'. In Jocelyn Wogan-Browne, Nicholas Watson, Andrew Taylor, and Ruth Evans (eds), *The Idea of the Vernacular: An Anthology of Middle English Literary Theory 1280–1520*. Exeter, 1999. 331–52.

Watson, Nicholas. '*Piers Plowman*, Pastoral Theology, and Spiritual Perfectionism: Hawkyn's Cloak and Patience's *Pater noster*'. *Yearbook of Langland Studies*, 21 (2007), 83–118.

Watt, David. '"Mescreantz", Schism, and the Plight of Constantinople: Evidence for Dating and Reading London, British Library, Additional MS 59495'. In Martha W. Driver, Derek Pearsall, and R. F. Yeager (eds), *John Gower in Manuscripts and Early Printed Books*. Cambridge, 2020. 131–52.

Weil, Simone. *Waiting for God*. Trans. Emma Craufurd. New York, 1951.

Weinberg, Bernard. *A History of Literary Criticism in the Italian Renaissance*. 2 vols. Chicago, IL, 1961.

Weiskott, Eric. 'Before Prosody: Early English Poetics in Practice and Theory'. *Modern Language Quarterly*, 77 (2016), 473–98.

Weiskott, Eric. *English Alliterative Verse: Poetic Tradition and Literary History*. Cambridge, 2016.

Weiskott, Eric. '"Seinte Loy": A Metrical Non-Problem in Chaucer's *General Prologue*'. *Notes & Queries*, 63 (2019), 361–3.

Weiskott, Eric. *Meter and Modernity in English Verse, 1350–1650*. Philadelphia, PA, 2021.

Wells, John Edwin. *A Manual of the Writings in Middle English, 1050–1500*. Rev. J. Burke Severs and Albert E. Hartung (eds). 11 vols. New Haven, CT, 1967–2005.

Wenzel, Siegfried. *Verses in Sermons: Fasciculus Morum and Its Middle English Poems*. Cambridge, MA, 1978.

Wenzel, Siegfried. *Preachers, Poets, and the Early English Lyric*. Princeton, NJ, 1986.

Wenzel, Siegfried (ed. and trans.). *Fasciculus Morum: A Fourteenth-Century Preacher's Handbook*. University Park, PA, 1989.

Wetherbee, Winthrop. *Platonism and Poetry in the Twelfth Century: The Literary Influence of the School of Chartres*. Princeton, NJ, 1972.

Wetherbee, Winthrop. 'Latin Structure and Vernacular Space: Gower, Chaucer and the Boethian Tradition'. In R. F. Yeager (ed.), *Chaucer and Gower: Difference, Mutuality, Exchange*. Victoria, BC, 1991. 7–35.

Wetherbee, Winthrop. 'Gower and the Epic Past'. In Ana Sáez-Hidalgo and R. F. Yeager (eds), *John Gower in England and Iberia: Manuscripts, Influences, Reception*. Cambridge, 2014. 165–79.

Whatley, E. Gordon. 'The Uses of Hagiography: The Legend of Pope Gregory and the Emperor Trajan in the Middle Ages'. *Viator*, 15 (1984), 25–64.

Whatley, E. Gordon. 'Heathens and Saints: *Saint Erkenwald* in Its Legendary Context'. *Speculum*, 61 (1986), 330–63.

Whatley, E. Gordon, Anne B. Thompson, and Robert K. Upchurch (eds). *Saints' Lives in Middle English Collections*. Kalamazoo, MI, 2004.

White, Hugh. *Nature, Sex, and Goodness in a Medieval Literary Tradition*. Oxford, 2000.

Whiteacre, Nigel. In Graydon W. Regenos (trans.), *The Book of Daun Burnel the Ass: Nigellus Wireker's Speculum stultorum*. Austin, TX, 1959.

Whiteacre, Nigel. In John H. Mozley and Robert R. Raymo (eds), *Nigel de Longchamps Speculum Stultorum*. Berkeley, CA, 1960.

Whitehead, Christiania. 'Middle English Religious Lyrics'. In Thomas G. Duncan (ed.), *A Companion to the Middle English Lyric*. Cambridge, 2005. 96–119.

Whitehead, Christiania, 'The Marian Voice: Female Pedagogy and Laudation in the Early Vernacular *Hymns* of St Godric of Finchale and the *Meditaciones* of the Monk of Farne'. Boston Symposium, *Medieval Women and the Literary Canon*. July 2017.

Whitman, Jon (ed.). *Romance and History: Imagining Time from the Medieval to the Early Modern Period*. Cambridge, 2015.

514 COMPLETE BIBLIOGRAPHY

Whitty, J. R. 'The Rhyming Charter of Beverley'. *Transactions of the Yorkshire Dialect Society*, 22 (1921), 36–44.

Wickert, Maria. *Studien zu John Gower*. Köln, 1953; trans. Robert J. Meindl, *Maria Wickert: Studies in John Gower*. 2nd edn. Tempe, AZ, 2016.

Wiggins, Alison. 'Are Auchinleck Manuscript Scribes 1 and 6 the Same Scribe? Whole-Data Analysis and the Advantages of Electronic Texts'. *Medium Ævum*, 73 (2004), 10–26.

Wiggins, Alison (ed.). *Stanzaic Guy of Warwick*. Kalamazoo, MI, 2004.

Willard, Charity Canon. *Christine de Pizan: Her Life and Works*. New York, 1984.

William of Palerne. In G. H. V. Bunt (ed.), *William of Palerne: An Alliterative Romance*. Groningen, 1985.

Williams, Ann. *The English and the Norman Conquest*. Woodbridge, 1995.

Williams, O. T. 'Another Welsh Phonetic Copy of the Early English Hymn to the Virgin from a British Museum MS No. 14866'. *Anglia*, 32 (1909), 295–300.

Williamson, Keith. 'Middle English: Dialects'. In Alexander Bergs and Laurel J. Brinton (eds), *English Historical Linguistics: An International Handbook*. 2 vols. Berlin, 2012. I.480–505.

Wilson, Edward (ed.). *A Descriptive Index of the English Lyrics in John of Grimestone's Preaching Book*. Medium Ævum Monographs n.s. 2. Oxford, 1973.

Wilson, R. M. *The Lost Literature of Medieval England*. London, 1952, 1970.

Wimsatt, James I. *Chaucer and His French Contemporaries: Natural Music in the Fourteenth Century*. Toronto, 1991.

Wimsatt, W. K. and Cleanth Brooks. *Literary Criticism: A Short History*. New York, 1957, 1975.

Windeatt, Barry. 'The Scribes as Chaucer's Early Critics'. *Studies in the Age of Chaucer*, 1 (1979), 119–41.

Windeatt, Barry. 'Chaucer and Fifteenth-Century Romance: *Partonope of Blois*'. In Ruth Morse and Barry Windeatt (eds), *Chaucer Traditions: Studies in Honour of Derek Brewer*. Cambridge, 1990. 62–80.

Windeatt, Barry. 'Literary Structures in Chaucer'. In Piero Boitani and Jill Mann (eds), *The Cambridge Chaucer Companion*. 2nd edn. Cambridge, 2003. 214–32.

Winstead, Karen A. 'John Capgrave and the Chaucer Tradition'. *Chaucer Review*, 30 (1996), 389–400.

Winstead, Karen A. *Virgin Martyrs: Legends of Sainthood in Late Medieval England*. Ithaca, NY, 1997.

Winstead, Karen A. *The Oxford History of Life-Writing, Vol. 1: The Middle Ages*. Oxford, 2018.

Wirtjes, Hanneke (ed.). *The Middle English Physiologus*, EETS, o.s. 299. Oxford, 1991.

Witalisz, Władysław. *The Trojan Mirror: Middle English Narratives of Troy as Books of Princely Advice*. Frankfurt/Main, 2011.

Wittig, Joseph S. '*Piers Plowman* B, Passus IX–XII: Elements in the Design of the Inward Journey'. *Traditio*, 28 (1972), 211–80.

Wittig, Susan. *Stylistic and Narrative Structures in the Middle English Romance*. Austin, TX, 1978.

Wogan-Browne, Jocelyn. 'The Apple's Message: Some Post-Conquest Hagiographic Accounts of Textual Transmission'. In A. J. Minnis (ed.), *Late-Medieval Religious Texts and Their Transmission: Essays in Honour of A. I. Doyle*. Cambridge, 1994. 39–53.

Wogan-Browne, Jocelyn. *Saints' Lives and Women's Literary Culture: Virginity and Its Authorizations*. Oxford, 2001.

Wogan-Browne, Jocelyn. 'General Introduction: What's in a Name—The "French" of "England"'. In Jocelyn Wogan-Browne, Carolyn Collette, Maryanne Kowaleski, Linne Mooney, Ad Putter, and David Trotter (eds), *Language and Culture in Medieval Britain: The French of England c.1100–c.1500*. Woodbridge, 2009. 1–13.

Wogan-Browne, Jocelyn, Thelma Fenster, and Delbert Russell (eds). *Vernacular Literary Theory from the French of Medieval England: Texts and Translations*. Cambridge, 2016.

Wood, Sarah. 'A Prose Redaction of *The Prick of Conscience* Part VI in Bodleian Library MS Laud Misc. 23'. *Medium Ævum*, 80 (2011), 1–17.

Wood, Sarah. 'Two Annotated *Piers Plowman* Manuscripts from London and the Early Reception of the B and C Versions'. *Chaucer Review*, 43 (2017), 274–97.

Woodman, D. A. 'The Forging of the Anglo-Saxon Past in Fourteenth-Century Beverley'. *English Manuscript Studies*, 17 (2012), 26–42.

Woods, Marjorie Curry. *Classroom Commentaries: Teaching the Poetria Nova Across Medieval and Renaissance Europe*. Columbus, OH, 2010.

Woods, Marjorie Curry. *Weeping for Dido: The Classics in the Medieval Classroom*. Princeton, NJ, 2019.

Woods, William F. *Chaucerian Spaces: Spatial Poetics in Chaucer's Opening Tales*. Albany, NY, 2008.

Woolf, Rosemary. *The English Religious Lyric in the Middle Ages*. Oxford, 1968.

Worley, Meg. 'Using the *Ormulum* to Redefine Vernacularity'. In Fiona Somerset and Nicholas Watson (eds), *The Vulgar Tongue: Medieval and Postmedieval Vernacularity*. University Park, PA, 2003. 19–30.

Worley, Meg. 'Forr þeȝȝre sawle need: The *Ormulum*, Vernacular Theology and a Tradition of Translation in Early England'. *English Studies*, 95 (2014), 256–77.

Wright, Neil (ed. and trans.). *The Historia Regum Britannie of Geoffrey of Monmouth, V, Gesta Regum Britannie*. Cambridge, 1991.

Wright, William Aldis (ed.). *The Metrical Chronicle of Robert of Gloucester*. 2 vols. Rolls Series 86.1–2. London, 1887.

Wulff, Friedrich and Emile Walberg (eds). *Les Vers de la Mort par Hélinant, Moine de Froidmont*. SATF. Paris, 1905.

Wülfing, Ernst. 'Das Laud-Troybook: Hs. Bodl. Laud 595 (früher K. 76)'. *Englische Studien*, 29 (1901), 374–96.

Wyclif, John. In Thomas Arnold (ed.), *Select English Works of John Wyclif*. 3 vols. Oxford, 1869–71.

Yeager, R. F. 'English, Latin, and the Text as "Other": The Page as Sign in the Work of John Gower'. *Text*, 3 (1987), 251–67.

Yeager, R. F. 'Pax Poetica: On the Pacifism of Chaucer and Gower'. *Studies in the Age of Chaucer*, 9 (1987), 97–121.

Yeager, R. F. 'Did Gower Write Cento?'. In R. F. Yeager (ed.), *John Gower: Recent Readings*. Kalamazoo, MI, 1989. 113–32.

Yeager, R. F. *John Gower's Poetic: The Search for a New Arion*. Cambridge, 1990.

Yeager, R. F. '*Scripture Veteris Capiunt Exempla Futuri*: John Gower's Transformation of a Fable of Avianus'. In Thomas Hahn (ed.), *Essays and Studies in Honor of Russell A. Peck*. Rochester, 1996. 341–54.

Yeager, R. F. 'John Gower's Images: "The Tale of Constance" and "The Man of Law's Tale"'. In R. F. Yeager and Charlotte C. Morse (eds), *Speaking Images: Essays in Honor of V.A. Kolve*. Asheville, NC, 2000. 525–57.

Yeager, R. F. 'John Gower's Audience: The Ballades'. *Chaucer Review*, 40 (2005), 81–105.

Yeager, R. F. 'John Gower's Audience: The *Mirour de l'Omme*'. *Chaucer Review*, 41 (2006), 111–37.

Yeager, R. F. 'Twenty-First Century Gower: The Theology of Marriage in John Gower's *Traitié* and the Turn toward French'. In Thelma Fenster and Carolyn Collette (eds), *Essays on the French of England in Honour of Jocelyn Wogan-Browne*. Cambridge, 2016. 257–71.

Yeager, R. F. 'Gower's Religions'. In Ana Sáez–Hidalgo, Brian Gastle, and R. F. Yeager (eds), *The Routledge Research Companion to John Gower*. New York, 2017. 56–74.

Yeager, R. F. 'The '*Strophe d'Hélinand*' and John Gower'. In Silvère Menegaldo (ed.), *Une forme médiévale à succès: La strophe d'Hélinand. Cahiers de recherches médiévales et humanistes* 36. Paris, 2018. 115–33.

Yeager, Stephen M. *From Lawmen to Plowmen: Anglo-Saxon Legal Tradition and the School of Langland*. Toronto, 2014.

Yeager, Stephen M. 'Diplomatic Antiquarianism and the Manuscripts of Laȝamon's Brut'. *Arthuriana*, 26.1 (2016), 124–40.

Younge, George. 'Monks, Money, and the End of Old English'. *New Medieval Literatures*, 16 (2016), 39–82.

Yvain and Gawain. In Mary Flowers Braswell (ed.), *Sir Perceval of Galles and Ywain and Gawain*. Kalamazoo, MI, 1995. 77–202.

Zarins, Kim. 'Rich Words: Gower's Rime Riche in Dramatic Action'. In Elisabeth Dutton, with John Hines and R.F. Yeager (eds), *John Gower, Trilingual Poet: Language, Translation and Tradition*. Cambridge, 2010. 239–53.

Zechmeister, Joseph (ed.). *Scholia Vindobonensia ad Horatii Artem Poeticam*. Vienna, 1977.

Zeeman, Nicolette. Piers Plowman *and the Medieval Discourse of Desire*. Cambridge, 2006.

Zeeman, Nicolette. '*Piers Plowman* in Theory'. In Andrew Cole and Andrew Galloway (eds), *Cambridge Companion to* Piers Plowman. Cambridge, 2014. 214–29.

Zeeman, Nicolette. *The Arts of Disruption: Allegory and* Piers Plowman. Oxford, 2020.

Zettl, Ewald (ed.). *An Anonymous Short English Metrical Chronicle*. London, 1935.

Zieman, Katherine. *Singing the New Song: Literacy, Liturgy, and Literature in Late Medieval England*. Philadelphia, PA, 2008.

Zieman, Katherine. 'Compiling the Lyric: Richard Rolle, Textual Dynamism and Devotional Song in London, British Library, Additional MS 37049'. In Julia Boffey and Christiana Whitehead (eds), *Middle English Lyrics: New Readings of Short Poems*. Cambridge, 2018. 158–73.

Zumthor, Paul. *Essai de poétique médiévale*. Paris, 1972.

Zuwiyya, Z. David (ed.). *A Companion to Alexander Literature in the Middle Ages*. Leiden, 2011.

Zwicky, Arnold. '"Well, This Rock and Roll Has Got to Stop. Junior's Head Is Hard as a Rock"'. In Salikoko S. Mufwene, Carol A Walker, and Sanford B Steever (eds), *Papers from the Twelfth Regional Meeting of the Chicago Linguistic Society*. Chicago, IL, 1976. 676–97.

Index

Adgar (*Le gracial*) 108
Ælfric 16, 21, 32, 75, 172, 228
Æthelred II, King 15
Against the King's Taxes 194–5
Alain de Lille 92, 93, 98, 100, 147–8, 150, 153
Alberic of Monte Cassino 149
Albinus, Abbot of Canterbury 105
Aldhelm 207
Alexander romances 7, 316–22
allegory 5, 93, 98, 114, 147, 148, 150, 155, 156, 190,
    204, 208, 210, 299–300, 399, 400, 402
    and exegesis 156
    in Gower 162, 443, 446, 453
    in Langland 9, 153, 375, 377–9, 383
alliteration 5, 41, 100, 140–3, 198–9, 206, 225, 304,
    317, 324, 342
    alliterative poetics 404
    in Arthurian romance 334–5, 338
    in *Gawain*-poet 141–3, 396–7, 399–402, 403–4
    in Katherine Group 228, 232
    in Laȝamon 30, 171–2
    in Langland 377
    in *St Erkenwald* 239–40
    vocabulary 85–6
    see also William of Palerne; 'Winnere and Wastour'
Alliterative Morte Arthur 31, 41, 67, 184, 324, 335–6,
    468
Alliterative Revival 5, 86, 110, 130–1, 140–4, 238,
    239, 404
Alysoun 57, 287–8
Amis and Amiloun 294–5, 301–3, 308
Amoryus and Cleopes 135
Ancrene Wisse 262
Anglo-Latin 88–103
Anglo-Norman 40–1, 114
    terminology for 105
Anglo-Saxon Chronicle 16, 107, 167
Anglo-Scottish poetry 4. *see also* Barbour, John
'Annot and John' 119–20, 287, 288
anthologies 54, 57, 61 n. 31, 229, 421. *see also*
    miscellanies
Aristotle 149, 151
Arthour and Merlin 319, 324–5
Arthur 93, 169, 170–3, 176–8, 180–1, 295–6
Arthurian romance 4, 7–8, 218, 323–38
'Arts of Poetry' 146–51
    absence of English 5
Arundel, Thomas, Archbishop of Canterbury 458
Athelston 359, 360
Auchinleck Manuscripts 31, 52, 53, 59–64, 170, 171,
    174–5, 184, 195, 221, 223, 230, 232, 233, 235, 299,

301, 318, 325, 327, 363, 393. *see also* Manuscripts
    cited
Audelay, John 143, 468
Augustine, St 105, 156, 354, 383, 385, 400
authorship 5, 7, 104, 105, 116–17, 146, 156, 158–63,
    171, 309, 310, 380–1, 462
    female authorship 3
Avianus 246–7, 254
awdl 122, 126–7
Awntyrs of Arthur 331–5, 338

ballade 116, 409, 466, 467
    and Chaucer 413, 414, 417, 438
    Deschamps to Chaucer 410, 412, 423
    and Gower 443, 445
Barbour, John 4, 182–6, 459
beast fable 95, 276, 427
Bede 2, 105, 171
Benedeit 108, 185
Benedictines 22, 23, 260
Benoît de Sainte-Maure 108, 311
Beowulf 1, 71–5, 78, 188, 245, 324, 360
Bernard of Chartres 145
Bernard of Clairvaux 261, 268, 270
Bernardus Silvestris 92, 93, 100
Béroul 109
Bersuire, Pierre 162
Berthelette, Thomas 449
Bestiary 204
Bevis of Hampton 52–3, 184, 312, 347–8, 356, 357,
    359, 360, 364, 367–8
Bible 6, 155, 156–7, 200, 458
    and *Gawain*-poet 393, 398, 399, 401
    and poetry 212–26
    Wycliffe, John 66
A Bird in Bishopswood 459
'Le Blasme des femmes' 57, 58
bob and wheel 9, 141, 142–3, 193, 225, 238, 324, 325,
    336, 338, 403
Boccaccio, Giovanni 116, 300, 409, 412, 417, 419–20,
    421, 422, 424, 426, 427, 428, 430
Bodel, Jean 7, 90, 183, 309, 310, 342
Boethius 89, 108, 207, 208, 300, 418–19, 420, 421,
    423. *see also* Walton, John
Bokenham, Osbern 240, 461–2
Bonaventure 159, 161
Le Bone Florence of Rome 294, 297
Boniface, St 207
Bozon, Nicholas 42, 112, 234–5, 269
Brut narratives 5, 30, 31–4, 36, 66, 121, 160, 168–70,
    171. *see also* Barbour, John; Laȝamon
Burgwine 260

518 INDEX

Byrd on Brere 278–9
'Bytuene Mersh ant Averil' 57

Canticum de Creatione 221, 222–4
Capgrave, John 241
Castle of Perseverance 468
Castleford's Chronicle 167, 170, 178–9, 184, 459
Caxton, William 40, 449
Chanson d'Aspremont 109
chanson de geste 4, 108, 109, 340–2, 344, 351, 352, 355
Chanson de Roland 24, 109, 110
chansonniers 108, 115
Chardri 112
Charles d'Orléans 108
Charnel amour est folie 268
The Charter of the Abbey of the Holy Ghost 205
The Charter of Christ 205
Chaucer, Geoffrey 1, 8, 61–2, 64–5, 67, 93, 96, 131, 133–5, 140, 162–3
    Anelida and Arcite 415–16, 422
    Boece 463
    Book of the Duchess 64, 134, 154, 158, 254, 413
    Canterbury Tales 158, 417, 425–39. *see also* individual tales
    'Complaint of Venus' 410
    complaint poetry 415–17
    Complaint Unto Pity 413
    dream poems 409–14
    fabliaux 255–6
    in fifteenth century 462–7, 469
    'Franklin's Tale' 154, 155, 407, 416
    'Friar's Tale' 157
    House of Fame 64, 90, 103, 159, 309, 318, 413–14, 423–4, 427
    'Knight's Tale' 348, 407, 463, 464
    Legend of Good Women 3, 309, 410–11, 413–14, 416, 423, 426, 427, 464
    'Man of Law's Tale' 236
    'Manciple's Tale' 158, 256
    'Merchant's Tale' 255, 412
    'Miller's Tale' 255
    'Monk's Tale' 236, 316, 463
    'Nun's Priest's Tale' 96, 154, 204, 247, 256
    Parliament of Fowls 64, 411, 413, 414, 417, 425, 464, 469
    'Parson's Tale' 158, 192, 256, 324
    'Prioress's Tale' 98, 236
    'Reeve's Tale' 255
    Retraction 158, 162, 200
    'Second Nun's Tale' 235–6
    'Shipman's Tale' 255
    'Squire's Tale' 82–5, 416
    'Summoner's Tale' 255
    'Tale of Sir Thopas' 7, 139, 229, 296, 307, 326–7, 331, 356, 357–8, 365
    Troilus and Criseyde 9, 61, 64–5, 134, 135, 154, 159, 162, 236, 309, 393, 412, 417–24, 462, 463
    'Wife of Bath's Tale' 411
Child reste þe a þrowe 291–2

Chrétien de Troyes 66, 109, 120, 323, 326, 327, 328, 329, 330, 338, 363
Christine de Pizan 157, 445
chronicle 20, 21, 27
    Anglo-Saxon Chronicle 107
    chronicle tradition 323
    in fifteenth century 460
    see also Brut narratives; *Castleford's Chronicle*
Cicero, Marcus Tullius 149, 152, 246
Cistercians 65, 260, 261, 264, 268
Clanvowe, Sir John 464–5
Clemence of Barking 3
Com Shuppere, Holy Ghost, ofsech our þouhtes 270, 271
Comestor, Peter 6, 33, 219
Compendium Historiae TroianaeRomanae 312
complaint 6, 20, 101, 154, 187, 193–9, 465, 467
    in Chaucer 409–10, 415–17, 422–3, 429–30
    in Gower 96
Conrad of Hirsau 155–6
contrafacta 280, 281, 286, 287, 291
Cotton Nero A.x 9, 55, 142, 392. *see also* Manuscripts cited
couplets 1, 5, 133, 170, 322, 468
    in Chaucer 414, 426–7
    elegiac 95, 447, 449
    four-beat 10, 137, 178, 208, 324
    hexameter 440
    irregular 175, 180, 262, 361
    in Katherine Group 228
    see also rhyming couplets; septenary verse; tetrameter
'Crist and Sainte Marie swa on scamel me iledde' 260
Crowned King 459
Crusades 8, 339–40, 348, 351
Cursor Mundi 47, 49, 50, 67, 114, 130, 217–21, 460, 469
Curtius Rufus, Quintus 93, 316
Cynewulf 135–6, 138
cynghanedd 119, 125, 126
cywydd 121–4

Daffyd ap Gwilym 118, 121–5
Dame Sirith 58, 115, 136–8, 139–40, 245, 250–1, 253, 281
Dan Michel of Northgate 40
Dante Alighieri 116, 157, 159, 410, 422, 433
Dares Phrygius 90, 309, 311, 312, 315, 316
David II, king of Scotland 192, 193
Death's Wither Clench 280
debate poetry 9, 20, 57, 59, 201, 207–11, 281, 290, 377, 378, 407, 465
    in *Gawain*-poet 398, 406
    in Langland 377–8, 380
    see also Clanvowe, Sir John; *The Owl and the Nightingale*; *The Thrush and the Nightingale*; 'Winnere and Wastour'
Deguileville, Guillaume de 423, 464

INDEX 519

Deschamps, Eustache 116, 409, 410, 412–13, 423, 440, 443, 454
La Destruction de Rome 348
Destruction of Troy 183, 310, 313–16
Dictys Cretensis 90, 309, 311, 315, 316
didactic verse 1, 3, 21, 28, 107, 108, 112, 115, 117, 201–5, 257, 338, 417
Digby 86 28, 43, 58–9, 60, 63, 111–12, 115, 137, 281, 286. *see also* Manuscripts cited
Distichs of Cato 109
'Le Dit des femmes' 57
Doctrinal Sauvage 112
'Doll thi ale' 139
Domesday Book 16, 20
Duke Roland and Sir Otuel of Spain (*Roland and Otuel*) 343, 344–6, 347, 351
Dum ludis floribus 268
Duns Scotus 156

Earth upon Earth 274–5, 277, 279, 285, 289
Edward I 17, 60, 189
Edward II 17, 18, 192
Edward III 15, 17, 187, 192, 194, 210, 307, 467
Edward the Confessor 15
Eleanor of Aquitaine 16, 27
Emaré 294, 297–9
Emma of Norway 15
English, early development 2, 4, 72–82, 104–5
  influence on Welsh 124–7
  see also Old English
epic 4, 7, 24, 32, 90–5, 151, 154, 183, 306, 320, 324, 340, 343, 344, 351, 365–7, 417. *see also* chanson de geste
Erle of Tolous 295–6, 297
Eustace, St 229
Excidium Troiae 312
exegesis 146, 156–63, 213–14, 215

fable 20, 115, 152, 155, 245–50, 251–6, 381
fabliau 115, 247–53, 255, 277, 362, 427, 435, 463
Ferroy chaunson 268
fictional narrative 6. *see also* fable; romance
Firumbras 346, 350
Floris and Blauncheflur 60, 134, 300–2, 305, 307
flyting (poetic contest) 188, 207
Folie Tristan 109
Foliot, Gilbert 149
Fortune (lyric) 293
The Four Foes of Mankind 63
'Foweles in þe frith' 283–4, 285–6, 292
The Fox and the Wolf 58, 115, 245, 249–50, 281
French 2, 9, 20, 27, 33, 40, 54, 56, 81, 84–5, 86, 104–7
  Anglo-Norman 41, 105, 107
  and Gower 441–6, 453
  hagiography 228
  in Harley 2253 277, 279, 281, 285, 286, 288–9
  as language of governance 1, 16
  precocity 104, 107–9
  romance sources for English writers 324

terminology 105–6
  in *Sir Gawain and the Green Knight* 404
Froidmont, Hélinand de 441–2
Froissart, Jean 116, 410, 411, 415, 440, 464
Fuerre de Gadres 317

Gaimar, Geffrei 16, 107, 108, 167, 185
Gamelyn 360, 469
Gawain–poet 8, 64, 392–5
  Cleanness 399–401
  Patience 9, 55, 393, 399, 401–3, 404, 405
  Pearl 9, 55, 143–4, 395–9, 402, 403, 405, 406
  Sir Gawain and the Green Knight 9, 55, 82–5, 86, 121, 140–4, 183, 197, 238, 312, 324, 331, 333, 335, 356, 358, 403–8
Genesis and Exodus 212–13, 219
genre 21, 60, 359–61, 377–8, 427, 434–6. *see also* Genre Poetics chapters
Geoffrey of Monmouth 31, 32, 35, 90, 104, 121, 167–8, 178, 182, 183, 311, 323
Geoffrey of Vinsauf 92, 93, 150–1, 154, 248, 254–5, 315
Geoffrey of Viterbo 448
Gerald of Wales 26, 279
Gest Hytoriale of the Destruction of Troy 183–4
Gilte Legend 239, 240, 241
Godric, St 257, 258–61, 263, 265
Godwine, earl of Wessex 15
Gospel of Nicodemus 192, 217
Gower, John 1, 2, 3, 5, 8, 9, 10, 55, 61, 65, 67, 88–9, 93, 96, 101, 116, 133–5, 140, 151, 154, 162–3, 192, 255, 392, 409, 423, 440
  Cinkante Balades 409, 443–6
  Confessio Amantis 64, 162, 255, 297, 316, 412, 441, 448–56
  '*Eneidos, Bucolis,* que *Georgica*' 440
  in fifteenth century 462–4
  'In Praise of Peace' 414, 441, 443, 444, 446, 456
  Mirour de l'Omme 441–3
  Traitié selonc les auctours pour essampler les amantz marietz 443–4
  Vox Clamantis 64, 95, 96, 440, 441, 442, 443, 446–8, 452, 453
Guernes de Pont-Sainte-Maixence 109
Guibert of Nogent 149
Guido delle Colonne 183, 309, 311, 312, 313, 314, 315, 463
Guillaume de Normandie 112
Guy of Warwick 350, 356, 359, 360, 363–4, 368. *see also* Stanzaic *Guy of Warwick*

hagiography 96, 117, 168, 227–41, 303
Harley 2253 3–4, 29, 43, 44, 55–63, 111, 115, 118–22, 132–3, 174, 187, 188–90, 193–4, 258, 265–9, 273, 274, 277–9, 281–9, 291. *see also* Manuscripts cited; miscellanies
Harley lyrics 56–8, 115, 131, 132, 174, 265–9, 277–8

520 INDEX

Havelok the Dane 1, 8, 71–5, 77, 85, 109, 114, 184, 312, 356, 357, 358, 359, 360, 362–3, 365–7, 369–70, 371
Hayl, Leuedy, sestœrre bryht 270, 271
Hayl mari!/I am sori 144
Hending 58, 206, 207, 281, 289, 292
Henry II 16, 27, 62, 114, 152
Henry III 17, 20, 96, 114, 189
Henry IV 190, 191, 395, 441, 444, 445, 449
Henry of Avranches 96
Henry of Ghent 156–7
Henry of Huntington 99–100, 103, 177
Herebert, William 42, 44, 54, 112, 269–71, 459
Herkne to my ron 267
Heye Louerd, thou here my bone 266–7
Higden, Ranulf 48, 149, 353, 354, 394
Hilton, Walter 65
History of William Marshal 33
Hoccleve, Thomas 157, 192, 414, 454, 463–4, 466, 467
Homer 90, 203, 309, 310, 311, 314
Horace (Quintus Horatius Flaccus) 147, 149, 150, 151, 158, 159
Horn Childe and Maiden Rimnild 53
household 3, 39–44, 45, 48, 56, 265–6, 314, 394
Hue de Rotelande 109
Humphrey de Bohun, earl of Hereford 41, 114, 304, 307
Hundred Years' War 15, 187, 310, 458

'I syke when I singe' 131
Ieuan ap Hywel Swrdwal 126–7
inventio/invention 90–1, 314
Ipomedon 114, 306
Isidore of Seville 145–6, 147, 152, 167, 246, 314, 319
Islam 339–40, 341, 351. *see also* Muslim

Jacob and Joseph 224–5
James I, king of Scotland 458, 465
Jean de Hauteville 92, 93
Jean de Saint-Pierre 445
Jerome, St 97
Jesu, suete is the love of the (Dulcis Jesu memoria) 268–9
John II 193
John of Garland 89, 96, 97–8, 99, 188
John of Grimestone 42–3, 44, 152
John of Howden 98
John of Salisbury 145, 146–7, 149
John of Tynemouth (*Historia Aurea*) 353
Joseph of Exeter 90–2, 103
Josephus 353
Judas 130, 276
Julius Valerius 316
Justinus, Marcus Julianus 316
Juvenal (Decimus Junius Juvenalis) 433

Katherine, St 60
Katherine Group 6, 79, 228–9, 231–2

Kildare poems 4
King Alisaunder 53, 316, 318–22, 465
King Horn 8, 109, 114, 128, 132–3, 184, 356–7, 358, 359, 360, 361–2
King of Tars 350
Kingis Quair 465

Laȝamon 5, 8, 30–5, 59
    Brut 2, 44, 104–5, 110, 140–1, 151, 160–1, 167, 168, 169, 170–3, 181–2, 184–6, 208
Land of Cockaygne 251–2
Langland, William 2, 3, 8, 41, 64, 67
    Piers Plowman 37–9, 44, 61, 65–6, 86, 150, 153, 157, 191, 198, 201, 210, 253–4, 290, 307, 348, 375–91, 459
Lateran Council, Fourth 5, 25, 40
Latin 2, 27, 40, 54, 56, 81, 88–9, 107, 110
    and Gower 446–8, 449–52
    in Harley 2253 277, 279, 282, 285, 288
    as language of governance 1, 16
Latini, Brunetto 154
Laud Troy Book 312–13
Laurent de Premierfait 410
Lawrence of Durham 99, 100–3
lay (*lai*) 265, 276, 298–300
legend 108. *see also* hagiography
Legenda Aurea 229, 230, 353
leonine 97, 447
    hexameters 453, 456
Lichfield 46–53, 66, 67, 394–5
Life of Adam 221–3
lineated verse 4, 181
literary theory 145–63
Little Sooth Sermon 281
Le Livre de Cent Ballades 445
Lollards 157, 212, 376
Lombard, Peter 156, 159, 161
London 52–3, 67
Lorens of Orléans 40, 41, 44, 45
Loue is selkud wodenesse 285–6
Lovelich, Henry 468
The Lover's Complaint 287–8
Luscombe lyrics 4
'Lustneth, lordynges, bothe yonge ant olde' 190
Lybeaus desconus 114, 326
Lydgate, John 4, 116, 135, 203, 240–1, 411, 414, 463–6, 469
    Siege of Thebes 463, 464, 469
    Troy Book 311, 463, 464
lyric 3, 4, 6, 10, 20, 26–30, 108, 112, 115, 117, 257
    criticism 275–9
    religious lyric 7, 257–73
    secular lyric 7, 274–93
    and Welsh 4
'Lystneth, lordynges' 190

macaronic poetry 2, 4, 20, 28, 112–13, 118, 124–6, 127, 268, 269, 285–6, 288
    in Gower 449

Machaut, Guillaume de 116, 413, 440, 443, 454, 464
Macrobius, Ambrosius Theodosius 246-8
Magna Carta 18
Maiden in the mor lay 280
Malacy (Irish Franciscan) 42
Malory, Sir Thomas 294, 323, 324, 335, 336, 338, 406, 407
Mannyng, Robert 19-20, 44, 88, 114, 170, 179-81, 183, 184, 185, 203-4, 248-9, 255, 460, 469
manuscripts 54-67
   Anglo-French 110-12
   see also Manuscripts cited
Map, Walter 42, 299
Margaret, St 6, 230, 231
   in Auchinleck 60, 230, 232-3, 235
   in Katherine Group 228
   in Nicholas Bozon 234-5
   in *South English Legendary* 233-4
Marie de France 3, 109, 265, 298-9, 326
'Mary Magdalene' 230
Matter of Britain 183, 323-38, 356, 359
Matter of England 8, 114, 309, 356-71
Matter of France 8, 294-5, 339-55, 359
Matter of Rome 7, 90, 183, 309-16, 359
Matthew of Vendôme 149-50
Maxims (Old English) 203
Metham, John 135
Middle English Metrical Paraphrase of the Old Testament 219
Minot, Lawrence 66, 187, 192-3
'Mirie it is while sumer ilast' 283
Mirk, John 48, 457-8
miscellanies 3, 7, 27 n. 46, 54, 57, 98, 111, 192, 278, 290, 416, 464 n. 40. *see also* anthologies; Manuscripts cited, especially: London, British Library MS Additional 22,283 (Simeon); Harley 2253; Edinburgh, National Library of Scotland, Advocates' MS 19.2.1 (Auchinleck); Oxford, Bodleian Library, Eng.poet.a.1 (Vernon), Digby 86; Oxford, Jesus College 29
'Most I riden by Ribblesdale' 43, 57, 288
mouvance 52, 115, 340
Mum and the Sothsegger 191, 198
Muslim 8, 24, 295, 300-1, 339-52. *see also* Islam

Nennius 168
Nine Worthies 210, 211, 295, 316
Norman Conquest 1, 15-17, 78, 89, 167, 177, 187, 203, 206, 359
North English Legendary 230
The Northern Homily Cycle 46, 47, 67, 114, 215-17
Northern Passion 460
'Now goth sonne under wod' 10

Occitan verse 16, 27, 108, 116, 410
Odo of Cheriton 248-9, 254
Of Arthour and of Merlin 53, 318-19, 324-5
'Of rybauds y ryme' 188-9
Old English 1, 15-16, 71-87, 104-5, 107

Old Norse 1, 15, 74, 78, 81, 85, 86, 109, 207, 404
On god ureisun of ure lefde 257, 262-5
Ordene de chevalrie 112
An Orisoun to Our Lady 280
Orm 8, 21-6, 31, 82, 84, 85
   Ormulum 2, 5, 79-82, 104, 128-32, 142, 202-3, 213-15
Orosius 316, 317
Oton de Granson 409-10, 445
Otuel 63, 343, 344, 347. *see also Duke Roland and Sir Otuel of Spain* (*Roland and Otuel*)
Ovid (Publius Ovidius Naso) 89, 162, 256, 309, 311, 413, 414, 420, 423, 424, 440, 447-8, 452
   Epistulae Ex Ponto 448
   Heroides 154, 311, 412, 416, 423
   Metamorphoses 156, 162, 254, 256, 412, 413, 432
   Tristia 448
Ovide moralisé 156, 162. *see also* Bersuire, Pierre
The Owl and the Nightingale 5, 44, 59, 112, 114, 138, 152-3, 160, 208-10, 280-1, 290

Paris, William 228, 236-8, 241
The Parlement of Thre Ages 210-11
Partonope of Blois 468-9
Passio Sanctae Margaretae Martyris 231
Passion of Our Lord 138
Pater Noster (alliterative poem) 143
patronage 3, 4, 15, 16, 27, 28, 35, 47, 53, 56, 116, 185, 412
   Chaucer 409, 411
   English-language 63, 66
   female 107, 108
   Gawain-poet 394, 403
   William of Palerne 304, 307
Pecham, John 98
Penllyn, Tudur 125-6
A Penniworth of Wit 245, 252-3
periodisation 2-3, 72-5, 211
Peter of Cornwall 149
Peter Lombard 156, 159
Peterborough Chronicle 1, 16, 81, 104, 167
Petit Bruit 176
Le petit plet 112
Petrarch, Francis 116, 154, 159, 420, 422, 423, 426, 435, 443
Philip IV, king of France 192, 193
Philippe de Thaon 109, 185
The Phoenix 108
Physiologus 204
Pierce the Ploughman's Creed 157, 187, 198, 459
Pierre d'Abernon of Fetcham 161
Piers Plowman. see Langland, William
The Pistel of Susan 142-3, 224, 225-6
Plato 245-6
Poema Morale 2, 25-6, 130, 136, 137, 138
poetic handbooks 5. *see also* literary theory
poetics 1-2, 8, 9, 10-11, 146, 149-55, 163, 203, 309, 310, 314, 322, 342, 364-71
   Chaucer 309, 413-14, 417

522   INDEX

poetics (*Continued*)
  'feminine' 305
  Gower 440–3, 447–8, 453–5
  Langland 380
  Pearl 396
  Welsh 122, 127
Prick of Conscience 45–6, 47, 49–52, 65, 66–7, 192,
    203, 204, 460
Pride of Life 468
'Prophecy of Thomas of Erceldoune' 58
prose 107, 185, 227–8, 262, 272, 287
prosody 4, 9, 109–10, 125, 131, 134, 179–80, 258,
    296–9, 307, 403, 414, 446, 453–5
proverb 205–7, 289–93
The Proverbs of Alfred 2, 141, 172, 206–7, 209, 281,
    289–90, 292
Proverbs of Hendyng 206, 207, 281, 289, 292

Quant fu en ma juvente 268
Quintilian 248

Reginald of Canterbury 89, 96–7, 98
Reginald of Durham 258
regionalism 37–53, 54–67, 324, 459
'Le regret de Maximian' 28–30, 58, 281
Religious lyric 7, 21, 27–30, 55, 115
Renart, Jean 410
Rhetorica ad Herennium 149, 152
rhyme royal 135, 235–6, 241, 417, 467–8
  in *Canterbury Tales* 425–6
  in Gower 453–4, 456
rhyming couplets 25, 60, 109, 110, 133, 134, 175, 180,
    181, 190, 209, 216, 262, 343, 365
  in *Canterbury Tales* 425–6
  see also couplets; septenary verse; tetrameter
Rich, Edmund, St 10
Richard I 18, 19, 60, 184
Richard II 8, 18, 190, 394–5, 411, 448, 467
Richard Coeur de Lion 184, 318, 339, 350, 351–3
Richard of Cornwall 189
Richard of Devizes 19
Richard the Redeless 187, 191–2, 198
Riga, Peter 448
'Rime of King William' 1
Robert of Basevorn 149
Robert of Gloucester 114, 168, 169, 170, 176–8, 179,
    184, 186
  in fifteenth century 460
Robert of Jumièges 15
Roger of Argenteuil (*Bible en François*) 353
Rolle, Richard 47, 48, 49, 51, 66, 203, 271–3
roman antique 4, 108, 183
Roman d'Eneas 306
Roman de la rose 116, 150, 157, 301, 393, 398, 410,
    412, 423, 426–7, 432, 442
Roman de Thèbes 319
romance 3, 4, 7–8, 9, 16, 21, 27, 28, 29, 30, 35, 52,
    53, 59–60, 63–4, 97, 108, 109, 114, 117, 183–5,
    218–19, 340–1

Crusade romance 339–55
  in fifteenth century 459–60
  non–cycle 294–308
  tradition 323
  Troy romances 310–15
  see also Alexander romances; Arthurian romance

Saint Erkenwald 232, 235, 238–40, 241, 348, 459
St Patrick's Purgatory 60
satire 6, 20, 96, 187–93
Satire on the Consistory Courts 187, 195
Scottish legendary 4, 230, 233
Scrope, Richard 394–5, 405
secular lyric 7, 20, 26–7, 55, 56, 115, 257, 263, 274–93
Seege or Batayle of Troye 312
Seneca (Lucius Annaeus Seneca, the Younger) 92, 93
septenary verse 5, 6, 21, 79, 82, 129–31, 136, 138, 169,
    177, 181, 202, 214, 224, 229–30, 234, 461, 462
The Seven Sages of Rome 66
Shirley, John 411
Short Metrical Chronicle 60, 63, 169–70, 171, 173–6,
    181, 184, 186
Siege of Jerusalem 339, 353–5, 459
Siege of Milan 347, 350–1
Simeon manuscript 46–9, 203, 267. *see also*
    Manuscripts cited; Vernon manuscript
Simon de Fresne 112
The Simonie 63, 187, 196
Sir Degrevant 295–6
Sir Eglamour 296–7
Sir Ferumbras 343, 346–7
Sir Launfal 326
Sir Orfeo 174, 299–300, 308
Sir Percyvell of Gales 296, 327–31, 338
Sir Tristrem 179, 185, 294, 325
Skelton, John 468
Solomon and Saturn I and II 207
'The song of the husbandman' 43, 57, 187, 193–5
Song of Jesus' Precious Blood 288
The Song of Lewes 189
Soul and Body I 76, 77, 78
The Soul's Address to the Body 75–9, 80, 84, 172
South English Legendary 6, 114, 130, 172–3, 176, 181,
    229, 230, 234, 241, 460–1
Speculum Guy of Warwick 63
Speculum Vitae 40, 44, 45, 46, 47, 65, 67
Spring ('Lenten is come with loue to toune') 284–5
A Spring Song on the Passion 288
Stanley, Sir John 395
Stanzaic *Guy of Warwick* 357, 364, 365
Stanzaic *Morte Arthur* 336–8
Statius (Publius Papinius Statius) 154, 158–9, 320,
    420
'Stond wel, moder, vnder rode' 58
Sultan of Babylon 347, 348–50
'Sumer is icumen in' 132, 282–3
Sutton, Katherine 3

tail-rhyme stanza 5, 8, 110, 136–7, 138, 144, 180, 181, 185, 190, 223, 230, 250, 266, 270, 281, 295–6, 297, 304 n. 36, 324, 326–7, 342, 343, 350, 365, 426, 468
tetrameter 4, 5, 6, 10, 52, 132, 202, 208, 210, 230, 237, 253, 324
  in Chaucer 134
  in *Gawain*-poet 143
  in Gower 133–4, 414, 415, 423
'Ther is a busch that is forgrowe' 190–1
Thomas (author of *Tristan*) 109
Thomas of Hales 27–8, 281
Thomas of Kent 109
The Thrush and the Nightingale 30, 281
Torrent of Portyngale 297, 468
translation 5, 8, 36, 40, 99, 114, 160, 212, 213, 269, 270, 273, 311, 315, 316, 340, 417, 418, 420, 426, 468–9
Tremulous Hand of Worcester 1, 75
trochaic verse 5, 91, 131–4, 202, 282
Trogus, Pompeius 316
trouvères 108, 116, 257, 263, 410
Troy 7, 90, 168, 170, 183, 309–16, 322, 361, 405, 434

Þe wohunge of ure lauerd 262
Þis nome ys also on honi komb 271
Þou wommon boute uére 270–1

Valerius Maximus 433
Venez Dames, Venez Avant 129, 130
Vernon Golden Legend 230
Vernon Manuscript 3–4, 46–9, 51, 65–6, 67, 203, 230, 267, 466–8. *see also* Manuscripts cited; Simeon manuscript
verse forms 4–5, 7, 8, 24, 51–2, 109–10, 119, 137, 140, 181, 202, 225, 257, 258, 338, 340, 342, 365, 460, 464, 465
  in Chaucer 409, 413–14, 425–6
  in *Gawain*-poet 395, 400
  in romances 324–7
  'unrhyming' 462
  see also Ormulum; tail-rhyme stanza
Vie de Saint Alexis 108

Vindicta Salvatoris 353
Virgil (Publius Vergilius Maro) 145, 309, 311, 320, 420, 423–4, 440, 447, 452
  Aeneid 90, 151, 158, 168, 306, 311, 320, 366–7, 395, 440
Vita Adae 221, 222
voicing 9, 258, 270–1, 272, 273
  in *Canterbury Tales* 429–30
  female 7, 92, 260, 262, 264, 265, 268, 288
  in Gower 444, 449

Wace 2, 30, 31, 32, 33, 34, 59, 104–5, 108, 140, 160–1, 167, 171, 172, 179, 180, 185
Walling of New Ross 112
Walter of Châtillon 90, 92–4, 151, 316, 319
Walter of England 147–8
Walter of Wimborne 98
Walton, John 462, 463, 466
'The Way of Christ's Love' 57
Way of Love 286, 287, 291
'The Way of Woman's Love' 57
Weal 290–1
Welsh poetry 118–27
What Love Is Like 286
'When þe nyhtegale singes' 43
'Whi wepistou so sore' 291–2, 293
Whiteacre (Wireker), Nigel 95–6, 103, 448
Will and Wit 290–1
William de Longchamp 17–19, 95
William of Conches 145
William the Conqueror 15–16
William of Palerne 41, 114, 304–7
William of Waddington 44, 114, 203, 248, 442
'Winnere and Wastour' 41, 187, 196–8, 210, 312
Wooing Group 257, 261–5
'Worcester Fragments' 75
Worldes Blis 278–9
Wulfstan 172, 228
Wyclif, John 157, 212, 376

York mystery cycle 217
Ywain and Gawain 66, 114, 192, 326